ספר ההפטרות

THE
HAFTARAH
COMMENTARY

by
W. Gunther Plaut

translation by
Chaim Stern
with the assistance of Philip D. Stern

S. David Sperling, Consulting Editor

UAHC Press
New York

LIBRARY OF CONGRESS CATALOGING-IN-PUBLICATION DATA

Plaut, W. Gunther, 1912–
    [Sefer ha-haftarot] = The Haftarah commentary / W. Gunther Plaut ; a new
translation by Chaim Stern ; S. David Sperling, consulting editor.
        p. cm.
    Includes text of the haftarot with English translation.
    Includes bibliographical references.
    ISBN 0–8074–0551–5 (cloth : alk. paper)
    1. Haftarot—Commentaries. I. Stern, Chaim. II. Sperling, S. David.
III. Haftarot. English & Hebrew. IV. Title.
BM670.H3P58 1996
296.4—dc20   96–5140
                                                                     CIP

This book is printed on acid-free paper
Copyright © 1996 by the UAHC Press

Manufactured in the United States of America

10 9 8 7 6 5 4 3 2 1

CONTENTS

*About the haftarot; about the prophets; about this Commentary
(a synopsis of each prophetic book, its composition and author).*

Haftarot

FOREWORD

The publication of this monumental new work of modern Jewish scholarship is a milestone in the history of the Jewish people, as well as a source of enormous pride to the Union of American Hebrew Congregations, the central body of Reform synagogues throughout the United States and Canada. Fifteen years in the making, *The Haftarah Commentary* will serve as the companion piece to *The Torah: A Modern Commentary*, which was also authored by W. Gunther Plaut and was published by the UAHC in 1981. Rabbi Plaut, the foremost Reform commentator of the modern era, has now completed his commentary project with a revolutionary new look at haftarah from the perspective of contemporary society. In so doing, he has provided us with a volume that is certain to be used extensively by scholar and layperson, both at home and in the synagogue.

The first haftarah commentary in modern idiom, this work contains a number of significant innovations. It draws on contemporary scholarship in such fields as archaeology, history, linguistics, and literature; it features a new gender-neutral, vernacular translation by Rabbi Chaim Stern, poet laureate of the Reform movement, replacing the stilted, arcane, and sexist translations previously used; and it offers both recent and traditional commentaries and gleanings from ancient and modern sources that bear on the text, all scrupulously checked for accuracy by our consulting editor, Professor S. David Sperling of the Hebrew Union College-Jewish Institute of Religion.

The publication of *The Haftarah Commentary* has special meaning for other reasons as well. All Jews have looked to the prophetic vision as a means of sustaining their faith and have seen the prophetic writings as a source of comfort in times of distress. For Reform Jews, however, the prophetic books have always held a special prominence. Ever since the Pittsburgh Platform in 1885 defined "the great task of modern times" as solving "on the basis of justice and righteousness the problems presented by the contrasts and evils of the present organization of society," Reform Jews have embraced the prophetic call for justice and peace and have identified with the prophetic view that anything that robs human beings of their dignity is an insult to the Divine. This volume represents Reform Judaism's reaffirmation of the universal, human prophetic agenda and of the call for social justice that agenda demands. It reaffirms as well the fundamental optimism of the prophetic message: our faith in God and humanity, and in its limitless possibilities.

Finally, coming at a time of a change in leadership in all branches of the Reform movement, this commentary reflects the new emphasis that I and others have placed on what we consider the central task of our movement as we proceed into the next century: lifelong Jewish study as the key to Jewish survival. Judaism imposes upon us a multiplicity of obligations, including the obligation to pray, to observe ritual mitzvot, and to improve our world in response to our tradition's ethical mandates. But the obli-

gation to study is fundamental to them all because it is from study of Torah and text that all other obligations flow. Reform Judaism has, therefore, committed itself anew to educating Jews in a serious and sustained way and to giving every Jewish child and adult the gift of Jewish competence. Just as *The Torah: A Modern Commentary* advanced this goal by serving as a study resource for tens of thousands of Jews in North America and around the world, so we hope and pray that *The Haftarah Commentary* will continue this tradition by reaching the increasing number of Jews who today are eager to embrace Jewish texts and Jewish learning. We hope and pray that *The Haftarah Commentary* will, through constant use, remind the modern Jew yet again that study must be our burning passion—our first duty and our greatest joy.

Rabbi Eric H. Yoffie
President-Elect, Union of American Hebrew Congregations

PREFACE

Separate books dealing with the prophetic readings in the Jewish liturgy are rare. Chief among them are Ludwig Philippson's (1859) and Mendel Hirsch's (1896) commentaries, both written in German, and Issachar Jacobson's more recent volumes (1959), written in Hebrew. The works of Hirsch and Jacobson are strictly traditional in approach, and both lack textual comment. Philippson explains the text broadly, but without an extended discussion of difficulties or variant interpretations, and with a minimum of historical references. The comments on the haftarot that are part of the commentary on the Torah edited by Joseph H. Hertz are quite brief and clearly not meant to stand on their own.

Our book is intended as a companion volume to *The Torah—A Modern Commentary*, which contains haftarot but—with the exception of a few sentences of introduction—presents the reader with no explanatory material. This volume attempts to fill this lacuna and, like the Torah Commentary, is aimed at the reader who wants to sample a significant portion of prophetic writings, although we trust that the volume will pass scholarly inspection as well.

The lectionary we present is the traditional one, chosen by our Sages many centuries ago. It contains the Ashkenazic selections used in the Diaspora, and includes those for the extra days not observed in Israel or in most Reform congregations. Sephardic selections that differ are noted in the Table of Haftarot and in the Commentary. Since some of the customary haftarot are quite difficult for modern readers to appreciate (even when a commentary is provided), or may not be relevant to the particular portion of the sidra read on the Shabbat in question, we have added some additional selections at the end of the volume. They are drawn from the prophetic books and also from *K'tuvim* ("Writings"), the third part of the Tanach.

Readers familiar with the Torah Commentary will note that the *Gleanings* in this book are, in comparison, briefer and less wide-ranging. In contrast to the immensity of sources that concern themselves with the Torah, prophetic selections have elicited not nearly the amount of midrashic or other comments.

We also present a new translation of all the haftarot.

There are, of course, many translations of the Bible, and our translation has benefited from its predecessors. All translation is interpretation, yet we hope we have been able to capture the essence of the text and to render it in idiomatic English. We have paid due attention to the work of our traditional commentators and to contemporary biblical scholars who by their labors have illuminated much that would otherwise have remained obscure. Where we have deviated from conventional understandings or literal

meanings, we have noted it. It has been our aim throughout to provide a readable text in contemporary English that remains faithful to the Hebrew.

It is worth noting that we have chosen to render the divine name יהוה (YHVH), for which most other translations have "Lord," by "Eternal" or "Eternal One." We believe that "the Eternal"—a rendering that goes back to Moses Mendelssohn—more accurately reflects the biblical understanding of יהוה, for the four-letter root of the divine name is derived from the verb "to be," while "Lord" translates the traditional substitute for it, *Adonai.*

The appearance of this book has been spurred on by the encouragement of Rabbi Daniel Syme and the devoted assistance of Seymour Rossel, both of the Union of American Hebrew Congregations. We have had the benefit of perceptive and scholarly advice from Professor S. David Sperling, of Hebrew Union College-Jewish Institute of Religion in New York, who served as consulting editor, and from Philip D. Stern, Ph.D., who assisted with the translation and the *Gleanings.* Both of these scholars contributed immensely to our work, and our sincere thanks are extended to them. We also thank Melvin Wolfson, our copy editor, for his meticulous and sensitive work and his numerous valuable suggestions.

Fall-Winter 5756/1995-1996.   תודה לאל

W.G.P. and C.S.

A Note on the Hebrew Text

Many times a Hebrew word is followed by a variant inserted by the Sages. The bracketed word is the one to read (*k'ré*), and not the one that precedes the brackets (*k'tiv*), "written," so called because it preserves an old textual tradition. See our further discussion on p. 506.

TABLE OF HAFTAROT

Sephardic readings are frequently shorter than those found in the Ashkenazic tradition, and the difference is listed in the footnotes. If the Sephardic reading is from the same prophet, only the verse numbers are indicated; otherwise, the full citation is given. Differences between various Jewish traditions are also noted, but not all variations could be included.

xiii

***

Notes

[1] 42:5-21.

[2] 54:1-10.

[3] 4:1-23.

[4] 12:7-13:5.

[5] Sephardim always read Obadiah, as do many Ashkenazic congregations.

[6] Jeremiah 1:1-2:3 for Matot.

[7] 5:1-31.

[8] 6:1-13.

[9] 18:20-39.

[10] 7:13-26.

[11] 7:40-50; see haftarah for Vayakhel.

[12] 6:1-19.

[13] 22:1-16.

[14] Ezekiel 20:2-20

[15] 2:4-28; 4:1-2.

[16] 1:1-9.

[17] II Kings 11:17-12:17.

[18] 15:1-34.

[19] 36:16-36.

[20] 45:18-46:15.

[21] Plus Numbers 29:1-6 from second scroll.

[22] *Gates of Repentance,* the Reform High Holy Day prayer book, also offers a selection from Nehemiah chapter 8 as an alternative haftarah.

[23] When the weekly sidra is Ha'azinu, Joel is read; when it is Vayeilech, Micah is read. Sephardim generally read Micah in either case.

[24] Traditional: plus Numbers 29:12-16.

[25] See the haftarah for Pikudei.

[26] Traditional: plus daily section from Numbers chapter 29.

[27] Most Reform congregations observe the Israeli calendar and celebrate Sh'mini Atzeret and Simchat Torah together, and generally read the Simchat Torah selections.

[28] Traditional: plus Numbers 29:35-30:1.

[29] Traditional: plus Numbers 29:35-30:1.

[30] 1:1-9.

[31] Traditional: plus Numbers 28:16-25.

[32] 5:2-6:1.

[33] Traditional: plus Numbers 28:16-25.

[34] 37:1-14.

[35] Traditional: plus Numbers 28:19-25.

[36] Traditional: plus Numbers 28:19-25.

[37] Traditional: plus Numbers 28:26-31.

[38] If the day falls on Shabbat: Deuteronomy 14:22-16:17. Traditional: plus Numbers 28:16-31.

[39] 2:20-3:19.

[40] The ninth day of Av, when the First and Second Temples were destroyed.

[41] Haftarah for Vayeilech; Sephardim read from Hosea and Micah as on Shabbat Shuvah.

[42] Sephardim read no haftarah.

[43] Traditional: plus Numbers 7:1-11 and verses regarding the prince, according to the day during the Chanukah observance.

[44] See previous note.

[45] Holocaust Remembrance Day.

[46] Israel Independence Day.

ALPHABETICAL LIST OF HAFTAROT

ABBREVIATIONS AND GLOSSARY

Abbreviations and Glossary

Abarbanel (also Abravanel), Isaac, medieval Jewish commentator (15th century).

Aggadah (אגדה), non-legal interpretations and tales relating to the Bible (see also *Midrash*).

Akkadian, old Semitic tongue, preserved in Babylonian and Assyrian dialects.

Aleinu, one of the concluding prayers in the worship service.

Amidah (עמידה, literally "standing"), the core prayers of the Jewish service. They are said while standing.

B., Babylonian Talmud, followed by the name of the tractate.

B.C.E., "Before the Common Era," usually referred to as B.C. by non-Jews.

Canon, the collection of books admitted to the Hebrew Bible.

C.E., "Common Era," usually referred to as A.D. by non-Jews.

Christian Scripture, usually referred to as "New Testament."

Eliezer of Beaugency, 12th century Jewish Bible commentator.

Festivals (חגים, *chagim*), Sukkot, Pesach (Passover), Shavuot.

Halachah (הלכה, also transliterated "Halakhah"), the Jewish legal system.

HUCA, Hebrew Union College Annual, a scholarly publication.

Ibn Ezra, Abraham, 12th century Jewish Bible commentator.

J., Jerusalem Talmud, followed by the name of the tractate.

JBL, Journal of Biblical Literature, a scholarly periodical.

Josephus, Flavius, Jewish historian (1st century C.E.) who witnessed the Jewish war against the Romans and wrote a book about it.

JPS, Jewish Publication Society; refers here to the translation of the Hebrew Scriptures (from 1964 on).

Judah, the Southern Kingdom (see there).

Judea, the Roman province of Palestine.

Kashrut, Jewish dietary law (from כשר, *kasher*, "fit to be eaten").

K'ré (קרי), the text as it ought to be read; see the explanation on p. iv.

K'tiv (כתיב), the preserved text as written, but to be read differently (see previous entry).

M., Mishnah, followed by the name of the tractate.

Machar Chodesh, "tomorrow is the new month," words from the haftarah that is read on a Sabbath when the new month is observed the next day.

Maimonides, Moses, also called Rambam (12th century), the leading Jewish philosopher and codifier.

Malbim, acronym for Rabbi Meir Lev ben Yechiel Michael, 19th century Jewish Bible commentator.

Masorah (מסורה, "tradition"), the traditionally accepted Hebrew text of the Tanach is referred to as the "masoretic text."

Metzudat David and Metzudat Zion, two-part commentary on the prophets by David Altschuler and his son Jechiel Hillel (18th century).

Metzudat Zion, see previous entry.

Midrash (מדרש), a vast collection of ethical, legendary, linguistic, and legal comments on the biblical text, referred to as "Midrash" (uppercase); a single comment from the collection is referred to as a "midrash" (lowercase). See also *Aggadah*.

Mitzvah (plural mitzvot), literally "commandment(s)"; tradition enumerates 613 mitzvot as the basis of Jewish ethical and ritual practice.

NEB, the New English Bible, a translation of the Bible (1970) published in Great Britain under the auspices of the Christian churches. Revised in 1989 and given a new title: The Revised English Bible.

NJPS, see JPS.

Northern Kingdom, the ten tribes that split off from the united nation and were known as Israel following the death of King Solomon (10th century B.C.E.).

NRSV, the New Revised Standard Verson of the Bible (1989), a revision of the 1952 Revised Standard Version of the Bible.

Parashah (פרשה), often used for "sidra" (see there).

Pentateuch, the five books of Moses. The term is derived from the Greek (see *Torah*).

Philo, Egyptian-Jewish philosopher and polemicist (1st century C.E.).

Radak, acronym for Rabbi David Kimchi, 12-13th century Jewish Bible commentator.

Ralbag, acronym for Rabbi Levi ben Gershom, medieval Jewish commentator (13-14th century).

Rambam, acronym for Rabbi Moshe ben Maimon (see under *Maimonides*).

Rashi (Rabbi Shelomo Yitzhaki), the most famous of all Jewish commentators (11-12th century C.E.).

Rosh Chodesh (ראש חדש, "New Month"), the day on which the New Moon is celebrated.

RSV, see NRSV.

Saadia ben Joseph, Jewish commentator and philosopher (10th century C.E.).

Septuagint, Greek translation of the Hebrew Bible (3rd-2nd century B.C.E.).

Shabbat Hagadol (שבת הגדול, "the Great Sabbath"), the Sabbath before Passover.

Shabbat Nachamu (שבת נחמו, "the Sabbath of Consolation"), the Sabbath after Tisha b'Av, so named after the first word of the haftarah.

Shabbat Shuvah (שבת שובה, "the Sabbath of Return"), the Sabbath before Yom Kippur, so named after the opening word of the haftarah.

Sidra (סדרה), the weekly Torah portion read in the synagogue (also called "parashah").

Southern Kingdom, the two tribes of Judah and Benjamin, known as "Judah" after the united nation split apart following the death of King Solomon (10th century B.C.E.). Destroyed by the Babylonians in 587 B.C.E.

Tanach (תנ״ך), acronym for the three parts of the Hebrew Bible, usually called "Old Testament" by non-Jews (see p. xvii).

Targum (תרגום), Aramaic translation of the Prophets, ascribed to Jonathan ben Uzziel (1st century C.E.).

Torah, the five books of Moses, the written foundation of Judaism.

Torah Commentary, see Bibliography under "Plaut."

UAHC, Union of American Hebrew Congregations.

Ugaritic, Semitic language in ancient Ugarit, a city on the site of Ras Shamra, in modern Syria.

Yehud, name for the area of Israel, Syria, and Jordan while under Persian dominance (6-4th century B.C.E.).

General Introduction

Preliminary Note on Terminology

In this book, the term *Tanach* (תַּנַ״ךְ) is used to denote the Hebrew Bible, an acronym that takes the first letters of the book's three parts and adds two vowels to make the term pronounceable. The three parts are:

תורה, נביאים, כתובים

Torah, *Nevi'im* (Prophets), and *K'tuvim* (Writings).[1]

About Haftarot

Haftarot (singular *haftarah*, from the root פטר (*p-t-r*), "to conclude") is the name given to certain biblical selections that are read after the Torah portion of the day, at Shabbat and festival services. They are always recited at morning worship, and only twice (on Yom Kippur and Tisha b'Av) also in the afternoon. In the traditional liturgy, all of them come from that section of the Tanach called "Prophets" (נביאים, *nevi'im*). In addition, we have provided some alternate haftarot, some of which are taken from the third part of the Tanach.

All readings represent portions of a prophet's writings, except that on Yom Kippur afternoon all of the book of Jonah is read,[2] and on Shabbat Vayishlach (when Genesis 32 and following provides the weekly Torah portion), all 21 verses that constitute the preserved writings of the prophet Obadiah are recited by the Sephardim and also by many Ashkenazim.

Haftarot are of varying lengths, but why some are short and others are long is not clear. There is even a report in an ancient source that at one time one haftarah consisted of only a single verse.[3]

The custom of reading haftarot is quite old, though its beginnings can only be surmised. One possibility is that a haftarah was introduced in order to isolate the Samaritans, who did not believe that the books of the prophets were Holy Writ. Another theory suggests that when the Syrian rulers forbade the teaching of Torah, prophetic readings served as a substitute and were retained in the liturgy even after the prohibition had been lifted. We know that by the year 100 C.E., the reading of haftarot was already firmly established, for the Christian Gospels (written at that time) tell us that Paul visited a Diaspora synagogue and spoke to the worshippers "after the readings from Torah and Prophets."[4]

The ancient Sages[5] attempted to select haftarot that had a special relation to the Torah readings of the day. Sometimes this relationship is obvious, as, for instance, when the Torah reading brings us Moses' Song at the Sea (Exodus 15), and the haftarah the Song of Deborah (Judges 5). Sometimes only a single word that occurs in both

haftarah and sidra[6] provides the link; at other times the connection is hard to discern; at still others it is the special nature of the day that provides the reason for its choice.

In traditional synagogues the person who will read the haftarah is also assigned to read the concluding verses of the sidra and is called *maftir*, "the one who concludes." The custom of having a bar/bat mitzvah read the haftarah is of fairly recent origin.

Ashkenazim and Sephardim usually, but not always, read the same haftarot. Our book will note the variations.[7]

There is also a divergence between the practices of Israel and those of the Diaspora. In the latter, an extra day is added to the festivals, while in Israel, Pesach, Shavuot, and Sukkot have no added days. Reform Jews also do not generally observe these extra days and therefore, like Israeli Jews, do not read the haftarot assigned to them.

Finally, while Torah is always to be read from a handwritten scroll, haftarot are usually read from printed books, although in some congregations, especially in Israel, written scrolls are used for them as well.[8]

About the Prophets

Prophetic books in the Tanach

All haftarot are taken from the second part, the prophetic books.[9] These fall into two parts:

Early Prophets is the name for the historical books (Joshua, Judges, Samuel, and Kings). They are listed among the Prophets because prophetic figures like Joshua, Deborah, Samuel, Nathan, Elijah, and Elisha appear in them. However, with few exceptions,[10] the Early Prophets contain no body of literary material.

Later or *Literary Prophets* are those ascribed to fifteen individuals who left us prophetic legacies identified by the name of a specific prophet. The three who bequeathed us extensive writings are often called the "Major Prophets" (Isaiah, Jeremiah, and Ezekiel), while the other twelve are referred to either as "The Twelve" or the "Minor Prophets," because their surviving literary heritage is relatively small, in some cases only a few pages. However, some of the most often-quoted orations stem from prophets like Hosea, Amos, and Micah, which makes it clear that the term "minor" refers to the *quantity* but not to the *quality* of their literary work.

Further in this Introduction will be found brief descriptions of each prophetic book, as well as of the political and social climate in which the people heard the message. Similarly, in the historical books the reader will find an overview of the times and circumstances from which these writings came.

Who were the Prophets?

We tend to think of them primarily as people who foretold the future. Such foretelling was indeed an important part of their message, but they were not soothsayers or fortune-tellers. Their message was usually: *"If* you continue on your current paths and disregard God's ways, *then* disaster lies ahead. But," they would continue, "if you turn from your evil ways you will live and enjoy God's favor." They would describe both misfortune and good fortune in vivid and memorable imagery.

Thus the prophet usually predicts what *should* be and delivers this prediction with a sense of certainty. "This rule applies even to the vision of messianic redemption: It is what should be, but whether it will be depends, at least to some extent, on us."[11]

What the prophets said was sometimes highly unpopular. For example, Jeremiah courted death and was jailed for announcing impending doom. At other times, when the people faced depression and despair, the prophet would give them hope by stressing that repentance was possible and that divine mercy was always available.

True prophets (there were false ones too[12]) knew that they spoke as messengers of God. Possessed with divine fire, they were convinced that God's spirit guided their speech. The Bible usually called the prophet *navee*, a word probably related to the Akkadian *nabû*, having the meaning of calling out or proclaiming.[13] The Greek translation (known as the Septuagint[14]) rendered the term as *prophetes*, which described a spokesperson for God. The true prophet did not convey a personal opinion, but rather proclaimed a divinely initiated message.

"And after all is said and done ... just words. But in those words, the invisible God, the Creator, the great mystery, becomes audible. The prophet helps us to hear, helps us to see. But it is up to us to believe and to think."[15]

Sheldon H. Blank, therefore, considered that the word *navee* originally meant "one who has been divinely called," and that in this sense the word was older than the Tanach. Being called, the prophet spoke as a mouthpiece of God and announced, without further explanation, "Thus says God ...." In turn, the listeners understood that they were urged to lead a God-pleasing life, though none of the prophets depicted this as an easy course to follow.[16]

On the contrary, they painted reality with unvarnished colors. They spoke as teachers, not philosophers. Abraham Joshua Heschel put it this way:

"Instead of dealing with the timeless issues of being and becoming, of matter and form, of definitions and demonstrations, [the prophet] is thrown into orations about widows and orphans, about the corruption of judges and affairs of the market place. Instead of showing us a way through the elegant mansions of the mind, the prophets

take us to the slums. The world is a proud place, full of beauty, but the prophets are scandalized and rave as if the whole world were a slum ....

"Why such immoderate excitement? Why such intense indignation? The things that horrified the prophets are now daily occurrences all over the world ...."[17]

Because of this, the prophetic challenges remain relevant today. They apply to all human beings and to all societies, and with special urgency they address Jews, who are the inheritors of the Covenant, which demands devotion to God and Torah and carries its own rewards. It is fitting, therefore, that Torah readings are concluded with prophetic haftarot.[18]

About This Commentary

The Hebrew and English texts of the haftarot are accompanied by four distinct forms of commentary.

1. Each haftarah is preceded by a brief *Introduction*, which highlights the setting as well as the major message(s) of the selection, and suggests the connection between it and the Torah reading that preceded it.

2. Below the text proper will be found a *Commentary* containing brief notes that explain difficult words or tell the reader where the original Hebrew is not clear, and that the English translation gives the most likely meaning. These notes attempt to show how the text was heard in the prophet's own day, and at times will also indicate how the biblical text was understood in later ages, which may not be the same as the prophet's contemporaries heard it.

3. Following Text, Translation, and Commentary, are brief *Essays* about the prophet or another personage mentioned in the text (for example, Cyrus), or about questions raised by the prophet's message. For instance, in the first haftarah in the book, Isaiah speaks of Israel as "a light to the nations," and a mini-essay is devoted to exploring this subject, asking: What did Isaiah mean to say thereby, and what might this message say to us?

4. Then follow *Gleanings*, providing excerpts from Jewish and also non-Jewish sources that explore the haftarah or expand upon its theme.

Readers of *The Torah—A Modern Commentary*[19] will be familiar with these features and methods. As in that Commentary, there also are selected *Notes* (at the end of each haftarah) as well as a *Bibliography* (p. 867) and a combined list of *Abbreviations and Glossary* (p. xiv).

Biblical Books
from which the haftarot are drawn
according to their order in the Tanach

JOSHUA

This book, consisting of 24 chapters, follows the Torah. After the death of Moses, Joshua has assumed the leadership and now prepares for the invasion of Canaan.

Chapters 1-12 describe the conquest of the land; chapters 13-21, its division among the tribes and the establishment of the Cities of Refuge; and chapters 22-24 conclude the book, especially with the farewell of Joshua and his death.

The book of Joshua covers the latter part of the 13th century B.C.E. and early decades of the 12th.[20] Tradition ascribes authorship of the book to Joshua himself (except for the last verses, relating to his death).[21] Rashi and other medieval commentators were of the opinion that some portions of the book were written later, and Isaac Abarbanel went even further and assigned the authorship of the book to Samuel.[22]

Many moderns take the book to be a pious reconstruction of the past rather than a trustworthy historical narrative, especially since the book of Judges (which follows Joshua) knows nothing of a unified Israelite campaign to conquer the country. Furthermore, it is said, Joshua reveals the same theological thrust as Deuteronomy, and therefore scholars have spoken of a Hexateuch (six books, consisting of Torah plus Joshua) as a unit, enlarging the traditional Pentateuch (five books or *Chumash*).

The scholarly debate remains unresolved, and a discussion of these issues goes beyond the scope of this commentary. The tales that the ancient Sages selected from the book of Joshua for inclusion in the cycle of haftarot have become part of Jewish folk tradition and as such have their independent value.

It is noteworthy that the book ends by reporting the death of Joshua at the age of 110, as well as of the burial of the bones of Joseph, who had reached that very same age.[23] Quite clearly, the tradition embedded in these figures means to indicate that Joseph and Joshua had a special relation to one another: Joseph brought his people from Canaan to a foreign country, and Joshua restored them to the Promised Land. The identical number of their life spans symbolizes the closing of the circle.

JUDGES

Among the post-Torah books, Judges has a special literary distinction: its text is unusually well preserved and generally not hard to read and understand. The one exception is the Song of Deborah, which is a long poem of great antiquity (see the haftarah for B'shalach).

xxxi

The book's title is a translation of שופטים (shof'tim), but the Hebrew term has a wider meaning than "judiciary officers." In the book, the shof'tim are also military leaders, administrators, and, in a general sense, persons to whom the people looked for guidance. Some served for a short time, others for as long as forty years.

The book presents traditions covering the 12th and 11th centuries B.C.E., an age of constant warfare with Canaanites and rare times of peace. Its stories differ significantly from the book of Joshua, which tells of the invasion of Canaan as a campaign of twelve tribes acting as a unified people. In Judges the picture is very different: the tribes proceed separately and with differing failures and successes, and at the end of the book combine to attack the tribe of Benjamin.

The text clearly draws on different sources. For instance, in one tradition, Jerusalem is captured and destroyed; in another, the attempt to conquer it fails (which accords with the later story of David capturing the city from the Jebusites).

The bulk of the 21 chapters deals with a succession of men and one woman who are listed as shof'tim: Othniel, Ehud, Shamgar, Deborah and Barak, Gideon (also called Jerubbaal), Abimelech, Tola and Jair, Jephthah, Ibzan, Elon and Abdon, and finally, Samson. The tales of Judges end here, and the text turns to the priest Micah (chapter 17), the migration of the tribe of Dan from the south to the north (chapter 18), and the terrible story of the tribal war with the Benjaminites (chapters 19-21). The book concludes with the telling statement: "In those days there was no king in Israel; people did as they pleased, everyone of them."

It is likely that Judges represents a variety of traditions that were collected at a much later time, and it is also likely that the story of Ruth once belonged to this cycle but then became a separate book.[24]

Samuel, whose book follows Judges, is often considered the last of the shof'tim, the bridge from the tribal divisions to a unified monarchy.

SAMUEL

The two books of Samuel were originally one single book, which, for convenience, was divided in two by the Septuagint. This led to the anomaly that the name of the prophet Samuel, who is the commanding figure in the first part, no longer appears in the second part.

The first book describes the birth and youth of Samuel and his rise to the leadership of the twelve tribes, who had not as yet formed a cohesive nation. Because of continued external troubles the people demanded of Samuel to provide them with a king, which he did unwillingly and only when God asked him to yield.[25] The history of King Saul and of the rise of David to the kingship occupies the rest of the first book.

Second Samuel is devoted entirely to the reign of David, and the external and internal developments of the young state, and especially the establishment of Jerusalem as its capital. (The death of David, however, is told at the beginning of Kings.)

I and II Samuel are in effect the story of the consolidation of the tribal confederation. Until then the Philistines had been a constant threat, but after David had defeated them decisively their remaining presence at the Mediterranean seashore no longer mattered.[26]

Throughout the two books, the role of the prophet is stressed. He remains the spiritual guide of the people, and although he yields his erstwhile secular power to the king, he remains his counselor and, when needed, his severe critic. In Saul's time, Samuel himself filled this role; in David's age, it was Nathan who called the king to account.

Tradition held that Samuel authored his own book.[27] Modern scholarship, however, considers it to have been written many centuries later. The author(s), probably using the royal archives, proceeded from the belief that the fate of Israel and its rulers stood in direct relation to their religious faithfulness. Hence, Samuel (and later, Nathan) were God's representatives on earth, whose major task was to remind both people and king that God's will was supreme.

Unfortunately, the text of Samuel is often in disarray, because the book was probably neglected after the books of Chronicles appeared (which represented an idealized version of Israelite history). However, the text can often be understood by a comparison with the Septuagint, which apparently used a copy that was better preserved.[28]

On the personality and influence of the prophet Samuel, see the haftarah for Korach.

KINGS

Kings, like Samuel, was originally a single book, divided in two by the Septuagint,[29] probably for the sake of easier handling. It begins with the death of King David and the succession of Solomon to the throne. After Solomon's death the kingdom split into Israel (the north, with ten tribes), with Samaria as its capital; and Judah (the south, consisting of the tribes of Judah and Benjamin), with Jerusalem as its capital. The histories of the two kingdoms are described chronologically and end with the destruction of the Temple and of Jerusalem by the Babylonians in 587 B.C.E.[30]

The bulk of the book was most likely composed about the year 615, shortly after the religious reforms instituted by King Josiah. The last part of Kings (relating the destruction of Jerusalem) was of course written after 587. According to Jewish tradition the entire book was authored by the prophet Jeremiah.[31]

The book has a central perspective: Jewish history is judged by its acknowledgment of the God of the Covenant. The kings of Israel and Judah either did or did not do "what was right in the eyes of the Eternal One."

The haftarot chosen by the Rabbis deal with memorable moments in the history of Israel, and frequently concentrate on outstanding figures.

ISAIAH

Sixty-six chapters have come down to us as the work of Isaiah. But there is general scholarly agreement that only the first 39 chapters could possibly have been authored by the man identified in the first sentence of the book as "Isaiah son of Amoz." The verse goes on to tell exactly when the Prophet lived and worked, which was during the reign of four kings of Judah, all of them living in the 8th century B.C.E.

With chapter 40, however, the tone of the book changes dramatically. The author of chapters 1-39 lived in Judah, generations before that kingdom was destroyed; the Isaiah of chapters 40-66 preached in Babylon in the 6th century B.C.E., as an exile whose homeland lay in ruins. The "first" Isaiah warns and scolds as well as counsels the court about what lies ahead, and his tone is often joyous and confident; the "second" addresses himself to a people that are sorely bereft, and he brings them comfort and hope.

As in so many matters affecting the Tanach, this division of the book into two major parts separated by centuries is not accepted unanimously. Traditional Jews and Christians tend to hold to the idea that "Isaiah" represents one single book and one single author. To be sure, they recognize that chapters 40 and following speak clearly of Jews in exile, but they believe that these words were spoken as a prophecy of things to come.

Abraham ibn Ezra (1189-1264) doubted this long ago,[32] and for the past two hundred years most scholars have agreed that chapters 1-39 were composed by an 8th century prophet called Isaiah, and chapters 40-66 by one (or possibly two) anonymous author(s) who lived in the 6th century. We will not enter the scholarly debate about a Third (or Trito-) Isaiah, to whom chapters 56-66 are ascribed, for his prophecies closely resemble those of chapters 40-55. We therefore simply call all of chapters 40-66 "Second Isaiah."[33]

The First Isaiah

His father's name was Amoz, who is otherwise unknown to us, although a tradition recorded in the Talmud says that he was a brother of King Amaziah, the father of King Uzziah, during whose reign Isaiah began to prophesy.[34] In any case, Isaiah seems to

have been close to the court and free to speak to the king, and his critique of state poli-cies did not cause him political difficulties—at least not any of which we are aware. The Talmud, however, records a tradition that he met a violent end at the hands of King Manasseh.[35]

The Prophet lived in Jerusalem, capital of the Southern Kingdom, called Judah (the Northern being called Israel).[36] He was active during the second half of the 8th century and witnessed two wars against his own nation as well as the destruction of the Northern Kingdom by the Assyrians (722/721 B.C.E.), followed by the exile of the ten tribes, who would never again be heard from. In those troubled days he counseled against war and asserted that trust in God rather than arms would protect the Holy City from devastation.

When he heard God's summons to preach to king and people, he did not hesitate and answered, "Here am I, send me."[37] While he spoke of his nation's penchant for idolatry, he was more concerned with social justice and bitterly criticized the lifestyle of the rich. Above all, God wanted charity, compassion, and faith; without them, sacrifice was an empty rite.

God's people had a special task to perform, and when the time was right, a descen-dant of David would lead the world into an age of universal amity, peace, and justice. Even the animal kingdom would be drawn into the magic circle: "The wolf shall dwell with the lamb, the leopard lie down with the kid .... The land shall be filled with devo-tion to the Eternal, as the waters cover the sea."[38]

The essence of Isaiah's teachings has been described as follows:[39]

> an emphasis on the holiness of God;
> total reliance on God rather than on human schemes;
> Jerusalem was holy to God and therefore inviolable, and in days to come would symbolize the world's acceptance of the One God;
> still, the possibility of destruction existed, and if it occurred, a remnant of the people of Israel would remain to preserve and revitalize the ancient faith;
> ritual without a moral life is an abomination in the eyes of God;
> a king would arise under whose guidance all creation would live in permanent peace and bliss.

Isaiah was a realist. Though he was convinced of the truth of his message, he did not expect the people to follow it readily. Old habits were not easily changed, and be-cause of this so much of what he preached retains its relevance and urgency.[40]

The Second Isaiah

The man we call the Second Isaiah, who composed chapters 40-66,[41] lived during the 6th century B.C.E. in Babylon. We know nothing about his personal life. Not even his name has come down to us, so that at some time after his death (perhaps a few hundred years later) his orations, poems, and prophecies were appended to the book of the First Isaiah.

In the Near East during the 6th century, there was no single great power that dominated all others. Rome was still only a promising town, and in Greece various cities like Athens and Sparta vied for dominance. The big powers of the time (not counting China and India) were Egypt and Babylon.

The Babylonians, led by Nebuchadnezzar, had plundered Jerusalem in 597 B.C.E. and destroyed it ten years later.[42] They had carried the members of the political, religious, and intellectual classes into exile, hoping that in time they would be assimilated and that the land from which they had been forcibly separated would no longer present a political or military threat. It had worked very well for the Assyrians some 130 years before, when they had conquered the Northern Kingdom of Israel and carried the ten tribes away. The latter did not retain their national and religious identity and disappeared from history. (Many peoples in various parts of the globe have claimed descent from the ten tribes, but no such claim has ever been proven.)

Fortunately, the pattern of assimilating with the captors was not repeated by the exiled Jews from the kingdom of Judah.[43] They managed to keep alive their sense of identity and continued to practice their religion. Of course, their Temple had been destroyed, and sacrifices were no longer possible, but the exiles developed substitute rituals, with readings from the sacred texts and with newly created prayers. These became the foundations for the institution known as the synagogue.[44]

Among the spiritual leaders who urged the people not to forget their traditions and to remember the God of Israel was the unknown person we call the Second Isaiah. His theme was simple: Jews had a special relationship to God, but because of their sins the Temple had been destroyed and the nation's leaders had been exiled from their land. Still, if they would repent and return to God in sincerity they would be pardoned, for the Almighty was unfailingly merciful and forgiving.

A powerful simile was at hand, one that all could understand: the people of Israel had once before been purified by trouble and trial. They had to spend forty years in the desert before they were permitted to enter the Promised Land. So this time too: God would forgive them in due time and return them to the Land. "It is prophecy tempered with human tears, mixed with a joy that heals all scars, clearing a way for understand-

ing the future in spite of the present. No words have ever gone further in offering comfort when the sick world cries."[45]

The Second Isaiah has been called the first Hebrew monotheist, who preached that, because other gods had no reality, the Eternal One would in time be worshipped by all the nations.

Rich in imagination, he was highly innovative in his literary work. For example, he employed female imagery for the Almighty,[46] and of all the prophets he was the most poetic.

His message of consolation came at a crucial time. Not only did his people need comfort, but there was also a real hope that Israel's prayers might be answered in the near future. Hope was on the horizon at last; exile might be near its end.

For the Babylonian empire was in trouble after Nebuchadnezzar's death. A new force, the Persians and Medes, had arisen on its borders, and Cyrus, their king, had a record of dealing generously with conquered nations. Isaiah perceived Cyrus as a tool of the Almighty and an agent of divine forgiveness who would let the Jews return to their homeland.

In 539 B.C.E., Cyrus overran Babylon and indeed, not long thereafter, allowed the Jews to start their trek homeward. We cannot be certain that the Second Isaiah was still alive at that time. We know only of his orations and visions, and nothing more. We do not even know whether he himself committed his thoughts to writing. Happily, the Second Isaiah's prophecies were preserved by a grateful people, and we read far more haftarot from his book than we do from any other.

JEREMIAH

Jeremiah came from Anatot, a little town not far from Jerusalem. His life was filled with so much trial and travail, that at one point he cried out, "Cursed be the day when I was born."[47]

At the end of the 7th century B.C.E., a spirit of doom lay over the nation, which found itself squeezed by the two superpowers of the era, Egypt in the south and Babylon in the north. The kingdom of Israel had already been destroyed, and a wrong move could visit the same fate on Judah and Jerusalem.

In 605 B.C.E., Egypt was decisively defeated by the Babylonians in the battle of Carchemish on the Euphrates River. Jerusalem thus came under the rule of Nebuchadnezzar, king of the Babylonians, but the city's political leaders were not satisfied with that outcome, and in the end they brought destruction on both city and nation. In 597 the capital was plundered by the Babylonians, and ten years later, on the day commemorated by the fast of Tisha b'Av, it was razed and many of the little nation's cultural, re-

ligious, and political elite were exiled to Babylon. Jeremiah was left behind, but when Gedaliah, the governor installed by Nebuchadnezzar, was assassinated,[48] most of the Jewish remnant in the city fled to Egypt and took the Prophet with them, quite against his will. He probably died as an exile in the land of the pharaohs.

Jeremiah has left us with many references to his life.

"First of all, there is a record of the actual events as they occurred: Jeremiah put into the stocks, put into a cell, put into a muddy pit; Jeremiah dictating his sermons to his friend and secretary, Baruch; the text of the scroll cut up and burned in the presence of the king; Jeremiah dictating a larger text of his prophecy; Jeremiah buying some land in his home town of Anatot; the method by which he preserved the legal papers involved; his conversation with the general of the conquering Babylonian army; his being virtually kidnapped and taken away by the Judean refugees to Egypt."[49]

Along with these and other events in his life we learn also of his innermost feelings: he was unmarried and lonely, given to despair and depression, and loathed his endless struggles with the king and his advisers. He counseled peace and submission, while they wanted to gain an illusory independence by means of war. Jeremiah pleaded with them, yet he knew that they would not listen. He preached the need for renewing the covenant with God; they wanted nothing more than to renew the good life. He was thus, in every respect, a tragic figure.

He often considered himself a failure, yet the ages have shown that this man who put his life at risk in order to preach God's will has had an enduring influence that is felt by everyone who reads his writings.

E Z E K I E L

We know a few facts about Ezekiel: he was exiled to Babylon at the time of the first conquest of Jerusalem by Nebuchadnezzar, in 597 B.C.E.; he had his first revelation about 593, and continued his ministry until about 571. He was married, then widowed, and had no children. We do not know the year of his birth or of his death.

At some time before the final destruction of Jerusalem in 587, he may have preached in the Holy City, foretelling its doom.[50] Jewish tradition was inclined toward that view, since it considered all prophets to have received their first inspiration in the Land of Israel. Ezekiel does in fact speak of a journey back and forth from Babylon to Jerusalem, but that could have been a spiritual journey only, and not a physical one.

His book may be divided into two distinct parts, chapters 1-24 and 25-48; the former preaches the doom of Jerusalem, and the latter its future restoration.[51]

The exiles in Babylon who were his primary audience probably belonged to the upper classes whom Nebuchadnezzar had deported. Their deep concern for the fate and

future of the Holy Land had remained constant. We can easily imagine how they hung on every word he spoke, and that his mystical allusions became a subject of intense discussions.

In fact, his visions were often so complex that some modern scholars have considered the Prophet to have been mentally disturbed. But that kind of judgment tries to measure God-intoxication against the cold rational standards of everyday thinking. Certainly Ezekiel's contemporaries and the many generations who studied his work considered him an authentic figure who deserved the deepest respect, though present-day attitudes may make it difficult to appreciate his mind-set. If nothing else, Ezekiel's social and ethical concerns (which do not appear prominently in the haftarot) as well as his grand visions (like the valley of the dry bones, read on the Shabbat during Passover) are gems that defy the passing of time.

Ezekiel's rhetoric is marked by extreme metaphors, and it may be said that he pushes earlier prophetic images to their limit. Isaiah has his lips touched (see Isaiah chapter 6); Ezekiel eats a scroll. Hosea has Israel whoring after paramours; Ezekiel follows them into the bedroom and watches. Jeremiah portrays Israel's journey of sin as starting in the Holy Land; Ezekiel has it sinning already in Egypt.

Judaism saw in him a man who combined a burning concern for social justice with a strong emphasis on the need for ritual observance. "Ezekiel pioneered the principle that ritual and righteousness need not compete for the soul of the true worshipper of God."[52]

HOSEA

Hosea's name denotes "[God] has saved." He lived during the 8th century B.C.E., the same century that also produced Amos, the First Isaiah, and Micah. While Isaiah resided and preached in the Southern Kingdom (Judah, with Jerusalem as its capital), Amos and Hosea challenged the Northern Kingdom (Israel, with Samaria as its capital),[53] and Micah inveighed against both.

The middle of the 8th century was a prosperous time for both the south and the north, especially the latter, which had expanded its borders considerably. But with material affluence came moral laxity and growing paganism. Hosea, a deeply religious man, perceived that the aura of well-being that surrounded him was the forerunner of disaster. The moral fiber of the nation had decayed, and, for him, it was clear that God's judgment would come in the form of terrible punishment. Hosea looked to the northeast and beheld the rising star of Assyria, which he saw as the power that would destroy his beloved land.[54]

We know next to nothing about Hosea's background. At the beginning of his book he mentions that "the word of the Eternal came to me." But he does not speak of having had a dramatic vision, as did Isaiah and Ezekiel.[55] Instead, Hosea's career begins with a command concerning his personal life: he tells us that God asked him to marry Gomer, a promiscuous woman. Their turbulent relationship became the metaphor for much of his preaching, with Israel as God's bride who had gone astray and lusted after other gods.[56] It is not clear, however, whether Gomer was a real person whom he divorced and took back, or whether her existence was extrapolated from the metaphor.[57] In any case, Hosea is the first biblical writer who pictured Israel as God's bride.

The Prophet warns that there will be terrible consequences for this breach of marital trust. Withal, Israel's heavenly husband has never ceased to love her and only waits for some sign that she will change her ways. When she does, she will be forgiven and taken back.

The fourteen chapters of the book of Hosea are not arranged in any particular sequence and may be seen as a kind of anthology.[58] Though Amos preceded Hosea, the latter's prophecies are placed first in the sequence of the Twelve Prophets.

JOEL

The book, consisting of four chapters, is placed second in the order of the Twelve (or "Minor") Prophets. Its text gives the reader no hint of the time when it was written, nor does it contain any information about the author, except that his name was Joel son of Pethuel.

Scholars have come to widely divergent conclusions about the time of the book's composition. Some believe that the first two and last two chapters belong to different times and authors. The Sages, by inserting the prophecies between Hosea and Amos, both living in the 8th century, apparently assumed that Joel was their contemporary.

A major theme of the opening chapters is a devastating plague of locusts, which Joel uses as a metaphor of destruction sent by God. The Prophet further speaks of the "Day of the Eternal," that is, the end of days. His call to repentance has been made part of the High Holy Day liturgy and is read on Shabbat Shuvah as a haftarah together with a selection from Hosea. (This is done when Ha'azinu is the sidra for the day; but when Vayeilech is the sidra, a selection from Micah is read instead.)

The best-known verse of the book comes from 3:1 (2:28 in most translations):

Your elders shall dream dreams
and your youth shall see visions.

AMOS

Historically, Amos is the first of the literary prophets. He came from a little place called Tekoa, in Judah, and described himself as "a sheep breeder[59] and a tender of sycamore figs."[60] The Midrash compares him to Moses and suggests that his very name, Amos, meant that he was *amoos*, heavy (of tongue), a stutterer like Moses.[61]

The ministry of Amos fell in the middle of the 8th century B.C.E., which makes him an older contemporary of the First Isaiah and Micah, and preceding Hosea by about a generation.

The call he received from God bade him to preach to the Northern Kingdom, and to inveigh against the irreligious and immoral practices of its leadership. He did so with courage and in words that made people forget his speech handicap (if in fact he had one). His primary message was social justice, and in memorable metaphors or unvarnished harangues he predicted utter destruction for the nation. People that exploited the poor without remorse had incurred the wrath of God, which was sure to descend upon a wicked nation.

Yet what he said fell on deaf ears, for it was a time when the rich became richer[62] and when prosperity for the few masked the poverty of the many.

"As an expounder of the moral and ethical aspects of religion Amos is pre-eminent. He is most emphatic when denouncing the delusion that the ritual itself can have the approval of God. Society, if it is to exist, must rely on justice between man and man as well as between nations."[63]

While the Rabbis used his preachings for only two haftarot, these selections contain his major themes: social justice and God's care for all human beings. Such prophecies became the battle cry of Emancipation and found eager listeners among the Jewish reformers. For them, Amos—the first of the literary prophets—set the tone both for basic human concerns and a broad universalism.

Although we do not know when or how Amos died, his words have given him immortality.[64]

OBADIAH

The shortest prophetic book in the Tanach gives the reader no information concerning the personality of the author and his time, nor does it contain any reference to specific events that can be identified with some certainty. The Talmud says[65] that Obadiah ("servant of the Eternal") was the same person who lived at the time of the prophet Elijah, functioned as an official of King Ahab, and protected God's prophets from the persecution of Queen Jezebel. He is mentioned in the book of Kings.[66]

But the prophet Obadiah could have been a different person, who lived at a different age and, if so, most probably after the destruction of the First Temple in 587 B.C.E.

For his oracle deals with Edom as the incarnation of Israel's enemies, and this focus is generally attributed to the role the Edomites played in the ravaging of the Holy City, when they helped the Babylonians and cut off many refugees.

In this respect, Obadiah speaks very much like Jeremiah, who also inveighs against Edom.[67] In Jeremiah, however, Edom is only one of the foreign nations exposed to prophetic obloquy, while Obadiah makes Edom the only target of his condemnation and prognostication. Of course, we do not know whether the 21 verses of Obadiah were originally part of a much larger book, whose text has been lost.

Obadiah climaxes his brief oracle with his prophecy of the Day of the Eternal that will judge Edom even as it will justify and glorify Israel.

J O N A H

This familiar book, read in all synagogues on Yom Kippur afternoon, actually contains only a few words of prophecy, which Jonah speaks to the inhabitants of Nineveh: "Forty days more, and Nineveh shall be overthrown!"[68] Beyond this proclamation, the book is the story of Jonah son of Amittai: how God asked him to prophesy to the wicked city of Nineveh; how Jonah tried to evade the charge and failed in his attempt; and how in the end he does God's bidding, but only reluctantly and petulantly. The book ends with a question posed by God.

Who was Jonah? Elsewhere the Tanach mentions a prophet by that name who lived in the 8th century B.C.E.,[69] and probably for that reason the book was included in the prophetic part of the biblical canon. However, we do not know whether this was the person of whom our book tells. In fact, despite its easy-to-read, straightforward story, there is wide disagreement about when and how the book was composed; whether it describes a historical event or is religious fiction; whether there was one author or whether we have before us a basic document with a number of additions.

As our commentary will point out, it is also not fully clear just what the main purpose of the story is, and this uncertainty makes it impossible to fix the date of the book's composition. Most likely it was after the year 612 B.C.E., when Nineveh was destroyed, for in Jonah 3:3 we read that Nineveh *was* an enormously large city— evidently describing the past. Many scholars put the time of the book's creation several centuries after this event.

xlii

MICAH

The name is probably a shortened form of Micaiah, "who is like the Eternal."[70] The Prophet was active in the last part of the 8th century and was a contemporary of the First Isaiah.

He was from a little place called Moreshet, in the foothills of the Judean mountains. In a crucial moment of his life he felt impelled to go to Jerusalem, where his outspoken prophecies earned him the enmity of the establishment.[71]

Two sayings of the Prophet are among the most often quoted passages in the Tanach:

[God] has told you, O mortal, what is good,
and what the Eternal requires of you—
Only this: to do justly,
and love mercy,
and walk humbly with your God.[72]

The other passage (almost identical with one appearing in Isaiah[73]) speaks of days to come when many nations shall worship at God's Mountain:

For from Zion shall go forth Torah,
And the word of the Eternal from Jerusalem.[74]

The text goes on to speak of a time when swords will be beaten into plowshares and spears into pruning hooks, and universal peace will reign. The passage ends:

Though all peoples may walk in the names of their gods,
We will walk in the name of the Eternal our God
Forever and ever.[75]

HABAKKUK

We know the Prophet only through his brief three chapters (56 verses), which reveal virtually nothing about his life and times. His name seems to have been derived from an Akkadian (Assyro-Babylonian) word, *hambakuku* (a flower), but Jewish tradition connected it to the root חבק (*ch-b-k*, embrace) and considered Habakkuk to have been the Shunammite woman's child whom Elisha revived.[76]

Ancient Jewish sources about Habakkuk differ widely. The historian Flavius Josephus says that he ministered during the reign of King Jotham (8th century),[77] while one midrash assigns him to the time of King Manasseh (7th century),[78] and another suggests that he belonged to those who comforted Jerusalem after its destruction.[79] Modern scholars believe that the last-named theory comes closest to the likely date of his prophecies, which places his ministry just before the destruction of the Temple in 587 B.C.E.

But all of this is conjecture, and the problem is exacerbated by a find that was made in 1947-1948 in a cave at the Dead Sea. It contained two chapters of Habakkuk with a commentary, but chapter 3 of the book was missing—even though the scroll was rolled in such a way that the chapter could not have been accidentally detached. Therefore, many scholars concluded that this chapter (which forms the haftarah for the second day of Shavuot) was authored by someone else. Still, the style and content of chapter 3 imply that it could have been from the same hand as chapters 1 and 2, and the issue remains unresolved.

Whatever its origins, this little book raises questions of belief. Chapters 1 and 2 wonder about God's presence in history, and chapter 3 is a poem of faith, in which the Prophet proclaims that, despite his low material fortunes, he will delight and rejoice in God.

This accords with his most often cited statement, "The righteous shall live by their faith."[80] In a talmudic discussion this formulation of trust was considered the best condensation of Jewish religious teaching.[81]

ZECHARIAH

The exiles who returned home from Babylon in 538 B.C.E. began plans for rebuilding the Temple, but adverse economic and political conditions delayed the project. Nothing happened until two prophets, Haggai and Zechariah, passionately pleaded with the people to continue and complete the building. Zechariah (his name means "the Eternal has remembered") was active between 520 and 518, and the sacred task was at last taken up again and finished in 516-515.

"Haggai and Zechariah ... must be given enormous credit for using their prophetic ministries to foster the transition of a people from national autonomy to an existence which transcended political definition and which centered upon a view of God and his moral demands."[82]

We know nothing about the personal life of the Prophet, except that he was the son of Berachiah and the grandson of Iddo.[83] We have only the book that goes under his name, and it happens to be one of the most difficult in the Tanach. Rashi and Ibn Ezra long ago noted its problems, which are exacerbated by a clearly visible difference between the first eight chapters and the last six. It appears to many scholars that chapters 1-8 are by one person (called First or Proto-Zechariah) and 9-14 by another (called Second or Deutero-Zechariah).[84] The former relate eight visions suffused with angels and other rich symbolism, with ethical pronouncements and a spirit of hope. These chapters also take note of the two most important personages of Yehud,[85] the high priest Joshua and the governor Zerubbabel, a descendant of the House of David.

Chapters 9-14 lack most of these features. Instead, they contain a series of pronouncements against other nations and prophecies about the end of days. The Temple is not mentioned (probably because it was already completed); and where the First Zechariah extols the governor, the Second Zechariah heavily criticizes him. The fact that Greece (*yavan*) is mentioned suggests that this portion of the book was written after the time of Alexander the Great (died 323 B.C.E.).

But the controversy has not been fully resolved, and there is a renewed tendency to see the two parts of the book as having a closer relation than was previously assumed.[86]

MALACHI

Malachi stands at the end of the prophetic books in the Tanach, and tradition held that after him prophecy ceased in Israel.[87] He thus represents a watershed in the development of Judaism: until then, God would speak to selected individuals and charge them with a mission to exhort and predict. But from then on, humans and not God would identify the truth. They would be called *sof'rim* (scribes) at first, because they belonged to those who guarded the literary tradition of the people, and later were known as *rabbanim* (rabbis), whose primary function was to teach and elucidate God's law.

We do not know Malachi's identity; the name simply means "My (that is, God's) Messenger," although some ancient sources identified him as Ezra and others as Mordecai. The whole spirit of the book suggests that the Temple had been rebuilt (516-515 B.C.E.). Yet it also suggests the disappearance of the enthusiasm shown during the building. Malachi describes a priesthood that is forgetful of its duties, a Temple that is underfunded because the people have lost interest in it, and a society in which Jewish men divorce their Jewish wives to marry out of the faith. The Prophet lived probably sometime after the year 500, perhaps as late as 450. It was an era of spiritual disillusionment, for the glorious age that earlier prophets had foreseen had not materialized.

Malachi urges his contemporaries to engage in a religious revival. Remember God and Torah, he tells them; make the Temple once again a center of your affection and attention; and purify your family life. The very last lines of his book speak of the "great day" that will bring reconciliation between the generations—and with this old-and-modern challenge he leaves us (see the haftarah for Shabbat Hagadol).

Notes

[1] We never call the book "Old Testament," a Christian term that contrasts the Tanach with the "New Testament," which was meant to denote that the former was fulfilled and superseded by the latter. Instead of "New Testament" we use "Christian Scriptures."

[2] Because of its length, Jonah has been commented upon only to a limited extent.

[3] Details in Ismar Elbogen, *Jewish Liturgy,* p.145.

[4] Acts 13:15.

[5] Also referred to as the Rabbis (with a capital R).

[6] We use this word (סדרה) for "Torah portion."

[7] Differences also exist in Italian and Yemenite traditions, but this book does not take special note of them.

[8] Traditional synagogues require ten men (a *minyan*) for a reading from the scroll; without the minyan, the reading takes place from a printed book. Reform synagogues vary in this respect.

[9] Non-Jewish editions of the biblical books follow various other arrangements.

[10] The Song of Deborah and Barak (Judges 5); the Prayer of Hannah (I Samuel 2); a few fragments of Samuel's sayings (I Samuel 15); the prayer of David (II Samuel 22); and the prayer of Solomon (I Kings 8).

[11] Yeshayahu Leibowitz, "No Guarantees," *Jerusalem Report*, August 11, 1994, p. 36. "They prophesied what should be, but we were evidently not fit to have these promises fulfilled."

[12] See Deuteronomy chapter 13.

[13] Other terms are רואה (*ro-eh*) and חוזה (*chozeh*), both meaning "seer."

[14] A word from the Greek denoting seventy. According to the pseudo-historical *Letter of Aristeas*, the king of Egypt brought 72 Jewish scholars to Alexandria during the 3rd century B.C.E. to create a biblical text in the Greek language.

[15] Harry Rasky, introduction to his film "Prophecy" (Toronto, December 1, 1994).

[16] *Understanding the Prophets,* p. 40.

[17] *The Prophets*, p. 3. According to M. A. Cohen, much of prophetic teaching could be called revolutionary; see his article "The Prophets as Revolutionaries—A Sociopolitical Analysis," *Biblical Archaeology Review*, May/June 1979, pp. 12-19.

[18] With the exception of the Additional Readings provided in this volume, some of which are taken from the third part of the Tanach.

[19] See Bibliography; it is referred to as "the Torah Commentary." Although the present commentary stands on its own, frequent reference will be made to relevant sections of the Torah Commentary.

[20] Historians differ on these dates; some put them much earlier. Others believe the whole book, including the personality of Joshua, to be later reconstructions of history.

[21] *B. Baba Batra* 14b-15a.

[22] In his *Introduction to the Early Prophets.*

[23] So the last verse of Genesis.

[24] The book of Ruth begins with the words, "In the days of the Judges ...." While the Talmud (*B. Baba Batra* 14b) assigns it a separate place in the third section of the Tanach (*K'tuvim*), Josephus reports that it was attached to Judges (*Contra Apion*, I:39). In non-Jewish editions of the Tanach, Ruth follows Judges.

[25] This subject was extensively explored by David Polish in his book *Give Us a King.*

[26] See the haftarah for Ha'azinu, which brings us David's thanksgiving prayer for the security he and his nation were then enjoying.

[27] *B. Baba Batra* 14b; according to one version, he also composed Judges.

[28] Among the Dead Sea Scrolls are Samuel fragments, which bear out the reliability of the Septuagint.

[29] See note 14.

[30] This is the currently accepted dating of the event; formerly it was generally believed to have happened a year later, in 586 (a date that the Torah Commentary adopted).

[31] *B. Baba Batra* 15a.

[32] In his commentary on chapter 40, where he says guardedly: הַמֵּבִין יָבִין, "The wise will understand."

[33] Among the reasons for assigning chapters 56-66 to a "third" Isaiah is the polemic in chapter 66 (haftarah for Shabbat Rosh Chodesh); see there for details.

[34] *B. Megillah* 10b.

[35] *B. Yevamot* 49b; *J. Sanhedrin* 10:2, 28c.

[36] "Israel" thus may refer to the Northern Kingdom, but it also describes the Jewish people as a whole. The context should make clear which of the two is meant.

[37] 6:8.

[38] 11:6, 9. It is noteworthy that this famous chapter is not included among the haftarot read in Israel, and is used in the Diaspora only on the 8th day of Pesach. The reason is probably that, when the selections were finalized by the Rabbis, the Christian schism had already occurred, and the new religion relied heavily on chapter 11 as a prediction of Jesus. The same is true for the 53rd chapter in the book, which was also excluded from the haftarot, no doubt for the same reason.

[39] Theodore Friedman, *Encyclopaedia Judaica*, vol. 9, col. 48.

[40] See also Solomon B. Freehof's commentary in his *Book of Isaiah*, pp. 9-13.

[41] Also called Deutero-Isaiah, from the Greek *deuteros*, meaning "second." (A similar term is used for the fifth book of the Torah, "Deuteronomy," literally, "the Second

Law," so called because the book contains many repetitions of the rest of the Torah.) About assigning chapters 56-66 to a Third (or Trito-) Isaiah, see our discussion under the heading "Isaiah," p. xxiv.

[42] Recent scholarship suggests that the older counting of 596 should be corrected to read 597.

[43] They were not yet called Jews, but for brevity's sake we will call them that.

[44] They did adopt some Babylonian customs. For instance, they began calling the months of the year by Babylonian names, and to this day the Jewish calendar uses Babylonian names rather than the older ones mentioned in the Torah. Thus, Tammuz is one of our summer months, even though that name goes back to a (now long forgotten) Babylonian deity. Also, the square Hebrew script we use today is still called "Assyrian"; and Aramaic, prevalent in much of the Near East, became the people's language and remained so even after they returned to their homeland.

[45] Abraham J. Heschel, *The Prophets*, p. 145.

[46] See the haftarah for B'reishit, with the notes on Isaiah 42:14.

[47] 20:14.

[48] This happened on the 3rd day of Tishri, which to this day is observed as a fast day by Orthodox Jews.

[49] Freehof, *Book of Jeremiah*, p. 9.

[50] See chapters 8 and 11.

[51] Some scholars consider chapters 25-32 a separate section, because they are prophecies against other nations; and still others have made more radical suggestions.

[52] Freehof, *Book of Ezekiel*, p.11.

[53] Its Hebrew name was Shomron.

[54] This would happen in 721, at which time Hosea was probably no longer alive. After the Assyrians razed Samaria, the city remained a ruin for centuries, until Herod rebuilt it in 25 B.C.E. and renamed it Sebaste.

[55] Isaiah chapter 6; Ezekiel chapter 1.

[56] The metaphor of the faithful husband and the unfaithful wife is also a commentary on male/female relationships during his time: unfaithfulness was identified with the female sex, while loyalty and steadfastness were identified with the male.

[57] On this problem, see H. L. Ginsberg in *Encyclopaedia Judaica*, vol. 8, pp. 1010-1024.

[58] So Andersen and Freedman, in *Anchor Bible Series*, p. 52.

[59] The Hebrew says he was a בוֹקֵר (*boker*, cattle breeder), but a better reading, with the Septuagint, is נוֹקֵד (*noked*, sheep breeder), which accords with the very first verse in the book, where he is described to have been one of the נוֹקְדִים (*nok'dim*), a word paralleled

by the Akkadian *naqidu* (shepherd) and reflected in the Arabic *nakad*, which describes small sheep with rich wool.

[60] Amos 7:14. But no sycamores grow in the area; they are found in the north. In fact, there was a Tekoa in the Galilee as well. Radak was the first to locate the Prophet exclusively in the Northern Kingdom.

[61] Leviticus Rabbah 10:2.

[62] Their wealth has been affirmed by archaeological finds in Samaria.

[63] S. M. Lehrman, *Soncino Bible*, The Twelve Prophets, p. 81.

[64] The young Reform movement in the 19th and 20th centuries C.E. embraced the teachings of Amos with special fervor. He became the inspiration for the movement's continuing dedication to social justice.

[65] *B. Sanhedrin* 39b.

[66] I Kings 18; haftarah for Ki Tissa. "Obadiah" may not have been the name of the prophet, but instead the description of the prophet, much as "Malachi" may be either a personal name or mean "My Messenger" (see haftarah for Tol'dot).

[67] Jeremiah 49:7 ff.

[68] Jonah 3:4; the prophecy consists of only five words in Hebrew.

[69] II Kings 14:25.

[70] An earlier prophet bore the full name Micaiah; he lived at the time of King Ahab (early 9th century B.C.E.; I Kings 22).

[71] However, King Hezekiah was so impressed with Micah's warnings that he implored God to avert disaster from his country. See haftarah for Balak. Jeremiah 26:18 makes reference to his influence.

[72] Micah 6:8.

[73] Isaiah 2:2-4.

[74] Micah 4:2. This saying has been made part of the synagogue's Torah service.

[75] Micah 4:5.

[76] II Kings 4:16; see *Zohar* B'shalach, 1:7, 2:44. An apocryphal fragment, *Bel and the Dragon*, tells of Habakkuk helping Daniel who was in a pit with seven lions (verses 33 ff.). See also the haftarah for Vayeira.

[77] *Antiquities* IX 11:3.

[78] *Seder Olam* 20.

[79] Pesikta deRav Kahana 16:8, translated by W. G. Braude and I. J. Kapstein, p. 296.

[80] 2:4.

[81] *B. Makkot* 23b-24a. It is also worth noting that the last verse of chapter 2 was the theme of a popular English hymn, familiar to worshippers in Reform temples a genera-

tion ago: "God is in His holy temple; earthly thoughts be silent now ...." The composer was H. W. Hawkes (*Union Hymnal*, p. 4).

[82] C. Meyers, *Haggai, Zechariah 1-8*, in *Anchor Bible Series*, p. xliii.

[83] Ezra 5:1 and 6:14 list him as the son of Iddo, which may be a different tradition or, more likely, the frequent habit of the ancients to list someone as the "son" (meaning descendant) of a well-known person.

[84] The controversy may be compared to that surrounding the 66 chapters of Isaiah (see our discussion of Isaiah).

[85] The Aramaic name by which the province of the former Judah was known. It was part of one of the Persian satrapies (Ever Nahara, beyond the river)

[86] Brevard S. Childs, *Introduction to the Old Testament as Scripture*, pp. 484-486, stresses that joining these two dissimilar segments into one book would affect the interpretation of both.

[87] *B. Yoma 9b.*

THE
HAFTARAH
COMMENTARY

בראשית

Isaiah, chapter 42, verse 5 to chapter 43, verse 11
Introduction

Connection of haftarah and sidra:
The weekly Torah portion opens the annual cycle of biblical readings. It begins with God's creation of the world, climaxing in the creation of humanity. The haftarah too opens with this theme. It reminds us that the same God who brought heaven and earth into being is also the One who created the people of Israel, to be a "covenant people, a light to the nations."

The setting:
The Prophet and his people had for decades been exiles in Babylon (6th century B.C.E.). They desperately wanted to return to their homeland and wondered whether it would ever happen. With the defeat of the Babylonians by the Persians and Medes, there was new hope among the exiles that their release might be at hand, and the Prophet strongly reinforced this hope and gave it a theological frame.

For more on Second Isaiah, his life and time, see our *General Introduction.*

The message:
1. By linking Israel's birth to that of the universe, Isaiah stresses Israel's importance to the world. Being God's partner means special responsibilities as well as opportunities. At all times the people must testify to God's greatness and be ready to "sing a new song to the Eternal." (42:5-12)
2. But because Israel was not true to the Covenant, it suffered exile from its land. The Prophet challenges his people by asking whether they are ready to change: "Who among you will listen to this?" (42:13-25)
3. God is our hope, and this hope will not be disappointed. Therefore, "have no fear, for I will redeem you." (43:1-10)

1

42:5. Thus says the Eternal God,

the One who created the heavens and stretched them out,

who made the earth

and all that grows in it,

who gives breath to its people

and spirit to all who walk on it:

6. I, the Eternal, have called you in righteousness,

and taken you by the hand.

I am the One who created you

and made you a covenant people,

a light to the nations:

7. to open eyes that are blind,

to bring the captive out of confinement,

those who sit in darkness,

out of the dungeon,

8. I am the Eternal—that is My name.

I will not share My glory with another,

My praise with idols.

כֹּה־אָמַ֞ר הָאֵ֣ל ׀ יְהֹוָ֗ה 42:5

בּוֹרֵ֤א הַשָּׁמַ֙יִם֙ וְנ֣וֹטֵיהֶ֔ם

רֹקַ֥ע הָאָ֖רֶץ וְצֶאֱצָאֶ֑יהָ

נֹתֵ֤ן נְשָׁמָה֙ לָעָ֣ם עָלֶ֔יהָ

וְר֖וּחַ לַהֹלְכִ֥ים בָּֽהּ׃

6 אֲנִ֧י יְהֹוָ֛ה קְרָאתִ֥יךָֽ בְצֶ֖דֶק

וְאַחְזֵ֣ק בְּיָדֶ֑ךָ

וְאֶצׇּרְךָ֗

וְאֶתֶּנְךָ֛ לִבְרִ֥ית עָ֖ם

לְא֥וֹר גּוֹיִֽם׃

7 לִפְקֹ֖חַ עֵינַ֣יִם עִוְר֑וֹת

לְהוֹצִ֤יא מִמַּסְגֵּר֙ אַסִּ֔יר

מִבֵּ֥ית כֶּ֖לֶא יֹ֥שְׁבֵי חֹֽשֶׁךְ׃

8 אֲנִ֥י יְהֹוָ֖ה ה֣וּא שְׁמִ֑י

וּכְבוֹדִי֙ לְאַחֵ֣ר לֹֽא־אֶתֵּ֔ן

וּתְהִלָּתִ֖י לַפְּסִילִֽים׃

Commentary

5. *Thus says the Eternal God.* The Prophet is certain that God's voice speaks through him (see our *General Introduction*).

6. *Covenant people.* Our translation reads the Hebrew as if it read עם ברית (*am b'rith*), with *am* meaning Israel, who will lead everyone on earth to a covenant with God.[1] But since the order in the text is ברית עם (*b'rith am*, literally "covenant of people"), some understand *am* to refer to humanity as a whole, which provides the meaning: "I have appointed you [Israel] to provide a covenant for humanity, a light to the nations."[2]

A light to the nations. See the essay below. Rashi believes that the charge is addressed to Isaiah himself: he is to lead the nations to see the divine light.

7. *To open eyes that are blind.* From lack of light in the dungeon of despair where the people dwell. (The dungeon was also very real for some; thus, King Jehoiachin was jailed for thirty-seven years.)[3]

8. *That is My name.* The name by which God revealed the Divine Presence to Moses (see Exodus 3:15).[4]

2

9. My earlier promises have come to pass,

and now I tell you new things;

before they appear, I tell you of them.

10. Sing a new song to the Eternal;

sing God's praise, all the earth.

Let the sea roar and all it contains,

you islands and all who live there!

11. Let the wilderness and its towns re-

joice,

and villagers of Kedar in their settlements;

let those who live in Sela sing out,

and shout from the mountaintops!

12. Let them give honor to the Eternal,

and praise God in the islands.

13. The Eternal goes out like a warrior,

like a soldier in fury ready for battle;

shouting and roaring, to prevail over the

foe.

14. Long enough have I held My peace;

I have kept still and held Myself back;

now, I cry out like a woman in labor;

I pant and I gasp.

9 הָרִאשֹׁנוֹת הִנֵּה־בָאוּ

וַחֲדָשׁוֹת אֲנִי מַגִּיד

בְּטֶרֶם תִּצְמַחְנָה אַשְׁמִיע אֶתְכֶם:

10 שִׁירוּ לַיהוָה שִׁיר חָדָשׁ

תְּהִלָּתוֹ מִקְצֵה הָאָרֶץ

יוֹרְדֵי הַיָּם וּמְלֹאוֹ

אִיִּים וְיֹשְׁבֵיהֶם:

11 יִשְׂאוּ מִדְבָּר וְעָרָיו

חֲצֵרִים תֵּשֵׁב קֵדָר

יָרֹנּוּ יֹשְׁבֵי סֶלַע

מֵרֹאשׁ הָרִים יִצְוָחוּ:

12 יָשִׂימוּ לַיהוָה כָּבוֹד

וּתְהִלָּתוֹ בָּאִיִּים יַגִּידוּ:

13 יְהוָה כַּגִּבּוֹר יֵצֵא

כְּאִישׁ מִלְחָמוֹת יָעִיר קִנְאָה

יָרִיע אַף־יַצְרִיחַ עַל־אֹיְבָיו יִתְגַּבָּר:

14 הֶחֱשֵׁיתִי מֵעוֹלָם

אַחֲרִישׁ אֶתְאַפָּק

כַּיּוֹלֵדָה אֶפְעֶה

אֶשֹּׁם וְאֶשְׁאַף יָחַד:

Commentary

10. *Let the sea roar.* Reading ירעם (*yir'am*) instead of יורדי (*yordei*). The emendation preserves the parallel structure of the prophecy, and that is the way Psalm 98:7 also has it.[5]

11. *Kedar ... Sela.* Even people living in these places (which are located outside of Judah's borders) will hear of it and marvel.

13. *The Eternal ... like a warrior.* Here and in subsequent verses, God's power is depicted in highly anthropomorphic terms. While this kind of language was quite acceptable in ancient times, it jars the modern ear.[6] The meaning is clear: God must not be trifled with.

14. *I cry out like a woman in labor.* One of the Prophet's distinguishing characteristics is his employment of female imagery for God.[7] (See also under *Gleanings*.)

15. I will destroy mountains and hills,
dry up their grass and their trees;
I will turn the riverbeds into desert-land,
and empty their pools of water.

16. I will lead the blind by roads they do
not know,
and guide them along roads they have not
traveled.
I will turn their darkness into light,
and make straight their twisting ways.
These things will I do; I will not forgo them.

17. All who trust in idols
and call metal things their gods
shall fall back in shame.

18. Listen, you deaf ones! You sightless,
look and see!

19. Who is as blind as My servant,
as deaf as My own messenger?
Who is as blind as the one whose heart is
whole,
as blind as the servant of the Eternal?

20. Seeing a lot, you notice naught;
your ears are open, yet you do not hear.

21. The Eternal delights,
for righteousness' sake,
to make the Teaching glorious and great.

22. But now this people has been plundered and despoiled,
trapped in holes, all of them,
and immured in dungeons.

אַחֲרִיב הָרִים וּגְבָעֹות 15
וְכָל־עֶשְׂבָּם אֹובִישׁ
וְשַׂמְתִּי נְהָרֹות לָאִיִּים
וַאֲגַמִּים אֹובִישׁ:

וְהֹולַכְתִּי עִוְרִים בְּדֶרֶךְ לֹא יָדָעוּ 16
בִּנְתִיבֹות לֹא־יָדְעוּ אַדְרִיכֵם
אָשִׂים מַחְשָׁךְ לִפְנֵיהֶם לָאֹור
וּמַעֲקַשִּׁים לְמִישֹׁור
אֵלֶּה הַדְּבָרִים עֲשִׂיתִם וְלֹא עֲזַבְתִּים:

נָסֹגוּ אָחֹור יֵבֹשׁוּ בֹשֶׁת הַבֹּטְחִים בַּפָּסֶל 17
הָאֹמְרִים לְמַסֵּכָה אַתֶּם אֱלֹהֵינוּ:

הַחֵרְשִׁים שְׁמָעוּ וְהַעִוְרִים 18
הַבִּיטוּ לִרְאֹות:

מִי עִוֵּר כִּי אִם־עַבְדִּי 19
וְחֵרֵשׁ כְּמַלְאָכִי אֶשְׁלָח
מִי עִוֵּר כִּמְשֻׁלָּם
וְעִוֵּר כְּעֶבֶד יְהוָה:

רָאִיתָ [רָאֹות] רַבֹּות וְלֹא תִשְׁמֹר 20
פָּקֹוחַ אָזְנַיִם וְלֹא יִשְׁמָע:

יְהוָה חָפֵץ 21
לְמַעַן צִדְקֹו
יַגְדִּיל תֹּורָה וְיַאְדִּיר:

וְהוּא עַם־בָּזוּז וְשָׁסוּי 22
הָפֵחַ בַּחוּרִים כֻּלָּם
וּבְבָתֵּי כְלָאִים הָחְבָּאוּ

Commentary

19. *Whose heart is whole.* משלם (*meshullam*). The meaning is uncertain; perhaps it is a proper name. Our translation suggests that the word is used paradoxically.

20. *You do not hear.* Construing the 3rd person ישמע (*yishma*) as though it were the 2nd person תשמע (*tishma*).

4

They are spoil, and no one comes to save
   them;

they are plundered, and no one says: Give
   it back.

23. Who among you will listen to this?

Who, listening, will take heed for the time
   to come?

24. Who allowed Jacob to be plundered?

Who gave Israel to the despoilers?

It was none other than the Eternal,

against whom they sinned,

in whose ways they would not walk,

to whose Teaching they would not listen!

25. Therefore God poured out on them

venomous wrath and violent war.

It burned all around them,

and they failed to understand;

it scorched them,

yet they did not take it to heart.

43:1. Now thus says the Eternal One,

your Creator, O Jacob; your Maker,
   O Israel:

Have no fear, for I will redeem you;

I have called you by name, you are Mine.

2. When you pass through the waters, I am
   with you;

when you pass through the rivers, they
   shall not overwhelm you;

הָיוּ לָבַז וְאֵין מַצִּיל

מְשִׁסָּה וְאֵין־אֹמֵר הָשַׁב׃

23 מִי בָכֶם יַאֲזִין זֹאת

יַקְשֵׁב וְיִשְׁמַע לְאָחוֹר׃

24 מִי־נָתַן לִמְשׁוֹסָה [לִמְשִׁסָּה] יַעֲקֹב

וְיִשְׂרָאֵל לְבֹזְזִים

הֲלוֹא יְהֹוָה

זוּ חָטָאנוּ לוֹ

וְלֹא־אָבוּ בִדְרָכָיו הָלוֹךְ

וְלֹא שָׁמְעוּ בְּתוֹרָתוֹ׃

25 וַיִּשְׁפֹּךְ עָלָיו חֵמָה אַפּוֹ

וֶעֱזוּז מִלְחָמָה

וַתְּלַהֲטֵהוּ מִסָּבִיב

וְלֹא יָדָע

וַתִּבְעַר־בּוֹ

וְלֹא־יָשִׂים עַל־לֵב׃

43:1 וְעַתָּה כֹּה־אָמַר יְהֹוָה

בֹּרַאֲךָ יַעֲקֹב וְיֹצֶרְךָ יִשְׂרָאֵל

אַל־תִּירָא כִּי גְאַלְתִּיךָ

קָרָאתִי בְשִׁמְךָ לִי־אָתָּה׃

2 כִּי־תַעֲבֹר בַּמַּיִם אִתְּךָ־אָנִי

וּבַנְּהָרוֹת לֹא יִשְׁטְפוּךָ

Commentary

24. *Jacob ... Israel*. Jacob was given the name Israel after he had struggled with the divine messenger.[8]

25. *Venomous wrath*. Literally, "His venomous wrath."

43:1. *Now*. After having subjected Israel to dire punishments, God now turns to it in mercy and will redeem the captives.[9]

when you walk through fire, you shall not
   be scorched,
the flame shall not consume you.

3. For I, the Eternal, am your God, the
   Holy One of Israel, your Deliverer.
I give Egypt as ransom for you,
Ethiopia and Saba in exchange for you.

4. Because you are precious to Me, and
   honored, and I love you,
I give up peoples and nations in exchange
   for your life.

5. Have no fear, for I am with you;
I will bring your offspring from the east,
I will gather you in from the west;

6. to the north I will say: Give back!
and to the south: Do not hold back!
Bring My sons from afar,
My daughters from the ends of the earth—

7. all who are called by My name,
whom I created for My glory,
whom I formed and made—

כִּי־תֵלֵךְ בְּמוֹ־אֵשׁ לֹא תִכָּוֶה
וְלֶהָבָה לֹא תִבְעַר־בָּךְ:
3 כִּי אֲנִי יְהוָה אֱלֹהֶיךָ קְדוֹשׁ יִשְׂרָאֵל
מוֹשִׁיעֶךָ
נָתַתִּי כָפְרְךָ מִצְרַיִם
כּוּשׁ וּסְבָא תַּחְתֶּיךָ:
4 מֵאֲשֶׁר יָקַרְתָּ בְעֵינַי נִכְבַּדְתָּ וַאֲנִי אֲהַבְתִּיךָ
וְאֶתֵּן אָדָם תַּחְתֶּיךָ
וּלְאֻמִּים תַּחַת נַפְשֶׁךָ:
5 אַל־תִּירָא כִּי אִתְּךָ־אָנִי
מִמִּזְרָח אָבִיא זַרְעֶךָ
וּמִמַּעֲרָב אֲקַבְּצֶךָּ:
6 אֹמַר לַצָּפוֹן תֵּנִי
וּלְתֵימָן אַל־תִּכְלָאִי
הָבִיאִי בָנַי מֵרָחוֹק
וּבְנוֹתַי מִקְצֵה הָאָרֶץ:
7 כֹּל הַנִּקְרָא בִשְׁמִי
וְלִכְבוֹדִי בְּרָאתִיו
יְצַרְתִּיו אַף־עֲשִׂיתִיו:

Commentary

3. *Egypt ... Ethiopia ... Saba*. Isaiah (speaking in God's name) sees the restoration of Israel to its homeland as a territorial sacrifice that the Persians will make, but they will be compensated by lands they will conquer in North Africa and elsewhere, a theme that is carried forward in verse 4.[10] Ezekiel, in 29:17-20, makes a prediction similar to that of Isaiah.

Saba. Its identity is much in doubt; recent archaeological investigations suggest that it was the area of Yemen, in southern Arabia.

6. *South*. תימן (*teiman*), one of the three biblical expressions for the south (the others are *darom* and *negev*). The word is connected with ימין (*yamin*, right), for when one faces east (toward the rising sun), the south is at one's right.

8. bring forth this people,

[once} blind, who [now] have eyes;

[once] deaf, who [now] have ears.

9. Let all the nations come together,

let all the peoples assemble:

who among them can explain this,

who foretold this to us?

Let them bring witnesses and be proved
    right,

that all may say: It is true!

10. You are *My* witnesses, says the Eternal
    One,

My servant whom I have chosen;

know Me, therefore, and put your trust in
    Me;

understand that I am the One.

Before Me no god was formed,

and after Me none shall be.

11. Be sure that I am the Eternal [God],

and I alone can deliver you.

8 הוֹצִיא עַם־עִוֵּר

וְעֵינַיִם יֵשׁ

וְחֵרְשִׁים וְאָזְנַיִם לָמוֹ:

9 כָּל־הַגּוֹיִם נִקְבְּצוּ יַחְדָּו

וְיֵאָסְפוּ לְאֻמִּים

מִי בָהֶם יַגִּיד זֹאת

וְרִאשֹׁנוֹת יַשְׁמִיעֻנוּ

יִתְּנוּ עֵדֵיהֶם וְיִצְדָּקוּ

וְיִשְׁמְעוּ וְיֹאמְרוּ אֱמֶת:

10 אַתֶּם עֵדַי נְאֻם־יְהֹוָה

וְעַבְדִּי אֲשֶׁר בָּחָרְתִּי

לְמַעַן תֵּדְעוּ וְתַאֲמִינוּ לִי

וְתָבִינוּ כִּי־אֲנִי הוּא

לְפָנַי לֹא־נוֹצַר אֵל

וְאַחֲרַי לֹא יִהְיֶה:

11 אָנֹכִי אָנֹכִי יְהֹוָה

וְאֵין מִבַּלְעָדַי מוֹשִׁיעַ:

Commentary

9. *It is true!* An ironic challenge: If there are any human beings who foretold all this and can testify to the reality of their gods, let them come forward and prove their case, so that all the nations might agree and say *emet*, "It is true." But of course they cannot bring proof, and verse 10 affirms in ringing language that now Israel, God's own witness, will testify.

10. *You are My witnesses.* See the essay on p. 8.

7

Essays

"A light to the nations" (42:6)

This oft-quoted expression is generally understood to mean that God has created Israel to be a light to humanity, a messenger of good tidings, who will lead the world to acknowledge the One God and thereby guide it to unity, peace, and justice.

This is a daunting task, and for some centuries prior to and during the rise of Christianity, Jews were indeed actively engaged in bringing their religion to pagan nations. Many thousands were converted at that time or became sympathizers, some of them belonging to the leadership of the Roman empire. Christianity's missionary efforts were greatly aided by the presence of these enclaves of new Jews around the Mediterranean Sea, who formed the springboard for the expansion of the nascent Christian-Jewish sect. The Romans thereupon prohibited these efforts, and in later centuries, when Christians had achieved dominance in Europe, the Church too forbade Jews, on pain of death, to conduct missionary activities.[11] In time Jewish tradition stayed away from any conversionary efforts, and in effect discouraged all conversions.

A change occurred in the 19th century, when Reform Judaism elevated the message of Isaiah to one of its central teachings: Jews were chosen by God to bring the divine light into the world, and their dispersion gave them a wonderful opportunity to let this light shine upon all nations. It was, in fact, a view already expressed in rabbinic literature.[12] Judaism had much to give, and carrying out the prophetic task became a modern challenge.

Reform leaders, in fact, from time to time have called for an active renewal of missionary efforts, but so far without noticeable effect. (See also under *Gleanings*.)

"You are My witnesses" (43:10)

The idea that Israel is to be a witness to God's reality and goodness is closely related to the task of being a light to the nations. For how was this noble goal to be achieved? Not by missionary effort, but only by Israel being true to the Covenant and becoming an example to the gentiles. Jews who themselves live up to the high ideals of Judaism will encourage others to follow the path of Torah and thus move humanity closer to the messianic age.

A rabbinic saying captures the significance of witnessing to God in a memorable, if extravagant, way. It interprets the verse as meaning: "If you are My witnesses I am God; but if you are not My witnesses, then (if this were possible) I would not be God."[13]

However, with religious convictions weakening, many Jews have become uncomfortable with the idea that they were singled out to be a model for others. Such a thought does not seem to fit with the egalitarian spirit of modern times. Many, if not most, modern Jews rarely refer to themselves as chosen or being "God's witnesses," and leave that cognomen to various Christian groups who choose to refer to themselves as witnessing for their faith.

While being a witness in this sense is no longer part of current Jewish parlance, it has nonetheless been part of Jewish fate. For when Jews died for the sanctification of God's name (*kiddush ha-shem*) they believed that they were witnessing for God in a godless world.

In Jewish history, our people's survival has always been both an end in itself and the prerequisite for achieving a higher purpose. That message is as old as the call at Sinai, and it has not lost its force for those who hear it today. "You are My witnesses," Isaiah said and issued a challenge to his generation as he does to ours. (See also the essay on "The Chosen People"; haftarah to Vayikra.)[14]

Gleanings

Words to Remember

[I] made you a covenant people,
a light to the nations. (42:6)
You are My witnesses, says the Eternal One,
My servant whom I have chosen. (43:10)

To open eyes that are blind (42:7)

When people eat too much, drink too much, and become arrogant in spirit, all kinds of mishaps take place. Only when their eyes are opened to the spirit of Torah do they appreciate that they were like prisoners sitting in darkness.

Midrash[15]

In biblical speech, "opening the eyes" refers always to uncovering mental vision.

Maimonides[16]

Sing a new song to the Eternal (42:10)

In the Hereafter, when the generations [of Israel] assemble and ask God who should be the first to sing, God answers: "The generation that sang to Me at the Sea will be the first to sing now."

(This is said in comment on Ecclesiastes 1:9, "That which has been shall be," and as proof text the words of Isaiah are cited, which speak of song and sea in the same sentence.)

Midrash[17]

Unwavering faith

Rabbi Joshua ben Chananya (2nd century) once visited Rome and heard that a Jewish child was languishing in jail. The Rabbi visited the boy and found him uncomplaining and firmly believing that it was God's will that he suffer. In support he quoted Isaiah 42:24. Witnessing such faith, Rabbi Joshua knew that this child could be a great leader for his people, and he managed to persuade the authorities to let him go. The boy grew up and became a rabbi, the famous Ishmael ben Elisha.

Midrash[18]

Isaiah's female imagery of God

It appears that not only the fact that the women were kept at a distance from the official Israelite cult but also the fact that the great prophets [like Jeremiah and Ezekiel] continually compared the Lord to a husband and Israel to a wife and never used explicitly feminine expressions for the Lord, may have contributed to Israelite women becoming attracted to cults in which femaleness existed as a positive value with which divinity could identify itself. Perhaps, as a result of this realization, our prophet deliberately made use of both masculine and feminine similes for God.

Mayer I. Gruber[19]

The simile of a travailing woman is employed because the poet has perceived within the exaggerated breaths which are characteristic of women in labor a striking image by which to convey a sense of the force of the breath of God. Here the simile "like a travailing woman" has been transformed from one connoting fear-induced pain to one bespeaking power and might—an image which is equal in intensity to the warrior image that precedes it.

K. I. P. Darr[20]

The mission

The Holy One performed an act of *tz'dakah* [toward the gentiles] by causing Israel to be dispersed.

Talmud[21]

This then is our task: to maintain Judaism within the Jewish people and at the same time spread Judaism amongst the nations; to protect the sense of unity with all men; to nourish the love for Judaism without diminishing the love of man. We pray that God may give us further strength to search out the way of truth and not to stray from the path of love.

Samuel Holdheim[22]

Emphasis on the universal character of Judaism brought in its train a reformation of Israel's destiny. To bring all nations to the house of God, to lead them in a climb to higher moral standards, to bring about peace and brotherhood—these were the goals which Liberal leaders saw for their people. Israel was the leaven of mankind, its mentor in religion and ethics. It was a grand mission which was to be accomplished not by conversion but by example, a mission which could be fulfilled only in dispersion.

W. G. Plaut[23]

* * *

Notes

[1] See Rashi.

[2] So Radak, and among modern scholars, Karl Elliger.

[3] II Kings 25:27-30.

[4] See the Torah Commentary, pp. 404-405.

[5] The words of the Psalm have found their way into a popular Hebrew song.

[6] On this subject see the essay on "God's anger," p.19.

[7] See Mayer I. Gruber, "The Motherhood of God ..."; Andrea L. Weiss, "Female Imagery in the Book of Isaiah," with many references in the Notes. See also the haftarah for Shabbat Rosh Chodesh.

[8] Genesis 32:29.

[9] So Ibn Ezra.

[10] Ibn Ezra and others.

[11] See Bernard J. Bamberger, *Proselytism in the Talmudic Period*.

[12] *B.* Pesachim 87b; see also Song of Songs Rabbah 1:4; Seder Eliyahu Rabbah 11:54.

[13] Pesikta deRav Kahana 12:6 (end); similarly Midrash Tehillim 123:2.

[14] See also the author's *The Case for the Chosen People*.

[15] Tanna deBei Eliyahu, chapter 18.

[16] *Guide of the Perplexed*, 1:2. Maimonides gives a number of examples—such as Genesis 3:7 (of Adam and Eve), Genesis 21:19 (of Hagar).

[17] Midrash Ecclesiastes (Kohelet) Rabbah 9:1.

[18] Yalkut Shimoni on verse 24.

[19] "The Motherhood of God ...," p. 358.

[20] "Like Warrior, like Woman: Destruction and Deliverance in Isaiah 42:10-17," *Catholic Biblical Quarterly*, vol. 49 (October 1987), p. 570.

[21] *B.* Pesachim 87b.

[22] In W. G. Plaut, *The Rise of Reform Judaism*, p. 139.

[23] Ibid., p.137.

נח

Isaiah, chapter 54, verse 1 to chapter 55, verse 5

Introduction

Note that portions of today's reading from Isaiah also form the haftarot for two other Shabbatot: twelve verses from it will be read on Shabbat R'ei (54:11-55:5), and ten on Shabbat Ki Teitzei (54:1-10).

Connection of haftarah and sidra:

The weekly Torah portion tells the story of the great Flood, which God brings upon humankind because its violence has burst all bounds. Isaiah's parallel: Israel too has sinned against its Creator and has broken the Covenant agreed to at Sinai. Just as God made a new start with Noah and his descendants, so is divine mercy now extended to Israel.

> *This is like the days of Noah to Me.*
> *I promised then never again to cover the earth*
> *with the waters of Noah('s days).*
> *So now I promise never again to be angry*
> *with you or rebuke you. (54:9)*

The setting:

The Prophet and his people had for decades been exiles in Babylon (6th century B.C.E.). They desperately wanted to return to their homeland and wondered whether it would ever happen. With the defeat of the Babylonians by the Persians and Medes, there was new hope among the exiles that their release might be at hand, and Isaiah strongly reinforced this hope and gave it a theological frame.

For more on Isaiah, his life and time, see our *General Introduction*.

The message:

The haftarah has three parts, and all of them speak to the same theme: the time of redemption from exile is at hand.

1. Make ready to assume your former place, for "great shall be the happiness of your children." (54:4-13)

2. A brief reassurance that no enemy shall succeed in thwarting God's salvation. (54:14-17)

3. Water, bread, and wine are used as figures of speech for the teachings of God. They can be had without money if and when the people are ready to obtain them. (55:1-5)

HAFTARAH FOR NOACH

Isaiah, chapter 54, verse 1 to chapter 55, verse 5

54:1. Sing, O barren woman who has never given birth;

break out in song, you who have never been in labor.

The desolate woman shall have more children

than a woman who is married!
—says the Eternal One.

2. Enlarge the space for your tent;

do not spare the canvas for your dwelling-place;

do not hold back: lengthen your ropes, drive in your pegs!

3. For you shall spread out to the right (the south) and the left (the north):

your offspring shall dispossess nations,

cities now deserted shall again be settled.

4. Have no fear: you shall not be put to shame;

do not cringe: your disgrace is at an end.

You shall forget the shame of your youth;

no more shall you remember your disgrace as a widow.

54:1 רָנִּי עֲקָרָה לֹא יָלָדָה

פִּצְחִי רִנָּה וְצַהֲלִי לֹא־חָלָה

כִּי־רַבִּים בְּנֵי־שׁוֹמֵמָה

מִבְּנֵי בְעוּלָה

אָמַר יְהוָה:

2 הַרְחִיבִי מְקוֹם אָהֳלֵךְ

וִירִיעוֹת מִשְׁכְּנוֹתַיִךְ יַטּוּ

אַל־תַּחְשֹׂכִי הַאֲרִיכִי מֵיתָרַיִךְ וִיתֵדֹתַיִךְ חַזֵּקִי:

3 כִּי־יָמִין וּשְׂמֹאול תִּפְרֹצִי

וְזַרְעֵךְ גּוֹיִם יִירָשׁ

וְעָרִים נְשַׁמּוֹת יוֹשִׁיבוּ:

4 אַל־תִּירְאִי כִּי־לֹא תֵבוֹשִׁי

וְאַל־תִּכָּלְמִי כִּי לֹא תַחְפִּירִי

כִּי בֹשֶׁת עֲלוּמַיִךְ תִּשְׁכָּחִי

וְחֶרְפַּת אַלְמְנוּתַיִךְ לֹא תִזְכְּרִי־עוֹד:

Commentary

54:1. *Sing, O barren woman.* Israel in exile—a nation barred from its land—is like "a desolate woman" who was divorced before she had children. But when she is taken back, her offspring will be more numerous than those of the married one (a metaphor for those who—like Babylon—had displaced Israel and temporarily gained God's favor.)[1]

2. *Enlarge the space for your tent.* Anticipate the coming restoration to your land, when your offspring will multiply.

3. *Shall dispossess nations.* Those who occupied your land, when the Northern Kingdom was destroyed some 200 years before.[2]

4. *Your disgrace as a widow.* אלמנה (*almanah*), usually rendered "widow," is properly "a once married woman who has no means of financial support and who is thus in need of special protection."[3] It appears that Isaiah takes "widow" in a wider sense, as a woman

14

5. For Your husband is your Maker, the
   One called *God of the hosts of heaven*,
and your Redeemer is the Holy One of
   Israel, called *God of all the earth*.

6. The Eternal calls you "wife" again, O
   [once] abandoned and brokenhearted;
once rejected, says your God, but a young
   wife still.

7. For a brief moment I forsook you;
with abiding love I take you back.

8. In a moment of flooding anger I hid My
   face from you,
but [now], with love unending I take you in
—says your Redeemer, the Eternal One.

9. This is like the days of Noah to Me—
I promised then never again to cover the
   earth
with the waters of Noah('s days).
So now I promise never again to be angry
   with you or rebuke you.

5 כִּי בֹעֲלַיִךְ עֹשַׂיִךְ
יְהֹוָה צְבָאוֹת שְׁמוֹ
וְגֹאֲלֵךְ קְדוֹשׁ יִשְׂרָאֵל
אֱלֹהֵי כָל־הָאָרֶץ יִקָּרֵא:
6 כִּי־כְאִשָּׁה עֲזוּבָה וַעֲצוּבַת רוּחַ
קְרָאֵךְ יְהֹוָה
וְאֵשֶׁת נְעוּרִים כִּי תִמָּאֵס אָמַר אֱלֹהָיִךְ:
7 בְּרֶגַע קָטֹן עֲזַבְתִּיךְ
וּבְרַחֲמִים גְּדֹלִים אֲקַבְּצֵךְ:
8 בְּשֶׁצֶף קֶצֶף הִסְתַּרְתִּי פָנַי רֶגַע מִמֵּךְ
וּבְחֶסֶד עוֹלָם רִחַמְתִּיךְ
אָמַר גֹּאֲלֵךְ יְהֹוָה:
9 כִּי־מֵי נֹחַ זֹאת לִי
אֲשֶׁר נִשְׁבַּעְתִּי מֵעֲבֹר מֵי־נֹחַ
עוֹד עַל־הָאָרֶץ
כֵּן נִשְׁבַּעְתִּי מִקְּצֹף עָלַיִךְ וּמִגְּעָר־בָּךְ:

Commentary

who has been abandoned and divorced by her husband and has thus been publicly shamed. (Note that the English language also expands the word "widow" when it describes a married woman who is temporarily alone as a "grass widow."). The expression reflects an old tradition (still alive in today's strict application of the Halachah) that allows men to divorce their wives, but gives wives no reciprocal right.

In general, a widowed woman was without the protection of her husband and was thereby socially disadvantaged. She therefore was placed under the protection of God, and numerous times in the Torah the people are bidden to take care of widows, orphans, and strangers—the weakest members of society.

8. *In a moment of flooding anger.* Portraying God in human terms, an anthropomorphism that Isaiah used occasionally (see the essay below.) The momentary exasperation of God is contrasted in the next line by "love unending."

9. *Like the days of Noah.* כִּמֵי (kiy'mei) is so rendered in some manuscripts, instead of מֵי (mei, waters).

10. Though the mountains may depart
and the hills be removed,
My love shall never depart from you,
and My covenant of peace
shall not be removed
—says the One who loves you, the Eternal.

11. Ah, unhappy, storm-tossed soul,
with none to comfort you:
I will make garnets your building-stones,
and sapphires your foundations.

12. I will build your towers with rubies,
your gates with precious stones,
your border with gems.

13. All your children shall be taught by the
Eternal,
and great shall be the happiness of your
children.

14. You shall be established in righteousness,
safe from oppression, and unafraid;
safe from terror—it shall not come near
you.

10 כִּ֤י הֶֽהָרִים֙ יָמ֔וּשׁוּ
וְהַגְּבָע֖וֹת תְּמוּטֶ֑נָה
וְחַסְדִּ֞י מֵאִתֵּ֣ךְ לֹֽא־יָמ֗וּשׁ
וּבְרִ֤ית שְׁלוֹמִי֙ לֹ֣א תָמ֔וּט
אָמַ֥ר מְרַחֲמֵ֖ךְ יְהֹוָֽה׃

11 עֲנִיָּ֥ה סֹעֲרָ֖ה
לֹ֣א נֻחָ֑מָה
הִנֵּ֨ה אָנֹכִ֜י מַרְבִּ֤יץ בַּפּוּךְ֙ אֲבָנַ֔יִךְ
וִיסַדְתִּ֖יךְ בַּסַּפִּירִֽים׃

12 וְשַׂמְתִּ֤י כַּֽדְכֹד֙ שִׁמְשֹׁתַ֔יִךְ
וּשְׁעָרַ֖יִךְ לְאַבְנֵ֣י אֶקְדָּ֑ח
וְכׇל־גְּבוּלֵ֖ךְ לְאַבְנֵי־חֵֽפֶץ׃

13 וְכׇל־בָּנַ֖יִךְ לִמּוּדֵ֣י יְהֹוָ֑ה
וְרַ֖ב שְׁל֥וֹם בָּנָֽיִךְ׃

14 בִּצְדָקָ֖ה תִּכּוֹנָ֑נִי
רַחֲקִ֤י מֵעֹ֙שֶׁק֙ כִּי־לֹ֣א תִירָ֔אִי
וּמִ֨מְּחִתָּ֔ה כִּ֥י לֹֽא־תִקְרַ֖ב אֵלָֽיִךְ׃

Commentary

10. *Says the One who loves you* …. Note the concluding phrases of verses 8 and 10. The parallelism is especially striking in the Hebrew text.

11. *Garnets.* פּוּךְ (*puch*); others, carbuncles.[4]

Sapphires. ספירים (*sappirim*). The Hebrew and English words have the same linguistic origin.[5] The Prophet uses the imagery of precious stones to depict the wondrous restoration of Israel to its home.

13. *All your children….* A famous rabbinic wordplay is based on this verse (see under *Gleanings*).

Happiness. שלום (*shalom*) means more than "peace"; it conveys total well-being.

15. Should any attack you, it will not be
My doing;

whoever attacks you will fall on your
account.

16. It is I who created the smith who fans
the coal in the fire and forges weapons
by his work;

I also create the destroyer to wreak havoc.

17. No weapon fashioned against you can
succeed;

you shall defeat all who rise to accuse you.

That is the heritage of the Eternal's
servants, and I am the Source of their
vindication, says the Eternal.

55:1. Come, all who are thirsty, come for
water;

even if you have no money, come buy food
and eat:

come buy food without money, wine and
milk without cost.

15 הֵן גּוֹר יָגוּר אֶפֶס מֵאוֹתִי
מִי־גָר אִתָּךְ עָלַיִךְ יִפּוֹל:

16 הֵן [הִנֵּה] אָנֹכִי בָּרָאתִי חָרָשׁ נֹפֵחַ בְּאֵשׁ
פֶּחָם וּמוֹצִיא כְלִי לְמַעֲשֵׂהוּ
וְאָנֹכִי בָּרָאתִי מַשְׁחִית לְחַבֵּל:

17 כָּל־כְּלִי יוּצַר עָלַיִךְ לֹא יִצְלָח
וְכָל־לָשׁוֹן תָּקוּם־אִתָּךְ לַמִּשְׁפָּט תַּרְשִׁיעִי
זֹאת נַחֲלַת עַבְדֵי יְהוָה וְצִדְקָתָם מֵאִתִּי
נְאֻם־יְהוָה:

55:1 הוֹי כָּל־צָמֵא לְכוּ לַמַּיִם
וַאֲשֶׁר אֵין־לוֹ כֶּסֶף לְכוּ שִׁבְרוּ וֶאֱכֹלוּ
וּלְכוּ שִׁבְרוּ בְּלוֹא־כֶסֶף וּבְלוֹא מְחִיר יַיִן
וְחָלָב:

Commentary

15. The verse features a wordplay on גור (gur), but its meaning is not clear. The Prophet apparently warns that whatever danger may lie ahead will come from within the people, and not from external enemies.

17. *That is the heritage.* Ibn Ezra takes this to be a messianic reference: the heritage of the Children of Israel will be the universal acceptance of the One God.

55:1. *Come, all who are thirsty.* The Prophet literally advertises his spiritual wares.[6] He does not here speak of physical water, bread, and choice food, but of God's teachings, which truly satisfy and are available without money. The figure of speech employs an image first uttered by the prophet Amos (8th century):

> *The days will come, says God, my Sovereign,*
> *When I will send famine to the land,*
> *But it will not be a hunger for bread*
> *Or a thirst for water:*
> *It will be [a yearning] to hear the words of the Eternal One (8:11).*

Buy. שברו (shivru), literally "break"; compare the English expression "to break bread."[7]

2. Why spend money for what is not bread?

Why spend your wages for what does not satisfy?

Listen well to Me, and you shall eat what is good,

and your souls shall delight in abundance.

3. Open your ears and come to Me;

hearken and you shall live.

I will make an everlasting covenant with you,

(like) the true love I extended to David.

4. As once I made him a witness to the world,

a prince and commander of nations,

5. so now you shall summon people you do not know,

and people that do not know you shall come running to you,

because of the Eternal your God,

the Holy One of Israel,

who has given you glory.

2 לָמָּה תִשְׁקְלוּ־כֶסֶף בְּלוֹא־לֶחֶם

וִיגִיעֲכֶם בְּלוֹא לְשָׂבְעָה

שִׁמְעוּ שָׁמוֹעַ אֵלַי וְאִכְלוּ־טוֹב

וְתִתְעַנַּג בַּדֶּשֶׁן נַפְשְׁכֶם:

3 הַטּוּ אָזְנְכֶם וּלְכוּ אֵלַי

שִׁמְעוּ וּתְחִי נַפְשְׁכֶם

וְאֶכְרְתָה לָכֶם בְּרִית עוֹלָם

חַסְדֵי דָוִד הַנֶּאֱמָנִים:

4 הֵן עֵד לְאוּמִּים נְתַתִּיו

נָגִיד וּמְצַוֵּה לְאֻמִּים:

5 הֵן גּוֹי לֹא־תֵדַע תִּקְרָא

וְגוֹי לֹא־יְדָעוּךָ אֵלֶיךָ יָרוּצוּ

לְמַעַן יְהוָה אֱלֹהֶיךָ

וְלִקְדוֹשׁ יִשְׂרָאֵל

כִּי פֵאֲרָךְ:

Commentary

3-5. In these verses, the connection of the covenant that God made with Israel is related to the covenant that was made with David. The allusion is to Psalm 89 and especially to verse 29:[8]

Forever will My unending love attend to him,
And My covenant with him be established.

Isaiah expects not only the reestablishment of the exiles in their ancestral land, but also that they will be ruled by a king from the House of David. The renewal of the covenant did indeed take place after the return, when Ezra led the people in a ceremony of formal rededication (Nehemiah chapter 8).[9] (See the essay following.)

3. *(Like) the true love....* A difficult verse; our translation follows Rashi and Metzudat David.

I made him a witness to the world. Referring to David or possibly to Zerubbabel, who became the civil head of the returnees and who was a descendant of the House of David.

5. *So now you shall summon people.* In that day your example will cause even those you do not know to seek the One God.

Essay

God's anger and disappointment

"I hid My face from you in a moment of anger" (54:8) are words put by the Prophet in God's mouth. Already the Sages of old were troubled by such anthropomorphisms that the Bible uses to explain the actions of God. If the Creator of All is beyond our world, how can we speak of divine anger (54:8) and even wrath, or in contrast, of God being long-suffering and patient?

Though troubled about such language, the Sages realized that ultimately there is no other way to speak of the living God than from the viewpoint of human experience. We can philosophize about the Almighty and use abstract terms, but a personal relationship requires words that denote empathy and mutuality: we weep and rejoice; hope and are disappointed—and we picture God as a living, caring Presence, not as a nebulous force or power.

In fact, one may describe God's experiment in creating humanity (against which, according to a midrash, angels argued vigorously) as a series of bitter disappointments:

The first humans were placed in the Garden of Eden and were given but one command, not to eat of the Tree of Knowledge. They began their journey in this world by defying God and were driven out of Eden.

From then on, God's disappointments increase, with Cain slaying Abel, people inventing implements of war and becoming steadily more violent—until God decides to start afresh and, after the great Flood, begins all over again, this time with Noah and his family. Yet note what they do when they leave the Ark: they engage in alcohol abuse and sexual perversion.[10]

The next divine disappointment occurs when humans attempt to build a tower that will reach the heavens. God scatters them across the globe and decides to make another start, at least spiritually. Abraham is chosen to father a new people that will serve God in perfecting rather than destroying the world.

Unfortunately, the people of Israel, though saved from slavery and exposed to the Presence at Sinai, wavered in their faithfulness. Idolatry, corruption, and all manner of moral evil characterized them, and God must now suffer the further disappointment of having to punish Israel with the destruction of the Temple and with exile to Babylon.

The Prophet knows of God's deep disappointment, though he describes the divine anger as being only "slight." But he cannot imagine that God has no emotion, and therefore revives the metaphor of which Hosea was so fond: the jilted and disappointed husband who remembers the love of his youth and, seeing that his beloved has changed her ways, is happy to take her back.[11]

We might be inclined to disallow the image of an angry God, but would we also be unwilling to think of a merciful and loving God? Hardly. Using language to which we can personally relate is the only way we know to make the Divine Presence real to ourselves.

19

Gleanings

Words to Remember

Though the mountains may depart
and the hills be removed,
My love shall never depart from you,
and my covenant of peace shall not be removed. (54:10)

All your children shall be taught by the Eternal,
and great shall be the happiness of your children. (54:13)

Why spend money for what is not bread?
Why spend your wages for what does not satisfy? (55:2)

Come, all who are thirsty, come for water (55:1)

Rabbi Chanina bar Pappa noted a seeming contradiction between two verses in the book of Isaiah. In one verse he says that everyone who is thirsty should go and find water (that is, Torah), while earlier he urges that we "meet the thirsty with water" (21:14). In one instance we are to bring it to them; in the other we ask them to find it for themselves.

The Sages' answer to this puzzle is rather cryptic, and Rashi explains it as follows: If a teacher of Torah is authentic he will bring water to the thirsty; but if he is not, students will have to search for themselves until they find it.

Talmud[12]

In the school of Rabbi Ishmael they taught:

If your evil inclination tempts you, by all means bring it with you to the place where water is dispensed (that is, to the house of study where Torah is taught). Even if the inclination is hard as stone it will be overcome by the living waters of Torah, as it is said, "Water wears away stone" (Job 14:19).

Talmud[13]

A play on words

The Prophet says, "All your children shall be taught by the Eternal, and great shall be the happiness *(shalom)* of your children" (54:13).

Rabbi Eleazar said in the name of Rabbi Chanina: "Those who study Torah help to build peace in the world." This conclusion is supported by a wordplay on בָּנַיִךְ, *banayich,* "your children." By pronouncing it בּוֹנַיִךְ, *bonayich,* we obtain the meaning "your builders." Those who learn and teach Torah become *bonayich,* building *shalom* for your children.

Talmud[14]

"All your children shall be taught by the Eternal" hints at the world-to-come. In this world we have human teachers, but in messianic days we shall have the Eternal One as our teacher.

Midrash[15]

This verse is an important landmark in the history of civilization. In obedience to it, Israel led the world in universal education. "The Jewish religion, because it was a literature-sustained religion, led to the first efforts to provide elementary instruction for all children of the community" (H. G.. Wells).

[The wordplay] proclaims a wonderful truth: the *children* of a nation are the *builders* of its future. And every Jewish child must be reared to become such a builder of his people's better future.

Joseph H. Hertz[16]

Allusions

The Shabbat hymn *L'chah Dodi,* by Solomon Alkabets, employs two images taken from this haftarah:

Its seventh verse (not counting the refrain) takes imagery from 54:4 ("You shall not be put to shame"), and its ninth from 54:3 ("You shall spread out to the right and the left").

***

Notes

[1] Targum and traditional commentaries identify Jerusalem as the "barren woman."

[2] See II Kings 17:24.

[3] Chaim Cohen, *Journal of the Ancient Near East Society*, vol. 5 (1973), p. 77; Martha Roth, "The Neo-Babylonian Widow," *Journal of Cuneiform Studies*, vols. 43-45 (1991-1993), pp. 1-126.

[4] For example, JPS.

[5] Probably Old Indian. Others render the word as "lapis lazuli."

[6] Westermann, p. 282, calls it the Prophet's "market place invitation" to listen to his words.

[7] The term first appears in Genesis 42:2, in the Joseph story in the meaning of "buy."

[8] Assuming it to be earlier than Isaiah and to have been known to him.

[9] See also Westermann, p. 285, who sees David as the mediator of the blessing bestowed on Israel as a people. For Ibn Ezra, the prophecy refers to messianic days.

[10] See Genesis 9:20 and following.

[11] On the quality of God remembering, see the Torah Commentary, p. 62.

[12] Ta'anit 7a.

[13] Sukkah 52b.

[14] B. Berachot 64a (end); Keritot 28b. In fact, the Dead Sea manuscript of Isaiah reads *bonayich*, "your builders."

[15] Pesikta deRab Kahana, 12:22.

[16] *Pentateuch and Haftorahs*, p. 818.

Isaiah, chapter 40, verse 27 to chapter 41, verse 16

Introduction

Connection of haftarah and sidra:

The weekly Torah portion begins the story of Abraham: how God selected him from among all the people of the earth, so that he might father a nation dedicated to the service of God. Isaiah compares God's choice of Israel to that of Abraham: "I have taken hold of you from the ends of the earth and called you from its far corners" (Isaiah 41:9). Just as God's promise to Abraham was fulfilled, so will Israel's faith be rewarded.

The setting:

Isaiah and his people have for decades been exiles in Babylon (6th century B.C.E.). They desperately want to go back to their homeland, and despair has led them to wonder whether it will ever happen. "It will," the Prophet tells them, "the time is coming and we will be redeemed; for Cyrus, king of the Medes and Persians, will set us free."

The Babylonian environment to which the Prophet was exposed is reflected repeatedly in his language; see, for example, our comment on "coastlands" at chapter 41, verse 1.

For more on Isaiah, his life and his time, see our *General Introduction;* on the life and time of Cyrus, see the essay below.

The message:

The haftarah brings us one overriding message: God has not forgotten Israel, and its troubles are always a matter of divine concern. Indeed, help is on the way; the rising star, Cyrus the Persian, is an agent of Providence, and through him Israel will be set free.

The haftarah may be divided into three parts:

1. Take courage! God remembers and cares for you; time will not thwart the divine plan, for God "never grows faint, never weary." (40:27-31)

2. God's greatness and power are beyond all comparisons and descriptions. Yet there are those who do not recognize God and still waste their time fashioning idols. They are described with biting irony: When they view their own creation they pronounce it as good, imitating God when the world was created—what fools! (41:1-7) [1]

3. Israel, as God's servant, need not be afraid of the future. Those who hold you in bondage today will be crushed, and the time will come when you will look around and can no longer find them. (41:8-16)

40:27. Why do you say, O Jacob,

Why do you assert, O Israel,

My way is hidden from the Eternal,

my claim is ignored by my God?

28. Do you not know?

Have you not heard?

The everlasting God, the Eternal,

Creator of the earth from end to end,

never grows faint, never grows weary.

Measureless in understanding is the One

29. who gives strength to the faint,

adds power to those whose who have none.

30. Even the young grow faint and weary;

the young may stumble and fall—

31. but all who trust in the Eternal

renew their strength,

they soar on wings like eagles,

they run and never grow weary,

they march and never grow faint.

40:27 לָמָּה תֹאמַר יַעֲקֹב

וּתְדַבֵּר יִשְׂרָאֵל

נִסְתְּרָה דַרְכִּי מֵיְהוָה

וּמֵאֱלֹהַי מִשְׁפָּטִי יַעֲבוֹר:

28 הֲלוֹא יָדַעְתָּ

אִם־לֹא שָׁמַעְתָּ

אֱלֹהֵי עוֹלָם יְהוָה

בּוֹרֵא קְצוֹת הָאָרֶץ

לֹא יִיעַף וְלֹא יִיגָע

אֵין חֵקֶר לִתְבוּנָתוֹ:

29 נֹתֵן לַיָּעֵף כֹּחַ

וּלְאֵין אוֹנִים עָצְמָה יַרְבֶּה:

30 וְיִעֲפוּ נְעָרִים וְיִגָעוּ

וּבַחוּרִים כָּשׁוֹל יִכָּשֵׁלוּ:

31 וְקוֹיֵ יְהוָה

יַחֲלִיפוּ כֹחַ

יַעֲלוּ אֵבֶר כַּנְּשָׁרִים

יָרוּצוּ וְלֹא יִיגָעוּ

יֵלְכוּ וְלֹא יִיעָפוּ:

Commentary

40:27. *My way is hidden from the Eternal.* But you, Israel, should know that nothing is hidden from God, whose power you must not doubt even in your exile.[2]

Measureless in understanding is the One. Literally, "Measureless is His understanding."

30. *Even the young grow faint and weary.* Verses 30 and 31 should be read as connected by contrast: Though youths get weary, the Eternal never does.[3]

יָעֵף (*ya-ef*, weary) is a poetic form of עָיֵף (*ayef*). This reversion of letters occurs occasionally in the Tanach; see, for instance, the words for sheep: כֶּשֶׂב (*kesev*) and כֶּבֶשׂ (*keves*).

31. *Soar on wings like eagles.* Tur-Sinai suggests that Isaiah here alludes to the old belief that when eagles molt they acquire new wings—a parallel to the mythic phoenix who arises rejuvenated from the ashes.

41:1. Listen in silence before Me, you
coastlands;

the peoples shall renew their strength.

Let them approach and state their case:

let us come together at the seat of
judgment.

2. Who has roused [a champion] from the
east

[One] whom triumph meets at every step,

putting nations at his feet,

laying rulers low before him,

making them like dust with his sword,

like windblown straw with his bow?

3. Pursuing them

he marches securely,

though never before has he taken that
road!

41:1 הַחֲרִישׁוּ אֵלַי אִיִּים

וּלְאֻמִּים יַחֲלִיפוּ כֹחַ

יִגְּשׁוּ אָז יְדַבֵּרוּ

יַחְדָּו לַמִּשְׁפָּט נִקְרָבָה:

2 מִי הֵעִיר מִמִּזְרָח

צֶדֶק יִקְרָאֵהוּ לְרַגְלוֹ

יִתֵּן לְפָנָיו גּוֹיִם

וּמְלָכִים יַרְדְּ

יִתֵּן כֶּעָפָר חַרְבּוֹ

כְּקַשׁ נִדָּף קַשְׁתּוֹ:

3 יִרְדְּפֵם

יַעֲבוֹר שָׁלוֹם

אֹרַח בְּרַגְלָיו לֹא יָבוֹא:

Commentary

41:1. *Listen in silence.* The verb illustrates the special dimensions of the Hebrew language. הַחֲרִישׁוּ comes from the root חרש (ch-r-sh), from which comes the word for deaf, חֵרֵשׁ (cheresh). Thus the overtone, "Be like one who can neither hear nor speak."

Coastlands. אִיִּים (iyyim) shows the Prophet's awareness of the cosmology of the Babylonians, who believed themselves to be living at the center of the earth, surrounded entirely by water. Accordingly, lands distant from them were "coastlands"; note verse 5 below, where the word betokens "ends of earth." [4]

Let us come together. This takes up the imagery of Isaiah 1:18. One can *plead* with God, as Abraham did for the condemned cities of Sodom and Gomorrah, [5] but one cannot *argue* with God on an equal footing. The verses that follow are similar to Isaiah's earlier words, which are read as the haftarah on the Shabbat after Tisha b'Av. [6] Both passages remind one of Job's argument with God, which ends with the Voice from the whirlwind that proclaims the inexpressible uniqueness of God's power. [7]

2. *A champion from the east.* The Targum [8] interprets this as a reference to Abraham, whom God selected from the east (from Ur in Mesopotamia [9]) and brought to the Land of Promise. Abraham is seen as the "champion from the east," because he fought four kings who had invaded the country and abducted his nephew Lot. [10]

But for other commentators, the champion is Cyrus, who sweeps all peoples before him. [11] (See the essay on Cyrus, below.)

4. Who set out to do this?

Who made this happen,

summoning the generations from the
  beginning?

I, the Eternal,

am the First;

and with the last, I am the One.

5. The coastlands see and are afraid,

the ends of earth tremble.

They draw near, they approach;

6. each helps the other,

saying: Be strong.

7. The artisan encourages the goldsmith.

The one who hammers the metal smooth

compliments the one who strikes the anvil,

saying, *The soldering is good,*

and they fasten it in place with nails:

it cannot be moved.

8. But you, Israel, My servant,

Jacob, My chosen one,

offspring of Abraham My friend—

9. I have taken hold of you from the ends
  of the earth,

and called you from its far corners,

and said to you: You are My servant,

I have chosen you, and not rejected you.

4 מִי־פָעַל וְעָשָׂה

קֹרֵא הַדֹּרוֹת מֵרֹאשׁ

אֲנִי יְהוָה רִאשׁוֹן

וְאֶת־אַחֲרֹנִים אֲנִי־הוּא:

5 רָאוּ אִיִּים וְיִירָאוּ

קְצוֹת הָאָרֶץ יֶחֱרָדוּ

קָרְבוּ וַיֶּאֱתָיוּן:

6 אִישׁ אֶת־רֵעֵהוּ יַעְזֹרוּ

וּלְאָחִיו יֹאמַר חֲזָק:

7 וַיְחַזֵּק חָרָשׁ אֶת־צֹרֵף

מַחֲלִיק פַּטִּישׁ אֶת־הוֹלֶם פָּעַם

אֹמֵר לַדֶּבֶק טוֹב הוּא

וַיְחַזְּקֵהוּ בְמַסְמְרִים

לֹא יִמּוֹט:

8 וְאַתָּה יִשְׂרָאֵל עַבְדִּי

יַעֲקֹב אֲשֶׁר בְּחַרְתִּיךָ

זֶרַע אַבְרָהָם אֹהֲבִי:

9 אֲשֶׁר הֶחֱזַקְתִּיךָ מִקְצוֹת הָאָרֶץ

וּמֵאֲצִילֶיהָ קְרָאתִיךָ

וָאֹמַר לְךָ עַבְדִּי־אַתָּה

בְּחַרְתִּיךָ וְלֹא מְאַסְתִּיךָ:

Commentary

6-8. An ironic description of idol makers. They are oblivious of the one God before whom the whole earth trembles.[12]

8. *But you, Israel, My servant.* You know that you are God's servant, destined for a special role. Isaiah often calls Israel "God's servant"; see the essay in the haftarah to Ekev.

Offspring of Abraham. זרע (zera) refers not only to a biological relationship, but carries also the legal connotation of "designated heir." The phrase resonates with God's promise to Abraham in the sidra: " … for through Isaac shall your offspring be called."[13]

10. Have no fear, for I am with you;

do not be afraid, for I am your God;

I will give you strength,

I will help you,

I will uphold you with My victorious hand.

11. All who assail you in anger shall be
    humiliated and shamed;

all who contend with you shall fade and
    disappear.

12. When you look for your tormentors,

you shall not find them;

those who war against you shall be less
    than nothing.

13. For I, the Eternal your God,

hold you by the hand;

and I say to you:

Have no fear; I will help you.

14. Have no fear, you worm Jacob,

you maggot Israel!

Here is My promise, says the Eternal One:

I, your Redeemer, the Holy One of Israel,

will help you.

10 אַל־תִּירָא֙ כִּי עִמְּךָ־אָ֔נִי

אַל־תִּשְׁתָּ֖ע כִּי־אֲנִ֣י אֱלֹהֶ֑יךָ

אִמַּצְתִּ֙יךָ֙ אַף־עֲזַרְתִּ֔יךָ

אַף־תְּמַכְתִּ֖יךָ בִּימִ֥ין צִדְקִֽי׃

11 הֵ֤ן יֵבֹ֙שׁוּ֙ וְיִכָּ֣לְמ֔וּ כֹּ֖ל הַנֶּחֱרִ֣ים בָּ֑ךְ

יִֽהְי֥וּ כְאַ֛יִן וְיֹאבְד֖וּ אַנְשֵׁ֥י רִיבֶֽךָ׃

12 תְּבַקְשֵׁם֙ וְלֹ֣א תִמְצָאֵ֔ם

אַנְשֵׁ֖י מַצֻּתֶ֑ךָ

יִהְי֥וּ כְאַ֛יִן וּכְאֶ֖פֶס אַנְשֵׁ֥י מִלְחַמְתֶּֽךָ׃

13 כִּ֗י אֲנִ֛י יְהוָ֥ה אֱלֹהֶ֖יךָ

מַחֲזִ֣יק יְמִינֶ֑ךָ

הָאֹמֵ֥ר לְךָ֖

אַל־תִּירָ֥א אֲנִ֥י עֲזַרְתִּֽיךָ׃

14 אַל־תִּֽירְאִי֙ תּוֹלַ֣עַת יַעֲקֹ֔ב

מְתֵ֖י יִשְׂרָאֵ֑ל

אֲנִ֥י עֲזַרְתִּ֖יךָ

נְאֻם־יְהוָ֔ה וְגֹאֲלֵ֖ךְ קְד֥וֹשׁ יִשְׂרָאֵֽל׃

Commentary

13. *Hold you by the hand.* Literally, by the right hand. In a Babylonian inscription, Cyrus tells how the god Marduk searched for a just ruler "whom he could grasp by the hand."[14]

14-16. The Prophet compares Israel to the helpless worm, which, left to its own resources, is easy prey for all predators. But God gives strength to the weak, and those who were threshed in the past will now in their turn "thresh the mountains to dust."

14. *Have no fear, you worm Jacob.* This is the imagery that David used when he was in distress: "But I am a worm, less than human."[15]

You maggot Israel. This is the kind of parallel to the first half of the verse one would expect, the image of another small, helpless creature. But to achieve this, the masoretic text needs the addition of one letter. Presently, the text reads מתי ישראל (*metei yisra'el*, men of Israel), which does not provide a parallel to "worm." We assume that the original Hebrew in this line read: רמתי ישראל (*rimmati yisra'el*, my [little] maggot Israel). But the ר in רמתי was omitted in the copying and the word became מתי, [little] men.[16]

27

15. I will make you like a threshing-sledge,
new, with sharp teeth;
you will thresh the mountains to dust,
and crumble the hills to chaff.
16. When you winnow them,
the wind shall carry them away,
the tempest shall scatter them.
Then shall you rejoice in the Eternal,
and glory in the Holy One of Israel.

15 הִנֵּה שַׂמְתִּיךְ לְמוֹרַג חָרוּץ
חָדָשׁ בַּעַל פִּיפִיּוֹת
תָּדוּשׁ הָרִים וְתָדֹק
וּגְבָעוֹת כַּמֹּץ תָּשִׂים:
16 תִּזְרֵם וְרוּחַ תִּשָּׂאֵם
וּסְעָרָה תָּפִיץ אוֹתָם
וְאַתָּה תָּגִיל בַּיהוָה
בִּקְדוֹשׁ יִשְׂרָאֵל תִּתְהַלָּל:

Commentary

15. *Threshing-sledge.* An image of strength.

16. *Then shall you rejoice in the Eternal.* The exaltation of God is the ultimate purpose of Israel's existence, for thereby all humanity will be led to obey the divine will.

Essay

Cyrus the Great

The oblique allusion to the "champion from the east" (41:2) is today generally understood as a reference to Cyrus, king of the Persians and Medes, who reigned from 559 to 529 B.C.E. and played a great role in the history of the Jewish exiles in Babylon. In fact, he became quite a legendary figure in his time, and not until Alexander the Great, 200 years later, would another such commanding personage appear on the stage of Near Eastern history.

He was born into the royal family of Persia, gained power by rebelling against his grandfather, and in 550 conquered the kingdom of Media, thereby establishing himself as a rival to Lydia in the west and Babylon in the east. The king of Lydia was Croesus, whose great wealth was legendary, and after he was overcome by Cyrus, the Babylonians were the next to be defeated. At the height of his power the reign of Cyrus extended from the Aegean Sea all the way to India. Also, since the Babylonians had ruled over Syria and Palestine, these lands too fell to Cyrus.

What made Cyrus "the Great" was not merely the extent of his conquests but how he dealt with the conquered lands. Instead of forcing them into the cultural and religious patterns of his own country, he allowed them the greatest freedom to adhere to their own traditional ways. Moreover, he was eager to learn from them—and not surprisingly, his subjects admired him greatly and, in fact, spun stories about him that ascribed to him supernatural powers. The Greek historian Herodotus held him up to his readers as the ideal king.

Isaiah reflects the same judgment in his prophecies. So profound was his admiration of Cyrus that he called him "God's anointed one" (45:1), although he was neither a Jew nor in any way related to the House of David. He was the exiles' great hope, and this hope was not disappointed. In the year 538 he permitted the Jews to return to their homeland, and thereby earned for himself an honored place in Jewish history as well. The very last verses in the Tanach (II Chronicles, end of chapter 36) pay tribute to him:

"The Eternal One roused the spirit of King Cyrus of Persia to issue a proclamation throughout his realm by word of mouth and in writing, as follows: 'Thus says King Cyrus of Persia: The Eternal One, the God of Heaven, has given me all the kingdoms of the earth, and has charged me with building a House of God in Jerusalem, which is in Judah. The Eternal One be with all God's people and let them go up [to build it].'"

Gleanings

Words to Remember

But all who trust in the Eternal
renew their strength,
they soar on wings like eagles,
they run and never grow weary,
they march and never grow faint. (40:31)
Have no fear, for I am with you;
do not be afraid, for I am your God. (41:10)

"My way is hidden from the Eternal" (40:27)

(The people complain that God pays no attention to their suffering. From this and other passages, Isaiah and later theologians have developed the doctrine of the "hidden God," meaning that at certain periods of history God "hides," so to speak (Isaiah 54:8), and history takes its own course.)

Isaiah's words are echoed in Job's complaint. How long will God hide His face? When shall we be allowed to see Him again? The Prophet expresses the despairing complaint of the faithful remnant which thinks that because God hides Himself, Israel's "way" is also "hid" from Him, and He pays no more attention to it...

Other nations too will address God reverently and say: "You are indeed a God who hides Himself."[17]

Martin Buber[18]

"My claim is ignored by my God" (40:27)

Never before had the Eternal One spoken in such a way by the lips of a prophet. Never before had God come so close to his people when he addressed them, laying aside anything which might alarm them in case he should terrify one of those who had lost heart. In these dialogues the prophet brings every possible means of persuasion into play. He appeals now to reason, now to emotion. He gives arguments and proofs. As Deutero-Isaiah entices and woos the heart of Israel, hardened by excessive suffering, he uses terms which expose the heart of his God....

Gerhard von Rad[19]

Tzedek (41:2)

Our translation renders the word as "champion," though usually it means righteousness or justice.[20] Isaiah says that God will raise *tzedek* from the east, and *tzedek* will rule nations and kings. Tradition took it to refer to Abraham,[21] or—as in talmudic and modern Hebrew—to the planet Jupiter.[22]

Our interpretation, following the majority of modern scholars, sees the word as referring to Cyrus. In this view, Isaiah uses the word *tzedek* in the sense of "victor," for he considers the defeat that Cyrus inflicted on his foes to be due to his righteousness. It has been

suggested that these verses were written or spoken about the year 546, when Cyrus had defeated Croesus of Lydia.

I am Cyrus

I am Cyrus, king of the world, great king, legitimate king, king of Babylon, king of Sumer and Akkad, king of the four rims (of the earth)....

(The text goes on to describe how Cyrus allowed the conquered nations to continue their traditional worship, how he improved their social condition, and that he did not allow his troops to terrorize the inhabitants.)[23]

Cyrus in legend

The Greek historian Herodotus tells various legends about Cyrus, some of which resemble stories told about Moses. Thus, when he was born his grandfather dreamt that Cyrus would some day rebel against him and usurp the throne. He thereupon charged a servant to take the baby into the mountains, there to expose him to certain death. But a shepherd found Cyrus, pitied him, and took him home. His wife was just then giving birth to a stillborn child, and the parents substituted it for Cyrus, keeping the latter as their own. The dead child was dressed in Cyrus' royal robe and returned to the place where the real Cyrus had been left. There the child was found, and the king's fear calmed. But in time the king's dream proved to be prophetic, for when Cyrus grew up he did rebel and gain the throne.[24]

Cyrus in the Midrash

Cyrus was chosen for great things by God, for he had wept when he heard that the Temple had been destroyed.[25]

His very name in Hebrew, כרש (*koresh*) suggests, by an inversion of consonants, that he was כשר (*kasher*, religiously fit).[26]

It should be noted that in Roman times the Palestinian Rabbis remembered Cyrus favorably, while the Babylonian sages did not. Oppressed Jews in Palestine looked at the Persians as friends, while the Babylonian Jews were suffering at the hands of the Mazdic priests, whose roots they traced to Babylon's conquest by Cyrus. Various midrashim composed in those years reflect these different perspectives.[27]

***

Notes

[1] See Genesis chapter 1:10 and following.

[2] Rashi.

[3] In grammar, this contrast is called prostasis and apodosis.

[4] See W. Horowitz, "The Islands of the Nations: Genesis 10 and Babylonian Geography," *Supplements to Vetus Testamentum,* vol. 41 (1990), pp. 35-43.

[5] Genesis chapter 18.

[6] Isaiah 40:12 and following.

[7] Job chapter 38.

[8] The Aramaic translation of the Tanach, which is followed by Rashi and Radak.

[9] Genesis 11:28.

[10] Genesis chapter 14.

[11] So Ibn Ezra and most modern commentators. Later on, Isaiah calls Cyrus by name (44:28; 45:1).

[12] Isaiah 40:16-20 uses the same imagery.

[13] Genesis 21:12. See H. Orlinsky, *Eretz Israel,* vol. 18 (1985), p. 53.

[14] See S. Paul, *Journal of the American Oriental Society,* vol. 88 (1968), p. 182.

[15] Psalm 22:7.

[16] So Elliger, following Ewald; Jerome T. Walsh, *Vetus Testamentum,* vol. xliii, no. 3 (1993), p. 357, who translates "you grub." The worm/maggot parallel is also found in Isaiah 14:11 and Job 25:6. But others believe that מתי (*metei*) means "little men," which satisfies the parallel and makes the emendation unnecessary.

[17] Isaiah 45:15.

[18] *The Prophetic Faith*, pp. 194, 217.

[19] *The Message of the Prophets,* p. 217.

[20] So in Deuteronomy 16:20: "Justice, justice shall you pursue."

[21] So Targum, Tanna deBei Eliyahu 28, Rashi.

[22] Pesikta deRab Kahana, supplement 4:3: God lifted Abraham above the heavenly bodies, and Jupiter (*tzedek)* was "summoned to his service" and served as his lamp..

[23] Pritchard, *Ancient Near Eastern Texts,* p. 316.

[24] *The History of Herodotus,* tr. by George Rawlinson, pp. 41 ff.; see also the survey of legends in *The New Century Classical Handbook,* pp. 352 ff.

[25] Seder Eliyahu Rabba 20.

[26] B. Talmud, Rosh Hashanah 3b. Note that in the late 20th century, a notorious cult leader in Waco, Texas, took on the name Koresh to enhance his special status. He and his followers were killed in a disastrous fire in 1992.

[27] For details, see Ginzberg, *Legends of the Jews,* vol. 6, pp. 433 ff.

ויֵרָא

Second Kings, chapter 4, verses 1 to 37

Introduction

Connection of sidra and haftarah:

In the sidra, Sarah is promised a son, although, she says, her husband is old; in the haftarah, a Shunammite woman, whose husband is also advanced in years, is promised by the prophet Elisha that she will embrace a son.

The setting:

Elisha was the chief disciple of his illustrious mentor, Elijah, and was active for about fifty years (850-800 B.C.E.). While Elijah was an outsider, engaged in confrontation with corrupt power and religion, Elisha was a man whose counsel the rulers of Israel tended to seek. He had been a farmer before becoming a follower of Elijah, and his concern for ordinary folk never left him. He became the subject of folktales, and many miracles were ascribed to him (about this, see the essay below).

For more on the books of Kings, see our *General Introduction*.

The stories:

1. The tale of the oil jars that were miraculously refilled. (1-7)
2. The tale of the Shunammite woman: the birth and death of her son, and his revival through the intercession of the Prophet. (8-37)

HAFTARAH FOR VAYEIRA

Second Kings, chapter 4, verses 1 to 37

4:1. The wife of one of the prophetic disciples cried out to Elisha, saying: Your servant my husband has died. You know how your servant always revered the Eternal. Now a creditor is coming to take away my two sons to be his slaves.

2. Elisha said to her: What can I do for you? Tell me what you have in the house. She replied: Your maidservant has nothing at home but a small oil jar.

3. Go outside to your neighbors, said Elisha, and borrow as many empty jars as you can.

4. Then you and your sons shut yourselves in and pour oil into all these jars; when one is full, set it aside.

5. She went away and did this, shutting herself and her sons in. They kept bringing jars and she kept pouring.

6. When these jars were full, she said to one of her sons: Bring me another jar. But he answered: There aren't any more. And the oil stopped [flowing].

4:1 וְאִשָּׁה אַחַת מִנְּשֵׁי בְנֵי־הַנְּבִיאִים צָעֲקָה אֶל־אֱלִישָׁע לֵאמֹר עַבְדְּךָ אִישִׁי מֵת וְאַתָּה יָדַעְתָּ כִּי עַבְדְּךָ הָיָה יָרֵא אֶת־יְהוָה וְהַנֹּשֶׁה בָּא לָקַחַת אֶת־שְׁנֵי יְלָדַי לוֹ לַעֲבָדִים׃

2 וַיֹּאמֶר אֵלֶיהָ אֱלִישָׁע מָה אֶעֱשֶׂה־לָּךְ הַגִּידִי לִי מַה־יֶּשׁ־לְכִי [לָךְ] בַּבָּיִת וַתֹּאמֶר אֵין לְשִׁפְחָתְךָ כֹל בַּבַּיִת כִּי אִם־אָסוּךְ שָׁמֶן׃

3 וַיֹּאמֶר לְכִי שַׁאֲלִי־לָךְ כֵּלִים מִן־הַחוּץ מֵאֵת כָּל־שְׁכֵנָכִי [שְׁכֵנָיִךְ] כֵּלִים רֵקִים אַל־תַּמְעִיטִי׃

4 וּבָאת וְסָגַרְתְּ הַדֶּלֶת בַּעֲדֵךְ וּבְעַד־בָּנַיִךְ וְיָצַקְתְּ עַל כָּל־הַכֵּלִים הָאֵלֶּה וְהַמָּלֵא תַּסִּיעִי׃

5 וַתֵּלֶךְ מֵאִתּוֹ וַתִּסְגֹּר הַדֶּלֶת בַּעֲדָהּ וּבְעַד בָּנֶיהָ הֵם מַגִּשִׁים אֵלֶיהָ וְהִיא מֵיצָקֶת [מוֹצָקֶת]׃

6 וַיְהִי כִּמְלֹאת הַכֵּלִים וַתֹּאמֶר אֶל־בְּנָהּ הַגִּישָׁה אֵלַי עוֹד כֶּלִי וַיֹּאמֶר אֵלֶיהָ אֵין עוֹד כֶּלִי וַיַּעֲמֹד הַשָּׁמֶן׃

Commentary

1. *The wife.* Her name is not given, but Jewish tradition identified her as the wife of Obadiah, himself a prophet and a servant of King Ahab of the Northern Kingdom.[1]

Prophetic disciples. בני נביאים (*b'nei nevi'im*), literally "sons of the prophets," denoting men given to prophesying, but having minor status.[2]

Take away my two sons to be his slaves. Exodus 21:7 deals with a woman whose father had sold her for some reason.

4. *Shut yourselves in.* This was not to be a public miracle.

7. She went and told the man of God, who said: Go sell the oil and pay your debt; you and the children can live on what remains.

8. One day Elisha went to Shunem. A rich woman who lived there prevailed on him to have a meal, and from then on he would stop for a meal whenever he was passing through.

9. The woman said to her husband: I am sure that this man who comes here so often is a holy man of God.

10. Let's build a small room on the roof, put a bed, a table, a chair and a lamp in it, and he can stay there whenever he visits us.

11. One day he came there and went to the upper room to rest.

12. He told his servant Gehazi to call the Shunammite woman. He called to her and she presented herself [before Elisha],

7 וַתָּבֹא וַתַּגֵּד לְאִישׁ הָאֱלֹהִים וַיֹּאמֶר לְכִי מִכְרִי אֶת־הַשֶּׁמֶן וְשַׁלְּמִי אֶת־נִשְׁיֵכִי [נִשְׁיֵךְ] וְאַתְּ בָּנַיְכִי [וּבָנַיִךְ] תִּחְיִי בַּנּוֹתָר:

8 וַיְהִי הַיּוֹם וַיַּעֲבֹר אֱלִישָׁע אֶל־שׁוּנֵם וְשָׁם אִשָּׁה גְדוֹלָה וַתַּחֲזֶק־בּוֹ לֶאֱכָל־לָחֶם וַיְהִי מִדֵּי עָבְרוֹ יָסֻר שָׁמָּה לֶאֱכָל־לָחֶם:

9 וַתֹּאמֶר אֶל־אִישָׁהּ הִנֵּה־נָא יָדַעְתִּי כִּי אִישׁ אֱלֹהִים קָדוֹשׁ הוּא עֹבֵר עָלֵינוּ תָּמִיד:

10 נַעֲשֶׂה־נָּא עֲלִיַּת־קִיר קְטַנָּה וְנָשִׂים לוֹ שָׁם מִטָּה וְשֻׁלְחָן וְכִסֵּא וּמְנוֹרָה וְהָיָה בְּבֹאוֹ אֵלֵינוּ יָסוּר שָׁמָּה:

11 וַיְהִי הַיּוֹם וַיָּבֹא שָׁמָּה וַיָּסַר אֶל־הָעֲלִיָּה וַיִּשְׁכַּב־שָׁמָּה:

12 וַיֹּאמֶר אֶל־גֵּחֲזִי נַעֲרוֹ קְרָא לַשּׁוּנַמִּית הַזֹּאת וַיִּקְרָא־לָהּ וַתַּעֲמֹד לְפָנָיו:

Commentary

7. *The man of God.* איש אלהים (*ish elohim*) is a term used more often of Elisha than of anyone else. It appears to reflect the popular belief that some persons possess inherent divine powers (David too is so spoken of).[3]

8. *Shunem.* Located in the valley of Jezreel.[4]

A rich woman. אשה גדולה (*ishah gedolah*). The adjective usually means "great," but occasionally indicates social esteem or wealth.[5] She had enough money to build an addition to her house in order to honor the Prophet (verse 10).

9. *Holy man.* The only time a prophet is so spoken of in the Tanach. Usually the expression is reserved for specially consecrated groups, like Nazirites.[6]

10. *On the roof.* Houses usually had flat roofs. The use of the word קיר (*kir*, literally wall) may indicate that the room was walled off, or by the wall, to give Elisha privacy.[7]

12. *Gehazi.* The servant appears here and in chapter 8 as a faithful associate of the Prophet, but in chapter 5 we are told that he was cursed by Elisha and contracted leprosy. The name signifies "valley of vision."

13. who said to Gehazi: Ask her what we can do for her in return for all the trouble she has taken on our account. Can I speak on your behalf with the king or the army commander?

I live among my kin, she replied.

14. What can we do for her, then? said Elisha [to Gehazi], who answered: Well, she has no son, and her husband is an old man.

15. Call her back, he said. He called to her, and she stood in the door. When she had returned,

16. [Elisha] said: At this time next year, you will be holding a son in your arms. She said: My lord, [you are] a man of God; do not, do not delude your maidservant.

17. But, as Elisha had promised her, the woman gave birth to a son at that season the next year.

18. The boy grew up. One day, he went out to see his father, who was among the reapers.

13 וַיֹּ֣אמֶר ל֗וֹ אֱמָר־נָ֣א אֵלֶ֘יהָ֘ הִנֵּ֣ה חָרַ֣דְתְּ אֵלֵינוּ֮ אֶת־כָּל־הַחֲרָדָ֣ה הַזֹּאת֒ מֶ֚ה לַעֲשׂ֣וֹת לָ֔ךְ הֲיֵ֤שׁ לְדַבֶּר־לָךְ֙ אֶל־הַמֶּ֔לֶךְ א֖וֹ אֶל־שַׂ֣ר הַצָּבָ֑א וַתֹּ֕אמֶר בְּת֥וֹךְ עַמִּ֖י אָנֹכִ֥י יֹשָֽׁבֶת׃

14 וַיֹּ֕אמֶר וּמֶ֖ה לַעֲשׂ֣וֹת לָ֑הּ וַיֹּ֣אמֶר גֵּיחֲזִ֗י אֲבָ֛ל בֵּ֥ן אֵֽין־לָ֖הּ וְאִישָׁ֥הּ זָקֵֽן׃

15 וַיֹּ֖אמֶר קְרָא־לָ֑הּ וַיִּקְרָא־לָ֔הּ וַֽתַּעֲמֹ֖ד בַּפָּֽתַח׃

16 וַיֹּ֗אמֶר לַמּוֹעֵ֤ד הַזֶּה֙ כָּעֵ֣ת חַיָּ֔ה [אַ֖תְּ] [אַ֖תְּ] חֹבֶ֣קֶת בֵּ֑ן וַתֹּ֗אמֶר אַל־אֲדֹנִי֙ אִ֣ישׁ הָאֱלֹהִ֔ים אַל־תְּכַזֵּ֖ב בְּשִׁפְחָתֶֽךָ׃

17 וַתַּ֤הַר הָֽאִשָּׁה֙ וַתֵּ֣לֶד בֵּ֔ן לַמּוֹעֵ֤ד הַזֶּה֙ כָּעֵ֣ת חַיָּ֔ה אֲשֶׁר־דִּבֶּ֥ר אֵלֶ֖יהָ אֱלִישָֽׁע׃

18 וַיִּגְדַּ֖ל הַיָּ֑לֶד וַיְהִ֣י הַיּ֔וֹם וַיֵּצֵ֥א אֶל־אָבִ֖יו אֶל־הַקֹּצְרִֽים׃

Commentary

13. *Who said to Gehazi.* Gehazi must have opened the door, but she did not enter, and the Prophet conveyed his message through him (see also verse 15).[8]

Or the army commander. Perhaps your military tax is too high.[9]

I live among my kin. A modest refusal of the Prophet's offer. If she needed anything, her family would take care of it. After making her reply she leaves the two men.

14. *She has no son.* Gehazi displays great insight into the woman's real need.

16. *Holding a son in your arms.* חבקת (*choveket*, literally embrace). The word resembles the name of the prophet Habakkuk (חבקוק), and tradition deduced from this that the prophet was the Shunammite's child.[10] (The sidra begins with a similar promise to Sarah, which is the reason the Rabbis chose this haftarah.)

19. [Suddenly] he cried out to his father: *My head! My head!* He said to a servant: Carry him to his mother.

20. The servant took the boy to his mother, who held him on her lap until noon, when he died.

21. She took him up and laid him on the bed of the man of God, Elisha, and left, closing the door behind her.

22. Then she called to her husband: Send me one of the servants and a donkey. I must hurry to the man of God, and come back.

23. Why go to him today? he asked. It is neither New Moon nor Sabbath.

Don't worry about it, she answered.

24. She saddled the donkey and said to her servant: Drive (the donkey) and get going, and don't slow down unless I tell you to.

19 וַיֹּ֥אמֶר אֶל־אָבִ֖יו רֹאשִׁ֣י ׀ רֹאשִׁ֑י וַיֹּ֨אמֶר֙ אֶל־הַנַּ֔עַר שָׂאֵ֖הוּ אֶל־אִמּֽוֹ׃

20 וַיִּשָּׂאֵ֔הוּ וַיְבִיאֵ֖הוּ אֶל־אִמּ֑וֹ וַיֵּ֧שֶׁב עַל־בִּרְכֶּ֛יהָ עַד־הַֽצׇּהֳרַ֖יִם וַיָּמֹֽת׃

21 וַתַּ֕עַל וַתַּשְׁכִּבֵ֔הוּ עַל־מִטַּ֖ת אִ֣ישׁ הָאֱלֹהִ֑ים וַתִּסְגֹּ֥ר בַּעֲד֖וֹ וַתֵּצֵֽא׃

22 וַתִּקְרָא֮ אֶל־אִישָׁהּ֒ וַתֹּ֗אמֶר שִׁלְחָ֨ה נָ֥א לִי֙ אֶחָ֣ד מִן־הַנְּעָרִ֔ים וְאַחַ֖ת הָאֲתֹנ֑וֹת וְאָר֛וּצָה עַד־אִ֥ישׁ הָאֱלֹהִ֖ים וְאָשֽׁוּבָה׃

23 וַיֹּ֗אמֶר מַ֠דּ֠וּעַ אַ֣תְּ [אַ֣תְּ] הֹלֶ֤כְתִּי [הֹלֶ֤כֶת] אֵלָיו֙ הַיּ֔וֹם לֹֽא־חֹ֖דֶשׁ וְלֹ֣א שַׁבָּ֑ת וַתֹּ֖אמֶר שָׁלֽוֹם׃

24 וַֽתַּחֲבֹשׁ֙ הָֽאָת֔וֹן וַתֹּ֥אמֶר אֶֽל־נַעֲרָ֖הּ נְהַ֣ג וָלֵ֑ךְ אַל־תַּעֲצׇר־לִ֣י לִרְכֹּ֔ב כִּ֖י אִם־אָמַ֥רְתִּי לָֽךְ׃

Commentary

19. *My head! My head!* Possibly a sunstroke. The book of Judith (in the Apocrypha) tells that Manasseh, her husband, had died from a sunstroke at the time of the barley harvest.[11]

21. *Bed of the man of God.* Which she had furnished for Elisha.

23. *Why go to him today?* Apparently it was customary to visit a prophet on special occasions, and New Moon or Sabbath must have been days when this custom was observed.

Don't worry. An idiomatic rendering of her one-word response: שלום (*shalom*). She does not tell her husband what has happened and quickly reassures him.

24. *Don't slow down.* She rides the donkey while the boy drives it with his stick. The journey from Shunem to Mount Carmel was some 20 miles (32 kilometers).

25. She went to Mount Carmel and found the man of God. Seeing her while she was still some distance away, the man of God said to his servant Gehazi: There is that Shunammite woman.

26. Run to meet her and ask her whether she, her husband, and her son are all well. She told him they were well,

27. but when she reached the man of God on the mountain, she took hold of his feet. Gehazi was about to push her away, but the man of God said: Let her be; her heart is bitter, and the Eternal kept it from me.

28. She said: Did I ask for a son from my lord? Did I not say, *Don't deceive me?*

29. He said to Gehazi: Hurry up. Take my staff and go. Do not stop to greet anyone and do not reply to anyone's greeting. Go and put my staff on the boy's face.

30. And the boy's mother said: As the Eternal lives and as you live, I will not leave you. So he got up and followed her.

25 וַתֵּ֙לֶךְ֙ וַתָּבֹ֤א אֶל־אִישׁ הָאֱלֹהִ֖ים אֶל־הַ֣ר הַכַּרְמֶ֑ל וַ֠יְהִי כִּרְא֨וֹת אִישׁ־הָאֱלֹהִ֤ים אֹתָהּ֙ מִנֶּ֔גֶד וַיֹּ֙אמֶר֙ אֶל־גֵּיחֲזִ֣י נַעֲר֔וֹ הִנֵּ֖ה הַשּׁוּנַמִּ֥ית הַלָּֽז׃

26 עַתָּ֞ה רֽוּץ־נָ֣א לִקְרָאתָ֗הּ וֶאֱמָר־לָ֛הּ הֲשָׁל֥וֹם לָ֛ךְ הֲשָׁל֥וֹם לְאִישֵׁ֖ךְ הֲשָׁל֣וֹם לַיָּ֑לֶד וַתֹּ֖אמֶר שָׁלֽוֹם׃

27 וַתָּבֹ֞א אֶל־אִ֤ישׁ הָאֱלֹהִים֙ אֶל־הָהָ֔ר וַֽתַּחֲזֵ֖ק בְּרַגְלָ֑יו וַיִּגַּ֨שׁ גֵּֽיחֲזִ֜י לְהָדְפָ֗הּ וַיֹּ֩אמֶר֩ אִ֨ישׁ הָאֱלֹהִ֤ים הַרְפֵּֽה־לָהּ֙ כִּֽי־נַפְשָׁ֣הּ מָֽרָה־לָ֔הּ וַֽיהוָה֙ הֶעְלִ֣ים מִמֶּ֔נִּי וְלֹ֥א הִגִּ֖יד לִֽי׃

28 וַתֹּ֕אמֶר הֲשָׁאַ֥לְתִּי בֵ֖ן מֵאֵ֣ת אֲדֹנִ֑י הֲלֹ֣א אָמַ֔רְתִּי לֹ֥א תַשְׁלֶ֖ה אֹתִֽי׃

29 וַיֹּ֨אמֶר לְגֵֽיחֲזִ֜י חֲגֹ֣ר מָתְנֶ֗יךָ וְקַ֨ח מִשְׁעַנְתִּ֣י בְיָדְךָ֮ וָלֵךְ֒ כִּֽי־תִמְצָ֨א אִ֜ישׁ לֹ֣א תְבָרְכֶ֗נּוּ וְכִֽי־יְבָרֶכְךָ֥ אִישׁ֙ לֹ֣א תַעֲנֶ֔נּוּ וְשַׂמְתָּ֥ מִשְׁעַנְתִּ֖י עַל־פְּנֵ֥י הַנָּֽעַר׃

30 וַתֹּ֙אמֶר֙ אֵ֣ם הַנַּ֔עַר חַי־יְהוָ֥ה וְחֵֽי־נַפְשְׁךָ֖ אִם־אֶעֶזְבֶ֑ךָּ וַיָּ֖קָם וַיֵּ֥לֶךְ אַחֲרֶֽיהָ׃

Commentary

25. *That Shunammite woman.* The Hebrew הַלָּז (hallaz, that) is masculine, instead of the feminine הַלָּזֶה. Such mixture of genders occurs a number of times in the Tanach.

26. *She told him they were well.* She wanted to bring her plight to Elisha personally.

27. *The Eternal kept it from me.* Said in puzzlement by the Prophet.

29. *He said to Gehazi.* The Shunammite's outburst told him everything he needed to know. The boy was dead, and she had come to ask for a miracle.

30. *I will not leave you.* She wants none but the master himself to ask God's help for the boy.

31. Gehazi went on ahead of them and laid the staff on the boy's face, but there was no sound and no sign of life. He turned back to meet Elisha and told him: The boy has not awakened.

32. Elisha went into the house, and there was the dead boy lying on his bed.

33. He went in, shut the door on the two of them, and prayed to the Eternal.

34. Then he stretched himself over the boy, placing his mouth, eyes, and hands on the boy's mouth, hands, and eyes. He crouched over him and the boy's body grew warm.

35. Elisha got up, walked to and fro about the house, and again crouched over the boy. The boy then sneezed seven times and opened his eyes.

36. Elisha called Gehazi and told him to call the Shunammite woman. When she came, he said: Lift up your son.

37. She threw herself down at his feet and bowed low to the ground. Then she lifted up her son and left.

31 וְגֵחֲזִי עָבַר לִפְנֵיהֶם וַיָּשֶׂם אֶת־הַמִּשְׁעֶנֶת עַל־פְּנֵי הַנַּעַר וְאֵין קוֹל וְאֵין קָשֶׁב וַיָּשָׁב לִקְרָאתוֹ וַיַּגֶּד־לוֹ לֵאמֹר לֹא הֵקִיץ הַנָּעַר:

32 וַיָּבֹא אֱלִישָׁע הַבָּיְתָה וְהִנֵּה הַנַּעַר מֵת מֻשְׁכָּב עַל־מִטָּתוֹ:

33 וַיָּבֹא וַיִּסְגֹּר הַדֶּלֶת בְּעַד שְׁנֵיהֶם וַיִּתְפַּלֵּל אֶל־יְהֹוָה:

34 וַיַּעַל וַיִּשְׁכַּב עַל־הַיֶּלֶד וַיָּשֶׂם פִּיו עַל־פִּיו וְעֵינָיו עַל־עֵינָיו וְכַפָּיו עַל־כַּפּוֹ [כַּפָּיו] וַיִּגְהַר עָלָיו וַיָּחָם בְּשַׂר הַיָּלֶד:

35 וַיָּשָׁב וַיֵּלֶךְ בַּבַּיִת אַחַת הֵנָּה וְאַחַת הֵנָּה וַיַּעַל וַיִּגְהַר עָלָיו וַיְזוֹרֵר הַנַּעַר עַד־שֶׁבַע פְּעָמִים וַיִּפְקַח הַנַּעַר אֶת־עֵינָיו:

36 וַיִּקְרָא אֶל־גֵּיחֲזִי וַיֹּאמֶר קְרָא אֶל־הַשֻּׁנַמִּית הַזֹּאת וַיִּקְרָאֶהָ וַתָּבוֹא אֵלָיו וַיֹּאמֶר שְׂאִי בְנֵךְ:

37 וַתָּבֹא וַתִּפֹּל עַל־רַגְלָיו וַתִּשְׁתַּחוּ אָרְצָה וַתִּשָּׂא אֶת־בְּנָהּ וַתֵּצֵא:

Commentary

33. *Shut the door*. Elisha wanted, literally, to be alone with God. He did not know whether he too, like Gehazi, might not be answered.

Essay

Elisha's miracles

While the prophet Elijah was credited with eight miracles, his disciple Elisha performed double that number[12]—two of them being recounted in our haftarah.

Miracles are generally understood to be divinely authored events that defy the laws of nature, and the Tanach is the repository of many such tales. The crossing of the Reed (Red) Sea by the Israelites and the ten plagues visited upon the Egyptians are famous examples. The ancients had no trouble believing extraordinary events of this kind, for God's power was seen as unlimited.[13]

But in modern days, miracles have fallen out of favor, because faith in an omnipotent God has greatly diminished. There is a tendency to say: what the ancients thought to have been miracles were really events whose nature was imperfectly understood. A confluence of unusual meteorological circumstances caused the Reed Sea to retreat, and the plagues were disasters experienced as supernatural but were in fact perfectly natural, though unusual.

Similarly with the story of the revived son in the haftarah. Perhaps, it might be argued, the boy had a severe sunstroke, which caused him to be comatose, with very shallow breathing, so that the mother thought he had died.[14] When the Prophet arrived and tried CPR (cardiopulmonary resuscitation), he succeeded. No wonder that the attempt to revive the boy through placing the prophetic rod on his forehead brought no result.

There is of course no way of establishing what "really" happened. All history is an interpretation of events, and the events themselves are not "facts" but reports seen through the eyes of contemporaries. We know today that what television presents as the day's fare is based on selected images by telejournalists and the news value that the studio assigns to them. And just as today's media shape the news, so did oral transmissions in ancient days.

People wanted to believe that Elisha, like his master, had extraordinary gifts, and they lovingly embellished what they learned about him. The text brings us legendary exploits of a great and revered man, who had the ear of kings, and whose prophetic power was wedded to a pervasive concern for the downtrodden.

Whatever we wish to make of these tales, it is clear that Elisha's contemporaries experienced them as having happened as told. They believed in the capacity of a few chosen individuals to exercise some of God's power on occasion. Note that the accounts are as bare and matter-of-fact as they can be. The Prophet does what needs to be done, and the stories end almost abruptly, leaving out all encomia. The writer did not feel that the obvious needed to be stressed: that God, and not Elisha, was the motive force in these happenings. The storyteller belonged to a time that was used to "radical amazement"[15]—a constant wonder at the marvelous presence of the Divine in their lives and the life of the world.

This sense is preserved in our daily prayer, when we give thanks for God's "wondrous gifts at all times, morning, noon, and night."[16]

40

Gleanings

The curse

After Elisha had performed the miracle of purifying the springs of Jericho,[17] he was assailed by the purveyors of fresh drinking water for interfering with their trade. The Prophet was greatly angered and cursed the water salesmen, whereupon they were attacked by bears. God was angry with Elisha and he was visited by a severe illness.

Talmud[18]

Elisha's prayer

The biblical story merely says that Elisha delivered a prayer when he was about to bring the Shunammite's child back to life.[19] However, the text does not give the prayer, and tradition fills in the 'missing text':

"Eternal One, sovereign of the world, as you performed wonders through my master Elijah and helped him to revive the dead, so, I pray, work a miracle through me, and let me restore life to this boy."

Midrash[20]

***

Notes

[1] Obadiah is mentioned in I Kings 18:3, and a brief fragment ascribed to the prophet Obadiah is found in the Tanach, and is read by the Sephardim as well as many Ashkenazim as the haftarah for the sidra Vayishlach. The tradition that the woman was Obadiah's wife is found in the Targum to the story and was already known in the 1st century C.E. The historian Flavius Josephus treats this tale as a historical fact (*Antiquities* IX 4:2); see further in Ginzberg, *Legends of the Jews,* vol. 6, p. 345, note 7.

[2] "The prophetic groups spoken of here appear as loosely organized brotherhoods living together in the towns of northern Israel" (*Anchor Bible,* II Kings, p. 31, note 3).

[3] Concerning David: Nehemiah 12:24, 36. See H. Orlinsky, *Essays in Biblical Culture ...,* p. 60; A. Rofé, *Introduction to the Prophetic Literature,* p. 57.

[4] In Joshua 18:18 it is listed as belonging to the tribe of Issachar.

[5] In Leviticus 19:15 the word is used as a contrast to "poor."

[6] One midrash speculates how the woman knew that he was a man of God and suggests that he was overwhelmingly awe-inspiring (*Pirke deRabbi Eliezer* 33), while another source says that a sacred (incense-like?) fragrance issued from him and that flies could not approach him; see Ginzberg, *Legends,* vol. 6, p. 346, note 12.

[7] So Radak.

[8] Similarly Ralbag.

[9] Suggested by J. Gray in *I and II Kings,* p. 486.

[10] Zohar I 7b; II 44a.

[11] Judith 8:3. The parallel is suggested by Cogan and Tadmor (*Anchor Bible,* II Kings), citing the commentary of O. Thenius (1873). Perhaps Psalm 121:6 has a sunstroke in mind when it says: "The sun shall not smite you by day."

[12] See Radak, in his comment on II Kings 2:14.

[13] The Rabbis of the mishnaic/talmudic age, as well as later Jewish philosophers, tried to soften the conception of miracles as contra-nature events. Rather, they said, these were built into the very process of creation and therefore part of nature from the beginning. See, for example, Mishnah Avot 5:6; or the midrash of Moses who refused to lift up his rod over the Reed Sea because he believed this to be contrary to God's natural laws. Only when God assured him that this was already foreseen when the world was created, did he proceed (Exodus Rabbah 21:6). For an example of medieval philosophers on this subject, see Maimonides, *Guide of the Perplexed,* 3:25.

[14] In fact, a talmudic passage suggests that he died of the heat (J. Yevamot 15:14d).

[15] The term was coined by Abraham J. Heschel; see his *God in Search of Man,* p. 43.

[16] From the 17th benediction of the *Amidah.*

[17] II Kings 2:19 ff.

[18] *B. Sota* 46b-47a. The tradition also suggests that the little boys who jeered at Elisha because he was bald (II Kings 2:23-24) were really grown men who behaved like little

children—an intepretation that makes his cursing them (with its disastrous results) not quite as gruesome a tale, but does not exculpate him.

[19] II Kings 4:33.

[20] *Pirke deRabbi Eliezer* 33. One tradition has it that the revived son was the prophet Habakkuk: *Zohar* B'shalach 1:7, 2:44.

חיי שרה

First Kings, chapter 1, verses 1 to 31

Introduction

Connection of sidra and haftarah:

Sarah has been buried, and the aged Abraham wants to find a proper wife for his son Isaac, so that the future of the family, which is the bearer of God's promise, will be secured. The haftarah tells us of King David's old age and the way Solomon was chosen as his successor.

The setting:

The haftarah brings us the opening story of the First Book of Kings.[1] David has reigned for forty years (from about 1010 B.C.E. on). He has now become feeble, and his son Adonijah, the heir apparent, does not want to wait for his father's demise and declares himself king. But a counter-faction favors Solomon, a younger son, and we learn how David is persuaded to name him as the next king.

For more on the book of Kings, see our *General Introduction*.

The story:

1. David's infirmity. (1-4)

2. Adonijah's grab for power. (5-10)

3. How David learned of Adonijah's action and was importuned by his wife Bathsheba and the prophet Nathan to keep an old promise and name Solomon as his successor. (11-27)

4. David decides that Solomon will succeed him. (28-31; the story of David's death is told in the haftarah for the sidra Va-y'chi.)

HAFTARAH FOR CHAYEI SARAH

First Kings, chapter 1, verses 1 to 31

1:1. King David was old, well advanced in years; and even though they covered him with (bed-)clothes, he never felt warm.

2. For this reason, his servants suggested that they seek out a young virgin for the king, to serve him, to be his nurse; she would lie close to him and warm the king.

3. So they searched all the territory of Israel for a beautiful girl, and they found Abishag the Shunammite and brought her to the king.

4. The girl was exceedingly beautiful; she became the king's nurse and attended to him; but the king had no (sexual) knowledge of her.

1:1 וְהַמֶּ֙לֶךְ֙ דָּוִד֙ זָקֵ֔ן בָּ֖א בַּיָּמִ֑ים וַיְכַסֻּ֙הוּ֙
בַּבְּגָדִ֔ים וְלֹ֥א יִחַ֖ם לֽוֹ:

2 וַיֹּ֧אמְרוּ ל֣וֹ עֲבָדָ֗יו יְבַקְשׁ֞וּ לַאדֹנִ֤י הַמֶּ֙לֶךְ֙
נַעֲרָ֣ה בְתוּלָ֔ה וְעָֽמְדָה֙ לִפְנֵ֣י הַמֶּ֔לֶךְ וּתְהִי־ל֖וֹ
סֹכֶ֑נֶת וְשָׁכְבָ֣ה בְחֵיקֶ֔ךָ וְחַ֖ם לַאדֹנִ֥י הַמֶּֽלֶךְ:

3 וַיְבַקְשׁוּ֙ נַעֲרָ֣ה יָפָ֔ה בְּכֹ֖ל גְּב֣וּל יִשְׂרָאֵ֑ל
וַיִּמְצְא֗וּ אֶת־אֲבִישַׁג֙ הַשּׁ֣וּנַמִּ֔ית וַיָּבִ֥אוּ אֹתָ֖הּ
לַמֶּֽלֶךְ:

4 וְהַֽנַּעֲרָ֖ה יָפָ֣ה עַד־מְאֹ֑ד וַתְּהִ֤י לַמֶּ֙לֶךְ֙
סֹכֶ֙נֶת֙ וַתְּשָׁ֣רְתֵ֔הוּ וְהַמֶּ֖לֶךְ לֹ֥א יְדָעָֽהּ:

Commentary

1. *King David was old.* He had reached the age of seventy and was very feeble. Generally, seventy was considered old, and people considered it the life span they hoped to reach. "The span of our life is seventy years," says the Psalmist.[2] The high ages of pre-historic humanity and of the ancestors of the Jewish people are legendary expressions of the idea of devolution, meaning to show that in the course of time humans have descended from a higher, purer state of being.[3]

Well advanced in years. The same words were used to describe the last stage of Abraham's life.[4]

2. *She would lie close to him.* Literally, at your bosom. The word is in the second person, though the rest of the address to the king is in the respectful third.

And warm the king. Many commentators take this literally: Abishag was to warm the king with her body heat; but others understand it as an attempt to arouse David sexually (hence, she had to be a virgin). If indeed the king was no longer virile (see verse 4), his capacity to rule was clearly at an end.[5]

3. *Abishag the Shunammite.* She was from Shunem, in the Jezreel valley.[6]

4. *No (sexual) knowledge of her.* The Rabbis, ever anxious to stress David's attention to tradition, explain this as follows: The Torah says that a king should not have many wives,[7] but David already had the limit of eighteen, and so he refrained from intercourse.[8]

5. Now Adonijah son of Haggit exalted himself [beyond his station], proclaiming: I will be king; he raised an escort of chariots, horsemen, and fifty men to run before him.

6. He had been born after Absalom. Never in his life had his father rebuked him, by asking him, *Why did you act in such a way?* Also, he was very handsome.

7. He met with Joab son of Zeruiah and Abiathar the priest, and they agreed to support him.

8. But Zadok the priest, Benaiah son of Jehoiadah, Nathan the prophet, Shim'i, Friend of David, and the elite warriors did not side with Adonijah.

5 וַאֲדֹנִיָּה בֶן־חַגִּית מִתְנַשֵּׂא לֵאמֹר אֲנִי אֶמְלֹךְ וַיַּעַשׂ לוֹ רֶכֶב וּפָרָשִׁים וַחֲמִשִּׁים אִישׁ רָצִים לְפָנָיו:

6 וְלֹא־עֲצָבוֹ אָבִיו מִיָּמָיו לֵאמֹר מַדּוּעַ כָּכָה עָשִׂיתָ וְגַם־הוּא טוֹב־תֹּאַר מְאֹד וְאֹתוֹ יָלְדָה אַחֲרֵי אַבְשָׁלוֹם:

7 וַיִּהְיוּ דְבָרָיו עִם יוֹאָב בֶּן־צְרוּיָה וְעִם אֶבְיָתָר הַכֹּהֵן וַיַּעְזְרוּ אַחֲרֵי אֲדֹנִיָּה:

8 וְצָדוֹק הַכֹּהֵן וּבְנָיָהוּ בֶן־יְהוֹיָדָע וְנָתָן הַנָּבִיא וְשִׁמְעִי וְרֵעִי וְהַגִּבּוֹרִים אֲשֶׁר לְדָוִד לֹא הָיוּ עִם־אֲדֹנִיָּהוּ:

Commentary

5. *Adonijah son of Haggit.* He was the fourth of David's sons,[9] and his older brothers had died: Amnon and Absalom suffered violent deaths; of Chileab's demise we know nothing, but it must be surmised that he was no longer alive.

Exalted himself. He decided not to wait and made himself king before his father died. Perhaps he feared that his younger brother Solomon would cause civil strife once David was dead. Or Adonijah proceeded because he had heard that his father was no longer virile and therefore no longer fit to rule. In either case, it is clear that David had not yet arranged for his succession.

6. *Never ... had his father rebuked him.* He had spoiled him, and therefore Adonijah assumed that, when faced with a fait accompli, David would not object, especially since he was so feeble.[10]

7. *Joab son of Zeruiah.* The army's commander in chief.

Abiathar the priest. The son of Ahimelech. He was an old supporter of David and alone had escaped the slaughter of his father and all the priests at Nob.[11]

8. *Zadok the priest.* He was a custodian of the Ark and the Tent of Meeting.

Benaiah. The chief of the palace guard, professional soldiers who were foreigners and owed allegiance only to David.

Nathan. The king's conscience, who had rebuked him after his affair with Bathsheba and the killing of her husband.[12]

Shim'i, Friend of David. Reading the text ושמעי רעה דוד (*v'shim'i r'eih david*). "Friend of the King" was apparently an established position.[13]

9. Then Adonijah sacrificed sheep, oxen, and fatted calves at the Stone of Zoheleth, near Ein-rogel; he invited all his brothers, the king's sons, and all the royal officials who were from Judah,

10. but he did not invite Nathan the prophet, or Benaiah, or the elite warriors, or his brother Solomon.

11. Nathan then went to see Solomon's mother, Bathsheba, and said to her: Have you not heard that Adonijah son of Haggit is calling himself king, and David knows nothing about it?

12. Now, look: let me give you advice that will save your life and the life of your son Solomon.

9 וַיִּזְבַּח אֲדֹנִיָּהוּ צֹאן וּבָקָר וּמְרִיא עִם אֶבֶן הַזֹּחֶלֶת אֲשֶׁר־אֵצֶל עֵין רֹגֵל וַיִּקְרָא אֶת־כָּל־אֶחָיו בְּנֵי הַמֶּלֶךְ וּלְכָל־אַנְשֵׁי יְהוּדָה עַבְדֵי הַמֶּלֶךְ:

10 וְאֶת־נָתָן הַנָּבִיא וּבְנָיָהוּ וְאֶת־הַגִּבּוֹרִים וְאֶת־שְׁלֹמֹה אָחִיו לֹא קָרָא:

11 וַיֹּאמֶר נָתָן אֶל־בַּת־שֶׁבַע אֵם־שְׁלֹמֹה לֵאמֹר הֲלוֹא שָׁמַעַתְּ כִּי מָלַךְ אֲדֹנִיָּהוּ בֶן־חַגִּית וַאֲדֹנֵינוּ דָוִד לֹא יָדָע:

12 וְעַתָּה לְכִי אִיעָצֵךְ נָא עֵצָה וּמַלְּטִי אֶת־נַפְשֵׁךְ וְאֶת־נֶפֶשׁ בְּנֵךְ שְׁלֹמֹה:

Commentary

9. *Zoheleth ... Ein-rogel.* The Stone of Zoheleth was evidently a well-known place: its closeness to the Fuller's Spring (Ein-Rogel)[14] locates it near Jerusalem, on the border between Benjamin and Judah. The spring waters were to symbolize the renewal of the kingdom: there would be no break in the monarchical succession.

11. *Solomon's mother, Bathsheba.* She had been the object of David's desire, when he observed her bathing. He proceeded to become intimate with her and arranged for her husband to be killed. The prophet Nathan came and rebuked the king, who repented—but this misdeed cost him the opportunity to build the Temple.[15] Bathsheba became one of his wives, but the illicitly conceived child died. Solomon was born thereafter.[16]

12. *Save your life.* מלטי (*malti*, save). The name Malta is derived from the common Semitic root of this word, "the island being a port of refuge in Phoenician navigation."[17] Nathan appeals not only to Bathsheba's hope for Solomon's accession, but warns that, should Adonijah become king, she and her son would be in danger, which most likely they would have been.

13. Go at once to King David and say, *My lord king, did you not swear to your servant, saying: Your son Solomon will follow me as king and sit on my throne? Why then has Adonijah become king?*

14. And while you are standing there talking with the king, I will join you and confirm your words.

15. So Bathsheba went to see the king in his bedroom. The king was very old, and Abishag the Shunammite was attending him.

16. Bathsheba bowed low before the king, who said: What do you want?

17. She answered him: My lord, you swore to me by the Eternal your God that *Solomon your son will follow me as king, he will sit on my throne.*

18. And now, look—Adonijah is acting as king, and you, my lord the king, do not even know it!

19. He has sacrificed oxen, fatted calves, sheep—many of them—and invited all the king's sons and Abiathar the priest and Joab son of Zeruiah, the army's commander—but your servant Solomon he did not invite.

20. Now, my lord king, the eyes of all Israel are upon you to see who will sit on your throne when you are gone.

13 לְכִי וּבֹ֙אִי֙ אֶל־הַמֶּ֣לֶךְ דָּוִ֔ד וְאָמַ֖רְתְּ אֵלָ֑יו הֲלֹא־אַתָּ֞ה אֲדֹנִ֣י הַמֶּ֗לֶךְ נִשְׁבַּ֤עְתָּ לַאֲמָֽתְךָ֙ לֵאמֹ֔ר כִּֽי־שְׁלֹמֹ֤ה בְנֵךְ֙ יִמְלֹ֣ךְ אַחֲרַ֔י וְה֖וּא יֵשֵׁ֣ב עַל־כִּסְאִ֑י וּמַדּ֖וּעַ מָלַ֥ךְ אֲדֹנִיָּֽהוּ׃

14 הִנֵּ֗ה עוֹדָ֛ךְ מְדַבֶּ֥רֶת שָׁ֖ם עִם־הַמֶּ֑לֶךְ וַאֲנִי֙ אָב֣וֹא אַחֲרַ֔יִךְ וּמִלֵּאתִ֖י אֶת־דְּבָרָֽיִךְ׃

15 וַתָּבֹ֣א בַת־שֶׁ֩בַע֩ אֶל־הַמֶּ֨לֶךְ הַחַ֜דְרָה וְהַמֶּ֣לֶךְ זָקֵ֣ן מְאֹ֑ד וַֽאֲבִישַׁג֙ הַשּׁ֣וּנַמִּ֔ית מְשָׁרַ֖ת אֶת־הַמֶּֽלֶךְ׃

16 וַתִּקֹּ֣ד בַּת־שֶׁ֔בַע וַתִּשְׁתַּ֖חוּ לַמֶּ֑לֶךְ וַיֹּ֥אמֶר הַמֶּ֖לֶךְ מַה־לָּֽךְ׃

17 וַתֹּ֣אמֶר ל֗וֹ אֲדֹנִי֙ אַתָּ֨ה נִשְׁבַּ֤עְתָּ בַּֽיהֹוָ֣ה אֱלֹהֶ֔יךָ לַֽאֲמָתֶ֔ךָ כִּֽי־שְׁלֹמֹ֥ה בְנֵ֖ךְ יִמְלֹ֣ךְ אַחֲרָ֑י וְה֖וּא יֵשֵׁ֥ב עַל־כִּסְאִֽי׃

18 וְעַתָּ֕ה הִנֵּ֥ה אֲדֹנִיָּ֖ה מָלָ֑ךְ וְעַתָּ֛ה אֲדֹנִ֥י הַמֶּ֖לֶךְ לֹ֥א יָדָֽעְתָּ׃

19 וַ֠יִּזְבַּח שׁ֥וֹר וּֽמְרִיא־וְצֹאן֘ לָרֹב֒ וַיִּקְרָא֙ לְכָל־בְּנֵ֣י הַמֶּ֔לֶךְ וּלְאֶבְיָתָר֙ הַכֹּהֵ֔ן וּלְיֹאָ֖ב שַׂ֣ר הַצָּבָ֑א וְלִשְׁלֹמֹ֥ה עַבְדְּךָ֖ לֹ֥א קָרָֽא׃

20 וְאַתָּה֙ אֲדֹנִ֣י הַמֶּ֔לֶךְ עֵינֵ֥י כָל־יִשְׂרָאֵ֖ל עָלֶ֑יךָ לְהַגִּ֣יד לָהֶ֔ם מִ֗י יֵשֵׁ֛ב עַל־כִּסֵּ֥א אֲדֹנִי־הַמֶּ֖לֶךְ אַחֲרָֽיו׃

Commentary

13. *Did you not swear.* The oath is not mentioned in earlier accounts; probably a small circle that included Bathsheba and Nathan knew about it, but Adonijah did not. "There is room, however, for the hypothesis that David's oath was known and that Adonijah's backers were the legitimists who opposed David's arbitrary choice of the son of his favorite wife." In fact, the Torah states expressly that the older son may not be deprived of his inheritance.[18]

20. *To see.* Literally, to tell, make known.

21. If you do not tell them, then as soon as you are lying down with your ancestors, my son Solomon and I will be treated as rebels.

22. While she was still speaking with the king, Nathan the prophet arrived.

23. The king was told that Nathan the prophet was there, and Nathan came in and bowed low before the king.

24. Nathan said: My lord king, have you said that Adonijah should rule after you and sit on your throne?

25. Today he has gone down and sacrificed many oxen, fatted calves, and sheep. He invited all the king's sons and the army officers and Abiathar the priest. Right now they are eating and drinking and shouting: *Long live King Adonijah!*

26. But as for your servant—as for me—and Zadok the priest and Benaiah son of Jehoiadah and your servant Solomon—us he did not invite!

27. Could it be that my lord the king ordered this, without telling your servant who will sit on the throne after you?

כא וְהָיָה כִּשְׁכַב אֲדֹנִי־הַמֶּלֶךְ עִם־אֲבֹתָיו
וְהָיִיתִי אֲנִי וּבְנִי שְׁלֹמֹה חַטָּאִים:

כב וְהִנֵּה עוֹדֶנָּה מְדַבֶּרֶת עִם־הַמֶּלֶךְ וְנָתָן
הַנָּבִיא בָּא:

כג וַיַּגִּידוּ לַמֶּלֶךְ לֵאמֹר הִנֵּה נָתָן הַנָּבִיא
וַיָּבֹא לִפְנֵי הַמֶּלֶךְ וַיִּשְׁתַּחוּ לַמֶּלֶךְ עַל־אַפָּיו
אָרְצָה:

כד וַיֹּאמֶר נָתָן אֲדֹנִי הַמֶּלֶךְ אַתָּה אָמַרְתָּ
אֲדֹנִיָּהוּ יִמְלֹךְ אַחֲרָי וְהוּא יֵשֵׁב עַל־כִּסְאִי:

כה כִּי יָרַד הַיּוֹם וַיִּזְבַּח שׁוֹר וּמְרִיא־וְצֹאן
לָרֹב וַיִּקְרָא לְכָל־בְּנֵי הַמֶּלֶךְ וּלְשָׂרֵי הַצָּבָא
וּלְאֶבְיָתָר הַכֹּהֵן וְהִנָּם אֹכְלִים וְשֹׁתִים לְפָנָיו
וַיֹּאמְרוּ יְחִי הַמֶּלֶךְ אֲדֹנִיָּהוּ:

כו וְלִי אֲנִי־עַבְדֶּךָ וּלְצָדֹק הַכֹּהֵן וְלִבְנָיָהוּ
בֶן־יְהוֹיָדָע וְלִשְׁלֹמֹה עַבְדְּךָ לֹא קָרָא:

כז אִם מֵאֵת אֲדֹנִי הַמֶּלֶךְ נִהְיָה הַדָּבָר הַזֶּה
וְלֹא הוֹדַעְתָּ אֶת־עֲבָדֶיךָ [עַבְדְּךָ] מִי יֵשֵׁב
עַל־כִּסֵּא אֲדֹנִי־הַמֶּלֶךְ אַחֲרָיו:

Commentary

21. *Lying down with your ancestors.* A biblical expression for dying.

Rebels. Literally, "sinners."

24. *My lord king.* Nathan does not here speak as the prophet, but rather as a loyal servant who has the king's interest at heart. (See the essay below.)

27. *Without telling your servant.* This can also be understood in the opposite sense: "And did you not tell your servant who would sit on the throne after you" (that is, you already told me that Solomon would succeed you).[19]

Nathan and Bathsheba have played their parts perfectly and have managed to appear as if they were independent of one another. While she speaks of the promise that David made to her, Nathan stresses the inappropriateness of Adonijah's behavior and the way the king's most trusted lieutenants have been excluded. The repetition of phrases and arguments gives the story an epic quality.

28. This was King David's answer: Bring Bathsheba back. So she came back and stood before the king.

29. David then took an oath, saying: As the Eternal lives, who has rescued me from every distress:

30. just as I once swore to you by the Eternal, the God of Israel, that your son Solomon would rule after me and sit on my throne, I will carry it out this very day!

31. Then Bathsheba bowed low to the ground and paid homage to the king and said: Let my lord king David live forever.

כח וַיַּעַן הַמֶּלֶךְ דָּוִד וַיֹּאמֶר קִרְאוּ־לִי לְבַת־שֶׁבַע וַתָּבֹא לִפְנֵי הַמֶּלֶךְ וַתַּעֲמֹד לִפְנֵי הַמֶּלֶךְ:

כט וַיִּשָּׁבַע הַמֶּלֶךְ וַיֹּאמַר חַי־יְהֹוָה אֲשֶׁר־פָּדָה אֶת־נַפְשִׁי מִכָּל־צָרָה:

ל כִּי כַּאֲשֶׁר נִשְׁבַּעְתִּי לָךְ בַּיהֹוָה אֱלֹהֵי יִשְׂרָאֵל לֵאמֹר כִּי־שְׁלֹמֹה בְנֵךְ יִמְלֹךְ אַחֲרַי וְהוּא יֵשֵׁב עַל־כִּסְאִי תַּחְתָּי כִּי כֵּן אֶעֱשֶׂה הַיּוֹם הַזֶּה:

לא וַתִּקֹּד בַּת־שֶׁבַע אַפַּיִם אֶרֶץ וַתִּשְׁתַּחוּ לַמֶּלֶךְ וַתֹּאמֶר יְחִי אֲדֹנִי הַמֶּלֶךְ דָּוִד לְעֹלָם:

Commentary

28. *This was King David's answer.* He is roused from his lethargy and acts with his former dispatch.

Bring Bathsheba back. She evidently had left when Nathan arrived.

31. *Let my lord king David live forever.* The haftarah ends here, but the biblical story goes on to tell of what happened. Solomon is named by his father, the priest Zadok anoints him, and the public acclaims Solomon. When the news reaches Adonijah, he and his supporters realize that they have failed. Adonijah flees to the Tent of Meeting and promises Solomon to be his loyal servant. But after David's death and an incident involving Abishag the Shunammite, Solomon orders his brother's execution.

Essay

Prophet or politician?

Readers unaware that Nathan was a prophet would likely see him as a clever schemer. He plays on Bathsheba's natural instincts of a mother who wants the best for her son. Nathan knows the king's weakness for this particular wife, and he appears to use her for his own political plans. Since he favors Solomon over Adonijah, the latter's self-proclamation as king requires him to make haste; tomorrow will be too late.

One might further surmise that David had never promised Bathsheba to make Solomon his successor; Nathan merely suggests this to the king whose memory—along with his other physical powers—is probably failing. Altogether, this is a clever political ploy on Nathan's part, and it is crowned with success.

Actually, of course, we do not know whether David had made the crucial promise or whether this was Nathan's invention. But there are two reasons to believe that David had indeed wanted Solomon to be king.

For one, he knew that the young man had all the makings of a great ruler. He was unusually bright and had good judgment, and was also ruthless if the occasion demanded it.

Even more important: Nathan was not the type of man who would have fed a patent lie to his sovereign. For Nathan was not only a politician, he was also a prophet. It was he who had confronted David after the king had arranged the death of Uriah, Bathsheba's husband. It was Nathan who by this action had risked his life and had caused the king to admit his wrongdoing. And it was he who, speaking in God's name, had pronounced divine punishment on David.

Was Nathan then both politician and prophet? Indeed, for the terms are not mutually exclusive. Prophets were not hermits, engaged continuously in meditation and prayer. They earned their livelihood in various ways, and Nathan (like Isaiah a hundred years later) was a counselor to the king. In that capacity he must have advised him on mundane political matters.

Yet he was also the king's conscience, and we have every reason to assume that lying to him was not part of his makeup. He probably knew the king very well, and was fairly sure that David would honor an oath. Nathan's approach shows his keen psychological insight, a capacity that made his prophetic activity especially successful. He was indeed a man of both political and moral capacity, and in a crucial moment in Israel's history he assured his nation of a promising future under Solomon.

Gleanings

A good age

Since David died at seventy years of age, this became accepted as a good age to reach.

Talmud[20]

Nathan's courage

After Nathan had confronted the king with his crime of having Uriah killed, he lived in constant danger. A cadre of the king's servants watched him day and night to make sure that he did not divulge anything he had said to David. If he had talked about the matter, he would have been killed.

Midrash[21]

The lost book of Nathan

We read in I Chronicles 29:29: "The acts of King David, early and late, are recorded in the history of Samuel the seer, the history of Nathan the prophet, and the history of Gad the seer." And in II Chronicles 9:29 we find: "The other events of Solomon's reign, early and late, are recorded in the chronicle of the prophet Nathan and in the prophecies of Ahijah the Shilonite and in the visions of Jedo the seer ...." None of these books has survived.

***

Notes

[1] In the Septuagint, it is called the Third Book of Kingdoms, while I and II Samuel are called I and II Kingdoms.

[2] Psalm 90:10. Older English translations, following the King James, rendered it, "The days of our years are three score years [that is, three times twenty] and ten."

[3] At the time of Cicero (106-43 B.C.E.), the life expectancy of Roman males was about 35 years.

[4] Genesis 24:1. Radak, living more than 2,000 years later, thought David's weakness unusual and traced it to his hard life and many wars.

[5] So J. Gray, *I and II Kings*.

[6] Another Shunammite woman plays a role in the life of Elisha (II Kings 4:12; see the haftarah for Veyeira).

[7] Deuteronomy 17:17.

[8] So *B. Sanhedrin* 22a; Rashi and Radak.

[9] I Samuel 3:4.

[10] So Ralbag.

[11] The killing had been ordered by Saul; I Samuel 22:20.

[12] II Samuel 12.

[13] So Gray, following the reading by Josephus, and based on I Kings 4:5, which lists רעה המלך (*r'eih hamelech*) as an established position, probably a court counselor. Shim'i son of Ela is mentioned in I Kings 4:18, while R'eih is an unknown in this list of important figures (which suggests the emendation).

[14] Scholars have not been able to agree on the meaning of the name.

[15] II Samuel chapters 11 and 12.

[16] The Talmud, attempting to exonerate David, suggested that Uriah, like every soldier, had to write a bill of divorce before going into battle. Hence Bathsheba did not commit adultery with the king (*B. Shabbat* 56a and elsewhere; on a midrash disagreeing with this, see Ginzberg, *Legends of the Jews*, vol. 6, p. 264, note 92).

[17] Suggested by Gray.

[18] Deuteronomy 21:16. For the citation, see Leo L. Honor, comment on verse 13, in *Book of Kings*. Defenders of the king's privilege to choose his successor hold that the Torah law applied only to possessions. They base their view on the wording of the Torah, which speaks of the "double portion" that is due to the older son.

[19] So Leo L. Honor, *Book of Kings*, citing Abarbanel.

[20] *B. Yevamot* 64b.

[21] Only a secondary reference is available; see Ginzberg, *Legends*, vol. 6, p. 265, note 92.

Malachi, chapter 1, verse 1 to chapter 2, verse 7

Introduction

Connection of haftarah and sidra:

The sidra begins with the struggle of Esau and Jacob in the womb of their mother, a struggle that was perpetuated in later history. The haftarah recalls this tension in its opening section.

The setting:

The anonymous prophet called Malachi (My Messenger) lived about the middle of the 5th century B.C.E. Judea was still a Persian province ruled by a governor. The Prophet addressed himself to the social and religious conditions of his time, which were not unlike what many societies at the end of the 20th century have come to know. People doubted God and divine justice; their Temple service was perfunctory; divorce and intermarriage rates were rising; and a general sense of instability prevailed. Malachi's critique helped to bring about the reforms by Ezra and Nehemiah.

For more on Malachi and his time, see our *General Introduction*.

The message:

1. Authorship and call by God. (1:1)

2. The fate of Esau reflects God's continuing attention to history. (1:2-5)

3. The main part of the haftarah deals with the neglect and corruption of the Temple service. (1:6-2:7)

HAFTARAH FOR TOL'DOT

Malachi, chapter 1, verse 1 to chapter 2, verse 7

1:1. The message of the Eternal to Israel through Malachi:

2. I have loved you, says the Eternal One.

But you say: *How have You shown Your love for us?*

Is not Esau Jacob's brother? says the Eternal One.

But I have loved Jacob,

3. and hated Esau,

making his hills a desolation,

giving his heritage to jackals.

4. Were Edom to say:

We are shattered,

but we shall rebuild the ruins,

1:1 מַשָּׂא דְבַר־יְהֹוָה אֶל־יִשְׂרָאֵל בְּיַד
מַלְאָכִי:

2 אָהַבְתִּי אֶתְכֶם אָמַר יְהֹוָה
וַאֲמַרְתֶּם בַּמָּה אֲהַבְתָּנוּ
הֲלוֹא־אָח עֵשָׂו לְיַעֲקֹב נְאֻם־יְהֹוָה
וָאֹהַב אֶת־יַעֲקֹב:

3 וְאֶת־עֵשָׂו שָׂנֵאתִי
וָאָשִׂים אֶת־הָרָיו שְׁמָמָה
וְאֶת־נַחֲלָתוֹ לְתַנּוֹת מִדְבָּר:

4 כִּי־תֹאמַר אֱדוֹם
רֻשַּׁשְׁנוּ וְנָשׁוּב
וְנִבְנֶה חֳרָבוֹת

Commentary

1:1. *Malachi.* מלאכי (*mal'achi*, My Messenger) is probably not a personal name, but merely indicates that the speaker was commissioned by God.

2-3. *But you say.* Malachi is often didactic and makes his points through questions and answers. This style is observable throughout the haftarah, and especially from verse 6 on.

I have loved Jacob and hated Esau. The Torah describes God's preference for Jacob, but speaks nowhere of God hating Esau. Malachi's statement reflects national feelings in Israel that centuries of tension had produced. They grew into hatred when Edom (the other name of Esau,[1]) had rejoiced in the downfall of Jerusalem and had participated in its pillage. The prophet Obadiah had expressed this outrage, when he described how Edom had looted Jerusalem and later killed its refugees.

> *How could you enter the gate of My people on the day disaster struck it,*
> *Gaze gleefully with others on its misfortune on its day of disaster ....*
> *As you did, so shall it be done to you; there will be retribution for your actions.*[2]

This retribution must have taken place in Malachi's time; historians believe that the Edomites were displaced by Nabateans, an Arabic tribe that flourished east of the Jordan for many centuries.[3]

4. *Were Edom to say.* If its people think they will return to their land, this hope will be shattered.[4] In fact, they settled permanently in the Negev, and their habitat was in Roman times called Idumea, a province of Judea. By a strange turn of fate, Herod, an Idumean by descent, was to rule in Jerusalem from 40 to 4 B.C.E.

תולדות

כֹּה אָמַר֙ יְהֹוָ֣ה צְבָא֔וֹת

הֵ֤מָּה יִבְנוּ֙ וַאֲנִ֣י אֶהֱר֔וֹס

וְקָרְא֤וּ לָהֶם֙ גְּב֣וּל רִשְׁעָ֔ה

וְהָעָ֛ם אֲשֶׁר־זָעַ֥ם יְהֹוָ֖ה עַד־עוֹלָֽם׃

5 וְעֵינֵיכֶ֖ם תִּרְאֶ֑ינָה וְאַתֶּ֣ם תֹּֽאמְר֔וּ

יִגְדַּ֣ל יְהֹוָ֔ה מֵעַ֖ל לִגְב֥וּל יִשְׂרָאֵֽל׃

6 בֵּ֛ן יְכַבֵּ֥ד אָ֖ב וְעֶ֣בֶד אֲדֹנָ֑יו

וְאִם־אָ֣ב אָ֣נִי אַיֵּ֣ה כְבוֹדִ֗י

וְאִם־אֲדוֹנִ֨ים אָ֜נִי אַיֵּ֤ה מוֹרָאִי֙

אָמַ֣ר ׀ יְהֹוָ֣ה צְבָא֗וֹת

לָכֶם֙ הַכֹּ֣הֲנִ֔ים בּוֹזֵ֖י שְׁמִ֑י

וַאֲמַרְתֶּ֕ם

בַּמֶּ֥ה בָזִ֖ינוּ אֶת־שְׁמֶֽךָ׃

7 מַגִּישִׁ֤ים עַֽל־מִזְבְּחִי֙ לֶ֣חֶם מְגֹאָ֔ל וַאֲמַרְתֶּ֕ם

בַּמֶּ֥ה גֵֽאַלְנ֑וּךָ

בֶּאֱמׇרְכֶ֕ם שֻׁלְחַ֥ן יְהֹוָ֖ה נִבְזֶ֥ה הֽוּא׃

the God of heaven's hosts would say:

They may build, but I will tear down.

People shall call them the Evil Territory,

the people whom God has cursed forever.

5. Your own eyes shall see this, and you shall say:

God is great [even] beyond the borders of Israel!

6. Children honor their parents, servants their masters.

Now, if I am a parent to you—where is the honor owed to Me?

If I am your master—where is the reverence owed to Me?

—says the God of heaven's hosts to you, the priests who despise My Name.

And yet you say:

How have we despised Your name?

7. You offer contemptible food on My altar and ask:

How have we held You in contempt?

—By saying that God's table is to be despised!

Commentary

5. *Beyond the borders of Israel.* For Malachi, God rules the world, and in time others too will recognize it or have already done so (see verse 11). In fact, the Prophet uses "God of Israel" only once,[5] and finds "God of heaven's hosts" an appealing alternate term.

6. *Children honor their parents.* The Hebrew is in the singular, using the male gender.

7. *Contemptible.* Literally, made dirty, unclean. Perhaps this is traceable to the conception that something sacred would be unfit (ritually "unclean") for ordinary use.

To be despised. Meaning, it doesn't really matter that much.

8. The God of heaven's hosts says:

When you bring a blind animal to sacrifice,

is it not a wrong?

When you bring one that is lame or sick,

is it not a wrong?

Try offering one (like that) to the governor!

Will he be pleased with you or show you

favor?

9. *Now entreat God to show us favor!*

Will God be gracious to us?

You were responsible for this—

Will God show favor to any of you?

—says the God of heaven's hosts.

10. O that one of you would close My

doors,

and not kindle fires on My altar in vain.

I have no pleasure in you—

says the God of heaven's hosts—

and I will not accept an offering from your

hands.

11. For from the rising of the sun to its

setting

My name is great among the nations.

8 וְכִי־תַגִּשׁוּן עִוֵּר לִזְבֹּחַ אֵין רָע

וְכִי תַגִּישׁוּ פִּסֵּחַ וְחֹלֶה אֵין רָע

הַקְרִיבֵהוּ נָא לְפֶחָתֶךָ הֲיִרְצְךָ

אוֹ הֲיִשָּׂא פָנֶיךָ

אָמַר יְהוָה צְבָאוֹת:

9 וְעַתָּה חַלּוּ־נָא פְנֵי־אֵל וִיחָנֵנוּ

מִיֶּדְכֶם הָיְתָה זֹּאת

הֲיִשָּׂא מִכֶּם פָּנִים

אָמַר יְהוָה צְבָאוֹת:

10 מִי גַם־בָּכֶם וְיִסְגֹּר דְּלָתַיִם

וְלֹא־תָאִירוּ מִזְבְּחִי חִנָּם

אֵין־לִי חֵפֶץ בָּכֶם

אָמַר יְהוָה צְבָאוֹת

וּמִנְחָה לֹא־אֶרְצֶה מִיֶּדְכֶם:

11 כִּי מִמִּזְרַח־שֶׁמֶשׁ וְעַד־מְבוֹאוֹ

גָּדוֹל שְׁמִי בַּגּוֹיִם

Commentary

8. *Blind .... lame ... sick.* Such animals were unfit for offering, else they would hardly be sacrifices in the meaning of "giving something up."

Governor. One would not think of presenting him with a defective gift, but for God it did not seem to matter. (The word was borrowed from the Akkadian.)

Or show you favor. It could also mean "or take your head off,"[6] which would make the use of the same verb in the next verse a play on words.

9. *You have done this to yourselves.* Literally, this came from your (own) hands.

11. *From the rising of the sun to its setting.* From east to west, that is to say, everywhere. These words are also part of Psalm 113 (verse 3), which is recited as the opening psalm of the Hallel prayers.

Everywhere incense and pure sacrifices are
    offered to My name,

for My name is great among the nations,

says the God of heaven's hosts.

12. But you profane it,

by saying that the altar of the Eternal is
    contemptible

and that its food can be despised.

13. And you said: *This is too much trouble!*

and you sniffed in contempt,

says the God of heaven's hosts.

You bring what has been stolen with
    violence,

lame animals, sickly ones—

this is what you bring as an offering.

Will I accept this from your hands?

says the Eternal One.

14. Cursed is the cunning knave

who has in his flocks a healthy beast,

and promises it with a vow,

then sacrifices to the Eternal an animal
    that is spoiled!

For I am a great Sovereign,

says the God of heaven's hosts,

and My name is feared among the nations.

2:1. Now, then, this command is for you,
    the priests:

וּבְכָל־מָקוֹם מֻקְטָר מֻגָּשׁ לִשְׁמִי וּמִנְחָה
טְהוֹרָה

כִּי־גָדוֹל שְׁמִי בַּגּוֹיִם

אָמַר יְהוָה צְבָאוֹת:

12 וְאַתֶּם מְחַלְּלִים אוֹתוֹ

בֶּאֱמָרְכֶם שֻׁלְחַן אֲדֹנָי מְגֹאָל הוּא

וְנִיבוֹ נִבְזֶה אָכְלוֹ:

13 וַאֲמַרְתֶּם הִנֵּה מַתְּלָאָה

וְהִפַּחְתֶּם אוֹתוֹ

אָמַר יְהוָה צְבָאוֹת

וַהֲבֵאתֶם גָּזוּל

וְאֶת־הַפִּסֵּחַ וְאֶת־הַחוֹלֶה

וַהֲבֵאתֶם אֶת־הַמִּנְחָה

הַאֶרְצֶה אוֹתָהּ מִיֶּדְכֶם

אָמַר יְהוָה:

14 וְאָרוּר נוֹכֵל

וְיֵשׁ בְּעֶדְרוֹ זָכָר וְנֹדֵר

וְזֹבֵחַ מָשְׁחָת לַאדֹנָי

כִּי מֶלֶךְ גָּדוֹל אָנִי

אָמַר יְהוָה צְבָאוֹת

וּשְׁמִי נוֹרָא בַגּוֹיִם:

2:1 וְעַתָּה אֲלֵיכֶם הַמִּצְוָה הַזֹּאת הַכֹּהֲנִים:

Commentary

13. *This is too much trouble*. To do it the way it ought to be done.

Stolen with violence. That in addition to the animal's physical defect makes the whole offering a triple sham.

14. *Healthy beast*. Literally, "male beast," which was on certain occasions required by the Torah.

2. Give honor to My name.

If you do not listen,

if you do not take it to heart,

says the God of heaven's hosts,

I will send a curse upon you,

and turn your blessings to curses.

In fact, I have [already] turned them into
curses,

because you do not take it to heart.

3. Behold, I will rebuke your seed

and spread dung on your faces,

the dung of your (feast-day) sacrifices,

and drive you away from My presence.

4. Then, says the God of heaven's hosts,
you shall know that I have sent you this
command

to keep alive My covenant with Levi,

5. My covenant of life and well-being that
was with him;

that I had given him, so that he stood in
awe of My name.

2 אִם־לֹא תִשְׁמְעוּ

וְאִם־לֹא תָשִׂימוּ עַל־לֵב

לָתֵת כָּבוֹד לִשְׁמִי

אָמַר יְהוָה צְבָאוֹת

וְשִׁלַּחְתִּי בָכֶם אֶת־הַמְּאֵרָה

וְאָרוֹתִי אֶת־בִּרְכוֹתֵיכֶם

וְגַם אָרוֹתִיהָ

כִּי אֵינְכֶם שָׂמִים עַל־לֵב:

3 הִנְנִי גֹעֵר לָכֶם אֶת־הַזֶּרַע

וְזֵרִיתִי פֶרֶשׁ עַל־פְּנֵיכֶם

פֶּרֶשׁ חַגֵּיכֶם

וְנָשָׂא אֶתְכֶם אֵלָיו:

4 וִידַעְתֶּם כִּי שִׁלַּחְתִּי אֲלֵיכֶם אֵת־הַמִּצְוָה
הַזֹּאת

לִהְיוֹת בְּרִיתִי אֶת־לֵוִי

אָמַר יְהוָה צְבָאוֹת:

5 בְּרִיתִי הָיְתָה אִתּוֹ הַחַיִּים וְהַשָּׁלוֹם

וָאֶתְּנֵם־לוֹ מוֹרָא וַיִּירָאֵנִי וּמִפְּנֵי שְׁמִי נִחַת
הוּא:

Commentary

2:2. *Give honor to My name.* The translation has been rearranged for clarity.

3. *Cut off your posterity.* Leave you without offspring.

Dung on your faces. An earthy tit-for-tat.

And cast you on the dung heap. A speculative translation. [7]

4. *Keep alive ...* Reading לחיות (*Lichyot*) instead of להיות (*lih'yot*).

My covenant with Levi. The covenant assuring the tribe of the exclusive right to priestly service. [8]

6. A teaching of truth was in his mouth,
and no wrong was found on his lips;
he walked with Me in peace and equity,
and turned many away from iniquity.
7. For the lips of a priest should faithfully
  speak knowledge,
so that people look to him for instruction—
for he is a messenger of the God of
  heaven's hosts.

6 תּוֹרַת אֱמֶת הָיְתָה בְּפִיהוּ
וְעַוְלָה לֹא־נִמְצָא בִשְׂפָתָיו
בְּשָׁלוֹם וּבְמִישׁוֹר הָלַךְ אִתִּי
וְרַבִּים הֵשִׁיב מֵעָוֺן:
7 כִּי־שִׂפְתֵי כֹהֵן יִשְׁמְרוּ־דַעַת
וְתוֹרָה יְבַקְשׁוּ מִפִּיהוּ
כִּי מַלְאַךְ יְהֹוָה־צְבָאוֹת הוּא:

Commentary

7. *Should faithfully speak*. Repeat faithfully.[9] The priests were to be the primary
teachers of the people, something Ezekiel had stressed strongly.

He is a messenger. Rashi calls the priest God's deputy.

Essay

Pagans as monotheists?

The eleventh verse of Malachi's first chapter is puzzling and thought-provoking. At a time when idolatry was nearly universal and belief in the One God was rare outside of Israel (and even there was shaky and diluted), the Prophet makes the statement that the Eternal's name is great among the nations, and that everywhere pure sacrifices are offered to the God of Israel.

Though he knew that paganism and not monotheism was regnant everywhere, he proceeded with his startling announcement. By doing this he expanded the meaning of religion and gave Judaism a dimension it had not as yet enjoyed.

Malachi confirms the concept that when people worship in sincerity—even though they be pagans—they honor the Sovereign of the world. "The offerings which they thus present (indirectly) unto Me are animated by a pure spirit, God looking to the heart of the worshipper." [10]

It is likely that Malachi saw pagans adding the Eternal to their pantheon, as a first stage (he hoped) on the road to the recognition of God as the sole deity. By incorporating the worship of the Eternal into their practices they showed respect and deference—even though they did not thereby abandon the worship of other gods. Malachi does not discuss this issue; what is on his mind is the lack of respect his own people have shown for God and tradition. Comparing Jews and gentiles, the Israelites come off second best, and in the Prophet's harangue a sincere pagan is considered better than an insincere Jew. [11]

When pagans adore the pantheon of their gods, they do so because they believe that there is something beyond themselves. Thus, when they engage in sincere worship of their deities they are in fact engaged in a search for God. Therefore, the Prophet says, God prefers them to an Israel that does not take its God seriously.

Some centuries later the Rabbis would phrase this teaching in their own way, when they said: "The righteous of all nations have a share in the world to come." [12] Judaism is not the only way to salvation.

Gleanings

Words to Remember

From the rising of the sun to its setting
My name is great among the nations. (1:11)

Who was Malachi?

Since the name means "My Messenger," but does not identify the Prophet, tradition speculates on who he really was. The Talmud suggests that Malachi was another name for Ezra the scribe. [13]

The end of prophecy

After Haggai, Zechariah, and Malachi, the Holy Spirit departed from Israel; that is, there were no other prophets in the biblical sense.

Talmud[14]

* * *

Notes

[1] Genesis 25:30; he was so called because he had red (*adom*) hair.

[2] Obadiah verses 12-15 (there is only one chapter). Psalm 137:7 also preserves this memory.

[3] To this day, the ruins of Petra testify to their civilization.

[4] Targum and Rashi render this sense: "We [Edomites] were impoverished, but now have become rich (from the spoils of a destroyed Jerusalem) and thus will be able to return and rebuild the ruins."

[5] In 2:16.

[6] Compare Genesis 40:19, where ישא is used in this way.

[7] The Septuagint has, "and drive you away from My presence."

[8] It has been suggested that the mention of Levi instead of Aaron shows that in Malachi's time the book of Leviticus had not as yet become part of the Torah. For, so the argument goes, the P document speaks of Aaron's house as the priests and of the levites as their attendants. (See *Interpreter's Bible*, vol. 6, p. 1131.) However, theories concerning the age of Leviticus are much in dispute, and Malachi's expression should not be given any weight in this discussion.

[9] This use of שמר (usually, to guard) is found in Numbers 23:12.

[10] J. H. Hertz, *The Pentateuch and Haftorahs*, p. 103 (in comment on this haftarah).

[11] That term was not yet in existence, but we use it here to describe members of the covenanted people.

[12] *Tosefta* Sanhedrin 13:2; see also Maimonides, *Yad*, Hilchot Melachim (Laws Concerning Kings) 8:11, and Hilchot Teshuvah (Laws Concerning Repentance) 3:5.

[13] B. Megillah 16b.

[14] B. Yoma 9b-10a.

וַיֵּצֵא

Hosea, chapter 12, verse 13 to chapter 14, verse 10

Introduction

Connection of haftarah and sidra:

The weekly sidra tells of Jacob's sojourn in Aram, and the first two verses of the haftarah recall that event. Otherwise, the content of the prophecy that follows has little to do with the tale of Jacob.[1]

The setting:

Hosea lived in the 8th century B.C.E., and was a contemporary of Amos. He resided and preached in the Northern Kingdom, which bore the name of Israel. However, Hosea calls it Ephraim, because its first king, Jeroboam (who had seceded from the united monarchy after Solomon's death) had belonged to the tribe of Ephraim. Hosea addresses himself unsparingly to the social and religious ills of his society, though in the end he holds out God's forgiveness if the people will mend their ways.

For more on Hosea and his time, see our *General Introduction.*

The message:

1. A historical note about Jacob and Moses. (12:13-14)
2. The sinfulness of Ephraim. (12:15-13:3)
3. God's past problems with Israel. (13:4-13)
4. The destruction that lies ahead for an unrepentant nation. (13:14-14:1)
5. A repentant Israel will enjoy God's favor once again. (14:2-10) This section of the prophecy forms also the bulk of the haftarah for the Shabbat between Rosh Hashanah and Yom Kippur (Shabbat Shuvah).

The text of the haftarah consists of different thoughts whose meaning is often unclear, and its meaning is often unclear.

HAFTARAH FOR VAYEITZEI

Hosea, chapter 12, verse 13 to chapter 14, verse 10

12:13. Jacob fled to the land of Aram,
Israel served for a wife;
and for a wife he kept watch [of sheep].

14. By a prophet the Eternal brought Israel
   up from Egypt,
and by a prophet they were watched.

15. Ephraim caused bitter anger,
and because of his (blood)guilt his
   Sovereign abandoned him,
and paid him back for his scorn.

13:1. When Ephraim spoke with trembling,
he was lifted high in Israel;
but through Baal he incurred guilt, and
   died.

12:13 וַיִּבְרַח יַעֲקֹב שְׂדֵה אֲרָם
וַיַּעֲבֹד יִשְׂרָאֵל בְּאִשָּׁה
וּבְאִשָּׁה שָׁמָר:

14 וּבְנָבִיא הֶעֱלָה יְהוָה אֶת־יִשְׂרָאֵל מִמִּצְרָיִם
וּבְנָבִיא נִשְׁמָר:

15 הִכְעִיס אֶפְרַיִם תַּמְרוּרִים
וְדָמָיו עָלָיו יִטּוֹשׁ
וְחֶרְפָּתוֹ יָשִׁיב לוֹ אֲדֹנָיו:

13:1 כְּדַבֵּר אֶפְרַיִם רְתֵת
נָשָׂא הוּא בְּיִשְׂרָאֵל
וַיֶּאְשַׁם בַּבַּעַל וַיָּמֹת:

Commentary

12:13. *Aram.* A state (or confederation of states) during the 11th to 8th centuries B.C.E. in the Near East. It was often at war with Israel, and though it disappeared in time, its language, Aramaic, became the popular tongue of the area. Jews spoke it at the time of the Romans (relegating Hebrew to religious and learning environments), and it entered the Tanach and both the Palestinian and Babylonian Talmuds.

Jacob set out for Haran in western Aram, when he fled from Esau.[2]

Israel served for a wife. The names Israel and Jacob are used interchangeably, even though at the time of his serving for Rachel[3] he had not yet been given his new name.[4]

14. *By a prophet.* Moses, who watched over Israel as he had watched over the flock of his father-in-law, Jethro.[5]

13:1. *Trembling.* רתת (r'tet) occurs nowhere else in the Tanach; the translation is an educated guess.[6]

He was lifted high. Ephraim had a preferred status in the Northern Kingdom.

Through Baal he incurred guilt. The reference is to Baal Peor, where Israel committed grievous sexual offenses,[7] as did Ephraim in Hosea's time.

And died. God caused many to die in the desert when the transgressions took place, and the same fate awaits Ephraim now.

2. They add sin to sin,

making for themselves molten images,

skillfully making idols,

the work of artisans throughout.

They speak to them:

to [images of] calves, which people sacrifice, they offer kisses!

3. Therefore, they shall be like the morning
cloud,

like the dew so quickly gone,

like straw driven as by a storm from a
threshing-floor,

like smoke out of a hole in the wall.

4. Yet I, the Eternal, have been your God

ever since the land of Egypt;

you have known no [real] God but Me,

there is no Savior besides Me.

5. I knew you in the wilderness,

in a land of blazing heat.

6. When you grazed and were sated,

sated, you grew proud

and therefore you forgot Me.

7. So I have become like a lion to you,

like a leopard lurking near the road;

2 וְעַתָּה יוֹסִפוּ לַחֲטֹא

וַיַּעֲשׂוּ לָהֶם מַסֵּכָה

מִכַּסְפָּם כִּתְבוּנָם עֲצַבִּים

מַעֲשֵׂה חָרָשִׁים כֻּלֹּה

לָהֶם הֵם אֹמְרִים

זֹבְחֵי אָדָם עֲגָלִים יִשָּׁקוּן׃

3 לָכֵן יִהְיוּ כַּעֲנַן־בֹּקֶר

וְכַטַּל מַשְׁכִּים הֹלֵךְ

כְּמֹץ יְסֹעֵר מִגֹּרֶן

וּכְעָשָׁן מֵאֲרֻבָּה׃

4 וְאָנֹכִי יְהוָה אֱלֹהֶיךָ

מֵאֶרֶץ מִצְרָיִם

וֵאלֹהִים זוּלָתִי לֹא תֵדָע

וּמוֹשִׁיעַ אַיִן בִּלְתִּי׃

5 אֲנִי יְדַעְתִּיךָ בַּמִּדְבָּר

בְּאֶרֶץ תַּלְאֻבוֹת׃

6 כְּמַרְעִיתָם וַיִּשְׂבָּעוּ

שָׂבְעוּ וַיָּרָם לִבָּם

עַל־כֵּן שְׁכֵחוּנִי׃

7 וָאֱהִי לָהֶם כְּמוֹ־שָׁחַל

כְּנָמֵר עַל־דֶּרֶךְ אָשׁוּר׃

Commentary

2. *Which people sacrifice.* Many understand זֹבְחֵי אָדָם (*zovchei adam*) as "those who sacrifice men," and assume that such practices existed in Hosea's time.

6-8. *When you grazed.* Here, and in the next two verses, the ancient Israelites are compared to a flock guarded by the shepherd. But their very guardian becomes their pursuer when they forget from whom their safety and well-being derive. In these three verses God addresses Israel in the third person, but our translation remains in the second.

8. Like a bear robbed of his cubs I will
   meet you,
and tear away the casing of your heart;
there like a lion I will devour you;
wild beasts shall tear you to pieces.
9. You are done for, Israel,
for who can help you!
10. Where then is your king? Let him save
   you
in all your towns!
Where are the leaders of your towns,
for whom you asked, saying:
Give me a king, give me leaders!
11. In My wrath I gave you a king;
in My fury I removed him!
12. Ephraim's iniquity is stored up;
his sin is preserved.
13. Birth pains came for him,
but he is an unwise babe,
for when the time comes he does not
   present himself at the birthplace of
   babes.

8 אֶפְגְּשֵׁם כְּדֹב שַׁכּוּל

וְאֶקְרַע סְגוֹר לִבָּם

וְאֹכְלֵם שָׁם כְּלָבִיא

חַיַּת הַשָּׂדֶה תְּבַקְּעֵם:

9 שִׁחֶתְךָ יִשְׂרָאֵל כִּי־בִי בְעֶזְרֶךָ:

10 אֱהִי מַלְכְּךָ אֵפוֹא וְיוֹשִׁיעֲךָ

בְּכָל־עָרֶיךָ

וְשֹׁפְטֶיךָ אֲשֶׁר אָמַרְתָּ

תְּנָה־לִּי מֶלֶךְ וְשָׂרִים:

11 אֶתֶּן־לְךָ מֶלֶךְ בְּאַפִּי

וְאֶקַּח בְּעֶבְרָתִי:

12 צָרוּר עֲוֺן אֶפְרָיִם

צְפוּנָה חַטָּאתוֹ:

13 חֶבְלֵי יוֹלֵדָה יָבֹאוּ לוֹ

הוּא־בֵן לֹא חָכָם

כִּי־עֵת לֹא־יַעֲמֹד בְּמִשְׁבַּר בָּנִים:

Commentary

8. *Like a bear robbed of his cubs.* Hosea now shifts from past to present: the Children of Israel are God's "cubs," and those who destroy the relationship will suffer bitter consequences.

9. *You are done for, Israel.* The Hebrew is difficult. Rashi explains: You have destroyed yourself, O Israel, by sinning and rebelling against your God.

10. *Give me a king.* Hosea recalls the tale of the prophet Samuel who tried to resist the people's demand for a king and reprimanded them for substituting an earthly ruler for the Eternal. Eventually he gave in, at God's behest.[8]

11. *In My wrath....* God gave them Saul as king, but eventually had to replace him with David.[9] Though the Hebrew is in the future tense, the past is intended. This dual use of tenses occurs regularly in the Tanach.

13. *At the birthplace of babes.* A speculative rendering, probably meaning "at the mouth of the womb." A metaphor for Ephraim's lack of consideration: by tarrying at the time of birth, the emerging child endangers not only itself but its mother as well.[10] The verse seems out of sequence.

14. I will redeem them from the grave;

I will save them from death!

Where are your plagues, O Death?

Where is your pestilence, O grave?

Vengeance shall be hidden from My eyes,

15. for he [only] among the reeds

shall be fruitful.

An east wind shall come,

a divine wind up from the wilderness,

so that his fountain shall dry up

and his spring shall be parched;

it shall pillage treasures,

every choice thing.

14:1. Samaria must bear her guilt,

for she has rebelled against her God.

They will fall to the sword,

their little ones dashed in pieces,

their women with child ripped open.

2. Return, O Israel, to the Eternal your
   God,

for you have stumbled in your iniquity.

14 מִיַּ֤ד שְׁאוֹל֙ אֶפְדֵּ֔ם

מִמָּ֖וֶת אֶגְאָלֵ֑ם

אֱהִ֤י דְבָרֶ֙יךָ֙ מָ֔וֶת

אֱהִ֥י קָטָבְךָ֖ שְׁא֑וֹל

נֹ֖חַם יִסָּתֵ֥ר מֵעֵינָֽי׃

15 כִּ֣י ה֤וּא בֵּ֤ן אַחִים֙ יַפְרִ֔יא

יָב֣וֹא קָדִ֗ים

ר֤וּחַ יְהֹוָה֙ מִמִּדְבָּ֣ר עֹלֶ֔ה

וְיֵב֣וֹשׁ מְקוֹר֗וֹ

וְיֶחֱרַ֣ב מַעְיָנ֔וֹ

ה֥וּא יִשְׁסֶ֖ה אוֹצַ֑ר

כָּל־כְּלִ֥י חֶמְדָּֽה׃

14:1 תֶּאְשַׁם֙ שֹׁ֣מְר֔וֹן

כִּ֥י מָרְתָ֖ה בֵּֽאלֹהֶ֑יהָ

בַּחֶ֣רֶב יִפֹּ֔לוּ

עֹלְלֵיהֶ֣ם יְרֻטָּ֔שׁוּ

וְהָרִיּוֹתָ֖יו יְבֻקָּֽעוּ׃

2 שׁ֚וּבָה יִשְׂרָאֵ֔ל עַ֖ד יְהֹוָ֣ה אֱלֹהֶ֑יךָ

כִּ֥י כָשַׁ֖לְתָּ בַּעֲוֺנֶֽךָ׃

Commentary

14. *The grave.* Literally, "Sheol," the netherworld, a biblical term for the abode of the dead, which is elsewhere described as a place of utter darkness. Unlike later Jewish and Christian teaching that differentiated between the postmortem fates of the righteous and the wicked, the Tanach teaches that issues of reward and punishment are settled before death. In consequence, everyone—good or bad—descends into Sheol, which was known also as "the grave" and "the forgotten land."[11] The end of the verse is not clear.

15. *Among the reeds.* Reading אחו (*achu*, reeds) for אחים (*achim*, brothers).[12]

14:1. *Samaria.* The kingdom of Israel is represented by its capital.

Women with child ripped open. They will fall prey to barbaric cruelty.[13]

2. *Return, O Israel.* The last nine verses of the haftarah are also the last in the book of Hosea. They are read again on Shabbat Shuvah, the first Shabbat of the new religious year.

Stumbled in your iniquity. Or, "because of your iniquity."

3. Take words with you

and return to the Eternal,

and say:

Forgive all iniquity and accept the good;

and we shall offer the fruit of our lips.

4. *Assyria cannot save us;*

we shall ride on horses no more;

never again shall we say "Our God"

to the works of our hands.

For in You [alone] the orphan finds com-

    passion.

5. *I will heal their disloyalty;*

I will love them freely;

for My wrath has turned away from them.

6. *I will be like dew to Israel.*

They shall blossom like a lily

and strike roots like [the trees of] Lebanon.

7. *Their shoots shall spread out wide,*

their splendor like an olive-tree's,

their fragrance like that of Lebanon.

3 קְחוּ עִמָּכֶם דְּבָרִים

וְשׁוּבוּ אֶל־יְהוָה

אִמְרוּ אֵלָיו

כָּל־תִּשָּׂא עָוֹן וְקַח־טוֹב

וּנְשַׁלְּמָה פָרִים שְׂפָתֵינוּ:

4 אַשּׁוּר לֹא יוֹשִׁיעֵנוּ

עַל־סוּס לֹא נִרְכָּב

וְלֹא־נֹאמַר עוֹד אֱלֹהֵינוּ

לְמַעֲשֵׂה יָדֵינוּ

אֲשֶׁר־בְּךָ יְרֻחַם יָתוֹם:

5 אֶרְפָּא מְשׁוּבָתָם

אֹהֲבֵם נְדָבָה

כִּי שָׁב אַפִּי מִמֶּנּוּ:

6 אֶהְיֶה כַטַּל לְיִשְׂרָאֵל

יִפְרַח כַּשּׁוֹשַׁנָּה

וְיַךְ שָׁרָשָׁיו כַּלְּבָנוֹן:

7 יֵלְכוּ יֹנְקוֹתָיו

וִיהִי כַזַּיִת הוֹדוֹ

וְרֵיחַ לוֹ כַּלְּבָנוֹן:

Commentary

3. *Take words with you.* Come prepared to confess your sins.

The fruit of our lips. Our earnest prayers. Reading פְּרִי (*p'ri*, fruit) instead of פָרִים (*parim*, bulls). [14]

4. *On horses no more.* Alluding to the use of horses by Egypt's armies: Israel will no longer rely on an alliance with Egypt. [15]

5. *I will heal their disloyalty.* A wordplay on verse 2: I will heal your מְשׁוּבָה (*meshuvah*, disloyalty) if you heed My plea, "שׁוּבָה" (*shuvah*, return).

From them. Here and in the following verse the Hebrew is in the singular; apparently Hosea had in mind the word *am*, which is a singular for people.

וַיֵּצֵא

8. Those who sit in their shade shall return
[to Me],

they shall grow [their] corn,

and blossom like a vine,

renowned as the wine of Lebanon.

9. Ephraim [shall say]: *What are idols to
me now?*

I will respond and look to him.

[For] I am a luxuriant cypress,

from which your fruit is found.

10. The wise shall understand these things,

the discerning shall know them:

that straight are the ways of the Eternal;

while the righteous walk in them,

transgressors stumble on them.

7. Their shoots shall spread out wide,

their splendor like an olive-tree's,

their fragrance like that of Lebanon.

8 יָשֻׁבוּ יֹשְׁבֵי בְצִלּוֹ

יְחַיּוּ דָגָן

וְיִפְרְחוּ כַגָּפֶן

זִכְרוֹ כְּיֵין לְבָנוֹן:

9 אֶפְרַיִם מַה־לִּי עוֹד לָעֲצַבִּים

אֲנִי עָנִיתִי וַאֲשׁוּרֶנּוּ

אֲנִי כִּבְרוֹשׁ רַעֲנָן

מִמֶּנִּי פֶּרְיְךָ נִמְצָא:

10 מִי חָכָם וְיָבֵן אֵלֶּה

נָבוֹן וְיֵדָעֵם

כִּי־יְשָׁרִים דַּרְכֵי יְהֹוָה

וְצַדִּקִים יֵלְכוּ בָם

וּפֹשְׁעִים יִכָּשְׁלוּ בָם:

7 יֵלְכוּ יֹנְקוֹתָיו

וִיהִי כַזַּיִת הוֹדוֹ

וְרֵיחַ לוֹ כַּלְּבָנוֹן:

Commentary

10. *Transgressors stumble on them.* Because a haftarah was not to end on a negative note, the Rabbis ordained that verse 7 be repeated as the finale.

Essay

"Return, O Israel" (14:2)

In Hosea's language, to turn to God is an act of contrition or, as we would say, repentance. One of his most often-cited orations begins with the word "return," and its Hebrew original (שובה, *shuvah*) has given the Shabbat between Rosh Hashanah and Yom Kippur its name, "Shabbat Shuvah." Repentance is returning to God in true contrition.

The root *shuv* combines in itself both requisites of repentance: to turn from the evil and turn to the good. The motion of turning implies that sin is not an ineradicable stain but a straying from the right path. By the effort of turning, all sinners can redirect their destiny.[16]

It is noteworthy that the Hebrew word for repentance, תשובה (*t'shuvah*), was known neither to Hosea nor to the rest of the Tanach in that meaning. It was so employed by the Rabbis and has been used in our theology ever since.

When Hosea and the other prophets spoke, they addressed the need for *national* regeneration. It was Israel as a people that had to turn to the Eternal, so that the nation might live. It was a collective concept, which became an *individual* one only after the Temple and the commonwealth had been destroyed. The nation was gone, and the need for returning now rested on each person.

Of course, Hosea did not address an abstract community whom he urged to acknowledge its sins; it was individuals, especially the leaders. They had to mend their ways, and their joint turning would accomplish the desired goal. While each one thus had a responsibility, there had to be enough of them to change the community's course. The focus of the prophets was on Israel's fate: the common decision to repent would spell well-being for all, even as the failure to heed the call for repentance would mean doom for the entire community, the guilty and the innocent.

In a democratic society, where each citizen has a share in the decision making of the community, something of the biblical setting is re-created: we are all part of the need for turning. This applies wherever Jews live, in the Diaspora where they must exert whatever influence for good they can muster, and especially in Israel, where each citizen can help to shape the fate of the nation.

In this way, we can imagine Hosea speaking to our time, confronting us with our shortcomings and spelling out the consequences that await us if we fall short of our responsibilities and opportunities.

Gleanings

Before Creation

Repentance, say the Rabbis, was created before the world was created.

Talmud[17]

All your days

What does Rabbi Eliezer mean when he says, "Repent one day before your death?" How can one know when that day comes? Since no person can know this, one must repent every day of one's life.

Talmud[18]

The culminating idea

To act out of love and to be willing to bear the suffering which the good and true person must inevitably bear in a world like ours, in a world which is only partly divine and which must be won for God through our efforts—that is the deepest utterance of the Rabbis and the culminating idea of of Jewish religiosity and of Jewish prayer.

Henry M. Slonimsky[19]

Hosea takes sides

The Prophet makes it clear that God has a controversy with Israel (4:1). Whose part does the Prophet take in the divine controversy? ... Hosea never tries to plead for the people or to dwell upon the reasons for the people's alienation from God. He has only one perspective: the divine partner. As a result there is little understanding for human weakness. ... God is in love with Israel, but also has a passionate love of right and a burning hatred of wrong.

Abraham J. Heschel[20]

***

Notes

[1] The suggestion has been made that this is an allusion to Hosea's prediction that at some future time Israel will again have to leave its home, but if that happens it will eventually return (like the Forefather) well endowed with earthly goods and God's grace (see commentary by A. Cohen in the *Soncino Bible*).

[2] Genesis 28:10.

[3] Genesis 29:15.

[4] The new name, Israel, was bestowed on him after he wrestled with the mysterious opponent (Genesis 32:29).

[5] Exodus 3:1.

[6] Andersen and Freedman (*Anchor Bible,* Hosea) translate "terrifyingly," making God the speaker and giving the verse an entirely different thrust.

[7] Numbers 25:1-3.

[8] I Samuel 8:4 and following.

[9] I Samuel 31.

[10] So A. Cohen, *Soncino Bible*.

[11] See T. Gaster, *Interpreter's Dictionary of the Bible*, vol. 1, pp. 787-788.

[12] So New JPS, RSV, and NEB.

[13] See II Kings 8:12; 15:16; Amos 1:13. Note that though the subject is "women" the verb is in the masculine, a grammatical dissonance also found in the Song of Songs 2:7 and 3:5.

[14] So the Septuagint and the Syriac translation.

[15] Compare II Kings 18:24; the same in Isaiah 36:9: "Relying on Egypt for chariots and horsemen."

[16] Jacob Milgrom, *Encyclopaedia Judaica*, vol. 14, p. 73.

[17] B. Pesachim 54a.

[18] B. Shabbat 153a.

[19] *Essays*, p.128.

[20] *The Prophets*, pp. 49-50.

וישלח א

Hosea, chapter 11, verse 7 to chapter 12, verse 12

Introduction

Connection of haftarah and sidra:

The weekly sidra's climax is Jacob's struggle with the angel, a scene that Hosea retells as a metaphor for his own time.

The setting:

Hosea lived in the 8th century B.C.E., and was a contemporary of Amos. He resided and preached in the Northern Kingdom, which bore the name of Israel. However, Hosea calls it Ephraim, because its first king, Jeroboam (who had seceded from the united monarchy after Solomon's death), had belonged to the tribe of Ephraim. The Prophet addresses himself unsparingly to the social and religious ills of his society, though in the end he holds out God's forgiveness if the people will mend their ways.

For more on Hosea and his time, see our *General Introduction*.

The message:

1. God's abiding compassion. (11:7-11)
2. Ephraim's defection from God and its need to return. (12:1-6)
3. All that Ephraim prizes is from God. (12:7-11)
4. A brief oracle about Gilead. (12:12)

Verse 13 is the beginning of the haftarah for the preceding sidra, Vayeitzei.

HAFTARAH FOR VAYISHLACH

Hosea, chapter 11, verse 7 to chapter 12, verse 12

11:7. My people are bent on turning from
  Me;

they invoke him [Baal] on the heights,

but he cannot lift them up!

8. How can I give you up, Ephraim?

How can I let you go, O Israel?

How can I make you like Admah,

or treat you like Zeboim?

My heart has changed in Me,

all My pity stirs.

9. I will not act upon My wrath,

I will not turn to destroy Ephraim:

for I am God and no mortal,

the Holy One in your midst;

I will not come with anger.

10. They shall follow the Eternal,

who will roar like a lion;

When God roars

children shall flutter from the west.

11:7 וְעַמִּי תְלוּאִים לִמְשׁוּבָתִי
וְאֶל־עַל יִקְרָאֻהוּ יַחַד
לֹא יְרוֹמֵם:
8 אֵיךְ אֶתֶּנְךָ אֶפְרַיִם
אֲמַגֶּנְךָ יִשְׂרָאֵל
אֵיךְ אֶתֶּנְךָ כְאַדְמָה
אֲשִׂימְךָ כִּצְבֹאיִם
נֶהְפַּךְ עָלַי לִבִּי
יַחַד נִכְמְרוּ נִחוּמָי:
9 לֹא אֶעֱשֶׂה חֲרוֹן אַפִּי
לֹא אָשׁוּב לְשַׁחֵת אֶפְרָיִם
כִּי אֵל אָנֹכִי וְלֹא־אִישׁ
בְּקִרְבְּךָ קָדוֹשׁ
וְלֹא אָבוֹא בְּעִיר:
10 אַחֲרֵי יְהוָה יֵלְכוּ
כְּאַרְיֵה יִשְׁאָג
כִּי־הוּא יִשְׁאַג
וְיֶחֶרְדוּ בָנִים מִיָּם:

Commentary

11:7. *On the heights.* אל על (*el-al*) became the name for Israel's national airline.

But he cannot lift them up. The translation is speculative.

8. *Admah ... Zeboim.* Hosea represents the northern tradition, which related that the two cities that God overturned for their sins were Admah and Zeboim, while in the south the tradition was that this happened to Sodom and Gomorrah.[1]

10. *Roar like a lion.* The ancients did not hesitate to use highly anthropomorphic expressions and metaphors when speaking about God.

11. They shall come from Egypt
fluttering like a bird,
from the land of Assyria
[trembling] like a dove,
and I will settle them in their homes,
says the Eternal One.

12:1. Ephraim surrounds Me with lies,
the House of Israel with deceit,
while Judah still stands firm
with God
and keeps faith with the holy [angels].

2. Ephraim tends the wind,
pursuing the east wind,
ever multiplying falsehood and violence:
now making a covenant with Assyria,
and then sending oil to Egypt.

3. The Eternal has arraigned Judah,
and will punish Jacob according to his
   ways,
repaying him according to his deeds.

4. In the womb he seized his brother's
   heel;
grown up, he wrestled with a divine being.

11 יֶחֶרְדוּ כְצִפּוֹר מִמִּצְרַיִם

וּכְיוֹנָה מֵאֶרֶץ אַשּׁוּר

וְהוֹשַׁבְתִּים עַל־בָּתֵּיהֶם

נְאֻם־יְהוָה:

12:1 סְבָבֻנִי בְכַחַשׁ אֶפְרַיִם

וּבְמִרְמָה בֵּית יִשְׂרָאֵל

וִיהוּדָה עֹד רָד עִם־אֵל

וְעִם־קְדוֹשִׁים נֶאֱמָן:

2 אֶפְרַיִם רֹעֶה רוּחַ

וְרֹדֵף קָדִים

כָּל־הַיּוֹם כָּזָב וָשֹׁד יַרְבֶּה

וּבְרִית עִם־אַשּׁוּר יִכְרֹתוּ

וְשֶׁמֶן לְמִצְרַיִם יוּבָל:

3 וְרִיב לַיהוָה עִם־יְהוּדָה

וְלִפְקֹד עַל־יַעֲקֹב כִּדְרָכָיו

כְּמַעֲלָלָיו יָשִׁיב לוֹ:

4 בַּבֶּטֶן עָקַב אֶת־אָחִיו

וּבְאוֹנוֹ שָׂרָה אֶת־אֱלֹהִים:

Commentary

12:1. *Stands firm.* רד (*rad*) has been understood in many ways; our translation follows Rashi.

2. *Assyria … Egypt.* Covenanting with them rather than with God.

Sending oil. Used in oath and treaty ceremonies in the ancient Near East.[2]

3. *Has arraigned Israel.* The text says "Judah," but this is no doubt due to an old scribal error, which was copied faithfully. The parallelism of the stanza requires "Israel," and so does the context.

5. He wrestled with an angel and prevailed;

he cried out and entreated him,

who met him at Beth El

and there spoke with us.

6. But [in truth it was] the Eternal, the God

　　of heaven's hosts,

whose designation is *the Eternal.*

7. Now, then, you must [truly] turn back to

　　your God:

hold fast to steadfast love and justice,

and wait continually for your God!

8. [Like] a trader who uses dishonest

　　scales, who loves to oppress,

9. Ephraim says:

How rich I have become,

I have found wealth for myself!

And in all my labors

they cannot find an offense

that is (really) a sin.

10. But I, the Eternal, have been your God

　　since the land of Egypt;

I can make you live in tents again, as in

　　the days of the Tabernacle.

5 וַיָּ֤שַׂר אֶל־מַלְאָךְ֙ וַיֻּכָ֔ל

בָּכָ֖ה וַיִּתְחַנֶּן־ל֑וֹ

בֵּֽית־אֵל֙ יִמְצָאֶ֔נּוּ

וְשָׁ֖ם יְדַבֵּ֥ר עִמָּֽנוּ׃

6 וַֽיהֹוָ֖ה אֱלֹהֵ֣י הַצְּבָא֑וֹת

יְהֹוָ֖ה זִכְרֽוֹ׃

7 וְאַתָּ֖ה בֵּאלֹהֶ֣יךָ תָשׁ֑וּב

חֶ֤סֶד וּמִשְׁפָּט֙ שְׁמֹ֔ר

וְקַוֵּ֥ה אֶל־אֱלֹהֶ֖יךָ תָּמִֽיד׃

8 כְּנַ֗עַן בְּיָד֛וֹ מֹאזְנֵ֥י מִרְמָ֖ה

לַעֲשֹׁ֥ק אָהֵֽב׃

9 וַיֹּ֣אמֶר אֶפְרַ֔יִם אַ֣ךְ עָשַׁ֔רְתִּי

מָצָ֥אתִי א֖וֹן לִ֑י

כָּל־יְגִיעַ֕י

לֹ֥א יִמְצְאוּ־לִ֖י עָוֺ֥ן

אֲשֶׁר־חֵֽטְא׃

10 וְאָ֣נֹכִ֔י יְהֹוָ֥ה אֱלֹהֶ֖יךָ מֵאֶ֣רֶץ מִצְרָ֑יִם

עֹ֛ד אוֹשִֽׁיבְךָ֥ בׇאֳהָלִ֖ים כִּימֵ֥י מוֹעֵֽד׃

Commentary

12:5. *He cried out.* A detail not mentioned in the account of Jacob's wrestling with the angel.[3]

And there spoke with us. Hosea identifies his nation with the ancestor Jacob and therefore says "us." Jacob wrestled with the angel there, and was given a new name, Israel.

7. A new section begins here.

8. *Trader.* In Hosea's time, כנען (*kena'an,* Canaan) was no longer used as a name for the country, but had come to mean trader or merchant (compare Zephaniah 2:5).

10. *Live in tents again.* As in desert days.

Tabernacle. Taking מועד (*mo'ed*) to be a short form for אהל מועד (*ohel mo'ed,* tent or tabernacle of meeting). Hosea asks his listeners: Would you prefer to live again as you did during our people's forty years of wandering? Would you not rather keep what you enjoy, which you can do if you turn to God? (Other very different translations have been suggested for this difficult verse.)

11. I spoke to the prophets, I heaped up
     visions;

and through the prophets I spoke in parables.

12. In Gilead there is wickedness:
they have become worthless;
in Gilgal they sacrifice bulls.
Their altars too shall be like heaps of stone
on the furrows of open fields.

11 וְדִבַּ֙רְתִּי֙ עַל־הַנְּבִיאִ֔ים וְאָנֹכִ֖י חָז֣וֹן הִרְבֵּ֑יתִי

וּבְיַ֥ד הַנְּבִיאִ֖ים אֲדַמֶּֽה׃

12 אִם־גִּלְעָ֣ד אָ֗וֶן

אַךְ־שָׁ֙וְא֙ הָי֔וּ

בַּגִּלְגָּל֙ שְׁוָרִ֣ים זִבֵּ֔חוּ

גַּ֥ם מִזְבְּחוֹתָם֙ כְּגַלִּ֔ים

עַ֖ל תַּלְמֵ֥י שָׂדָֽי׃

Commentary

12. *Gilead.* A region in Jordan; its northern portion had been settled by the tribe of
Manasseh.

Gilgal. A town near Jericho, where Saul had been crowned king. Here, a sanctuary had
been erected where, in Hosea's time, pagan rites were performed.

(It is highly unusual for a haftarah to end on such a negative note. In fact, the last verse
cannot be understood by itself; it belongs to what follows in the book of Hosea. See p. 65.)

Essay

Jacob or Israel?

Central to this haftarah (as well as to the sidra) is the figure of Jacob. In 12:3-5 the Prophet identifies his nation's fate with that of the ancestor.

He begins with a preamble (verse 3): The nation that calls itself after the forefather has not lived up to its responsibilities and opportunities and is due for punishment. Hosea then proceeds to sketch the life of the ancestor and challenges his compatriots to become like Jacob/Israel of old.

He selects three highlights:

In his mother's womb, Jacob seizes his twin brother's heel, as if trying to prevent him from being born first. Hence his name Jacob, "heel-grabber."[4]

Grown up, he wrestles with the angel and is named Israel, "God-wrestler."[5]

At God's behest Jacob/Israel moves to Beth El, where he had his first vision of God when he was fleeing from his brother Esau. After removing all alien images and gods from his household, he builds an altar to God at Beth El.[6]

These three way stations are chosen to show the ancestor's journey from a scheming, self-serving child and young man to a mature person who sincerely strives to merit the blessing of his father. He wrestles with his base inclinations and overcomes them, disposes of all idols, and devotes the rest of his life to the service of the Eternal.

Hosea recounts this tale, which of course was familiar to all his hearers, because he wants to impress them with the fact that they are Israel. The very name of the kingdom underscores the identity they must feel with the past. If they do and return to their true Sovereign, their past sins will be forgiven, but if the new Beth El will be like Gilgal, a place of pagan corruption, divine punishment is sure to follow.

The student of Hosea's orations must remember that, while we require explanations of his meanings, his contemporaries hardly did. They knew what he was talking about; the images he drew for them were familiar and readily understandable, certainly by those who were responsible for the leadership of the people. Unfortunately, they did not respond to his pleading, and in 721 B.C.E. the Assyrians conquered the country, exiled its leaders, and settled the land with strangers. The ten tribes were never heard of again; they disappeared into the shadows of history.

It is worth noting that modern Israel chose its name as a sign of Jewish continuity.

Gleanings

Like a lion

Rabbi Zeira said: It used to be, that when I saw the sages running to attend a lecture on the Sabbath I would think: They are profaning the Sabbath. But I changed my mind and joined those who ran when I heard Rabbi Tanchum say this in the name of Rabbi Joshua ben Levi: "One should always run to fulfill the Halachah, even on the Sabbath, as it is said (Hosea 11:10): They shall follow the Eternal One,/who will roar like a lion;/When God roars/children shall flutter from the west."

Talmud[7]

A unique prophetic vision

"Nor has there arisen in Israel since a prophet like Moses." (Deuteronomy 34:10) It is taught: All the other prophets saw through dark glass, as it is said: "... and through the prophets I spoke in parables." (Hosea 12:11) But Moses our Teacher saw through clear glass, as it is said: "He (Moses) looks upon the likeness of the Eternal." (Numbers 12:8)

Talmud[8]

***

Notes

[1] Genesis 10:19. The Hebrew spelling of Zeboim varies slightly in Genesis 14:2.

[2] See S. Parpola and K. Watanabe, *Neo-Assyrian Vassal Treaties and Loyalty Oaths,* vol. 2, p. 35.

[3] Genesis 32:26.

[4] Genesis 25: 26.

[5] Genesis 32:25-30.

[6] Genesis 35:1-7.

[7] *B. 'Erubin 6b*

[8] *B. Yevamot 49b*

וישלח ב

Obadiah

Introduction

Another Haftarah for Vayishlach: Obadiah 1-21.
This is the haftarah selection according to the Sephardic tradition, and is also
the choice of many Ashkenazic communities.

Connection of haftarah and sidra:

The sidra reports the reconciliation of Jacob and Esau (Esau's other name was Edom);
the haftarah brings us Obadiah's prophecy concerning Edom. In the sidra, the two brothers
end their long period of estrangement; the haftarah is witness to the enmity and hatred
between the two peoples that characterized later centuries.

The setting:

Since we do not know when the Prophet lived, we cannot determine the setting in
which he delivered his message. We find it likely that the destruction of Jerusalem, in which
the Edomites had a hand, caused the old hatred to flare up and engendered a desire for
retribution. Perhaps Obadiah was, like Jeremiah, one of those who were not exiled to
Babylon and who, living amidst ruins, bitterly resented the role that Edom had played in
ravaging the city (see verse 11 ff.).

For more on the book of Obadiah, see our *General Introduction.*

The prophecy:

1. A brief introduction. (verse 1)
2. Edom's sin of pride. (2-4)
3. God's severe judgment upon Edom and the reasons for it. (2-14)
4. The Day of the Eternal One. (15-18)
5. A map of victory when judgment comes and favors Israel. (19-21)

HAFTARAH FOR VAYISHLACH (Sephardic Ritual)

Obadiah

1:1. This is the vision of Obadiah:

We have heard a report from the Eternal,

and an envoy has been sent out among the nations:

Up! Let us rise up against her in battle!

Thus says the Eternal God about Edom:

2. Behold, I will make you the least of nations,

one utterly despised.

3. Your heart's presumption has led you astray,

you who dwell in crannies among the rocks,

who make your abode in the heights,

you who say to yourself:

Who can throw me to the ground?

1:1 חֲזוֹן עֹבַדְיָה

כֹּה־אָמַר אֲדֹנָי יְהֹוִה לֶאֱדוֹם

שְׁמוּעָה שָׁמַעְנוּ מֵאֵת יְהֹוָה

וְצִיר בַּגּוֹיִם שֻׁלָּח

קוּמוּ וְנָקוּמָה עָלֶיהָ לַמִּלְחָמָה:

2 הִנֵּה קָטֹן נְתַתִּיךָ בַּגּוֹיִם

בָּזוּי אַתָּה מְאֹד:

3 זְדוֹן לִבְּךָ הִשִּׁיאֶךָ

שֹׁכְנִי בְחַגְוֵי־סֶלַע

מְרוֹם שִׁבְתּוֹ

אֹמֵר בְּלִבּוֹ מִי יוֹרִדֵנִי אָרֶץ:

Commentary

1. *Obadiah.* "Servant of the Eternal" may be a personal name or a reference to an (unnamed) prophet's piety. The same uncertainty exists with regard to the book of Malachi, which could be a name or mean simply "My Messenger."

We have heard. Obadiah may here refer to God's prophets to whose guild he belongs. In the nearly identical passage, Jeremiah says, "I have heard."[1]

Against her. Against Edom.

Thus says the Eternal God about Edom. In the Hebrew text this line comes directly after the opening two words, and has been transferred to the end of the verse for greater clarity.[2]

Edom is the alternate name for Esau, Jacob's older twin. The Torah derives the name from the word *adom,* red, because Esau referred to the stew that he traded for his birthright as "that red stuff."[3]

The land that Edom occupied is, broadly speaking, the kingdom of Jordan of today.

3-4. The topography has been taken metaphorically by some, as a reference to Edom's desire for "splendid isolation,"[4] but more likely it is an accurate description of the area, not unlike the Qumran caves by the Dead Sea.

Among the rocks. The Hebrew *sela'* was formerly identified with Petra, the capital of the Nabateans, but this has lately been doubted, and another site farther north has been proposed instead.[5]

4. Though you soar high as an eagle
and make your nest among the stars,
I will force you down from there,
says the Eternal One.
5. Were thieves to come upon you,
or robbers by night,
—how you would be undone!—
surely they would steal only what they
　　need!
Were grape-pickers to come upon you,
surely they would leave some gleanings!
6. Yet Esau has been searched out,
its secret stores discovered!
7. Your [former] allies have driven you to
　　the border;
your confederates have betrayed and
　　overcome you,
your companions have put a snare under
　　your feet:
Is this not beyond understanding?
8. On that day, says the Eternal One,
it is I who will destroy the wise of Edom
and [remove] understanding from Mount
　　Esau.

4 אִם־תַּגְבִּיהַּ כַּנֶּשֶׁר
וְאִם־בֵּין כּוֹכָבִים שִׂים קִנֶּךָ
מִשָּׁם אוֹרִידְךָ
נְאֻם־יְהוָה:
5 אִם־גַּנָּבִים בָּאוּ־לְךָ
אִם־שׁוֹדְדֵי לַיְלָה
אֵיךְ נִדְמֵיתָה
הֲלוֹא יִגְנְבוּ דַּיָּם
אִם־בֹּצְרִים בָּאוּ לָךְ
הֲלוֹא יַשְׁאִירוּ עֹלֵלוֹת:
6 אֵיךְ נֶחְפְּשׂוּ עֵשָׂו
נִבְעוּ מַצְפֻּנָיו:
7 עַד־הַגְּבוּל שִׁלְּחוּךָ כֹּל אַנְשֵׁי בְרִיתֶךָ
הִשִּׁיאוּךָ יָכְלוּ לְךָ אַנְשֵׁי שְׁלֹמֶךָ
לַחְמְךָ יָשִׂימוּ מָזוֹר תַּחְתֶּיךָ
אֵין תְּבוּנָה בּוֹ:
8 הֲלוֹא בַּיּוֹם הַהוּא נְאֻם־יְהוָה
וְהַאֲבַדְתִּי חֲכָמִים מֵאֱדוֹם
וּתְבוּנָה מֵהַר עֵשָׂו:

Commentary

5. *Were thieves to come upon you.* What happened to you was of a far more disastrous dimension.

6. *Searched out.* Possibly a euphemism for being stripped naked.[6]

7. *Your [former] allies.* Possibly the ancestors of the Nabateans, who would later occupy all of Edom and establish a flourishing civilization, with Petra as its capital.

A snare. So most modern translators of מזור (*mazor*). The origin of the word may denote a braid, so that the image would be: They have made braids (nets?) out of your bread and thus turned it into a snare.[7]

8. *Mount Esau.* A term appearing only here and referring apparently to the entire territory on both sides of the Aravah (the north-south rift extending southward from the Dead Sea). The topography makes it understandable that the Edomites believed themselves to be unassailable.[8]

9. Your warriors, Teman, shall be
   dismayed,

as every man on Mount Esau is cut down
   in a massacre.

10. Because of your violence against your
    brother Jacob

shame shall cover you

and you shall be cut off forever.

11. On the day when you stood apart,

on the day when barbarians carried off
    their wealth,

and strangers entered their gates to cast
    lots for Jerusalem,

you too were like one of them.

12. You should not have gloated over your
    kin

on the day of their calamity!

You should not have rejoiced over the
    people of Judah

on the day of their ruin!

And you should not have opened your big
    mouth

on the day of [their] distress!

9 וְחַתּוּ גִבּוֹרֶיךָ תֵּימָן

לְמַעַן יִכָּרֶת־אִישׁ מֵהַר עֵשָׂו מִקָּטֶל:

10 מֵחֲמַס אָחִיךָ יַעֲקֹב

תְּכַסְּךָ בוּשָׁה וְנִכְרַתָּ לְעוֹלָם:

11 בְּיוֹם עֲמָדְךָ מִנֶּגֶד בְּיוֹם שְׁבוֹת זָרִים חֵילוֹ

וְנָכְרִים בָּאוּ שַׁעֲרוֹ [שְׁעָרָיו]

וְעַל־יְרוּשָׁלַם יַדּוּ גוֹרָל

גַּם־אַתָּה כְּאַחַד מֵהֶם:

12 וְאַל־תֵּרֶא בְיוֹם־אָחִיךָ

בְּיוֹם נָכְרוֹ

וְאַל־תִּשְׂמַח לִבְנֵי־יְהוּדָה

בְּיוֹם אָבְדָם

וְאַל־תַּגְדֵּל פִּיךָ

בְּיוֹם צָרָה:

Commentary

9. *Teman.* A city in Edom,[9] here standing for the whole country, a stylistic device called synecdoche.

10. *Your brother Jacob.* The progenitors of the peoples of Edom and Israel were brothers, and therefore their enmity is doubly hurtful. Compare the Torah warning: "You shall not abhor an Edomite, for he is your brother."[10]

12. *Opened your big mouth.* In derision; literally, "widened your mouth."

13. You should not have entered my people's gate

on the day of their disaster!

You should not have been among those who gloated over their misery

on the day of their calamity!

And you should not have laid hands on their wealth

on the day of their calamity!

14. And you should not have stood at the crossroads

to cut off their fugitives!

And you should not have betrayed their survivors

on the day of [their] distress!

15. For the day of the Eternal draws near for all the nations:

as you have done, so shall it be done to you;

your deeds shall come back to haunt you.

13 אַל־תָּבוֹא בְשַׁעַר־עַמִּי

בְּיוֹם אֵידָם

אַל־תֵּרֶא גַם־אַתָּה בְּרָעָתוֹ

בְּיוֹם אֵידוֹ

וְאַל־תִּשְׁלַחְנָה בְחֵילוֹ

בְּיוֹם אֵידוֹ:

14 וְאַל־תַּעֲמֹד עַל־הַפֶּרֶק

לְהַכְרִית אֶת־פְּלִיטָיו

וְאַל־תַּסְגֵּר שְׂרִידָיו

בְּיוֹם צָרָה:

15 כִּי־קָרוֹב יוֹם־יְהוָה עַל־כָּל־הַגּוֹיִם

כַּאֲשֶׁר עָשִׂיתָ יֵעָשֶׂה לָּךְ

גְּמֻלְךָ יָשׁוּב בְּרֹאשֶׁךָ:

Commentary

13. *Disaster.* אֵיד (*eid*) is employed three times in this verse, to produce a memorable litany of betrayal. The first time the plural possessive is used, thereby producing the word אֵידָם (*edam*), in assonance with Edom. The possessive ending then shifts back to the singular אֵידוֹ (*eido*).

14. *Crossroads* פֶּרֶק (*perek*), a word used today in many other meanings, all denoting a division or departure of some kind—for example, chapter, puberty, season.

Cut off their fugitives. The same kind of sin that exposed the Amalekites to eternal obloquy.

15. *Day of the Eternal.* When Israel will at last be justified and relieved of its enemies. At first the concept was to evoke confidence in a coming historical redemption by God, but later it took on eschatological meaning—that is, the expectation was shifted to post-historic, messianic times. Of the fifteen literary prophets in the Tanach, seven speak of such a judgment day. [11]

As you have done. The classical formulation of the doctrine of retribution. (See the essay below.)

16. As you drank upon My holy mountain,

so shall all the nations drink for evermore,

drinking and gulping—

only to become as though they had never
　been.

17. And on Mount Zion there shall be a
　surviving remnant;

and it shall be holy;

the House of Jacob shall dispossess those
　who dispossessed them.

18. The House of Jacob shall be fire

and the House of Joseph a flame,

while the House of Esau shall be stubble

that they shall kindle and consume.

No vestige shall remain of the House of
　Esau—

the Eternal One has spoken.

16 כִּי כַּאֲשֶׁר שְׁתִיתֶם֙ עַל־הַ֣ר קׇדְשִׁ֔י

יִשְׁתּ֧וּ כׇל־הַגּוֹיִ֛ם תָּמִ֖יד

וְשָׁת֣וּ וְלָע֑וּ

וְהָי֖וּ כְּל֥וֹא הָיֽוּ׃

17 וּבְהַ֥ר צִיּ֛וֹן תִּהְיֶ֥ה פְלֵיטָ֖ה

וְהָ֣יָה קֹ֑דֶשׁ

וְיָֽרְשׁוּ֙ בֵּ֣ית יַעֲקֹ֔ב אֵ֖ת מוֹרָֽשֵׁיהֶֽם׃

18 וְהָיָה֩ בֵית־יַעֲקֹ֨ב אֵ֜שׁ

וּבֵ֧ית יוֹסֵ֣ף לֶהָבָ֗ה

וּבֵ֤ית עֵשָׂו֙ לְקַ֔שׁ

וְדָלְק֥וּ בָהֶ֖ם וַאֲכָל֑וּם

וְלֹא־יִֽהְיֶ֤ה שָׂרִיד֙ לְבֵ֣ית עֵשָׂ֔ו

כִּ֥י יְהֹוָ֖ה דִּבֵּֽר׃

Commentary

16. *As you drank.* Addressed to Edom: As you celebrated in honor of Israel's distress, so other nations will do at your expense—and share your fate as well.

Holy mountain. Set apart and inviolable.

17. *It shall be holy.* Like the purified "holy seed" of which Isaiah spoke.[12]

18. *House of Jacob ... House of Joseph.* The southern and northern states, respectively. Obadiah foresees the reunion of the twelve tribes. The basic message, however, is clear: Israel will possess all of the land, and Esau—which delivered the remnant of Judah to destruction—will itself remain without a remnant.[13]

19. They shall possess the Negev, the
Mount of Esau, and the Shephelah of the
Philistines;

they shall possess the countryside of
Ephraim and Samaria,

and Benjamin [shall possess] Gilead.

20.　And the exiles of this host of Israel
who are among the Canaanites as far as
Zarephat, and the exiles of Jerusalem who
are in Sepharad shall possess the cities of
the Negev.

21. Liberators shall ascend Mount Zion
to hold sway over Mount Esau,
and the kingdom shall belong to the
Eternal.

19 וְיָרְשׁ֣וּ הַנֶּ֗גֶב אֶת־הַ֣ר עֵשָׂ֞ו

וְהַשְּׁפֵלָה֙ אֶת־פְּלִשְׁתִּ֔ים וְיָרְשׁוּ֙

אֶת־שְׂדֵ֣ה אֶפְרַ֔יִם וְאֵ֖ת שְׂדֵ֣ה שֹׁמְר֑וֹן

וּבִנְיָמִ֖ן אֶת־הַגִּלְעָֽד׃

20 וְגָלֻ֣ת הַֽחֵל־הַ֠זֶּה לִבְנֵ֨י יִשְׂרָאֵ֤ל אֲשֶׁר־

כְּנַעֲנִים֙ עַד־צָ֣רְפַ֔ת וְגָלֻ֥ת יְרוּשָׁלַ֖͏ִם אֲשֶׁ֣ר

בִּסְפָרַ֑ד יִֽרְשׁ֕וּ אֵ֖ת עָרֵ֥י הַנֶּֽגֶב׃

21 וְעָל֤וּ מֽוֹשִׁעִים֙ בְּהַ֣ר צִיּ֔וֹן

לִשְׁפֹּ֖ט אֶת־הַ֣ר עֵשָׂ֑ו

וְהָיְתָ֥ה לַֽיהֹוָ֖ה הַמְּלוּכָֽה׃

Commentary

19-21. The three verses present considerable difficulties and have been interpreted in various ways.[14]

Negev. The south.

Shephelah. The coastal lowlands.

Gilead. The land east of the Jordan, north of Edom.

20 *Exiles.* גלות (*galut*) became the common term for Diaspora, and its long duration conveyed God's continuing displeasure with Israel (*gólus* in Yiddish).[15]

Zarephat. A coastal city in today's Lebanon, where the village of Sarafand is located.[16] Medieval Jewish scholars identified Zarephat with France, which they pronounced *tzorfat* and which has remained the name for France in modern Hebrew. Obadiah foresaw a united kingdom holding territory that ancient Israel never had.

Sepharad. Most likely the Aramaic name for Sardis in Asia Minor, near Ismir (formerly Smyrna). Obadiah's mention of Sepharad is the earliest witness to an ancient Jewish community in Sardis.[17]

Traditional interpreters, following Targum Jonathan, understood Sepharad to mean Spain. In the Middle Ages, Spanish Jews were called Sephardim (often spelled Sefardim), and German Jews, Ashkenazim,[18] a distinction between two traditions that—without the old geographic meanings—persists to this day.

21. *Liberators.* מושעים (*moshi'im*). The scroll found at Qumran read *noshi'im*, "redeemed ones."

Mount Esau. The ultimate contrast to Mount Zion. Esau here has come to stand for evil, which will be overcome at last.

Essay

Vengeance or retribution?

Obadiah's message that "as you have done, so shall it be done to you" (verse 15) is often cited by critics of the Bible as "the law of vengeance," and the God who exacts it as "the God of vengeance." Those who phrase their assessment in this way are likely to contrast their critique of Judaism and its Bible with the "law of love" and the "God of love" of the Christian faith.

Without engaging in apologetic argument, the cited passage of the haftarah requires further discussion.

To begin with, neither divine *vengeance* nor divine *retribution* are expressed by any biblical terms, but the idea that God rewards and punishes are part and parcel of the Tanach. Amos was the first prophet to develop the thought that God's control over history was total, and that doing right or doing wrong determined a nation's fate. That is to say, God's presence made a decisive difference: it guaranteed that evil would not become dominant.

The prophets of Israel are unanimous in preaching the message of God's careful watch over Israel. Both the fortunes and misfortunes of the nation depend on its own doing and the expected response from God. In other words, Israelite history does not proceed in secret. Its progress is written in God's book of remembrance and is judged accordingly.

Obadiah's focus on Edom's unbrotherly behavior and God's expected response are not some isolated pieces of vengeful behavior, but a mirror of the underlying philosophy of the Tanach. One can't get away with injuring others, and that is especially true for Edom, of whom better is expected than siding with the enemies of the House of Jacob. But the adversities befalling God's people caused the prophetic doctrine to recede and make room for other perceptions. One was the post-historical application of the doctrine: reward and punishment will be exacted in the world-to-come, if they have not become visible in this world.

From there it was but one step to the statement of Ben Azzai, which is preserved in the Mishnah: "One mitzvah brings another in its train, even as one sin brings on another sin; for the reward of a mitzvah is doing another mitzvah, and the consequence of sin is further sin."[19]

God's motivation is not vengeance, but the need to keep evil in its bounds and to fulfill the terms of the divine covenant with Israel. The bottom line of divine retribution is justice, a balance in which right and wrong are clearly distinguished. After Auschwitz these concepts have undergone close scrutiny and reevaluation. Expressions like "the eclipse of God" or "the God who has withdrawn" have taken center stage, along with the warning that by abandoning God one rewards Hitler's madness.

The name Israel denotes "wrestling with God,"[20] implying both a description and a challenge.

Gleanings

Words to Remember

And on Mount Zion there shall be a surviving remnant;
and it shall be holy. (17a)

Classical sources

The expression מדה כנגד מדה *(middah k'neged middah)*, "measure for measure," is a principle seen in God's design for humanity.

Talmud[21]

Hillel saw a skull floating upon the water and said, "Because you drowned someone, you were drowned, and the one that drowned you will be drowned in turn."

Midrash[22]

A powerful counter motif

The often expressed faith that God's redemptive purpose is neither a denial of the seriousness of God's opposition to evil in any form, nor failure to recognize the moral relationship of human deeds to their consequences. But it is a powerful counter motif to the notion that God is bound to exact payment in kind from sinners. In confrontation with God's holiness and mercy, biblical figures repeatedly discover, not only their own unworthiness and culpability, but also his determination to redeem and restore them.

W. S. Towner[23]

***

Notes

1 Jeremiah 49:14.

2 So also NJPS.

3 Genesis 25:30.

4 So S. Goldman, *The Twelve Prophets*, Soncino Bible Commentary, p. 129.

5 It is in fact called Sela today; see W. N. Fanwar in the *Anchor Bible Dictionary*, vol. 6, p. 1074. Note also a passage from the annals of King Sennacherib of Assyria (704-681 B.C.E.): "I pitched my camp against the (enemy) troops, whose emplacement was on the peak of steep Mt. Nippur like the eagle's nest." (Cited by M. Cogan and U. Simon, *Mikra LeYisrael*, p. 22.)

6 Suggested by S. D. Sperling (personal communication).

7 Rashi understands the verse to say that Edom's allies accompanied it to the border and then deserted it; while Ibn Ezra reads: Your allies could not help you, but went with you into exile. S. D. Sperling (in personal communication) suggests that לחמך (*lachm'cha*, your bread) might be elliptical for "those who eat your bread," that is, "your allies" (see the idiom in Psalm 41:10).

8 So M. Cogan and U. Simon, *Mikra LeYisrael*, p. 25.

9 Compare Amos 1:12.

10 Deuteronomy 23:8.

11 See the well-annotated survey by K. J. Cathcart in the *Anchor Bible Dictionary*, vol. 2, pp. 84 ff.

12 Isaiah 6:13 (haftarah for Yitro).

13 So Eliezer of Beaugency, medieval Franco-Jewish scholar.

14 Our translation of verse 19 follows NEB.

15 The parallel term *golah* did not acquire this connotation.

16 See further R. L. Roth, *Anchor Bible Dictionary*, vol. 6, p. 1041.

17 So J. G. Pedley, *Anchor Bible Dictionary* vol. 5, pp. 982-984. The identification was first made by E. Littmann in 1916; see *Encyclopaedia Mikra'it*, vol. 5, p. 1099.

18 From *ashkenaz*, the word for pre-modern German lands (though in the Torah it referred to the land of the Scythians, an Iranian people (see the Torah Commentary, p. 74). When from the 15th century on, German Jews migrated to Poland and eastward, the term Ashkenazim was applied to them as well.

19 Pirkei Avot 4:2.

20 Genesis 32:29.

21 *B*. Sanhedrin 90a.

22 Genesis Rabbah 9:11.

23 *Interpreter's Dictionary of the Bible*, Supplementary Volume, p. 744.

Amos, chapter 2, verse 6 to chapter 3, verse 8

Introduction

Connection of haftarah and sidra:

The sidra relates how young Joseph was sold into slavery by his brothers, and in the first verse of the haftarah Amos castigates Israel for selling a *tzaddik* (righteous person) for silver. In the Talmud, Joseph is called *tzaddik*,[1] and therefore the Rabbis assumed that Amos must have had a person like Joseph in mind when he used the term.

The setting:

Though Amos was a native of Tekoa, a little place probably near Jerusalem (capital of Judah), he moved to Israel and preached in Samaria (its capital) and Bethel, where a shrine existed that featured immoral practices under the guise of religion. He was deeply shocked at what he saw: moral laxity, legal and social corruption, and religious rites that had little to do with the God of Israel. Conspicuous wealth and social injustice lived side by side.

For more on Amos and his time, see our *General Introduction*.

The message:

1. The sins of Israel. (2:6-8)
2. What God has done for Israel, and how its people have forgotten it. (2:6-8)
3. The looming punishment. (13-15)
4. A dramatic, poetic appeal to the people. (3:1-8)

2:6. Thus says the Eternal One:

For Israel's three transgressions,

and for four,

I will not revoke [judgment]:

because they sell the innocent for silver,

the needy for a pair of sandals;

7. they who trample the heads of the poor

   into the earth's dust,

and make crooked the road of the meek.

Father and son go to the same girl:

thus [they] profane My holy name.

כֹּה אָמַר יְהֹוָה 2:6

עַל־שְׁלֹשָׁה פִּשְׁעֵי יִשְׂרָאֵל

וְעַל־אַרְבָּעָה לֹא אֲשִׁיבֶנּוּ

עַל־מִכְרָם בַּכֶּסֶף צַדִּיק

וְאֶבְיוֹן בַּעֲבוּר נַעֲלָיִם:

7 הַשֹּׁאֲפִים עַל־עֲפַר־אֶרֶץ בְּרֹאשׁ דַּלִּים

וְדֶרֶךְ עֲנָוִים יַטּוּ

וְאִישׁ וְאָבִיו יֵלְכוּ אֶל־הַנַּעֲרָה

לְמַעַן חַלֵּל אֶת־שֵׁם קָדְשִׁי:

Commentary

2:6. *For three … and for four.* A stylistic device (denoting "one too many"²) with which Amos begins his denunciation of sins that various nations have committed. He uses this formula eight times in succession, beginning in chapter 1 with his castigation of Damascus, and then in turn of Gaza, Tyre, Edom, and Ammon, and in chapter 2 of Moab and Judah. After having thus established the supremacy of God's moral law in all these nations, gentiles and Children of the Covenant, the Prophet focuses on his main subject, the sins of Israel.³

I will not revoke [judgment]. An alternative rendering is, "I will not take him back."

The innocent. צדיק (*tzaddik*) here describes persons who innocently trust people and lose their very liberty in the process.

A pair of sandals. The poetic image can be translated into prose to convey: "For Israel's three trangressions—and now a fourth!— I will not take him back. Because they sell the innocent (needy) for (only) the price of sandals." "They" are the corrupt judges who do not care about the guilt or innocence of poor people.⁴

7. *Trample.* Reading it שפים (*shafim*) instead of שאפים (*sho'afim*, yearn for). So the Septuagint, Vulgate and Ibn Ezra, JPS. The rest of the Hebrew is also not clear.

Go to the same girl. While technically not incest, these sexual acts are highly reminiscent of behavior prohibited in Leviticus 18:15-17. The Hebrew נערה (*na'arah*) stresses the youth of the woman.⁵

8. Near every altar they lie

on clothing taken in pledge;

[with the proceeds]

of those who have been fined

they drink wine

in the house of their God.

9. Yet it was I

who destroyed the Amorites before them,

who were tall as cedars,

and sturdy as oaks!

I destroyed their fruit on top,

and cut off their roots beneath.

10. And it was I who brought you up out of
    the land of Egypt,

and led you in the wilderness forty years,

to take possession of the land of the
Amorites!

11. I raised up prophets from among your
    children,

and Nazirites from among your young.

Is this not so, people of Israel?

—says the Eternal One.

8 וְעַל־בְּגָדִים חֲבֻלִים יַטּוּ

אֵצֶל כָּל־מִזְבֵּחַ

וְיֵין עֲנוּשִׁים יִשְׁתּוּ בֵּית אֱלֹהֵיהֶם:

9 וְאָנֹכִי הִשְׁמַדְתִּי אֶת־הָאֱמֹרִי מִפְּנֵיהֶם

אֲשֶׁר כְּגֹבַהּ אֲרָזִים גָּבְהוֹ

וְחָסֹן הוּא כָּאַלּוֹנִים

וָאַשְׁמִיד פִּרְיוֹ מִמַּעַל

וְשָׁרָשָׁיו מִתָּחַת:

10 וְאָנֹכִי הֶעֱלֵיתִי אֶתְכֶם מֵאֶרֶץ מִצְרַיִם

וָאוֹלֵךְ אֶתְכֶם בַּמִּדְבָּר אַרְבָּעִים שָׁנָה

לָרֶשֶׁת אֶת־אֶרֶץ הָאֱמֹרִי:

11 וָאָקִים מִבְּנֵיכֶם לִנְבִיאִים

וּמִבַּחוּרֵיכֶם לִנְזִרִים

הַאַף אֵין־זֹאת בְּנֵי יִשְׂרָאֵל

נְאֻם־יְהֹוָה:

Commentary

8. *Clothing taken in pledge*. In contravention of the law: "If you take your neighbor's garment in pledge, you must return it to him before the sun sets."[6] Amos castigates the hypocrites who exploit the poor and lie down in religious places on garments that they have acquired through unethical means.

9. *The Amorites*. One of the peoples whom Israel displaced when they conquered the land.

Tall as cedars. Recalling the report that the spies brought back when they scouted the land for Moses: "All the people we saw were of great size."[7]

11. *Nazirites*. Persons under special vows to observe certain restrictions in their personal lives.[8]

12. But you made the Nazirites drink wine,

and prohibited the prophets from prophesying.

13. Now I will make you totter

as a wagon totters under a full load of
newly-cut grain.

14. Flight shall fail the swift,

the strong shall find no strength,

warriors shall not escape with their lives.

15. The archer shall not stand firm,

the swift runner shall not escape,

nor shall the horseman escape with his life.

16. On that day, says the Eternal One,

even the bravest of soldiers

shall flee away naked.

3:1. People of Israel,

hear this word the Eternal has spoken
about you,

about the whole crowd that I brought up
out of the land of Egypt:

12 וַתַּשְׁקוּ אֶת־הַנְּזִרִים יָיִן
וְעַל־הַנְּבִיאִים צִוִּיתֶם לֵאמֹר לֹא תִּנָּבְאוּ:
13 הִנֵּה אָנֹכִי מֵעִיק תַּחְתֵּיכֶם
כַּאֲשֶׁר תָּעִיק הָעֲגָלָה הַמְלֵאָה לָהּ עָמִיר:
14 וְאָבַד מָנוֹס מִקָּל
וְחָזָק לֹא־יְאַמֵּץ כֹּחוֹ
וְגִבּוֹר לֹא־יְמַלֵּט נַפְשׁוֹ:
15 וְתֹפֵשׂ הַקֶּשֶׁת לֹא יַעֲמֹד
וְקַל בְּרַגְלָיו לֹא יְמַלֵּט
וְרֹכֵב הַסּוּס לֹא יְמַלֵּט נַפְשׁוֹ:
16 וְאַמִּיץ לִבּוֹ בַּגִּבּוֹרִים
עָרוֹם יָנוּס בַּיּוֹם־הַהוּא
נְאֻם־יְהוָה:
3:1 שִׁמְעוּ אֶת־הַדָּבָר הַזֶּה אֲשֶׁר דִּבֶּר יְהוָה
עֲלֵיכֶם בְּנֵי יִשְׂרָאֵל
עַל כָּל־הַמִּשְׁפָּחָה אֲשֶׁר הֶעֱלֵיתִי מֵאֶרֶץ
מִצְרַיִם לֵאמֹר:

Commentary

12. *But you made the Nazirites drink wine.* Thus causing them to violate one of the restrictions (to abstain from alcohol, from cutting their hair, and from touching a corpse).

Prohibited the prophets from prophesying. Amos himself was "encouraged" to cease his preaching.[9]

13. *Totters.* Reading מפיק (*mefik*) instead of מעיק (*me'ik,* hinder, slow down).

3:1. *About the whole crowd.* Usually, משפחה (*mishpachah*) means family, and appears in that meaning in the next verse. But here, Amos uses it disparagingly and applies it to Judah as well as to Israel. Micah and Jeremiah also employ it in this sense.[10]

2. You alone have I known

of all the families of the earth—

therefore I will punish you

for all your iniquities.

3. Do two walk together

without having arranged it?

4. Does a lion in the forest roar

when it has no prey?

Does a young lion growl in its den

without having caught something?

5. Does a bird fall into a trap on the ground

that has no bait?

Does a trap spring up from the ground

when there is nothing to capture?

6. When the shofar is sounded in the town

do not the people tremble?

When evil falls on a city

did not the Eternal make it happen?

7. The Eternal God does nothing

without revealing its purpose

to God's servants, the prophets.

2 רַק אֶתְכֶם יָדַעְתִּי

מִכֹּל מִשְׁפְּחוֹת הָאֲדָמָה

עַל־כֵּן אֶפְקֹד עֲלֵיכֶם

אֵת כָּל־עֲוֺנֹתֵיכֶם:

3 הֲיֵלְכוּ שְׁנַיִם יַחְדָּו

בִּלְתִּי אִם־נוֹעָדוּ:

4 הֲיִשְׁאַג אַרְיֵה בַּיַּעַר

וְטֶרֶף אֵין לוֹ

הֲיִתֵּן כְּפִיר קוֹלוֹ מִמְּעֹנָתוֹ

בִּלְתִּי אִם־לָכָד:

5 הֲתִפֹּל צִפּוֹר עַל־פַּח הָאָרֶץ

וּמוֹקֵשׁ אֵין לָהּ

הֲיַעֲלֶה־פַּח מִן־הָאֲדָמָה

וְלָכוֹד לֹא יִלְכּוֹד:

6 אִם־יִתָּקַע שׁוֹפָר בְּעִיר

וְעָם לֹא יֶחֱרָדוּ

אִם־תִּהְיֶה רָעָה בְּעִיר

וַיהוָה לֹא עָשָׂה:

7 כִּי לֹא יַעֲשֶׂה אֲדֹנָי יְהוִה דָּבָר

כִּי אִם־גָּלָה סוֹדוֹ

אֶל־עֲבָדָיו הַנְּבִיאִים:

Commentary

2. *You alone have I known.* In your unique relationship with God.

Therefore I will punish you. For violating your special trust. Belonging to God's people does not guarantee privileged treatment; on the contrary, it entails added obligation.

3. *Do two walk together.* The first of three examples of cause and effect, which are explained in dramatic fashion in verses 7 and 8.

4. *Does a lion ... roar.* The roar of the lion is a metaphor for God's voice ringing in the ears of a prophet (as verse 8 has it).[11]

8. The lion has roared,

who will not fear?

The Eternal God has spoken,

who can but prophesy?

8 אַרְיֵ֣ה שָׁאָ֔ג

מִ֖י לֹ֣א יִירָ֑א

אֲדֹנָ֤י יְהוִה֙ דִּבֶּ֔ר

מִ֖י לֹ֥א יִנָּבֵֽא׃

Commentary

8. *Who can but prophesy?* God's warning of inevitable doom is so overwhelming that it leaves the Prophet no choice but to confront the people with it. Will they listen, or will they pretend that all is in order?

Essay

The prophet of social justice

No one among the prophets was as appalled at what he saw as was Amos. Time and again the Prophet denounced the immorality that surrounded him.

When he appeared in the north there was pride, plenty, and splendor in the land, elegance in the cities, and might in the palaces. The rich had their summer and winter mansions adorned with costly ivory, gorgeous couches with damask pillows, on which they reclined at their sumptuous feasts. They planted pleasant vineyards, anointed themselves with precious oils; their women, compared by Amos to the fat cows of Bashan, were addicted to wine.

At the same time there was no justice in the land, the poor were afflicted, exploited, even sold into slavery, and the judges were corrupt. In the midst of this atmosphere arose Amos, a shepherd, to exclaim: "Woe to those who are at ease in Zion, and those who feel secure in the mountains of Samaria."[12]

It has been said that to Amos, social justice was religion. That is both right and wrong. Right, because all pretense to religious observance is a sham without just living. Wrong, because social ethics cannot take the place of religion; it is an essential aspect but not the whole of it.

For it is God who stands behind the whole edifice of existence. It is God who commands us to love our neighbor, to distinguish right from wrong, and to act accordingly. In the view of Amos and all of the Tanach, God wants Israel not only to *remember* the Covenant, but above all to *live* by it. This means to order one's existence in such a way that we constantly remember God's presence (with ritual and prayer the mainstays of remembrance) and at the same time order our relationships with others—personally or as members of society—in accordance with ethical principles. Religion without ethics is not religion. The two are obverse and reverse of the same coin that bears God's signature.

Adherents of traditional Judaism often picture Reform Jews as people who have forgotten God and the divine law. In return, Reform Jews have frequently created an image of Orthodoxy as form without moral content. Both judgments are only partial truths. Indeed, there are Jews who deem themselves observant but are unethical; and there those who believe they are leading ethical lives, while forgetting about God and Covenant. The truth lies with neither of these extremes.

Amos reminds us of this. He decries injustice because God abhors it. To be sure, the shepherd from Tekoa is the prophet of social justice, but he is also the voice of the Living God who cares for Jerusalem and Samaria. Amos urges us to requite God's love for the House of Jacob by caring for the unfortunate and at the same time by remembering the opening line of the *Shema*: "You shall love your Eternal God with all your heart, with all your soul and with all your might."[13]

Gleanings

They sell the innocent for silver,
the needy for a pair of sandals. (2:6)

The lion has roared,
who will not fear?
The Eternal God has spoken,
who can but prophesy? (3:8)

The outsider

Amos was a peasant, and the amenities of life among the well-to-do and leisured classes were no doubt shocking to him, as they have always been to those who were not brought up with them. And coming from a region and particularly from a background where there was, as yet, no great wealth and no fixed line of demarcation between rich and poor, he found the inequalities in Israel especially noticeable. The biting irony and scorn of his comments must have enraged his hearers, who felt they were living pretty much like the rest of the world, as no doubt they were. Why, they wondered, should they be singled out for vituperation just because some out-of-date fanatic from the backwoods had a quaint outmoded conception of God which he wished to substitute for their own.

Brooke Peters Church[14]

The essential point

The great message, with all its variety and differences in imagery and details, is that God will not finally abandon his people, even if he is responsible for judging and destroying them, even if that action is necessary and there is no way to escape it. Without repentance there is no possibility of forgiveness.

F.I. Andersen and David Noel Freedman[15]

* * *

Notes

[1] *B.* Ketuvot 111a.

[2] See M. Barré, *Journal of Biblical Literature,* vol. 105 (1986), p. 621.

[3] "Three and four" occurs also in Proverbs 30:15; "six and seven" in Proverbs 6:16; "two and three" in Isaiah 17:6; "one and two" in Psalm 62:12. Note that all of these, when added, produce prime numbers, which the ancients knew well and which were accorded mystical power—especially the sacred seven. (The one exception to this is the "four and five" mentioned also in Isaiah 17:6.) On the subject of prime numbers, see the Torah Commentary on Genesis chapter 14 (p. 104, note 14).

[4] S. M. Lehrman, in his commentary on Amos in the *Soncino Bible Commentay,* notes that shoes were used as legal symbols in the transfer of property (compare Ruth 4:7). "The sense would then be that the exploiters cloaked their unscrupulous transactions with legal formality."

[5] See K. van der Toorn, *Anchor Bible Dictionary,* vol. 5, pp. 510-513.

[6] Exodus 22:25.

[7] Numbers 13:32.

[8] See Numbers 6:1-7.

[9] Amos 7:13, 16.

[10] Micah 2:3; Jeremiah 8:3.

[11] So Rashi's second explanation. His first choice is to identify the lion with Nebuchadnezzar, even though the Babylonian king reigned well over a hundred years later.

[12] Amos 6:1; A.J. Heschel, *The Prophets,* pp. 27-28.

[13] Deuteronomy 6:5.

[14] *The Private Lives of the Prophets,* p. 67.

[15] Commentary on Amos, *Anchor Bible,* p. 81.

מקץ

First Kings, chapter 3, verses 15 to 28 and chapter 4, verse 1

Introduction

Connection between sidra and haftarah:

The dream of Pharaoh in the sidra has its parallel in the dream of Solomon in the haftarah. As with Joseph, who ascribes his ability to interpret the dream to God, so Solomon's wisdom too is derived from its divine source.

The setting:

Solomon had succeeded to the throne (about 970 B.C.E.), when God appeared to him in a dream and asked him what gift he desired. Solomon asked not for material things but for an understanding heart, which was granted to him.[1] His wisdom was widely hailed, and the story of the two mothers is a prime example of his intuition.

For more on the book of Kings, see our *General Introduction;* and on Solomon, see the essay below.

The story:

1. Solomon awakes from his dream and brings thanks offerings to God. (3:15)
2. The adjudication of the quarrel between two mothers. (3:16-27)
3. Epilogue: Solomon is admired for his wisdom, and his reign is established in all Israel. (3:28-4:1)

3:15. Then Solomon woke; it was a dream! He went to Jerusalem, and stood before the Ark of the Covenant of the Eternal; there he offered burnt-offerings and peace-offerings. After that, he gave a banquet for all his officials.

16. Sometime later two prostitutes presented themselves before the king.

17. One said: Please, my lord, this woman and I live in the same house. She was there with me when I gave birth to a child.

18. Three days later, this woman also had a child. We were alone; no one else was with us, just the two of us were in the house.

19. During the night she lay on it, and her son died.

20. She got up in the middle of the night while your maidservant was asleep, took my child and put it in her bosom, and put her dead child in mine!

3:15 וַיִּקַ֣ץ שְׁלֹמֹ֔ה וְהִנֵּ֖ה חֲל֑וֹם וַיָּב֣וֹא יְרוּשָׁלַ֗ם וַֽיַּעֲמֹ֞ד לִפְנֵ֣י ׀ אֲר֣וֹן בְּרִית־אֲדֹנָ֗י וַיַּ֤עַל עֹלוֹת֙ וַיַּ֣עַשׂ שְׁלָמִ֔ים וַיַּ֥עַשׂ מִשְׁתֶּ֖ה לְכָל־עֲבָדָֽיו׃

16 אָ֣ז תָּבֹ֗אנָה שְׁתַּ֛יִם נָשִׁ֥ים זֹנ֖וֹת אֶל־הַמֶּ֑לֶךְ וַֽתַּעֲמֹ֖דְנָה לְפָנָֽיו׃

17 וַתֹּ֜אמֶר הָאִשָּׁ֤ה הָֽאַחַת֙ בִּ֣י אֲדֹנִ֔י אֲנִי֙ וְהָאִשָּׁ֣ה הַזֹּ֔את יֹשְׁבֹ֖ת בְּבַ֣יִת אֶחָ֑ד וָאֵלֵ֥ד עִמָּ֖הּ בַּבָּֽיִת׃

18 וַיְהִ֞י בַּיּ֤וֹם הַשְּׁלִישִׁי֙ לְלִדְתִּ֔י וַתֵּ֖לֶד גַּם־הָאִשָּׁ֣ה הַזֹּ֑את וַאֲנַ֣חְנוּ יַחְדָּ֗ו אֵֽין־זָ֤ר אִתָּ֙נוּ֙ בַּבַּ֔יִת זֽוּלָתִ֥י שְׁתַּֽיִם־אֲנַ֖חְנוּ בַּבָּֽיִת׃

19 וַיָּ֛מָת בֶּן־הָאִשָּׁ֥ה הַזֹּ֖את לָ֑יְלָה אֲשֶׁ֥ר שָׁכְבָ֖ה עָלָֽיו׃

20 וַתָּ֩קָם֩ בְּת֨וֹךְ הַלַּ֜יְלָה וַתִּקַּ֧ח אֶת־בְּנִ֣י מֵֽאֶצְלִ֗י וַאֲמָֽתְךָ֙ יְשֵׁנָ֔ה וַתַּשְׁכִּיבֵ֖הוּ בְּחֵיקָ֑הּ וְאֶת־בְּנָ֥הּ הַמֵּ֖ת הִשְׁכִּ֥יבָה בְחֵיקִֽי׃

Commentary

3:15. *It was a dream!* Dreams of kings are found frequently in Near East royal annals.[2] *Peace-offerings.* Or offerings of well-being.[3]

16. *Presented themselves before the king.* He was as accessible as his father, who received a woman of Tekoa forthwith.[4]

17. *Please.* בִּי (*bi*) is a term of uncertain derivation, probably from אבה (*avah*, to consent).[5] It occurs twice in this story and altogether twelve times in the Tanach, mostly as part of the expression בִּי אֲדֹנִי (*bi adoni*, please, my lord).

18. *No one else.* In ancient Israel it would be unusual to find two unmarried women living together without the presence of male family members. The story virtually requires the women to be prostitutes. זר (*zar*) means "stranger," and the feminine form of the word could be used for "prostitute."[6]

21. When I got up in the morning to nurse my son, I saw that he was dead! But when I looked more closely by the morning [light], I saw that the [dead] baby was not the one born to me.

22. The other woman broke in: No, the living one is my son—yours is the dead one! But the first insisted: No, the dead boy is yours; mine is the live one. Thus they continued to argue before the king.

23. The king said: One says, *The live one is my son, and the dead one is yours,* and the other says, *No, your son is dead and mine is alive.*

24. So the king said: Fetch me a sword. They brought a sword into the king's presence.

25. Then the king said: Cut the living child in two, and give half to the one, half to the other.

26. But the real mother was churning with compassion for her son, so she pleaded with the king: Please, my lord, give her the living bairn; whatever you do, don't kill him! But the other said: No, it will be neither yours nor mine; cut it in two.

21 וָאָקֻם בַּבֹּקֶר לְהֵינִיק אֶת־בְּנִי וְהִנֵּה־מֵת וָאֶתְבּוֹנֵן אֵלָיו בַּבֹּקֶר וְהִנֵּה לֹא־הָיָה בְנִי אֲשֶׁר יָלָדְתִּי:

22 וַתֹּאמֶר הָאִשָּׁה הָאַחֶרֶת לֹא כִי בְּנִי הַחַי וּבְנֵךְ הַמֵּת וְזֹאת אֹמֶרֶת לֹא כִי בְּנֵךְ הַמֵּת וּבְנִי הֶחָי וַתְּדַבֵּרְנָה לִפְנֵי הַמֶּלֶךְ:

23 וַיֹּאמֶר הַמֶּלֶךְ זֹאת אֹמֶרֶת זֶה־בְּנִי הַחַי וּבְנֵךְ הַמֵּת וְזֹאת אֹמֶרֶת לֹא כִי בְּנֵךְ הַמֵּת וּבְנִי הֶחָי:

24 וַיֹּאמֶר הַמֶּלֶךְ קְחוּ לִי־חָרֶב וַיָּבִאוּ הַחֶרֶב לִפְנֵי הַמֶּלֶךְ:

25 וַיֹּאמֶר הַמֶּלֶךְ גִּזְרוּ אֶת־הַיֶּלֶד הַחַי לִשְׁנָיִם וּתְנוּ אֶת־הַחֲצִי לְאַחַת וְאֶת־הַחֲצִי לְאֶחָת:

26 וַתֹּאמֶר הָאִשָּׁה אֲשֶׁר־בְּנָהּ הַחַי אֶל־הַמֶּלֶךְ אֶל־הַמֶּלֶךְ כִּי־נִכְמְרוּ רַחֲמֶיהָ עַל־בְּנָהּ וַתֹּאמֶר בִּי אֲדֹנִי תְּנוּ־לָהּ אֶת־הַיָּלוּד הַחַי וְהָמֵת אַל־תְּמִיתֻהוּ וְזֹאת אֹמֶרֶת גַּם־לִי גַם־לָךְ לֹא יִהְיֶה גְּזֹרוּ:

Commentary

23. *The king said.* He repeats the testimony in order to make sure that he has it right.

25. *Cut the living child.* He had of course no intention of killing the child; he anticipated that the real mother would protest.[7]

26. *Churning with compassion.* The mother who carried the child in her womb (רחם, *rechem*) feels deep compassion (רחמים, *rachamim*) for her son.

Give her the living bairn. Instead of ילד (*yeled,* child) she uses ילוד (*yalud,* one born [by me]). "Bairn" is a Scottish and North English word for child, and parallels the Hebrew exactly.[8]

27. The king spoke up: On no account kill the child—give him to the first woman— she is the real mother.

28. When Israel heard of the decision of the king, they held him in awe, seeing that he had within him divine wisdom to do justice.

4:1. And king Solomon was now king over all Israel.

27 וַיַּעַן הַמֶּלֶךְ וַיֹּאמֶר תְּנוּ־לָהּ אֶת־הַיָּלוּד הַחַי וְהָמֵת לֹא תְמִיתֻהוּ הִיא אִמּוֹ:

28 וַיִּשְׁמְעוּ כָל־יִשְׂרָאֵל אֶת־הַמִּשְׁפָּט אֲשֶׁר שָׁפַט הַמֶּלֶךְ וַיִּרְאוּ מִפְּנֵי הַמֶּלֶךְ כִּי רָאוּ כִּי־ חָכְמַת אֱלֹהִים בְּקִרְבּוֹ לַעֲשׂוֹת מִשְׁפָּט:

4:1 וַיְהִי הַמֶּלֶךְ שְׁלֹמֹה מֶלֶךְ עַל־כָּל־יִשְׂרָאֵל:

Essay

The many sides of Solomon

The new king had two names, Solomon (*Sh'lomo*, connected with *shalom*) and Jedediah (*y'didyah*, beloved of God).[9]

The kingdom he inherited from his father reached from the borders of Egypt to the river Euphrates in Mesopotamia, and Solomon preserved it peaceably through treaties and economic development.[10] He established mining operations in the southern Negev, and the port of Ezion-geber (near today's Eilat) became the focal point of his shipping trade. By his domination of the major trade routes between East and West he made his nation a central factor in the economic and political life of the Near East, expanding his trade to southern Arabia and Africa, whence he imported gold, spices, and exotic animals, while horses were bought from Anatolia and chariots from Egypt. The visit of the Queen of Sheba and his friendship with Hiram, king of Tyre, are testimony to his international stature.[11] He began his royal career by marrying the daughter of Egypt's pharaoh,[12] and followed this marital policy with other international alliances.

He was also an innovative organizer at home. He divided the country into districts and created an administrative structure that crossed tribal lines and was firmly controlled from Jerusalem. His building programs were legendary: he began by constructing a splendid Temple; then followed this with the erection of his own palace close by, and by the building of fortified cities at crucial entry points to the country. All this was done through high taxes and the employment of forced labor, which created serious disaffection, especially in the north. As long as he lived he managed to keep his nation together, but as soon as he died it split into Israel and Judah (ten northern and two southern tribes). They were never united again.[13]

Solomon was a highly gifted man, and Jewish tradition ascribed to him the authorship of three books in the Tanach.[14]

Though he was greatly admired for his wisdom, he did not gain the affection of his people in the way his father did. His introduction of pagan practices, his many wives, his ostentatious opulence, and, above all, his ruthless administrative measures did not endear him to his subjects. A large body of folklore arose around his life and character, his exploits and his failures. He was said to command the spirit world and had the use of a worm-like creature, named Shamir, with which he could cut the hardest stone and which enabled him to build the Temple in only seven years. But this same tradition also told tales of his giving up the kingship and ending his life as a private person, wandering incognito among his people.

In sum, he was a complex man who acted the absolute monarch, who had a sense of justice, yet also dealt harshly with his subjects. The ambivalence of later generations was perhaps best seen in the controversy engendered by two of the books ascribed to him, the Song of Songs and Koheleth. Both were eventually admitted to the biblical canon, but not without much resistance. This ambivalence is a faithful image of how Jewish tradition evaluated King Solomon.

Gleanings

The riddles of the Queen of Sheba

Many legends arose around the visit of the Queen of Sheba to Solomon. Sometimes they had sexual overtones and suggestions of unsolved mysteries, but more often they exalted the wisdom of the king. The most famous of these encounters is enlarged by a tale that details the questions the queen asked of Solomon.

Thus, the seventh of her twenty-two questions was this: "There is an enclosure with ten doors; when one is open, nine are shut; when nine are open, one is shut."

The king's answer was: "That enclosure is the womb; the ten doors are the ten orifices of every human being—eyes, ears, nostrils, mouth, the apertures for the discharge of stool and urine, and the navel. When the child is in the womb, the navel is open and the other apertures are closed; but when it issues from the womb the navel is closed and the others are opened."

Midrash[15]

Midrashic samples of Solomon's wisdom

He solved the mystery arising from the claim of a slave who averred that he was his master's son,[16] and he settled the demand of a double-headed child for a double portion of its inheritance.[17] He was so perceptive that he planned to dispense with any witnesses at a trial, because he felt he did not need them to make his decision, but a heavenly voice prevented him from flouting the accepted rules of justice.[18]

The wages of sin—talmudic views

Solomon sinned in a number of ways: he especially offended against the Torah command not to amass women (many of them foreign, to boot) and acquire excessive numbers of horses.[19] He was punished by losing his throne, but opinions vary on this. One tradition says that he traveled the road from king to poor citizen and back to king upon his repentance; and another, that he began as a private person, became king, and then returned to his earlier state.[20]

The author

According to tradition, Solomon was the author of three books found in the Tanach: Song of Songs, which he wrote in his youth; Proverbs, composed in middle age; and Koheleth (Ecclesiastes), a product of his old age.

Midrash[21]

***

Notes

[1] II Kings 3:9; the dream is told in the verses that precede our haftarah in chapter 3. Radak repeats the tradition that a wise heart preserves what it has learned, and the understanding heart knows how to draw the right conclusions.

[2] Cyrus H. Gordon, *Introduction to Old Testament Times,* p. 67.

[3] See the Torah Commentary, p. 365.

[4] II Samuel 14:4.

[5] So Gray, *I and II Kings,* quoting A. M. Honeyman.

[6] In popular lore, such a woman was referred to as an אשה זרה (*ishah zarah*, a "strange woman"); so in Proverbs 2:16 and other passages.

[7] So Malbim, in his commentary.

[8] The Hebrew word occurs elsewhere too; for example, Job 14:4.

[9] The latter name was given him by Nathan; II Samuel 12:25.

[10] However, he did not possess Gaza and the surrounding area dominated by the Philistines.

[11] I Kings 10.

[12] I Kings 3:1.

[13] I Kings 11:9-13 reports that this was God's punishment of Solomon.

[14] Modern scholarship is divided over the amount of his contribution to Song of Songs and Proverbs, but is unanimous in assigning Koheleth (Ecclesiastes) to the time of Greek dominance some 600 years later.

[15] Quoted from Ginzberg, *Legends of the Jews,* vol. 4, pp. 145-147.

[16] *Beit haMidrash* (Jellinek, 1967 ed.), vol. 2, pp. 85-86.

[17] Ibid., vol. 4, pp. 151-152.

[18] *B*. Rosh Hashanah 21b.

[19] *J*. Sanhedrin 2b, 20c.

[20] *B*. Sanhedrin 20b.

[21] Song of Songs Rabbah 1:1 (#10).

Ezekiel, chapter 37, verses 15 to 28

Introduction

Connection of haftarah and sidra:

The sidra tells us of the reunification of Joseph with his brothers. Ezekiel foretells that the lost ten tribes will be reunited with the tribe of Judah, which, with Benjamin, had formed the Southern Kingdom.

The setting:

Ezekiel—master of metaphors and mystical visions—lived in the days before and after the destruction of the First Temple and preached to his fellow exiles in Babylon in the early part of the 6th century B.C.E. They were captives in a foreign country, and they never ceased to hope for an eventual return to their homeland.

For more on Ezekiel and his time, see our *General Introduction*.

The message:

The first part of chapter 37 (read as the haftarah for the Shabbat during Passover) brings the Prophet's listeners the metaphor of the dried bones that will be resuscitated. Now, Ezekiel changes his imagery and illustrates his message with a visual demonstration. He takes two sticks—one representing the Northern Kingdom and one the Southern—and puts them one upon the other, so that they appear as one. He thus illustrates his message: David's throne will be reestablished; Israel will once again be one people; and the Eternal's Presence will forever dwell in its midst.

37:15 וַיְהִי דְבַר־יְהוָה אֵלַי לֵאמֹר:

37:15. The word of the Eternal came to me, saying:

16 וְאַתָּה בֶן־אָדָם קַח־לְךָ עֵץ אֶחָד וּכְתֹב עָלָיו לִיהוּדָה וְלִבְנֵי יִשְׂרָאֵל חֲבֵרָו [חֲבֵרָיו] וּלְקַח עֵץ אֶחָד וּכְתוֹב עָלָיו לְיוֹסֵף עֵץ אֶפְרַיִם וְכָל־בֵּית יִשְׂרָאֵל חֲבֵרָו [חֲבֵרָיו]:

16. Mortal, take a stick and write on it, *For Judah and Israelites associated with it;* and take another stick and write on it, *Joseph's—Ephraim's stick—and all the House of Israel associated with it.*

17 וְקָרַב אֹתָם אֶחָד אֶל־אֶחָד לְךָ לְעֵץ אֶחָד וְהָיוּ לַאֲחָדִים בְּיָדֶךָ:

17. Bring them together, every one of them, as one stick, that they may be as one in your hand.

18 וְכַאֲשֶׁר יֹאמְרוּ אֵלֶיךָ בְּנֵי עַמְּךָ לֵאמֹר הֲלוֹא־תַגִּיד לָנוּ מָה־אֵלֶּה לָּךְ:

18. And when any of your people say to you, Will you not tell us what you mean by what you are doing?

19 דַּבֵּר אֲלֵהֶם כֹּה־אָמַר אֲדֹנָי יְהוִה הִנֵּה אֲנִי לֹקֵחַ אֶת־עֵץ יוֹסֵף אֲשֶׁר בְּיַד־אֶפְרַיִם וְשִׁבְטֵי יִשְׂרָאֵל חֲבֵרָו [חֲבֵרָיו] וְנָתַתִּי אוֹתָם עָלָיו אֶת־עֵץ יְהוּדָה וַעֲשִׂיתִם לְעֵץ אֶחָד וְהָיוּ אֶחָד בְּיָדִי:

19. Say to them: Thus says the Eternal God: Behold, I am taking the stick of Joseph, which is in the hand of Ephraim and the tribes of Israel associated with it, and placing them on him, along with the stick of Judah, making them one stick, so that they become a single stick in My hand.

20 וְהָיוּ הָעֵצִים אֲשֶׁר־תִּכְתֹּב עֲלֵיהֶם בְּיָדְךָ לְעֵינֵיהֶם:

20. Before their eyes, hold in your hand the sticks on which you have written,

Commentary

37:16. *Mortal.* בֶן־אָדָם (*ben-adam*) is a term that in the Tanach occurs only in the books of Daniel and Ezekiel, with the latter using it over eighty times. Jewish tradition generally explained it as a reminder to the Prophet that he was only human, even though he was privileged to see supernatural visions. Christian tradition divided the idiom בֶן־אָדָם (*ben-adam*), that is "mortal," into its components, בֶן (son) and אָדָם (man or human) and applied it to Jesus, as the one who combined the natural and the supernatural.[1]

19. *Joseph ... Ephraim ... Judah.* The first two represent the Northern Kingdom, whose capital was Samaria and which, in Ezekiel's time, had been destroyed by the Assyrians over a hundred years before. Judah (with Jerusalem its capital) had been conquered and destroyed by the Babylonians in 587. (See the essay below.)

21. and tell them: Thus says the Eternal God: Behold, I am about to take the people of Israel from the nations where they went; I will gather them from all around and bring them back to their soil.

22. There, on the hills of Israel, I will make them into a single nation in the land, with a single king to rule them. Never again shall they be two nations; never again shall they be divided into two kingdoms;

23. never again shall they defile themselves with their idols, with their abominable images and with their other transgressions; I will save them from all their backslidings wherein they have sinned, and I will cleanse them: then they shall be My people, and I will be their God.

24. My servant David shall rule them; they shall all have one shepherd. They shall follow My ordinances, and faithfully keep My laws.

25. They shall live in the land that I gave to My servant Jacob, the land of your ancestors; they, their children and their children's children shall live there forever, and My servant David shall be their head forever.

כא וְדַבֵּר אֲלֵיהֶם כֹּה־אָמַר אֲדֹנָי יְהֹוִה הִנֵּה אֲנִי לֹקֵחַ אֶת־בְּנֵי יִשְׂרָאֵל מִבֵּין הַגּוֹיִם אֲשֶׁר הָלְכוּ־שָׁם וְקִבַּצְתִּי אֹתָם מִסָּבִיב וְהֵבֵאתִי אוֹתָם אֶל־אַדְמָתָם:

כב וְעָשִׂיתִי אֹתָם לְגוֹי אֶחָד בָּאָרֶץ בְּהָרֵי יִשְׂרָאֵל וּמֶלֶךְ אֶחָד יִהְיֶה לְכֻלָּם לְמֶלֶךְ וְלֹא יִהְיֶה [יִהְיוּ־] עוֹד לִשְׁנֵי גוֹיִם וְלֹא יֵחָצוּ עוֹד לִשְׁתֵּי מַמְלָכוֹת עוֹד:

כג וְלֹא יִטַּמְּאוּ עוֹד בְּגִלּוּלֵיהֶם וּבְשִׁקּוּצֵיהֶם וּבְכֹל פִּשְׁעֵיהֶם וְהוֹשַׁעְתִּי אֹתָם מִכֹּל מוֹשְׁבֹתֵיהֶם אֲשֶׁר חָטְאוּ בָהֶם וְטִהַרְתִּי אוֹתָם וְהָיוּ־לִי לְעָם וַאֲנִי אֶהְיֶה לָהֶם לֵאלֹהִים:

כד וְעַבְדִּי דָוִד מֶלֶךְ עֲלֵיהֶם וְרוֹעֶה אֶחָד יִהְיֶה לְכֻלָּם וּבְמִשְׁפָּטַי יֵלֵכוּ וְחֻקֹּתַי יִשְׁמְרוּ וְעָשׂוּ אוֹתָם:

כה וְיָשְׁבוּ עַל־הָאָרֶץ אֲשֶׁר נָתַתִּי לְעַבְדִּי לְיַעֲקֹב אֲשֶׁר יָשְׁבוּ־בָהּ אֲבוֹתֵיכֶם וְיָשְׁבוּ עָלֶיהָ הֵמָּה וּבְנֵיהֶם וּבְנֵי בְנֵיהֶם עַד־עוֹלָם וְדָוִד עַבְדִּי נָשִׂיא לָהֶם לְעוֹלָם:

Commentary

23. *Backslidings.* Reading משובתיהם (*m'shuvotéhem*) instead of מושבתיהם (*moshvotéhem, their dwellings*).

26. I will make a covenant of peace with them, an everlasting covenant with them. I will make them safe and increase their numbers, and place My sanctuary in their midst forever.

27. My Presence will be with them; I will be their God, and they shall be My people.

28. And when My sanctuary remains among them forever, the nations shall know that I am the Eternal, who sanctifies Israel.

26 וְכָרַתִּ֤י לָהֶם֙ בְּרִ֣ית שָׁל֔וֹם בְּרִ֥ית עוֹלָ֖ם יִהְיֶ֣ה אוֹתָ֑ם וּנְתַתִּים֙ וְהִרְבֵּיתִ֣י אוֹתָ֔ם וְנָתַתִּ֧י אֶת־מִקְדָּשִׁ֛י בְּתוֹכָ֖ם לְעוֹלָֽם׃

27 וְהָיָ֤ה מִשְׁכָּנִי֙ עֲלֵיהֶ֔ם וְהָיִ֥יתִי לָהֶ֖ם לֵֽאלֹהִ֑ים וְהֵ֖מָּה יִהְיוּ־לִ֥י לְעָֽם׃

28 וְיָֽדְעוּ֙ הַגּוֹיִ֔ם כִּ֚י אֲנִ֣י יְהֹוָ֔ה מְקַדֵּ֖שׁ אֶת־יִשְׂרָאֵ֑ל בִּהְי֧וֹת מִקְדָּשִׁ֛י בְּתוֹכָ֖ם לְעוֹלָֽם׃

Commentary

26. *I will make them safe.* Others render ונתתים (*u-n'tatim*) as "I will establish them." Both translations are guesswork; a word probably has been omitted from the masoretic text.

27. *My Presence.* Literally, My dwelling place. The word hints at the reestablishment of the Temple where the Divine Presence will be manifest.

Essay

A single nation (verse 22)

The imagery of the two sticks must have struck a powerful chord in the minds of the Prophet's listeners. He probably preached this sermon after the destruction of the Temple in the year 587 B.C.E., when he and the élite of Jerusalem found themselves in Babylonian exile. Do not despair, he pleaded, you will return to your patrimony; God will see to it. In fact, not you alone but also that portion of our people who were exiled long before our time, those of the Northern Kingdom.

In the year 721 B.C.E., Samaria/Israel had been sacked and its leaders deported to Assyria. Those who remained behind intermingled with the foreign settlers whom the conquerors imported; but what happened to the deportees is shrouded in mystery. They disappeared from history, and to this day there are claims that certain nations (the Scots, for instance, or the B'nai Israel of India) are the descendants of what came to be known as the Ten Lost Tribes. But so far, no credible historical evidence has supported any such claims. Most likely the exiles were assimilated in Assyrian territory.

Now, almost a century and a half later, this territory was ruled by the Babylonians among whom Ezekiel and the exiles from Jerusalem/Judah were living. Perhaps at that time there were still people who identified themselves as descendants of the "lost tribes," and they may have been in the Prophet's audience. If so, he wanted to give them hope as well, by assuring them that God had not forgotten them. They, too, would be returned to their homeland when the time for redemption was at hand.

As we know today, history did not bear out the Prophet's hope. The "one people" vision saw fulfillment only for Jerusalem/Judah, and we today are known as *yehudim* (Jews) because we are the inheritors of *yehudah* (Judah).[2]

Our traditional interpreters were unwilling to admit the possibility that any prediction of a great prophet like Ezekiel could fail of fulfillment. So they spiritualized the message and interpreted "Israel united" as united in a return to God and in faithful adherence to Torah law.[3]

Gleanings

Words to Remember

I will make a covenant of peace with them,
an everlasting covenant. (verse 26)

Symbolic actions

Although most prophetic books include some dramatic actions performed by the prophet, Ezekiel uses them regularly. He acts out dramatizations of his message as a motivation or basis on which to interpret coming events. They are to be seen as a form of teaching aid; they have a performative character that makes them a kind of street theater to provoke the people to listen.

Lawrence Boadt[4]

The ingathering of Israel

By gathering Israel and bringing her back to her own land, the Eternal manifests his holiness in the sight of the nations. It is an event which comes about in the full glare of the political scene, and which can be noticed by foreign nations as well as by Israel. The Eternal owes it to his honour that the covenant profaned by all the heathen should be reestablished. There is an unmistakable element of reason in this method of argument. In order to make the whole saving work comprehensible, Ezekiel takes the radical course of relating it to the Eternal's honour, which must be restored in the sight of the nations.

Gerhard von Rad[5]

The vision of 37:28 was to him no vague dream of the distant future. He envisaged a speedy return and an actual brick and mortar temple in his lifetime, and one can picture him busied for the next weeks or months with compass and rule as he planned temple and city for the theocracy of his dreams.

Brooke Peters Church[6]

***

Notes

[1] Rashi and Radak represent the mainstream of Jewish interpretation; for an extensive survey of the Christian use of the term, see *Anchor Bible Dictionary,* vol. 6, pp. 137-150.

[2] The German language preserves this derivation more clearly, for it calls a Jew "Jude."

[3] So J.H. Hertz, *Pentateuch and Haftorahs,* p. 179.

[4] *Anchor Bible Dictionary,* vol. 2, pp. 716-717.

[5] *The Message of the Prophets,* pp. 204-205.

[6] *The Private Lives of the Prophets,* p. 211.

ויחי

First Kings, chapter 2, verses 1 to 12

Introduction

Connection of sidra and haftarah:

In the sidra, Jacob delivers his last charge to his children, and in the haftarah, David leaves instructions with his son Solomon, who will succeed him on the throne.

The setting:

The haftarah, taken from the First Book of Kings,[1] is one of the briefest in the yearly cycle. It brings us the last words of David, whose forty-year reign (from about 1010 B.C.E. on) is nearing its end. He has appointed Solomon as his successor (see the haftarah to Chayei Sarah) and now shares with him some final matters that have been on his mind. Solomon is asked to settle a few old scores and to be generous to one particular person. The haftarah raises serious questions about David; see the essay below.

For more on the book of Kings, see our *General Introduction*.

The story:

1. David's life is drawing to a close, and he gives last instructions to Solomon: Religious/moral charges. (1-4)

2. Outstanding personal matters: Solomon is asked to execute vengeance on Joab and Shim'i, something David could not do; and David reminds his son that Barzillai of Gilead must be treated with kindness. (5-9)

3. David's death and Solomon's accession. (10-12)

HAFTARAH FOR VA-Y'CHI

First Kings, chapter 2, verses 1 to 12

2:1. When the time came near for David to die, he gave this instruction to his son Solomon:

2. I am going the way of all the earth; you must now be strong; show yourself a man

3. and keep faith with the Eternal your God, walking in God's ways, carrying out the laws, commandments, rules of justice and directions of God, as written in the Torah of Moses, so that you may succeed in all that you do and whatever you turn to.

4. In that way the Eternal will see to it that the promise about me comes true. As God said: *If your children are careful how they live, and walk before Me faithfully with all their heart and soul, one of your descendants will always rule Israel.*

וַיִּקְרְבוּ יְמֵי־דָוִד לָמוּת וַיְצַו אֶת־שְׁלֹמֹה 2:1
בְנוֹ לֵאמֹר:

אָנֹכִי הֹלֵךְ בְּדֶרֶךְ כָּל־הָאָרֶץ וְחָזַקְתָּ וְהָיִיתָ 2
לְאִישׁ:

וְשָׁמַרְתָּ אֶת־מִשְׁמֶרֶת יְהוָה אֱלֹהֶיךָ לָלֶכֶת 3
בִּדְרָכָיו לִשְׁמֹר חֻקֹּתָיו מִצְוֹתָיו וּמִשְׁפָּטָיו
וְעֵדְוֹתָיו כַּכָּתוּב בְּתוֹרַת מֹשֶׁה לְמַעַן תַּשְׂכִּיל
אֵת כָּל־אֲשֶׁר תַּעֲשֶׂה וְאֵת כָּל־אֲשֶׁר תִּפְנֶה
שָׁם:

לְמַעַן יָקִים יְהוָה אֶת־דְּבָרוֹ אֲשֶׁר דִּבֶּר 4
עָלַי לֵאמֹר אִם־יִשְׁמְרוּ בָנֶיךָ אֶת־דַּרְכָּם
לָלֶכֶת לְפָנַי בֶּאֱמֶת בְּכָל־לְבָבָם וּבְכָל־נַפְשָׁם
לֵאמֹר לֹא־יִכָּרֵת לְךָ אִישׁ מֵעַל כִּסֵּא
יִשְׂרָאֵל:

Commentary

1. He gave this instruction. וַיְצַו (*va-y'tzav*), implies commanding his son. מִצְוָה (*mitzvah*, commandment) and צַוָּאָה (*tzava'ah*, testament) come from the same root. Of the dying Jacob too it is said that he finished לְצַוֺּת (*l'tzavvot*, to instruct) his children.[2]

2. The way of all the earth. The way of all flesh—that is, I am going to die.

4. The promise about me. To Nathan the prophet and conveyed to David.[3]

Your descendants will always rule Israel. Literally, will never be cut off from the throne of Israel. David is speaking of the promise that ended with the words, "Your throne shall be established forever."

5. Moreover, you know what Joab son of Zeruiah did to me, what he did to the two commanders of Israel's army, Abner son of Ner and Amasa son of Jether, killing them, shedding war-blood in peacetime, and spilling war-blood upon the girdle hitched over his loins and upon the sandals on his feet.

6. Do what you know is wise, and do not allow his gray head to descend in peace to Sheol.

7. But be kind to the family of Barzillai of Gilead, and let them be among those who eat at your table [whom you support], because they showed me friendship when I had to flee from your brother Absalom.

5 וְגַם אַתָּה יָדַעְתָּ אֵת אֲשֶׁר־עָשָׂה לִי יוֹאָב בֶּן־צְרוּיָה אֲשֶׁר עָשָׂה לִשְׁנֵי־שָׂרֵי צִבְאוֹת יִשְׂרָאֵל לְאַבְנֵר בֶּן־נֵר וְלַעֲמָשָׂא בֶן־יֶתֶר וַיַּהַרְגֵם וַיָּשֶׂם דְּמֵי־מִלְחָמָה בְּשָׁלֹם וַיִּתֵּן דְּמֵי מִלְחָמָה בַּחֲגֹרָתוֹ אֲשֶׁר בְּמָתְנָיו וּבְנַעֲלוֹ אֲשֶׁר בְּרַגְלָיו:

6 וְעָשִׂיתָ כְּחָכְמָתֶךָ וְלֹא־תוֹרֵד שֵׂיבָתוֹ בְּשָׁלֹם שְׁאֹל:

7 וְלִבְנֵי בַרְזִלַּי הַגִּלְעָדִי תַּעֲשֶׂה־חֶסֶד וְהָיוּ בְּאֹכְלֵי שֻׁלְחָנֶךָ כִּי־כֵן קָרְבוּ אֵלַי בְּבָרְחִי מִפְּנֵי אַבְשָׁלוֹם אָחִיךָ:

Commentary

5. *What Joab son of Zeruiah did to me*. When he killed the rebellious Absalom, David's favorite son, against the king's explicit instruction. The king mourned bitterly, and his last words to Solomon make clear that he never forgave Joab.[4]

Abner son of Ner. One of David's generals, who was killed by Joab.[5]

Amasa son of Jether. Killed by Abner and avenged by Joab.[6]

6. *Do what you know is wise*. David repeats it in verse 9; see comment on that verse.

Sheol. "The shadowy, insubstantial underworld, the destination of all, good or bad without discrimination, where existence is wholly undesirable. The Hebrews in the classical period had no comfortable prospect of the hereafter."[7]

7. *But be kind*. Extend חסד (*chesed*), a word that has no exact English equivalent. It is a relational term, that is, the kindness that proceeds from a relationship, which might exist because of blood, marriage, alliance, or covenant with the divine (manifested in the Eternal's special relationship with Israel). When kindness was extended in the absence of a relationship it was termed חן (*chen*), given "freely"," out of grace," or "gratis."

Barzillai. Who had supplied David and his troops with food during the rebellion of Absalom.[8]

Who eat at your table. Either literally so, or who receive a royal stipend. Sometimes the king also kept people at his table whom he wanted to keep under close scrutiny.[9]

8. There is also Shim'i son of Gera the Benjamite, from Bahurim. He cursed me with a terrible curse the time I went to Mahanaim; then he came to meet me at the river Jordan, and I swore to him by God that I would not put him to the sword.

9. But you must not treat him as though he were innocent; you are wise and know what to do with him: send his bloody gray head down to Sheol.

10. Then David slept with his ancestors, and was buried in the City of David.

11. David ruled Israel for forty years; he ruled seven years in Hebron and thirty-three years in Jerusalem.

12. Now Solomon sat on the throne of his father David, and his rule was secure and strong.

8 וְהִנֵּה עִמְּךָ שִׁמְעִי בֶן־גֵּרָא בֶן־הַיְמִינִי מִבַּחֻרִים וְהוּא קִלְלַנִי קְלָלָה נִמְרֶצֶת בְּיוֹם לֶכְתִּי מַחֲנָיִם וְהוּא־יָרַד לִקְרָאתִי הַיַּרְדֵּן וָאֶשָּׁבַע לוֹ בַיהוָה לֵאמֹר אִם־אֲמִיתְךָ בֶּחָרֶב:

9 וְעַתָּה אַל־תְּנַקֵּהוּ כִּי אִישׁ חָכָם אָתָּה וְיָדַעְתָּ אֵת אֲשֶׁר תַּעֲשֶׂה־לּוֹ וְהוֹרַדְתָּ אֶת־שֵׂיבָתוֹ בְּדָם שְׁאוֹל:

10 וַיִּשְׁכַּב דָּוִד עִם־אֲבֹתָיו וַיִּקָּבֵר בְּעִיר דָּוִד:

11 וְהַיָּמִים אֲשֶׁר מָלַךְ דָּוִד עַל־יִשְׂרָאֵל אַרְבָּעִים שָׁנָה בְּחֶבְרוֹן מָלַךְ שֶׁבַע שָׁנִים וּבִירוּשָׁלַםִ מָלַךְ שְׁלֹשִׁים וְשָׁלֹשׁ שָׁנִים:

12 וּשְׁלֹמֹה יָשַׁב עַל־כִּסֵּא דָּוִד אָבִיו וַתִּכֹּן מַלְכֻתוֹ מְאֹד:

Commentary

8. *Bahurim*. Near Jerusalem.

When I went to Mahanaim. Located east of the Jordan. This incident too happened during the revolt of Absalom. Shim'i was a member of Saul's family and pelted David with stones and curses as he marched by, shouting: "Get out, get out, you criminal, you villain! The Eternal is paying you back for all your crimes against Saul's family, whose throne you grabbed. But now the Eternal is handing your throne to your son Absalom. You're in deep trouble, you criminal!"[10] The curse was deemed still operative, and so was the promise that David had given to Shim'i, not to harm him.[11]

9. *You are wise and know what to do*. After David's death, Solomon ordered Shim'i to move to Jerusalem, where he put him under house arrest. When Shim'i broke the ban, he was killed.[12] Solomon also found occasion to kill Adonijah and Joab.[13]

10. *Then David slept with his ancestors*. An idiom signifying originally "buried with one's family," as opposed to being "cut off."

Buried in the City of David. This was the name of the oldest part of Jerusalem, which he had wrested from the Jebusites. It was located south of the Temple Mount, on a fortified ridge called Ophel.

Essay

David's bloody testament

"There is little else in the frankly told story of David's life and reign which so seriously impairs his reputation as the blemish in his character revealed by his last charge to Solomon." [14] This blemish is affixed to David's order to do away with Joab and Shim'i. As a deathbed wish, it was something Solomon would feel bound to carry out, which indeed he did. [15]

How do these last requests square with the character of David, the God-fearing man and composer of psalms? A number of attempts were made by traditional interpreters to exculpate the dying king in some way. Thus, Radak says that David did not ask Solomon to find a pretext to kill an old enemy. [16] Rather, he cautioned him to be watchful for any future transgression that Shim'i might commit and then do what needed to be done. [17] It is noteworthy that the account in Chronicles, which deals much more elaborately with Solomon's succession, omits the deathbed wish entirely. [18]

However, there is no need to put these requests into a rosy light, nor should we judge them by the standards of a peaceful democratic society of modern times. Such an attempt does not do justice to the nature of biblical writing, and in addition it is well to remember that David's age was not peaceful, nor was Israel's society democratic.

The heroes of the Tanach are not depicted as saints; rather, they are flesh-and-blood human beings who have great qualities and are poets, prophets, and intimates of God. But they remain human and exhibit weaknesses that are often glaring.

With all his spiritual capacities, David was also a warrior who spent his life fighting and therefore was used to spilling blood. The Rabbis suggest that because of this he became enfeebled at seventy. In addition to inimical nations at his borders, he had internal enemies, and his preference for Benjamin and Judah was not appreciated in the northern part of the country. His last charge was in part politically motivated, for he wanted to make sure that Solomon's reign would be firmly established.

David was a complex personality: generous and vengeful, spiritual and lustful, desiring peace but waging war. He had a hard life: in his youth, forced to become a refugee and bereaved of his best friend; elevated to a throne that was never quite secure; a father who had terrible troubles with three of his sons. His last request is not that of a philosopher; it is the charge of an embattled man.

His contemporaries remembered him with admiration and affection and saw no need to hide his faults. For them, he was the king *par excellence*, and as the generations went by, his name was connected not only with the past but with the future. "David, king of Israel, lives!" goes a popular Hebrew folk song, and when the messianic days arrive, a descendant of the House of David is hoped to be its standard-bearer.

Gleanings

The midrash of Josephus

(In his history of the Jewish people, the politician-turned-historian, Flavius Josephus (about 37-100 C.E.), retells the substance of our haftarah. His account is considerably more elaborate than the biblical text.)

When David was assailed by weakness due to old age, he became ill and felt that death was approaching. He called Solomon and said to him: "My son, I am about to depart from this world and join my ancestors. I am on the way that all humans have to travel, those who are now living or those yet to come. No one returns from there to find out how things are going here. But seeing I am still alive, yet with death near at hand, do remember what I have told you earlier: be just to your subjects and loyal to God ...."

Antiquities[19]

Extremely strange

We find three instructions given by David, two of which, considered superficially, seem extremely strange.

Here is David, who in the words of his psalms has given us an insight into his innermost feelings, into the most secret emotions of his heart. This is the David who, with the most intensive self-control, had worked himself up by hard struggles above all feelings of the bitterness that must have filled him, when so often he experienced ingratitude and black treachery on the part of those who were close to him. Is this then the man who, in the clarifying repose of age and facing death, would allow feelings of low revenge to dictate his last instructions? Surely not.

Mendel Hirsch[20]

(The commentator goes on to explain at great length that David's command to do away with old enemies was intended to fortify Solomon's hold on the throne and guard him against insurrections that David was sure would otherwise occur.)

* * *

Notes

[1] In the Septuagint, it is called the Third Book of Kingdoms, while I and II Samuel are called I and II Kingdoms.

[2] Genesis 49:33.

[3] II Samuel 7:12-16.

[4] II Samuel 18:1-18; 19:2-9.

[5] II Samuel 3:24-34.

[6] II Samuel 2:17-25.

[7] Gray, p. 99. On *Sheol*, see the haftarah to *Vayeitzei,* with comment on Hosea 13:14.

[8] II Samuel 17:27-29.

[9] Thus, David kept a surviving member of Saul's family at his table; II Samuel 9:11-13.

[10] II Samuel 16:7-8.

[11] II Samuel 19:24.

[12] I Kings 2:36-46.

[13] I Kings 2: 23-25; 28-34. According to Malbim, there was always a danger of these men staging a revolt.

[14] Honor, p.45.

[15] See also comment on verse 1 above, for the Hebrew meaning of "instructed."

[16] Comment on verse 9.

[17] Shim'i was a much discussed person. He was thought to be the teacher of Solomon. Some Rabbis regarded him as an evil influence and others as the opposite. See Ginzberg, *Legends of the Jews,* vol. 4, p. 128 and vol. 6, p. 279, note 11. Also, by reading "my girdle" and "my sandals" David would say that the stain was upon him and his offspring; hence the command to do away with Joab.

[18] I Chronicles, chapters 29 and 30.

[19] VII 15:1.

[20] *Haftoroth*, p. 115.

שמות

Isaiah, chapter 27, verse 6 to chapter 28, verse 13 and chapter 29, verses 22 to 23
Introduction

Connection of haftarah and sidra:

The weekly portion tells the story of the people's enslavement in Egypt and of the eventual deliverance that God has planned. The haftarah too deals with Israel's misfortunes and the salvation that is bound to come.

The setting:

Isaiah lived in the kingdom of Judah (of which Jerusalem was the capital), during the second half of the 8th century B.C.E. The Northern Kingdom, called Israel, with Samaria as its capital, had been destroyed by the Assyrians in 721 B.C.E. Isaiah traces its demise to the thorough corruption of the upper classes, with drink and gluttony serving as his prime examples. But in the Southern Kingdom, too, such malfeasance was common and did not escape the Prophet's scalpel.

For more on Isaiah, see our *General Introduction*.

The message:

1. Preamble: A prediction of future happiness precedes the sorry tale of past events. (27:6)

2. Part 1: A lament for the Northern Kingdom, and a hope for the future. (27:7-13)

3. Part 2: A scathing analysis of the kingdom's downfall and the prescription for moral regeneration that had to take place. It would be slow and painful, and only then would Jerusalem again be the center of a reconstructed people. (28:1-13)

4. Postscript: The Rabbis added these two verses from another chapter as a consoling conclusion to the haftarah. (29:22-23)

HAFTARAH FOR SH'MOT

Isaiah, chapter 27, verse 6 to chapter 28, verse 13 and chapter 29, verses 22 to 23

27:6. Jacob shall come to take root,
Israel shall blossom and bloom.
They shall fill the earth with fruit
like a medlar when it sends forth runners.

7. Did God strike [Israel] down
like others who were struck?
Was [Israel] slain as [God] slew the
slayers?

8. God contended with them, sending them
off with a hot blast,
as on the day the east wind comes.

9. See, now: thus shall Jacob's sin be
atoned,
and this will be the result of removing its
guilt:
when they grind all their altar-stones
into powdered limestone,
when none of the sacred posts
and incense-altars are left standing.

27:6 הַבָּאִים֙ יַשְׁרֵ֣שׁ יַֽעֲקֹ֔ב

יָצִ֥יץ וּפָרַ֖ח יִשְׂרָאֵ֑ל

וּמָלְא֥וּ פְנֵי־תֵבֵ֖ל תְּנוּבָֽה׃

7 הַכְּמַכַּ֥ת מַכֵּ֖הוּ הִכָּ֑הוּ

אִם־כְּהֶ֥רֶג הֲרֻגָ֖יו הֹרָֽג׃

8 בְּסַאסְּאָ֖ה בְּשַׁלְּחָ֣הּ תְּרִיבֶ֑נָּה

הָגָ֛ה בְּרוּח֥וֹ הַקָּשָׁ֖ה

בְּי֥וֹם קָדִֽים׃

9 לָכֵ֗ן בְּזֹאת֙ יְכֻפַּ֣ר עֲוֺֽן־יַֽעֲקֹ֔ב

וְזֶ֕ה כָּל־פְּרִ֖י הָסִ֣ר חַטָּאת֑וֹ

בְּשׂוּמ֣וֹ ׀ כָּל־אַבְנֵ֣י מִזְבֵּ֗חַ

כְּאַבְנֵי־גִר֙

מְנֻפָּצ֔וֹת לֹֽא־יָקֻ֥מוּ אֲשֵׁרִ֖ים וְחַמָּנִֽים׃

Commentary

27:6-8. The text is in disarray. Our translation is based on Tur-Sinai, who divides verse 6 into three stanzas and follows them with the beginning of verse 8. [1]

6. *Medlar*. A form of apple tree.

7. *God*. Literally, He.

9. This verse probably stood originally before verse 6, so that verses 7-8, 10-11 read as a continuum. For the sequence of verses as suggested, see Notes. [2]

Sacred posts. In design they may have been comparable to Indian totem poles; they served as holy markers in pagan rites, which probably were connected to the ancient cult of the goddess Asherah, known from the second millennium B.C.E. [3]

10. The fortified city is empty,

its homes deserted, forsaken like a wilderness;

there calves graze, and there lie down,

and consume [the] branches [of the trees].

11. When the crown withers, they crack;

women come and use them to kindle fires.

Since this people has no understanding,

their Maker will show them no pity,

their Creator will show them no mercy.

12. But there will come a day

when, from the river Euphrates

to Egypt's Nile,

God will beat out [the peoples like grain]

and you will be picked up one by one,

O people of Israel.

13. And on that day

a great shofar shall be sounded:

Those lost in Assyria, those banished to
Egypt, shall come back

and worship the Eternal

on the holy mountain, in Jerusalem.

10 כִּי עִיר בְּצוּרָה בָּדָד

נָוֶה מְשֻׁלָּח וְנֶעֱזָב כַּמִּדְבָּר

שָׁם יִרְעֶה עֵגֶל וְשָׁם יִרְבָּץ

וְכִלָּה סְעִפֶיהָ:

11 בִּיבֹשׁ קְצִירָהּ תִּשָּׁבַרְנָה

נָשִׁים בָּאוֹת מְאִירוֹת אוֹתָהּ

כִּי לֹא עַם־בִּינוֹת הוּא

עַל־כֵּן לֹא־יְרַחֲמֶנּוּ עֹשֵׂהוּ

וְיֹצְרוֹ לֹא יְחֻנֶּנּוּ:

12 וְהָיָה בַּיּוֹם הַהוּא

יַחְבֹּט יְהֹוָה מִשִּׁבֹּלֶת הַנָּהָר

עַד־נַחַל מִצְרָיִם

וְאַתֶּם תְּלֻקְּטוּ לְאַחַד אֶחָד

בְּנֵי יִשְׂרָאֵל:

13 וְהָיָה בַּיּוֹם הַהוּא

יִתָּקַע בְּשׁוֹפָר גָּדוֹל

וּבָאוּ הָאֹבְדִים בְּאֶרֶץ אַשּׁוּר וְהַנִּדָּחִים

בְּאֶרֶץ מִצְרָיִם

וְהִשְׁתַּחֲווּ לַיהֹוָה

בְּהַר הַקֹּדֶשׁ בִּירוּשָׁלָ͏ִם:

Commentary

10. *The fortified city.* Samaria, capital of the Northern Kingdom.

And consume [the] branches. The Hebrew is difficult. A better understanding is obtained by adding the letter א (aleph) to וכלה (v'chillah, and consume), which would produce the word וכאלה (u-ch'-elah, and like a terebinth). The verse then would read: "... and like a terebinth whose branches break when the crown is withered."[4]

13. *Those lost in Assyria ... shall come back.* Unfortunately, Isaiah's hope was never realized; the exiled people became the "Ten Lost Tribes" and disappeared into the mists of history. (See the essay in the haftarah for Vayigash, p. 112.)

28:1. Ah, the proud garlands of the drunkards of Ephraim,

whose glorious beauty is but fading flowers

on the proud heads of gluttons and drunkards.

2. See now: my Sovereign has something strong and mighty in store,

like a stream of hail, a destructive storm,

a downpour of mighty waters overflowing the land.

3. They shall be trampled underfoot—

the proud garlands of the drunkards of Ephraim.

4. The faded flowers

whose glorious beauty is

on the heads of those gluttons!

They shall be

like an early fig

before the summer harvest:

who sees it swallows it

as soon as it comes to hand.

5. But a day will come when the God of heaven's hosts

will be a garland of beauty,

a diadem of loveliness

for the remnant of God's people,

28:1 הֹוֹי עֲטֶרֶת גֵּאוּת שִׁכֹּרֵי אֶפְרַיִם

וְצִיץ נֹבֵל צְבִי תִפְאַרְתֹּו

אֲשֶׁר עַל־רֹאשׁ גֵּיא־שְׁמָנִים הֲלוּמֵי יָיִן:

2 הִנֵּה חָזָק וְאַמִּץ לַאדֹנָי

כְּזֶרֶם בָּרָד שַׂעַר קָטֶב

כְּזֶרֶם מַיִם כַּבִּירִים שֹׁטְפִים הִנִּיחַ לָאָרֶץ בְּיָד:

3 בְּרַגְלַיִם תֵּרָמַסְנָה

עֲטֶרֶת גֵּאוּת שִׁכֹּורֵי אֶפְרָיִם:

4 וְהָיְתָה צִיצַת נֹבֵל

צְבִי תִפְאַרְתֹּו

אֲשֶׁר עַל־רֹאשׁ גֵּיא שְׁמָנִים

כְּבִכּוּרָהּ בְּטֶרֶם קַיִץ

אֲשֶׁר יִרְאֶה הָרֹאֶה אֹותָהּ

בְּעֹודָהּ בְּכַפֹּו יִבְלָעֶנָּה:

5 בַּיֹּום הַהוּא יִהְיֶה יְהוָה צְבָאֹות

לַעֲטֶרֶת צְבִי

וְלִצְפִירַת תִּפְאָרָה

לִשְׁאָר עַמֹּו:

Commentary

28:1. *Ephraim.* The leading tribe of the Northern Kingdom whose downfall and its causes are the subject of this chapter.

2. *Has something strong and mighty [in store].* Namely Assyria, which is seen as God's instrument.[5] The words "in store" are taken from the end of the verse (ביד, *b'yad*).

5. *God's people.* Literally, "His people." A remnant who were spared the Assyrian destruction will return; but they too will in the end revert to evil ways and be punished accordingly.[6]

6. a spirit of justice for those who sit as
    judges,

and courage for those who defend the city.

7. But these too are reeling with wine

and dazed by liquor:

Priest and prophet reel with liquor,

are besotted with wine and totter in
    judgment.

8. Yes, every table is covered with vomit
    and filth,

not a place is left [clean].

9.]The drunkards say:]

To whom is he teaching his revelation?

To those newly weaned from milk?

10. Therefore [teach them]:

one command and then another,

one line and then another,

a little here, a little there!

11. So he [the prophet] must talk to this
    crowd

with slow speech and simple words,

6 וּלְרוּחַ מִשְׁפָּט לַיּוֹשֵׁב עַל־הַמִּשְׁפָּט

וְלִגְבוּרָה מְשִׁיבֵי מִלְחָמָה שָׁעְרָה:

7 וְגַם־אֵלֶּה בַּיַּיִן שָׁגוּ

וּבַשֵּׁכָר תָּעוּ

כֹּהֵן וְנָבִיא שָׁגוּ בַשֵּׁכָר

נִבְלְעוּ מִן־הַיַּיִן

תָּעוּ מִן־הַשֵּׁכָר

שָׁגוּ בָרֹאֶה פָּקוּ פְּלִילִיָּה:

8 כִּי כָּל־שֻׁלְחָנוֹת מָלְאוּ קִיא צֹאָה

בְּלִי מָקוֹם:

9 אֶת־מִי יוֹרֶה דֵעָה וְאֶת־מִי יָבִין שְׁמוּעָה

גְּמוּלֵי מֵחָלָב עַתִּיקֵי מִשָּׁדָיִם:

10 כִּי צַו לָצָו צַו לָצָו

קַו לָקָו קַו לָקָו

זְעֵיר שָׁם זְעֵיר שָׁם:

11 כִּי בְּלַעֲגֵי שָׂפָה וּבְלָשׁוֹן אַחֶרֶת

יְדַבֵּר אֶל־הָעָם הַזֶּה:

Commentary

7. *Priest and prophet.* The mention of drunken leaders calls to mind the Torah's command that priests must abstain from intoxicating drink before officiating.[7]

8. *Vomit.* Alcohol abuse is known also from older Near East civilizations, and is strongly condemned in the book of Proverbs and rabbinic writings (see *Gleanings*).

9. *Whom is he teaching.* יורה דעה (*yoreh de'ah*) became the title of one of the sections of the *Shulchan Aruch* (tradition's primary law code).[8] A thorough knowledge of Yoreh De'ah is a prerequisite for Orthodox rabbinic ordination.

10. *One command and then another.* צו לצו ... קו לקו (*tzav latzav ... kav lakav*), a memorable litany in Hebrew.

11. *Simple words.* Literally, different words; that is, simpler than speech that adults ordinarily use. It is also possible that *tzav* and *kav* were old names for the letters צ (*tzade*) and ק (*kof*). In either case, the text suggests that people ought to be treated like little children who are learning one word or letter at a time.[9]

12. and say to them:

Here is rest; rest for the weary; repose is here.

[Still] they refuse to listen.

13. To them the word of the Eternal will
   come:

one command and then another,

one line and then another,

a little here, a little there!

But instead [of listening]

they will march forward, only to fall back
   hurt;

they will be snared and taken captive.

29:22. The Eternal, the One who saved
   Abraham,

therefore says to the House of Jacob:

No more shall Jacob be put to shame,

no more shall his face grow pale.

23. For when his children see

what I am doing in their midst,

they shall hallow My name,

hallowing the Holy One of Jacob

and holding Israel's God in awe.

12 אֲשֶׁר אָמַר אֲלֵיהֶם

זֹאת הַמְּנוּחָה֙ הָנִ֣יחוּ לֶעָיֵ֔ף וְזֹ֖את הַמַּרְגֵּעָ֑ה

וְלֹ֥א אָב֖וּא שְׁמֽוֹעַ׃

13 וְהָיָ֙ה לָהֶ֜ם דְּבַר־יְהֹוָ֗ה

צַ֤ו לָצָו֙ צַ֣ו לָצָ֔ו

קַ֤ו לָקָו֙ קַ֣ו לָקָ֔ו

זְעֵ֥יר שָׁ֖ם זְעֵ֥יר שָֽׁם

לְמַ֣עַן יֵלְכ֗וּ וְכָשְׁל֤וּ אָחוֹר֙ וְנִשְׁבָּ֔רוּ

וְנוֹקְשׁ֖וּ וְנִלְכָּֽדוּ׃

29:22 לָכֵ֗ן כֹּה־אָמַ֤ר יְהֹוָה֙ אֶל־בֵּ֣ית יַעֲקֹ֔ב

אֲשֶׁ֥ר פָּדָ֖ה אֶת־אַבְרָהָ֑ם

לֹֽא־עַתָּ֤ה יֵבוֹשׁ֙ יַעֲקֹ֔ב

וְלֹ֥א עַתָּ֖ה פָּנָ֥יו יֶחֱוָֽרוּ׃

23 כִּ֣י בִרְאֹת֗וֹ יְלָדָ֛יו

מַעֲשֵׂ֥ה יָדַ֖י בְּקִרְבּ֑וֹ

יַקְדִּ֣ישׁוּ שְׁמִ֑י

וְהִקְדִּ֙ישׁוּ֙ אֶת־קְד֣וֹשׁ יַעֲקֹ֔ב

וְאֶת־אֱלֹהֵ֥י יִשְׂרָאֵ֖ל יַעֲרִֽיצוּ׃

Commentary

13. God repeats the Prophet's speech, and is disdained just as much.

But instead … למען (*l'ma-an*) usually conveys a sense of consequence; here it introduces
the consequences of disobedience.

Essay

The drunkards of Ephraim

The picture that Isaiah paints of the evils of alcohol is unparalleled in literature. Not only are the effects of drunkenness on individuals described in the most vivid language, they are also depicted as the causes of national disaster. Is this to be taken literally as a historically accurate assessment, or does the Prophet use it as a metaphor in order to illumine a dark side of the nation's character?

There are several reasons why the chapter must be seen as a metaphor for Israel's society rather than be understood literally.

For one, the Prophet's description of actual addicts appears excessive:

> ... *every table is covered with vomit and filth,*
> *not a place is left [clean].* (28:8)

Second, the denunciation of humanity's most popular and pervasive drug is here linked to gluttony. Then as now, extravagant consumption of food was not available to the masses. Isaiah would not have used this image if he wanted to describe a whole nation's behavior.

Third, it is unlikely that he believed the downfall of the Northern Kingdom to be a result of excessive drinking and eating

Therefore we must conclude that Isaiah used these images of excess as a metaphor for the corruption of the upper classes, whose priests and prophets are given as outstanding examples. They had the responsibility of guiding the nation morally and had failed dismally. They were rich and indulged their whims; God and ethics were not on their agenda. The idols of the pagans were supplemented by the idols of pleasure and power; the covenant at Sinai was furthest from their minds.

Their disastrous disregard of responsibility aroused God's ire; Assyria was summoned to destroy a nation that allowed itself to stray so far from its national purpose. And even if a remnant would return, its leaders would learn nothing from the past and therefore require moral reconstruction from the ground up. They would have to be taught like little children, in simple language, step by step.

Unfortunately, history took a harsher course, for not even a remnant returned. The ten tribes disappeared permanently and vanished like Sodom and Gomorrah, having forfeited their right to existence.

Isaiah's prophecy is thus more than a historical assessment; it is above all a potent warning for Judah, the Southern Kingdom. Its leaders must revamp their ways if they are to merit God's care and compassion.

The Prophet did not live see the day when—a little over a hundred years later—the judgment on Ephraim would visit Judah as well; but then a saving remnant would indeed return and, after decades of exile, re-create a new nation centered once again on Jerusalem and the worship of God.

(The Torah deals with alcohol in various contexts. See the Torah Commentary, pp. 793-794 and 1060-1061, with further references.)

Gleanings

The antiquity of alcohol abuse

An old text from the Syrian city of Ugarit describes how the god El, the head of the pantheon, became horribly drunk and collapsed under the table in his own filth.[10]

On drunkenness and gluttony

Hear, my son, and be wise,
and guide yourself accordingly:
Don't be among the winebibbers
or the gluttonous flesh eaters.
For the drunkard and glutton shall end up poor,
and their clouded thought end up in anger.

Book of Proverbs [11]

Three things show what people are: their drinking, their way of handling money, and their anger.

Talmud[12]

Wine goes in, understanding goes out.

Midrash[13]

Prudence should not be expected from someone who is never sober.

Cicero[14]

I have very poor and unhappy brains for drinking: I could wish courtesy would invent some other custom of entertainment.

Shakespeare[15]

We were to do much more business after dinner; but after dinner is after dinner—an old saying and true, "much drinking, little thinking."

Jonathan Swift[16]

Love of drinking and love of eating are here put on the same level. Our modern culture with its emphasis on external appearances has come to invest overeating and overweight with the sort of opprobrium once reserved for alcohol abuse. Commercial advertising regularly employs the language of sin, reward and punishment to sell both food and weight loss programs. In fact, excessive drinking and excessive eating have been found to be expressions of unresolved emotional problems.

S. David Sperling[17]

* * *

Notes

[1] *The Language and the Book*, p. 399. He relates הבאים (*haba'im*) to the Syriac הבא, flower; and סאסה (*sas'ah*) to the Syriac סאסא, medlar. Many other solutions have been proposed to make this cryptic text understandable; thus, סאסה has been understood to be a shepherd's cry.

[2] 9. See, now: thus shall Jacob's sin be atoned,
and this will be the result of removing its guilt:
when they grind all their altar-stones
into powdered limestone,
when none of the sacred posts
and incense-altars are left standing.
6. Jacob shall come to take root,
Israel shall blossom and bloom.
They shall fill the earth with fruit
like a medlar when it sends forth runners.
7. Did God strike [Israel] down
like others who were struck?
Was [Israel] slain as [God] slew the slayers?
Verses 10-11 (p. 124) follow.

[2] See J. Day, "Asherah," in the *Anchor Bible Dictionary*, vol. 1, pp. 483-487.

[3] Suggested by the JPS translation.

[4] So Krauss, *Isaiah*.

[5] Radak and others believe that verses 5 and 6 are an insertion referring to Judah and Jerusalem.

[6] Leviticus 10:8-11.

[7] Compiled by Joseph Caro in the 16th century.

[8] See W. W. Hallo, *Journal of Biblical Literature*, vol. 77 (1958), pp. 324-338. Rashi and Radak interpret differently: As they were taught so they will be punished: for one transgression at a time.

[9] S. Loewenstamm, *Comparative Studies in Ancient and Oriental Literatures*, pp. 369-381.

[10] 23:19-21.

[11] B. Eruvin 65b. The Hebrew is in the form of a wordplay, in that people are known by כוס, כיס and כעס (*kos, kis, ka'as*, cup, wallet, anger).

[12] *Midrash Tanhuma*, Sh'mini 7.

[13] Non est ab homine nunquam sobrio postulanda prudentia; *Philippics* II: 32.

[14] *Othello* Act 2, Scene 3.

[15] *Journal to Stella*, 26 February 1712.

[16] In personal communication (printed with his permission). See also W. G. Plaut, *The Book of Proverbs*, pp. 241 ff.

וארא

Ezekiel, chapter 28, verse 25 to chapter 29, verse 21

Introduction

Connection of haftarah and sidra:

The sidra tells us of the plagues inflicted on Egypt when it refused to release the Children of Israel from slavery; the haftarah predicts the forthcoming humiliation of Egypt, because it has forsaken Jerusalem in its time of trouble.

The setting:

Ezekiel lived in the days before and after the destruction of the First Temple and preached in the early part of the sixth century B.C.E. Egypt had promised to support the kingdom of Judah, but when the Babylonians laid their first siege to Jerusalem, no help came from Egypt. The city was conquered, and Ezekiel was among the deportees.

For more on Ezekiel and his time, see our *General Introduction*.

The message:

The haftarah brings us two of the six orations that the Prophet preached against Egypt. The first (29:1-16) chides Egypt for its perfidy, and was probably also meant to warn the powers in Jerusalem to rely no longer on its southern neighbor. The second oration (17-20) predicts a Babylonian invasion of Egypt.

The text begins and ends with words of comfort for Jerusalem.

HAFTARAH FOR VA'EIRA

Ezekiel, chapter 28, verse 25 to chapter 29, verse 21

28:25. Thus says the Eternal God: When I have gathered the House of Israel from the peoples among whom they have been scattered, and have made manifest My holiness there in the sight of the nations, they shall dwell on their own soil, that I gave to My servant Jacob.

26. They shall dwell on it in safety, and build houses, and plant vineyards. When I execute judgments on all the surrounding peoples who have shown them contempt, they shall dwell in safety. And they shall know that I, the Eternal, am their God.

29:1. On the twelfth day of the tenth month of the tenth year, the word of the Eternal came to me, saying:

2. Mortal, set your face against Pharaoh king of Egypt, and prophesy against him and against all Egypt.

28:25 כֹּה־אָמַר֩ אֲדֹנָ֨י יְהוִ֜ה בְּקַבְּצִ֣י אֶת־בֵּ֣ית יִשְׂרָאֵ֗ל מִן־הָֽעַמִּים֙ אֲשֶׁ֣ר נָפֹ֣צוּ בָ֔ם וְנִקְדַּ֥שְׁתִּי בָ֖ם לְעֵינֵ֣י הַגּוֹיִ֑ם וְיָֽשְׁבוּ֙ עַל־אַדְמָתָ֔ם אֲשֶׁ֥ר נָתַ֖תִּי לְעַבְדִּ֥י לְיַעֲקֹֽב׃

26 וְיָֽשְׁב֣וּ עָלֶיהָ֘ לָבֶטַח֒ וּבָנ֤וּ בָתִּים֙ וְנָֽטְע֣וּ כְרָמִ֔ים וְיָֽשְׁב֖וּ לָבֶ֑טַח בַּעֲשׂוֹתִ֣י שְׁפָטִ֗ים בְּכֹ֨ל הַשָּׁאטִ֤ים אֹתָם֙ מִסְּבִֽיבוֹתָ֔ם וְיָ֣דְע֔וּ כִּ֛י אֲנִ֥י יְהוָ֖ה אֱלֹהֵיהֶֽם׃

29:1 בַּשָּׁנָה֙ הָעֲשִׂירִ֔ית בָּעֲשִׂרִ֕י בִּשְׁנֵ֥ים עָשָׂ֖ר לַחֹ֑דֶשׁ הָיָ֥ה דְבַר־יְהוָ֖ה אֵלַ֥י לֵאמֹֽר׃

2 בֶּן־אָדָ֕ם שִׂ֥ים פָּנֶ֖יךָ עַל־פַּרְעֹ֣ה מֶ֣לֶךְ מִצְרָ֑יִם וְהִנָּבֵ֣א עָלָ֔יו וְעַל־מִצְרַ֖יִם כֻּלָּֽהּ׃

Commentary

28:26. *Plant vineyards.* Expecting long-term security.

29:1. *Tenth year.* That is, after King Jehoiachin's removal and King Zedekiah's installation, one year before the final destruction of Jerusalem in 587 B.C.E.

2. *Pharaoh king of Egypt.* Pharaoh was the title but not the name of the ruler who at that time was Hophra (also known as Apries).

3. Speak these words:

Thus says the Eternal God:

Behold, I am against you, Pharaoh king of
 Egypt,

you [are like the] great crocodile, crouching
 in its River branches,

thinking: *My River is mine,*

I made it for myself.

4. I will put hooks through your jaws,

and make the fish of your streams stick to
 your scales.

I will pull you up out of your River
 branches

with all the fish of your River branches
 sticking to your scales.

5. I will throw you out into the wilderness

you and all the fish of your River branches.

You shall fall on dry ground

ungathered and unburied.

3 דַּבֵּ֤ר וְאָמַרְתָּ֙

כֹּה־אָמַ֖ר אֲדֹנָ֣י יְהֹוִ֑ה

הִנְנִ֤י עָלֶ֙יךָ֙ פַּרְעֹ֣ה מֶֽלֶךְ־מִצְרַ֔יִם

הַתַּנִּים֙ הַגָּד֔וֹל הָרֹבֵ֖ץ בְּת֣וֹךְ יְאֹרָ֑יו

אֲשֶׁ֥ר אָמַ֛ר לִ֥י יְאֹרִ֖י

וַאֲנִ֥י עֲשִׂיתִֽנִי׃

4 וְנָתַתִּ֣י חַחִ֣ים [חַחִים֙] בִּלְחָיֶ֔יךָ

וְהִדְבַּקְתִּ֛י דְּגַת־יְאֹרֶ֖יךָ בְּקַשְׂקְשֹׂתֶ֑יךָ

וְהַעֲלִיתִ֙יךָ֙ מִתּ֣וֹךְ יְאֹרֶ֔יךָ

וְאֵת֙ כׇּל־דְּגַ֣ת יְאֹרֶ֔יךָ בְּקַשְׂקְשֹׂתֶ֖יךָ תִּדְבָּֽק׃

5 וּנְטַשְׁתִּ֣יךָ הַמִּדְבָּ֗רָה

אֽוֹתְךָ֙ וְאֵת֙ כׇּל־דְּגַ֣ת יְאֹרֶ֔יךָ

עַל־פְּנֵ֤י הַשָּׂדֶה֙ תִּפּ֔וֹל

לֹ֥א תֵאָסֵ֖ף וְלֹ֥א תִקָּבֵ֑ץ

Commentary

3. *Speak these words.* Literally, "speak and say."

River branches. The river Nile, when reaching the Mediterranean Sea, spreads out into a delta with many branches. יאר (*ye'or*) denotes a river generally, but when applied to Egypt it means the Nile. In verses 3 to 5, *ye'or* is used five times—once for the River itself and four times for its branches, which are in many places quite shallow.

Crocodile. This understanding of תנים (*tannim*, a variant of the usual *tannin*) was suggested by Luzzatto; *tannin* has this meaning in modern Hebrew.[1] The animal becomes the metaphor for Egypt and its ruler.

My River is mine. Pharaoh prides himself as the River's master, but his powers end when he comes into conflict with God. For "pride goes before the fall; arrogance before destruction."[2]

4. *The fish.* Meaning the people and its army, who will share the fate of the crocodile (Pharaoh) when it is dragged out of the River.

5. *Unburied.* Reading תקבר (*tikkaver*) for תקבץ (*tikkavetz*).[3]

I have given you as food

to the beasts of the earth and the birds of
the sky.

6. Then all who dwell in Egypt shall know
that I am the Eternal.

For you were a staff of reed to the House of
Israel:

7. when they took hold of you, you
splintered,

cutting their palms;

when they leaned on you, you broke,

rattling all their bones.

8. Therefore, thus says the Eternal God:
Behold, I will bring a sword upon you,

and deprive you of people and beasts.

9. Because you thought:

The River is mine, I made it,

Egypt will be a desolation, a ruin,

and they shall know that I am the Eternal!

10. Therefore, I am against you and your
streams. I will make of the land of Egypt an
utterly ruined desolation, from Migdol to
Aswan, all the way to the border of Kush.

לְחַיַּ֤ת הָאָ֨רֶץ֙ וּלְע֣וֹף הַשָּׁמַ֔יִם
נְתַתִּ֖יךָ לְאׇכְלָֽה:

6 וְיָֽדְעוּ֙ כׇּל־יֹשְׁבֵ֣י מִצְרַ֔יִם כִּ֖י אֲנִ֣י יְהֹוָ֑ה
יַ֚עַן הֱיוֹתָ֣ם מִשְׁעֶ֣נֶת קָנֶ֔ה לְבֵ֖ית יִשְׂרָאֵֽל:

7 בְּתׇפְשָׂ֨ם בְּךָ֤ בכפך [בַכַּף֙] תֵּר֔וֹץ
וּבָקַעְתָּ֥ לָהֶ֖ם כׇּל־כָּתֵ֑ף
וּבְהִשָּֽׁעֲנָ֤ם עָלֶ֨יךָ֙ תִּשָּׁבֵ֔ר
וְהַעֲמַדְתָּ֥ לָהֶ֖ם כׇּל־מׇתְנָֽיִם:

8 לָכֵ֗ן כֹּ֤ה אָמַר֙ אֲדֹנָ֣י יְהֹוִ֔ה
הִנְנִ֛י מֵבִ֥יא עָלַ֖יִךְ חָ֑רֶב
וְהִכְרַתִּ֥י מִמֵּ֖ךְ אָדָ֥ם וּבְהֵמָֽה:

9 וְהָיְתָ֤ה אֶֽרֶץ־מִצְרַ֨יִם֙ לִשְׁמָמָ֣ה וְחׇרְבָּ֔ה
וְיָדְע֖וּ כִּֽי־אֲנִ֣י יְהֹוָ֑ה
יַ֚עַן אָמַ֣ר יְאֹ֣ר לִ֔י וַאֲנִ֖י עָשִֽׂיתִי:

10 לָכֵ֛ן הִנְנִ֥י אֵלֶ֖יךָ וְאֶל־יְאֹרֶ֑יךָ וְנָתַתִּ֞י אֶת־
אֶ֣רֶץ מִצְרַ֗יִם לְחׇרְבוֹת֙ חֹ֣רֶב שְׁמָמָ֔ה מִמִּגְדֹּ֥ל
סְוֵנֵ֖ה וְעַד־גְּב֥וּל כּֽוּשׁ:

Commentary

6. *You were a staff of reed.* Literally, "*they* were". A sarcastic description of Pharaoh,
upon whom Israel had leaned with disastrous results. The same description of Egypt's
Pharaoh was already used by the First Isaiah.[4]

7. *Cutting their palms.* Reading כף (*kaf*) instead of כתף (*katef*, shoulder).[5]

Rattling all their bones. Literally, making all their limbs shake. Reading the verb as מעד
(*ma'ad*) instead of עמד (*amad*, stand).[6]

10. *Migdol.* A town or military installation in the delta area of the Nile.

Aswan. An old locale near today's dam.

Kush. Probably meaning Ethiopia,[7] though occasionally referring to other locations.
Today it stands only for Ethiopia.

11. No human foot shall pass through it; no animal foot shall pass through it; it shall be uninhabited for forty years.

12. I will make Egypt a desolation surpassing other desolate lands; her cities will lie desolate for forty years, surpassing other ruined cities; I will scatter the Egyptians among the nations and disperse them among the countries.

13. For thus says the Eternal God: At the end of forty years, I will gather the Egyptians from the peoples among whom they were scattered,

14. and I will restore Egypt's fortunes and let them return to the land they came from, the land of Pathros. There they shall be a lowly kingdom,

15. the lowliest of all the kingdoms, one that no longer exalts itself among the nations. I will make them too few ever again to rule other nations.

16. Never again shall [Egypt] be the reliance of the House of Israel; [it shall be] a reminder of the wrong they did by turning to it. Then they shall know that I am the Eternal God.

Commentary

12. *Forty years*. Ezekiel evokes the Israelites' forty-year trek in the desert.[8]

14. *Pathros*. In southern Egypt.[9] The Prophet suggests that this was the original home of the Egyptians. A Jewish colony sprang up in the city and remained active for several hundred years.

16. *Never again*. Israel's reliance on Egypt should never be repeated; it was a grievous error for which both nations paid heavily.

17. On the first day of the first month of the twenty-seventh year, the word of the Eternal came to me, saying:

18. Mortal, Nebuchadnezzar king of Babylon has made his army work so hard [in a war] against Tyre, that all their heads were made bald and all their shoulders rubbed bare; but neither he nor his army got any reward from Tyre for all this hard labor against it.

19. Therefore, says the Eternal God, I am giving Nebuchadnezzar king of Babylon the land of Egypt; he shall carry off its wealth, despoil it and plunder it: it shall be his army's wages.

20. As his reward for which he labored, I am giving him the land of Egypt, for what they have done for Me, says the Eternal God.

21. On that day I will make the House of Israel strong, and I will give you courage to speak in their midst. Then they shall know that I am the Eternal.

17 וַיְהִי בְּעֶשְׂרִים וָשֶׁבַע שָׁנָה בָּרִאשׁוֹן בְּאֶחָד לַחֹדֶשׁ הָיָה דְבַר־יְהוָה אֵלַי לֵאמֹר:

18 בֶּן־אָדָם נְבוּכַדְרֶאצַּר מֶלֶךְ־בָּבֶל הֶעֱבִיד אֶת־חֵילוֹ עֲבֹדָה גְדֹלָה אֶל־צֹר כָּל־רֹאשׁ מֻקְרָח וְכָל־כָּתֵף מְרוּטָה וְשָׂכָר לֹא־הָיָה לוֹ וּלְחֵילוֹ מִצֹּר עַל־הָעֲבֹדָה אֲשֶׁר־עָבַד עָלֶיהָ:

19 לָכֵן כֹּה אָמַר אֲדֹנָי יְהוִה הִנְנִי נֹתֵן לִנְבוּכַדְרֶאצַּר מֶלֶךְ־בָּבֶל אֶת־אֶרֶץ מִצְרָיִם וְנָשָׂא הֲמֹנָהּ וְשָׁלַל שְׁלָלָהּ וּבָזַז בִּזָּהּ וְהָיְתָה שָׂכָר לְחֵילוֹ:

20 פְּעֻלָּתוֹ אֲשֶׁר־עָבַד בָּהּ נָתַתִּי לוֹ אֶת־אֶרֶץ מִצְרָיִם אֲשֶׁר עָשׂוּ לִי נְאֻם אֲדֹנָי יְהוִה:

21 בַּיּוֹם הַהוּא אַצְמִיחַ קֶרֶן לְבֵית יִשְׂרָאֵל וּלְךָ אֶתֵּן פִּתְחוֹן־פֶּה בְּתוֹכָם וְיָדְעוּ כִּי־אֲנִי יְהוָה:

Commentary

17. *Twenty-seventh year*. 570 B.C.E., the last year of Ezekiel's prophecies.

18. *Nebuchadnezzar*. This is the way the Tanach speaks most frequently of the Babylonian king, while Ezekiel always calls him Nebuchadrezzar (which accurately reflects the Babylonian name). We use the more common English rendering throughout this commentary.

Tyre. Located on the coast of today's Lebanon. Ezekiel refers to its lengthy siege by the Babylonians, which appears to have been broken off after thirteen years. Since the Prophet considers Nebuchadnezzar and his people as God's agents (verse 20) he assures them that they will receive their due when they defeat Egypt and acquire its wealth.

21. *Courage to speak*. The Israelites are exiles and guests in Egypt, but in time they will be established sufficiently to find their voice. During the centuries to follow, the Egyptian-Jewish community grew exceedingly large and established vibrant religious and cultural institutions. The Greek translation of the Tanach (known as the Septuagint, because tradition ascribed it to the combined labor of seventy persons) became its lasting monument.

Essay

Are prophets always right?

Ezekiel has been recognized as one of Israel's great prophets, yet a number of his predictions were proven wrong by later history. Thus, in this haftarah Ezekiel speaks of the coming destruction of Egypt: Babylon will conquer it and condemn its people to exile, and only after a while will they be able to return. But when they do, their new state will be small and insignificant.

However, history did not quite go the way of the Prophet's vision. While Egypt was defeated by the Babylonians and subsequently lost its place as one of the predominant powers of the Near East, it did not suffer the kind of devastation the Prophet speaks about, nor were its people ever exiled.

Must not true prophecy always be validated by history? The answer would be yes if biblical prophecy were nothing more than prediction. The English word "prophet" (derived from the Greek) has become a synonym for "forecaster of events," but the Hebrew נביא (*navee*) has a different thrust. The *navee* speaks as one possessed by the Divine Presence, and always and primarily calls the people to religious behavior.[10]

While all true prophets were sure that their utterances were God's own words, we can never forget that all prophets were human vessels through which the divine message had to filter. They were sure that they knew what God wanted, but they had to put it into their own language and apply the message to their own time.

Thus the core of prophecy was religious, the application often social and political, and it was mixed with each prophet's hopes and dreams. Divine inspiration and human judgment stood side by side. Not surprisingly, therefore, prophets occasionally differed in their views.

Ezekiel's interpretation of Egypt's future was flawed in detail, but not in its long-range view. The nation would lose its former influence and even its independence; it would be dominated first by the Greeks and then the Romans, and never again emerge as the power it had been politically and culturally in antiquity.

Gleanings

Egypt—a different vision

A passage in Isaiah speaks of Egypt in very different tones than does Ezekiel. It foresees the nation to be a pillar of stability, allied in friendship with Israel:

The Eternal will first afflict and then heal the Egyptians ....

In that day, Israel shall be a third partner with Egypt and Assyria as a benediction on earth; for the God of heaven's hosts will bless them and say: "Blessed be My people Egypt, My handiwork Assyria, and My very own Israel."

Isaiah [11]

Ezekiel and Jeremiah

In our haftarah, Ezekiel castigates Egypt and predicts for it a dreary future. He reflects to some degree the oracles against Egypt delivered by his older contemporary Jeremiah. An example of the latter is represented in the haftarah that follows (haftarah for the sidra Bo).

An unfulfilled prophecy

This is one of the many Biblical prophecies that the exile to Babylon will be the last, that Israel will dwell securely in her own land once she has been brought back to it. We have seen that the hopes thus raised have not been fulfilled. Why? Two reasons may be offered. First, all such promises contain an implicit condition, they presume that those who return have learned their lesson and will remain faithful. Second, if security is man's natural desire, he is mistaken in thinking it God's most precious boon. God gives us something better, the power to win and maintain inward serenity even in the face of dire insecurity. [12]

* * *

Notes

[1] Others render *tannim* as "great sea dragon," a mythic beast appearing in various prophetic passages; for example, Ezekiel 32:2 and Isaiah 27:1. Crocodiles were hunted with hooks (verse 4), a practice attested by Herodotus, *History* II 70.

[2] Proverbs 16:18.

[3] So the Targum and JPS.

[4] 36:6. Isaiah's words are repeated in II Kings 18:21.

[5] So the Greek and the Syriac versions of the text.

[6] So the Syriac version.

[7] Compare Amos 9:7, haftarah for K'doshim.

[8] Malbim believes that "forty" is to be read as a round number. See also the midrash in *Gleanings*, which Rashi cites in his explanation of the text.

[9] Mentioned in Isaiah 11:11, in the haftarah for the 8th day of Pesach; also Jeremiah 44:1, 15.

[10] See also our *General Introduction*.

[11] 19:22, 24, 25. Some scholars believe that, while this passage appears as a part of the First Isaiah's prophecies, it is in fact a post-exilic addition.

[12] E. L. Allen, *Interpreter's Bible*, "Ezekiel," pp. 222ff.

Jeremiah, chapter 46, verses 13 to 28

Introduction

Connection of haftarah and sidra:

The weekly portion tells of the ancient Pharaoh's struggle with God, and the haftarah updates the tale: a modern Pharaoh of Egypt will also suffer a bitter defeat.

The setting:

In the year 609 B.C.E., Egypt had defeated Judah at the battle of Megiddo, Pharaoh Necho had slain King Josiah, then deposed his successor and set young Jehoiachin on the throne (see II Kings 23:29-34). Jeremiah foresaw that eventually Egypt would clash with Babylon, and indeed, in 605, Pharaoh Necho fought with Babylon's Nebuchadnezzar and was defeated at the battle of Carchemish, which settled the fate of the Near East for a long time to come.

For more on Jeremiah, see our *General Introduction*.

The message:

This is the first of Jeremiah's oracles against foreign nations; they occupy the rest of the book. In the first part of chapter 46 (1-12), we find Jeremiah taunting Egypt over its defeat at Carchemish; in the verses following (13-26), which have been selected by the Rabbis for the haftarah, the Prophet predicts the invasion of Egypt by the Babylonians.

Other prophets, too, preached about foreign powers and their fate: Isaiah (chapters 13-25), Amos (chapter 1), and Ezekiel (chapters 25-32).[1] All of them exalt the power of God, who rules the whole world and not just Israel.

An encouraging message for Israel is appended to the prophecy (verses 27 and 28).

Jeremiah, chapter 46, verses 13 to 28

46:13. This is the word the Eternal spoke to Jeremiah the prophet concerning an attack on Egypt by Nebuchadnezzar king of Babylon:

14. Declare it in Egypt!

Announce it in Migdol,

and in Memphis and Tahpanhes!

Say: Take your stand, be ready,

for the sword is devouring

all around you.

15. Why did Chaf flee?

הַדָּבָר֙ אֲשֶׁ֣ר דִּבֶּ֣ר יְהֹוָ֔ה אֶֽל־יִרְמְיָ֖הוּ 46:13
הַנָּבִ֑יא לָב֗וֹא נְבֽוּכַדְרֶאצַּר֙ מֶ֣לֶךְ בָּבֶ֔ל לְהַכּ֖וֹת
אֶת־אֶ֥רֶץ מִצְרָֽיִם׃

הַגִּ֣ידוּ בְמִצְרַ֔יִם 14
וְהַשְׁמִ֖יעוּ בְמִגְדּ֑וֹל
וְהַשְׁמִ֥יעוּ בְנֹ֖ף וּבְתַחְפַּנְחֵ֑ס
אִמְר֕וּ הִתְיַצֵּב֙ וְהָכֵ֣ן לָ֔ךְ
כִּֽי־אָכְלָ֥ה חֶ֖רֶב סְבִיבֶֽיךָ׃

מַדּ֖וּעַ נִסְחַ֣ף 15

Commentary

13. *Nebuchadnezzar*. Though in his mention of the Babylonian king, Jeremiah most often calls him *Nebuchadrezzar*, we follow the spelling that other parts of the Tanach use, and that Jeremiah also uses on occasion.

14. *Egypt*. The Hebrew מצרים (*mitzrayim*) is a Semitic rendition of the native name, which meant "the two lands." The English comes to us via the Greek, which pronounced the name of the chief temple in Memphis (the nation's capital) as *Aigyptos*.

Migdol. Originally a Semitic word for "tower," it is one of the many Semitic loanwords in Egyptian, reflecting the constant contact with the nation's northern neighbors.

Memphis. נֹף (*Nof*), capital of ancient Egypt, located some 13 miles (21 kilometers) south of today's Cairo. The various Hebrew and Greek forms that have resulted in the English "Memphis" reflect the Egyptian *mn-nfr*, "firm and fair." The city was the religious and political capital of Egypt during the 7th and 6th centuries B.C.E., which is the reason that the Hebrew prophets always named Memphis in their predictions of Egyptian doom.[2]

Tahpanhes. An outpost in the eastern Nile delta, which was called Daphne by the Greeks.[3] Jeremiah probably spent his last days there.

15. *Chaf*. The bull-god of the Egyptian pantheon. We arrive at this meaning through a small emendation, and in so doing follow the Septuagint. It apparently did not have the masoretic נסחף (*nis-chaf*), but instead had a text with two separate words, reading נס חף (*nas chaf*), meaning "Chaf has fled." Chaf was Apis, believed to be the incarnation of the god Ptah and, later, of Osiris. In Jeremiah's time, the worship of Apis had become the national cult, so that the flight of Apis symbolized the downfall of Egypt.[4]

Your champion did not stand fast,

for the Eternal has driven him away.

16. He made many stumble,

one falling over the next,

and they said:

Quick, let us go back to our people,

to the land where we were born,

away from the flashing sword.

17. There they called Pharaoh king of Egypt:

Big Noise Who Has Missed His Chance.

18. As I live, says the Eternal One,

the Sovereign God of heaven's hosts,

as Tabor is among the mountains,

as Carmel is by the sea,

so shall he [Nebuchadnezzar] come.

19. Pack your bags for exile,

Fair Egypt, dwelling so safe and sound!

Memphis will become a desolation,

an uninhabited ruin!

אַבִּירֶיךָ לֹא עָמַד

כִּי יְהוָה הֲדָפוֹ:

16 הִרְבָּה כּוֹשֵׁל

גַּם־נָפַל אִישׁ אֶל־רֵעֵהוּ

וַיֹּאמְרוּ קוּמָה וְנָשֻׁבָה אֶל־עַמֵּנוּ

וְאֶל־אֶרֶץ מוֹלַדְתֵּנוּ

מִפְּנֵי חֶרֶב הַיּוֹנָה:

17 קָרְאוּ שָׁם פַּרְעֹה מֶלֶךְ־מִצְרַיִם

שָׁאוֹן הֶעֱבִיר הַמּוֹעֵד:

18 חַי־אָנִי נְאֻם־הַמֶּלֶךְ

יְהוָה צְבָאוֹת שְׁמוֹ

כִּי כְּתָבוֹר בֶּהָרִים

וּכְכַרְמֶל בַּיָּם

יָבוֹא:

19 כְּלֵי גוֹלָה עֲשִׂי לָךְ

יוֹשֶׁבֶת בַּת־מִצְרָיִם

כִּי־נֹף לְשַׁמָּה תִהְיֶה

וְנִצְּתָה מֵאֵין יוֹשֵׁב:

Commentary

Your champion. Literally, "your strong one," referring to Chaf/Apis. The literal meaning of אביר (*abir*) is "bull," which suits the bovine character of the god. See also verse 20, where Egypt is called "a lovely heifer," and verse 21, where the Egyptian mercenaries are described as "fatted calves."

16. *Flashing.* The translation is speculative.

17. *Has missed his chance.* An idiomatic translation.[5]

18. *Tabor … Carmel.* Tabor, though only 1800 feet (550 meters) high, stands in a plain and can be seen from afar. Carmel, only a third its height, is the location of today's Haifa and stands out as a cliff by the seashore. The traveler seems to come suddenly upon them, and just so will Nebuchadnezzar's appearance be precipitate and seem to arrive out of nowhere.[6]

19. *Fair Egypt.* Literally, "Daughter of Egypt." So JPS and others.

20. Egypt is a lovely heifer

upon whom a gadfly from the north
   (has descended).

21. Even the mercenaries in her
   midst

were like fatted calves;

for they too have turned and fled as
   one,

making no stand.

For their day of disaster had come
   upon them,

their hour of doom.

22. Hear her hiss like a snake

when [the Babylonians] come in
   force

to attack her with axes,

like woodchoppers.

23. Says the Eternal One:

They cut down her forest,

impenetrable though it is,

for they outnumber the locusts,

and cannot be counted.

20 עֶגְלָ֥ה יְפֵֽה־פִיָּ֖ה מִצְרָ֑יִם

קֶ֥רֶץ מִצָּפ֖וֹן בָּ֥א בָֽא׃

21 גַּם־שְׂכִרֶ֤יהָ בְקִרְבָּהּ֙

כְּעֶגְלֵ֣י מַרְבֵּ֔ק

כִּֽי־גַם־הֵ֧מָּה הִפְנ֛וּ נָ֥סוּ יַחְדָּ֖יו

לֹ֣א עָמָ֑דוּ

כִּ֣י י֥וֹם אֵידָ֛ם בָּ֥א עֲלֵיהֶ֖ם

עֵ֥ת פְּקֻדָּתָֽם׃

22 קוֹלָ֖הּ כַּנָּחָ֣שׁ יֵלֵ֑ךְ

כִּֽי־בְחַ֣יִל יֵלֵ֔כוּ

וּבְקַרְדֻּמּוֹת֙ בָּ֣אוּ לָ֔הּ

כְּחֹטְבֵ֖י עֵצִֽים׃

23 כָּרְת֤וּ יַעְרָהּ֙ נְאֻם־יְהֹוָ֔ה

כִּ֖י לֹ֣א יֵֽחָקֵ֑ר

כִּ֤י רַבּוּ֙ מֵֽאַרְבֶּ֔ה

וְאֵ֥ין לָהֶ֖ם מִסְפָּֽר׃

Commentary

20. *A gadfly.* A metaphor for Babylon, which had stung Egypt, the "heifer." The word קֶרֶץ (*keretz*) occurs nowhere else in the Tanach.[7]

Upon whom. Following the Septuagint, whose text apparently read בא בה (*ba bah*), making the second word a prepositional phrase instead of repeating the first word.[8]

From the north. Clearly, the reference is to Babylon (present-day southern Iraq), which actually lay southeast of Israel. But because Babylonian troops could not cross the desert, they had to march northward along the Euphrates into Syria and then turn southward to Israel.

22. *Hear her.* That is, Egypt.

Hiss. A free translation of a difficult verse. ילך (*yelech;* literally, go by) is taken to mean the sound of a snake slithering by.

23. *Cannot be counted.* So Rashi and Radak.

24. Fair Egypt shall be put to shame,

given over to a northern people.

25. The God of heaven's hosts, the God of
Israel, says:

Behold, I punish Amon, [god] of [the town
of] No,

and Pharaoh, and Egypt, her gods

and her kings—Pharaoh and all who trust
in him.

26. I am handing them over to those who
seek their lives,

to Nebuchadnezzar king of Babylon and
his army.

But later on, it will be inhabited as in days
of old.

That is the word of the Eternal One.

27. But you,

have no fear, Jacob, My servant;

do not despair, O Israel!

For, behold, I will save you from that
distant place,

and your offspring from the land of your
captivity;

24 הֹבִישָׁה בַּת־מִצְרָיִם

נִתְּנָה בְּיַד עַם־צָפוֹן:

25 אָמַר יְהֹוָה צְבָאוֹת אֱלֹהֵי יִשְׂרָאֵל

הִנְנִי פוֹקֵד אֶל־אָמוֹן מִנֹּא

וְעַל־פַּרְעֹה וְעַל־מִצְרַיִם וְעַל־אֱלֹהֶיהָ

וְעַל־מְלָכֶיהָ וְעַל־פַּרְעֹה וְעַל הַבֹּטְחִים בּוֹ:

26 וּנְתַתִּים בְּיַד מְבַקְשֵׁי נַפְשָׁם

וּבְיַד נְבוּכַדְרֶאצַּר מֶלֶךְ־בָּבֶל וּבְיַד־עֲבָדָיו

וְאַחֲרֵי־כֵן תִּשְׁכֹּן כִּימֵי־קֶדֶם

נְאֻם־יְהֹוָה:

27 וְאַתָּה אַל־תִּירָא עַבְדִּי יַעֲקֹב

וְאַל־תֵּחַת יִשְׂרָאֵל

כִּי הִנְנִי מוֹשִׁעֲךָ מֵרָחוֹק

וְאֶת־זַרְעֲךָ מֵאֶרֶץ שִׁבְיָם

Commentary

24. *Northern people.* Babylon. See comment on verse 20.

25. *Amon, god of No.* The Hebrew נֹא (No) reflects the Egyptian *niwt*, meaning "city." Jeremiah prophesied during an age when No (called "Thebes" by the Greeks) and its god Amon enjoyed great prestige in the country.

Egypt, her gods. The Torah also speaks of the punishment of the nation's gods,[9] but never mentions them by name.

26. *His army.* Literally, his officers.

27. *Have no fear.* The expression, repeated in verse 28, occurs also in 30:10 and in Isaiah 44:2.

Jacob shall return; and be quiet and

  tranquil,

and none shall make [you] afraid.

28. Have no fear, O Jacob My servant,

for I am with you,

says the Eternal One.

I will bring to an end

all the nations

to whose lands I have driven you,

but I will not make an end of you.

Though I do not let you go unpunished,

I will chastise you justly.

וְשָׁב יַעֲקֹב וְשָׁקַט וְשַׁאֲנַן

וְאֵין מַחֲרִיד:

28 אַתָּה אַל־תִּירָא עַבְדִּי יַעֲקֹב נְאֻם־יְהֹוָה

כִּי אִתְּךָ אָנִי

כִּי אֶעֱשֶׂה כָלָה בְּכָל־הַגּוֹיִם

אֲשֶׁר הִדַּחְתִּיךָ שָׁמָּה

וְאֹתְךָ לֹא־אֶעֱשֶׂה כָלָה

וְיִסַּרְתִּיךָ לַמִּשְׁפָּט

וְנַקֵּה לֹא אֲנַקֶּךָ:

Commentary

28. *Unpunished.* Divine forgiveness mitigates but does not annul punishment, for divine justice must be served in some (if limited) way.[10]

Essay

Babylon and Egypt

Nebuchadnezzar, king of Babylon in the first part of the 6th century B.C.E., was a dominant figure in his time. He was in constant struggle with his archenemy, the pharaoh of Egypt, while Judah and Jerusalem played second fiddle to his plans. Nebuchadnezzar had defeated the Egyptians in the decisive battle of Carchemish and at various times thereafter made advances toward their territory. His eventual victory and the humiliation of the Egyptians were foreseen by Jeremiah, as recorded in our haftarah and in one of his last orations (43:8-13). It is likely that these two passages belong together, and that they were composed by the Prophet while he was languishing as an exile in Egypt, before death overtook him.

The prophecy must be understood in the light of Jeremiah's bitter opposition to the flight of his fellow Jews to Egypt. He had counseled them to stay put in Jerusalem, but they had not heeded his pleading and instead had left for the presumed safety of Egypt and had taken the Prophet with them. Jeremiah thought the flight futile and prophesied that Nebuchadnezzar would conquer Egypt as well.

"He will come and attack the land of Egypt, delivering those destined [to be struck by] the plague, to the plague; those destined for captivity, to captivity; and those destined for [death by] the sword, to the sword."[11]

The actual invasion of Egypt by Nebuchadnezzar did not occur until several decades later, most likely after Jeremiah had died. The incursion was meant to keep the empire on the Nile from meddling in Near Eastern affairs, and indeed from then on Egypt ceased to be a player in the Near East, which was dominated by Babylon and its successors, the Medes and Persians.

Gleanings

Words to Remember

Have no fear, O Jacob My servant,
for I am with you,
says the Eternal One. (verse 28)

The mercenaries (verse 21)

The mercenaries here mentioned are the Ionians and Carians,[12] introduced into his service by pharaoh Psammetichus and retained by his successors. They failed to secure him victory over Amasis of Babylon.

Harry Freedman[13]

Jerusalem's destruction

(After Nebuchadnezzar's defeat of Judah) the land was a shambles. As archaeological evidence testifies, all, or virtually all, of the fortified towns of Judah's heartland had been razed to the ground, most of them not to be rebuilt for generations to come. Only in the Negev, which had probably separated from Judah in 597, and in the district north of Jerusalem, did towns escape destruction. The population that remained was sparse indeed. Aside from those deported to Babylon, thousands must have died in battle or of starvation and disease; a considerable number—surely more than we know of—had been executed, while others had fled for their lives. Those left in the land were mostly poor peasants[14] whom Nebuchadnezzar considered incapable of stirring up trouble.

John Bright[15]

* * *

Notes

[1] Note the preceding haftarah (Va'eira), an oracle against Egypt delivered by Ezekiel.

[2] On these names and their backgrounds, see D. Redford, *Anchor Bible Dictionary,* vol. 4, pp. 689-691.

[3] Reflected in the modern Tel-ed-Defenna.

[4] Redford, *Anchor Bible Dictionary,* vol. 4, p. 278.

[5] Suggested by John Bright (*Anchor Bible,* Jeremiah).

[6] Arnold B. Ehrlich, *Mikra ki–Pheshuto III,* p. 272.

[7] Our translation follows several old manuscripts. Others understand "butcher," that is, Babylon, which will destroy Egypt.

[8] Others understand the repetition to be purposeful, as an emphasis, as in Psalm 96:13: "[The Eternal] has come—yes, [the Eternal] has come!" "[יהוה...] כי בא כי בא"

[9] Exodus 12:12; Numbers 33:4.

[10] The phrase occurs in similar form in Jeremiah 30:11, reflecting the thought of the Torah in Exodus 34:7 and Numbers 14:18. Jonah, however, believes that punishment can be averted altogether (4:2), which fits the hope of Yom Kippur and is the reason for its selection as the haftarah for the afternoon service.

[11] Jeremiah 43:11.

[12] And not the Cushites, Putites, and Ludites whom Jeremiah had mentioned earlier (verse 9). The Ionians were Greeks, whence their Hebrew name יון (*yavan*).

[13] In his Commentary on Jeremiah (*Soncino Bible Commentary*), citing Herodotus II:152 ff.

[14] II Kings 25:12; Jeremiah 52:16.

[15] In his Commentary on Jeremiah (*Soncino Bible Commentary*), p. liii.

Judges, chapter 4, verse 4 to chapter 5, verse 31

Introduction

Connection of sidra and haftarah:

Both sidra and haftarah bring us tales of confrontation with an enemy of Israel, and when victory is won the leaders celebrate the occasion with song. But while the *shirah* of Moses is a paean to God alone, Deborah sings of both God and of her people, thereby providing us with insight into the life and relationships of the tribes some hundred years later.

The setting:

The turbulent history of Israel between the death of Joshua and the time of the prophet Samuel is covered by the book of Judges. It describes the long years during which the tribes struggled with Canaanites and Philistines and then sank roots into the land assigned to them. They considered themselves partners in a loose confederation, bound together by historical memory and a common religious cult. Especially in times of external and internal crises (which occurred frequently), they elected a military-judicial head, called judge, to ward off the enemy and to foster their common interests. Deborah was such a leader, one of the five women whom the Tanach calls "prophet." In the annual cycle of haftarot, this is the longest and—because of its many historical allusions—one of the most challenging.

For more on the book of Judges, see our *General Introduction.*

Content of the haftarah:

    1. Introducing Deborah (4:4-5)

    2. The battle with Sisera, general of King Jabin of Hazor:

        Preparation for the battle with Sisera (4:6-8)

        Decisive victory over the Canaanites (4:9-16)

        The death of Sisera at the hand of Jael (4:17-22)

        Postscript to the battle (4:23-24)

    3. The Song of Deborah

        Hymn to the God of Israel (5:1-11)

        Assessment of the contribution of the tribes (5:12-23)

        In praise of Jael (5:24-30)

        Postscript (5:31)

HAFTARAH FOR B'SHALACH

Judges, chapter 4, verse 4 to chapter 5, verse 31

4:4. Deborah, wife of Lapidoth, a woman, was a prophet; at that time, she was the leader of Israel.

5. She used to sit under Deborah's Palm, between Ramah and Beth El in the hill country of Ephraim, when the people of Israel came to her for decisions.

6. So she sent for Barak son of Abinoam of Kedesh [in the territory] of Naphtali and said to him: The Eternal, the God of Israel, commands you to draw up at Mount Tabor; take with you ten thousand men from the tribes of Naphtali and Zebulun.

4:4 וּדְבוֹרָה֙ אִשָּׁ֣ה נְבִיאָ֔ה אֵ֖שֶׁת לַפִּיד֑וֹת הִ֛יא שֹׁפְטָ֥ה אֶת־יִשְׂרָאֵ֖ל בָּעֵ֥ת הַהִֽיא׃

5 וְ֠הִיא יוֹשֶׁ֨בֶת תַּֽחַת־תֹּ֜מֶר דְּבוֹרָ֗ה בֵּ֧ין הָרָמָ֛ה וּבֵ֥ין בֵּֽית־אֵ֖ל בְּהַ֣ר אֶפְרָ֑יִם וַיַּעֲל֥וּ אֵלֶ֛יהָ בְּנֵ֥י יִשְׂרָאֵ֖ל לַמִּשְׁפָּֽט׃

6 וַתִּשְׁלַ֗ח וַתִּקְרָא֙ לְבָרָ֣ק בֶּן־אֲבִינֹ֔עַם מִקֶּ֖דֶשׁ נַפְתָּלִ֑י וַתֹּ֨אמֶר אֵלָ֜יו הֲלֹ֥א צִוָּ֣ה ׀ יְהוָ֣ה אֱלֹהֵֽי־יִשְׂרָאֵ֗ל לֵ֣ךְ וּמָֽשַׁכְתָּ֙ בְּהַ֣ר תָּב֔וֹר וְלָקַחְתָּ֣ עִמְּךָ֗ עֲשֶׂ֤רֶת אֲלָפִים֙ אִ֔ישׁ מִבְּנֵ֥י נַפְתָּלִ֖י וּמִבְּנֵ֥י זְבֻלֽוּן׃

Commentary

The Prose Tale

4:4. *Deborah, wife of Lapidoth.* Her name means "bee"; her father's and mother's names are omitted, and after this initial notation so is any further mention of her husband. The reason, some say, may be that Lapidoth ("flames" or "torches") was a nickname for Barak ("lightning"), her general.[1]

A woman. The text points this out specifically; she was clearly an exception to the other judges, all of whom were men. Four other women are called prophets: Miriam, sister of Aaron and Moses, a leader of the exodus from Egypt; the unnamed wife of Isaiah was called a "woman prophet";[2] Hulda played a leading role in the religious reformation under King Josiah of Judah, at the end of the 7th century B.C.E.;[3] and a prophet named Noadiah was an opponent of Nehemiah.[4]

Leader of Israel. The last verse of the haftarah says that she held the office for forty years. This number occurs several times as the tenure of judges and is therefore considered by modern scholars to have been a round number, meaning "for a whole generation."[5]

5. *Deborah's Palm.* That seems to have been the popular name for the tree. Trees were important landmarks for public business and often served as shrines; two of Abraham's revelations came to him in such a locale.[6]

6. *Sent for Barak.* His name means "lightning" (see comment on verse 4). The formality of the text makes it doubtful that he was indeed Deborah's husband.[7]

Kedesh. In the area of today's Tiberias.

150

7. Then I will draw Sisera, Jabin's army commander, with his chariots and troops, to the Wadi Kishon, and I will hand him over to you.

8. Barak answered: I will go only if you come with me; if you don't, I won't go either.

9. I will most certainly go with you, she said, but you will gain no glory on the path you are taking, for now the Eternal will hand Sisera over to a woman. So Deborah went with Barak to Kedesh.

10. Barak called the tribes of Naphtali and Zebulun to Kedesh. Ten thousand men then followed him on his march, and Deborah too went up with him.

7 וּמָשַׁכְתִּ֣י אֵלֶ֗יךָ אֶל־נַ֤חַל קִישׁוֹן֙ אֶת־סִֽיסְרָא֙ שַׂר־צְבָ֣א יָבִ֔ין וְאֶת־רִכְבּ֖וֹ וְאֶת־הֲמוֹנ֑וֹ וּנְתַתִּ֖יהוּ בְּיָדֶֽךָ׃

8 וַיֹּ֤אמֶר אֵלֶ֨יהָ֙ בָּרָ֔ק אִם־תֵּלְכִ֥י עִמִּ֖י וְהָלָ֑כְתִּי וְאִם־לֹ֥א תֵלְכִ֛י עִמִּ֖י לֹ֥א אֵלֵֽךְ׃

9 וַתֹּ֜אמֶר הָלֹ֧ךְ אֵלֵ֣ךְ עִמָּ֗ךְ אֶ֚פֶס כִּי֩ לֹ֨א תִֽהְיֶ֜ה תִּֽפְאַרְתְּךָ֗ עַל־הַדֶּ֨רֶךְ֙ אֲשֶׁ֣ר אַתָּ֣ה הוֹלֵ֔ךְ כִּ֣י בְֽיַד־אִשָּׁ֔ה יִמְכֹּ֥ר יְהוָ֖ה אֶת־סִֽיסְרָ֑א וַתָּ֧קָם דְּבוֹרָ֛ה וַתֵּ֥לֶךְ עִם־בָּרָ֖ק קֶֽדְשָׁה׃

10 וַיַּזְעֵ֨ק בָּרָ֜ק אֶת־זְבוּלֻ֤ן וְאֶת־נַפְתָּלִי֙ קֶ֔דְשָׁה וַיַּ֣עַל בְּרַגְלָ֔יו עֲשֶׂ֥רֶת אַלְפֵ֖י אִ֑ישׁ וַתַּ֥עַל עִמּ֖וֹ דְּבוֹרָֽה׃

Commentary

Naphtali. The tribal territory in central Galilee, west and northwest of Lake Kinneret. Some believe Deborah to have been a Naphtalite; others, that she belonged to Ephraim, in whose territory Deborah's Palm stood.

Mount Tabor. Which commands the plain of Jezreel.

7. Sisera. He is the luckless center of the story that follows. Nothing further is known about him, but the Midrash was extravagant in its speculation about his prowess and gigantic stature (see *Gleanings*).

9. I will most certainly go with you. She will go with Barak, but there will be a price: for Barak will not obtain the glory of a victor in the battle to come.

A woman. She agrees, but warns Barak that, if she goes along, people will think her the real leader and that she, instead of Barak, will be the one who will be remembered—an accurate prediction, as it turned out.[8]

10. Naphtali and Zebulun. Barak's headquarters were in Kedesh, located in Naphtali, which therefore supplied part of the army. The tribe of Zebulun lived to the west of Naphtali and volunteered many of its fighting men, while some other tribes declined altogether to participate in the campaign (see the song that follows, 5:2 ff.).

11. Now it happened that Heber the Kenite had moved away from the other Kenites, the descendants of Hobab, Moses' father-in-law; he had pitched his tent by Kedesh, at Oak of Beza'ananim.

12. When [his scouts] told Sisera that Barak had gone up to Mount Tabor,

13. he called out his chariots—he had nine hundred iron chariots—and his troops from Haroshet-Goyim to the Wadi Kishon.

11 וְחֶבֶר הַקֵּינִי נִפְרָד מִקַּיִן מִבְּנֵי חֹבָב חֹתֵן מֹשֶׁה וַיֵּט אָהֳלוֹ עַד־אֵלוֹן בַּצְעַנִּים [בְּצַעֲנַנִּים] אֲשֶׁר אֶת־קֶדֶשׁ:

12 וַיַּגִּדוּ לְסִיסְרָא כִּי עָלָה בָרָק בֶּן־אֲבִינֹעַם הַר־תָּבוֹר:

13 וַיַּזְעֵק סִיסְרָא אֶת־כָּל־רִכְבּוֹ תְּשַׁע מֵאוֹת רֶכֶב בַּרְזֶל וְאֶת־כָּל־הָעָם אֲשֶׁר אִתּוֹ מֵחֲרֹשֶׁת הַגּוֹיִם אֶל־נַחַל קִישׁוֹן:

Commentary

11. *Heber the Kenite*. This notation comes now, before the drama unfolds in which his wife plays the major role. The Kenites were a wandering tribe of smiths and general "fixers" (not unlike modern-day Gypsies), who were loosely affiliated with Israel. Their general habitat was in the Negev and Sinai, but Heber had moved away and lived in the Jezreel valley.

Hobab, Moses' father-in-law. This is one of his names; others are Jethro and Reuel.[9]

Oak of Beza'ananim. Another tree that plays a cultic role, like Deborah's Palm. Its location is uncertain, for while it is said to be near Kedesh, this raises a strategic problem. As the story to follow reveals, Sisera, the general of the defeated Canaanite army, flees to this place. But would he flee here, near Barak's headquarters? Perhaps there was another place called Kedesh.[10] *Beza'ananim* is the way tradition says the text ought to be read.

13. *He called out*. וַיַּזְעֵק (*vayaz'ek*). The root זעק usually denotes "to cry" and suggests that his troops were summoned either by the war-cry of bugles, or by "town criers" who informed the people of the call-up.

Iron chariots. These instruments of war are elsewhere depicted as giving the Canaanites a distinct military advantage over Israel.[11] So far, however, archaeologists have not found even fragmentary remains of chariots from ancient Canaan.[12]

Haroshet-Goyim. Called Haroshet-hagoyim in an earlier verse,[13] it may have been near the point where Wadi Kishon flows into the Mediterranean (north of Haifa).

14. Then Deborah said to Barak: Up! This is the day on which the Eternal will put Sisera in your hands: the Eternal is marching ahead of you.

So Barak went down from Mount Tabor along with ten thousand men.

15. And the Eternal threw Sisera, his chariots and his whole army, into disarray, because of Barak's onslaught; Sisera got down out of his chariot and ran away on foot

16. as Barak pursued the [remaining] chariots and soldiers as far as Haroshet-Goyim. All of Sisera's soldiers fell by the sword; not one was left alive.

17. Sisera, however, escaped on foot and came to the tent of Jael, wife of Heber the Kenite, because there was peace between King Jabin of Hazor and the family of Heber the Kenite.

14 וַתֹּ֩אמֶר֩ דְּבוֹרָ֨ה אֶל־בָּרָ֜ק ק֗וּם כִּ֣י זֶ֤ה הַיּוֹם֙ אֲשֶׁר֩ נָתַ֨ן יְהֹוָ֤ה אֶת־סִֽיסְרָא֙ בְּיָדֶ֔ךָ הֲלֹ֥א יְהֹוָ֖ה יָצָ֣א לְפָנֶ֑יךָ וַיֵּ֤רֶד בָּרָק֙ מֵהַ֣ר תָּב֔וֹר וַעֲשֶׂ֥רֶת אֲלָפִ֛ים אִ֖ישׁ אַחֲרָֽיו:

15 וַיָּ֣הָם יְ֠הֹוָה אֶת־סִֽיסְרָ֨א וְאֶת־כָּל־הָרֶ֜כֶב וְאֶת־כָּל־הַֽמַּחֲנֶ֛ה לְפִי־חֶ֖רֶב לִפְנֵ֣י בָרָ֑ק וַיֵּ֧רֶד סִֽיסְרָ֛א מֵעַ֥ל הַמֶּרְכָּבָ֖ה וַיָּ֥נָס בְּרַגְלָֽיו:

16 וּבָרָ֗ק רָדַ֞ף אַחֲרֵ֤י הָרֶ֙כֶב֙ וְאַחֲרֵ֣י הַֽמַּחֲנֶ֔ה עַ֖ד חֲרֹ֣שֶׁת הַגּוֹיִ֑ם וַיִּפֹּ֞ל כָּל־מַחֲנֵ֤ה סִֽיסְרָא֙ לְפִי־חֶ֔רֶב לֹ֥א נִשְׁאַ֖ר עַד־אֶחָֽד:

17 וְסִֽיסְרָ֗א נָ֤ס בְּרַגְלָיו֙ אֶל־אֹ֣הֶל יָעֵ֔ל אֵ֖שֶׁת חֶ֣בֶר הַקֵּינִ֑י כִּ֣י שָׁל֗וֹם בֵּ֚ין יָבִ֣ין מֶֽלֶךְ־חָצ֔וֹר וּבֵ֕ין בֵּ֖ית חֶ֥בֶר הַקֵּינִֽי:

Commentary

14. *The Eternal is marching ahead of you.* The credit for the victory that Barak and Deborah achieve is not credited to them but to God.

15. From here on the imagery and language resemble those of Israel's salvation at the Reed (Red) Sea, which is related in the sidra (see Exodus 14:24.).

Ran away on foot. Heber's encampment was probably close to the battlefield, and Sisera may have hoped to be sheltered there (but see comment on verse 11).

16. *Not one was left alive.* Virtually identical with the sidra's report of Egypt's defeat. The regular appearance of this phrase in the annals of Assyrian kings suggests that it may be an idiomatic way of describing an overwhelming military victory.

17. *Jael.* The name means "mountain goat." She, like Deborah, is identified by the name of her husband and not by her ancestry. Up to her marriage, she would have been called by her father's name, and thereafter she was under the tutelage of her husband.[14]

Peace. Here *shalom* conveys the sense of military alliance, which explains why Sisera felt safe in Jael's tent.

18. Jael came out to greet Sisera. She said: Come here, my lord, come here; there is nothing to be afraid of. So he went into the tent and she covered him with a blanket.

19. He said to her: Let me have a little water, if you please; I'm thirsty. So she opened a skin of milk, gave him some to drink, and covered him again.

20. He said: Stand at the door of the tent, and if anyone comes and asks if anyone is here, tell him no, there is no one here.

21. Sisera was exhausted and fell asleep. Then Jael took a tent-peg and a mallet. Quietly she went up to him and drove the peg into the side of his head right through to the ground. So it was that he died.

22. When Barak came in pursuit of Sisera, Jael came out to greet him. She said: Come here; I will show you the man you are looking for.

He came after her and found Sisera lying dead, with the tent-peg in the side of his head.

18 וַתֵּצֵא יָעֵל לִקְרַאת סִיסְרָא וַתֹּאמֶר אֵלָיו
סוּרָה אֲדֹנִי סוּרָה אֵלַי אַל־תִּירָא וַיָּסַר אֵלֶיהָ
הָאֹהֱלָה וַתְּכַסֵּהוּ בַּשְּׂמִיכָה:

19 וַיֹּאמֶר אֵלֶיהָ הַשְׁקִינִי־נָא מְעַט־מַיִם כִּי
צָמֵאתִי וַתִּפְתַּח אֶת־נֹאוד הֶחָלָב וַתַּשְׁקֵהוּ
וַתְּכַסֵּהוּ:

20 וַיֹּאמֶר אֵלֶיהָ עֲמֹד פֶּתַח הָאֹהֶל וְהָיָה אִם־
אִישׁ יָבוֹא וּשְׁאֵלֵךְ וְאָמַר הֲיֵשׁ־פֹּה אִישׁ
וְאָמַרְתְּ אָיִן:

21 וַתִּקַּח יָעֵל אֶת־יְתַד הָאֹהֶל וַתָּשֶׂם אֶת־הַמַּקֶּבֶת בְּיָדָהּ וַתָּבוֹא אֵלָיו
בַּלָּאט וַתִּתְקַע אֶת־הַיָּתֵד בְּרַקָּתוֹ וַתִּצְנַח
בָּאָרֶץ וְהוּא־נִרְדָּם וַיָּעַף וַיָּמֹת:

22 וְהִנֵּה בָרָק רֹדֵף אֶת־סִיסְרָא וַתֵּצֵא יָעֵל
לִקְרָאתוֹ וַתֹּאמֶר לוֹ לֵךְ וְאַרְאֶךָּ אֶת־הָאִישׁ
אֲשֶׁר־אַתָּה מְבַקֵּשׁ וַיָּבֹא אֵלֶיהָ וְהִנֵּה סִיסְרָא
נֹפֵל מֵת וְהַיָּתֵד בְּרַקָּתוֹ:

Commentary

18. *There is nothing to be afraid of.* In earlier days, Joshua was encouraged with the same words when he faced the forces of Hazor.[15]

She covered him. In the poem that follows, Sisera does not lie down (see 5:25).

19. *Milk.* Though Sisera had asked only for water. One commentator suggests that goat milk has a soporific effect, so that Sisera was both "doped and duped."[16] But see the song (5:25-27), which, with its older version of this incident, knows nothing of the deception.

20. *Stand at the door.* עמד (*amod*) can be either an imperative (to a male person) or an infinitive (occasionally denoting a command, as here).

21. *Peg ... mallet.* Why these? The Targum says it was because a woman was not supposed to use weapons.[17]

154

23. That day God humbled Jabin king of Canaan before the people of Israel.

24. The power of the Israelites bore on Jabin king of Canaan with increasing severity, until they destroyed him.

5:1. On that day Deborah and Barak son of Abinoam sang this song:

2. When Israelites let their hair grow loose, when people volunteer themselves, praise the Eternal.

23 וַיַּכְנַע אֱלֹהִים בַּיּוֹם הַהוּא אֵת יָבִין מֶלֶךְ־כְּנָעַן לִפְנֵי בְּנֵי יִשְׂרָאֵל:

24 וַתֵּלֶךְ יַד בְּנֵי־יִשְׂרָאֵל הָלוֹךְ וְקָשָׁה עַל יָבִין מֶלֶךְ־כְּנָעַן עַד אֲשֶׁר הִכְרִיתוּ אֵת יָבִין מֶלֶךְ־כְּנָעַן:

5:1 וַתָּשַׁר דְּבוֹרָה וּבָרָק בֶּן־אֲבִינֹעַם בַּיּוֹם הַהוּא לֵאמֹר:

2 בִּפְרֹעַ פְּרָעוֹת בְּיִשְׂרָאֵל בְּהִתְנַדֵּב עָם בָּרֲכוּ יְהֹוָה:

Commentary

23. *God humbled Jabin.* The ultimate credit is God's.

24. *Jabin king of Canaan.* Referring to the kings or princes that fought with him; see our comment on verse 19 below.

The Song of Deborah

5:1. Here the song is introduced. Most scholars agree that it is older than the preceding prose part. It is one of the most heavily analyzed poems in world literature and features archaic expressions that are also found in Ugaritic sources (see further the essay below).[18] The poem features six partners in the Israelite campaign, while the prose knows only of Naphtali and Zebulun. The Wadi Kishon figures in both versions, but Mount Tabor is absent from the poem. Further, Jael overcomes a waking Sisera in the poem, while in the prose tale Sisera is asleep.

Deborah and Barak. Because Deborah is mentioned first, the song has always been primarily identified with her.[19]

2. *Let their hair grow loose.* Many soldiers had evidently taken the vow of a Nazir, which prevented them from trimming their hair until their time of service was completed or victory was achieved.[20]

3. Listen, kings!

Hear, you rulers!

I sing, to the Eternal I sing,

I chant to the Eternal, the God of Israel.

4. Eternal One, when You went forward
from Seir,

when You marched from the land of Edom,

earth shook, sky dripped,

yes, the clouds poured down water.

5. The mountains quaked before the
Eternal;

the One of Sinai,

before the Eternal, the God of Israel.

6. In the time of Shamgar son of Anat,

in the time of Jael,

roads had fallen into disuse,

travelers had taken the back-roads.

7. All governance had left Israel,

till you rose up, Deborah,

you rose, a Mother in Israel!

3 שִׁמְעוּ מְלָכִים

הַאֲזִינוּ רֹזְנִים

אָנֹכִי לַיהֹוָה

אָנֹכִי אָשִׁירָה

אֲזַמֵּר לַיהֹוָה אֱלֹהֵי יִשְׂרָאֵל׃

4 יְהֹוָה בְּצֵאתְךָ מִשֵּׂעִיר

בְּצַעְדְּךָ מִשְּׂדֵה אֱדוֹם

אֶרֶץ רָעָשָׁה גַּם־שָׁמַיִם נָטָפוּ

גַּם־עָבִים נָטְפוּ מָיִם׃

5 הָרִים נָזְלוּ מִפְּנֵי יְהֹוָה

זֶה סִינַי

מִפְּנֵי יְהֹוָה אֱלֹהֵי יִשְׂרָאֵל׃

6 בִּימֵי שַׁמְגַּר בֶּן־עֲנָת

בִּימֵי יָעֵל

חָדְלוּ אֳרָחוֹת

וְהֹלְכֵי נְתִיבוֹת יֵלְכוּ אֳרָחוֹת עֲקַלְקַלּוֹת׃

7 חָדְלוּ פְרָזוֹן בְּיִשְׂרָאֵל חָדֵלּוּ

עַד שַׁקַּמְתִּי דְּבוֹרָה

שַׁקַּמְתִּי אֵם בְּיִשְׂרָאֵל׃

Commentary

3. *I chant.* אזמר (*azammer*) is probably an onomatopoetic word, which tries to evoke a particular quality of singing, possibly as an accompaniment to some instrument (compare the English "hum").[21]

4. *Seir ... Edom.* The two terms are synonyms and describe the territory east and southeast of the Dead Sea, which is one of the possible locations of Mount Sinai (see the next verse).[22]

6. *Shamgar.* The judge preceding Deborah. Little is known about him except for one Samson-like feat against the Philistines.[23]

In the time of Jael. That is, before the war, when people were afraid to venture into open country. Inasmuch as the poem places her as a parallel to Shamgar, Rashi suggested that Jael too was a judge, but she is not otherwise so attested.

7. *You rose.* An antique poetic form of the verb. But most traditional interpreters understood: "*I rose*, a Mother in Israel."[24]

8. [Israel] chose new gods—

there was war in the gates—

(among) forty thousand in Israel,

no shield nor spear was to be seen!

9. My heart goes out to Israel's leaders,

those of the people who offered them-

selves:

praise the Eternal!

10. You riders on white donkeys,

you who sit on saddles,

(and) you who walk the roads

ponder this well!

11. Hark, the bards strike up among the

water troughs;

there they tell of the victories of the

Eternal,

the victorious rule of the Eternal in Israel.

the people of the Eternal God march down

to the gates [and call]:

12. Rouse yourself, Deborah, rouse your-

self,

rouse yourself and sing a song!

Arise, Barak;

son of Abinoam, take your captives!

13. Thereupon the survivors defeated the

mighty;

8 יִבְחַר֙ אֱלֹהִ֣ים חֲדָשִׁ֔ים

אָ֖ז לָחֶ֣ם שְׁעָרִ֑ים

מָגֵ֤ן אִם־יֵֽרָאֶה֙ וָרֹ֔מַח

בְּאַרְבָּעִ֥ים אֶ֖לֶף בְּיִשְׂרָאֵֽל׃

9 לִבִּי֙ לְחֹוקְקֵ֣י יִשְׂרָאֵ֔ל

הַמִּֽתְנַדְּבִ֖ים בָּעָ֑ם

בָּרֲכ֖וּ יְהוָֽה׃

10 רֹכְבֵי֩ אֲתֹנ֨וֹת צְחֹרֹ֜ות

יֹשְׁבֵ֧י עַל־מִדִּ֛ין

וְהֹלְכֵ֥י עַל־דֶּ֖רֶךְ שִֽׂיחוּ׃

11 מִקֹּ֣ול מְחַֽצְצִ֗ים בֵּ֚ין מַשְׁאַבִּ֔ים

שָׁ֤ם יְתַנּוּ֙ צִדְקֹ֣ות יְהוָ֔ה

צִדְקֹ֥ת פִּרְזֹנֹ֖ו בְּיִשְׂרָאֵ֑ל

אָ֛ז יָרְד֥וּ לַשְּׁעָרִ֖ים עַם־יְהוָֽה׃

12 עוּרִ֤י עוּרִי֙ דְּבֹורָ֔ה

ע֥וּרִי ע֖וּרִי דַּבְּרִי־שִׁ֑יר

ק֥וּם בָּרָ֛ק

וּֽשֲׁבֵ֥ה שֶׁבְיְךָ֖ בֶּן־אֲבִינֹֽעַם׃

13 אָ֚ז יְרַ֣ד שָׂרִ֔יד לְאַדִּירִ֖ים

Commentary

9. *Praise the Eternal!* We might say, "Thank God!"

10. *Sit on saddles.* Or, "who ride camels." Those are the rich and the leaders, while "you who walk the roads" are the poor. The poet thus says "rich and poor," which means everybody.[25]

12. *Sing a song.* The poet who composed the Shabbat hymn *L'chah Dodi* used this phrase when he wrote: עורי, עורי, שיר דברי (*uri uri, shir dabberi*), "awake, awake, sing a song."

13. *The mighty.* Sisera and Jabin.[26]

the people of the Eternal defeated the warriors for me!

14. Out of the land of Ephraim

—that once was Amalek's—

[they came,] and then Benjamin after you,

with your troops.

Leaders came down from Machir,

and out of Zebulun, bearers of the ruler's scepter.

15. The leaders of Issachar were with Deborah,

as Issachar, so Barak—

they followed his charge down the valley.

And in Reuben's divisions were [some] leaders

of resolute mind.

16. Why then do you [others] stay behind among the sheepfolds,

listening to the piping to the flocks?

Reuben's divisions had chiefs

who wrestled [only] in their minds!

17. Gilead stayed east of the Jordan;

why did Dan keep to their ships?

Asher remained at the shore of the sea,

sticking to their landfalls.

עַם יְהוָה יְרַד־לִי בַּגִּבּוֹרִים׃

14 מִנִּי אֶפְרַיִם

שָׁרְשָׁם בַּעֲמָלֵק

אַחֲרֶיךָ בִנְיָמִין בַּעֲמָמֶיךָ

מִנִּי מָכִיר יָרְדוּ מְחֹקְקִים

וּמִזְּבוּלֻן מֹשְׁכִים בְּשֵׁבֶט סֹפֵר׃

15 וְשָׂרַי בְּיִשָּׂשכָר עִם־דְּבֹרָה

וְיִשָּׂשכָר כֵּן בָּרָק

בָּעֵמֶק שֻׁלַּח בְּרַגְלָיו

בִּפְלַגּוֹת רְאוּבֵן גְּדֹלִים

חִקְקֵי־לֵב׃

16 לָמָּה יָשַׁבְתָּ בֵּין הַמִּשְׁפְּתַיִם

לִשְׁמֹעַ שְׁרִקוֹת עֲדָרִים

לִפְלַגּוֹת רְאוּבֵן גְּדוֹלִים

חִקְרֵי־לֵב׃

17 גִּלְעָד בְּעֵבֶר הַיַּרְדֵּן שָׁכֵן

וְדָן לָמָּה יָגוּר אֳנִיּוֹת

אָשֵׁר יָשַׁב לְחוֹף יַמִּים

וְעַל מִפְרָצָיו יִשְׁכּוֹן׃

Commentary

14. *Machir.* A poetic appellation for the western portion of the tribe of Manasseh (the eastern part residing on the other side of the Jordan).[27]

Scepter. סֹפֵר (*sofer*) usually means "scribe," but here is to be understood as an antique term related to the Akkadian *shaparu,* "to rule."[28]

16. *In their minds.* But not on the battlefield, where they should have been.

17. *Gilead.* A general term for much of the trans-Jordanian land; here it denotes the eastern portion of the tribe of Manasseh.

18. [But] Zebulun was a troop that scorned
   death,

along with Naphtali on the open heights.

19. Kings came and fought,

the kings of Canaan fought:

in Taanach, by Megiddo's waters—

yet won no spoil or silver there.

20. From heaven itself they fought—

the stars in their courses fought against
   Sisera.

21. The Wadi Kishon swept them away,

the raging waters of Wadi Kishon—

March on, my soul, with might!

22. Then the hoofs were pounding,

as the stallions came galloping, galloping
   along.

23. *Curse Meroz, says God's angel.*

Curse bitterly all who live there.

They never came to the aid of the Eternal,

to help the Eternal against the warriors.

18 זְבֻלוּן עַם חֵרֵף נַפְשׁוֹ לָמוּת

וְנַפְתָּלִי עַל מְרוֹמֵי שָׂדֶה:

19 בָּאוּ מְלָכִים נִלְחָמוּ

אָז נִלְחֲמוּ מַלְכֵי כְנַעַן

בְּתַעְנַךְ עַל־מֵי מְגִדּוֹ

בֶּצַע כֶּסֶף לֹא לָקָחוּ:

20 מִן־שָׁמַיִם נִלְחָמוּ

הַכּוֹכָבִים מִמְּסִלּוֹתָם נִלְחֲמוּ עִם־סִיסְרָא:

21 נַחַל קִישׁוֹן גְּרָפָם

נַחַל קְדוּמִים נַחַל קִישׁוֹן

תִּדְרְכִי נַפְשִׁי עֹז:

22 אָז הָלְמוּ עִקְּבֵי־סוּס

מִדַּהֲרוֹת דַּהֲרוֹת אַבִּירָיו:

23 אוֹרוּ מֵרוֹז אָמַר מַלְאַךְ יְהֹוָה

אֹרוּ אָרוֹר יֹשְׁבֶיהָ

כִּי לֹא־בָאוּ לְעֶזְרַת יְהֹוָה

לְעֶזְרַת יְהֹוָה בַּגִּבּוֹרִים:

Commentary

18. *On the open heights.* Where the enemy had an advantage.

19. *Taanach, by Megiddo's waters.* The waters are those of Wadi Kishon and refer to the impact that the overflowing stream had on Sisera's campaign, miring his troops in deep mud (see verse 21). Megiddo, site of large-scale excavations, was a town that controlled access to the valley of Jezreel; it was located some 20 miles (32 kilometers) southeast of today's Haifa. Neither Taanach nor Megiddo was then in the hands of any tribe of Israel.[29]

21. *Swept them away.* In time of heavy rains, wadis overflow and often turn the countryside into a quagmire. Sisera was apparently unable to deploy his army, which suffered the fate that befell Pharaoh's army at the Reed (Red) Sea. The downpour was seen by the contemporaries as an act of God, who took sides with Israel.

March on. The passage has been rendered in various ways.[30]

22. *Galloping.* דהרות דהרות (*daharot daharot*). Like the English rendering, the Hebrew is onomatopoetic, imitating the clattering sound of horses' hooves.

24. Most blessed of women be Jael,

wife of Heber the Kenite;

most blessed of the women in tents.

25. He asked for water, she gave him milk;

she brought him curds in a bowl fit for the
    mighty.

26. One hand reached for the tent-peg,

the other took a laborer's hammer;

she hammered Sisera

and smashed his head,

piercing and passing right through his
    temples.

27. He sinks, falls, lies at her feet;

he sinks, he falls at her feet;

where he sank, there he fell down dead.

28. Out of the window looks Sisera's
    mother;

she peers through the lattice:

Why is his chariot so long in coming?

Why are his chariot's hoofbeats delayed?

29. Her wisest ladies answer her,

and she tells herself the same:

24 תְּבֹרַךְ מִנָּשִׁים יָעֵל

אֵשֶׁת חֶבֶר הַקֵּינִי

מִנָּשִׁים בָּאֹהֶל תְּבֹרָךְ:

25 מַיִם שָׁאַל חָלָב נָתָנָה

בְּסֵפֶל אַדִּירִים הִקְרִיבָה חֶמְאָה:

26 יָדָהּ לַיָּתֵד תִּשְׁלַחְנָה

וִימִינָהּ לְהַלְמוּת עֲמֵלִים

וְהָלְמָה סִיסְרָא

מָחֲקָה רֹאשׁוֹ

וּמָחֲצָה וְחָלְפָה רַקָּתוֹ:

27 בֵּין רַגְלֶיהָ כָּרַע נָפַל שָׁכָב

בֵּין רַגְלֶיהָ כָּרַע נָפָל

בַּאֲשֶׁר כָּרַע שָׁם נָפַל שָׁדוּד:

28 בְּעַד הַחַלּוֹן נִשְׁקְפָה

וַתְּיַבֵּב אֵם סִיסְרָא בְּעַד הָאֶשְׁנָב

מַדּוּעַ בֹּשֵׁשׁ רִכְבּוֹ לָבוֹא

מַדּוּעַ אֶחֱרוּ פַּעֲמֵי מַרְכְּבוֹתָיו:

29 חַכְמוֹת שָׂרוֹתֶיהָ תַּעֲנֶינָּה

אַף־הִיא תָּשִׁיב אֲמָרֶיהָ לָהּ:

Commentary

23. *Curse Meroz.* Meroz is mentioned nowhere else in the Tanach; it seems to have been a tribal group that refused outright to participate in the campaign, even though it lived close to the scene of battle. The curse recalls a Mari parallel, which reads: "The king is going on a campaign. All (men) down to the youngest (soldiers) shall be used. The administrator whose troops have not all been used, who exempts (even) a single man, shall be cursed."[31]

25. *Bowl fit for the mighty.* Rashi understands this as a reference to water,[32] so that Sisera was deceived when he drank the soporific libation from a water bowl.

28-30. Sisera's mother, rather than a wife, takes the limelight; perhaps the general was a fairly young man.

29. *Her wisest ladies.* However wise, they did not suspect the truth. It is also possible that "ladies" is a title, referring either to a princess or minister.

30. *They're dividing the spoil they have found,*

a girl or two for each man,

dyed cloth as Sisera's spoil,

embroidered cloth, and dyed,

two for every spoiler's neck.

31. Let all Your enemies, Eternal One, end like that;

but let those who love You be as the sun rising in its might!

And the land was at rest for forty years.

30 הֲלֹא יִמְצְאוּ יְחַלְּקוּ שָׁלָל

רַחַם רַחֲמָתַ֫יִם לְרֹאשׁ גֶּ֫בֶר

שְׁלַל צְבָעִים לְסִיסְרָא

שְׁלַל צְבָעִים רִקְמָה

צֶבַע רִקְמָתַ֫יִם לְצַוְּארֵי שָׁלָל:

31 כֵּן יֹאבְדוּ כָל־אוֹיְבֶ֫יךָ יְהֹוָה

וְאֹהֲבָיו כְּצֵאת הַשֶּׁ֫מֶשׁ בִּגְבֻרָתוֹ

וַתִּשְׁקֹט הָאָ֫רֶץ אַרְבָּעִים שָׁנָה:

Commentary

30. *Spoiler's neck.* Reading שֹׁלֵל (*sholel*) for שָׁלָל (*shalal*, spoil).

31. *Let all Your enemies* … These words became a popular Israeli song.

Essay

Some problems raised by the haftarah

This, the longest haftarah in the synagogue cycle, has been analyzed more thoroughly than most portions of the Tanach. Modern scholars especially have given it a great deal of attention. The major problems raised by the text are linguistic, historical, and moral.

Linguistic: While the prose section of the haftarah is relatively clear, the poem is not, and translations occasionally will differ widely. Of course, poetry—by its very imagery—is often difficult to understand, and that is especially true when it comes to very ancient texts. The Song of Deborah is particularly difficult, because—though it originated in a period close to the events it describes—linguistic studies show that redaction(s) took place in later times.

Much of the understanding reflected in our translation has been facilitated by scholarly study of Near Eastern texts, especially from Ugaritic sources. Also, we have today a much clearer grasp of the nature of biblical poetry, which is characterized by accentuation patterns, and above all, by parallel images in the first and second parts of each verse, and by an abundant amount of repetition. These features assisted the memory of the hearer, for it must be remembered that the Song was heard and not read. Chapter 5, verse 27 demonstrates these features:

> *He sinks, falls, lies at her feet;*
> *He sinks, he falls at her feet,*
> *Where he sank, there he fell down dead.*

Historical: Scholars agree that the Song is older than the prose version. It provides more on-the-scene detail, and its language is much more archaic. Among the differences between the two, one stands out: the Song knows nothing of Sisera being asleep, after having been "doped and duped." In the Song, Jael attacks him while he is awake, possibly drinking his milk.

Why did the editor of these chapters not choose one version over the other, or combine both into one consistent account? This question is often asked with regard to other contradictory passages in the Tanach, and the answer is simple: The editor was highly respectful of received traditions; and when there were contradictions, both versions would most likely be preserved.

Moral: Why do both versions exult in the deed of a woman who deceives her victim through feigned kindness, and then proceeds to kill him in cold blood? Because, obviously, this is what happened, and the death of Sisera assured that Israel was saved, at least for the time being. War was (and remains) a dreadfully brutal business. The defeated were usually killed—soldiers and civilians alike—unless they could be of use to the victor. To judge a war of survival by the rules of peaceful intercourse is to compare situations that are not

comparable or is an example of latter-day moral arrogance. In the ancient view, Jael's action saved the nation, and that was enough to admire her courage and daring.

"Judged by the standards of peace, [Jael's] act was one of treacherous cruelty; but every nation glorifies similar, and worse, deeds in its history. Our own age [about 1930], in which the most enlightened nations have, for reasons of policy or patriotism, committed or condoned crimes and inhumanities on an immeasurably greater scale, is not entitled to condemn the praise bestowed upon the fierce deed of this wild Bedouin woman."[33]

Gleanings

An authentic song

The Song of Deborah is almost universally regarded as a genuine historical song, that is to say a spontaneous poetical outbreak of the heart of a woman, who having taken part in a mighty historical event is now impelled to master it in rhythmical form, to express, to transmit it.

(The Song's) character is apparent as soon as we look at it: a special poetic means here serves an utterly religious purpose. This means is repetition.

Martin Buber[34]

Deborah's Palm

Deborah's judgments were rendered in the open air, for wrong impressions might arise if men were to visit her at home.

Talmud[35]

Mallet and peg

Why did Jael use mallet and peg to kill Sisera? Because the Torah says, "A woman must not put on man's apparel," and apparel includes weapons. (Hence, he was unsuspecting. The Targum assumes, of course, that Sisera was familiar with Torah law.[36])

Targum Jonathan[37]

Negative judgments on Deborah

(Traditional texts contain a number of negative comments on Deborah because, being a woman, she was supposed to adhere to standards designed by a male-dominated society.)

In comment on 4:6, which says that Deborah "sent for Barak," the Talmud characterizes this as inappropriate for her, and says that pride is unbecoming a woman.[38] Consequently, the prophetic spirit left her temporarily, while she was composing her famed song.[39]

About Jael

Though her thoughts are never revealed, she is clearly a woman caught in the middle. The Israelites have obviously won. They cannot be far behind Sisera, and they are likely to take unkindly to a family that has allied itself to the enemy. Jael does what she has to do.

Jael not only wins her security, but in the Song of Deborah and Barak she wins Israel's praise as well ... and becomes larger than life.

Danna Nolan Fewell[40]

* * *

Notes

1 This was one traditional view: see *B. Megillah* 14a; Exodus Rabbah 10:48. Another interpretation of the expression *eshet lapidot*: she was a wick maker for the sanctuary (see Rashi and Radak), or a "spirited woman" (Metzudat David; NEB also adopts this meaning).

2 Isaiah 8:3.

3 II Kings 22:14.

4 Nehemiah 6:14.

5 One of them, Ehud, is said to have served for two times forty years.

6 Genesis 12:6-7 (terebinth of Moreh); 18:1 (terebinths of Mamre).

7 One midrashic source speculates that Deborah and Barak/Lapidoth did not live together, due to her prophetic status. For since she had to be always ready for divine communication, she could not indulge in sexual relations. A precedent for this interpretation was the problem that arose out of Moses' relations with his wife (see the Torah Commentary on Numbers chapter 12, p. 1101). Some considered her sending for Barak a sign of her arrogance (see *Gleanings)*.

8 So Ralbag, while Metzudat David believes that "a woman" refers to Jael, who will kill Sisera. Boling (*Anchor Bible,* Judges), comments: "Deborah is thus represented as speaking better than she knows, an example of unconscious prediction, which adds poignancy to the outcome" (p. 96).

9 Biblical critics assign these names to different sources of the Moses tradition.

10 So Y. Aharoni (p. 36), who locates a Kenite splinter group in the Galilee. Boling (*Anchor Bible,* Judges, pp. 96-97) locates it between the tribes of Asher and Naphtali.

11 Joshua 17:17-18.

12 See M. Littauer and J. Crouwel, *Anchor Bible Dictionary,* vol. 1, pp. 888-892.

13 Verse 2, which precedes the haftarah.

14 The traditional word for husband was *ba'al,* master. For that reason, Deborah's position as a judge was highly unusual; see above, at verse 4, which emphasizes that, though a woman, she was a leader of Israel.

15 Joshua 5:25.

16 So Boling (*Anchor Bible,* Judges pp. 97-98), citing C. F. Burney's commentary on Judges (2nd ed. 1930; reprinted New York: Ktav, 1970; p. 93).

17 Deuteronomy 22:5.

18 For a survey of major contributions to its study, see Boling (*Anchor Bible,* Judges, pp. 105-106).

19 Similarly, the *Shirah* (read in the sidra to which our haftarah is attached; Exodus 15:1), is considered a song by Moses, although it begins: "Then Moses and the children of Israel sang. ..."

20 On the vows of a Nazir, see Numbers 6:5 and the haftarah for Naso. But the phrase has received many other translations; see, for example, the Targum and Radak, who understand it as "avenged themselves."

21 Akkadian uses *zamaru* in this sense.

[22] See pp. 478 and 520 of the Torah Commentary.

[23] Judges 3:31. In modern Israel, Shamgar was the name of a chief judge of the nation's highest court.

[24] So Ralbag. On the judgment that she thus lauded herself unbecomingly, see *Gleanings*.

[25] It is called a merism, like "young and old," "length and breadth."

[26] So Ralbag.

[27] The Torah lists Machir as the son of Manasseh; Numbers 26:29.

[28] Mattityahu Tsevat, "Some Biblical Notes," *HUCA*, XXIV (1952-1953), p. 107.

[29] Megiddo was settled by Israel at the time of David and Solomon. The Targum says that Sisera's camp was pitched between Taanach and Megiddo.

[30] Boling renders: "You shall trample the throat of the mighty" (p. 113).

[31] Quoted by Boling, pp. 114, 116.

[32] Compare the sidra, Exodus 15:10.

[33] J. H. Hertz, *Pentateuch and Haftorahs*, vol. 1, p. 286. This was written prior to the Holocaust, or the killing fields of Vietnam, Bosnia, and Rwanda. But the argument does not gain by characterizing Jael as "wild" and "Bedouin."

[34] *The Prophetic Faith*, p. 6.

[35] *B. Megillah* 14a. The Rabbis discussed the problem of women dispensing justice when women were ineligible as witnesses; see Tosafot on *B. Niddah* 50a.

[36] Deuteronomy 32:5.

[37] On Judges 5:26.

[38] *B. Megillah* 14b.

[39] *B. Pesachim* 66b.

[40] "Judges," in *The Women's Bible Commentary*, ed. Newman and Ringe, p. 69.

Isaiah, chapter 6, verse 1 to chapter 7, verse 6 and chapter 9, verses 5 and 6

Introduction

Connection of haftarah and sidra:

The weekly portion contains the revelation at Sinai, an event that was witnessed by the entire people of Israel. The haftarah brings us the personal revelation of God to Isaiah and the beginning of his prophetic career.

The setting:

Isaiah lived in the kingdom of Judah (of which Jerusalem was the capital) during the second half of the 8th century B.C.E. The Northern Kingdom, called Israel (with Samaria as its capital), was the larger of the two kingdoms and had designs on Judah, hoping to conquer it and thereby once again to unite the twelve tribes. It was a time of military and political confrontation.

Meanwhile, idolatry was rampant; the upper classes lived in ostentatious luxury; and the God of the Covenant was all but forgotten by large masses of the people.

For more on Isaiah, see our *General Introduction*.

The message:

Rashi believed that chapter 6 of Isaiah should have opened the book. The haftarah may be divided into three clearly delineated parts:

1. The divine challenge to Isaiah, which contains the threefold call of the angels: קדוש קדוש קדוש (*kadosh, kadosh, kadosh...*), "Holy, holy, holy is the God of heaven's hosts, whose Presence fills all the earth." (6:1-8)

2. The message that Isaiah is to deliver to the people. (6:9-13)

3. A historical interlude. (7:1-6)

4. Two sentences chosen by the Sages to end the haftarah. Taken from a different chapter of the book and not connected to Parts 1-3, they relate a messianic vision. (9:5-6)

HAFTARAH FOR YITRO

Isaiah, chapter 6, verse 1 to chapter 7, verse 6 and chapter 9, verses 5 and 6

6:1. In the year that King Uzziah died,
I saw my Liege
seated on a throne, high and exalted,
with a robe whose train filled the temple.

2. Seraphim stood about,
each with six wings—two covering the face,
two covering the body, and two to fly with.

3. And each called to the other:
Holy, holy, holy is the God of heaven's
hosts, whose Presence fills all the earth!

4. At the sound of the call,
the foundations shook and the temple
filled with smoke.

6:1 בִּשְׁנַת־מוֹת הַמֶּלֶךְ עֻזִּיָּהוּ
וָאֶרְאֶה אֶת־אֲדֹנָי יֹשֵׁב עַל־כִּסֵּא רָם
וְנִשָּׂא וְשׁוּלָיו מְלֵאִים אֶת־הַהֵיכָל:
2 שְׂרָפִים עֹמְדִים מִמַּעַל לוֹ
שֵׁשׁ כְּנָפַיִם שֵׁשׁ כְּנָפַיִם לְאֶחָד בִּשְׁתַּיִם יְכַסֶּה פָנָיו
וּבִשְׁתַּיִם יְכַסֶּה רַגְלָיו וּבִשְׁתַּיִם יְעוֹפֵף:
3 וְקָרָא זֶה אֶל־זֶה וְאָמַר
קָדוֹשׁ קָדוֹשׁ קָדוֹשׁ יְהוָה צְבָאוֹת
מְלֹא כָל־הָאָרֶץ כְּבוֹדוֹ:
4 וַיָּנֻעוּ אַמּוֹת הַסִּפִּים מִקּוֹל הַקּוֹרֵא
וְהַבַּיִת יִמָּלֵא עָשָׁן:

Commentary

6:1. *In the year that King Uzziah died.* The exact date of his death is not known; it was most likely sometime between 742 and 733 B.C.E. The Sages asked: How could Isaiah know that the king would die that year? (The text can be read to suggest that possibility.) One answer: Uzziah "died" meant that he was stricken with leprosy (as reported in II Kings 15:5), and a leper was considered like one about to die.[1] A simpler explanation would assume that Isaiah wrote this chapter in his later years, as an autobiographical recollection.

Whose train filled the temple. Note the continuing use of "fill." In verse 1, God's train fills the temple; in verse 3, the Divine Presence fills all the earth; in verse 4, the temple is filled with smoke.

Seraphim stood about. The Prophet perceives angelic creatures who were attending the Eternal.

Covering the body. Literally, "the legs," which by extension covers "the nakedness." Seraphim must be modest in the Divine Presence, as must human officiants.[2]

3. *Holy, holy, holy.* The call has become a climactic part of the daily and holy day liturgy,. This part of the public prayer service is called קדושה (*k'dushah*, holiness), and the congregation stands when it is recited.[3]

Presence. In the Tanach, כבוד (*kavod*) often describes the [radiant] glory of God.

4. The *foundations shook.* This was the earthquake, says Rashi, that occurred during Uzziah's reign.[4]

168

5. Woe is me, said I,

I am lost; for I am a man of unclean lips,

and I live among a people of unclean lips,

yet these eyes of mine have seen the
    Sovereign,

the God of heaven's hosts.

6. But one of the seraphim flew over to me

with a live coal, which he had taken

from the altar with a pair of tongs.

7. He touched my lips with it, saying:

Now that this has touched your lips,

your guilt is gone, your sin is wiped clean.

8. Then I heard the voice of my Liege
    saying:

Whom shall I send? Who shall go on Our
    behalf?

And I said: Here I am; send me.

5 וָאֹמַ֞ר אֽוֹי־לִ֣י כִֽי־נִדְמֵ֗יתִי

כִּ֣י אִ֣ישׁ טְמֵֽא־שְׂפָתַ֜יִם אָנֹ֗כִי

וּבְתוֹךְ֙ עַם־טְמֵ֣א שְׂפָתַ֔יִם אָנֹכִ֖י יוֹשֵׁ֑ב

כִּ֗י אֶת־הַמֶּ֛לֶךְ יְהֹוָ֥ה צְבָא֖וֹת רָא֥וּ עֵינָֽי׃

6 וַיָּ֣עָף אֵלַ֗י אֶחָד֙ מִן־הַשְּׂרָפִ֔ים

וּבְיָד֖וֹ רִצְפָּ֑ה בְּמֶ֨לְקַחַ֔יִם לָקַ֖ח מֵעַ֥ל הַמִּזְבֵּֽחַ׃

7 וַיַּגַּ֣ע עַל־פִּ֔י וַיֹּ֕אמֶר

הִנֵּ֛ה נָגַ֥ע זֶ֖ה עַל־שְׂפָתֶ֑יךָ

וְסָ֣ר עֲוֺנֶ֔ךָ וְחַטָּאתְךָ֖ תְּכֻפָּֽר׃

8 וָאֶשְׁמַ֞ע אֶת־ק֤וֹל אֲדֹנָי֙ אֹמֵ֔ר

אֶת־מִ֥י אֶשְׁלַ֖ח וּמִ֣י יֵֽלֶךְ־לָ֑נוּ

וָאֹמַ֖ר הִנְנִ֥י שְׁלָחֵֽנִי׃

Commentary

5. *Unclean lips*. A metaphor of speech and its misuse. When first called to prophesy, Moses demurred by describing his lips as "uncircumcised,"[5] which in biblical Hebrew is virtually synonymous with "unclean."[6] Zephaniah uses the opposite expression "pure of lips" to convey "pure speech."[7]

Have seen the Sovereign. Biblical texts treat the consequence of "seeing God" differently. Thus, the Torah says in one place that no one, not even Moses, could behold the Divine Presence and live, but in another he is said to behold the likeness of God, who speaks to him "mouth to mouth."[8] In still another place, Moses, Aaron, Nadav, Abihu, and seventy elders saw God, yet remained unharmed.[9] In his vision, Isaiah feels he is doomed, but is spared nonetheless when the seraph proceeds to wipe away his sin (verse 7).

6. *Live coal*. A metaphor: God's challenge was like a burning coal.[10]

8. *Send me*. Unlike Moses, who tried to escape God's challenge to him, Isaiah volunteers without hesitation. It is ironic that his own willingness contrasts with God's objective to dull the people's minds against hearing the import of his message.

9. God said: Go and tell this people:

Hear again and again—but without
   understanding;

Look again and again—but without
   perceiving.

10. Dull this people's mind,

stop its ears and cloud its eyes,

or it may see with its eyes

and hear with its ears

and understand with its mind,

and return to Me, and be healed.

11. My Liege, said I, how long?

And God said:

Till cities are desolate, without people,

and houses are empty,

and the land is an utter desolation.

9 וַיֹּאמֶר לֵךְ וְאָמַרְתָּ לָעָם הַזֶּה
שִׁמְעוּ שָׁמוֹעַ וְאַל־תָּבִינוּ
וּרְאוּ רָאוֹ וְאַל־תֵּדָעוּ:
10 הַשְׁמֵן לֵב־הָעָם הַזֶּה
וְאָזְנָיו הַכְבֵּד וְעֵינָיו הָשַׁע
פֶּן־יִרְאֶה בְעֵינָיו
וּבְאָזְנָיו יִשְׁמָע
וּלְבָבוֹ יָבִין
וָשָׁב וְרָפָא לוֹ:
11 וָאֹמַר עַד־מָתַי אֲדֹנָי
וַיֹּאמֶר
עַד אֲשֶׁר אִם־שָׁאוּ עָרִים מֵאֵין יוֹשֵׁב
וּבָתִּים מֵאֵין אָדָם
וְהָאֲדָמָה תִּשָּׁאֶה שְׁמָמָה:

Commentary

9. *Hear again and again—but without understanding.* The divine command must be understood as a parallel to the story of Moses confronting Pharaoh. Moses was asked to urge Pharaoh to liberate the enslaved Israelites. Yet, at the same time, Moses is told that the Egyptian king will not listen, for God has "hardened his heart"—which is to say that he won't be able to listen. His previous crimes have rendered him incapable of doing what is right.[11] Nonetheless, Moses is bidden to go and plead with the king.

So here too. Isaiah must speak to the people, but in the very speaking he will "stop its ears" (that is, his rebuke will harden them against hearing God's word; verse 10). The transgressors don't want to be confronted with the truth, and when someone tries to tell it to them, they close their minds and become incapable of listening any further. Just as the word כבד (*kabbéd*, harden) is used in the story of Moses, so it is in the vision of Isaiah as a warning that the Prophet's task will be frustrating, for the people will simply turn away from his message. Nonetheless, he must say what needs to be said. In the end, God alone knows when the ensuing punishment of Israel will have run its course and a saving remnant will guarantee a renewed future.

11. *How long?* This is the language of lamentation, revealing the prophetic anguish of preaching to people who hear the sounds but not the meaning.[12]

God said. Literally, "He said." Also in verse 9.

12. For the Eternal will drive the people far
   away,

and many places in the land shall be
abandoned.

13. And even when a tenth of the people is
   left,

in its turn it shall be burned off like an oak
   or terebinth,

cut down, yet leaving a stump,

a stump that shall be a holy seed.

7:1. When Ahaz son of Jotham, grandson
of Uzziah, ruled Judah, Rezin, king of
Aram and Pekah son of Remaliah, king of
Israel, went up to attack Jerusalem, but
they could not manage it.

12 וְרִחַ֤ק יְהוָה֙ אֶת־הָ֣אָדָ֔ם

וְרַבָּ֥ה הָעֲזוּבָ֖ה בְּקֶ֥רֶב הָאָֽרֶץ׃

13 וְע֥וֹד בָּהּ֙ עֲשִׂ֣רִיָּ֔ה

וְשָׁ֖בָה וְהָיְתָ֣ה לְבָעֵ֑ר כָּאֵלָ֣ה

וְכָאַלּ֗וֹן אֲשֶׁ֤ר בְּשַׁלֶּ֙כֶת֙ מַצֶּ֣בֶת בָּ֔ם

זֶ֥רַע קֹ֖דֶשׁ מַצַּבְתָּֽהּ׃

7:1 וַיְהִ֡י בִּימֵ֣י אָ֠חָז בֶּן־יוֹתָ֨ם בֶּן־עֻזִּיָּ֜הוּ מֶ֣לֶךְ

יְהוּדָ֗ה עָלָ֣ה רְצִ֣ין מֶֽלֶךְ־אֲרָ֡ם וּפֶ֣קַח בֶּן־

רְמַלְיָ֣הוּ מֶֽלֶךְ־יִשְׂרָאֵ֤ל יְרוּשָׁלִַ֙ם֙ לַמִּלְחָמָ֣ה

עָלֶ֔יהָ וְלֹ֥א יָכֹ֖ל לְהִלָּחֵ֥ם עָלֶֽיהָ׃

Commentary

13. *Yet leaving a stump.* The tree is the nation of Israel, but from the stump that
remains—the righteous among the people—a new nation will rise. This is the only hope held
out by the Prophet. Some scholars, however, have pointed out that the original may not
have contained this verse, for it is missing in the Septuagint (the translation into Greek),
which was composed about 200 B.C.E. in Egypt. If so, verse 13 may have been added to the
manuscript by an annotator of the text, who believed that this consoling note was indeed
Isaiah's meaning, for, after all, he had named his own son She'ar Yashuv ("a remnant shall
return"). "No blows struck against the people of Israel will ever destroy it and Israel will
always find the power to begin new growth and new life."[13]

7:1-6. The opening verses of chapter 7 present a historical vignette, which has
occasioned a large literature of political interpretation. The Northern Kingdom had designs
on its Southern neighbor and allied itself with Aram (whose capital was Damascus). As
Isaiah predicted, the attack came to naught. The "stump" of the previous chapter and the
naming of Isaiah's son, She'ar Yashuv, provide the bridge between these otherwise unrelated
accounts.

1. *Ahaz … grandson of Uzziah.* He is mentioned in Assyrian annals by his full name,
Jehoahaz ("the Eternal held secure").

2. When the House of David learned that Aram and Ephraim had joined forces, the hearts of Ahaz and the hearts of all his people shook, as trees of the forest shake in the wind.

3. Then the Eternal One said to Isaiah: Go now with your son She'ar Yashuv to meet Ahaz. He is at the end of the conduit of the Upper Pool, by the road to Fuller's Field.

4. Say to him: Be very calm, have no fear, do not lose heart because of the fury of Rezin and his Arameans, and the son of Remaliah. They are spent torches, nothing but smoke.

5. Aram and Ephraim and the son of Remaliah are plotting evil against you. They say:

6. Let us go up against Judah, invade, tear it asunder, break her spirit and make the son of Tabeel its king.

2 וַיֻּגַּ֣ד לְבֵ֣ית דָּוִד֮ לֵאמֹר֒ נָ֥חָֽה אֲרָ֖ם עַל־אֶפְרָ֑יִם וַיָּ֤נַע לְבָבוֹ֙ וּלְבַ֣ב עַמּ֔וֹ כְּנ֥וֹעַ עֲצֵי־יַ֖עַר מִפְּנֵי־רֽוּחַ׃

3 וַיֹּ֣אמֶר יְהֹוָה֮ אֶֽל־יְשַֽׁעְיָהוּ֒ צֵא־נָא֙ לִקְרַ֣את אָחָ֔ז אַתָּ֕ה וּשְׁאָ֖ר יָשׁ֣וּב בְּנֶ֑ךָ אֶל־קְצֵ֗ה תְּעָלַת֙ הַבְּרֵכָ֣ה הָעֶלְיוֹנָ֔ה אֶל־מְסִלַּ֖ת שְׂדֵ֥ה כוֹבֵֽס׃

4 וְאָמַרְתָּ֣ אֵ֠לָ֠יו הִשָּׁמֵ֨ר וְהַשְׁקֵ֜ט אַל־תִּירָ֗א וּלְבָבְךָ֙ אַל־יֵרַ֔ךְ מִשְּׁנֵ֨י זַנְב֧וֹת הָאוּדִ֛ים הָעֲשֵׁנִ֖ים הָאֵ֑לֶּה בׇּחֳרִי־אַ֛ף רְצִ֥ין וַאֲרָ֖ם וּבֶן־רְמַלְיָֽהוּ׃

5 יַ֗עַן כִּֽי־יָעַ֥ץ עָלֶ֛יךָ אֲרָ֖ם רָעָ֑ה אֶפְרַ֥יִם וּבֶן־רְמַלְיָ֖הוּ לֵאמֹֽר׃

6 נַעֲלֶ֤ה בִֽיהוּדָה֙ וּנְקִיצֶ֔נָּה וְנַבְקִעֶ֖נָּה אֵלֵ֑ינוּ וְנַמְלִ֥יךְ מֶ֙לֶךְ֙ בְּתוֹכָ֔הּ אֵ֖ת בֶּן־טָֽבְאַֽל׃

Commentary

3. *To meet Ahaz.* Isaiah seems to have had free access to the king, because he probably belonged to the royal family or the aristocracy of the court (see our *General Introduction*).

Upper Pool. Part of Jerusalem's irrigation system.

Fuller's Field. שדה כובס (*s'deh kovés*, field of the cleaner), the area where communal washing was done.[14]

4. *Nothing but smoke.* Literally, two smoldering stumps of firewood.

6. *The son of Tabeel.* Referring to a person only by the name of an ancestor was deliberately insulting. See, for instance, Saul's reference to David as "the son of Jesse."[15]

9:5. For a child has been born to us,   9:5 כִּי־יֶ֤לֶד יֻלַּד־לָ֙נוּ֙

a son has been given us.   בֵּ֚ן נִתַּן־לָ֔נוּ

Authority has settled on his shoulders,   וַתְּהִ֥י הַמִּשְׂרָ֖ה עַל־שִׁכְמ֑וֹ

and the wonderful Counselor, God
  Almighty,   וַיִּקְרָ֨א שְׁמ֜וֹ פֶּ֠לֶא יוֹעֵץ֙ אֵ֣ל גִּבּ֔וֹר

will call his name   אֲבִיעַ֖ד שַׂר־שָׁלֽוֹם:

Avi-ad, Sar-shalom,

Eternal Progenitor, Ruler of Peace,   6 לְם רַבֵּ֤ה [לְמַרְבֵּ֨ה] הַמִּשְׂרָ֜ה

6. to add strength to his authority,

and peace without end   וּלְשָׁל֣וֹם אֵֽין־קֵ֗ץ

for the throne of David and his kingdom,   עַל־כִּסֵּ֤א דָוִד֙ וְעַל־מַמְלַכְתּ֔וֹ

establishing it and supporting it,   לְהָכִ֤ין אֹתָהּ֙ וּֽלְסַעֲדָ֔הּ

based on justice and right   בְּמִשְׁפָּ֤ט וּבִצְדָקָ֔ה מֵעַתָּ֖ה וְעַד־עוֹלָ֑ם

now and forever.

The passionate determination of the God of
heaven's hosts   קִנְאַ֛ת יְהֹוָ֥ה צְבָא֖וֹת

will bring this about.   תַּעֲשֶׂה־זֹּֽאת:

Commentary

9:5-6. The Rabbis added these verses to the haftarah, in order to give it a messianic thrust. These passages, as well as the rest of chapter 7 (not included in the haftarah) have been interpreted by traditional Christian theology as foretelling the coming of Jesus. Jewish tradition identified the child as Hezekiah, son of Ahaz.

The Hebrew text is difficult; our translation is based on interpretations by the Targum and Ibn Ezra.

Progenitor. Literally, "father."

Essay

Holy, holy, holy

Three times does the voice of the angel cry out that God is קָדוֹשׁ (*kadosh*, holy), and in subsequent Jewish tradition the Eternal is often referred to as הקדוש ברוך הוא (*ha-kadosh baruch hu*), "The Holy One, the Blessed One."[16]

Holiness is a concept that plays a basic role in the Tanach and in Jewish thought thereafter. It appears in various forms: *kodesh*, holiness; *kadosh*, holy; *k'dushah* (the section of the prayer service that contains the words of Isaiah's vision); *kaddish* (the memorial prayer); *kiddush*, the blessing of Shabbat or holy day; *kiddushin*, the wedding ceremony; and others—all derived from the root קדשׁ (*k-d-sh*).

The basic meaning of the word means "to set aside, to be apart." Clearly, God is set apart from creation. This conception negates pantheism, which posits all of nature to be infused with divinity (and therefore often seen to be indistinguishable from it). The biblical books see the Eternal as *kadosh*, uniquely set apart.

It is important to keep this underlying meaning of holiness in mind. Shabbat is holy, because it is set apart from the week; Israel is called a *goy kadosh*, a holy people, because it was set apart from the rest of humanity to be a witness to the Eternal. And holy days are unlike any other: they are special occasions to serve God.

Of late, popular speech has used the word "holy" in a variety of ways. It may describe pious people ("he is a holy man") and in that sense is applied by Chasidim to describe some of their rabbis. At the other end of the scale, "holy" may be used for expletives ("holy cow") or in derogatory fashion for certain types of highly emotional worshippers (who are called "holy rollers"), or become cheapened from holy days to holidays.

Such usage is of course far from the biblical model where, especially regarding God, a deep sense of awe and fundamental otherness is expressed by the word. Israel is bidden to remain *kadosh* because God is *kadosh*, and service to the Almighty creates its own *k'dushah*: "You shall be holy, for I, the Eternal your God, am holy," says the Torah.[17]

But this apartness does not mean separation from the rest of creation and its creatures. The holiness of God does not imply disinterest in and remoteness from the world. Quite the contrary: we believe that God is deeply concerned with creation and with humanity. When we are open to the Divine, it can enter our souls; when we shut it out, it appears indeed remote. Prayer is a means of drawing the Presence into our lives. Thus, God is both apart and near.

The same is true for human holiness. In biblical thought, a hermit would not fit the concept of *k'dushah*.

So it is with the Jewish people. It remains *kadosh* when it preserves its identity—but only when it does so for the sake of God. Therefore, it must not stand aside from God's creation, but be involved in it as a partner with the Eternal to make it better and more habitable in every way. Self-ghettoization, removing one's community from society, is not *k'dushah*; but identity for the sake of shaping it in God's image is the true way to holiness.

Gleanings

Holy, holy, holy
is the God of heaven's hosts,
whose Presence fills all the earth! (chapter 6, verse 3)

Then I heard the voice of my Liege saying:
Whom shall I send? Who shall go on Our behalf?
And I said: Here I am; send me. (chapter 6, verse 8)

Unclean lips

Isaiah beheld the Presence, a sight fraught with danger, and he exclaimed:

I am lost; for I am a man of unclean lips,

and I live among a people of unclean lips. (verse 5)

Thereupon God rebuked him, for while Isaiah was free to speak of himself in derogatory terms, he was not free to do so with regard to Israel. As a punishment, a seraph flew to him and scorched his lips with a live coal.

Isaiah repented forthwith and became Israel's staunchest advocate. For this he was rewarded and escaped physical injury; moreover, he received more divine revelations than any other prophet, and he received them not through a teacher but directly from God.

Midrash[18]

Beloved

Holiness is what is loved by all the gods. It is loved because it is holy, and not holy because it is loved.

Ascribed to Plato

Holiness

The duty of holiness is not specifically enjoined by the prophets, among ethical duties. The omission may suggest that the concept of holiness had not yet attained fully its ethical content. It may, however, be inferred from Isaiah's general teaching that holiness includes moral excellence.

Israel I. Mattuck[19]

Standing before God

God ... Who with the single word has made the world, hanging before us the heavens like an unrolled scroll, and the earth an old manuscript, and the murmurous sea, each, all-allusive to Thy glory, so that from them we might conjecture and surmise and almost know thee:

Whom only angels know
Who in Thy burning courts
Cry: Holy! Holy! Holy!
While mortal voice below
With seraphim consorts
To murmur: Holy! Holy!
Yet holiness not know.

A. M. Klein[20]

* * *

Notes

[1] So the Targum; see also Song of Songs Rabbah 1:34.

[2] Exodus 20:23.

[3] It also served as a model for the Christian mass, in which *kadosh* is also thrice repeated (in the Latin translation, *sanctus, sanctus, sanctus*).

[4] See Amos 1:1; Zechariah 14:5.

[5] Exodus 6:12, 30.

[6] See Isaiah 52:1.

[7] Zephaniah 3:9.

[8] Exodus 33:20 and Numbers 12:8. The former passage gave rise to midrashic discussions about the alleged transgression of the Prophet who—by making this and other statements—seems to have contradicted the teachings of the Torah. After all, Moses had said that no one could see God and live. See B. Yevamot 49b and the sources cited in Ginzberg, *Legends of the Jews*, vol. 6, p. 373.

[9] Exodus 24:10-11.

[10] Malbim, following the Targum.

[11] See the Torah Commentary, pp. 416 ff.

[12] See Psalm 6:4. The lamentation formula has a long history, appearing in Akkadian and Ugaritic.

[13] See Freehof, *Book of Isaiah*, following Krauss.

[14] See, for example, S. Irvine, *Isaiah, Ahab and the Syro-Ephraimitic Crisis* (Atlanta: Scholars Press, 1990).

[15] I Samuel 20:27, 30, 31; 22:7.

[16] The Name stands for God's identity, which by definition is inexpressible.

[17] Leviticus 19:2.

[18] Ginzberg, *Legends*, vol. 4, p. 263; Pesikta deRab Kahana, piska 16 (Braude and Kapstein, pp. 292 ff.). Various midrashim go so far as to compare Isaiah to Moses, stating that he too lived to be 120 years.

[19] *The Thought of the Prophets*, pp. 73-74.

[20] From "Stance of the Amidah," *Collected Poems*, p. 345.

Jeremiah, chapter 34, verses 8 to 22 and chapter 33, verses 25 and 26

Introduction

Connection of haftarah and sidra:

The weekly portion opens with rules about the release of Hebrew slaves; the haftarah reports how, in Jeremiah's time, the ruling classes of Judah reversed their previous release of Jewish slaves, and how the Prophet dealt with this reversal.

The setting:

In the year 589 B.C.E. the Babylonians, under King Nebuchadnezzar, invaded Judah and laid siege to Jerusalem. Its Jewish elite agreed to a wholesale release of Hebrew slaves, in order to induce God's forgiveness (the slaves should have been released long ago; see below). But when, in 588, the siege was suddenly lifted, the former owners canceled the release and returned the slaves to their previous status. Jeremiah severely condemns this perfidious act and predicts the direst consequences.

For more on Jeremiah and his time, see our *General Introduction*.

The message:

1. The historical stage is set. It is told in the objective-biographical form that characterizes much of the book. (34:8-11)

2. The Prophet's reaction to the perfidy: speaking in God's name, he predicts that the Babylonians will return and take up the siege, conquer Jerusalem, and burn it down. (12-22)

3. The haftarah concludes with an encouraging message, with two verses added from the preceding chapter of the book. (33:25-26)

HAFTARAH FOR MISHPATIM

Jeremiah, chapter 34, verses 8 to 22 and chapter 33, verses 25 and 26

34:8. The word of the Eternal that came to Jeremiah after King Zedekiah had made a covenant with the people of Jerusalem to proclaim liberty there:

9. They were to set free their Hebrew slaves, both men and women; no fellow Judean would serve as a slave to another.

10. The people and their officials who had made this covenant, agreeing to set free their male and female slaves and never again to enslave them, carried it out and freed them;

11. but afterward they turned around and took the people whom they had set free and forced them once again into bondage.

12. Then the word of the Eternal came to Jeremiah:

13. Thus says the Eternal One, the God of Israel: When I brought your ancestors out of the land of Egypt, out of the House of Bondage, I made this covenant with them:

8 הַדָּבָר אֲשֶׁר־הָיָה אֶל־יִרְמְיָהוּ מֵאֵת יְהֹוָה אַחֲרֵי כְּרֹת הַמֶּלֶךְ צִדְקִיָּהוּ בְּרִית אֶת־כָּל־הָעָם אֲשֶׁר בִּירוּשָׁלַ͏ִם לִקְרֹא לָהֶם דְּרוֹר:

9 לְשַׁלַּח אִישׁ אֶת־עַבְדּוֹ וְאִישׁ אֶת־שִׁפְחָתוֹ הָעִבְרִי וְהָעִבְרִיָּה חָפְשִׁים לְבִלְתִּי עֲבָד־בָּם בִּיהוּדִי אָחִיהוּ אִישׁ:

10 וַיִּשְׁמְעוּ כָל־הַשָּׂרִים וְכָל־הָעָם אֲשֶׁר־בָּאוּ בַבְּרִית לְשַׁלַּח אִישׁ אֶת־עַבְדּוֹ וְאִישׁ אֶת־שִׁפְחָתוֹ חָפְשִׁים לְבִלְתִּי עֲבָד־בָּם עוֹד וַיִּשְׁמְעוּ וַיְשַׁלֵּחוּ:

11 וַיָּשׁוּבוּ אַחֲרֵי־כֵן וַיָּשִׁבוּ אֶת־הָעֲבָדִים וְאֶת־הַשְּׁפָחוֹת אֲשֶׁר שִׁלְּחוּ חָפְשִׁים וַיִּכְבִּישׁוּם [וַיִּכְבְּשׁוּם] לַעֲבָדִים וְלִשְׁפָחוֹת:

12 וַיְהִי דְבַר־יְהֹוָה אֶל־יִרְמְיָהוּ מֵאֵת יְהֹוָה לֵאמֹר:

13 כֹּה־אָמַר יְהֹוָה אֱלֹהֵי יִשְׂרָאֵל אָנֹכִי כָּרַתִּי בְרִית אֶת־אֲבוֹתֵיכֶם בְּיוֹם הוֹצִאִי אוֹתָם מֵאֶרֶץ מִצְרַיִם מִבֵּית עֲבָדִים לֵאמֹר:

Commentary

34:8. *To proclaim liberty*. In accordance with the Torah's command to release Hebrew slaves at the end of six years (see the essay below).[1]

Liberty. דרור (*d'ror*), the same word that occurs in Leviticus 25:10, the verse that was inscribed on the Liberty Bell in Philadelphia. The term and the institution have Babylonian antecedents.[2]

9. *Hebrew slaves*. Who had sold themselves or (in the case of females) had been sold by their fathers. The sidra Mishpatim ("Laws") is clearly aimed at the abolition of servitude among the covenant people and emphasizes this purpose by setting the provision at the head of the section.

12. *Then the word of the Eternal came to Jeremiah:* The Hebrew continues with ... "from the Eternal."

14. *In the seventh year you must set free your fellow Hebrews who sell themselves to you. When they have served you six years, you must let them go free.* But your ancestors did not obey Me; they paid no heed.

15. Then you recently turned around and did the right thing in My sight by proclaiming liberty for your neighbors; and you made a covenant in My presence, in the house that bears My name.

16. Yet then you turned around and profaned My name by taking back the men and women whom you had set free as they desired, and forcing them again to be your slaves.

17. Therefore, says the Eternal One, because you did not proclaim [permanent] liberty for your kinfolk and your neighbors, and thereby refused to obey Me, I tell you that I will [now] give *you* a proclamation of liberty: [a liberty] of the sword, of plague and of famine; I will make you a horror to all the kingdoms of the world!

18. Those who broke My covenant, who did not fulfill the terms of the covenant that they made in My presence, I will make

14 מִקֵּץ שֶׁבַע שָׁנִים תְּשַׁלְּחוּ אִישׁ אֶת־אָחִיו הָעִבְרִי אֲשֶׁר־יִמָּכֵר לְךָ וַעֲבָדְךָ שֵׁשׁ שָׁנִים וְשִׁלַּחְתּוֹ חָפְשִׁי מֵעִמָּךְ וְלֹא־שָׁמְעוּ אֲבוֹתֵיכֶם אֵלַי וְלֹא הִטּוּ אֶת־אָזְנָם:

15 וַתָּשֻׁבוּ אַתֶּם הַיּוֹם וַתַּעֲשׂוּ אֶת־הַיָּשָׁר בְּעֵינַי לִקְרֹא דְרוֹר אִישׁ לְרֵעֵהוּ וַתִּכְרְתוּ בְרִית לְפָנַי בַּבַּיִת אֲשֶׁר־נִקְרָא שְׁמִי עָלָיו:

16 וַתָּשֻׁבוּ וַתְּחַלְּלוּ אֶת־שְׁמִי וַתָּשִׁבוּ אִישׁ אֶת־עַבְדּוֹ וְאִישׁ אֶת־שִׁפְחָתוֹ אֲשֶׁר־שִׁלַּחְתֶּם חָפְשִׁים לְנַפְשָׁם וַתִּכְבְּשׁוּ אֹתָם לִהְיוֹת לָכֶם לַעֲבָדִים וְלִשְׁפָחוֹת:

17 לָכֵן כֹּה־אָמַר יְהֹוָה אַתֶּם לֹא־שְׁמַעְתֶּם אֵלַי לִקְרֹא דְרוֹר אִישׁ לְאָחִיו וְאִישׁ לְרֵעֵהוּ הִנְנִי קֹרֵא לָכֶם דְּרוֹר נְאֻם־יְהֹוָה אֶל־הַחֶרֶב אֶל־הַדֶּבֶר וְאֶל־הָרָעָב וְנָתַתִּי אֶתְכֶם לְזַעֲוָה [לְזַעֲוָה] לְכֹל מַמְלְכוֹת הָאָרֶץ:

18 וְנָתַתִּי אֶת־הָאֲנָשִׁים הָעֹבְרִים אֶת־בְּרִתִי אֲשֶׁר לֹא־הֵקִימוּ אֶת־דִּבְרֵי הַבְּרִית אֲשֶׁר

Commentary

14. *In the seventh year.* Of servitude. Each indentured serf was to be freed after six years; but apparently the owners had disregarded the law entirely, and none had been released.[3]

15. *Recently.* היום (*ha-yom*, literally "today") here stands for "as if it were today," that is, recently. When the city was besieged, the slave owners had at last obeyed the Torah law.

[like] the calf they cut in two in order to pass between the halves.

19. I will give the leaders of Judah and Jerusalem, the officials, and all the people of the land who passed between the halves of the calf

20. to their enemies, to their mortal foes; their dead bodies shall become food for the birds of the sky and the beasts of the earth.

21. I will give Zedekiah king of Judah and his officials to their enemies, those who seek their lives—to the army of the king of Babylon, which has pulled back from you.

22. I will give the command, says the Eternal One, and I will return them to this city. They shall fight against it and capture it and burn it down. I will make the cities of Judah a desolation, uninhabited.

כָּרְתוּ לְפָנֵי הָעֵגֶל אֲשֶׁר כָּרְתוּ לִשְׁנַיִם וַיַּעַבְרוּ בֵּין בְּתָרָיו:

19 שָׂרֵי יְהוּדָה וְשָׂרֵי יְרוּשָׁלַ͏ִם הַסָּרִסִים וְהַכֹּהֲנִים וְכֹל עַם הָאָרֶץ הָעֹבְרִים בֵּין בִּתְרֵי הָעֵגֶל:

20 וְנָתַתִּי אוֹתָם בְּיַד אֹיְבֵיהֶם וּבְיַד מְבַקְשֵׁי נַפְשָׁם וְהָיְתָה נִבְלָתָם לְמַאֲכָל לְעוֹף הַשָּׁמַיִם וּלְבֶהֱמַת הָאָרֶץ:

21 וְאֶת צִדְקִיָּהוּ מֶלֶךְ יְהוּדָה וְאֶת שָׂרָיו אֶתֵּן בְּיַד אֹיְבֵיהֶם וּבְיַד מְבַקְשֵׁי נַפְשָׁם וּבְיַד חֵיל מֶלֶךְ בָּבֶל הָעֹלִים מֵעֲלֵיכֶם:

22 הִנְנִי מְצַוֶּה נְאֻם יְהֹוָה וַהֲשִׁבֹתִים אֶל הָעִיר הַזֹּאת וְנִלְחֲמוּ עָלֶיהָ וּלְכָדוּהָ וּשְׂרָפֻהָ בָאֵשׁ וְאֶת עָרֵי יְהוּדָה אֶתֵּן שְׁמָמָה מֵאֵין יֹשֵׁב:

Commentary

18. *The calf they cut in two.* An ancient ritual by which parties to an agreement passed between the halves of a slaughtered animal and thereby bound themselves solemnly to the terms of the covenant.[4] The cutting ritual may have symbolized that the contracting parties were now the guarantors of wholeness. It has been suggested that the present-day ceremony of cutting a ribbon when new facilities are opened or dedicated may derive from such traditions.[5]

21. *Zedekiah.* His eventual capture by the Babylonians had been predicted earlier,[6] but Jeremiah had still hoped that the king would surrender peacefully and thereby escape the bitter fate that he—disregarding the Prophet's plea—was sure to suffer. His sons were killed before his eyes, and then he himself was blinded (the picture of such punishment has been preserved in an Assyrian source).

33:25. Thus says the Eternal One:

If I did not create day and night,

or fix the laws that govern heaven and earth,

26. then would I reject the descendants of Jacob and My servant David,

or not choose a descendant of David to rule the descendants of Abraham, Isaac, and Jacob.

For I will restore their fortunes, and take them back in love.

33:25 כֹּה אָמַ֣ר יְהֹוָ֔ה

אִם־לֹ֥א בְרִיתִ֖י יוֹמָ֣ם וָלָ֑יְלָה

חֻקּ֛וֹת שָׁמַ֥יִם וָאָ֖רֶץ לֹא־שָֽׂמְתִּי׃

26 גַּם־זֶ֣רַע יַעֲקוֹב֩ וְדָוִ֨ד עַבְדִּ֜י אֶמְאַ֗ס

מִקַּ֤חַת מִזַּרְעוֹ֙ מֹֽשְׁלִ֔ים אֶל־זֶ֖רַע אַבְרָהָ֑ם

יִשְׂחָ֖ק וְיַעֲקֹ֑ב

כִּֽי־אָשׁ֥וּב [אָשִׁ֛יב] אֶת־שְׁבוּתָ֖ם וְרִחַמְתִּֽים׃

Commentary

Verses 25 and 26 are added to the haftarah from the previous chapter because the Sages did not wish to dismiss the congregation on a negative note.

25. *If I did not create day and night.* The masoretic text reads awkwardly and does not provide the intended parallelism. We arrive at our translation by substituting an aleph (א) for a yod (י), thereby obtaining בראתי (*barati*, I did create) instead of בריתי (*beriti*, My covenant).

26. *Take them back in love.* Or, "show them mercy." רחם (*rachem*), which is related to the word for "womb," often has the sense of love, with even the forensic nuance of the formal acknowledgment of the child as one's own.[7]

182

Essay

Sin and history

The haftarah tells us of a serious breach of Torah law. Hebrew men and women who had become indentured because of family or personal debts were to serve no more than six years and then (like the soil that was not be worked in the seventh year) were to be released. But their masters had never complied with these rules. Then, in a moment of mortal danger to the nation, they bethought themselves and, led by King Zedekiah, granted liberty to their serfs, making a solemn covenant to abide by the law.

Indeed, Jerusalem's siege was suddenly lifted, and the Babylonians were turned away. But what was at first experienced as divine intervention was soon evaluated in political terms. When the city's leaders learned that the Babylonians had abandoned the siege in order to deal with an approaching Egyptian army, they reasoned that this, and not divine intervention, had brought about the relief of Jerusalem. Now that the danger seemed to have passed, they reverted to their former habits and enslaved the serfs once again.

Jeremiah evaluated the situation differently. He was convinced that the timely arrival of Egyptian troops had not been accidental, but was a sign from God. The release of the serfs had been a religious act, and its immoral reversal was bound to engender the direst consequences. God would no longer suffer the people's continued defiance. Zedekiah, the king who had let it happen, would pay dearly for it, and Jerusalem would feel the divine wrath to the fullest. The Prophet was sure that destruction would ensue and the Jewish state would cease to exist.

He did not hesitate to let the leaders of Judah know what awaited them. As a last resort he counseled them to surrender to Nebuchadnezzar, in order to assuage him if possible. This caused the king's advisers, who saw their situation only through the lens of politics, to consider Jeremiah a puppet of the Babylonians and a traitor to the state. They heard him condemn Zedekiah and his court, which they believed was sheer treason. The moral direction of the Prophet's imprecations was beyond their ken.

Did Jeremiah divorce himself from all political judgments and listen only to what he knew was a message from on high? We must see him as a person both of deep spiritual sensitivity and of uncanny judgment, a man convinced that only peace and religious living could guarantee the security of Jerusalem. When the cords of morality were irrevocably sundered, the ship of state was sure to sink.

For Jeremiah, God and Israel played a joint role in human history. Israel prospered when it followed the way of Torah; it suffered when it contravened the divine law and will. This was the choice that Moses had laid before the people, and the consequences were of the people's own choosing. The incident of revoking the freedom of the serfs was the last straw, and God decreed that Jerusalem would be razed and the people exiled. They had squandered their inheritance.

Gleanings

The calf cut in two

The symbolism of the ceremony is articulated in political treaties of the 8th century B.C.E. A treaty from Syria (written in Aramaic) reads in part: "Just as this calf is cut in two, so may [King] Matiel be cut in two, and so may his nobles be cut in two."[8]

The king also signed a second treaty, which describes how a "spring lamb has been brought from the fold, not for sacrifice ... but to sanction the treaty ...."[9]

The destruction of Jerusalem

Nebuzaradan, chief of the [Babylonian] guards, burned down God's House, the king's palace, and the houses of all important people in Jerusalem. Then his entire force tore down the walls of Jerusalem in their entirety. The remnant of the people were taken into exile by Nebuzaradan; only the poorest in the land were left behind, so that they might be vine-dressers and laborers.

Thus Judah was exiled from its land. King Nebuchadnezzar put Gedaliah in charge of the people left in the land. But in the seventh month some Jews came to Mizpah [the new seat of government] and struck down Gedaliah, and he died. And the [remaining] people, young and old, fled to Egypt for fear of the Babylonians.

II Kings 25 (extracts)

Another version

They burned down the House of God, razed the city wall of Jerusalem and all its fine mansions with all their treasurers until everything was destroyed. Those who escaped the sword were taken to Babylon as prisoners and became the king's slaves, [and remained so] until the Persians came to power.

II Chronicles 36 (extracts)

The lesson

(After telling the story of the Temple's destruction the author continues:)

I have told all this in order to explain God's nature to those who do not as yet know it. For God has arranged it so that all prophecies, however varied, will be fulfilled at the fixed time precisely as predicted. From this we also learn something about the ignorance and gullibility of people, who cannot foresee the future and therefore plunge blindly into disaster, without a chance of escaping it.

Flavius Josephus[10]

***

Notes

[1] Exodus 21:1ff. and Deuteronomy 15:12.

[2] See the Torah Commentary, p. 943.

[3] So Rashi.

[4] See Genesis 15:9-10, 17-20.

[5] See the Torah Commentary, p. 113.

[6] Jeremiah 34:4-5.

[7] S. David Sperling, *Journal of the Ancient Near Eastern Society,* vol. 19 (1989), pp. 149-159.

[8] See W. Holladay, *Jeremiah,* vol. 2, p. 243.

[9] Text in J. Pritchard, *Ancient Near Eastern Texts*, p. 532.

[10] *Antiquities* X: 8:3. The Jewish historian also described the destruction of the Second Temple in the year 70, in his book *History of the Jewish War.*

First Kings, chapter 5, verse 26 to chapter 6, verse 13

Introduction

Connection of sidra and haftarah:

Both sidra and haftarah deal with the construction of a sanctuary to honor God: one in the desert and the other in Jerusalem. Both describe how the Torah's challenge was met: "Let them make Me a sanctuary, and I will dwell among them."[1]

The setting:

Soon after his accession to the throne (about 970 B.C.E.), Solomon began to build the Temple. In this enterprise he was aided by his ally, King Hiram of Tyre, who supplied him with skilled labor and with wood from the forests of Lebanon.

The story:

The haftarah, taken from the First Book of Kings, consists of only 15 verses. [2]

1. Introduction: Solomon's wisdom and his alliance with Hiram. (5:26)

2. The labor force and its administration. (27-31)

3. Construction details. (6:1-10)

4. Postscript: the Divine Presence will dwell among the people as long as they—represented by the king[3]— observe the Covenant. (11-13)

HAFTARAH FOR T'RUMAH

First Kings, chapter 5, verse 26 to chapter 6, verse 13

5:26. The Eternal gave Solomon wisdom, as promised. There was peace between Hiram and Solomon, and the two of them made a treaty.

27. King Solomon drafted 30,000 men from all over Israel as forced labor.

28. He sent them by relays of 10,000 to Lebanon; each group worked there one month and stayed home for two. Adoniram was in charge of the labor force.

29. Solomon employed 70,000 who carried the loads and 80,000 quarry workers in the hill country,

30. apart from the 3,300 foremen responsible for the assigned tasks, who directed the people engaged in the work.

5:26 וַיהוָ֗ה נָתַ֤ן חָכְמָה֙ לִשְׁלֹמֹ֔ה כַּאֲשֶׁ֖ר דִּבֶּר־לֹ֑ו וַיְהִ֣י שָׁלֹ֗ם בֵּ֤ין חִירָם֙ וּבֵ֣ין שְׁלֹמֹ֔ה וַיִּכְרְת֥וּ בְרִ֖ית שְׁנֵיהֶֽם׃

27 וַיַּ֨עַל הַמֶּ֧לֶךְ שְׁלֹמֹ֛ה מַ֖ס מִכָּל־יִשְׂרָאֵ֑ל וַיְהִ֣י הַמַּ֔ס שְׁלֹשִׁ֖ים אֶ֥לֶף אִֽישׁ׃

28 וַיִּשְׁלָחֵ֣ם לְבָנֹ֗ונָה עֲשֶׂ֨רֶת אֲלָפִ֤ים בַּחֹ֨דֶשׁ֙ חֲלִיפֹ֔ות חֹ֚דֶשׁ יִהְי֣וּ בַלְּבָנֹ֔ון שְׁנַ֥יִם חֳדָשִׁ֖ים בְּבֵיתֹ֑ו וַאֲדֹנִירָ֖ם עַל־הַמַּֽס׃

29 וַיְהִ֧י לִשְׁלֹמֹ֛ה שִׁבְעִ֥ים אֶ֖לֶף נֹשֵׂ֣א סַבָּ֑ל וּשְׁמֹנִ֥ים אֶ֖לֶף חֹצֵ֥ב בָּהָֽר׃

30 לְ֠בַד מִשָּׂרֵ֨י הַנִּצָּבִ֤ים לִשְׁלֹמֹה֙ אֲשֶׁ֣ר עַל־הַמְּלָאכָ֔ה שְׁלֹ֥שֶׁת אֲלָפִ֖ים וּשְׁלֹ֣שׁ מֵאֹ֑ות הָרֹדִ֣ים בָּעָ֔ם הָעֹשִׂ֖ים בַּמְּלָאכָֽה׃

Commentary

5:26. *As promised.* Literally, "as He had promised."

27. *Forced labor.* מס (*mas*), also known as corvée, a throwback to the practices of ancient Egypt. The same word was used by Pharaoh's representatives to describe their forced labor practices in Canaan in the 14th century B.C.E., when the land was part of the Egyptian empire. By reviving the institution of *mas* Solomon stirred up resentment, which led to revolt in the reign of his son. [4] The later notation (9:22) that the Israelites did not become bondsmen stems either from another source or indicates that only foreigners were permanently indentured. [5]

28. *Relays.* חליפות (*chalifot*), one contingent succeeding the other. The word is related to the Arabic *chalifa*, whence the term Caliph (who was considered a successor of the prophet Mohammed).

29. *Adoniram.* Son of Avda; so mentioned in 4:6.

In the hill country. Of Israel. The limestone was soft when quarried and gradually hardened under exposure. [6]

30. *3,300 foremen.* The figure in II Chronicles 2:1 and 17 is 3,600 men. [7]

31. By the king's command they cut large blocks of costly stone, in order to lay the foundation of the Temple with ashlar.

31 וַיְצַו הַמֶּלֶךְ וַיַּסִּעוּ אֲבָנִים גְּדֹלוֹת אֲבָנִים יְקָרוֹת לְיַסֵּד הַבָּיִת אַבְנֵי גָזִית:

32. Solomon's and Hiram's builders and builders from [the city of] Gebal shaped them; they made ready the timber and stones for the building of the Temple.

32 וַיִּפְסְלוּ בֹּנֵי שְׁלֹמֹה וּבֹנֵי חִירוֹם וְהַגִּבְלִים וַיָּכִינוּ הָעֵצִים וְהָאֲבָנִים לִבְנוֹת הַבָּיִת:

6:1. Four hundred and eighty years after the people of Israel left Egypt, in the fourth year of Solomon's rule over Israel, in the second month, the month of Ziv, Solomon [began to] build the Temple of the Eternal.

6:1 וַיְהִי בִשְׁמוֹנִים שָׁנָה וְאַרְבַּע מֵאוֹת שָׁנָה לְצֵאת בְּנֵי־יִשְׂרָאֵל מֵאֶרֶץ־מִצְרַיִם בַּשָּׁנָה הָרְבִיעִית בְּחֹדֶשׁ זִו הוּא הַחֹדֶשׁ הַשֵּׁנִי לִמְלֹךְ שְׁלֹמֹה עַל־יִשְׂרָאֵל וַיִּבֶן הַבַּיִת לַיהוָה:

2. The Temple that Solomon built for [the worship of] the Eternal was sixty cubits

2 וְהַבַּיִת אֲשֶׁר בָּנָה הַמֶּלֶךְ שְׁלֹמֹה לַיהוָה

Commentary

31. *Costly stone*. Even though they served for the foundation and therefore could not be seen, they were to be of the best quality.[8]

Ashlar. Hewn stones that were made to fit precisely and without bonding materials. "There were several degrees of finish: sometimes only the four fitting surfaces were accurately squared and dressed, leaving the outer surface in the rough; very often the margins of the outer face were finely chiseled to a breadth of a few inches; and at other times the whole outer surface (with or without a depressed margin) was smoothed."[9]

32. *Gebal*. The Greek name of the city was Byblos, some 20 miles (32 kilometers) north of today's Beirut.[10]

Shaped them. The root of the verb is פסל (*p-s-l*), from which פֶּסֶל (*pesel*, graven image) is derived.

6:1. *Four hundred and eighty years*. The author(s) of Kings would thereby place the Exodus from Egypt in the 15th century B.C.E., while modern scholarship is agreed that the pharaoh of the Exodus was most likely Ramses II, who lived in the 13th century.

In the second month, the month of Ziv. Usually, months were called by numerals; the counting started with the spring month. Babylonian names came into use later on and have remained part of the Jewish calendar. Today, the second month is called Iyyar.[11]

2. *The Temple that Solomon built*. The actual location of the building is nowhere mentioned, though it is generally agreed to have been on the Temple Mount.[12] A recent study locates the Holy of Holies inside the Mosque of Omar.[13]

long, twenty cubits wide, and thirty cubits high.

3. The porch in front of the main hall of the Temple was as long as the Temple itself was wide, twenty cubits, and it was ten cubits deep.

4. He made windows and latticed shutters for the Temple.

5. Against the wall of the Temple—the outside walls of the main hall and the Holy of Holies—he built an annex all around with side rooms in it.

6. The lowest story [of the annex] was five cubits wide, the middle one was six cubits wide, and the top one was seven cubits wide: on the outside of the Temple, all around, he had provided recesses, so that [the beams] did not have a hold on the outside walls of the Temple [in order to have support].

שִׁשִּׁים־אַמָּה אָרְכּוֹ וְעֶשְׂרִים רָחְבּוֹ וּשְׁלֹשִׁים אַמָּה קוֹמָתוֹ:

3 וְהָאוּלָם עַל־פְּנֵי הֵיכַל הַבַּיִת עֶשְׂרִים אַמָּה אָרְכּוֹ עַל־פְּנֵי רֹחַב הַבָּיִת עֶשֶׂר בָּאַמָּה רָחְבּוֹ עַל־פְּנֵי הַבָּיִת:

4 וַיַּעַשׂ לַבָּיִת חַלּוֹנֵי שְׁקֻפִים אֲטֻמִים:

5 וַיִּבֶן עַל־קִיר הַבַּיִת יָצוֹעַ [יָצִיעַ] סָבִיב אֶת־קִירוֹת הַבַּיִת סָבִיב לַהֵיכָל וְלַדְּבִיר וַיַּעַשׂ צְלָעוֹת סָבִיב:

6 הַיָּצוֹעַ [הַיָּצִיעַ] הַתַּחְתֹּנָה [הַתַּחְתֹּנָה] חָמֵשׁ בָּאַמָּה רָחְבָּהּ וְהַתִּיכֹנָה שֵׁשׁ בָּאַמָּה רָחְבָּהּ וְהַשְּׁלִישִׁית שֶׁבַע בָּאַמָּה רָחְבָּהּ כִּי מִגְרָעוֹת נָתַן לַבַּיִת סָבִיב חוּצָה לְבִלְתִּי אֲחֹז בְּקִירוֹת־הַבָּיִת:

Commentary

Sixty cubits long. Most likely these figures came from the royal archives; but another source supplied the writer of the book of Chronicles with different figures.[14] The length of a cubit was the distance from the elbow to the finger tips, an imprecise measurement, estimated to be about 17 1/2 inches (45 centimeters). The building would therefore have been 90 feet long, 30 feet wide, and 45 feet high (27 x 9 x 13.5 meters), measuring the inside dimensions. The walls were about 5 cubits thick (about 7 feet, or 2 meters).[15] It was thus not a very large building; but then the population was not large either.

3. *The porch.* A gateway to the Temple.

4. *Windows ... latticed shutters.* The Hebrew is obscure. Jewish tradition understood the words to mean "windows broad within and narrow outside," because God's place did not need outside light, being illuminated from within.[16]

5. *Side rooms.* צלעות (*tz'la'ot*). The same term is prominently featured in the sidra.[17]

Main hall. היכל (*hechal*), from an Akkadian word meaning "great house." (Today's Chief Rabbinate of Israel is located in a structure named Hechal Shelomo, that is, Great Hall of Solomon.)

7. When the Temple was built, it was built with unhewn stones prepared at the quarry, so that no hammer or ax or any other iron tool was heard in the Temple while it was being built.

8. The entrance to the lowest story was on the right side of the Temple; and there were winding stairs to the middle story, and from there to the third story.

9. When he finished building the Temple, he paneled it with beams and planks of cedar.

10. He built the storied annex all around the Temple, each story five cubits high; they held fast to the Temple by beams of cedar.

11. Then the word of the Eternal came to Solomon:

12. *Concerning this Temple that you have been building [I tell you this:]— if you obey My statutes and carry out My rules of justice and take care to keep all My commandments, I will fulfill My promise, the one I made to your father David,*

13. and I will dwell among the people of Israel, and never forsake My people Israel.

7 וְהַבַּ֙יִת֙ בְּהִבָּ֣נֹת֔וֹ אֶֽבֶן־שְׁלֵמָ֥ה מַסָּ֖ע נִבְנָ֑ה וּמַקָּב֤וֹת וְהַגַּרְזֶן֙ כׇּל־כְּלִ֣י בַרְזֶ֔ל לֹֽא־נִשְׁמַ֥ע בַּבַּ֖יִת בְּהִבָּנֹתֽוֹ׃

8 פֶּ֗תַח הַצֵּלָע֙ הַתִּ֣יכֹנָ֔ה אֶל־כֶּ֥תֶף הַבַּ֖יִת הַיְמָנִ֑ית וּבְלוּלִּ֗ים יַֽעֲלוּ֙ עַל־הַתִּ֣יכֹנָ֔ה וּמִן־הַתִּֽיכֹנָ֖ה אֶל־הַשְּׁלִשִֽׁים׃

9 וַיִּ֥בֶן אֶת־הַבַּ֖יִת וַיְכַלֵּ֑הוּ וַיִּסְפֹּ֤ן אֶת־הַבַּ֙יִת֙ גֵּבִ֔ים וּשְׂדֵרֹ֖ת בָּאֲרָזִֽים׃

10 וַיִּ֤בֶן אֶת־[הַיָּצ֙וּעַ֙] עַל־כׇּל־הַבַּ֔יִת חָמֵ֥שׁ אַמּ֖וֹת קֽוֹמָת֑וֹ וַיֶּאֱחֹ֥ז אֶת־הַבַּ֖יִת בַּעֲצֵ֥י אֲרָזִֽים׃

11 וַֽיְהִי֙ דְּבַר־יְהֹוָ֔ה אֶל־שְׁלֹמֹ֖ה לֵאמֹֽר׃

12 הַבַּ֨יִת הַזֶּ֜ה אֲשֶׁר־אַתָּ֣ה בֹנֶ֗ה אִם־תֵּלֵ֤ךְ בְּחֻקֹּתַי֙ וְאֶת־מִשְׁפָּטַ֣י תַּֽעֲשֶׂ֔ה וְשָׁמַרְתָּ֥ אֶת־כׇּל־מִצְוֺתַ֖י לָלֶ֣כֶת בָּהֶ֑ם וַהֲקִמֹתִ֤י אֶת־דְּבָרִי֙ אִתָּ֔ךְ אֲשֶׁ֥ר דִּבַּ֖רְתִּי אֶל־דָּוִ֥ד אָבִֽיךָ׃

13 וְשָׁ֣כַנְתִּ֔י בְּת֖וֹךְ בְּנֵ֣י יִשְׂרָאֵ֑ל וְלֹ֥א אֶעֱזֹ֖ב אֶת־עַמִּ֥י יִשְׂרָאֵֽל׃

Commentary

8. *Lowest story.* Following the Targum and the Septuagint; the masoretic text has "middle story."

Winding stairs. So the Septuagint. The Hebrew is unclear.

9. *He paneled it with beams and planks.* A conjectural rendering.[18]

12. *If you obey My statutes.* God's promise is clearly conditional, which appears to be in conflict with the promise made to David, that God's favor would never be withdrawn from Solomon.[19]

Essay

Architecture and religion

The details about the building of the Temple, which the book of Kings has preserved, and which are read as our haftarah, may puzzle many a reader. Why should later generations be interested in recessed beams, the dimensions of the front porch, or the way the stones were cut? What purpose do statistics about the number of quarry workers serve, or details of the accoutrements described in the haftarah that follows?

To begin with, we should look into how and why these architectural descriptions were preserved altogether. All ancient courts had royal archives, which kept a running record of the most important events of a sovereign's rule. They would describe military victories (but few if any defeats), note financial data, and describe in detail the king's building projects. The book of Kings was compiled and edited many centuries after Solomon, when the Temple he had built had already been destroyed by the Babylonians. The available court archives—along with oral traditions or personal memories—were the sources that could give the readers an idea how the Temple had looked. Apparently the architectural plans survived the sack of Jerusalem, and they served the writer(s) as the major historical sources.

Though the Temple was a fairly modest structure when measured by modern standards,[20] it was central to the account of Solomon's reign. In fact, except for legendary embellishments of his life and accomplishments, it was the building of the Temple that above all concerned the composer(s) of the book of Kings.

For the Temple was the heart of the new nation; its erection had been denied to David and was a privilege conferred on his son. The sanctuary—like the wilderness Tabernacle of which the sidra speaks—represented the assurance that God was dwelling in the people's midst.

The writer(s) of Kings, reflecting the theology of the book of Deuteronomy, perceived the importance of Solomon's kingship to have been primarily religious: the king had helped to make the service of the Eternal the national religion and had taken it beyond tribal traditions and local shrines. To be sure, Solomon himself and a number of his successors in Judah and Israel did not meet the standard of the exclusive worship of the Eternal, which the Torah (in the book of Deuteronomy) demands. But the Temple remained the symbol of the ideal religion, and its building was regarded as Solomon's most significant contribution to history. The architectural data and statistics emphasized this view, and therefore every detail was recorded with loving care and must be seen as a description of how God was served in holiness.

Gleanings

The Eternal gave Solomon wisdom (5:26)

Legends embellished the extent of Solomon's wisdom (see haftarah for Mikeitz), which in some respects was deemed akin to the very wisdom of God. Thus, the king could penetrate the secret thoughts of others and therefore could dispense with the presence of witnesses.

Midrash[21]

The Temple that Solomon built

The text does not tell us the exact location of the building site (see comment on 6:2, in our haftarah). A famous story tells of a vision he had, which directed him to build it on Mount Zion, in a field owned jointly by two brothers.

One was poor and single; the other rich and a family man. Each one wanted to ease the lot of the other and each night secretly added to the grain bin of his brother. The result was that each morning the two brothers found their bins undiminished and ascribed it to a miracle. Their brotherly love was deemed worthy of divine recognition, and thus their field became the site of the Temple.

Folktale[22]

Self-built

An old tradition stated that the Temple was not really built by human hands. Actually, it had, so to speak, built itself: the stones broke themselves loose from the quarry and assembled themselves according to plan.

Midrash[23]

* * *

Notes

[1] Exodus 25:8.

[2] In the Septuagint, it is called the Third Book of Kingdoms, while I and II Samuel are called I and II Kingdoms.

[3] This is in keeping with the biblical and extra-biblical thinking that the fate of the people is determined by the piety or impiety of the king; see II Samuel 24; II Kings 23:26-27.

[4] I Kings 12. Some commentators blame Solomon's reintroduction of corvée on his marriage to a daughter of the ruling pharaoh; so Hertz, who also contrasts this practice with the building of the desert Tabernacle, which was done through voluntary participation of all the people.

[5] Rashi suggests that מס (mas) does not mean forced labor but a monetary tribute laid on all citizens (the word is so used in Esther 10:1).

[6] So I. W. Slotki, in *Soncino Bible Commentary*, and Gray.

[7] The divergence is probably due to different sources utilized, but Rashi tries to harmonize the figures by suggesting that the extra 300 men were supervisors of the foremen.

[8] So Malbim.

[9] I. W. Slotki, in *Soncino Bible Commentary*, citing Skinner.

[10] But Targum and Septuagint consider the word גבלים (givlim) to denote special artisans.

[11] Ziv appears in the Tanach only here. A thorough analysis of the calendar has been provided by Julian Morgenstern in *HUCA* I, pp. 13-78; III, pp. 77-108; X, pp. 1-148.

[12] For a detailed description, with illustrations, see C. Meyers, *Anchor Bible Dictionary*, vol. 6, pp. 350-369.

[13] Leon Ritmeyer, "The Ark of the Covenant," BAR (January-February 1996), pp. 46 ff.

[14] See II Chronicles, chapter 3.

[15] So Ezekiel 41:5.

[16] B. Menachot 86b, but the Targum reverses the shape of the windows.

[17] Exodus 26:20 ff.

[18] So also JPS.

[19] II Samuel 7:12-16. Metzudat David and Malbim reconcile this by suggesting that the promise made to David has to be read together with the above passage: Only if Solomon would follow godly ways, would his house stand forever.

[20] It has been suggested that the Temple had originally been planned as a kind of prayer-annex to the much more magnificent royal palace.

[21] *Midrash Tehillim* (ed. Buber, 1891), 72, p. 324.

[22] Its origins are unclear, as is its age. There is also a German rendering of it and one in Russia, both in the 19th century, and both may have been based on oral tradition. On this issue see Ginzberg, *Legends of the Jews*, vol. 6, pp. 293 ff., note 57.

[23] A number of midrashim tell this tale; see, for example, *Numbers Rabbah* 14:13; *Song of Songs Rabbah* (Vilna, 1887), 1:1, 5.

Ezekiel, chapter 43, verses 10 to 27

Introduction

Connection of haftarah and sidra:

The sidra concludes with a description for building an incense altar in the desert Tabernacle. The haftarah is drawn from a section of Ezekiel (chapters 40-48) that describes the future sanctuary and its cult in detail, and gives detailed provisions for settlement in the restored land. Following on the description of the Prophet's visionary transportation to the new Temple (beginning in chapter 40; see the essay below), the haftarah presents Ezekiel's vision of an altar to be placed in the new Temple that will be built after the exile is over. Our haftarah begins immediately after the Prophet's declaration of the divine word, that the Israelites will not pollute this new Temple as they had the old one (44:9).

The setting:

Ezekiel lived in the days before and after the destruction of the First Temple and preached in the early part of the 6th century B.C.E. The haftarah belongs to the last nine chapters of his book, which contain Ezekiel's final prophecies. In 40:1 the prophecies are dated as having been delivered in the twenty-fifth year of the first exile, which began in 597.[1] Thus the year of this vision was 572.

For more on Ezekiel and his time, see our *General Introduction*.

The message:

After a brief introduction (verses 10 and 11) the Prophet relates his vision of the altar in minute detail (12 to 18), and then concludes with a description of the dedication ceremonies that are required. The haftarah specifies that only the levitical priests descended from Zadok will remain full priests. All the others whom Ezekiel holds to have been unfaithful are to be degraded (see the haftarah for Emor).

43:10. Now you, mortal, describe the Temple to the House of Israel. Let them measure its design. And let them be ashamed of their iniquities.

11. And when they are ashamed of what they have done, show them the plan of the Temple: its arrangement, its exits and entrances, and all its rules and regulations. Write it down in their sight, so that they can follow and keep its entire plan and its rules.

12. This is the law of the Temple: the whole area on top of the mountain, all around it, is most holy. Such is the law of the Temple.

13. Here are the dimensions of the altar, in cubits whose length is a cubit and a handbreadth. Its foundation shall be one cubit deep and a cubit wide, with a border around the edge measuring a span in width. This is the height of the altar.

43:10 אַתָּה בֶן־אָדָם הַגֵּד אֶת־בֵּית־יִשְׂרָאֵל אֶת־הַבַּיִת וְיִכָּלְמוּ מֵעֲוֺנוֹתֵיהֶם וּמָדְדוּ אֶת־תָּכְנִית:

11 וְאִם־נִכְלְמוּ מִכֹּל אֲשֶׁר־עָשׂוּ צוּרַת הַבַּיִת וּתְכוּנָתוֹ וּמוֹצָאָיו וּמוֹבָאָיו וְכָל־צוּרֹתָו וְאֵת כָּל־חֻקֹּתָיו וְכָל־צוּרֹתָו [צוּרֹתָיו] וְכָל־תּוֹרֹתָו [תּוֹרֹתָיו] הוֹדַע אוֹתָם וּכְתֹב לְעֵינֵיהֶם וְיִשְׁמְרוּ אֶת־כָּל־צוּרָתוֹ וְאֶת־כָּל־חֻקֹּתָיו וְעָשׂוּ אוֹתָם:

12 זֹאת תּוֹרַת הַבָּיִת עַל־רֹאשׁ הָהָר כָּל־גְּבֻלוֹ סָבִיב סָבִיב קֹדֶשׁ קָדָשִׁים הִנֵּה־זֹאת תּוֹרַת הַבָּיִת:

13 וְאֵלֶּה מִדּוֹת הַמִּזְבֵּחַ בָּאַמּוֹת אַמָּה אַמָּה וָטֹפַח וְחֵיק הָאַמָּה וְאַמָּה־רֹחַב וּגְבוּלָהּ אֶל־שְׂפָתָהּ סָבִיב זֶרֶת הָאֶחָד וְזֶה גַּב הַמִּזְבֵּחַ:

Commentary

43:10. *The Temple*. The Hebrew has simply הבית (*habayit*), literally, "the house" or "the dwelling." Elsewhere, biblical writers refer to "the House of the Eternal."[2]

Let them be ashamed. The exquisite nature of the design will awaken in the viewers a sense of guilt that they had forfeited so beautiful a structure through their past sins, which brought about the destruction of the Temple.

11. *Show them the plan*. Which was divinely revealed, as was the sanctuary that Moses erected.[3]

13. *Here are the dimensions*. They are, however, no longer clear, perhaps because the text became corrupted in the process of copying it over the centuries. Many interpreters have tried to visualize what Ezekiel had in mind, but have not been able to agree.

Cubits. The distance from a person's elbow to the tip of the middle finger. Since persons are of different sizes, one can speak only of averages. Generally, cubits were about 17 to 18 inches (43 to 46 centimeters) long, but Ezekiel specifies that the cubit he speaks about is a handbreadth larger, bringing it to about 20 1/2 inches (52 centimeters).

14. From the foundation on the ground to the lower ledge, two cubits, with a width of one cubit; from the smaller to the larger ledge, four cubits, with a width of one cubit.

15. The hearth shall be four cubits; and four horns are to rise up from the hearth.

16. The hearth shall be twelve cubits long and twelve cubits wide, squared in its four equal sides.

17. The ledge shall be a square of fourteen cubits by fourteen, with four equal sides, with a surrounding border of a half-cubit, and the surrounding base one cubit. Its ramp shall face the east.

18. Then God said to me: Mortal, thus says the Eternal God: These are the rules for the altar, on the day it is built, for offering whole burnt-offerings and for sprinkling blood on it:

14 וּמֵחֵיק הָאָרֶץ עַד־הָעֲזָרָה הַתַּחְתּוֹנָה שְׁתַּיִם אַמּוֹת וְרֹחַב אַמָּה אֶחָת וּמֵהָעֲזָרָה הַקְּטַנָּה עַד־הָעֲזָרָה הַגְּדוֹלָה אַרְבַּע אַמּוֹת וְרֹחַב הָאַמָּה:

15 וְהַהַרְאֵל אַרְבַּע אַמּוֹת וּמֵהָאֲרִאֵיל [וּמֵהָאֲרִיאֵל] וּלְמַעְלָה הַקְּרָנוֹת אַרְבַּע:

16 וְהָאֲרִאֵיל [וְהָאֲרִיאֵל] שְׁתֵּים עֶשְׂרֵה אֹרֶךְ בִּשְׁתֵּים עֶשְׂרֵה רֹחַב רָבוּעַ אֶל אַרְבַּעַת רְבָעָיו:

17 וְהָעֲזָרָה אַרְבַּע עֶשְׂרֵה אֹרֶךְ בְּאַרְבַּע עֶשְׂרֵה רֹחַב אֶל אַרְבַּעַת רְבָעֶיהָ וְהַגְּבוּל סָבִיב אוֹתָהּ חֲצִי הָאַמָּה וְהַחֵיק־לָהּ אַמָּה סָבִיב וּמַעֲלֹתֵהוּ פְּנוֹת קָדִים:

18 וַיֹּאמֶר אֵלַי בֶּן־אָדָם כֹּה אָמַר אֲדֹנָי יְהֹוִה אֵלֶּה חֻקּוֹת הַמִּזְבֵּחַ בְּיוֹם הֵעָשׂוֹתוֹ לְהַעֲלוֹת עָלָיו עוֹלָה וְלִזְרֹק עָלָיו דָּם:

Commentary

14. *Foundation on the ground.* Literally, "bosom of the earth." Ezekiel's expression reflects the idiom of his environment, which often referred to temples in such fashion.[4] We have here a metaphor standing for the idea that the altar's depth went to the bosom of the earth, while its top—the hearth, where the fire burnt—represented the heavens and was called *har-el,* mountain of God (verse 15). Ezekiel seems to have seen the ideal altar as a form of miniature temple, shaped like a ziggurat.[5] The Temple itself is a miniature of what later would be called "the universe."[6]

15. *Hearth.* Where the fire was built. The verse has two terms for it: הראל (*har-el,* mountain of God) and אריאל (*ari-el,* lion of God). Isaiah 29:1 uses Ariel as a metaphor for Jerusalem; and a Progressive synagogue in modern Jerusalem calls itself Har-El.

Four horns. As prescribed for the desert Tabernacle.[7] The horns, like the horns of a bull, represented strength. A horned altar has been excavated at Tel Beersheba.[8]

17. *Ramp.* Building an altar with steps was prohibited by the Torah.[9]

18. *Then God said to me.* Literally, "He." Since this vision is part of one large revelation that begins with chapter 40, the "He" may refer to the supernatural figure that spoke to the Prophet on top of the mountain.[10]

19. To the levitical priests who are descended from Zadok and therefore draw near to serve Me, says the Eternal God, give a young bull of the herd for a sin-offering.

20. Take some of its blood and put it on the four horns of the altar, the four corners of the ledge, and the surrounding border; thus shall you purify it and wipe it clean.

21. Then take the bull of the sin-offering and burn it in the appointed place in the Temple, outside the sanctuary.

22. On the next day, you shall offer a goat without blemish as a sin-offering, purifying the altar from sin as you purified it with the bull.

23. When you are done with the purification, offer a young bull of the herd and a ram from the flock, both without blemish.

24. Offer them to the Eternal. Let the priests throw salt on them, and sacrifice them as a whole burnt-offering to the Eternal.

25. Every day, for seven days, you shall provide a goat as a sin-offering, as well as a young bull of the herd and a ram from the flock; all of them must be without blemish.

19 וְנָתַתָּה אֶל־הַכֹּהֲנִים הַלְוִיִּם אֲשֶׁר הֵם מִזֶּרַע צָדוֹק הַקְּרֹבִים אֵלַי נְאֻם אֲדֹנָי יְהֹוִה לְשָׁרְתֵנִי פַּר בֶּן־בָּקָר לְחַטָּאת:

20 וְלָקַחְתָּ מִדָּמוֹ וְנָתַתָּה עַל־אַרְבַּע קַרְנֹתָיו וְאֶל־אַרְבַּע פִּנּוֹת הָעֲזָרָה וְאֶל־הַגְּבוּל סָבִיב וְחִטֵּאתָ אוֹתוֹ וְכִפַּרְתָּהוּ:

21 וְלָקַחְתָּ אֵת הַפָּר הַחַטָּאת וּשְׂרָפוֹ בְּמִפְקַד הַבַּיִת מִחוּץ לַמִּקְדָּשׁ:

22 וּבַיּוֹם הַשֵּׁנִי תַּקְרִיב שְׂעִיר־עִזִּים תָּמִים לְחַטָּאת וְחִטְּאוּ אֶת־הַמִּזְבֵּחַ כַּאֲשֶׁר חִטְּאוּ בַּפָּר:

23 בְּכַלּוֹתְךָ מֵחַטֵּא תַּקְרִיב פַּר בֶּן־בָּקָר תָּמִים וְאַיִל מִן־הַצֹּאן תָּמִים:

24 וְהִקְרַבְתָּם לִפְנֵי יְהֹוָה וְהִשְׁלִיכוּ הַכֹּהֲנִים עֲלֵיהֶם מֶלַח וְהֶעֱלוּ אוֹתָם עֹלָה לַיהֹוָה:

25 שִׁבְעַת יָמִים תַּעֲשֶׂה שְׂעִיר־חַטָּאת לַיּוֹם וּפַר בֶּן־בָּקָר וְאַיִל מִן־הַצֹּאן תְּמִימִם יַעֲשׂוּ:

Commentary

23. *Without blemish.* Only the best was to be offered; it was to be a "sacrifice," giving up something that had value.

24. *Whole burnt-offering.* An עלה (*olah*) was an offering that required the total burning of the animal (except for the skin), and nothing was to be eaten of it. The King James translation (written in 1611) rendered the word as "holocaust."

26. For seven days you are to purify the altar and cleanse it; then consecrate it.

27. When those days are past, from the eighth day onward, the priests shall present your burnt-offerings and your peace-offerings on the altar; and I will show you favor, says the Eternal God.

26 שִׁבְעַת יָמִים יְכַפֵּר עַל־הַמִּזְבֵּחַ וְטִהַרְתָּ אֹתוֹ וּמִלֵּאתָ יָדוֹ [יָדָיו]:

27 וִיכַלּוּ אֶת־הַיָּמִים וְהָיָה בַיּוֹם הַשְּׁמִינִי וָהָלְאָה יַעֲשׂוּ הַכֹּהֲנִים עַל־הַמִּזְבֵּחַ אֶת־עוֹלוֹתֵיכֶם וְאֶת־שַׁלְמֵיכֶם וְרָצִאתִי אֶתְכֶם נְאֻם אֲדֹנָי יְהֹוִה:

Commentary

26. *For seven days*. Repeating almost verbatim the prescription given in the Torah for consecrating the altar.[11]

Consecrate it. Literally, fill its hands, an expression derived from the ceremony of consecrating a priest.

27. *Peace-offerings*. שלמים (*sh'lamim*) were brought as thanksgiving offerings, as payment of vows or as a voluntary gifts.[12]

Others translate *sh'lamim* as "offerings of well-being"; both renderings reflect the root *sh-l-m*. Still another interpretation considers *sh'lamim* as a sacred gift of greeting, "offered when one greets another by saying 'shalom'!"[13] God is, so to speak, greeted as a guest at the meal.[14]

Essay

Verbalizing a vision

The two words "verbalizing" and "vision" reflect two different senses, and put together they represent an oxymoron. They are used here in order to demonstrate the impossibility of fully expressing in words what the eye has seen. However hard we try, we will at best come close, but seeing is a special sense, even as speaking is, and they are never congruous.

Therefore, when Ezekiel tried to tell the world what he had seen in a vision, he had to fall short of succeeding entirely. We do not know the true nature of his supernatural experience; it was in any case something utterly personal. He tells us at the beginning of chapter 40 that in his vision he had been transported from Babylon to Jerusalem, and there, on top of Mount Zion, a heavenly being who shone like copper had shown him the future Temple in all its glory. Our haftarah brings us a small part of this mystic happening, and when afterward the Prophet attempted to cast it into words he wanted to make sure that nothing he had seen would be lost—hence the meticulous details.

The rebuilding of the Temple was a matter of utmost importance to Ezekiel and therefore occupied an important part of his teachings. To him, ritual and ceremony were a vital aspect of Judaism, and the rebuilt Temple would concretize it.

To be sure, Ezekiel preached the central need for righteousness and personal responsibility as the core of religious living, but insisted on surrounding the core with fixed ritual, which served as a constant reminder of God's presence. Ritual without moral living was an empty gesture, and similarly, ethics without ritual was like a core without a protective shell and therefore bound for disintegration.

Thus, our haftarah challenges us to understand the thrust of the Prophet's mystic experience. The details of the altar may in themselves be without meaning today to most people, but to the Prophet's contemporaries his vision said a great deal. They hoped to return to their homeland and there rebuild God's holy shrine, and the very details that they heard confirmed the likelihood of its happening.

Gleanings

You, mortal

(Ezekiel is frequently addressed as *Ben Adam*, literally "son of Adam," which our translation renders as "mortal.") This appellation indicates that Ezekiel and all Israel in the Diaspora have a mission: to be priests to humanity and to bring it to a realization of the highest ideals of human beings given them with the name of Adam ["human"].

Mendel Hirsch[15]

A discrepancy

The builders of the Second Temple should have followed the prescriptions of Ezekiel's vision. But they had not sufficiently changed their Diaspora ways and went their own way.

Rashi, following the Talmud[16]

We cannot explain why in the actual building of the Second Temple by the returnees from Babylonian exile the prescriptions of this vision were not heeded. There can only be one explanation: Ezekiel's vision speaks of a messianic Third Temple.

Radak

The way the First Temple was built was clearly explained in the Book of Kings. But Ezekiel's vision was not fully clear to the builders of the Second Temple, and so they followed the model of the First.

Maimonides[17]

* * *

201

Notes

[1] See 40:1.

[2] The specialized term for the Jerusalem Temple, *Beit ha-Mikdash*, is first found in the Mishnah (3rd century C.E.), and was based on usage such as Ezekiel 44:7, in which *mikdash* (sacred precinct) and *bayit* (house) occur together in poetic parallelism.

[3] The divine revelation of Temple plans has ancient, pre-Israelite roots. See M. Weinfeld, *Deuteronomy and the Deuteronomic School*, pp. 246-250.

[4] The idiom "bosom of the earth" is Akkadian—that is, Assyro-Babylonian.

[5] The old Mesopotamian temple structure. This interpretation was suggested by W.F. Albright, *JBL*, vol. 39 (1920), pp. 137-142.

[6] J. Levenson, *Sinai and Zion*, pp. 142 ff.

[7] Exodus 27:2

[8] For details see the Torah Commentary, pp. 609-610.

[9] Exodus 20:23.

[10] Ezekiel 40:3.

[11] Exodus 29:37.

[12] A description of such offerings made by King Ahaz of Judah (late 8th century B.C.E.) is found in II Kings 16:12 ff.

[13] Baruch Levine in the JPS Torah Commentary, *Leviticus*, pp. 14-15. See also the explanation of Bernard J. Bamberger in the Torah Commentary, p. 765.

[14] On *sh'lamim*, see the Torah Commentary, p. 765.

[15] *The Haftoroth*, pp. 194-195.

[16] B. Sota 36a. Similarly the explanation by Rabbi Yom Tov Lipman Heller: "The builders of the Second Temple could not follow the prescriptions of Ezekiel. Their sinful ways prevented them, for they had not fulfilled the conditions laid down in Ezekiel 43:10-11." (Quoted by Issachar Jacobson, *Chazon Hamikra*, vol. 1, p. 211.)

[17] *Yad*, Hilchot Beit Habechirah 1:4.

First Kings, chapter 18, verses 1 to 39

Introduction

Connection of sidra and haftarah:

Both Torah and haftarah deal with seminal crises in the religious life of Israel. Moses confronts the consequences of the worship of the Golden Calf, and Elijah battles the priests of Baal whom Queen Jezebel had installed.

There is another connection. "The parallel is found in Israel's irresolution, in their halting between two opinions, between following God and Baal .... In accordance with the Sephardic rite, the haftarah is limited to verses 20-39, thus focusing on this parallelism more directly."[1]

The setting:

Along with King David, the prophet Elijah is the most popular hero in Jewish history. He lived in the 9th century B.C.E. amid the semi-nomads in Gilead, east of the Jordan, and beheld with horror the official introduction of the Baal cult in his nation. The ruling king of Israel (which comprised the northern ten tribes) was Ahab, who had married Jezebel, a princess from Tyre. She brought into the union strong convictions about her own religion, and soon Baal worship became a common feature of the nation. For Elijah, battling the foreign cult and preserving a measure of social justice were the prime goals of his ministry.

The haftarah is taken from the First Book of Kings.[2] For more on the book see our *General Introduction*; on Elijah, see the essay below.

Content of the haftarah:

1. In the midst of a crippling drought, the King and his servant Obadiah go on a search for water sources. (1-6)
2. Obadiah meets the Prophet Elijah and is requested to arrange a meeting between the Prophet and the King. (7-15)
3. The two meet and Elijah asks the King to set up a contest between God's Prophet and the priests of Baal. (16-19)
4. The dramatic contest. (20-39)

HAFTARAH FOR KI TISSA

First Kings, chapter 18, verses 1 to 39

1. After many days, in the third year [of the drought], the word of the Eternal came to Elijah: Go, show yourself to [King] Ahab, and I will send rain onto the earth.

2. Elijah went to present himself to Ahab. The famine in Samaria was severe.

3. So Ahab had called in Obadiah, the man in charge of the Palace—Obadiah was a man who greatly honored the Eternal:

4. for example, when [Queen] Jezebel was persecuting the prophets loyal to the Eternal, Obadiah took one hundred of them of them and hid them, fifty to a cave, and sustained them with food and drink.

5. Now Ahab said to Obadiah: Go around the country, to every spring and wadi; perhaps we may find enough grass to keep alive the horses and mules, so that we do not lose all our animals.

6. They then divided up the land between them for the search; Ahab would go one way, Obadiah the other.

18:1 וַיְהִי֙ יָמִ֣ים רַבִּ֔ים וּדְבַר־יְהֹוָ֗ה הָיָה֙ אֶל־אֵ֣לִיָּ֔הוּ בַּשָּׁנָ֥ה הַשְּׁלִישִׁ֖ית לֵאמֹ֑ר לֵ֚ךְ הֵֽרָאֵ֣ה אֶל־אַחְאָ֔ב וְאֶתְּנָ֥ה מָטָ֖ר עַל־פְּנֵ֥י הָאֲדָמָֽה:

2 וַיֵּ֙לֶךְ֙ אֵ֣לִיָּ֔הוּ לְהֵרָא֖וֹת אֶל־אַחְאָ֑ב וְהָרָעָ֖ב חָזָ֥ק בְּשֹׁמְרֽוֹן:

3 וַיִּקְרָ֣א אַחְאָ֔ב אֶל־עֹבַדְיָ֖הוּ אֲשֶׁ֣ר עַל־הַבָּ֑יִת וְעֹבַדְיָ֗הוּ הָיָ֥ה יָרֵ֛א אֶת־יְהֹוָ֖ה מְאֹֽד:

4 וַיְהִי֙ בְּהַכְרִ֣ית אִיזֶ֔בֶל אֵ֖ת נְבִיאֵ֣י יְהֹוָ֑ה וַיִּקַּ֨ח עֹבַדְיָ֜הוּ מֵאָ֣ה נְבִאִ֗ים וַֽיַּחְבִּיאֵ֞ם חֲמִשִּׁ֥ים אִישׁ֙ בַּמְּעָרָ֔ה וְכִלְכְּלָ֖ם לֶ֥חֶם וָמָֽיִם:

5 וַיֹּ֤אמֶר אַחְאָב֙ אֶל־עֹ֣בַדְיָ֔הוּ לֵ֥ךְ בָּאָ֖רֶץ אֶל־כָּל־מַעְיְנֵ֤י הַמַּ֙יִם֙ וְאֶ֣ל כָּל־הַנְּחָלִ֔ים אוּלַ֣י ׀ נִמְצָ֣א חָצִ֗יר וּנְחַיֶּה֙ ס֣וּס וָפֶ֔רֶד וְל֥וֹא נַכְרִ֖ית מֵהַבְּהֵמָֽה:

6 וַֽיְחַלְּק֥וּ לָהֶ֛ם אֶת־הָאָ֖רֶץ לַֽעֲבָר־בָּ֑הּ אַחְאָ֞ב הָלַ֨ךְ בְּדֶ֤רֶךְ אֶחָד֙ לְבַדּ֔וֹ וְעֹבַדְיָ֛הוּ הָלַ֥ךְ בְּדֶֽרֶךְ־אֶחָ֖ד לְבַדּֽוֹ:

Commentary

1. *I will send rain.* Though the Prophet had issued a warning that no rain would come to the land until he, Elijah, would say so.[3] A severe drought was mentioned also in the chronicles of neighboring Tyre.

3. *Obadiah.* Because there is also a prophet by that name (a fragment of whose writings is included in the Tanach), the Talmud speculates that the two were the same person.[4]

4. *One hundred of them.* They appear to have been an organized religious underground movement.

To a cave. Probably in the caves of Atlit, near Mount Carmel.

5-6. The story of King Ahab and his counselor searching for water, each one proceeding alone, has a fairy-tale flavor that underlines their utter desperation.

7. Once on his way, Obadiah was unexpectedly met by Elijah. Recognizing him, Obadiah bowed low, saying: Is it really you, my lord Elijah?

8. He answered: It is I. Go tell your master that Elijah has come.

9. Obadiah said: How have I wronged you, that you are handing me over to Ahab to be killed?

10. As the Eternal your God, lives, I tell you that there is not a nation or a country to which my lord [Ahab] has not sent to look for you. When they said you were not there, he made them swear to it.

11. And now you say: *Go tell your master that Elijah has come!*

12. The minute I leave you the spirit of the Eternal might carry you off, who knows where; and when I go tell Ahab [that you have returned] and he cannot find you, he will surely kill me, I who from childhood on have revered the Eternal.

7 וַיְהִי עֹבַדְיָהוּ בַּדֶּרֶךְ וְהִנֵּה אֵלִיָּהוּ לִקְרָאתוֹ וַיַּכִּרֵהוּ וַיִּפֹּל עַל־פָּנָיו וַיֹּאמֶר הַאַתָּה זֶה אֲדֹנִי אֵלִיָּהוּ:

8 וַיֹּאמֶר לוֹ אָנִי לֵךְ אֱמֹר לַאדֹנֶיךָ הִנֵּה אֵלִיָּהוּ:

9 וַיֹּאמֶר מֶה חָטָאתִי כִּי־אַתָּה נֹתֵן אֶת־עַבְדְּךָ בְּיַד־אַחְאָב לַהֲמִיתֵנִי:

10 חַי יְהוָה אֱלֹהֶיךָ אִם־יֶשׁ־גּוֹי וּמַמְלָכָה אֲשֶׁר לֹא־שָׁלַח אֲדֹנִי שָׁם לְבַקֶּשְׁךָ וְאָמְרוּ אָיִן וְהִשְׁבִּיעַ אֶת־הַמַּמְלָכָה וְאֶת־הַגּוֹי כִּי לֹא יִמְצָאֶכָּה:

11 וְעַתָּה אַתָּה אֹמֵר לֵךְ אֱמֹר לַאדֹנֶיךָ הִנֵּה אֵלִיָּהוּ:

12 וְהָיָה אֲנִי אֵלֵךְ מֵאִתָּךְ וְרוּחַ יְהוָה יִשָּׂאֲךָ עַל אֲשֶׁר לֹא־אֵדָע וּבָאתִי לְהַגִּיד לְאַחְאָב וְלֹא יִמְצָאֲךָ וַהֲרָגָנִי וְעַבְדְּךָ יָרֵא אֶת־יְהוָה מִנְּעֻרָי:

Commentary

7. *Unexpectedly.* Elijah had a way of coming suddenly into view and then disappearing again. It is precisely this unpredictability of the Prophet's movements that worries Obadiah (verses 9-12).

10. *Nation.* גוֹי (goy) is a term that in the Tanach is applied equally to Israel and other nations; its sole application to non-Jewish people is a post-biblical development.

When they said you were not there. Obadiah seems to imply that there were extradition treaties between Israel and other nations, but no such contracts have been discovered. There is an example of an extradition clause in a much older agreement between the Hittites and Egyptians.[5]

12. *He will surely kill me.* He will use whatever means available to get his way,[6] which makes Elijah's coming confrontation with the King that much more remarkable.

13. Have you not heard what I did when Jezebel was slaughtering the prophets loyal to the Eternal, how I hid a hundred of them in a cave, in two groups of fifty, and sustained them with food and drink?

14. Yet now you say: *Go tell your master that Elijah has come.* He will surely kill me.

15. Elijah answered: As the Eternal, the God of heaven's hosts, lives, and before whom I stand [as servant], I tell you that today I will appear before him.

16. So Obadiah went to find Ahab, and told him [that Elijah had returned]; and Ahab went to meet Elijah.

17. The minute Ahab saw Elijah he said: Is this indeed you, the troubler of Israel!

18. And Elijah answered: I am not the one who has made trouble for Israel—you have, you and your father's house, by turning away from the commandments of the Eternal, and following the Baals.

13 הֲלֹא־הֻגַּד לַאדֹנִי אֵת אֲשֶׁר־עָשִׂיתִי בַּהֲרֹג אִיזֶבֶל אֵת נְבִיאֵי יְהֹוָה וָאַחְבִּא מִנְּבִיאֵי יְהֹוָה מֵאָה אִישׁ חֲמִשִּׁים חֲמִשִּׁים אִישׁ בַּמְּעָרָה וָאֲכַלְכְּלֵם לֶחֶם וָמָיִם:

14 וְעַתָּה אַתָּה אֹמֵר לֵךְ אֱמֹר לַאדֹנֶיךָ הִנֵּה אֵלִיָּהוּ וַהֲרָגָנִי:

15 וַיֹּאמֶר אֵלִיָּהוּ חַי יְהֹוָה צְבָאוֹת אֲשֶׁר עָמַדְתִּי לְפָנָיו כִּי הַיּוֹם אֵרָאֶה אֵלָיו:

16 וַיֵּלֶךְ עֹבַדְיָהוּ לִקְרַאת אַחְאָב וַיַּגֶּד־לוֹ וַיֵּלֶךְ אַחְאָב לִקְרַאת אֵלִיָּהוּ:

17 וַיְהִי כִּרְאוֹת אַחְאָב אֶת־אֵלִיָּהוּ וַיֹּאמֶר אַחְאָב אֵלָיו הַאַתָּה זֶה עֹכֵר יִשְׂרָאֵל:

18 וַיֹּאמֶר לֹא עָכַרְתִּי אֶת־יִשְׂרָאֵל כִּי אִם־אַתָּה וּבֵית אָבִיךָ בַּעֲזָבְכֶם אֶת־מִצְוֹת יְהֹוָה וַתֵּלֶךְ אַחֲרֵי הַבְּעָלִים:

Commentary

15. *The Eternal, the God of heaven's hosts.* יהוה צבאות (*adonai tz'va'ot*), literally "God of the armies." The term was at first meant to describe the divine protector of Israel's soldiers,[7] but later became a figure of speech denoting God's rule over the angelic hosts, or "all-powerful God."[8]

17. *Troubler of Israel.* Either a reference to Elijah having caused the drought or, more likely, to the Prophet's interference with royal privilege.

18. *Baals.* There were a number of different gods who were called Baal (literally, master or ruler). Thus, Hadad was adored as the Baal who defeated the rebellious waters.[9] Some scholars believe that the name "Carmel" originally described a rain-Baal of that name who was identified with the mountain, and that Elijah wanted to demonstrate the Eternal's superiority in the very domain of a Baal. In Assyrian annals, Mount Carmel is referred to as Ba'li-ra'si, meaning "Baal of the (head-shaped) promontory."[10]

19. Now send, gather for me all Israel at Mount Carmel, and the four hundred and fifty prophets of Baal and the four hundred prophets of Asherah who dine at Jezebel's table.

20. Ahab called all Israel together and gathered the prophets at Mount Carmel.

21. Elijah stepped forward and said to the people: How long are you going to hop between two opinions? If the Eternal is God, follow the Eternal; if Baal is God, follow Baal!

The people made no answer.

22. Then Elijah said: I am the only prophet of the Eternal left, and there are four hundred and fifty prophets of Baal.

23. Let us have a couple of bulls. They can choose one, chop it up and lay the pieces on the wood, but do not put a fire underneath it, and I will prepare the other bull, lay it on the wood without putting fire under it.

19 וְעַתָּ֗ה שְׁלַ֞ח קְבֹ֤ץ אֵלַי֙ אֶת־כָּל־יִשְׂרָאֵ֔ל אֶל־הַ֖ר הַכַּרְמֶ֑ל וְאֶת־נְבִיאֵ֨י הַבַּ֜עַל אַרְבַּ֧ע מֵא֣וֹת וַחֲמִשִּׁ֗ים וּנְבִיאֵ֤י הָאֲשֵׁרָה֙ אַרְבַּ֣ע מֵא֔וֹת אֹכְלֵ֖י שֻׁלְחַ֥ן אִיזָֽבֶל׃

20 וַיִּשְׁלַ֥ח אַחְאָ֖ב בְּכָל־בְּנֵ֣י יִשְׂרָאֵ֑ל וַיִּקְבֹּ֥ץ אֶת־הַנְּבִיאִ֖ים אֶל־הַ֥ר הַכַּרְמֶֽל׃

21 וַיִּגַּ֨שׁ אֵלִיָּ֜הוּ אֶל־כָּל־הָעָ֗ם וַיֹּ֙אמֶר֙ עַד־מָתַ֞י אַתֶּ֣ם פֹּסְחִים֮ עַל־שְׁתֵּ֣י הַסְּעִפִּים֒ אִם־יְהוָ֤ה הָאֱלֹהִים֙ לְכ֣וּ אַחֲרָ֔יו וְאִם־הַבַּ֖עַל לְכ֣וּ אַחֲרָ֑יו וְלֹא־עָנ֥וּ הָעָ֛ם אֹת֖וֹ דָּבָֽר׃

22 וַיֹּ֤אמֶר אֵלִיָּ֙הוּ֙ אֶל־הָעָ֔ם אֲנִ֞י נוֹתַ֤רְתִּי נָבִ֣יא לַיהוָ֖ה לְבַדִּ֑י וּנְבִיאֵ֣י הַבַּ֔עַל אַרְבַּע־מֵא֥וֹת וַחֲמִשִּׁ֖ים אִֽישׁ׃

23 וְיִתְּנוּ־לָ֜נוּ שְׁנַ֣יִם פָּרִים֮ וְיִבְחֲר֣וּ לָהֶ֣ם הַפָּ֣ר הָאֶחָד֒ וִינַתְּחֻ֗הוּ וְיָשִׂ֙ימוּ֙ עַל־הָ֣עֵצִ֔ים וְאֵ֖שׁ לֹ֣א יָשִׂ֑ימוּ וַאֲנִ֞י אֶעֱשֶׂ֣ה ׀ אֶת־הַפָּ֣ר הָאֶחָ֗ד וְנָֽתַתִּי֙ עַל־הָ֣עֵצִ֔ים וְאֵ֖שׁ לֹ֥א אָשִֽׂים׃

Commentary

19. *All Israel*. As many as would come, but especially the leadership.

Asherah. A Near Eastern goddess whose worship is documented as early as the second millennium B.C.E. She is depicted as a creator and mother of many gods. (See further under *Gleanings*, below.)

Who dine at Jezebel's table. Who were financially supported by the Queen. However, they did not appear to take part in the ensuing contest.[11]

20. Sephardim start the haftarah here.

21. *Hop between two opinions*. The Hebrew means literally "two branches"; Elijah evokes the image of a hopping bird.[12]

Follow the Eternal. Literally "Him."

23. *They can choose one*. Thereby making sure that neither bull has been tampered with.

24. You then call upon your god and I will call upon the Eternal; the one who answers by fire is the real God.

The people answered: Well said!

25. Then Elijah said to the prophets of Baal: Since there are so many of you, you take a bull and prepare it first. Call on your god, but don't set fire to the wood.

26. They took the bull that was given them, prepared it, and called on Baal from morning to noon, shouting: *Answer us, Baal!* But there was no sound, no answer, as they did their hopping dance around the altar that had been set up.

27. At midday, Elijah began to mock them, saying: Call louder—he is a god: maybe he's thinking, or has gone off to the privy, or maybe he's asleep and will wake up!

28. So they raised their voices, cutting themselves with knives and lances, as was their practice, until blood flowed.

29. And they raved on from noon until [mid-afternoon,] the time when grain is offered [in the Temple]; but there was no voice, no sound, no sign of attention.

כד וּקְרָאתֶ֞ם בְּשֵׁ֣ם אֱלֹֽהֵיכֶ֗ם וַֽאֲנִי֙ אֶקְרָ֣א בְשֵׁם־יְהֹוָ֔ה וְהָיָ֧ה הָֽאֱלֹהִ֛ים אֲשֶׁר־יַֽעֲנֶ֥ה בָאֵ֖שׁ ה֣וּא הָֽאֱלֹהִ֑ים וַיַּ֧עַן כָּל־הָעָ֛ם וַיֹּֽאמְר֖וּ ט֥וֹב הַדָּבָֽר:

כה וַיֹּ֨אמֶר אֵֽלִיָּ֜הוּ לִנְבִיאֵ֣י הַבַּ֗עַל בַּֽחֲר֨וּ לָכֶ֜ם הַפָּ֤ר הָֽאֶחָד֙ וַֽעֲשׂ֣וּ רִֽאשֹׁנָ֔ה כִּ֥י אַתֶּ֖ם הָֽרַבִּ֑ים וְקִרְאוּ֙ בְּשֵׁ֣ם אֱלֹֽהֵיכֶ֔ם וְאֵ֖שׁ לֹ֥א תָשִֽׂימוּ:

כו וַ֠יִּקְח֠וּ אֶת־הַפָּ֨ר אֲשֶׁר־נָתַ֣ן לָהֶם֮ וַֽיַּעֲשׂוּ֒ וַיִּקְרְא֣וּ בְשֵׁם־הַבַּ֡עַל מֵֽהַבֹּ֣קֶר וְעַד־הַצָּהֳרַ֩יִם֩ לֵאמֹ֨ר הַבַּ֤עַל עֲנֵ֨נוּ֙ וְאֵ֥ין ק֖וֹל וְאֵ֣ין עֹנֶ֑ה וַֽיְפַסְּח֔וּ עַל־הַמִּזְבֵּ֖חַ אֲשֶׁ֥ר עָשָֽׂה:

כז וַיְהִ֨י בַֽצָּהֳרַ֜יִם וַיְהַתֵּ֧ל בָּהֶ֣ם אֵֽלִיָּ֗הוּ וַיֹּ֨אמֶר֙ קִרְא֤וּ בְקֽוֹל־גָּדוֹל֙ כִּֽי־אֱלֹהִ֣ים ה֔וּא כִּ֣י שִׂ֧יחַ וְכִי־שִׂ֛יג ל֖וֹ וְכִי־דֶ֣רֶךְ ל֑וֹ אוּלַ֛י יָשֵׁ֥ן ה֖וּא וְיִקָֽץ:

כח וַיִּקְרְאוּ֙ בְּק֣וֹל גָּד֔וֹל וַיִּתְגֹּֽדְד֗וּ כְּמִשְׁפָּטָ֛ם בַּֽחֲרָב֖וֹת וּבָֽרְמָחִ֑ים עַד־שְׁפָךְ־דָּ֖ם עֲלֵיהֶֽם:

כט וַיְהִ֗י כַּֽעֲבֹר֙ הַצָּ֣הֳרַ֔יִם וַיִּֽתְנַבְּא֔וּ עַ֖ד לַֽעֲל֣וֹת הַמִּנְחָ֑ה וְאֵֽין־ק֥וֹל וְאֵֽין־עֹנֶ֖ה וְאֵ֥ין קָֽשֶׁב:

Commentary

24. *Who answers by fire.* God had been revealed to Israel in the midst of fire when they stood at Mount Sinai. [13]

27. *Maybe he's thinking or ... off to the privy.* Others, "in conversation or detained."

28. *Until blood flowed.* This mantic practice, believed to induce a state of ecstasy, was expressly forbidden by the Torah, as unbefitting a holy people. [14] (See further under *Gleanings*, below.)

29. *Raved on.* The verb form suggests "prophesying in ecstasy."

30. Then Elijah said to all the people:
Come closer to me, and they gathered
around him. Elijah then repaired the
damaged altar of the Eternal.

31. He took twelve stones, one for each of
the tribes of the sons of Jacob—to whom
the word of the Eternal had come, saying:
Your name shall be Israel—

32. and with these stones he built an altar
in the name of the Eternal. Around the
altar he made a trench large enough [to
plant] two measures of seed.

33. He then arranged the wood, sliced up
the bull, and laid the pieces on the wood.

34. Then he said: Fill four jars of water and
pour it over the burnt-offering and the
wood. Then he said: Do it again; and they
did it a second time. Do it a third time, he
said; and they did it a third time.

35. The water ran down around the altar
and even filled the trench.

36. At the time of the [afternoon] grain-
offering, the prophet Elijah came forward
and said: Eternal One, God of Abraham,
Isaac, and Israel, make it known today that
You are God in Israel, and that I am Your
servant, that I have done all these things at
Your command.

30 וַיֹּ֨אמֶר אֵלִיָּ֤הוּ לְכָל־הָעָם֙ גְּשׁ֣וּ אֵלַ֔י וַיִּגְּשׁ֥וּ
כָל־הָעָ֖ם אֵלָ֑יו וַיְרַפֵּ֛א אֶת־מִזְבַּ֥ח יְהוָ֖ה
הֶהָרֽוּס׃

31 וַיִּקַּ֣ח אֵלִיָּ֗הוּ שְׁתֵּ֤ים עֶשְׂרֵה֙ אֲבָנִ֔ים
כְּמִסְפַּ֖ר שִׁבְטֵ֣י בְנֵֽי־יַעֲקֹ֑ב אֲשֶׁר֩ הָיָ֨ה דְבַר־
יְהוָ֤ה אֵלָיו֙ לֵאמֹ֔ר יִשְׂרָאֵ֖ל יִהְיֶ֥ה שְׁמֶֽךָ׃

32 וַיִּבְנֶ֧ה אֶת־הָאֲבָנִ֛ים מִזְבֵּ֖חַ בְּשֵׁ֣ם יְהוָ֑ה וַיַּ֣עַשׂ
תְּעָלָ֗ה כְּבֵית֙ סָאתַ֣יִם זֶ֔רַע סָבִ֖יב לַמִּזְבֵּֽחַ׃

33 וַֽיַּעֲרֹ֖ךְ אֶת־הָֽעֵצִ֑ים וַיְנַתַּח֙ אֶת־הַפָּ֔ר וַיָּ֖שֶׂם
עַל־הָעֵצִֽים׃

34 וַיֹּ֗אמֶר מִלְא֨וּ אַרְבָּעָ֤ה כַדִּים֙ מַ֔יִם וְיִֽצְק֥וּ
עַל־הָעֹלָ֖ה וְעַל־הָעֵצִ֑ים וַיֹּ֤אמֶר שְׁנוּ֙ וַיִּשְׁנ֔וּ
וַיֹּ֥אמֶר שַׁלֵּ֖שׁוּ וַיְשַׁלֵּֽשׁוּ׃

35 וַיֵּלְכ֣וּ הַמַּ֔יִם סָבִ֖יב לַמִּזְבֵּ֑חַ וְגַ֥ם אֶת־
הַתְּעָלָ֖ה מִלֵּא־מָֽיִם׃

36 וַיְהִ֣י ׀ בַּעֲל֣וֹת הַמִּנְחָ֗ה וַיִּגַּ֞שׁ אֵלִיָּ֣הוּ הַנָּבִיא֮
וַיֹּאמַר֒ יְהוָ֗ה אֱלֹהֵי֙ אַבְרָהָם֙ יִצְחָ֣ק וְיִשְׂרָאֵ֔ל
הַיּ֣וֹם יִוָּדַ֗ע כִּֽי־אַתָּ֧ה אֱלֹהִ֛ים בְּיִשְׂרָאֵ֖ל וַאֲנִ֣י
עַבְדֶּ֑ךָ וּבִדְבָרֶ֖יךָ [וּבִדְבָֽרְךָ] עָשִׂ֔יתִי אֵ֖ת כָּל־
הַדְּבָרִ֥ים הָאֵֽלֶּה׃

Commentary

30. *Repaired the damaged altar.* Rashi suggests that it had been built by Saul,[15] but
apparently had been damaged later on or used for pagan sacrifices. The repair performed by
Elijah may have been of a spiritual nature, accomplished by rededicating it anew to God.[16]

31. *Twelve stones.* Symbolizing the rededication.

37. Answer me, Eternal One, answer me, and let this people know that You, the Eternal, are God, and that You were the One who turned their hearts backward.

38. The lightning of the Eternal came down and burned up the sacrifice, the wood, the stones, and the dust; it licked up the water in the trench as well.

39. When they saw this, all the people threw themselves to the ground and cried out: *The Eternal alone is God; the Eternal alone is God!*

37 עֲנֵנִי יְהֹוָה עֲנֵנִי וְיֵדְעוּ הָעָם הַזֶּה כִּי־אַתָּה יְהֹוָה הָאֱלֹהִים וְאַתָּה הֲסִבֹּתָ אֶת־לִבָּם אֲחֹרַנִּית:

38 וַתִּפֹּל אֵשׁ־יְהֹוָה וַתֹּאכַל אֶת־הָעֹלָה וְאֶת־הָעֵצִים וְאֶת־הָאֲבָנִים וְאֶת־הֶעָפָר וְאֶת־הַמַּיִם אֲשֶׁר־בַּתְּעָלָה לִחֵכָה:

39 וַיַּרְא כָּל־הָעָם וַיִּפְּלוּ עַל־פְּנֵיהֶם וַיֹּאמְרוּ יְהֹוָה הוּא הָאֱלֹהִים יְהֹוָה הוּא הָאֱלֹהִים:

Commentary

37. *You were the One.* See NJPS. Elijah boldly makes God co-responsible for the aberration of Israel, an argument reminiscent of Abraham confronting God;[17] and also recalling the story of the Egyptian plagues, where we are told that God "hardened Pharaoh's heart."[18] He now forces God's hand, so to speak, to perform the miracle that validates both God and the Prophet. The text can, however, be construed differently: "You are the One who will turn their hearts back [to You]."[19]

38. *Lightning … came down.* See the haftarah for Va'eira for a discussion of prophetic miracles.

The trench. The altar was built after the biblical model.[20]

39. *The Eternal alone is God.* This confession of faith is recited seven times at the conclusion of the Yom Kippur service, and is also spoken by a dying person.

Essay

The man Elijah

Who was this man who captured the imagination of his people as no one else did—not even Moses or David?

He appears in the book of Kings quite suddenly and without introduction; there is only a brief note in 17:1, which gives us not even the name of his progenitor but a mere (and unclear) indication where he came from. He is simply called Elijah the Tishbite אליהו התשבי (*eliyahu ha-tishbi*); but "Tishbi" is not—as the Septuagint and later translations have it—the name of any city. The biblical text explains it by using the consonants of תשב, explaining that he belonged to the תשבי גלעד (*toshavei gil'ad*, the sojourners of Gilead).[21]

The vagueness of these references, his sudden appearances and disappearances, added to the mystique that surrounded him, and legends were spun about his deeds and miracles. His assumption into heaven on a fiery chariot convinced the people that he would return to earth, and the final words of the prophet Malachi stamped him as a forerunner of the day of judgment. While there were various talmudic statements that tried to counter the cult of Elijah, they did not succeed, and the Talmud itself repeatedly recorded the saying that all difficult legal questions will in time be solved by Elijah. Legends have him appear in many places and times, and the Passover Haggadah includes the well-known ritual of setting aside a cup for Elijah and opening the door for him, so that he may join the celebrants.

However, it was not the miracles ascribed to him that endeared him to his people—more miracles were ascribed to his disciple, Elisha. It was not even his purist loyalty to the One God, to whom he had committed his life. What distinguished him above all was his unequaled courage to stand up to a king and queen who sought his life, and his advocacy of the rights of the ordinary citizen who, like Naboth, was helpless when facing royal power.

Elijah was in every way a warrior for the common folk. He was hunted and became a refugee, never to be found twice in the same place. His very attire bespoke the simple man: he would confront the authorities dressed in leather loin cloth and haircloth mantle. He came from the periphery of society and always preserved the perspective that an outsider's stance afforded him.

When Malachi, in his final oration, identified him as an immortal who would be the harbinger of end-time, he confirmed the superhuman stature of the guarantor of future generations:

Behold, I will send you Elijah the prophet,
before the coming of the great and terrible day of the Eternal,
to turn the hearts of parents to their children,
and the hearts of children to their parents ....[22]

Gleanings

Words to Remember

יהוה הוא האלהים (*adonai hu ha-elohim*), The Eternal alone is God! (18:39)

The archaeological trail

In the late 1970s, Israeli archaeologists discovered Hebrew inscriptions from the biblical period in the Sinai desert and in the vicinity of Hebron, one of which reads: "I have blessed you by YHVH [the Eternal] of Samaria and *ashrth*." This last word has been variously understood as "His [the Eternal's] Asherah"; or "its [the city of Samaria's] Asherah"; or as "Asheratah," a variant pronunciation of Asherah. The matter is further complicated by the attestation in the Torah of *asherah* as an illicit cultic object. [23]

In our haftarah, the association of Ahab and Jezebel (whose capital was the city of Samaria, named in the inscription) with Asherah is significant. Whereas the haftarah links Asherah to Baal, the ancient Hebrew inscriptions may show that some Israelites believed that the Eternal had a consort, a notion that would have been anathema to Elijah.

S. D. Sperling[24]

In praise of the Prophet

How wonderful you were, Elijah, in your miracles!
Who else could boast of such deeds?
By the word of the Almighty
You redeemed a corpse from death and the grave ....
You were taken to heaven in a storm of fire,
In a chariot drawn by horses of fire ....
It is written:
You will come without warning at the appointed time,
To soften the divine wrath before its final fury,
To reconcile parents and children,
And restore the tribes of Jacob.

Ben Sirach[25]

Our animals

Ahab and Obadiah go out to find grass for horses and mules (verse 5). Even though people may not be worthy of rain, it comes for the sake of animals. They, unlike humans, have no choice between good and evil, and therefore nature must provide for them, even though this may also benefit undeserving humans.

Malbim

The willing and the unwilling

"Ahab called all Israel together and gathered the prophets at Mount Carmel" (verse 20).

Ahab "called" the people, and they came of their own accord. But he "gathered" the prophets of Baal, which means that he had to bring them against their will.

Radak

Self-mutilation

The practice of self-mutilation by Tyrian priests as a means of inducing ecstasy is attested by ancient writers. It is interesting to compare the inscription of a Roman eyewitness with 19th century accounts of fanatical dervishes who rouse themselves to a state of ecstasy through music, shouting, and self-mutilation.

The gulf that separates Hebrew prophecy (from such activities) goes far beyond stimulating inspiration. Hebrew prophecy has moved human conscience because the Hebrew prophets have identified themselves with the will of a God of Justice who wants us to build a just and humane society.

Leo L. Honor[26]

Elijah was not alone

Elijah's power of intercession would not have brought about the miracle had not the people hoped that God would be vindicated. But because *"all* the people" (verse 39) were prepared to shout "The Eternal One alone is God!" the fire fell from heaven.

Talmud[27]

Elijah in Christian and Muslim traditions

Jesus proclaimed John the Baptist to have been a reincarnation of Elijah.[28]

In Islam, Elijah (Ilyas) was one of the messengers sent by God to admonish people not to worship Baal, and he is mentioned among the righteous.[29]

* * *

Notes

[1] Leo L. Honor, *Book of Kings I*, p. 254.

[2] In the Septuagint, it is called the Third Book of Kingdoms, while I and II Samuel are called I and II Kingdoms.

[3] I Kings 17:1. While some traditional commentators see this as a demonstration of God's compassion, in view of the people's suffering, others tried to harmonize the Prophet's stern announcement with the divine order. Thus, Malbim says that the divine command really means: Go to Ahab, persuade him that he and his people must repent, and I will provide rain for the country.

[4] *B.* Sanhedrin 39b. See also the haftarah for Vayishlach (2).

[5] Pritchard, pp. 201-205. The Talmud (*B.* Megillah 11a) is therefore most likely right when it interprets the text as meaning that Ahab had made friendly inquiries; see also Radak and Ralbag.

[6] Ahab would, for instance, frame an innocent man to get hold of his property (I Kings 21).

[7] See I Samuel 17:45.

[8] So Gray, p. 349, citing Wambacq.

[9] So the cuneiform texts found in Ras Shamra (Ugarit), on the Mediterranean Sea.

[10] M. Astour, *Interpreter's Dictionary*, Supplement, p.141; also Noth, p. 242, note 6. Tacitus refers to a Carmel sanctuary; *Histories* II 78. Queen Jezebel's personal god was likely Baal Melkart, the divinity of her hometown, Tyre.

[11] Radak and Ralbag speculate that Jezebel did not allow them to participate.

[12] Compare Job 4:13; 20:2. But the Septuagint translates: "How long will you be lame on both knee joints," taking the meaning of the verb from II Samuel 4:4.

[13] Exodus 19:18.

[14] Leviticus 19:28; Deuteronomy 14:1. For such practices in Tyre, see Honor, p. 262.

[15] See I Samuel 15:12.

[16] So Radak and Metzudat David.

[17] Genesis 18:23 and following.

[18] Exodus 4:21 and similar passages in the story; for an explanation, see the Torah Commentary, pp. 416-417. The question of human free will is not at issue; see Maimonides, *Yad*, Hilchot Teshuvah, 6:3. Elijah pleads with God to reopen the gates of repentance, which had been shut because the sins of the people had become too great.

[19] Compare NEB, NRSV.

[20] Leviticus 9:24.

[21] Nelson Glueck suggested that there had been a transposition of consonants, and that the text had not read *tishbi* but *yibshi*, and that Elijah stemmed from Jabesh-Gilead ("Explorations ..." part I, pp. 218, 225-227).

[22] Malachi 3:23-24; see the haftarah for Shabbat Hagadol.

[23] Deuteronomy 16:21.

[24] In private communication; see his article in *Jewish Quarterly Review* 81 (1990), pp. 207-212; and J. Day, *Anchor Bible Dictionary* vol. 1, pp. 481-487.

[25] Ecclesiasticus (Ben Sira) 48:4 and following (excerpts).

[26] *Book of Kings 1,* pp. 262-263, quoting Kittel, p. 159, and other sources.

[27] J. Ta'anit 3:4.

[28] Matthew 11:10 ff.; 17:10 ff.; Mark 9:1 ff.

[28] Sura 37:123-130; 6:85.

ויקהל

First Kings, chapter 7, verses 40 to 50

Introduction

Connection of sidra and haftarah:

Both sidra and haftarah deal with the construction of a sanctuary to honor God: one in the desert and the other in Jerusalem. Moses has the support of his chief architect, Bezalel; Solomon has Hiram, his own gifted artisan.

The setting:

Solomon accedes to the throne (about 970 B.C.E.) and soon thereafter begins to build the Temple. In this enterprise he has the valuable aid of Hiram, who supplies him not only with wood from the forests of Lebanon but also with skilled labor, which was not as yet available in Israel.

The haftarah is fully understandable only in the context of previous chapters, for it is but a small excerpt of the story of construction, which relates the making of the outside of the Temple and of the holy vessels and other small items within the sanctuary. For another segment of the account, see the haftarot for T'rumah and Pikudei. The records are part of ancient royal archives, and their meticulous detail is characteristic of this literary genre.

For more on the book of Kings, see our *General Introduction;* on Solomon, see the haftarah for Va-y'chi.

Content of the haftarah:

Taken from the First Book of Kings,[1] the haftarah consists of only 11 verses.
1. Enumeration of various aspects of the building project. (40-45)
2. Construction methods; the metals used. (46-50)
The records are repeated in II Chronicles 4:11-18 almost verbatim; and the various items are enumerated also in II Kings 25:13-17, as well as in a Babylonian account that lists their loot from the sack of Jerusalem in 587 B.C.E.

7:40. Hiram also made the pots, the shovels, and the basins [for the Temple]. With that, Hiram finished all the work he was doing for Solomon in the House of the Eternal:

41. the two columns, the two bowl-shaped capitals on top of the columns, and the two pieces of network to cover the bowl-shaped capitals;

42. the four hundred pomegranates for the pieces of latticework, two rows of pomegranates for each latticework, to cover the two rounded capitals on top of the columns;

43. the ten stands and the ten pots that stood on them;

7:40 וַיַּעַשׂ חִירוֹם אֶת־הַכִּירוֹת וְאֶת־הַיָּעִים וְאֶת־הַמִּזְרָקוֹת וַיְכַל חִירָם לַעֲשׂוֹת אֶת־כָּל־הַמְּלָאכָה אֲשֶׁר עָשָׂה לַמֶּלֶךְ שְׁלֹמֹה בֵּית יְהוָה:

41 עַמֻּדִים שְׁנַיִם וְגֻלֹּת הַכֹּתָרֹת אֲשֶׁר־עַל־רֹאשׁ הָעַמּוּדִים שְׁתָּיִם וְהַשְּׂבָכוֹת שְׁתַּיִם לְכַסּוֹת אֶת־שְׁתֵּי גֻּלֹּת הַכֹּתָרֹת אֲשֶׁר עַל־רֹאשׁ הָעַמּוּדִים:

42 וְאֶת־הָרִמֹּנִים אַרְבַּע מֵאוֹת לִשְׁתֵּי הַשְּׂבָכוֹת שְׁנֵי־טוּרִים רִמֹּנִים לַשְּׂבָכָה הָאֶחָת לְכַסּוֹת אֶת־שְׁתֵּי גֻּלֹּת הַכֹּתָרֹת אֲשֶׁר עַל־פְּנֵי הָעַמּוּדִים:

43 וְאֶת־הַמְּכֹנוֹת עָשֶׂר וְאֶת־הַכִּיֹרֹת עֲשָׂרָה עַל־הַמְּכֹנוֹת:

Commentary

40. *Hiram also made* .... An ellipsis: Hiram (Solomon's artisan/counselor from Tyre) had his artisans make these items. He bore the same name as the king of Tyre, and was the son of a Tyrian father and Israelite mother from the tribe of Naphtali.[2] His name is here spelled חִירֹם (*Hirom*, instead of חִירָם, *Hiram*), which faithfully renders the pronunciation of the Phoenician language of his native Tyre.

The shovels. For removing the ashes of the sacrificed animals from the altar.

The basins. For the ritual sprinkling of blood.

43. *Ten pots.* Often rendered as "lavers," vessels probably placed at various points of the hall. It appears that they contained water for cleansing purposes.

44. the tank with the twelve oxen supporting it;

45. and the pots, shovels and basins. All these articles that Hiram made for King Solomon in the House of the Eternal were of polished bronze.

46. The king had them cast on the plain of Jordan, between Sukkot and Zaretan, in clay molds.

47. There were so many articles that Solomon left them unweighed; so the weight of the bronze was never determined.

44 וְאֶת־הַיָּם הָאֶחָד וְאֶת־הַבָּקָר שְׁנֵים־עָשָׂר תַּחַת הַיָּם:

45 וְאֶת־הַסִּירוֹת וְאֶת־הַיָּעִים וְאֶת־הַמִּזְרָקוֹת וְאֵת כָּל־הַכֵּלִים הָאֹהֶל [הָאֵלֶּה] אֲשֶׁר עָשָׂה חִירָם לַמֶּלֶךְ שְׁלֹמֹה בֵּית יְהוָה נְחֹשֶׁת מְמֹרָט:

46 בְּכִכַּר הַיַּרְדֵּן יְצָקָם הַמֶּלֶךְ בְּמַעֲבֵה הָאֲדָמָה בֵּין סֻכּוֹת וּבֵין צָרְתָן:

47 וַיַּנַּח שְׁלֹמֹה אֶת־כָּל־הַכֵּלִים מֵרֹב מְאֹד מְאֹד לֹא נֶחְקַר מִשְׁקַל הַנְּחֹשֶׁת:

Commentary

44. *Tank.* Literally "the sea," so called because of its large size (15 feet in diameter and 7 1/2 feet [4.6 x 2.3 meters] in depth.)[3] It was used for the ablutions of the priests. "Such a laver would weigh from twenty-five to thirty tons or one and one-half times the weight of the great bell in St. Paul's Cathedral. It is small wonder that a modern historian refers to it as a 'triumph in bronze working.'"[4] It has been suggested that "the sea" had mythic roots, alluding to the Eternal's command over the waters of the sea.[5]

Twelve oxen. Literally, cattle. They were grouped in threesomes, each facing in a different direction.[6] This novel embellishment was introduced by Solomon despite its similarity to the Baal/bull cult, but apparently he thought that it posed no danger to the adoration of the One God. However, his confidence was misplaced, for when after his death his kingdom was divided, King Jeroboam of Israel set up a rival sanctuary in Bethel and installed two bull images in it and proclaimed, "These are your gods, O Israel, who brought you out of the land of Egypt!"[7]

45. *Polished bronze.* נחשת (n'choshet) was also the material used in the desert Tabernacle and was there rendered as "copper,"[8] since no facilities existed for smelting and creating an alloy. In Solomon's time the word is used for an alloy of copper and tin, which was much more costly. (נחשת is often mistakenly rendered as "brass," an alloy composed of copper and zinc, which however was not known in biblical times.)

46. *Between Sukkot and Zaretan.* The exact location of these cities is the subject of scholarly dispute. A good deal of evidence suggests that it was somewhere along the river Jabbok (on the east side of the Jordan). The soil is rich in clay, and charcoal deposits attest to the likelihood that kilns for clay molds were operated in this area.

Clay molds. Literally, "in the thick of the earth," suggesting the density of clay.

48. King Solomon [also] made all the articles that were used in the House of the Eternal: the golden altar, the table that held the loaves of [God's] Presence, also of gold;

49. the lamp stands of pure gold that stood in front of the inner Sanctuary, five on the right and five on the left, with their gold flowers, lamps, and tongs;

50. and the pure gold cups, lamp-snuffers, bowls, ladles, and fire-pans; and the gold hinges for the doors of the innermost room of the Temple, the Holy of Holies, and for the golden doors of the Main Hall of the Temple.

48 וַיַּעַשׂ שְׁלֹמֹה אֵת כָּל־הַכֵּלִים אֲשֶׁר בֵּית יְהֹוָה אֵת מִזְבַּח הַזָּהָב וְאֶת־הַשֻּׁלְחָן אֲשֶׁר עָלָיו לֶחֶם הַפָּנִים זָהָב:

49 וְאֶת־הַמְּנֹרוֹת חָמֵשׁ מִיָּמִין וְחָמֵשׁ מִשְּׂמֹאול לִפְנֵי הַדְּבִיר זָהָב סָגוּר וְהַפֶּרַח וְהַנֵּרֹת וְהַמֶּלְקַחַיִם זָהָב:

50 וְהַסִּפּוֹת וְהַמְזַמְּרוֹת וְהַמִּזְרָקוֹת וְהַכַּפּוֹת וְהַמַּחְתּוֹת זָהָב סָגוּר וְהַפֹּתוֹת לְדַלְתוֹת הַבַּיִת הַפְּנִימִי לְקֹדֶשׁ הַקֳּדָשִׁים לְדַלְתֵי הַבַּיִת לַהֵיכָל זָהָב:

Commentary

48. *Golden altar.* The desert altar was *overlaid* with gold,[9] while here "golden" is not qualified.

49. *Lamp stands.* Only one was mentioned in the Torah,[10] while Chronicles and Jeremiah know of more than one candelabrum.[11] Josephus suggests that the plural includes lamps for illumination, in addition to the one and only sacred appurtenance.[12]

Essay and Gleanings

Since our haftarah and that for the earlier sidra T'rumah are part of one story which relates the building of the Temple by Solomon, the *Essays* and *Gleanings* for the two haftarot have been combined and are found in the haftarah for T'rumah.

* * *

Notes

[1] In the Septuagint, it is called the Third Book of Kingdoms, while I and II Samuel are called I and II Kingdoms.

[2] See I Kings 5:26 (haftarah for T'rumah) and I Kings 7:14.

[3] I Kings 7:23.

[4] II Chronicles 4:6, and Honor, *Book of Kings 1*, p.104. But since it was so tall, and therefore would have been inconvenient for the priestly use, it has been suggested that it had unknown, extra-religious purposes (for details see Gray, *I and II Kings*, p.177). But others do not perceive the tank to have syncretistic significance; see, for example, De Vaux, *Ancient Israel*, p. 328.

[5] J. Levenson, *Sinai and Zion*, pp. 138 ff. See also the poetic reflexes of ancient tales of divine forces battling the powers of the deep, in Psalm 93 and Job 26.

[6] I Kings 7:25.

[7] I Kings 12:28.

[8] See Exodus 27:19.

[9] Exodus 30:3.

[10] Exodus 37:17-24.

[11] I Chronicles 28:15; Jeremiah 52:19.

[12] *Antiquities* VIII 3:7. The Arch of Titus, depicting some of the goods that the Romans removed from the Temple (70 C.E.), shows one candelabrum only, but that in itself is not conclusive evidence.

פְּקוּדֵי

First Kings, chapter 7, verse 51 to chapter 8, verse 21

Introduction

Connection of sidra and haftarah:

The sidra recounts the completion of the Tabernacle; the haftarah, the completion of the Temple. But while in the Torah, *God* had chosen Bezalel to do the work; in the haftarah, *Solomon* had chosen Hiram to be his chief architect and adviser.[1]

The setting:

Solomon, who succeeded his father David on the throne of Israel about the year 970 B.C.E., began his large-scale building program by erecting the First Temple, which his father had hoped to build, but could not (see commentary on 8:19). The project took only seven years (then considered a brief time), and its completion was observed with elaborate ceremonies. They served to make Jerusalem the spiritual and political center of the nation and also to fortify and legitimate Solomon's reign.

The haftarah is taken from the First Book of Kings.[2] For more on the book, see our *General Introduction;* on Solomon, see the haftarah for Va-y'chi.

Content of the haftarah:

The text begins where the haftarah for Vayakhel left off and ends with verse 21 of chapter 8. Verses 54-66 of that chapter constitute the haftarah for Sh'mini Atzeret. Also, 8:2-21 serve as the haftarah for the second day of Sukkot. When the weekly readings Vayakhel and Pikudei are combined (as is often the case), the haftarah for Pikudei is used.

1. The consecrated items that David had set aside for a sanctuary are now transferred to the Temple. (7:51)

2. The people are assembled and the Ark of the Covenant is conveyed to the Temple. (8:1-5)

3. The Ark, with its cherubim and tablets, is installed. (6-9)

4. The descent of the cloud of God. (10-11)

5. Solomon's opening recitation. (12-13)

6. His review of the project and a tribute to his father. (14-21)

The haftarah ends here, but the chapter continues with Solomon's prayer and benediction.

HAFTARAH FOR PIKUDEI

First Kings, chapter 7, verse 51 to chapter 8, verse 21

7:51. When all King Solomon's work in building the House of the Eternal was done, Solomon brought all the things that his father David had consecrated—the silver, gold, and the vessels—and deposited them into the treasury of the House of the Eternal.

8:1. Solomon then assembled the elders of Israel and all the heads of the tribes and clans of Israel to come to him in Jerusalem. They were to bring up the Ark of the Covenant of the Eternal from the City of David, that is, Zion.

2. All the men of Israel came together before King Solomon at the festival (of Sukkot) in the seventh month, Etanim.

7:51 וַתִּשְׁלַם֙ כָּל־הַמְּלָאכָ֔ה אֲשֶׁ֥ר עָשָׂ֖ה הַמֶּ֣לֶךְ שְׁלֹמֹ֑ה בֵּ֣ית יְהוָ֑ה וַיָּבֵ֣א שְׁלֹמֹ֗ה אֶת־קָדְשֵׁ֣י ׀ דָּוִ֣ד אָבִ֗יו אֶת־הַכֶּ֤סֶף וְאֶת־הַזָּהָב֙ וְאֶת־הַכֵּלִ֔ים נָתַ֕ן בְּאֹצְר֖וֹת בֵּ֥ית יְהוָֽה׃

8:1 אָ֣ז יַקְהֵ֣ל שְׁלֹמֹ֡ה אֶת־זִקְנֵ֣י יִשְׂרָאֵ֣ל אֶת־כָּל־רָאשֵׁ֣י הַמַּטּוֹת֩ נְשִׂיאֵ֨י הָאָב֜וֹת לִבְנֵ֣י יִשְׂרָאֵ֗ל אֶל־הַמֶּ֥לֶךְ שְׁלֹמֹ֖ה יְרוּשָׁלָ֑͏ִם לְהַעֲלֹ֞ות אֶת־אֲר֧וֹן בְּרִית־יְהוָ֛ה מֵעִ֥יר דָּוִ֖ד הִ֥יא צִיּֽוֹן׃

2 וַיִּקָּֽהֲל֞וּ אֶל־הַמֶּ֤לֶךְ שְׁלֹמֹה֙ כָּל־אִ֣ישׁ יִשְׂרָאֵ֔ל בְּיֶ֥רַח הָאֵתָנִ֖ים בֶּחָ֑ג ה֖וּא הַחֹ֥דֶשׁ הַשְּׁבִיעִֽי׃

Commentary

8:1. *Bring up the Ark*. Which David had brought from the house of Obed-edom to the City of David, located on the lower part of the Temple hill.[3] (See the essay below.)

City of David, that is, Zion. Later, Zion denoted the entire city of Jerusalem.

2. *In the seventh month*. In 6:38 we are told that the Temple was completed in the *eighth* month. Many suggestions have been made to explain this discrepancy, one being that the dedication ceremonies took place eleven months after the completion of the Temple.

Etanim. The writer makes two points: one, the festival is to be celebrated in the seventh month (a rule that the rebellious King Jeroboam I had defied);[4] and further, that the pre-exilic name of the month had been Etanim, as in Phoenician. Since the books of Kings were written after 587 B.C.E. (see our *General Introduction*), readers would have known only the later name, Tishri, on the fifteenth day of which the festival of Sukkot is celebrated.[5]

"Etanim" implies either strength (coming from a completed harvest that supplies one's needs) or running water (denoting the early rains of this season).

3. When all the elders of Israel had come, the priests took up the Ark.

4. The priests and levites together took up the Ark of God, the Tent of Meeting, and all the holy articles of the Tent.

5. Meantime, King Solomon and all the community of Israel with him were sacrificing countless, innumerable sheep and oxen.

6. Then the priests brought the Ark of the Covenant of the Eternal to its place in the Inner Sanctuary of the Temple, the Holy of Holies, under the wings of the cherubim,

3 וַיָּבֹאוּ כֹּל זִקְנֵי יִשְׂרָאֵל וַיִּשְׂאוּ הַכֹּהֲנִים
אֶת־הָאָרוֹן:

4 וַיַּעֲלוּ אֶת־אֲרוֹן יְהוָה וְאֶת־אֹהֶל מוֹעֵד
וְאֶת־כָּל־כְּלֵי הַקֹּדֶשׁ אֲשֶׁר בָּאֹהֶל וַיַּעֲלוּ אֹתָם
הַכֹּהֲנִים וְהַלְוִיִּם:

5 וְהַמֶּלֶךְ שְׁלֹמֹה וְכָל־עֲדַת יִשְׂרָאֵל הַנּוֹעָדִים
עָלָיו אִתּוֹ לִפְנֵי הָאָרוֹן מְזַבְּחִים צֹאן וּבָקָר
אֲשֶׁר לֹא־יִסָּפְרוּ וְלֹא יִמָּנוּ מֵרֹב:

6 וַיָּבִאוּ הַכֹּהֲנִים אֶת־אֲרוֹן בְּרִית־יְהוָה אֶל־
מְקוֹמוֹ אֶל־דְּבִיר הַבַּיִת אֶל־קֹדֶשׁ הַקֳּדָשִׁים
אֶל־תַּחַת כַּנְפֵי הַכְּרוּבִים:

Commentary

4. *Priests and levites.* This is the only time the levites are mentioned in the book of Kings, while in Chronicles their role is repeatedly emphasized. This notable difference reflects the changing status of the levites. In earlier days (reflected in Kings) all levites were priests, but later only the Aaronide/Zadokite levites were recognized as such, and the other levites became their assistants. Their single mention in this verse must be considered a later gloss, designed to stress the distinction between the two groups of Temple servants.

Tent of Meeting. Tradition said that this was the same portable sanctuary that Moses had used during desert days.[6]

5. *Commmunity of Israel.* עדת ישראל (*adath yisrael*) describes the people as a religious community, and therefore many synagogues have been so named.

Innumerable sheep and oxen. These sacrifices during the procession replayed what had taken place in David's time, when he brought up the Ark. During the solemn processional, sacrifices were offered after the first six steps taken by the Ark bearers.[7]

This is not the kind of celebratory rite that moderns would choose, but it must be understood as an expression of religious fervor in days when such offerings were an integral part of religious expression. Also, animals represented a substantial part of people's wealth, and giving them up for sacrifice was their way of showing how much the Ark meant to them.

6. *Cherubim.* Angelic, winged beings that protected the entrance to the Garden of Eden.[8] Images of two such creatures symbolized the throne of God and were mounted on the Ark in the Tent.[9] In Solomon's Temple, too, they were prominent: the Ark featured two large cherubim, and they served as decorative motifs throughout the Sanctuary.[10] The word cherubim is probably related to the Akkadian *karabu*, "to pray or bless."

7. whose outstretched wings covered the place where the Ark was standing, so that they hid the Ark and its poles.

8. The poles were so long that their tops could be seen from the Sanctuary in front of the Innermost Sanctuary, but could not be seen from outside; they are [standing] there to this day.

9. There was nothing in the Ark but the two stone tablets that Moses had placed there at Horeb, where the Eternal had made a covenant with the people of Israel after they had come out of Egypt.

10. As soon as the priests filed out of the Sanctuary, the cloud [of God] filled the House of the Eternal—

11. for on account of the cloud the priests were unable to stand and do their service: the glory of God filled the House of the Eternal.

7 כִּי הַכְּרוּבִים פֹּרְשִׂים כְּנָפַיִם אֶל־מְקוֹם הָאָרוֹן וַיָּסֹכּוּ הַכְּרֻבִים עַל־הָאָרוֹן וְעַל־בַּדָּיו מִלְמָעְלָה:

8 וַיַּאֲרִכוּ הַבַּדִּים וַיֵּרָאוּ רָאשֵׁי הַבַּדִּים מִן־הַקֹּדֶשׁ עַל־פְּנֵי הַדְּבִיר וְלֹא יֵרָאוּ הַחוּצָה וַיִּהְיוּ שָׁם עַד הַיּוֹם הַזֶּה:

9 אֵין בָּאָרוֹן רַק שְׁנֵי לֻחוֹת הָאֲבָנִים אֲשֶׁר הִנִּחַ שָׁם מֹשֶׁה בְּחֹרֵב אֲשֶׁר כָּרַת יְהוָֹה עִם־בְּנֵי יִשְׂרָאֵל בְּצֵאתָם מֵאֶרֶץ מִצְרָיִם:

10 וַיְהִי בְּצֵאת הַכֹּהֲנִים מִן־הַקֹּדֶשׁ וְהֶעָנָן מָלֵא אֶת־בֵּית יְהוָֹה:

11 וְלֹא־יָכְלוּ הַכֹּהֲנִים לַעֲמֹד לְשָׁרֵת מִפְּנֵי הֶעָנָן כִּי־מָלֵא כְבוֹד־יְהוָֹה אֶת־בֵּית יְהוָֹה:

Commentary

In poetic language, the Eternal could be depicted as riding a cherub (see the haftarah for Ha'azinu).

7. *Its poles.* They served originally to carry the Ark, and were left in place even though portability was no longer a problem.

To this day. That is, when the book of Kings was composed.[11]

9. *The two stone tablets.* There were two major traditions about the inscription written on them: one, that it was the Ten Commandments; and another, that all 613 mitzvot were miraculously incised thereon.

Horeb. A synonym for Sinai. Many biblical scholars believe that Horeb and Sinai point to two different ancient traditions about the holy mountain.

10. *Cloud [of God].* Which had led the people through the wilderness years. It symbolized the Divine Presence, which was hidden from sight.[12]

12. Then Solomon said: The Eternal said: *I choose to dwell in thick darkness;*

13. *now I have truly built for You a royal mansion, a place where You may dwell forever.*

14. With all Israel standing there, the king turned around [to face them] and blessed them.

15. He said: Praised be the Eternal, the God of Israel, whose mouth made a promise to my father David and whose hand has fulfilled it.

16. God had said: *From the time I brought My people Israel out of Egypt, I did not choose a city from all the tribes of Israel for My House to be built there, for My Presence to be there; but I have chosen David to rule My people Israel.*

17. My father David set his heart on building a House for the Presence of the Eternal, the God of Israel.

18. But God said to my father David: *You have done well to set your heart on building a Temple for My Presence,*

12 אָז אָמַר שְׁלֹמֹה יְהֹוָה אָמַר לִשְׁכֹּן
בָּעֲרָפֶל:

13 בָּנֹה בָנִיתִי בֵּית זְבֻל לָךְ מָכוֹן לְשִׁבְתְּךָ
עוֹלָמִים:

14 וַיַּסֵּב הַמֶּלֶךְ אֶת־פָּנָיו וַיְבָרֶךְ אֵת כָּל־
קְהַל יִשְׂרָאֵל וְכָל־קְהַל יִשְׂרָאֵל עֹמֵד:

15 וַיֹּאמֶר בָּרוּךְ יְהֹוָה אֱלֹהֵי יִשְׂרָאֵל אֲשֶׁר
דִּבֶּר בְּפִיו אֵת דָּוִד אָבִי וּבְיָדוֹ מִלֵּא לֵאמֹר:

16 מִן־הַיּוֹם אֲשֶׁר הוֹצֵאתִי אֶת־עַמִּי אֶת־
יִשְׂרָאֵל מִמִּצְרַיִם לֹא־בָחַרְתִּי בְעִיר מִכֹּל
שִׁבְטֵי יִשְׂרָאֵל לִבְנוֹת בַּיִת לִהְיוֹת שְׁמִי שָׁם
וָאֶבְחַר בְּדָוִד לִהְיוֹת עַל־עַמִּי יִשְׂרָאֵל:

17 וַיְהִי עִם־לְבַב דָּוִד אָבִי לִבְנוֹת בַּיִת לְשֵׁם
יְהֹוָה אֱלֹהֵי יִשְׂרָאֵל:

18 וַיֹּאמֶר יְהֹוָה אֶל־דָּוִד אָבִי יַעַן אֲשֶׁר הָיָה
עִם־לְבָבְךָ לִבְנוֹת בַּיִת לִשְׁמִי הֱטִיבֹתָ כִּי הָיָה
עִם־לְבָבֶךָ:

Commentary

12. *Then Solomon said.* The Septuagint here has an addition, saying that the king recited these lines from an otherwise unknown work, the Book of Song. Such a title would read in Hebrew, ספר השיר (*sefer hashir*). By transposing the letters י and שׁ in the Hebrew text that the translators used, השיר would become הישר, and one would obtain ספר הישר (*sefer hayashar*), a book that is elsewhere quoted in the Tanach.[13] It apparently contained war songs and other poetry, but no copies have survived.

In thick darkness. Meaning, God cannot be seen.[14]

15. *Whose mouth made a promise.* Literally, "whose mouth spoke." God spoke through the prophet Nathan.[15]

16. *My Presence.* Literally, "My Name."[16] So through verse 20.

19. *and yet it is not you, but your son, your own offspring, who will build that House for My Presence.*

20. See how that promise has now been kept! I have risen to succeed my father David, and I now sit on Israel's throne, as God promised, and I have built that House for the Presence of the Eternal, the God of Israel.

21. And I have made a place there for the Ark which contains the covenant that the Eternal, leading led them out of Egypt, made with our ancestors

19 רַק אַתָּה לֹא תִבְנֶה הַבָּיִת כִּי אִם־בִּנְךָ הַיֹּצֵא מֵחֲלָצֶיךָ הוּא־יִבְנֶה הַבַּיִת לִשְׁמִי:

20 וַיָּקֶם יְהֹוָה אֶת־דְּבָרוֹ אֲשֶׁר דִּבֵּר וָאָקֻם תַּחַת דָּוִד אָבִי וָאֵשֵׁב עַל־כִּסֵּא יִשְׂרָאֵל כַּאֲשֶׁר דִּבֶּר יְהֹוָה וָאֶבְנֶה הַבַּיִת לְשֵׁם יְהֹוָה אֱלֹהֵי יִשְׂרָאֵל:

21 וָאָשִׂם שָׁם מָקוֹם לָאָרוֹן אֲשֶׁר־שָׁם בְּרִית יְהֹוָה אֲשֶׁר כָּרַת עִם־אֲבֹתֵינוּ בְּהוֹצִיאוֹ אֹתָם מֵאֶרֶץ מִצְרָיִם:

Commentary

19. *And yet it is not you.* Solomon delicately omits the reason why David was not permitted to build the Temple, namely, because he had committed adultery with Bathsheba (Solomon's own mother) and had her husband (Uriah the Hittite) killed. (Tradition partially excuses David by asserting that Bathsheba was divorced.)

Essay

The Ark

The ארון (*aron*), which David had brought to Jerusalem and which his son Solomon installed in the Temple, went by three names: Ark of the Eternal, Ark of God, and Ark of the Covenant. It contained the two stone slabs upon which the divine commandments were inscribed and, according to tradition, the fragments of the first tablets as well.[17] There were also traditions that other objects were preserved in the Ark (see *Gleanings*); and some biblical scholars believe that it was the place where were kept the Urim and Thummim, used by the High Priest to search out the will of God.

With two cherubim guarding it from above, the Ark became the symbolic footstool of the Almighty (see the commentary on verses 6 and 7 above).

Popular belief invested the Ark with miraculous qualities. Armies took it with them into battle to vouchsafe victory, and it was carried around the walls of Jericho during Joshua's assault on the city.[18] Terrible punishment was visited on those who desecrated it in any fashion.[19]

The book of Samuel contains several chapters that deal with events affecting the Ark, including its capture by the Philistines.[20] When David defeated them he recaptured the Ark and brought it to his new capital.[21] There he housed it in a special Tent, and it remained there until Solomon made it into the centerpiece of the Temple's dedication ceremonies.

After the Babylonians destroyed the Temple in 587 B.C.E., the Ark disappeared from extant historical annals, and Ezekiel, in his extended vision of the new Temple, does not foresee it as part of the reconstituted edifice.[22] Only Jeremiah deals with it in a remarkable passage:

"[At some future time] people shall no longer speak of the Ark of the Eternal, and shall not give it any thought. They shall not mention it or miss it, nor shall they fashion another. At that time, they shall call Jerusalem 'Throne of the Eternal,' and all nations shall gather there ...."[23]

Meanwhile, the Ark has survived as a symbolic presence in every synagogue. It is usually placed in or by the wall that faces Jerusalem, and an Eternal Light burns nearby or above it. The Ark contains one or more handwritten scrolls of the Torah, and in days gone by the number of scrolls would testify to the affection of the community for the sacred parchments. Most often the synagogue Ark is a recess in the wall, but in some places of worship it is a free-standing receptacle, like the portable shrine in the Tent or the permanent one in Solomon's Temple.

Then as now, it is the focus of the congregation, and the reading from the scroll remains at the center of the religious service.

Gleanings

Midrashic musings

After the destruction of the Temple, many legends were spun about the fate of the Ark. One, recorded in the Apocrypha, tells of Jeremiah hiding it in a secret place, where it will remain undiscovered "until God finally gathers the people [of Israel] together and shows mercy upon them."[24]

King Josiah, fearing that sometime soon the city and Temple would be destroyed, hid the Ark and holy objects, lest they be desecrated by the enemy. In addition, he also hid the holy oil, the jars of manna, the rod of Aaron, and other objects.[25]

Another tradition holds that Solomon provided a secret place in the newly erected Temple, so that in cases of emergency, holy objects could be hidden there.[26]

What the Ark contained

Beyond the second curtain was the tent called The Most Holy Place. Here was a golden altar of incense, and the ark of the covenant all plated over with gold, in which were a golden jar containing the manna, and Aaron's staff which once budded,[27] and the tablets of the covenant; and above it, the cherubim of God's glory.

Christian Scriptures[28]

The voice of the poet

> Lord, with what glory wast Thou served of old,
> When Solomon's temple stood and flourished!
> Where most things were of purest gold;
> The wood was all embellished
> With flowers and carvings, mystical and rare:
> All showed the builders, craved the seers care.

George Herbert[29]

* * *

Notes

[1] Jacobson, *Chazon Hamikra*, vol. 1, pp. 229-230, considers this to be *the* fundamental difference between the two building projects.

[2] In the Septuagint, it is called the Third Book of Kingdoms, while I and II Samuel are called I and II Kingdoms.

[3] II Samuel 6:17. The City of David was a fort that he had wrested from the Jebusites.

[4] I Kings 12:32.

[5] It was in ancient days characterized by water ceremonies, celebrating the rainy season.

[6] See *Tosefta* Sota 13:1; the Tent is described in Exodus 33:7-10; II Chronicles 1:3-4 states that it had been housed in Gibeon, while the Ark had been brought up already by David, who made a temporary Tent to house it.

[7] II Samuel 6:13.

[8] Genesis 3:24.

[9] Exodus 25:18-20

[10] I Kings 6:25.

[11] On the time of composition, see our *General Introduction*.

[12] See Exodus 33:9-11; 40:34.

[13] Joshua 10:13; II Samuel 1:18.

[14] The expression is also found in Psalms 18:12 and 97:2 (see under *Gleanings*). The Septuagint reads: The Eternal One established the sun in the heavens,/but God said that thick darkness would be the divine abode/I have built a royal house for You,/an established place for you forever. The Targum has still another version: The Eternal One has been pleased to establish the Divine Presence in Jerusalem.

[15] II Samuel 7:11-15.

[16] See the corresponding rendering in II Chronicles 6:6.

[17] In the Torah (Deuteronomy 10:2, 5), Moses tells how God asked him to deposit the tablets in the Ark, and how he had carried out the command. The story of the broken tablets is found in many rabbinic sources—for example, *B. Baba Batra* 14a-b; *Sh'kalim* 49b. But another tradition is cited in *Talmud Yerushalmi*, Sotah 8:22b-c, which says that there were two arks in the Tent, one with the whole tablets and one with the broken ones. Only the latter was carried into battle.

[18] Joshua chapter 6.

[19] I Samuel 6:19; II Samuel 6:6-7.

[20] I Samuel 4:1-7:2

[21] II Samuel 6.

[22] Ezekiel 40-48.

[23] Jeremiah 3:15-17. Some biblical scholars believe this to have been written in post-exilic times and inserted into the text.

[24] II Maccabees 2:4-8.

[25] This tradition is found frequently in the Talmudim—for example, *B.* Yoma 52b, *J.* Sh'kalim 6:59c.

[26] Reported by Radak on I Kings 6:19 and II Chronicles 35:3. However, the manuscript he used has been lost. See Ginzberg, *Legends of the Jews,* vol. 6, pp. 377-378, footnote 118.

[27] Numbers 17:8.

[28] Hebrews 9:3-5 (NEB translation).

[29] *Chapters into Verse*, p. 235.

ויקרא

Isaiah, chapter 43, verse 21 to chapter 44, verse 23

Introduction

Connection of haftarah and sidra:

The weekly portion begins the third book of the Torah, Vayikra (Leviticus), which contains the bulk of the laws on sacrifice and priesthood. Since sacrifices were no longer possible for the people dwelling in Babylonian exile, Isaiah urges his listeners to bring God their offerings of the heart.

The setting:

Isaiah[1] and his people lived as exiles in Babylon (6th century B.C.E.). Undoubtedly there were many among them who doubted that God would redeem them, and they began to revert to the worship of idols. For Isaiah this was a dreadful aberration, and he attacked it with devastating sarcasm, reminding them at the same time that God's mercy will wipe away the sins of the past and restore Israel to its glory as God's servants.

For more on Isaiah and his time, see our *General Introduction*.

The message:

The haftarah may be divided into three parts: a prologue, speaking of Israel's past transgressions; the main message, dealing with the folly of idol worship; and an epilogue, sketching the redemption that Israel will experience.

1. Though the people of Israel were chosen by God, they did not even bring the required sacrifices and instead have burdened God with their sins. (43: 21-28)

2. Israel had been chosen to exalt the glory of the Eternal and thereby to bear witness to the folly of idolatry. The description of the childish efforts of an idol maker forms the core of this section. (41:1-20)

3. A brief postscript. The foolish make an idol that can do nothing, but God has fashioned Israel (with all its potential), a feat that nature itself will acclaim. (41:21-23)

HAFTARAH FOR VAYIKRA

Isaiah, chapter 43, verse 21 to chapter 44, verse 23

43:21. This people I formed for Myself,

to recount My praise.

22. Yet you have not called upon Me, O Jacob,

or wearied yourself for Me, O Israel.

23. You brought Me no sheep for burnt-offerings,

nor honored Me with your sacrifices.

I did not burden you with grain-offerings,

nor weary you by demanding incense.

24. You have not spent your coin to give Me sweet cane,

nor sated Me with the fat of your sacrifices:

instead, you have burdened Me with your sins,

and wearied Me with your offenses.

25. I, I am the One who blots out your transgressions, for My own sake,

and your sins will I remember no more.

26. Now [if you think I don't recall your merits]

help Me remember!

43:21 עַם־זוּ יָצַרְתִּי לִי

תְּהִלָּתִי יְסַפֵּרוּ:

22 וְלֹא־אֹתִי קָרָאתָ יַעֲקֹב

כִּי־יָגַעְתָּ בִּי יִשְׂרָאֵל:

23 לֹא־הֵבֵיאתָ לִּי שֵׂה עֹלֹתֶיךָ

וּזְבָחֶיךָ לֹא כִבַּדְתָּנִי

לֹא הֶעֱבַדְתִּיךָ בְּמִנְחָה

וְלֹא הוֹגַעְתִּיךָ בִּלְבוֹנָה:

24 לֹא־קָנִיתָ לִּי בַכֶּסֶף קָנֶה

וְחֵלֶב זְבָחֶיךָ לֹא הִרְוִיתָנִי

אַךְ הֶעֱבַדְתַּנִי בְּחַטֹּאותֶיךָ

הוֹגַעְתַּנִי בַּעֲוֹנֹתֶיךָ:

25 אָנֹכִי אָנֹכִי הוּא מֹחֶה פְשָׁעֶיךָ לְמַעֲנִי

וְחַטֹּאתֶיךָ לֹא אֶזְכֹּר:

26 הַזְכִּירֵנִי

Commentary

43:23. *You brought Me no sheep.* In Babylon you don't have to worry about sacrifices, but instead of prayers and good deeds "you have burdened Me with your sins."[2]

24. *Coin ... cane.* Our translation tries to come close to the Hebrew wordplay קָנִית and קָנֶה . Coins had been invented slightly before the Prophet's time, roughly about 600 B.C.E.

Sweet cane. Mentioned in Exodus 30:23 as an ingredient of spice-offerings.

Sated Me with the fat of your sacrifices. Compare this to the opposite sentiment of the First Isaiah; see the haftarah for D'varim.

25. *I, I am the One ....* The verse is recited repeatedly on Yom Kippur.

For My own sake. To put an end to the profanation of My holy Name.[3]

Let us arrive at judgment!

State your case and justify yourself!

27. Your first ancestor sinned,

and your leaders have rebelled against Me.

28. So I degraded the Temple's chiefs,

made Jacob an outcast,

surrendered Israel to mockery.

44:1. Listen to Me now, O Jacob, My servant,

Israel, My chosen one:

2. Thus says the Eternal One, your Maker,

who formed you from the womb

[and] will help you:

Have no fear, Jacob My servant,

Jeshurun, My chosen one.

נִשָּׁפְטָה יָחַד

סַפֵּר אַתָּה לְמַעַן תִּצְדָּק:

27 אָבִיךָ הָרִאשׁוֹן חָטָא

וּמְלִיצֶיךָ פָּשְׁעוּ בִי:

28 וַאֲחַלֵּל שָׂרֵי קֹדֶשׁ

וְאֶתְּנָה לַחֵרֶם יַעֲקֹב

וְיִשְׂרָאֵל לְגִדּוּפִים:

44:1 וְעַתָּה שְׁמַע יַעֲקֹב עַבְדִּי

וְיִשְׂרָאֵל בָּחַרְתִּי בוֹ:

2 כֹּה־אָמַר יְהוָה עֹשֶׂךָ

וְיֹצֶרְךָ מִבֶּטֶן יַעְזְרֶךָ

אַל־תִּירָא עַבְדִּי יַעֲקֹב

וִישֻׁרוּן בָּחַרְתִּי בוֹ:

Commentary

26. *Let us arrive at judgment* A frequent image in Isaiah: Israel is invited to plead with God, for thereby it will become clear what its folly has been. See our comment on Isaiah 43:1 in the haftarah for Lech L'cha.

27. *Your first ancestor sinned.* There is no way to tell whom Isaiah had in mind. Some believe he had Adam in mind, but since Adam is never referred to as Israel's forebear, that is improbable. Most likely Abraham is meant, and the sin he committed was to have doubted God's promise, when he fled Canaan and went to Egypt.

28. *Degraded.* Literally, "profaned." They are no longer God's "holy princes."

The Temple's chiefs. Literally, "holy princes," שָׂרֵי קֹדֶשׁ (*sarei kodesh*), a poetic reference to the priests.[4] Because of Israel's sins, God allowed the Temple to be destroyed.

44:2. *Who formed you from the womb.* This is not a reference to Jacob, who struggled in the womb with his brother Esau (Genesis 25:22 ff.),[5] but to the whole people, as the parallel of the second half of the verse makes clear. So also Jeremiah 1:5 has God saying: "Before I created you in the womb I selected you ... I appointed you a prophet concerning the nations." (See the haftarah to the weekly portion Matot.) The whole people are selected to assume a prophetic role in the world.[6]

Jeshurun. A poetic name for Israel.[7] The word is probably derived from *yashar*, upright.

3. As I pour water on thirsty soil,

and streams on dry ground,

so will I pour My spirit on your descen-

dants,

My blessing upon your offspring.

4. They shall flourish amidst the grass,

like willows by flowing streams.

5. One shall say: *I am the Eternal's,*

and take the name *Jacob.*

Another shall write *For the Eternal* on his

hand,

and be known as *Israel.*

6. Thus says the Eternal God, Israel's Sov-

ereign

and Redeemer, the God of heaven's hosts:

I am the first, I am the last;

there is no God but Me.

7. Who is like Me?

[If there is someone,] declare it,

proclaim it, and confront Me:

Since I founded the ancient people,

and [created] things yet to come,

let them foretell what they shall be.

3 כִּי אֶצָּק־מַ֙יִם֙ עַל־צָמֵ֔א

וְנֹזְלִ֖ים עַל־יַבָּשָׁ֑ה

אֶצֹּ֤ק רוּחִי֙ עַל־זַרְעֶ֔ךָ

וּבִרְכָתִ֖י עַל־צֶאֱצָאֶֽיךָ׃

4 וְצָמְח֖וּ בְּבֵ֣ין חָצִ֑יר

כַּעֲרָבִ֖ים עַל־יִבְלֵי־מָֽיִם׃

5 זֶ֤ה יֹאמַר֙ לַיהֹוָ֣ה אָ֔נִי

וְזֶ֥ה יִקְרָ֖א בְשֵׁם־יַעֲקֹ֑ב

וְזֶ֗ה יִכְתֹּ֤ב יָדוֹ֙ לַֽיהֹוָ֔ה

וּבְשֵׁ֥ם יִשְׂרָאֵ֖ל יְכַנֶּֽה׃

6 כֹּֽה־אָמַ֤ר יְהֹוָה֙ מֶֽלֶךְ־יִשְׂרָאֵ֔ל

וְגֹאֲל֖וֹ יְהֹוָ֣ה צְבָא֑וֹת

אֲנִ֤י רִאשׁוֹן֙ וַאֲנִ֣י אַחֲר֔וֹן

וּמִבַּלְעָדַ֖י אֵ֥ין אֱלֹהִֽים׃

7 וּמִֽי־כָמ֣וֹנִי

יִקְרָ֗א

וְיַגִּידֶ֤הָ וְיַעְרְכֶ֙הָ֙ לִ֔י

מִשּׂוּמִ֖י עַם־עוֹלָ֑ם וְאֹתִיּ֛וֹת

וַאֲשֶׁ֥ר תָּבֹ֖אנָה יַגִּ֥ידוּ לָֽמוֹ׃

Commentary

4. *They shall flourish amidst the grass.* Among the idolaters.[8]

5. *On his hand.* Tattoo it like a servant who is branded with the master's name.

6. *I am the first.* ראשון (*rishon*), an ascription used in the synagogue hymn *Yigdal.*[9] An unequivocal monotheistic statement, which leaves no room for the worship of other gods.

7. The traditional text is difficult to understand; the translation is speculative.

Ancient people. Referring to Israel or to humanity as a whole. If the latter, the text would be saying: Go back to the earliest human records and you will find that no one could ever match My knowledge of the future.

Let them foretell what they shall be. Which they can't.

8. Do not be afraid; do not tremble.
You are My witnesses:
did I not tell you from of old?
Did I not declare [it]?
Is there any God or any Power but Me?
I know of none.
9. Those who make idols—
the things they are so fond of, all of them
    naught—
They are themselves witnesses that their
    gods cannot see nor think,
and they shall be put to shame.
10. What good does it do
to carve a god, to cast an idol?
11. All its devotees shall be put to shame,
for those who make it are but human.
Let them gather, let them stand up!
Together they shall be afraid and put to
shame.

8 אַל־תִּפְחֲדוּ וְאַל־תִּרְהוּ
הֲלֹא מֵאָז הִשְׁמַעְתִּיךָ וְהִגַּדְתִּי
וְאַתֶּם עֵדָי
הֲיֵשׁ אֱלוֹהַּ מִבַּלְעָדַי וְאֵין צוּר
בַּל־יָדָעְתִּי:
9 יֹצְרֵי־פֶסֶל
כֻּלָּם תֹּהוּ וַחֲמוּדֵיהֶם בַּל־יוֹעִילוּ
וְעֵדֵיהֶם הֵמָּה בַּל־יִרְאוּ וּבַל־יֵדְעוּ
לְמַעַן יֵבֹשׁוּ:
10 מִי־יָצַר אֵל וּפֶסֶל נָסָךְ
לְבִלְתִּי הוֹעִיל:
11 הֵן כָּל־חֲבֵרָיו יֵבֹשׁוּ
וְחָרָשִׁים הֵמָּה מֵאָדָם
יִתְקַבְּצוּ כֻלָּם יַעֲמֹדוּ
יִפְחֲדוּ יֵבֹשׁוּ יָחַד:

Commentary

8. *You are My witnesses.* As in Isaiah 43:10. See the essay in the haftarah to *B'reishit.* Note the contrast with the worshippers of false gods in verse 9: they themselves are witnesses to the inefficacy of their gods.

9-20. The Prophet's critique is a mixture of exquisite poetry and caustic humor. But did the ancients—and especially Mesopotamians who had a highly developed civilization— really believe that the statues they had fashioned were indeed divine? What many did believe was that gods could choose to make an image their place of habitation. But the representation of gods through images led to and reinforced polytheism, and the less sophisticated among the people would indeed confuse image and reality.[10]

12. A smith takes metal, works on an implement in glowing coal, and shapes it with hammers, working it with his strong arm; yet hunger makes his strength fail; without water, he grows faint.

13. A carpenter measures with a line, makes an outline with a stylus, shapes it with scrapers, marks it out with a compass, giving it a human form, with human beauty, to be placed in a shrine.

14. He cuts down cedars, or plane trees, or oaks. He sets aside trees in the forest, or plants a fir and the rain makes it grow.

15. People use the wood for fuel. They use some of it to warm themselves; they kindle a fire and bake bread; and they make a god and bow down [to it], an idol to whom they prostrate themselves.

16. Half [the wood] they throw into the fire; with that half they roast meat and eat till they are full. They warm themselves, too, and say: *I can feel the heat.*

17. With the rest they make gods, idols to whom they prostrate themselves and bow down, to whom they pray, saying: *Save me; you are my god.*

18. They do not know, they do not understand, for their eyes are too clouded to see; their minds, to understand.

12 חָרַשׁ בַּרְזֶל מַעֲצָד וּפָעַל בַּפֶּחָם וּבַמַּקָּבוֹת יִצְּרֵהוּ וַיִּפְעָלֵהוּ בִּזְרוֹעַ כֹּחוֹ גַּם־רָעֵב וְאֵין כֹּחַ לֹא־שָׁתָה מַיִם וַיִּיעָף:

13 חָרַשׁ עֵצִים נָטָה קָו יְתָאֲרֵהוּ בַשֶּׂרֶד יַעֲשֵׂהוּ בַּמַּקְצֻעוֹת וּבַמְּחוּגָה יְתָאֲרֵהוּ וַיַּעֲשֵׂהוּ כְּתַבְנִית אִישׁ כְּתִפְאֶרֶת אָדָם לָשֶׁבֶת בָּיִת:

14 לִכְרָת־לוֹ אֲרָזִים וַיִּקַּח תִּרְזָה וְאַלּוֹן וַיְאַמֶּץ־לוֹ בַּעֲצֵי־יָעַר נָטַע אֹרֶן וְגֶשֶׁם יְגַדֵּל:

15 וְהָיָה לְאָדָם לְבָעֵר וַיִּקַּח מֵהֶם וַיָּחָם אַף־יַשִּׂיק וְאָפָה לָחֶם אַף־יִפְעַל־אֵל וַיִּשְׁתָּחוּ עָשָׂהוּ פֶסֶל וַיִּסְגָּד־לָמוֹ:

16 חֶצְיוֹ שָׂרַף בְּמוֹ־אֵשׁ עַל־חֶצְיוֹ בָּשָׂר יֹאכֵל יִצְלֶה צָלִי וְיִשְׂבָּע אַף־יָחֹם וְיֹאמַר הֶאָח חַמּוֹתִי רָאִיתִי אוּר:

17 וּשְׁאֵרִיתוֹ לְאֵל עָשָׂה לְפִסְלוֹ יִסְגּוֹד [יִסְגָּד־] לוֹ וְיִשְׁתַּחוּ וְיִתְפַּלֵּל אֵלָיו וְיֹאמַר הַצִּילֵנִי כִּי אֵלִי אָתָּה:

18 לֹא יָדְעוּ וְלֹא יָבִינוּ כִּי טַח מֵרְאוֹת עֵינֵיהֶם מֵהַשְׂכִּיל לִבֹּתָם:

Commentary

12-13. These verses are of special interest to students of ancient art and technology.

16. *I can feel the heat.* Literally, "see" the heat. The faculty of seeing stands here for perception in general, as when the people of Israel standing at Sinai are said to have "seen" the thundering.[11] Similarly, in English, a blind person may be heard to say, "Yes, I see it."

19. They never take it to heart, and have neither sense nor insight to say: *I burned half the wood in the fire, and baked bread on the coals, and roasted meat and ate it: should I make the rest into an idol and prostrate myself to a block of wood?*

20. They busy themselves with ashes;

they are deluded and gone astray;

they cannot save themselves,

yet never admit: *I am holding a fake!*

21. Remember these things, O Jacob,

for you are My servant, O Israel:

I formed you, You are My servant.

O Israel, do not forget Me!

22. I have swept away your transgressions like a cloud,

your sins like a thick cloud;

return to Me,

for I have redeemed you.

23. Shout for joy, you heavens,

for the Eternal has acted!

Shout in triumph, you depths of the earth!

Break out in joyful song, O hills,

O forests and all its trees!

For the Eternal has redeemed Jacob,

and is glorified in Israel.

19 וְלֹא־יָשִׁיב אֶל־לִבּוֹ וְלֹא דַעַת וְלֹא־תְבוּנָה לֵאמֹר חֶצְיוֹ שָׂרַפְתִּי בְמוֹ־אֵשׁ וְאַף אָפִיתִי עַל־גֶּחָלָיו לֶחֶם אֶצְלֶה בָשָׂר וְאֹכֵל וְיִתְרוֹ לְתוֹעֵבָה אֶעֱשֶׂה לְבוּל עֵץ אֶסְגּוֹד:

20 רֹעֶה אֵפֶר

לֵב הוּתַל הִטָּהוּ

וְלֹא־יַצִּיל אֶת־נַפְשׁוֹ

וְלֹא יֹאמַר הֲלוֹא שֶׁקֶר בִּימִינִי:

21 זְכָר־אֵלֶּה יַעֲקֹב

וְיִשְׂרָאֵל כִּי עַבְדִּי־אָתָּה

יְצַרְתִּיךָ עֶבֶד־לִי אַתָּה

יִשְׂרָאֵל לֹא תִנָּשֵׁנִי:

22 מָחִיתִי כָעָב פְּשָׁעֶיךָ

וְכֶעָנָן חַטֹּאותֶיךָ

שׁוּבָה אֵלַי

כִּי גְאַלְתִּיךָ:

23 רָנּוּ שָׁמַיִם

כִּי־עָשָׂה יְהוָה

הָרִיעוּ תַּחְתִּיּוֹת אָרֶץ

פִּצְחוּ הָרִים רִנָּה

יַעַר וְכָל־עֵץ בּוֹ

כִּי־גָאַל יְהוָה יַעֲקֹב

וּבְיִשְׂרָאֵל יִתְפָּאָר:

Commentary

20 *With ashes.* Tending them as a shepherd tends the flock—as if they were worth guarding and worrying about.

21. *My servant.* An expression frequent in Second Isaiah. (See the essay, "The Chosen People," below.) Scholars have tried to isolate in these prophecies a series of "servant songs." (See the haftarah for Ekev.)

22. *I have swept away your transgressions.* The verse, combined with 43:25 (above), is recited repeatedly in the Yom Kippur service.[12]

Essay

The Chosen People

The Prophet addresses the exiled remnant. They are depressed and wonder whether the Eternal still remembers them. Isaiah reassures his people by invoking the image of Israel as God's servant.[13]

The image reinforces the idea of Israel's chosenness. In the Torah, the people are referred to as the Eternal's "treasured possession," and are to be "a kingdom of priests and a holy nation."[14] Because they were mysteriously chosen for divine service, they have a duty to separate themselves from the idolatry that surrounds them, and unswerving faith in the Holy One is their obligation. For this they are singled out from all other nations—strange as that concept must have struck many persons then and still does so today.

Yet it is around this very concept that Jewish history revolves. To be a Jew was and is a privilege, and in daily Jewish worship the idea is repeated time and again: We praise the Maker of heaven and earth who has set us apart from the other families of the earth, giving us a destiny unique among the nations.[15]

The choice of Israel goes back to Abraham and was confirmed at Sinai and acknowledged by the people, who affirmed: "All that the Eternal has spoken we will do."[16] In this grand view, God's plan for humanity can be put into effect only if Israel is faithful, and then the world at large will see salvation. God and Israel are forever intertwined and depend on each other.

In a direct way, then, human history is the responsibility of the Jews, for it is ultimately they to whom human fate is entrusted. God and the world await the perfection of the Jewish people.

It is without question a grand, if "unreasonable," conception. But then, is grandeur ever reasonable? Against all odds, Jews have played a role quite out of proportion to their numbers.

They have nonetheless not fared materially better than others. Rather, their task has exposed them to persecution and oppression, to anti-Semitism and the Holocaust. Yet their belief in the divinely appointed task has never disappeared, even when it has been difficult to maintain it. It was difficult in Isaiah's day, among conditions of exile, and modern times have not eased the problem of believing in a God who chose this people for divine service despite all appearances that would deny such a choice.

This is the burden of belief. Isaiah faced it among his contemporaries, and in this respect conditions are not much different today. Many Jews (as well as many gentiles) think that such a concept has become outmoded. It once served Jews as a survival mechanism, they say, but that does not work any longer in an open, egalitarian society, and consequently there is no further need for it, and all it does is to raise the resentment of others.

However, Jews and Christians who see Torah as a holy book centered in God, will counter that the only privilege that this belief entails is the self-assumed obligation to be God's servant at all times and with full devotion. In antiquity, all Israelites took this task upon themselves, not because they were in any way superior to others, but only because God's mysterious plan had so provided.

To the ears of the disbelievers, Isaiah's voice sounds strange and disconnected from an often harsh reality; for those who continue to believe in the divine promise, being a member of the Jewish people is an infinite privilege, which is grounded in special obligations, called *mitzvot*. For them, there is nothing more glorious than to be a servant of the Holy One.[17]

Gleanings

Words to Remember

I, I am the One who blots out your transgressions, for My own sake,
and your sins will I remember no more. (43:25)
As I pour water on thirsty soil,
and streams on dry ground,
so will I pour My spirit on your descendants,
My blessing upon your offspring. (44:3)
I am the first, I am the last;
there is no God but Me. (44:6)

Chosen?

Israel is an essential part of creation. By its life and history, Israel is to set forth the existence of spiritual values and a Divine purpose in the Universe; without which spiritual values life would be meaningless; and without which the Divine purpose, the material Universe, would, morally speaking, be no better than primeval chaos, *tohu va-vohu*.

Joseph H. Hertz[18]

Does chosenness mean that God is exclusively concerned with Israel and is totally oblivious of the fate of other nations? The prophet Amos [who stresses Israel's chosenness] has this to say (9:7):

To me, O Israelites, you are just like the Ethiopians—declares the Eternal.
True, I brought Israel up from the land of Egypt,
But also the Philistines from Caphtor and the Arameans from Kir.

The color of the Ethiopians is black, and in those days many of them were sold on the slave markets. The Philistines were the archenemies of Israel, and the Arameans continued to be a menace to Israel, the Northern Kingdom. The God of Israel is the God of all nations, and all men's history is His concern.

Abraham J. Heschel[19]

The doctrine is not of a Herrenvolk whom others must serve but on the contrary of a folk dedicated to the service of others.

As a powerful spur to Jewish survival, as providing a sense of destiny, as a reaffirmation of the covenant with its demands, responsibilities and obligations, the doctrine of the chosen people still possesses much value. As a temptation to narrowness and exclusiveness it still has its dangers. The modern Jew must learn to avail himself of the values inherent in the doctrine while taking due caution against its degeneration .... It is altogether right and proper that Jews should be concerned with the difficulties in the doctrine of Israel's chosenness. It may be that the Jew never comes closer to the truth in the doctrine of

chosenness than when he is severely critical of how and why God can choose the Jewish people.

Louis Jacobs[20]

Improbable history

Jewish history is a succession of vast improbabilities. It is studded with unlikely heroes, impossible coincidences, enormous failures, and astounding successes. It has received more attention, more literary, historic, and philosophic treatments—to say nothing of theological considerations—than any comparable group in history. Proponents and opponents have described its subjects in extreme terms, reaching from the "chosen of God" to the "devils incarnate." The Jews have been called mankind's greatest blessing by some, and mankind's greatest scourge by others .... Scholars of many kinds have tried their hands at describing or solving the puzzle of this people's existence.

Chosenness is one answer, and it certainly is worthy of serious consideration.

W. G. Plaut[21]

* * *

Notes

[1] Though we deal here with the Second Isaiah, we call him "Isaiah" for the sake of brevity.

[2] So Ibn Ezra. Rashi and Radak interpret differently They read the text as a reference to the past: In your own land you did not bring your sacrifices to *Me*, but instead to the idols.

[3] See Isaiah 48:9-11.

[4] Genesis chapter 12; So Rashi, followed by Freehof (*Book of Isaiah*); Radak believes the reference is to Adam; Hertz (*Pentateuch and Haftorahs*) and others, to Jacob.

[5] So also in I Chronicles 24:5.

[6] So Freehof, *Book of Isaiah*.

[7] So Freehof, *Book of Isaiah*.

[8] Deuteronomy 32:15.

[9] Rashi: They will attract many proselytes.

[10] Exodus 25:8.

[11] For a discussion of the dynamism of Mesopotamian beliefs, see W. W. Hallo and others, eds., *Scripture in Context II*, pp. 11-17.

[14] Exodus 20:15, in the Hebrew text.

[15] See, for example, The following prayerbooks: Singer, *The Authorized Prayer Book*, New York: Bloch (1957), p. 380; Silverman, *High Holiday Prayer Book*, Hartford: Prayer Book Press (1939), p. 240; Stern, *Gates of Repentance*, New York: Central Conference of American Rabbis (1978), p. 265.

[16] Isaiah 43:21.

[17] Exodus 19:5-6.

[18] So the *Aleinu* (also referred to as "Adoration"), a prayer that is recited near the end of every service.

[19] Exodus 19:8.

[20] W. Gunther Plaut has devoted an entire book to this subject: *The Case for the Chosen People* (see Bibliography).

[21] *Pentateuch and Haftorahs*, p. 424.

[22] *The Prophets*, p. 33.

[23] *A Jewish Theology*, pp. 274 ff.

[24] *The Case for the Chosen People*, p. 4.

Jeremiah, chapter 7, verse 21 to chapter 8, verse 3 and chapter 9, verses 22 to 23

Introduction

Connection of haftarah and sidra:

The weekly portion speaks of sacrifices, and so does the haftarah. The Prophet warns his people not to believe that sacrifices by themselves will please the Almighty; they must be accompanied by godly deeds.

The setting:

The haftarah is part of Jeremiah's "Temple sermon," so called because the people of Jerusalem mistakenly believed that they were forever protected by the nearness of the Temple. They endlessly repeated, "The Temple of the Eternal, the Temple of the Eternal" (7:4, not read as part of the haftarah). The sermon was probably preached at the beginning of King Jehoiakim's reign (609/608 B.C.E.), at a time of approaching political turmoil.

For more on Jeremiah and his time, see our *General Introduction*.

The message:

1. The Prophet is asked to preach a message of repentance and is told in advance that the people will not listen. (7:21-27)

2. A recital of the misdeeds of the people and of the ensuing terrible consequences. (7:28-8:3)

3. Added by the Rabbis from another chapter, so that the reading would conclude on a positive note. The two verses are among Jeremiah's most frequently quoted utterances. (9:22-23)

HAFTARAH FOR TZAV

Jeremiah, chapter 7, verse 21 to chapter 8, verse 3 and chapter 9, verses 22 to 23

7:21. Thus says the God of heaven's hosts, the God of Israel: Add your (whole) burnt-offerings to your other sacrifices and eat the meat!

22. But when I brought your ancestors out of the land of Egypt, I neither spoke to them nor commanded them about burnt-offerings or sacrifices.

23. But this is the command I gave them: *Listen to Me, and I will be your God, and you shall be My people; walk only in the way that I have commanded you, and it shall go well with you.*

24. But they neither listened nor paid heed; in the stubbornness of their evil hearts, they walked in their own counsels. They went backward instead of forward.

כֹּה אָמַר יְהֹוָה צְבָאוֹת אֱלֹהֵי יִשְׂרָאֵל 7:21
עֹלוֹתֵיכֶם סְפוּ עַל־זִבְחֵיכֶם וְאִכְלוּ בָשָׂר:

כִּי לֹא־דִבַּרְתִּי אֶת־אֲבוֹתֵיכֶם וְלֹא צִוִּיתִים 22
בְּיוֹם הוֹצִיא [הוֹצִיאִי] אוֹתָם מֵאֶרֶץ מִצְרָיִם
עַל־דִּבְרֵי עוֹלָה וָזָבַח:

כִּי אִם־אֶת־הַדָּבָר הַזֶּה צִוִּיתִי אוֹתָם לֵאמֹר 23
שִׁמְעוּ בְקוֹלִי וְהָיִיתִי לָכֶם לֵאלֹהִים וְאַתֶּם
תִּהְיוּ־לִי לְעָם וַהֲלַכְתֶּם בְּכָל־הַדֶּרֶךְ אֲשֶׁר
אֲצַוֶּה אֶתְכֶם לְמַעַן יִיטַב לָכֶם:

וְלֹא שָׁמְעוּ וְלֹא־הִטּוּ אֶת־אָזְנָם וַיֵּלְכוּ 24
בְּמֹעֵצוֹת בִּשְׁרִרוּת לִבָּם הָרָע וַיִּהְיוּ לְאָחוֹר
וְלֹא לְפָנִים:

Commentary

7:21. *Add your (whole) burnt-offerings....* The phrase can be understood only in reference to Deuteronomy 12:27. There, the Torah provides that the burnt-offering (*olah*) be totally consumed on the altar, with no food benefit to anyone; while in other offerings (*z'vachim*) the eating of the meat was permitted. Jeremiah castigates his audience by asserting that their disregard of God's law is such that these distinctions between *olah* and *z'vachim* are irrelevant.

22. *When I brought your ancestors out of the land of Egypt.* The Passover sacrifice that was commanded served a special purpose, while the regular schedule of offerings came later in Israel's history. Jeremiah's statement refers to the latter. He himself was of priestly descent and may have had access to particular traditions about these distinctions.[1]

Burnt-offerings. Which were set aside from all other offerings because (except for the hide) they had to be totally consumed by fire, and nothing of them could be eaten.

Nor commanded them about burnt-offerings. See the essay below.

The command I gave them. Though it does not occur in the Torah, it represents the Prophet's understanding of God's will.

24. *Own counsels.* Relying on oneself rather than God is for Jeremiah a grievous sin.[2]

24. *Backward instead of forward.* Regressing morally.

25. From the day your ancestors left the land of Egypt to this day, I have been sending you My servants, the prophets, sending them day in, day out.

26. But they would not listen to Me, they paid no heed; they stiffened their necks and did even worse than did their ancestors.

27. When you speak all these words to them, they shall not listen; when you call to them, they shall not answer you.

28. Therefore say to them:

Here is the nation that would not listen to
   the voice of the Eternal, their God,
that would not accept instruction.
Faithfulness is lost, banished from their
   mouths.

29. Cut off your locks, throw them away,
and on the heights raise your voice in lamentation:

25 לְמִן־הַיּוֹם אֲשֶׁר יָצְאוּ אֲבוֹתֵיכֶם מֵאֶרֶץ מִצְרַיִם עַד הַיּוֹם הַזֶּה וָאֶשְׁלַח אֲלֵיכֶם אֶת־ כָּל־עֲבָדַי הַנְּבִיאִים יוֹם הַשְׁכֵּם וְשָׁלֹחַ:

26 וְלוֹא שָׁמְעוּ אֵלַי וְלֹא הִטּוּ אֶת־אָזְנָם וַיַּקְשׁוּ אֶת־עָרְפָּם הֵרֵעוּ מֵאֲבוֹתָם:

27 וְדִבַּרְתָּ אֲלֵיהֶם אֶת־כָּל־הַדְּבָרִים הָאֵלֶּה וְלֹא יִשְׁמְעוּ אֵלֶיךָ וְקָרָאתָ אֲלֵיהֶם וְלֹא יַעֲנוּכָה:

28 וְאָמַרְתָּ אֲלֵיהֶם
זֶה הַגּוֹי אֲשֶׁר לוֹא־שָׁמְעוּ בְּקוֹל יְהוָה אֱלֹהָיו
וְלֹא לָקְחוּ מוּסָר
אָבְדָה הָאֱמוּנָה וְנִכְרְתָה מִפִּיהֶם:

29 גָּזִּי נִזְרֵךְ וְהַשְׁלִיכִי
וּשְׂאִי עַל־שְׁפָיִם קִינָה

Commentary

25. *Day in, day out.* Literally, early in the day and onward.

26. Worse *than did their ancestors.* A hint of the Prophet's displeasure with the religious reformation:[3] it started well enough and people were very proud about it, only to slide back into their former ways.

27. *They shall not listen.* No more than they listened to Me.

28. *Instruction.* מוסר (*musar*), teaching a moral life.

Faithfulness. אמונה (*emunah*). The word is difficult to translate, for it reflects a combination of truth and steadfastness, and is often applied to God (who is called *El emunah*). The basic Hebrew assertion of something being true and right is אמן (*amen*, which is of the same root).

29. *Cut off your locks.* In antiquity, a sign of mourning;[4] the Prophet is to address Jerusalem. In addition, Jeremiah's term for "locks" (*nezer*) alludes to Nazirite vows. People are hypocrites: they wear long hair to show their devotion to God, yet their outward observance has no value, and they might as well cast their shorn locks away instead of burning them in accordance with Torah law.[5]

The Eternal has rejected and abandoned the generation [that provoked] God's wrath.

30. The people of Judah have done what is evil in My sight, says the Eternal One: They have placed their idols in the house that bears My name, and defiled it.

31. They have built the shrine of Tophet in the Valley of Ben-Hinnom, to sacrifice their sons and daughters by burning—something I never commanded them to do, something that never entered My mind!

32. Therefore, says the Eternal One, the days are coming when this place will no longer be called Tophet or the Valley of Ben-Hinnom, but the Valley of Slaughter; they shall bury in Tophet till no room remains.

כִּי מָאַס יְהֹוָה וַיִּטֹּשׁ אֶת־דּוֹר עֶבְרָתוֹ:

30 כִּי־עָשׂוּ בְנֵי־יְהוּדָה הָרַע בְּעֵינַי נְאוּם־יְהֹוָה שָׂמוּ שִׁקּוּצֵיהֶם בַּבַּיִת אֲשֶׁר־נִקְרָא־שְׁמִי עָלָיו לְטַמְּאוֹ:

31 וּבָנוּ בָּמוֹת הַתֹּפֶת אֲשֶׁר בְּגֵיא בֶן־הִנֹּם לִשְׂרֹף אֶת־בְּנֵיהֶם וְאֶת־בְּנֹתֵיהֶם בָּאֵשׁ אֲשֶׁר לֹא צִוִּיתִי וְלֹא עָלְתָה עַל־לִבִּי:

32 לָכֵן הִנֵּה־יָמִים בָּאִים נְאֻם־יְהֹוָה וְלֹא־יֵאָמֵר עוֹד הַתֹּפֶת וְגֵיא בֶן־הִנֹּם כִּי אִם־גֵּיא הַהֲרֵגָה וְקָבְרוּ בְתֹפֶת מֵאֵין מָקוֹם:

Commentary

31. *Shrine*. Or "high place." במות (*bamot*) is a plural form, but is here treated as a singular. Conventionally, the word is rendered as "high place," but in fact we do not know what precisely a *bamah* was. The Moabite king Mesha in the mid-9th century left an inscription that mentions the building of a *bamah*, but no traces of it have been found. The word בימה, *bimah*, which designates a stage or the elevated pulpit area in the synagogue, is unconnected to the Hebrew *bamah* and is derived from the Greek *bema*, which meant "raised place to speak from in a public assembly."

Tophet. Located just outside Jerusalem, in a valley that featured a rise where the rite took place.[6]

Ben-Hinnom. Probably named after a former owner, it later became the common place for the burial of Jerusalemites, and was referred to as the "Valley of Hinnom" (Ge-Hinnom).[7]

Burning. The altars of Ben-Hinnom were associated with sacrificing children to the god Molech (and also Baal).[8]

Never entered My mind. An anthropomorphism, bringing to the hearer's mind the story of the sacrifice of Isaac, which showed that human sacrifice was contrary to divine will.[9]

33. The bodies of this people will be food for birds and beasts; there will be no one to frighten them away.

34. And in the towns of Judah and the street of Jerusalem I will silence

the sounds of joy and the sounds of gladness,

the voice of the bridegroom and the voice of the bride,

for the land shall be a ruin.

8:1. At that time, says the Eternal One, the bones of the kings of Judah, the leaders, priests, prophets, and all the people of Jerusalem shall be taken out of their graves.

2. They shall be spread out under the sun, moon, and the hosts of heaven which they loved and served, which they followed and consulted and worshipped; instead of being gathered up and buried, they shall be dung, fertilizing the ground.

3. And the remnant that remains of this evil folk in all the remaining places to which I have driven them will prefer death to life, says the God of heaven's hosts.

33 וְהָיְתָ֞ה נִבְלַ֤ת הָעָם֙ הַזֶּ֔ה לְמַֽאֲכָ֕ל לְע֥וֹף הַשָּׁמַ֖יִם וּלְבֶהֱמַ֣ת הָאָ֑רֶץ וְאֵ֖ין מַחֲרִֽיד׃

34 וְהִשְׁבַּתִּ֣י ׀ מֵעָרֵ֣י יְהוּדָ֗ה וּמֵֽחֻצוֹת֙ יְר֣וּשָׁלִַ֔ם ק֤וֹל שָׂשׂוֹן֙ וְק֣וֹל שִׂמְחָ֔ה ק֥וֹל חָתָ֖ן וְק֣וֹל כַּלָּ֑ה כִּ֥י לְחׇרְבָּ֖ה תִּהְיֶ֥ה הָאָֽרֶץ׃

8:1 בָּעֵ֣ת הַהִ֣יא נְאֻם־יְהֹוָ֗ה [וְיֹצִ֜יאוּ] וְיֹצִ֜יאוּ אֶת־עַצְמ֣וֹת מַלְכֵֽי־יְהוּדָ֣ה וְאֶת־עַצְמוֹת־שָׂרָיו֮ וְאֶת־עַצְמ֣וֹת הַכֹּהֲנִ֣ים וְאֵ֣ת עַצְמ֣וֹת הַנְּבִיאִ֗ים וְאֵ֛ת עַצְמ֥וֹת יֽוֹשְׁבֵי־יְרוּשָׁלָ֖͏ִם מִקִּבְרֵיהֶֽם׃

2 וּשְׁטָח֣וּם לַשֶּׁ֣מֶשׁ וְלַיָּרֵ֗חַ וּלְכֹ֣ל ׀ צְבָ֣א הַשָּׁמַ֡יִם אֲשֶׁ֣ר אֲהֵב֡וּם וַאֲשֶׁ֣ר עֲבָדוּם֩ וַאֲשֶׁ֨ר הָלְכ֜וּ אַֽחֲרֵיהֶ֗ם וַאֲשֶׁ֤ר דְּרָשׁוּם֙ וַאֲשֶׁ֣ר הִֽשְׁתַּחֲו֣וּ לָהֶ֔ם לֹ֤א יֵאָֽסְפוּ֙ וְלֹ֣א יִקָּבֵ֔רוּ לְדֹ֛מֶן עַל־פְּנֵ֥י הָאֲדָמָ֖ה יִֽהְיֽוּ׃

3 וְנִבְחַ֥ר מָ֙וֶת֙ מֵֽחַיִּ֔ים לְכֹ֗ל הַשְּׁאֵרִית֙ הַנִּשְׁאָרִ֔ים מִן־הַמִּשְׁפָּחָ֥ה הָֽרָעָ֖ה הַזֹּ֑את בְּכׇל־הַמְּקֹמ֤וֹת הַנִּשְׁאָרִים֙ אֲשֶׁ֣ר הִדַּחְתִּ֣ים שָׁ֔ם נְאֻ֖ם יְהֹוָ֥ה צְבָאֽוֹת׃

Commentary

33. *Food for birds and beasts*. Similar to the dire threats of Deuteronomy 28:26.

34. *Sounds of joy*. The prophecy speaks of silencing the happy sounds in a sinful land, but these very words have entered the Jewish wedding ceremony as a joyful blessing (see further under *Gleanings*, below).

8:1. *Bones of the kings* …. The Hebrew of the sentence features a constant repetition of the words "the bones of …" and creates a rhythm of emphasis.

Shall be taken out of their graves. By the enemy.

2. *Fertilizing the ground*. Literally, "lying upon the ground."[10]

9:22. Thus says the Eternal One:
Let not the wise glory in their wisdom,
let not the mighty glory in their might,
let not the rich glory in their riches;
23. but let them who glory, glory in this:
that they understand and know Me,
that I, the Eternal,
practice kindness, justice,
and righteousness in the earth,
for in these things do I delight,
says the Eternal One.

9:22 כֹּה אָמַר יְהֹוָה
אַל־יִתְהַלֵּל חָכָם בְּחָכְמָתוֹ
וְאַל־יִתְהַלֵּל הַגִּבּוֹר בִּגְבוּרָתוֹ
אַל־יִתְהַלֵּל עָשִׁיר בְּעָשְׁרוֹ:
23 כִּי אִם־בְּזֹאת יִתְהַלֵּל הַמִּתְהַלֵּל
הַשְׂכֵּל וְיָדֹעַ אוֹתִי
כִּי אֲנִי יְהֹוָה עֹשֶׂה חֶסֶד מִשְׁפָּט
וּצְדָקָה בָּאָרֶץ
כִּי־בְאֵלֶּה חָפַצְתִּי נְאֻם־יְהֹוָה:

Essay

Preaching despite likely failure

Jeremiah's life as a prophet was one continuous trial. Not only did he repeatedly suffer incarceration and constant threats of death, but the very message he was to deliver was—so it would appear—contradictory. Nowhere else is this highlighted more clearly than in this haftarah.

To go and preach what he knew to be God's message was one thing. He was, like all true prophets, obeying a command he could not escape. "Preach to the people, tell them of their shortcomings, urge them to repent and mend their ways both personally and as a community"—that was the content of every prophet's admonitions. In Jeremiah's case, the divine behest was, in addition, accompanied by physical danger and misery, and it all ended with forced exile to a strange land.

Still, he would have found his trials more bearable had there been even the slightest possibility that some persons in positions of responsibility would heed his warnings. However unpopular his message, however "politically incorrect" it was, he could always hope that somehow the voice of God would be heard above the tumult of corruption, exploitation, and idolatry.

But even this hope was taken away from him, for (as our haftarah tells us) God says to him: You must tell them the truth, but you should also know that you will fail. They will not hear you; they will be deaf to what you will tell them:

When you speak all these words to them, they shall not listen;
when you call them they shall not answer you. (7:27)

In other words, the Prophet was to discharge his dangerous and difficult task in the certainty of failure. "Why am I doing this and to what purpose?" he must have asked himself time and again.

Yet preach he did, at mortal danger to himself, for refusing to heed the divine behest was impossible for him. But why would God decide to expose him to this terrible trial altogether? No answer can be more than a surmise, and it is well to keep the words of another prophet in mind: "My thoughts are not your thoughts, says the Eternal."[11]

This commentary reads verse 27 ('they [the people] shall not listen') not as a given fact but as a divine assessment of reality that Jeremiah should know in advance: "Go and remind the people of their duty, but know also that the *chances* of your success are minimal. Still,

you must go, for they need to hear your message. There is always a chance, however small, that they will turn back from their evil ways. I don't think you will have any success—*but even I cannot tell the decisions that human beings will make, for I have given them free will. I want to grant them one more chance to repent.*"[12]

We believe that this is the way the Prophet understood the challenge. He knew that the likelihood of his success was severely limited; and yet he felt he had to proceed. This heroic optimism was a hallmark of his faith and of his loyalty to the One who sent him.

Gleanings

Words to Remember

In the towns of Judah and the streets of Jerusalem
will be heard the sounds of joy and the sounds of gladness,
the voice of the bridegroom and the voice of the bride.
(Extracted from 7:34 and recited in the seventh benediction at the wedding ceremony.)

Let not the wise glory in their wisdom, let not the mighty glory in their might, let not the rich glory in their riches; but let them who glory, glory in this: that they know and understand Me, that I, the Eternal, practice kindness, justice, and righteousness in the earth, for in these things do I delight, says the Eternal One. (9:22-23)

About child sacrifice

Generally, the pagan god Molech (also Molek or Moloch) was associated with child sacrifices offered to him. However, a number of questions remain about the practices.

For instance, some medieval Jewish scholars wondered whether children were actually burned or whether this was a ceremony at which youngsters had to go through a fire ritual. This theory has lately been revived.[13]

An older proposal denied that Molech was a god, but that Molech (or a related form) was the name of the ceremony that had its parallels in North Africa (Carthage, for instance). The majority of contemporary scholars accept the biblical evidence, that indeed there was child sacrifice and that the godhead to whom it was dedicated was Molech (and sometimes Baal). However, those favoring this interpretation "must concede that the portrait of a god Molek remains frustratingly difficult to draw with precision, and that the ultimate 'why' of the cult occasions much speculation but little certainty."[14]

* * *

Notes

[1] S. D. Sperling, "Jeremiah," *Encyclopedia of Religion*, vol. 8, pp. 1-6.

[2] See W. Holladay, *Jeremiah 1*, p. 121.

[3] II Kings chapters 22 and 23; see also our *General Introduction*.

[4] See Micah 1:16; Job 1:20.

[5] Numbers chapter 6; Amos 2:11. See the haftarah for Vayeishev, and the Torah Commentary, pp. 1060 ff.

[6] Compare II Kings 23:10.

[7] In later parlance, Gehinnom (or Gehenna in many translations) became identified as a hellish place of the dead.

[8] Jeremiah refers to it also in 19:5 and 32:35; see also Leviticus 18:21. See the Torah Commentary, pp. 883 ff., and under *Gleanings*.

[9] See Genesis chapter 22.

[10] Translation suggested by John Bright (*Anchor Bible*, Jeremiah).

[11] Isaiah 55:8.

[12] The possibility that human freedom and God's foreknowledge could exist side by side was expressed by Rabbi Akiba in this manner: "Everything is foreseen, yet freedom of choice is given" (Pirkei Avot 3:15; and see the Rambam's commentary thereon). But in Akiba's view, God *does* know how humans will decide.

[13] See M. Weinfeld, "The Worship of Molech and of the Queen of Heaven and Its Background," *Ugarit-Forschungen* (1972), vol. 4, pp. 133-154.

[14] G. C. Heider in a survey of the theories, *Anchor Bible Dictionary*, vol. 4, pp. 895-898.

שְׁמִינִי

Second Samuel, chapter 6, verse 1 to chapter 7, verse 17

Introduction

Connection of sidra and haftarah:

Both sidra and haftarah report tragic incidents involving the Tabernacle and the Ark, respectively, and both portions raise questions: Why did Nadab, Abihu, and Uzzah die? And what was Uzzah's transgression?

The setting:

David's wars with the Philistines had ended in victory for Israel, and now—with peace reigning at last—the king wanted the long-exiled Ark of the Covenant brought to Jerusalem. This symbolic act was to give the tribal confederacy a religious center and was meant to unite it into a nation with a secular and religious capital. This happened in the early part of the 10th century B.C.E.

For more on the two books of Samuel, see our *General Introduction;* on David and his time, see the haftarah for Chayei Sarah.

The story:

1. David starts to bring the Ark to Jerusalem, but a tragic incident mars the triumphant return. (6:1-8)

2. In consequence, David abandons his plan and temporarily houses the Ark with Obed-Edom. (9-11)

3. When Obed-Edom prospers, David interprets it as a sign that he should resume his plan, and this time sees it through. The Ark is now installed in Jerusalem. (2-19)

4. Interlude: Michal, David's wife, is displeased with the way her husband comported himself during the celebration. (20-23)

5. David now wants to build a temple to house the Ark, but God (through the prophet Nathan) aborts the plan. Still, there is long-term compensation for David, for God promises him that his royal house shall reign forever. (7:1-17)

HAFTARAH FOR SH'MINI

Second Samuel, chapter 6, verse 1 to chapter 7, verse 17

6:1. Once more David brought together Israel's best men, thirty thousand in all.

2. Then David and all the people with him went up from Baalei-Judah, to take up from there the Ark of God, on which is written the Name—the Name *God of Heaven's Hosts*—Enthroned on the Cherubim.

3. They put the Ark of God on a new cart and took it out of the house of Abinadab on the hill; Uzzah and Achio, Abinadab's sons, drove the new cart.

4. As they brought it out of Abinadab's house on the hill, with the Ark of God [on it], Achio was walking in front of the Ark,

5. while David and the rest of the Israelites were dancing before God [to the sound of] all kinds of [instruments of] cedar-wood—harps, lyres, tambourines, rattles, and cymbals.

6:1 וַיֹּסֶף עוֹד דָּוִד אֶת־כָּל־בָּחוּר בְּיִשְׂרָאֵל שְׁלֹשִׁים אָלֶף:

2 וַיָּקָם וַיֵּלֶךְ דָּוִד וְכָל־הָעָם אֲשֶׁר אִתּוֹ מִבַּעֲלֵי יְהוּדָה לְהַעֲלוֹת מִשָּׁם אֵת אֲרוֹן הָאֱלֹהִים אֲשֶׁר־נִקְרָא שֵׁם שֵׁם יְהוָה צְבָאוֹת יֹשֵׁב הַכְּרֻבִים עָלָיו:

3 וַיַּרְכִּבוּ אֶת־אֲרוֹן הָאֱלֹהִים אֶל־עֲגָלָה חֲדָשָׁה וַיִּשָּׂאֻהוּ מִבֵּית אֲבִינָדָב אֲשֶׁר בַּגִּבְעָה וְעֻזָּא וְאַחְיוֹ בְּנֵי אֲבִינָדָב נֹהֲגִים אֶת־הָעֲגָלָה חֲדָשָׁה:

4 וַיִּשָּׂאֻהוּ מִבֵּית אֲבִינָדָב אֲשֶׁר בַּגִּבְעָה עִם אֲרוֹן הָאֱלֹהִים וְאַחְיוֹ הֹלֵךְ לִפְנֵי הָאָרוֹן:

5 וְדָוִד וְכָל־בֵּית יִשְׂרָאֵל מְשַׂחֲקִים לִפְנֵי יְהוָה בְּכֹל עֲצֵי בְרוֹשִׁים וּבְכִנֹּרוֹת וּבִנְבָלִים וּבְתֻפִּים וּבִמְנַעַנְעִים וּבְצֶלְצֶלִים:

Commentary

6:1. *Thirty thousand.* The original meaning of אֶלֶף (*elef*, thousand) was "unit," and described a flexible number of men who formed the basic military unit, usually about nine to ten soldiers.[1] Most likely, David's choicest soldiers did not number thirty thousand, but thirty units, or about three thousand men.

2. *Baalei-Judah.* Another name for Kiriat-Ye'arim, some 6 miles (10 kilometers) west of Jerusalem.[2]

On which is written the Name. There is no other reference to God's Name being written on the Ark. It has therefore been suggested that this identification was made when the Ark was in the possession of the Philistines.[3]

Cherubim. See our comment on I Kings 8:6 (haftarah for Pikudei).

3. *New cart.* Because of the significance of the occasion. The Philistines, too, in possession of the Ark for some time, had made a new cart for it.[4]

Abinadab. In whose keeping the Ark had been after its liberation from the Philistines.[5]

Uzzah and Achio. The unfortunate tale of Uzzah follows; about Achio (אַחְיוֹ) we know nothing. The word was possibly mis-vocalized and originally read אָחִיו (*achiv*, his brother).[6]

6. But when they got to the threshing-floor of Nachon, the oxen nearly upset [the cart], and Uzzah reached out for and seized hold of the Ark of God,

7. and the Eternal grew furious with Uzzah and God struck him down on the spot, because of his disrespect; there he died, next to the Ark of God.

8. David, distressed because the Eternal had broken out there against Uzzah, named that place Peretz-Uzzah, and so it is called to this day.

9. That day David was terrified of the Eternal, and he said: How can I let the Ark of the Eternal come to me?

6 וַיָּבֹאוּ עַד־גֹּרֶן נָכוֹן וַיִּשְׁלַח עֻזָּא אֶל־אֲרוֹן הָאֱלֹהִים וַיֹּאחֶז בּוֹ כִּי שָׁמְטוּ הַבָּקָר:

7 וַיִּחַר־אַף יְהֹוָה בְּעֻזָּה וַיַּכֵּהוּ שָׁם הָאֱלֹהִים עַל־הַשַּׁל וַיָּמָת שָׁם עִם אֲרוֹן הָאֱלֹהִים:

8 וַיִּחַר לְדָוִד עַל אֲשֶׁר פָּרַץ יְהֹוָה פֶּרֶץ בְּעֻזָּה וַיִּקְרָא לַמָּקוֹם הַהוּא פֶּרֶץ עֻזָּה עַד הַיּוֹם הַזֶּה:

9 וַיִּרָא דָוִד אֶת־יְהֹוָה בַּיּוֹם הַהוּא וַיֹּאמֶר אֵיךְ יָבוֹא אֵלַי אֲרוֹן יְהֹוָה:

Commentary

6. *Nachon.* In the parallel account in I Chronicles 13:9, his name is Kidon.

The oxen nearly upset [the cart]. Others interpret it as "stumbled"; a few understand it as "defecated";[7] in any case, the meaning of the Hebrew is in doubt.

7. *The Eternal ... struck him down.* See the essay below.

Because of his disrespect. So the Targum; the account in Chronicles says that he laid a hand on the Ark.[8]

8. *Distressed.* It is noteworthy that the storyteller uses the same Hebrew word for God's anger and for David's distress (ויחר, *va-yichar*), and therefore some translators render both the divine and the human reaction as "anger"—suggesting that David was angry with God, even as God was angry with Uzzah. But this sentiment does not fit David, who was at all times submissive to God and did not, like Abraham or Moses, question the divine judgment. Indeed, the text—though using *va-yichar* in both instances—introduces a subtle difference: In David's case it says ויחר לדוד (*va-yichar* **le**-david), which elsewhere indicates distress rather than anger.[9] As the next verse indicates, David was terrified.

10. So David was not willing to have the Ark brought to him at the City of David; instead, David diverted it to the house of Obed-Edom the Gittite.

11. The Ark of the Eternal remained at the house of Obed-Edom for three months, and [during that time] the Eternal blessed Obed-Edom and all his family.

12. When David was told that the Eternal had blessed Obed-Edom and all his family because of the Ark of God, David went and had the Ark of God brought up from the house of Obed-Edom to the City of David, with rejoicing.

13. When the Ark bearers had gone six steps, he sacrificed an ox and a fatling.

14. David, dressed in a linen tunic, skipped before the Eternal with all his might.

10 וְלֹא־אָבָה דָוִד לְהָסִיר אֵלָיו אֶת־אֲרוֹן יְהֹוָה עַל־עִיר דָּוִד וַיַּטֵּהוּ דָוִד בֵּית עֹבֵד־אֱדוֹם הַגִּתִּי:

11 וַיֵּשֶׁב אֲרוֹן יְהֹוָה בֵּית עֹבֵד אֱדֹם הַגִּתִּי שְׁלֹשָׁה חֳדָשִׁים וַיְבָרֶךְ יְהֹוָה אֶת־עֹבֵד אֱדֹם וְאֶת־כָּל־בֵּיתוֹ:

12 וַיֻּגַּד לַמֶּלֶךְ דָּוִד לֵאמֹר בֵּרַךְ יְהֹוָה אֶת־בֵּית עֹבֵד אֱדֹם וְאֶת־כָּל־אֲשֶׁר־לוֹ בַּעֲבוּר אֲרוֹן הָאֱלֹהִים וַיֵּלֶךְ דָּוִד וַיַּעַל אֶת־אֲרוֹן הָאֱלֹהִים מִבֵּית עֹבֵד אֱדֹם עִיר דָּוִד בְּשִׂמְחָה:

13 וַיְהִי כִּי צָעֲדוּ נֹשְׂאֵי אֲרוֹן־יְהֹוָה שִׁשָּׁה צְעָדִים וַיִּזְבַּח שׁוֹר וּמְרִיא:

14 וְדָוִד מְכַרְכֵּר בְּכָל־עֹז לִפְנֵי יְהֹוָה וְדָוִד חָגוּר אֵפוֹד בָּד:

Commentary

10. *City of David.* It was located to the east and south of the present walls. This is the name often given to the Jerusalem of the early days, after it had been captured by David from the Jebusites.

Obed-Edom the Gittite. The name suggests that the new caretaker was a non-Israelite,[10] commandeered by David to take on this task.[11] But this view is not unanimous; see further under *Gleanings.*

13. *Six steps.* The first steps were crucial, and after David saw that things were going well he brought a sacrifice of thanksgiving.[12]

An ox and a fatling. In the parallel account he sacrificed seven bulls and seven rams, stressing not only the extravagance of numbers but also the maleness of the animals.[13]

14. *Linen tunic.* The text speaks of an ephod, the shape of which is not fully clear. Neither Torah nor other biblical writings explain it further, which suggests that it was a well-known garment It may have been a kind of pinafore, or a type of loincloth, worn to emphasize that Israelite priests were forbidden the kind of cultic nakedness of certain pagan practices.[14] Its wearing emphasized the king's role as a priest, in which capacity he proceeded to bless the people (verse 18).

15. And so David and the whole House of Israel brought up the Ark of the Eternal with shouting and blasts of the shofar.

16. As the Ark of the Eternal entered the City of David, Michal, Saul's daughter, was looking out the window; when she observed King David leaping and skipping before the Eternal, she came to despise him.

17. They brought in the Ark of the Eternal and set it in its place, in the tent that David had prepared for it; then David sacrificed burnt-offerings and peace-offerings in honor of the Eternal.

18. When David was done with his offerings, he blessed the people in the name of the God of heaven's hosts,

19. and he distributed to every one of the large number of Israelites, men and women alike, a loaf of bread, fruit cake, and a flask (of wine). Then the people returned to their homes.

15 וְדָוִד וְכָל־בֵּית יִשְׂרָאֵל מַעֲלִים אֶת־אֲרוֹן
יְהֹוָה בִּתְרוּעָה וּבְקוֹל שׁוֹפָר:

16 וְהָיָה אֲרוֹן יְהֹוָה בָּא עִיר דָּוִד וּמִיכַל
בַּת־שָׁאוּל נִשְׁקְפָה בְּעַד הַחַלּוֹן וַתֵּרֶא אֶת־
הַמֶּלֶךְ דָּוִד מְפַזֵּז וּמְכַרְכֵּר לִפְנֵי יְהֹוָה וַתִּבֶז
לוֹ בְּלִבָּהּ:

17 וַיָּבִאוּ אֶת־אֲרוֹן יְהֹוָה וַיַּצִּגוּ אֹתוֹ בִּמְקוֹמוֹ
בְּתוֹךְ הָאֹהֶל אֲשֶׁר נָטָה־לוֹ דָּוִד וַיַּעַל דָּוִד
עֹלוֹת לִפְנֵי יְהֹוָה וּשְׁלָמִים:

18 וַיְכַל דָּוִד מֵהַעֲלוֹת הָעוֹלָה וְהַשְּׁלָמִים
וַיְבָרֶךְ אֶת־הָעָם בְּשֵׁם יְהֹוָה צְבָאוֹת:

19 וַיְחַלֵּק לְכָל־הָעָם לְכָל־הֲמוֹן יִשְׂרָאֵל
לְמֵאִישׁ וְעַד־אִשָּׁה לְאִישׁ חַלַּת לֶחֶם אַחַת
וְאֶשְׁפָּר אֶחָד וַאֲשִׁישָׁה אֶחָת וַיֵּלֶךְ כָּל־הָעָם
אִישׁ לְבֵיתוֹ:

Commentary

17. *The tent.* A new but temporary abode, for David expected to build a temple.

19. *The large number.* Of those present.

Fruit cake. So the meaning in modern Hebrew. But some understand אשפר (*eshpar*) to be a portion of meat, which would mean that David distributed the three basics of a festive meal: bread, meat, and wine.[15]

A flask (of wine). In modern Hebrew אשישה (*ashishah*); more generally in the shortened form אשיש (*ashish*) can mean either flask or fruit cake.

20. When David went home to greet his household, Michal, Saul's daughter, went out to greet him. She said: The king of Israel really honored himself today! He showed himself off before every slave girl like an empty-headed lout!

21. David answered Michal: Before the Eternal, who chose me over your father and all his family to be the leader of Israel, the people of the Eternal! I shall dance before the Eternal,

22. and "dishonor" myself even more, and lower myself even more—and, yet, I shall be honored by those slave girls you were talking about!

23. And Michal, Saul's daughter, never bore a child till the day she died.

20 וַיָּשָׁב דָּוִד לְבָרֵךְ אֶת־בֵּיתוֹ וַתֵּצֵא מִיכַל
בַּת־שָׁאוּל לִקְרַאת דָּוִד וַתֹּאמֶר מַה־נִּכְבַּד
הַיּוֹם מֶלֶךְ יִשְׂרָאֵל אֲשֶׁר נִגְלָה הַיּוֹם לְעֵינֵי
אַמְהוֹת עֲבָדָיו כְּהִגָּלוֹת נִגְלוֹת אַחַד הָרֵקִים:

21 וַיֹּאמֶר דָּוִד אֶל־מִיכַל לִפְנֵי יְהֹוָה אֲשֶׁר
בָּחַר־בִּי מֵאָבִיךְ וּמִכָּל־בֵּיתוֹ לְצַוֹּת אֹתִי נָגִיד
עַל־עַם יְהֹוָה עַל־יִשְׂרָאֵל וְשִׂחַקְתִּי לִפְנֵי
יְהֹוָה:

22 וּנְקַלֹּתִי עוֹד מִזֹּאת וְהָיִיתִי שָׁפָל בְּעֵינָי
וְעִם־הָאֲמָהוֹת אֲשֶׁר אָמַרְתְּ עִמָּם אִכָּבֵדָה:

23 וּלְמִיכַל בַּת־שָׁאוּל לֹא־הָיָה לָהּ יָלֶד עַד
יוֹם מוֹתָהּ:

Commentary

20. *Michal.* David's first wife.

To greet. The Hebrew ברך (*b-r-ch*) can mean both to bless (as in verse 18) and, more rarely, to greet. [16]

She said. Sarcastically.

Showed himself off. By his ecstatic dancing, which she considered lacking in royal dignity.

21. *Chose me over your father.* In retaliation, David reminds her that God replaced her father with the very man she now despises.

23. *Never bore a child.* Having children was considered a reward for piety, [17] and the writer clearly disapproved of Michal's reproach—yet the Torah appears to support her critique when it says: "Do not ascend My altar by steps, lest your nakedness may be exposed." [18] In fact, a variant tradition reports that she had five children. [19]

7:1. When the king had settled in his palace, and the Eternal had made him safe from his enemies in the surrounding countries,

2. the king said to Nathan the prophet: Look, now—I live in a cedar palace, while the Ark of the Eternal stays in a tent!

3. Nathan said to the king: The Eternal is with you; do all that is in your heart.

4. That night, however, the word of the Eternal came to Nathan [in a dream]:

5. Go tell My servant David: *Is it you who shall build Me a temple to dwell in?*

6. I have not had a temple from the time I brought the people of Israel up out of Egypt to this day; I have moved about in a tent and a tabernacle.

7:1 וַיְהִי כִּי־יָשַׁב הַמֶּלֶךְ בְּבֵיתוֹ וַיהוָה הֵנִיחַ לוֹ מִסָּבִיב מִכָּל־אֹיְבָיו:

2 וַיֹּאמֶר הַמֶּלֶךְ אֶל־נָתָן הַנָּבִיא רְאֵה נָא אָנֹכִי יוֹשֵׁב בְּבֵית אֲרָזִים וַאֲרוֹן הָאֱלֹהִים יֹשֵׁב בְּתוֹךְ הַיְרִיעָה:

3 וַיֹּאמֶר נָתָן אֶל־הַמֶּלֶךְ כֹּל אֲשֶׁר בִּלְבָבְךָ לֵךְ עֲשֵׂה כִּי יְהוָה עִמָּךְ:

4 וַיְהִי בַּלַּיְלָה הַהוּא וַיְהִי דְּבַר־יְהוָה אֶל־נָתָן לֵאמֹר:

5 לֵךְ וְאָמַרְתָּ אֶל־עַבְדִּי אֶל־דָּוִד כֹּה אָמַר יְהוָה הַאַתָּה תִּבְנֶה־לִּי בַיִת לְשִׁבְתִּי:

6 כִּי לֹא יָשַׁבְתִּי בְּבַיִת לְמִיּוֹם הַעֲלֹתִי אֶת־בְּנֵי יִשְׂרָאֵל מִמִּצְרַיִם וְעַד הַיּוֹם הַזֶּה וָאֶהְיֶה מִתְהַלֵּךְ בְּאֹהֶל וּבְמִשְׁכָּן:

Commentary

7:1. *Made him safe.* Literally, gave him rest. He had decisively defeated his enemies, and especially the Philistines, and now could turn to matters close to his heart.

2. *Nathan the prophet.* This is his first appearance in the Tanach. The fact that he is mentioned without explanation or background indicates that his figure had become a household word by the time the book was written. He severely rebuked the king for arranging the death of Uriah (the husband of Bathsheba, with whom he had committed adultery[20]), and played a crucial role in securing the kingship for Solomon.[21] He wrote down his experiences, but the book has been lost.[22]

3. Nathan wrongly anticipates God's approval.

6. *I have not had a temple.* This and the following verses are highly anthropomorphic, but were clearly quite acceptable to the contemporary reader. The writer (possibly Nathan himself) projected very human feelings upon God. The underlying sense is important: God was not and is not bound to or identified with one place only.

A tent and a tabernacle. The two Torah terms for the portable sanctuary: אהל (*ohel*) and משכן (*mishkan*).

7. In all My wanderings with the people of Israel, have I ever said a word of complaint to any of the leaders I have appointed to take care of My people Israel, that they did not build Me a cedar temple?

8. And say this, too, to My servant David: Thus says the God of heaven's hosts: I took you from the pasture, from following the flock, to be the leader of My people Israel.

9. I have been with you wherever you have gone, and cut down all your enemies for you; I will make your name great, like that of the greatest on earth.

10. And I am establishing a [secure] place for My people Israel, and planting them there, so that they can live without having to be afraid; nor shall evildoers oppress them, as they have been doing

7 בְּכֹל אֲשֶׁר־הִתְהַלַּכְתִּי בְּכָל־בְּנֵי יִשְׂרָאֵל הֲדָבָר דִּבַּרְתִּי אֶת־אַחַד שִׁבְטֵי יִשְׂרָאֵל אֲשֶׁר צִוִּיתִי לִרְעוֹת אֶת־עַמִּי אֶת־יִשְׂרָאֵל לֵאמֹר לָמָּה לֹא־בְנִיתֶם לִי בֵּית אֲרָזִים:

8 וְעַתָּה כֹּה־תֹאמַר לְעַבְדִּי לְדָוִד כֹּה אָמַר יְהוָה צְבָאוֹת אֲנִי לְקַחְתִּיךָ מִן־הַנָּוֶה מֵאַחַר הַצֹּאן לִהְיוֹת נָגִיד עַל־עַמִּי עַל־יִשְׂרָאֵל:

9 וָאֶהְיֶה עִמְּךָ בְּכֹל אֲשֶׁר הָלַכְתָּ וָאַכְרִתָה אֶת־כָּל־אֹיְבֶיךָ מִפָּנֶיךָ וְעָשִׂתִי לְךָ שֵׁם גָּדוֹל כְּשֵׁם הַגְּדֹלִים אֲשֶׁר בָּאָרֶץ:

10 וְשַׂמְתִּי מָקוֹם לְעַמִּי לְיִשְׂרָאֵל וּנְטַעְתִּיו וְשָׁכַן תַּחְתָּיו וְלֹא יִרְגַּז עוֹד וְלֹא־יֹסִיפוּ בְנֵי־עַוְלָה לְעַנּוֹתוֹ כַּאֲשֶׁר בָּרִאשׁוֹנָה:

Commentary

7. *Cedar temple.* Wood from the cedars of Lebanon was prized as especially fine. Later, Solomon would arrange with King Hiram of Tyre to float the wood down the coast to Israelite territory, whence it was hauled overland to Jerusalem.[23] An ancient myth told of the gods going to Lebanon in order to secure wood for the palace of Baal.

10. *Without having to be afraid.* A free translation; the Hebrew is difficult.[24] ושכן תחתיו (*v'shachan tachtav*) means literally, "dwell under it" or "in place of it." It is most likely an elliptical expression that fits the context: "I will plant (Israel securely) and it will dwell (with firm ground) under it."[25]

11. ever since I appointed leaders over My people Israel [to defend them]. But I will make you safe from all your enemies—and the Eternal guarantees you to build up your house.

12. For when your days are done and you sleep with the ancestors, I will appoint your child, your offspring, to succeed you, and establish his kingdom.

13. He is the one who shall build a temple for Me, and I will establish his royal throne for eternity.

14. I will be a parent to him, as he shall be a child to Me, so that when he does wrong, I will punish him with the rod [I apply] to human beings, with the afflictions of mortals;

15. but My steadfast love will never go away from him, as I took it away from Saul when I removed him in your favor.

16. Your house and your kingdom shall always be secure; your throne shall be set firm for all time.

17. In accordance with all these words, and in accordance with this entire vision, so did Nathan transmit [it all] to David.

11 וּלְמִן־הַיּוֹם אֲשֶׁר צִוִּיתִי שֹׁפְטִים עַל־עַמִּי יִשְׂרָאֵל וַהֲנִיחֹתִי לְךָ מִכָּל־אֹיְבֶיךָ וְהִגִּיד לְךָ יְהוָֹה כִּי־בַיִת יַעֲשֶׂה־לְּךָ יְהוָֹה:

12 כִּי יִמְלְאוּ יָמֶיךָ וְשָׁכַבְתָּ אֶת־אֲבֹתֶיךָ וַהֲקִימֹתִי אֶת־זַרְעֲךָ אַחֲרֶיךָ אֲשֶׁר יֵצֵא מִמֵּעֶיךָ וַהֲכִינֹתִי אֶת־מַמְלַכְתּוֹ:

13 הוּא יִבְנֶה־בַּיִת לִשְׁמִי וְכֹנַנְתִּי אֶת־כִּסֵּא מַמְלַכְתּוֹ עַד־עוֹלָם:

14 אֲנִי אֶהְיֶה־לּוֹ לְאָב וְהוּא יִהְיֶה־לִּי לְבֵן אֲשֶׁר בְּהַעֲוֺתוֹ וְהֹכַחְתִּיו בְּשֵׁבֶט אֲנָשִׁים וּבְנִגְעֵי בְּנֵי אָדָם:

15 וְחַסְדִּי לֹא־יָסוּר מִמֶּנּוּ כַּאֲשֶׁר הֲסִרֹתִי מֵעִם שָׁאוּל אֲשֶׁר הֲסִרֹתִי מִלְּפָנֶיךָ:

16 וְנֶאְמַן בֵּיתְךָ וּמַמְלַכְתְּךָ עַד־עוֹלָם לְפָנֶיךָ כִּסְאֲךָ יִהְיֶה נָכוֹן עַד־עוֹלָם:

17 כְּכֹל הַדְּבָרִים הָאֵלֶּה וּכְכֹל הַחִזָּיוֹן הַזֶּה כֵּן דִּבֶּר נָתָן אֶל־דָּוִד:

Commentary

11. *Will ... build up your house.* A wordplay on verse 5: You shall not be able to build Me a (physical, but destructible) house, but I will build you an (indestructible) house, in that your throne shall be established for all future generations. This promise became a firm part of Israel's hope and made it essential (though difficult) for the later prophets to emphasize that God's assurance was dependent on the people's loyalty.

14. *I will punish him.* As a human father would.

Essay

The death of Uzzah

While in the sidra the deaths of Nadab and Abihu can be explained by a ritual violation they committed (in that they brought a "strange fire" to the altar), no such explanation will do in the tale of Uzzah. After all, so the text seems to say, he tried to steady the Ark to keep it from falling. His intent was noble, and anyone else would likely have done the same thing. Wherefore, then, the extreme reaction of God?

Rashi's cryptic comment refers to a passage in the Talmud that tries to explain Uzzah's transgression.[26] There we read first of all of how the Ark was carried across the Jordan at the time of the invasion. The priests carried the Ark and stood in the middle of the Jordan, until all the people had crossed over, and then they resumed their place at the head of the train.[27] How was this accomplished? Because of a miracle: the Ark floated across, carrying its porters, and not the other way around.

The meaning of this tale is simple: When God wants to protect the Ark, no human hand is necessary to steady it. Uzzah sinned because he lacked confidence in the efficacy of divine help. Such is the traditional interpretation, which Rashi supports. At the same time Rabbi Jochanan, while he considered Uzzah's action a transgression, nonetheless asserted that because Uzzah was accompanying the Ark and the Ark is eternal, he too would partake of eternal life. Which is to say that Uzzah died prematurely, only to be granted immortality.[28]

These discussions reveal the trouble that tradition had with the text. When all was said and done, the divine action (which the text says it was) remained inexplicable. The Talmud even goes on to say that God's anger (6:7) wasn't really any anger at all—but it does not explain just what it was.

In our view, the explanation is less complicated. The celebration was in full swing, the joy was immense—and suddenly the man who guided the cart fell down dead. Death is all too often inexplicable, and sudden death especially so. The storyteller believed that everything that happens is God's will; thus, what happened to Uzzah must have been deserved—even though the reason was not at all clear. It seemed simplest to treat this as a case of transgressing priestly privilege, with God as its zealous Guardian. That it was God who "struck down" the hapless Uzzah was the chronicler's interpretation of the inexplicable, and it is only natural that David too interpreted this incident as a bad omen and therefore discontinued the journey. Thus, even as God's actions are often beyond human understanding, so is death. Both speak of the fundamental limitation of mortals.

There is still another aspect to this strange tale. The storyteller as well as the audience had a deep sense of awe when it came to God. The Ark represented the Divine Presence, and touching it haphazardly, however innocently, was like playing with fire. In Hebrew, this awe is expressed by the word for fear. The "fear of God"[29] is not just reverence (as it is frequently rendered) but another dimension of the meeting between the Divine and the human. Uzzah was seen to have trespassed the line of demarcation.

Gleanings

Uzzah and the Ark

The death of Uzzah was so puzzling to the Sages that they tried to explain God's actions in ways that could find but weak support from the text itself. We have already alluded to Rabbi Jochanan's semi-defense of Uzzah, which compensates the hapless man with the gift of immortality, and the same talmudic passage also reports the opinion of Rabbi Eliezer, who looked for a more earthly and earthy explanation: Uzzah had to relieve himself and did it right by the Ark—thereby denigrating its special status. He apparently derived this from the word *shal* in 6:6, which he read as *nashal*, to throw out or down.[30]

A modern interpreter goes a similarly imaginative linguistic route, which circumvents the question by ascribing the incident to purely physical reasons. The text speaks of the oxen stumbling, which is our rendering of *shamtu*, the meaning of which is not certain. G.B. Caird, however, leaves God out of the equation. He understands *shamtu* as defecating, and he suggests that Uzzah, who walked behind the oxen, stepped into the offal, slipped and fell, and struck his head on a rock.[31]

One tradition traces the whole unfortunate incident to David himself. Instead of having the Ark carried by priests as the Torah provides, he loaded it on a wagon and thus committed a sin.[32]

About Obed-Edom

The Talmud treats him as an Edomite, and he reminds us of the Torah prescription, "You shall not think badly of the Edomite, for he is your brother."[33] He was rewarded by many offspring. He had eight sons, whose wives each gave birth to sextuplets.[34]

But others treat him as a "pious levite," who lit the lamp twice a day before the Ark.[35]

* * *

Notes

[1] See the Torah Commentary, pp. 1034 ff.

[2] See Joshua 15:9; I Samuel 6:21; also Targum and Rashi.

[3] So Radak.

[4] I Samuel 6:7.

[5] I Samuel 17:1; I Chronicles 13:7.

[6] Whose name was Eleazar (I Samuel 7:1).

[7] So, apparently, Slotki (in the *Soncino Bible Commentary* on the verse in Chronicles).

[8] I Chronicles 13:10. Rashi says, "because of his error."

[9] I Samuel 15:10, and so Metzudat David.

[10] He combined two foreign elements into his name, "Edom" and the Philistine "Gath" (hence he was called a Gittite).

[11] So Hertzberg, *I and II Samuel*, p. 279.

[12] Some understand that he did not bring sacrifices after *every* six steps.

[13] I Chronicles 15:26.

[14] See our commentary on Exodus 28:6, where the ephod is first introduced.

[15] So the Vulgate and Radak.

[16] As in I Kings 4:29.

[17] Compare Psalm 127:3.

[18] Exodus 20:23.

[19] II Samuel 21:8 But some ancient versions have Merab instead of Michal. The Talmud (*B. Sanhedrin* 19b) reconciles the difference by saying that Michal adopted her sister's children and was thus considered the actual parent.

[20] II Samuel chapters 11 and 12. But tradition manages to exonerate David.

[21] I Kings chapter 1 (see the haftarah for Chayei Sarah).

[22] See I Chronicles 29:29. He was also instrumental in arranging the musical liturgy for the Temple priests, but this record too is not extant (see II Chronicles 29:25).

[23] I Kings 5:20 ff. "Cedar temple" has a reproachful undertone—see Jeremiah 22:13-14.

[24] It follows the sense of the Targum.

[25] Radak has a different rendering: Israel will have security because it will have people to rule over ("beneath them," instead of being ruled by others).

[26] *B. Sotah* 35a.

[27] Joshua 4:10-11.

[28] *B. Sota* 35a.

[29] יראת שמים (*yir'at shamayim*).

[30] *B. Sota* 35a.

[31] See *Interpreter's Bible, vol. 2*, comment on that verse.

[32] See Josephus, *Antiquities* VII 4:2.

[33] Deuteronomy 23:8.

[34] *B.* Berachot 63b-64a.

[35] Ginzberg, *Legends of the Jews*, vol. 6, p. 275, note 135, based on the Midrash; see also Josephus, *Antiquities* VII 4:20.

תזריע

Second Kings, chapter 4, verse 42 to chapter 5, verse 19

Introduction

Connection of sidra and haftarah:

The sidra deals with the treatment of skin diseases (often referred to as "leprosy"), and the bulk of the haftarah tells the tale of Naaman, a Syrian general, who was healed from some such disease by the waters of the Jordan and through the mediation of the prophet Elisha. (See also the haftarah for Vayeira.)

The setting:

Elisha was the chief disciple of his illustrious mentor, Elijah, and was active for about fifty years (850-800 B.C.E.). While Elijah was an outsider, engaged in confrontation with corrupt power and religion, Elisha was the man whose counsel the rulers of Israel tended to seek. He had been a farmer before he became a follower of Elijah, and his concern for ordinary folk never left him. He was the subject of folktales, and many miracles were ascribed to him.

The haftarah is taken from the Second Book of Kings. For more on the book, see our *General Introduction.*

The stories:

1. A hundred men are fed by the miraculous multiplication of a few loaves of bread. (4:42-44)

2. An Aramean general, Naaman, is afflicted by a skin disease and healed. In consequence he acknowledges God as the sole ruler of the world. (5:1-19)

HAFTARAH FOR TAZRI'A

Second Kings, chapter 4, verse 42 to chapter 5, verse 19

4:42. A man came from Baal-Shalishah, bringing the man of God some bread made of the first barley harvest—twenty loaves—and fresh grain with ears of new corn. So Elisha said: Give it to the people to eat.

43. His servant said: How can I put this [small amount] in front of a hundred people? But he insisted: Give it to the people to eat; the Eternal has said that they will eat and have some left over.

44. So he gave it to them; they ate and had some left over, as the Eternal had said.

5:1. Naaman, the commander of the Aramean army, was important to the king, who valued him highly, because through him the Eternal had given Aram victory. He was a valiant soldier, who had a skin disease.

וְאִישׁ בָּא מִבַּעַל שָׁלִשָׁה וַיָּבֵא לְאִישׁ 4:42
הָאֱלֹהִים לֶחֶם בִּכּוּרִים עֶשְׂרִים־לֶחֶם שְׂעֹרִים
וְכַרְמֶל בְּצִקְלֹנוֹ וַיֹּאמֶר תֵּן לָעָם וְיֹאכֵלוּ:

וַיֹּאמֶר מְשָׁרְתוֹ מָה אֶתֵּן זֶה לִפְנֵי מֵאָה אִישׁ 43
וַיֹּאמֶר תֵּן לָעָם וְיֹאכֵלוּ כִּי כֹה אָמַר יְהֹוָה
אָכֹל וְהוֹתֵר:

וַיִּתֵּן לִפְנֵיהֶם וַיֹּאכְלוּ וַיּוֹתִרוּ כִּדְבַר יְהֹוָה: 44

וְנַעֲמָן שַׂר־צְבָא מֶלֶךְ־אֲרָם הָיָה אִישׁ 5:1
גָּדוֹל לִפְנֵי אֲדֹנָיו וּנְשֻׂא פָנִים כִּי־בוֹ נָתַן־יְהֹוָה
תְּשׁוּעָה לַאֲרָם וְהָאִישׁ הָיָה גִּבּוֹר חַיִל מְצֹרָע:

Commentary

4:42. *Baal-Shalishah.* A family property located in the tribe of Ephraim, in the Northern Kingdom (Israel).

Ears of new corn. The translation is based on the Ugaritic *bsql*, stalk. The word appears nowhere else in the Tanach.

5:1. *The Eternal had given Aram victory.* God's power extends over Aram (Syria), as it does over all nations. Similarly, the prophet Amos says (speaking in God's name): "Did I not bring Israel up from the land of Egypt, and the Philistines from Crete, and the Arameans from Kir?"[1]

A skin disease. The disease called צרעת (*tzara'at*) comprises a group of skin ailments.[2] Naaman did not have true leprosy (Hansen's disease), else he would not have been able to function in his post; he would have been quarantined and banished from the community (see the next haftarah).

2. Once, when the Arameans went out on a raid, they carried off a young girl from the land of Israel as a captive, and she became a servant to Naaman's wife.

3. She said to her mistress: If only my lord could go to the prophet in Samaria! He would cure him of his skin disease.

4. [Hearing this,] Naaman went to his master and told him: *This is what the girl from Israel said.*

5. So the king of Aram said: Go, and take this letter to the king of Israel. So he went, taking along ten talents of silver, six thousand shekels of gold, and ten changes of clothing.

6. He brought the letter to the king of Israel. It said: *This letter will introduce my servant Naaman, that you may cure him of his skin disease.*

7. When the king of Israel read the letter, he tore his clothes and said: Am I God, with power over life and death, that this fellow wants me to cure a man of a skin disease? He is obviously looking to pick a quarrel with me.

2 וַאֲרָם יָצְאוּ גְדוּדִים וַיִּשְׁבּוּ מֵאֶרֶץ יִשְׂרָאֵל נַעֲרָה קְטַנָּה וַתְּהִי לִפְנֵי אֵשֶׁת נַעֲמָן:

3 וַתֹּאמֶר אֶל־גְּבִרְתָּהּ אַחֲלֵי אֲדֹנִי לִפְנֵי הַנָּבִיא אֲשֶׁר בְּשֹׁמְרוֹן אָז יֶאֱסֹף אֹתוֹ מִצָּרַעְתּוֹ:

4 וַיָּבֹא וַיַּגֵּד לַאדֹנָיו לֵאמֹר כָּזֹאת וְכָזֹאת דִּבְּרָה הַנַּעֲרָה אֲשֶׁר מֵאֶרֶץ יִשְׂרָאֵל:

5 וַיֹּאמֶר מֶלֶךְ־אֲרָם לֶךְ־בֹּא וְאֶשְׁלְחָה סֵפֶר אֶל־מֶלֶךְ יִשְׂרָאֵל וַיֵּלֶךְ וַיִּקַּח בְּיָדוֹ עֶשֶׂר כִּכְּרֵי־כֶסֶף וְשֵׁשֶׁת אֲלָפִים זָהָב וְעֶשֶׂר חֲלִיפוֹת בְּגָדִים:

6 וַיָּבֵא הַסֵּפֶר אֶל־מֶלֶךְ יִשְׂרָאֵל לֵאמֹר וְעַתָּה כְּבוֹא הַסֵּפֶר הַזֶּה אֵלֶיךָ הִנֵּה שָׁלַחְתִּי אֵלֶיךָ אֶת־נַעֲמָן עַבְדִּי וַאֲסַפְתּוֹ מִצָּרַעְתּוֹ:

7 וַיְהִי כִּקְרֹא מֶלֶךְ־יִשְׂרָאֵל אֶת־הַסֵּפֶר וַיִּקְרַע בְּגָדָיו וַיֹּאמֶר הַאֱלֹהִים אָנִי לְהָמִית וּלְהַחֲיוֹת כִּי־זֶה שֹׁלֵחַ אֵלַי לֶאֱסֹף אִישׁ מִצָּרַעְתּוֹ כִּי אַךְ־דְּעוּ־נָא וּרְאוּ כִּי־מִתְאַנֶּה הוּא לִי:

Commentary

2. *Went out on a raid.* גדודים (g'dudim; literally, bands); they had staged raids, even though Aram and Israel were not at war.[3] A related Phoenician word refers to paramilitary groups not under centralized control.

3. *If only.* אחלי (achalei) occurs one other time in the Tanach.[4] A closely related term is found in Akkadian (Assyro-Babylonian) in the meaning of "pardon" or "mercy."

5. *Ten talents of silver.* The exact weight of these gifts is disputed. According to one counting, each talent weighed 2,500 shekels, or 66 pounds (30 kilograms).[5]

Six thousand shekels. Equal to 158 pounds (72 kilograms).

Ten changes of clothing. Rich cloth was a valued possession.[6]

8. But when Elisha, the man of God, heard that the king of Israel had torn his clothes, he sent the king the following message: Why have you torn your clothes? Let this man come to me, and he will learn that there is a prophet in Israel!

9. So Naaman came with his horses and chariots, and waited for Elisha at the entrance of the house.

10. Elisha sent him this message: Go bathe seven times in the (river) Jordan, and your flesh will be cleansed and return to normal.

11. This made Naaman angry and he left, saying: I thought he would come out and stand here and call out in the name of the Eternal his God, and wave his hand at the spot and cure the disease.

12. Aren't the waters of the Amanah and the Pharpar, the rivers of Damascus, better than all the waters of Israel? Can't I wash in them and get clean?

So he walked off in a fury.

8 וַיְהִ֞י כִּשְׁמֹ֣עַ ׀ אֱלִישָׁ֣ע אִישׁ־הָאֱלֹהִ֗ים כִּֽי־קָרַ֤ע מֶֽלֶךְ־יִשְׂרָאֵל֙ אֶת־בְּגָדָ֔יו וַיִּשְׁלַח֙ אֶל־הַמֶּ֣לֶךְ לֵאמֹ֔ר לָ֥מָּה קָרַ֖עְתָּ בְּגָדֶ֑יךָ יָבֹֽא־נָ֣א אֵלַ֔י וְיֵדַ֕ע כִּ֛י יֵ֥שׁ נָבִ֖יא בְּיִשְׂרָאֵֽל׃

9 וַיָּבֹ֥א נַֽעֲמָ֖ן בְּסוּסָ֣ו [בְּסוּסָ֔יו] וּבְרִכְבּ֑וֹ וַֽיַּעֲמֹ֥ד פֶּֽתַח־הַבַּ֖יִת לֶאֱלִישָֽׁע׃

10 וַיִּשְׁלַ֥ח אֵלָ֛יו אֱלִישָׁ֖ע מַלְאָ֣ךְ לֵאמֹ֑ר הָל֗וֹךְ וְרָחַצְתָּ֤ שֶֽׁבַע־פְּעָמִים֙ בַּיַּרְדֵּ֔ן וְיָשֹׁ֧ב בְּשָׂרְךָ֛ לְךָ֖ וּטְהָֽר׃

11 וַיִּקְצֹ֥ף נַֽעֲמָ֖ן וַיֵּלַ֑ךְ וַיֹּ֗אמֶר הִנֵּ֤ה אָמַ֙רְתִּי֙ אֵלַ֔י יֵצֵ֣א יָצ֗וֹא וְעָמַד֙ וְקָרָא֙ בְּשֵׁם־יְהוָ֣ה אֱלֹהָ֔יו וְהֵנִ֥יף יָד֛וֹ אֶל־הַמָּק֖וֹם וְאָסַ֥ף הַמְּצֹרָֽע׃

12 הֲלֹ֡א טוֹב֩ אֲבָנָ֨ה [אֲמָנָ֜ה] וּפַרְפַּ֗ר נַהֲר֣וֹת דַּמֶּ֔שֶׂק מִכֹּ֖ל מֵימֵ֣י יִשְׂרָאֵ֑ל הֲלֹֽא־אֶרְחַ֥ץ בָּהֶ֖ם וְטָהָ֑רְתִּי וַיִּ֖פֶן וַיֵּ֥לֶךְ בְּחֵמָֽה׃

Commentary

10. *Elisha sent him this message.* He frequently carried on his conversations through his servant. (In this manner he also conversed with the Shunammite woman; see the haftarah for Vayeira.)

Go bathe seven times. The number seven had a sacred connotation.

13. Naaman's servants went up to him and said: Sir, had the prophet asked you to do something elaborate, surely you would have done it; why not do it, then, when he only asks you to wash and be clean?

14. Naaman then went down and dipped himself into the Jordan seven times, as the man of God had said; and his flesh became clean as the flesh of a young child.

15. He and his men returned to the man of God. Standing in front of him, Naaman said: Now I know that the God of Israel is the only God in the whole world; please, now, accept a present from me.

16. But Elisha answered: As the Eternal, whom I serve, lives, I tell you that I will not accept a gift. Naaman entreated him to accept, but he refused.

17. Then Naaman said: If not, please let me have two mule-loads of earth [on which to build an altar back home]; because I will never again offer a burnt-offering or sacrifice to any god but the Eternal.

13 וַיִּגְּשׁוּ עֲבָדָיו וַיְדַבְּרוּ אֵלָיו וַיֹּאמְרוּ אָבִי דָּבָר גָּדוֹל הַנָּבִיא דִּבֶּר אֵלֶיךָ הֲלוֹא תַעֲשֶׂה וְאַף כִּי־אָמַר אֵלֶיךָ רְחַץ וּטְהָר:

14 וַיֵּרֶד וַיִּטְבֹּל בַּיַּרְדֵּן שֶׁבַע פְּעָמִים כִּדְבַר אִישׁ הָאֱלֹהִים וַיָּשָׁב בְּשָׂרוֹ כִּבְשַׂר נַעַר קָטֹן וַיִּטְהָר:

15 וַיָּשָׁב אֶל־אִישׁ הָאֱלֹהִים הוּא וְכָל־מַחֲנֵהוּ וַיָּבֹא וַיַּעֲמֹד לְפָנָיו וַיֹּאמֶר הִנֵּה־נָא יָדַעְתִּי כִּי אֵין אֱלֹהִים בְּכָל־הָאָרֶץ כִּי אִם־בְּיִשְׂרָאֵל וְעַתָּה קַח־נָא בְרָכָה מֵאֵת עַבְדֶּךָ:

16 וַיֹּאמֶר חַי־יְהוָה אֲשֶׁר־עָמַדְתִּי לְפָנָיו אִם־אֶקָּח וַיִּפְצַר־בּוֹ לָקַחַת וַיְמָאֵן:

17 וַיֹּאמֶר נַעֲמָן וָלֹא יֻתַּן־נָא לְעַבְדְּךָ מַשָּׂא צֶמֶד־פְּרָדִים אֲדָמָה כִּי לוֹא־יַעֲשֶׂה עוֹד עַבְדְּךָ עֹלָה וָזֶבַח לֵאלֹהִים אֲחֵרִים כִּי אִם־לַיהוָה:

Commentary

13. *Sir.* אָבִי (*avee*), literally "my father." An unusual appellation to be used by servants It has been suggested that the original reading was בִּי (*bee*), which has the meaning of "please." [7]

15. *Accept a present.* ברכה (*b'rachah*), literally a blessing, of which the gift was to be the tangible expression.

17. *Two mule-loads of earth.* Naaman believes that the Eternal, whom he has made his God, rules over the land of Israel only, and so he wants to take along some of its soil.

18. And I hope that God will pardon me in one thing: when my master goes to the Temple of [the god] Rimmon to worship there, and he leans on my arm, so that I have to bow down in the Temple of Rimmon—I hope God will forgive me this one thing, that I have to bow down in the Temple of Rimmon.

19. And Elisha said to him: Go in peace.

18 לַדָּבָר הַזֶּה יִסְלַח יְהוָה לְעַבְדֶּךָ בְּבוֹא אֲדֹנִי בֵית־רִמּוֹן לְהִשְׁתַּחֲוֹת שָׁמָּה וְהוּא נִשְׁעָן עַל־יָדִי וְהִשְׁתַּחֲוֵיתִי בֵּית רִמֹּן בְּהִשְׁתַּחֲוָיָתִי בֵּית רִמֹּן יִסְלַח־נא יְהוָה לְעַבְדְּךָ בַּדָּבָר הַזֶּה:

19 וַיֹּאמֶר לוֹ לֵךְ לְשָׁלוֹם.

Commentary

18. *Rimmon.* More usually called Rammon, the thunder and weather god of Assyria, also known as Hadad.

God will forgive me this one thing. Naaman repeats his explanation, for he wants Elisha to understand that he has no choice in the matter. The second time the text reads יסלח־נא יהוה (*yislach-na adonai*). Note that the second word, נא (please), is not vocalized, and tradition provides that it not be read, for there should be no appearance that Naaman's plea was addressed to Elisha, as if he were in God's place. Instead, Naaman begs Elisha silently to pray to God that he be forgiven when this situation arises.[8]

19. *Go in peace.* The haftarah ends in the middle of verse 19.

Essay

Naaman's conversion

The Aramean general has no doubt that it was Israel's God who healed him of his illness. "Now I know (he says) that the God of Israel is the only God in the whole world." From now on he considers himself a monotheist.

Why then would he need a load of Israeli earth to take with him? Surely, the Eternal is approachable in prayer wherever people seek the Divine Presence? Evidently, Naaman is not quite sure, for in his conception, gods belong to specific places—mountains, rivers, shrines, or lands—and outside of these precincts and borders other gods preside. He reasons that a bit of Israel's soil will make it possible for him to approach the God of Israel even after his return to Aram. The soil of the land of Israel is the bridge between a spiritual conception of the Divine and a visual perception of its reality. It is a tale of ancient Israelite universalism.[9]

Naaman's acknowledgment of God's uniqueness and his forswearing of other gods meant, in effect, a religious conversion (to use a term not then in existence). Even so, no one would have considered him a Jew, least of all he himself. For such belonging related to descent and family ties, and they did not exist in his case.

It was different with Ruth, for she had been married to a Jew and thereby had established links with the Jewish people. To be sure, she acknowledged that God would be her God and Israel would be her people, but even without this declaration she would have become part of her late husband's tribal family once she returned to his home.

But neither Naaman nor Ruth underwent "conversion" in the later sense, when certain ritual requirements became established: acceptance of the Covenant and its mitzvot, immersion, and (with males) circumcision.[10]

At the time of Elisha, and for many centuries thereafter, no attempt was made to go out and convert gentiles to Judaism. Only during the last two centuries B.C.E. did emissaries travel abroad and gain proselytes. With the rise of Christianity and then of Islam, conversion to Judaism became illegal, and proselytism disappeared from the Jewish agenda.

It has tentatively resurfaced during the second half of the 20th century, but no organized proselytizing activities have been undertaken so far. However, with the rise of intermarriages in the Diaspora, conversions to Judaism have been steadily increasing.

Early Reform Jews, deeming ritual a secondary aspect of spiritual religion, considered a verbal affirmation (of the kind made by Naaman and Ruth) to be sufficient for acceptance to the Jewish faith and people. Lately, however, ancient history is being replayed, and the three-fold demands of traditional conversion are replacing the merely verbal affirmation.

Gleanings

About Elisha

Elisha declined the gifts offered to him by Naaman, and for this he was rewarded by God. He was allowed to remain Israel's spiritual guide for many years.

Midrash[11]

About Naaman

Naaman was a great warrior and proud of it, and was punished with leprosy for his arrogance. But when he was stricken, and especially after he acknowledged the Eternal One as his God, he became a modest person.

Thus, when he met with Elisha he came as a simple man, rather than as the famous general. This is derived from the word בסוסו (*b'susav*, with his horses), which ordinarily would be written בסוסיו. By leaving out the *yud* (suggesting that he came with a smaller entourage than was his wont), the text calls attention to Naaman's humility.[12]

Midrash[13]

* * *

Notes

[1] Amos 9:7; see the haftarah for K'doshim.

[2] As well as molds in garments and houses. See Bernard Bamberger's discussion of the illness in the Torah Commentary (Leviticus), p. 828; Baruch Levine, in his commentary on Leviticus, *JPS Torah Commentary*, pp. 75 ff.

[3] The size of גדודים would vary; see the article on it in the *Encyclopedia Mikra'it*.

[4] In Psalm 119:5, with slightly different vocalization.

[5] By another counting, which has a talent equal 3,600 shekel, the gift would have weighed 95 pounds (43.2 kilograms).

[6] See Judges 14:12.

[7] See Cogan and Tadmor, in *Anchor Bible,* II Kings.

[8] So Radak.

[9] Cogan and Tadmor, in *Anchor Bible*, II Kings, citing Yehezkel Kaufmann (*Toledot,* vol. 2, pp. 277-279).

[10] Pious historians, however, will aver that Ruth underwent formal conversion, even though such a process cannot be shown to have existed at the time.

[11] *Sefer Hasidim* (ed. Wistinetzki, 1891), No. 328.

[12] Without the *yud* the word would ordinarily be read *b'suso*, with his (one) horse.

[13] On the reason for Naaman's leprosy, see Numbers Rabbah 7:4-5; the derivation of Naaman's later simple ways is found in *Midrash Chaserot Viy'terot* (ed. Wertheimer, 1900), No. 35.

First Kings, chapter 7, verses 3 to 20

Introduction

Connection of sidra and haftarah:

The sidra (like the previous one) deals with the treatment of skin diseases (often referred to as "leprosy"), and the haftarah tells the tale of four lepers and their role during the siege of Samaria. Like the previous haftarah it belongs to the cycle of Elisha tales; in this case, how his prediction of a dramatic turn of events would come true.

The setting:

Israel, the Northern Kingdom, is engaged in a war with Syria (Aram), which has been strengthened by its alliance with Judah. The war goes badly for Israel, and its capital is under siege. The famine is so terrible that mothers are forced to eat their children. Samaria's reigning king is Jehoahaz (second part of the 9th century B.C.E.), and no salvation is in sight. But the prophet Elisha predicts a dramatic turn of events and foretells that the king's counselor who doubts his words will be punished for his lack of faith. Thus, the story unfolds as told in 6:24 and following; the fate of the counselor is predicted in 7:1 and 2; and the man's end is told at the end of the haftarah.

However, no records exist that make an alliance of Judah and Syria and their joint war on Israel likely at the time in which these events are said to have taken place. Prevailing scholarship holds therefore that this is a tale woven around the wondrous works of Elisha.

The haftarah is taken from the First Book of Kings. For more on the book, see our *General Introduction* and the haftarah for the previous sidra, Tazri'a.

The story:

Note that the story covers the events of one single day.

1. The discovery of the lepers. (3-9)
2. The delivery of Samaria. (10-16)
3. The death of the king's counselor, which Elisha had predicted. (17-20)

HAFTARAH FOR M'TZORA

First Kings, chapter 7, verses 3 to 20

7:3. At the entrance to the gate were four men, all lepers. They said to one another. Why should we sit here until we die?

4. If we decide to go into the city, we will die of the famine; and if we remain here, we will die as well; better to desert to the Aramean camp: if they let us live, we will live; if they put us to death, we will be dead.

5. At twilight they made their way toward the Aramean camp. When they reached the edge of the camp, they found not a soul.

6. The Eternal had caused the Arameans to hear the sounds of horses and chariots, the sounds of a large army, so they had thought: *The king of Israel must have paid the kings of the Hittites and of Egypt to attack us.*

7. And they had run away at twilight: leaving their tents, their horses, their mules, everything in their camp, just as it was, they had fled for their lives.

וְאַרְבָּעָה אֲנָשִׁים הָיוּ מְצֹרָעִים פֶּתַח הַשָּׁעַר 7:3 וַיֹּאמְרוּ אִישׁ אֶל־רֵעֵהוּ מָה אֲנַחְנוּ יֹשְׁבִים פֹּה עַד־מָתְנוּ:

אִם־אָמַרְנוּ נָבוֹא הָעִיר וְהָרָעָב בָּעִיר וָמַתְנוּ 4 שָׁם וְאִם־יָשַׁבְנוּ פֹה וָמָתְנוּ וְעַתָּה לְכוּ וְנִפְּלָה אֶל־מַחֲנֵה אֲרָם אִם־יְחַיֻּנוּ נִחְיֶה וְאִם־יְמִיתֻנוּ וָמָתְנוּ:

וַיָּקוּמוּ בַנֶּשֶׁף לָבוֹא אֶל־מַחֲנֵה אֲרָם וַיָּבֹאוּ 5 עַד־קְצֵה מַחֲנֵה אֲרָם וְהִנֵּה אֵין־שָׁם אִישׁ:

וַאדֹנָי הִשְׁמִיעַ אֶת־מַחֲנֵה אֲרָם קוֹל רֶכֶב 6 קוֹל סוּס קוֹל חַיִל גָּדוֹל וַיֹּאמְרוּ אִישׁ אֶל־אָחִיו הִנֵּה שָׂכַר־עָלֵינוּ מֶלֶךְ יִשְׂרָאֵל אֶת־מַלְכֵי הַחִתִּים וְאֶת־מַלְכֵי מִצְרַיִם לָבוֹא עָלֵינוּ:

וַיָּקוּמוּ וַיָּנוּסוּ בַנֶּשֶׁף וַיַּעַזְבוּ אֶת־אָהֳלֵיהֶם 7 וְאֶת־סוּסֵיהֶם וְאֶת־חֲמֹרֵיהֶם הַמַּחֲנֶה כַּאֲשֶׁר־הִיא וַיָּנֻסוּ אֶל־נַפְשָׁם:

Commentary

3. *All lepers.* They were suffering from true leprosy (Hansen's disease) and were therefore excluded from contact with the rest of the population. They had little to lose by going over to the Arameans. (On leprosy, see the essay below.)

6. *Egypt.* Doubts about the historicity of the whole tale are strengthened by the mention of Egypt. The Arameans' belief that Egypt had conspired against them by making an alliance with the Hittites is seen by most scholars as an unlikely state of mind. Hence, they think that *Mitzrayim* (usually Egypt) read originally *Mutzri*, a nation in Western Asia.[1]

8. These lepers came to the edge of the camp, went into one tent, and ate and drank. They carried off some silver, some gold and clothing, and went and hid it; then they came back, entered another tent, took what they could find there, and hid it.

9. Then they said to one another: We're not doing right. This is a red-letter day, and we are keeping quiet about it. If we wait till daybreak, we will pay for it; we had better go now and let the king's household know what has happened.

10. They went and called to the gatekeepers of the city and told them that they had come to the Aramean camp and found no one there, not a single human voice, only tethered horses and mules, and tents left as is.

11. The gatekeepers called out, and the news was passed on into the inner court of the palace.

8 וַיָּבֹאוּ הַמְצֹרָעִים הָאֵלֶּה עַד־קְצֵה הַמַּחֲנֶה וַיָּבֹאוּ אֶל־אֹהֶל אֶחָד וַיֹּאכְלוּ וַיִּשְׁתּוּ וַיִּשְׂאוּ מִשָּׁם כֶּסֶף וְזָהָב וּבְגָדִים וַיֵּלְכוּ וַיַּטְמִנוּ וַיָּשֻׁבוּ וַיָּבֹאוּ אֶל־אֹהֶל אַחֵר וַיִּשְׂאוּ מִשָּׁם וַיֵּלְכוּ וַיַּטְמִנוּ:

9 וַיֹּאמְרוּ אִישׁ אֶל־רֵעֵהוּ לֹא־כֵן אֲנַחְנוּ עֹשִׂים הַיּוֹם הַזֶּה יוֹם־בְּשֹׂרָה הוּא וַאֲנַחְנוּ מַחְשִׁים וְחִכִּינוּ עַד־אוֹר הַבֹּקֶר וּמְצָאָנוּ עָווֹן וְעַתָּה לְכוּ וְנָבֹאָה וְנַגִּידָה בֵּית הַמֶּלֶךְ:

10 וַיָּבֹאוּ וַיִּקְרְאוּ אֶל־שֹׁעֵר הָעִיר וַיַּגִּידוּ לָהֶם לֵאמֹר בָּאנוּ אֶל־מַחֲנֵה אֲרָם וְהִנֵּה אֵין־שָׁם אִישׁ וְקוֹל אָדָם כִּי אִם־הַסּוּס אָסוּר וְהַחֲמוֹר אָסוּר וְאֹהָלִים כַּאֲשֶׁר־הֵמָּה:

11 וַיִּקְרָא הַשֹּׁעֲרִים וַיַּגִּידוּ בֵּית הַמֶּלֶךְ פְּנִימָה:

Commentary

10. *They went and called.* From afar, for their leprosy prevented them from coming too near.

The gatekeepers. The Hebrew is a collective that looks like a singular noun but commands a plural verb.

11. *The gatekeepers called out.* Here, the exact reverse of the previous comment applies: the verb is singular and the noun is plural.[2]

12. The king rose up in the night and said to his officials: I'll tell you what the Arameans are doing to us: they know that we're starving, so they've hidden in the fields, saying: *They [Israel] will go out of the city, and then we can take them alive, and march into the city.*

13. One of his officials answered, saying: Let some of the remaining horses be taken—they are [but few] like the remainder—[few, alas] like the remainder of the multitude of Israel that has perished. So let us send [the horses] and see.

14. So they took two mounted riders, and the king sent them after the Aramean army, saying: Go reconnoiter.

15. They followed the [Aramean] trail as far as the (river) Jordan; all along the way there were clothes and weapons that the Arameans had thrown away in their haste. The scouts returned and told the king.

וַיָּ֤קָם הַמֶּ֙לֶךְ֙ לַ֔יְלָה וַיֹּ֙אמֶר֙ אֶל־עֲבָדָ֔יו 12
אַגִּֽידָה־נָּ֣א לָכֶ֔ם אֵ֛ת אֲשֶׁר־עָ֥שׂוּ לָ֖נוּ אֲרָ֑ם יָדְע֞וּ
כִּֽי־רְעֵבִ֣ים אֲנַ֗חְנוּ וַיֵּצְא֤וּ מִן־הַֽמַּחֲנֶה֙ לְהֵחָבֵ֣ה
בְהַשָׂדֶ֣ה [בַשָׂדֶ֣ה] לֵאמֹ֔ר כִּֽי־יֵצְא֣וּ מִן־הָעִ֗יר
וְנִתְפְּשֵׂ֤ם חַיִּים֙ וְאֶל־הָעִ֖יר נָבֹֽא׃

וַיַּ֩עַן֩ אֶחָ֨ד מֵעֲבָדָ֜יו וַיֹּ֗אמֶר וְיִקְחוּ־נָ֞א חֲמִשָּׁ֣ה 13
מִן־הַסּוּסִים֮ הַֽנִּשְׁאָרִים֮ אֲשֶׁ֣ר נִשְׁאֲרוּ־בָהּ֒ הִנָּ֗ם
כְּכָל־הֲֽהָמוֹן֙ [הֲמ֤וֹן] יִשְׂרָאֵל֙ אֲשֶׁ֣ר נִשְׁאֲרוּ־בָ֔הּ
הִנָּ֕ם כְּכָל־הֲמ֥וֹן יִשְׂרָאֵ֖ל אֲשֶׁר־תָּ֑מּוּ וְנִשְׁלְחָ֖ה
וְנִרְאֶֽה׃

וַיִּקְח֕וּ שְׁנֵ֖י רֶ֣כֶב סוּסִ֑ים וַיִּשְׁלַ֨ח הַמֶּ֜לֶךְ 14
אַחֲרֵ֧י מַחֲנֵֽה־אֲרָ֛ם לֵאמֹ֖ר לְכ֥וּ וּרְאֽוּ׃

וַיֵּלְכ֣וּ אַחֲרֵיהֶם֮ עַד־הַיַּרְדֵּן֒ וְהִנֵּ֣ה כָל־ 15
הַדֶּ֗רֶךְ מְלֵאָ֤ה בְגָדִים֙ וְכֵלִ֔ים אֲשֶׁר־הִשְׁלִ֥יכוּ
אֲרָ֖ם בְּהֵחָפְזָם֙ [בְּחָפְזָ֑ם] וַיָּשֻׁ֙בוּ֙ הַמַּלְאָכִ֔ים
וַיַּגִּ֖דוּ לַמֶּֽלֶךְ׃

Commentary

12. *In the fields.* This is an example of the care that the scribes took with the text. Note that the Hebrew בהשדה contains a superfluous ה that slipped into the text in error and is therefore neither vocalized nor pronounced, but copied nonetheless. The word is read בשדה (*va-sadeh*).

13. This verse is considered by most scholars to be both repetitious and corrupted. Our translation has tried to render it by adding explanatory brackets, without emending the text. Again, a superfluous ה has slipped into the text and is not pronounced.

Let some of the remaining horses. Literally, "five," which functions here as an indefinite number, similar to certain English expressions ("A million thanks" or "A couple of people").

15. *In their haste.* As in verses 12 and 13, there is a superfluous ה in בהחפזם (*b'chofzam*, in their haste), which is neither vocalized nor pronounced.

16. Then the people went out and looted the Aramean camp. So it came about that a bushel of the best flour was sold for [only] a shekel and two bushels of barley cost [only] a shekel, just as the Eternal had promised.

17. Now the king had appointed the adjutant on whose arm he leaned to be in charge of the gate, and the people there trampled him to death, just as the man of God had predicted, when the king had gone down to talk to him.

18. For when the man of God had said to the king that at the same time the next day two bushels of barley would be sold for a shekel, and a bushel of the best flour would be sold for a shekel,

19. this officer had said to the man of God: Even if God made windows in the sky, would something like this happen? And he had answered: You'll see it happen, but you won't eat any of it.

20. And that's what happened to him. The people trampled him to death in the gate.

16 וַיֵּצֵא הָעָם וַיָּבֹזּוּ אֵת מַחֲנֵה אֲרָם וַיְהִי סְאָה־סֹלֶת בְּשֶׁקֶל וְסָאתַיִם שְׂעֹרִים בְּשֶׁקֶל כִּדְבַר יְהוָה:

17 וְהַמֶּלֶךְ הִפְקִיד אֶת־הַשָּׁלִישׁ אֲשֶׁר־נִשְׁעָן עַל־יָדוֹ עַל־הַשַּׁעַר וַיִּרְמְסֻהוּ הָעָם בַּשַּׁעַר וַיָּמֹת כַּאֲשֶׁר דִּבֶּר אִישׁ הָאֱלֹהִים אֲשֶׁר דִּבֶּר בְּרֶדֶת הַמֶּלֶךְ אֵלָיו:

18 וַיְהִי כְּדַבֵּר אִישׁ הָאֱלֹהִים אֶל־הַמֶּלֶךְ לֵאמֹר סָאתַיִם שְׂעֹרִים בְּשֶׁקֶל וּסְאָה־סֹלֶת בְּשֶׁקֶל יִהְיֶה כָּעֵת מָחָר בְּשַׁעַר שֹׁמְרוֹן:

19 וַיַּעַן הַשָּׁלִישׁ אֶת־אִישׁ הָאֱלֹהִים וַיֹּאמַר וְהִנֵּה יְהוָה עֹשֶׂה אֲרֻבּוֹת בַּשָּׁמַיִם הֲיִהְיֶה כַּדָּבָר הַזֶּה וַיֹּאמֶר הִנְּךָ רֹאֶה בְּעֵינֶיךָ וּמִשָּׁם לֹא תֹאכֵל:

20 וַיְהִי־לוֹ כֵּן וַיִּרְמְסוּ אֹתוֹ הָעָם בַּשַּׁעַר וַיָּמֹת:

Commentary

16. *As the Eternal had promised.* Referring to 7:1-2, repeated in verses 18 and 19.

17. *On whose arm he leaned.* That is, his most trusted lieutenant.[3]

Trampled him to death. Probably in their mad rush to get a share of the loot.

Essay

Facts and fables

The disease that the Torah calls צרעת (*tzara'at*) is generally rendered as leprosy.[4] However, it should be kept in mind that both the Hebrew and English terms cover different afflictions—from Hansen's disease (true "leprosy") to temporary skin ailments. Only the former, if untreated, affects the deeper layers of the skin and produces permanent disintegration of membranes and leads to serious disfiguration. In the following, "leprosy" refers only to this illness.

Formerly it was believed that leprosy was highly contagious, and therefore lepers were isolated from the community. Josephus describes such people as "in effect dead persons."[5] The fatalistic attitude of the four men in our haftarah shows that they so considered themselves. The only other case of true leprosy mentioned in the Tanach is that of King Uzziah, who had to live in a separate house.[6]

Since illness was generally believed to be divine visitation, leprosy was seen as pointing to a particularly odious transgression, for which God had sent appropriate punishment. It is noteworthy that our Sages identified slander as the sin that would draw leprosy as a punishment. They deduced it from the story of Miriam, Moses' sister, who had spoken ill of her brother and in consequence was stricken in dramatic fashion and had to be removed temporarily from society.[7]

This interpretation was fortified by an aggadic play on words. A slanderer is described as מוציא שם רע (*motzi shem ra*, one who brings someone into ill repute), and the first and last two consonants produce the word מצרע (*m'tzora*, leper), the name of our sidra.[8]

Modern medicine has shed much light on leprosy, and the old fear of leprous contagion is disappearing. The haftarah deals with it in a matter-of-fact fashion and portrays the four lepers as persons who lead a life of despair, yet become the saviors of their nation.

Gleanings

Midrashim about leprosy

Leprosy was the punishment meted out to those whose major interest in life is to acquire things. This was the failing of Cain, Job, and Uzziah.[9]

Egyptian folklore would not admit that Pharaoh had to let the Israelites go, but turned the story on its head by claiming that Israel was expelled from the country because its people were leprous. Jewish folklore retaliated by suggesting that Pharaoh himself was leprous.[10]

Leprosy was the potential punishment for thirteen sins: blasphemy, unchastity, murder, suspecting others falsely, pride, unlawful acquisition of other people's rights, slander, theft, perjury, dragging down God's holy name, idolatry, envy, and contempt for Torah.[11]

* * *

Notes

[1] For example, Norman H. Snaith, *Interpreter's Bible*, vol. 3, pp. 100 and 222. However, this view is not unanimous. Thus, Cogan and Tadmor (in *Anchor Bible*, I Kings) point out (in their comment on this verse) that Mutzri had lost its independence already a hundred years before and therefore could hardly be believed to be making war on Aram.

[2] The translation follows the Targum and most modern versions. But Radak and Ralbag interpret: The gatekeeper (noted in the previous verse) called to (the other) gatekeepers, who passed the news on.

[3] The identical expression is used of Naaman, the Aramean general, in II Kings 5:18 (haftarah for Tazri'a).

[4] See B. J. Bamberger's essay in the Torah Commentary, pp. 828-829.

[5] *Antiquities* III:261 and following. The Mishnah (as well as the Tosefta) devotes the tractate N'ga'im to the disease.

[6] II Chronicles 26:19-21.

[7] Numbers chapter 12. Her affliction was not true leprosy but most likely leucodermia.

[8] *B. Shabbat 97a.*

[9] Numbers Rabbah 22:12-13. King Uzziah was indeed so afflicted (II Chronicles 26:21), but the biblical text does not mention that this applied also to Cain and Job. The midrash suggests that the "mark of Cain" was leprosy, and that the "severe skin ailment" of Job was the punishment for acquiring great wealth. (This does not, however, agree with the text itself, which makes Job's illness the result of a wager between God and Satan.)

[10] See Josephus, *Contra Apionem* I:26. The Egyptian claim is cited in Ginzberg, *Legends of the Jews*, vol. 5, p. 413, footnote 101.

[11] Numbers Rabbah 7:4-5, which gives examples for each of the thirteen transgressions.

Ezekiel, chapter 22, verses 1 to 19

Introduction

Connection of haftarah and sidra:

The sidra contains a detailed catalogue of forbidden sexual relations, and in the haftarah the Prophet denounces Jerusalem for its sexual licentiousness (as well as other transgressions).

The setting:

Ezekiel lived in the days before and after the destruction of the First Temple and preached in the early part of the 6th century B.C.E. He was exiled to Babylon after Nebuchadnezzar first occupied Jerusalem in the year 597 (without destroying it at that time), but seems to have returned to the city sometime before its final seizure and destruction in 587. During his visit—either in the flesh or in a vision—he was evidently horror-struck with what he saw and roundly denounced the city's leadership for their moral turpitude. He did so in the manner of extreme rhetoric, of which H. M. Orlinsky once wrote: "If one reads the book of Ezekiel, one gathers that the government and the people of Judah were on the greatest sinning binge in the history of Judah and Israel, if not in all of history."[1]

For more on Ezekiel, his rhetoric, and his time, see our *General Introduction.*

The message:

Two sins occupy center stage: Jerusalem is a city of blood and of sexual perversion.

1. Introduction. (22:1-2)

2. A catalogue of transgressions. (23:3-16)

3. Words of solace. The Rabbis so arranged it that no haftarah ever concluded on a negative, pessimistic note. (17)

HAFTARAH FOR ACHAREI MOT

Ezekiel, chapter 22, verses 1 to 19

22:1. The word of the Eternal came to me, saying:

2. Now you, mortal, are you ready to arraign the city of blood? Make her know all her abominable deeds?

3. Now say: Thus says the Eternal God: City in whose midst blood is shed, whose time will come! City where idols are made, to her own defilement!

4. You are guilty for the blood of your own that you have shed; you are defiled by the idols you have made. Your time is up, your day [of doom] has come. Therefore I have made you a disgrace to the nations, and a derision to all the countries.

5. Near and far alike will deride you, who have sullied your [own] name and have shown no restraint.

6. Every one of the leaders of Israel among you uses his strength to act the bloodsucker.

22:1 וַיְהִי דְבַר־יְהֹוָה אֵלַי לֵאמֹר:

2 וְאַתָּה בֶן־אָדָם הֲתִשְׁפֹּט הֲתִשְׁפֹּט אֶת־עִיר הַדָּמִים וְהוֹדַעְתָּהּ אֵת כָּל־תּוֹעֲבוֹתֶיהָ:

3 וְאָמַרְתָּ כֹּה אָמַר אֲדֹנָי יֱהוִֹה עִיר שֹׁפֶכֶת דָּם בְּתוֹכָהּ לָבוֹא עִתָּהּ וְעָשְׂתָה גִלּוּלִים עָלֶיהָ לְטָמְאָה:

4 בְּדָמֵךְ אֲשֶׁר־שָׁפַכְתְּ אָשַׁמְתְּ וּבְגִלּוּלַיִךְ אֲשֶׁר־עָשִׂית טָמֵאת וַתַּקְרִיבִי יָמַיִךְ וַתָּבוֹא עַד־שְׁנוֹתָיִךְ עַל־כֵּן נְתַתִּיךְ חֶרְפָּה לַגּוֹיִם וְקַלָּסָה לְכָל־הָאֲרָצוֹת:

5 הַקְּרֹבוֹת וְהָרְחֹקוֹת מִמֵּךְ יִתְקַלְּסוּ־בָךְ טְמֵאַת הַשֵּׁם רַבַּת הַמְּהוּמָה:

6 הִנֵּה נְשִׂיאֵי יִשְׂרָאֵל אִישׁ לִזְרֹעוֹ הָיוּ בָךְ לְמַעַן שְׁפָךְ־דָּם:

Commentary

22:2. *Mortal.* On the expression *ben-adam*, see haftarah for Vayigash.

Are you ready ....? Possibly a warning that the fate of Jeremiah might befall Ezekiel as well. Jeremiah had denounced the leaders of Jerusalem and had suffered grievously for it. If, as we suggest, this took place before 587, both prophets were in the city at the same time.

4. *Your time is up, your day [of doom] has come.* Literally, you have brought your days near and have entered into your year.

5. *Have shown no restraint.* Literally, are full of disorder (or tumult).

6. *Uses his strength to act the bloodsucker.* Verses 6 and 7 speak of the élite of the city who have used their power to despoil the people. Though literally the text speaks of shedding blood, it assumes a figurative sense here—just as the English word "bloodsucker" connotes economic exploitation.

7. They have treated your fathers and mothers with contempt; they have practiced extortion on the strangers in your midst; they have oppressed widows and orphans;

8. you despise My holy things, and you profane My Sabbaths;

9. you have slanderers among you, intent on shedding blood; people eat [sacrifices to idols] on mountaintops; they do lewd things among you.

10. They uncover their fathers' nakedness, and ravish menstruating women.

11. One man commits an abominable act with his neighbor's wife; another obscenely defiles his daughter-in-law; a third rapes his own sister, his father's daughter.

12. People among you take bribes to suck blood; you take usurious interest, and you have injured your neighbors through extortion—[completely] forgetting Me, says the Eternal God.

7 אָב וָאֵם הֵקַלּוּ בָךְ לַגֵּר עָשׂוּ בַעֹשֶׁק בְּתוֹכֵךְ יָתוֹם וְאַלְמָנָה הוֹנוּ בָךְ:

8 קָדָשַׁי בָּזִית וְאֶת־שַׁבְּתֹתַי חִלָּלְתְּ:

9 אַנְשֵׁי רָכִיל הָיוּ בָךְ לְמַעַן שְׁפָךְ־דָּם וְאֶל־הֶהָרִים אָכְלוּ בָךְ זִמָּה עָשׂוּ בְתוֹכֵךְ:

10 עֶרְוַת־אָב גִּלָּה־בָךְ טְמֵאַת הַנִּדָּה עִנּוּ־בָךְ:

11 וְאִישׁ אֶת־אֵשֶׁת רֵעֵהוּ עָשָׂה תּוֹעֵבָה וְאִישׁ אֶת־כַּלָּתוֹ טִמֵּא בְזִמָּה וְאִישׁ אֶת־אֲחֹתוֹ בַת־אָבִיו עִנָּה־בָךְ:

12 שֹׁחַד לָקְחוּ־בָךְ לְמַעַן שְׁפָךְ־דָּם נֶשֶׁךְ וְתַרְבִּית לָקַחַתְּ וַתְּבַצְּעִי רֵעַיִךְ בַּעֹשֶׁק וְאֹתִי שָׁכַחַתְּ נְאֻם אֲדֹנָי יְהוִה:

Commentary

7. Contempt of parents is decried in the language of the Torah.[2]

9. The association of slander and blood is found in the Torah.[3]

Eat on mountaintops. The sequence of worship and feasting replays the story of the Golden Calf.[4]

10. *Uncover their father's nakedness.* Sleep with women who once were married to their fathers—strictly forbidden by the Torah (see the sidra at Leviticus 18:6 ff.).

Ravish menstruating women. The Torah considers a menstruating woman (נדה, *niddah*) ritually unclean and unfit for intercourse;[5] however, the emphasis here is not on women's ritual status, but rather on the men who purposely pick menstruating women to ravish. (A talmudic tractate, *Niddah*, deals with the subject of menstruation, and its laws retain their force in present-day Orthodoxy.)

11. *Daughter-in-law.* Outlawed in the sidra at Leviticus 18:16.

13. Now, then, I clap My hand at the dishonest profits you have made, and the bloodletting you have caused.

14. Will your heart remain steady, and your hand be firm, when the days come for Me to deal with you? I, the Eternal, have spoken and I will do it.

15. I will scatter you among the nations and disperse you in foreign lands; I will purge you of your unclean ways.

16. When you are profaned before the nations, you shall know that I am the Eternal.

17. The word of the Eternal came to me, saying:

18. Mortal, the House of Israel has become base metal to Me: all of them—copper, tin, iron, lead, even silver—have come into the furnace.

19. Therefore, says the Eternal God: Because you all became base metal, I will gather you up into the midst of Jerusalem.

13 וְהִנֵּה֙ הִכֵּ֣יתִי כַפִּ֔י אֶל־בִּצְעֵ֖ךְ אֲשֶׁ֣ר עָשִׂ֑ית וְעַל־דָּמֵ֔ךְ אֲשֶׁ֥ר הָי֖וּ בְּתוֹכֵֽךְ׃

14 הֲיַעֲמֹ֤ד לִבֵּךְ֙ אִם־תֶּחֱזַ֣קְנָה יָדַ֔יִךְ לַיָּמִ֕ים אֲשֶׁ֥ר אֲנִ֖י עֹשֶׂ֣ה אוֹתָ֑ךְ אֲנִ֧י יְהֹוָ֛ה דִּבַּ֖רְתִּי וְעָשִֽׂיתִי׃

15 וַהֲפִיצוֹתִ֤י אוֹתָךְ֙ בַּגּוֹיִ֔ם וְזֵרִיתִ֖יךְ בָּאֲרָצ֑וֹת וַהֲתִמֹּתִ֥י טֻמְאָתֵ֖ךְ מִמֵּֽךְ׃

16 וְנִחַ֥לְתְּ בָּ֖ךְ לְעֵינֵ֣י גוֹיִ֑ם וְיָדַ֖עַתְּ כִּֽי־אֲנִ֥י יְהֹוָֽה׃

17 וַיְהִ֥י דְבַר־יְהֹוָ֖ה אֵלַ֥י לֵאמֹֽר׃

18 בֶּן־אָדָ֕ם הָֽיוּ־לִ֥י בֵֽית־יִשְׂרָאֵ֖ל לְסֻ֑וג [לְסִ֣יג] כֻּלָּ֗ם נְחֹ֨שֶׁת וּבְדִ֤יל וּבַרְזֶל֙ וְעוֹפֶ֙רֶת֙ בְּת֣וֹךְ כּ֔וּר סִגִ֥ים כֶּ֖סֶף הָיֽוּ׃

19 לָכֵ֗ן כֹּ֤ה אָמַר֙ אֲדֹנָ֣י יְהֹוִ֔ה יַ֛עַן הֱי֥וֹת כֻּלְּכֶ֖ם לְסִגִ֑ים לָכֵן֙ הִנְנִ֣י קֹבֵ֣ץ אֶתְכֶ֔ם אֶל־תּ֖וֹךְ יְרוּשָׁלָֽ͏ִם׃

Commentary

13. *I clap My hand.* Either in mockery or, more likely, in sorrow.[6]

18. *Base metal … silver.* Imagery recalling Isaiah 1:22. Having purified Israel, God will give it another chance.

Essay

The city of blood (verse 2)

Eight times in this short haftarah, Jerusalem and its people are accused of violating the strict Torah laws dealing with blood. This includes rules about menstruation (verse 10) and, figuratively, about the "blood" of commerce (verse 6). Blood is Ezekiel's metaphor for total corruption.

He delivered his indictment to an audience that understood the metaphor, for blood was considered equivalent to life itself[7] and its consumption was strictly forbidden[8]—a law that was deemed incumbent upon non-Jews as well, for blood belongs to God.[9] To this day, the dietary laws concerning meat consumption center on draining the blood from the animal during the slaughter, and on further draining procedures before consumption.

It appears certain that Ezekiel was in Jerusalem when he delivered this oracle. It resembles similar indictments by Jeremiah, who was his older contemporary and who preached in the city at the same time. Though we have no record of the two men having met, one may surmise that Ezekiel was inspired by Jeremiah's bold speeches (which landed him in jail and nearly cost him his life). But despite the same burning conviction about the city's moral corruption, Ezekiel's rhetoric is very different from Jeremiah's. He spells everything out in detail, and in this oration he uses "blood" as his verbal vehicle.

That is why he includes acts of sexual immorality that have to do with menstruating women and blood relations (verses 10 and 11), and he treats extortion, dishonesty, and similar depravities as bloodsucking. Even slander is mentioned, for the slanderer is intent on killing the reputation of another person, and was therefore considered by the Rabbis as equivalent to a murderer—neither had a share in the world to come.[10]

The connection of city life with bloodshed and corruption is very old in Jewish tradition. Cain, the original murderer, is also said to have been the founder of the first city.[11] It is an identification that moderns find as compelling as did the ancients.

For Ezekiel, who had returned to Jerusalem from Babylon and had hoped to bask in the glory of the Holy City, the sight of a community bent on idolatry and "bloodshed" in all its forms must have been a terrible shock. The message he delivered to his contemporaries therefore had an inescapable conclusion: Jerusalem will be destroyed, and not until it has gone through the smelter of purification will God restore it to divine favor.

Gleanings

Words to Remember

I will scatter you among the nations
and disperse you in foreign lands. (15)

Taking interest (verse 12)

All interest is forbidden on loans to the poor. In modern times money is commonly lent for commercial purposes, to enable the borrower to increase his capital and develop his business; and it is as natural and proper that a reasonable payment should be made for this accommodation, as that it should be made for the loan (i.e. the hire) of a house, or any other commodity. But this use of loans is a modern development: in ancient times money was commonly lent for the relief of poverty brought about by misfortune or debt; it partook thus of the nature of charity; to take interest on money thus lent was felt to be making gain out of a neighbor's need.

Samuel R. Driver[12]

The power of the sexual urge

Though far removed from the Freudian concept of sex as the ultimate key to normal and abnormal behaviour in childhood as in mature life, the Rabbis often asserted the predominance of the sex urge and the effort needed to control it.

"Who is mighty? He who subdues his lust" (*M.* Avot 4:1) and "For most people there is nothing harder in the entire Torah than to abstain from sex and forbidden relations" (Maimonides, *Mishneh Torah*, Issurei Bi'ah, 22:18) are typical statements. Characteristic, too, is the interpretation given to the rite of circumcision, the "covenant" between God and Israel and the first law enjoined upon the first Jew, as symbolising the primacy of hallowing the sex act by an operation "to weaken the organ of generation as far as possible, and thus cause man to be moderate" (Maimonides, *Guide of the Perplexed*, 3:39).

Immanuel Jakobovits[13]

***

Notes

[1] Harry M. Orlinsky, *Essays in Biblical Culture and Biblical Translation*, pp. 215 ff.

[2] Exodus 21 :17.

[3] Leviticus 19:16.

[4] So D. N. Freedman, in *Anchor Bible*, Ezekiel 1-20, p. 329. He follows the interpretation by M. Greenberg,

[5] Leviticus 20:18.

[6] The latter interpretation is favored by Rashi and Radak. See the similar expression, "slap the thigh" in Jeremiah 31:19 (haftarah for the Second Day of Rosh Hashanah).

[7] Leviticus 17:11 and 14; Deuteronomy 12:23.

[8] Leviticus 3:17; 7:26, and elsewhere in the Torah.

[9] Genesis 3:4.

[10] *B.* Baba Metzi'a 58b; *M.* Avot 3:12.

[11] Genesis 4:17.

[12] Quoted by J.H. Hertz, *Pentateuch and Haftorahs*, p. 314.

[13] *Encyclopaedia Judaica*, vol. 14, p. 1206.

קְדֹשִׁים

Amos, chapter 9, verses 7 to 15

Introduction

Connection of haftarah and sidra:

Opinions are divided over the reasons for the selection of this haftarah.

According to one view, the sidra deals prominently and memorably with the ethical prerequisites of the kingdom of priests that Israel was meant to be, while the haftarah shows how widely, at the time of Amos, Israel diverged from its destined path.

Another opinion finds the reason for the selection at the end of the sidra, which contains the warning that a sinful nation will be plucked from its land. Amos speaks in like tones, though in the end he holds out the vision of a brighter future.

The setting:

Though Amos was a native of Tekoa, a little place near Jerusalem, he moved north, to the kingdom of Israel, and preached in Samaria (its capital) as well as in Bethel, where a shrine existed that featured immoral practices under the guise of religion. He was deeply shocked at what he saw: moral laxity, legal and social corruption, and religious rites that had little to do with the God of Israel. Conspicuous wealth and social injustice lived side by side.

For more on Amos and his time, see our *General Introduction.*

The message:

1. The universal God has not lost sight of Israel's misdeeds, and its punishment is inevitable. (9:7-10)

2. But after the punishment will come a glorious reversal and restoration. This ends the book of Amos. (11-15)

HAFTARAH FOR K'DOSHIM

Amos, chapter 9, verses 7 to 15

9:7 הֲלֹ֣וא כִבְנֵי֩ כֻשִׁיִּ֨ים אַתֶּ֥ם לִ֛י

בְּנֵ֥י יִשְׂרָאֵ֖ל

נְאֻם־יְהֹוָ֑ה

הֲל֣וֹא אֶת־יִשְׂרָאֵ֗ל הֶעֱלֵ֙יתִי֙ מֵאֶ֣רֶץ מִצְרַ֔יִם

וּפְלִשְׁתִּיִּ֥ים מִכַּפְתּ֖וֹר

וַאֲרָ֥ם מִקִּֽיר׃

8 הִנֵּ֞ה עֵינֵ֣י ׀ אֲדֹנָ֣י יְהֹוִ֗ה

בַּמַּמְלָכָה֙ הַֽחַטָּאָ֔ה

וְהִשְׁמַדְתִּ֣י אֹתָ֔הּ

מֵעַ֖ל פְּנֵ֣י הָאֲדָמָ֑ה

אֶ֗פֶס כִּ֠י לֹ֣א הַשְׁמֵ֥יד אַשְׁמִ֛יד

אֶת־בֵּ֥ית יַעֲקֹ֖ב

נְאֻם־יְהֹוָֽה׃

9:7. Are you not to Me,
O people of Israel,
like the Cushites?
says the Eternal One.
Did I not bring Israel up from the land of
  Egypt,
and the Philistines from Crete,
and the Arameans from Kir?

8. Look, now:
the eyes of the Eternal God
are on the sinful kingdom,
and I will destroy it
from the face of the earth—
though I will not utterly destroy
the House of Jacob,
says the Eternal One.

Commentary

7. *Cushites.* In the Tanach, כוש (*cush*) refers to a cultural and political entity originating in Nubia, which came to power in Egypt as the twenty-fifth dynasty. Under the Cushites, the country experienced a notable revival (about 780-656 B.C.E.).[1] In modern Hebrew, Cush stands for Ethiopia.

Crete. כפתור (*kaphtor*). Archaeologists believe that the Philistines came to Canaan partly by sea (by way of Crete) and partly by land (via Anatolia). Their geographic origins— somewhere in the Aegean—are unknown.[2]

Kir. Its location is unknown; Mesopotamia, northern Syria, and Armenia have been suggested.[3] Apparently, the peoples involved told their own tales of relocation from an original homeland, even as Israel remembered its migrations. We do not know what details were familiar to Amos; in any case, he attributed these wanderings to God.

8. *The sinful kingdom.* Traditional commentators say that this refers to the Northern Kingdom, while the further prophecy, "I will not utterly destroy," refers to the House of Jacob, which will survive destruction and exile.[4]

9. For at My command

I will shake the House of Israel among all
 the nations

as one shakes in a sieve,

yet not a pebble shall fall to the ground.

10. The sinners of My people

shall die by the sword,

saying [all the while]:

No harm shall overtake us, nor meet us.

11. On that day

I will raise up David's fallen shelter.

I will rebuild the breaches in its walls

and raise up its ruins

and build it up as in days of old.

9 כִּי־הִנֵּה אָנֹכִי מְצַוֶּה

וַהֲנִעוֹתִי בְכָל־הַגּוֹיִם אֶת־בֵּית יִשְׂרָאֵל

כַּאֲשֶׁר יִנּוֹעַ בַּכְּבָרָה

וְלֹא־יִפּוֹל צְרוֹר אָרֶץ:

10 בַּחֶרֶב יָמוּתוּ

כֹּל חַטָּאֵי עַמִּי

הָאֹמְרִים

לֹא־תַגִּישׁ וְתַקְדִּים בַּעֲדֵינוּ הָרָעָה:

11 בַּיּוֹם הַהוּא

אָקִים אֶת־סֻכַּת דָּוִיד הַנֹּפֶלֶת

וְגָדַרְתִּי אֶת־פִּרְצֵיהֶן

וַהֲרִסֹתָיו אָקִים

וּבְנִיתִיהָ כִּימֵי עוֹלָם:

Commentary

9. *Not a pebble shall fall to the ground.* The conclusion of the Prophet's metaphor: God will shake us up as if we were pebbles in a sieve, but the purpose is not to winnow us but to awaken our consciences.[5]

10. *The sinners of My people.* The winnowing will result in the death of the wicked, implying that the righteous will be saved, much like the "holy seed" of Isaiah 6:13 (haftarah for Yitro).

11. *On that day.* When destruction is rampant, God will relent and will reestablish the united kingdom with a Davidic head.

David's fallen shelter. The circumstances did not apply to the time of Amos, and the same applies to the promise to return Israel's exiles whose cities were destroyed. Tradition therefore sees the text as a prophecy, while others believe that later disciples or editors wanted to give the book a visionary conclusion.

The סכה (*sukkah*) is a metaphor for the impermanence of the old kingdom, but its successor will be built up and endure "as in the days of old." (Note that the name of David is spelled not as usual, דוד, but דויד. This so-called "full" spelling does not occur often in the Tanach.[6])

12. They shall possess what is left of Edom
and all the nations that were called by My
  name,
says the Eternal God, who does this.
13. The time is coming, says the Eternal
  One,
when the one who plows the field
will overtake the one who reaps it,
and the treader of grapes will overtake the
  one who sows seeds,
when the mountains shall drip sweet wine,
and all the hills shall overflow.
14. I will restore the fortunes of My people
  Israel:
They shall rebuild the desolate cities, and
  dwell [in them];
they shall plant vineyards, and drink their
  wine;
make gardens, and eat their fruit.
15. I will plant them on their soil,
never again to be uprooted from the soil
  that I have given them,
says the Eternal One, your God.

12 לְמַ֙עַן֙ יִֽירְשׁ֔וּ אֶת־שְׁאֵרִ֖ית אֱד֑וֹם
וְכָל־הַגּוֹיִ֗ם אֲשֶׁר־נִקְרָ֥א שְׁמִ֖י עֲלֵיהֶ֑ם
נְאֻם־יְהֹוָ֖ה עֹ֥שֶׂה זֹּֽאת׃
13 הִנֵּ֨ה יָמִ֤ים בָּאִים֙ נְאֻם־יְהֹוָ֔ה
וְנִגַּ֥שׁ חוֹרֵ֖שׁ בַּקֹּצֵ֑ר
וְדֹרֵ֤ךְ עֲנָבִים֙ בְּמֹשֵׁ֣ךְ הַזָּ֔רַע
וְהִטִּ֤יפוּ הֶֽהָרִים֙ עָסִ֔יס
וְכָל־הַגְּבָע֖וֹת תִּתְמוֹגַֽגְנָה׃
14 וְשַׁבְתִּי֙ אֶת־שְׁב֣וּת עַמִּ֣י יִשְׂרָאֵ֔ל
וּבָנ֞וּ עָרִ֤ים נְשַׁמּוֹת֙ וְיָשָׁ֔בוּ
וְנָטְע֣וּ כְרָמִ֔ים וְשָׁת֖וּ אֶת־יֵינָ֑ם
וְעָשׂ֣וּ גַנּ֔וֹת וְאָכְל֖וּ אֶת־פְּרִיהֶֽם׃
15 וּנְטַעְתִּ֖ים עַל־אַדְמָתָ֑ם
וְלֹ֨א יִנָּתְשׁ֜וּ ע֗וֹד מֵעַ֤ל אַדְמָתָם֙ אֲשֶׁ֣ר נָתַ֣תִּי
  לָהֶ֔ם
אָמַ֖ר יְהֹוָ֥ה אֱלֹהֶֽיךָ׃

Commentary

13. *Will overtake.* The yield of the land will be so rich that even while the harvest is not yet in, the sowing for the next crop has already begun. The same image is also part of the Torah.[7]

Essay

Questions of prejudice

In the first verse of the haftarah, the children of Israel are compared to the Cushites, that is, to inhabitants of northern Africa. Amos takes it for granted that God's mastery encompasses all human beings, and while Israel may have a special place, it is not the only one to whom the divine concern extends.

Just what does Amos mean when he states this equation? Does his reference to the Cushites imply, negatively, that Israel is no better than the Cushites, or, positively, that God makes no distinction between them?

Some commentators opt for the negative explanation. For instance, J. H. Hertz says: "Degenerate Israel is no more to God than the despised inhabitants of distant Ethiopia, the descendants of Ham."[8]

In our view, there is no warrant for this kind of assessment. True, the Genesis tales of prehistoric humanity paint a negative image of the Hamites, but among these are, in addition to the Cushites, people from one end of the Fertile Crescent to the other: Egyptians, Canaanites, Philistines, Assyrians, and Babylonians—the traditional enemies of Israel. In no wise are the Cushites singled out for special opprobrium.

For the Tanach knows of no racial prejudice. Moses himself married a Cushite. The Torah, in its catalogue of the nations of the world, describes them according to language and location, but never race.[9] And even though Israel was repeatedly enslaved in the course of its history, its homes devastated and its people exiled, such events were traced to the mysterious designs that God had mapped out for the people of the Covenant, and not any inherent characteristics of its enemies.

The prophecy of Amos proclaims that God is the God of all humanity and that, as humans, the Children of Israel are no different from the inhabitants of Africa (Cushites), or Asia (Arameans), or Europe (Philistines). Israel's special relationship with the Divine stems not from any innate capacities or race, but from its historic commitment to know and do God's will. The reverse of this commitment is God's extra attention to Israel's sins, as well as a special concern for its moral future. In Amos, as in all prophets, this is both the burden and the joy of belonging to the House of Jacob.[10]

Gleanings

Words to Remember

Are you not to Me, O people of Israel,
like the Cushites? (9:7)
On that day
I will raise up David's fallen shelter.
I will rebuild the breaches in its walls
and raise up its ruins
and build it up as in days of old. (9:11)

The God of all nations

The prophecies against, or about, the nations included in nearly all the books of the prophets, are not merely casual additions, they belong integrally to the framework of prophecy. Not only the history of the Hebrews but the history of all nations comes under God's sovereignty. The God from whom he (Amos) brought a message rules all the nations and judges their conduct. Sometimes the prophets predict disaster for a nation because of its treatment of, or attitude to, the Jews, but more often they attribute a nation's misfortunes to its overweening pride, idolatry, or general unrighteousness.

Israel I. Mattuck[11]

A special relationship

The universalism thus enunciated [in verse 7] is no mere impartial unconcern with the course of human history but an actual positive control of the destinies of them all. It is a universalism that had learned from the particularism of the past, Israel's sense of all that its unique relationship to God had meant for its history, its realization of the intimacy of God's loving care.

H. E. W. Fosbroke[12]

***

Notes

[1] D. Redford, *Anchor Bible Dictionary*, vol. 4, p. 110; see also Andersen and Freedman, *Anchor Bible*, Amos, p. 869.

[2] B. Katzenstein, *Anchor Bible Dictionary*, vol. 5, p. 326.

[3] Note the occurrences in II Kings 16:9 and Isaiah 22:5.

[4] So Rashi and Radak. According to Andersen and Freedman, in their commentary on Amos (*Anchor Bible*, Amos), p. 870, the expression "House of Jacob" refers to all of Israel. It is also possible that the "further prophecy" was from the hand of a later editor.

[5] Most commentators, however, suggest that the pebbles stand for the God-fearing, who will be preserved, while the sinners will be destroyed (verse 10).

[6] It is possible that the "full" spelling is intentional here, to underscore the extended possession that the restored monarchy will enjoy.

[7] Leviticus 26:5.

[8] *Pentateuch and Haftorahs*, p. 509. Ham is listed in Genesis as the second son of Noah (9:18) and as the progenitor of many peoples, chief amongst them Cush and Mitzraim (Egypt), that is, the Africa known to the Bible. Jeremiah's saying (13:23) that Cushites cannot change their skin or leopards their spots has also nothing to do with race. It illustrates the Prophet's main point: that there are some unchangeable things in life.

[9] Genesis 10.

[10] It is noteworthy that—with the exception of Deborah (see the haftarah for B'shalach), who mentions "Sinai," and Malachi (see the haftarah for Shabbat Hagadol), who mentions "Horeb"— there are no prophetic references to the covenant mountain(s).

[11] *The Thought of the Prophets*, pp. 148 ff.

[12] *Interpreter's Bible*, vol. 6, p. 648.

Ezekiel, chapter 44, verses 15 to 31

Introduction

Connection of haftarah and sidra:

The sidra speaks of priestly duties, and the entire haftarah is devoted to the status, practices, and privileges of the priesthood.

The setting:

Ezekiel lived in the days before and after the destruction of the First Temple and preached in the early part of the 6th century B.C.E. He was exiled to Babylon and lived through a period of great despair after the destruction of the Temple in 587. The haftarah is part of the last nine chapters of Ezekiel's book. By describing in great detail the service in the new Temple, which would be built after their return to Jerusalem, he reinforced the people's hope that this would happen in their lifetime.

For more on Ezekiel and his time, see our *General Introduction.*

The message:

1. The descendants of Zadok are the legitimate priests. (44:15-17)
2. The priestly garments. (17-19)
3. Various laws. (20-27)
4. Gifts due to the priests. (28-30)
5. A warning not to eat the flesh of animals that are found dead. (31)

44:15. But the levitical priests who are descendants of Zadok faithfully kept charge of My Sanctuary when the people of Israel were unfaithful to Me. They may come near to Me and serve Me by offering Me the fat and blood of sacrifices, says the Sovereign God.

16. They alone may enter My sanctuary and draw near to My table to serve Me and keep My charge.

17. They must wear linen clothing when they come through the gates to the inner courtyard, and wear nothing woolen when they serve in the gates of the inner courtyard or in the Temple.

44:15 וְהַכֹּהֲנִים הַלְוִיִּם בְּנֵי צָדוֹק אֲשֶׁר שָׁמְרוּ

אֶת־מִשְׁמֶרֶת מִקְדָּשִׁי בִּתְעוֹת בְּנֵי־יִשְׂרָאֵל

מֵעָלַי הֵמָּה יִקְרְבוּ אֵלַי לְשָׁרְתֵנִי וְעָמְדוּ לְפָנַי

לְהַקְרִיב לִי חֵלֶב וָדָם נְאֻם אֲדֹנָי יֱהֹוִה:

16 הֵמָּה יָבֹאוּ אֶל־מִקְדָּשִׁי וְהֵמָּה יִקְרְבוּ אֶל־

שֻׁלְחָנִי לְשָׁרְתֵנִי וְשָׁמְרוּ אֶת־מִשְׁמַרְתִּי:

17 וְהָיָה בְּבוֹאָם אֶל־שַׁעֲרֵי הֶחָצֵר הַפְּנִימִית

בִּגְדֵי פִשְׁתִּים יִלְבָּשׁוּ וְלֹא־יַעֲלֶה עֲלֵיהֶם צֶמֶר

בְּשָׁרְתָם בְּשַׁעֲרֵי הֶחָצֵר הַפְּנִימִית וָבָיְתָה:

Commentary

44:15. *The levitical priests.* Ezekiel legitimates only those stemming from the tribe of Levi, reflecting the fact that the priesthood in Israel had over the centuries been contested by other claimants.

Descendants of Zadok. Zadok ben Ahitub was a supporter of King David when his son Absalom rebelled against him, and successfully supported Solomon to become David's successor (about 970 B.C.E.).[1] Zadok's family thereupon became the unchallenged priests in the First Temple as well as in the rebuilt Second Temple. Their hold on the office ended during the second century.

Fat and blood of sacrifices. Biblical writers considered them to be the essence of animal life, and consequently they were assigned to God and forbidden to Israelites.[2] The assignment symbolized God's control over life.

16. *My table.* The altar.[3]

17. *Linen … woolen ….* One fabric is cool, the other warm. A perspiring priest was an unsightly officiant. But otherwise priests did wear garments made of linen and wool,[4] a mixture (called *sha'atnez*) prohibited for lay people.[5]

18. Let them wear linen turbans and trousers, but nothing that makes them sweat.

19. And when they go to the outer courtyard where the people are, they must take off the clothing in which they serve, leaving them in the holy chambers. They must then put on other garments, so that they do not make the people holy through [the touch of] their garments.

20. They are not to shave their heads, nor let their hair grow too long; they are only to trim their hair.

21. No priest may drink wine before entering the inner courtyard.

18 פַּאֲרֵי פִשְׁתִּים יִהְיוּ עַל־רֹאשָׁם וּמִכְנְסֵי פִשְׁתִּים יִהְיוּ עַל־מָתְנֵיהֶם לֹא יַחְגְּרוּ בַּיָּזַע:

19 וּבְצֵאתָם אֶל־הֶחָצֵר הַחִיצוֹנָה אֶל־הֶחָצֵר הַחִיצוֹנָה אֶל־הָעָם יִפְשְׁטוּ אֶת־בִּגְדֵיהֶם אֲשֶׁר־הֵמָּה מְשָׁרְתִם בָּם וְהִנִּיחוּ אוֹתָם בְּלִשְׁכֹת הַקֹּדֶשׁ וְלָבְשׁוּ בְּגָדִים אֲחֵרִים וְלֹא־יְקַדְּשׁוּ אֶת־הָעָם בְּבִגְדֵיהֶם:

20 וְרֹאשָׁם לֹא יְגַלֵּחוּ וּפֶרַע לֹא יְשַׁלֵּחוּ כָּסוֹם יִכְסְמוּ אֶת־רָאשֵׁיהֶם:

21 וְיַיִן לֹא־יִשְׁתּוּ כָּל־כֹּהֵן בְּבוֹאָם אֶל־הֶחָצֵר הַפְּנִימִית:

Commentary

18. *Turbans.* This reflected no rule that heads had to be covered at worship. The turban (פְּאֵר, *p'er*), was a decoration,[6] mentioned by Isaiah as special head wear for bridegrooms (Isaiah 61:13) and as women's finery (Isaiah 3:20).

Trousers. An Iranian invention that caught on about the 6th century B.C.E. Wearing them solved the problem of inadvertent immodesty, against which the Torah warns.[7]

19. *Make the people holy.* יְקַדְּשׁוּ (*y'kadd'shu*), from the root קדשׁ (*k-d-sh*). The sacred garments confer special status on the wearers.

20. *Too long.* Extremes were to be avoided.

21. *No priest may drink wine.* In accordance with Torah law.[8]

22. They must not marry widowed or divorced women; they may marry only Israelite virgins or the widows of priests.

23. They are to teach My people the difference between the holy and the common, and let them know how to tell the clean from the unclean.

24. When there are disputes, they are to be the judges; and in judging, they are to follow My laws of justice. On all My religious festivals they are to carry out My Teachings and My laws, and they are to keep My Sabbaths holy.

25. They are not to make themselves unclean by coming into contact with a dead body, except in the case of a father or mother, a son or daughter, a brother or an unmarried sister.

26. After a priest has made himself clean, seven days are to be counted off for him.

22 וְאַלְמָנָה וּגְרוּשָׁה לֹא־יִקְחוּ לָהֶם לְנָשִׁים כִּי אִם־בְּתוּלֹת מִזֶּרַע בֵּית יִשְׂרָאֵל וְהָאַלְמָנָה אֲשֶׁר תִּהְיֶה אַלְמָנָה מִכֹּהֵן יִקָּחוּ:

23 וְאֶת־עַמִּי יוֹרוּ בֵּין קֹדֶשׁ לְחֹל וּבֵין־טָמֵא לְטָהוֹר יוֹדִעֻם:

24 וְעַל־רִיב הֵמָּה יַעַמְדוּ לשְׁפֹט [לְמִשְׁפָּט] בְּמִשְׁפָּטַי וּשְׁפָטֻהוּ [יִשְׁפְּטֻהוּ] וְאֶת־תּוֹרֹתַי וְאֶת־חֻקֹּתַי בְּכָל־מוֹעֲדַי יִשְׁמֹרוּ וְאֶת־שַׁבְּתוֹתַי יְקַדֵּשׁוּ:

25 וְאֶל־מֵת אָדָם לֹא יָבוֹא לְטָמְאָה כִּי אִם־לְאָב וּלְאֵם וּלְבֵן וּלְבַת לְאָח וּלְאָחוֹת אֲשֶׁר־לֹא הָיְתָה לְאִישׁ יִטַּמָּאוּ:

26 וְאַחֲרֵי טָהֳרָתוֹ שִׁבְעַת יָמִים יִסְפְּרוּ־לוֹ:

Commentary

22. *They must not marry widowed or divorced women*. This is one of the passages that caused tradition much difficulty, for the Torah (in the sidra at Leviticus 21:14) restricts only the High Priest in this fashion.[9] Some said that God (through the Prophet) had decided to amend the Torah law, because the new Temple needed an extra degree of sanctity to protect it from the abuses of the past.[10]

25. *Unclean*. The word טמא (*tamé*, here in the infinitive form *tam'ah*) does not mean dirty, but always conveys a state of *ritual* impurity. Priests were to avoid it as much as possible. Touching a corpse was equivalent to having come too close to the mystery of death, and required special ablution. The rules were suspended for close relatives of the priest, whose wife was not mentioned by Ezekiel or the Torah,[11] but whom the Rabbis included.[12]

Unmarried sister. Once she married she was considered to have moved into the family of her husband.

26. *Seven days*. Another of Ezekiel's additions to the Torah law.

27. On the day when he returns to the inner courtyard to serve in the sanctuary, he must offer his sin-offering, says the Sovereign God.

28. This is to be their inheritance: *I am their inheritance;* you are to give them no property in Israel: *I am their property.*

29. They shall eat the grain-offering, the sin-offering, and the guilt-offering; and everything in Israel that has been set aside shall be theirs.

30. The priests shall also get the best of the first fruits of all kinds, and every offering of whatever you offer. You shall also give the priest the first loaf of whatever you bake, and a blessing will rest on your home.

31. And priests are not to eat any bird or animal that dies [a natural death] or is killed by another animal.

27 וּבְיוֹם בֹּאוֹ אֶל־הַקֹּדֶשׁ אֶל־הֶחָצֵר הַפְּנִימִית לְשָׁרֵת בַּקֹּדֶשׁ יַקְרִיב חַטָּאתוֹ נְאֻם אֲדֹנָי יְהוִה:

28 וְהָיְתָה לָהֶם לְנַחֲלָה אֲנִי נַחֲלָתָם וַאֲחֻזָּה לֹא־תִתְּנוּ לָהֶם בְּיִשְׂרָאֵל אֲנִי אֲחֻזָּתָם:

29 הַמִּנְחָה וְהַחַטָּאת וְהָאָשָׁם הֵמָּה יֹאכְלוּם וְכָל־חֵרֶם בְּיִשְׂרָאֵל לָהֶם יִהְיֶה:

30 וְרֵאשִׁית כָּל־בִּכּוּרֵי כֹל וְכָל־תְּרוּמַת כֹּל מִכֹּל תְּרוּמוֹתֵיכֶם לַכֹּהֲנִים יִהְיֶה וְרֵאשִׁית עֲרִסוֹתֵיכֶם תִּתְּנוּ לַכֹּהֵן לְהָנִיחַ בְּרָכָה אֶל־בֵּיתֶךָ:

31 כָּל־נְבֵלָה וּטְרֵפָה מִן־הָעוֹף וּמִן־הַבְּהֵמָה לֹא יֹאכְלוּ הַכֹּהֲנִים:

Commentary

28. *No property in Israel.* The priests had the sole responsibility of looking after the Sanctuary, and were to be supported entirely from the proceeds of their Temple service. Hence, the tribe of Levi did not receive a land apportionment.[13]

29. *Set aside.* חרם (*cherem*), like first fruits that were removed from use by others.[14] The word later assumed the meaning of "ban"; an excommunicated person was "in *cherem*."

31. *And priests are not to eat* .... However, according to the Torah,[15] the prohibition was general and not just for priests. Traditionalists were hard put to reconcile this verse with the Torah. Thus J. H. Hertz says that it represents a "half-ideal and half-allegorical programme of the New Jerusalem." Modern biblical critics would suggest that at the time of Ezekiel the general prohibition had not yet become a part of the Torah.

Essay

The priesthood

The history of the Israelite priesthood is not at all clear, and scholars have come to various conclusions about it. There is agreement that its nature changed during the centuries of settlement in the land. The most probable development was as follows:

When Israel arose as a new people in Canaan, it did not at once have a central sanctuary. Instead, local shrines were distributed around the country, with members of the clan of Levi the usual officiants when people brought their offerings. But many people had private altars, and they sacrificed to God or (for many centuries) to idols without priestly benefit.

After the Temple in Jerusalem was established, sacrificial service—especially on the three Pilgrim Festivals, Pesach, Shavuot, and Sukkot—was supposed to be concentrated in the central Sanctuary. Nevertheless, private offerings and competing shrines continued to exist until the reform of King Josiah in the 7th century B.C.E. [16]

Ezekiel himself was a *kohen*, a priest, a status that was hereditary, handed down by father to son. The family of Zadok had been in control of the office ever since their forebear had supported Solomon for the throne. Ezekiel wanted to make sure that this privilege continued, and the haftarah reflects this purpose. All priests were levites, but not all levites were priests.

The *kohen* (always a man) officiated at the sacrificial cult; pronounced the priestly benediction; carried the holy Ark when it was to be moved; cast the sacred lots (Urim and Thummim); functioned as a judge; and was the principal teacher of Torah. He was also there to cleanse people from ritual impurities caused by certain diseases, and thereby functioned in addition as a physician—of the soul as well as of the body.

His status was so exalted that holiness was assumed to be attached to him: merely touching his garments was enough to gain a part of that status, and therefore the Prophet commands priests to leave their garments in a special chamber, inaccessible to outsiders.

The *kohen* received 27 types of benefits: he shared in the sacrificial meal; and people were expected to set aside a portion of their first fruits and baked goods (*challot*) for them, and give them a portion of their tithes.

After the destruction of the Second Temple (70 C.E.), traditional Judaism preserved some of the priestly privileges and restrictions: only a *kohen* speaks the priestly blessing during the service; he is the first to be called the Torah, and he officiates at the redemption of the firstborn (*pidyon ha-ben*).

Along with these privileges go a number of restrictions: a *kohen* may not marry a divorced woman or a proselyte (see comment on verse 22, above); he may not come too close to the dead and must refrain from entering any closed space in which a dead body is kept. (He may therefore not visit funeral homes, unless their buildings conform to certain rules.)

Levites who were not priests did not officiate at the altar; instead, they sang in the choir, played sacred music, and functioned as gatekeepers. Today, a levite is called to the Torah after the *kohen*, and levites perform ablutions for the *kohanim*, as the latter prepare for the priestly benediction.

Conservative Judaism has in some instances lightened the restrictions placed upon the *kohen*, while Reform Judaism has abandoned them altogether as incompatible with egalitarian principles.

Gleanings

Words to Remember

I am their inheritance. (from verse 28)

A presumptive status

Since there are no reliable registers of who is a priest, his status is only presumptive. Therefore, when he receives money at a *pidyon ha-ben,* he will return it or give it to charity.

Family names

Today, family names are often the best indicators of who was most likely a member of priestly or levitical origin.

Thus, in addition to Cohen, Cohn, Kahane, Kogan or Kagan, the name Katz will usually indicate priestly descent: it is an acronym of the first letters of the Hebrew **k**ohen **t**zedek (righteous priest).

Levites are most often known as Levy or Levine and will often bear anglicized names such as Lewis.

The true importance of Ezekiel

The core of Ezekiel's goal was religious organization. It could combine opposites. It could appeal at the same time to the desire of being superior to others and to the inner imperative of human sympathy, to selfishness and unselfishness. It could sustain the best in men as well as the poorest.

Century after century has proved the strength of this combination, in many forms, over all the world. As Ezekiel shaped it, it has endured storms as have visited no other. The history of the Jewish people is one long record of terror and agony, but after two thousand years of unparalleled suffering their organization still appears indestructible. That is primarily Ezekiel's achievement, and beside it the empires and the conquests of the heroes of history seem impermanent superficialities.

Edith Hamilton[17]

***

Notes

[1] I Kings 1:8, 32.

[2] Leviticus 3:4; Ezekiel 44:7, the section preceding the haftarah.

[3] So called also in 41:22.

[4] See *Mishnah* Kilayim 9:1.

[5] Leviticus 19:19; Deuteronomy 22:11.

[6] So Radak. See also Hertz, *Pentateuch and Haftorahs.*

[7] Exodus 20:23.

[8] Leviticus 10:9.

[9] Leviticus 21:14. The Talmud records (*B.* Shabbat 13b) that—because of variations like these—some Sages considered excluding the book of Ezekiel from the curriculum of instruction.

[10] See, for instance, Radak, who stresses the need for increased purity.

[11] Leviticus 21:2-3.

[12] *B.* Yevamot 22b.

[13] Deuteronomy 10:8-9; Joshua 13:33.

[14] Leviticus 27:26.

[15] Leviticus 7:24.

[16] See II Kings chapters 22-23.

[17] *Spokesmen for God,* pp. 194 ff.

Jeremiah, chapter 32, verses 6 to 27

Introduction

Connection of haftarah and sidra:

The weekly portion contains a law aimed at preserving a family's title to the land it owns. The haftarah tells of Jeremiah fulfilling the terms of the Torah commandment and thereby teaching the despairing people of Jerusalem an important lesson.

The setting:

While the haftarah begins with verse 6 of chapter 32, the first five verses provide the setting. The incident took place in the tenth year of King Zedekiah, which was the eighteenth year of King Nebuchadnezzar of Babylon. The latter was besieging Jerusalem (588/587 B.C.E.), and Jeremiah, who had counseled surrender, was considered by many a traitor and was imprisoned by the king in the guardhouse of the palace. However, the Prophet was given the opportunity to receive visitors and also had access to his friend and secretary, Baruch ben Neriah (who may have been imprisoned with him).

For more on Jeremiah and his time, see our *General Introduction*.

The message:

1. The acquisition of a parcel of land is used by the Prophet as a symbolic act, speaking to the future of the people who were in dire straits. (32:6-15)
2. A prayer that recounts the incident and the reasons for God's stern judgment. (16-25)
3. A few upbeat words to end the haftarah. In the full text of the book of Jeremiah, these two verses form the opening parts of a new prophecy. (26-27)

HAFTARAH FOR B'HAR SINAI

Jeremiah, chapter 32, verses 6 to 27

32:6. Jeremiah said: The word of the Eternal came to me:

7. Your uncle Shallum's son Chanam'el will come to you, saying: Buy my land in Anatot, because you have the redemption-right to buy it.

8. And just as the Eternal had foretold, my cousin Chanam'el came to me in the court of the guard and said: *Please buy my land in Anatot, in the territory of Benjamin; you have the right of possession and [the duty of] redemption—so buy it.*

32:6 וַיֹּאמֶר יִרְמְיָהוּ הָיָה דְבַר־יְהֹוָה אֵלַי לֵאמֹר:

7 הִנֵּה חֲנַמְאֵל בֶּן־שַׁלֻּם דֹּדְךָ בָּא אֵלֶיךָ לֵאמֹר קְנֵה לְךָ אֶת־שָׂדִי אֲשֶׁר בַּעֲנָתוֹת כִּי לְךָ מִשְׁפַּט הַגְּאֻלָּה לִקְנוֹת:

8 וַיָּבֹא אֵלַי חֲנַמְאֵל בֶּן־דֹּדִי כִּדְבַר יְהֹוָה אֶל־חֲצַר הַמַּטָּרָה וַיֹּאמֶר אֵלַי קְנֵה נָא אֶת־שָׂדִי אֲשֶׁר־בַּעֲנָתוֹת אֲשֶׁר בְּאֶרֶץ בִּנְיָמִין כִּי־לְךָ מִשְׁפַּט הַיְרֻשָּׁה וּלְךָ הַגְּאֻלָּה קְנֵה־לָךְ וָאֵדַע כִּי דְבַר־יְהֹוָה הוּא:

Commentary

32:6. Jeremiah said. Perhaps to King Zedekiah, but more likely the two words introduce a prophecy that had been spoken earlier.[1] What follows is the record of an important incident in Jeremiah's life.

7. The redemption-right to buy it. Based on the prescriptions in the sidra at Leviticus 25:25-28 (for the text, see under *Gleanings*). According to the Torah, land was supposed to remain with the family that had possessed it at the time of the first land allotment after the conquest. Therefore, when someone wanted to sell property it had to be offered first to the next of kin. Here, Jeremiah seems to be next in line to his cousin who wishes to sell. (A similar scenario is recounted in Ruth 4:1-10, where Boaz exercises his right of redemption.) The symbolic thrust of the procedure is explained in verse 15:

> *For thus says the God of heaven's hosts, the God of Israel:*
> *Houses, fields and vineyards shall again be bought in this land.*

To be sure, the country would be destroyed, as Jeremiah had preached, but someday its children would return to it and rebuild it. His own purchase was therefore an investment in the future he knew would be theirs. The word for the "redemption" of the field, גאלה (ge'ullah), is regularly employed to describe the divine redemption of the people.

Anatot. A place not far from Jerusalem, where Jeremiah was born.

8. Court of the guard. The prison compound of the palace guard.

...and [the duty of] redemption. Though there was no *legal* duty to buy the land, a *familial* duty existed if such redemption was the only way to keep the land in the family.

Then I knew that this was truly the word of the Eternal.

9. So I bought the land in Anatot from my cousin Chanam'el; I weighed the money out for him, seventeen shekels of silver.

10. I wrote a deed, sealed it, and had it witnessed; and I weighed out the silver on scales.

11. Then I took the deed of purchase—the sealed copy containing the terms and conditions, and the open one—

12. and gave the deed to Baruch son of Neriah and grandson of Machseiah in the presence of my cousin Chanam'el, of the witnesses who had signed the deed of

9 וָאֶקְנֶה אֶת־הַשָּׂדֶה מֵאֵת חֲנַמְאֵל בֶּן־דֹּדִי

אֲשֶׁר בַּעֲנָתוֹת וָאֶשְׁקֲלָה־לּוֹ אֶת־הַכֶּסֶף שִׁבְעָה

שְׁקָלִים וַעֲשָׂרָה הַכָּסֶף:

10 וָאֶכְתֹּב בַּסֵּפֶר וָאֶחְתֹּם וָאָעֵד עֵדִים וָאֶשְׁקֹל

הַכֶּסֶף בְּמֹאזְנָיִם:

11 וָאֶקַּח אֶת־סֵפֶר הַמִּקְנָה אֶת־הֶחָתוּם

הַמִּצְוָה וְהַחֻקִּים וְאֶת־הַגָּלוּי:

12 וָאֶתֵּן אֶת־הַסֵּפֶר הַמִּקְנָה אֶל־בָּרוּךְ בֶּן־

נֵרִיָּה בֶּן־מַחְסֵיָה לְעֵינֵי חֲנַמְאֵל דֹּדִי וּלְעֵינֵי

Commentary

Then I knew. That God was the originator of the redemption and its symbolic thrust. We know from other references in Jeremiah that the Prophet was very much concerned with the question of distinguishing true prophecy from self-delusion and dreaming[2]—even when it came to his own prophecies!

9. *Seventeen shekels.* We do not know whether this was the usual price for such property, or whether the amount was low because of the precarious military situation (see under *Gleanings*).

... *of silver.* כסף (*kesef*) came to stand also for "money" in general, because most currencies of the ancient Near East were evaluated in terms of silver.

11-14. The most detailed biblical description of the legal specifics of a land sale. For the protection of both parties two copies of the contract were made (something done to this day). However, instead of delivering one set to each, the symbolic nature of the procedure required a somewhat different approach. One copy (the sealed one) was put into an earthen jar, the ideal container for such long-term usage. The open copy was for ready reference, and if there was any suspicion that the terms had been tampered with, the sealed contract could be broken to establish the correct wording.[3] (See under *Gleanings* for documents written on clay and for those written on papyri).

12. *My cousin Chanam'el.* The text says "my uncle," which—in view of verse 7—is probably due to a scribal error.[4]

purchase, and in the presence of all the Judeans who were present in the court of the guard.

13. In the presence of them all I gave Baruch this instruction:

14. Thus says the God of heaven's hosts, the God of Israel: Take these deeds, both the sealed deed of purchase and the open copy, and put them in a clay jar, so that they will last a long time.

15. For thus says the God of heaven's hosts, the God of Israel: Houses, fields, and vineyards shall again be bought in this land.

16. Then I prayed to the Eternal after giving the deed of purchase to Baruch son of Neriah:

17. O! Eternal God, by Your tremendous power and outstretched arm, You made heaven and earth; nothing is too difficult for You.

18. You act with love to thousands [of generations], but make their children after them pay for the sins of their parents. You are the great and mighty God, whose name is *the God of heaven's hosts*,

הָעֵדִים הַכְּתֻבִים בְּסֵפֶר הַמִּקְנֶה לְעֵינֵי כָּל־ הַיְּהוּדִים הַיֹּשְׁבִים בַּחֲצַר הַמַּטָּרָה:

13 וָאֲצַוֶּה אֶת־בָּרוּךְ לְעֵינֵיהֶם לֵאמֹר:

14 כֹּה־אָמַר יְהֹוָה צְבָאוֹת אֱלֹהֵי יִשְׂרָאֵל לָקוֹחַ אֶת־הַסְּפָרִים הָאֵלֶּה אֵת סֵפֶר הַמִּקְנָה הַזֶּה וְאֵת הֶחָתוּם וְאֵת סֵפֶר הַגָּלוּי הַזֶּה וּנְתַתָּם בִּכְלִי־חָרֶשׂ לְמַעַן יַעַמְדוּ יָמִים רַבִּים:

15 כִּי כֹה אָמַר יְהֹוָה צְבָאוֹת אֱלֹהֵי יִשְׂרָאֵל עוֹד יִקָּנוּ בָתִּים וְשָׂדוֹת וּכְרָמִים בָּאָרֶץ הַזֹּאת:

16 וָאֶתְפַּלֵּל אֶל־יְהֹוָה אַחֲרֵי תִתִּי אֶת־סֵפֶר הַמִּקְנָה אֶל־בָּרוּךְ בֶּן־נֵרִיָּה לֵאמֹר:

17 אֲהָהּ אֲדֹנָי יֱהוִֹה הִנֵּה אַתָּה עָשִׂיתָ אֶת־ הַשָּׁמַיִם וְאֶת־הָאָרֶץ בְּכֹחֲךָ הַגָּדוֹל וּבִזְרֹעֲךָ הַנְּטוּיָה לֹא־יִפָּלֵא מִמְּךָ כָּל־דָּבָר:

18 עֹשֶׂה חֶסֶד לַאֲלָפִים וּמְשַׁלֵּם עֲוֺן אָבוֹת אֶל־חֵיק בְּנֵיהֶם אַחֲרֵיהֶם הָאֵל הַגָּדוֹל הַגִּבּוֹר יְהֹוָה צְבָאוֹת שְׁמוֹ:

Commentary

17. *O!* אהה (*aha*). The Hebrew conveys a plea, while the English word "aha" is of Middle English provenance and conveys sudden discovery and understanding.

Difficult. Literally, wondrous or marvelous.

18. *You act with love.* Jeremiah here quotes Exodus 34:7, the words that Moses heard in his special encounter with God.

The great and mighty God. The words appear in the first benediction of the *Amidah*, the central prayer of the Jewish service.

19. great in counsel and mighty in action; whose eyes are open to see all the ways of mortals, giving to all according to their ways and according to the fruit of their deeds.

20. To this day You have worked signs and wonders in the land of Egypt, in Israel, and among all the world's people; You have made Your name renowned to this very day.

21. You brought Israel, Your people, out of the land of Egypt with signs and wonders, with a strong hand and an outstretched arm, and with great terror.

22. You gave them this land, the one You promised to give to their ancestors, a land flowing with milk and honey.

23. But when they came and took possession of it, they did not listen to You or follow Your Teaching, they did not do as You had commanded them: so You brought on them all this trouble.

24. Behold the siege-mounds have arrived at the city to capture it; and the city, because of the sword, starvation and disease, is at the mercy of the Chaldeans who are attacking it. What You announced has happened, and now You look at it.

19 גְּדֹל֙ הָֽעֵצָ֔ה וְרַ֖ב הָעֲלִֽילִיָּ֑ה אֲשֶׁר־עֵינֶ֣יךָ פְקֻח֗וֹת עַל־כׇּל־דַּרְכֵי֙ בְּנֵ֣י אָדָ֔ם לָתֵ֤ת לְאִישׁ֙ כִּדְרָכָ֔יו וְכִפְרִ֖י מַעֲלָלָֽיו׃

20 אֲשֶׁר־שַׂ֠מְתָּ אֹת֨וֹת וּמֹפְתִ֤ים בְּאֶֽרֶץ־מִצְרַ֙יִם֙ עַד־הַיּ֣וֹם הַזֶּ֔ה וּבְיִשְׂרָאֵ֖ל וּבָֽאָדָ֑ם וַתַּעֲשֶׂה־לְּךָ֥ שֵׁ֖ם כַּיּ֥וֹם הַזֶּֽה׃

21 וַתֹּצֵ֤א אֶֽת־עַמְּךָ֙ אֶת־יִשְׂרָאֵ֔ל מֵאֶ֖רֶץ מִצְרָ֑יִם בְּאֹת֣וֹת וּבְמ֣וֹפְתִ֗ים וּבְיָ֤ד חֲזָקָה֙ וּבְאֶזְר֣וֹעַ נְטוּיָ֔ה וּבְמוֹרָ֖א גָּדֽוֹל׃

22 וַתִּתֵּ֤ן לָהֶם֙ אֶת־הָאָ֣רֶץ הַזֹּ֔את אֲשֶׁר־נִשְׁבַּ֥עְתָּ לַאֲבוֹתָ֖ם לָתֵ֣ת לָהֶ֑ם אֶ֛רֶץ זָבַ֥ת חָלָ֖ב וּדְבָֽשׁ׃

23 וַיָּבֹ֜אוּ וַיִּרְשׁ֣וּ אֹתָ֗הּ וְלֹֽא־שָׁמְע֤וּ בְקוֹלֶ֙ךָ֙ וּבְתֹרוֹתְךָ֣ [וּבְתוֹרָתְךָ֣] לֹא־הָלָ֔כוּ אֵת֩ כׇּל־אֲשֶׁ֨ר צִוִּ֧יתָה לָהֶ֛ם לַעֲשׂ֖וֹת לֹ֣א עָשׂ֑וּ וַתַּקְרֵ֣א אֹתָ֔ם אֵ֥ת כׇּל־הָרָעָ֖ה הַזֹּֽאת׃

24 הִנֵּ֣ה הַסֹּלְל֗וֹת בָּ֣אוּ הָעִיר֮ לְלׇכְדָהּ֒ וְהָעִ֣יר נִתְּנָ֗ה בְּיַ֤ד הַכַּשְׂדִּים֙ הַנִּלְחָמִ֣ים עָלֶ֔יהָ מִפְּנֵ֛י הַחֶ֥רֶב וְהָרָעָ֖ב וְהַדָּ֑בֶר וַאֲשֶׁ֥ר דִּבַּ֛רְתָּ הָיָ֖ה וְהִנְּךָ֥ רֹאֶֽה׃

Commentary

20. *Renowned*. Literally, You have made Yourself a name.

21. Jeremiah here quotes Deuteronomy 26:8.

24. *Now You look at it*. While the inevitable consequences of our sins take their course.

25. Yet you, O Eternal God, have said to me, *Buy the land for money in the presence of witnesses*—when the city is about to fall to the Chaldeans!

26. Then the word of the Eternal came to Jeremiah:

27. I am the Eternal, the God of all flesh—is anything too difficult for Me?

25 וְאַתָּה אָמַרְתָּ אֵלַי אֲדֹנָי יְהוִֹה קְנֵה־לְךָ הַשָּׂדֶה בַּכֶּסֶף וְהָעֵד עֵדִים וְהָעִיר נִתְּנָה בְּיַד הַכַּשְׂדִּים:

26 וַיְהִי דְּבַר־יְהוָֹה אֶל־יִרְמְיָהוּ לֵאמֹר:

27 הִנֵּה אֲנִי יְהוָֹה אֱלֹהֵי כָּל־בָּשָׂר הֲמִמֶּנִּי יִפָּלֵא כָּל־דָּבָר:

Essay

Baruch the scribe (verse 12)

The name Baruch, so common today as a first or family name, appears for the first time in our haftarah, and thereafter more than twenty times in the book of Jeremiah. In the Tanach we hear of two other men by that name, both living much later, at the time of Nehemiah, after the exiles had returned from Babylonian captivity.[5] Baruch the scribe is one of the few biblical figures who can be documented from records of his own time. A stamp-seal impression, currently in the Israel Museum in Jerusalem, bears the inscription:

לברכיהו בן נריהו הספר ,

"Property of Berachyahu ben Neriyahu, the scribe."[6]

Baruch (an abbreviation of the full name, possibly a nickname), son of Neriah and grandson of Machseiah, was the Prophet's friend and scribe. Since no other prophet employed such help, may we therefore conclude that Jeremiah himself could not read or write? Hardly, for verse 10 says quite unequivocally that the Prophet himself wrote the deed. Why then did he employ a scribe?

Because, so it would appear, he could afford this special luxury. He could afford to spend 17 shekels on a symbolic action, and this, coupled with his free access to the court, may indicate that he was a man of means.

To be sure, Baruch and his master lived in an age when the ability to read and write was rare, but many prophets—much like medieval Christian and Muslim clergy—were most likely literate, and their lack of scribal assistance may have been a matter of personal choice and/or financial restraint. Kings had official scribes who kept records; and King Ahasuerus had the state's annals read to him (acquainting him with the story of an attempt on his life).[7]

In any case, we owe Baruch much; his name (which means "blessed") was surely a fitting cognomen, especially since it was probably he who composed the biographical notations about the Prophet, which appear in the book.

He shared his master's fate in every respect. They were hunted as fugitives from the king's wrath, and when Jerusalem was destroyed both he and Jeremiah were permitted by the conquerors to stay behind and were not exiled to Babylon. But after the assassination of Gedaliah both he and Jeremiah were forced by their fleeing countrymen to accompany them to Egypt, where the two of them are likely to have died.[8]

Baruch's loyalty and steadfastness earned him the love of his people. Legends were spun about him, and several apocalyptic books—containing visions and miracles—were either attributed to him or told of his wondrous experiences. First Baruch became part of

Christian Bibles, and Second Baruch reports that God took him alive into the heavenly realm, much like Elijah.[9] In a way the popular affection accorded him rather than his master resembles that lavished upon the memory of Moses' brother, Aaron. Moses and Jeremiah were far more influential than Aaron and Baruch, yet they remained somewhat remote. They were towering figures, enormously esteemed and admired, but the people's love was bestowed on Aaron and Baruch.

Gleanings

Words to Remember

I am the Eternal, the God of all flesh—
is anything too difficult for Me? (verse 27)

The law of redemption (Leviticus 25:25)

If your brother is in difficulty and has to sell part of his holdings, the nearest redeemer [that is, the nearest relative able to keep the land in the family] shall come and redeem what his brother is selling.

Legal customs

Weighing out money: Coined money did not come into use until the post-exilic period; gold and silver were valued by weight. Since we know nothing of the size or quality of the field Jeremiah bought, or of then current land values or the purchasing power of money, we cannot say whether seventeen shekels was much or little. Presumably, however, the symbolic nature of the act would require that a fair, normal price was paid.

Sealed and open contracts: Examples of such documents are known from Elephantine in Egypt. The text of these documents was written in duplicate on the two halves of a single sheet of papyrus. One half of the sheet was then rolled up, tied with strips running through holes in the middle of the sheet, and sealed; the other half was then loosely rolled, but not sealed. Thus the sealed copy protected the document from fraudulent alteration, while the open copy was available for ready reference …. Legal documents in Judah were written with ink on papyrus, or even parchment.

John Bright[10]

***

316

Notes

[1] So Rashi and Metzudat David. The former emphasizes that when it says here, "Jeremiah said ..." it was *not* to Zedekiah.

[2] See 23:25-32; 27:14-18.

[3] The remarkable durability of manuscripts sealed in clay jars was proven by the finds at Qumran, among which were fragments of the oldest copies of Jeremiah's prophecies. Unfortunately, Jeremiah's contracts have not yet been found.

[4] The Septuagint and some old Hebrew manuscripts support this reading, as does Radak, but others, among them Rashi, suggest that this Chanam'el was a different man by the same name. JPS renders, "my kinsman."

[5] Nehemiah 3:20; 10:7; 11:5.

[6] For a photograph of the impression and of one belonging to his brother, see S. Ahituv, *Handbook of Ancient Hebrew Inscriptions*, p. 129.

[7] Esther 6:1; and see S. D. Sperling, *Encyclopedia of Religion*, vol. 8, pp. 1-6. Paul, chief disciple of Jesus, also dictated to a scribe, though he was no illiterate. According to Acts 28:30, he lived in Rome for two years "at his own expense," so it may supposed that he had money.

[8] The apocryphal book of Baruch, however, says that he was transported to Babylon.

[9] For a brief survey of traditional sources and the apocalyptic books dealing with Baruch, see *Encyclopaedia Judaica*, vol. 4, pp. 270-273.

[10] *Anchor Bible Commentary to Jeremiah*, pp. 237-238. See also Yigal Yadin, *Israel Exploration Journal*, vol. 12 (1962), pp. 236-238, and plate 48B. The Dead Sea Scrolls found in earthen jars in Qumran were written on leather. The Talmud describes the treatment of contract copies in great detail; see *B. Baba Bathra* 160 a-b.

בְּחֻקֹּתַי

Jeremiah, chapter 16, verse 19 to chapter 17, verse 14

Introduction

Connection of haftarah and sidra:

The sidra presents Israel with a choice between blessings and curses. The haftarah brings us Jeremiah's assurance that, after God's people make their choice for God, they can be certain of divine favor: "Blessed are those whose trust in the Eternal." (17:7)

The setting:

Jeremiah lived at a time of turbulence and danger. We cannot tell at what stage of his life he delivered the observations and warnings contained in our haftarah. Most likely they stem from various periods of his career.

For more on Jeremiah and his time, see our *General Introduction.*

The message:

We can distinguish eight individual sets of sayings, which may have been culled from Jeremiah's notes by his scribe and friend, Baruch. Some of them have become famous sayings, and one has been incorporated into the daily prayer service.

1. The peoples of the earth will come to acknowledge the Eternal. (16:19)
2. Pagan deities are not divine. (16:20-21)
3. Israel's sins will cause it to lose its inheritance. (17:1-4)
4. The cursed contrasted with the blessed. (17:5-7)
5. The human heart is deceitful, but God knows its ways. (17:9-10)
6. On wealth unjustly acquired. (17:11)
7. The consequence of forsaking the Fountain of Living Waters. (17:12-13)
8. A short prayer for healing. (17:14)

HAFTARAH FOR B'CHUKOTAI

Jeremiah, chapter 16, verse 19 to chapter 17, verse 14

16:19. Eternal One, my strength and my
stronghold,

my refuge in time of trouble—
nations from the ends of earth
shall come to You and say:
Our ancestors inherited false gods,
empty and utterly useless.

20. How can human beings make gods?
They are not gods at all!

21. Therefore, I am letting them know:
once and for all I will make them know
My might and power—
and they shall know that I am called *the*
Eternal.

17:1. Judah's sin is inscribed with an iron
pen,

engraved with a diamond point
on the tablet of their hearts
and the horns of their altars,

2. to remind their children
of their altars and sacred poles
near leafy trees, on the high hills.

16:19 יְהֹוָה עֻזִּי וּמָעֻזִּי
וּמְנוּסִי בְּיוֹם צָרָה
אֵלֶיךָ גּוֹיִם יָבֹאוּ מֵאַפְסֵי־אָרֶץ וְיֹאמְרוּ
אַךְ־שֶׁקֶר נָחֲלוּ אֲבוֹתֵינוּ הֶבֶל
וְאֵין־בָּם מוֹעִיל:
20 הֲיַעֲשֶׂה־לּוֹ אָדָם אֱלֹהִים
וְהֵמָּה לֹא אֱלֹהִים:
21 לָכֵן הִנְנִי מוֹדִיעָם
בַּפַּעַם הַזֹּאת אוֹדִיעֵם
אֶת־יָדִי וְאֶת־גְּבוּרָתִי
וְיָדְעוּ כִּי־שְׁמִי יְהֹוָה:
17:1 חַטַּאת יְהוּדָה כְּתוּבָה בְּעֵט בַּרְזֶל
בְּצִפֹּרֶן שָׁמִיר חֲרוּשָׁה
עַל־לוּחַ לִבָּם
וּלְקַרְנוֹת מִזְבְּחוֹתֵיכֶם:
2 כִּזְכֹּר בְּנֵיהֶם
מִזְבְּחוֹתָם וַאֲשֵׁרֵיהֶם
עַל־עֵץ רַעֲנָן עַל גְּבָעוֹת הַגְּבֹהוֹת:

Commentary

17:1. *Diamond.* The translation is not secure; the Hebrew *shamir* may have denoted
some other hard substance (like an adamant or lodestone). Shamir was also the name of two
places mentioned in the Tanach, in the territories of Judah (and Ephraim).[1] In folk tradition,
Shamir was a creature that could cut the hardest substances and served King Solomon in the
building of the Temple.[2]

Their altars. The masoretic text reads "*your* altars"; our translation follows the reading
of some old manuscripts.

2. *Sacred poles.* Dances and other pagan rites were held around these *asherim.*

3. I will give your wealth, all your
treasures,

as spoil to a country bumpkin, the
Hararite,

because of the sin of your high places
throughout your borders.

4. You yourself will lose the heritage I
gave you,

and I will make you serve your enemies

in a land you do not know:

for you have kindled the flame of My
wrath,

to burn a long time.

5. Thus says the Eternal One:

Cursed are those who trust in mortals,

making mortal flesh their strength,

turning their hearts from the Eternal!

6. They shall be like a [stunted] tree in the
desert,

never seeing when good comes,

dwelling in dry places in the wilderness,

in a salt land where no one dwells.

הֲרָרַי֙ בַּשָּׂדֶ֔ה 3

חֵילְךָ֧ כָל־אוֹצְרוֹתֶ֛יךָ לָבַ֥ז אֶתֵּ֖ן

בָּמֹתֶ֖יךָ בְּחַטָּ֑את

בְּכָל־גְּבוּלֶֽיךָ׃

וְשָׁמַטְתָּ֗ה וּבְךָ֙ מִנַּחֲלָֽתְךָ֙ אֲשֶׁ֣ר נָתַ֣תִּי לָ֔ךְ 4

וְהַעֲבַדְתִּ֙יךָ֙ אֶת־אֹ֣יְבֶ֔יךָ

בָּאָ֖רֶץ אֲשֶׁ֣ר לֹֽא־יָדָ֑עְתָּ

כִּֽי־אֵ֛שׁ קְדַחְתֶּ֥ם בְּאַפִּ֖י

עַד־עוֹלָ֥ם תּוּקָֽד׃

כֹּ֣ה ׀ אָמַ֣ר יְהֹוָ֗ה 5

אָר֤וּר הַגֶּ֙בֶר֙ אֲשֶׁ֣ר יִבְטַ֣ח בָּֽאָדָ֔ם

וְשָׂ֥ם בָּשָׂ֖ר זְרֹע֑וֹ

וּמִן־יְהֹוָ֖ה יָס֥וּר לִבּֽוֹ׃

וְהָיָה֙ כְּעַרְעָ֣ר בָּעֲרָבָ֔ה 6

וְלֹ֥א יִרְאֶ֖ה כִּי־יָב֣וֹא ט֑וֹב

וְשָׁכַ֤ן חֲרֵרִים֙ בַּמִּדְבָּ֔ר

אֶ֥רֶץ מְלֵחָ֖ה וְלֹ֥א תֵשֵֽׁב׃

Commentary

3. *Hararite.* Mentioned as an inconsequential group in other places in the Tanach.[3] The translation is uncertain; others connect *harari* with "mountain."[4] In the annals of Assyrian kings of that time, "mountain dweller" was a pejorative term like "country bumpkin" or "hillbilly."

High places. Where pagan rites were held.

4. *To burn a long time.* Occasionally, as here, עולם (*olam*) denotes a prolonged period of time,[5] though usually it means "forever." The latter understanding would contradict the consistent message of the Prophet, who preached that God's mercy would in time return to a repentant people.

5. *Those.* The Hebrew is in the singular, but means everyone.

6. *[Stunted] tree.* ערער (*ar'ar*) referred to the tamarisk, which played a role in Ugaritic symbolism as a "tree of death."[6]

7. Blessed are those who trust in the
    Eternal,

whose trust is in the Eternal!

8. They shall be like a tree planted near
    water,

sinking its roots by a stream,

never noticing when the heat comes,

its leaves green,

careless of times of drought,

never failing to bear fruit.

9. The human heart

is of all things the most deceitful,

so perverse—

who can understand it?

10. I, the Eternal, search the heart and
     test the spirit,

giving to all according to their ways,

according to the fruit of their doings.

11. Those who gain wealth by unjust
     means

are like a partridge hatching eggs it never
    laid:

in the middle of life it will forsake them,

at the end they are [known to be] fools.

7 בָּרוּךְ הַגֶּבֶר אֲשֶׁר יִבְטַח בַּיהוָה
וְהָיָה יְהוָה מִבְטַחוֹ:

8 וְהָיָה כְּעֵץ שָׁתוּל עַל־מַיִם
וְעַל־יוּבַל יְשַׁלַּח שָׁרָשָׁיו
וְלֹא יִרְא [יִרְאֶה] כִּי־יָבֹא חֹם
וְהָיָה עָלֵהוּ רַעֲנָן
וּבִשְׁנַת בַּצֹּרֶת לֹא יִדְאָג
וְלֹא יָמִישׁ מֵעֲשׂוֹת פֶּרִי:

9 עָקֹב הַלֵּב מִכֹּל
וְאָנֻשׁ הוּא
מִי יֵדָעֶנּוּ:

10 אֲנִי יְהוָה חֹקֵר לֵב בֹּחֵן כְּלָיוֹת
וְלָתֵת לְאִישׁ כִּדְרָכוֹ [כִּדְרָכָיו]
כִּפְרִי מַעֲלָלָיו:

11 קֹרֵא דָגַר וְלֹא יָלָד
עֹשֶׂה עֹשֶׁר וְלֹא בְמִשְׁפָּט
בַּחֲצִי יָמוֹ [יָמָיו] יַעַזְבֶנּוּ
וּבְאַחֲרִיתוֹ יִהְיֶה נָבָל:

Commentary

7. Blessed are those …. Literally, "Blessed is the man." The saying resembles the first words of Psalm 1 (see under *Gleanings*). Scholars debate who influenced whom.[7]

9-10. Heart … spirit. The Tanach considers the heart as the seat of intelligence, and the kidneys as the seat of the spirit and the emotions. Though the Hebrew is in the singular, we translate verses 10-11 into the plural.

According to the fruit of their doings. Although we cannot always observe this result.

11. The translation is speculative. Others suggest, "the partridge broods but doesn't hatch." Equally uncertain is the underlying thought: does ill-gotten wealth result in eventual poverty, or is early death the penalty?[8]

12. A Throne of Glory, exalted from the
  beginning,
is our holy Shrine!

13. O Hope of Israel, Eternal One:
those who forsake You shall be put to
  shame,
those who turn from You
are written in the dust,
for they have forsaken the Fountain of
  Living Waters,
the Eternal.

14. Heal me, Eternal One;
(only) then shall I be healed.
Save me;
(only) then shall I be saved:
for You are my praise.

12 כִּסֵּא כָבוֹד מָרוֹם מֵרִאשׁוֹן
מְקוֹם מִקְדָּשֵׁנוּ:

13 מִקְוֵה יִשְׂרָאֵל יְהֹוָה
כָּל־עֹזְבֶיךָ יֵבֹשׁוּ
יְסוּרַי [וְסוּרַי] בָּאָרֶץ יִכָּתֵבוּ
כִּי עָזְבוּ מְקוֹר מַיִם־חַיִּים
אֶת־יְהֹוָה:

14 רְפָאֵנִי יְהֹוָה
וְאֵרָפֵא
הוֹשִׁיעֵנִי
וְאִוָּשֵׁעָה
כִּי תְהִלָּתִי אָתָּה:

Commentary

12. *Throne of Glory.* The Temple was believed to have been directly aligned with God's own Throne of Glory.[9]

13. *Hope of Israel.* Mikveh Israel was the name given to one of the oldest Jewish congregations in North America (Philadelphia, 18th century), and to a modern Israeli agricultural school.

Written in the dust. The meaning of the passage is not certain; our translation follows Bright.[10]

Fountain of Living Waters. That is, God.[11]

14. *Heal me ....* The prayer has become part of the 18 benedictions of the Jewish service, where it is cast in plural form.

Essay

And they shall know that I am called the Eternal (16:21)

It is often said by those who are unfamiliar with Jewish literature that Judaism is not a universalistic religion in that it concentrates on the Jewish people alone. True, Jews have considered themselves to be the bearers of a special mission: to witness to God in the world. But precisely because of this, the ultimate goal has always been to let all nations know of the One Universal God. On occasion (as in Roman times) we went out to convert others to our religion; but during the last two thousand years we have generally not imitated Christian and Muslim missionary activity. Rather, we have stressed that "the righteous of all nations have a share in the world to come"[12]—which is to say that one need not be a Jew in order to partake of divine grace and salvation.

Jeremiah too believed that the victory of God was inevitable, but his immediate focus was on his own people, who had both the obligation and opportunity to be servants of the Almighty. While Jeremiah knew that they would fall short of their task and, in consequence, suffer grievously, they would learn their lesson in due time and by their example inspire others to search out the Eternal.

Did Jeremiah hope to witness such a day in his own lifetime? Probably not, and in that sense the opening verse of the haftarah may be called messianic—that is, a vision of a post-historic age. It is this kind of dream that has preserved the universalistic strand of Jewish thinking as an important part of its worldview.

In Jeremiah's time, the hope that someday the nations of the world would abjure their false beliefs in idols and acknowledge the Eternal as their God had become a firm part of Jewish thinking. Isaiah and Micah had already sung:

> *Many nations shall go and say:*
> *Come, let us go up to the Mount of the Eternal,*
> *to the House of the God of Jacob.*[13]

This had been also the teaching of the unknown prophet (whose writings were attached to those of Zechariah) that the day would come when God would rule over the whole earth: "On that day, God and God's Name will be one"—meaning that it alone will be called upon by all humanity.[14]

This latter phrase has been incorporated into every daily, Shabbat, and holy day worship, where it forms the end of the *Aleinu* prayer, and on the High Holy Days the idea is expressed in a stirring poem by an unknown medieval writer. Known in Hebrew as *V'ye'etayu*, it was popularized by Israel Zangwill's translation, "All the world shall come to serve Thee" (see under *Gleanings*).

Gleanings

Words to Remember

Eternal One, my strength and my stronghold,
my refuge in time of trouble. (16:19)

Cursed are those who trust in mortals ....
Blessed are those who trust in the Eternal. (17:5, 7)

The human heart is of all things the most deceitful,
so perverse—who can understand it?
I, the Eternal, search the heart
and test the spirit. (17:9-10)

The Fountain of Living Waters, the Eternal. (17:13)

Heal me, Eternal One;
(only) then shall I be healed.
Save me;
(only) then shall I be saved:
for You are my praise. (17:14)

A play on words

   (*Mikveh* means both hope and the ritual bath.) Rabbi Akiba said: It says, *mikveh yisrael* (Jeremiah 17:13), which means that just as the ritual bath cleans the unclean, so does the Holy One cleanse Israel.

Mishnah [15]

The day will come

   The day will come when the nations of the world will convert themselves to Judaism.

Talmud [16]

A broad definition

   Whoever repudiates idolatry is called a Jew.

Talmud [17]

The messianic vision

   It is a distinctive feature of Biblical teaching, and flows from the exalted concept of the Brotherhood of Man, which will be realized as the sequel of all nations acknowledging the One God. It is worthy of note that the prophet conceived of this conversion as a spontaneous act brought about neither by compulsion nor even persuasion.

Harry Freedman [18]

324

A medieval poem

> All the world shall come to serve Thee
> And bless Thy glorious Name,
> And Thy righteousness triumphant
> The islands shall acclaim.
> And the people shall go seeking
> Who knew Thee not before,
> And the ends of earth shall praise Thee,
> And tell Thy greatness o'er.

> *V'ye'etayu*, translated by Israel Zangwill[19]

A tree planted near water (17:8)

[Those whose delight is the Eternal's Teaching]
are like a tree planted by streams of water
that yields its fruit in due season
and whose leaves do not wither;
they prosper in all that they do.

> Psalm 1:3

***

325

Notes

[1] Joshua 15:48; Judges 10:1-2.

[2] See *B. Sota* 48b. In our time, Shamir is the name of a kibbutz in northern Israel, of a novelist (Moshe Shamir), and an Israeli prime minister (Yitzhak Shamir).

[3] II Samuel 23:11 and 33; I Chronicles 11:34 ff.

[4] Rashi reads it as referring to the elevated location of Jerusalem.

[5] See, for example, Rashi's comment on Isaiah 9:5, where the words מעתה ועד עולם (*mé-atah v'ad olam*) are applied to a limited span in Israel's history.

[6] See S. Loewenstamm, *Comparative Studies in Biblical and Ancient Oriental Literatures*, p. 224. *Arar* has the meaning of tamarisk in current Arabic.

[7] Compare W. Holladay, *Jeremiah 1*, p. 490; see also J. Pritchard, *Ancient Near Eastern Texts*, p. 422.

[8] See also Psalm 55:24 and W. McKane, pp. 398-402.

[9] So Radak; Jeremiah 14:21 extends the expression "Throne of Glory" to the city of Jerusalem.

[10] In his *Anchor Bible Commentary to Jeremiah*, p. 118, note 13.

[11] See also Jeremiah 2:3.

[12] *Tosefta*, Sanhedrin 13:10.

[13] Isaiah 2:3; Micah 4:2.

[14] Zechariah 14:9. About the time of this prophecy, see the haftarah for the First Day of Sukkot and our *General Introduction*.)

[15] Yoma 8:9 (at the very end of the tractate).

[16] *B.* Avodah Zarah 3b.

[17] *B.* Megillah 13a.

[18] In his *Anchor Bible Commentary to Jeremiah*, on 16:19.

[19] See *Gates of Repentance*, pp. 160-161.

Hosea, chapter 2, verses 1 to 22

Introduction

It should be noted that many translations number this chapter differently. The Masorah (the traditional Hebrew text on which our translation is based) has nine verses in chapter 1, and then begins chapter 2. Other editions of Hosea join the first three verses of chapter 2 to the nine verses of chapter 1, making the numbering of chapter 2 different.

Connection of haftarah and sidra:

The weekly sidra tells of Israel's numbers in the wilderness, and the haftarah begins with the promise that the people of Israel will be "like the sands of the sea, not to be measured or counted."

The setting:

Hosea lived in the 8th century B.C.E., and was a younger contemporary of Amos. He resided and preached in the Northern Kingdom, whose irreligious practices had become an abhorrence to God. Baal worship was common, and the God of the Covenant was increasingly forgotten.

For more on Hosea and his time, see our *General Introduction.*

The message:

The meaning of the haftarah can be understood only in conjunction with the first chapter of Hosea. At the behest of God, the Prophet had married Gomer, a prostitute, and had children with her. Her unfaithfulness becomes a metaphor for Israel's love affairs with other gods. But the Eternal will be like a forgiving husband, taking Israel (the faithless wife) back if she forswears her wanton ways.

1. A promise that foretells the happy conclusion. (1-3)
2. Israel portrayed as a harlot. (4-9)
3. The terrible consequences of faithlessness. (10-15)
4. The restoration. (16-22)

HAFTARAH FOR B'MIDBAR

Hosea, chapter 2, verses 1 to 22

2:1. The number of the people of Israel shall be like the sands of the sea,
not to be measured or counted;
and where they were called, *You are Not My People,*
they shall be called *The Children of the Living God.*

2. The people of Judah and Israel shall be gathered together
and choose for themselves a single head and rise up from the ground,
for the day of Jezreel will be great.

3. Call your brothers *My people,* and your sisters *Loved [by God].*

4. Complain against your mother, complain,
for she is no longer My wife,
and I am not her husband.
Let her remove her whorings from her face,

וְהָיָ֞ה מִסְפַּ֤ר בְּנֵֽי־יִשְׂרָאֵל֙ כְּח֣וֹל הַיָּ֔ם 2:1

אֲשֶׁ֥ר לֹֽא־יִמַּ֖ד וְלֹ֣א יִסָּפֵ֑ר

וְֽהָיָ֞ה בִּמְק֣וֹם אֲשֶׁר־יֵאָמֵ֤ר לָהֶם֙ לֹֽא־עַמִּ֣י אַתֶּ֔ם

יֵאָמֵ֥ר לָהֶ֖ם בְּנֵ֥י אֵל־חָֽי׃

וְֽנִקְבְּצ֞וּ בְּנֵֽי־יְהוּדָ֣ה וּבְנֵֽי־יִשְׂרָאֵל֮ יַחְדָּו֒ 2

וְשָׂמ֤וּ לָהֶם֙ רֹ֣אשׁ אֶחָ֔ד וְעָל֖וּ מִן־הָאָ֑רֶץ

כִּ֥י גָד֖וֹל י֥וֹם יִזְרְעֶֽאל׃

אִמְר֥וּ לַאֲחֵיכֶ֖ם עַמִּ֑י וְלַאֲחֽוֹתֵיכֶ֖ם רֻחָֽמָה׃ 3

רִ֤יבוּ בְאִמְּכֶם֙ רִ֔יבוּ 4

כִּי־הִיא֙ לֹ֣א אִשְׁתִּ֔י

וְאָנֹכִ֖י לֹ֣א אִישָׁ֑הּ

וְתָסֵ֤ר זְנוּנֶ֙יהָ֙ מִפָּנֶ֔יה

Commentary

1. *You are Not My People.* This follows directly after verse 9 of the preceding chapter, where one of the Prophet's children (born to his wife, a prostitute) is called לא עמי (*lo-ammi,* Not-My-People), and the other לא רחמה (*lo-ruchama,* Not-Loved or Unacknowledged, Disowned.)[1] The names are symbols of Israel's errant ways

Children of the Living God. בני אל חי (*b'nei el-chai*). See further in verse 3.

2. *Judah and Israel.* Hosea foresees the day when the division into a northern and a southern kingdom (which happened after the death of Solomon, in the 10th century B.C.E.) will come to an end, and the people of the Covenant will once again be united under one head.

The day of Jezreel will be great. A reference to Hosea's oldest child whose name was chosen by God. The name means "God sows."

3. *Loved.* Or "Acknowledged."[2]

4. *Complain against your mother.* That is, Israel.

Her whorings. Or "makeup." Prostitutes could be recognized by the way they painted their faces.[3]

וְנַאֲפוּפֶיהָ מִבֵּין שָׁדֶיהָ:

5 פֶּן־אַפְשִׁיטֶנָּה עֲרֻמָּה וְהִצַּגְתִּיהָ

כְּיוֹם הִוָּלְדָהּ

וְשַׂמְתִּיהָ כַמִּדְבָּר

וְשַׁתִּהָ כְּאֶרֶץ צִיָּה

וַהֲמִתִּיהָ בַּצָּמָא:

6 וְאֶת־בָּנֶיהָ לֹא אֲרַחֵם

כִּי־בְנֵי זְנוּנִים הֵמָּה:

7 כִּי זָנְתָה אִמָּם

הֹבִישָׁה הוֹרָתָם

כִּי אָמְרָה אֵלְכָה אַחֲרֵי מְאַהֲבַי

נֹתְנֵי לַחְמִי וּמֵימַי

צַמְרִי וּפִשְׁתִּי שַׁמְנִי וְשִׁקּוּיָי:

8 לָכֵן הִנְנִי־שָׂךְ אֶת־דַּרְכֵּךְ בַּסִּירִים

וְגָדַרְתִּי אֶת־גְּדֵרָהּ וּנְתִיבוֹתֶיהָ לֹא תִמְצָא:

her adulteries from between her breasts,

5. or I will strip her naked and expose her
as on the day she was born,
and make her like the wilderness,
turn her into a dry land
and kill her with thirst.

6. And I will show her children no love,
for they are children of whoring.

7. Their mother played the whore;
she who bore them acted shamefully,
saying: I will go after my lovers,
who give me my bread and my water,
my wool and my linen, my oil and my
   drink.

8. So I am blocking her path with thorns,
walling her in: she shall not find her way.

Commentary

Between her breasts. Probably a bunch of myrrh, esteemed as an aphrodisiac.[4]

5. *I will strip her.* The wilderness is a metaphor for Israel being reduced to utter poverty. This is the formal language of divorce. In remote antiquity, a wife could be subjected to a proceeding in which the husband declared, "You are not my wife," that is, she was no longer under his protection. She had, literally, lost bed and board.

6. *No love.* Or "will not acknowledge her." Therefore Israel's offspring—born in harlotry—will be known as *lo-ruchama*, Not-Loved or Unacknowledged, Disowned (see 1:6 and verse 1 of this chapter).

7. *Who give me my bread. . . .* She is of course mistaken: her lovers are not the source of her permanent nourishment. In addition, this may also be an allusion to an old custom that was mentioned already in the law code of the Sumerian king Lipit Ishtar (20th century B.C.E.). It stipulated that a man who was married to a barren woman and then proceeded to have children with a prostitute had to provide her with grain, oil, and clothes.[5]

8. *Blocking her path.* She will have to find other ways of practicing her profession, but will not be successful. She (Israel) will then perforce return to her rightful lover (God).[6]

329

9. However hard she pursues her lovers—
she shall not catch them;
she will look for them, but shall not find them;
then she will say:
Let me go back to my first husband;
I was better off then than now.

10. She did not consider
that I was the one who gave her the grain,
the wine, and the oil;
I gave her abundant silver and gold,
which they used for Baal.

11. Therefore I am taking back My grain in its time,
My wine in its season;
I take away My wool and linen
that she uses to cover her nakedness.

12. I will uncover her shame in the sight of her lovers,
and none will save her from My hand.

13. I will make an end to her rejoicing:
her pilgrim-feasts, her new moons and sabbaths,
all her festivals.

9 וְרִדְּפָה אֶת־מְאַהֲבֶ֫יהָ
וְלֹא־תַשִּׂיג אֹתָם
וּבִקְשָׁתַם וְלֹא תִמְצָא
וְאָמְרָה
אֵלְכָה וְאָשׁ֫וּבָה אֶל־אִישִׁי הָרִאשׁ֫וֹן
כִּי ט֫וֹב לִי אָז מֵעָתָּה׃

10 וְהִיא לֹא יָדְעָה
כִּי אָנֹכִי נָתַתִּי לָהּ הַדָּגָן וְהַתִּירוֹשׁ וְהַיִּצְהָר
וְכֶ֫סֶף הִרְבֵּ֫יתִי לָהּ וְזָהָב
עָשׂוּ לַבָּעַל׃

11 לָכֵן אָשׁוּב וְלָקַחְתִּי דְגָנִי בְּעִתּוֹ
וְתִירוֹשִׁי בְּמוֹעֲדוֹ
וְהִצַּלְתִּי צַמְרִי וּפִשְׁתִּי
לְכַסּוֹת אֶת־עֶרְוָתָהּ׃

12 וְעַתָּה אֲגַלֶּה אֶת־נַבְלֻתָהּ לְעֵינֵי מְאַהֲבֶ֫יהָ
וְאִישׁ לֹא־יַצִּילֶ֫נָּה מִיָּדִי׃

13 וְהִשְׁבַּתִּי כָּל־מְשׂוֹשָׂהּ
חַגָּהּ חָדְשָׁהּ וְשַׁבַּתָּהּ
וְכֹל מוֹעֲדָהּ׃

Commentary

10-15. By depriving her of all the necessities and luxuries of life, the Eternal will demonstrate who the real source of her sustenance is.

10. *Baal.* The god was widely worshipped in the ancient Near East. As a thunder god, called "Rider of the Clouds," he was associated with the fertility of the soil, of beasts and humans.

11. The verse would read better if it followed on verse 12.

In its time ... in its season. When grain and wine are ready to be harvested.

14. And I will destroy her vines and her fig-
trees,

of which she said:

They are my hire,

given me by my lovers;

I will turn them into a forest,

and wild animals shall consume them.

15. So I will punish her for all the [feast]
days

when she offered incense to the [various]
Baals,

and, putting on her rings and her jewels,

she ran after her lovers,

forgetting Me,

says the Eternal One.

16. That is when I will entice her to Me,

lead her to the wilderness,

and speak to her heart.

17. From there I will give her back her
vineyards,

and make the Valley of Trouble

the Door of Hope;

there she shall respond as when she was
young,

when she came up out of Egypt.

14 וַהֲשִׁמֹּתִי֙ גַּפְנָהּ֙ וּתְאֵנָתָ֔הּ

אֲשֶׁ֣ר אָֽמְרָ֗ה

אֶתְנָ֥ה הֵ֨מָּה֙ לִ֔י

אֲשֶׁ֥ר נָֽתְנוּ־לִ֖י מְאַֽהֲבָ֑י

וְשַׂמְתִּ֣ים לְיַ֔עַר

וַאֲכָלָ֖תַם חַיַּ֥ת הַשָּׂדֶֽה׃

15 וּפָקַדְתִּ֣י עָלֶ֗יהָ אֶת־יְמֵ֤י הַבְּעָלִים֙

אֲשֶׁ֣ר תַּקְטִ֣יר לָהֶ֔ם

וַתַּ֤עַד נִזְמָהּ֙ וְחֶלְיָתָ֔הּ

וַתֵּ֖לֶךְ אַחֲרֵ֣י מְאַהֲבֶ֑יהָ

וְאֹתִ֥י שָׁכְחָ֖ה

נְאֻם־יְהֹוָֽה׃

16 לָכֵ֗ן הִנֵּ֤ה אָֽנֹכִי֙ מְפַתֶּ֔יהָ

וְהֹֽלַכְתִּ֖יהָ הַמִּדְבָּ֑ר

וְדִבַּרְתִּ֖י עַל־לִבָּֽהּ׃

17 וְנָתַ֨תִּי לָ֤הּ אֶת־כְּרָמֶ֨יהָ֙ מִשָּׁ֔ם

וְאֶת־עֵ֥מֶק עָכ֖וֹר

לְפֶ֣תַח תִּקְוָ֑ה

וְעָ֤נְתָה שָּׁ֨מָּה֙ כִּימֵ֣י נְעוּרֶ֔יהָ

וּכְי֖וֹם עֲלֹתָ֥הּ מֵאֶֽרֶץ־מִצְרָֽיִם׃

Commentary

16. *Lead her to the wilderness.* And thence back to the ravaged homeland.

17. *Valley of Trouble.* עמק עכור (*emek achor*). The valley was so named because of the troubling incident described in Joshua 7:25-26.[7]

Door of Hope. פתח תקוה (*petach tikvah*). In the 1870s, Jewish pioneers founded the first agricultural settlement in what was then Ottoman Palestine and named it Petach Tikvah after this passage in Hosea. In 1883 the village was moved to its present site and later became a suburb of Tel Aviv.

Respond as when she was young. With song, as Israel did after its rescue at the Reed (Red) Sea.[8]

18. And on that day, says the Eternal One,
you will call Me *My Man*,
and no longer call Me *My Baal*.

19. For I will erase the names of the Baals
from her mouth,

and they shall no longer be mentioned by
name.

20. On that day I will make a covenant for
them

with beasts of the field, birds of the air,

and with creeping things on the ground;

I will remove the bow, the sword,

and war from the land,

and make them lie down in safety.

21. I will betroth you to Me forever;

I will betroth you to Me

in righteousness and justice,

in steadfast love and compassion.

22. I will betroth you to Me
in faithfulness,

and you shall know the Eternal.

18 וְהָיָה בַיּוֹם־הַהוּא נְאֻם־יְהֹוָה

תִּקְרְאִי אִישִׁי

וְלֹא־תִקְרְאִי־לִי עוֹד בַּעְלִי:

19 וַהֲסִרֹתִי אֶת־שְׁמוֹת הַבְּעָלִים מִפִּיהָ

וְלֹא־יִזָּכְרוּ עוֹד בִּשְׁמָם:

20 וְכָרַתִּי לָהֶם בְּרִית בַּיּוֹם הַהוּא

עִם־חַיַּת הַשָּׂדֶה וְעִם־עוֹף הַשָּׁמַיִם

וְרֶמֶשׂ הָאֲדָמָה

וְקֶשֶׁת וְחֶרֶב

וּמִלְחָמָה אֶשְׁבּוֹר מִן־הָאָרֶץ

וְהִשְׁכַּבְתִּים לָבֶטַח:

21 וְאֵרַשְׂתִּיךְ לִי לְעוֹלָם

וְאֵרַשְׂתִּיךְ לִי

בְּצֶדֶק וּבְמִשְׁפָּט

וּבְחֶסֶד וּבְרַחֲמִים:

22 וְאֵרַשְׂתִּיךְ לִי בֶּאֱמוּנָה

וְיָדַעַתְּ אֶת־יְהֹוָה:

Commentary

18. *My Man ... My Baal.* בעלי (*ba'ali*) has the dual meaning of "my husband" and "my Baal." God will be henceforth be referred to only as אישי (*ishi*), which also means "my man" or "my husband," but avoids any confusion with Baal.

In modern Israel these terms have become the backdrop of social controversy (see the essay below).

20. *Lie down in safety.* Evoking the idyll described by Isaiah.[9]

21. *I will betroth you.* The verse recounts the gifts that will be the bride-price affirming the betrothal. God will confer these gifts on Israel, so that faithfulness will become her very constitution.[10]

Verses 21 and 22 are recited when a person puts on tefillin. The thrice repeated "I will betroth you" connotes an extra-strong marital bond, for "the triple cord will not be easily broken."[11]

Essay

Israel compared to a prostitute

The opening chapters of Hosea are both memorable and troubling. Memorable, because they report that the Prophet was asked by God to marry Gomer, a woman of questionable ways, so that the paternity of their children would be in question. Troubling, because Israel is depicted as a woman who whores and forsakes her master/husband.

To begin with, Hosea tells us that it was God who made him marry Gomer. They had three children: the first (Jezreel) was probably fathered by him, the next two (*lo-ruchama* and *Lo-Ammi*) by other men. The prophecy of Israel's return may indicate that Gomer repented of her ways and that Hosea took her back—but we cannot be certain.

This succession of events in his personal life was without doubt devastating for the Prophet and his children. Did God need to ruin the life of a family in order for Hosea to be able to preach about an adulterous Israel? Did this paradigm require Gomer and Hosea to experience the consequences of unfaithfulness in their own lives?

Hardly. It seems much more likely that Hosea, having suffered the breakup of his marriage, began to see it as a metaphor of God's relationship to Israel. He now believed it to have been prearranged by Providence, and so interpreted it in chapter 1. It is also possible that the divine promise of Israel's restoration to God's favor may have encouraged him to take back his own wife. [12]

While we may account for the metaphor by recalling that Hosea was the first prophet to speak of Israel as the God's bride,[13] we cannot overlook that the metaphor itself presents a vexing problem.

For the identification of God as the master and husband and Israel as the adulterous wife reflects a view of male-female relationships that have been all too real in much of human history, but are now being increasingly abandoned in Western societies and questioned in the modern State of Israel.

Aside from all else, husbands commit adultery far more frequently than their wives. Male promiscuity is the engine of female prostitution, while male prostitution is, in comparison, quite rare. Thus, the metaphor of God as the trusting husband and master, and Israel as the whoring wife, represents a reversal of human experience and tends to reinforce a cultural stereotype. The current attempt by many Israelis to replace the expression *ba'ali* ("my master/husband") with *ishi* ("my man") reflects the desire to make marriage a partnership in which no one is master. (See also above at verse 18.)

In theology, too, the Eternal—though sovereign—is seen increasingly in terms of partnership: God needs us to perfect the world, even as we need God to make our lives whole and meaningful.

Thus, Hosea's metaphor, powerful and memorable as it is, reflects the language and perception of his time. We today would express it differently, but the underlying recognition remains: as we turn to God, God turns to us. It is an eternally reciprocal relationship.

Gleanings

Words to Remember

I will betroth you to Me forever;
I will betroth you to Me in righteousness and justice,
in steadfast love and compassion.
I will betroth you to Me in faithfulness,
and you shall know the Eternal. (2:21-22)

An argument with God

When Hosea became unhappy with his wife's unfaithfulness, God asked him: "Why don't you imitate Moses, who had no relations with his wife when he was in constant contact with Me?"[14] Hosea answered that he could not do this because Gomer had given him children. "How much more so," said God, "can I separate Myself from My children." Hosea then asked the Eternal to forgive him his forwardness.

Talmud[15]

Prostitution

Israel's intolerance of prostitution was probably influenced by several factors. First, paternity would be largely unknown with regard to the children of a prostitute .... A society which valued the patrilineal bloodline so highly would logically have a real abhorrence of children with no known paternity and of the mother who bred them. These offspring would have no proper inheritance and no patronym. Also, unknown paternity could lead to unwitting incest.

Second, Israel was to aspire to be a "holy nation," and this included a strict code of sexual morality. A comparison of the sexual ethics in biblical law with those reflected in Mesopotamian law reveals the absolute nature of the former .... Israel's God was highly intolerant of sexual relations outside of narrowly prescribed circumstances. The activities of a prostitute certainly fell outside of these limitations.

Elaine Adler Goodfriend[16]

* * *

Notes

[1] The word רחם (*r-ch-m*) conveys both pity and compassion, and also accepting love, which has a forensic overtone. *Lo-ruchama* can thus mean a child who has been rejected (because it was born in whoredom). According to H. L. Ginsberg (*Encyclopaedia Judaica*, vol. 8, pp. 1010 ff.), Hosea's metaphor equates the mother with the upper classes of Israel, who, by tolerating their leaders' whoring after Baal, suffer the effects of God divorcing the mother and thus making the children "unaccepted." See also the discussion in *B. Pesachim* 87b.

[2] Some translate *ruchama* as "one to whom compassion is extended." God is called אל רחום (*el rachum*), God of compassion or mercy. See also note 1, above.

[3] Compare Jeremiah 4:30; Ezekiel 23:40. NEB renders: ... forswear her wanton looks.

[4] So Andersen and Freedman, in *Anchor Bible*, Hosea, citing Song of Songs 1:13.

[5] Pritchard, *Ancient Near Eastern Texts*, p. 160. The Tanach mentions the three commodities as mainstays of existence; see Numbers 18:12, Deuteronomy 7:13.

[6] The Hebrew has "*your* path."

[7] Isaiah 65:10 says that even the Valley of Achor will be turned into a pleasant pasture when the time for Israel's salvation comes.

[8] Exodus 15:21; so Radak.

[9] 11:6 ff.

[10] So JPS translation, p. 768, footnote l-l.

[11] Ecclesiastes 4:12.

[12] The Talmud (*B. Pesachim* 87a-b) is clearly aware of the problem and makes Hosea rather than God the originator of the Gomer alliance. It has God say to the Prophet: "Your people have strayed." Hosea should have answered: "They are *Your* children, the children of Your beloved, Abraham, Isaac, and Jacob." But he didn't say this; instead he replied: "So exchange this people for another." Whereupon God decided to have Hosea himself experience unfaithfulness by ordering him to marry a prostitute. The exchange reveals also that the Rabbis considered Hosea a true intimate of God. In the passage immediately preceding, Hosea, Isaiah, Amos, and Micah are listed as contemporaries, and Hosea is called the greatest among them.

[13] It has been suggested that Hosea, consciously or unconsciously, co-opted aspects of the sexual symbolism of the Near East's fertility cults.

[14] This was the midrashic explanation of the quarrel that Aaron and Miriam had with Moses (Numbers 12); see Sifre Numbers 99 and the Torah Commentary, p. 1101.

[15] *B. Pesachim* 87a-b.

[16] *Anchor Bible Dictionary*, vol. 5, p. 508.

נשא

Judges, chapter 13, verses 2 to 25

Introduction

Connection of sidra and haftarah:

Both sidra and haftarah deal with Nazirites, that is, persons under special vows. They are obligated not to trim their hair, not to touch alcoholic beverages, and not to defile themselves with ritually unclean matters. For some, the vow is temporary, for others—as with Samson—it was valid for life. (For details, see Numbers chapter 6.)

The setting:

The turbulent history of Israel between the death of Joshua and the time of the prophet Samuel is covered by the book of Judges. It describes the long years during which the tribes struggled with Canaanites and Philistines and then sank roots into the land assigned to them. They considered themselves partners in a loose confederation, bound together by historical memory and a common religious cult. Especially in times of crisis—a frequent occurrence—whether external or internal, they elected a military-judicial head, called "judge," to ward off the enemy and to foster their common interests. Samson was one of these men, whose exploits against the Philistines (Israel's constant enemies and often their oppressors) spawned tales of miraculous birth and supra-human strength.

For more on the book of Judges, see our *General Introduction.*

Content of the haftarah:

1. An angel visits Manoah's wife and announces the birth of a son who will begin to liberate Israel from its Philistine yoke. (2-7)
2. Manoah prays for and obtains a second angelic visit. (8-22)
3. A son is born and is called Samson, and God's spirit rests on him. (22-25)

13:2. There was a man named Manoah from Zorah. He was of a Danite clan, and his wife was barren, never having given birth.

3. [One day] an angel of the Eternal appeared to the woman and said to her: Yes, you are barren and unable [till now] to have children, but you shall be pregnant and give birth to a son.

4. Take care not to drink wine or beer, or eat anything unclean,

13:2 וַיְהִי֩ אִ֨ישׁ אֶחָ֧ד מִצָּרְעָ֛ה מִמִּשְׁפַּ֥חַת הַדָּנִ֖י וּשְׁמ֣וֹ מָנ֑וֹחַ וְאִשְׁתּ֥וֹ עֲקָרָ֖ה וְלֹ֥א יָלָֽדָה:

3 וַיֵּרָ֥א מַלְאַךְ־יְהוָֹ֖ה אֶל־הָאִשָּׁ֑ה וַיֹּ֣אמֶר אֵלֶ֗יהָ הִנֵּה־נָ֤א אַתְּ־עֲקָרָה֙ וְלֹ֣א יָלַ֔דְתְּ וְהָרִ֖ית וְיָלַ֥דְתְּ בֵּֽן:

4 וְעַתָּה֙ הִשָּׁ֣מְרִי נָ֔א וְאַל־תִּשְׁתִּ֖י יַ֣יִן וְשֵׁכָ֑ר וְאַל־תֹּֽאכְלִ֖י כָּל־טָמֵֽא:

Commentary

2. *Manoah.* The name means "rest" and predicts the role that his son will have in bringing rest to Israel.

From Zorah. A town on the tribal border between Judah and Dan, about halfway between Jerusalem and the sea. At this time it belonged to Dan, but earlier it was in Judah's possession.[1] "*From Zorah*" could have two different meanings: one, a simple identification that this was his hometown; or two, that once he had lived in Zorah and had come from there.[2] For in their allotted territory, the Danites had not been able to displace much of the resident population and had moved north (hence the subsequent description of Israelite settlements as reaching "from Dan to Beersheba"). The last verse in our haftarah would suggest that the family was still living in Zorah.

His wife was barren. Her name is not mentioned; Jewish tradition identified her with Hazlelponi of the tribe of Judah.[3]

3. *An angel ... appeared.* Sarah and Hannah are the two other biblical figures who received divine announcements of their pregnancy.[4]

4. *Wine or beer.* יַיִן וְשֵׁכָר (*yayin v'shechar*) covers the fermented products of grapes as well as those of grains or fruit.[5] The words are often mentioned together and may possibly mean "all intoxicants." These provisions raise problems, for while in the sidra (at Numbers 6:6) the Nazir is forbidden contact with the dead, Samson is not, which makes it possible for him to kill so many of the enemy. Further, Samson's parents were not bidden to keep their son away from grapes, wine, or beer. (For additional discussion of the Nazir, see the haftarah for Vayeishev, Amos 2:11 ff.)

Anything unclean. That is ritually forbidden. While this obtains for any Israelite, it is an especially strong prohibition for the Nazir.[6] The rules are generally meant to apply to the Nazir, but, in addition, are here imposed on the pregnant mother, an illuminating precursor of modern-day medical caution.

5. for you shall soon be pregnant, and give birth to a boy. His hair is never to be cut, because from the womb he is God's Nazirite; he will begin to liberate Israel from the hand of the Philistines.

6. The woman went and told her husband: A man of God came to me; he looked like an angel of God—very frightening. I didn't ask him where he had come from, and he didn't tell me his name.

7. All he said to me was this: *You shall soon be pregnant, and give birth to a boy; you are not to drink wine or beer, nor eat unclean food, because the boy shall be God's Nazirite from the womb to the day of his death.*

8. Manoah then turned to the Eternal in prayer, saying: Eternal One, please let Your messenger return to us and teach us how to bring up our child.

9. God listened to Manoah's prayer, and the angel of God returned to the woman as she was sitting in the field; [and again] her husband Manoah was not there.

5 כִּי הִנָּךְ הָרָה וְיֹלַדְתְּ בֵּן וּמוֹרָה לֹא־יַעֲלֶה עַל־רֹאשׁוֹ כִּי־נְזִיר אֱלֹהִים יִהְיֶה הַנַּעַר מִן־הַבָּטֶן וְהוּא יָחֵל לְהוֹשִׁיעַ אֶת־יִשְׂרָאֵל מִיַּד פְּלִשְׁתִּים:

6 וַתָּבֹא הָאִשָּׁה וַתֹּאמֶר לְאִישָׁהּ לֵאמֹר אִישׁ הָאֱלֹהִים בָּא אֵלַי וּמַרְאֵהוּ כְּמַרְאֵה מַלְאַךְ הָאֱלֹהִים נוֹרָא מְאֹד וְלֹא שְׁאִלְתִּיהוּ אֵי־מִזֶּה הוּא וְאֶת־שְׁמוֹ לֹא־הִגִּיד לִי:

7 וַיֹּאמֶר לִי הִנָּךְ הָרָה וְיֹלַדְתְּ בֵּן וְעַתָּה אַל־תִּשְׁתִּי יַיִן וְשֵׁכָר וְאַל־תֹּאכְלִי כָּל־טֻמְאָה כִּי־נְזִיר אֱלֹהִים יִהְיֶה הַנַּעַר מִן־הַבֶּטֶן עַד־יוֹם מוֹתוֹ:

8 וַיֶּעְתַּר מָנוֹחַ אֶל־יְהוָה וַיֹּאמַר בִּי אֲדוֹנָי אִישׁ הָאֱלֹהִים אֲשֶׁר שָׁלַחְתָּ יָבוֹא־נָא עוֹד אֵלֵינוּ וְיוֹרֵנוּ מַה־נַּעֲשֶׂה לַנַּעַר הַיּוּלָּד:

9 וַיִּשְׁמַע הָאֱלֹהִים בְּקוֹל מָנוֹחַ וַיָּבֹא מַלְאַךְ הָאֱלֹהִים עוֹד אֶל־הָאִשָּׁה וְהִיא יוֹשֶׁבֶת בַּשָּׂדֶה וּמָנוֹחַ אִישָׁהּ אֵין עִמָּהּ:

Commentary

5. *He will begin liberating.* The task was not completed for another two generations, when David finally laid to rest the Philistine danger.

6. *Man of God.* אישׁ אלהים (*ish elohim*) is a title also bestowed on the prophet Elisha (see haftarah for Tazri'a).

8. *Let Your messenger return to us.* Perhaps he did not quite believe her story.[7]

9. *Her husband.* אישה (*ishah*). This is the way contemporary Hebrew refers to a woman's spouse, rather than calling him בעלה (*ba'alah*, literally, her master), which was common usage for a long time.

10. The woman ran quickly and told her husband: The man who came here that day has shown up again!

11. So Manoah followed his wife and came to the man, saying to him: Are you the man who spoke to my wife?

Yes, I am, he answered.

12. May your words come true! said Manoah. What do you prescribe for the boy? What is he to do?

13. The angel of the Eternal said to Manoah: Your wife must do exactly as I instructed her.

14. She must eat nothing that comes from a grapevine, she must not drink wine or beer, she must eat nothing unclean—let her do exactly as I instructed her.

15. Then Manoah said to the angel of the Eternal: Please let us detain you, while we cook a kid for you.

16. The angel of the Eternal said to him: Even if you were to detain me, I could not eat your food. If you want to make a burnt-offering, offer it up to the Eternal. Manoah had not realized that this was an angel of the Eternal.

10 וַתְּמַהֵר֙ הָֽאִשָּׁ֔ה וַתָּ֖רָץ וַתַּגֵּ֣ד לְאִישָׁ֑הּ וַתֹּ֣אמֶר אֵלָ֔יו הִנֵּ֨ה נִרְאָ֤ה אֵלַי֙ הָאִ֔ישׁ אֲשֶׁר־בָּ֥א בַיּ֖וֹם אֵלָֽי׃

11 וַיָּ֛קׇם וַיֵּ֥לֶךְ מָנ֖וֹחַ אַחֲרֵ֣י אִשְׁתּ֑וֹ וַיָּבֹא֙ אֶל־הָאִ֔ישׁ וַיֹּ֣אמֶר ל֗וֹ הַאַתָּ֥ה הָאִ֛ישׁ אֲשֶׁר־דִּבַּ֥רְתָּ אֶל־הָאִשָּׁ֖ה וַיֹּ֥אמֶר אָֽנִי׃

12 וַיֹּ֣אמֶר מָנ֔וֹחַ עַתָּ֖ה יָבֹ֣א דְבָרֶ֑יךָ מַה־יִּֽהְיֶ֥ה מִשְׁפַּט־הַנַּ֖עַר וּמַעֲשֵֽׂהוּ׃

13 וַיֹּ֛אמֶר מַלְאַ֥ךְ יְהֹוָ֖ה אֶל־מָנ֑וֹחַ מִכֹּ֛ל אֲשֶׁר־אָמַ֥רְתִּי אֶל־הָאִשָּׁ֖ה תִּשָּׁמֵֽר׃

14 מִכֹּ֣ל אֲשֶׁר־יֵצֵא֩ מִגֶּ֨פֶן הַיַּ֜יִן לֹ֣א תֹאכַ֗ל וְיַ֤יִן וְשֵׁכָר֙ אַל־תֵּ֔שְׁתְּ וְכׇל־טֻמְאָ֖ה אַל־תֹּאכַ֑ל כֹּ֥ל אֲשֶׁר־צִוִּיתִ֖יהָ תִּשְׁמֹֽר׃

15 וַיֹּ֥אמֶר מָנ֖וֹחַ אֶל־מַלְאַ֣ךְ יְהֹוָ֑ה נַעְצְרָה־נָּ֣א אוֹתָ֔ךְ וְנַעֲשֶׂ֥ה לְפָנֶ֖יךָ גְּדִ֥י עִזִּֽים׃

16 וַיֹּ֩אמֶר֩ מַלְאַ֨ךְ יְהֹוָ֜ה אֶל־מָנ֗וֹחַ אִם־תַּעְצְרֵ֙נִי֙ לֹא־אֹכַ֣ל בְּלַחְמֶ֔ךָ וְאִם־תַּעֲשֶׂ֣ה עֹלָ֔ה לַֽיהֹוָ֖ה תַּעֲלֶ֑נָּה כִּ֚י לֹא־יָדַ֣ע מָנ֔וֹחַ כִּֽי־מַלְאַ֥ךְ יְהֹוָ֖ה הֽוּא׃

Commentary

12-14. The man of God does not answer the question of what the boy is to do.

14. *Let her do exactly as I instructed her.* By concentrating exclusively on what the mother ought to do, the messenger's response is an indirect reprimand to Manoah, for he implies: Why do you ask? Your wife knows what she must do. Manoah's original request, which was to guide the parents in the upbringing of their child, is disregarded.[8]

17. Manoah then said to the angel: What is your name? We would like to honor you when your words come true.

18. Why is it, said the angel of the Eternal, that you ask my name? It belongs to another order!

19. So Manoah took the kid and some grain, put it on a rock, and offered it up to the Eternal. As Manoah and his wife watched, they saw something extraordinary!

20. As the flame rose skyward from the altar, the angel of the Eternal went up in the flame. Seeing this, Manoah and his wife threw themselves to the ground, face downward.

21. Only then did Manoah understand that this was truly an angel of the Eternal. Never again did the angel of the Eternal appear to Manoah and his wife.

22. So Manoah said to his wife: We shall surely die, because we have seen a divine being!

17 וַיֹּאמֶר מָנוֹחַ אֶל־מַלְאַךְ יְהוָה מִי שְׁמֶךָ כִּי־
יָבֹא דְבָרְיךָ [דְבָרְךָ] וְכִבַּדְנוּךָ:

18 וַיֹּאמֶר לוֹ מַלְאַךְ יְהוָה לָמָּה זֶּה תִּשְׁאַל
לִשְׁמִי וְהוּא־פֶלִאי:

19 וַיִּקַּח מָנוֹחַ אֶת־גְּדִי הָעִזִּים וְאֶת־הַמִּנְחָה
וַיַּעַל עַל־הַצּוּר לַיהוָה וּמַפְלִא לַעֲשׂוֹת וּמָנוֹחַ
וְאִשְׁתּוֹ רֹאִים:

20 וַיְהִי בַעֲלוֹת הַלַּהַב מֵעַל הַמִּזְבֵּחַ הַשָּׁמַיְמָה
וַיַּעַל מַלְאַךְ־יְהוָה בְּלַהַב הַמִּזְבֵּחַ וּמָנוֹחַ וְאִשְׁתּוֹ
רֹאִים וַיִּפְּלוּ עַל־פְּנֵיהֶם אָרְצָה:

21 וְלֹא־יָסַף עוֹד מַלְאַךְ יְהוָה לְהֵרָאֹה אֶל־
מָנוֹחַ וְאֶל־אִשְׁתּוֹ אָז יָדַע מָנוֹחַ כִּי־מַלְאַךְ יְהוָה
הוּא:

22 וַיֹּאמֶר מָנוֹחַ אֶל־אִשְׁתּוֹ מוֹת נָמוּת כִּי
אֱלֹהִים רָאִינוּ:

Commentary

17. *What is your name?* A replay of Jacob wrestling with an angel and asking his name. Both questioners receive an evasive answer.[9]

18. *It belongs to another order.* And is, for mortals, unknowable. The Hebrew word usually describes a divine wonder.[10]

20. *As the flame rose skyward.* A supernatural experience of this kind is told about the judge Gideon, who belonged to an earlier age.[11]

21. *Only then.* This second part of the verse has been put first for easier reading.

23. But his wife answered him: Had the Eternal intended to take our lives, God would not have taken from us a burnt-offering and a meal-offering, and would not have shown us all this, and given such a message just now.

24. [In time] the woman gave birth to a child. She called him Samson. The boy grew up with the blessing of the Eternal.

25. The spirit of the Eternal first began to move him in the encampment of Dan, between Zorah and Eshtaol.

23 וַתֹּאמֶר לוֹ אִשְׁתּוֹ לוּ חָפֵץ יְהֹוָה לַהֲמִיתֵנוּ לֹא־לָקַח מִיָּדֵנוּ עֹלָה וּמִנְחָה וְלֹא הֶרְאָנוּ אֶת־כָּל־אֵלֶּה וְכָעֵת לֹא הִשְׁמִיעָנוּ כָּזֹאת:

24 וַתֵּלֶד הָאִשָּׁה בֵּן וַתִּקְרָא אֶת־שְׁמוֹ שִׁמְשׁוֹן וַיִּגְדַּל הַנַּעַר וַיְבָרְכֵהוּ יְהֹוָה:

25 וַתָּחֶל רוּחַ יְהֹוָה לְפַעֲמוֹ בְּמַחֲנֵה־דָן בֵּין צָרְעָה וּבֵין אֶשְׁתָּאֹל:

Commentary

23. *God.* Literally, "He."

24. *She called him Samson.* Mothers were the ones who usually gave names to their children. She calls him Samson (שמשון, *shimshon*) giving him a heavenly name (derived from שמש, *shemesh,* sun), thus recalling the celestial being who visited her.[12]

25. *Eshtaol.* Close to Zorah and several times named together with it. It was apparently not far from Gaza.

Essay

The tales of Samson

Everything in the haftarah points to the future hero who will begin to deliver his people from the Philistines. When the boy grew up and became known for spectacular exploits he became a leader for twenty years, but we are not told whether—like others before and after him—he was raised to leadership by the will of the people. In fact, he seems to have acted as a private member of his clan who involved himself in several acts of personal vendetta, which earned him acclaim and admiration. His strength and daring were the stuff from which folk legends are made.

The Torah tells the story of Abraham who was visited by three divine messengers who promised that his wife Sarah, though much beyond her normal childbearing years, would conceive. The story has much in common with the Manoah tale, but while in one case the child that will be born becomes an ancestor of his people, Samson assumes no such exalted role. In fact we hear little of his character except that he was easily attracted to women, which got him into trouble and eventually led to his downfall and tragic end. He is listed among the judges, but just how and when he exercised the functions of leadership remains untold.

We are made aware that he was capable of his feats of strength because he was a Nazir and therefore specially endowed with power not vouchsafed to others. When the spirit of God rested upon him, the otherwise impossible became possible. His strength was legendary, and his very size was said to have been gigantic. He was able to take the gates of Gaza from their hinges and carry them on his shoulders, and he could handle wild beasts and scores of men all by himself.

His contemporaries and later generations loved to tell stories about him, and in time these grew into wondrous events. As so often happened in world history, a tragic and premature end of a well-beloved leader is likely to make him into a hero, and Samson was a prime example of this trend. But neither he nor Jewish tradition ever forgot that his physical prowess was the gift of God, and was on loan. When he breached his trust he was captured and mutilated, but God gave him one last chance to strike at his foes. He clutched the pillars of the great Philistine temple and brought it down, crushing more people than he had killed in all the years before. [13]

Gleanings

The midrash of Josephus

A certain Manoah, a distinguished Danite, and without question the most important man in the country, had an exceptionally beautiful wife, whose figure excelled that of all other women. But because he was greatly in love with his wife he was also very jealous, and when she said that she had been visited by an angel in the form of a slender young man, who had promised that her barrenness would come to an end and a remarkable child would emerge who had to be dedicated to God, Manoah was not sure about the angel tale and became suspicious. (The author goes on to retell the biblical story in embellished detail; of course, Manoah was eventually convinced that the visitor was indeed an angel.)

His wife became pregnant and observed everything the angel had told her to do. The boy was named Samson, which means "the brave (or mighty) one."[14] He grew up quickly, and because he lived simply and did not cut his hair, he gave every indication that he was destined to be a prophet.

Flavius Josephus[15]

Shorn of his strength

> There is a poor, blind Samson in this land,
> Shorn of his strength and bound in bonds of steel,
> Who may, in some grim revel, raise his hand,
> And shake the pillars of this Commonweal,
> Till the vast Temple of our liberties
> A shapeless mass of wreck and rubbish lies.

Henry Wadsworth Longfellow[16]

Rabbinic censure

The Rabbis explain several incidents in Samson's life as well as his tragic end by the severe faults that he exhibited.

Once, when he was thirsty he was miraculously provided with water springing from the jawbone of an ass, for as the ass is (ritually) unfit, so was Samson lusting after women unfit for marriage. Also, since his eyes were constantly on women not of his people, he eventually lost his eyesight.

Talmud and Midrash[17]

***

Notes

1 Joshua 15:33.

2 Comparable to the custom in 18th-19th century Europe, when names like Wiener, Frankfurter, Wormser, or Leipziger became family names indicating that their bearers had once lived in these cities but had moved away. The migration is told in Joshua 19:40 and in detail in Judges chapter 18.

3 *B. Baba Bathra* 91a; *Tanhuma B* 4:160. The name appears as Hazlelponit in these and other sources.

4 See Genesis 16:11 and I Samuel 1:11 (which is the haftarah for the first day of Rosh Hashanah in the traditional cycle). Christian Scriptures too tell of an angel visiting Mary and forecasting the birth of Jesus (Luke 1:26-38).

5 The Aramaic Targum and Rashi translate *yayin* as "new wine" and *shéchar* as "old wine."

6 The Torah law prohibits a Nazir also from eating anything from the grape, fresh or dried (Numbers 6:3-4.; on the significance of hair and alcohol see the Torah Commentary on this chapter).

7 Boling, (*Anchor Bible*, Judges, p. 221) calls this a skillful literary build-up. But Josephus (*Antiquities* V 8:2-3) believes that Manoah loved his wife dearly and was very jealous of her, thinking she had met some man.

8 In the imperfect tense the second person masculine has the same form as the third person feminine. Therefore, the text can also be understood to apply to Manoah, who would then have been bidden to observe whatever had been imposed upon his wife.

9 The Hebrew does not say "*What* is your name" but "*Who....*" Radak says that this reveals Manoah's desire to know the stranger's essence (the name representing the essence). Boling (*Anchor Bible*, Judges, p. 220) understands "Who" as the opening word of what he really wanted to say, namely, "Who are you?" but then bethinks himself and asks for the name.

10 In the song that Moses and Israel sang at after they had been saved at the Reed Sea, God is described as עשה פלא (*oseh féle*, who does wondrous things); the song is part of the daily liturgy of the Jewish people (Exodus 15:11).

11 Judges 6:19-24.

12 So *B. Sotah* 10a, but there are other suggested derivations as well.

13 Judges 16:23-30.

14 A dubious explanation. See comment on verse 24 above in accordance with the Talmud, which derives it from *shemesh*, sun, connecting it with Psalm 84:12, "The Eternal God is a sun and a shield." *B. Sota* 10a.

15 *Antiquities* V 8:3-4. The author describes the events of Samson's life in great and loving detail. The Rabbis are hesitant to call him a prophet, though they agree that the divine spirit rested on him.

16 "The Warning," from *Poems on Slavery* (1842).

[17] B. Sota 9b and Numbers Rabbah 9:24. The interpretation derives from Judges 15:15-17, which tells the story of Samson slaying a thousand men with the jawbone (*lechi*) of an ass. The miracle (verse 19) also speaks of *l'chi*, but is probably a wordplay and signifies a place, "the hollow at Lechi."

Zechariah, chapter 2, verse 14 to chapter 4, verse 7

Introduction

Connection of sidra and haftarah:

The sidra begins with instructions for the seven-branched candlestick in the Tabernacle; the haftarah ends with a vision of the candelabrum in the Jerusalem Temple. This was one of the reasons that caused the Rabbis to choose this haftarah also for the Shabbat during the Chanukah week.[1]

The setting:

Zechariah lived in an exciting time. In the year 538 B.C.E. the Persian ruler, Cyrus, had permitted the Judean exiles to return to their homeland, and the work on the new Temple had begun shortly thereafter. But after a while it lagged; other priorities emerged for the people. Two prophets, Haggai and his younger contemporary Zechariah, urged the completion of the task, and they were the major reason that the work was taken up again and eventually completed.[2] Zechariah's visions illustrate his commitment to the Temple as the community's central institution. It was presided over by Joshua, a high priest of distinguished ancestry, while the secular polity was headed by Zerubbabel, a descendant of the Davidic line, who was appointed to his position as governor by King Darius of Persia.

For more on Zechariah and his time, see our *General Introduction.*

The message:

1. Four introductory verses of encouragement: the Presence of the Eternal will once again make Jerusalem its dwelling place. (2:14-17)

2. The vision and parable of the high priest's old and new garments. (3:1- 5)

3. The importance of following the divine instructions. (6-10)

4. The vision and parable of the candelabrum, ending with a puzzle. (4:1-7)

HAFTARAH FOR B'HA-ALOT'CHA

Zechariah, chapter 2, verse 14 to chapter 4, verse 7

2:14. Sing joyfully and be glad, fair Zion:
for behold, I am coming
to dwell in your midst,
says the Eternal One,

15. On that day many nations shall join
themselves to the Eternal
and become My people,
and I will dwell in your midst.
Then you shall know that the God of
heaven's hosts has sent me to you.

16. The Eternal will take possession of
Judah—
God's portion in the holy land—
and will again choose Jerusalem.

17. Be silent, all flesh, before the Eternal,
who is roused from God's [own] holy
dwelling place.

2:14 רָנִּי וְשִׂמְחִי בַּת־צִיּוֹן

כִּי הִנְנִי־בָא

וְשָׁכַנְתִּי בְתוֹכֵךְ

נְאֻם־יְהֹוָה:

15 וְנִלְווּ גוֹיִם רַבִּים אֶל־יְהֹוָה בַּיּוֹם הַהוּא

וְהָיוּ לִי לְעָם

וְשָׁכַנְתִּי בְתוֹכֵךְ

וְיָדַעַתְּ כִּי־יְהֹוָה צְבָאוֹת שְׁלָחַנִי אֵלָיִךְ:

16 וְנָחַל יְהֹוָה אֶת־יְהוּדָה

חֶלְקוֹ עַל אַדְמַת הַקֹּדֶשׁ

וּבָחַר עוֹד בִּירוּשָׁלָ͏ִם:

17 הַס כָּל־בָּשָׂר מִפְּנֵי יְהֹוָה

כִּי נֵעוֹר מִמְּעוֹן קָדְשׁוֹ:

Commentary

"Verses 14-17 contain elements of thought which perhaps seem contradictory to the modern reader, but which posed no such difficulty for the ancients. Although there seems to be a tension between universalism and particularism and between God's immanence and transcendence in the oracle ... such notions were complementary and not incompatible."[3]

15. *On that day.* While the expression points to a messianic time, it must have evoked in his hearers the hope that they themselves would live to experience it. Zechariah, like some other prophets of his period, here suggests the possibility of converting gentiles. The expression "become My people" was probably unsettling for many of his listeners, but in any case the message likely helped to stir the people to advance the building of the Temple.

17. *Be silent.* Perhaps the Prophet was becoming impatient with those who did not share his enthusiasm for the speedy completion of the Sanctuary.

Who is roused. An anthropomorphic phrase, suggesting that God takes a personal interest in the project.

God's [own] holy dwelling place. An image taken from the Torah;[4] because of God's incorporeal nature, it remains vague.

3:1. God showed me Joshua the high priest standing in front of the angel of the Eternal. The Accuser was standing on the right side, to accuse him.

2. The Eternal said to the Accuser: The Eternal rebukes you, Satan! The Eternal who chooses Jerusalem rebukes you! Is not [Joshua] a brand plucked out of the fire?

3. Now Joshua stood before the angel dressed in filthy clothing.

3:1 וַיַּרְאֵנִי אֶת־יְהוֹשֻׁעַ הַכֹּהֵן הַגָּדוֹל עֹמֵד לִפְנֵי מַלְאַךְ יְהוָה וְהַשָּׂטָן עֹמֵד עַל־יְמִינוֹ לְשִׂטְנוֹ:

2 וַיֹּאמֶר יְהוָה אֶל־הַשָּׂטָן יִגְעַר יְהוָה בְּךָ הַשָּׂטָן וְיִגְעַר יְהוָה בְּךָ הַבֹּחֵר בִּירוּשָׁלָ͏ִם הֲלוֹא זֶה אוּד מֻצָּל מֵאֵשׁ:

3 וִיהוֹשֻׁעַ הָיָה לָבֻשׁ בְּגָדִים צוֹאִים וְעֹמֵד לִפְנֵי הַמַּלְאָךְ:

Commentary

3:1. *God showed me*. Literally, "He showed me."

Joshua the high priest. His full name was Joshua ben Yehozadak,[5] and "high priest" was a title now coming into use. It has been suggested that his father, while exiled in Babylon, was the person who put the final editing touches to the text of the Torah and Early Prophets.[6]

The angel. Standing before God in the heavenly court. Zechariah refers frequently to angels. The concept of angels or messengers who mediate the divine message occurs in various parts of the Tanach, but the Major Prophets speak of direct rather than mediated revelation.

The Accuser. השטן (*ha-satan*). Sometimes rendered "Satan," as if it were a proper name,[7] he is one of God's servants; he plays the role of prosecuting attorney but acts only with the permission of God.[8] We are not told what the Accuser says; most likely he represents those who opposed Temple building and Joshua's elevation to the high priesthood.[9]

2. *The Eternal rebukes you, Satan.* For what he will say or has already said. The phrase became a standard incantation formula in medieval Jewish magic to ward off evil spirits.

4. The angel spoke up and said to his attendants: Take those filthy clothes off of him. And to [Joshua] he said: See, I have taken off your iniquity and am giving you something new to wear.

5. Then I said: Have them put a clean turban on his head. They gave him a clean turban and new clothing, while the angel of the Eternal stood by.

6. Then the angel of the Eternal solemnly exhorted Joshua:

7. Thus says the God of heaven's hosts:

If you follow My ways and carry out the service due to Me,

then you shall govern My House and have charge of My courts,

and I will allow you access among these attendants of Mine.

4 וַיַּעַן וַיֹּאמֶר אֶל־הָעֹמְדִים לְפָנָיו לֵאמֹר
הָסִירוּ הַבְּגָדִים הַצֹּאִים מֵעָלָיו וַיֹּאמֶר אֵלָיו
רְאֵה הֶעֱבַרְתִּי מֵעָלֶיךָ עֲוֹנֶךָ וְהַלְבֵּשׁ אֹתְךָ
מַחֲלָצוֹת:

5 וָאֹמַר יָשִׂימוּ צָנִיף טָהוֹר עַל־רֹאשׁוֹ וַיָּשִׂימוּ
הַצָּנִיף הַטָּהוֹר עַל־רֹאשׁוֹ וַיַּלְבִּשֻׁהוּ בְּגָדִים
וּמַלְאַךְ יְהֹוָה עֹמֵד:

6 וַיָּעַד מַלְאַךְ יְהֹוָה בִּיהוֹשֻׁעַ לֵאמֹר:

7 כֹּה־אָמַר יְהֹוָה צְבָאוֹת
אִם־בִּדְרָכַי תֵּלֵךְ וְאִם אֶת־מִשְׁמַרְתִּי תִשְׁמֹר
וְגַם־אַתָּה תָּדִין אֶת־בֵּיתִי וְגַם תִּשְׁמֹר אֶת־חֲצֵרָי
וְנָתַתִּי לְךָ מַהְלְכִים בֵּין הָעֹמְדִים הָאֵלֶּה:

Commentary

4. *Filthy clothes.* The Accuser is answered by the angel, who proceeds to legitimate Joshua's position by an act of purification.[10] Joshua is now cleansed of the sin that afflicted his people, which caused the destruction of the First Temple and their exile. The ritual of clothing the priest resembles the consecration rites in Exodus chapter 9 and Leviticus chapter 8, though the customary anointing is absent. We may assume that Joshua had been anointed previously.

5. *Then I said.* Some older versions have "he said,"[11] which better fits the context. But a vision (like a dream) does not follow a straight line. The "I" shows that the Prophet, who has been a bystander, suddenly enters the proceedings with his suggestion. Ibn Ezra considers "I said" to be Zechariah's unexpressed wish, which is fulfilled at once.

7. *Access among these attendants of Mine.* Like the angels, he will be able to have privileged communication with God.

8. Listen well, High Priest Joshua, you and your companions who sit before you: these men are a sign that I am bringing forward My servant, The Seedling.

9. Look at the stone that I have set before Joshua, a single stone with seven facets; now I am going to put an engraving on it, says the God of heaven's hosts, and in a single day remove the iniquity of this land.

10. On that day, says the God of heaven's hosts, you shall all invite each other to sit under your vines and your fig-trees.

4:1. The angel who had been talking with me came back and wakened me as a sleeper is awakened.

2. He said to me: What do you see? I said: I see a lampstand all of gold with a bowl on its top; there are seven lamps on it, and, on its top, there are seven pipes for the lamps.

8 שְׁמַע־נָ֞א יְהוֹשֻׁ֣עַ ׀ הַכֹּהֵ֣ן הַגָּד֗וֹל אַתָּה֙ וְרֵעֶ֙יךָ֙ הַיֹּשְׁבִ֣ים לְפָנֶ֔יךָ כִּֽי־אַנְשֵׁ֥י מוֹפֵ֖ת הֵ֑מָּה כִּֽי־הִנְנִ֥י מֵבִ֛יא אֶת־עַבְדִּ֖י צֶֽמַח:

9 כִּ֣י ׀ הִנֵּ֣ה הָאֶ֗בֶן אֲשֶׁ֤ר נָתַ֙תִּי֙ לִפְנֵ֣י יְהוֹשֻׁ֔עַ עַל־אֶ֥בֶן אַחַ֖ת שִׁבְעָ֣ה עֵינָ֑יִם הִנְנִ֧י מְפַתֵּ֣חַ פִּתֻּחָ֗הּ נְאֻם֙ יְהוָ֣ה צְבָא֔וֹת וּמַשְׁתִּ֛י אֶת־עֲוֺ֥ן הָאָֽרֶץ־הַהִ֖יא בְּי֥וֹם אֶחָֽד:

10 בַּיּ֣וֹם הַה֗וּא נְאֻם֙ יְהוָ֣ה צְבָא֔וֹת תִּקְרְא֖וּ אִ֣ישׁ לְרֵעֵ֑הוּ אֶל־תַּ֥חַת גֶּ֖פֶן וְאֶל־תַּ֥חַת תְּאֵנָֽה:

4:1 וַיָּ֕שָׁב הַמַּלְאָ֖ךְ הַדֹּבֵ֣ר בִּ֑י וַיְעִירֵ֕נִי כְּאִ֖ישׁ אֲשֶׁר־יֵע֥וֹר מִשְּׁנָתֽוֹ:

2 וַיֹּ֣אמֶר אֵלַ֔י מָ֥ה אַתָּ֖ה רֹאֶ֑ה וַיֹּאמַר [וָאֹמַ֡ר] רָאִ֣יתִי ׀ וְהִנֵּ֣ה מְנוֹרַת֩ זָהָ֨ב כֻּלָּ֜הּ וְגֻלָּ֣הּ עַל־רֹאשָׁ֗הּ וְשִׁבְעָ֤ה נֵרֹתֶ֙יהָ֙ עָלֶ֔יהָ שִׁבְעָ֤ה וְשִׁבְעָה֙ מֽוּצָק֔וֹת לַנֵּר֖וֹת אֲשֶׁ֥ר עַל־רֹאשָֽׁהּ:

Commentary

8. *My servant, The Seedling.* Also rendered as shoot, sprout, branch, something that will grow. It recalls the vision of Isaiah 11:1: "A shoot shall spring forth from the stump of Jesse. ..."[12] The reference is to a future king of the Davidic line (Jesse being David's father). The message is the same in our passage, but it does not have messianic overtones. Rather, Zechariah foresees a nation with a legitimate king of the House of David,[13] and probably has Zerubbabel in mind (see comment on 4:6).

9. *Stone with seven facets.* Literally, eyes. Radak reports an interpretation by his father, who suggested that the seven facets were the seven persons who were responsible for the revitalization of Judaism.[14] More likely, such engraved stones were believed to have special powers to withstand the wiles of enemies, and the sacred number seven helped to assure this.[15]

10. *Under your vines and your fig-trees.* An image made popular by Micah's vision of a world without war.[16]

351

3. By it are two olive trees, one on the right of the bowl, and the other on its left.

4. Then I said to the angel who had been talking with me: What are these, my lord?

5. And the angel who had been talking with me answered, saying: Don't you know what these things are? No, my lord, I do not, I said.

6. Then he explained it to me, saying:

This is the word of the Eternal to Zerubbabel:

Not by might, nor by power,

but by My spirit,

says the God of heaven's hosts.

7. What are you, you great mountain? Before Zerubbabel, you shall become a plain. He shall bring out the topmost stone and [seeing it] all shall cry: Beautiful! Beautiful!

3 וּשְׁנַיִם זֵיתִים עָלֶיהָ אֶחָד מִימִין הַגֻּלָּה וְאֶחָד עַל־שְׂמֹאלָהּ:

4 וָאַעַן וָאֹמַר אֶל־הַמַּלְאָךְ הַדֹּבֵר בִּי לֵאמֹר מָה־אֵלֶּה אֲדֹנִי:

5 וַיַּעַן הַמַּלְאָךְ הַדֹּבֵר בִּי וַיֹּאמֶר אֵלַי הֲלוֹא יָדַעְתָּ מָה־הֵמָּה אֵלֶּה וָאֹמַר לֹא אֲדֹנִי:

6 וַיַּעַן וַיֹּאמֶר אֵלַי לֵאמֹר

זֶה דְּבַר־יְהוָה אֶל־זְרֻבָּבֶל לֵאמֹר

לֹא בְחַיִל וְלֹא בְכֹחַ

כִּי אִם־בְּרוּחִי

אָמַר יְהוָה צְבָאוֹת:

7 מִי־אַתָּה הַר־הַגָּדוֹל לִפְנֵי זְרֻבָּבֶל לְמִישֹׁר וְהוֹצִיא אֶת־הָאֶבֶן הָרֹאשָׁה תְּשֻׁאוֹת חֵן חֵן לָהּ:

Commentary

4:6. *Then he explained.* The explanation, however, is not contained in verses 6 and 7, which appear as an insertion into the text. (The angel's answer begins with the last half of verse 10 and continues to verse 14. These are not part of the haftarah.)

Zerubbabel. The governor of the province. זרבבל is a contraction of זרע (*zera*, seed) and בבל (*bavel*, Babylon). He was the grandson of Jehoiachin, the former king of Judah who was exiled to Babylon. Zechariah says that Zerubbabel will finish the Temple building, and will do it because of God and not through political might.

Not by might .... One of the most often quoted phrases in the Tanach; see the essay below. חיל (*chayil*) represents military force; in modern Hebrew it can denote the army.

7. *You great mountain.* Mount Zion. Now, says the angel, it contains only the ruins of the old Temple, but it will be leveled ("you shall become a plain"), so that the new Temple can be constructed on the same site.

Beautiful! Literally, "grace." The Temple, a gift of God's grace, is beautiful to behold.

Essay

Not by might (4:6)

Zechariah heard the angel say, "Not by might, nor by power, but by My spirit." To him the message, addressed to Zerubbabel, the governor of the province, was clear:

You are deeply worried over the slow progress of the Temple project, and indeed there are obstructionist forces, inside the province and outside as well. They would prefer the cancelation of the whole project, believing it to be politically dangerous. Today your province, which the Persians call Yehud, is integrated into the satrapy of Ever Nahara ("beyond the river") and a secure part of their empire. They fear that the Temple will kindle new hopes among the Jews that Yehud will become Judah once more, an independent nation. These are the arguments that the opposition advances.

You want the Temple to be built and may be inclined to squash your opponents through political counteraction. I am telling you that in truth the cornerstone will be laid and the structure will arise, but not because of power ploys. It shall come to pass because God desires it. Trust in the Eternal and you will succeed.

There is little question that this oracle, in highly condensed form, was inserted into the vision of the seven-branched candelabrum, because its light stood for the illuminated, God-centered spirit.

To readers no longer familiar with the times and problems of Zechariah, the message seems mysterious and complex, whereas those whom the Prophet addressed understood well what he was saying. Political circumstances did not allow him to say it outright, but the vision made it quite clear to his contemporaries.

Many centuries later, when the Rabbis fixed the order of the haftarot, they chose these passages from Zechariah not only for the sidra that describes the original candelabrum but also for the Shabbat of Chanukah.[17] When they did this, the conditions were of course vastly different from those of Zechariah's time. Chanukah was instituted as the festival to celebrate the recovery of religious freedom and the rededication of the Temple in 164 B.C.E. But while commemorating military successes was natural as long as the Maccabean kings were in their glory, this was hardly feasible under Roman rule. Therefore, the Rabbis wanted to shift the emphasis away from the military and political ("not by might, nor by power") to the spiritual ("but by My spirit"); and so they chose this haftarah, even though they had many other prophetic portions from which they might have selected the reading for Shabbat Chanukah. For them, Zechariah said most clearly what they wanted to convey—both to Jews and to the governing powers.

Since then, conditions have again changed, and changed often, and the Prophet's message—stripped of its original meanings—has become a reminder of the power of God's spirit. While people still think that the forces that move society are primarily material, the Prophet's words come to strengthen the conviction that we can have recourse to a greater Power in order to accomplish our goals.

Gleanings

Words to Remember

A brand plucked out of the fire (3:2).[18]

Not by might, nor by power, but by My Spirit (4:6).

Not by might

Zechariah's vision meant to warn Zerubbabel not to attempt a re-institution of the kingdom at that time.

Eli Casdan[19]

In the ancient world a "nation" comprised a religion, political unity and often common descent. For the Prophets, religion had the central place in the Hebrew nation. All their thought about Israel has to be understood in the light of their belief that it was a people of religion. Hence its election. Hence, too, religion was its life as a people. It had to live by faith: "Not by might, nor by power, but by My spirit, says the God of heaven's hosts."

Israel Mattuck[20]

But by My spirit

Just as the cadelabrum was supernaturally replenished, so will the Temple be restored, not by your strength but by the fact that God will inspire Darius (the king of Persia) to allow you to build the Temple in peace.

Rashi

Angels

The most characteristic feature of the prophecies of Zechariah is the visions. Prophecy was a different function to Zechariah from what it had been in the golden days of the past. The older prophets, too, saw visions, but in them angels hardly ever appear .... With Zechariah angels are a constant feature, and there is an interpreting angel present throughout the visions who takes no part in the action, his sole function being to explain what goes on.

Eli Casdan[21]

In praise of Zechariah

According to the Talmud, the prophet was adept at explaining difficult biblical texts and helped Jonathan ben Uzziel to create his Targum to the Prophets.

After the death of Zechariah, Haggai, and Malachi—all contemporaries—the Holy Spirit of prophecy departed from Israel.[22]

* * *

Notes

[1] When there are two Shabbatot during the week, the haftarah from Zechariah is read on the first Shabbat and another on the second (I Kings 7:40-50).

[2] The Temple was rededicated about 516/515 B.C.E.

[3] C. and E. Meyers, *Haggai, Zechariah 1-8*, p. 176.

[4] Deuteronomy 26:15.

[5] Ezra and Nehemiah call him Jeshua.

[6] The theory is advanced by David Noel Freeedman; see the summary in C. and E. Meyers, *Haggai, Zechariah 1-8*, p.16.

[7] The Hebrew usually says *ha-satan*, that is, "the *satan*," indicating that *satan* is a noun and not a proper name.

[8] Except for the opening two chapters of the book of Job, he does not play an important role in biblical or post-biblical theology.

[9] So Ibn Ezra.

[10] For a similar act, see Isaiah 6:5-7 (haftarah for Yitro). According to A. B. Ehrlich (*Mikra ki-Pheshuto III*), it was customary for accused persons to wear black or soiled clothing.

[11] So the Vulgate and Peshitta.

[12] In our haftarah the word for seedling is צמח (*tzemach*), while Isaiah uses חטר (*choter*). The expression *tzemach tzedek* occurs in a 3rd century B.C.E. Phoenician inscription, where it denotes the legitimate royal offspring. Similar terms are used of Davidic kings in Jeremiah 23:5 and 33:15.

[13] To this day, the traditional Amidah of the daily service contains a prayer for the restoration of *tzemach david*, a sprout of the House of Jesse.

[14] Joshua, Zerubbabel, Ezra, Nehemiah, Haggai, Zechariah, and Malachi.

[15] C. and E. Meyers believe that the stone referred to was either the gemstone in the turban of Joshua or a stone of the future national identity, and that the ambiguity may have been purposeful. At a time when Judah (or Yehud as it was called) was a small province in the large Persian empire, Zechariah combined the permissible (religious independence) with the secular (which was risky). Political independence was out of the question, but hidden in his visions and couched in messianic terms he expressed hope for a future nation. By stressing neither "he accommodated both the ideology and the actuality" (*Haggai, Zechariah 1-8*, pp. 205-207).

[16] Micah 4:4.

[17] See above, at note 1.

[18] The expression אוד מצל מאש (*ood mutzal mé-eish*) is often applied to a survivor of the Holocaust.

[19] *Soncino Books of the Bible,* The Twelve Prophets, p. 284.
[20] *The Thought of the Prophets,* pp. 105-106.
[21] *Soncino Books of the Bible,* The Twelve Prophets, p. 268.
[22] B. Eruvin 21a-b; Megillah 3a. Yoma 9b.

שְׁלַח לְךָ

Joshua, chapter 2, verses 1 to 24

Introduction

Connection between sidra and haftarah:

Both sidra and haftarah tell of spies, sent out to explore the land that Israel was destined to occupy. In the sidra, Joshua bin-Nun is one of the twelve spies; in the haftarah, as the successor of Moses in the leadership of the people, he follows his mentor's example, but the new mission turns out to be quite different. (The story of the dramatic conquest of Jericho is told later, in chapter 6, which is not utilized as a haftarah.)

The setting:

Joshua's assumption of leadership and the beginning of the invasion occurred about the year 1200 B.C.E., which archaeologists also consider the beginning of the Iron Age.[1] The people were poised on the east side of the Jordan, and were now ready to cross over and start the campaign.

For more on the book of Joshua, see our *General Introduction;* on Joshua and his time, see the essay in the haftarah for Simchat Torah (V'zot Hab'rachah).

The story:

    1. Two appointed spies come to the dwelling of Rahab. (2:1)

    2. The king wants to question the spies, but Rahab hides them. (2-7)

    3. Why Rahab decides to do this. (8-11)

    4. The compact that Rahab and the spies make. (12-21)

    5. The spies' escape and return to Joshua. (22-24)

HAFTARAH FOR SH'LACH L'CHA

Joshua, chapter 2, verses 1 to 24

2:1. Joshua son of Nun secretly sent two spies from Shittim, saying: Go, explore the countryside of Jericho. When they got to Jericho, they came to the house of a prostitute named Rahab and stayed there.

2. Someone told the king of Jericho that some Israelites had come that night to spy out the country,

3. so he sent word to Rahab: The men who have just arrived and are in your house have come to spy out the whole country; bring them out!

4. But [instead] the woman had taken the two men and hidden them, so she answered: Yes, indeed, the men did come to me, but I didn't know where they were from.

וַיִּשְׁלַח יְהוֹשֻׁעַ־בִּן־נוּן מִן־הַשִּׁטִּים שְׁנַיִם־ 2:1
אֲנָשִׁים מְרַגְּלִים חֶרֶשׁ לֵאמֹר לְכוּ רְאוּ אֶת־
הָאָרֶץ וְאֶת־יְרִיחוֹ וַיֵּלְכוּ וַיָּבֹאוּ בֵּית־אִשָּׁה
זוֹנָה וּשְׁמָהּ רָחָב וַיִּשְׁכְּבוּ־שָׁמָּה:
וַיֵּאָמַר לְמֶלֶךְ יְרִיחוֹ לֵאמֹר הִנֵּה אֲנָשִׁים בָּאוּ 2
הֵנָּה הַלַּיְלָה מִבְּנֵי יִשְׂרָאֵל לַחְפֹּר אֶת־הָאָרֶץ:
וַיִּשְׁלַח מֶלֶךְ יְרִיחוֹ אֶל־רָחָב לֵאמֹר הוֹצִיאִי 3
הָאֲנָשִׁים הַבָּאִים אֵלַיִךְ אֲשֶׁר־בָּאוּ לְבֵיתֵךְ כִּי
לַחְפֹּר אֶת־כָּל־הָאָרֶץ בָּאוּ:
וַתִּקַּח הָאִשָּׁה אֶת־שְׁנֵי הָאֲנָשִׁים וַתִּצְפְּנוֹ 4
וַתֹּאמֶר כֵּן בָּאוּ אֵלַי הָאֲנָשִׁים וְלֹא יָדַעְתִּי
מֵאַיִן הֵמָּה:

Commentary

1. *Secretly.* Or quietly. The word חרש (*chéresh*, accented on the first syllable) occurs nowhere else in the Tanach, and is related to חרש (*cherésh*, accented on the second syllable), meaning deaf.

Shittim. Literally, the acacias. The definite article suggests that the reference is not to the town that bore this name but to an area known by its trees.[2] In any case, the location must have been east of the river Jordan, not too far from Jericho.

Jericho. See the essay below.

Prostitute. זונה (*zonah*), the usual meaning of the word. But because there was a tradition that afterward Rahab became the wife of Joshua (see *Gleanings*) the Targum, Rashi, and others explain that the word *zonah* here denotes an innkeeper, because a similar sounding word means "to feed."[3]

The Torah does not outlaw prostitution as such, unless there are particular circumstances that prohibit it.[4]

Rahab. The Hebrew means "wide" or "broad," and occurs in such names as Rehoboam and Rehabiah (the former the successor of Solomon, and the latter a nephew of Moses).[5]

3. *Bring them out!* That demand was also made by the people of Sodom, when they asked Lot to produce his guests.[6]

4. *The men did come to me.* As a prostitute, she would have no reason to know the comings and goings of her patrons.

5. They left as it was getting dark, just before the city gates were closed. I don't know where they were going, but if you hurry after them, you can catch them.

6. Actually, she had taken them up to the roof and hidden them under some stalks of flax she had arranged for herself.

7. The pursuers went as far as the Jordan, as far as the fords, and as soon as they left the town the gate was shut.

8. Before [the spies] settled down for the night, Rahab went up to them, onto the roof,

9. and said to them: I know that the Eternal has given you this land. Dread of you has fallen on us, and all the inhabitants of this land are scared to death of you.

10. We have heard how the Eternal dried up the waters of the Reed [Red] Sea for you when you were leaving Egypt, and how you dealt with Sihon and Og, the two Amorite kings east of the Jordan, whom you wiped out.

5 וַיְהִי הַשַּׁעַר לִסְגּוֹר בַּחֹשֶׁךְ וְהָאֲנָשִׁים יָצָאוּ לֹא יָדַעְתִּי אָנָה הָלְכוּ הָאֲנָשִׁים רִדְפוּ מַהֵר אַחֲרֵיהֶם כִּי תַשִּׂיגוּם:

6 וְהִיא הֶעֱלָתַם הַגָּגָה וַתִּטְמְנֵם בְּפִשְׁתֵּי הָעֵץ הָעֲרֻכוֹת לָהּ עַל־הַגָּג:

7 וְהָאֲנָשִׁים רָדְפוּ אַחֲרֵיהֶם דֶּרֶךְ הַיַּרְדֵּן עַל הַמַּעְבְּרוֹת וְהַשַּׁעַר סָגָרוּ אַחֲרֵי כַּאֲשֶׁר יָצְאוּ הָרֹדְפִים אַחֲרֵיהֶם:

8 וְהֵמָּה טֶרֶם יִשְׁכָּבוּן וְהִיא עָלְתָה עֲלֵיהֶם עַל־הַגָּג:

9 וַתֹּאמֶר אֶל־הָאֲנָשִׁים יָדַעְתִּי כִּי־נָתַן יְהוָה לָכֶם אֶת־הָאָרֶץ וְכִי־נָפְלָה אֵימַתְכֶם עָלֵינוּ וְכִי נָמֹגוּ כָּל־יֹשְׁבֵי הָאָרֶץ מִפְּנֵיכֶם:

10 כִּי שָׁמַעְנוּ אֵת אֲשֶׁר־הוֹבִישׁ יְהוָה אֶת־מֵי יַם־סוּף מִפְּנֵיכֶם בְּצֵאתְכֶם מִמִּצְרָיִם וַאֲשֶׁר עֲשִׂיתֶם לִשְׁנֵי מַלְכֵי הָאֱמֹרִי אֲשֶׁר בְּעֵבֶר הַיַּרְדֵּן לְסִיחֹן וּלְעוֹג אֲשֶׁר הֶחֱרַמְתֶּם אוֹתָם:

Commentary

7. *Fords.* מעברות (*ma'berot*), from the root "to pass through." The same word was used in Israel in the 1960s for the temporary housing units built for new immigrants.

9. *Scared to death.* Literally, faint with fear.

10. *Wiped out.* From the root חרם (*ch-r-m*), ban.[7] The Hebrew denotes the utter destruction of something unfit for human use, because it is consecrated and at God's exclusive disposal. If a city was so marked, even people living in it were doomed.[8]

11. Our hearts sank as soon as we heard about it; and because of you our spirits are low, for the Eternal your God is God in heaven above and here on earth.

12. Now swear by the Eternal that you will treat my family as well as I have treated you, and give me a sign I can trust

13. that you will save my father and mother, my brothers and sisters, and all their families. Save us from death!

14. The men said to her: [We give] our lives for yours; as long as you do not betray what we have been doing, we shall treat you well and faithfully when the Eternal gives us this land.

15. Rahab lived in a house built into the city wall, so she let the men down from the window by a rope.

16. She said to them: Head for the hills, so that the pursuers don't run into you. Hide there for three days, until they come back; then go your way.

11 וַנִּשְׁמַע֙ וַיִּמַּ֣ס לְבָבֵ֔נוּ וְלֹא־קָ֨מָה ע֥וֹד ר֛וּחַ בְּאִ֖ישׁ מִפְּנֵיכֶ֑ם כִּ֚י יְהֹוָ֣ה אֱלֹֽהֵיכֶ֔ם ה֤וּא אֱלֹהִים֙ בַּשָּׁמַ֣יִם מִמַּ֔עַל וְעַל־הָאָ֖רֶץ מִתָּֽחַת׃

12 וְעַתָּ֗ה הִשָּֽׁבְעוּ־נָ֥א לִי֙ בַּֽיהֹוָ֔ה כִּֽי־עָשִׂ֥יתִי עִמָּכֶ֖ם חָ֑סֶד וַעֲשִׂיתֶ֨ם גַּם־אַתֶּ֜ם עִם־בֵּ֤ית אָבִי֙ חֶ֔סֶד וּנְתַתֶּ֥ם לִ֖י א֥וֹת אֱמֶֽת׃

13 וְהַחֲיִתֶ֞ם אֶת־אָבִ֣י וְאֶת־אִמִּ֗י וְאֶת־אַחַי֙ וְאֶת־אַחְיוֹתַ֣י [אַחְיוֹתַ֔י] וְאֵ֖ת כׇּל־אֲשֶׁ֣ר לָהֶ֑ם וְהִצַּלְתֶּ֥ם אֶת־נַפְשֹׁתֵ֖ינוּ מִמָּֽוֶת׃

14 וַיֹּ֧אמְרוּ לָ֣הּ הָאֲנָשִׁ֗ים נַפְשֵׁ֤נוּ תַחְתֵּיכֶם֙ לָמ֔וּת אִ֚ם לֹ֣א תַגִּ֔ידוּ אֶת־דְּבָרֵ֖נוּ זֶ֑ה וְהָיָ֗ה בְּתֵת־יְהֹוָ֥ה לָ֙נוּ֙ אֶת־הָאָ֔רֶץ וְעָשִׂ֥ינוּ עִמָּ֖ךְ חֶ֥סֶד וֶאֱמֶֽת׃

15 וַתּוֹרִדֵ֥ם בַּחֶ֖בֶל בְּעַ֣ד הַֽחַלּ֑וֹן כִּ֤י בֵיתָהּ֙ בְּקִ֣יר הַֽחוֹמָ֔ה וּבַֽחוֹמָ֖ה הִ֥יא יוֹשָֽׁבֶת׃

16 וַתֹּ֤אמֶר לָהֶם֙ הָהָ֣רָה לֵּ֔כוּ פֶּֽן־יִפְגְּע֥וּ בָכֶ֖ם הָרֹדְפִ֑ים וְנַחְבֵּתֶ֨ם שָׁ֜מָּה שְׁלֹ֣שֶׁת יָמִ֗ים עַ֚ד שׁ֣וֹב הָרֹֽדְפִ֔ים וְאַחַ֖ר תֵּלְכ֥וּ לְדַרְכְּכֶֽם׃

Commentary

11. *God in heaven above and here on earth*. This quotation from the Torah[9] was put in Rahab's mouth by the writer of the story.

12. *Treat my family well*. A free translation of the literal, "as I have shown mercy to you so you will show mercy to my family" (also in verse 14). חסד (*chesed*) has no parallel in English. It is often rendered as "mercy" or "loyalty" or "grace."

17. The men had warned her: We shall be free of the oath you made us swear,

18. unless, when we invade the country, you tie this cord of red thread outside the window through which you let us down. Bring your father and your mother, your brothers, and all your family together in your house.

19. If anyone goes out of your house, his blood shall be on his own head, and we shall not be responsible; but if any harm comes to anyone who remains in your house, we shall be responsible.

20. And if you tell anyone what we have been doing, we will be free of the oath you made us swear.

21. Just as you say, she had said. She sent them on their way. When they had gone, she tied the red cord to the window.

22. They went straight to the hills and stayed there three days until their pursuers, who had searched all along the road without success, returned to Jericho.

17 וַיֹּאמְרוּ אֵלֶיהָ הָאֲנָשִׁים נְקִיִּם אֲנַחְנוּ מִשְּׁבֻעָתֵךְ הַזֶּה אֲשֶׁר הִשְׁבַּעְתָּנוּ:

18 הִנֵּה אֲנַחְנוּ בָאִים בָּאָרֶץ אֶת־תִּקְוַת חוּט הַשָּׁנִי הַזֶּה תִּקְשְׁרִי בַּחַלּוֹן אֲשֶׁר הוֹרַדְתֵּנוּ בּוֹ וְאֶת־אָבִיךְ וְאֶת־אִמֵּךְ וְאֶת־אַחַיִךְ וְאֵת כָּל־בֵּית אָבִיךְ תַּאַסְפִי אֵלַיִךְ הַבָּיְתָה:

19 וְהָיָה כֹּל אֲשֶׁר־יֵצֵא מִדַּלְתֵי בֵיתֵךְ הַחוּצָה דָּמוֹ בְרֹאשׁוֹ וַאֲנַחְנוּ נְקִיִּם וְכֹל אֲשֶׁר יִהְיֶה אִתָּךְ בַּבַּיִת דָּמוֹ בְרֹאשֵׁנוּ אִם־יָד תִּהְיֶה־בּוֹ:

20 וְאִם־תַּגִּידִי אֶת־דְּבָרֵנוּ זֶה וְהָיִינוּ נְקִיִּם מִשְּׁבֻעָתֵךְ אֲשֶׁר הִשְׁבַּעְתָּנוּ:

21 וַתֹּאמֶר כְּדִבְרֵיכֶם כֶּן־הוּא וַתְּשַׁלְּחֵם וַיֵּלֵכוּ וַתִּקְשֹׁר אֶת־תִּקְוַת הַשָּׁנִי בַּחַלּוֹן:

22 וַיֵּלְכוּ וַיָּבֹאוּ הָהָרָה וַיֵּשְׁבוּ שָׁם שְׁלֹשֶׁת יָמִים עַד־שָׁבוּ הָרֹדְפִים וַיְבַקְשׁוּ הָרֹדְפִים בְּכָל־הַדֶּרֶךְ וְלֹא מָצָאוּ:

Commentary

17. *The men had warned her.* Rendered here in the past-perfect tense, for otherwise one would have to imagine this discussion as taking place while the men were, literally, on the ropes.

23. Then two spies came down from the hills, crossed the river, and went back to Joshua. They told him everything that had happened to them.

24. They said to Joshua: The Eternal has put the whole country in our hands; all the people there are scared to death of us.

23 וַיָּשֻׁבוּ שְׁנֵי הָאֲנָשִׁים וַיֵּרְדוּ מֵהָהָר וַיַּעַבְרוּ וַיָּבֹאוּ אֶל־יְהוֹשֻׁעַ בִּן־נוּן וַיְסַפְּרוּ־לוֹ אֵת כָּל־הַמֹּצְאוֹת אוֹתָם:

24 וַיֹּאמְרוּ אֶל־יְהוֹשֻׁעַ כִּי־נָתַן יְהוָה בְּיָדֵנוּ אֶת־כָּל־הָאָרֶץ וְגַם־נָמֹגוּ כָּל־יֹשְׁבֵי הָאָרֶץ מִפָּנֵינוּ:

Commentary

23. *They told him everything.* The most important item they carried back with them was the knowledge that the people of Jericho were fainthearted.

24. *Scared to death.* See comment for verse 9.

Essay

About Jericho

Jericho was built first in the Mesolithic period (8th millennium B.C.E.), the oldest town in the Promised Land. Located east of Jerusalem, just north of where the Jordan flows into the Dead Sea, it has a subtropical climate and lies some 820 feet (250 meters) below sea level. Settlers found it to be a site with rich soil and abundant opportunities for agriculture, and especially the growing of dates and persimmons. The prophets Elijah and Elisha both spent some time there.

In addition, it provided easy access to the land east of the Jordan, and soon became a prize object of invaders. Time and again, the walls of the city along with all habitable buildings were razed, only to be rebuilt by another generation and to suffer destruction again. In consequence, Jericho's archaeological remains reveal much about cultures long gone.

The book of Joshua recounts (in chapter 6) how the invading Israelites encircled the city repeatedly and eventually blew the shofar, wherewith the walls collapsed. This folktale, unfortunately, is not backed up by archaeological evidence: no ruins of a 12th century B.C.E. wall (when the invasion is reckoned to have begun) have been found so far. Perhaps the fact that the city remained uninhabited for many centuries—presumed to have been the result of a curse pronounced upon it by Joshua[10]—gave nature its opportunity to erase all traces of the wall.

The intersection between folktale and history cannot be drawn with certainty. The attempt to find causes for existing conditions ("etiology") is the engine that drives the inquiring mind, whether in science or any other area of life. Thus, people always want to know "how things came to be the way they are," and the answers are often found in reconstructions that in time take on the mantle of authenticated history. The fact that Jericho lay in ruins for a long time led people to believe that there must have been a cogent reason for it, and the story of Joshua's curse provided a ready, popular explanation.

In the Six Day War of 1967, Jericho fell to the State of Israel and became the locus for significant refugee aggregations. In late 1993, Israel agreed with the Palestine Liberation Organization to make it the headquarters of the new self-rule area, and Jericho once more assumed its historic role in the Near East.

Gleanings

Rahab the prostitute

Though she spent the early part of her life in following a disreputable profession, she repented and converted to Judaism, and was rewarded by gaining none other than Joshua himself as her husband, and became the ancestor of nine prophets.

Talmud[11]

Because she took the spies into her house and rescued them, she was rewarded by the Holy One as if she had done this because of God.

Midrash[12]

The Christian Scriptures, too, honor Rahab: she is said to have been the ancestor of Jesus and was an example of a person living by faith.[13]

Secretly (verse 1)

Why did send Joshua send the spies secretly? Because he remembered what happened when he and Caleb had been among the spies, and when the people were disheartened by the report of the other ten and refused to fight. But since he needed information he sent the two men quietly, without letting it become public knowledge.

Radak[14]

The outsider

From Israel's perspective Madame Rahab is the epitome of the outsider. She is a woman, a prostitute and a foreigner. As a prostitute she is marginal even in her own culture, and her marginality is symbolized by her dwelling in the city wall, in the very boundary between the inside and the outside. And it is Rahab who saves the lives of the feeble Israelite spies, who willingly cavort with foreigners, indeed with a woman whom they would have eventually slaughtered in combat.

Donna Nolan Fewell[15]

* * *

Notes

[1] On the dating of the invasion, see the essay above.

[2] So Boling (*Anchor Bible*, Judges), p.144.

[3] They come, however, from two different roots: זוּן (*zun*, to feed; whence *mazon*, food) and זנה (*zanah*, to prostitute oneself). It happens that in their participles the verbs are identical, perhaps hinting that prostitutes often provided food and lodging in addition to sexual services. Radak notes the first meaning as a possibility both here and in Judges 11:1, where it is said that Jephthah, one of the judges, was also the son of a *zonah*. See haftarah for Chukkat for further details.

[4] See, for example, Leviticus 21:9 (regarding a priest's daughter); also 19:29 (selling one's own daughter into prostitution); and of course a married woman was not allowed to prostitute herself, since that would make her commit adultery. See also the haftarah for B'midbar, under *Gleanings*.

[5] I Kings 11:43 and I Chronicles 23:17, respectively.

[6] Genesis 19:5.

[7] Being "in *cherem*" came to mean "excommunicated."

[8] See Deuteronomy 2:34-35. The institution has been studied by Philip D. Stern, *The Biblical Herem*.

[9] Deuteronomy 4:39, which is recited daily in the Aleinu prayer.

[10] Joshua (6:26) swore an oath that no one should rebuild the wall, lest firstborn and last-born be taken by death.

[11] B. Megillah 14b.

[12] Numbers Rabbah 8:9. "Legend paints Rahab in very black colors to bring out the effect of repentance" (Ginzberg, *Legends of the Jews*, vol. 6, p. 171, note 12; and see there for additional sources).

[13] Matthew 1:5; Hebrews 11:31; Epistle of James 2:25.

[14] Comment on verse 1. Some midrashim say that Caleb was one of the two spies, with Phinehas being the other; Numbers Rabbah 16:1.

[15] "Joshua," *The Women's Bible Commentary* (1992), ed. Newman and Ringe, p. 66.

קֹרַח

First Samuel, chapter 11, verse 14 to chapter 12, verse 22

Introduction

Connection of sidra and haftarah:

The sidra deals with Korach's attempt to replace Moses in the leadership of the people, and in the haftarah the people try to displace God as their sovereign and want instead to have an earthly king. There are other parallels: both Moses and Samuel defend themselves by saying that they have not taken for themselves a single donkey that did not belong to them, and miracles occur in both tales to justify the status of the prophet. (There is also a significant difference: Moses appeals to God, while Samuel appeals to the people.)

The setting:

Samuel was the last and greatest hero of the tumultuous pre-monarchical period in Israel's history (second part of the 11th century B.C.E.). He served as military leader, judge, and prophet, and laid the foundations for uniting the twelve tribes into a religious nation. He anointed Saul to be Israel's first king, and the book (in chapters 9, 10, and 12) tells of three separate ceremonies devoted to this purpose. The last of these is told in our haftarah.

For more on the two books of Samuel, see our *General Introduction*; on Samuel and his time, see the essay below.

The story:

1. Preparations for the public crowning of Saul. (11:14-15)
2. Samuel defends his leadership. (12: 1-5)
3. He defends God's guidance of Israel. (6-11)
4. He reminds the people that their desire for a king was tantamount to a rejection of God. (12-18)
5. The people admit their lack of faith, and Samuel warns them not to fail God again. (13-22)

11:14. Samuel said to the people: Let us all go up to Gilgal and there renew the kingship.

15. So all the people went to Gilgal, and there at Gilgal, before the Eternal, they crowned Saul king. Then they offered up peace-offerings to God, and, along with Saul, they all held a great celebration.

12:1. Then Samuel said to all Israel: I have listened to your pleas and done everything you asked of me, and set a king over you.

2. From now on, the king will be your leader. As for me, I am old and gray. My [grown-up] sons are among you, and I have been your leader since my youth.

3. Here I am! Testify against me in the presence of the Eternal and in the presence of God's anointed [king]: have I taken anyone's ox or anyone's donkey? Have I maltreated or oppressed anyone?

11:14 וַיֹּ֤אמֶר שְׁמוּאֵל֙ אֶל־הָעָ֔ם לְכ֖וּ וְנֵלְכָ֣ה הַגִּלְגָּ֑ל וּנְחַדֵּ֥שׁ שָׁ֖ם הַמְּלוּכָֽה׃

15 וַיֵּלְכ֨וּ כָל־הָעָ֜ם הַגִּלְגָּ֗ל וַיַּמְלִ֨כוּ שָׁ֤ם אֶת־שָׁאוּל֙ לִפְנֵ֤י יְהוָה֙ בַּגִּלְגָּ֔ל וַיִּזְבְּחוּ־שָׁ֛ם זְבָחִ֥ים שְׁלָמִ֖ים לִפְנֵ֣י יְהוָ֑ה וַיִּשְׂמַ֨ח שָׁ֥ם שָׁא֛וּל וְכָל־אַנְשֵׁ֥י יִשְׂרָאֵ֖ל עַד־מְאֹֽד׃

12:1 וַיֹּ֤אמֶר שְׁמוּאֵל֙ אֶל־כָּל־יִשְׂרָאֵ֔ל הִנֵּה֙ שָׁמַ֣עְתִּי בְקֹֽלְכֶ֔ם לְכֹ֥ל אֲשֶׁר־אֲמַרְתֶּ֖ם לִ֑י וָאַמְלִ֥יךְ עֲלֵיכֶ֖ם מֶֽלֶךְ׃

2 וְעַתָּ֞ה הִנֵּ֥ה הַמֶּ֣לֶךְ ׀ מִתְהַלֵּ֣ךְ לִפְנֵיכֶ֗ם וַאֲנִי֙ זָקַ֣נְתִּי וָשַׂ֔בְתִּי וּבָנַ֖י הִנָּ֣ם אִתְּכֶ֑ם וַאֲנִי֙ הִתְהַלַּ֣כְתִּי לִפְנֵיכֶ֔ם מִנְּעֻרַ֖י עַד־הַיּ֥וֹם הַזֶּֽה׃

3 הִנְנִ֣י עֲנ֣וּ בִי֩ נֶ֨גֶד יְהוָ֜ה וְנֶ֣גֶד מְשִׁיח֗וֹ אֶת־שׁוֹר֩ ׀ מִ֨י לָקַ֜חְתִּי וַחֲמ֧וֹר מִ֣י לָקַ֗חְתִּי וְאֶת־מִ֤י עָשַׁ֙קְתִּי֙

Commentary

11:14. *Gilgal.* A town just east of Jericho, which played an important part as a cultic center in the time of Samuel and Saul.

Renew the kingship. Saul already had been anointed (chapter 9) and acclaimed (chapter 10), but had not yet been fully accepted by all the tribes.[1]

A great celebration. During which Samuel felt obligated to reinforce his own role as God's representative. The celebration turns into a public confession of wrongdoing on the people's part.

12:2. *Your leader.* Literally, "the one who walks before you."

My [grown-up] sons. Samuel illustrates his advanced years by pointing to his sons who are now part of the decision-making populace.

To God. Literally, "to the Eternal."

God's. Literally, "His." Also in verse 5 below

Have I taken a bribe to turn a blind eye to anyone? Tell me, and I will return it!

4. They answered: You have not maltreated or oppressed us, you have taken nothing from anyone.

5. He said to them: Then the Eternal is witness and God's anointed [king] is witness this day that you have found nothing sticking to my hand. They answered: *Witness.*

6. And Samuel said to the people: The Eternal [is witness], the One who chose Moses and Aaron, and who brought your ancestors out of Egypt.

7. Now stand here, and in the presence of the Eternal I will put the case to you concerning all the victorious acts that the Eternal has done for you and your ancestors.

8. When Jacob [and his family] came to Egypt, [the Egyptians oppressed them, and] your ancestors cried out for help to the Eternal, who sent Moses and Aaron, who brought them out of Egypt and settled them in this place.

אֶת־מִי רַצּוֹתִי וּמִיַּד־מִי לָקַחְתִּי כֹפֶר וְאַעְלִים עֵינַי בּוֹ וְאָשִׁיב לָכֶם:

4 וַיֹּאמְרוּ לֹא עֲשַׁקְתָּנוּ וְלֹא רַצּוֹתָנוּ וְלֹא לָקַחְתָּ מִיַּד־אִישׁ מְאוּמָה:

5 וַיֹּאמֶר אֲלֵיהֶם עֵד יְהֹוָה בָּכֶם וְעֵד מְשִׁיחוֹ הַיּוֹם הַזֶּה כִּי לֹא מְצָאתֶם בְּיָדִי מְאוּמָה וַיֹּאמֶר עֵד:

6 וַיֹּאמֶר שְׁמוּאֵל אֶל־הָעָם יְהֹוָה אֲשֶׁר עָשָׂה אֶת־מֹשֶׁה וְאֶת־אַהֲרֹן וַאֲשֶׁר הֶעֱלָה אֶת־אֲבֹתֵיכֶם מֵאֶרֶץ מִצְרָיִם:

7 וְעַתָּה הִתְיַצְּבוּ וְאִשָּׁפְטָה אִתְּכֶם לִפְנֵי יְהֹוָה אֵת כָּל־צִדְקוֹת יְהֹוָה אֲשֶׁר־עָשָׂה אִתְּכֶם וְאֶת־אֲבוֹתֵיכֶם:

8 כַּאֲשֶׁר־בָּא יַעֲקֹב מִצְרָיִם וַיִּזְעֲקוּ אֲבוֹתֵיכֶם אֶל־יְהֹוָה וַיִּשְׁלַח יְהֹוָה אֶת־מֹשֶׁה וְאֶת־אַהֲרֹן וַיּוֹצִיאוּ אֶת־אֲבֹתֵיכֶם מִמִּצְרַיִם וַיֹּשִׁבוּם בַּמָּקוֹם הַזֶּה:

Commentary

3. *A bribe.* Reflecting the language of the Torah: "You shall not take bribes, for bribes blind the eyes of the wise and upset the plea of the just. Justice, justice shall you pursue ...."[2]

6. *[is witness].* The bracketed words are lacking in the Hebrew.[3]

The Eternal ... chose Moses and Aaron. Literally, "made." עשה (*asah*) is the key word in God's creative process. Israel exists because God "made" something of this people.[4]

8. *And settled them.* Meaning, Moses and Aaron were the ones who made it possible.

9. But they forgot the Eternal their God, who then gave them into the hand of Sisera, Hazor's commanding general, into the hand of the Philistines, and into the hand of the king of Moab, and they had to fight them.

10. They cried out to the Eternal, saying: *We did wrong by turning away from the Eternal and serving the Baals and Astartes; save us now from our enemies, and we will serve You.*

11. Then the Eternal sent Jerubaal and Bedan and Jephthah and Samuel and saved you from the enemies around you, and you lived in safety.

9 וַיִּשְׁכְּחוּ אֶת־יְהֹוָה אֱלֹהֵיהֶם וַיִּמְכֹּר אֹתָם בְּיַד סִיסְרָא שַׂר־צְבָא חָצוֹר וּבְיַד־פְּלִשְׁתִּים וּבְיַד מֶלֶךְ מוֹאָב וַיִּלָּחֲמוּ בָּם:

10 וַיִּזְעֲקוּ אֶל־יְהֹוָה וַיֹּאמֶר [וַיֹּאמְרוּ] חָטָאנוּ כִּי עָזַבְנוּ אֶת־יְהֹוָה וַנַּעֲבֹד אֶת־הַבְּעָלִים וְאֶת־הָעַשְׁתָּרוֹת וְעַתָּה הַצִּילֵנוּ מִיַּד אֹיְבֵינוּ וְנַעַבְדֶךָּ:

11 וַיִּשְׁלַח יְהֹוָה אֶת־יְרֻבַּעַל וְאֶת־בְּדָן וְאֶת־יִפְתָּח וְאֶת־שְׁמוּאֵל וַיַּצֵּל אֶתְכֶם מִיַּד אֹיְבֵיכֶם מִסָּבִיב וַתֵּשְׁבוּ בֶּטַח:

Commentary

10. *Astarte.* עשתרות (*ashtarot*, singular *ashtoret*), the goddess better known by her Akkadian (Assyro-Babylonian) name Ishtar. She was the goddess of the morning star as well as commanding fertility and love. She was worshipped at Ugarit (North Syria) before 1200 B.C.E., and her worship persisted in Phoenicia (where she was identified with Aphrodite) throughout the biblical period.[5]

11. *Jerubaal.* Known as Gideon, a judge who defeated the Midianites.[6] Samuel names him first because Gideon, when asked to make his rulership hereditary, replied: "I will not rule over you, and my son will not rule over you."[7]

Bedan. Otherwise unknown. The reference is either to Samson,[8] or to Barak, the victorious judge/general who served with the prophet Deborah.[9]

Jephthah. Another judge who defeated Israel's enemies.[10]

Samuel. It seems strange for Samuel to name himself as a savior of his people. Radak suggests that he delivered his speech in a prophetic trance and spoke words that came from God, and not from him.[11] But, in fact, Samuel is defending his leadership and therefore lets the people know that he is part of an illustrious group.

12. But when you saw Nahash king of the Ammonites marching against you, you said to me: *No, we must have a king to rule us*, though the Eternal your God is your [true] king.

13. Now, then, there is the king you chose, whom you requested; now the Eternal has given you a king.

14. If you revere, serve and listen to God, and do not rebel against the word of the Eternal, then you and your king will be followers of the Eternal your God [and all will be well].

15. But if you do not listen to the voice of the Eternal, but rebel against the word of the Eternal, then the hand of the Eternal will be against you and against your kings.

16. Now stand here and see the great thing that the Eternal is going to do before your very eyes.

17. This is the time of the wheat harvest, is it not? I am going to call to the Eternal, who will send thunder and rain. This will show you what a wrong you have done in the eyes of the Eternal by asking for a king.

18. So Samuel called to the Eternal, who sent thunder and rain that very day. Then the people were greatly in fear of the Eternal, and of Samuel.

12 וַתִּרְא֗וּ כִּי־נָחָ֞שׁ מֶ֣לֶךְ בְּנֵי־עַמּוֹן֮ בָּ֣א עֲלֵיכֶם֒ וַתֹּ֣אמְרוּ לִ֔י לֹ֕א כִּי־מֶ֖לֶךְ יִמְלֹ֣ךְ עָלֵ֑ינוּ וַיהֹוָ֥ה אֱלֹהֵיכֶ֖ם מַלְכְּכֶֽם׃

13 וְעַתָּ֗ה הִנֵּ֥ה הַמֶּ֛לֶךְ אֲשֶׁ֥ר בְּחַרְתֶּ֖ם אֲשֶׁ֣ר שְׁאֶלְתֶּ֑ם וְהִנֵּ֗ה נָתַ֨ן יְהֹוָ֧ה עֲלֵיכֶ֖ם מֶֽלֶךְ׃

14 אִם־תִּֽירְא֣וּ אֶת־יְהֹוָ֗ה וַעֲבַדְתֶּ֤ם אֹתוֹ֙ וּשְׁמַעְתֶּ֣ם בְּקֹל֔וֹ וְלֹ֥א תַמְר֖וּ אֶת־פִּ֣י יְהֹוָ֑ה וִהְיִתֶ֣ם גַּם־אַתֶּ֗ם וְגַם־הַמֶּ֙לֶךְ֙ אֲשֶׁ֣ר מָלַ֣ךְ עֲלֵיכֶ֔ם אַחַ֖ר יְהֹוָ֥ה אֱלֹהֵיכֶֽם׃

15 וְאִם־לֹ֤א תִשְׁמְעוּ֙ בְּק֣וֹל יְהֹוָ֔ה וּמְרִיתֶ֖ם אֶת־ פִּ֣י יְהֹוָ֑ה וְהָיְתָ֧ה יַד־יְהֹוָ֛ה בָּכֶ֖ם וּבַאֲבֹתֵיכֶֽם׃

16 גַּם־עַתָּ֗ה הִֽתְיַצְּבוּ֙ וּרְא֔וּ אֶת־הַדָּבָ֥ר הַגָּד֖וֹל הַזֶּ֑ה אֲשֶׁ֥ר יְהֹוָ֖ה עֹשֶׂ֥ה לְעֵינֵיכֶֽם׃

17 הֲל֤וֹא קְצִיר־חִטִּים֙ הַיּ֔וֹם אֶקְרָא֙ אֶל־יְהֹוָ֔ה וְיִתֵּ֥ן קֹל֖וֹת וּמָטָ֑ר וּדְע֣וּ וּרְא֗וּ כִּי־רָעַתְכֶ֤ם רַבָּה֙ אֲשֶׁ֤ר עֲשִׂיתֶם֙ בְּעֵינֵ֣י יְהֹוָ֔ה לִשְׁא֥וֹל לָכֶ֖ם מֶֽלֶךְ׃

18 וַיִּקְרָ֤א שְׁמוּאֵל֙ אֶל־יְהֹוָ֔ה וַיִּתֵּ֧ן יְהֹוָ֛ה קֹלֹ֥ת וּמָטָ֖ר בַּיּ֣וֹם הַה֑וּא וַיִּירָ֨א כָל־הָעָ֥ם מְאֹ֖ד אֶת־ יְהֹוָ֖ה וְאֶת־שְׁמוּאֵֽל׃

Commentary

15. *Against your kings*. So the Septuagint; the Hebrew has, "against your ancestors."

370

19. The people all said to Samuel: Pray for us to the Eternal your God, so that we do not die, for we have added to all our other sins a [new] evil, by asking for a king.

20. But Samuel said to the people: Do not be afraid. It is true that you have done all this evil; just do not turn away from the Eternal your God, but serve the Eternal with all your heart;

21. Do not turn to "no-things" that cannot help or save you, because they are nothing,

22. because the Eternal will never give you up, for the sake of God's great Name, for the Eternal has willed [it] to make you God's own people.

19 וַיֹּאמְרוּ כָל־הָעָם אֶל־שְׁמוּאֵל הִתְפַּלֵּל בְּעַד־עֲבָדֶיךָ אֶל־יְהֹוָה אֱלֹהֶיךָ וְאַל־נָמוּת כִּי־יָסַפְנוּ עַל־כָּל־חַטֹּאתֵינוּ רָעָה לִשְׁאֹל לָנוּ מֶלֶךְ:

20 וַיֹּאמֶר שְׁמוּאֵל אֶל־הָעָם אַל־תִּירָאוּ אַתֶּם עֲשִׂיתֶם אֵת כָּל־הָרָעָה הַזֹּאת אַךְ אַל־תָּסוּרוּ מֵאַחֲרֵי יְהֹוָה וַעֲבַדְתֶּם אֶת־יְהֹוָה בְּכָל־לְבַבְכֶם:

21 וְלֹא תָּסוּרוּ כִּי אַחֲרֵי הַתֹּהוּ אֲשֶׁר לֹא־יוֹעִילוּ וְלֹא יַצִּילוּ כִּי־תֹהוּ הֵמָּה:

22 כִּי לֹא־יִטֹּשׁ יְהֹוָה אֶת־עַמּוֹ בַּעֲבוּר שְׁמוֹ הַגָּדוֹל כִּי הוֹאִיל יְהֹוָה לַעֲשׂוֹת אֶתְכֶם לוֹ לְעָם:

Commentary

19. *The Eternal your God.* They say "your," as if Samuel had a proprietary relation with God.

21. *"No-things."* תהו (*tohu*) occurs for the first time in the second verse of the Torah, where it describes a world devoid of any form. Samuel subtly links the desire for a king to a worship of תהו.

Essay

About Samuel

The twelve tribes of Israel had found that their occupation of the Promised Land was fraught with far greater difficulty than they had anticipated. Joshua had led the invasion, and a variety of Judges had been chosen by the tribal leaders to repel imminent dangers or reverse the results of devastating defeats by the Philistines who inhabited the land along the Mediterranean coast.

Samuel was the last of these Judges. Born to Elkanah and Hannah of the tribe of Ephraim, he entered the service of the priest Eli, who officiated at Shiloh, the most prominent of Israel's sanctuaries. After Shiloh was destroyed by the Philistines, the tribes were once more leaderless, and it was then that Samuel assumed the role he was to occupy for many years: judge, military leader, and prophet.

Pressures mounted among the people for the appointment of a king who would forge the loose tribal confederation into a nation. Samuel yielded reluctantly, and with divine guidance anointed Saul, son of Kish, a Benjaminite, as king.

The first book of Samuel has no fewer than three accounts of the way the kingship was established. They show Samuel generally as a staunch opponent of the monarchy, yet he was the very person who at God's behest had to choose Saul and, later on, David to preside over Israel's fortunes. Even during the public ceremonies at Gilgal, described in our haftarah, he castigated the people for having forced him to agree to the monarchy.

He saw in it a diminution of God's stature as the sole sovereign of the people, and at the same time the ascension of a king was bound to restrict his own role. From now on, the king would be the supreme judge and general, and Samuel would be the nation's prophetic voice. He would tell Saul that God would wrest the throne from him, and it was he who anointed David.

Jewish tradition softened his opposition to the kingship by saying that he agreed in principle to a king, but balked only because the people wanted him primarily so that they would be like other nations.[12]

We know little about Samuel's personal life, except that he was married and had two sons. He led Israel into a new period and thus was the last of the Judges and the first of the settled nation's great prophets. His grave is said to be on top of the highest peak that overlooks Jerusalem,[13] but the authenticity of the site is in doubt.

Gleanings

The law of kingship

If, after you have entered the land that the Eternal One has given you, and you occupied and settled it, you decide [and say], "I want to set a king over me, like all the nations around me," you shall be free to set a king over yourself, one whom the Eternal your God will choose. Be sure to set one of your own kin as king over you; you must not set a foreigner over you who is not of your kin.

Torah[14]

There was a dispute among the Rabbis about the meaning of this law. Some held that kingship was in fact commanded by it, but that the people sinned by asking for it before the time was ripe. Others believed that God never approved of human kingship, but yielded in the matter in case the people wanted it. Again, the people sinned by asking for it, because they should have waited until the Temple was built.

Talmud[15]

Resistance to the kingship

(A response to Yehezkel Kaufmann, who was one of those who considered Samuel's opposition to the monarchy a transient condition in Israel's history.)

Antimonarchy did not vanish from biblical and rabbinic thought. Jewish history quite obviously adopted kingship, but Jewish religious thought continued to wrestle with the issue. This is manifest in the speeches by Samuel condemning kingship, which were not edited out of the Samuel and Saul sagas. While the nation turned toward kingship, the retention in the Bible of Samuel's condemnations indicates a significant resistance to kingship. Even more, with the transition to monarchy, the inclusion of both the resistance and the ready acceptance of kingship indicates that, theologically, the issue had not been totally resolved and had been left ambivalent.

David Polish[16]

* * *

Notes

[1] So Ralbag.

[2] Deuteronomy 17:20-21.

[3] Our rendering follows the Septuagint.

[4] See Ralbag's extended discussion.

[5] *Ashtoret* also has the meaning of "womb of the sheep," which may preserve the original name of the goddess. Astartes and Baals are a good foil for the Eternal who sends rain during the harvest (verse 18).

[6] For an explanation, see Judges 6:32.

[7] Judges 8:23.

[8] So the Targum, followed by Radak, who reads the name as if it were "ben Dan," son of the tribe of Dan, which description would fit Samson.

[9] The Septuagint reads Barak. For his story, see the haftarah on B'shalach (II Samuel 4:4 and following).

[10] Judges 10:6-12:7 (see the haftarah on Chukkat).

[11] According to Radak, Samuel "did not know what he was saying." Some scholars have suggested that perhaps the original text did not read "Samuel" but "Samson."

[12] *B.* Sanhedrin 20b.

[13] Generally called by its Arabic name, Nebi Samwil (or Nabi Samuil).

[14] Deuteronomy 17:14 ff. The text goes on to restrict the king with regard to the number of wives and the wealth he is allowed to amass. Modern scholars assign this passage (like the book as a whole) to a much later time than that of Samuel.

[15] *B.* Sanhedrin 20b.

[16] *Give Us a King,* p. 24.

חקת

Introduction

Connection of sidra and haftarah:

Usually the connection arises from a repetition of a single name or the similarity of themes, while here we find an unusual link: verses 19-22 in the haftarah are a recitation of verses 21-25 in the sidra. The verses deal with the request that Moses made of King Sihon of the Amorites, a request that serves as a historical remembrance in the haftarah. (Note that many of the names in the haftarah occur also in the sidra, and have been more fully discussed in our commentary thereon.)

The setting:

The turbulent history of Israel between the death of Joshua and the time of the prophet Samuel is covered by the book of Judges. It describes the long years during which the tribes struggled with Canaanites and Philistines and then sank roots into the land assigned to them. They considered themselves partners in a loose confederation, bound together by historical memory and a common religious cult. Especially in times of external or internal crises (which occurred frequently), they elected a military-judicial head, called judge, to ward off the enemy and to foster their common interests. Jephthah was such a leader, who is remembered not so much for his considerable exploits as for the vow he made and its disastrous consequence (see the essay below).

For more on the book of Judges, see our *General Introduction*.

Content of the haftarah:

1. Jephthah's background. (1-3)
2. His election as general and judge. (4-11)
3. His futile negotiations with the Ammonites. (12-29)
4. Jephthah's dubious vow and his victory in battle. (30-33)

HAFTARAH FOR CHUKAT

Judges, chapter 11, verses 1-33

11:1. Jephthah of Gilead was a mighty warrior. Though he was the son of a prostitute, Gilead had fathered him.

2. Gilead's [legal] wife had sons; when they grew up, they drove Jephthah out, saying to him: You are not going to inherit our father's property, because you are the son of another woman.

3. So Jephthah fled from his brothers and settled in the area of Tob, where some outlaws joined him and went out [raiding] with him.

11:1 וְיִפְתָּח הַגִּלְעָדִי הָיָה גִּבּוֹר חַיִל וְהוּא בֶּן־אִשָּׁה זוֹנָה וַיּוֹלֶד גִּלְעָד אֶת־יִפְתָּח:

2 וַתֵּלֶד אֵשֶׁת־גִּלְעָד לוֹ בָּנִים וַיִּגְדְּלוּ בְנֵי־הָאִשָּׁה וַיְגָרְשׁוּ אֶת־יִפְתָּח וַיֹּאמְרוּ לוֹ לֹא־תִנְחַל בְּבֵית־אָבִינוּ כִּי בֶּן־אִשָּׁה אַחֶרֶת אָתָּה:

3 וַיִּבְרַח יִפְתָּח מִפְּנֵי אֶחָיו וַיֵּשֶׁב בְּאֶרֶץ טוֹב וַיִּתְלַקְּטוּ אֶל־יִפְתָּח אֲנָשִׁים רֵיקִים וַיֵּצְאוּ עִמּוֹ:

Commentary

1. *Jephthah.* The Hebrew means "he opens" but does not say what, and therefore may be an abbreviation of an originally longer name. He is introduced as a person from Gilead, but shortly thereafter it is said that "Gilead sired him," for Gilead served both as the personal name of its eponymous founder and the region.[1]

Gilead. The name probably meant "rugged country" and described the then heavily wooded, mountainous region known in modern days as the kingdom of Jordan. In the time of the Judges it was settled by the tribes of Gad and Reuben in the south (between the Arnon and Jabbok rivers) and Manasseh in the north (between the Arnon and Yarmuk rivers).[2]

Prostitute. This is the usual meaning of the word. The Targum interprets it, however, as "innkeeper," just as it does in the case of Rahab.[3] Another Jewish tradition took זונה (*zonah*) as an epithet rather than a description of her occupation: she was *like* a harlot because she lived with her husband without proper documents.[4] In any case, as the story shows, Jephthah was socially unacceptable.

Gilead's [legal] wife had sons. Like Jephthah's mother, she is left nameless.

Son of another woman. This may have been the classical term for "illegitimate child," whose mother did not have the recognized status of either wife or concubine. It did not, however, carry the opprobrium of *mamzer.*

3. *Area of Tob.* Probably the city that in Roman times was known as Hippos,[5] just outside the border of Gilead.

Outlaws. Literally, "empty" men.[6]

[Raiding.] The word is not in the text, but the context suggests it: The band made their living by raiding settlements,[7] and must have given their leader a reputation as a successful fighter.

4. Time passed, and the Ammonites went to war against Israel.

5. When the Ammonites attacked Israel, the elders of Gilead went to bring Jephthah back from the area of Tob.

6. They said to Jephthah: Come, lead us in battle against Ammon.

7. Jephthah said to the elders of Gilead: You hated me; you drove me out of my father's house; now, when you're in trouble, why do you come to me?

8. The elders of Gilead answered him: But we have now turned back to you. If you come with us to fight the Ammonites, you will be in command of all Gilead.

9. Jephthah replied to the elders of Gilead: If you do bring me back to [lead the] fight against Ammon, and the Eternal hands them over to me, I will be your commander.

4 וַיְהִי מִיָּמִים וַיִּלָּחֲמוּ בְנֵי־עַמּוֹן עִם־יִשְׂרָאֵל:

5 וַיְהִי כַּאֲשֶׁר־נִלְחֲמוּ בְנֵי־עַמּוֹן עִם־יִשְׂרָאֵל וַיֵּלְכוּ זִקְנֵי גִלְעָד לָקַחַת אֶת־יִפְתָּח מֵאֶרֶץ טוֹב:

6 וַיֹּאמְרוּ לְיִפְתָּח לְכָה וְהָיִיתָה לָּנוּ לְקָצִין וְנִלָּחֲמָה בִּבְנֵי עַמּוֹן:

7 וַיֹּאמֶר יִפְתָּח לְזִקְנֵי גִלְעָד הֲלֹא אַתֶּם שְׂנֵאתֶם אוֹתִי וַתְּגָרְשׁוּנִי מִבֵּית אָבִי וּמַדּוּעַ בָּאתֶם אֵלַי עַתָּה כַּאֲשֶׁר צַר לָכֶם:

8 וַיֹּאמְרוּ זִקְנֵי גִלְעָד אֶל־יִפְתָּח לָכֵן עַתָּה שַׁבְנוּ אֵלֶיךָ וְהָלַכְתָּ עִמָּנוּ וְנִלְחַמְתָּ בִּבְנֵי עַמּוֹן וְהָיִיתָ לָּנוּ לְרֹאשׁ לְכֹל יֹשְׁבֵי גִלְעָד:

9 וַיֹּאמֶר יִפְתָּח אֶל־זִקְנֵי גִלְעָד אִם־מְשִׁיבִים אַתֶּם אוֹתִי לְהִלָּחֵם בִּבְנֵי עַמּוֹן וְנָתַן יְהוָה אוֹתָם לְפָנָי אָנֹכִי אֶהְיֶה לָכֶם לְרֹאשׁ:

Commentary

4. *Time passed.* According to the text immediately preceding our haftarah, the Ammonites had been threatening Gilead with war, and the leaders came to the conclusion that they needed a proven fighter to oppose the enemy.[8]

Ammonites. Who inhabited the area known in earlier times as Moab, south of Gilead. In biblical genealogy, they were close relatives of the Israelites,[9] but their relationship was not always amicable, despite the specific injunction of the Torah.[10] Today's Amman, capital of the kingdom of Jordan, takes its name from the ancient people.

7. *You drove me out.* You helped my brothers, or in any case tolerated their behavior, and now you come to me.[11]

8. *But we have now turned back.* They acknowledge thereby that they wronged Jephthah.[12]

10. The elders said to Jephthah: The Eternal will witness between us if we do not act as you say.

11. Jephthah went with the elders of Gilead, and the people confirmed him as their commander and chief. In the presence of the Eternal, at Mizpah, Jephthah repeated all the terms of the agreement.

12. Jephthah sent messengers to the king of the Ammonites, saying: What quarrel lies between us, that you have come to my land to fight me?

13. The king of Ammon said to Jephthah's emissaries: Because when Israel went up from Egypt they took away my land from the Arnon [River] to the Yabbok [River], as far as the Jordan [River]. Now, give it back peacefully.

14. Jephthah sent still more messengers to the king of the Ammonites,

10 וַיֹּאמְרוּ זִקְנֵי־גִלְעָד אֶל־יִפְתָּח יְהוָֹה יִהְיֶה שֹׁמֵעַ בֵּינוֹתֵינוּ אִם־לֹא כִדְבָרְךָ כֵּן נַעֲשֶׂה:

11 וַיֵּלֶךְ יִפְתָּח עִם־זִקְנֵי גִלְעָד וַיָּשִׂימוּ הָעָם אוֹתוֹ עֲלֵיהֶם לְרֹאשׁ וּלְקָצִין וַיְדַבֵּר יִפְתָּח אֶת־כָּל־דְּבָרָיו לִפְנֵי יְהוָה בַּמִּצְפָּה:

12 וַיִּשְׁלַח יִפְתָּח מַלְאָכִים אֶל־מֶלֶךְ בְּנֵי־עַמּוֹן לֵאמֹר מַה־לִּי וָלָךְ כִּי־בָאתָ אֵלַי לְהִלָּחֵם בְּאַרְצִי:

13 וַיֹּאמֶר מֶלֶךְ בְּנֵי־עַמּוֹן אֶל־מַלְאֲכֵי יִפְתָּח כִּי־לָקַח יִשְׂרָאֵל אֶת־אַרְצִי בַּעֲלוֹתוֹ מִמִּצְרַיִם מֵאַרְנוֹן וְעַד־הַיַּבֹּק וְעַד־הַיַּרְדֵּן וְעַתָּה הָשִׁיבָה אֶתְהֶן בְּשָׁלוֹם:

14 וַיּוֹסֶף עוֹד יִפְתָּח וַיִּשְׁלַח מַלְאָכִים אֶל־מֶלֶךְ בְּנֵי עַמּוֹן:

Commentary

10. *Will witness.* Literally, is among us, listening. God hears the oath and therefore becomes a witness.

11. *Commander and chief.* ראש (*rosh*), as permanent head of Gilead, and קָצִין (*katzin*), as military leader for the war with the Ammonites. The latter term denotes "officer" in modern Hebrew.

Mizpah. Where the people were encamped. [13]

13. *Arnon [River].* Now known as Mojib, it empties from the east into the Dead Sea.

Yabbok [River]. Now called Zarka, it flows from the east into the Jordan, roughly halfway between the northern end of the Dead Sea and Lake Kinneret. The two rivers mark the southern and northern borders of the territory to which the Ammonites laid claim. At the time, the land was inhabited by the tribes of Reuben and Gad.

15. saying: Israel took no land from Moab and Ammon.

16. When they went up from Egypt, Israel traveled through the wilderness to the Reed [Red] Sea until they reached Kadesh.

17. Then Israel sent a message to the king of Edom asking to be allowed to pass through his land; the king of Edom refused. They also sent a message to the king of Moab, but he too refused, so Israel remained in Kadesh.

18. Then they went by way of the wilderness, making a circle around the lands of Edom and Moab, keeping east of Moab. They camped on the other side of the Arnon [River], Moab's border, but they never crossed that border.

19. Then Israel sent messengers to the Amorite king Sihon, king of Heshbon, saying: *Please let us cross your land to our own.*

15 וַיֹּאמֶר לוֹ כֹּה אָמַר יִפְתָּח לֹא־לָקַח
יִשְׂרָאֵל אֶת־אֶרֶץ מוֹאָב וְאֶת־אֶרֶץ בְּנֵי עַמּוֹן:

16 כִּי בַּעֲלוֹתָם מִמִּצְרָיִם וַיֵּלֶךְ יִשְׂרָאֵל
בַּמִּדְבָּר עַד־יַם־סוּף וַיָּבֹא קָדֵשָׁה:

17 וַיִּשְׁלַח יִשְׂרָאֵל מַלְאָכִים אֶל־מֶלֶךְ אֱדוֹם
לֵאמֹר אֶעְבְּרָה־נָּא בְאַרְצֶךָ וְלֹא שָׁמַע מֶלֶךְ
אֱדוֹם וְגַם אֶל־מֶלֶךְ מוֹאָב שָׁלַח וְלֹא אָבָה
וַיֵּשֶׁב יִשְׂרָאֵל בְּקָדֵשׁ:

18 וַיֵּלֶךְ בַּמִּדְבָּר וַיָּסָב אֶת־אֶרֶץ אֱדוֹם וְאֶת־
אֶרֶץ מוֹאָב וַיָּבֹא מִמִּזְרַח־שֶׁמֶשׁ לְאֶרֶץ מוֹאָב
וַיַּחֲנוּן בְּעֵבֶר אַרְנוֹן וְלֹא־בָאוּ בִּגְבוּל מוֹאָב כִּי
אַרְנוֹן גְּבוּל מוֹאָב:

19 וַיִּשְׁלַח יִשְׂרָאֵל מַלְאָכִים אֶל־סִיחוֹן מֶלֶךְ־
הָאֱמֹרִי מֶלֶךְ חֶשְׁבּוֹן וַיֹּאמֶר לוֹ יִשְׂרָאֵל
נַעְבְּרָה־נָּא בְאַרְצֶךָ עַד־מְקוֹמִי:

Commentary

15. *Took no land from Moab and Ammon.* The land that Ammon claims was, in Moses' time, in control of Moab. Being denied passage through it, Israel left it alone. Later, the land was conquered by the Amorites, and when they in turn engaged in war with Israel, were defeated. Israel's possession of the territory therefore derived not from any quarrel with either Moab or Ammon. Further details are provided in verses 19-21.

16. *Kadesh.* Also known as Kadesh-Barnea. Located some 50 miles (80 km) south of Beersheba, it was the chief halting place of the Israelites during their forty years after their liberation from Egypt and before their invasion of Canaan.

17. *Message to the king of Moab.* This is not mentioned in the Torah account.

18. *On the other side of the Arnon [River].* North of the river that constituted Moab's border.

19. *Amorite king Sihon.* Who had conquered Moab. He was king of Heshbon, apparently identical with Tel Hesban, some 17 miles (27 kilometers) southeast of modern Amman.

20. But Sihon did not believe the Israelites would [merely] pass through his territory; so he mustered his army, encamped at Jahaz, and attacked Israel.

21. But the Eternal, the God of Israel, put Sihon and his army into the hands of Israel, who defeated them. In that way Israel took over the land of the Amorites, who lived in that territory.

22. They took possession of the territory of the Amorites, from the Arnon [River] to the Jabbok [River], from the wilderness all the way to the Jordan [River].

23. And now that the Eternal, the God of Israel, dispossessed the Amorites in favor of Israel, the people of the Eternal, are you going to take it over?

24. Do you not hold whatever your god Chemosh has given you as a holding? So will we hold whatever land the Eternal our God has given to us.

25. Are you really any better than Balak son of Zippor, king of Moab? Did he dare contend with Israel? Did he dare wage war against them?

20 וְלֹא־הֶאֱמִין סִיחֹן אֶת־יִשְׂרָאֵל עֲבֹר בִּגְבֻלוֹ וַיֶּאֱסֹף סִיחֹן אֶת־כָּל־עַמּוֹ וַיַּחֲנוּ בְּיָהְצָה וַיִּלָּחֶם עִם־יִשְׂרָאֵל:

21 וַיַּכֵּהוּ יְהוָה אֱלֹהֵי־יִשְׂרָאֵל אֶת־סִיחֹן וְאֶת־כָּל־עַמּוֹ בְּיַד יִשְׂרָאֵל וַיַּכּוּם וַיִּירַשׁ יִשְׂרָאֵל אֶת כָּל־אֶרֶץ הָאֱמֹרִי יוֹשֵׁב הָאָרֶץ הַהִיא:

22 וַיִּירְשׁוּ אֵת כָּל־גְּבוּל הָאֱמֹרִי מֵאַרְנֹן וְעַד־הַיַּבֹּק וּמִן־הַמִּדְבָּר וְעַד־הַיַּרְדֵּן:

23 וְעַתָּה יְהוָה אֱלֹהֵי יִשְׂרָאֵל הוֹרִישׁ אֶת־הָאֱמֹרִי מִפְּנֵי עַמּוֹ יִשְׂרָאֵל וְאַתָּה תִּירָשֶׁנּוּ:

24 הֲלֹא אֵת אֲשֶׁר יוֹרִישְׁךָ כְּמוֹשׁ אֱלֹהֶיךָ אוֹתוֹ תִירָשׁ וְאֵת כָּל־אֲשֶׁר הוֹרִישׁ יְהוָה אֱלֹהֵינוּ מִפָּנֵינוּ אוֹתוֹ נִירָשׁ:

25 וְעַתָּה הֲטוֹב טוֹב אַתָּה מִבָּלָק בֶּן־צִפּוֹר מֶלֶךְ מוֹאָב הֲרוֹב רָב עִם־יִשְׂרָאֵל אִם־נִלְחֹם נִלְחַם בָּם:

Commentary

20. *Jahaz.* A town at the edge of the wilderness, which had changed hands several times.[14]

24. *Your god Chemosh.* This appears to be a sarcastic remark: You Ammonites adore Chemosh, the national god of the Moabites, and he could not prevent Moab from falling to the Amorites. So, you go with your god and we will go with ours.[15]

25. *Balak.* The Torah devotes several chapters to his attempt to defeat Israel through the incantations of Balaam.[16]

26. Three hundred years Israel has been settled in Heshbon and Aroer and the towns surrounded them, and the cities along the Arnon [River]: why didn't you try to take them back all that time?

27. No, I have done you no wrong; it is you who are wronging me by making war on me. The Eternal, the Judge, will decide this day between the people of Israel and the people of Ammon.

28. But the king of Ammon paid no attention to the message Jephthah had sent to him.

29. Then the spirit of the Eternal settled on Jephthah. He went through Gilead and Manasseh, passing Mizpeh of Gilead, and from there he passed to the army of Ammon.

30. Jephthah made this vow to the Eternal: If You hand the people of Ammon over to me,

26 בְּשֶׁבֶת יִשְׂרָאֵל בְּחֶשְׁבּוֹן וּבִבְנוֹתֶיהָ וּבְעַרְעוֹר וּבִבְנוֹתֶיהָ וּבְכָל־הֶעָרִים אֲשֶׁר עַל־יְדֵי אַרְנוֹן שְׁלֹשׁ מֵאוֹת שָׁנָה וּמַדּוּעַ לֹא־הִצַּלְתֶּם בָּעֵת הַהִיא:

27 וְאָנֹכִי לֹא־חָטָאתִי לָךְ וְאַתָּה עֹשֶׂה אִתִּי רָעָה לְהִלָּחֶם בִּי יִשְׁפֹּט יְהוָה הַשֹּׁפֵט הַיּוֹם בֵּין בְּנֵי יִשְׂרָאֵל וּבֵין בְּנֵי עַמּוֹן:

28 וְלֹא שָׁמַע מֶלֶךְ בְּנֵי עַמּוֹן אֶל־דִּבְרֵי יִפְתָּח אֲשֶׁר שָׁלַח אֵלָיו:

29 וַתְּהִי עַל־יִפְתָּח רוּחַ יְהוָה וַיַּעֲבֹר אֶת־הַגִּלְעָד וְאֶת־מְנַשֶּׁה וַיַּעֲבֹר אֶת־מִצְפֵּה גִלְעָד וּמִמִּצְפֵּה גִלְעָד עָבַר בְּנֵי עַמּוֹן:

30 וַיִּדַּר יִפְתָּח נֶדֶר לַיהוָה וַיֹּאמַר אִם־נָתוֹן תִּתֵּן אֶת־בְּנֵי עַמּוֹן בְּיָדִי:

Commentary

26. *Three hundred years.* The book of Judges notes the number of years during which the various leaders occupied their office, but scholars agree that many of these data are schematic and not reliable.[17] Thus, it is likely that Jephthah's remark meant, "a very long time."[18]

Heshbon and Aroer. Cities in the tribal land of Reuben. Aroer (the Hebrew has the variant Ar'or) was located on the Arnon, and Heshbon lay farther north.

29. *Mizpeh.* A variant of Mizpah; its exact location is not known.

31. Then I will offer to the Eternal as a (whole) burnt-offering whatever comes out of my house to meet me when I come home safe from the Ammonites.

32. Jephthah then crossed over to do battle against the Ammonites, and the Eternal put them into his grasp.

33. He routed them with a terrible slaughter from Aroer as far as Minith, all the way to Abel Keramin—twenty towns. So the Ammonites were subdued by the people of Israel.

31 וְהָיָה הַיּוֹצֵא אֲשֶׁר יֵצֵא מִדַּלְתֵי בֵיתִי לִקְרָאתִי בְּשׁוּבִי בְשָׁלוֹם מִבְּנֵי עַמּוֹן וְהָיָה לַיהֹוָה וְהַעֲלִיתֵהוּ עוֹלָה:

32 וַיַּעֲבֹר יִפְתָּח אֶל־בְּנֵי עַמּוֹן לְהִלָּחֶם בָּם וַיִּתְּנֵם יְהֹוָה בְּיָדוֹ:

33 וַיַּכֵּם מֵעֲרוֹעֵר וְעַד־בּוֹאֲךָ מִנִּית עֶשְׂרִים עִיר וְעַד אָבֵל כְּרָמִים מַכָּה גְּדוֹלָה מְאֹד וַיִּכָּנְעוּ בְּנֵי עַמּוֹן מִפְּנֵי בְּנֵי יִשְׂרָאֵל:

Commentary

31. Whatever *comes out*. This is the wording of Jephthah's tragic oath, for when he does return home after his victory, his own daughter meets him. (The haftarah does not include that part of the story; see the essay following.)

Minith ... Abel Keramim. Towns in Ammon whose exact location remains unknown. They were probably in the neighborhood of today's Amman.

Essay

About Jephthah

It is to be noted that the Rabbis, in arranging the haftarah readings, excluded the most famous part of the Jephthah story, and did so doubtlessly because of the problems it raised: the victorious soldier coming home, expecting to be met by one of his animals, is greeted by his only daughter. Thus, victory turns into tragedy, for Jephthah considers his vow to be holy and irreversible, and his unfortunate daughter agrees that he has no choice but to carry it out.

She begs for, and receives, a two months' reprieve "to bewail her maidenhood" (because she would die childless) and mourn with her friends. Then "she returned to her father, and he did to her as he had vowed."[19]

The text does not detail how the vow was carried out, but seems to leave little doubt that the daughter was killed. (Still, a modern study argues that the text permits an ambiguous reading.[20]) The Sages did not hesitate to condemn Jephthah for his act. They blamed him for the hasty and imprecise way in which he made his vow, and went on to emphasize that such a vow was in any case illegal and could have been annulled by the regnant priestly authority.[21]

The whole tale is unpalatable to our sensibilities. Not only is the daughter treated as an object that can be disposed of, but Jephthah's piety too is so literal that it regards a vow as more important than a human life.[22] While he ascribed his accomplishments to God, his religion also did not prevent him from being cruel to his own countrymen, allowing the slaughter of forty-two thousand Ephraimites.[23]

Modern psychology would predict that Jephthah's early years would make him the kind of person he grew up to be. In his youth, he was despised because of his mother and was abused by his siblings. Pushed out of his familiar environment he became an outlaw, and the desperation that led the Gileadites to appoint him their judge and leader did not transform him into a different person. He served his people as best as he could, and in an age of turbulence and constant warfare he was known as a successful, though cruel, fighter. In the end, he emerges as a tragic figure.

One might finally remember that mass slaughter and misapplication of religion were not confined to ancient times.

Gleanings

The outcast as leader

It is a dramatic incident, the outcast become the chief, scorn replaced by applause. The crises of experience often reveal the true leaders of a people. Unseen and disregarded in placid times, they seem to attract attention like a magnet, and men move toward them with a sure instinct .... In Jephthah Israel found the man for her need.

P. P. Elliott[24]

The result of Jephthah's vow

Two famous rabbis disagreed. Rabbi Jochanan said that, since Jephthah had made a pledge which he could not and should not carry out, he was obligated to make a monetary contribution instead. Resh Lakish said, he was not even obligated to do that, for the vow was null and void.[25]

In any case, couldn't Phineas the High Priest have absolved Jephthah from his vow? He could indeed have done that, but thought that his dignity demanded that Jephthah should come to him. But Jephthah did not come because, since he was the head of Israel's leaders, Phineas should come to him. Between the two of them the maiden perished. Hence the popular saying, "Between the midwife and the woman in labor the young woman's child is lost."

Midrash[26]

The Jephthah saga

> I have read that many years agoe,
> When Jephthah, judge of Israel,
> Had one fair daughter and no moe,
> Whom he loved passing well;
> As by lot, God wot,
> It came to pass, most like it was,
> Great warrs there should be,
> And who should be the chiefe but he, but he.

Old English Ballad[27]

The heart of the tragedy

The male-oriented narrator, who has all along neglected to reveal the young woman's name, is now concerned to tell that she had never known a man (11:39), as if this somehow makes her end more tragic. A woman reader might reply that she had known men, at least one all too well, and that is the heart of her tragedy.

Donna Nolan Fewell[28]

* * *

Notes

[1] See, for instance, Shechem, the name of a city and of the king's son (Genesis 34:2).

[2] In Genesis 31:47, Gilead is etymologized as "stone heap of witness."

[3] Joshua 2:1; see the haftarah for Sh'lach L'cha, for the etymology of the Hebrew term.

[4] See Radak, who was unaware that marital documentation was introduced at a much later time. There was also another interpretation, that the mother belonged to another tribe, which was considered highly inappropriate; see Josephus, *Antiquities* V 7:8 (who may have had a text reading *zarah*, strange, foreign, instead of *zonah*, harlot. See also *B*. Ketubot 28b; *J*. Ketubot 2:26d).

[5] One of the cities in the Roman province of Decapolis (established in 63 B.C.E. by Pompey), which encompassed some of the area of biblical Gilead; see *J*. Shevi'it 6:36c. According to another tradition, Tob was a person of ill repute, who was congenial to Jephthah and the fellows around him (*B*. Baba Kamma 92b). Radak and Metzudat Zion also take Tob to be a person, and take Ruth 3:12 as proof. The Targum, on the other hand, understands that *tov* means goodness, that is, it was a good land (*ar'a tov*).

[6] Boling (*Anchor Bible,* Judges), suggests that they were mercenaries. JPS has "men of low character"; and NEB, "idle men."

[7] So Ralbag.

[8] Judges 10:17-18.

[9] They traced their ancestry to Lot, nephew of Abraham (Genesis 19:37 f.).

[10] Deuteronomy 2:19 and 3:16; but see the battles of Saul (I Samuel 11) and David (II Samuel 11-12).

[11] So Metzudat David, A. Cohen, in the *Soncino Bible Commentary.*

[12] The Septuagint reads the text slightly differently: לכן (*lachén*) as לא כן (*lo chen*, not so).

[13] Judges 10:17.

[14] It is noted on the Mesha stele; see Pritchard, *Ancient Near Eastern Texts,* pp. 320-321.

[15] Similarly Radak.

[16] Numbers chapter 22-24.

[17] The number 40 recurs several times (for Othniel, Deborah, and Gideon), and one judge, Ehud, is said to have ruled for 80 years. But the number 300 became part of the traditional biblical chronology and was incorporated in the medieval work *Seder Olam.*

[18] Metzudat David adds: "So why did no one claim the land all this time?"

[19] Judges 11:39. The text goes on to say that it became an annual custom for young maidens to observe a period of four days when they would chant dirges for the daughter of Jephthah. See the analysis by Jacobson, *Chazon Hamikra,* vol. 1, pp. 395 ff.

[20] D. Marcus, *Jephthah and His Vow.*

[21] However, Radak avers that Jephthah did not sacrifice his daughter, but built a house for her, where she lived out her days, unmarried and in isolation. According to Ginzberg, *Legends of the Jews,* vol. 6, p. 203, "the midrashic and talmudic literature does not know of this rationalistic view, and it strongly condemns Jephthah and his contemporaries for having

offered a human sacrifice." (See Ginzberg's note 109 for the many rabbinic references.)

[22] Jewish tradition too considered Jephthah very negatively; the Midrash reports that he contracted leprosy for slaughtering the Ephraimites.

[23] Judges 12:6. This was after a civil war in which Ephraimites were identified by their opponents through their inability of pronouncing "Shibboleth" (which they called "Sibboleth").

[24] "Judges," *Interpreter's Bible*, pp. 765-766.

[25] The two sages taught in Palestine in the 3rd century C.E..

[26] Genesis Rabbah 60:3, in comment on the vow that Abraham's servant, Eliezer, made (Genesis 24:13 ff.). The midrash is not bothered by the fact that Phineas belonged to the time of Moses and Joshua, and would therefore be unbelievably old. It also goes on the tell that both he and Jephthah were punished for their transgression.

[27] The ballad was called "Jephtha, Judge of Israel," and one of its phrases was cited by Shakespeare in Hamlet, Act II, Scene 2, lines 440 ff., "One fair daughter ...."

[28] "Judges," *The Women's Bible Commentary*, ed. Newman and Ringe, p. 71.

בָּלָק

Micah, chapter 5, verse 6 to chapter 6, verse 8

Introduction

Connection of haftarah and sidra:

The sidra tells the story of King Balak of Moab engaging Balaam, son of Be'or, to curse Israel—a plan that God turned into its opposite. In the haftarah (6:5), Micah recalls this famous event in Jewish history.

The setting:

Micah was a younger contemporary of the First Isaiah, and lived toward the end of the 8th century B.C.E. in a small town in Judah. The Northern Kingdom had been destroyed by the Assyrians, who now threatened Judah as well. Micah, like Amos before him, was convinced that the terrible social injustices that existed in the country and especially in Jerusalem would cause God to allow the downfall of the nation and the destruction of the Holy City. What God demanded was not more sacrifices but ethical living, "to do justly, and love mercy, and walk humbly with your God" (6:8).

For more on Micah and his time, see our *General Introduction.*

The message:

The haftarah contains five diverse and unrelated orations that have been assembled by the editor. They deal with subjects of mission, idolatry, war and peace, with an argument between God and Israel, and end with a memorable summation of God's ultimate demand.

1. Israel's mission. (5:6)
2. The destruction of Israel's foes. (5:7)
3. The destruction of the implements of war and idolatry. (5:8-14)
4. How God dealt with Israel in the past. (6:1-5)
5. What God demands of us. (6:6-8)

HAFTARAH FOR BALAK

Micah, chapter 5, verse 6 to chapter 6, verse 8

5:6. The remnant of Jacob
shall be among the many nations
like dewdrops from the Eternal,
like showers on the grass
which don't tarry for mortals,
or wait for human beings.

7. The remnant of Jacob shall be among
   the nations
—in the midst of many peoples—
like a lion among the animals of the forest,
a young lion among flocks of sheep,
that roams and tramples and tears,
with none to save.

8. Your hand shall overcome your foes,
your enemies shall all be cut off.

9. On that day, says the Eternal One,

5:6 וְהָיָה שְׁאֵרִית יַעֲקֹב
בְּקֶרֶב עַמִּים רַבִּים
כְּטַל מֵאֵת יְהֹוָה
כִּרְבִיבִים עֲלֵי־עֵשֶׂב
אֲשֶׁר לֹא־יְקַוֶּה לְאִישׁ
וְלֹא יְיַחֵל לִבְנֵי אָדָם:

7 וְהָיָה שְׁאֵרִית יַעֲקֹב בַּגּוֹיִם
בְּקֶרֶב עַמִּים רַבִּים
כְּאַרְיֵה בְּבַהֲמוֹת יַעַר
כִּכְפִיר בְּעֶדְרֵי־צֹאן
אֲשֶׁר אִם עָבַר וְרָמַס וְטָרַף
וְאֵין מַצִּיל:

8 תָּרֹם יָדְךָ עַל־צָרֶיךָ
וְכָל־אֹיְבֶיךָ יִכָּרֵתוּ:

9 וְהָיָה בַיּוֹם־הַהוּא נְאֻם־יְהֹוָה

Commentary

5:6. *The remnant of Jacob.* Micah anticipates that in the coming destruction of the nation only a few will survive. Ibn Ezra sees this verse as forecasting that a portion of the people will continue to live in the Diaspora.

Like dewdrops ... like showers. Israel's presence among the nations will have a refreshing and sustaining effect, which stems ultimately—like dew and showers—from God.[1] A different interpretation would understand "dew" not in a beneficent but a hostile sense, as in II Samuel 17:12: Israel's superior numbers will overwhelm the enemy like dew in the morning, which covers everything.[2]

7. The verse has the same opening phrase as the preceding one, which is probably the reason that these two dissimilar messages are standing side by side.

9-14. Reliance on horses, chariots, fortifications and the like, rather than on God, is a form of idolatry.[3]

9. *On that day.* If one reads this verse directly after verse 6, the day to which Micah refers is probably the time when the predicted exile will end and Israel will assume its beneficent role among the nations.

I will cut off your war-horses from your
  midst,

and do away with your chariots.

10. I will cut off the cities of your land,

and tear down all your fortresses.

11. I will cut off the sorceries you practice;

no longer shall you have soothsayers.

12. I will cut off your idols and pillars from
  your midst;

no longer shall you bow down to the work
  of your hands.

13. I will uproot the asherim from your
  midst,

I will destroy your idols;

14. in anger and wrath I will execute
  vengeance upon the nations

that did not obey [Me].

6:1. Hear now what the Eternal is saying:

Rise, put your case to the mountains;

let the hills hear your voice.

2. Hear the case of the Eternal, you
  mountains;

give ear, you foundations of the earth!

וְהִכְרַתִּי סוּסֶיךָ מִקִּרְבֶּךָ

וְהַאֲבַדְתִּי מַרְכְּבֹתֶיךָ:

10 וְהִכְרַתִּי עָרֵי אַרְצֶךָ

וְהָרַסְתִּי כָּל־מִבְצָרֶיךָ:

11 וְהִכְרַתִּי כְשָׁפִים מִיָּדֶךָ

וּמְעוֹנְנִים לֹא יִהְיוּ־לָךְ:

12 וְהִכְרַתִּי פְסִילֶיךָ וּמַצֵּבוֹתֶיךָ מִקִּרְבֶּךָ

וְלֹא־תִשְׁתַּחֲוֶה עוֹד לְמַעֲשֵׂה יָדֶיךָ:

13 וְנָתַשְׁתִּי אֲשֵׁירֶיךָ מִקִּרְבֶּךָ

וְהִשְׁמַדְתִּי עָרֶיךָ:

14 וְעָשִׂיתִי בְּאַף וּבְחֵמָה נָקָם אֶת־הַגּוֹיִם

אֲשֶׁר לֹא שָׁמֵעוּ:

6:1 שִׁמְעוּ־נָא אֵת אֲשֶׁר־יְהוָה אֹמֵר

קוּם רִיב אֶת־הֶהָרִים

וְתִשְׁמַעְנָה הַגְּבָעוֹת קוֹלֶךָ:

2 שִׁמְעוּ הָרִים אֶת־רִיב יְהוָה

וְהָאֵתָנִים מֹסְדֵי אָרֶץ

Commentary

10. *I will cut off*. The same word, הכרתי (*hichratti*), leads off each of the next three verses, giving the oration a cumulative effect.

13. *Asherim*. Idols probably connected with the Canaanite goddess Asherah. Made of wood, they represented sacred trees.[4]

Idols. Reading עצביך (*otzbecha*) instead of עריך (*arecha*, cities), which provides the parallel apparently intended, but changed due to a scribal error.

6:1. *Put your case*. This is the language of a lawsuit by God against Israel, for its breach of the Covenant.

2. *Give ear*. Reading האזינו (*ha'azinu*) instead of האתנים (*ha'etanim*, enduring).

The Eternal has a case against our people,
and will contend with Israel:

3. My people!
What [wrong] have I done to you?
Have I exhausted your patience?
Answer Me!

4. In fact,
I brought you up from the land of Egypt,
redeemed you from the house of bondage,
and sent Moses, Aaron, and Miriam to lead
   you.

5. My people,
remember what Balak king of Moab
   planned,
and how Balaam son of Be'or answered
   him.

[Remember your journey]
from Shittim to Gilgal,
and you will understand God's victorious
   acts.

כִּי רִיב לַיהוָה עִם־עַמּוֹ

וְעִם־יִשְׂרָאֵל יִתְוַכָּח:

3 עַמִּי

מֶה־עָשִׂיתִי לְךָ

וּמָה הֶלְאֵתִיךָ

עֲנֵה בִי:

4 כִּי הֶעֱלִתִיךָ מֵאֶרֶץ מִצְרַיִם

וּמִבֵּית עֲבָדִים פְּדִיתִיךָ

וָאֶשְׁלַח לְפָנֶיךָ אֶת־מֹשֶׁה אַהֲרֹן וּמִרְיָם:

5 עַמִּי

זְכָר־נָא מַה־יָּעַץ בָּלָק מֶלֶךְ מוֹאָב

וּמֶה־עָנָה אֹתוֹ בִּלְעָם בֶּן־בְּעוֹר

מִן־הַשִּׁטִּים עַד־הַגִּלְגָּל

לְמַעַן דַּעַת צִדְקוֹת יְהוָה:

Commentary

4. *I brought you up.* A wordplay between העלתיך (*he'eleticha*, brought you up) and הלאתיך (*hel'eticha*, exhausted your patience) in the previous verse.

5. *Balak ... Balaam.* The story told in the sidra. An inscription found at Deir Alla in Jordan (8th century B.C.E.) refers to Balaam as "a seer of gods," though there is no reference to the biblical story.

[Remember your journey]. A suggested replacement for an omitted line.

Shittim to Gilgal. When you crossed the Jordan to conquer the land.[5] The expression can also be understood as a reference to a period of time: from Israel's crossing the Jordan to the rise of the monarchy (Saul was crowned at Gilgal[6]).

6. With what should I come to the Eternal,
and bow down before God on high?
Should I come before God with burnt-
offerings,
with yearling calves?

7. Would the Eternal be pleased with
thousands of rams,
with ten thousand rivers of oil?
Should I give my firstborn for my transgression,
the fruit of my body for my own sin?

6 בַּמָּה אֲקַדֵּם יְהֹוָה
אִכַּף לֵאלֹהֵי מָרוֹם
הַאֲקַדְּמֶנּוּ בְעוֹלוֹת
בַּעֲגָלִים בְּנֵי שָׁנָה:

7 הֲיִרְצֶה יְהֹוָה בְּאַלְפֵי אֵילִים
בְּרִבְבוֹת נַחֲלֵי־שָׁמֶן
הַאֶתֵּן בְּכוֹרִי פִּשְׁעִי
פְּרִי בִטְנִי חַטַּאת נַפְשִׁי:

Commentary

6. *With what should I come* .... Beginning a series of rhetorical questions, to be answered in the climactic response of verse 8.

Before God. Literally, before Him.

Yearling calves. Required at the dedication of the wilderness tabernacle.[7]

7. *Be pleased*. ירצה (*yirtzeh*) conveys technical acceptability in the cult—an oxymoron when it comes to child sacrifice.

Should I give my firstborn. Should I sacrifice my firstborn child to atone for my transgression? One might conclude from this that in Micah's time child sacrifice was practiced in Judah, but there is no ancient source to bear this out. The books of Kings would have mentioned it, and the prophets would have inveighed against it. Only one case of such offering is recorded in II Kings 21:6, where we are told that King Manasseh had his son burned in some heathen ritual. But—unless this passage is a later addition to the book as some claim—that happened long after Micah's prophetic career was over.

Therefore the verse must be understood as a rhetorical question: Would God be pleased with even the most extreme examples of religious zeal?

8. It has been told you, O mortal, what is
   good,

and what the Eternal requires of you—
Only this: to do justly,

and love mercy,

and walk humbly with your God.

8 הִגִּיד לְךָ אָדָם מַה־טּוֹב

וּמָה־יְהֹוָה דּוֹרֵשׁ מִמְּךָ

כִּי אִם־עֲשׂוֹת מִשְׁפָּט

וְאַהֲבַת חֶסֶד

וְהַצְנֵעַ לֶכֶת עִם־אֱלֹהֶיךָ׃

Commentary

8. *It has been told you.* This verse is often cited as the summation of Judaism (see the essay below). But the Hebrew text is somewhat unclear, because the opening words הגיד לך (*higgid l'cha*, has told you) lack a precise subject. The common assumption is that God does the telling. But it is also possible to see the word אדם (*adam*, mortal or mortals) as the subject, and then the opening of the verse would read: Mortals/People have told you what is good, but what does the Eternal require of you?[8]

Mercy. חסד (*chesed*) also means lovingkindness or goodness.

Humbly. Or modestly, aware before God that we are only human.[9] A talmudic passage understands "walk" in the literal sense: go and do mitzvot, like bringing a bride to the chuppah (making it possible for her to be married) or walking with the dead to their grave (seeing to it that they are buried).[10]

Essay

A controversy

In the concluding verse Micah defines the essence of religion: God requires not sacrifice but righteous living. Does Micah thereby suggest that sacrifice (and, by implication, all ritual) was unnecessary, and that the real essence of Judaism was expressed by justice toward others, by loving and caring relationships, and by suitable modesty?

The answer is "no," just as it is for the other prophets who inveighed against mere external observance. It is in the nature of oratory and moral harangue to employ extremes of speech in order to make essential points. Micah does not advocate the abolition of the Temple worship; rather, he censures external observance by persons who lack devotion to social and ethical principles. Judaism has always been an integrated system of form and substance, of ritual and spirituality, for neither is viable without the other.

It happens, however, that the passage in question became part of a controversy that involved an oft-quoted passage in the Talmud.[11] We are told that Rabbi Simla'i taught that there were 613 mitzvot in the Torah—365 negative and 248 positive commandments.[12] Thereupon King David came and condensed the 613 to eleven, as we may read in Psalm 15; Isaiah then reduced the number even farther, to six (see 33:15-17); he was followed by Micah, who contracted the number to three; but in Isaiah (56:1) the number became two ("Observe the right and do the just"); and finally the prophet Habakkuk reduced it all to one single precept: "The righteous shall live by their faith" (2:4).

But how can this catalogue of contractions be reconciled with the regime of 613 mitzvot? Why strive to do the many when a few will do? There were some spirited discussions on this subject,[13] all intent on maintaining the importance of maximum observance. The answer must ultimately be this: David, Isaiah, Micah, and Habakkuk try to distill the basic principles of the mitzvot, without in any way attempting to have their contractions substitute for all observance.

Basing ourselves on the verse in Micah, we would say: Observe as much as you can, and do it in the spirit of the threefold objective of justice, mercy, and modesty. It is not one or the other, but rather both: one in the spirit of the other.

Gleanings

It has been told you, O mortal, what is good,
and what the Eternal requires of you—
Only this: to do justly,
and love mercy,
and walk humbly with your God. (6:8)

The most important utterance

Verse 8 has been called the most important utterance in the prophetic literature. It is in fact an epitome of the whole of Scripture. 'In opposition to the most awful mockery of religion is set the purest expression of it, and out of the corruption of the age there shines like a star the purest light of prophecy.'

Joseph H. Hertz[14]

More precious than sacrifice

The prophets disparaged the cult when it became a substitute for righteousness. It is precisely the implied recognition of the value of the cult that lends force to their insistence that there is something far more precious than sacrifice.

Abraham J. Heschel[15]

* * *

Notes

[1] Rashi interprets the verse as follows: Israel must place its hope not in mortals but only in God, for its salvation will have the same source as dew and rain.

[2] See D. Hillers, *Micah*, p. 71.

[3] Compare Hosea 14:4 (haftarah for Shabbat Shuvah).

[4] See Deuteronomy 16:21 and the Torah Commentary, p. 1377, as well as our comments on I Kings 18:21 (haftarah for Ki Tissa).

[5] As told in Joshua chapters 3 and 4.

[6] I Samuel 11:14; see the haftarah for Korach.

[7] Leviticus 9:3.

[8] First suggested by A. B. Ehrlich, *Mikra ki-Pheshuto*.

[9] Others translate as "wisely" (NEB).

[10] B. Makkot 24a.

[11] B. Makkot 23b-24a.

[12] The former to parallel the days of the year; the latter, to correspond to the number of specific human body parts (as counted by tradition).

[13] See the account in I. Jacobson's *Chazon Hamikra*, vol. 1, pp. 403-410.

[14] *Pentateuch and Haftorahs*, p. 683, quoting Claude Montefiore.

[15] *The Prophets*, p. 196.

First Kings, chapter 18, verse 46 to chapter 19, verse 21

Introduction

Connection of sidra and haftarah:

The sidra is named for Phineas (Pinchas in Hebrew), who was zealous about the moral state of his people and was rewarded with the crown of priesthood for his descendants. The haftarah tells of Elijah, whose devotion earned him the everlasting affection of his people. In both sidra and haftarah we are told what happened *after* they had publicly shown their zeal.[1]

In addition, there was also another reason for connecting the stories of Pinchas (a contemporary of Moses) and Elijah (who lived almost 400 years later): in Jewish folklore the two were actually one and the same person in some mystical and inexplicable way.[2]

The setting:

Along with King David, the prophet Elijah is the most popular hero in Jewish history. He lived in the 9th century B.C.E. amid the semi-nomads in Gilead, east of the Jordan, and beheld with horror the official introduction of the Baal cult in his nation. In a memorable confrontation with the priests of Baal he had demonstrated the superiority of the Eternal (see the haftarah for Ki Tissa). The subsequent killing of the heretic priests forced Elijah to flee from their protector, Queen Jezebel, wife of King Ahab (about 869-850 B.C.E.).

Our haftarah—taken from First Kings[3]—recounts the events that followed. For more on the book, see our *General Introduction*.

Content of the haftarah:

1. A one-sentence bridge between the events on Mount Carmel and those to follow. (18:46)
2. Elijah's flight to the kingdom of Judah. (19:1-3)
3. Weary unto death he is met by an angel who revives his spirit. (4-8)
4. The revelation at Mount Horeb. (9-18)
5. Elisha is chosen as Elijah's successor. (19-21)

HAFTARAH FOR PINCHAS

First Kings, chapter 18, verse 46 to chapter 19, verse 21

18:46. The hand of the Eternal settled on Elijah, and he girded up his loins and ran ahead of [King] Ahab all the way to Jezreel.

19:1. When Ahab told [Queen] Jezebel all that Elijah had done, and how he had put all the prophets [of Baal] to the sword,

2. Jezebel sent a messenger to Elijah, who said: May the gods do this to me and more if by this time tomorrow I have not done the same thing to your life as you did to the life of one of them.

3. Fearing this, Elijah fled at once for his life. He came to Beersheba, in [the territory of] Judah, and there he left his servant behind.

18:46 וְיַד־יְהֹוָה הָיְתָה אֶל־אֵלִיָּהוּ וַיְשַׁנֵּס מָתְנָיו

וַיָּרָץ לִפְנֵי אַחְאָב עַד־בֹּאֲכָה יִזְרְעֶאלָה:

19:1 וַיַּגֵּד אַחְאָב לְאִיזֶבֶל אֵת כָּל־אֲשֶׁר עָשָׂה

אֵלִיָּהוּ וְאֵת כָּל־אֲשֶׁר הָרַג אֶת־כָּל־הַנְּבִיאִים

בֶּחָרֶב:

2 וַתִּשְׁלַח אִיזֶבֶל מַלְאָךְ אֶל־אֵלִיָּהוּ לֵאמֹר

כֹּה־יַעֲשׂוּן אֱלֹהִים וְכֹה יוֹסִפוּן כִּי־כָעֵת מָחָר

אָשִׂים אֶת־נַפְשְׁךָ כְּנֶפֶשׁ אַחַד מֵהֶם:

3 וַיַּרְא וַיָּקָם וַיֵּלֶךְ אֶל־נַפְשׁוֹ וַיָּבֹא בְּאֵר שֶׁבַע

אֲשֶׁר לִיהוּדָה וַיַּנַּח אֶת־נַעֲרוֹ שָׁם:

Commentary

18:46. *Ran ahead ... to Jezreel.* Apparently Elijah did this to demonstrate that his battle with the priests of Baal did not diminish his loyalty to the King. Jewish tradition considered this be another of Elijah's supernatural feats (see *Gleanings*), but if he ran only to the entrance of the valley, he could have kept pace with chariots that had to traverse difficult terrain and roads broken apart by the prolonged drought.[4]

19:2. *May the gods do this.* Let them kill me if I don't carry out my oath and take your life.[5]

3. *Fearing this.* וַיַּרְא (*va-yar*, he saw) was read by the Septuagint as וַיִּרָא (*va-yira*, he was afraid), which better fits the context.

Judah. The Southern Kingdom, where he had a better chance of being protected from the reach of Jezebel—yet he knew he would not feel safe even there, for the royal houses of north and south were maritally connected with one another. Perhaps this is why he was so depressed and wished for death (see the next verse).

He left his servant behind. As the next verse indicates, he was hoping for death and, like many a creature, wanted to die alone.

4. He went on a day's journey into the wilderness. He came and sat under a broom-bush and prayed for death, saying: *It is too much! Take my life now, Eternal One; I am no better than my forebears.*

5. He lay down under the bush and fell asleep. Suddenly an angel touched him and said: Get up and eat!

6. He looked around and there, beside his head, was a cake baked on hot stones and a jar of water! After eating and drinking, he lay down again and slept.

7. The angel of the Eternal came a second time and woke him up, saying: Get up and eat, or the journey will be too much for you.

8. He got up and ate and drank, and that meal gave him enough strength to walk forty days and nights as far as the mountain of God at Horeb.

4 וְהֽוּא־הָלַ֤ךְ בַּמִּדְבָּר֙ יוֹם֙ וַיָּבֹ֔א וַיֵּ֕שֶׁב תַּ֖חַת רֹ֣תֶם אֶחָ֑ד [אֶחָ֑ת] וַיִּשְׁאַ֤ל אֶת־נַפְשׁוֹ֙ לָמ֔וּת וַיֹּ֣אמֶר רַ֗ב עַתָּ֤ה יְהֹוָה֙ קַ֣ח נַפְשִׁ֔י כִּֽי־לֹא־ט֥וֹב אָנֹכִ֖י מֵאֲבֹתָֽי:

5 וַיִּשְׁכַּב֙ וַיִּישַׁ֔ן תַּ֖חַת רֹ֣תֶם אֶחָ֑ד וְהִנֵּֽה־זֶ֤ה מַלְאָךְ֙ נֹגֵ֣עַ בּ֔וֹ וַיֹּ֥אמֶר ל֖וֹ ק֥וּם אֱכֽוֹל:

6 וַיַּבֵּ֕ט וְהִנֵּ֧ה מְרַאֲשֹׁתָ֛יו עֻגַ֥ת רְצָפִ֖ים וְצַפַּ֣חַת מָ֑יִם וַיֹּ֣אכַל וַיֵּ֔שְׁתְּ וַיָּ֖שָׁב וַיִּשְׁכָּֽב:

7 וַיָּ֩שָׁב֩ מַלְאַ֨ךְ יְהֹוָ֤ה ׀ שֵׁנִית֙ וַיִּגַּע־בּ֔וֹ וַיֹּ֖אמֶר ק֣וּם אֱכֹ֑ל כִּ֛י רַ֥ב מִמְּךָ֖ הַדָּֽרֶךְ:

8 וַיָּ֖קָם וַיֹּ֣אכַל וַיִּשְׁתֶּ֑ה וַיֵּ֜לֶךְ בְּכֹ֣חַ ׀ הָאֲכִילָ֣ה הַהִ֗יא אַרְבָּעִ֥ים יוֹם֙ וְאַרְבָּעִ֣ים לַ֔יְלָה עַ֛ד הַ֥ר הָאֱלֹהִ֖ים חֹרֵֽב:

Commentary

4. *Broom-bush.* A fabaceous plant (legume), which grows high enough to give some shade. A somewhat similar scenario is found in the book of Jonah, who also sought the shade of a desert plant and who, when it died, prayed for death.[6]

I am no better than my forebears. I deserve no special treatment; I have reached the end of my tether and am of no more use to You.[7]

6. *Baked on hot stones.* To this day, *pitah* is baked in this way.

8. *Forty days and nights.* Assuming that Horeb (Sinai) is located in the southern part of the peninsula, it would not require a journey of that length. Clearly, therefore, we deal here with a symbolic figure, meant to show that Elijah replayed the role of Moses, who spent forty days and nights without food on the mountain (while he wrote down the Covenant), and who was granted an insight into the nature of God.[8]

9. There he went into a cave and spent the night. Then the word of the Eternal came to him: What are you doing here, Elijah?

10. He answered: Eternal One, God of heaven's hosts, I have always been devoted to You, only to You. But the people of Israel have broken their covenant with You, torn down Your altars, and killed Your prophets. I am the only one left— and now they are trying to kill me!

11. And God said: Go out and stand before [Me], the Eternal, on the mountaintop. Then the Eternal passed by. A furious wind split mountains and shattered rocks in the presence of the Eternal, but the Eternal was not in the wind. After the wind, an earthquake—but the Eternal was not in the earthquake.

12. After the earthquake, fire—but the Eternal was not in the fire. And after the fire, a still, small voice.

9 וַיָּבֹא־שָׁם אֶל־הַמְּעָרָה וַיָּלֶן שָׁם וְהִנֵּה דְבַר־
יְהֹוָה אֵלָיו וַיֹּאמֶר לוֹ מַה־לְּךָ פֹה אֵלִיָּהוּ:

10 וַיֹּאמֶר קַנֹּא קִנֵּאתִי לַיהֹוָה אֱלֹהֵי צְבָאוֹת
כִּי־עָזְבוּ בְרִיתְךָ בְּנֵי יִשְׂרָאֵל אֶת־מִזְבְּחֹתֶיךָ
הָרָסוּ וְאֶת־נְבִיאֶיךָ הָרְגוּ בֶחָרֶב וָאִוָּתֵר אֲנִי
לְבַדִּי וַיְבַקְשׁוּ אֶת־נַפְשִׁי לְקַחְתָּהּ:

11 וַיֹּאמֶר צֵא וְעָמַדְתָּ בָהָר לִפְנֵי יְהֹוָה וְהִנֵּה
יְהֹוָה עֹבֵר וְרוּחַ גְּדוֹלָה וְחָזָק מְפָרֵק הָרִים
וּמְשַׁבֵּר סְלָעִים לִפְנֵי יְהֹוָה לֹא בָרוּחַ יְהֹוָה
וְאַחַר הָרוּחַ רַעַשׁ לֹא בָרַעַשׁ יְהֹוָה:

12 וְאַחַר הָרַעַשׁ אֵשׁ לֹא בָאֵשׁ יְהֹוָה וְאַחַר
הָאֵשׁ קוֹל דְּמָמָה דַקָּה:

Commentary

9. *A cave.* The Hebrew text says *the* cave, which Rashi therefore identifies as the cave (or cleft) where Moses had stood.[9]

What are you doing here? A rhetorical question, like God's words to Adam: "Where are you?"[10]

10. *Thrown down your altars.* Elijah had to rebuild the altar of the Eternal on Mount Carmel.[11]

I am the only one left. Hyperbole; Obadiah had managed to save some prophets.

11. *Great and mighty wind.* רוח (*ru'ach*, wind) also doubles for spirit, and especially the spirit of God.

12. *A still, small voice.* Literally, the voice of thin stillness. Others render the phrase as "a soft, murmuring sound," or "a sound of gentle stillness." (See the essay below.)

13. When Elijah heard it, he wrapped his mantle about his face and went out, standing at the entrance of the cave. A voice came to him, saying: What are you doing here, Elijah?

14. He said: I have been full of zeal for the Eternal, the God of heaven's hosts. The people of Israel have broken Your covenant, thrown down Your altars and killed Your prophets; I am the last one left, and they are looking to take my life, too.

15. The Eternal said to him: Go back the way you came to the wilderness of Damascus; there anoint Hazael as king of Aram,

13 וַיְהִי כִּשְׁמֹעַ אֵלִיָּהוּ וַיָּלֶט פָּנָיו בְּאַדַּרְתּוֹ וַיֵּצֵא וַיַּעֲמֹד פֶּתַח הַמְּעָרָה וְהִנֵּה אֵלָיו קוֹל וַיֹּאמֶר מַה־לְּךָ פֹה אֵלִיָּהוּ:

14 וַיֹּאמֶר קַנֹּא קִנֵּאתִי לַיהוָה אֱלֹהֵי צְבָאוֹת כִּי־עָזְבוּ בְרִיתְךָ בְּנֵי יִשְׂרָאֵל אֶת־מִזְבְּחֹתֶיךָ הָרָסוּ וְאֶת־נְבִיאֶיךָ הָרְגוּ בֶחָרֶב וָאִוָּתֵר אֲנִי לְבַדִּי וַיְבַקְשׁוּ אֶת־נַפְשִׁי לְקַחְתָּהּ:

15 וַיֹּאמֶר יְהוָה אֵלָיו לֵךְ שׁוּב לְדַרְכְּךָ מִדְבַּרָה דַמָּשֶׂק וּבָאתָ וּמָשַׁחְתָּ אֶת־חֲזָאֵל לְמֶלֶךְ עַל־אֲרָם:

Commentary

13. *He wrapped his mantle about his face.* Like Moses, "he was afraid to look at God." [12]

What are you doing here? Returning to the same question asked previously (verse 9). The repetitive back-and-forth underscores the dreamlike nature of the vision.

15. *Hazael.* Attested in contemporary Aramaic inscriptions. In one of them he is referred to as the "son of a nobody who seized the throne." [13]

King of Aram. It appears that the meaning is: Make Hazael king, and he will attack Israel to bring it to its senses. God uses other nations to punish Israel if needed. Thus, some 400 years later, "the Eternal let loose against [King Jehoiakim] the raiding bands of the Chaldeans, Arameans, Moabites, and Ammonites." [14] The anointing of Hazael was carried out by Elisha, Elijah's successor, after the latter's death. [15]

16. and anoint Jehu son of Nimshi as king of Israel, and anoint Elisha son of Shafat of Abel Meholah as prophet to take your place.

17. Anyone who escapes death at the hands of Hazael will be killed by Jehu, and anyone who escapes Jehu will be put to death by Elisha.

18. I will leave in Israel only seven thousand—all those who did not kneel to Baal, whose lips did not kiss him.

19. He left that place and found Elisha son of Shafat, who was plowing; there were twelve pairs of oxen before him; he was with the twelfth. Elijah went over to him and tossed his mantle onto him.

16 וְאֵת֙ יֵה֣וּא בֶן־נִמְשִׁ֔י תִּמְשַׁ֥ח לְמֶ֖לֶךְ עַל־יִשְׂרָאֵ֑ל וְאֶת־אֱלִישָׁ֤ע בֶּן־שָׁפָט֙ מֵאָבֵ֣ל מְחוֹלָ֔ה תִּמְשַׁ֥ח לְנָבִ֖יא תַּחְתֶּֽיךָ׃

17 וְהָיָ֗ה הַנִּמְלָ֛ט מֵחֶ֥רֶב חֲזָאֵ֖ל יָמִ֣ית יֵה֑וּא וְהַנִּמְלָ֛ט מֵחֶ֥רֶב יֵה֖וּא יָמִ֥ית אֱלִישָֽׁע׃

18 וְהִשְׁאַרְתִּ֥י בְיִשְׂרָאֵ֖ל שִׁבְעַ֣ת אֲלָפִ֑ים כָּל־הַבִּרְכַּ֗יִם אֲשֶׁ֤ר לֹֽא־כָֽרְעוּ֙ לַבַּ֔עַל וְכָ֨ל־הַפֶּ֔ה אֲשֶׁ֥ר לֹֽא־נָשַׁ֖ק לֽוֹ׃

19 וַיֵּ֣לֶךְ מִשָּׁ֔ם וַיִּמְצָ֥א אֶת־אֱלִישָׁ֖ע בֶּן־שָׁפָ֑ט וְה֣וּא חֹרֵ֗שׁ שְׁנֵים־עָשָׂ֤ר צְמָדִים֙ לְפָנָ֔יו וְה֖וּא בִּשְׁנֵ֣ים הֶעָשָׂ֑ר וַיַּעֲבֹ֤ר אֵלִיָּ֨הוּ֙ אֵלָ֔יו וַיַּשְׁלֵ֥ךְ אַדַּרְתּ֖וֹ אֵלָֽיו׃

Commentary

16. *Jehu.* The only king of whom there is a contemporary pictorial representation. On a slab celebrating the triumph of Shalmanezer III, an artist showed Jehu bowing in submission before the Assyrian king. [16]

Jehu too was not anointed by Elijah, but by a member of a prophetic band who did it at the behest of Elisha. [17] While Elijah did not personally carry out these tasks, he must have instructed Elisha to see to them.

Anoint Elisha. Meaning, "establish him as your successor." Prophets did not gain their status by anointing, as kings did.

17. *Will be put to death by Elisha.* However, no such action by him has been recorded.

18. *Only seven thousand.* Seven here serves as the indefinite number of the epic.

Kiss him. Kissing sacred objects has been and is part of many religions, including Judaism. Thus Jews will kiss their prayer books or the Torah scroll.

19. *Tossed his mantle onto him.* Having been close to the person of the Prophet, it was believed to have been endowed with some of his qualities. In the story that tells of Elijah being taken up to heaven, the mantle dropped down and became Elisha's. [18]

20. He left the oxen and ran after Elijah and said: Let me please go kiss my father and mother, and then I will follow you.
Go back, said he. For what would I do to you?

21. Elisha went back and took the pair of oxen and slaughtered them; using [the wood] from the ox harness, he boiled the meat and gave it to the people to eat. Then he got up and went after Elijah, and became his apprentice.

20 וַיַּעֲזֹב אֶת־הַבָּקָר וַיָּרָץ אַחֲרֵי אֵלִיָּהוּ וַיֹּאמֶר אֶשְּׁקָה־נָּא לְאָבִי וּלְאִמִּי וְאֵלְכָה אַחֲרֶיךָ וַיֹּאמֶר לוֹ לֵךְ שׁוּב כִּי מֶה־עָשִׂיתִי לָךְ׃

21 וַיָּשָׁב מֵאַחֲרָיו וַיִּקַּח אֶת־צֶמֶד הַבָּקָר וַיִּזְבָּחֵהוּ וּבִכְלִי הַבָּקָר בִּשְּׁלָם הַבָּשָׂר וַיִּתֵּן לָעָם וַיֹּאכֵלוּ וַיָּקָם וַיֵּלֶךְ אַחֲרֵי אֵלִיָּהוּ וַיְשָׁרְתֵהוּ׃

Commentary

20. *"What would I do to you?"* This cryptic remark has been interpreted in various ways. It probably was a colloquialism; Elijah is saying: "I won't stand in your way; go right ahead!"[19]

21. *Ox harness.* A similar use of ox's gear is recorded about David.[20]

Essay

The sound of God

Wind, earthquake, and fire were natural events that, in their grandeur and mystery, were often seen as manifestations of the Divine. The Torah was given at Sinai amid thunderclaps and lightning.

Still, the essence of the Eternal was not to be found in sound and fury; it was to be an expression of their very opposite: the sound of stillness. While linguistically this is an oxymoron, theologically it reflects the inexpressibility of God. Neither Moses nor Elijah could see God's face; that is, they could not see with their eyes what could or should not be seen, for God is, literally, too awesome to behold (one may not even look into the sun with the naked eye).

Yet the Divine can be experienced by the ear, and that comes close to the meaning of Elijah's experience. As we listen, the very stillness may speak to us, and in that stillness God may be heard. It is noteworthy that Judaism's emphasis has always been on our auditory capacity. We say "Hear O Israel," and consider these words as beginning our confession of faith. Only when we hear properly can we continue and say with conviction, "The Eternal is God, the Eternal alone."

None of this denies the possibility of experiencing the Presence in other ways; it does however assign a place of preeminence to quietude and stillness. We pray silently when we want to pray with special fervor, and in so doing we reenact the moment at Horeb when the Prophet heard what has come to be known as "the still, small voice."

Gleanings

קוֹל דְּמָמָה דַקָּה (*kol d'mamah dakkah*), "a still small voice."

Running like a horse

Elijah was clothed with divine strength when he ran before the chariot (18:46).

Targum[21]

The four gates

(In a prayer ascribed to Ezra, God is addressed as the ultimate seat of power.)

You rescued [Jacob's] descendants from Egypt and brought them to Mount Sinai. There You bent the sky, fixed the earth, moved the world, made the depths tremble, and turned creation upside down. Your majesty passed through the four gates of fire and earthquake, wind and frost; and You gave the Torah to the Israelites.

Second Book of Esdras[22]

Analyzing Elijah

(In his despair, the Prophet wants to die and says, "I am no better than my forebears"; 19:5).

Wrestling with himself, balancing this new feeling [that God wants him to keep on living] against the feeling that all his previous efforts have been of no avail, and that to continue to struggle is utterly pointless, he comes to the conclusion that in order to find the answer to the question which is troubling him, he must commune further with God. What better place could there be for such communion than Horeb, the mountain of God, where the great teacher Moses communed for forty days and forty nights and where God stood revealed before all Israel?

Leo L. Honor[23]

An accessible God

The revelation of God in an intelligible communication rather than in the spectacular phenomena described marks an advance in the conception of God as personally accessible and intelligible within the framework of human experience.

John Gray[24]

The four phenomena

God sent wind, earthquake, fire and a still small voice to help Elijah understand human destiny, for these four are the various stages which await us. The wind represents the fleeting nature of life; the earthquake symbolizes the agony of death; the fire burns for us if we descend to Gehinnom; and the still small voice is God's judgment.

Midrash[25]

The still small voice

> Not in levin, not in thunder
> Shall I behold the sign and wonder,
> > But in the still small voice,
> > Let me rejoice.
> Wherefore Thy will is manifest, O Lord,
> Thy will be done.
> > > A. M. Klein[26]

The weariness of the prophet Elijah

> Lord
> You know the weariness of your prophets
> You wake them with a jolt of new hurt
> to place a new desert beneath their feet
> to give them a new mouth a new voice
> and a new name.
> > > A. Kamienska[27]

* * *

Notes

[1] This connection is emphasized by Jacobson, *Chazon Hamikra,* vol. 2, p. 412.

[2] See, for example, Pirke deRabbi Eliezer 44; Numbers Rabbah 21:3.

[3] In the Septuagint, it is called the Third Book of Kings, while I and II Samuel are called I and II Kings.

[4] So Gray, *I and II Kings,* p. 360, who believes that the distance Elijah ran was 17 miles (27 kilometers).

[5] This formula of swearing was also used by Saul (I Samuel 14:44). Note that אלהים (*elohim*) can mean "God" or "gods." In Saul's formulation, *elohim* is followed by a verb form in the singular, for he believed in one God; while Jezebel uses it with a plural verb form, for she believed in many gods.

[6] Jonah 4:8.

[7] It has been suggested that "my forebears" refers to the prophets who preceded him and who had been slaughtered by Jezebel (see I Kings 18:13; haftarah for Ki Tissa). So M. Garsiel, *Olam HaTanach* 10:180 ff.

[8] Exodus 33:21; 34: 5-7; 34:28.

[9] Exodus 33:22.

[10] Genesis 3:9.

[11] I Kings 18:13; haftarah for Ki Tissa.

[12] Exodus 3:6.

[13] Cogan and Tadmor (*Anchor Bible,* II Kings), p. 334. II Kings 8:7-15 relates how he obtained the throne by killing his master.

[14] II Kings 24:2.

[15] II Kings 8: 7-15.

[16] Cogan and Tadmor (*Anchor Bible,* II Kings), plates 6 and 7.

[17] II Kings 9:1-6. Jehu reigned from 849 to 843 B.C.E.

[18] About the magic qualities ascribed to the mantle, see II Kings 2:6-8, 13-15.

[19] Radak considers this passage as a test for Elisha; Slotki (*Soncino Bible*) reads it an elliptic statement: *Go (and do as you suggest, but come) back.*

[20] II Samuel 22:24.

[21] Elaborated by the Midrash (*Mekhilta* Pischa 13:70), Rashi, and Radak.

[22] 3:17-19. An apocryphal work ascribed to Ezra (Esdras), it was composed about the first century C.E.

[23] *Book of Kings 2,* p. 271.

[24] *I and II Kings,* p. 365.

[25] Tanchuma Pekudei 2.

[26] "Rabbi Yom-Tob of Mayence Petitions His God," *Poems,* p. 58.

[27] Translated from the Polish by G. Drabik and D. Curzon, in *Modern Poems on the Bible,* p. 233.

מטות

Jeremiah, chapter 1, verse 1 to chapter 2, verse 3

Introduction

Connection of haftarah and sidra:

There is no connection between the two; rather, this is the first of three haftarot that are usually read between the seventeenth day of Tammuz (when the Babylonians breached the city walls) and the ninth of Av (when they razed the Temple). All three deal with the punishment that will be meted out to a people that forgets the God of the Covenant, and are known to tradition by an Aramaic name, תלת דפרענותא (*t'lat d'fur'anuta*), the "three [haftarot] of affliction."[1]

The setting:

The first three verses give us the where and when of Jeremiah's call to prophecy. Josiah was Judah's king in the last quarter of the 7th century B.C.E., when the struggle between Egypt and Assyria, the two contending superpowers of the Near East, was nearing its climax. The Northern Kingdom (Israel and its capital, Samaria) had already been destroyed and its inhabitants deported. Now it was the turn of the Southern Kingdom (Judah and its capital, Jerusalem) to be in mortal danger—a danger which Jeremiah understood to be due more to spiritual than political failures.

For more on Jeremiah and his time, see our *General Introduction*.

The message:

1. The setting of the divine call to young Jeremiah. (1:1-3)
2. Jeremiah learns about the message he is deliver to the people. He is warned that though his mission will not be without danger, God will sustain him. (1:4-19)
3. The opening verses of the next chapter are not related to the preceding, but are added in order to provide the kind of hopeful message that the Rabbis always arranged for the end of a haftarah. (2:1-3)

HAFTARAH FOR MATOT

Jeremiah, chapter 1, verse 1 to chapter 2, verse 3

1:1. The words of Jeremiah son of Hilkiah, one of the priests of Anatot in the territory of Benjamin.

2. The word of the Eternal came to him in the time of King Josiah son of Amon of Judah, in the thirteenth year of his rule,

3. and during the rule of King Jehoiakim son of Josiah of Judah, and until the end of the eleventh year of the rule of King Zedekiah son of Josiah of Judah, when, in the fifth month, Jerusalem went into exile.

4. The word of the Eternal came to me, saying:

5. Before I formed you in the womb, I knew you;

דִּבְרֵי יִרְמְיָהוּ בֶּן־חִלְקִיָּהוּ מִן־הַכֹּהֲנִים 1:1
אֲשֶׁר בַּעֲנָתוֹת בְּאֶרֶץ בִּנְיָמִן:

2 אֲשֶׁר הָיָה דְבַר־יְהוָה אֵלָיו בִּימֵי יֹאשִׁיָּהוּ
בֶן־אָמוֹן מֶלֶךְ יְהוּדָה בִּשְׁלֹשׁ־עֶשְׂרֵה שָׁנָה
לְמָלְכוֹ:

3 וַיְהִי בִּימֵי יְהוֹיָקִים בֶּן־יֹאשִׁיָּהוּ מֶלֶךְ
יְהוּדָה עַד־תֹּם עַשְׁתֵּי עֶשְׂרֵה שָׁנָה לְצִדְקִיָּהוּ
בֶן־יֹאשִׁיָּהוּ מֶלֶךְ יְהוּדָה עַד־גְּלוֹת יְרוּשָׁלַ͏ִם
בַּחֹדֶשׁ הַחֲמִישִׁי:

4 וַיְהִי דְבַר־יְהוָה אֵלַי לֵאמֹר:

5 בְּטֶרֶם אֶצּוֹרְךָ [אֶצָּרְךָ] בַבֶּטֶן יְדַעְתִּיךָ

Commentary

1:1. *The words.* דברי (*divrei,* singular *davar*) can mean "words" or "matters." The book of Jeremiah contains not only the sayings of the Prophet but also the story of his times and of his life.[2]

Hilkiah. Not the high priest by that name who lived in Jerusalem, but one who seems to have belonged to a priestly clan that, three hundred years earlier, had opposed the accession of King Solomon to the throne and had been banished to Anatot.[3] Thus it is likely that Jeremiah was raised in an environment that habitually took a critical view of the government.

3. *Josiah.* He became king in 637 B.C.E., so that Jeremiah's call came to him in 625/624. Since he remonstrated with God and claimed to be unprepared because of his youth (verse 6), he was probably born about the year 640.

In the fifth month. The month of Av, after the Temple had been destroyed by the Babylonians, on the ninth day (Tisha b'Av).

5. *Before I formed you.* Jeremiah was thus predestined to be a spokesman for God (see further below). The Second Isaiah spoke of himself in like fashion: "The Eternal called me while I was yet in the womb."[4]

before you were born, I set you apart;

I have appointed you a prophet to the
   nations.

6. And I said:

O! Eternal God:

I do not know how to speak;

for I am only a youth.

7. The Eternal One said to me:

Do not say I am only a youth,

for wherever I send you, you must go,

and whatever I command you, you must
   speak.

8. Have no fear of them,

for I am with you to keep you safe,

says the Eternal One.

9. The Eternal then reached out and
   touched my mouth,

and (the Eternal) said to me:

Behold, I have put My words in your
   mouth!

10. See, I have appointed you this day

[to speak] to nations and kingdoms,

to uproot, to pull down,

to destroy, to root out,

[but also] to build and to plant.

וּבְטֶרֶם תֵּצֵא מֵרֶחֶם הִקְדַּשְׁתִּיךָ
נָבִיא לַגּוֹיִם נְתַתִּיךָ:
6 וָאֹמַר
אֲהָהּ אֲדֹנָי יְהֹוִה
הִנֵּה לֹא־יָדַעְתִּי דַּבֵּר
כִּי־נַעַר אָנֹכִי:
7 וַיֹּאמֶר יְהֹוָה אֵלַי
אַל־תֹּאמַר נַעַר אָנֹכִי
כִּי עַל־כָּל־אֲשֶׁר אֶשְׁלָחֲךָ תֵּלֵךְ
וְאֵת כָּל־אֲשֶׁר אֲצַוְּךָ תְּדַבֵּר:
8 אַל־תִּירָא מִפְּנֵיהֶם
כִּי־אִתְּךָ אֲנִי לְהַצִּלֶךָ
נְאֻם־יְהֹוָה:
9 וַיִּשְׁלַח יְהֹוָה אֶת־יָדוֹ וַיַּגַּע עַל־פִּי
וַיֹּאמֶר יְהֹוָה אֵלַי
הִנֵּה נָתַתִּי דְבָרַי בְּפִיךָ:
10 רְאֵה הִפְקַדְתִּיךָ הַיּוֹם הַזֶּה
עַל־הַגּוֹיִם וְעַל־הַמַּמְלָכוֹת
לִנְתוֹשׁ וְלִנְתוֹץ
וּלְהַאֲבִיד וְלַהֲרוֹס
לִבְנוֹת וְלִנְטוֹעַ:

Commentary

I set you apart. This is the original meaning of the root קדש (*k-d-sh*), which also signifies consecration and holiness. (Terms like Kaddish and Kiddush are derived from it.)

Prophet to the nations. Not only did Jeremiah's preaching often have a universal thrust, but beginning with chapter 46 he addresses the gentiles directly.[5]

6. *I am only a youth.* נער (*na'ar*). The word can mean child or boy, but also youth, which is the more likely understanding here.[6] Rashi compares Jeremiah's hesitation with the protestation of Moses to God's challenge: "Please, O Eternal, I have never been a man of words .... I am slow of speech and slow of tongue."[7]

8. *Keep you safe.* Literally, to rescue you.

9. *Touched my mouth.* Similar to the way a seraph touched Isaiah's mouth.[8]

11. And the word of the Eternal came to
me saying:
What do you see, Jeremiah?
And I said: I see the branch of an almond
tree.
12. The Eternal then said to me:
You see well; I am like an almoner
[dispensing] My word to be fulfilled.
13. The word of the Eternal came to me a
second time:
What do you see?
And said
I see a boiling pot whose face
is tipped away from the north.
14. And the Eternal One said to me:
Out of the north shall disaster break forth
over all the people of the land.
15. I am calling all the kings of the north
(says the Eternal One); each one will set
up his throne facing the gates of Jerusalem,
and all its surrounding walls, and all the
cities of Judah.
16. I will deliver My verdict against them
for all their evil deeds, for they have
forsaken Me, and have sacrificed to other
gods, and prostrated themselves before the
work of their own hands.

11 וַיְהִ֤י דְבַר־יְהוָה֙ אֵלַ֣י לֵאמֹ֔ר

מָה־אַתָּ֥ה רֹאֶ֖ה יִרְמְיָ֑הוּ

וָאֹמַ֕ר מַקֵּ֥ל

שָׁקֵ֖ד אֲנִ֥י רֹאֶֽה׃

12 וַיֹּ֧אמֶר יְהוָ֛ה אֵלַ֖י

הֵיטַ֣בְתָּ לִרְא֑וֹת כִּֽי־שֹׁקֵ֥ד אֲנִ֛י

עַל־דְּבָרִ֖י לַעֲשֹׂתֽוֹ׃

13 וַיְהִ֨י דְבַר־יְהוָ֤ה אֵלַי֙ שֵׁנִ֣ית לֵאמֹ֔ר

מָ֥ה אַתָּ֖ה רֹאֶ֑ה

וָאֹמַ֗ר סִ֤יר נָפ֙וּחַ֙ אֲנִ֣י רֹאֶ֔ה

וּפָנָ֖יו מִפְּנֵ֥י צָפֽוֹנָה׃

14 וַיֹּ֥אמֶר יְהוָ֖ה אֵלָ֑י

מִצָּפוֹן֙ תִּפָּתַ֣ח הָרָעָ֔ה

עַ֥ל כָּל־יֹשְׁבֵ֖י הָאָֽרֶץ׃

15 כִּ֣י הִנְנִ֣י קֹרֵ֗א לְכָֽל־מִשְׁפְּח֛וֹת מַמְלְכ֥וֹת

צָפ֖וֹנָה נְאֻם־יְהוָ֑ה וּבָ֡אוּ וְֽנָתְנוּ֩ אִ֨ישׁ כִּסְא֜וֹ פֶּ֣תַח

שַׁעֲרֵ֣י יְרוּשָׁלִַ֗ם וְעַ֤ל כָּל־חוֹמֹתֶ֙יהָ֙ סָבִ֔יב וְעַ֖ל

כָּל־עָרֵ֥י יְהוּדָֽה׃

16 וְדִבַּרְתִּ֤י מִשְׁפָּטַי֙ אוֹתָ֔ם עַ֖ל כָּל־רָעָתָ֑ם

אֲשֶׁ֣ר עֲזָב֗וּנִי וַֽיְקַטְּרוּ֙ לֵֽאלֹהִ֣ים אֲחֵרִ֔ים

וַיִּֽשְׁתַּחֲו֖וּ לְמַעֲשֵׂ֥י יְדֵיהֶֽם׃

Commentary

11. *Almond tree.* שקד (*shakéd*), a harbinger of spring.

12. *Like an almoner.* שקד (*shokéd*). Our translation has imitated the Hebrew wordplay *shakéd/shokéd* by rendering it almond/almoner. (More precisely, *shokéd* means to be wakeful or watchful.)

14. *Out of the north.* See our comment on Jeremiah 46:25 (haftarah for Bo).

15. *Each one will set up his throne.* The probable meaning is: By coming from everywhere to assemble before the gates of Jerusalem, they will emphasize the importance of God's judgment on the city.

16. *Against them.* Against Judah and Jerusalem.

17. So you, gird your loins, get up and speak to them all that I have commanded you. Do not lose your nerve because of them, or *I* will unnerve you before them!

18. I am making you this day a fortified city, an iron pillar, and [like] bronze walls against the whole land, against the kings of Judah, against its leaders, priests, and people of the land.

19. They shall attack you, but they shall not overcome you, for I am with you to keep you safe, says the Eternal One.

2:1. The word of the Eternal came to me, saying:

2. Go, cry out to the people of Jerusalem, saying:

Thus says the Eternal One:

I remember the devotion

of your youth,

your love as a bride,

how you followed Me in the wilderness

in a land not sown.

17 וְאַתָּה תֶּאְזֹר מָתְנֶיךָ וְקַמְתָּ וְדִבַּרְתָּ אֲלֵיהֶם אֵת כָּל־אֲשֶׁר אָנֹכִי אֲצַוֶּךָ אַל־תֵּחַת מִפְּנֵיהֶם פֶּן־אֲחִתְּךָ לִפְנֵיהֶם:

18 וַאֲנִי הִנֵּה נְתַתִּיךָ הַיּוֹם לְעִיר מִבְצָר וּלְעַמּוּד בַּרְזֶל וּלְחֹמוֹת נְחֹשֶׁת עַל־כָּל־הָאָרֶץ לְמַלְכֵי יְהוּדָה לְשָׂרֶיהָ לְכֹהֲנֶיהָ וּלְעַם הָאָרֶץ:

19 וְנִלְחֲמוּ אֵלֶיךָ וְלֹא־יוּכְלוּ לָךְ כִּי־אִתְּךָ אֲנִי נְאֻם־יְהוָה לְהַצִּילֶךָ:

2:1 וַיְהִי דְבַר־יְהוָה אֵלַי לֵאמֹר:

2 הָלֹךְ וְקָרָאתָ בְאָזְנֵי יְרוּשָׁלַ͏ִם לֵאמֹר

כֹּה אָמַר יְהוָה

זָכַרְתִּי לָךְ חֶסֶד נְעוּרַיִךְ

אַהֲבַת כְּלוּלֹתָיִךְ

לֶכְתֵּךְ אַחֲרַי בַּמִּדְבָּר

בְּאֶרֶץ לֹא זְרוּעָה:

Commentary

18. *Bronze walls.* An ancient figure of protection.[9]

People of the land. In the Bible עם הארץ (*am ha-aretz*) can mean "landholder" of high or low rank; it gradually came to mean "unlettered," much like in English, where "peasant" came to signify an unsophisticated person.

2:2. *Devotion of your youth.* Jeremiah's image of Israel having been faithful in the desert contrasts with the Torah's emphasis on Israel's faithlessness.

411

3. [For] Israel is holy to the Eternal,

the first fruit of God's harvest.

All who eat it shall bear their guilt;

ill shall befall them,

says the Eternal One.

3 קֹדֶשׁ יִשְׂרָאֵל לַיהוָה

רֵאשִׁית תְּבוּאָתֹה

כָּל־אֹכְלָיו יֶאְשָׁמוּ

רָעָה תָּבֹא אֲלֵיהֶם

נְאֻם־יְהוָה:

Commentary

2:3. *Shall bear their guilt.* Israel is "the first fruit of humanity,"[10] and is compared to the first harvest of the farmer who may not consume all of it but must set aside a portion for God's Temple. Thus a nation that would try to "consume" Israel and destroy it utterly would trespass on God's privilege. Though God may summon such a nation to punish Israel, the agent of divine judgment will itself be punished if it will attempt to annihilate God's people.

Ill shall befall them. Isaac had blessed his son Jacob with this prediction: "Those who will curse you will themselves be cursed ...."[11]

Essay

"Before you were born..."(1:5)

The idea that a person like Jeremiah had his destiny determined even before he was born is troublesome. Are we not the masters of our own fate; don't we ourselves determine how we live and shape our years?

Our tradition was ambivalent on this subject. A midrash says that already in Adam's time, that is, at the beginning of human existence, God had shown him the future leaders of the world—among them Jeremiah.[12] In later centuries such a concept was called predestination: whatever happens is already determined by God. This became an important view in the Christian theology of divine grace, which played a minor role in Judaism.

It held, rather, that all people have the capacity to fashion their own fate, though God already knows what decisions they will reach. Thus, God knew that Abraham's descendants would some day be enslaved; still, Pharaoh and his counselors had the freedom to decide otherwise. God did not influence them, yet—knowing them in every respect—knew what they would do.[13]

But how can it be said that, even before he was born, Jeremiah was destined to be a prophet?

Medieval philosophers understood that human beings come into the world with certain propensities, but what use they will make of them is their own doing.[14] We today can back this insight with scientific proof: we are born with a certain genetic structure that puts our existence into a fairly predetermined framework. We enter the world as males or females and inherit some (but not all) physiological and psychological traits from our parents; we may be afflicted with or prone to certain illnesses or, on the contrary, enjoy the likelihood of good health and longevity. We are apparently endowed with a certain IQ and have, say, a propensity for music. Withal, what we do with these inborn capacities is, to a significant degree, up to us. This capability we call free will, and biblical teaching is squarely based on its crucial role.

Some of us exploit our possibilities, and others waste them. There is much in us we cannot change, but there is enough freedom to make something of the potential we have. Judaism accords the teaching of free will a central place, while Islam lays greater weight on the factor of predetermination. Christianity has generally followed Judaism in this debate, although some of its branches have not.[15]

The call to Jeremiah may thus be seen to express both predetermination and freedom: the child was born with particular gifts and a high degree of religious sensitivity. But giving his life to a pursuit of the divine call—with all its rewards, difficulties and dangers—was a decision that Jeremiah had to make for himself. The possibilities of prophecy may therefore be said to have been a divine gift; while being and living as a prophet were his own choice.

Gleanings

Words to Remember

Before I formed you in the womb, I knew you;
before you were born, I set you apart. (1:5)
I remember the devotion
of your youth,
your love as a bride,
how you followed Me in the wilderness
in a land not sown. (2:2)
Israel is holy to the Eternal,
the first fruit of God's harvest. (2:3)

Prophet to the nations (1:5)

The Prophets spoke to the Hebrews but their thought took the nations, which they knew, individually and all mankind collectively within its purview. Israel was the centre of their world, but the whole world was their concern as it was the concern of the One God. The prophecies in nearly all the books of the Prophets about, or to, the nations show that they interpreted with a universal scope their mission to spread the knowledge of God and the divine law.

Israel I. Mattuck[16]

First fruits

(It says in 2:3: "Israel is ... the first fruit of God's harvest. All who eat it shall bear their guilt.")

In a special sense, Israel is dedicated to God, just as the first fruits belonged to the priests as God's representatives .... As the first fruits of a field are sacred, so is Israel, "the first fruits of humanity," sacred to God.

Harry Freedman[17]

"Ill shall befall them" (2:3)

The story of European history during the past centuries teaches one uniform lesson: that the nations which have received and in any way dealt fairly and mercifully with the Jew have prospered; and that the nations that have tortured and oppressed him have written out their own curse.

Olive Schreiner[18]

* * *

Notes

[1] Some translate as "retribution," and others as "rebuke." The Raban (Abraham ben Nathan of Lunel, 12th century) said: "From the sidra *B'reishit* until the 17th of Tammuz, the haftarot allude to their respective Torah portions; thereafter, the calendar dates take over." (*Sefer Hamanhig*, Hilchot Ta'anit, # 16.) Thus, the seven weeks after Tisha b'Av feature seven haftarot of consolation.

[2] See Radak.

[3] I Kings 2:26 ff. Thus Luzzato, opposing Radak who identified Hilkiah with the high priest.

[4] Isaiah 49:1. Kings of Mesopotamia and Egypt also claimed this distinction; see W. Holladay, *Jeremiah 1*, p. 28.

[5] Similarly Malbim; Rashi explains it differently: Jeremiah was to preach to his own people who were acting like other nations (*goyim*).

[6] As in Genesis 14:24; 34:19.

[7] Exodus 4:10.

[8] Isaiah 6:7; haftarah for Yitro.

[9] In a text from Egypt almost a millennium before Jeremiah; see Alt, cited in McKane, *Jeremiah*, vol. *1*, p. 22.

[10] So Philo.

[11] Genesis 27:29.

[12] B. Sanhedrin 38b. Rashi follows this explanation without questioning it.

[13] This is pithily expressed by the saying of R. Akiba: הכל צפוי והרשות נתונה "All is foreseen, yet freedom of choice is given" (*Mishnah*, Pirke Avot 3:15; in prayer books it appears as 3:19). This may be called a form of determinism (as distinct from predestination), for God knows everything there is to be known and therefore perceives the course of events as a logical consequence. In Omar Khayyam's formulation: "And the first morning of Creation wrote / What the last Dawn of Reckoning shall read."

[14] So the Rambam, whom Radak cites on this passage.

[15] Presbyterians, for example, have stressed the theology of predestination.

[16] *The Thought of the Prophets*, p. 33.

[17] Comment on the passage in the *Soncino Bible Commentary*.

[18] Cited by Freedman in the *Soncino Bible Commentary*.

מסעי

Jeremiah, chapter 2, verses 4 to 28 and chapter 3, verse 4

Introduction

Connection of haftarah and sidra:

There is no connection between the two; rather, this is the second of three haftarot that are usually read between the seventeenth day of Tammuz (when the Babylonians breached the city walls) and the ninth of Av (when they razed the Temple). All three deal with the punishment that will be meted out to a people that forgets the God of the Covenant, and are known to tradition by an Aramaic name, תלת דפרענותא (*t'lat d'fur'anuta*), the "three [haftarot] of affliction."[1]

The setting:

Josiah was king of Judah in the last quarter of the 7th century B.C.E., when the struggle between Egypt and Assyria, the two contending superpowers of the Near East, was nearing its climax. The Northern Kingdom (Israel and its capital, Samaria) had already been destroyed and its inhabitants deported. Now it was the turn of the Southern Kingdom (Judah and its capital, Jerusalem) to be in mortal danger—a danger that Jeremiah understood to be due more to spiritual than political failures.

We cannot tell at what stage of his life the Prophet delivered these warnings. Many scholars believe that it was during the earlier part of his ministry, at a time when he became disenchanted with the effectiveness of Josiah's reforms.

For more on Jeremiah and his time, see our *General Introduction.*

The message:

1. A historical prelude. (2:4-8)
2. An exposition of Israel's idolatry by comparing it to other nations. (2:9-13)
3. Current and future events will bear out the Prophet's warnings. (2:14-19)
4. Metaphors to illustrate the message. (2:20-28)
5. Conclusion. In the Ashkenazic rite, a one-sentence upbeat message is added, which is unconnected to the main text. (3:4) In the Sephardic rite, two verses from chapter 4 are appended. The Rabbis never wanted to dismiss the congregation on a pessimistic note. (4:1-2)

HAFTARAH FOR MAS'EI

Jeremiah, chapter 2, verses 4 to 28 and chapter 3, verse 4

2:4 שִׁמְע֥וּ דְבַר־יְהֹוָ֖ה בֵּ֣ית יַעֲקֹ֑ב
וְכׇל־מִשְׁפְּח֖וֹת בֵּ֥ית יִשְׂרָאֵֽל׃

5 כֹּ֣ה ׀ אָמַ֣ר יְהֹוָ֗ה
מַה־מָּצְא֨וּ אֲבוֹתֵיכֶ֥ם בִּי֙ עָ֔וֶל
כִּ֥י רָחֲק֖וּ מֵעָלָ֑י
וַיֵּ֛לְכ֥וּ אַחֲרֵ֥י הַהֶ֖בֶל
וַיֶּהְבָּֽלוּ׃

6 וְלֹ֣א אָמְר֔וּ
אַיֵּ֣ה יְהֹוָ֔ה
הַמַּעֲלֶ֥ה אֹתָ֖נוּ מֵאֶ֣רֶץ מִצְרָ֑יִם
הַמּוֹלִ֨יךְ אֹתָ֜נוּ בַּמִּדְבָּ֗ר
בְּאֶ֨רֶץ עֲרָבָ֤ה וְשׁוּחָה֙
בְּאֶ֨רֶץ צִיָּ֣ה וְצַלְמָ֔וֶת
בְּאֶ֗רֶץ לֹא־עָ֤בַר בָּהּ֙ אִ֔ישׁ
וְלֹא־יָשַׁ֥ב אָדָ֖ם שָֽׁם׃

7 וָאָבִ֤יא אֶתְכֶם֙ אֶל־אֶ֣רֶץ הַכַּרְמֶ֔ל
לֶאֱכֹ֥ל פִּרְיָ֖הּ וְטוּבָ֑הּ

2:4. Hear the word of the Eternal, O House
of Jacob
and all the clans of the House of Israel.

5. Thus says the Eternal One:
What wrong did your ancestors find in Me,
that they moved away from Me,
and went after empty things
and themselves became empty?

6. They never said:
Where is the Eternal,
who brought us up from the land of Egypt,
who led us in the wilderness,
a land of desert and pits,
a land of drought and darkness,
a land that none had crossed,
where no one had lived?

7. I brought you to a fruitful land
to enjoy its bountiful fruit;

Commentary

The haftarah presents considerable linguistic difficulties, and the meaning of the text is frequently uncertain.

2:5. *Themselves became empty.* Psalm 115:8 uses the same image: "... all who trust in them [the idols] shall become like them."[2]

6. *Darkness.* The word צלמות (*tzalmavet*) is familiar from the 23rd Psalm (verse 4), where it is usually rendered as "shadow of death," in accordance with its presumed components, צל and מות. However, it derives from an ancient Semitic root *tz-l-m*, which means "blackness" and conveys the sense of total darkness.[3]

7. *Fruitful land.* Literally, "Carmel-land." The area of Mount Carmel features lush growth; the name itself comes from *kerem*, vineyard.[4]

but you came and defiled My land;

you turned My heritage into an abomination.

8. And the priests did not say:

Where is the Eternal?

Those who should take hold of the Torah

did not know Me;

the [secular] rulers rebelled against Me,

[like] the prophets who prophesied in the
name of Baal

and followed things that have no use.

9. Therefore I will go on accusing you,

says the Eternal One,

and I will accuse your children's children!

10. Cross over to Cyprus and see,

send to Kedar and consider well:

see—was there ever the like?

וַתָּבֹ֙אוּ֙ וַתְּטַמְּא֣וּ אֶת־אַרְצִ֔י

וְנַחֲלָתִ֥י שַׂמְתֶּ֖ם לְתוֹעֵבָֽה׃

8 הַכֹּהֲנִ֗ים לֹ֤א אָֽמְרוּ֙

אַיֵּ֣ה יְהֹוָ֔ה

וְתֹפְשֵׂ֤י הַתּוֹרָה֙ לֹ֣א יְדָע֔וּנִי

וְהָרֹעִ֖ים פָּ֣שְׁעוּ בִ֑י

וְהַנְּבִיאִים֙ נִבְּא֣וּ בַבַּ֔עַל

וְאַחֲרֵ֥י לֹֽא־יוֹעִ֖לוּ הָלָֽכוּ׃

9 לָכֵ֗ן עֹ֛ד אָרִ֥יב אִתְּכֶ֖ם

נְאֻם־יְהֹוָ֑ה

וְאֶת־בְּנֵ֥י בְנֵיכֶ֖ם אָרִֽיב׃

10 כִּ֣י עִבְר֞וּ אִיֵּ֤י כִתִּיִּים֙ וּרְא֔וּ

וְקֵדָ֛ר שִׁלְח֥וּ וְהִתְבּוֹנְנ֖וּ מְאֹ֑ד

וּרְא֕וּ הֵ֥ן הָֽיְתָ֖ה כָּזֹֽאת׃

Commentary

My land. It belongs to God and is given to Israel in trust.

Defiled … abomination. Cultic terms that bespeak Jeremiah's own family tradition and lead naturally into the next verse, in which faithless priests are the first target of the Prophet's ire.

8. *Rulers.* Literally, "shepherds."

Prophesied in the name of Baal. As they did in Elijah's time.[5]

Things that have no use. The followers of Baal are like empty bowls—see the image evoked in verse 4.

10. *Cyprus.* Literally, "isles of the Kittites," a name derived from the city-state Kition (today's Lanarka) on Cyprus.

Kedar. A son of Ishmael (considered the father of the Arabs).[6] Kedar stands here for Arabia in general.

11. Has a nation ever exchanged its gods,

even though they were unreal gods?

Yet My people has exchanged its glory

for what has no use!

12. You heavens, shake with horror at this,

bristle with horror, be stunned! says the
      Eternal One.

13. For My people have done a double
      wrong:

they have forsaken *Me*,

the Fountain of Living Waters,

and have hewn for themselves cisterns,

cracked cisterns that cannot hold water.

14. Is Israel a slave,

a homeborn serf,

[If not,] why has he become a prey

15. over which lions roar,

growling aloud,

11 הַהֵימִיר גּוֹי אֱלֹהִים

וְהֵמָּה לֹא אֱלֹהִים

וְעַמִּי הֵמִיר כְּבוֹדוֹ

בְּלוֹא יוֹעִיל:

12 שֹׁמּוּ שָׁמַיִם עַל־זֹאת

וְשַׂעֲרוּ חָרְבוּ מְאֹד נְאֻם־יְהוָה:

13 כִּי־שְׁתַּיִם רָעוֹת עָשָׂה עַמִּי

אֹתִי עָזְבוּ

מְקוֹר מַיִם חַיִּים

לַחְצֹב לָהֶם בֹּארוֹת

בֹּארֹת נִשְׁבָּרִים אֲשֶׁר לֹא־יָכִלוּ הַמָּיִם:

14 הַעֶבֶד יִשְׂרָאֵל

אִם־יְלִיד בַּיִת הוּא

מַדּוּעַ הָיָה לָבַז:

15 עָלָיו יִשְׁאֲגוּ כְפִרִים

נָתְנוּ קוֹלָם

Commentary

11. *Has a nation ever exchanged its gods...?* Though pagan nations had good reason to forsake their useless idols, they did not do so out of loyalty and respect for their forebears—how much more so, then, should Israel cherish its Sovereign. Yet "they forgot the God who saved them."[7] Logic is stood on its head: pagans are loyal to what is useless and even harmful, while Israel's God is the only Reality, yet is abandoned by a faithless people.

13. *Fountain of Living Waters.* A metaphor for the Eternal; sometimes also used for Torah. The metaphor has a special thrust: you exchange fresh water (for which you don't have to labor) for broken vessels, which demand your effort (literally, "quarrying") but can't hold a even a drop of water. (Ironically, the Prophet's courage landed him in a muddy cistern, where he was cast by his enemies and almost met his death.[8])

14. *Is Israel a slave?* The metaphor changes and "Israel is described as if it was a child of a slave whom nobody cares about, wandering around to Egypt or to Assyria, looking hopelessly for help."[9] "Slave" and "homeborn serf" describe two technically different types of servitude.

15. *Lions.* Foreign nations; but it is not clear precisely who is meant. (Assyria and Egypt are named in verse 18.)

making the land desolate,

their towns unpeopled ruins.

16. The people of Memphis and Tahpan-
    hes will break your head;

17. Did you not bring this on yourselves
    by forsaking the Eternal your God,
    while God led you on your way?

18. Now, then: What good will it do you to
    go to Egypt
    to drink the waters of the Nile?
    And what good will it do you to go to
    Assyria
    to drink the waters of the Euphrates?

19. Your own wickedness rebukes you,

and your betrayals reprove you.

Know and see how bad it is, and bitter,

to forsake the Eternal your God,

to hold Me in awe no more,

says the Eternal One, God of heaven's
    hosts.

20. For long ago I broke your yoke,

shattered your bonds,

וַיָּשִׁ֤יתוּ אַרְצוֹ֙ לְשַׁמָּ֔ה

עָרָ֛יו נִצְּתָ֥ה [נִצְּת֖וּ] מִבְּלִ֥י יֹשֵֽׁב׃

16 גַּם־בְּנֵי־נֹ֖ף וְתַחְפְּנֵ֑ס [וְתַחְפַּנְחֵ֑ס] יִרְע֖וּךְ

קָדְקֹֽד׃

17 הֲלוֹא־זֹ֖את תַּעֲשֶׂה־לָּ֑ךְ

עׇזְבֵךְ֙ אֶת־יְהֹוָ֣ה אֱלֹהַ֔יִךְ

בְּעֵ֖ת מוֹלִיכֵ֥ךְ בַּדָּֽרֶךְ׃

18 וְעַתָּ֗ה מַה־לָּךְ֙ לְדֶ֣רֶךְ מִצְרַ֔יִם

לִשְׁתּ֖וֹת מֵ֣י שִׁח֑וֹר

וּמַה־לָּךְ֙ לְדֶ֣רֶךְ אַשּׁ֔וּר

לִשְׁתּ֖וֹת מֵ֥י נָהָֽר׃

19 תְּיַסְּרֵ֣ךְ רָעָתֵ֗ךְ

וּמְשֻׁבוֹתַ֙יִךְ֙ תּוֹכִחֻ֔ךְ

וּדְעִ֤י וּרְאִי֙ כִּי־רַ֣ע וָמָ֔ר

עׇזְבֵ֖ךְ אֶת־יְהֹוָ֣ה אֱלֹהָ֑יִךְ

וְלֹ֤א פַחְדָּתִי֙ אֵלַ֔יִךְ

נְאֻם־אֲדֹנָ֥י יְהֹוִ֖ה צְבָאֽוֹת׃

20 כִּ֣י מֵעוֹלָ֞ם שָׁבַ֣רְתִּי עֻלֵּ֗ךְ

נִתַּ֙קְתִּי֙ מוֹסְרֹתַ֔יִךְ

Commentary

16. *Memphis and Tahpanhes.* Memphis (Hebrew *Nof*) was the capital of ancient Egypt, and Tahpanhes (called Daphne by the Greeks) a fortified town that guarded eastern approaches to the country. The Prophet speaks of these cities also in 46:14; see the haftarah for *Bo.*

Break your head. A speculative rendering.

18. *Egypt … Assyria.* Trust in political alliances is not only useless, it is tantamount to idolatry. [10]

Nile. שחור (*shichor*) is not the usual biblical term for Nile. Egyptologists see it as meaning "waters of Horus" (the god with the body of a man and the head of a falcon). Neither Nile nor Euphrates is a "fountain of living waters."

and you said: I will not transgress;

yet now on every high hill,

under every leafy tree

you lie sprawling as a harlot.

21. I planted you a choice vine

with the right kind of seed;

how putrid you have become,

so strange a vine!

22. Though you wash yourself with lye,

and use more and more soap,

the stain of your guilt remains before Me,

says the Eternal God.

23. How can you say: I am not defiled,

I have not gone after the Baalim?

Look at your way into the Valley,

וַתֹּאמְרִי לֹא אֶעֱבֹד [אֶעֱבוֹר]

כִּי עַל־כָּל־גִּבְעָה גְּבֹהָה

וְתַחַת כָּל־עֵץ רַעֲנָן

אַתְּ צֹעָה זֹנָה:

21 וְאָנֹכִי נְטַעְתִּיךְ שֹׂרֵק

כֻּלֹּה זֶרַע אֱמֶת

וְאֵיךְ נֶהְפַּכְתְּ לִי

סוּרֵי הַגֶּפֶן נָכְרִיָּה:

22 כִּי אִם־תְּכַבְּסִי בַּנֶּתֶר

וְתַרְבִּי־לָךְ בֹּרִית

נִכְתָּם עֲוֹנֵךְ לְפָנַי

נְאֻם אֲדֹנָי יְהוִה:

23 אֵיךְ תֹּאמְרִי לֹא נִטְמֵאתִי

אַחֲרֵי הַבְּעָלִים לֹא הָלַכְתִּי

רְאִי דַרְכֵּךְ בַּגַּיְא

Commentary

20. *Sprawling as a harlot*. Contradicting her status as God's bride.

21. *How putrid you have become*. Our translation contracts three Hebrew words into two, and realigns the masoretic division. Instead of לִי, סוּרֵי הַגֶּפֶן (*lee, surei ha-gefen*), we read לסוריה גפן (*l'soriyyah gefen*).[11]

22. *Lye*. נתר (*neter*), probably related to the Akkadian *nitiru;* the English natron, niter, and nitrate are of the same root.[12]

The stain of your guilt remains. A related image appears in Jeremiah 13:23: "Can the Ethiopian change his skin, or the leopard his spots?"

23. *Your way into the Valley*. The Valley of Ben-Hinnom, where children were sacrificed.[13] Note that the Prophet finds it necessary to emphasize that this practice has nothing to do with the Eternal, which suggests that there were Israelites who did indeed hold such beliefs.

know what you have done:

You are a young camel

running wild;

24. a wild ass used to the desert,

eagerly snuffing the breeze,

—at rutting time who can restrain her?

Those who are after her never grow tired,

in her [mating] season they'll easily find
her.

25. Keep your feet from going bare,

and your throat from thirst!

But it's no use, you say;

I have loved strange [gods],

and after them I must go.

26. Like a thief found out and disgraced,

so is the House of Israel disgraced—

all of them—their kings and leaders,

their priests and prophets:

27. all who call wood *My Father,*

and say to stone: *You gave birth to me.*

And they turn their backs to Me, not their
faces.

Then in their hour of trouble they say:

Rise up and save us!

דְּעִי מֶה עָשִׂית
בִּכְרָה קַלָּה
מְשָׂרֶכֶת דְּרָכֶיהָ:

24 פֶּרֶה לִמֻּד מִדְבָּר
בְּאַוַּת נַפְשׁוֹ [נַפְשָׁהּ] שָׁאֲפָה רוּחַ
תַּאֲנָתָהּ מִי יְשִׁיבֶנָּה
כָּל־מְבַקְשֶׁיהָ לֹא יִיעָפוּ
בְּחָדְשָׁהּ יִמְצָאוּנְהָ:

25 מִנְעִי רַגְלֵךְ מִיָּחֵף
וּגְורֹנֵךְ [וּגְרוֹנֵךְ] מִצִּמְאָה
וַתֹּאמְרִי נוֹאָשׁ לוֹא
כִּי־אָהַבְתִּי זָרִים
וְאַחֲרֵיהֶם אֵלֵךְ:

26 כְּבֹשֶׁת גַּנָּב כִּי יִמָּצֵא
כֵּן הֹבִישׁוּ בֵּית יִשְׂרָאֵל
הֵמָּה מַלְכֵיהֶם שָׂרֵיהֶם
וְכֹהֲנֵיהֶם וּנְבִיאֵיהֶם:

27 אֹמְרִים לָעֵץ אָבִי אַתָּה
וְלָאֶבֶן אַתְּ יְלִדְתָּנִי [יְלִדְתָּנוּ]
כִּי־פָנוּ אֵלַי עֹרֶף וְלֹא פָנִים
וּבְעֵת רָעָתָם יֹאמְרוּ
קוּמָה וְהוֹשִׁיעֵנוּ:

Commentary

25. *Keep your feet from going bare.* As if you were a young camel or wild ass. The phrase can also be read as a metaphor for spiritual poverty. Tradition took this to stand for the consequence of practicing idolatry: if you persist in it you will suffer exile and wander about without footwear or water.[14]

27. *Their backs.* Literally, "their necks."

28. And where are your gods that you have
made for yourselves?

Let them rise up and save you, in your
hour of trouble!

Judah, you have as many gods as you have
towns!

3:4. And yet not long ago you cried out to
Me:

My Father, Friend of my youth!

וְאַיֵּה אֱלֹהֶ֙יךָ֙ אֲשֶׁ֣ר עָשִׂ֣יתָ לָּ֔ךְ 28

יָק֕וּמוּ אִם־יוֹשִׁיע֖וּךָ בְּעֵ֣ת רָעָתֶ֑ךָ

כִּ֚י מִסְפַּ֣ר עָרֶ֔יךָ הָי֥וּ אֱלֹהֶ֖יךָ יְהוּדָֽה:

הֲל֣וֹא מֵעַ֔תָּה קָרָ֥אתי [קָרָ֖את] לִ֑י 3:4

אָבִ֕י אַלּ֥וּף נְעֻרַ֖י אָֽתָּה:

Commentary

28. *As many gods as towns*. Likely a piece of prophetic rhetoric.

The Sephardim do not add 3:4 but add instead 4:1-2

4:1. The Eternal One says:

If you return, O Israel,

if you return to Me

and remove your abominations from before
  Me,

and do not go astray,

2. and if you swear by the living God

in truth, justice, and righteousness,

then nations shall find blessing in you,

and glory in you.

אִם־תָּשׁוּב יִשְׂרָאֵל 4:1

נְאֻם־יְהֹוָה

אֵלַי תָּשׁוּב

וְאִם־תָּסִיר שִׁקּוּצֶיךָ מִפָּנַי

וְלֹא תָנוּד:

וְנִשְׁבַּעְתָּ חַי־יְהֹוָה 2

בֶּאֱמֶת בְּמִשְׁפָּט וּבִצְדָקָה

וְהִתְבָּרְכוּ בוֹ גּוֹיִם

וּבוֹ יִתְהַלָּלוּ:

Commentary

2. By the living God. Literally, "as the Eternal lives" or "by the life of the Eternal."

Essay

Who is to blame for our suffering?

The terrible destruction that the haftarah foretells is attributed squarely to Israel's own failings. It represents God's punishment of a recalcitrant, disloyal people. Israel is its own worst enemy.

This teaching became the very foundation of Jewish self-perception. The causes of persecutions, exile, and even mass slaughter were laid primarily at our own door, for had we acted differently none of this would have befallen us. "Because of our sins we were exiled," says the traditional prayer. In this view, God sent us these dreadful afflictions to bring us back to the path we should tread; and our persecutors were divine messengers to teach us the basic lesson.

One cannot quarrel with the basic assumption that we are responsible for what we do or fail to do, and that there are inevitable consequences. We are masters of our fate, both positively and negatively. But was the cruelty of our oppressors part of the divine plan? Can all the evils that befell our people be traced to the will of the Eternal?

There are those who, even after the Holocaust, would answer "yes." As a people we had fallen short of our potential, had betrayed our trust, and had violated our covenant with God. The result was terrible, but we, and not God, are to blame for the consequences.

However, only a small minority of our people would assent to this theology. To be sure, there were some rabbis who, after a terrorist attack killed more than score of children in Ma'alot in Israel's north, blamed the tragedy on uninspected mezuzot in the town. The overwhelming majority of Jews (and especially in Israel) rejected this explanation as a perversion of religion.

But, one may argue, is this not after all what Jeremiah and other prophets preached? Does not this train of thought make God responsible for Auschwitz?

We think not. Jeremiah warns and pleads so that his vision of disaster may *not* come to pass. He depicts the coming terror in order to sway his listeners. We read his predictions as warnings; and after the fact, he and the other post-exilic prophets turn to consolation. But at the same time they say: continue to act as once you did, and the same consequences will ensue.

We thus understand prophecy to have one emphasis before the fact, and another afterward. Jeremiah identified God as the One who would punish Israel; but not as the One who allowed women to be raped and children to be slaughtered. However, he probably would have agreed that, once the wild beasts of terror and war are unleashed, there is no telling what will happen next.

Jeremiah's own life and his tragic end mirrored his view of history's unfolding.

Gleanings

Words to Remember

My people have done a double wrong:
they have forsaken *Me*, the Fountain of Living Waters,
and have hewn for themselves cisterns,
cracked cisterns that cannot hold water. (2:13)

Though you wash yourself with lye, and use more and more soap,
the stain of your guilt remains before Me,
says the Eternal God. (2:22)

and if you swear by the living God in truth, justice, and righteousness,
then nations shall find blessing in you,
and glory in you. (4:2)

Israel
    I hear the voice
        of David and Bathsheba
     and the judgment
       on the continual
   backslidings
      of the kings of Israel
   I have stumbled
      on the ancient voice
  of honesty
    and tremble
 at the voice
    of my people.

Carl Rakosi[15]

Use more and more soap (2:22)

This idea is used elsewhere by Jeremiah (4:14) and means that the strain of sin is now so deep that it cannot be eradicated by soap or lye. The same theme was borrowed by Shakespeare in *Macbeth*, when Lady Macbeth tries in vain to wash the bloodstain from her hand: "Out, damned spot!"[16]

Solomon B. Freehof[17]

* * *

Notes

[1] Some translate as "retribution" and others as "rebuke." The Raban (Abraham ben Nathan of Lunel, 12th century) said: "From the sidra *B'reishit* until the 17th of Tammuz, the haftarot allude to their respective Torah portions; thereafter, the calendar dates take over" (*Sefer Hamanhig*, Hilchot Ta'anit, No. 16). Thus, the seven weeks after Tisha b'Av feature seven haftarot of consolation.

[2] Some believe that וַיֶּהְבָּלוּ הֶהֶבֶל (*ha-hevel va-yeh'balu*) is a wordplay on *baal*, the (empty) god of the pagans. A similar assonance is detectable in verse 8.

[3] Rashi, who in turn based himself on the grammarian Dunash, so interpreted the text.

[4] The image is also used in 48:33.

[5] I Kings 18:19; haftarah for Ki Tissa.

[6] Genesis 25:13.

[7] Psalm 106:21.

[8] Jeremiah 38:3-13.

[9] S. B. Freehof's *Book of Jeremiah*.

[10] See Hosea 14:4; haftarah for Shabbat Shuvah.

[11] So Bright (*Anchor Bible*, Jeremiah), following B. Duhm.

[12] The word occurs only once more in the Tanach, in Proverbs 25:20.

[13] See Jeremiah 7:31; haftarah for Tzav.

[14] So Rashi and Metzudat David.

[15] In *Chapters into Verse*, pp. 410-411.

[16] *Macbeth* Act V, Scene 1.

[17] Commentary on Jeremiah 2:22.

דברים

(Shabbat Chazon)

Isaiah, chapter 1, verses 1 to 27

Introduction

Connection of haftarah and sidra:

There is no connection between the two; rather, this is the third and last of three haftarot that are read between the seventeenth day of Tammuz (when the Babylonians breached the city walls) and the ninth of Av (when they razed the Temple). All three haftarot deal with the punishment that will be meted out to a people that forgets the God of the Covenant, and are known to tradition by an Aramaic name, תלת דפרענותא (*t'lat d'fur'anuta*), the "three [haftarot] of affliction."[1]

The haftarah is always read on the Shabbat before Tisha b'Av and, since it begins with the word *chazon* (vision), the Shabbat is called *Shabbat Chazon*.

The setting:

We cannot determine at which particular period of Isaiah's career these words were spoken. In view of verses 5-9 it would appear that the Northern Kingdom (with Samaria as its capital) had already been destroyed, and that the Assyrian troops had also invaded and devastated parts of Judah and were threatening Jerusalem.

For more on Isaiah and his time, see our *General Introduction*.

The message:

1. After the introductory sentence, part 1 (verses 2-9) conveys an image of devastation.

2. A detailed list of spiritual remedies. (10-17)

3. A prophecy on what will happen if Israel does not heed the divine call. (18-25)

4. Conclusion. Verses 26 and 27 take up the theme foreshadowed in verse 18: Return to God and make Zion a city of righteousness; then true redemption will be yours.

HAFTARAH FOR D'VARIM

Isaiah, chapter 1, verses 1 to 27

1:1. The vision of Isaiah son of Amoz, that he beheld concerning Judah and Jerusalem in the reigns of Uzziah, Jotham, Ahaz, and Hezekiah, kings of Judah.

2. Hear, O heavens, and listen, O earth,

for the Eternal has spoken:

I reared children and brought them up,

and they have rebelled against Me!

3. The ox knows its owner,

and the ass its master's stall,

but Israel does not know,

My people does not consider.

4. Ah, sinful nation,

people weighed down by iniquity!

Brood of evildoers! Destructive children

who have forsaken the Eternal,

despised the Holy One of Israel,

estranged themselves [from God].

1:1 חֲזוֹן יְשַׁעְיָהוּ בֶן־אָמוֹץ אֲשֶׁר חָזָה עַל־
יְהוּדָה וִירוּשָׁלָ͏ִם בִּימֵי עֻזִּיָּהוּ יוֹתָם אָחָז
יְחִזְקִיָּהוּ מַלְכֵי יְהוּדָה:
2 שִׁמְעוּ שָׁמַיִם וְהַאֲזִינִי אֶרֶץ
כִּי יְהוָה דִּבֵּר
בָּנִים גִּדַּלְתִּי וְרוֹמַמְתִּי
וְהֵם פָּשְׁעוּ בִי:
3 יָדַע שׁוֹר קֹנֵהוּ
וַחֲמוֹר אֵבוּס בְּעָלָיו
יִשְׂרָאֵל לֹא יָדַע
עַמִּי לֹא הִתְבּוֹנָן:
4 הוֹי גּוֹי חֹטֵא
עַם כֶּבֶד עָוֺן
זֶרַע מְרֵעִים בָּנִים מַשְׁחִיתִים
עָזְבוּ אֶת־יְהוָה
נִאֲצוּ אֶת־קְדוֹשׁ יִשְׂרָאֵל
נָזֹרוּ אָחוֹר:

Commentary

1. *Uzziah, Jotham* .... See our *General Introduction.*

2. *Hear, O heavens.* Using the imagery of the first words of the penultimate Torah portion, Ha'azinu,[2] but reversing the verbs.

The Eternal has spoken. It is not I who am originating this speech, but God.[3]

They have rebelled. The corrupt practices of the times are mentioned in the last book of the Tanach.[4]

3. *Israel does not know.* It does not even *want* to know God's will.[5]

4. *Brood of evildoers.* This generation has learned its evil ways from its parents.[6]

5. Why invite yet more beatings,

that you continue your rebellion?

The whole head is sick, the whole heart is
ill.

6. From head to foot, nothing is sound:

injuries, bruises, fresh wounds,

not dressed, nor bound, nor softened with
oil.

7. Your land is desolate,

your cities burnt down;

strangers consume your land before your
eyes;

it is desolation, like Sodom overthrown.

8. Only fair Zion is left;

she is like a booth in a vineyard,

like a hut in a cucumber-field,

like a city under siege.

5 עַל מֶה תֻכּוּ עוֹד

תּוֹסִיפוּ סָרָה

כָּל־רֹאשׁ לָחֳלִי וְכָל־לֵבָב דַּוָּי:

6 מִכַּף־רֶגֶל וְעַד־רֹאשׁ אֵין־בּוֹ מְתֹם

פֶּצַע וְחַבּוּרָה וּמַכָּה טְרִיָּה

לֹא־זֹרוּ וְלֹא חֻבָּשׁוּ וְלֹא רֻכְּכָה בַּשָּׁמֶן:

7 אַרְצְכֶם שְׁמָמָה

עָרֵיכֶם שְׂרֻפוֹת אֵשׁ

אַדְמַתְכֶם לְנֶגְדְּכֶם זָרִים אֹכְלִים אֹתָהּ

וּשְׁמָמָה כְּמַהְפֵּכַת זָרִים:

8 וְנוֹתְרָה בַת־צִיּוֹן

כְּסֻכָּה בְכָרֶם

כִּמְלוּנָה בְמִקְשָׁה

כְּעִיר נְצוּרָה:

Commentary

5. *The whole head is sick.* As suggested in our *Introduction* ("The Setting"), Samaria had already fallen, the Israelites of the Northern Kingdom had been exiled, and parts of Judah too had been devastated—yet all this had made no difference. People went on as if nothing needed to change.

7. *Sodom.* The second זרים (*zarim*) in the verse is most likely due to a scribal error and originally read סדום, that is Sodom, the city that was destroyed by God because of its evil-doing; see verse 10.[7]

8. *City under siege.* Jerusalem was beleaguered by King Sennacherib of Assyria in 701 B.C.E., though the city was not taken at that time.[8] It also possible to read the expression as a figure of speech: the city remained in the shadow of Assyrian power and, in that sense, under siege.

9. Had not the God of heaven's hosts

left us a remnant,

we should have already been like Sodom,

we should have seemed like Gomorrah.

10. Hear the word of the Eternal,

you rulers of Sodom;

listen to the teaching of our God,

you people of Gomorrah:

11. What are your many sacrifices to Me?

says the Eternal One.

I am sated with the rams you bring as

burnt-offerings,

with the fat of your fine animals;

I take no delight in the blood of bulls or

lambs or goats.

12. When you come to seek My presence,

who asked this of you,

to trample My courts?

9 לוּלֵי יְהֹוָה צְבָאוֹת

הוֹתִיר לָנוּ שָׂרִיד כִּמְעָט

כִּסְדֹם הָיִינוּ

לַעֲמֹרָה דָּמִינוּ:

10 שִׁמְעוּ דְבַר־יְהֹוָה

קְצִינֵי סְדֹם

הַאֲזִינוּ תּוֹרַת אֱלֹהֵינוּ

עַם עֲמֹרָה:

11 לָמָה־לִּי רֹב־זִבְחֵיכֶם

יֹאמַר יְהֹוָה

שָׂבַעְתִּי עֹלוֹת אֵילִים

וְחֵלֶב מְרִיאִים

וְדַם פָּרִים וּכְבָשִׂים וְעַתּוּדִים לֹא חָפָצְתִּי:

12 כִּי תָבֹאוּ לֵרָאוֹת פָּנָי

מִי־בִקֵּשׁ זֹאת מִיֶּדְכֶם

רְמֹס חֲצֵרָי:

Commentary

9. *A remnant.* The image of a surviving remnant recurs often in Isaiah. He even named his son She'ar Yashuv ("a remnant shall return").[9]

11-17. This ringing denunciation of hypocritical religion has sometimes been read as if Isaiah denounced ritual in general and said: Forget about sacrifices and Temple, do the right thing, for that is all that God demands. But this is a complete misreading of the Prophet's message. What he does say is: If sacrifice or prayer are not accompanied by righteous living and pure intent they are abhorrent to God.[10] (See also the essay following, and *Gleanings*.)

The prophet's language is highly instructive: he uses the central terms of the ritual to reject its hypocritical observance. Thus he condemns blood and fat offerings, though they were essential to the cult and their proper use was later on praised by Ezekiel.[11] Incense, which in the Torah is called "holy," is condemned as an "abomination" when it is accompanied by evil ways.[12]

13. Bring Me no more futile offerings;

incense is an abomination to Me.

New moon and sabbath,

the calling of assemblies:

I cannot endure festivities

along with evil.

14. I hate your new moons, your festival
    days:

they are a burden to Me;

I can bear [them] no more.

15. When you stretch out your hands,

I will avert My eyes from you;

however much you pray,

I will not listen,

while your hands are filled with blood.

16. Wash yourselves; cleanse yourselves,

put your evil doings away from My sight.

Cease to do evil,

17. learn to do good,

seek justice; relieve the oppressed.

Uphold the orphan's rights;

take up the widow's cause.

13 לֹא תוֹסִיפוּ הָבִיא מִנְחַת־שָׁוְא

קְטֹרֶת תּוֹעֵבָה הִיא לִי

חֹדֶשׁ וְשַׁבָּת

קְרֹא מִקְרָא

לֹא־אוּכַל אָוֶן וַעֲצָרָה:

14 חָדְשֵׁיכֶם וּמוֹעֲדֵיכֶם שָׂנְאָה נַפְשִׁי

הָיוּ עָלַי לָטֹרַח

נִלְאֵיתִי נְשֹׂא:

15 וּבְפָרִשְׂכֶם כַּפֵּיכֶם

אַעְלִים עֵינַי מִכֶּם

גַּם כִּי־תַרְבּוּ תְפִלָּה

אֵינֶנִּי שֹׁמֵעַ

יְדֵיכֶם דָּמִים מָלֵאוּ:

16 רַחֲצוּ הִזַּכּוּ

הָסִירוּ רֹעַ מַעַלְלֵיכֶם מִנֶּגֶד עֵינָי

חִדְלוּ הָרֵעַ:

17 לִמְדוּ הֵיטֵב

דִּרְשׁוּ מִשְׁפָּט אַשְּׁרוּ חָמוֹץ

שִׁפְטוּ יָתוֹם רִיבוּ אַלְמָנָה:

Commentary

13. *New moon.* The observance of Rosh Chodesh, the arrival of the new moon, was a festival of major importance in biblical times (see the explanations accompanying the haftarah for Shabbat Rosh Chodesh).

15. *Stretch out your hands.* A reference to the blessings spoken by the priests. If they are unrighteous, the blessings will be no more than empty words.

18. Come now, says the Eternal One,

let us reason together:

though your sins be scarlet,

they can become white as snow;

though they be dyed crimson,

they can become like fleece.

19. If you are willing and obey,

you shall eat the good things of the earth;

20. but if you refuse and rebel,

you shall be devoured by the sword—

for the Eternal One has spoken.

21. O how the faithful city played the

whore!

Once [she was] so full of justice;

righteousness dwelt there;

and now—murderers!

22. Your silver has turned to dross,

your wine is diluted with water.

18 לְכוּ־נָ֣א וְנִוָּֽכְחָ֔ה יֹאמַ֖ר יְהוָ֑ה

אִם־יִהְי֨וּ חֲטָאֵיכֶ֤ם כַּשָּׁנִים֙

כַּשֶּׁ֣לֶג יַלְבִּ֔ינוּ

אִם־יַאְדִּ֥ימוּ כַתּוֹלָ֖ע

כַּצֶּ֥מֶר יִהְיֽוּ:

19 אִם־תֹּאב֖וּ וּשְׁמַעְתֶּ֑ם

ט֥וּב הָאָ֖רֶץ תֹּאכֵֽלוּ:

20 וְאִם־תְּמָאֲנ֖וּ וּמְרִיתֶ֑ם

חֶ֖רֶב תְּאֻכְּל֑וּ

כִּ֛י פִּ֥י יְהוָ֖ה דִּבֵּֽר:

21 אֵיכָה֙ הָיְתָ֣ה לְזוֹנָ֔ה קִרְיָ֖ה נֶאֱמָנָ֑ה

מְלֵאֲתִ֣י מִשְׁפָּ֔ט

צֶ֛דֶק יָלִ֥ין בָּ֖הּ

וְעַתָּ֥ה מְרַצְּחִֽים:

22 כַּסְפֵּ֖ךְ הָיָ֣ה לְסִיגִ֑ים

סָבְאֵ֖ךְ מָה֥וּל בַּמָּֽיִם:

Commentary

18. *Become white as snow.* Jeremiah, using the same metaphor, was less generous and hopeful; see the preceding haftarah for Mas'ei.[13] The expression "white as snow" occurs frequently in the Tanach. Some understand the verse as an imperative: If your sins are scarlet, you must make them white as snow.

Scarlet ... fleece. The verse served as a source for a Yom Kippur custom in the Second Temple: a crimson thread was tied to the head of the (Torah-commanded) scapegoat, in order to symbolize the community's dispatch of its sins.[14]

21. *O how.* The book of Lamentations opens with this same word, איכה (*echah*), and with the same tone of mourning.

22. Traditional commentators connect this verse with the one following and consider the reference to silver and dross as a metaphor: people cheat in business, debase the currency, and lead immoral lives.[15]

23. Your rulers are rebels,

cronies of thieves;

everyone of them loves bribes and is avid
    for graft;

they do not decide the orphan's case;

the widow's cause never comes before
    them.

24. Therefore, says the Sovereign,

the God of heaven's hosts,

the Mighty One of Israel:

Enough! I will rid Myself of My foes,

and revenge Myself on My enemies;

25. Again and again I will [raise] My hand
    to you,

smelt away your dross as if with lye

and rid you of your slag.

26. And I will restore your judges as in the
    beginning,

and your counselors as in days of old.

Then shall you be called

Righteous City, Faithful Town.

27. Zion shall be redeemed by justice,

and its repentant people by righteousness.

שָׂרַיִךְ סוֹרְרִים 23

וְחַבְרֵי גַּנָּבִים

כֻּלּוֹ אֹהֵב שֹׁחַד וְרֹדֵף שַׁלְמֹנִים

יָתוֹם לֹא יִשְׁפֹּטוּ

וְרִיב אַלְמָנָה לֹא־יָבוֹא אֲלֵיהֶם:

לָכֵן נְאֻם הָאָדוֹן 24

יְהוָה צְבָאוֹת

אֲבִיר יִשְׂרָאֵל

הוֹי אֶנָּחֵם מִצָּרַי

וְאִנָּקְמָה מֵאוֹיְבָי:

וְאָשִׁיבָה יָדִי עָלַיִךְ 25

וְאֶצְרֹף כַּבֹּר סִיגָיִךְ

וְאָסִירָה כָּל־בְּדִילָיִךְ:

וְאָשִׁיבָה שֹׁפְטַיִךְ כְּבָרִאשֹׁנָה 26

וְיֹעֲצַיִךְ כְּבַתְּחִלָּה

אַחֲרֵי־כֵן יִקָּרֵא לָךְ

עִיר הַצֶּדֶק קִרְיָה נֶאֱמָנָה:

צִיּוֹן בְּמִשְׁפָּט תִּפָּדֶה 27

וְשָׁבֶיהָ בִּצְדָקָה:

Commentary

24. *And revenge Myself.* Passages like these have led critics of the Hebrew Bible to charge that its Divinity is a vengeful God. This characterization is wide of the mark. Rather, evil has its consequences (though we cannot always see them), for God balances the scales in retributive justice—and this retribution falls on Jews and gentiles alike.

25. *I will [raise] My hand.* An interpretation favored by earlier commentators.

27. The verse admits of various interpretations. For שביה (*shave'ha*) can convey spiritual returning (repentance) or physical going back (to Jerusalem).[16]

Essay

An exaltation of justice (verse 27)

If one wonders what makes Israel unique, an answer is found in this haftarah. The core of the people's obligation is justice. Without it, all ritual acts, including prayer, count for little. We cannot love God without loving human beings; we cannot expect justice from the Eternal without practicing it ourselves in our relations with others.

As indicated in the comment on verses 11-17, Isaiah is not an anti-ritualist. His denunciation of sacrificial rites is directed not against the rites but against the religious hypocrisy with which they are performed. The same holds true for any celebration—be it Shabbat or New Moon or any festival occasion. Form without substance is useless, and especially so in one's relationship with God.

A well-known Chasidic saying goes as follows: "The way to loving God is through loving God's children." And, in Isaiah's view (as indeed in the view of biblical religion in general), being just is an essential component of love. Ritual is the way by which we remind ourselves daily of the Divine Presence and what it betokens, and thereby reinforce our decision to live in accordance with God's will. The message of the Prophet is that God demands of us a life dedicated to just action.

He looks at the city he loves and sees it infested with injustice. He is convinced that the Northern Kingdom fell because of its iniquity, and he fears that the same fate will befall his beloved city and country. He is afraid that God will allow it to be conquered and destroyed, though in time it will be rebuilt by the small remnant that will survive destruction. When that happens, justice must be the cornerstone of the new Jerusalem.

This theme, expressed in the 8th century B.C.E., has not lost its potency for our day. Is there another nation that perceives its very right to existence in such terms? For Torah and prophets see justice as the heartbeat of this people's life, whose future is conditioned less by allies and arms than by its adherence to a national ethic. This represents both a singular assignment from God and an unparalleled self-perception. Social justice is a prerequisite for Israel's survival.

Gleanings

Words to Remember

The ox knows its owner, and the ass its master's stall,
but Israel does not know (God). (3)

Wash yourselves, cleanse yourselves,
put your evil doings away from My sight.
Cease to do evil,
learn to do good,
seek justice, relieve the oppressed. (16-17)

Zion shall be redeemed by justice,
and its repentant people by righteousness. (27)

I hate ... your festivals (verse 14)

A pagan asked Rabbi Akiba: Why do you celebrate your festivals? Did not the Holy One (through Isaiah) say to you: "I *hate* your festivals"?

Rabbi Akiba answered: If God had said, "I hate *My* new moons and *My* festivals," you might have had a point. But God said *"your* new moons and *your* festivals"—yours, not Mine.

(God hates the corruption of our observance, but wants us to celebrate festive occasions in a true religious spirit.)

Midrash[17]

"Your hands are filled with blood" (verse 15)

Even repeated prayer will not be heard when your hands are dripping with blood. The image has special strength because of its utter simplicity.

Ludwig Philippson[18]

Righteousness

Isaiah measured faithfulness in terms of righteousness and justice, even as justice and righteousness were the vintage which God awaited from Judah, His vineyard.

If God did not want the pomp and ceremony that went with the Temple cult, that did not mean that He made no demands. The prophets looked for religion beyond the sacred precincts: in the stores and warehouses, in the courtrooms and the legislatures, on the farms and in the households; and not alone on holy days and solemn assemblies but on ordinary weekdays as well.

Sheldon Blank[19]

Divine sorrow

Significantly, the speech that opens the book of Isaiah, and which sets the tone for all the utterances of this prophet, deals not with the anger, but with the sorrow of God. The prophet pleads with us to understand the plight of a parent whom his children have abandoned:

> *I reared children and brought them up,*
> *and they have rebelled against Me.* (verse 2)

The weariness of God (the expression occurs again in 43:24), an important theological category in Isaiah's thinking, brings about a greater concealment of God's personal involvement in history.

Abraham J. Heschel[20]

* * *

Notes

[1] Some translate as "retribution" and others as "rebuke." The Raban (Abraham ben David of Lunel, 12th century) said: "From the sidra *B'reishit* until the 17th of Tammuz, the haftarot allude to their respective Torah portions; thereafter, the calendar dates take over" (*Sefer Hamanhig*, Hilchot Ta'anit, No. 16). Thus, the seven weeks after Tisha b'Av feature seven haftarot of consolation.

[2] Deuteronomy 32:1.

[3] Metzudat David.

[4] II Chronicles 27:2 and 28:1 and following.

[5] Rashi.

[6] So Ibn Ezra, but other commentators differ.

[7] The tale of the destruction of Sodom and Gomorrah is found in Genesis 18:22 and following.

[8] II Kings 19:36; see also Pritchard, *Ancient Near Eastern Texts*, pp. 287 ff.

[9] Isaiah 7:3.

[10] H. L. Ginsberg (*Encyclopaedia Judaica*, vol. 9, p. 50) infers from this that Isaiah must have been a rather frequent visitor to the Temple—whence also his famous vision of the Eternal on the throne (Isaiah 6; haftarah for Yitro).

[11] Ezekiel 44:15; haftarah for Emor.

[12] Verse 13; and see Exodus 30:37.

[13] Jeremiah 2:22.

[14] See *Mishnah* Shabbat 9:3, and the Torah Commentary, p. 868.

[15] See Rashi, Radak, Ibn Ezra.

[16] Rashi and Ibn Ezra prefer the former; Radak and Malbim, the latter. The *New English Bible* translates as "Zion will be redeemed by justice/ and her returning people by righteousness."

[17] Numbers Rabbah 25:21.

[18] *Das Buch der Haphthoroth*, p. 158.

[19] *Understanding the Prophets*, pp. 170 ff.

[20] *The Prophets*, pp. 80 ff.

ואתחנן

(Shabbat Nachamu)

Isaiah, chapter 40, verses 1 to 26

Introduction

This haftarah is the first of seven that are called *sheva de-nechamta*, "the seven [haftarot] of consolation." Six others will follow, all from the Second Isaiah, the last one to be recited on the Shabbat before Rosh Hashanah. (See the essay below.)

As most modern scholars see it, chapter 40 opens the prophecies of the Second Isaiah. This unknown preacher-poet lived among the exiles in Babylon (6th century B.C.E.), and at some later time his writings were attached to those of the First Isaiah, who lived well over a century earlier. (See our *General Introduction*.)[1]

Connection of haftarah and Shabbat:

The weekly portion is read on the Shabbat after Tisha b'Av, the traditional fast that commemorates the destruction of the Temple in Jerusalem in 587 B.C.E. The haftarah begins with words of comfort: the term of Israel's exile is over, for God not only desires to liberate them but can and will do so.

The setting:

Undoubtedly there were many among the exiles who doubted that God could redeem them, the promises of the prophets notwithstanding. But with Cyrus about to conquer Babylon and (so the Prophet hoped) willing to let the exiles return to their native land, Isaiah preaches that God will surely proceed to make good on the divine promise.

For more on Isaiah and his time, see our *General Introduction*.

The message:

The haftarah may be divided into three parts:

1. A brief general introduction setting out Isaiah's theme: he has been charged by God to deliver a message of hope. (43:1-2)

2. God's might is unbounded, and this power will now be demonstrated in the redemption of Israel. (40:1-20)

3. Conclusion. God's might is such that Israel's oppressors will crumble, "bringing princes to naught, making earth's rulers as nothing." (40: 21-26)

HAFTARAH FOR VA'ET-CHANAN

Isaiah, chapter 40, verses 1 to 26

40:1. Comfort My people, comfort them,
says your God.

2. Speak tenderly to Jerusalem;

say to her

that she has served her term,

that her sin is pardoned

for she has received from the hand of the
Eternal

more than enough punishment for her sins.

3. A voice calls:

*Prepare a road for the Eternal through the
wilderness,*

clear a highway in the desert for our God.

40:1 נַחֲמוּ נַחֲמוּ עַמִּי

יֹאמַר אֱלֹהֵיכֶם:

2 דַּבְּרוּ עַל־לֵב יְרוּשָׁלַם

וְקִרְאוּ אֵלֶיהָ

כִּי מָלְאָה צְבָאָהּ

כִּי נִרְצָה עֲוֹנָהּ

כִּי לָקְחָה מִיַּד יְהוָה

כִּפְלַיִם בְּכָל־חַטֹּאתֶיהָ:

3 קוֹל קוֹרֵא

בַּמִּדְבָּר פַּנּוּ דֶּרֶךְ יְהוָה

יַשְּׁרוּ בָּעֲרָבָה מְסִלָּה לֵאלֹהֵינוּ:

Commentary

40:1. Comfort My people. נחמו (*nachamu*) gives to this Shabbat the name *Shabbat Nachamu*. Most likely the divine plea is addressed to the prophets and leaders: they have the task of speaking words of consolation and hope to the people.

Says your God. The Hebrew is in the future tense, but that tense has different uses and sometimes means the past (when preceded by the letter ו, *vav*), and sometimes denotes the present as here. The context determines the meaning.

2. *She has served her term.* For Cyrus is about to overthrow Babylon and will liberate you. The people's enslavement is considered the consequence of their sinfulness.

She has received ... more than enough punishment. Literally "double." Why would God mete out excessive retribution to Israel? Even as a leader is judged more severely than others, so is Israel because of its special role as God's servant. The Targum adds that therefore Israel will also receive double comfort from God.

3. Music lovers will recall that Handel's "Messiah" opens with a recitative composed of these verses of our haftarah.[2]

Prepare a road ... through the wilderness. God will take Israel through the desert for a second exodus, this time from Babylon. In Isaiah's day, travelers would proceed northward from Babylon in present-day Iraq, enter what is now Syria, and from there turn south to Israel.[3] But God would lead the Jews by a more direct route, by a way that would lead through the wilderness.

4. Every valley shall be exalted,

every mountain and hill made low;

the uneven ground shall be made level,

the rough places a plain.

5. The Eternal's Presence shall be revealed,

and, united, all shall see it;

for the Eternal One has spoken.

6. A voice rings out: Announce!

Another asks: What shall I announce?

All flesh is grass,

and all its grace like a flower in the field:

7. Grass withers and flowers fade

when God's breath blows on them.

Yes, the people are grass:

8. Grass withers and flowers fade,

but our God's word holds good forever.

4 כָּל־גֶּיא יִנָּשֵׂא
וְכָל־הַר וְגִבְעָה יִשְׁפָּלוּ
וְהָיָה הֶעָקֹב לְמִישׁוֹר
וְהָרְכָסִים לְבִקְעָה:
5 וְנִגְלָה כְּבוֹד יְהֹוָה
וְרָאוּ כָל־בָּשָׂר יַחְדָּו
כִּי פִּי יְהֹוָה דִּבֵּר:
6 קוֹל אֹמֵר קְרָא
וְאָמַר מָה אֶקְרָא
כָּל־הַבָּשָׂר חָצִיר
וְכָל־חַסְדּוֹ כְּצִיץ הַשָּׂדֶה:
7 יָבֵשׁ חָצִיר נָבֵל צִיץ
כִּי רוּחַ יְהֹוָה נָשְׁבָה בּוֹ
אָכֵן חָצִיר הָעָם:
8 יָבֵשׁ חָצִיר נָבֵל צִיץ
וּדְבַר־אֱלֹהֵינוּ יָקוּם לְעוֹלָם:

Commentary

5. *For the Eternal One has spoken.* Literally, "the mouth of the Eternal One has spoken." The Prophet emphasizes that these words are not his own imaginings, but came out of God's own mouth, as it were.

6. *What shall I announce?* Following the text of an Isaiah manuscript discovered at the Dead Sea, which reads "I" instead of "He."[4]

Its grace ... Others translate as "goodness," "glory," "constancy," etc. Whatever we prize is impermanent. Compare the words of Psalm 90:6.

7. *Grass withers ....* This verse and the one following are very similar to Psalm 90:5-6: "At daybreak they are like grass that renews itself; at daybreak it flourishes anew, by dusk it withers and dries up." The psalm is ascribed to Moses.

God's breath. A metaphor for the hot winds that dry up the land.

8. *Holds good forever.* In Second Isaiah's prophecies the promise of Israel's restoration and its fulfillment are fundamental.[5]

9. Ascend a high mountain,

O herald of good tidings to Zion:

raise your voice with power;

O herald of good tidings to Jerusalem—

speak up without fear;

Say to the cities of Judah:

Behold your God!

10. Behold the Eternal God coming in

might,

coming to rule with [outstretched] arm,

bringing [divine] reward

and recompense [from on high],

11. like a shepherd tending a flock,

gathering the lambs in his arms,

carrying them,

and gently leading the ewes.

12. Who can measure the oceans in the

palm of their hand,

or gauge the skies with a span,

9 עַל הַר־גָּבֹהַ עֲלִי־לָךְ

מְבַשֶּׂרֶת צִיּוֹן

הָרִימִי בַכֹּחַ קוֹלֵךְ

מְבַשֶּׂרֶת יְרוּשָׁלָ͏ִם

הָרִימִי אַל־תִּירָאִי

אִמְרִי לְעָרֵי יְהוּדָה

הִנֵּה אֱלֹהֵיכֶם:

10 הִנֵּה אֲדֹנָי יֱהֹוִה בְּחָזָק יָבוֹא

וּזְרֹעוֹ מֹשְׁלָה לוֹ

הִנֵּה שְׂכָרוֹ אִתּוֹ

וּפְעֻלָּתוֹ לְפָנָיו:

11 כְּרֹעֶה עֶדְרוֹ יִרְעֶה

בִּזְרֹעוֹ יְקַבֵּץ טְלָאִים

וּבְחֵיקוֹ יִשָּׂא

עָלוֹת יְנַהֵל:

12 מִי־מָדַד בְּשָׁעֳלוֹ מַיִם

וְשָׁמַיִם בַּזֶּרֶת תִּכֵּן

Commentary

9. *Herald of good tidings.* מבשרת ציון (*m'vaseret tziyon*). A suburb of Jerusalem bears that name today.

10. *The Eternal God.* אדני יהוה (pronounced *Adonai Elohim*). Ordinarily, the Divine Name יהוה, which we never attempt to pronounce as such, is expressed as *Adonai* (my Sovereign) and vocalized יְהֹוָה. But when יהוה is coupled with the actual Hebrew word *Adonai* (אדני), as here, we do not read *Adonai Adonai*, but *Adonai Elohim*, the Eternal God. In such cases, יהוה is vocalized יֱהֹוִה (indicating the vowels that go with *Elohim*).[6]

11. *[outstretched] arm* ... Evoking the image of a warrior wielding sword and spear; see Exodus 6:6.

Like a shepherd. God is often depicted as a shepherd, who was the symbol of watchful care; see Psalm 23 and *Gleanings*, below.

A flock. Literally, "his" flock.

442

or put all earth's dust in a bushel,

or weigh the mountains in a scale,

the hills in a balance?

13. Who can assess the mind of the
Eternal,

or act as God's adviser?

14. Whom has God consulted,

from whom has God taken instruction

to learn the path of right,

Who has guided God in knowledge,

teaching God the way of understanding?

15. Why, the nations are but a drop in the
bucket,

no more than dust on a scale;

to God, whole islands are but fine dust!

16. All Lebanon could not provide fuel
enough,

nor are all its beasts enough for burnt-
offerings.

17. The nations are nothing before God,

who considers them as less than nothing!

18. To whom, then, can you liken God?

What can you imagine that compares to
God?

19. An idol?

A metalworker poured it,

a smith plated it with gold

and forged silver links.

וְכָל בַּשָּׁלִשׁ עֲפַר הָאָרֶץ
וְשָׁקַל בַּפֶּלֶס הָרִים
וּגְבָעוֹת בְּמֹאזְנָיִם:

13 מִי־תִכֵּן אֶת־רוּחַ יְהוָה
וְאִישׁ עֲצָתוֹ יוֹדִיעֶנּוּ:

14 אֶת־מִי נוֹעָץ
וַיְבִינֵהוּ
וַיְלַמְּדֵהוּ בְּאֹרַח מִשְׁפָּט
וַיְלַמְּדֵהוּ דַעַת
וְדֶרֶךְ תְּבוּנוֹת יוֹדִיעֶנּוּ:

15 הֵן גּוֹיִם כְּמַר מִדְּלִי
וּכְשַׁחַק מֹאזְנַיִם נֶחְשָׁבוּ
הֵן אִיִּים כַּדַּק יִטּוֹל:

16 וּלְבָנוֹן אֵין דֵּי בָּעֵר
וְחַיָּתוֹ אֵין דֵּי עוֹלָה:

17 כָּל־הַגּוֹיִם כְּאַיִן נֶגְדּוֹ
מֵאֶפֶס וָתֹהוּ נֶחְשְׁבוּ־לוֹ:

18 וְאֶל־מִי תְּדַמְּיוּן אֵל
וּמַה־דְּמוּת תַּעַרְכוּ לוֹ:

19 הַפֶּסֶל
נָסַךְ חָרָשׁ
וְצֹרֵף בַּזָּהָב יְרַקְעֶנּוּ
וּרְתֻקוֹת כֶּסֶף צוֹרֵף:

Commentary

12. *Bushel*. A metaphor. שלש (*shalish*, third) probably refers to a third of an ephah, a common volume measure.

15. *Drop in the bucket*. The English idiom derives from this phrase; the Hebrew reads literally "drop *from* a bucket." (So still the King James translation, 1611.)

20. As a gift, someone chooses mulberry—
a wood that does not rot—
then finds a skillful woodworker
to make an idol that won't fall down.

21. Do you not know?
Have you not heard?
Were you not told from the beginning?
Have you not grasped how the the world
  began?

22. It is God, enthroned beyond the horizon,
to whom we all seem like grasshoppers;
it is God who spreads the heavens out like
  a curtain,
and stretches them like a tent to live in,

23. bringing princes to naught,
making earth's rulers as nothing.

24. Scarcely are they planted, hardly sown,
scarcely has their stem taken root in earth,
when God blows on them and they wither,
and the tempest carries them off like
  stubble.

25. To whom, then, will you compare Me,
who is My equal? says the Holy One.

20 הַמְסֻכָּן תְּרוּמָה
עֵץ לֹא־יִרְקַב יִבְחָר
חָרָשׁ חָכָם יְבַקֶּשׁ־לוֹ
לְהָכִין פֶּסֶל לֹא יִמּוֹט׃

21 הֲלוֹא תֵדְעוּ
הֲלוֹא תִשְׁמָעוּ
הֲלוֹא הֻגַּד מֵרֹאשׁ לָכֶם
הֲלוֹא הֲבִינֹתֶם מוֹסְדוֹת הָאָרֶץ׃

22 הַיֹּשֵׁב עַל־חוּג הָאָרֶץ
וְיֹשְׁבֶיהָ כַּחֲגָבִים
הַנּוֹטֶה כַדֹּק שָׁמַיִם
וַיִּמְתָּחֵם כָּאֹהֶל לָשָׁבֶת׃

23 הַנּוֹתֵן רוֹזְנִים לְאָיִן
שֹׁפְטֵי אֶרֶץ כַּתֹּהוּ עָשָׂה׃

24 אַף בַּל־נִטָּעוּ אַף בַּל־זֹרָעוּ
אַף בַּל־שֹׁרֵשׁ בָּאָרֶץ גִּזְעָם
וְגַם־נָשַׁף בָּהֶם וַיִּבָשׁוּ
וּסְעָרָה כַּקַּשׁ תִּשָּׂאֵם׃

25 וְאֶל־מִי תְדַמְּיוּנִי
וְאֶשְׁוֶה יֹאמַר קָדוֹשׁ׃

Commentary

20. *Mulberry—a wood that does not rot.* The Hebrew is difficult and its meaning uncertain. The "wood that does not rot" is likely a reference to either mulberry or teak; מסכן (*mesukkan*) appears to have been borrowed from the Akkadian (Assyro-Babylonian) *musukkanu*, which conveys the quality of permanence.[7]

21. *Were you not told?* The emphasis is on "you": of all peoples, Israel should have known, for it had prophets and scriptures and knew the true account of creation (details of which Isaiah rehearses in the verses following).

23-24. Reminiscent of Job 12:16-25. We cannot be sure whether Isaiah lived before or after Job. Modern scholars would generally consider Isaiah the earlier of the two.

VA'ET-CHANAN

26. Lift up your eyes on high, and see:
Who created these [stars]?
The One who leads out their host by
   number,

calling them each by name;
by whose great might and vast power
not one is missing!

26 שְׂאוּ־מָרוֹם עֵינֵיכֶם וּרְאוּ
מִי־בָרָא אֵלֶּה
הַמּוֹצִיא בְמִסְפָּר צְבָאָם
לְכֻלָּם בְּשֵׁם יִקְרָא
מֵרֹב אוֹנִים וְאַמִּיץ כֹּחַ
אִישׁ לֹא נֶעְדָּר:

Essay

Why has God forsaken us?
The cry for divine help—whether coming from the heart of an individual or of a collective—is as old as the religious quest itself. And since such prayers are sometimes answered and sometimes not, the question "Why not?" is likely to shake the very foundations of faith. It is found in the Bible, as it is in other scriptures. David asked it in his distress:

My God, my God,
why have You forsaken me;
why [are You] so far from delivering me
and from my anguished outcry?
My God, I cry by day—
You answer not;
[I cry] by night, and have no rest.[8]

It is this anguish of Israel that Isaiah expresses also in the beginning of next week's haftarah:

Zion says:
The Eternal has forsaken me,
My God has forgotten me.[9]

It was the cry of Job and the pleading of the victims of persecution, from ancient times to the Holocaust and beyond. The failure to receive a clear answer has turned many a believer into an unbeliever. The bridge from "Why doesn't God help?" to "God cannot help" and "There is no God" is all too easily crossed.

Yet in the end there is no answer that will stand the proof of the scientist. Faith is strengthened or weakened by the experiences we have, but whether *we* believe in a God who can save us is far removed from the actual existence of the Divine. One is a personal attitude, the other a reality that does not depend on how we feel about it.

There is also an intermediate position, which is that of doubt: "We'd like to believe, but are not sure how we can." This is the situation that the Second Isaiah faced in this opening chapter of his book. He reassures his people that God desires not only to save Israel, but is also capable of doing it. The Eternal is not merely a divine friend with goodwill, but a power beyond all powers who can rescue the beleaguered nation.[10]

Withal, Isaiah does not pretend to know why the rescue has been so long delayed. For ultimately a believer knows that there are limits to human understanding. We are not God, and our human mind operates on a level different from the Divine.

Who can assess the mind of the Eternal,
or act as God's adviser? (verse 13)

The border of human understanding is the door to faith. We cannot know God's plans, but we can trust God as our friend. All true relationships are ultimately based on such trust.

Gleanings

Words to Remember

Comfort My people, comfort them,
says your God. (40:1)

All flesh is grass,
and all its grace like a flower in the field (40:6)

Grass withers and flowers fade,
but our God's word holds good forever. (40:8)

The divine and human shepherd

God watched Moses and saw how tenderly he cared for the sheep of his father-in-law, Jethro. Once a kid escaped from the flock, and when Moses found it he saw it drinking at a brook. "I did not know it was so thirsty," he thought, "it must be tired now." He then carried it back on his shoulder.

Thereupon God said: "Because you have compassion upon a kid you are fit to pasture Israel, My people."

Midrash[11]

Human and divine comfort

Joseph could comfort his brothers, who were little more than strangers to him,[12] and Boaz comforted Ruth, who had come as an alien not long before.[13] How much more so will the Holy One comfort Israel, God's own people.

Midrash[14]

Why twice?

God says "Comfort My people, comfort them" (40:1). Why is "comfort" said twice? Because (as stated in the next verse) Israel received a double portion of punishment, and therefore a double portion of comfort is due her now. For that reason also God reassures Israel twice: "I, I am the One who comforts you" (51:12).

Midrash[15]

Together

The prophets came before the Holy One and reported that Jerusalem refused to be comforted by them. God then said, "Then you and I will go together to comfort her."

Midrash[16]

God too needs comforting

The first three words of the haftarah, נחמו נחמו עמי (*nachamu nachamu ammi,* Comfort, O comfort My people), gave rise to several wordplays:

Instead of עַמִּי, *ammi*, my people, a midrash reads עִמִּי (*immi*), with Me—hence, "Comfort, O comfort [Jerusalem] together with Me," says God.

Rabbi Berachiah the Priest read the words "Comfort My people," as "Comfort Me, comfort Me, O My people." [Reading נחמוני עמי (*nachamuni ammi*) instead of נחמו עמי (*nachamu ammi*.)]

Midrash[17]

From lament to comfort

Jeremiah struck terror in the hearts of the people when he said, "Zion spreads out her hands, there is no one to comfort her."[18] But Isaiah came and said, "Comfort, O comfort My people, says your God."

Midrash[19]

God's mind

To say that YHVH is Creator does not afford a complete understanding of the divine mind. What the prophet means is that God communicates to those who believe some of the unfailing strength of His eternity. They receive the power to do what they must do; they can live in a hope which is as strong as He in whom they hope. Israel must face its future with a conviction that the divine promises are not dimmed or frustrated. The Creator has not yielded His sovereignty to another.

John L. McKenzie[20]

The promise of liberation

(In their exile in Babylon the Jews watch the advance of Cyrus, the Persian ruler who will return them to their homeland.)

Against their enslaver and oppressor, they saw uplifted the irresistible sword of God's instrument, this Persian prince to whose religion the Babylonian idolatry was hateful; a victorious warrior, a wise and just statesman favorable to Babylon's prisoners and victims, and disposed to restore the exiles of Judah to their land.

Matthew Arnold[21]

The steed bit its master

(Popular wit occasionally used a biblical text, as in the anonymous ditty based on Isaiah 40:6, "All flesh is grass.")

> The steed bit its master:
> How came this to pass?
> He heard the good pastor
> Cry, "All flesh is grass."[22]

* * *

449

Notes

[1] For the sake of brevity, in our commentary on the "Seven [Haftarot] of Consolation," Second Isaiah is simply called Isaiah.

[2] To be sure, Handel understood verse 3 in its Christian revision as it appears in Matthew 2:3, which speaks of "the voice of him that cries in the wilderness" and applies it to John the Baptist.

[3] See our comments on Jeremiah 46:24; haftarah for Bo.

[4] So also the Septuagint.

[5] See, for example, Isaiah 44:7; haftarah for Vayikra; this feature is shared by other post-exilic writers.

[6] Prayer books will usually write the Name as ״. About the care that Jews accord to the Name, see the Torah Commentary, p. 31.

[7] N. Tur-Sinai, *The Language and the Book*, vol. 2, p. 119, suggests that *t'rumah* is a scribal error for the original *t'marah*, date-palm.

[8] Psalm 22:1-3. The Christian Bible reports that Jesus uttered these words (in Aramaic) on the cross; Matthew 27:46; Mark 15:34.

[9] Isaiah. 49:14. This is the topic of a comment by Resh Lakish (a rabbi in the 3rd century C.E.), found in Pesikta deRav Kahana 17:2.

[10] See the interpretation of the seven haftarot of consolation by Rabbi Mark Dov Shapiro, in *Journal of Reform Judaism*, Spring 1984, pp. 68 ff. He shows how with each passing week the Prophet's answer touches on various areas of Israel's doubt, so that in the end, when the New Year is about to come, the people will face it with hope and confidence.

[11] The theme of Moses the shepherd is treated in Sh'mot Rabbah 2:2-3. A section of the Zohar is called "The Faithful Shepherd."

[12] Genesis 50:21.

[13] Ruth 2:13.

[14] Pesikta deRav Kahana 16:1.

[15] Lamentations Rabbah 1, no. 23.

[16] Pesikta deRav Kahana 16:8. The 16th *piska* (chapter) of the book is entirely devoted to a midrashic contemplation of Isaiah 40:1. So also Pesikta Rabbati, Piska 29/30A (ed. Braude and Kapstein, p. 586). This and the following piska deal with the theme of comforting Israel.

[17] Pesikta Rabbati, Nachamu, 29/30:3.

[18] The quotation is from Lamentations (1:17), one of the biblical books believed by some to have been authored by Jeremiah.

[19] Pesikta Rabbati, Piska 29/30A [end].

[20] In his *Anchor Bible* commentary on Isaiah, p. 25.

[21] Cited by J. H. Hertz, *Pentateuch and Haftorahs*, p. 776.

[22] Found in *Chapters into Verse*, p. 400.

Isaiah, chapter 49, verse 14 to chapter 51, verse 3

Introduction

Connection of haftarah and sidra:

The weekly portion is read on the second Shabbat after Tisha b'Av and is the second of the *sheva de-nechamta,* the "seven [haftarot] of consolation," which are read until the arrival of Rosh Hashanah (see the Introduction to the previous haftarah).

The setting:

The Second Isaiah, author of this prophecy, lived among his people in Babylonian exile (6th century B.C.E.). The Israelites had begun to doubt that God would ever free them from the yoke of exile, and the first verse of the haftarah expresses this theme:

> Zion says,
>
> The Eternal has forsaken me,
>
> My Sovereign has forgotten me.

Isaiah comforts the people, prophesying that their present misery will turn to glory.

As most modern scholars see it, chapter 40 opens the prophecies of the Second Isaiah. This unknown preacher-poet lived among the exiles in Babylon (6th century B.C.E.), and at some later time his writings were attached to those of the First Isaiah, who lived well over a century earlier.

For more on Second Isaiah, see our *General Introduction*.[1]

The message:

The haftarah is unusually long and consists of a number of subthemes:

1. God can no more forget Israel than a mother can abandon her child. (49:14-21)
2. God will bring about a reversal of fortunes, and the oppressors will suffer a ghastly fate, which is set forth in extreme images. (49:22-26)
3. Not God but Israel itself is the author of its misfortune. (50:1-3)
4. Isaiah uses his own life as an example of how he was vindicated by God. (50:4-11)
5. A final trumpet blast of hope and encouragement, cast in memorable poetry. (51:1-4)

HAFTARAH FOR EKEV

Isaiah, chapter 49, verse 14 to chapter 51, verse 3

49:14. Zion says:

The Eternal has forsaken me;

my Sovereign has forgotten me.

15. Can a mother forget her babe,

or stop loving the child of her womb?

Even these could forget,

but I could not forget you!

16. Indeed, I have inscribed you on the

palms of My hands;

your safety is continually in My thoughts.

17. Your builders drive out your destroyers,

and those who wrought havoc with you

depart from you.

18. Look up and see:

they are gathering and coming to you, all of

them!

As I live, says the Eternal One,

you shall put all of them on like

ornaments,

you shall bind them on yourself like a

bride.

49:14 וַתֹּאמֶר צִיּוֹן

עֲזָבַנִי יְהֹוָה

וַאדֹנָי שְׁכֵחָנִי:

15 הֲתִשְׁכַּח אִשָּׁה עוּלָהּ

מֵרַחֵם בֶּן־בִּטְנָהּ

גַּם־אֵלֶּה תִשְׁכַּחְנָה

וְאָנֹכִי לֹא אֶשְׁכָּחֵךְ:

16 הֵן עַל־כַּפַּיִם חַקֹּתִיךְ

חוֹמֹתַיִךְ נֶגְדִּי תָּמִיד:

17 מִהֲרוּ בָּנָיִךְ מְהָרְסַיִךְ

וּמַחֲרִבַיִךְ מִמֵּךְ יֵצֵאוּ:

18 שְׂאִי־סָבִיב עֵינַיִךְ וּרְאִי

כֻּלָּם נִקְבְּצוּ בָאוּ־לָךְ

חַי־אָנִי נְאֻם־יְהֹוָה

כִּי כֻלָּם כָּעֲדִי תִלְבָּשִׁי

וּתְקַשְּׁרִים כַּכַּלָּה:

Commentary

49:14. *The Eternal has forsaken me.* See the essay "Why has God forsaken us?" in the previous haftarah.

15. *Stop loving.* מְרַחֵם (*m'rachem*), comes from the same root as רֶחֶם (*rechem*, womb). A woman cannot forget that her womb brought forth the child. (From this root also comes the word for compassion, רַחֲמָנוּת, *rachmanut*.)

16. *On the palms of My hands.* Another of Isaiah's startling anthropomorphisms, the more so since he declares God to be incomparable.[2]

Your safety. Literally, "Your walls," a metaphor for Israel's security.

17. *Your builders.* Reading בּוֹנַיִךְ (*bonayich*, your builders) instead of בָּנַיִךְ (*banayich*, your children).[3] See the comment to Isaiah 62:5 in the haftarah for Nitzavim and the wordplay discussed on p. 468.

19. Your ruins, your abandoned places,
    your desolated land,

shall soon be crowded with people,

while those who sought to devour you shall
    be far off.

20. Then children you have mourned

shall yet say in your hearing:

This place is too crowded for us;

make room for us to dwell in.

21. And you shall think:

Who bore all these children for me,

when I was in mourning, and childless,

exiled and left by the road?

And who brought these up?

I was all alone: where did they come from?

22. Thus says the Eternal God:

I lift My hand to the nations,

I raise My ensign to the peoples:

They shall cradle your sons in their arms,

and carry your daughters on their shoul-
    ders.

23. Kings shall serve them,

their queens shall nurse them;

they shall bow down to you, faces to the
    ground,

and lick the dust of your feet;

then you shall know that I am the Eternal,

that none who trust in Me are put to
    shame.

19 כִּי חָרְבֹתַיִךְ וְשֹׁמְמֹתַיִךְ וְאֶרֶץ הֲרִסֻתֵיךְ

כִּי עַתָּה תֵּצְרִי מִיּוֹשֵׁב

וְרָחֲקוּ מְבַלְּעָיִךְ:

20 עוֹד יֹאמְרוּ בְאָזְנַיִךְ

בְּנֵי שִׁכֻּלָיִךְ

צַר־לִי הַמָּקוֹם

גְּשָׁה־לִּי וְאֵשֵׁבָה:

21 וְאָמַרְתְּ בִּלְבָבֵךְ

מִי יָלַד־לִי אֶת־אֵלֶּה

וַאֲנִי שְׁכוּלָה וְגַלְמוּדָה

גֹּלָה וְסוּרָה

וְאֵלֶּה מִי גִדֵּל

הֵן אֲנִי נִשְׁאַרְתִּי לְבַדִּי אֵלֶּה אֵיפֹה הֵם:

22 כֹּה־אָמַר אֲדֹנָי יְהוִֹה

הִנֵּה אֶשָּׂא אֶל־גּוֹיִם יָדִי

וְאֶל־עַמִּים אָרִים נִסִּי

וְהֵבִיאוּ בָנַיִךְ בְּחֹצֶן

וּבְנֹתַיִךְ עַל־כָּתֵף תִּנָּשֶׂאנָה:

23 וְהָיוּ מְלָכִים אֹמְנַיִךְ

וְשָׂרוֹתֵיהֶם מֵינִיקֹתַיִךְ

אַפַּיִם אֶרֶץ יִשְׁתַּחֲווּ לָךְ

וַעֲפַר רַגְלַיִךְ יְלַחֵכוּ

וְיָדַעַתְּ כִּי־אֲנִי יְהוָה

אֲשֶׁר לֹא־יֵבֹשׁוּ קוָֹי:

Commentary

22-26. This prophecy, which foretells Israel's expected rise from being oppressed to being honored, is spoken in the name of *Adonai Elohim*. (On this expression see the comment in the previous haftarah, on Isaiah 40:10.)

24. Can spoil be taken away from a
   warrior?
Can a victor's captives escape?
25. And yet, says the Eternal One,
the warrior's captives shall be taken away,
the tyrant's spoil shall be retrieved,
for I will contend with those who contend
   with you,
and I will save your children.
26. I will make your oppressors eat their
   own flesh;
they shall be drunk on their own blood as
   though it were wine,
and all flesh shall know that I, the Eternal,
am your Savior, your Redeemer,
the Mighty One of Jacob.

24 הֲיֻקַּח מִגִּבּוֹר מַלְקוֹחַ

וְאִם־שְׁבִי צַדִּיק יִמָּלֵט:

25 כִּי־כֹה אָמַר יְהוָה

גַּם־שְׁבִי גִבּוֹר יֻקָּח

וּמַלְקוֹחַ עָרִיץ יִמָּלֵט

וְאֶת־יְרִיבֵךְ אָנֹכִי אָרִיב

וְאֶת־בָּנַיִךְ אָנֹכִי אוֹשִׁיעַ:

26 וְהַאֲכַלְתִּי אֶת־מוֹנַיִךְ אֶת־בְּשָׂרָם

וְכֶעָסִיס דָּמָם יִשְׁכָּרוּן

וְיָדְעוּ כָל־בָּשָׂר כִּי אֲנִי יְהוָה

מוֹשִׁיעֵךְ וְגֹאֲלֵךְ

אֲבִיר יַעֲקֹב:

Commentary

24. *Can spoil be taken …?* A rhetorical question reminiscent of the prophecies of Amos 3:3 ff.

Victor צדיק (*tzaddik*). In Isaiah's verbal imagery, being righteous leads to being victorious. The Septuagint and a Qumran manuscript read עריץ (*aritz*, tyrant) instead of *tzaddik*, victor, providing a better parallel to what follows.

26. The fate with which a faithless Israel is threatened in the Torah (Deuteronomy chapter 28), is—with the same harsh language—now foretold for Israel's enemies.

Drunk on their own blood. This image may be based on an actual practice, attested to by the Greek historian Herodotus, who lived close to the time of Isaiah and reported that Scythian warriors drank the blood of their first victims.[4]

The Mighty One of Jacob. אביר יעקב (*Avir ya'acov*), one of the descriptive names given to God.[5]

50:1. Where is your mother's bill of divorce

with which I sent her away?

asks the Eternal One.

Which of My creditors was it,

to whom I sold you?

You were sold because of your own sins,

for your own transgressions your mother

    was sent away.

2. Why, when I came, was no one there,

no one to answer, when I called?

Is My hand really too weak to redeem?

Do I lack the power to save?

With My rebuke I dry up the sea,

and turn rivers into desert.

Fish stink from lack of water

and die on parched ground.

כֹּה אָמַר יְהֹוָה 50:1

אֵי זֶה סֵפֶר כְּרִיתוּת אִמְּכֶם

אֲשֶׁר שִׁלַּחְתִּיהָ

אוֹ מִי מִנּוֹשַׁי

אֲשֶׁר־מָכַרְתִּי אֶתְכֶם לוֹ

הֵן בַּעֲוֹנֹתֵיכֶם נִמְכַּרְתֶּם

וּבְפִשְׁעֵיכֶם שֻׁלְּחָה אִמְּכֶם:

מַדּוּעַ בָּאתִי וְאֵין אִישׁ 2

קָרָאתִי וְאֵין עוֹנֶה

הֲקָצוֹר קָצְרָה יָדִי מִפְּדוּת

וְאִם־אֵין־בִּי כֹחַ לְהַצִּיל

הֵן בְּגַעֲרָתִי אַחֲרִיב יָם

אָשִׂים נְהָרוֹת מִדְבָּר

תִּבְאַשׁ דְּגָתָם מֵאֵין מַיִם

וְתָמֹת בַּצָּמָא:

Commentary

50:1. *Divorce.* כריתות (*k'ritut*) means literally "cutting." To this day, the traditional divorce ceremony ends with the document (the *get*) being cut apart. Israel's exile is described by the metaphor of divorce, an image first used by Hosea. Jeremiah applies this terminology to the fall of the Northern Kingdom, calling it the Eternal's "bill of divorce."[6]

I sold you. Selling a daughter's services to pay a debt is mentioned in Exodus 21:7. The indenture lasted a fixed number of years.

2. *When I came.* When My Presence became known to you, you turned away and did not respond to Me. The Targum avoids the anthropomorphic expression and translates: "When I sent My prophets."

Is My hand really too weak? Literally, "too short." Isaiah here uses an expression found in the Torah.[7]

With My rebuke I dry up the sea. Isaiah employs ancient imagery known in Ugaritic myths, which told of the fertility god Baal rebuking the sea. The Ugaritic word for "rebuke" in that context is *ga'ar*, just as here.[8]

And die on parched ground. This reading provides a parallel to the first half of the verse, by substituting צמאון (*tzima'on*, parched ground) for צמא (*tzama*, thirst) as in Isaiah 35:7.[9] The literal text, unemended, reads, "and die of thirst."

3. I shroud the skies in blackness,

and make their clothing sackcloth.

4. The Eternal God has taught me how to
   speak,

even to those tired of speech.

Morning by morning God awakens me,

awakens my ear,

teaching me to listen.

5. The Eternal God opened my ear;

and I did not rebel, I did not turn away.

6. I gave my back to those who beat me,

my cheeks to those who tore out my hair.

I did not hide my face from insult and
   spitting.

7. For the Eternal God will help me,

and therefore I feel no disgrace,

but have set my face like flint,

knowing that I shall not be put to shame.

8. My champion is near,

who dare contend with me?

Let us stand up together [to be judged]!

Who are my adversaries?

Let them confront me!

9. With the Eternal God to help me,

who can declare me wrong?

They shall wear out like a garment,

like moth-eaten cloth.

3 אַלְבִּישׁ שָׁמַיִם קַדְרוּת

וְשַׂק אָשִׂים כְּסוּתָם:

4 אֲדֹנָי יֱהֹוִה נָתַן לִי לְשׁוֹן לִמּוּדִים

לָדַעַת לָעוּת אֶת־יָעֵף דָּבָר יָעִיר

בַּבֹּקֶר בַּבֹּקֶר יָעִיר לִי אֹזֶן

לִשְׁמֹעַ כַּלִּמּוּדִים:

5 אֲדֹנָי יֱהֹוִה פָּתַח־לִי אֹזֶן

וְאָנֹכִי לֹא מָרִיתִי אָחוֹר לֹא נְסוּגֹתִי:

6 גֵּוִי נָתַתִּי לְמַכִּים

וּלְחָיַי לְמֹרְטִים

פָּנַי לֹא הִסְתַּרְתִּי מִכְּלִמּוֹת וָרֹק:

7 וַאדֹנָי יֱהֹוִה יַעֲזָר־לִי

עַל־כֵּן לֹא נִכְלָמְתִּי

עַל־כֵּן שַׂמְתִּי פָנַי כַּחַלָּמִישׁ

וָאֵדַע כִּי־לֹא אֵבוֹשׁ:

8 קָרוֹב מַצְדִּיקִי

מִי־יָרִיב אִתִּי

נַעַמְדָה יָּחַד

מִי־בַעַל מִשְׁפָּטִי

יִגַּשׁ אֵלָי:

9 הֵן אֲדֹנָי יֱהֹוִה יַעֲזָר־לִי

מִי־הוּא יַרְשִׁיעֵנִי

הֵן כֻּלָּם כַּבֶּגֶד יִבְלוּ

עָשׁ יֹאכְלֵם:

Commentary

4-9. These verses are quite different from the surrounding text and strike a special note.
See the essay below, *The Mystery of the "Servant."*

4. Our translation is a free rendering of the Prophet's message. The Hebrew is difficult.

5. *Opened my ear.* An example of Isaiah borrowing an idiom from Akkadian, the ancient
language spoken in Babylon, where the Prophet lived.

10. Who among you reveres the Eternal,

and respects the words of God's servant,

who walks in darkness,

though he has no light,

who trusts in the Eternal

and leans upon God?

11. But you—all of you— who kindle [your

own] fire,

who set torches alight,

go walk by the blaze of your fire,

by the torches you have lit.

This comes to you from My hand:

you shall lie down in pain.

51:1. Listen to Me, all who pursue justice,

all who seek the Eternal:

Look to the rock from which you were

hewn,

the quarry from which you were cut.

2. Look back to Abraham your father,

and to Sarah who bore you.

When I called him he was alone,

but I blessed him and made him many.

3. Just so the Eternal will comfort Zion,

comforting all her ruins:

making her wilderness like Eden,

her desert like the Eternal's garden,

where joy and gladness are found,

thanksgiving and the strains of song.

10 מִי בָכֶם יְרֵא יְהֹוָה

שֹׁמֵעַ בְּקוֹל עַבְדּוֹ

אֲשֶׁר ׀ הָלַךְ חֲשֵׁכִים

וְאֵין נֹגַהּ לוֹ

יִבְטַח בְּשֵׁם יְהֹוָה

וְיִשָּׁעֵן בֵּאלֹהָיו:

11 הֵן כֻּלְּכֶם קֹדְחֵי אֵשׁ

מְאַזְּרֵי זִיקוֹת

לְכוּ ׀ בְּאוּר אֶשְׁכֶם

וּבְזִיקוֹת בִּעַרְתֶּם

מִיָּדִי הָיְתָה־זֹּאת לָכֶם

לְמַעֲצֵבָה תִּשְׁכָּבוּן:

51:1 שִׁמְעוּ אֵלַי רֹדְפֵי צֶדֶק

מְבַקְשֵׁי יְהֹוָה

הַבִּיטוּ אֶל־צוּר חֻצַּבְתֶּם

וְאֶל־מַקֶּבֶת בּוֹר נֻקַּרְתֶּם:

2 הַבִּיטוּ אֶל־אַבְרָהָם אֲבִיכֶם

וְאֶל־שָׂרָה תְּחוֹלֶלְכֶם

כִּי־אֶחָד קְרָאתִיו

וַאֲבָרְכֵהוּ וְאַרְבֵּהוּ:

3 כִּי־נִחַם יְהֹוָה צִיּוֹן

נִחַם כָּל־חָרְבֹתֶיהָ

וַיָּשֶׂם מִדְבָּרָהּ כְּעֵדֶן

וְעַרְבָתָהּ כְּגַן־יְהֹוָה

שָׂשׂוֹן וְשִׂמְחָה יִמָּצֵא בָהּ

תּוֹדָה וְקוֹל זִמְרָה:

Commentary

51:1-3. The concluding verses of the haftarah evoke Torah images: the story of the Garden of Eden (Genesis 3) and Genesis 17, which tells of God's promise to make the descendants of Abraham and Sarah a great people.[10]

Essay

The mystery of the "servant"

Verses 4-9 in chapter 50 of this haftarah are clearly different from the surrounding text. The voice that speaks here seems to belong to one that suffers and desperately asks for help from God. The tone reminds one of Job and his challenge to his Maker to let him know why he was so sorely stricken.

The question arises: Who is the subject of this tearful inquiry? Is it Isaiah himself who, like Jeremiah, has suffered persecution because of his prophecies? Possibly so, but nowhere in his book does the Prophet identify himself as the one who has suffered. Rather, this passage and three others like it have a wider sweep than voicing the cry of the author (42:1-4; 49:1-6; and a long passage, 52:13-53:12. These three are not included among the haftarot).

Although in Second Isaiah these poems are scattered, scholars have grouped them together because they pursue the same theme. They have called them the "servant songs," since the first one sets the theme by beginning:

> See, My servant whom I uphold,
> My chosen one in whom I delight. (42:1).

Just who is the servant? This question has given rise to lengthy discussions between biblical commentators of earlier and modern days, as well as theologians of Judaism and Christianity.

Throughout Isaiah's book, Israel as a people is called God's servant, but the four songs do not carry that identification. They appear to point to an individual in that they are highly personal in tone, and especially the 53rd chapter seems to suggest a messianic figure. Did the Prophet here refer to himself? Possibly, though nowhere is there any hint in the rest of his book that he, a member of the royal family, was exposed to the kind of suffering that Jeremiah endured. [11]

The Aramaic translation by Jonathan ben Uzziel and many midrashim interpret the passsages as referring to the Messiah, and Christian theologians of the past saw them as predictions of the coming of Jesus. While Jewish and non-Jewish commentators of our time have abandoned any messianic identification, they have not been able to agree on whom the Prophet might have had in mind.

Jewish tradition staunchly held that Israel was a collective, rather than an individual; that Israel was the servant who suffered and was "cut off from the land of the living" (53:9). This reading has overwhelmingly been the Jewish view,[12] and is predominant today among non-Jewish scholars as well.[13]

This understanding must be supported, in contrast to Christian interpretations that continue to identify the servant as the Jesus of the Gospels. It is worth noting that the whole concept of the "suffering servant" is not developed in the Gospels, and only the verses in

Isaiah 53:7-8 are applied to Jesus by Philip the almoner.[14] Later Christian literature, however, did lay much emphasis on this identification and built a significant portion of its theology around it. Whether Jesus saw himself in this light is doubtful.

While today the controversy has run its course, it did agitate the Rabbis for centuries. A whole collection of Jewish comments on Isaiah chapter 53 reflects this concern.[15] When the haftarot were selected (a process that stretched over several generations) the controversy was still heated, and it is not suprising, therefore, that three of the four "servant songs," among them the most controversial one from chapter 53, were not included in the selections for the haftarot.[16]

Even though Isaiah did not generally think in messianic terms, his prophecies did lift Israel beyond the scope of the here and now. His people had a task to fulfill that was difficult even as it was glorious. That task existed then, and it continues into time unbounded.[17]

Gleanings

Words to Remember

look to the rock from which you were hewn,
the quarry from which you were cut.
Look back to Abraham your father,
and to Sarah who bore you. (51:1-2)

The mystery of the "servant".

Our opponents [the Christian theologians] say that these passages refer to their God, supposing the "servant" to signify him. If their view be correct, then he should have had offspring and have long life (Isaiah 53:10). The proof of the proper meaning lies in the passages immediately before (52:12, where 'you' signifies Israel) and immediately afterward (54:1, where 'the barren one' signifies Israel).

"My servant" means each individual belonging to Israel, and thus God's servant, who is in exile.

Abraham ibn Ezra[18]

The Servant is conceived as an individual figure, but he is the figure who recapitulates in himself all the religious gifts and the religious mission of Israel.

John L. McKenzie[19]

The New Testament shared a broad understanding with contemporary rabbinic interpretation. For both communities the message of Second Isaiah was not tied to a sixth century referent, but was understood to address an eschatological hope to future Israel. The disagreement between Jews and Christians in the use of Isaiah remains a theological one—what is the nature of the promise and who is Israel?—and cannot be resolved by appeals to 'objective, scientific exegesis.'

Brevard S. Childs[20]

There is very little in the Gospels to support the traditional view that Jesus identified his mission with that of the Servant of the Songs.

Morna D. Hooker[21]

* * *

Notes

[1] For the sake of brevity, in our commentary on the "Seven [Haftarot] of Comfort," Second Isaiah is simply called Isaiah.

[2] See Isaiah 40:45; haftarah for D'varim. It has been suggested that כפים ought to be read and understood as "stone," based on the Targum's use of *tzar*, which would also provide a parallel to the verse.

[3] Suggested by S.D. Sperling, in a written communication.

[4] *Histories* IV:65.

[5] See the Torah Commentary, p. 31.

[6] Jeremiah 3:6-8, where he speaks of a *sefer keritut*.

[7] Numbers 11:23.

[8] A few verses hence (after the haftarah, 51:9) Isaiah is even more graphic when he describes how the arm of the Eternal slew the primeval sea monsters before drying up the sea.

[9] So JPS Notes; also A. S. Herbert, *The Book of the Prophet Isaiah* (1975). Another suggestion, made by Bernhard Duhm, *Das Buch Jesaja* (1968), is to insert the word *b'hemtam* (their cattle) into the text. The reading then is: "Their cattle die of thirst."

[10] Reminiscent of Isaiah 54:9; haftarah for Noah. Rashi and Radak emphasize that even as Abraham was alone in a strange land when the divine promise was made, so is the promise now issued to a people alone in a land not theirs.

[11] The most elaborate defense of identifying Isaiah as the servant was mounted by Harry M. Orlinsky, "The So-called Servant of the Lord," *Supplements to Vetus Testamentum*, XIV (1967) pp. 1-133. There were also attempts to identify the servant with other biblical figures such as Moses, Jeremiah (so none other than Rav Saadia Gaon, on 52:15), Zerubbabel, or even Cyrus.

[12] So Rashi, Radak, and particularly Isaac Abarbanel, who devotes a lengthy discourse to this matter. (See the translation in Neubauer and Driver (cited below), pp. 153-197.

[13] There is also a frequently voiced opinion that these songs were not authored by Isaiah at all and were added to the book at a later time.

[14] Acts 7:33-34.

[15] See A. Neubauer and S. R. Driver, *The 53rd Chapter of Isaiah According to the Jewish Interpreters* (originally published 1876; reprinted 1969). The first volume contains the texts in Hebrew; the second provides the translations.

[16] This conclusion suggests itself, though ancient sources make no reference to it. No doubt our haftarah was admitted because its context clearly points to Israel as God's servant.

[17] Brevard S. Childs, *Introduction to the Old Testament as Scripture*, pp. 336 ff. calls the songs "meta-historical" (see *Gleanings*). See also Issachar Jacobson, *Chazon Hamikra*, vol. 2, pp. 57 ff., for an analysis by Joseph Carlebach (*Die drei grossen Propheten*, 1932, pp. 28-40). Carlebach holds that the central theme of the songs is the search for certainty: Israel wants to know not so much *why* it is exposed to suffering but that it suffers for God's sake. It is a

question that reaches beyond one particular incident in history, but is Israel's existential question.

[18] Comments on Isaiah 53; however, he also gives weight to Rav Saadia's view that Isaiah may have meant the prophet Jeremiah.

[19] *Introduction to the Old Testament*, p. LIII.

[20] *Introduction to the Old Testament as Scripture*, p. 338.

[21] *The Influence of the Servant Concept of Deutero-Isaiah in the New Testament*, p.102.

רְאֵה

Isaiah, chapter 54, verse 11 to chapter 55, verse 5

Introduction

This is the third of the *sheva de-nechamta,* the "seven [haftarot] of consolation." Four others will follow, all from the Second Isaiah, the last one to be recited on the Shabbat before Rosh Hashanah. (See the Introduction to the haftarah for Va'et-chanan, the first of the seven). This haftarah serves also as part of the haftarah for Noach.

Connection of haftarah and Shabbat:

The theme of consolation rather than the connection with the sidra seems to be the main reason for this haftarah to have been chosen by the Sages. It appears that at one time another haftarah was read on this Shabbat, a selection from Zechariah 9, but since its ninth verse was interpreted by Christians to be a direct forecasting of Jesus, its recitation in the synagogue ceased, and the haftarah for Noach replaced it.[1]

The setting:

The Second Isaiah, author of this prophecy, lived among his people in Babylonian exile (6th century B.C.E.). The people had suffered grievously and were now in Babylonian exile; many despaired of ever returning to their homeland. But now—with the expected victory of the Persians over the Babylonians—there was hope that their fortunes might be reversed.

For more on Second Isaiah, see our *General Introduction.*[2]

The message:

The selection for this Shabbat consists of only 12 verses (while the haftarah to Noach is almost twice as long). God's abiding promise to turn the present, unhappy fate of Israel's exiles into glorious happiness is the main theme, as it is in all the "seven [haftarot] of consolation."

1. Israel's enemies will not prevail; instead, God's people will be safe from oppression. (54:11-17)

2. All that is needed for this glorious fate to be realized is Israel's true return to God, who will renew the everlasting covenant and fulfill the promise made to David. (55:1-5)

54:11. Ah, unhappy, storm-tossed soul,
with none to comfort you:
I will make garnets your building-stones,
and sapphires your foundations.

12. I will build your towers with rubies,
your gates with precious stones,
your border with gems.

13. All your children shall be taught by the
Eternal,
and great shall be the happiness of your
children.

14. You shall be established in righteousness,
safe from oppression, and unafraid;
safe from terror—it will not come near you.

15. Should any attack you, it will not be
My doing;
whoever attacks you will fall on your
account.

16. It is I who created the smith
who fans the coal in the fire and forges
weapons by his work;

54:11 עֲנִיָּה סֹעֲרָה

לֹא נֻחָמָה

הִנֵּה אָנֹכִי מַרְבִּיץ בַּפּוּךְ אֲבָנַיִךְ

וִיסַדְתִּיךְ בַּסַּפִּירִים:

12 וְשַׂמְתִּי כַּדְכֹד שִׁמְשֹׁתַיִךְ

וּשְׁעָרַיִךְ לְאַבְנֵי אֶקְדָּח

וְכָל־גְּבוּלֵךְ לְאַבְנֵי־חֵפֶץ:

13 וְכָל־בָּנַיִךְ לִמּוּדֵי יְהוָה

וְרַב שְׁלוֹם בָּנָיִךְ:

14 בִּצְדָקָה תִּכּוֹנָנִי

רַחֲקִי מֵעֹשֶׁק כִּי־לֹא תִירָאִי

וּמִמְּחִתָּה כִּי לֹא־תִקְרַב אֵלָיִךְ:

15 הֵן גּוֹר יָגוּר אֶפֶס מֵאוֹתִי

מִי־גָר אִתָּךְ עָלַיִךְ יִפּוֹל:

16 הֵן [הִנֵּה] אָנֹכִי בָּרָאתִי חָרָשׁ

נֹפֵחַ בְּאֵשׁ פֶּחָם וּמוֹצִיא כְלִי לְמַעֲשֵׂהוּ

Commentary

11. *Garnets.* פוּךְ (*puch*); others translate as carbuncles.[3]

Sapphires. ספירים (*sappirim*). The Hebrew and English words have the same linguistic origin.[4] The Prophet uses the imagery of precious stones to depict the wondrous restoration of Israel to its home.

13. *All your children....* A famous rabbinic wordplay is based on this verse (see *Gleanings*).

Happiness. שלום (*shalom*) means more than "peace"; it conveys total well-being.

15. The verse features a wordplay on גור (*gur*), but its meaning is not clear. The Prophet apparently warns that whatever danger may lie ahead will come from within the people, and not from external enemies.

I also create the destroyer to wreak havoc.

17. No weapon fashioned against you can succeed;

you shall defeat all who rise to accuse you.

That is the heritage of the Eternal's servants,

and I am the Source of their vindication,

says the Eternal.

55:1. Come, all who are thirsty, come for water;

even if you have no money, come buy food and eat:

come buy food without money, wine and milk without cost.

2. Why spend money for what is not bread?

Why spend your wages for what does not satisfy?

Listen well to Me, and you shall eat what is good,

and your souls shall delight in abundance.

וְאָנֹכִי בָּרָאתִי מַשְׁחִית לְחַבֵּל:

17 כָּל־כְּלִי יוּצַר עָלַיִךְ לֹא יִצְלָח

וְכָל־לָשׁוֹן תָּקוּם־אִתָּךְ לַמִּשְׁפָּט תַּרְשִׁיעִי

זֹאת נַחֲלַת עַבְדֵי יְהֹוָה

וְצִדְקָתָם מֵאִתִּי נְאֻם־יְהֹוָה:

55:1 הוֹי כָּל־צָמֵא לְכוּ לַמַּיִם

וַאֲשֶׁר אֵין־לוֹ כָּסֶף לְכוּ שִׁבְרוּ וֶאֱכֹלוּ

וּלְכוּ שִׁבְרוּ בְּלוֹא־כֶסֶף

וּבְלוֹא מְחִיר יַיִן וְחָלָב:

2 לָמָּה תִשְׁקְלוּ־כֶסֶף בְּלוֹא־לֶחֶם

וִיגִיעֲכֶם בְּלוֹא לְשָׂבְעָה

שִׁמְעוּ שָׁמוֹעַ אֵלַי וְאִכְלוּ־טוֹב

וְתִתְעַנַּג בַּדֶּשֶׁן נַפְשְׁכֶם:

Commentary

17. *That is the heritage.* Ibn Ezra takes this to be a messianic reference: The heritage of the Children of Israel will be the universal acceptance of the One God.

55:1. *Come, all who are thirsty.* The Prophet literally advertises his spiritual wares.[5] He does not here speak of physical water, bread and choice food, but of God's teachings, which truly satisfy and are available without money. The figure of speech employs an image first uttered by the prophet Amos (8th century B.C.E.):

> *The days will come, says the Eternal One,*
> *When I will send famine to the land,*
> *But it will not be a hunger for bread*
> *Or a thirst for water:*
> *It will be [a yearning] to hear the words of the Eternal* (8:11).

Buy. שברו (*shivru*), literally "break"; compare the English expression "to break bread."[6]

3. Open your ears and come to Me;
hearken and you shall live.
I will make an everlasting covenant with
   you,
(like) the true love I extended to David.
4. As once I made him a witness to the
   world,
a prince and commander of nations,
5. so now you shall summon a people you
   do not know,
and people that do not know you shall
   come running to you,
because of the Eternal your God,
the Holy One of Israel,
who has given you glory.

3 הַטּוּ אָזְנְכֶם וּלְכוּ אֵלַי

שִׁמְעוּ וּתְחִי נַפְשְׁכֶם

וְאֶכְרְתָה לָכֶם בְּרִית עוֹלָם

חַסְדֵי דָוִד הַנֶּאֱמָנִים:

4 הֵן עֵד לְאוּמִּים נְתַתִּיו

נָגִיד וּמְצַוֵּה לְאֻמִּים:

5 הֵן גּוֹי לֹא־תֵדַע תִּקְרָא

וְגוֹי לֹא־יְדָעוּךָ אֵלֶיךָ יָרוּצוּ

לְמַעַן יְהוָה אֱלֹהֶיךָ

וְלִקְדוֹשׁ יִשְׂרָאֵל

כִּי פֵאֲרָךְ:

Commentary

3-5. In these verses, the connection of the covenant that God made with Israel is related to the covenant that was made with David. The allusion is to Psalm 89 and especially to verse 29:

> Forever will My unending love attend to him,
> And My covenant with him be established.[7]

Isaiah expects not only the reestablishment of the exiles in their ancestral land, but also that they will be ruled by a king from the House of David. The renewal of the covenant did indeed take place after the return, when Ezra led the people in a ceremony of formal rededication (Nehemiah chapter 8).[8] (See the essay following.)

3. *(Like) the true love....* A difficult verse; our translation follows Rashi and Metzudat David.

4. *I made him a witness to the world.* Referring to David or possibly to Zerubbabel, who became the civil head of the returnees and who was a descendant of the House of David.

5. *So now you shall summon a people.* In that day, by your example, even those you do not know will cause others to seek the One God.

466

Essay

The promise to David (55:3)

When Isaiah talked of renewing the covenant that God had made with David, he touched on an old popular tradition. The fabled king had already been dead for 400 years and more, but his memory was as fresh as when he lived—perhaps even more so. He had been warrior, poet, and ruler. He had lived a tumultuous life that knew tragedy and happiness; he had been a refugee fleeing from a jealous and mad king; he had lost Jonathan, his dearest friend, and Absalom, his favorite son. He had risen from humble beginnings as a shepherd boy to become the absolute monarch of his people, whose boundaries he enlarged and secured. David was the one who wrested the city of Jerusalem from the Jebusites and made it the capital of his united nation.

He was a passionate believer in the One God, to whom he ascribed all his successes and to whom he sang songs we still sing today.[9] He was thoroughly human and had serious character flaws, but he was distinguished by his capacity for repentance. After he had committed a particularly grievous sin and was confronted by the prophet Nathan, he humbly acknowledged his failing and asked forgiveness. He was granted his request, but he did not escape punishment. The goal that above all else he wanted to achieve was denied him: the building of a Temple to God in Jerusalem would be left to his son and successor, Solomon.[10]

Withal, and most important, God had promised an everlasting kingdom to David and his descendants. Though during the Babylonian exile, the rule of the House of David was inoperative, there was a general belief among the people that this was but a temporary interruption. Had not the prophet Nathan spoken in the name of God: "Your throne shall be established forever"?[11] And had not the Psalmist phrased this promise in words known to every Jew:

> *I will maintain My unending love for him always,*
> *My covenant with him shall endure.*
> *I will establish his line forever,*
> *his throne, as long as the heavens last.*[12]

As the centuries went by, Jews came to believe that even the Messiah would be a descendant of David.[13]

David had begun his rule about the year 1000 B.C.E. Instead of a remote figure consigned to history books, he has remained alive the in the hearts of his people. Like the prophet Elijah whose presence is evoked at the Seder table, so David too is recalled in a popular folk song: דוד מלך ישראל חי וקים (*david, melech yisra'el, chai v'kayam*), "David, king of Israel, lives now and forever!"

467

Gleanings

All your children shall be taught by the Eternal,
and great shall be the happiness of your children. (54:13)

Why spend money for what is not bread?
Why spend your wages for what does not satisfy? (55:2)

Come, all who are thirsty, come for water (55:1)

Rabbi Chanina bar Pappa noted a seeming contradiction between two verses in the book of Isaiah. In one verse he says that everyone who is thirsty should go and find water (that is, Torah), while earlier he urges us that we "meet the thirsty with water" (21:14). In one instance we are to bring it to them; in the other, we ask them to find it for themselves.

The Sages' answer to this puzzle is rather cryptic, and Rashi explains it as follows: If a teacher of Torah is authentic, he will bring water to the thirsty; but if he is not, students will have to search for themselves until they find it.

Talmud[14]

In the school of Rabbi Ishmael they taught:

If your evil inclination tempts you, by all means bring it with you to the place where water is dispensed (that is, to the house of study where Torah is taught). Even if the inclination is hard as stone it will be overcome by the living waters of Torah, as it is said, "Water wears away stone" (Job 14:19).

Talmud[15]

A play on words

The Prophet says, "All your children shall be taught by the Eternal, and great shall be the *shalom* of your children" (54:13).

Rabbi Eleazar said in the name of Rabbi Chanina: "Those who study Torah help to build peace in the world." This conclusion is supported by a wordplay on בָּנַיִךְ, *banayich*, "your children." By pronouncing it בּוֹנַיִךְ, *bonayich*, we obtain the meaning "your builders": Those who learn and teach Torah become *bonayich*, building *shalom* for your children.

Talmud[16]

"All your children shall be taught by the Eternal" hints at the world-to-come. In this world we have human teachers, but in messianic days we shall have the Eternal One as our teacher.

Midrash[17]

This verse is an important landmark in the history of civilization. In obedience to it, Israel led the world in universal education. "The Jewish religion, because it was a literature-sustained religion, led to the first efforts to provide elementary instruction for all children of the community" (H.G. Wells).

(The wordplay) proclaims a wonderful truth: the *children* of a nation are the *builders* of its future. And every Jewish child must be reared to become such a builder of his People's better future.

Joseph H. Hertz[18]

* * *

Notes

[1] Pesikta Rabbati, Piska 34, ed. Braude and Kapstein, p. 663, footnote 2 (citing Friedman).

[2] For the sake of brevity, in our commentary on the "Seven [Haftarot] of Consolation," Second Isaiah is simply called Isaiah.

[3] For example, JPS.

[4] Probably Old Indian. Others render as lapis lazuli.

[5] Westermann, p. 282, calls it the Prophet's "market place invitation" to listen to his words.

[6] The term first appears in the sense of "buy" in Genesis 42:2, in the Joseph story.

[7] Assuming it to be earlier than Isaiah and to have been known to him.

[8] See also Westermann, p. 285, who sees David as the mediator of the blessing bestowed on Israel as a people. For Ibn Ezra, the prophecy refers to messianic days.

[9] These songs are found in the book of Psalms. Many of them begin by stating "A Psalm of David." See Psalm 23, for example. Scholars have attempted to identify those poems that can with some certainty be traced to David.

[10] See II Samuel chapters 11 and 12.

[11] II Samuel 7:16.

[12] Psalm 89:29-30.

[13] The Christian Scriptures therefore present a genealogical line that traces the ancestry of Jesus to King David (see Matthew chapter 1).

[14] Ta'anit 7a.

[15] Sukkah 52b.

[16] *B.* Berachot 64a (end); Keritot 28b. In fact, the Dead Sea manuscript of Isaiah reads *bonayich*, your builders.

[17] Pesikta Rabbati deRab Kahana, 12:22.

[18] *Pentateuch and Haftorahs*, p. 818.

Isaiah, chapter 51, verse 12 to chapter 52, verse 12

Introduction

On this fourth Shabbat after Tisha b'Av, we read the fourth prophecy of the *sheva de-nechamta*, the "seven [haftarot] of consolation." Three others will follow, all from the Second Isaiah, the last one to be recited on the Shabbat before Rosh Hashanah. (See the Introduction to the haftarah for Va'et-chanan.)

Connection of haftarah and Shabbat:

The theme of consolation rather than the connection with the sidra appears to be the main reason for this haftarah to have been chosen by the Sages.

The setting:

The people were in Babylonian exile, and had suffered grievously. Now, however—with the expected victory of the Persians over the Babylonians—they had high hopes that their fortunes would be reversed and their present unhappy fate turned into glorious happiness.

The Second Isaiah, who is the author of this prophecy and whose real identity is unknown, lived among his people in Babylonian exile (6th century B.C.E.).

For more on Second Isaiah, see our *General Introduction*.[1]

The message:

1. "I, I am the One who comforts you," says God. (51:12-16)

2. The terror and misery that have befallen you came from God, and it is God who will end your trouble. (51:17-23)

3. An ode to Zion restored. (52:1-10; see the essay below)

4. Prepare yourselves spiritually to go back to your homeland. (52:11-12)

HAFTARAH FOR SHOF'TIM

Isaiah, chapter 51, verse 12 to chapter 52, verse 12

51:12. I, I am the One who comforts you:

what is wrong with you, that you are afraid
    of mortals,

of human beings who become like grass,

13. that you forget the Eternal your Maker,

who spread out the heavens and estab-
    lished the earth?

All day long you are in terror

of the fury of an oppressor

intent on your destruction.

Yet where is the oppressor's fury?

14. Neither death nor the grave for you
    who bend low:

you shall be free and lack nothing.

15. For I am the Eternal your God;

I stir up the sea and make its waves roar,

God of heaven's hosts is My name.

אָנֹכִי אָנֹכִי הוּא מְנַחֶמְכֶם 51:12

מִי־אַתְּ וַתִּירְאִי מֵאֱנוֹשׁ יָמוּת

וּמִבֶּן־אָדָם חָצִיר יִנָּתֵן׃

וַתִּשְׁכַּח יְהוָה עֹשֶׂךָ 13

נוֹטֶה שָׁמַיִם וְיֹסֵד אָרֶץ

וַתְּפַחֵד תָּמִיד כָּל־הַיּוֹם

מִפְּנֵי חֲמַת הַמֵּצִיק

כַּאֲשֶׁר כּוֹנֵן לְהַשְׁחִית

וְאַיֵּה חֲמַת הַמֵּצִיק׃

מִהַר צֹעֶה לְהִפָּתֵחַ וְלֹא־יָמוּת לַשַּׁחַת 14

וְלֹא יֶחְסַר לַחְמוֹ׃

וְאָנֹכִי יְהוָה אֱלֹהֶיךָ 15

רֹגַע הַיָּם וַיֶּהֱמוּ גַּלָּיו

יְהוָה צְבָאוֹת שְׁמוֹ׃

Commentary

51:12. Who *comforts you*. מנחמכם (*menachemchem*). In subsequent ages, Menachem ("one who comforts") became a popular Jewish name, as did its Yiddish diminutive, Mendel.

Like grass. חציר (*chatzir*). Elsewhere too the Second Isaiah likens humans to grass.[2]

13. This verse is one of many in Second Isaiah in which the creation of the world is a prominent motif. Living in a Diaspora that blended various traditions and was now strongly influenced by the Zoroastrianism of the Persian rulers, the Prophet may here be responding subtly to this new dominant religion, whose ruling deity was regularly called "the Creator Ahuramazda." The second phrase of this verse appears in the *Aleinu*.[3]

Your Maker. This expression has entered the English language as a synonym for God. In the book of Genesis, the verb עשה describes God as "making" the world; and the same word is used here to describe God as the Maker of Israel. It underscores the unlimited power of the Eternal.

Where is the oppressor's fury? The tyrants who rule today will be gone tomorrow.[4]

14. *Neither death nor the grave*. Our somewhat free translation attempts to render a rather obscure text, and transposes the Hebrew from the third masculine singular.

16. I have put My words in your mouth
and sheltered you with My hand;
I spread out the heavens and established
   the earth,
I say to Zion: You are My people.

17. Rouse yourself, rouse yourself,
rise up, Jerusalem,
you have drunk from the Eternal's hand
   the cup of wrath,
and drained to the dregs the bowl that
   made you stagger.

18. She has none to guide her, of all her
   children she bore;
none to take her by the hand, of all the
   children she raised.

19. These two things have befallen you:
devastation, destruction—who will console
   you?
famine and sword—who can comfort you?

16 וָאָשִׂים דְּבָרַי בְּפִיךָ

וּבְצֵל יָדִי כִּסִּיתִיךָ

לִנְטֹעַ שָׁמַיִם וְלִיסֹד אָרֶץ

וְלֵאמֹר לְצִיּוֹן עַמִּי־אָתָּה:

17 הִתְעוֹרְרִי הִתְעוֹרְרִי

קוּמִי יְרוּשָׁלַם

אֲשֶׁר שָׁתִית מִיַּד יְהֹוָה אֶת־כּוֹס חֲמָתוֹ

אֶת־קֻבַּעַת כּוֹס הַתַּרְעֵלָה שָׁתִית מָצִית:

18 אֵין־מְנַהֵל לָהּ מִכָּל־בָּנִים יָלָדָה

וְאֵין מַחֲזִיק בְּיָדָהּ מִכָּל־בָּנִים גִּדֵּלָה:

19 שְׁתַּיִם הֵנָּה קֹרְאֹתַיִךְ

מִי יָנוּד לָךְ הַשֹּׁד וְהַשֶּׁבֶר

וְהָרָעָב וְהַחֶרֶב מִי אֲנַחֲמֵךְ:

Commentary

16. *I have put My words in your mouth.* The Prophet emphasizes that he is but the mouthpiece of the Eternal.[5] The message of the One God has been committed to Israel as a sacred trust. Isaiah elaborates this later on: "My spirit is upon you, and My words which I have put in your mouth shall not depart from you, nor from your children or your children's children, henceforth and forever, says the Eternal One" (59:21).

You are My people. Repeating Hosea's formulation of God reclaiming Israel.[6]

17. *Cup of wrath.* The image is used frequently by Jeremiah.[7]

That made you stagger. From misfortune. Israel in exile, says Ibn Ezra, is like someone drunk, staggering about. Now is the time to awake from the stupor of exile.

18. *She has none to guide her.* The ultimate fear of the parent: her children will not be there when she needs them. The striking metaphor of a drunken Zion has ancient Near East roots, which list the duties of a good son toward his father. He "takes him by the hand when he's drunk, carries him when he is sated with wine."[8]

20. On every street corner your children lie
    senseless

like antelopes in a net,

glutted with the wrath of the Eternal,

your God's rebuke.

21. Therefore listen to this, you who are
    afflicted,

drunk, but not with wine:

22. Thus says the Eternal One, your
    Sovereign,

your God who defends you:

I am taking from your hand the cup of
    staggering;

no more shall you drink from the bowl of
    My wrath.

23. I will put it into the hands of your
    tormentors,

those who said: *Lie down for us to trample*
    you,

so that you made your backs like the
    ground,

like a street for passers-by.

52:1. Awake, awake!

clothe yourself in strength, O Zion;

array yourself in robes of splendor,

O Holy City of Jerusalem!

Never again shall the uncircumcised and
    unclean enter you.

2. Shake off the dust

and rise up, captive Jerusalem;

strip the chain off your neck,

O captive daughter of Zion.

20 בָּנַיִךְ עֻלְּפוּ שָׁכְבוּ בְּרֹאשׁ כָּל־חוּצוֹת

כְּתוֹא מִכְמָר

הַמְלֵאִים חֲמַת־יְהֹוָה

גַּעֲרַת אֱלֹהָיִךְ:

21 לָכֵן שִׁמְעִי־נָא זֹאת עֲנִיָּה

וּשְׁכֻרַת וְלֹא מִיָּיִן:

22 כֹּה־אָמַר אֲדֹנַיִךְ יְהֹוָה

וֵאלֹהַיִךְ יָרִיב עַמּוֹ

הִנֵּה לָקַחְתִּי מִיָּדֵךְ אֶת־כּוֹס הַתַּרְעֵלָה

אֶת־קֻבַּעַת כּוֹס חֲמָתִי

לֹא־תוֹסִיפִי לִשְׁתּוֹתָהּ עוֹד:

23 וְשַׂמְתִּיהָ בְּיַד־מוֹגַיִךְ

אֲשֶׁר־אָמְרוּ לְנַפְשֵׁךְ שְׁחִי וְנַעֲבֹרָה

וַתָּשִׂימִי כָאָרֶץ גֵּוֵךְ

וְכַחוּץ לַעֹבְרִים:

52:1 עוּרִי עוּרִי

לִבְשִׁי עֻזֵּךְ צִיּוֹן

לִבְשִׁי בִּגְדֵי תִפְאַרְתֵּךְ

יְרוּשָׁלַ͏ִם עִיר הַקֹּדֶשׁ

כִּי לֹא יוֹסִיף יָבֹא־בָךְ עוֹד עָרֵל וְטָמֵא:

2 הִתְנַעֲרִי מֵעָפָר

קוּמִי שְּׁבִי יְרוּשָׁלָ͏ִם

הִתְפַּתְּחוּ [הִתְפַּתְּחִי] מוֹסְרֵי צַוָּארֵךְ

שְׁבִיָּה בַּת־צִיּוֹן:

Commentary

52:1. Here begins the Ode to Zion.
Clothe yourself. Quoted in the Sabbath hymn *L'chah Dodi.*
Enter you. To despoil you.
2. *Shake off the dust.* So also the English idiom. This, too, is quoted in *L'chah Dodi.*

3. For thus says the Eternal One:

as you were sold for nothing,

so you shall be redeemed without money.

4. For thus says the Eternal God:

Long ago, My people went down to dwell
   in Egypt

[and later] Assyria oppressed them without
   cause.

5. Now, then, says the Eternal One, what
   do I find here?

My people are carried off for nothing,

their captors howl,

My name is reviled continually, all through
   the day!

6. Be sure, then, My people shall learn My
   Name;

be sure, on that day [they shall learn that]

I am the One who speaks; here I am.

7. How beautiful upon the mountains

are the feet of the herald

who brings good tidings,

who proclaims peace,

the messenger of good tidings

who proclaims deliverance;

who says to Zion: Your God reigns!

3 כִּי־כֹה֙ אָמַ֣ר יְהֹוָ֔ה

חִנָּ֖ם נִמְכַּרְתֶּ֑ם

וְלֹ֥א בְכֶ֖סֶף תִּגָּאֵֽלוּ׃

4 כִּ֣י כֹ֤ה אָמַר֙ אֲדֹנָ֣י יְהֹוִ֔ה

מִצְרַ֛יִם יָרַד־עַמִּ֥י בָרִֽאשֹׁנָ֖ה לָג֣וּר שָׁ֑ם

וְאַשּׁ֖וּר בְּאֶ֥פֶס עֲשָׁקֽוֹ׃

5 וְעַתָּ֤ה מַה־לִּי־פֹה֙ נְאֻם־יְהֹוָ֔ה

כִּֽי־לֻקַּ֥ח עַמִּ֖י חִנָּ֑ם

מֹשְׁלָ֤יו יְהֵילִ֙ילוּ֙ נְאֻם־יְהֹוָ֔ה

וְתָמִ֥יד כׇּל־הַיּ֖וֹם שְׁמִ֥י מִנֹּאָֽץ׃

6 לָכֵ֛ן יֵדַ֥ע עַמִּ֖י שְׁמִ֑י

לָכֵן֙ בַּיּ֣וֹם הַה֔וּא

כִּֽי־אֲנִי־ה֥וּא הַֽמְדַבֵּ֖ר הִנֵּֽנִי׃

7 מַה־נָּאו֨וּ עַל־הֶהָרִ֜ים

רַגְלֵ֣י מְבַשֵּׂ֗ר

מַשְׁמִ֧יעַ שָׁל֛וֹם

מְבַשֵּׂ֥ר ט֖וֹב

מַשְׁמִ֣יעַ יְשׁוּעָ֑ה

אֹמֵ֥ר לְצִיּ֖וֹן מָלַ֥ךְ אֱלֹהָֽיִךְ׃

Commentary

3. *Without money.* God received nothing for sending Israel into exile; hence, redemption too is without compensation.[9]

4. *Assyria oppressed them without cause.* Rashi and Radak understood Egypt and Assyria to be contrasted with each other. Egypt had invited Israel and (at least initially) had shown it hospitality. Assyria's oppression had no mitigating features.

5. *My name is reviled.* A recurring theme, found also in the Torah: One reason for God redeeming Israel is to prevent a diminution of the divine name and reputation.[10]

8. Listen! your sentinels raise their voices,

together they shout for joy;

for with their own eyes they see

the return of God to Zion.

9. Together break out in a paean of praise-

ful joy,

you ruins of Jerusalem;

the Eternal comforts your people,

and redeems Jerusalem.

10. The Eternal has bared the Holy Arm

in the sight of all the nations,

and all the ends of the earth

shall see the salvation of our God.

11. Depart, depart! Go out from there!

Touch nothing impure; go out from her

midst;

purify yourselves, you bearers of the

vessels of the Eternal.

12. But you shall not go out in haste,

or leave in flight;

for the Eternal will go before you,

the God of Israel will be your rear guard.

8 קוֹל צֹפַיִךְ נָשְׂאוּ קוֹל

יַחְדָּו יְרַנֵּנוּ

כִּי עַיִן בְּעַיִן יִרְאוּ

בְּשׁוּב יְהֹוָה צִיּוֹן:

9 פִּצְחוּ רַנְּנוּ יַחְדָּו

חָרְבוֹת יְרוּשָׁלָ‍ִם

כִּי־נִחַם יְהֹוָה עַמּוֹ

גָּאַל יְרוּשָׁלָ‍ִם:

10 חָשַׂף יְהֹוָה אֶת־זְרוֹעַ קָדְשׁוֹ

לְעֵינֵי כָּל־הַגּוֹיִם

וְרָאוּ כָּל־אַפְסֵי־אָרֶץ

אֵת יְשׁוּעַת אֱלֹהֵינוּ:

11 סוּרוּ סוּרוּ צְאוּ מִשָּׁם

טָמֵא אַל־תִּגָּעוּ צְאוּ מִתּוֹכָהּ

הִבָּרוּ נֹשְׂאֵי כְּלֵי יְהֹוָה:

12 כִּי לֹא בְחִפָּזוֹן תֵּצֵאוּ

וּבִמְנוּסָה לֹא תֵלֵכוּן

כִּי־הֹלֵךְ לִפְנֵיכֶם יְהֹוָה

וּמְאַסִּפְכֶם אֱלֹהֵי יִשְׂרָאֵל:

Commentary

10. *The Holy Arm.* Literally, "His holy arm." The image of God's outstretched arm as a synonym for power is used by Moses when he retells the story of the Exodus.[11] The expression "baring the arm" is reflected in the English idiom "rolling up one's sleeve."

11-12. The two verses impress on the people that the time of redemption is near. They are to sanctify themselves and be ready for the great day of return.

12. *In haste.* The parallel to the exodus from Egypt is underscored by the word חִפָּזוֹן (*chippazon*), used in the Torah to describe the great event.[12] By invoking the parallel—but saying " *not* in haste"—Isaiah assures his audience that the second exodus will involve fewer hardships than the first.

Rear guard. Literally, "the one who collects you [who fall behind]."

Essay

The Holy City (52:1)

In four other places in the Tanach is Jerusalem called עיר הקדש (*ir ha-kodesh*), "the holy city."[13] But long before Isaiah's time the idea that the city had a special relationship to both God and Israel was deeply embedded in the people's consciousness. Mount Zion was part of the old city enclave and was called "the holy mountain."[14] In Isaiah's time, "Zion" and "Jerusalem" were used to express the two aspects of the city. Zion was predominantly its spiritual identification, and Jerusalem its geographic. Tellingly, *Hatikvah*, Israel's national anthem, describes the country as the "land of Zion and Jerusalem" (see *Gleanings*). Older texts often call Israel itself "Fair Zion," also translatable as "Daughter (of) Zion".

Since David had wrested the city from the Jebusites (about the year 1000 B.C.E.), it had become the capital of the united kingdom and, after his son Solomon had built the Temple there, the Jewish people had forever after considered the city as the symbol of its hopes. It was affectionately thought of as the City of David; and the promise of an everlasting rule that God had promised to him and his descendants was for many centuries an ever-present dream and in later ages was transmuted into a messianic hope.

> *In days to come...*
> *many peoples shall go and say:*
> *"Come, let us go up to the Mount of the Eternal,*
> *to the House of the God of Jacob.*
> *For out of Zion shall go forth Torah,*
> *and the word of the Eternal from Jerusalem."*[15]

Zion/Jerusalem was part of the Jew's daily prayers; it was mentioned in the benedictions after every meal and when a couple stood under the marriage canopy; it became part of folklore and the subject of religious law. In Jewish consciousness it was in every way "the city of God."[16] In mystical musings, there was a heavenly and an earthly Jerusalem, and cartographers showed the city as the navel or center of the earth.[17] Ravaged by the Babylonians in the 6th century B.C.E., by the Romans in the first century C.E., object of political and religious warfare for nearly two thousand years, it remains the focus of Jewish prayer and hope to this day.

But for Christians and Muslims too the city is endowed with deep religious meaning. For Christians it is the place in which the life and death of Jesus became the beginning of a new worldwide faith, with sacred buildings and sites marking his journey. For Muslims, it is

the city of Mohammed's supernatural journey and of the holy Rock upon which Abraham offered his son.[18]

Jewish hope looks to a resolution of political and religious differences surrounding the Holy City, when it will be a symbol of universal peace, a time when nations

> *shall beat their swords into plowshares*
> *and their spears into pruning hooks;*
> *nation shall not lift sword*
> *against nation,*
> *and they shall study war no more."*[19]

Gleanings

How beautiful upon the mountains
are the feet of the herald,
who brings good tidings. (52:7)

Hatikvah

As long as in the inmost heart
a Jewish spirit sings,
as long as eyes look eastward,
fixed on Zion,
our hope's not lost:
that hope of two millennia,
to be a people free in our land,
the land of Zion and Jerusalem.

Naftali Herz Imber

In England's Realm

I will not cease from Mental Fight,
Nor shall my Sword sleep in my Hand,
Till we have built Jerusalem,
In England's green & pleasant Land.

William Blake[20]

L'chah Dodi

(The poem joins the image of the Sabbath bride to that of the City of David, and does so using the language of Isaiah.)

Rouse yourself, rouse yourself!
For your light has come, arise and shine!
Awake, awake! Break out in song,
For the glory of the Eternal is revealed through you.

Shelomo Halevi (Alkabetz)[21]

City of God

The Eternal is great, and greatly acclaimed
in the City of God, the holy mountain:
Fair-crested, joy of all the earth,
Mount Zion, summit of God's dwelling,
city of the great king.

Psalm 48:2-3

Prayer for Jerusalem

> Pray for the peace (*shalom*) of Jerusalem:
> *May those who love you be at peace.*
> *May shalom reign in your ramparts,*
> *Quiet in your citadels.*

> Psalm 122:6-7

Shir Ha-ma'alot, a Song of Ascents

(Sung on every Shabbat and holy day at the beginning of *birkat ha-mazon*, the grace after the meal.)

> When the Eternal restores the fortunes of Zion
> it will be like a dream fulfilled;
> our mouths shall be filled with laughter,
> our tongues, with songs of joy ....

> Psalm 126:1-2

Lament of the Exiles

(Sung before *birkat ha-mazon* on weekdays.)

> By the rivers of Babylon,
> there we sat, sat and wept,
> as we rememebred Zion ....
> If I forget you, O Jerusalem,
> let my right hand forget its cunning;
> let my tongue stick to the roof of my mouth
> if I cease to think of you,
> if I do not remember you,
> if I do not set Jerusalem above my greatest joy.

> Psalm 137:5-6

* * *

Notes

1 For the sake of brevity, in our commentary on the "Seven [Haftarot] of Consolation," Second Isaiah is simply called "Isaiah."

2 See Isaiah 40:6; haftarah for Va'et-chanan.

3 In the Reform prayerbook the English translation too became a familar recitation; see *Gates of Prayer*, p. 616.

4 So Rashi. Radak takes it as a reference to the Assyrian king, Sennacherib, who once besieged Jerusalem. Where is he now?

5 In the same way as did Jeremiah (1:9; haftarah for Matot).

6 Hosea 1:25.

7 See especially Jeremiah 25:15-29. See also Lamentations 4:21.

8 Pritchard, *Ancient Near Eastern Texts*, p. 150b.

9 So Ibn Ezra, Malbim.

10 Compare Moses' intercession in Exodus 32:12; and see the Torah Commentary, p. 647.

11 Deuteronomy 26:8. It is prominent in Isaiah chapters 51-63. On this subject see H. L. Ginsberg in *Journal of Biblical Literature*, vol. 77 (1958), pp. 152-156.

12 Exodus 12:11; Deuteronomy 16:3.

13 Literally "city of holiness": Isaiah 48:2; Zechariah 8:3; Nehemiah 11:1 and 18.

14 Isaiah 27:13.

15 Isaiah 2:2 and following; Micah 4:1 and following. The last two lines are recited in synagogue worship whenever the scrolls are taken from the Ark.

16 So often called in Psalms 46, 48, 76, 87.

17 See such a medieval map in *Encyclopaedia Judaica*, vol. 9, cols. 1547/8.

18 The Mosque of Omar is built over the site. In Jewish tradition too the Rock plays a role, and the Temple Mount is considered to have been Mount Moriah of the *Akedah*, the sacrifice of Isaac (Genesis 22). Muslims call Jerusalem al-Quds.

19 Isaiah 2:4; Micah 4:3.

20 In the Preface to his poem *Milton*. The stanza was used by the British Labour Party as its anthem.

21 Kabbalist and poet of the 16th century C.E. The poem, of which we quote one verse, is recited as part of the Shabbat eve service, and contains other allusions to this haftarah (see 52:1, 2).

כי תצא

Isaiah, chapter 54, verses 1 to 10

Introduction

This haftarah consists of only ten verses. If they are combined with the haftarah that was read two weeks before (R'ei), the two constitute the haftarah for Noach. However, in the Sephardic tradition the haftarot for Noach and Ki Teitzei are identical.

On this Shabbat, the fifth after Tisha b'Av, the prophecy becomes the fifth of the *sheva de-nechamta*, the "seven [haftarot] of consolation." Two others will follow, also from the Second Isaiah, the last one to be recited on the Shabbat before Rosh Hashanah. (See the Introduction to the haftarah for Va'et-chanan).

Connection of haftarah and Shabbat:

The theme of consolation rather than the connection with the sidra seems to be the main reason for this haftarah to have been chosen by the Sages. It appears that at one time another haftarah was read on this Shabbat, a selection from Zechariah 9, but since its ninth verse was interpreted by Christians to be a direct forecasting of Jesus, its recitation in the synagogue ceased, and the haftarah for Noach replaced it.[1]

The setting:

It was a time of deep despair. The exiles in Babylon felt that God had cast them off, but Isaiah reassured them: God will take you back, like a husband taking back his divorced wife.

As most modern scholars see it, chapter 40 opens the prophecies of the Second Isaiah. This unknown preacher-poet lived among the exiles (6th century B.C.E.), and at some later time his writings were attached to those of the First Isaiah, who lived about 150 years earlier.

For more on Second Isaiah, see our *General Introduction*.[2]

The message:

The image of the divorced woman whom her husband takes back dominates the haftarah. God will turn the present, unhappy fate of Israel's exiles into glorious happiness. This is the theme, as it is in all the "seven [haftarot[of consolation."

HAFTARAH FOR KI TEITZEI

Isaiah, chapter 54, verses 1 to 10

54:1. Sing, O barren woman who has never given birth;

break out in song, you who have never been in labor.

The desolate woman will have more children

than a woman who is married!
—says the Eternal One.

2. Enlarge the space for your tent;

do not spare the canvas for your dwelling-place;

do not hold back: lengthen your ropes, drive in your pegs!

3. For you shall spread out to the right [the south] and the left [the north]:

your offspring shall dispossess nations.

Cities now deserted shall again be settled.

רָנִּי עֲקָרָה לֹא יָלָדָה 54:1

פִּצְחִי רִנָּה וְצַהֲלִי לֹא־חָלָה

כִּי־רַבִּים בְּנֵי־שׁוֹמֵמָה

מִבְּנֵי בְעוּלָה

אָמַר יְהֹוָה:

הַרְחִיבִי מְקוֹם אׇהֳלֵךְ 2

וִירִיעוֹת מִשְׁכְּנוֹתַיִךְ יַטּוּ

אַל־תַּחְשֹׂכִי הַאֲרִיכִי מֵיתָרַיִךְ וִיתֵדֹתַיִךְ חַזֵּקִי:

כִּי־יָמִין וּשְׂמֹאול תִּפְרֹצִי 3

וְזַרְעֵךְ גּוֹיִם יִירָשׁ

וְעָרִים נְשַׁמּוֹת יוֹשִׁיבוּ:

Commentary

54:1. *Sing, O barren woman.* Israel in exile—a nation barred from its land—is like a "desolate woman" who was divorced before she had children. But when she is taken back, her offspring will be more numerous than those of the married one; it is a metaphor also for those who displaced Israel and temporarily gained God's favor.[3]

2. *Enlarge the space for your tent*. Anticipate the coming restoration to your land, when your offspring will multiply.

3. *Shall dispossess nations.* Those who occupied your land, when the Northern Kingdom was destroyed some 200 years before.[4]

4. Have no fear: you shall not be put to
   shame;

do not cringe: your disgrace is at an end.

You will forget the shame of your youth;

no more will you remember your disgrace
   as a widow.

5. For Your husband is your Maker, the
   One called *God of the hosts of heaven,*

and your Redeemer is the Holy One of
   Israel, called *God of all the earth.*

6. The Eternal calls you "wife" again, O
   [once] abandoned and brokenhearted;

once rejected, says your God, but a young
   wife still.

7. For a brief moment I forsook you;

with abiding love I take you back.

4 אַל־תִּירְאִי כִּי־לֹא תֵבֹושִׁי

וְאַל־תִּכָּלְמִי כִּי לֹא תַחְפִּירִי

כִּי בֹשֶׁת עֲלוּמַיִךְ תִּשְׁכָּחִי

וְחֶרְפַּת אַלְמְנוּתַיִךְ לֹא תִזְכְּרִי־עֹוד:

5 כִּי בֹעֲלַיִךְ עֹשַׂיִךְ יְהוָה צְבָאֹות שְׁמֹו

וְגֹאֲלֵךְ קְדֹושׁ יִשְׂרָאֵל אֱלֹהֵי כָל־הָאָרֶץ יִקָּרֵא:

6 כִּי־כְאִשָּׁה עֲזוּבָה וַעֲצוּבַת רוּחַ

קְרָאָךְ יְהוָה

וְאֵשֶׁת נְעוּרִים כִּי תִמָּאֵס אָמַר אֱלֹהָיִךְ:

7 בְּרֶגַע קָטֹן עֲזַבְתִּיךְ

וּבְרַחֲמִים גְּדֹלִים אֲקַבְּצֵךְ:

Commentary

4. *Your disgrace as a widow,* It appears that Isaiah takes "widow" in a wider sense, as a woman who has been abandoned and divorced by her husband and has thus been publicly shamed. (Note that the English language also expands the word "widow" when it describes a married woman who is temporarily alone as a "grass widow.") The expression reflects an old tradition (still alive in today's strict application of the Halachah) that allows men to divorce their wives but gives wives no reciprocal right.

In general, a widowed woman was without the protection of her husband and was thereby socially disadvantaged. She therefore was placed under the protection of God, and numerous times in the Torah the people are bidden to take care of widows, orphans, and strangers—the weakest members of society.

8. In a moment of flooding anger I hid My
    face from you,
but [now], with love unending I take you in
—says your Redeemer, the Eternal One.
9. This is like the days of Noah to Me—
I promised then never again to cover the
    earth
with the waters of Noah('s days).
So now I promise never again to be angry
    with you or rebuke you.
10. Though the mountains may depart
and the hills be removed,
My love shall never depart from you,
and My covenant of peace
shall not be removed
—says the One who loves you, the Eternal.

8 בְּשֶׁ֣צֶף קֶ֗צֶף הִסְתַּ֤רְתִּי פָנַי֙ רֶ֙גַע֙ מִמֵּ֔ךְ
וּבְחֶ֥סֶד עוֹלָ֖ם רִֽחַמְתִּ֑יךְ
אָמַ֥ר גֹּאֲלֵ֖ךְ יְהֹוָֽה:
9 כִּי־מֵ֥י נֹ֙חַ֙ זֹ֣את לִ֔י
אֲשֶׁ֣ר נִשְׁבַּ֗עְתִּי מֵעֲבֹ֥ר מֵי־נֹ֛חַ
ע֖וֹד עַל־הָאָ֑רֶץ
כֵּ֥ן נִשְׁבַּ֛עְתִּי מִקְּצֹ֥ף עָלַ֖יִךְ וּמִגְּעָר־בָּֽךְ:
10 כִּ֤י הֶֽהָרִים֙ יָמ֔וּשׁוּ
וְהַגְּבָע֖וֹת תְּמוּטֶ֑נָה
וְחַסְדִּ֞י מֵאִתֵּ֣ךְ לֹֽא־יָמ֗וּשׁ
וּבְרִ֤ית שְׁלוֹמִי֙ לֹ֣א תָמ֔וּט
אָמַ֥ר מְרַחֲמֵ֖ךְ יְהֹוָֽה:

Commentary

8. *In a moment of flooding anger.* Portraying God in human terms, an anthropomorphism that Isaiah used occasionally (see the essay below.) The momentary exasperation of God is contrasted in the next line by "love unending."

9. *Like the days of Noah.* כימי (*kiy'mei*). So some manuscripts, instead of מי (*mei*, waters).

10. *Says the One who loves you* .... Note the concluding phrases of verses 8 and 10. The parallelism is especially striking in the Hebrew text.

Essay

Divorce as a metaphor

In the Tanach, the relationship between God and Israel is often described in marital terms. God is depicted as the husband and Israel as the wife. Hosea, who lived in the 8th century and was contemporary of Amos, was fond of using this figure of speech.[5] When Israel observes the terms of marriage by doing God's will, the relationship is spoken of as one of love and affection. But when Israel breaks the covenant, God is said to have divorced Israel, as in the opening words of the 50th chapter of this prophet: "Where is the bill of divorce of your mother [Israel] whom I dismissed? And which of My creditors was it to whom I sold you [the children of Israel] off?" Since God has not formally divorced Israel and no sale of any children has taken place, there is no obstacle to full restoration. All that Israel has to do is to signify its willingness to serve God alone and do it with sincerity of heart.

Modern readers of these ancient prophecies will likely find this metaphor troubling. We tend to to think of God in more abstract terms or, when praying alone or as members of a congregation, to address God as children who address a parent. We would not think of a husband/wife relationship either prayerfully or intellectually.

There is another dimension of the divorce metaphor that is strange to us. In the biblical setting, husbands were free to divorce their partners at will, for marriage was not seen as a relationship of equals. In that light, God and Israel—certainly not equals—could be perceived as if they were engaged in marriage, and while God would not break the marital contract capriciously as a human husband might, the metaphor was potent in the sense that God *could* issue the separation decree at any time.

Thus, since God is ruler and sovereign, and Israel is the servant, the application of the divorce metaphor to our time has lost its force. But that does not negate the underlying thought: any relationship that involves commitment, trust, and love has an element of fragility built into it. When the terms of the relationship are breached, there are likely to be severe consequences. It is hard to say what an Isaiah, Jeremiah, or Hosea might use as figures of speech were they to preach to us today, but their theme would remain the same: when the covenant to which both partners agreed is broken, the consequences are painful and often catastrophic.

Thus, while the husband/wife metaphor is generally inappropriate for modern sensibilities, in one major respect it is as applicable today as it was in Isaiah's time. Love and trust need constant nurturing in human marriage, and faithlessness will destroy it. God is close to us when we nurture the relationship with love and *mitzvot,* and when we turn away, God becomes a distant partner. But true repentance will turn God back to us. That was Isaiah's message, and it remains in force for our time.

Gleanings

Words to Remember

Though the mountains may depart
and the hills be removed,
My love shall never depart from you,
and My covenant of peace shall not be removed. (54:10)

Divorce in biblical times

The Bible records only two types of situations in which the husband was stripped of his right to divorce. The first is the one in which he falsely accused his wife of prenuptial intercourse. The second is the result of his having ravished a virgin who had never been engaged to another man. These instances were the only limitations set on (a) man's authority to dissolve his marriage.

Still, there are no instances in the Bible when a man sent his wife away lightly. On the contrary, Abraham is depicted as resisting the expulsion of his concubine (Genesis 21:11-12). Paltiel wept when he had to give up Michal (II Samuel 3:14-16), and Ezra encountered significant opposition when he called on the men to give up their foreign wives (Ezra 10:3 ff.). The ideal of marriage was that of a permanent union, and conjugal fidelity was praised (Ecclesiastes 9:9). Divorce did remain a necessary evil and was probably resorted to most often in the event of the barrenness of the marital union.

The life of the divorcée was not a pleasant one. Generally she returned to her father's home, leaving her children with her former husband. Moral anguish speaks out of Malachi's denunciation of the frequency of divorce in Judea in the 5th century B.C.E. (Malachi 2:13-16).

David L. Lieber[6]

Allusions

The Shabbat hymn *L'chah Dodi,* by Solomon Alkabetz, employs two images taken from this haftarah:

Its seventh verse (not counting the refrain) takes imagery from 54:4 ("You shall not be put to shame"), and its ninth from 54:3 ("You shall spread out to the right and the left").

* * *

Notes

[1] Pesikta Rabbati, Piska 34, ed. Braude and Kapstein, p. 663, footnote 2 (citing Friedman).

[2] For the sake of brevity, in our commentary on the "Seven [Haftarot] of Consolation," Second Isaiah is simply called Isaiah.

[3] Similarly Rashi and Radak.

[4] See II Kings 17:24.

[5] See, for instance, chapter 3; also Jeremiah chapter 3.

[6] *Encyclopaedia Judaica*, vol. 6, pp. 123-124.

Isaiah, chapter 60, verses 1 to 22

Introduction

On this Shabbat, the sixth after Tisha b'Av, the prophecy continues the *sheva de-nechamta*, the "seven [haftarot] of consolation." One more will follow, which will be recited on the Shabbat before Rosh Hashanah. (See the Introduction to the haftarah for Va'et-chanan).

Connection of haftarah and Shabbat:

Consolation is the main thrust of the haftarah, as is expected during the seven Shabbatot before Rosh Hashanah. But it is doubly relevant as a counterweight to the sidra, which contains the dreaded catalogue of evils that will befall Israel if it fails to observe God's law. The haftarah lifts the gloom with a depiction of Israel's future glory.

The setting:

The Second Isaiah, the author of this prophecy, lived among his people in Babylonian exile (6th century B.C.E.). The exiles were suffering grievously; poverty and despair were their daily diet. Isaiah depicted for them a future marked by fabulous well-being, wealth, and happiness—a startling contrast to the reality the people were experiencing.

For more on Isaiah and his time, see our *General Introduction*.

The message:[1]

1. An introduction sets forth the theme: Today may be dark, but tomorrow God's light will shine on Israel. (60:1-2)
2. A description of the glorious future the people may expect. (3-20)
3. Summation: All this will come to pass in due time, and when it does, God will hasten its fulfillment. (21-22)

HAFTARAH FOR KI TAVO

Isaiah, chapter 60, verses 1 to 22

60:1. Arise, shine, [O Jerusalem,]

for your light has come, the glory of the
    Eternal is shining upon you!

2. Though darkness may cover the earth,

thick darkness [the] peoples—

upon you the Eternal will shine,

over you God's Presence will appear.

3. Nations shall walk toward your light,

and kings toward your sunrise.

4. Raise your eyes and see!

They are gathering, all of them,

they are coming to you.

Your sons shall come from afar,

your daughters borne securely.

5. You shall see it and beam with joy,

your heart will thrill with pride,

the sea's abundance shall shower you,

the wealth of nations shall come your way.

60:1 קוּמִי אוֹרִי

כִּי בָא אוֹרֵךְ וּכְבוֹד יְהוָה עָלַיִךְ זָרָח:

2 כִּי־הִנֵּה הַחֹשֶׁךְ יְכַסֶּה־אֶרֶץ

וַעֲרָפֶל לְאֻמִּים

וְעָלַיִךְ יִזְרַח יְהוָה

וּכְבוֹדוֹ עָלַיִךְ יֵרָאֶה:

3 וְהָלְכוּ גוֹיִם לְאוֹרֵךְ

וּמְלָכִים לְנֹגַהּ זַרְחֵךְ:

4 שְׂאִי־סָבִיב עֵינַיִךְ וּרְאִי

כֻּלָּם נִקְבְּצוּ

בָאוּ־לָךְ

בָּנַיִךְ מֵרָחוֹק יָבֹאוּ

וּבְנֹתַיִךְ עַל־צַד תֵּאָמַנָה:

5 אָז תִּרְאִי וְנָהַרְתְּ

וּפָחַד וְרָחַב לְבָבֵךְ

כִּי־יֵהָפֵךְ עָלַיִךְ הֲמוֹן יָם

חֵיל גּוֹיִם יָבֹאוּ לָךְ:

Commentary

1. *Arise, shine.* This verse is quoted in the Shabbat hymn *L'chah Dodi*, which uses other verses from Isaiah as well (see pp. 474, 479). The Hebrew uses the feminine gender for the one who is addressed. Clearly, that is Jerusalem, which is always spoken of as "she." The expression "Rise and shine!" comes from this verse.

The glory. Its radiance was considered an aspect of the Divine—even as in ancient Near East tradition it was connected with deities and royal personages. (The glow of Moses' face and the saintly halo of Christian depiction represent the divine quality of luminosity.[2])

2. That God's light shines only for Israel recalls the description of the plague of darkness.[3]

6. A horde of camels shall cover your land,

the young camels of Midian and Ephah,

all coming from Sheba

bearing gold and frankincense;

proclaiming the praises of God!

7. The flocks of Kedar shall be gathered to you,

the rams of Nevayot shall serve your need—

a sacrifice welcome on My altar,

adding glory to My glorious house.

8. Who are these that fly like a cloud,

like doves to their cotes?

6 שִׁפְעַת גְּמַלִּים תְּכַסֵּךְ

בִּכְרֵי מִדְיָן וְעֵיפָה

כֻּלָּם מִשְּׁבָא יָבֹאוּ

זָהָב וּלְבוֹנָה יִשָּׂאוּ

וּתְהִלֹּת יְהֹוָה יְבַשֵּׂרוּ:

7 כָּל־צֹאן קֵדָר יִקָּבְצוּ לָךְ

אֵילֵי נְבָיוֹת יְשָׁרְתוּנֶךְ

יַעֲלוּ עַל־רָצוֹן מִזְבְּחִי

וּבֵית תִּפְאַרְתִּי אֲפָאֵר:

8 מִי־אֵלֶּה כָּעָב תְּעוּפֶינָה

וְכַיּוֹנִים אֶל־אֲרֻבֹּתֵיהֶם:

Commentary

6. This verse begins an extravagant enumeration of the material wealth that will come Israel's way. Isaiah draws this picture as a dreamlike contrast to the misery of the day.

Midian. Referring not to a specific area but to a nomadic tribe or confederation of five tribes frequenting the Sinai peninsula, the southern Negev, and probably Arabia as well. Archaeological evidence of excavation in the Northern Hejaz (east of the Gulf of Aqaba) reveals a highly sophisticated civilization that may have been created by the Midianites. The Torah traces their origin to Abraham's marriage to Keturah.[4] The word "Midianites" was often used as a synonym for "traders."[5]

Ephah. Noted in Genesis as a descendant of Midian. Probably the name of a similar tribe.[6]

Sheba. A kingdom made famous by its wealth and by the queen who visited Solomon.[7] Though Josephus connected the nation with Ethiopia,[8] it was probably located in Arabia, and possibly identified with Saba in the southwest corner of the peninsula. It had an advanced culture in the early part of the first millennium B.C.E., and Ezekiel knew it as a source of gold and gems.[9]

Frankincense. An aromatic gum resin.

7. *Kedar ... Nevayot.* Nomadic tribes, probably in Arabia, for both names are mentioned in Genesis as the firstborn and second sons of Ishmael, who was considered the ancestor of the Arabs.[10] Kedar and Nevayot are also noted in Assyrian records of the time.

9. The coastlands' vessels wait for Me,

the ships of Tarshish in the lead,

to bring your children from afar,

along with their silver and gold,

to please the Eternal your God,

the Holy One of Israel,

who has given you glory.

10. Foreigners shall rebuild your walls,

and their kings shall serve you.

For in anger I struck you down,

but in favor I show you love [again].

11. Your gates shall be open always,

day or night they shall not be shut,

to bring in the wealth of nations,

their kings led as in procession.

12. Nations and kingdoms that refuse to
serve you shall vanish,

their people utterly destroyed.

9 כִּי־לִ֤י אִיִּים֙ יְקַוּ֔וּ
וָאֳנִיּ֤וֹת תַּרְשִׁישׁ֙ בָּרִֽאשֹׁנָ֔ה
לְהָבִ֥יא בָנַ֖יִךְ מֵרָח֑וֹק
כַּסְפָּ֥ם וּזְהָבָ֖ם אִתָּ֑ם
לְשֵׁם֙ יְהֹוָ֣ה אֱלֹהַ֔יִךְ
וְלִקְד֖וֹשׁ יִשְׂרָאֵ֑ל
כִּ֥י פֵאֲרָֽךְ׃

10 וּבָנ֤וּ בְנֵֽי־נֵכָר֙ חֹמֹתַ֔יִךְ
וּמַלְכֵיהֶ֖ם יְשָׁרְת֑וּנֶךְ
כִּ֤י בְקִצְפִּי֙ הִכִּיתִ֔יךְ
וּבִרְצוֹנִ֖י רִֽחַמְתִּֽיךְ׃

11 וּפִתְּח֨וּ שְׁעָרַ֧יִךְ תָּמִ֛יד
יוֹמָ֥ם וָלַ֖יְלָה לֹ֣א יִסָּגֵ֑רוּ
לְהָבִ֤יא אֵלַ֙יִךְ֙ חֵ֣יל גּוֹיִ֔ם
וּמַלְכֵיהֶ֖ם נְהוּגִֽים׃

12 כִּֽי־הַגּ֤וֹי וְהַמַּמְלָכָה֙ אֲשֶׁ֣ר לֹא־יַעַבְד֔וּךְ
יֹאבֵ֑דוּ
וְהַגּוֹיִ֖ם חָרֹ֥ב יֶחֱרָֽבוּ׃

Commentary

9. *Ships of Tarshish.* A seaport of unknown location, probably far away from Israel—possibly the port of Tartessus in Spain. When Jonah fled from God's command to preach to Nineveh he took a ship from Jaffa to Tarshish.[11] The Torah lists Tarshish as a son of Javan, who is the mythic ancestor of the Greeks.[12]

11. *Your gates shall be open always.* There will be no danger in leaving them open, for the threat of war will have disappeared.[13]

The wealth of nations. Adam Smith used these words for (part of) the title of his principal work.[14]

Their kings led. Understood by many as "brought in chains."[15]

13. The pride of Lebanon shall come to
 you—

juniper, box-tree, and cypress together,

to beautify the place of My sanctuary,

to glorify the place where I rest.

14. They shall come bowing before you—

the children of those who oppressed you;

they shall bow down at the soles of your
 feet,

all those who despised you.

They shall call you the City of God,

Zion, [abode] of Israel's Holy One.

15. As once you were abandoned and
 hated,

with no one passing through,

so now I make you a pride forever,

the joy of all generations.

16. You shall suck the milk of nations,

suck the breast of kingdoms,

and you shall know that I, the Eternal, am
 your Savior,

your Redeemer, the Mighty One of Jacob.

13 כְּבוֹד הַלְּבָנוֹן אֵלַיִךְ יָבוֹא

בְּרוֹשׁ תִּדְהָר וּתְאַשּׁוּר יַחְדָּו

לְפָאֵר מְקוֹם מִקְדָּשִׁי

וּמְקוֹם רַגְלַי אֲכַבֵּד:

14 וְהָלְכוּ אֵלַיִךְ שְׁחוֹחַ

בְּנֵי מְעַנַּיִךְ

וְהִשְׁתַּחֲווּ עַל־כַּפּוֹת רַגְלַיִךְ

כָּל־מְנַאֲצָיִךְ

וְקָרְאוּ לָךְ עִיר יְהֹוָה

צִיּוֹן קְדוֹשׁ יִשְׂרָאֵל:

15 תַּחַת הֱיוֹתֵךְ עֲזוּבָה וּשְׂנוּאָה

וְאֵין עוֹבֵר

וְשַׂמְתִּיךְ לִגְאוֹן עוֹלָם

מְשׂוֹשׂ דּוֹר וָדוֹר:

16 וְיָנַקְתְּ חֲלֵב גּוֹיִם

וְשֹׁד מְלָכִים תִּינָקִי

וְיָדַעַתְּ כִּי אֲנִי יְהֹוָה מוֹשִׁיעֵךְ

וְגֹאֲלֵךְ אֲבִיר יַעֲקֹב:

Commentary

13. *Pride of Lebanon.* A reference to cedars, which were also used to build the first Temple.[16]

The mention of valuable wood to be used in the new Temple is influenced by the Assyrian tradition (encapsuled in royal inscriptions) of enumerating trees brought as tribute to Assyrian kings.[17]

Where I rest. Literally, where My feet rest—a metaphor used in various ways. Here, it probably means (parallel to the preceding line) the Holy of Holies in the Temple.[18]

17. Instead of copper I will bring gold,
instead of iron, silver,
instead of wood, copper,
and iron instead of stones.
I will make Peace your government,
and Righteousness your rulers.

18. No more shall [the noise of] violence
be heard in your land,
desolation and destruction within your
borders.
You shall name your walls *Deliverance*,
and your gates *Praise*.

19. No more shall the sun be your light by
day,
nor shall the moon's glow brighten [your
night];
the Eternal will be your everlasting light,
and your God [will be] your glory.

20. No more shall your sun go down,
or your moon disappear;
for the Eternal will be your everlasting
light,
and your days of mourning shall be ended.

21. Your people shall be righteous, all of
them,
and possess the land forever:

17 תַּחַת הַנְּחֹשֶׁת אָבִיא זָהָב

וְתַחַת הַבַּרְזֶל אָבִיא כֶסֶף

וְתַחַת הָעֵצִים נְחֹשֶׁת

וְתַחַת הָאֲבָנִים בַּרְזֶל

וְשַׂמְתִּי פְקֻדָּתֵךְ שָׁלוֹם

וְנֹגְשַׂיִךְ צְדָקָה:

18 לֹא־יִשָּׁמַע עוֹד חָמָס בְּאַרְצֵךְ

שֹׁד וָשֶׁבֶר בִּגְבוּלָיִךְ

וְקָרָאת יְשׁוּעָה חוֹמֹתַיִךְ

וּשְׁעָרַיִךְ תְּהִלָּה:

19 לֹא־יִהְיֶה־לָּךְ עוֹד הַשֶּׁמֶשׁ לְאוֹר יוֹמָם

וּלְנֹגַהּ הַיָּרֵחַ לֹא־יָאִיר לָךְ

וְהָיָה־לָךְ יְהוָה לְאוֹר עוֹלָם

וֵאלֹהַיִךְ לְתִפְאַרְתֵּךְ:

20 לֹא־יָבוֹא עוֹד שִׁמְשֵׁךְ

וִירֵחֵךְ לֹא יֵאָסֵף

כִּי יְהוָה יִהְיֶה־לָּךְ לְאוֹר עוֹלָם

וְשָׁלְמוּ יְמֵי אֶבְלֵךְ:

21 וְעַמֵּךְ כֻּלָּם צַדִּיקִים

לְעוֹלָם יִירְשׁוּ אָרֶץ

Commentary

20. *Your everlasting light.* The prophecy begins and ends with light from the Eternal shining on Israel.

21. *Possess the land forever.* When the reason for Israel's losing the land because of sinfulness falls away, it will never be lost again. In the Mishnah, this verse is cited as proof text that "all Israel have a share (that is, a holding) in the world-to-come. [19]

they are the shoot that I have planted,

the work of My hands,

to display My glory.

22. The least of them shall become a thousand,

and the smallest a mighty nation;

I, the Eternal, will hasten it

when the time has come.

נֵצֶר מַטָּעַו [מַטָּעַי]

מַעֲשֵׂה יָדַי

לְהִתְפָּאֵר:

22 הַקָּטֹן יִהְיֶה לָאֶלֶף

וְהַצָּעִיר לְגוֹי עָצוּם

אֲנִי יְהֹוָה בְּעִתָּהּ אֲחִישֶׁנָּה:

Essay

When is the time of Deliverance?

Our haftarah concludes with the enigmatic verse 22. Referring to the time when all the magnificent events described in the prophecy will take place, it says:

> *I, the Eternal, will hasten it*
> *when the time has come.*

One could easily understand it if God would say only "Deliverance is on its way and I will make sure there is no delay. Therefore I will hasten it."

But Isaiah does not say this of God. Rather, there seems to be a qualification: Yes, it will happen according to the promise, but only "when its time has come." Will the Deliverance be hastened, or will God wait for the right time? And does the right time depend only on God's pleasure or also on human readiness?

Various attempts have been made by biblical commentators to elucidate the passage.

Radak says: Once the time has come, God will hasten Deliverance to its speedy completion.

Rashi, basing himself on the talmudic explanation,[20] separates the two expressions as follows: If Israel is deserving, I will hasten it; if it is not, it will happen when its time has come.

In this latter explanation, גאולה (*ge'ullah*, Deliverance or Redemption) depends on Israel's performance of God's will. This opinion became the predominant view of our Rabbis, and is often voiced today as well.

Some contemporary Jews, chief among them the Chasidim who professed (and profess) allegiance to the Rebbe of Lubavitch, see the signs of Redemption multiply: the return of Jews to their homeland; the defeat of fascism and the breakdown of communism, and other events suddenly changing the course of history. They hope that the Messiah may reveal himself now; the time has come, and so they pray that God may hasten the Deliverance.

Many other Jews too are gripped by the thought that, precisely because the world seems upside down, with violence and war taking center stage, with refugees roaming the continents, Redemption must be near. For tradition says that these cataclysmic events are its harbingers, "the birth pangs of the Messiah." Israel has already experienced the utmost in misery (the Holocaust), and the rest of the world goes through the trauma of terrible suffering. Now God *must* decide that the time has come, decide to put an end to it all.

Liberal Jews generally forswear such beliefs. They no longer hope for a personal Messiah from the House of David; rather, they look to a gradual evolution of humanity toward universal amity and peace. This they call the messianic age, which is unlikely to arrive in the lifetime of anyone alive today. It is a goal toward which we strive, without expecting fulfillment in any foreseeable historic period.

Do the people of Israel have a role to play in this slow advance? We believe they do. They are still the People of God and have a task to bring Redemption nearer—if only in a small and perhaps invisible measure. But God will know.[21]

None of this definitively illumines verse 22. In fact, it cannot be otherwise. Deliverance is partly in God's and partly in humanity's realm. It is a fluid rather than a fixed relationship, and we know not the future trek of history, nor can we plumb the mind of the Eternal. But this ignorance does not mean that our striving is in vain. We labor in God's vineyard as if Deliverance is in our hands, and we leave the rest to God. That is how the vision of Isaiah can speak to us in our day.[22]

Gleanings

Arise, shine, [O Jerusalem,] for your light has come,
the glory of the Eternal is shining upon you! (60:1)

No more shall [the noise of] violence be heard in your land,
desolation and destruction within your borders. (60:18)

Your people shall be righteous, all of them,
and possess the land forever. (60:21)

The light

The prophet sees Jerusalem as lighting a world of darkness; as the light grows in intensity, it illuminates the dark world and attracts the nations ....

The light, which is the presence of the Eternal, will outshine the sun and the moon, and it will never set. Nor will the world be illumined by any other light; those who are not illuminated by the light of the new Jerusalem will sit in perpetual darkness .... In this new Jerusalem the fullness of the promises of the Eternal to Abraham is achieved; this is the new and the whole Israel.

John L. McKenzie[23]

* * *

Notes

[1] On this chapter in the context of the Second Isaiah's thinking, see H. Orlinsky, *Essays in Biblical Culture and Biblical Translation*, pp. 173-175.

[2] A. L. Oppenheim, *Ancient Mesopotamia*, p.98.

[3] Exodus 10:23.

[4] Genesis 25:2.

[5] See G. Mendenhall in *Anchor Bible Dictionary*, vol. 4, p. 817.

[6] Genesis 25:4.

[7] I Kings 10:1-13.

[8] See *Antiquities* II 10:2.

[9] Ezekiel 7:22; see S. Ricks in *Anchor Bible Dictionary*, vol. 5, p. 1171; B. Oded in עולם התנ״ך (*Olam HaTanach*), 10: 108.

[10] Genesis 25:13.

[11] Jonah 1:3; afternoon haftarah for Yom Kippur; see N. Sarna, *JPS Torah Commentary*, Genesis, p. 71.

[12] Genesis 10:4.

[13] So Freehof, *Book of Isaiah*.

[14] Published in 1776, its full title was *An Inquiry into the Nature and Causes of the Wealth of Nations*. See also Isaiah 60:5 in this haftarah and Isaiah 66:12 (p. 588).

[15] So Rashi and Radak.

[16] I Kings 6:9; haftarah for T'rumah.

[17] See S. Paul in *Journal of the American Oriental Society*, vol. 88 (1968), pp. 182 ff.

[18] The Targum suggests this understanding. In another passage, Isaiah calls the earth itself God's footstool (66:1, which is read as the haftarah for Shabbat Rosh Chodesh).

[19] Sanhedrin 10:1.

[20] B. Sanhedrin 98a.

[21] See also the haftarah for B'reishit, with its essay on the expression "A light to the nations."

[22] Note the insightful discussion of this subject by Issachar Jacobson, *Chazon Hamikra*, vol. 2, pp. 99 ff.

[23] Commentary on Isaiah 60, in *Anchor Bible*, pp. 177 ff.

נצבים

Isaiah, chapter 61, verse 10 to chapter 63, verse 9

Introduction

This haftarah is the seventh after Tisha b'Av, the last of the *sheva de-nechamta*, the "seven [haftarot] of consolation." It is usually recited on the Shabbat before Rosh Hashanah. (See the Introduction to the haftarah for Va'et-chanan.)

Connection of haftarah and Shabbat:

Rosh Hashanah, the New Year, is at hand, and the haftarah depicts the dawning of a new era for Israel's exiles. It has been a long way from the wilderness to Canaan, then on to exile, and now to deliverance.

With this message the cycle of the seven haftarot of consolation reaches its climax.[1] Rosh Hashanah is at hand, the season of repentance and hope.

The setting:

The Second Isaiah, who is the author of this prophecy, lived among his people in Babylonian captivity (6th century B.C.E.). The exiles had suffered grievously; poverty and despair had been their daily diet. But now, with Cyrus having defeated Babylon, their return to the homeland seemed a distinct possibility. "Behold," the Prophet announces, "your Deliverer is coming!"[2]

For more on Isaiah and his time, see our *General Introduction*.

The message:

1. An introduction sets forth the theme: Israel's salvation is near and all the nations will see it. (61:10-11)

2. No longer will Israel be called by its former epithets, "Forsaken" or "Abandoned"; rather, it will be called "The Holy People," "The Redeemed of God," "Sought Out," "A City Not Forsaken." (62:1-12)

3. A highly anthropomorphic section in which God is depicted as a warrior who, having defeated Israel's enemies, is dripping with their blood. Behind this violent metaphor lies a divine confession: When God needed allies to save the world and save Israel, there was none to help. God too was wounded, "afflicted in their affliction." But then the Eternal "raised them and lifted them up as in the days of old." (63:1-6)

4. An upbeat message with which the Rabbis wanted to end the haftarah. (63:7-9)

61:10. I greatly rejoice in the Eternal,

my whole being exults in my God,

who has clothed me in triumph,

and robed me in victory,

as a bridegroom whose head is adorned,

as a bride bedecks herself in her finery.

11. For as the earth brings forth its blossoms,

as gardens spring into flower,

so the Eternal God

will make a glorious victory

spring up before all the nations.

62:1. For Zion's sake I will not be silent,

For Jerusalem's sake I will not be still,

till her victory goes forth like a flame,

and her triumph is like a blazing torch.

2. Nations shall see your deliverance,

every ruler shall see your glory;

and you shall be called by a new name,

a name conferred by the Eternal.

3. You shall be a crown of beauty in the hand of the Eternal,

a royal diadem in the palm of your God.

4. No more shall you be called *Forsaken*,

no more shall your land be called *Abandoned*.

61:10 שׂוֹשׂ אָשִׂישׂ בַּיהֹוָה

תָּגֵל נַפְשִׁי בֵּאלֹהַי

כִּי הִלְבִּישַׁנִי בִּגְדֵי־יֶשַׁע

מְעִיל צְדָקָה יְעָטָנִי

כֶּחָתָן יְכַהֵן פְּאֵר

וְכַכַּלָּה תַּעְדֶּה כֵלֶיהָ:

11 כִּי כָאָרֶץ תּוֹצִיא צִמְחָהּ

וּכְגַנָּה זֵרוּעֶיהָ תַצְמִיחַ

כֵּן אֲדֹנָי יֱהֹוִה

יַצְמִיחַ צְדָקָה וּתְהִלָּה

נֶגֶד כָּל־הַגּוֹיִם:

62:1 לְמַעַן צִיּוֹן לֹא אֶחֱשֶׁה

וּלְמַעַן יְרוּשָׁלַ͏ִם לֹא אֶשְׁקוֹט

עַד־יֵצֵא כַנֹּגַהּ צִדְקָהּ

וִישׁוּעָתָהּ כְּלַפִּיד יִבְעָר:

2 וְרָאוּ גוֹיִם צִדְקֵךְ

וְכָל־מְלָכִים כְּבוֹדֵךְ

וְקֹרָא לָךְ שֵׁם חָדָשׁ

אֲשֶׁר פִּי יְהֹוָה יִקֳּבֶנּוּ:

3 וְהָיִית עֲטֶרֶת תִּפְאֶרֶת בְּיַד־יְהֹוָה

וּצְנוּף [וּצְנִיף] מְלוּכָה בְּכַף־אֱלֹהָיִךְ:

4 לֹא־יֵאָמֵר לָךְ עוֹד עֲזוּבָה

וּלְאַרְצֵךְ לֹא־יֵאָמֵר עוֹד שְׁמָמָה

Commentary

62:4. *Forsaken.* Another way of expressing the idiom found in Isaiah 50:1 (haftarah for Ekev), where the Prophet asks rhetorically, "Where is your mother's bill of divorce?"[3]

For your name shall be *My Delight is in Her*,

and your land shall be called *Married*,

because God delights in you,

and your land shall be married.

כִּי לָךְ יִקָּרֵא חֶפְצִי־בָהּ
וּלְאַרְצֵךְ בְּעוּלָה
כִּי־חָפֵץ יְהֹוָה בָּךְ
וְאַרְצֵךְ תִּבָּעֵל:

5. As a young man and woman marry,

So will your Creator marry you.

And as a bridegroom rejoices in his bride,

So your God will rejoice in you.

5 כִּי־יִבְעַל בָּחוּר בְּתוּלָה
יִבְעָלוּךְ בָּנָיִךְ
וּמְשׂוֹשׂ חָתָן עַל־כַּלָּה
יָשִׂישׂ עָלַיִךְ אֱלֹהָיִךְ:

6. Upon your walls, O Jerusalem,

I have placed sentries.

They shall not be silent day or night.

They shall announce the Eternal

and never rest.

6 עַל־חוֹמֹתַיִךְ יְרוּשָׁלַ͏ִם
הִפְקַדְתִּי שֹׁמְרִים
כָּל־הַיּוֹם וְכָל־הַלַּיְלָה תָּמִיד לֹא יֶחֱשׁוּ
הַמַּזְכִּרִים אֶת־יְהֹוָה
אַל־דֳּמִי לָכֶם:

7. But neither does God rest,

until Jerusalem is restored,

until God makes Jerusalem the praise of all

the earth.

7 וְאַל־תִּתְּנוּ דֳמִי לוֹ
עַד־יְכוֹנֵן
וְעַד־יָשִׂים אֶת־יְרוּשָׁלַ͏ִם תְּהִלָּה בָּאָרֶץ:

Commentary

My Delight is in Her. חפצי בה (*cheftzi-vah*) became a first name for women and also for a well-known department store in Israel.

Married. בעולה (*be'ulah*), Like Hepzibah, Beulah is a woman's name. In the American Bible-reading culture of the 17th century and onward, both were commonly used names.

5. *Your Creator.* The traditional Hebrew reads בניך (*banayich*), your sons [will marry you]; obviously a corrupted text. If we vocalize the word as בונך (*bonech*), similar to a famous midrash in another verse of Isaiah,[4] we obtain the meaning: "the one who builds (or rebuilds) you," that is to say, God, your Creator.[5]

8. The Eternal swears

with all the divine power and strength:

Never again shall I give your new grain to

be food for your enemies,

never shall strangers drink your new wine,

for which you have labored.

9. But those who harvest it

shall eat it and praise the Eternal;

those who gather it in

shall drink it in My sacred courts.

10. Pass through, pass through the gates!

Clear a road for the people!

Build up, build up the highway; clear out

the stones;

put an ensign above the peoples [for all to

see].

11. Behold, the Eternal has proclaimed to

the ends of the earth:

Tell fair Zion:

Your Deliverance is coming!

bringing (divine) reward

and recompense [from on high].

12. They [Israel] shall be called:

The Holy People,

The Redeemed of God.

And you shall be called:

Sought Out,

A City Not Forsaken.

8 נִשְׁבַּע יְהֹוָה

בִּימִינוֹ וּבִזְרוֹעַ עֻזּוֹ

אִם־אֶתֵּן אֶת־דְּגָנֵךְ עוֹד מַאֲכָל לְאֹיְבַיִךְ

וְאִם־יִשְׁתּוּ בְנֵי־נֵכָר תִּירוֹשֵׁךְ

אֲשֶׁר יָגַעַתְּ בּוֹ:

9 כִּי מְאַסְפָיו

יֹאכְלֻהוּ וְהִלְלוּ אֶת־יְהֹוָה

וּמְקַבְּצָיו

יִשְׁתֻּהוּ בְּחַצְרוֹת קָדְשִׁי:

10 עִבְרוּ עִבְרוּ בַּשְּׁעָרִים

פַּנּוּ דֶּרֶךְ הָעָם

סֹלּוּ סֹלּוּ הַמְסִלָּה סַקְּלוּ מֵאֶבֶן

הָרִימוּ נֵס עַל־הָעַמִּים:

11 הִנֵּה יְהֹוָה הִשְׁמִיעַ אֶל־קְצֵה הָאָרֶץ

אִמְרוּ לְבַת־צִיּוֹן

הִנֵּה יִשְׁעֵךְ בָּא

הִנֵּה שְׂכָרוֹ אִתּוֹ

וּפְעֻלָּתוֹ לְפָנָיו:

12 וְקָרְאוּ לָהֶם

עַם־הַקֹּדֶשׁ

גְּאוּלֵי יְהֹוָה

וְלָךְ יִקָּרֵא

דְרוּשָׁה

עִיר לֹא נֶעֱזָבָה:

Commentary

8. *Power and strength.* Literally, His (God's) right hand and strong arm.

10. *Pass through.* To announce the good tidings to all.

11. *Bringing your reward.* Isaiah uses the same expression in 40:10.

12. *Sought out.* דרושה (*d'rushah*), a term that conveys divine care.[6]

63:1. I am the One proclaiming vindication,

mighty to save.

Who is this coming from Edom,

from Bozrah, stripped of clothing,

the one dressed in such splendor,

striding in such might?

2. Why is your clothing red,

your garments as though you were a
   treader of grapes?

3. All alone I have trodden the winepress,

and of the peoples no one was with Me;

in My anger I stepped on them,

in My wrath I trampled them,

spattering their blood on My garments,

staining all My clothes.

4. I intended a day of vengeance,

for the year of My redemption had come.

63:1 מִי־זֶה בָּא מֵאֱדוֹם

חֲמוּץ בְּגָדִים מִבָּצְרָה

זֶה הָדוּר בִּלְבוּשׁוֹ

צֹעֶה בְּרֹב כֹּחוֹ

אֲנִי מְדַבֵּר בִּצְדָקָה

רַב לְהוֹשִׁיעַ׃

2 מַדּוּעַ אָדֹם לִלְבוּשֶׁךָ

וּבְגָדֶיךָ כְּדֹרֵךְ בְּגַת׃

3 פּוּרָה דָּרַכְתִּי לְבַדִּי

וּמֵעַמִּים אֵין־אִישׁ אִתִּי

וְאֶדְרְכֵם בְּאַפִּי

וְאֶרְמְסֵם בַּחֲמָתִי

וְיֵז נִצְחָם עַל־בְּגָדַי

וְכָל־מַלְבּוּשַׁי אֶגְאָלְתִּי׃

4 כִּי יוֹם נָקָם בְּלִבִּי

וּשְׁנַת גְּאוּלַי בָּאָה׃

Commentary

63:1. *I am the One.* Moved up from near the end of the verse for clarity's sake.

Mighty to save. These words are quoted in the 2nd blessing of the *Amidah.* In the Hebrew they appear at the end of the verse, but for the sake of clarity they have been put forward in our translation.

Coming from Edom. An image of God already used in the book of Judges,[7] and finding its closest parallel in Isaiah 34. The harsh language comes from a time when Edom became the stereotypical enemy, probably because it had cooperated with the Babylonians when they destroyed Jerusalem in 587 B.C.E. In rabbinic days, Edom stood for the Roman empire and later for the Christian Church.[8] To achieve a clearer flow we have moved the last two (English) lines of this verse to the beginning of the verse.

Bozrah. An Edomite city.

3. *I have trodden the winepress.* Julia Ward Howe used the imagery for her *Battle Hymn of the Republic:* "Mine eyes have seen the coming of the Lord, He is trampling out the vintage where the grapes of wrath are stored."

5. I looked, but none would help;

I was amazed that none would uphold;

so My own arm brought Me victory,

My wrath was what upheld Me.

6. In My anger I trampled peoples;

I shattered them with My wrath.

I made their blood spill to the earth!

7. Let me recount the Eternal's loving acts,

the Eternal's praiseworthy deeds,

for all that the Eternal has done for us,

all the great goodness, mercy, and love

the Eternal has shown the House of Israel.

8. God said:

They alone are My people,

children who will not be false to Me.

So God became their Savior.

9. Afflicted in their affliction,

the Divine Presence saved them.

In love and pity God redeemed them,

carried them and raised them high

in all times past.

5 וְאַבִּיט וְאֵין עֹזֵר

וְאֶשְׁתּוֹמֵם וְאֵין סוֹמֵךְ

וַתּוֹשַׁע לִי זְרֹעִי

וַחֲמָתִי הִיא סְמָכָתְנִי:

6 וְאָבוּס עַמִּים בְּאַפִּי

וַאֲשַׁכְּרֵם בַּחֲמָתִי

וְאוֹרִיד לָאָרֶץ נִצְחָם:

7 חַסְדֵי יְהֹוָה אַזְכִּיר

תְּהִלֹּת יְהֹוָה

כְּעַל כֹּל אֲשֶׁר־גְּמָלָנוּ יְהֹוָה

וְרַב־טוּב לְבֵית יִשְׂרָאֵל

אֲשֶׁר־גְּמָלָם כְּרַחֲמָיו וּכְרֹב חֲסָדָיו:

8 וַיֹּאמֶר אַךְ־עַמִּי הֵמָּה

בָּנִים לֹא יְשַׁקֵּרוּ

וַיְהִי לָהֶם לְמוֹשִׁיעַ:

9 בְּכָל־צָרָתָם לֹא [לוֹ] צָר

וּמַלְאַךְ פָּנָיו הוֹשִׁיעָם

בְּאַהֲבָתוֹ וּבְחֶמְלָתוֹ הוּא גְאָלָם

וַיְנַטְּלֵם וַיְנַשְּׂאֵם

כָּל־יְמֵי עוֹלָם:

Commentary

6. *I shattered them.* We follow the Targum and other old manuscripts, substituting a ב for the כ, reading וַאֲשַׁבְּרֵם (*va'ashabrem*), "I shattered them," as in Isaiah 14:25. The masoretic text has וַאֲשַׁכְּרֵם (*va'ashakrem*), "I made them drunk."

9. *Afflicted.* Reading the bracketed לוֹ (*lo*); see the essay that follows.

The Divine Presence. Literally, "the angel of His face [that is, 'Presence']." The somewhat paradoxical sense seems to be that God alone, and not a messenger, redeemed them.[9]

Carried them. Recalling the image of Israel being borne "on eagles' wings."[10]

Essay

God too suffers (63:9)

This is the way the Sages wanted us to understand the verse, even though the actual (masoretic) text read one crucial letter differently. Before discussing the theological question of a "suffering God," it is well to explain the change that the Rabbis instituted. However, the process is not always clear.

1. For instance, it may be that sometimes the Rabbis were convinced that the scribe had erred in copying a word. But since they could not (and would not) actually alter the text, they arrived at a method that nonetheless would achieve their purpose. They indicated in the margin that the written text (*k'tiv*) should be disregarded and instead a different word should be read (*k'ré*). See the boxed note in our *Preface* (p. iv).

Thus, in 63:9 the *k'tiv* is בכל־צרתם לא צר (*b'chol tzaratam lo tzar*). Translated literally this says: "In all of their [Israel's] affliction [God] was *not* afflicted." The Rabbis were convinced that a scribal error was to blame for this strange theology of an unconcerned God, and that the error had occurred in copying the word לא (*lo*, "not"). They believed that the original and proper word had the same sound but had a different spelling, namely לו (*lo*, the personal pronoun for God). By this substitution, the negative was overcome and God's affliction, together with Israel's, was affirmed instead of denied. [11]

2. It is also possible that decisions about the proper text were reached on the basis of the number of reliable manuscripts available rather than on theological grounds—or perhaps these processes were intermingled and are no longer identifiable. In any case, *keré* and *k'tiv* are important masoretic notations. [12]

3. We now turn to the concept itself. What did Isaiah mean when he said that when Israel suffers so does God?

With this image he no doubt meant to convey the sense of God's closeness to Israel. When Israel is persecuted God is filled with anger, even wrath, especially when there is no one to help. In this sense, the Divine Presence too is afflicted.

But what does that say about God's omnipotence? Isn't the Almighty, as the name suggests, all-powerful? Why does an Almighty God have to suffer? And why would the Sovereign of the world allow the Holocaust to happen, an event of such proportions that it nearly wiped out the Torah's "chosen people"?

These are difficult questions, which cannot be answered in a brief comment. But they are important to ask, for on their answers depends the possibility of belief in a merciful and just God whose true nature will always escape human understanding.

But what about Isaiah and his perception? In the Prophet's imagery, God appears as *both powerful and vulnerable* (assuming, of course, that the text is read as the Sages said it should be). Clearly, in the Prophet's view, these two divine characteristic are compatible, even as they are compatible in a human being—and the poet uses human language to convey what is essentially inaccessible.

For Isaiah, God struggles forever with human evil and its consequences. Israel is not the only nation to suffer its effects, but Israel is of special divine concern. God interferes in history only when ultimate disaster may thwart the divine purpose—but in the process the Eternal too suffers. For the human race has from the beginning caused God anger and disappointment. Hence the metaphor of the Eternal who is afflicted while history takes its human course.

Gleanings

For Zion's sake I will not be silent,
for Jerusalem's sake I will not be still. (62:1)

God's anguish (63:9)

Ibn Ezra supports the k'ré, which says that even as Israel was afflicted, so was God. He considers this the correct reading and points out that in the book of Judges (10:6) God is pictured as saddened by Israel's suffering: "God's soul was anguished because of Israel's misery."

Outstanding among the dissenters is Rashi, who stays with the written text (*k'tiv*). He understands it to say that when Israel was afflicted God did not afflict them as much as they deserved.

Radak prefers not to choose between the readings, considering both to be possible.

Other commentators and translators amend the text by reading ציר (*tzir*), "emissary," for צר (*tzar*), "afflicted," thus giving the text yet another meaning: When Israel was afflicted, they were delivered not by an emissary but directly by the Divine Presence. [13]

The diffference

Judaism in its nonphilosophic form acknowledges the utter reality of evil and suffering. God Himself is often described as suffering with Man. Man is challenged to remedy suffering wherever it can be remedied, and to endure it wherever it is irremediable. Max Brod considers the attitude toward suffering the major distinguishing factor between Judaism and Christianity. [14]

* * *

Notes

[1] See the analysis of the seven haftarot by Rabbi Mark D. Shapiro, which has been noted in the haftarah to Va'et-chanan.

[2] Isaiah 62:12.

[3] Using עזובה (*azuvah*) in this sense derives from Isaiah being exposed to the Babylonian environment, where the Akkadian *ezebu* was so employed.

[4] See Isaiah 54:10, in the haftarah for Noach.

[5] Here too Isaiah's environment plays a role: *bonech* reflects the Akkadian word *banû* for "creator."

[6] Compare Deuteronomy 11:12.

[7] 5:4; haftarah for B'shallach.

[8] On this subject see H. Williamson, *The Book Called Isaiah*, p. 217.

[9] S.D. Sperling remarks that "מלאך פניו is a divine viceroy much like the one in whom the Divine Name dwells (Exodus 23:21). The distinction between the angel and the Divine Presence is blurred."

[10] Exodus 19:4.

[11] A similar *k'tiv/k'ré* substitution from לא to לו changed a famous passage in Job 13:15 into its opposite. However, it has been suggested that the א and ו were (as vowels) originally omitted from the text, and that the decision on which of the two was to be read was likely based on theological grounds. (S. D. Sperling in personal communication.)

[12] On the various theories, see E. Tov, *Textual Criticism of the Hebrew Bible*, pp. 58-64. See also H. M. Orlinsky, "The Origin of the Kethib-Qere System: A New Approach."

[13] See, for instance, NEB and J. L. McKenzie (*Anchor Bible*, Isaiah).

[14] *Encyclopaedia Judaica*, vol. 15, pp. 485-486. The reference to Brod is to his study, *Paganism, Christianity, Judaism* (University of Alabama Press, 1970. The German original appeared in 1922).

וַיֵּלֶךְ

Isaiah, chapter 55, verse 6 to chapter 56, verse 8

Introduction

This haftarah is read by Ashkenazim only when the sidra Vayeilech falls on the Shabbat before Rosh Hashanah. More often, that sidra will be recited on the Shabbat between Rosh Hashanah and Yom Kippur, and in that case the haftarah for Shabbat Shuvah will be from Hosea and Micah (or Joel).

Sephardim recite a different haftarah for Vayeilech when the sidra is read before Rosh Hashanah (Hosea 14:2-10 and Micah 7:18-20).

The haftarah is also read on the afternoon of Tisha b'Av.

Connection of haftarah and Shabbat:

The first sentence of the haftarah makes the connection obvious:

Seek the Eternal while there is still time,

call out while God is near.

Rosh Hashanah will soon come and begin the Ten Days of Repentance, climaxing in Yom Kippur. Get your life in order and do it now, the Prophet urges us.

The setting:

The Second Isaiah, who is the author of this prophecy, shared his people's exile in Babylon (6th century B.C.E.). The message of this haftarah seems to have been delivered at a time when redemption from exile was near; in fact, some of the exiles appear to have already started their trek home, as the last verse suggests.

For more on Isaiah and his time, see our *General Introduction*.

The message:

1. Introduction. Return to God while there is time. (55:6-7)

2. God's ways are inscrutable and cannot be compared to ours. Don't try to figure them out. (55:8-13)

3. Israel's task is to do right and practice justice—and also to live Jewishly. Observing Shabbat is the key to accomplishing it. (56:1-2)

4. Outsiders too are included in the opportunity to serve God fully. The two examples given are eunuchs and foreigners. (56:3-8)

HAFTARAH FOR VAYEILECH

Isaiah, chapter 55, verse 6 to chapter 56, verse 8

55:6. Seek the Eternal while there is still
time;

call out while God is near.

7. Let the wicked forsake their ways,

and the sinful their thoughts.

Let them return to the Eternal,

who will show them compassion;

to our God,

who is quick to forgive.

8. For My thoughts are not like yours,

nor are your ways like Mine,

says the Eternal One.

9. For high as the heavens above the earth,

so are My ways high above your ways,

and My thoughts above your thoughts.

10. Just as rain and snow come down from
the sky without returning,

but water the earth, making it blossom and
bear fruit,

yielding seed for sowing and bread to eat,

11. so it is with the word that comes from
My mouth:

it does not return to Me unfulfilled,

without having accomplished My desire;

and achieved what I send it to do.

55:6 דִּרְשׁ֥וּ יְהוָ֖ה בְּהִמָּצְא֑וֹ

קְרָאֻ֖הוּ בִּֽהְיוֹת֥וֹ קָרֽוֹב:

7 יַעֲזֹ֤ב רָשָׁע֙ דַּרְכּ֔וֹ

וְאִ֥ישׁ אָ֖וֶן מַחְשְׁבֹתָ֑יו

וְיָשֹׁ֤ב אֶל־יְהוָה֙

וִֽירַחֲמֵ֔הוּ

וְאֶל־אֱלֹהֵ֖ינוּ

כִּֽי־יַרְבֶּ֥ה לִסְלֽוֹחַ:

8 כִּ֣י לֹ֤א מַחְשְׁבוֹתַי֙ מַחְשְׁב֣וֹתֵיכֶ֔ם

וְלֹ֥א דַרְכֵיכֶ֖ם דְּרָכָ֑י

נְאֻ֖ם יְהוָֽה:

9 כִּֽי־גָבְה֥וּ שָׁמַ֖יִם מֵאָ֑רֶץ

כֵּ֣ן גָּבְה֤וּ דְרָכַי֙ מִדַּרְכֵיכֶ֔ם

וּמַחְשְׁבֹתַ֖י מִמַּחְשְׁבֹתֵיכֶֽם:

יֵרֵ֡ד הַגֶּשֶׁם֩ וְהַשֶּׁ֨לֶג מִן־הַשָּׁמַ֜יִם וְשָׁ֗מָּה לֹ֣א יָשׁ֔וּב

10 כִּ֚י כַֽאֲשֶׁ֣ר

כִּ֣י אִם־הִרְוָ֣ה אֶת־הָאָ֗רֶץ וְהֽוֹלִידָ֙הּ וְהִצְמִיחָ֔הּ

וְנָ֤תַן זֶ֙רַע֙ לַזֹּרֵ֔עַ וְלֶ֖חֶם לָֽאֹכֵֽל:

11 כֵּ֣ן יִֽהְיֶ֤ה דְבָרִי֙ אֲשֶׁ֣ר יֵצֵ֣א מִפִּ֔י

לֹֽא־יָשׁ֥וּב אֵלַ֖י רֵיקָ֑ם

כִּ֤י אִם־עָשָׂה֙ אֶת־אֲשֶׁ֣ר חָפַ֔צְתִּי

וְהִצְלִ֖יחַ אֲשֶׁ֥ר שְׁלַחְתִּֽיו:

Commentary

55:6. *While there is still time.* Don't wait until you have passed the point of no return. The Hebrew can also be understood to mean: Seek the Eternal in the way that God can be found. And the following verses give the direction: "Let the wicked forsake their ways .... Maintain justice and do what is right."[1]

7. *Quick to forgive.* Literally, "forgives generously" or "freely."

12. For you shall go out in joy;

you shall be led forth in peace.

Before you mountains and hills shall break
    out in joyous song,

and all the trees of the field shall clap their
    hands.

13. Cypresses shall grow instead of thorn-
    bushes,

myrtle instead of briar.

These shall be a monument to God,

an everlasting sign that will stand firm.

56:1. Thus says the Eternal One:

Maintain justice and do what is right,

for My salvation is close at hand,

and revealed shall be My vindication.

12 כִּי־בְשִׂמְחָה תֵצֵאוּ

וּבְשָׁלוֹם תּוּבָלוּן

הֶהָרִים וְהַגְּבָעוֹת יִפְצְחוּ לִפְנֵיכֶם רִנָּה

וְכָל־עֲצֵי הַשָּׂדֶה יִמְחֲאוּ־כָף:

13 תַּחַת הַנַּעֲצוּץ יַעֲלֶה בְרוֹשׁ

תַּחַת [וְתַחַת] הַסִּרְפַּד יַעֲלֶה הֲדַס

וְהָיָה לַיהוָה לְשֵׁם לְאוֹת עוֹלָם לֹא יִכָּרֵת:

56:1 כֹּה אָמַר יְהוָה

שִׁמְרוּ מִשְׁפָּט וַעֲשׂוּ צְדָקָה

כִּי־קְרוֹבָה יְשׁוּעָתִי לָבוֹא

וְצִדְקָתִי לְהִגָּלוֹת:

Commentary

13. *Myrtle instead of briar.* The Talmud takes this as a reference to messianic times when the righteous (myrtle) will replace the wicked (briar). [2]

That will stand firm. לֹא יִכָּרֵת (*lo yikaret*). Literally, "that will not be cut down." Isaiah uses the same expression a few sentences later, in 56:5.

56:1. Many scholars believe that with this chapter an entirely new note is struck, so different that they see here the beginning of a different work, authored by another unknown prophet. They call this person the "Third Isaiah" (or Trito-Isaiah). Still others see chapters 56–66 as the work of various prophets, whose sayings were collected and appended to the book of Isaiah. Then again, there are those who hold that chapters 40–66 were authored by one person (whom we call the "Second Isaiah"), and—as set forth in our *General Introduction*—there are traditionalists who see the whole book as the outpouring of one single person. As further indicated there, this commentary sees chapters 56–66 as the work of the Second Isaiah, but a full discussion of the subject exceeds the purposes of this volume.

2. Happy is the one who does this,

the person that holds fast to it—

who keeps the Sabbath lest it be profaned,

who keeps from all wrongdoing.

3. Never more let the foreigner who has

joined the Eternal say:

The Eternal will keep me apart from God's

people.

And nevermore let the eunuch say:

I am but a withered tree.

4. For thus says the Eternal One to those

eunuchs

who keep My Sabbaths

and choose what pleases Me

and hold fast to My covenant:

אַשְׁרֵי אֱנוֹשׁ יַעֲשֶׂה־זֹּאת 2

וּבֶן־אָדָם יַחֲזִיק בָּהּ

שֹׁמֵר שַׁבָּת מֵחַלְּלוֹ

וְשֹׁמֵר יָדוֹ מֵעֲשׂוֹת כָּל־רָע:

וְאַל־יֹאמַר בֶּן־הַנֵּכָר הַנִּלְוָה אֶל־יְהֹוָה לֵאמֹר 3

הַבְדֵּל יַבְדִּילַנִי יְהֹוָה מֵעַל עַמּוֹ

וְאַל־יֹאמַר הַסָּרִיס

הֵן אֲנִי עֵץ יָבֵשׁ:

כִּי־כֹה אָמַר יְהֹוָה 4

לַסָּרִיסִים אֲשֶׁר יִשְׁמְרוּ אֶת־שַׁבְּתוֹתַי

וּבָחֲרוּ בַּאֲשֶׁר חָפָצְתִּי

וּמַחֲזִיקִים בִּבְרִיתִי:

Commentary

2. Happy is the one ... who keeps the Sabbath. The subject of observing Shabbat has not been raised until now. But "do what is right" is so general that it calls for something more specific, and Shabbat was then, and remains, a central occasion for Jews to remember their covenant with God. Shabbat is thus a symbol of relating to the Eternal, and "maintain justice" is the measure of relating to human beings.[3]

3. God's people ... Literally, "His people."

Eunuch. Castrated men. In God's eyes they are as worthy as any other persons.

4. Hold fast to My covenant. Radak suggests that this refers to circumcision. At the time this chapter was written the Jewish community in Babylon was divided between those who favored mixed marriage and the incorporation of outsiders into the community, and those opposed to the admission of non-Jews. The Prophet here offers a compromise: Lack of Jewish birth can be overcome by righteous conduct (verses 1 and 2), observance of Shabbat, and male circumcision.[4]

5. In My House, within My walls,
I will give you a monument and a name
better than sons and daughters;
I will give you an everlasting name
that will never be cut off.

6. As for the foreigners who join themselves
to the Eternal in love and service, who
keep the Sabbath lest it be profaned, and
hold fast to My covenant:

7. I will bring them to My holy mountain
and make them joyful in My house of
prayer. [I will accept] the burnt-offerings
and sacrifices they offer on My altar: for
My House shall be called a house of prayer
for all peoples.

8. This is the promise of the Eternal God
who brings Israel's exiles home: I will yet
bring more home, besides those I have
already brought.

5 וְנָתַתִּי לָהֶם בְּבֵיתִי וּבְחוֹמֹתַי
יָד וָשֵׁם
טוֹב מִבָּנִים וּמִבָּנוֹת
שֵׁם עוֹלָם אֶתֶּן־לוֹ
אֲשֶׁר לֹא יִכָּרֵת:

6 וּבְנֵי הַנֵּכָר הַנִּלְוִים עַל־יְהוָה לְשָׁרְתוֹ
וּלְאַהֲבָה אֶת־שֵׁם יְהוָה לִהְיוֹת לוֹ לַעֲבָדִים
כָּל־שֹׁמֵר שַׁבָּת מֵחַלְּלוֹ וּמַחֲזִיקִים בִּבְרִיתִי:

7 וַהֲבִיאוֹתִים אֶל־הַר קָדְשִׁי וְשִׂמַּחְתִּים בְּבֵית
תְּפִלָּתִי עוֹלֹתֵיהֶם וְזִבְחֵיהֶם לְרָצוֹן עַל־מִזְבְּחִי
כִּי בֵיתִי בֵּית־תְּפִלָּה יִקָּרֵא לְכָל־הָעַמִּים:

8 נְאֻם אֲדֹנָי יְהוִה מְקַבֵּץ נִדְחֵי יִשְׂרָאֵל עוֹד
אֲקַבֵּץ עָלָיו לְנִקְבָּצָיו:

Commentary

5. *Monument and name.* יד ושם (*yad vashem*), meaning something that preserves a person's name, hence "memorial." יד means also "portion," and שם (name) carries the additional connotation of "permanence." God confirms the right of the eunuch to be part of the community (despite Deuteronomy 23:2) and makes the right permanent.[5]

Israel's Holocaust research and remembrance institution is called Yad Vashem.

56:7. *Make them joyful.* שמחתים (*simmachtim*) has the overtone of "making them celebrate festivals and rituals."

Essay

Universalist or particularist?

In a frequently cited passage, the Prophet says, "My house shall be called a house of prayer for all peoples."[6] Based on this, as well as on his emphasis on human righteousness, Isaiah has frequently been called a "universalist."

If this means merely that he saw the Eternal as the God of all nations, he was indeed a universalist.[7]

But "universalist" is usually perceived as something different and is considered the opposite of "particularist." The former is said to be the loftier idea, for it embraces all humanity; the latter the inferior conception, for it puts its emphasis on one group. Taking this argument into the realm of religious assessment, Christianity is said to concern itself with all humankind, while Judaism focuses on Jews, to the exclusion of all others.

This a misreading of Isaiah as well as of the nature of Judaism.

Isaiah's chief concern *is* with Israel. He himself was one of the exiles, and he saw as his main task to give comfort to his people, and to have them trust in God's promise of a better future. In this, he stood foursquare on the basis of his religious tradition. In this sense, he was indeed preoccupied with the particular, with those among whom he lived and of whom he was a part. His people were his starting point, the frame of reference that commanded his heart and his intellect.

But the particular did not function in opposition to the universal. It was the watch tower from which he could envisage—and teach his listeners to envisage—the wider horizons of all humanity. "Do what is right" was addressed to his environment, but the message was universal. Israel was held to strict account for its failure to do God's will, but the nation's ultimate task lay in the realm of the universal: by serving God faithfully Israel would carry out its universal task. Redemption would come not only to Zion but to the world, when God's temple "shall be called a house of prayer for all people." It was a hope already expressed by Solomon when he dedicated the Temple (see *Gleanings* below).

In his vision, the Second Isaiah is much like the First, and probably because of this, his work was appended to the existing Isaiah work. The later prophet's name is unknown, but his poetry has had a life of its own. It remains alive today, so many centuries after it was first uttered, and every reader is addressed by his message.

Gleanings

Words to Remember

My thoughts are not like yours
... says the Eternal. (55:8)

Thus says the Eternal one:
Maintain justice and do what is right. (56:1)

In My House, within My walls,
I will give you a monument and a name *[yad vashem]*. (56:5)

My House shall be called a house of prayer
for all peoples. (56:7)

The Prayer of Solomon

(King Solomon carried out the dream of his father, David, and built a splendid Temple to God. The work was completed after seven years, in 959 B.C.E. At the dedication ceremonies, Solomon delivered a long prayer, a segment of which is reflected in Isaiah's words, spoken some 400 years later.)

If a foreigner who is not of Your people comes from a distant land for the sake of Your name—for they shall hear about Your great name and your mighty hand and Your outstretched arm—when such a one comes to pray in this House, O hear it in Your heavenly abode and grant all that the foreigner asks You for. Thus all the peoples of the earth will know your name and revere You, as does Your people Israel; and they will recognize that Your name is attached to this House that I have built.

I Kings 8:41-43

Babylon

Babylon that was beautiful is Nothing now.
Once to the world it tolled a golden bell:
Belshazzar wore its blaze upon his brow,
Ruled, and to ruin fell.
Babylon—a blurred and blinded face of stone—
At dumb Oblivion bragged with trumpets blown;
Teemed, and while merchants strove and prophets dreamed,
Bowed before idols, and was overthrown.

Babylon the merciless, now a name of doom,
Built towers in Time, as we today, for whom
Auguries of self-annihilation loom.

Siegfried Sassoon[8]

* * *

516

Notes

[1] So Ibn Ezra and Radak (citing his father).

[2] *B. Megillah* 10b.

[3] So Malbim, followed by Freehof, *Book of Isaiah*.

[4] S. D. Sperling, *Biblica* 70 (1989), p. 71.

[5] S. Japhet, *Ma'arav* 8 (1992), pp. 969-980.

[6] Isaiah 56:7.

[7] See also Radak, in his comment on the verse.

[8] In *Chapters into Verse*, pp. 391-392.

האזינו

Second Samuel, chapter 22, verses 1 to 51

Introduction

Connection of sidra and haftarah:

The sidra brings us Moses' farewell song, and the haftarah a song by David. The haftarah is repeated on the seventh day of Pesach.

It must be noted that this poem is found also in the book of Psalms (Psalm 18); the two versions are largely identical, and some differences are helpful in understanding difficult passages.

The setting:

Verse 1 informs the reader that David spoke this prayer after he had been delivered from his enemies, and especially from Saul, who had sought his life. This superscription is problematic, for the last portion of the prayer depicts David as one whose rule is firmly established and whose battles are behind him. Traditional interpreters suggest this solution: David composed the prayer at the end of his life, but the sense of being saved was so real that it was as if it happened yesterday, and especially so with the remembrance of his escape from Saul.[1]

But perhaps the poem itself comes from a much later era, and the title was added by a pious editor. At one time, this opinion was widespread among scholars, while nowadays the case for the antiquity and the Davidic authorship of the text has been reasserted, although the presence of many archaic expressions is not in itself proof of early authorship.[2]

Just when David would have composed this prayer/poem cannot be ascertained; it may have been after he had brought the Ark of God to Jerusalem.[3]

For more on the book of Samuel, see our *General Introduction*.

Content of the haftarah:

Title (verse 1)

1. The cry of David. (2-7; continued in verse 17)
2. Interlude: in praise of God's power. (8-16)
3. How God protected David. (17-35)
4. A vision of victory. (36-46)
5. Finale: in praise of God. (47-51)

HAFTARAH FOR HA'AZINU

Second Samuel, chapter 22, verses 1 to 51

22:1. When the Eternal had saved him from the grasp of his enemies, and [especially] from the grasp of [King] Saul, David sang this song to the Eternal:

2. He sang: The Eternal is my rock, my fortress,
my refuge.

3. God is my rock where I seek shelter,
my shield, the source of my salvation.
My deliverer, You save me from violence.

4. Derided, I cry out to God,
and am saved from my foes.

5. The waves of Death surrounded me,
Destruction's floods frightened me;

6. the bonds of Sheol closed in on me,
Death's net entrapped me.

7. In my torment I called to the Eternal,
I called to my God:
in Your Temple You heard me,
my scream was in Your ears.

$$
\begin{array}{r}
\text{22:1} \quad \text{וַיְדַבֵּר דָּוִד לַיהוָה אֶת־דִּבְרֵי הַשִּׁירָה} \\
\text{הַזֹּאת בְּיוֹם הִצִּיל יְהוָה אֹתוֹ מִכַּף כָּל־} \\
\text{אֹיְבָיו וּמִכַּף שָׁאוּל:} \\
\text{2 וַיֹּאמַר יְהוָה סַלְעִי וּמְצֻדָתִי} \\
\text{וּמְפַלְטִי־לִי:} \\
\text{3 אֱלֹהֵי צוּרִי אֶחֱסֶה־בּוֹ} \\
\text{מָגִנִּי וְקֶרֶן יִשְׁעִי} \\
\text{מִשְׂגַּבִּי וּמְנוּסִי מֹשִׁעִי מֵחָמָס תֹּשִׁעֵנִי:} \\
\text{4 מְהֻלָּל אֶקְרָא יְהוָה} \\
\text{וּמֵאֹיְבַי אִוָּשֵׁעַ:} \\
\text{5 כִּי אֲפָפֻנִי מִשְׁבְּרֵי־מָוֶת} \\
\text{נַחֲלֵי בְלִיַּעַל יְבַעֲתֻנִי:} \\
\text{6 חֶבְלֵי שְׁאוֹל סַבֻּנִי} \\
\text{קִדְּמֻנִי מֹקְשֵׁי־מָוֶת:} \\
\text{7 בַּצַּר־לִי אֶקְרָא יְהוָה} \\
\text{וְאֶל־אֱלֹהַי אֶקְרָא} \\
\text{וַיִּשְׁמַע מֵהֵיכָלוֹ קוֹלִי} \\
\text{וְשַׁוְעָתִי בְּאָזְנָיו:}
\end{array}
$$

Commentary

1. *Saul.* Those who believe that this poem had little to do with David (see above, "The Setting," and footnote 2) read not שָׁאוּל (*sha'ul*, Saul), but שְׁאוֹל (*sheol*, netherworld).[4]

2. *My rock, my fortress.* "My rock" here has the function of an adjective and conveys the sense that the fortress is firm as a rock.

5. *Death.* בְלִיַּעַל (*b'liya'al*), the personification of the netherworld.[5]

6. *Sheol.* In classical biblical thought there was no heaven or hell, for God allocated rewards and punishments during one's earthly life. At death, everyone descended into Sheol, and David here expresses his fear of making the journey before his time.

7. *You heard me.* From here on, our translation speaks of God in the second person.[6]

In Your Temple. The poet conceives of God as dwelling in a heavenly Temple from which it is necessary to descend (see verse 10). Earthly temples were modeled after their perceived heavenly counterparts.

8. The earth trembled and shuddered,

the sky's foundations shook,

Your wrath made them shudder.

9. Smoke poured from Your nostrils,

a devouring fire from Your mouth,

blazing coals flamed forth from You.

10. You spread out the sky and came down,

with a thick cloud beneath Your feet.

11. You saddled a cherub and flew,

You swooped on the wings of the wind.

12. You tented Yourself around with darkness,

with rain clouds your pavilion.

13. Glowing coals flared forth from Your brilliance.

14. The Eternal thundered from heaven;

the voice of the Most High made itself heard.

15. You launched arrows and scattered them;

Your lightning confounded them.

8 וַתִּגְעַשׁ [וַיִּתְגָּעַשׁ] וַתִּרְעַשׁ הָאָרֶץ
מוֹסְדוֹת הַשָּׁמַיִם יִרְגָּזוּ
וַיִּתְגָּעֲשׁוּ כִּי־חָרָה לוֹ:

9 עָלָה עָשָׁן בְּאַפּוֹ
וְאֵשׁ מִפִּיו תֹּאכֵל
גֶּחָלִים בָּעֲרוּ מִמֶּנּוּ:

10 וַיֵּט שָׁמַיִם וַיֵּרַד
וַעֲרָפֶל תַּחַת רַגְלָיו:

11 וַיִּרְכַּב עַל־כְּרוּב וַיָּעֹף
וַיֵּרָא עַל־כַּנְפֵי־רוּחַ:

12 וַיָּשֶׁת חֹשֶׁךְ סְבִיבֹתָיו סֻכּוֹת
חַשְׁרַת־מַיִם עָבֵי שְׁחָקִים:

13 מִנֹּגַהּ נֶגְדּוֹ בָּעֲרוּ גַּחֲלֵי־אֵשׁ:

14 יַרְעֵם מִן־שָׁמַיִם יְהוָה
וְעֶלְיוֹן יִתֵּן קוֹלוֹ:

15 וַיִּשְׁלַח חִצִּים וַיְפִיצֵם
בָּרָק וַיְהֻמֵּם [וַיָּהֹם]:

Commentary

8. *The earth trembled.* According to Dahood (see note 2, p. 529), ארץ (*eretz*) does not here mean "earth," but netherworld.[7]

The sky's foundations. The mountains that, in ancient thinking, held up the sky.

11. *You saddled a cherub.* A mythic angelic figure, who appears first in the story of the Garden of Eden, and is prominent in the description of the Ark in the Tabernacle and in Ezekiel's visions. Here, cherubim drive the divine chariot.[8]

Swooped. Instead of וירא (*vayeira*, being seen), we read וידא (*vayeideh*), as in Psalm 18. This is an ancient word for the flight of birds, attested in Ugaritic before 1200 B.C.E.

15. *You launched arrows.* In this mythic language, God has a bow (compare Genesis 9:13) and launches lightning bolts as divine arrows.

And scattered them. David's foes.

16. The sea's channels could be seen,
earth's foundations were revealed.
By Your great roar, Eternal One,
by the blast of Your nostrils,

16 וַיֵּרָאוּ אֲפִקֵי יָם
יִגָּלוּ מֹסְדוֹת תֵּבֵל
בְּגַעֲרַת יְהוָה
מִנִּשְׁמַת רוּחַ אַפּוֹ:

17. You reached down from above and
took me,
pulling me out of the deep waters.

17 יִשְׁלַח מִמָּרוֹם יִקָּחֵנִי
יַמְשֵׁנִי מִמַּיִם רַבִּים:

18. You saved me from my powerful foe,
from enemies too strong for me.

18 יַצִּילֵנִי מֵאֹיְבִי עָז
מִשֹּׂנְאַי כִּי אָמְצוּ מִמֶּנִּי:

19. They advanced on me in my time of
calamity,
but the Eternal was my support.

19 יְקַדְּמֻנִי בְּיוֹם אֵידִי
וַיְהִי יְהוָה מִשְׁעָן לִי:

20. You brought me out [from trouble] to
the wide open space;
because You cherish me, You rescued me.

20 וַיֹּצֵא לַמֶּרְחָב אֹתִי
יְחַלְּצֵנִי כִּי־חָפֵץ בִּי:

21. You treated me as I deserved,
You rewarded me for my innocence.

21 יִגְמְלֵנִי יְהוָה כְּצִדְקָתִי
כְּבֹר יָדַי יָשִׁיב לִי:

22. I have kept the ways of the Eternal,
I have not turned wickedly from my God.

22 כִּי שָׁמַרְתִּי דַּרְכֵי יְהוָה
וְלֹא רָשַׁעְתִּי מֵאֱלֹהָי:

23. Your rules of justice are before me,
I have not turned away from Your laws.

23 כִּי כָל־מִשְׁפָּטוֹ [מִשְׁפָּטָיו] לְנֶגְדִּי
וְחֻקֹּתָיו לֹא־אָסוּר מִמֶּנָּה:

24. I have been blameless toward You,
I have kept guard against offense.

24 וָאֶהְיֶה תָמִים לוֹ
וָאֶשְׁתַּמְּרָה מֵעֲוֹנִי:

25. And You treated me as I deserved,
according to my purity in Your sight.

25 וַיָּשֶׁב יְהוָה לִי כְּצִדְקָתִי
כְּבֹרִי לְנֶגֶד עֵינָיו:

Commentary

16. *Roar.* Again using a mythic image, which was also applied to Baal, the god of storm.

20. *Wide open space.* מרחב (*merchav*) is the opposite of מצר (*metzar*), confining distress, and is used in a figurative sense.[9]

21. *My innocence.* Literally, the purity of my hands.

24. *Blameless.* תמים (*tamim*) describes a character that is simple and straightforward, and wholly righteous (so in verse 26).

26. You show Yourself faithful to the faithful;

with the (truly) upright You show Yourself upright.

27. To the pure You are pure,

and with the crooked You are cunning.

28. You give victory to the humble,

and You look at the proud, to humble them.

29. Eternal One, You are my lamp;

Eternal One, you make my darkness light.

30. With You I can run through a wall;

with my God, I can leap over a barrier.

31. God, Your way is perfect,

Eternal One, Your word is clear,

You are a shield to all who look to You for shelter.

32. Who is God beside the Eternal,

who is a Rock other than our God?

33. —the God who is my mighty shelter,

who maps out for me a noble path,

34. who has made my legs like a deer's,

who makes me stand on the heights,

26 עִם־חָסִיד תִּתְחַסָּד
עִם־גְּבוֹר תָּמִים תִּתַּמָּם:
27 עִם־נָבָר תִּתָּבָר
וְעִם־עִקֵּשׁ תִּתַּפָּל:
28 וְאֶת־עַם עָנִי תּוֹשִׁיעַ
וְעֵינֶיךָ עַל־רָמִים תַּשְׁפִּיל:
29 כִּי־אַתָּה נֵירִי יְהֹוָה
וַיהֹוָה יַגִּיהַּ חָשְׁכִּי:
30 כִּי בְכָה אָרוּץ גְּדוּד
בֵּאלֹהַי אֲדַלֶּג־שׁוּר:
31 הָאֵל תָּמִים דַּרְכּוֹ
אִמְרַת יְהֹוָה צְרוּפָה
מָגֵן הוּא לְכֹל הַחֹסִים בּוֹ:
32 כִּי מִי־אֵל מִבַּלְעֲדֵי יְהֹוָה
וּמִי צוּר מִבַּלְעֲדֵי אֱלֹהֵינוּ:
33 הָאֵל מָעוּזִּי חָיִל
וַיַּתֵּר תָּמִים דַּרְכּוֹ [דַּרְכִּי]:
34 מְשַׁוֶּה רַגְלָיו [רַגְלַי] כָּאַיָּלוֹת
וְעַל בָּמוֹתַי יַעֲמִדֵנִי:

Commentary

27. *You are cunning.* You know their deceit and can match them.

29. *You make my darkness light.* Elsewhere the Psalmist sings: "Darkness is not too dark for You; / night is as light as day."[10]

30. *Run through a wall.* Relating גדוד (*g'dud*) to the Aramaic גדא (*gudda*, wall),[11] but this reading is speculative.

31. *Your word is clear.* Literally, refined (like silver).

33. *My mighty shelter.* מעוזי (*ma'uzzi*). The image occurs in Psalm 31:3 (צור מעוז, *tzur-ma'oz*) and is reflected in the Chanukah hymn that begins with the words מעוז צור ישועתי (*ma'oz tzur y'shuati*), "A mighty Rock (God) is my salvation."

34. *Stand on the heights.* Habakkuk too uses this image.[12]

35. who trains my hands for battle,

my arms to bend a bow of bronze.

36. You have bestowed on me Your triumphant shield,

Your response [to me] enlarges [my
strength].

37. You lengthen my stride,

and my ankles do not waver.

38. I chase my foes and destroy them,

I do not turn back till they are no more.

39. I destroy them, I shatter them;

they cannot get up, they lie at my feet.

40. You have girded me with strength for
battle

and laid low my foes beneath me.

41. You make my enemies bare their
necks;

I rid myself of those who hate me.

42. They cry for help, but there is none;

[they cry] to the Eternal, but get no answer.

35 מְלַמֵּד יָדַי לַמִּלְחָמָה

וְנִחֲתָה קֶשֶׁת־נְחוּשָׁה זְרֹעֹתָי:

36 וַתִּתֶּן־לִי מָגֵן יִשְׁעֶךָ

וַעֲנֹתְךָ תַּרְבֵּנִי:

37 תַּרְחִיב צַעֲדִי תַחְתֵּנִי

וְלֹא מָעֲדוּ קַרְסֻלָּי:

38 אֶרְדְּפָה אוֹיְבַי וָאַשְׁמִידֵם

וְלֹא אָשׁוּב עַד־כַּלּוֹתָם:

39 וָאֲכַלֵּם וָאֶמְחָצֵם

וְלֹא יְקוּמוּן וַיִּפְּלוּ תַּחַת רַגְלָי:

40 וַתְּזַרְנִי חַיִל לַמִּלְחָמָה

תַּכְרִיעַ קָמַי תַּחְתֵּנִי:

41 וְאֹיְבַי נָתַתָּה לִּי עֹרֶף

מְשַׂנְאַי וָאַצְמִיתֵם:

42 יְשַׁוְּעוּ וְאֵין מוֹשִׁיעַ

אֶל־יְהוָה וְלֹא עָנָם:

Commentary

35. *Bow of bronze.* Bows of various kinds of metal were fashioned for decorative purposes in the ancient Near East. Their existence encourages the poet's hyperbole: Through God's gift of strength I could even draw a bronze bow. The same image is found in Job.[13]

37. *Ankles.* קרסל (*karsul*) occurs only here and in Psalm 18. Its meaning is attested in the Akkadian (Assyrian-Babylonian) *kursinnu*.

39. *They lie at my feet.* Literally, *under* my feet, as if placing one's foot on the neck of a defeated foe. This is what Joshua ordered his officers to do with the five kings captured in the cave of Makkedah.[14] (See also verse 41.)

42. *They cry for help.* This is the verb used in Psalm 18 (ישועו, *y'shav'u*) and provides a better parallel to the second half of the verse.[15]

43. Then I pound them like the dust of the
   earth,

like mud in the streets I trample and
pulverize them.

44. You have saved me from strife with
peoples,

You have preserved me to be the leader of
nations,

[so that] a people I never knew [now]
serves me.

45. Foreigners shall cringe before me,

obey me as soon as they hear me;

46. foreigners fade away,

they come quaking from their strongholds.

47. The Eternal lives! Praised be my Rock!

God is exalted,

the Rock of my salvation,

48. the God who gives me revenge,

who makes people subject to me,

49. who frees me from my foes,

who raises me above my enemies,

who rescues me from the violent.

50. So I thank you, Eternal One, among
   the nations,

and sing praises to Your name.

43 וְאֶשְׁחָקֵם כַּעֲפַר־אָרֶץ

כְּטִיט־חוּצוֹת אֲדִקֵּם אֶרְקָעֵם:

44 וַתְּפַלְּטֵנִי מֵרִיבֵי עַמִּי

תִּשְׁמְרֵנִי לְרֹאשׁ גּוֹיִם

עַם לֹא־יָדַעְתִּי יַעַבְדֻנִי:

45 בְּנֵי נֵכָר יִתְכַּחֲשׁוּ־לִי

לִשְׁמוֹעַ אֹזֶן יִשָּׁמְעוּ לִי:

46 בְּנֵי נֵכָר יִבֹּלוּ

וְיַחְגְּרוּ מִמִּסְגְּרוֹתָם:

47 חַי־יְהֹוָה וּבָרוּךְ צוּרִי

וְיָרֻם אֱלֹהֵי

צוּר יִשְׁעִי:

48 הָאֵל הַנֹּתֵן נְקָמֹת לִי

וּמוֹרִיד עַמִּים תַּחְתֵּנִי:

49 וּמוֹצִיאִי מֵאֹיְבָי

וּמִקָּמַי תְּרוֹמְמֵנִי

מֵאִישׁ חֲמָסִים תַּצִּילֵנִי:

50 עַל־כֵּן אוֹדְךָ יְהֹוָה בַּגּוֹיִם

וּלְשִׁמְךָ אֲזַמֵּר:

Commentary

44. *With peoples.* The text has עמי (*ammi*), "my people," which Rashi and others understand as referring to David's troubles with Saul and other internal enemies; our rendering follows the Septuagint.[16]

51 מַגְדִּיל [מִגְדּוֹל] יְשׁוּעוֹת מַלְכּוֹ
וְעֹשֶׂה־חֶסֶד לִמְשִׁיחוֹ
לְדָוִד וּלְזַרְעוֹ עַד־עוֹלָם:

51. You are a tower of victory to Your king,

You show love for Your anointed,

to David and his descendants forever.

Commentary

51. *Tower.* מִגְדּוֹל (*migdol*); so the [bracketed] *k'ré*, while the word is מַגְדִּיל (*magdil,* magnifies) in Psalm 18. Since this verse has been incorporated into the *birkat hamazon* (the blessing after the meal), the version from Psalms is recited on weekdays, and the one from our text on Sabbaths and festivals.

To David and his descendants forever. This conclusion appears to come from a time much later than David's.

Essay

About biblical poems

Both the sidra and haftarah are poetic creations. While the Torah contains only a few poems, the prophetic books, and especially the literary prophets, abound with them. The historical works, like the two named after Samuel, consist mostly of prose, and our haftarah is one of the exceptions. [17]

Poetry, says a dictionary, is the art of rhythmical composition, which features beautiful, imaginative or elevated thoughts.[18] Every reader will recognize at once that David's prayer fits this category, especially since the text has been printed in verse form.

Biblical poems rarely feature rhyme and instead are distinguished by their content and meter. While the latter forms an important part of its structure,[19] the poem's *content* is its distinguishing feature. Take the beginning of verse 3:

> *God is my rock where I seek shelter,*
> *my shield, the source of my salvation.*
> *My deliverer, You save me from violence.*

Note that each line (also called colon) contains basically the same thought. This is called synonymous parallelism, and the entire poem of our haftarah exhibits such parallels. [20]

Another type of this mode is called antithetic parallelism, the second colon being the opposite of the first:

> *For a brief moment I forsook you,*
> *in love I took you back.[21]*

A third type of is called synthetic parallelism, in which the succeeding line expands on what precedes:

> *You tread the sea with Your steeds,*
> *churning the mighty waters.[22]*

Another feature of biblical poetry is repetition, either of words or of the same thought. Take verses 38 and 39 of our haftarah:

> *I chase my foes and destroy them,*
> *I do not turn back till they are no more.*
> *I destroy them, I shatter them ....*

These are just a few of aspects of this mode of biblical writing, which has been studied extensively and has been shown to be highly complex. [23] It is also often quite difficult to distinguish between biblical poetry and prose, especially when the latter contains elevated speech.

Since the Hebrew of the Tanach contains few abstractions, its poetry teems with concrete images, and when they deal with God these images may strike moderns as highly anthropomorphic. The ancients took no umbrage at this, for it was the only way in which poets could express their thoughts. David's concept of God was no less lofty than ours; on the contrary, the extent to which he was suffused with the reality of God's Presence gives it its true religious significance. The poet ascribes nothing of his good fortune to himself; it was all God's doing, and to God he sings his grateful praise.

Gleanings

Words to Remember

God is my rock where I seek shelter,
my shield, the source of my salvation. (verse 3)

Eternal One, You are my lamp;
Eternal One, you make my darkness light. (verse 29)

David the poet

Once David had been freed from the constraints of war and danger, and enjoyed the rest of his life in peace, he turned to compose songs and hymns in several kinds of meters. He also made musical instruments and taught the Levites to sing them.

Josephus[24]

Original and translation

Poetry cannot be translated; and, therefore, it is the poets that preserve the languages; for we would not be at the trouble to learn a language if we could have all that is written in it just as well in a translation. But as the beauties of poetry cannot be preserved in any language except that in which it was originally written, we learn the language.

Samuel Johnson[25]

Biblical poetry

Hebrew biblical poetry conforms to Milton's familiar dictum that good poetry should be "simple, sensuous, and passionate." The lines are short; each line has an identity of its own and elicits a corresponding effect. Speech is concentrated to the barest minimum, and prolixity is rare. Repetitions, on the other hand, are common, but these usually have a special function in the composition of the poem. Verbs play a primary and strategic role and account in large part for the style and in the ordering of the words. The most characteristic features of biblical poetry are action, imagery, simplicity, vigor, and concreteness.

James Muilenberg[26]

* * *

Notes

[1] Rashi, followed by Radak, stresses that David's words came from the time of his old age.

[2] Mitchell Dahood (*Anchor Bible,* Psalms) dwells extensively on Ugaritic linguistic and cultic parallels; see the essay by F. M. Cross, Jr. and D. N. Freedman, noted in our bibliography. H. W. Hertzberg, too, in his commentary on Samuel, calls the text a poem of high antiquity (pp. 392-393). A chief proponent of the old school is Moses Buttenwieser, who, in his commentary on the Psalms, ascribes the prayer to the time of the Babylonian exile (pp. 456 ff.). To him, David was "a born soldier ... temperamentally incapable of such profound spiritual experience and transcendent faith" (p. 461). This represents a simplistic view of a gifted and complex personage, whom the Jewish people took to heart as one of its great men.

[3] See the haftarah for Sh'mini (II Samuel chapter 6); it appears that Hertzberg (p. 392) leans toward this dating. The fact that the text appears near the end of the books of Samuel (and might suggest therefore as belonging to the end of David's life) is not significant. It is generally recognized that this prayer is part of the final section of the book and consists of materials dealing with different periods in David's life.

[4] So, for example, Moses Buttenwieser, *The Psalms,* p. 453.

[5] The name is probably derived from two components, בלי and יעל ("without" and "use"); but others derive it from בלע (*bala*), to swallow—that is, the power that swallows up life; so Dahood, p. 105.

[6] This makes the poem more direct in translation, and also avoids male-gender pronouns for God.

[7] Based on Ugaritic parallels. See note 2.

[8] See Solomon B. Freehof's commentary on Psalm 18, in *Book of Psalms.* See also I Kings 8:6; haftarah for Pikudei.

[9] As in Psalm 118:5, מן־המצר קראתי יה ענני במרחב יה.

[10] Psalm 139:12.

[11] Dahood in his commentary on Psalm 18 (in the *Anchor Bible,* Psalms) relates *g'dud* to *gid* (sinew), and renders: "For through You, I run well-sinewed, and with my God I can scale any wall."

[12] Habakkuk 3:19 (see the haftarah for the second day of Shavuot).

[13] Job 20:24.

[14] Joshua 10:24.

[15] The Hebrew is very similar: ישעו (*yish'u,* they look), and ישועו (*yeshavvu,* they cry) in Psalm 18.

[16] Radak notes that *ammi* means "peoples" (plural) also in Psalm 144:2 (where the Targum so interprets it, as does Saadia).

[17] The other large poem is the Song of Deborah; see the haftarah for B'shalach.

[18] This is the basic definition in *The American College Dictionary* (New York: Random House, 1947).

[19] Mostly through the placement of accents.

[20] Our example consists of three stanzas or cola; two cola occur much more frequently.

[21] Isaiah 54:7; see the haftarah for Noach.

[22] Habakkuk 3:15; see the haftarah for the second day of Shavuot.

[23] See especially J. L. Kugel's work, *The Idea of Biblical Poetry*. Like older contributions to this field of scholarship, his study notes also the relation of biblical poetry to Canaanite, and especially Ugaritic literature (as does M. Dahood in his commentary on Psalms).

[24] See especially J. L. Kugel's work, *The Idea of Biblical Poetry*. Like older contributions to this field of scholarship, his study notes also the relation of biblical poetry to Canaanite, and especially Ugaritic literature (as does M. Dahood in his commentary on Psalms).

[25] Cited in *The International Dictionary of Thoughts*, ed. J. P. Bradley and others   (Chicago: J. G. Ferguson Pub. Co., 1969), p. 561.

[26] Poetry," *Encyclopaedia Judaica*, vol. 13, p. 671.

וזאת הברכה

Joshua, chapter 1, verses 1 to 18

Introduction

Connection of sidra and haftarah:

The sidra is always read on Simchat Torah and ends with the death of Moses. The haftarah, whose language and terminology are very much in the style of Deuteronomy, takes up the story of Joshua, his successor, under whose guidance the conquest of Canaan will take place.

The setting:

The people were poised on the east side of the Jordan and were now bidden by God, through Joshua, to start the campaign.

For more on the book of Joshua, see our *General Introduction*; on Joshua and his time, see the essay below.

The story:

1. The time of the events. (1)
2. God's charge to Joshua:
    Order to cross the Jordan and begin the conquest. (2-5)
    Moral instructions. (6-9).
3. Joshua's charge to the people. (10-15)
4. The people's response. (16-18)

1:1. After the death of Moses, the servant of the Eternal, the Eternal said to Joshua son of Nun, Moses' assistant:

2. My servant Moses is dead; come now, come across this (river) Jordan, you and all this people, and go into the land that I am giving to the people Israel.

3. As I promised Moses, I am giving you every foot of ground you step on.

4. Your borders [shall reach] from the desert [in the south] and the Lebanon [in the north] to the great River, the river

1:1 וַיְהִי אַחֲרֵי מוֹת מֹשֶׁה עֶבֶד יְהֹוָה וַיֹּאמֶר

יְהֹוָה אֶל־יְהוֹשֻׁעַ בִּן־נוּן מְשָׁרֵת מֹשֶׁה לֵאמֹר:

2 מֹשֶׁה עַבְדִּי מֵת וְעַתָּה קוּם עֲבֹר אֶת־

הַיַּרְדֵּן הַזֶּה אַתָּה וְכָל־הָעָם הַזֶּה אֶל־הָאָרֶץ

אֲשֶׁר אָנֹכִי נֹתֵן לָהֶם לִבְנֵי יִשְׂרָאֵל:

3 כָּל־מָקוֹם אֲשֶׁר תִּדְרֹךְ כַּף־רַגְלְכֶם בּוֹ לָכֶם

נְתַתִּיו כַּאֲשֶׁר דִּבַּרְתִּי אֶל־מֹשֶׁה:

4 מֵהַמִּדְבָּר וְהַלְּבָנוֹן הַזֶּה וְעַד־הַנָּהָר הַגָּדוֹל

Commentary

1. *The servant of the Eternal.* עבד יהוה (*eved adonai*). An honorific title, accorded to Abraham, Isaac, and Jacob, and occasionally affixed to others. In Second Isaiah, Israel as a people is called Servant of God (see the haftarah for Ekev).

Joshua. יהושע (*y'hoshua*, "the Eternal is salvation") was originally called Hosea (הושע, *hoshe'a*), but Moses changed his name to Joshua.[1] In later Hebrew, the name was often shortened to Jeshua.[2]

Son of Nun. יהושע בן־נון (*y'hoshua bin nun*). Usually "son of" is בֶּן (*ben*) but here it is בִּן (*bin*), probably because the two "n" sounds (נ, ן) follow each other and caused a diminution of the vowel sound.[3] Joshua's father, Nun, appears once as Non.[4]

Moses' assistant. Or "lieutenant." His appointment was at divine behest, and Moses installed him "in the sight of all Israel."[5]

2. *All this people.* Israel is called עם (*am*), a term that combines the familial and ethnic with the element of religious cohesion.

The people Israel. בני ישראל (*b'nei yisrael*) stresses the peoplehood of Israel and therefore is to be preferred over "Israelites" or the older and literal "Children of Israel."

3. *As I promised Moses.* The Promised Land would be Israel's, but only if it observed its part of the Covenant. "The gift was 'in fief,' not an outright grant."[6]

Euphrates [in the east]—[that is] all the land of the Hittites—to the Great Sea in the west.

5. As long as you live, no one shall be able to stand against you. I will be with you as I was with Moses. I will never fail you or leave you.

6. Be strong and of good courage, for you must bring this people into possession of the land that I swore to their ancestors to give to them.

7. Only be strong and of good courage in observing faithfully all the Torah that Moses My servant commanded you; do not turn away from it to the right or to the left: then you shall do well wherever you go.

8. Let the book of this Torah never depart from your mouth; meditate on it day and night, taking care to carry out all that

נְהַר־פְּרָת כֹּל אֶרֶץ הַחִתִּים וְעַד־הַיָּם הַגָּדוֹל מְבוֹא הַשָּׁמֶשׁ יִהְיֶה גְּבוּלְכֶם:

5 לֹא־יִתְיַצֵּב אִישׁ לְפָנֶיךָ כֹּל יְמֵי חַיֶּיךָ כַּאֲשֶׁר הָיִיתִי עִם־מֹשֶׁה אֶהְיֶה עִמָּךְ לֹא אַרְפְּךָ וְלֹא אֶעֶזְבֶךָּ:

6 חֲזַק וֶאֱמָץ כִּי אַתָּה תַּנְחִיל אֶת־הָעָם הַזֶּה אֶת־הָאָרֶץ אֲשֶׁר־נִשְׁבַּעְתִּי לַאֲבוֹתָם לָתֵת לָהֶם:

7 רַק חֲזַק וֶאֱמַץ מְאֹד לִשְׁמֹר לַעֲשׂוֹת כְּכָל־ הַתּוֹרָה אֲשֶׁר צִוְּךָ מֹשֶׁה עַבְדִּי אַל־תָּסוּר מִמֶּנּוּ יָמִין וּשְׂמֹאול לְמַעַן תַּשְׂכִּיל בְּכֹל אֲשֶׁר תֵּלֵךְ:

8 לֹא־יָמוּשׁ סֵפֶר הַתּוֹרָה הַזֶּה מִפִּיךָ וְהָגִיתָ בּוֹ יוֹמָם וָלַיְלָה לְמַעַן תִּשְׁמֹר לַעֲשׂוֹת כְּכָל־

Commentary

4. *Land of the Hittites.* Although the Hittite empire, which ruled much of the Near East for five hundred years, had collapsed by 1180 B.C.E., the designation "land of the Hittites" persisted. Here it corresponds to the usage found in Assyrian and Babylonian annals of the first millennium, where it meant essentially the areas of present-day Israel, Jordan, Syria, and Lebanon.

The Great Sea. The Mediterranean.

6. *Be strong and of good courage.* God here repeats the words spoken by Moses to Joshua.[7]

7. *Do not turn ... right or left.* This too is Torah language.[8]

8. *Meditate.* The Hebrew conveys more than an activity of the spirit and implies something that is audible, and often means "moan," "mutter," or "utter." Hence, "let the book ... never depart from your *mouth.*"[9]

Day and night. Repeating the instruction that is at the center of the *Shema:* "Speak of them when in your home and on your way, when you lie down and when you rise up." The book of Psalms begins in like fashion.[10]

is written in it. Then shall you be successful in your enterprise, and then shall you do well.

9. Have I not enjoined you? Be strong and of good courage, do not be afraid or disheartened, for I, the Eternal your God, am with you wherever you go.

10. Then Joshua gave these orders to the officers of the people:

11. Go through the camp and tell the people: Get provisions ready, for within three days you are going to cross the Jordan to take possession of the land that the Eternal your God, is giving you to possess.

12. Joshua also said to the tribes of Reuben and Gad and to half the tribe of Manasseh:

13. Remember the words of God's servant Moses, charging you that the Eternal your God would give you a place to rest by giving you this land.

14. Let your wives, your children, and your cattle stay here, in the territory that Moses gave you, east of the Jordan; but your ablest warriors, in battle array, must cross over ahead of your kinfolk, thus to help them,

הַכָּתוּב בּוֹ כִּי־אָז תַּצְלִיחַ אֶת־דְּרָכֶךָ וְאָז תַּשְׂכִּיל:

9 הֲלוֹא צִוִּיתִיךָ חֲזַק וֶאֱמָץ אַל־תַּעֲרֹץ וְאַל־תֵּחָת כִּי עִמְּךָ יְהוָה אֱלֹהֶיךָ בְּכֹל אֲשֶׁר תֵּלֵךְ:

10 וַיְצַו יְהוֹשֻׁעַ אֶת־שֹׁטְרֵי הָעָם לֵאמֹר:

11 עִבְרוּ בְּקֶרֶב הַמַּחֲנֶה וְצַוּוּ אֶת־הָעָם לֵאמֹר הָכִינוּ לָכֶם צֵידָה כִּי בְּעוֹד שְׁלֹשֶׁת יָמִים אַתֶּם עֹבְרִים אֶת־הַיַּרְדֵּן הַזֶּה לָבוֹא לָרֶשֶׁת אֶת־הָאָרֶץ אֲשֶׁר יְהוָה אֱלֹהֵיכֶם נֹתֵן לָכֶם לְרִשְׁתָּהּ:

12 וְלָראוּבֵנִי וְלַגָּדִי וְלַחֲצִי שֵׁבֶט הַמְנַשֶּׁה אָמַר יְהוֹשֻׁעַ לֵאמֹר:

13 זָכוֹר אֶת־הַדָּבָר אֲשֶׁר צִוָּה אֶתְכֶם מֹשֶׁה עֶבֶד־יְהוָה לֵאמֹר יְהוָה אֱלֹהֵיכֶם מֵנִיחַ לָכֶם וְנָתַן לָכֶם אֶת־הָאָרֶץ הַזֹּאת:

14 נְשֵׁיכֶם טַפְּכֶם וּמִקְנֵיכֶם יֵשְׁבוּ בָּאָרֶץ אֲשֶׁר נָתַן לָכֶם מֹשֶׁה בְּעֵבֶר הַיַּרְדֵּן וְאַתֶּם תַּעַבְרוּ חֲמֻשִׁים לִפְנֵי אֲחֵיכֶם כֹּל גִּבּוֹרֵי הַחַיִל וַעֲזַרְתֶּם אוֹתָם:

Commentary

11. *Within three days.* On the third day the people began to cross the Jordan.[11]

12. *Reuben and Gad.* They and half the tribe of Manasseh were allotted land on the east side of the Jordan, but they had to promise that they would participate in the conquest of Canaan, whenever it would begin.[12] A 9th century B.C.E. inscription of Mesha, king of Moab, speaks of the tribe of Gad having lived in the area "forever."

14. *In battle array.* חמשים (*chamushim*), a word of disputed meaning, which also describes the manner in which the people of Israel left Egypt.[13]

534

15. until the Eternal gives rest to your kin like yourselves, and they shall have taken possession of the land that the Eternal your God is giving them. Then you may go back and take possession of your rightful land east of the Jordan that Moses the servant of God gave to you.

16. They answered Joshua: We will do everything you have commanded us and go anywhere you send us.

17. We will listen to you, just as we always listened to Moses. Our only prayer is that, just as was the case with Moses, the Eternal your God may be with you!

18. Let anyone who rebels against your command and refuses to obey your words, who does not do as you command, be put to death. Only be strong and have courage!

15 עַ֣ד אֲשֶׁר־יָנִ֣יחַ יְהֹוָ֣ה ׀ לַאֲחֵיכֶם֮ כָּכֶם֒ וְיָרְשׁ֣וּ גַם־הֵ֔מָּה אֶת־הָאָ֕רֶץ אֲשֶׁר־יְהֹוָ֥ה אֱלֹהֵיכֶ֖ם נֹתֵ֣ן לָהֶ֑ם וְשַׁבְתֶּ֞ם לְאֶ֣רֶץ יְרֻשַּׁתְכֶ֗ם וִירִשְׁתֶּ֣ם אוֹתָ֔הּ אֲשֶׁ֣ר ׀ נָתַ֣ן לָכֶ֗ם מֹשֶׁה֙ עֶ֣בֶד יְהֹוָ֔ה בְּעֵ֖בֶר הַיַּרְדֵּ֑ן מִזְרַ֖ח הַשָּֽׁמֶשׁ׃

16 וַֽיַּעֲנ֔וּ אֶת־יְהוֹשֻׁ֖עַ לֵאמֹ֑ר כֹּ֤ל אֲשֶׁר־צִוִּיתָ֙נוּ֙ נַֽעֲשֶׂ֔ה וְאֶֽל־כׇּל־אֲשֶׁ֥ר תִּשְׁלָחֵ֖נוּ נֵלֵֽךְ׃

17 כְּכֹ֤ל אֲשֶׁר־שָׁמַ֙עְנוּ֙ אֶל־מֹשֶׁ֔ה כֵּ֖ן נִשְׁמַ֣ע אֵלֶ֑יךָ רַ֠ק יִהְיֶ֞ה יְהֹוָ֤ה אֱלֹהֶ֙יךָ֙ עִמָּ֔ךְ כַּאֲשֶׁ֥ר הָיָ֖ה עִם־מֹשֶֽׁה׃

18 כׇּל־אִ֞ישׁ אֲשֶׁר־יַמְרֶ֣ה אֶת־פִּ֗יךָ וְלֹֽא־יִשְׁמַ֧ע אֶת־דְּבָרֶ֛יךָ לְכֹ֥ל אֲשֶׁר־תְּצַוֶּ֖נּוּ יוּמָ֑ת רַ֖ק חֲזַ֥ק וֶאֱמָֽץ׃

Commentary

15. *Gives rest to your kin.* From doing battle.

18. *Only be strong.* Have no patience with or compassion for shirkers.[14]

Essay

Joshua and his time

Joshua assumed the leadership of his people at a crucial time in Near East history. From Egypt to the borders of India, the superpowers were tottering and had lost their ability to control their vassals. These in turn grasped the opportunity to cut themselves loose, thereby upsetting traditional structures and turning the birthplace of major civilizations into a cauldron of armed conflicts. It was also the time when the so-called Sea Peoples migrated eastward in the Mediterranean and settled along the coast of Canaan and Lebanon.

These upheavals coincided with the use of iron for fashioning various instruments, primary among them the plow. Its introduction propelled agriculture into a dominant position, displacing nomads and seminomads in the process. Thus, the events described in the book of Joshua fit the general picture of migrations and territorial struggles of the time, and describe what took place in a small strip of land, located between the eastern desert and the western sea. (On the history and theology of the book, see our *General Introduction*.)

Joshua's earlier life is described in the Torah: he was an Ephraimite who was one of the spies sent to explore the Promised Land and who (with Caleb) rendered an encouraging report.[15] He became Moses' trusted assistant and eventually was chosen by God to be his successor.[16] His military prowess bore the stamp of divine approval and was embellished by legends about the crumbling walls of Jericho and the sun standing still at his bidding.

Still, despite the book's detailed accounts of his leadership, he does not emerge as a distinct personality, and we know nothing about his personal life. Though called a prophet who could say with assurance, "Thus says the Eternal One,"[17] he remained in the shadow of his great predecessor. His overriding conviction was the same: Do God's will, and the land will be yours.

The book concludes by recording his death to have occurred at the age of 110, exactly duplicating the life span of Joseph. Thus, tradition closes the circle by linking Joseph and Joshua: one caused his people to leave Canaan, the other brought them back.

Gleanings

The man in the moon

Moses and Joshua occupied central places in Jewish legends, which compared Moses to the sun and Joshua to the moon.[18] From this arose the popular belief among Jews in Eastern Europe that Joshua was the man in the moon.[19]

The family man

Joshua married Rahab, who had saved the spies, had reformed her disorderly ways and had converted to Judaism. They had no sons, but their daughters became the forebears of nine prophets.

Talmud[20]

The credit

(The book of Joshua is seen by many biblical scholars as a reflection of the same theology that brought Deuteronomy into being, and is often considered as belonging to the Pentateuch [the five books of Moses], which then becomes the Hexateuch or "Six-Books.")

Joshua is God's charismatic leader for the task of leading the people in the conquest. He is especially chosen and empowered; he was not a son of Moses, nor did his office pass to his heirs. The victories are God's alone. Israel can claim no credit; the book does not enable one to fashion hero stories. Quite the contrary! The victory and the credit belong to God alone.

R. G. Boling and G. E. Wright[21]

* * *

Notes

[1] Numbers 13:8, 16. Hoshea (or Hosea) was also the name of the oft-cited prophet of the 8th century (see the haftarot on Vayeitzei and Vayishlach), as well as of the last ruler of the Northern Kingdom (Israel).

[2] Often in Ezra (for example, 2:2) and Nehemiah (for example, 3:19), and also in I Chronicles 24:11 and II Chronicles 31:15, and of course in Christian Scriptures ("Jesus" deriving from the Greek and Latin rendering of Jeshua).

[3] See Radak and Ralbag. Joshua is always called bin Nun; otherwise the use of *bin* is rare in the Tanach.

[4] I Chronicles 7:27.

[5] Deuteronomy 31:7.

[6] Boling (*Anchor Bible*, Joshua), p. 121.

[7] In our sidra, Deuteronomy 31:7.

[8] Deuteronomy 5:29; 17:11, 20; 28:14.

[9] See H. L. Ginsberg, *Supplements to Vetus Testamentum*, vol. XIV (1967), p. 80.

[10] Deuteronomy 6:7; Psalm 1:2.

[11] Joshua 3:2.

[12] Numbers 32:1-32.

[13] See the Torah Commentary on Exodus 13:18 (p. 478) for various interpretations.

[14] So Metzudat David.

[15] Numbers chapter 13.

[16] Numbers 27:15-23.

[17] Joshua 24:29.

[18] *B. Baba Batra* 75a.

[19] For sources of this belief see Ginzberg, *Legends of the Jews*, vol. 6, p. 170, note 6. See also note 2 for the legends about Joshua being the executioner of his own father.

[20] *B. Megillah* 14b. There is also a tradition that understood Rahab to have been an innkeeper and not a prostitute; see the haftarah for Sh'lach L'cha.

[21] In their commentary (*Anchor Bible*, Joshua), p. 51.

Second Kings, chapter 12, verses 1 to 17

Introduction

Connection of sidra and haftarah:

This is the first of four Shabbatot on which the regular sidra for the day is supplemented by an additional reading, the theme of which gives each Shabbat a special name.[1] Thus, Shabbat Sh'kalim features a reading from the opening verses of sidra Ki Tissa (Exodus 30:11-16), and the haftarah brings us the story of Temple dues in the days of King Jehoash of Judah.

The setting:

In the late 9th century B.C.E., the kingdom of Judah was going through turbulent days. Queen Athalia had occupied the throne after her son had been assassinated and she herself had killed his descendants, that is, her own grandchildren.[2] But one had a escaped, a small child, Jehoash, who was hidden in the Temple by the wife of the chief priest, Jehoiada, who had helped Jehoash to safety. When the boy was seven years old the priestly party proclaimed him king, and Athalia lost her life in the revolution. The young king began his reign in the year 835, under the tutelage of Jehoiada, who himself became a legendary figure (he was said to have lived for 130 years).[3]

For more on the books of Kings, see our *General Introduction*.

Content of the haftarah:

1. Jehoash becomes king. (1-4)
2. He relieves the priests of the duty to repair the Temple. (5-9)
3. Arrangements for the repair work and its funding. (10-17)

HAFTARAH FOR SHABBAT SH'KALIM

Second Kings, chapter 12, verses 1 to 17

12:1. Jehoash was seven years old when he began his reign;

2. and Jehoash began to rule in the seventh year of Jehu's reign, reigning in Jerusalem forty years. His mother was Zibiah of Beer-sheba.

3. All his days Jehoash did what was right in the sight of the Eternal, as Jehoiada the priest instructed him.

4. However, the high places were not removed; people continued to sacrifice and burn incense on the high places.

5. Jehoash said to the priests: Let all the money brought into the House of the Eternal as a sacred gift, whether it be money one is required to pay, money for which each person is assessed, or money brought as a free-will offering,

6. be taken by the priests, each from the one who is making the gift, and used by

1 בֶּן־שֶׁבַע שָׁנִים יְהוֹאָשׁ בְּמָלְכוֹ: 12:1

2 בִּשְׁנַת־שֶׁבַע לְיֵהוּא מָלַךְ יְהוֹאָשׁ וְאַרְבָּעִים שָׁנָה מָלַךְ בִּירוּשָׁלָ͏ִם וְשֵׁם אִמּוֹ צִבְיָה מִבְּאֵר שָׁבַע:

3 וַיַּעַשׂ יְהוֹאָשׁ הַיָּשָׁר בְּעֵינֵי יְהוָה כָּל־יָמָיו אֲשֶׁר הוֹרָהוּ יְהוֹיָדָע הַכֹּהֵן:

4 רַק הַבָּמוֹת לֹא־סָרוּ עוֹד הָעָם מְזַבְּחִים וּמְקַטְּרִים בַּבָּמוֹת:

5 וַיֹּאמֶר יְהוֹאָשׁ אֶל־הַכֹּהֲנִים כֹּל כֶּסֶף הַקֳּדָשִׁים אֲשֶׁר־יוּבָא בֵית־יְהוָה כֶּסֶף עוֹבֵר אִישׁ כֶּסֶף נַפְשׁוֹת עֶרְכּוֹ כָּל־כֶּסֶף אֲשֶׁר יַעֲלֶה עַל לֶב־אִישׁ לְהָבִיא בֵּית יְהוָה:

6 יִקְחוּ לָהֶם הַכֹּהֲנִים אִישׁ מֵאֵת מַכָּרוֹ וְהֵם

Commentary

2. *Jehu's reign.* In the Northern Kingdom. He was favored by the prophet Elijah for his opposition to Baal worship, and in 843 killed Jehoram, the reigning king of Israel. He also directed the slaying of King Ahaziah of Judah (the Southern Kingdom).[4]

His mother was Zibiah. His father was King Ahaziah, whom Jehu had killed.

3. *All his days.* The author(s) of the book of Kings thought highly of Jehoash, but the author(s) of Chronicles recorded that he returned to idolatrous practices after his mentor Jehoiada died.[5]

6. *The one who is making the gift.* מכרו (*makaro*), an interpretation based on relating the word to מכיר (*makir*, recognize, know), meaning: take personal donations from those who recognize their obligation to the priesthood.[6] Another understanding would derive the word from מכר (*m-k-r*), to sell or trade: the priest should take the money from a person responsible for financial affairs.[7] In either interpretation the priests, after receiving the money, would then be responsible for the repairs, but—as the next verse indicates—they did not make them.

יְחַזְּקוּ אֶת־בֶּדֶק הַבָּיִת לְכֹל אֲשֶׁר־יִמָּצֵא שָׁם
בָּדֶק:

7 וַיְהִי בִּשְׁנַת עֶשְׂרִים וְשָׁלֹשׁ שָׁנָה לַמֶּלֶךְ
יְהוֹאָשׁ לֹא־חִזְּקוּ הַכֹּהֲנִים אֶת־בֶּדֶק הַבָּיִת:

8 וַיִּקְרָא הַמֶּלֶךְ יְהוֹאָשׁ לִיהוֹיָדָע הַכֹּהֵן
וְלַכֹּהֲנִים וַיֹּאמֶר אֲלֵהֶם מַדּוּעַ אֵינְכֶם מְחַזְּקִים
אֶת־בֶּדֶק הַבָּיִת וְעַתָּה אַל־תִּקְחוּ־כֶסֶף מֵאֵת
מַכָּרֵיכֶם כִּי־לְבֶדֶק הַבַּיִת תִּתְּנֻהוּ:

9 וַיֵּאֹתוּ הַכֹּהֲנִים לְבִלְתִּי קְחַת־כֶּסֶף מֵאֵת
הָעָם וּלְבִלְתִּי חַזֵּק אֶת־בֶּדֶק הַבָּיִת:

10 וַיִּקַּח יְהוֹיָדָע הַכֹּהֵן אֲרוֹן אֶחָד וַיִּקֹּב חֹר
בְּדַלְתּוֹ וַיִּתֵּן אֹתוֹ אֵצֶל הַמִּזְבֵּחַ בְּיָמִין [מִיָּמִין]
בְּבוֹא־אִישׁ בֵּית יְהוָה וְנָתְנוּ־שָׁמָּה הַכֹּהֲנִים
שֹׁמְרֵי הַסַּף אֶת־כָּל־הַכֶּסֶף הַמּוּבָא בֵית־יְהוָה:

11 וַיְהִי כִּרְאוֹתָם כִּי־רַב הַכֶּסֶף בָּאָרוֹן וַיַּעַל
סֹפֵר הַמֶּלֶךְ וְהַכֹּהֵן הַגָּדוֹל וַיָּצֻרוּ וַיִּמְנוּ אֶת־
הַכֶּסֶף הַנִּמְצָא בֵית־יְהוָה:

them to make repairs in the Temple, whenever it is found that repairs are needed.

7. But by the twenty-third year of King Jehoash, the priests had not made any repairs in the Temple.

8. So King Jehoash called in Jehoiada and the other priests and said to them: Why haven't you been repairing the Temple? From now on, you are not to keep the money from your donors; you are to hand it over for the repair of the Temple.

9. The priests agreed that they would no longer receive money from the people, and that they would no longer be responsible for the repair of the Temple.

10. Then Jehoiada the priest took a chest, made a hole in its lid, and placed it to the right of the altar, as one enters the House of the Eternal. The priests on guard at the entrance put into it all the money that was brought into the House of the Eternal.

11. Whenever they saw that there was a good deal of money in the chest, the royal scribe and the high priest would go up and count the money found in the House of the Eternal and put it into bags.

Commentary

8. *From now on.* The king, realizing the priests would do nothing to repair the Temple, now takes a different approach. Priests would no longer take offerings as before, but would also be relieved of the responsibility for the repairs.

9. *The priests agreed.* They were, in fact, glad to shed their task, "which they considered as outside their priestly functions."[8]

12. After the money had been weighed out, they would give it to the artisans in charge of the work at the House of the Eternal; then they would pay the carpenters and the builders who worked there,

13. and the masons and stone-cutters. They also bought wood and cut stone for the repair of the House of the Eternal, and all the other expenses for the repair of the Temple.

14. But the money that was brought to the House of the Eternal was not used to make silver cups, snuffers, basins, trumpets, or any gold or silver vessels;

15. it was given to the artisans, using it to repair the House of the Eternal.

16. No detailed accounting was made with those to whom the silver was given to pay the artisans because they worked under contract.

17. The money given for guilt-offerings and sin-offerings was not brought into the House of the Eternal; it went to the priests.

12 וְנָתְנוּ אֶת־הַכֶּסֶף עַל־יַד [יְדֵי] עֹשֵׂי הַמְּלָאכָה הַמֻּפְקָדִים [הַמֻּפְקָדִים] בֵּית יְהֹוָה וַיּוֹצִיאֻהוּ לְחָרָשֵׁי הָעֵץ וְלַבֹּנִים הָעֹשִׂים בֵּית יְהֹוָה:

13 וְלַגֹּדְרִים וּלְחֹצְבֵי הָאֶבֶן וְלִקְנוֹת עֵצִים וְאַבְנֵי מַחְצֵב לְחַזֵּק אֶת־בֶּדֶק בֵּית־יְהֹוָה וּלְכֹל אֲשֶׁר־יֵצֵא עַל־הַבַּיִת לְחָזְקָה:

14 אַךְ לֹא יֵעָשֶׂה בֵּית יְהֹוָה סִפּוֹת כֶּסֶף מְזַמְּרוֹת מִזְרָקוֹת חֲצֹצְרוֹת כָּל־כְּלִי זָהָב וּכְלִי־כָסֶף מִן־הַכֶּסֶף הַמּוּבָא בֵּית־יְהֹוָה:

15 כִּי־לְעֹשֵׂי הַמְּלָאכָה יִתְּנֻהוּ וְחִזְּקוּ־בוֹ אֶת־בֵּית יְהֹוָה:

16 וְלֹא יְחַשְּׁבוּ אֶת־הָאֲנָשִׁים אֲשֶׁר יִתְּנוּ אֶת־הַכֶּסֶף עַל־יָדָם לָתֵת לְעֹשֵׂי הַמְּלָאכָה כִּי בֶאֱמֻנָה הֵם עֹשִׂים:

17 כֶּסֶף אָשָׁם וְכֶסֶף חַטָּאוֹת לֹא יוּבָא בֵּית יְהֹוָה לַכֹּהֲנִים יִהְיוּ:

Commentary

14. *But ....* Exceptions to these arrangements were the appurtenances that were made of precious metals. The traditional explanation is that the textile fabrics of the Sanctuary had priority, and public funds could be used only if there was a surplus; but others say that the purpose of the new rule was to prevent any misappropriation of funds.[9] The latter explanation is more likely.

16. *They worked under contract.* Or "dealt honorably."

17. *Guilt-offerings and sin-offerings.* Individual offerings that people made for special events in their lives, which were given to the priests for their personal sustenance.[10]

Essay

How the Temple was supported

The additional Torah reading for this Shabbat tells us that the maintenance of the national Sanctuary was the financial responsibility of the whole people, each of whom had to contribute a half-shekel annually. No distinction was made between rich and poor—a rule that was much discussed in rabbinic literature.[11] The duty to contribute a half-shekel did not cease when Jews migrated to other lands; being Jews they had to contribute their share wherever they lived.

Other forms of Temple taxation derived from the various offerings that were to be brought, and their values were assessed by the priests. The Torah states explicitly: "Whatever assessment is set by the priest shall stand."[12]

Apparently, there was rarely enough money to take care of capital expenses, and much of the Sanctuary had become seedy. Not enough people availed themselves of the Temple's facilities, neglecting their religious duties. Jehoash therefore tried a revolutionary approach: he asked the levites to go out into the countryside and collect the funds. But the levites dragged their feet.[13] They probably considered this assignment to be below their dignity, and they may also have felt that they would be considered like other tax collectors and thereby bring themselves and the Temple into bad repute.

The king realized that his plan had misfired and that he could collect money only if it were done on a totally voluntary basis. He removed the priests from the process altogether by placing a treasure chest in the Temple precincts and letting people make anonymous contributions, dropping their silver (there were as yet no coins or paper money) into the chest through the small hole bored at the top. When the box was full, it would be emptied and the proceeds reserved for the needed repairs. This plan worked; where compulsion had failed, the free-will system succeeded.

In this way, the maintenance of the building became the responsibility of everyone, and the people responded gladly and generously.[14] Also, relieving the priests of secular responsibilities—like money collection and building repair—allowed them to concentrate on their religious duties.

The unemotional narrative of the haftarah has a distinctly modern ring. Similar problems worry the leaders of our synagogues, and often they find the same kind of sometimes hesitant and sometimes ready response that Jehoash made in his day.

But neither he nor the custodians of today's temples could match the success of the first fund-raising campaign in the Sinai desert. Then, the people responded with such generosity that Moses had to make an announcement: "Let no man or woman make any further effort to collect gifts for the Sanctuary."[15]

Gleanings

About Jehoash

He was pious as long as Jehoiada, his mentor, was alive. But later, he listened to the flatterers who suggested that his miraculous escape from Athalia was proof that he had divine status. He was punished by meeting a horrible death.

Midrash[16]

The half-shekel tax

The modern Zionist movement revived the idea of a universal tax and asked all Jews to join the movement and pay an annual membership fee, which they dubbed "shekel." Even during the days of World War II, this voluntary system showed its vitality. Jews exiled to the island of Mauritius established a branch of the Zionist movement there and collected the shekel. A membership card of that enclave has survived.

W. Gunther Plaut

* * *

Notes

[1] The four Shabbatot are Sh'kalim, Zachor, Parah, and Hachodesh.

[2] She herself was the daughter of Queen Jezebel (King Ahab's wife), whose idolatrous practices the prophet Elijah had battled.

[3] So in the parallel story in II Chronicles 24:15-22.

[4] Because he was a close ally of Jehoram and supported his policies.

[5] II Chronicles 24:17 and following. There also the death of Jehoiada at age 130 (!) is noted.

[6] So Radak, JPS.

[7] So Gray, *I and II Kings,* p. 528.

[8] Ralbag; Cohen (*Soncino Bible Commentary*), p. 236.

[9] See Cohen (*Soncino Bible Commentary*), p. 237; also Gray, p. 529, note c.

[10] See Leviticus 5:15 and the Torah Commentary, pp. 774 ff.

[11] See the Torah Commentary, pp. 636 ff., for a discussion of this issue.

[12] Leviticus 27:12.

[13] II Chronicles 24:5.

[14] So the account in Chronicles 24:10-11.

[15] Exodus 36:5-7.

[16] See Ginzberg, *Legends of the Jews,* vol. 4, pp. 258-259 and vol. 6, p. 354, notes 12-16.

First Samuel, chapter 15, verses 2 to 34

Introduction

Connection of sidra and haftarah:

On the Shabbat before Purim, the regular sidra is augmented by three verses from the book of Deuteronomy (25:17-19), which ask us not to forget what Amalek did to us in days gone by. The haftarah deals with a war between Israel and Amalek in the days of Samuel. Its central figure is King Agag, the ancestor of Haman, about whose involvement with the Jewish people we read on Purim, in the scroll of Esther.

The setting:

Saul, Israel's first king (late 11th century B.C.E.), is a tested warrior, and he readily responds to the divine order, transmitted to him by the prophet Samuel, to make war on the people's archenemy, Amalek. This is more than another battle for land or power; it is described as a war in which the Almighty is involved—a war to right an old wrong.

For more on the books of Samuel, see our *General Introduction*.

Content of the haftarah:

1. Samuel transmits God's order, which includes the total destruction of people and things. (15:2-3)
2. Saul fights the war, but spares the best cattle and the king. (4-9)
3. God is deeply disappointed in Saul and—through Samuel—informs him that the One who chose him to be king has now resolved to reject him. (10-23).
4. Saul pleads in vain for divine forgiveness. (24-31)
5. Samuel kills Agag. (32-33)
6. Postscript: the two leaders part. (34)

(In the text that follows, but is not part of the haftarah, Samuel is bidden to anoint young David, chosen to succeed Saul.)

HAFTARAH FOR SHABBAT ZACHOR

First Samuel, chapter 15, verses 2 to 34

15:2. So says the God of heaven's hosts: I remember what Amalek did to Israel, attacking them on their way, as they went up out of Egypt.

3. Go, now, and attack Amalek; consign all that they have to destruction; spare no one, but kill them all—men, women, children, infants, oxen, sheep, camels, and donkeys.

4. Saul summoned the people and numbered them at Telaim: two hundred thousand foot-soldiers, and ten thousand soldiers from Judah.

5. When Saul reached the city of Amalek, he waited in the valley.

6. Saul said to the Kenites: Go away, go down, pull out from among the Amalekites, or I will destroy you along with them—and [yet] you acted kindly to all the people of Israel when they went up from Egypt. So the Kenites pulled out from Amalek.

15:2 כֹּה אָמַר יְהוָה צְבָאוֹת פָּקַדְתִּי אֵת אֲשֶׁר־עָשָׂה עֲמָלֵק לְיִשְׂרָאֵל אֲשֶׁר־שָׂם לוֹ בַּדֶּרֶךְ בַּעֲלֹתוֹ מִמִּצְרָיִם:

3 עַתָּה לֵךְ וְהִכִּיתָה אֶת־עֲמָלֵק וְהַחֲרַמְתֶּם אֶת־כָּל־אֲשֶׁר־לוֹ וְלֹא תַחְמֹל עָלָיו וְהֵמַתָּה מֵאִישׁ עַד־אִשָּׁה מֵעֹלֵל וְעַד־יוֹנֵק מִשּׁוֹר וְעַד־שֶׂה מִגָּמָל וְעַד־חֲמוֹר:

4 וַיְשַׁמַּע שָׁאוּל אֶת־הָעָם וַיִּפְקְדֵם בַּטְּלָאִים מָאתַיִם אֶלֶף רַגְלִי וַעֲשֶׂרֶת אֲלָפִים אֶת־אִישׁ יְהוּדָה:

5 וַיָּבֹא שָׁאוּל עַד־עִיר עֲמָלֵק וַיָּרֶב בַּנָּחַל:

6 וַיֹּאמֶר שָׁאוּל אֶל־הַקֵּינִי לְכוּ סֻּרוּ רְדוּ מִתּוֹךְ עֲמָלֵקִי פֶּן־אֹסִפְךָ עִמּוֹ וְאַתָּה עָשִׂיתָה חֶסֶד עִם־כָּל־בְּנֵי יִשְׂרָאֵל בַּעֲלוֹתָם מִמִּצְרָיִם וַיָּסַר קֵינִי מִתּוֹךְ עֲמָלֵק:

Commentary

3. *Consign to ... destruction.* הַחֲרַמְתֶּם (*hacharamtem*). The root is חרם (*ch-r-m*), which conveys something or someone exclusively dedicated to God, and therefore no longer allowed to humans. To be in חרם (*cherem*) later came to mean to be banned from the community, excommunicated.[1]

4. *Telaim.* Also called Telem,[2] a town in the southern part of Judah.

Two hundred thousand. This understanding of the Hebrew ("two hundred *elef*") is based on a misunderstanding of *elef*, which originally meant "contingent" and comprised about nine or ten persons. Saul's army therefore consisted of fewer than two thousand fighters, and the contribution of Judah was something less than a hundred men.[3]

5. *City of Amalek.* It cannot be located with certainty.

6. *Kenites.* A nomadic tribe who had a long history of friendship with Israel. Jethro, father-in-law of Moses, was a Kenite,[4] and so was Jael, the woman who contributed to the victory of Deborah and Barak over the Canaanites.[5]

7. Saul struck Amalek from Havilah all the way to Shur, near the Egyptian border.

8. He took Agag king of Amalek alive, while putting all the rest of the people to the sword.

9. But Saul and his men spared Agag, and the best of the sheep and the oxen, the fatlings and the lambs, and whatever had value. They were unwilling to destroy them; they consigned to destruction only what was despised and useless.

10. The word of the Eternal then came to Samuel:

11. I regret that I made Saul king of Israel; he has turned from following Me and has not carried out My command.
Samuel was distressed, and all night long he cried out to the Eternal.

7 וַיַּ֥ךְ שָׁא֖וּל אֶת־עֲמָלֵ֑ק מֵחֲוִילָ֔ה בּוֹאֲךָ֣ שׁ֔וּר אֲשֶׁ֖ר עַל־פְּנֵ֥י מִצְרָֽיִם׃

8 וַיִּתְפֹּ֛שׂ אֶת־אֲגַ֥ג מֶֽלֶךְ־עֲמָלֵ֖ק חָ֑י וְאֶת־כָּל־הָעָ֖ם הֶחֱרִ֥ים לְפִי־חָֽרֶב׃

9 וַיַּחְמֹל֩ שָׁא֨וּל וְהָעָ֜ם עַל־אֲגָ֗ג וְעַל־מֵיטַ֣ב הַצֹּאן֩ וְהַבָּקָ֨ר וְהַמִּשְׁנִ֤ים וְעַל־הַכָּרִים֙ וְעַל־כָּל־הַטּ֔וֹב וְלֹ֥א אָב֖וּ הַחֲרִימָ֑ם וְכָל־הַמְּלָאכָ֛ה נְמִבְזָ֥ה וְנָמֵ֖ס אֹתָ֥הּ הֶחֱרִֽימוּ׃

10 וַֽיְהִי֙ דְּבַר־יְהֹוָ֔ה אֶל־שְׁמוּאֵ֖ל לֵאמֹֽר׃

11 נִחַ֗מְתִּי כִּֽי־הִמְלַ֤כְתִּי אֶת־שָׁאוּל֙ לְמֶ֔לֶךְ כִּֽי־שָׁב֙ מֵאַֽחֲרַ֔י וְאֶת־דְּבָרַ֖י לֹ֣א הֵקִ֑ים וַיִּ֨חַר֙ לִשְׁמוּאֵ֔ל וַיִּזְעַ֥ק אֶל־יְהֹוָ֖ה כָּל־הַלָּֽיְלָה׃

Commentary

7. *Saul struck Amalek.* The text gives no further details about the way the victory was won, and hurries on to the main subject: Saul's disobedience of the divine order.

From Havilah all the way to Shur. That is, from east to west, wherever the tribe lived. In any case, the destruction was far from total, and warfare continued for another two hundred years.

8. *Agag king of Amalek.* The enmity between Amalek and Israel was extended by the author of the book of Esther, who traced its chief villain Haman to Agag king of Amalek.[6] Later Jewish parlance identified all enemies as quasi-descendants of Haman.

11. *Samuel was distressed.* Like Abraham and Moses, he had the courage to argue with God.

12. Early next morning Samuel went to look for Saul. He was told that Saul was at Carmel, where he had put up a monument for himself. Then he turned and went on down to Gilgal.

13. When Samuel came to Saul, Saul said to him: The Eternal bless you! I have carried out the Eternal's command!

14. Samuel said: How is it, then, that I hear sheep bleating and oxen bellowing?

15. Saul answered: They were brought from the Amalekites; the troops spared the best sheep and oxen to be a sacrifice to the Eternal your God. The rest we consigned to destruction.

16. Stop! Let me tell you what the Eternal said to me last night, said Samuel to Saul. Speak, he answered.

17. Then Samuel said: You may be small in your own eyes, but you are the head of the tribes of Israel; the Eternal anointed you king over Israel

12 וַיַּשְׁכֵּם שְׁמוּאֵל לִקְרַאת שָׁאוּל בַּבֹּקֶר וַיֻּגַּד לִשְׁמוּאֵל לֵאמֹר בָּא־שָׁאוּל הַכַּרְמֶלָה וְהִנֵּה מַצִּיב לוֹ יָד וַיִּסֹּב וַיַּעֲבֹר וַיֵּרֶד הַגִּלְגָּל:

13 וַיָּבֹא שְׁמוּאֵל אֶל־שָׁאוּל וַיֹּאמֶר לוֹ שָׁאוּל בָּרוּךְ אַתָּה לַיהוָה הֲקִימֹתִי אֶת־דְּבַר יְהוָה:

14 וַיֹּאמֶר שְׁמוּאֵל וּמֶה קוֹל־הַצֹּאן הַזֶּה בְּאָזְנָי וְקוֹל הַבָּקָר אֲשֶׁר אָנֹכִי שֹׁמֵעַ:

15 וַיֹּאמֶר שָׁאוּל מֵעֲמָלֵקִי הֱבִיאוּם אֲשֶׁר חָמַל הָעָם עַל־מֵיטַב הַצֹּאן וְהַבָּקָר לְמַעַן זְבֹחַ לַיהוָה אֱלֹהֶיךָ וְאֶת־הַיּוֹתֵר הֶחֱרַמְנוּ:

16 וַיֹּאמֶר שְׁמוּאֵל אֶל־שָׁאוּל הֶרֶף וְאַגִּידָה לְּךָ אֵת אֲשֶׁר דִּבֶּר יְהוָה אֵלַי הַלָּיְלָה וַיֹּאמְרוּ [וַיֹּאמֶר] לוֹ דַּבֵּר:

17 וַיֹּאמֶר שְׁמוּאֵל הֲלוֹא אִם־קָטֹן אַתָּה בְּעֵינֶיךָ רֹאשׁ שִׁבְטֵי יִשְׂרָאֵל אָתָּה וַיִּמְשָׁחֲךָ יְהוָה לְמֶלֶךְ עַל־יִשְׂרָאֵל:

Commentary

12. *Carmel.* Not at the site of today's Haifa, but a place in southern Judah, where Saul had erected a marker by which he would be remembered. The writer clearly wants to emphasize that the king considered himself, and not God, as the cause of his military success.

15. *Your God.* Saul does not say "my" or "our" God, but implies that the God *he* knows is less exacting. The same "your God" occurs again in verse 30.

17. *You are the head.* Don't tell me you couldn't have insisted that God's command of total destruction was to be obeyed. Samuel anticipates that Saul will say (as he does in verse 24) that he was afraid of his troops. But the king had not feared to criticize the people's impious consumption of blood.[7]

18. and sent you on a mission to consign those sinners, Amalek, to destruction, to wage war against them until you had made an end to them.

18 וַיִּשְׁלָחֲךָ יְהוָה בְּדָרֶךְ וַיֹּאמֶר לֵךְ וְהַחֲרַמְתָּה אֶת־הַחַטָּאִים אֶת־עֲמָלֵק וְנִלְחַמְתָּ בוֹ עַד כַּלּוֹתָם אֹתָם:

19. Why did you not obey the Eternal's voice? Why did you pounce on the spoil, doing what was evil in the eyes of the Eternal?

19 וְלָמָּה לֹא־שָׁמַעְתָּ בְּקוֹל יְהוָה וַתַּעַט אֶל־הַשָּׁלָל וַתַּעַשׂ הָרַע בְּעֵינֵי יְהוָה:

20. Saul said to Samuel: I *have* obeyed the Eternal! I did go on the mission the Eternal sent me on: I captured King Agag of Amalek and consigned Amalek to destruction.

20 וַיֹּאמֶר שָׁאוּל אֶל־שְׁמוּאֵל אֲשֶׁר שָׁמַעְתִּי בְּקוֹל יְהוָה וָאֵלֵךְ בַּדֶּרֶךְ אֲשֶׁר־שְׁלָחַנִי יְהוָה וָאָבִיא אֶת־אֲגַג מֶלֶךְ עֲמָלֵק וְאֶת־עֲמָלֵק הֶחֱרַמְתִּי:

21. And the people took of the spoil the best sheep and oxen, the best of what had been consigned to destruction, to sacrifice to the Eternal your God in Gilgal.

21 וַיִּקַּח הָעָם מֵהַשָּׁלָל צֹאן וּבָקָר רֵאשִׁית הַחֵרֶם לִזְבֹּחַ לַיהוָה אֱלֹהֶיךָ בַּגִּלְגָּל:

22. Samuel said:

Does the Eternal delight in burnt-offerings and sacrifices,
as in obeying the voice of the Eternal?
No, to obey is better than sacrifice,
To listen, than the fat of rams.

22 וַיֹּאמֶר שְׁמוּאֵל
הַחֵפֶץ לַיהוָה בְּעֹלוֹת וּזְבָחִים
כִּשְׁמֹעַ בְּקוֹל יְהוָה
הִנֵּה שְׁמֹעַ מִזֶּבַח
טוֹב לְהַקְשִׁיב מֵחֵלֶב אֵילִים:

23. Rebellion is as bad as witchcraft,
stubbornness is like wickedness and idolatry.
Because you rejected the word of the Eternal,
God has rejected you as king.

23 כִּי חַטַּאת־קֶסֶם מֶרִי וְאָוֶן וּתְרָפִים הַפְצַר יַעַן מָאַסְתָּ אֶת־דְּבַר יְהוָה וַיִּמְאָסְךָ מִמֶּלֶךְ:

Commentary

23. *Because you rejected the word of the Eternal.* By substituting your judgment for God's.

God has rejected you ... Literally, "He." Also in verse 29.

24. I have sinned, said Saul to Samuel. I should not have disobeyed the Eternal's command and your words. But I was afraid of the troops, so I obeyed their words.

25. Please pardon my sin and come back with me [to Gilgal], so that I can worship the Eternal.

26. But Samuel said to Saul: I will not go back with you; you rejected the word of the Eternal, and the Eternal has [therefore] rejected you as king of Israel.

27. As Samuel turned to leave, he [Saul] took hold of the hem of his cloak, and it tore.

28. Samuel said to him: The Eternal has torn the kingdom of Israel from you today, and given it to your neighbor, one better than you.

29. What is more, Israel's Glory does not lie or have a change of mind; God is not [like] human beings who change their minds.

30. He [Saul] said: I have sinned, but please honor me now before the leaders of my people and before Israel; come back with me, and let me worship the Eternal your God.

31. So Samuel went back after Saul, and Saul worshipped the Eternal.

כד וַיֹּאמֶר שָׁאוּל אֶל־שְׁמוּאֵל חָטָאתִי כִּי־עָבַרְתִּי אֶת־פִּי־יְהוָה וְאֶת־דְּבָרֶיךָ כִּי יָרֵאתִי אֶת־הָעָם וָאֶשְׁמַע בְּקוֹלָם:

כה וְעַתָּה שָׂא נָא אֶת־חַטָּאתִי וְשׁוּב עִמִּי וְאֶשְׁתַּחֲוֶה לַיהוָה:

כו וַיֹּאמֶר שְׁמוּאֵל אֶל־שָׁאוּל לֹא אָשׁוּב עִמָּךְ כִּי מָאַסְתָּה אֶת־דְּבַר יְהוָה וַיִּמְאָסְךָ יְהוָה מִהְיוֹת מֶלֶךְ עַל־יִשְׂרָאֵל:

כז וַיִּסֹּב שְׁמוּאֵל לָלֶכֶת וַיַּחֲזֵק בִּכְנַף־מְעִילוֹ וַיִּקָּרַע:

כח וַיֹּאמֶר אֵלָיו שְׁמוּאֵל קָרַע יְהוָה אֶת־מַמְלְכוּת יִשְׂרָאֵל מֵעָלֶיךָ הַיּוֹם וּנְתָנָהּ לְרֵעֲךָ הַטּוֹב מִמֶּךָּ:

כט וְגַם נֵצַח יִשְׂרָאֵל לֹא יְשַׁקֵּר וְלֹא יִנָּחֵם כִּי לֹא אָדָם הוּא לְהִנָּחֵם:

ל וַיֹּאמֶר חָטָאתִי עַתָּה כַּבְּדֵנִי נָא נֶגֶד זִקְנֵי־עַמִּי וְנֶגֶד יִשְׂרָאֵל וְשׁוּב עִמִּי וְהִשְׁתַּחֲוֵיתִי לַיהוָה אֱלֹהֶיךָ:

לא וַיָּשָׁב שְׁמוּאֵל אַחֲרֵי שָׁאוּל וַיִּשְׁתַּחוּ שָׁאוּל לַיהוָה:

Commentary

27. The tearing of Samuel's robe has its symbolic parallel in a later incident. The prophet Ahijah tears his cloak in twelve and tells Jeroboam to take ten of the pieces, indicating that he will rule ten tribes of Israel.[8]

29. *Israel's Glory.* נצח ישראל (*netzach yisra'el*), a name for God not found elsewhere in the Tanach.

32. Samuel then said: Bring Agag king of Amalek here to me. Agag came to him confidently, thinking: *Now the danger of bitter death is past.*

33. Samuel said: As your sword made women childless, so will your mother be childless among women. And in the presence of the Eternal at Gilgal, Samuel cut Agag to pieces.

34. Samuel then went to Ramah, and Saul went up to his home in Gibeah of Saul.

32 וַיֹּאמֶר שְׁמוּאֵל הַגִּישׁוּ אֵלַי אֶת־אֲגַג מֶלֶךְ עֲמָלֵק וַיֵּלֶךְ אֵלָיו אֲגַג מַעֲדַנֹּת וַיֹּאמֶר אֲגָג אָכֵן סָר מַר־הַמָּוֶת:

33 וַיֹּאמֶר שְׁמוּאֵל כַּאֲשֶׁר שִׁכְּלָה נָשִׁים חַרְבֶּךָ כֵּן־תִּשְׁכַּל מִנָּשִׁים אִמֶּךָ וַיְשַׁסֵּף שְׁמוּאֵל אֶת־אֲגָג לִפְנֵי יְהֹוָה בַּגִּלְגָּל:

34 וַיֵּלֶךְ שְׁמוּאֵל הָרָמָתָה וְשָׁאוּל עָלָה אֶל־בֵּיתוֹ גִּבְעַת שָׁאוּל:

Commentary

32. *Confidently,* מַעֲדַנֹּת (*ma'adannot*). A speculative translation of an otherwise unknown Hebrew word. We derive it from עֵדֶן (*eden*), but it could also come from מָעַד (*ma'ad*), to totter. Which of these contrasting meanings is chosen also determines the sense of Agag's words that follow. If the former, then our translation is likely; if the latter, one would render, "with faltering steps."

34. *Ramah ... Gibeah.* Located in the territories of Ephraim and Benjamin, respectively.

Essay

Remembering Amalek

The additional Torah reading that gives this Shabbat its name deals with Amalek and instructs us never to forget what was done to us by these ancient people. Our information about them is somewhat sketchy and has to be pieced together from the scattered biblical references to them, for no outside sources have been found that mention them.[9]

They were a nomadic tribe who ranged from Egypt to Arabia and for centuries were at war with Israel. They were the first to oppose Israel's entry into Canaan, and targeted its weakest elements for destruction. This was Israel's earliest encounter with warfare, and apparently it impressed itself so deeply on the nation's consciousness that "Amalek" came to mean "eternal and unrelenting enemy." The conviction grew that as long as Amalek remained a threat, Israel could never be at rest. Not until Hezekiah (who reigned 727-698 B.C.E.) defeated them decisively was their danger eliminated.

Samuel instructs King Saul to make war on Israel's traditional pursuer and adds a crucial warning: everybody and everything must be destroyed; nothing is to be left, neither people nor booty. Amalek belongs to God who wants to make sure that Israel will not appropriate anything that bears the stamp of Amalek. This is Samuel's understanding of the divine behest, and he demonstrates it before Saul and the people when he kills King Agag. On the personal level, he grieved for Saul,[10] though he was convinced that God wanted him to do what he did—a conviction that is not subject to objective verification.

In the millennia since, Amalek—epitomized by Haman, its infamous descendant—became the term for those who tried to exterminate Israel or return it in one form or another to a state of servitude.

To fight an enemy was then, as it would be today, a matter of life and death for the twelve tribes. It is difficult for us to put ourselves into their frame of mind, just as a present-day generation cannot appreciate the desperation of Jews in Nazi days and the conviction that life would never be secure lest the adversary be destroyed once and for all and an independent state be created that would end the scourge of Jewish homelessness.

The haftarah affirms that the command to exterminate the Amalekites came from God, though it is difficult for us to think of the All Merciful One as a destroyer of innocent children. Nonetheless, this is what the story tells us, that fighting the Amalekites was another of the "Wars of the Eternal."[11] What are we to say of this conception, when we consider with disdain the contending claims of Christians and Muslims in the Middle Ages, or of those who today speak of *jihad* and similar battles that are to be waged in behalf of a Supreme Being?

There are those, of course, who say that the book of Samuel is clear and must be believed in every respect. This is what God wanted, and who are we to second-guess the Almighty?

But others may look at the same facts differently and yet believe in God's guidance of Israel. They would say that Israel fought a war of survival and later ascribed its conduct to the will of God. They will also see Saul's punishment as the last battle for the supremacy of judge and prophet, for with Samuel that long and turbulent phase of Israel came to an end.

Our position is that the Tanach is not be judged but to be read for what it is: a record of our history that withholds little and whitewashes no one. One thing is sure: wars have not become more humane in our day, though we do not associate the killing of innocent people with God's will. (For Martin Buber's discussion of this theological problem, see *Gleanings*.)

Gleanings

The traditional view

It was clear to Samuel that the struggle with these ancient and ever-hostile opponents was a matter of life and death to Israel.

The moral difficulty in connection with this command is very real. It seems to be in violent contrast to the Divine law which forbids vengeance, private vengeance. However, the truest mercy sometimes lies in the dispensation of sternest justice, and Israel here was the instrument of Divine Retribution.

The charge [of this haftarah] to the generations in Israel is to blot out from the human heart the cruel Amalek spirit.

Joseph H. Hertz[12]

Samuel misunderstood God

Man is so created that he can understand, but does not have to understand, what God says to him. In the very hearing he already confuses the command of heaven and the statute of earth, revelation to the created being with the orientations that he himself has established. Even man's holy scriptures are not immune, not even the Bible.

What is involved here is, ultimately, not the fact that this or that form of biblical historical narrative has misunderstood God; what is involved is the fact that in the work of throats and pens out of which the text of the "Old Testament" has arisen, misunderstanding has again and again attached itself to understanding, the manufactured been mixed with the received. We have no objective criterion for distinguishing between the two; we have only faith—if we have it. Nothing can make me believe in a God who punishes Saul because he did not murder his enemy. And yet even today I cannot read the passage that tells this otherwise than with fear and trembling ... an inescapable tension between the word of God and the word of man.

Martin Buber[13]

* * *

Notes

[1] See further our comment on Joshua 2:10; haftarah for Sh'lach L'cha.

[2] Joshua 15:24.

[3] Later on, this meaning of *elef* was forgotten, and only the meaning of "thousand" was retained. On this whole subject see the Torah Commentary, pp. 1034 ff.

[4] Judges 1:16 and 4:11.

[5] Judges 4:11; 17-22 (see the haftarah for B'shalach).

[6] Esther 3:1; and see the Torah Commentary, p. 514.

[7] I Samuel 14:31-35; see P. Stern, *The Biblical Herem*, p. 173.

[8] I Kings 11:29-31.

[9] See the references in the essay, "The Memory of Amalek," in the Torah Commentary, pp. 511 ff.

[10] As expressed in the text following the haftarah.

[11] There was in fact a whole collection dealing with such wars, but it has not survived.

[12] *Pentateuch and Haftorahs*, p. 957.

[13] *Commentary*, January 1962, pp. 63 ff.

Ezekiel, chapter 36, verses 16 to 38

Introduction

Connection of haftarah and sidra:

The additional Torah reading of the Red Cow (*parah adummah*, Numbers 19:1-22), which gives this Shabbat its name, deals with ritual purification. The haftarah speaks of the purification of Israel and its restoration to moral health.

The setting:

Ezekiel lived in the days before and after the destruction of the First Temple and preached in the early part of the 6th century B.C.E. He was exiled to Babylon and, like the Second Isaiah after him, foresaw the day when the exiles would be restored to their homeland. The return, however, would require a reversal of their ways and practices.

For more on Ezekiel and his time, see our *General Introduction*.

The message:

    1. Israel's exile has brought God's name into disrepute. (verses 16-23)

    2. God therefore will give Israel a new heart and end the exile. (verses 24-26)

    3. The haftarah ends with a vision of Israel's glorious future. (verses 37-38)

HAFTARAH FOR SHABBAT PARAH

Ezekiel, chapter 36, verses 16 to 38

36:16. The word of the Eternal came to me, saying:

17. Mortal, when the people of Israel were living in their [own] land, they defiled it by their ways and their deeds; like the uncleanness of a menstruating woman was their behavior before Me.

18. So I poured out My wrath upon them on account of the blood they had poured on the earth, and for defiling it with their idols.

19. I scattered them among the nations; they were dispersed among the countries; I passed sentence upon them as their ways and deeds deserved.

20. But by their arrival among those nations they diminished My holy Name, because it was said of them: *These are the people of the Eternal, whose land they had to leave!*

21. So I became concerned for My holy Name, which the people of Israel have diminished among the nations to which they have gone.

36:16 וַיְהִי דְבַר־יְהֹוָה אֵלַי לֵאמֹר:

17 בֶּן־אָדָם בֵּית יִשְׂרָאֵל יֹשְׁבִים עַל־אַדְמָתָם וַיְטַמְּאוּ אוֹתָהּ בְּדַרְכָּם וּבַעֲלִילוֹתָם כְּטֻמְאַת הַנִּדָּה הָיְתָה דַרְכָּם לְפָנָי:

18 וָאֶשְׁפֹּךְ חֲמָתִי עֲלֵיהֶם עַל־הַדָּם אֲשֶׁר־שָׁפְכוּ עַל־הָאָרֶץ וּבְגִלּוּלֵיהֶם טִמְּאוּהָ:

19 וָאָפִיץ אֹתָם בַּגּוֹיִם וַיִּזָּרוּ בָּאֲרָצוֹת כְּדַרְכָּם וְכַעֲלִילוֹתָם שְׁפַטְתִּים:

20 וַיָּבוֹא אֶל־הַגּוֹיִם אֲשֶׁר־בָּאוּ שָׁם וַיְחַלְּלוּ אֶת־שֵׁם קָדְשִׁי בֶּאֱמֹר לָהֶם עַם־יְהֹוָה אֵלֶּה וּמֵאַרְצוֹ יָצָאוּ:

21 וָאֶחְמֹל עַל־שֵׁם קָדְשִׁי אֲשֶׁר חִלְּלוּהוּ בֵּית יִשְׂרָאֵל בַּגּוֹיִם אֲשֶׁר־בָּאוּ שָׁמָּה:

Commentary

36: 17. *Mortal.* On the expression *ben-adam*, see our discussion in the haftarah on Vayigash.

Uncleanness of a menstruating woman. The flow of blood created one of the conditions considered by Torah and tradition as ritual defilement. To this day, an observant Jewish woman will visit the *mikveh* (the ritual bath) at the end of her monthly period.

20. *They diminished My holy Name.* The verb חלל (*ch-l-l*) usually means "to profane," that is, to violate holiness and make it ordinary (as, for instance, when applied to Shabbat). God had punished Israel, and this divine action had a side effect: it led to a diminution of respect for God as the Protector of Israel.

22. Say, therefore, to the House of Israel: thus says the Eternal God: Not for your sake, O House of Israel, am I acting, but for My holy Name, which you have profaned among the nations to which you came.

23. I will sanctify My great Name, which has been profaned among the nations, which you have profaned among them; and the nations shall know that I am the Eternal—says the Eternal God—when I sanctify Myself through you before their very eyes.

24. And I will take you from among the nations, and gather you from all the lands [of your dispersion], and bring you [back] to your land.

25. I will sprinkle cleansing waters upon you, and you shall be cleansed of all your impurities; and I will cleanse you of all your idols.

26. I will give you a new heart, and a new spirit will I put within you; I will remove the heart of stone from your body, and give you a heart of flesh.

22 לָכֵן אֱמֹר לְבֵית־יִשְׂרָאֵל כֹּה אָמַר אֲדֹנָי יֱהֹוִה לֹא לְמַעַנְכֶם אֲנִי עֹשֶׂה בֵּית יִשְׂרָאֵל כִּי אִם־לְשֵׁם־קׇדְשִׁי אֲשֶׁר חִלַּלְתֶּם בַּגּוֹיִם אֲשֶׁר־בָּאתֶם שָׁם:

23 וְקִדַּשְׁתִּי אֶת־שְׁמִי הַגָּדוֹל הַמְחֻלָּל בַּגּוֹיִם אֲשֶׁר חִלַּלְתֶּם בְּתוֹכָם וְיָדְעוּ הַגּוֹיִם כִּי־אֲנִי יֱהֹוָה נְאֻם אֲדֹנָי יֱהֹוִה בְּהִקָּדְשִׁי בָכֶם לְעֵינֵיהֶם:

24 וְלָקַחְתִּי אֶתְכֶם מִן־הַגּוֹיִם וְקִבַּצְתִּי אֶתְכֶם מִכׇּל־הָאֲרָצוֹת וְהֵבֵאתִי אֶתְכֶם אֶל־אַדְמַתְכֶם:

25 וְזָרַקְתִּי עֲלֵיכֶם מַיִם טְהוֹרִים וּטְהַרְתֶּם מִכֹּל טֻמְאוֹתֵיכֶם וּמִכׇּל־גִּלּוּלֵיכֶם אֲטַהֵר אֶתְכֶם:

26 וְנָתַתִּי לָכֶם לֵב חָדָשׁ וְרוּחַ חֲדָשָׁה אֶתֵּן בְּקִרְבְּכֶם וַהֲסִרֹתִי אֶת־לֵב הָאֶבֶן מִבְּשַׂרְכֶם וְנָתַתִּי לָכֶם לֵב בָּשָׂר:

Commentary

22. *Not for your sake … but for My holy Name.* See the essay below.

24. *I will … gather you.* From the root קבץ (k-b-tz). In contemporary Hebrew, *kibbutz galuyot* signifies the "ingathering of the Diaspora communities."

25. *Cleansing waters.* A metaphor derived from the ritual of the Red Cow, which gives Shabbat Parah its name.[1]

26. *A heart of flesh*. One that is not dead but alive. In biblical language the heart is considered the seat of intelligence, and the bowels the seat of spirit or emotion. Israel's new heart will provide it with the capacity to understand God's ways and the reason for its own misfortunes.

27. I will put My spirit within you, thus bringing it about that you walk in My statutes and faithfully observe My edicts.

28. And you shall dwell in the land I gave to your ancestors; you shall be My people, and I will be your God.

29. I will deliver you from all your impurities; I will summon the grain and make it abundant; I will not bring famine on you.

30. I will make the fruit of the trees and the crops of the fields abound, so that never again shall you be disgraced among the nations by famine.

31. Then you shall remember your evil ways, your dealings that were not good, and you shall loathe yourselves for your iniquities and your abominable deeds.

32. I am not doing this for your sake, says the Eternal God; mark this well! Feel the shame, the disgrace, of your ways, O House of Israel.

33. Thus says the Eternal God: On the day that I cleanse you of all your iniquities, I will resettle your cities, and the ruins shall be rebuilt.

34. The desolated land shall be farmed, instead of being a desolation in the sight of every passerby.

27 וְאֶת־רוּחִי אֶתֵּן בְּקִרְבְּכֶם וְעָשִׂיתִי אֵת אֲשֶׁר־בְּחֻקַּי תֵּלֵכוּ וּמִשְׁפָּטַי תִּשְׁמְרוּ וַעֲשִׂיתֶם:

28 וִישַׁבְתֶּם בָּאָרֶץ אֲשֶׁר נָתַתִּי לַאֲבֹתֵיכֶם וִהְיִיתֶם לִי לְעָם וְאָנֹכִי אֶהְיֶה לָכֶם לֵאלֹהִים:

29 וְהוֹשַׁעְתִּי אֶתְכֶם מִכֹּל טֻמְאוֹתֵיכֶם וְקָרָאתִי אֶל־הַדָּגָן וְהִרְבֵּיתִי אֹתוֹ וְלֹא־אֶתֵּן עֲלֵיכֶם רָעָב:

30 וְהִרְבֵּיתִי אֶת־פְּרִי הָעֵץ וּתְנוּבַת הַשָּׂדֶה לְמַעַן אֲשֶׁר לֹא תִקְחוּ עוֹד חֶרְפַּת רָעָב בַּגּוֹיִם:

31 וּזְכַרְתֶּם אֶת־דַּרְכֵיכֶם הָרָעִים וּמַעַלְלֵיכֶם אֲשֶׁר לֹא־טוֹבִים וּנְקֹטֹתֶם בִּפְנֵיכֶם עַל עֲוֹנֹתֵיכֶם וְעַל תּוֹעֲבוֹתֵיכֶם:

32 לֹא לְמַעַנְכֶם אֲנִי־עֹשֶׂה נְאֻם אֲדֹנָי יְהוִֹה יִוָּדַע לָכֶם בּוֹשׁוּ וְהִכָּלְמוּ מִדַּרְכֵיכֶם בֵּית יִשְׂרָאֵל:

33 כֹּה אָמַר אֲדֹנָי יְהוִֹה בְּיוֹם טַהֲרִי אֶתְכֶם מִכֹּל עֲוֹנוֹתֵיכֶם וְהוֹשַׁבְתִּי אֶת־הֶעָרִים וְנִבְנוּ הֶחֳרָבוֹת:

34 וְהָאָרֶץ הַנְּשַׁמָּה תֵּעָבֵד תַּחַת אֲשֶׁר הָיְתָה שְׁמָמָה לְעֵינֵי כָּל־עוֹבֵר:

Commentary

30. *Disgraced ... by famine.* Which befalls only Israel and not other nations.

35. And they shall say: This land, that was desolate, is like the Garden of Eden; the ruined cities, desolate and torn down, are now fortified settlements.

36. Then the surviving nations around you shall know that I, the Eternal, have rebuilt the torn-down places; I have replanted the desolation. I, the Eternal, have spoken, and I will do it.

37. Thus says the Eternal God: This, in addition: I will let Myself be sought out by the House of Israel to do [things] for them: I will increase their numbers like a human flock of sheep.

38. As Jerusalem is filled with flocks, flocks for sacrifice at her appointed festivals, so shall Israel's ruined cities be filled with flocks of people. Then they shall know that I am the Eternal.

35 וְאָמְרוּ הָאָרֶץ הַלֵּזוּ הַנְּשַׁמָּה הָיְתָה כְּגַן־עֵדֶן וְהֶעָרִים הֶחֲרֵבוֹת וְהַנְשַׁמּוֹת וְהַנֶּהֱרָסוֹת בְּצוּרוֹת יָשָׁבוּ:

36 וְיָדְעוּ הַגּוֹיִם אֲשֶׁר יִשָּׁאֲרוּ סְבִיבוֹתֵיכֶם כִּי אֲנִי יְהוָה בָּנִיתִי הַנֶּהֱרָסוֹת נָטַעְתִּי הַנְּשַׁמָּה אֲנִי יְהוָה דִּבַּרְתִּי וְעָשִׂיתִי:

37 כֹּה אָמַר אֲדֹנָי יְהוִה עוֹד זֹאת אִדָּרֵשׁ לְבֵית־יִשְׂרָאֵל לַעֲשׂוֹת לָהֶם אַרְבֶּה אֹתָם כַּצֹּאן אָדָם:

38 כְּצֹאן קֳדָשִׁים כְּצֹאן יְרוּשָׁלַ͏ִם בְּמוֹעֲדֶיהָ כֵּן תִּהְיֶינָה הֶעָרִים הֶחֲרֵבוֹת מְלֵאוֹת צֹאן אָדָם וְיָדְעוּ כִּי־אֲנִי יְהוָה:

Commentary

35. *Like the Garden of Eden*. While the Torah never again mentions the story of the Garden (Genesis chapters 2 and 3) and its image appears once in Isaiah, Joel, and Amos, only Ezekiel uses it repeatedly, especially in chapter 31.

36. Sephardim conclude the haftarah with this verse.

38. *Flocks for sacrifice*. Literally, holy things (which are consecrated as gifts to God).

Essay

Questions about God

The haftarah contains a jarring image: it depicts the Eternal very much like ordinary humans who are first and foremost concerned for themselves and for their reputation. God (says Ezekiel) will restore Israel to its homeland, but "not for your sake, O House of Israel, am I acting, but for My holy Name" (verse 22).

The divine conundrum is brought about by the way God has punished Israel for its transgressions. The people were exiled and are now living among pagans, and these deride both the exiles and their God. Look at them, they say, their own God threw them out! What kind of a God is that? In consequence of these sentiments God will now reverse the edict of expulsion, in order to protect the Divine Name and its reputation.

This raises serious questions about the Prophet's view of God.

First, God appears in highly anthropomorphic terms, motivated by jealousy and self-love. Second, where is God's love for Israel? Does the covenant at Sinai or the promise made to the Ancestors play no role in the divine concern?

We have to remember the setting in which this oration was created. Ezekiel was not writing a philosophical essay, but was preaching to people who were fed up with their miserable fate and wondered whether their exile would ever end. It will, he assures them, but not because you have changed your ways and because God will therefore forgive you. In fact, you show no sign of change. Nonetheless, you will have another chance to lead a God-fearing life, because your being here does nothing for our religion. The people here don't understand that God is in fact all-powerful, and they diminish the Divine Name by their thoughts and comments. And because the Name must always be honored, you will have another opportunity to correct your behavior. You are undeserving beneficiaries of this situation.

We may assume that the Prophet's hearers knew what he was driving at. For he affirmed that God not only had *not* forgotten Israel, but continued to consider them part and parcel of the divine plan. God's holy Name was bound up with Israel: it was a mutual relationship that indeed went back to the Ancestors and was affirmed at Sinai.

What about the anthropomorphic imagery in which this oration is couched? To begin with, we all speak of God in human terms. We say that God "sees" and "hears," and the very idea that God "loves" us is a human expression. Short of philosophical abstraction there is no other way of relating us to the Divine.

Furthermore, Ezekiel was a preacher, and like all public orators he used images that were likely to have an emotional impact. He was addressing people in distress; he wanted to give them hope, but at the same time he did not want them to think that they deserved

God's grace—not yet anyway, for they had not mended their ways. So, the Prophet says, don't mistake your coming turn of fortune as an approval of your practices. I hope that you will understand just how great God's compassion is. Now act to deserve it!

The haftarah thus must be appreciated as having its origin in a particular setting. What message it might have for other times is a question each later generation has to contemplate.

Gleanings

I will give you a new heart,
and a new spirit will I put within you;
I will remove the heart of stone from your body,
and give you a heart of flesh. (26)

A new heart

The purpose of God's saving activity is the re-creation of a people able to obey the commandments perfectly. Ezekiel goes into very much greater detail over the human aspect than did Jeremiah—God takes away their hardened heart and gives in its stead a "new heart," a "heart of flesh." Moreover, God will bestow his spirit on Israel and, thus equipped, she will be able to walk in the path of the Divine ordinances.

By gathering Israel and bringing her back to her own land, God manifests his holiness in the sight of the nations. This manifestation is therefore much more than simply something inward or spiritual; it is an event which comes about in the full glare of the political scene, and which can be noticed by foreign nations as well as by Israel. The Eternal owes it to his honor that the covenant profaned by all the heathen should be re-established. There is an unmistakable element of reason in this method of argument. In order to make the whole theory work theologically and be comprehensible, Ezekiel takes the radical course of relating it to the Eternal's honor, which must be restored, in the sight of the nations ....

The final goal of the Divine activity is therefore that the Eternal should be recognized and worshipped by those who so far have not known him or who still do not know him properly.

Gerhard von Rad[2]

* * *

Notes

1 On the meaning of the rite, see the Torah Commentary, p.1146.
2 *The Message of the Prophets,* pp. 203 ff.

Ezekiel, chapter 45, verse 16 to chapter 46, verse 18

Introduction

Connection of haftarah and sidra:

The Shabbat derives its name from the additional selection read from the Torah, which begins: "This month (Hebrew, *Ha-chodesh ha-zeh*) ... shall be the first of the months of the year for you."[1] The month of Nisan marks the liberation of Israel from Egyptian slavery, and on the eve of its fifteenth day the festival of Passover is celebrated by a special offering.

The haftarah brings us Ezekiel's vision of the sacrifices to be offered in anticipation and observance of the festival that will take place in the new Temple, after the people have returned from captivity.

The setting:

Ezekiel lived in the days before and after the destruction of the First Temple and preached in the early part of the 6th century B.C.E. He was exiled to Babylon and, like the Second Isaiah after him, foresaw the day when the captives would be restored to their homeland.

For more on Ezekiel and his time, see our *General Introduction*.

The message:

The Prophet's message gave our traditional interpreters great difficulty. They asked: what kind of Temple did Ezekiel have in mind? If it was the actual edifice that was to be erected once the Jews returned to their homeland, then this was new legislation, since it was not mentioned in the Torah and, in fact, significantly differed from it. For that reason, some argued that one should understand Ezekiel's words as prophecies for a Third Temple, which would be built only when the Messiah comes.

Others were not satisfied and suggested that the book of Ezekiel should not be taught publicly because it contravened the Torah. Indeed, certain restrictions became customary with regard to reading it, especially chapter 1, with its mystical vision of the heavenly chariot (on this, see the haftarah for the first day of Shavuot).[2]

The haftarah belongs to the last nine chapters of the book (which contain the Prophet's vision of the rebuilt Temple) and begins in the middle of the 45th chapter. Its first part starts with a description of the location of the Temple, then proceeds to a reminder that moral behavior must be a cornerstone of the rebuilding, but also, once the Temple is rebuilt, that its ritual must take certain forms.

There are four parts to the haftarah:

1. A description of what needs to be done to prepare for the festival. (45:16-20)

2. What is to be done to celebrate the week's festivities, which are to take place on the feast of Sukkot as well. (21-25)

3. Rules for Shabbat, New Moon, and other festive celebrations in the Temple. (46:1-15)

4. An addendum on laws of inheritance. (16-18)

45:16. All the people of the land must join the prince of Israel in making this contribution.

17. But the prince's obligation for the (whole) burnt-offerings, the grain and drink offerings on festivals, on new moons, and on sabbaths, on all the appointed festivals of the House of Israel, is this: he must provide the sin-offering, the grain-offering, the (whole) burnt-offering, and the peace-offerings, to make atonement for the House of Israel.

18. Thus says the Eternal God: On the first day of the first month, take a young bull of the herd without blemish, and purify the sanctuary.

19. Let the priest take some of the blood of the sin-offering and put it on the doorposts of the Temple, on the four corners of the altar's base, and on the posts of the gate of the inner court.

45:16 כֹּל הָעָם הָאָרֶץ יִהְיוּ אֶל־הַתְּרוּמָה הַזֹּאת לַנָּשִׂיא בְּיִשְׂרָאֵל:

17 וְעַל־הַנָּשִׂיא יִהְיֶה הָעוֹלוֹת וְהַמִּנְחָה וְהַנֶּסֶךְ בַּחַגִּים וּבֶחֳדָשִׁים וּבַשַּׁבָּתוֹת בְּכָל־מוֹעֲדֵי בֵּית יִשְׂרָאֵל הוּא־יַעֲשֶׂה אֶת־הַחַטָּאת וְאֶת־הַמִּנְחָה וְאֶת־הָעוֹלָה וְאֶת־הַשְּׁלָמִים לְכַפֵּר בְּעַד בֵּית־יִשְׂרָאֵל:

18 כֹּה־אָמַר אֲדֹנָי יְהוִה בָּרִאשׁוֹן בְּאֶחָד לַחֹדֶשׁ תִּקַּח פַּר־בֶּן־בָּקָר תָּמִים וְחִטֵּאתָ אֶת־הַמִּקְדָּשׁ:

19 וְלָקַח הַכֹּהֵן מִדַּם הַחַטָּאת וְנָתַן אֶל־מְזוּזַת הַבַּיִת וְאֶל־אַרְבַּע פִּנּוֹת הָעֲזָרָה לַמִּזְבֵּחַ וְעַל־מְזוּזַת שַׁעַר הֶחָצֵר הַפְּנִימִית:

Commentary

45:16. *The people of the land.* עַם הָאָרֶץ (*am ha-aretz*) eventually came to mean "peasant," but in the Bible it can mean "landholder" of high or low rank.

The prince of Israel. נָשִׂיא (*nasee*) is often used by Ezekiel to describe a leader generally; here it seems to refer to the head of the anticipated reconstituted monarchy. Metzudat David, an 18th century commentary, says that "prince" means the Messiah, while the earlier Aramaic translation (Targum) renders *nasee* as *rabba*, that is, a person distinguished by learning. In contemporary Hebrew, *nasee* is used for "president."[3]

17. *Peace-offerings.* שְׁלָמִים (*sh'lamim*). They were brought as a tribute of thanksgiving, as payment of vows or as a voluntary offering.[4]

Others translate *sh'lamim* as "offerings of well-being"; both renderings reflect the root *sh-l-m*. A more recent interpretation: "The *sh'lamim* is offered when one greets another by saying 'shalom!'"[5] God is, so to speak, greeted as a guest at the meal.

20. On the seventh day of the month do the same thing, for those who have sinned accidentally or through inexperience. Thus shall you wipe the Temple clean.

21. The fourteenth day of the first month shall be your Passover; and during the seven-day festival, unleavened bread shall be eaten.

22. On that day, let the prince provide a bull as a sin-offering for himself and for all the common people.

23. Let him present a whole burnt-offering to the Eternal each of the seven days of the Festival, consisting of seven bulls and seven rams without blemish, and a goat each day as a sin-offering.

24. For each bull and each ram let him also provide an offering of an ephah of grain and a hin of oil.

25. He must do the same thing on the Festival beginning on the fifteenth day of the seventh month, providing the same sin-offering, (whole) burnt-offering, grain-offering, and oil for seven days.

46:1. Thus says the Eternal God: The eastern gate of the inner court must be kept closed on the six working days, and opened on the Sabbath and on the day of the New Moon.

20 וְכֵן תַּעֲשֶׂה בְּשִׁבְעָה בַחֹדֶשׁ מֵאִישׁ שֹׁגֶה וּמִפֶּתִי וְכִפַּרְתֶּם אֶת־הַבָּיִת:

21 בָּרִאשׁוֹן בְּאַרְבָּעָה עָשָׂר יוֹם לַחֹדֶשׁ יִהְיֶה לָכֶם הַפָּסַח חָג שְׁבֻעוֹת יָמִים מַצּוֹת יֵאָכֵל:

22 וְעָשָׂה הַנָּשִׂיא בַּיּוֹם הַהוּא בַּעֲדוֹ וּבְעַד כָּל־עַם הָאָרֶץ פַּר חַטָּאת:

23 וְשִׁבְעַת יְמֵי־הֶחָג יַעֲשֶׂה עוֹלָה לַיהוָה שִׁבְעַת פָּרִים וְשִׁבְעַת אֵילִים תְּמִימִם לַיּוֹם שִׁבְעַת הַיָּמִים וְחַטָּאת שְׂעִיר עִזִּים לַיּוֹם:

24 וּמִנְחָה אֵיפָה לַפָּר וְאֵיפָה לָאַיִל יַעֲשֶׂה וְשֶׁמֶן הִין לָאֵיפָה:

25 בַּשְּׁבִיעִי בַּחֲמִשָּׁה עָשָׂר יוֹם לַחֹדֶשׁ בֶּחָג יַעֲשֶׂה כָאֵלֶּה שִׁבְעַת הַיָּמִים כַּחַטָּאת כָּעֹלָה וְכַמִּנְחָה וְכַשָּׁמֶן:

46:1 כֹּה־אָמַר אֲדֹנָי יְהוִה שַׁעַר הֶחָצֵר הַפְּנִימִית הַפֹּנֶה קָדִים יִהְיֶה סָגוּר שֵׁשֶׁת יְמֵי הַמַּעֲשֶׂה וּבְיוֹם הַשַּׁבָּת יִפָּתֵחַ וּבְיוֹם הַחֹדֶשׁ יִפָּתֵחַ:

Commentary

24. *Ephah*. A dry measure, about three-eighths to two-thirds of a bushel.

Hin. A liquid measure of Egyptian origin, generally thought to be about a half quart; but Ezekiel 4:11 leads one to believe that it may have been as much as three quarts.

2. When the prince enters the porch of the gate from the outside, let him stand at the gatepost while the priests offer his (whole) burnt-offering and his peace-offerings, then let him bow down at the threshold of the gate and go out; but the gate may not be closed until evening.

3. On Sabbaths and New Moons the common people are to bow down to the Eternal at the entrance of that gate.

4. On the Sabbath let the prince offer to the Eternal God as a (whole) burnt-offering six lambs without blemish and one ram without blemish,

5. and an offering of an ephah of grain with the ram, and as much grain as he is willing to give with the lambs, and a hin of oil with each ephah of grain.

6. On the day of the New Moon, the offering must be a young bull without defects, six lambs, and a ram, all of these without defects.

7. He must also provide an offering of an ephah of grain with the bull, an ephah with the ram, and as much as he can afford to give with the lambs, as well as a hin of oil with every ephah of grain.

8. Whenever the prince enters he must come in by way of the porch of the gate and go out by the same way.

2 וּבָא הַנָּשִׂיא דֶּרֶךְ אוּלָם הַשַּׁעַר מִחוּץ וְעָמַד עַל־מְזוּזַת הַשַּׁעַר וְעָשׂוּ הַכֹּהֲנִים אֶת־עוֹלָתוֹ וְאֶת־שְׁלָמָיו וְהִשְׁתַּחֲוָה עַל־מִפְתַּן הַשַּׁעַר וְיָצָא וְהַשַּׁעַר לֹא־יִסָּגֵר עַד־הָעָרֶב:

3 וְהִשְׁתַּחֲווּ עַם־הָאָרֶץ פֶּתַח הַשַּׁעַר הַהוּא בַּשַּׁבָּתוֹת וּבֶחֳדָשִׁים לִפְנֵי יְהֹוָה:

4 וְהָעֹלָה אֲשֶׁר־יַקְרִב הַנָּשִׂיא לַיהֹוָה בְּיוֹם הַשַּׁבָּת שִׁשָּׁה כְבָשִׂים תְּמִימִם וְאַיִל תָּמִים:

5 וּמִנְחָה אֵיפָה לָאַיִל וְלַכְּבָשִׂים מִנְחָה מַתַּת יָדוֹ וְשֶׁמֶן הִין לָאֵיפָה:

6 וּבְיוֹם הַחֹדֶשׁ פַּר בֶּן־בָּקָר תְּמִימִם וְשֵׁשֶׁת כְּבָשִׂם וָאַיִל תְּמִימִם יִהְיוּ:

7 וְאֵיפָה לַפָּר וְאֵיפָה לָאַיִל יַעֲשֶׂה מִנְחָה וְלַכְּבָשִׂים כַּאֲשֶׁר תַּשִּׂיג יָדוֹ וְשֶׁמֶן הִין לָאֵיפָה:

8 וּבְבוֹא הַנָּשִׂיא דֶּרֶךְ אוּלָם הַשַּׁעַר יָבוֹא וּבְדַרְכּוֹ יֵצֵא:

Commentary

46:8-12. A detailed description of the way the worshippers were to enter and to leave the Temple. Ezekiel sees a stately progression, rather than crowds milling to and fro.

9. But when the common people come before the Eternal on the appointed festivals, whoever enters by the northern gate to worship must leave by the southern gate, and whoever enters by the southern gate must leave by the northern; one must not go out by way of the gate of entry, but shall go out straight ahead.

10. Let the prince come in when they come in, and go out when they go out.

11. The grain-offering on festivals and feast days is to be an ephah with each bull and an ephah with each ram, as much as one can afford to give with the lambs, and a hin of oil with each ephah.

12. Whenever the prince wants to provide a voluntary (whole) burnt-offering or peace-offering as a gift to the Eternal, let him open for himself the gate that faces east; let him offer them just as he does on the Sabbath; then, after he goes out, let him shut the gate.

13. Every day, each morning, you shall provide a yearling lamb without blemish as a (whole) burnt-offering to the Eternal,

14. and you shall provide a grain-offering every morning of a sixth of an ephah and a third of a hin of oil to be sprinkled on the fine flour as an offering to the Eternal: this is a law for all time, for always.

15. The lamb, the grain, and the oil are to be offered every morning as a regular burnt-offering.

9 וּבְב֣וֹא עַם־הָאָ֩רֶץ֩ לִפְנֵ֨י יְהֹוָ֜ה בַּמּֽוֹעֲדִ֗ים הַבָּ֞א דֶּֽרֶךְ־שַׁ֤עַר צָפוֹן֙ לְהִ֨שְׁתַּחֲוֺ֔ת יֵצֵא֙ דֶּֽרֶךְ־שַׁ֣עַר נֶ֔גֶב וְהַבָּא֙ דֶּֽרֶךְ־שַׁ֣עַר נֶ֔גֶב יֵצֵ֖א דֶּֽרֶךְ־שַׁ֣עַר צָפ֑וֹנָה לֹ֣א יָשׁ֗וּב דֶּ֤רֶךְ הַשַּׁ֙עַר֙ אֲשֶׁר־בָּ֣א ב֔וֹ כִּ֥י נִכְח֖וֹ יֵצֵ֥אוּ [יֵצֵֽא]:

10 וְהַנָּשִׂ֖יא בְּתוֹכָ֑ם בְּבוֹאָ֣ם יָב֔וֹא וּבְצֵאתָ֖ם יֵצֵֽאוּ:

11 וּבַחַגִּ֣ים וּבַמּֽוֹעֲדִ֗ים תִּֽהְיֶ֤ה הַמִּנְחָה֙ אֵיפָ֤ה לַפָּר֙ וְאֵיפָ֣ה לָאַ֔יִל וְלַכְּבָשִׂ֖ים מַתַּ֣ת יָד֑וֹ וְשֶׁ֖מֶן הִ֥ין לָאֵיפָֽה:

12 וְכִֽי־יַעֲשֶׂה֩ הַנָּשִׂ֨יא נְדָבָ֜ה עוֹלָ֣ה אֽוֹ־שְׁלָמִים֮ נְדָבָ֣ה לַֽיהֹוָה֒ וּפָ֣תַֽח ל֗וֹ אֶת־הַשַּׁ֙עַר֙ הַפֹּנֶ֣ה קָדִ֔ים וְעָשָׂ֤ה אֶת־עֹֽלָתוֹ֙ וְאֶת־שְׁלָמָ֔יו כַּאֲשֶׁ֥ר יַעֲשֶׂ֖ה בְּי֣וֹם הַשַּׁבָּ֑ת וְיָצָ֗א וְסָגַ֤ר אֶת־הַשַּׁ֙עַר֙ אַחֲרֵ֥י צֵאתֽוֹ:

13 וְכֶ֨בֶשׂ בֶּן־שְׁנָת֜וֹ תָּמִ֗ים תַּעֲשֶׂ֥ה עוֹלָ֛ה לַיּ֖וֹם לַֽיהֹוָ֑ה בַּבֹּ֥קֶר בַּבֹּ֖קֶר תַּעֲשֶׂ֥ה אֹתֽוֹ:

14 וּמִנְחָה֩ תַעֲשֶׂ֨ה עָלָ֤יו בַּבֹּ֙קֶר֙ בַּבֹּ֙קֶר֙ שִׁשִּׁ֣ית הָאֵיפָ֔ה וְשֶׁ֛מֶן שְׁלִישִׁ֥ית הַהִ֖ין לָרֹ֣ס אֶת־הַסֹּ֑לֶת מִנְחָה֙ לַֽיהֹוָ֔ה חֻקּ֥וֹת עוֹלָ֖ם תָּמִֽיד:

15 וַעֲשׂ֨וּ [יַעֲשׂ֜וּ] אֶת־הַכֶּ֧בֶשׂ וְאֶת־הַמִּנְחָ֛ה וְאֶת־הַשֶּׁ֖מֶן בַּבֹּ֣קֶר בַּבֹּ֑קֶר עוֹלַ֖ת תָּמִֽיד:

16. Thus says the Eternal God: If the prince makes a gift to any of his sons out of his inheritance, it belongs to his sons, it is their holding through inheritance.

17. But if he gives any of his inheritance to any of his slaves, [the slave] may keep it only until the Year of Release, when it reverts to the prince. His inheritance may pass on only to his sons.

18. But the prince must not take any of the inheritance of the people and rob them of their holdings. He may give his sons an inheritance only out of his own holding; that none of My people be thrown off their own holding.

16 כֹּה־אָמַר אֲדֹנָי יֱהֹוִה כִּי־יִתֵּן הַנָּשִׂיא מַתָּנָה לְאִישׁ מִבָּנָיו נַחֲלָתוֹ הִיא לְבָנָיו תִּהְיֶה אֲחֻזָּתָם הִיא בְּנַחֲלָה:

17 וְכִי־יִתֵּן מַתָּנָה מִנַּחֲלָתוֹ לְאַחַד מֵעֲבָדָיו וְהָיְתָה לּוֹ עַד־שְׁנַת הַדְּרוֹר וְשָׁבַת לַנָּשִׂיא אַךְ נַחֲלָתוֹ בָּנָיו לָהֶם תִּהְיֶה:

18 וְלֹא־יִקַּח הַנָּשִׂיא מִנַּחֲלַת הָעָם לְהוֹנֹתָם מֵאֲחֻזָּתָם מֵאֲחֻזָּתוֹ יַנְחִל אֶת־בָּנָיו לְמַעַן אֲשֶׁר לֹא־יָפֻצוּ עַמִּי אִישׁ מֵאֲחֻזָּתוֹ:

Commentary

15. Sephardim end the haftarah with this verse.

17. *Year of Release.* Also called "Jubilee"; every fiftieth year, when all real property was to revert to the original owners.[6] This law was to prevent the alienation of land, but whether it was ever observed or was an ideal is in doubt.

18. The haftarah concludes with the warning that royal privilege must never be abused, as was done once by King Ahab, who robbed one of his subjects of his vineyard and was castigated for this act by the prophet Elijah and severely punished by God.[7]

Essay

How relevant is this haftarah?

In Jerusalem today, there live a small group of ultra-Orthodox students, whose members occupy themselves with the laws of the Third Temple, which, they believe, the Messiah will cause to be built in our time. For them, the detailed descriptions of Ezekiel are of the utmost importance, for when the great event comes to pass they will have to give the rest of the Jewish people the necessary guidance. This thinking probably also animated the ancient Rabbis who selected the prophetic portions for the haftarot; they wanted to remind the hearers that Ezekiel's writings were not idle speculation, but divinely inspired forecasts of Redemption that was sure to come.

But what may the average modern reader, who does not share these expectations, glean from our haftarah?

First, that the Prophet's vision proceeds from an enormous respect for the House of God. No detail is too small, no procedure too unimportant, if it helps to assure its sanctity. It is a sentiment worth respecting in every age.

Second, form has its place in the structure of religion. Biblical religion was a combination of content and form. The prophets urged the people above all to lead a moral life, and their battle against idolatry was ultimately related to this purpose. But they also knew that their religion could not survive as mere idealism and spirituality; it had to be surrounded by a ritual that would remind the people of God.

All prophets shared these motivations. To be sure, Ezekiel goes much farther than the others in making form an outstanding component of his teaching; but elsewhere in his book he gives due attention to the ethical elements. Even in the midst of the details of Temple ritual, he injects a reminder that all merchants who sell sacred supplies must be scrupulously honest.[8] In the prophetic view, ritual empty of religious content is an abomination, and Ezekiel stands squarely within that tradition.

His emphasis on Temple ritual had an additional function in his own time. The meticulous care that he devotes to every detail acted as a powerful inspiration for his listeners. It assured them that their dream of a temple restored was not mere speculation, for his descriptions made it so utterly realistic. No one else, before or after him, managed to concretize a people's hope as well as Ezekiel did.

Gleanings

The prince must not take any of the inheritance of the people and rob them of their holdings.
(46:18)

God loves our study

Ezekiel received the revelation about the new Temple while he and his people languished in exile. He asked God of what use this revelation was. The answer: Let the people study the laws, for even their study compares to the actual rebuilding.

(The implied meaning is that God does not need the Temple as much as Israel does, and its study of the divine will is as meritorious as the Temple service itself.)

Midrash[9]

* * *

Notes

[1] Exodus 20:12.

[2] For instance, in his *Pentateuch and Haftorahs,* J. H. Hertz calls this haftarah "half-ideal, half-allegorical" (p. 964).

[3] It also carries a secondary meaning—already found in the Tanach—of "vapor" or "puff" (Proverbs 25:14).

[4] A description of such offerings made by King Ahaz of Judah (late 8th century B.C.E.) is found in II Kings 16:12 ff.

[5] Baruch Levine in his commentary on *Leviticus* (JPS Torah Commentary), pp. 14-15. See also the explanation of Bernard J. Bamberger in the UAHC Torah Commentary, p. 765.

[6] Leviticus 25:10.

[7] I Kings chapter 21.

[8] 45:10-12 (not part of our haftarah).

[9] Tanhuma Tzav 14.

Malachi, chapter 3, verses 4 to 24

Introduction

About the choice of this haftarah:

Opinions differ about the reasons for the choice of this haftarah. Most say that it is read on the Shabbat before Pesach, the festival of liberation from Egyptian servitude, because it deals with the ultimate liberation of Israel from oppression, which would come about when the "great day" arrives, with Elijah as its messenger—and Elijah is by long tradition connected with the Seder observance.[1]

Another opinion holds that Pesach is the great family festival of the Jewish people, and the concluding words of the haftarah speak of family unity.

The Shabbat itself is named the "Great Shabbat" because Malachi speaks of the arrival of the "great day."[2]

The setting:

The anonymous prophet called Malachi ("My Messenger") lived about the middle of the 5th century B.C.E. Judea was still a Persian province ruled by a governor. The Prophet addressed himself to the social and religious conditions of his time, which were not unlike what many societies at the end of the 20th century have come to know. People doubted God and divine justice; their temple service was perfunctory; divorce and intermarriage rates were rising; and a general sense of instability prevailed. Malachi's critique helped to bring about the reforms by Ezra and Nehemiah.

For more on Malachi and his time, see our *General Introduction*.

The message:

1. The opening verses of the haftarah are part of Malachi's vision of the distant future that precedes them in verses 1-3. On that day, God will see to it that justice reigns throughout the land. (3:4-5)

2. In order to turn your land into a place of delight, you must start by cleansing the Temple of its corruption. (6-12)

3. God takes note of the doubt that people have about divine justice. (14-16) See the essay below.

4. Taking up the theme of the opening lines, the Prophet now depicts the "great and terrible day" that the Eternal will bring about when the time is right. (17-24)

HAFTARAH FOR SHABBAT HAGADOL

Malachi, chapter 3, verses 4 to 24

3:4. Then the offerings of Judah and Jerusalem will be pleasing to the Eternal as they were in days of old, as in years long past.

5. Then I will draw near to you for justice. I Myself will be swift to witness against sorcerers, adulterers, those who swear falsely, those who extort the wages of workers, oppress widows and orphans, and who thrust aside strangers—

[all those] who do not fear Me,

says the God of heaven's hosts.

6. For I, the Eternal, have not changed, and thus you, the children of Jacob, have not ceased to be.

7. From the days of your ancestors you have strayed from My statutes, and have not observed [them];

return to Me, and I will return to you,

says the God of heaven's hosts.

Yet you say: *In what way do we need to return?*

וְעָרְבָה֙ לַֽיהוָ֔ה מִנְחַ֥ת יְהוּדָ֖ה וִירֽוּשָׁלָ֑ם 3:4
כִּימֵ֣י עוֹלָ֔ם וּכְשָׁנִ֖ים קַדְמֹנִיּֽוֹת:

וְקָרַבְתִּ֥י אֲלֵיכֶם֮ לַמִּשְׁפָּט֒ 5
וְהָיִ֣יתִי ׀ עֵ֣ד מְמַהֵ֗ר בַּֽמְכַשְּׁפִים֙ וּבַֽמְנָ֣אֲפִ֔ים
וּבַנִּשְׁבָּעִ֖ים לַשָּׁ֑קֶר וּבְעֹשְׁקֵ֣י שְׂכַר־שָׂכִ֡יר
אַלְמָנָ֤ה וְיָתוֹם֙ וּמַטֵּי־גֵ֔ר
וְלֹ֥א יְרֵא֖וּנִי
אָמַ֖ר יְהוָ֥ה צְבָאֽוֹת:

כִּ֛י אֲנִ֥י יְהוָ֖ה לֹ֣א שָׁנִ֑יתִי וְאַתֶּ֥ם בְּנֵֽי־יַעֲקֹ֖ב לֹ֥א 6
כְלִיתֶֽם:

לְמִימֵ֨י אֲבֹֽתֵיכֶ֜ם סַרְתֶּ֤ם מֵֽחֻקַּי֙ וְלֹ֣א שְׁמַרְתֶּ֔ם 7
שׁ֤וּבוּ אֵלַי֙ וְאָשׁ֣וּבָה אֲלֵיכֶ֔ם
אָמַ֖ר יְהוָ֣ה צְבָא֑וֹת
וַאֲמַרְתֶּ֖ם בַּמֶּ֥ה נָשֽׁוּב:

Commentary

3:4. *Then the offerings* .... As noted above, this can be understood only in conjunction with verses 1-3, which precede. They announce that God will send a messenger (Elijah?) to prepare for a golden age.

5. *I will draw near.* The messenger having prepared the way, God will be ready to acknowledge the Temple as authentic, and social justice will be a divine priority.

6. *You, the children of Jacob* .... God does not change but remains always the same, and the children of Jacob, too, have not changed their ways. They were deceitful, and they still are. Jacob dealt ill with his brother and cheated him, and his name betokened his character.[3] His Hebrew name is derived from עקב (*a-k-v*, supplant) and is used by Malachi as a wordplay on קבע (*k-v-a*, cheat, verse 8).

7. *Return to Me.* Reminiscent of Hosea's plea: "Return, O Israel ...." (See the comments on the haftarah for Shabbat Shuvah.)

8. Can anyone cheat God? Yet you do cheat Me.

And you say: *How have we cheated You?*

In regard to tithes and sacred contributions!

9. You are cursed with a curse, for you are cheating Me—the whole lot of you!

10. Bring the full tithe to the storehouse, so that there is food in My house; test Me in this, says the God of heaven's hosts—will I not open heaven's windows for you, and pour down for you a limitless blessing?

11. I will rebuke the devourer for you, so that it does not destroy the fruit of your soil; nor will the vine in the field be barren for you, says the God of heaven's hosts.

12. All the nations shall count you happy, for you shall be a land of delight, says the God of heaven's hosts.

13. Your words have been harsh against Me, says the Eternal,

yet you say: *What have we said to one another against You?*

14. You have said: *It's useless to serve God! What gain is there in observing God's service or in walking with mourner's attire before the God of heaven's hosts?*

8 הֲיִקְבַּע אָדָם אֱלֹהִים כִּי אַתֶּם קֹבְעִים אֹתִי
וַאֲמַרְתֶּם בַּמֶּה קְבַעֲנוּךָ
הַמַּעֲשֵׂר וְהַתְּרוּמָה:

9 בַּמְּאֵרָה אַתֶּם נֵאָרִים וְאֹתִי אַתֶּם קֹבְעִים
הַגּוֹי כֻּלּוֹ:

10 הָבִיאוּ אֶת־כָּל־הַמַּעֲשֵׂר אֶל־בֵּית הָאוֹצָר
וִיהִי טֶרֶף בְּבֵיתִי וּבְחָנוּנִי נָא בָּזֹאת אָמַר יְהוָה
צְבָאוֹת אִם־לֹא אֶפְתַּח לָכֶם אֵת אֲרֻבּוֹת
הַשָּׁמַיִם וַהֲרִיקֹתִי לָכֶם בְּרָכָה עַד־בְּלִי־דָי:

11 וְגָעַרְתִּי לָכֶם בָּאֹכֵל וְלֹא־יַשְׁחִת לָכֶם אֶת־
פְּרִי הָאֲדָמָה וְלֹא־תְשַׁכֵּל לָכֶם הַגֶּפֶן בַּשָּׂדֶה
אָמַר יְהוָה צְבָאוֹת:

12 וְאִשְּׁרוּ אֶתְכֶם כָּל־הַגּוֹיִם כִּי־תִהְיוּ אַתֶּם
אֶרֶץ חֵפֶץ אָמַר יְהוָה צְבָאוֹת:

13 חָזְקוּ עָלַי דִּבְרֵיכֶם אָמַר יְהוָה
וַאֲמַרְתֶּם מַה־נִּדְבַּרְנוּ עָלֶיךָ:

14 אֲמַרְתֶּם שָׁוְא עֲבֹד אֱלֹהִים
וּמַה־בֶּצַע כִּי שָׁמַרְנוּ מִשְׁמַרְתּוֹ וְכִי הָלַכְנוּ
קְדֹרַנִּית מִפְּנֵי יְהוָה צְבָאוֹת:

Commentary

9. *The whole lot of you!* Literally, "the whole nation." In the Tanach, גוי (*goy*) is generally a neutral word, but it is used here in a derogatory fashion.

10. *Storehouse.* A room in the Temple where people deposited their gifts, which were then distributed to priests and levites or used for capital improvements.

11. *The devourer.* Literally, the one who eats (everything), a term that means locusts. God will hold them back from Israel's farmlands.

14. *Mourner's attire.* Sackcloth and ashes, to indicate that they had repented—but it was for show only, not because they were serious about it.

15 וְעַתָּה אֲנַחְנוּ מְאַשְּׁרִים זֵדִים

גַּם־נִבְנוּ עֹשֵׂי רִשְׁעָה

גַּם בָּחֲנוּ אֱלֹהִים וַיִּמָּלֵטוּ:

16 אָז נִדְבְּרוּ יִרְאֵי יְהוָה אִישׁ אֶת־רֵעֵהוּ

וַיַּקְשֵׁב יְהוָה וַיִּשְׁמָע וַיִּכָּתֵב סֵפֶר זִכָּרוֹן לְפָנָיו

לְיִרְאֵי יְהוָה וּלְחֹשְׁבֵי שְׁמוֹ:

17 וְהָיוּ לִי

אָמַר יְהוָה צְבָאוֹת

לַיּוֹם אֲשֶׁר אֲנִי עֹשֶׂה

סְגֻלָּה

וְחָמַלְתִּי עֲלֵיהֶם כַּאֲשֶׁר יַחְמֹל אִישׁ עַל־בְּנוֹ

הָעֹבֵד אֹתוֹ:

18 וְשַׁבְתֶּם וּרְאִיתֶם בֵּין צַדִּיק לְרָשָׁע בֵּין

עֹבֵד אֱלֹהִים לַאֲשֶׁר לֹא עֲבָדוֹ:

15. *We account the arrogant happy;*
the evildoers are the ones who live on;
they even try God and get away with it.

16. Then those who revered the Eternal talked to each other. The Eternal listened and took note of it, and a scroll of remembrance was written before God concerning those who revered and valued God's name.

17. On the day that I am preparing—
says the God of heaven's hosts—
they shall be to Me My most precious
    possession;
I will be tender to them as parents are tender toward their children who serve them.

18. You shall turn back, and see the difference between the righteous and the wicked, between one who serves God and one who does not serve.

Commentary

16. *Scroll of remembrance.* Just like earthly sovereigns have their state annals,[4] so does God. "Erase me from the record You have written," Moses asks God; and in our High Holiday tradition we pray, "Inscribe us in the book of life."

Before God. Literally, "before Him."

17. *My most precious possession.* סגלה (*s'gullah*). That Israel will be God's own possession or treasure was promised to the people at Sinai when they prepared to receive the revelation (Exodus 19:5).[5] Malachi here applies this word to the remnant that will keep the faith.

19. For behold, the day is coming, burning like an oven.

Those who were so proud, who did so much evil, shall be stubble.

The day that comes will burn them up, leaving them neither root nor branch, says the God of heaven's hosts.

20. But for you who revere My name a sun of righteousness shall rise with healing on its wings. You shall break out and gambol like calves, like stall-fed calves.

21. You shall trample the wicked, for they shall be ashes under your feet, on the day that I am making, says the God of heaven's hosts.

22. Remember the Torah of Moses My servant, the statutes and ordinances I commanded him at Horeb for all Israel.

19 כִּי־הִנֵּה הַיּוֹם בָּא בֹּעֵר כַּתַּנּוּר
וְהָיוּ כָל־זֵדִים וְכָל־עֹשֵׂה רִשְׁעָה קַשׁ
וְלִהַט אֹתָם הַיּוֹם הַבָּא
אָמַר יְהוָה צְבָאוֹת
אֲשֶׁר לֹא־יַעֲזֹב לָהֶם שֹׁרֶשׁ וְעָנָף:

20 וְזָרְחָה לָכֶם יִרְאֵי שְׁמִי שֶׁמֶשׁ צְדָקָה
וּמַרְפֵּא בִּכְנָפֶיהָ וִיצָאתֶם וּפִשְׁתֶּם כְּעֶגְלֵי
מַרְבֵּק:

21 וְעַסּוֹתֶם רְשָׁעִים כִּי־יִהְיוּ אֵפֶר תַּחַת כַּפּוֹת
רַגְלֵיכֶם בַּיּוֹם אֲשֶׁר אֲנִי עֹשֶׂה אָמַר יְהוָה
צְבָאוֹת:

22 זִכְרוּ תּוֹרַת מֹשֶׁה עַבְדִּי אֲשֶׁר צִוִּיתִי אוֹתוֹ
בְחֹרֵב עַל־כָּל־יִשְׂרָאֵל חֻקִּים וּמִשְׁפָּטִים:

Commentary

19. *Burning like an oven*. According to Rashi's explanation, based on the Talmud,[6] on the day of judgment God will unleash the sun, which will burn the wicked and heal the righteous.

22. *Horeb*. Another name for Sinai.

23. Behold, I will send you Elijah the prophet,

before the coming of the great and terrible day of the Eternal,

24. to turn the hearts of parents to their children,

and the hearts of children to their parents—

lest I come, and smite the land with destruction.

23. Behold, I will send you Elijah the prophet,

before the coming of the great and terrible day of the Eternal.

23 הִנֵּה אָנֹכִי שֹׁלֵחַ לָכֶם אֵת אֵלִיָּה הַנָּבִיא

לִפְנֵי בּוֹא יוֹם יְהוָֹה הַגָּדוֹל וְהַנּוֹרָא:

24 וְהֵשִׁיב לֵב־אָבוֹת עַל־בָּנִים

וְלֵב בָּנִים עַל־אֲבוֹתָם

פֶּן־אָבוֹא וְהִכֵּיתִי אֶת־הָאָרֶץ חֵרֶם:

23 הִנֵּה אָנֹכִי שֹׁלֵחַ לָכֶם אֵת אֵלִיָּה הַנָּבִיא

לִפְנֵי בּוֹא יוֹם יְהוָֹה הַגָּדוֹל וְהַנּוֹרָא:

Commentary

23. *Elijah.* Malachi's evocation of the 9th century fiery prophet and folk hero helped to confirm his special stature in Jewish tradition: he will be the one to announce the coming of the Messiah; he will settle all outstanding talmudic disputes, and meanwhile he visits every Jewish home at Seder time.

The great and terrible day. Of the final judgment.

24. *To turn the hearts.* The book of Malachi (and therewith the section of the Tanach called "Prophets") ends with a vision of family unity and affection. Obviously, family life was not what it should be, and the Prophet's final hope is for parents and children to find a way to bridge the gap of generations—a phenomenon that apparently existed even then.

Because the verse ends on a negative note, the preceding verse is repeated to conclude the haftarah.[7] In many books, the repeated sentence is printed in a smaller size font.

Essay

It's useless to serve God! (verse 14)

As long as there has been belief in a higher power, there has also been doubt about its existence and especially its role in human affairs. Judaism was no exception. The Tanach contains two secular books (Esther and Koheleth[8]); another book is devoted to exploring whether God is just (Job); and there is Malachi, who raises the whole question but does not proceed to answer it.

Departing from his didactic style (which ordinarily has aspects of a Socratic method), he tells us merely what the non-believers say about God, and then goes on to assert that a small group of steadfast believers will in the end be justified, because God keeps a book of remembrance. He follows this with his prediction of the "great and terrible day" that will see the non-believers ("the wicked") literally burn, while the faithful will be "God's precious possession."

Even though Malachi does not respond with reasoned argument to the doubters of God's justice, he acquaints us with what many people thought. Then as today, there was waning belief in the traditional God, a deity that would punish the non-believers while taking care of Israel and all decent people. The believers were apparently in the minority; the majority neglected worship and married out of the faith. Family life was in a state of crisis, which caused Malachi to hope for the Great Day on which Elijah would appear, a day bringing about generational unity.

The Prophet does not argue the basic question: Why do good people suffer and the arrogant self-seekers prosper? He answers with a statement of traditional faith. He believes that Israel is God's beloved friend, that there is reward and punishment, and that at some future time everyone will behold the righting of the scales. (Job too asks about God's justice and in the end must admit that as a human being he cannot hope to know the mind of God.)

Malachi did not satisfy everyone who heard him, but he like all prophets expected that their prescriptions for a better life would meet resistance. Nonetheless, he spoke his mind and did so, trusting that this is what God wanted him to do.

The Rabbis say that after Malachi prophecy was taken away from Israel. His message therefore deserves a special hearing, as the last cry of those who were God-possessed and were in time acknowledged as such by a grateful people and its enduring tradition.

Gleanings

Words to Remember

Behold, I will send you Elijah the prophet,
before the coming of the great and terrible day of the Eternal,
to turn the hearts of parents to their children,
and the hearts of children to their parents. (23-24)

The great task

It is the home divided against itself, the estrangement of the youth from the elders, that especially fills the Prophet with pain and horror as something unnatural—a curse which, if unremoved, must blight the land. First reconciling parents and children, Elijah will turn the hearts of both to God.

Joseph H. Hertz[9]

Dating Malachi

The man who addresses us is exclusively concerned with abuses practiced by the community. He attacks priests who are careless in ritual matters. This suggests that he was writing after the religious revival under Haggai and Zechariah and the completion of the rebuilding of the Temple.

Gerhard von Rad[10]

Seeing the sun again

After a long illness I was permitted for the first time to step outdoors. And as I crossed the threshold, sunlight greeted me. So long as I live I shall never forget that moment. The sky overhead was very blue, very clear, and very, very high. A faint wind blew from off the western plains, cool and yet somehow tinged with warmth—like a dry chilled wine. And everywhere in the firmament above me, in the great vault between earth and sky, on the pavements, the buildings—the golden glow of sunlight. It touched me, too, with friendship, with warmth, with blessing. And as I basked in its glory there ran through my mind those wonderful words of the prophet Malachi: "For you who revere My name the sun of righteousness will rise with healing on its wings."[11]

And I remembered how often I had been indifferent to the sunlight, how often, preoccupied with petty and sometimes mean concerns, I had disregarded it. And I said to myself, How precious is the sunlight, but alas, how careless of it we are.

Milton Steinberg[12]

* * *

Notes

[1] It is unlikely, however, that the custom of inviting Elijah into one's home as part of the Seder ritual existed when the haftarot were arranged.

[2] There is even an opinion that the name arises from the custom of having rabbis lecture all day long, on the Shabbat before Pesach, on the laws of the festival, making it a very long ("great") day. This theory is anachronistic, for the custom of rabbinic lectures on Shabbat Hagadol did not arise until long after the order of haftarot had been fixed.

It may be noted that the Hebrew *shabbat hagadol* takes *shabbat* to be a masculine noun, which is quite rare in the Tanach; only Isaiah so uses it in a few instances (56:2 and 6; 58:13).

[3] Genesis 27:36.

[4] King Ahasuerus had such a scroll; see Esther 6:1.

[5] On the origin of *s'gullah*, see the Torah Commentary, p. 522, and the essay on the Chosen People, pp. 525-526.

[6] B. Avodah Zarah 3b.

[7] For a similar arrangement see the end of the book of Isaiah, read as the haftarah for Shabbat and Rosh Chodesh.

[8] Koheleth is also known by its Greek name, Ecclesiastes. To be sure, both books mention God—Esther indirectly (if at all) and Koheleth, despite the additions by a pious editor, remains a pessimistic and sometimes cynical book about the human condition. It is remarkable that despite many objections to their inclusion in the Tanach, these books were nonetheless admitted.

[9] *Pentateuch and Haftorahs*, p. 970.

[10] *The Message of the Prophets*, p. 254.

[11] Malachi 3:20.

[12] In Sidney Greenberg, ed., *A Treasury of Comfort*, p. 273.

Isaiah, chapter 66, verses 1-24

Introduction

Connection of haftarah and Shabbat:

This haftarah is read whenever Rosh Chodesh (the New Moon) falls on a Shabbat, and verse 23 provides the obvious link: "From new moon to new moon, and from sabbath to sabbath, says the Eternal One, all flesh shall come to worship Me."

The setting:

The Second Isaiah, the author of this prophecy, shared his people's exile in Babylon (6th century B.C.E.). We do not know his real name, and at some later time his writings were attached to those of the First Isaiah, who lived well over a century earlier.

The haftarah is taken from the last chapter of the book and seems to come from a time when delivery from exile had already begun. The Prophet's message in the previous chapter (65) appears as a denunciation of those who had disregarded King Cyrus' offer allowing Jews to return to their homeland. Now Isaiah addresses those who are prepared to go back.

For more on Second Isaiah, see our *General Introduction.*[1]

The message:

1. In view of God's greatness, what kind of temple will you build to encompass the Divine Glory? [This should be followed by verse 5, which apparently was misplaced due to a scribe's error:] When you do it with concern for God, you will rejoice, while those among you who choose not to participate will experience disgrace. (66:1-2, 5)
2. Illicit and repulsive pagan practices will bring shame on their practitioners. (66:3-4)
3. The marvelous birthing of Zion. (66:7-9)
4. The wonderful fate that awaits Israel upon the return of the exiles. (66:10-13)

Postscript. Every New Moon and every Shabbat, people everywhere will come to worship the God of Israel. (66:23)

HAFTARAH FOR ROSH CHODESH

Isaiah, chapter 66, verses 1-24

66:1. Thus says the Eternal One:

The heavens are My throne,

and the earth is My footstool;

where is the house you could build for Me,

and where might be My resting-place?

2. My own hand made all these things,

and they came to be, says the Eternal One.

Yet this is the one to whom I look —

the poor and the contrite spirit

who trembles at My word.

3. But some do as they choose,

taking pleasure in their perversions;

they slaughter oxen and kill humans;

they sacrifice sheep and break the necks of
   dogs;

they offer grain and the blood of pigs;

they burn incense and worship idols.

כֹּה אָמַר יְהֹוָה 66:1

הַשָּׁמַיִם כִּסְאִי

וְהָאָרֶץ הֲדֹם רַגְלָי

אֵי־זֶה בַיִת אֲשֶׁר תִּבְנוּ־לִי

וְאֵי־זֶה מָקוֹם מְנוּחָתִי:

וְאֶת־כָּל־אֵלֶּה יָדִי עָשָׂתָה 2

וַיִּהְיוּ כָל־אֵלֶּה נְאֻם־יְהֹוָה

וְאֶל־זֶה אַבִּיט

אֶל־עָנִי וּנְכֵה־רוּחַ

וְחָרֵד עַל־דְּבָרִי:

שׁוֹחֵט הַשּׁוֹר מַכֵּה־אִישׁ 3

זוֹבֵחַ הַשֶּׂה עֹרֵף כֶּלֶב

מַעֲלֵה מִנְחָה דַּם־חֲזִיר

מַזְכִּיר לְבֹנָה מְבָרֵךְ אָוֶן

גַּם־הֵמָּה בָּחֲרוּ בְּדַרְכֵיהֶם

וּבְשִׁקּוּצֵיהֶם נַפְשָׁם חָפֵצָה:

Commentary

66:1. *The earth is My footstool.* The image of the divine footstool is found several times in the Tanach. (Christian scriptures repeat this metaphor and quote the verse verbatim.[2])

Where is the house ... ? When Solomon dedicated the Temple he prayed: "Can God really dwell on earth? The heavens cannot contain You—how much less this house which I have built."[3]

Rebuilding the Temple in Jerusalem (a task that was no doubt eagerly anticipated by the returnees) without accompanying moral and religious commitment holds litle interest for God.[4] In addition to all else, the Temple must be an expression of human concern for the poor (verse 2).[5]

3. *Perversions.* The Prophet enumerates a series of pagan practices that are especially disgusting and that appear to have been imitated by Jews as well. Idolaters slaughter humans the way they slaughter oxen; and dogs as if they were sacrificial sheep.[6] (On pigs and dogs, see *Gleanings*.)

This passage is but one of the detailed denunciations of idolatrous rites that Isaiah describes;[7] he specifically denounces the practice of sacrificing children and of indulging in sexual orgies.[8]

4. I too will choose: to treat them ill

and bring upon them the very things they
  dread.

For I called but no one answered,

I spoke but no one listened.

They did what is evil in My sight,

and chose what is not to My liking.

5. Hear the word of the Eternal,

you who tremble at God's word!

Some of your own people hate you

and spurn you on My account.

They say:

Let God's glory be manifest,

so that we may see your joy!

They [who say this] shall be put to shame!

6. [Listen:] the city's uproar,

the Temple's thunder,

are the sound of the Eternal,

bringing retribution to such foes.

7. Can [a woman] give birth before going
  into labor?

Can she bear a son before she has pains?

8. Whoever heard of such a thing? Whoever saw the like?

Can a land be born in a day?

Is a nation born all at once?

4 גַּם־אֲנִי אֶבְחַר בְּתַעֲלֻלֵיהֶם

וּמְגוּרֹתָם אָבִיא לָהֶם

יַעַן קָרָאתִי וְאֵין עוֹנֶה

דִּבַּרְתִּי וְלֹא שָׁמֵעוּ

וַיַּעֲשׂוּ הָרַע בְּעֵינַי

וּבַאֲשֶׁר לֹא־חָפַצְתִּי בָּחָרוּ:

5 שִׁמְעוּ דְּבַר־יְהֹוָה

הַחֲרֵדִים אֶל־דְּבָרוֹ

אָמְרוּ אֲחֵיכֶם שֹׂנְאֵיכֶם

מְנַדֵּיכֶם לְמַעַן שְׁמִי

יִכְבַּד יְהֹוָה

וְנִרְאֶה בְשִׂמְחַתְכֶם

וְהֵם יֵבֹשׁוּ:

6 קוֹל שָׁאוֹן מֵעִיר

קוֹל מֵהֵיכָל

קוֹל יְהֹוָה

מְשַׁלֵּם גְּמוּל לְאֹיְבָיו:

7 בְּטֶרֶם תָּחִיל יָלָדָה

בְּטֶרֶם יָבוֹא חֵבֶל לָהּ וְהִמְלִיטָה זָכָר:

8 מִי־שָׁמַע כָּזֹאת מִי רָאָה כָּאֵלֶּה

הֲיוּחַל אֶרֶץ בְּיוֹם אֶחָד

אִם־יִוָּלֵד גּוֹי פַּעַם אֶחָת

Commentary

4. *No one answered.* Isaiah uses these expressions also in 50:2 (see haftarah for Ekev), but there, God unsuccessfully calls out to the nations, while here, the unanswered appeal is to idolatrous Israelites.

5. *You who tremble.* Who are filled with awe toward God. They are called חרדים (*charedim*), a term that today is used for ultra-Orthodox Jews, especially in Israel.

Yet Zion began her pains,
and at once she bore her children!

9. The Eternal One says: I bring on labor—
do I not [then] bring on birth?

Your God says: I bring on birth—do I
[then] shut the womb?

10. Rejoice with Jerusalem; be glad for her,
all you who love her!

You who once mourned over her, rejoice in
her rejoicing!

11. Suck then to the full from her consoling
breast;

drink in delight from her glorious bosom.

12. For thus says the Eternal One:

I will make well-being flow over her like a
river,

the wealth of nations like a stream in flood;

and you shall drink it;

you shall be like a child carried in her
mother's arms

and dandled on her knees.

13. As a mother comforts her child,

so will I comfort you;

You shall find comfort in Jerusalem.

כִּי־חָלָה גַּם־יָלְדָה צִיּוֹן אֶת־בָּנֶיהָ:

9 הַאֲנִי אַשְׁבִּיר וְלֹא אוֹלִיד יֹאמַר יְהוָה

אִם־אֲנִי הַמּוֹלִיד וְעָצַרְתִּי אָמַר אֱלֹהָיִךְ:

10 שִׂמְחוּ אֶת־יְרוּשָׁלַ͏ִם וְגִילוּ בָהּ כָּל־אֹהֲבֶיהָ

שִׂישׂוּ אִתָּהּ מָשׂוֹשׂ כָּל־הַמִּתְאַבְּלִים עָלֶיהָ:

11 לְמַעַן תִּינְקוּ וּשְׂבַעְתֶּם מִשֹּׁד תַּנְחֻמֶיהָ

לְמַעַן תָּמֹצּוּ וְהִתְעַנַּגְתֶּם מִזִּיז כְּבוֹדָהּ:

12 כִּי־כֹה אָמַר יְהוָה

הִנְנִי נֹטֶה־אֵלֶיהָ כְּנָהָר שָׁלוֹם

וּכְנַחַל שׁוֹטֵף כְּבוֹד גּוֹיִם

וִינַקְתֶּם

עַל־צַד תִּנָּשֵׂאוּ

וְעַל־בִּרְכַּיִם תְּשָׁעֳשָׁעוּ:

13 כְּאִישׁ אֲשֶׁר אִמּוֹ תְּנַחֲמֶנּוּ

כֵּן אָנֹכִי אֲנַחֶמְכֶם

וּבִירוּשָׁלַ͏ִם תְּנֻחָמוּ:

Commentary

8. *At once she bore her children.* A metaphor: unlike a woman in labor, Israel will give birth to its newborn nation without birth pangs. Some modern scholars have compared God's role to that of a midwife (see *Gleanings*).

10. *Rejoice with Jerusalem.* These words have been woven into a popular Israeli song.

12. *The wealth of nations.* See Isaiah 60:11 and our comment there (p. 492).

13. *So will I comfort you.* אנחמכם (*anachemchem*). In the haftarah for Shof'tim, God is similarly called מנחמכם (*m'nachemchem*), "the One who comforts you."[9]

14. You shall see, and your heart shall
   rejoice;

your limbs shall flourish like grass;

to servants of the Eternal, divine power
   shall be manifest;

to God's foes, divine anger.

15. For the Eternal comes in fire,

with chariots like a whirlwind,

to bring home divine anger with wrath,

and God's rebuke with fiery flames.

16. For with fire the Eternal will judge;

and the divine sword [judge] all flesh;

and those slain by God shall be many.

17. Those who sanctify and purify themselves

in their groves, following their leader,

eating swine's flesh, vermin, and rodents

shall meet their end together,

declares the Eternal One.

18. For I know their deeds and their
   thoughts,

and I come to gather in all the nations and
   peoples;

they [in turn] shall come and behold My
   Glory,

19. and as a sign

I will send survivors among them to the
   nations:

14 וּרְאִיתֶם֙ וְשָׂ֣שׂ לִבְּכֶ֔ם

וְעַצְמוֹתֵיכֶ֖ם כַּדֶּ֣שֶׁא תִפְרַ֑חְנָה

וְנוֹדְעָ֤ה יַד־יְהֹוָה֙ אֶת־עֲבָדָ֔יו

וְזָעַ֖ם אֶת־אֹיְבָֽיו:

15 כִּֽי־הִנֵּ֤ה יְהֹוָה֙ בָּאֵ֣שׁ יָב֔וֹא

וְכַסּוּפָ֖ה מַרְכְּבֹתָ֑יו

לְהָשִׁ֤יב בְּחֵמָה֙ אַפּ֔וֹ

וְגַעֲרָת֖וֹ בְּלַהֲבֵי־אֵֽשׁ:

16 כִּ֤י בָאֵשׁ֙ יְהֹוָ֣ה נִשְׁפָּ֔ט

וּבְחַרְבּ֖וֹ אֶת־כָּל־בָּשָׂ֑ר

וְרַבּ֖וּ חַלְלֵ֥י יְהֹוָֽה:

17 הַמִּֽתְקַדְּשִׁ֨ים וְהַמִּֽטַּהֲרִ֜ים

אֶל־הַגַּנּ֗וֹת

אַחַ֤ר אֶחָד֙ [אַחַ֣ת] בַּתָּ֔וֶךְ

אֹֽכְלֵי֙ בְּשַׂ֣ר הַחֲזִ֔יר וְהַשֶּׁ֖קֶץ וְהָעַכְבָּ֑ר

יַחְדָּ֥ו יָסֻ֖פוּ

נְאֻם־יְהֹוָֽה:

18 וְאָֽנֹכִ֗י מַעֲשֵׂיהֶם֙ וּמַחְשְׁבֹ֣תֵיהֶ֔ם

בָּאָ֕ה לְקַבֵּ֥ץ אֶת־כָּל־הַגּוֹיִ֖ם וְהַלְּשֹׁנ֑וֹת

וּבָ֖אוּ וְרָא֥וּ אֶת־כְּבוֹדִֽי:

19 וְשַׂמְתִּ֨י בָהֶ֜ם א֗וֹת

וְשִׁלַּחְתִּ֣י מֵהֶ֣ם פְּלֵיטִ֣ים אֶל־הַגּוֹיִ֡ם

Commentary

16. *The divine sword.* Likely an allusion to Genesis 3:24, which speaks of cherubim guarding the entrance to the Garden of Eden with "the fiery, ever-turning sword."

17. *Their leader.* Literally, "the one in the center," that is, the one who conducts these rites.[10]

18. *And I know.* So the Septuagint and Syriac versions.
I come to gather. The translation is based on ancient versions.

589

to Tarshish, Pul, and Lud,

and archers to Tubal and Yavan,

to the remote shores,

that have not heard of Me

or beheld My glory.

They shall declare My glory among the
nations.

20. And along with your kin from all the
distant nations

they shall bring an offering to the Eternal

on horses, in chariots, in wagons and on
mules,

and on dromedaries

to My holy mountain, Jerusalem,

says the Eternal One,

just as the people of Israel bring the grain-
offering

in a clean vessel to the House of God.

תַּרְשִׁישׁ פּוּל וְלוּד

מֹשְׁכֵי קֶשֶׁת תֻּבַל וְיָוָן הָאִיִּים הָרְחֹקִים

אֲשֶׁר לֹא־שָׁמְעוּ אֶת־שִׁמְעִי

וְלֹא־רָאוּ אֶת־כְּבוֹדִי

וְהִגִּידוּ אֶת־כְּבוֹדִי בַּגּוֹיִם:

20 וְהֵבִיאוּ אֶת־כָּל־אֲחֵיכֶם מִכָּל־הַגּוֹיִם

מִנְחָה לַיהוָה

בַּסּוּסִים וּבָרֶכֶב וּבַצַּבִּים וּבַפְּרָדִים

וּבַכִּרְכָּרוֹת

עַל הַר קָדְשִׁי יְרוּשָׁלַם

אָמַר יְהוָה

כַּאֲשֶׁר יָבִיאוּ בְנֵי יִשְׂרָאֵל אֶת־הַמִּנְחָה

בִּכְלִי טָהוֹר בֵּית יְהוָה:

Commentary

19. *Tarshish*. Its location is not clear; possibly it was Tartessus in Spain. [11]

Pul and Lud. Probably in North Africa.

Tubal. In Asia Minor.

Yavan. יָוָן. The biblical and contemporary name for Greece.

20. *An offering*. מנחה (minchah) is here used in the sense of "gift," as in Genesis 32:14. More specifically, it meant the grain-offering in the Temple, and after its destruction came to denote the afternoon prayer.

21. And from among them too I will choose
   priests and levites,

says the Eternal One.

22. For just as the new heavens and the
   new earth

that I am making shall abide by My will,

so shall your descendants and your name
   abide.

23. And from new moon to new moon,

and from sabbath to sabbath,

says the Eternal One,

all flesh shall come to worship Me.

24. They shall go and see the dead bodies

of those who rebelled against Me,

for worm and fire [that consumed them]

shall still be visible.

23. And from new moon to new moon,

and from sabbath to sabbath,

says the Eternal One,

all flesh shall come to worship Me.

21 וְגַם־מֵהֶם אֶקַּח לַכֹּהֲנִים לַלְוִיִּם
אָמַר יְהוָה:

22 כִּי כַאֲשֶׁר הַשָּׁמַיִם הַחֳדָשִׁים וְהָאָרֶץ
הַחֲדָשָׁה
אֲשֶׁר אֲנִי עֹשֶׂה עֹמְדִים לְפָנַי
נְאֻם־יְהוָה
כֵּן יַעֲמֹד זַרְעֲכֶם וְשִׁמְכֶם:

23 וְהָיָה מִדֵּי־חֹדֶשׁ בְּחָדְשׁוֹ
וּמִדֵּי שַׁבָּת בְּשַׁבַּתּוֹ
יָבוֹא כָל־בָּשָׂר לְהִשְׁתַּחֲוֹת לְפָנַי
אָמַר יְהוָה:

24 וְיָצְאוּ וְרָאוּ בְּפִגְרֵי הָאֲנָשִׁים
הַפֹּשְׁעִים בִּי
כִּי תוֹלַעְתָּם לֹא תָמוּת וְאִשָּׁם לֹא תִכְבֶּה
וְהָיוּ דֵרָאוֹן לְכָל־בָּשָׂר:

23 וְהָיָה מִדֵּי־חֹדֶשׁ בְּחָדְשׁוֹ
וּמִדֵּי שַׁבָּת בְּשַׁבַּתּוֹ
יָבוֹא כָל־בָּשָׂר לְהִשְׁתַּחֲוֹת לְפָנַי
אָמַר יְהוָה:

Commentary

23. *From new moon to new moon … from sabbath to sabbath.* That is, all year long.

All flesh shall come to worship Me. A messianic hope. Because in the following verse (the last in the book of Isaiah) the Prophet delivers a terrible imprecation against those who oppose God, the Sages arranged to repeat verse 23 and thus end the reading on an upbeat note. This rabbbinic practice applies also to the books of Malachi, Lamentations, and Koheleth (Ecclesiastes). In many editions, a repeated passage is printed in a smaller size font.

Essay

Celebrating Rosh Chodesh (the New Moon)

In biblical days, the waxing and waning of the moon provided people with the most accessible means of counting time. After an average of 29 1/2 days the moon, which had vanished from view, appeared again, and that event was celebrated with great joy. In fact, it was accorded a degree of attention rivaled only by Shabbat. It was customary not to do any work,[12] though in later centuries resting on this day became a privilege for women only—a symbolic acknowledgment of their monthly cycle.[13]

Since precise calendation was not yet perfected, the reappearance of the moon depended on people sighting it; and when two reliable witnesses reported having seen it the High Court in Jerusalem officially proclaimed Rosh Chodesh. By fire signals from one mountain to another (and later on, by messengers) communities throughout the land were informed. But since Jews living abroad could not be notified in time, they always observed the 30th day of the month as Rosh Chodesh, and when they learned that the new moon had not been sighted until the thirty-first day, they observed that day as well as the first of the new month. This addition of extra days became also the foundation for the Diaspora custom of celebrating Rosh Hashanah and the three Pilgrim festivals with one additional day, which was continued even after the calendar was fixed by the middle of the 4th century C.E., and the notification of communities was discontinued. (In Israel and in most Reform congregations the extra days are not observed.[14])

Since the average moon-year amounts to 354 days (12 times 29 1/2 days), it falls short by eleven days of the 365-day sun-year. In order to keep the Jewish festivals within their assigned seasons of the year, a special month is added every few years.[15]

People unacquainted with the Jewish year are frequently puzzled about the holy days "moving about." Of course they do so only in relation to the civic calendar, which is governed by the earth's rotation around the sun. All Jewish festivals are assigned fixed dates in the *lu'ach*, or Hebrew calendar. Thus, Rosh Hashanah falls always on the first of Tishri, Yom Kippur occurs always nine days later; and Sukkot begins another five days after that. Occasionally, Jewish and Christian festivals will coincide; at other times they will be far apart.

On the Shabbat before Rosh Chodesh an announcement is made that the festival is to be observed on such and such a day of the coming week; and when it arrives, special prayers (such as *Hallel* psalms) are inserted into the liturgy.

Mystics also observed the day before Rosh Chodesh, and did so by fasting. The occasion is known as *Yom Kippur Katan* (the Small Yom Kippur).

Gleanings

Words to Remember

The heavens are My throne,
and the earth is My footstool;
where is the house you could build for Me,
and where might be My resting-place? (66:1)

From new moon to new moon,
and from sabbath to sabbath,
says the Eternal One,
all flesh shall come to worship Me. (66:23)

Dogs and swine (verse 3)

Although in ancient Israel shepherds were known to use dogs to guard their flocks,[16] canines generally had a bad reputation. "Dog" was a derogatory word,[17] as it still is in English, despite the high esteem the species enjoys nowadays. Dogs were not fit to eat, and thus also unfit for sacrifice.

The same held true for swine, which, like dogs, do not meet the requirement of chewing their cud. The special abhorrence that Jews developed regarding eating swine's meat has been variously explained, but no scholarly consensus has been reached on the matter. By the time of the Maccabees (2nd century B.C.E.) the pig had become a symbol of anti-Judaism.[18]

Observance of the biblical prohibition has weakened in modern days, both in the Diaspora and in Israel (where pigs are raised in some kibbutzim and sold as "white meat").

God as a midwife?

(In her study of Isaiah 66:7-9, A. L. Weiss discusses the view of J. F. A. Sawyer and V. R. Mollenkott that the Prophet here sees God as acting in the role of a midwife.)[19]

Sawyer characterizes God in this scene as a humble midwife; Mollenkott elaborates on God's role:

God's ministrations toward Zion are like the acts of a midwife immediately after birth. She cleans up the infant and the mother, and then lays the new-born baby upon the mother's consoling breast to be suckled and filled.
But the accumulated force of the earlier birthing image of Isaiah suggests a different reading of our passages. In contrast to Sawyer and Mollenkott's image of a humble midwife, one can understand Isaiah 66 as portraying a manipulative, intrusive figure so powerful as to be able to control the most intimate parts of a woman's body.... Birthing involves not only characteristics of compassion, but also issues of power.

Andrea L. Weiss[20]

An end-note

(Abraham ibn Ezra wrote a commentary on Isaiah and here, at the end of the book, he added a personal observation.)

> Finished is [my commentary on] the book of the Prophet Isaiah.
> Thanks unnumbered to my father's God
> who taught me the book of the Prophet,
> and granted wisdom to my heart.
> May God hold my right hand,
> so that I may finish my writing.
> Iyar 905 [1145 C.E.], in Lucca [Italy], where I dwell.

Ibn Ezra[21]

* * *

Notes

[1] For the sake of brevity, Second Isaiah is simply called Isaiah in this haftarah.

[2] Acts 7:49.

[3] I Kings 8:27.

[4] Rashi: God does not need a temple.

[5] Some commentators (for example, McKenzie, in the *Anchor Bible,* Isaiah) see this prophecy as a repudiation of the sacrificial cult altogether, but such a conclusion is unwarranted. See the essay "An exaltation of justice" in the haftarah for D'varim.

[6] So Rashi.

[7] See Isaiah 65:1-12.

[8] Isaiah 57:5-8.

[9] Isaiah 50:12.

[10] So Maimonides, *Guide of the Perplexed,* 3:33.

[11] See the haftarah for Ki Tavo, on Isaiah 60:9.

[12] Amos 8: 5.

[13] The Rabbis explained this special status of women on Rosh Chodesh as a reward for not having surrendered their jewelry during the incident of the Golden Calf (Tosefta to Rosh Hashanah 23a). In recent years, Jewish women have reappropriated the old festival for themselves, and new liturgies have been created to celebrate it.

[14] The exception is Rosh Hashanah, which is celebrated for two days in Israel, as well as in increasing numbers of Reform congregations.

[15] It is added as "Second Adar," and the feast of Purim is observed in this extra month. Leap years occur seven times every nineteen years. The Muslim calendar has no leap years, and so the holy month of Ramadan may be observed during the summer in one year but in the winter some years later.

[16] See Isaiah 56:11.

[17] II Kings 8:13.

[18] See the Torah Commentary, pp. 1444-1445.

[19] Sawyer, "Daughter of Zion and Servant of the Lord in Isaiah: A Comparison," *Journal for the Study of the Old Testament,* vol. 44 (1989), p. 98; Mollenkott: *The Divine Feminine,* p. 33.

[20] "Female Imagery in the Book of Isaiah," *CCAR Journal* (Winter 1994), pp. 73-74.

[21] Based on a translation by Solomon B. Freehof in his *Book of Isaiah,* p. 331. The original is not found in my copy of the *Miqra'ot G'dolot.*

מחר חדש

First Samuel, chapter 20, verses 18 to 42

Introduction

Connection of haftarah and festival:

Whenever Rosh Chodesh (the festival of the New Moon) falls on Sunday, this haftarah is read on the day before, for its first sentence contains the words "Tomorrow is the New Moon." While this is the obvious reason for choosing the selection, the Sages may also have felt that the content of the haftarah speaks of true friendship, the ultimate harmony of human life. Similarly does the recurrence of the new moon bespeak the harmony of the heavens.

The setting:

Saul, Israel's first king, lived in the second half of the 11th century B.C.E. He was a forceful and intelligent ruler, but he was also possessed by an increasing sense of insecurity. He became jealous of the success of his eldest son, Jonathan, and especially of Jonathan's friend David, the rising star of the land. Saul determined to eliminate him and would have succeeded had Jonathan not protected his friend.

The haftarah begins in the middle of the 20th chapter of the First Book of Samuel. David and Jonathan are meeting, and both are aware that on the morrow, which is Rosh Chodesh, the king will hold a festive meal and will expect David to be in his customary seat at the table. David and his friend concoct a scheme by which David will learn whether Saul still seeks his life or whether he has relented. Meanwhile, David will stay in hiding.

For more on the book of Samuel, where this story appears, see our *General Introduction.*

The story:

1. The scheme. (20-23)
2. David is missed and Jonathan tries to explain his friend's absence. (24-29)
3. It becomes clear that Saul will try to kill David. (30-34)
4. David and Jonathan play out their charade and part tearfully. (35-42)

HAFTARAH FOR MACHAR CHODESH

First Samuel, chapter 20, verses 18 to 42

20:18. Jonathan said to him [David]: Tomorrow is the New Moon, and you will be missed, when your seat [at the king's table] is empty.

19. So on the third day, when you have gone down very far, come to the place where you hid on the day of the incident, and then stay close to the Ezel Stone.

20. I shall shoot three arrows to one side, as though I were aiming at a target;

21. Then I shall tell the [servant] boy to go find the arrows. If I tell the boy, *Look, the arrows are on this side of you,* take it [as a sign] and come out; it will be well with you, there is nothing wrong, as God lives.

22. But if I tell the lad, *Look, the arrows are beyond you,* then leave, because God wants you away.

23. The Eternal will be witness between you and me forever concerning the promise we made to each other.

24. David then hid in the field. The New Moon came, and the king sat down to eat the [special] meal.

20:18 וַיֹּאמֶר־לוֹ יְהוֹנָתָן מָחָר חֹדֶשׁ וְנִפְקַדְתָּ כִּי יִפָּקֵד מוֹשָׁבֶךָ:

19 וְשִׁלַּשְׁתָּ תֵּרֵד מְאֹד וּבָאתָ אֶל־הַמָּקוֹם אֲשֶׁר־נִסְתַּרְתָּ שָׁם בְּיוֹם הַמַּעֲשֶׂה וְיָשַׁבְתָּ אֵצֶל הָאֶבֶן הָאָזֶל:

20 וַאֲנִי שְׁלֹשֶׁת הַחִצִּים צִדָּה אוֹרֶה לְשַׁלַּח־לִי לְמַטָּרָה:

21 וְהִנֵּה אֶשְׁלַח אֶת־הַנַּעַר לֵךְ מְצָא אֶת־הַחִצִּים אִם־אָמֹר אֹמַר לַנַּעַר הִנֵּה הַחִצִּים מִמְּךָ וָהֵנָּה קָחֶנּוּ וָבֹאָה כִּי־שָׁלוֹם לְךָ וְאֵין דָּבָר חַי־יְהוָה:

22 וְאִם־כֹּה אֹמַר לָעֶלֶם הִנֵּה הַחִצִּים מִמְּךָ וָהָלְאָה לֵךְ כִּי שִׁלַּחֲךָ יְהוָה:

23 וְהַדָּבָר אֲשֶׁר דִּבַּרְנוּ אֲנִי וָאָתָּה הִנֵּה יְהוָה בֵּינִי וּבֵינְךָ עַד־עוֹלָם:

24 וַיִּסָּתֵר דָּוִד בַּשָּׂדֶה וַיְהִי הַחֹדֶשׁ וַיֵּשֶׁב הַמֶּלֶךְ עַל [אֶל־]הַלֶּחֶם לֶאֱכוֹל:

Commentary

18. *New Moon.* In ancient Israel, the appearance of the new moon was celebrated as a major festival. (For details, see the haftarah for Shabbat Rosh Chodesh.)

19. *On the day of the incident.* When Saul threw his spear at David, who then fled.[1]

Ezel Stone. Apparently a well-known landmark.

21. *Take it [as a sign].* This interpretation of קָחֶנּוּ (*kachennu*) is cited by Radak as having been suggested by his father.[2]

25. The king sat in his usual place by the wall. Jonathan got up [and sat opposite him] while Abner sat alongside Saul; David's place was empty.

26. That day, however, Saul said nothing, because he thought: *It's just an accident; he's probably unclean.*

27. But on the day after the New Moon—the second day—David's place was [again] empty, and Saul said to his son Jonathan: Why didn't the son of Jesse come to the meal yesterday or today?

28. David asked me for leave to go to Bethlehem, answered Jonathan.

29. He said: *Please let me go; we are going to have a family sacrifice in the town, and my brother ordered me [to come]. Now, if you are a friend of mine, let me slip away and see my brothers.* That's why he didn't come to the king's table.

25 וַיֵּ֣שֶׁב הַמֶּ֩לֶךְ֩ עַל־מ֨וֹשָׁב֜וֹ כְּפַ֣עַם ׀ בְּפַ֗עַם אֶל־מוֹשַׁב֙ הַקִּ֔יר וַיָּ֙קׇם֙ יְה֣וֹנָתָ֔ן וַיֵּ֥שֶׁב אַבְנֵ֖ר מִצַּ֣ד שָׁא֑וּל וַיִּפָּקֵ֖ד מְק֥וֹם דָּוִֽד׃

26 וְלֹֽא־דִבֶּ֥ר שָׁא֛וּל מְא֖וּמָה בַּיּ֣וֹם הַה֑וּא כִּ֤י אָמַר֙ מִקְרֶ֣ה ה֔וּא בִּלְתִּ֥י טָה֛וֹר ה֖וּא כִּֽי־לֹ֥א טָהֽוֹר׃

27 וַיְהִ֗י מִֽמׇּחֳרַ֤ת הַחֹ֙דֶשׁ֙ הַשֵּׁנִ֔י וַיִּפָּקֵ֖ד מְק֣וֹם דָּוִ֑ד וַיֹּ֤אמֶר שָׁאוּל֙ אֶל־יְה֣וֹנָתָ֣ן בְּנ֔וֹ מַדּ֜וּעַ לֹא־בָ֣א בֶן־יִשַׁ֛י גַּם־תְּמ֥וֹל גַּם־הַיּ֖וֹם אֶל־הַלָּֽחֶם׃

28 וַיַּ֥עַן יְהוֹנָתָ֖ן אֶת־שָׁא֑וּל נִשְׁאֹ֨ל נִשְׁאַ֥ל דָּוִ֛ד מֵֽעִמָּדִ֖י עַד־בֵּ֥ית לָֽחֶם׃

29 וַיֹּ֡אמֶר שַׁלְּחֵ֣נִי נָ֡א כִּ֣י זֶ֩בַח֩ מִשְׁפָּחָ֨ה לָ֜נוּ בָּעִ֗יר וְה֤וּא צִוָּה־לִי֙ אָחִ֔י וְעַתָּ֗ה אִם־מָצָ֤אתִי חֵן֙ בְּעֵינֶ֔יךָ אִמָּ֥לְטָה נָּ֖א וְאֶרְאֶ֣ה אֶת־אֶחָ֑י עַל־כֵּ֣ן לֹא־בָ֔א אֶל־שֻׁלְחַ֖ן הַמֶּֽלֶךְ׃

Commentary

25. *His usual place.* Literally, "his place [which he occupied] time after time."

26. *Unclean.* In a ritual sense. For instance, if he had come in touch with a dead body he would have been precluded until evening from participating in ritual occasions such as the festive Rosh Chodesh meal.[3]

27. *Son of Jesse.* Referring to a person in this manner was then, and still is, a way of expressing negative feelings about him/her.

30. Saul became furious with Jonathan and said: You son of a perverse, rebellious woman! Now I know that you are siding with the son of Jesse, to your own dishonor and to the dishonor of your mother's nakedness!

31. As long as the son of Jesse lives on earth, neither you nor your rule will be secure. Now go and have him brought to me—he deserves to die!

32. But Jonathan spoke up and said: Why should he be killed? What has he done?

33. Then Saul threw his spear at him to kill him, and Jonathan realized that his father was determined to kill David.

34. So Jonathan got up from the table in a rage and ate nothing on the second day of the new month, out of his hurt for David, and because his father had shamed him.

35. In the morning, Jonathan went out to the field as he and David had agreed; with him was a young boy.

36. He said to the boy: You run and find the arrows that I shoot. The boy ran, and he shot an arrow beyond him.

30 וַיִּחַר־אַף שָׁאוּל בִּיהוֹנָתָן וַיֹּאמֶר לוֹ בֶּן־נַעֲוַת הַמַּרְדּוּת הֲלוֹא יָדַעְתִּי כִּי־בֹחֵר אַתָּה לְבֶן־יִשַׁי לְבָשְׁתְּךָ וּלְבֹשֶׁת עֶרְוַת אִמֶּךָ:

31 כִּי כָל־הַיָּמִים אֲשֶׁר בֶּן־יִשַׁי חַי עַל־הָאֲדָמָה לֹא תִכּוֹן אַתָּה וּמַלְכוּתֶךָ וְעַתָּה שְׁלַח וְקַח אֹתוֹ אֵלַי כִּי בֶן־מָוֶת הוּא:

32 וַיַּעַן יְהוֹנָתָן אֶת־שָׁאוּל אָבִיו וַיֹּאמֶר אֵלָיו לָמָּה יוּמַת מֶה עָשָׂה:

33 וַיָּטֶל שָׁאוּל אֶת־הַחֲנִית עָלָיו לְהַכֹּתוֹ וַיֵּדַע יְהוֹנָתָן כִּי־כָלָה הִיא מֵעִם אָבִיו לְהָמִית אֶת־דָּוִד:

34 וַיָּקָם יְהוֹנָתָן מֵעִם הַשֻּׁלְחָן בָּחֳרִי־אָף וְלֹא־אָכַל בְּיוֹם־הַחֹדֶשׁ הַשֵּׁנִי לֶחֶם כִּי נֶעְצַב אֶל־דָּוִד כִּי הִכְלִמוֹ אָבִיו:

35 וַיְהִי בַבֹּקֶר וַיֵּצֵא יְהוֹנָתָן הַשָּׂדֶה לְמוֹעֵד דָּוִד וְנַעַר קָטֹן עִמּוֹ:

36 וַיֹּאמֶר לְנַעֲרוֹ רֻץ מְצָא נָא אֶת־הַחִצִּים אֲשֶׁר אָנֹכִי מוֹרֶה הַנַּעַר רָץ וְהוּא־יָרָה הַחֵצִי לְהַעֲבִרוֹ:

Commentary

30. *Dishonor of your mother's nakedness.* When thus you love your father's enemy, people will think that you are really not my son—which means that your mother must have conceived you in an adulterous act.[4]

34. *Second day of the new month.* Some take this as an indication that a second day of Rosh Chodesh was observed already in those days.

His father had shamed him. By throwing his spear at him.

37. When the boy reached to where the arrow shot by him had fallen, Jonathan shouted to him, saying: The arrow is further on.

38. And Jonathan shouted to the boy: Quick, hurry up, don't stand still! And the boy collected the arrows and returned to his master.

39. Only Jonathan and David understood what was happening; the boy who served him suspected nothing.

40. Then Jonathan gave his weapons to the boy and said: Take this back to town.

41. When the boy had gone, David got up out of his hiding place to the south [of the Ezel Stone], and bowed down to the ground three times. Then they kissed each other and wept together, David weeping uncontrollably.

42. And Jonathan said to David: Go in peace; we two have taken a binding oath, that the Eternal will be between us and between our descendants forever.

37 וַיָּבֹא הַנַּעַר עַד־מְקוֹם הַחֵצִי אֲשֶׁר יָרָה יְהוֹנָתָן וַיִּקְרָא יְהוֹנָתָן אַחֲרֵי הַנַּעַר וַיֹּאמֶר הֲלוֹא הַחֵצִי מִמְּךָ וָהָלְאָה:

38 וַיִּקְרָא יְהוֹנָתָן אַחֲרֵי הַנַּעַר מְהֵרָה חוּשָׁה אַל־תַּעֲמֹד וַיְלַקֵּט נַעַר יְהוֹנָתָן אֶת־הַחֵצִי [הַחִצִּים] וַיָּבֹא אֶל־אֲדֹנָיו:

39 וְהַנַּעַר לֹא־יָדַע מְאוּמָה אַךְ יְהוֹנָתָן וְדָוִד יָדְעוּ אֶת־הַדָּבָר:

40 וַיִּתֵּן יְהוֹנָתָן אֶת־כֵּלָיו אֶל־הַנַּעַר אֲשֶׁר־לוֹ וַיֹּאמֶר לוֹ לֵךְ הָבֵיא הָעִיר:

41 הַנַּעַר בָּא וְדָוִד קָם מֵאֵצֶל הַנֶּגֶב וַיִּפֹּל לְאַפָּיו אַרְצָה וַיִּשְׁתַּחוּ שָׁלֹשׁ פְּעָמִים וַיִּשְּׁקוּ אִישׁ אֶת־רֵעֵהוּ וַיִּבְכּוּ אִישׁ אֶת־רֵעֵהוּ עַד־דָּוִד הִגְדִּיל:

42 וַיֹּאמֶר יְהוֹנָתָן לְדָוִד לֵךְ לְשָׁלוֹם אֲשֶׁר נִשְׁבַּעְנוּ שְׁנֵינוּ אֲנַחְנוּ בְּשֵׁם יהוה לֵאמֹר יהוה יִהְיֶה בֵּינִי וּבֵינֶךָ וּבֵין זַרְעִי וּבֵין זַרְעֲךָ עַד־עוֹלָם:

Commentary

41. *David weeping uncontrollably.* Others, "David wept the longer."[5]

42. *A binding oath.* Literally, "an oath in the Eternal's Name."

Essay

Friendship

In Pirkei Avot, the Mishnah's collection of ethical norms (known as Ethics of the Fathers), we read:

> Whenever love depends on some material cause, with the passing of that cause, love too passes away; but if it is not dependent on such a cause, it will never pass away.
>
> Which love depended on a material cause? The love of Amnon and Tamar.[6]
>
> Which love depended on no such cause? The love of David and Jonathan. (5:16)

The Tanach has no difficulty in describing the relationship between the two friends as one of love. Some modern writers have wondered whether in fact their bond was purely an affection bereft of the sensual, or whether it had also a physical dimension.

But nothing we know of the two friends suggests the latter. The two were brothers-in-law, David having married Michal, Jonathan's sister. Jonathan was in line for the throne, and David paid him the homage due his liege.[7] While there is also reason to believe that in his heart Jonathan knew that sooner or later David would be king, he did not let this presage interfere with his friendship.

The two lived a thousand years prior to Cicero, the Roman senator, whose definition of friendship is applicable to them: "The real friend is, as it were, another self."[8]

Jonathan and his father died in the battle of Gilboa, and their bodies were desecrated by the enemy.[9] In an ode that he taught his people, David lamented their death as valiant patriots who had given their lives, and as a last gift to a friendship that had sustained him and saved his life he paid special homage to Jonathan:

> *I grieve for you, my brother Jonathan,*
> *Most dear were you to me, your love more wondrous*
> *Than the love of women.*[10]

Gleanings

Love and death

The Song of Songs says that "love is as strong as death" (8:6). This was a reference to Jonathan's love for David, for Jonathan risked his life when he spoke up for his friend and his father tried to spear him.

Midrash[11]

The tragedy of Nob

(The parting of David and Jonathan led to an unforeseen tragedy, recounted in I Samuel 21:2-8 and 22:9-19. David left his friend and arrived, utterly famished, in the city of Nob. He asked the priest Ahimelech for sustenance, but there was none available save the holy bread set aside for God. The priest, unaware of David's problem with the king, gave it to him and David ate it. But a servant of King Saul was present and reported the matter to Saul, who executed the innocent Ahimelech and his family for siding with David. Tradition comments as follows:)

The tragedy of the priests of Nob would not have happened had Jonathan given David some provisions for his flight. From this we may learn that failing to provide a departing guest with food for the journey is accounted as a sin, even though—as in Jonathan's case—it was not done deliberately, but was merely an oversight.

Talmud[12]

Eating the holy bread

(The fact that David ate consecrated bread is not held against him by tradition, for the need to sustain life is considered more important than almost any command. David's appearance in Nob is reflected in Christian scriptures. Disciples of Jesus felt hungry and plucked ears of corn on the Sabbath. When rebuked for doing this, Jesus defended his disciples:)

Have you not read what David did when he and his men were hungry? He went into the House of God and ate the sacred bread, though neither he nor his men had a right to eat it, but only the priests. [13]

Jonathan

There is hardly a more beautiful figure in history than Jonathan. Truly he was 'a very perfect knight,' the essence of chivalry. To the Rabbis, he stands for all time as the type of disinterested, self-denying friendship. His greatness was manifested in the very clash of duty between loyalty to his father and his love for David. Jonathan's was a task of rare difficulty, to combine duty to his father with devotion to his friend. Yet he fails in neither.

Joseph H. Hertz[14]

* * *

Notes

[1] I Samuel 19:10.

[2] JPS translates as "be reassured"; NEB and others take the word as a part of what Jonathan will say to the boy, and render "pick them [the arrows] up."

[3] See Leviticus 7:20.

[4] So Radak.

[5] So JPS. NEB expands on it and renders, "until David's grief was even greater than Jonathan's." We follow the sense of Rashi, who comments, "he wept a great deal."

[6] Both Amnon and Tamar were children of David, but born of different mothers. Amnon raped his sister, and afterward discarded her, even though they could have married under the laws then in force (II Samuel 13:1-29).

[7] I Samuel 20:7-8.

[8] *Of Friendship* (*De amicitia*), written 44 B.C.E..

[9] I Samuel 31.

[10] II Samuel 1:25-26.

[11] Song of Songs Rabbah 8:6; B. Arachin 16b. Not every talmudic reference is totally complimentary, however. One passage suggests that Jonathan, seeing how the people adored David, anticipated that the latter would someday be king and therefore curried his favor (J. Pesachim 6:1, 33a); see also the next selection, "The Tragedy of Nob."

[12] *B.* Sanhedrin 104a.

[13] Matthew 12:1-8 (NEB translation).

[14] J. H. Hertz, *Pentateuch and Haftorahs*, p. 952.

First Samuel, chapter 1, verse 1 to chapter 2, verse 10

Introduction

Why this haftarah was chosen:

Hannah, a childless woman, dominates the haftarah, and the Talmud says that she was one of the three women whose barrennness was ended by God, and that this happened on Rosh Hashanah.[1] Also, the traditional Torah reading of Genesis 21 speaks of the end of Sarah's barrennness, just as the haftarah records the end of Hannah's. The Rabbis taught that Rosh Hashanah is the birthday of the world, and that each time a woman gives birth to a child the miracle of creation is repeated.

Traditional synagogues observe two days of Rosh Hashanah. A number of Reform congregations also observe two days of the festival, but at this writing the majority do not. Their most widely used prayer book, שערי תשובה (*Gates of Repentance*), uses the traditional haftarah, but also provides an alternative.

The setting:

With the birth of Samuel, which is told in this haftarah, Israel's history enters a new chapter. The turbulent time of the Judges is coming to an end. Samuel will be the last of the prophet-judges, who combined religious and secular leadership. Thereafter, Israel united will become a monarchy. The haftarah does not concern the realm of public policy, but is an intensely personal account of a deeply religious woman, whose prayer is heard and whose son will lead his country for many years.

For more on the books of Samuel, see our *General Introduction;* on Samuel, see the haftarah for Korach.

The story:

1. Elkanah has two wives; one of them, Hannah, is barren. (1:1-8)
2. Hannah asks God for help; her silent prayer puzzles the priest Eli. (1:9-18)
3. A son, Samuel, is born and dedicated to God's service. (1:19-28)
4. Hannah's prayer of thanksgiving. (2:1-10)

HAFTARAH FOR THE FIRST DAY OF ROSH HASHANAH

First Samuel, chapter 1, verse 1 to chapter 2, verse 10

1:1. There was a man from Ramataim, a Zuphite of the line of Ephraim, from the hill country of Ephraim, whose name was Elkanah son of Jerocham, the son of Elihu, the son of Tohu, the son of Zuph man of Ephraim, and

2. he had two wives, one named Hannah and the other Peninah. Peninah had children, but Hannah had none.

3. This man used to go up from his town annually to worship and to offer sacrifice to the God of heaven's hosts in Shiloh. There, Eli's two sons, Hofni and Phineas, were priests of the Eternal.

1:1 וַיְהִי אִישׁ אֶחָד מִן־הָרָמָתַיִם צוֹפִים מֵהַר
אֶפְרָיִם וּשְׁמוֹ אֶלְקָנָה בֶּן־יְרֹחָם בֶּן־אֱלִיהוּא
בֶּן־תֹּחוּ בֶן־צוּף אֶפְרָתִי:

2 וְלוֹ שְׁתֵּי נָשִׁים שֵׁם אַחַת חַנָּה וְשֵׁם הַשֵּׁנִית
פְּנִנָּה וַיְהִי לִפְנִנָּה יְלָדִים וּלְחַנָּה אֵין יְלָדִים:

3 וְעָלָה הָאִישׁ הַהוּא מֵעִירוֹ מִיָּמִים יָמִימָה
לְהִשְׁתַּחֲוֺת וְלִזְבֹּחַ לַיהוָה צְבָאוֹת בְּשִׁלֹה
וְשָׁם שְׁנֵי בְנֵי־עֵלִי חָפְנִי וּפִנְחָס כֹּהֲנִים לַיהוָה:

Commentary

1:1. *Ramataim.* Hereafter referred to as Ramah (the singular of Ramataim); it was located in the district of Zuph, in the hillsides of Ephraim.[2] The geographic description follows the same pattern "from small to large" that we use today. Compare Ramataim-Zuph-Ephraim with Chicago-Cook County-Illinois.

2. *Hannah.* The name denotes grace or mercy.

3. *Annually.* מימים ימימה (*miyamim yamimah*) is generally so understood, though it could also mean "from one [festival] season to another."[3]

God of heaven's hosts. יהוה צבאות (*adonai tz'va'ot*) occurs here for the first time in the Tanach. It developed from a military image of God as fighting inimical forces with the help of the stars in heaven,[4] and later became spiritualized and described the ruler of all the world.

Shiloh. Along with Mizpah and Beth-El, one of the favorite locations where sacrifices to God were brought in the days of the Judges. The Ark of the Covenant was housed in Shiloh, until it was captured by the Philistines.

Shiloh was located a short distance east of the main road leading from Jerusalem to Shechem. The ruins of the city, known in Arabic as Khirbet Seilun, have been extensively excavated, most recently by Israeli archaeologists, and its ceramic remains are the richest yet found in any early Israelite site. They suggest that Shiloh was an ancient cultic locale before it became an Israelite shrine.[5]

Eli's two sons. They served as priests with their aged father, but were no credit to him.[6]

4. When Elkanah offered a sacrifice, he would give portions to Peninah his wife and to each of her sons and daughters;

5. but to Hannah he would give a special portion, for it was Hannah he loved, but the Eternal had shut her womb.

6. Her rival would torment her constantly, (in order to grieve her,) because the Eternal had shut her womb.

7. This went on year by year; when they went up to the House of the Eternal, her rival would so torment her that she would weep and not eat.

8. Elkanah would say to her: Hannah, why do you weep? Why don't you eat? Why are you so unhappy? Am I not dearer to you than ten sons?

9. Once, Hannah rose up after eating and drinking—it was in Shiloh and Eli the priest was sitting near the entrance of the Temple of the Eternal.

10. In bitter grief she prayed to the Eternal, weeping bitterly.

4 וַיְהִי הַיּוֹם וַיִּזְבַּח אֶלְקָנָה וְנָתַן לִפְנִנָּה אִשְׁתּוֹ וּלְכָל־בָּנֶיהָ וּבְנוֹתֶיהָ מָנוֹת:

5 וּלְחַנָּה יִתֵּן מָנָה אַחַת אַפָּיִם כִּי אֶת־חַנָּה אָהֵב וַיהֹוָה סָגַר רַחְמָהּ:

6 וְכִעֲסַתָּה צָרָתָהּ גַּם־כַּעַס בַּעֲבוּר הַרְּעִמָהּ כִּי־סָגַר יְהֹוָה בְּעַד רַחְמָהּ:

7 וְכֵן יַעֲשֶׂה שָׁנָה בְשָׁנָה מִדֵּי עֲלֹתָהּ בְּבֵית יְהֹוָה כֵּן תַּכְעִסֶנָּה וַתִּבְכֶּה וְלֹא תֹאכַל:

8 וַיֹּאמֶר לָהּ אֶלְקָנָה אִישָׁהּ חַנָּה לָמֶה תִבְכִּי וְלָמֶה לֹא תֹאכְלִי וְלָמֶה יֵרַע לְבָבֵךְ הֲלוֹא אָנֹכִי טוֹב לָךְ מֵעֲשָׂרָה בָּנִים:

9 וַתָּקָם חַנָּה אַחֲרֵי אָכְלָה בְשִׁלֹה וְאַחֲרֵי שָׁתֹה וְעֵלִי הַכֹּהֵן יֹשֵׁב עַל־הַכִּסֵּא עַל־מְזוּזַת הֵיכַל יְהֹוָה:

10 וְהִיא מָרַת נָפֶשׁ וַתִּתְפַּלֵּל עַל־יְהֹוָה וּבָכֹה תִבְכֶּה:

Commentary

5. *A special portion.* Taking the word אפים (*apayim*) to mean generous, as in the Torah's description of God as being ארך אפים (*erech apayim*, generously patient, long-suffering).[7] Radak so understands it, but also reports that his father had interpreted it in the opposite way: Even though Elkanah loved Hannah, he gave her only one portion, because she was childless.[8]

6. *Torment her constantly.* Literally, cause her aggravation upon aggravation.

Grieve. Note that the word הרעמה (*ha-re'imah*) has a *dagesh* in the *resh* (an unusual occurrence), as if to emphasize a "guttural" grief that possessed Hannah.

11. She took a vow, saying: *Eternal God, if You take notice of Your servant's affliction, if You keep me in mind and do not forget Your maidservant, giving Your maidservant a son, I will dedicate him to You for life, and no razor shall touch his head.*

12. As she continued to pray before the Eternal, Eli was observing her lips.

13. Hannah was talking to herself; though her lips were moving, she made no sound, so that Eli took her for a drunkard.

14. Eli said to her: *How long do you propose to carry on drunk like this! Get rid of your wine!*

15. *Not so, my lord,* Hannah replied. *I am a woman distressed in spirit; I have had neither wine nor beer, but have been pouring out my soul before the Eternal.*

11 וַתִּדֹּר נֶדֶר וַתֹּאמַר יְהוָה צְבָאוֹת אִם־רָאֹה תִרְאֶה בׇּעֳנִי אֲמָתֶךָ וּזְכַרְתַּנִי וְלֹא־תִשְׁכַּח אֶת־אֲמָתֶךָ וְנָתַתָּה לַאֲמָתְךָ זֶרַע אֲנָשִׁים וּנְתַתִּיו לַיהוָה כׇּל־יְמֵי חַיָּיו וּמוֹרָה לֹא־יַעֲלֶה עַל־רֹאשׁוֹ׃

12 וְהָיָה כִּי הִרְבְּתָה לְהִתְפַּלֵּל לִפְנֵי יְהוָה וְעֵלִי שֹׁמֵר אֶת־פִּיהָ׃

13 וְחַנָּה הִיא מְדַבֶּרֶת עַל־לִבָּהּ רַק שְׂפָתֶיהָ נָּעוֹת וְקוֹלָהּ לֹא יִשָּׁמֵעַ וַיַּחְשְׁבֶהָ עֵלִי לְשִׁכֹּרָה׃

14 וַיֹּאמֶר אֵלֶיהָ עֵלִי עַד־מָתַי תִּשְׁתַּכָּרִין הָסִירִי אֶת־יֵינֵךְ מֵעָלָיִךְ׃

15 וַתַּעַן חַנָּה וַתֹּאמֶר לֹא אֲדֹנִי אִשָּׁה קְשַׁת־רוּחַ אָנֹכִי וְיַיִן וְשֵׁכָר לֹא שָׁתִיתִי וָאֶשְׁפֹּךְ אֶת־נַפְשִׁי לִפְנֵי יְהוָה׃

Commentary

11. *Eternal God.* Literally, God of heaven's hosts.

A son. For a woman, having a son was a sign of having been favored by Providence, and constituted the condition for social acceptance.

Dedicate him to You. Making him a lifelong Nazir, who could not touch liquor and had to observe other restrictions, among them to leave the hair uncut.[9]

13. *Her lips were moving.* The Talmud derived several rules from her way of praying (see *Gleanings*).

14. *Get rid of your wine!* The Septuagint adds: "Remove yourself from the presence of the Eternal." In the Halachah a person is forbidden to pray while intoxicated.[10]

16. Do not take your servant for a wicked woman. All this time I have been speaking out of my abundant sorrow and torment.

17. Then Eli replied: Go in peace; and may the God of Israel grant your request.

18. May your maidservant find favor in your sight, she said. So the woman went on her way. She ate, and was downcast no longer.

19. Early in the morning they arose, prostrated themselves before the Eternal, and returned to their home in Ramah. Elkanah knew his wife, and the Eternal remembered her.

20. At the turn of the year, Hannah conceived and gave birth to a son, whom she named Samuel, saying: *I asked him of the Eternal (and was heard).*

16 אַל־תִּתֵּן אֶת־אֲמָתְךָ לִפְנֵי בַּת־בְּלִיָּעַל כִּי־מֵרֹב שִׂיחִי וְכַעְסִי דִּבַּרְתִּי עַד־הֵנָּה:

17 וַיַּעַן עֵלִי וַיֹּאמֶר לְכִי לְשָׁלוֹם וֵאלֹהֵי יִשְׂרָאֵל יִתֵּן אֶת־שֵׁלָתֵךְ אֲשֶׁר שָׁאַלְתְּ מֵעִמּוֹ:

18 וַתֹּאמֶר תִּמְצָא שִׁפְחָתְךָ חֵן בְּעֵינֶיךָ וַתֵּלֶךְ הָאִשָּׁה לְדַרְכָּהּ וַתֹּאכַל וּפָנֶיהָ לֹא־הָיוּ־לָהּ עוֹד:

19 וַיַּשְׁכִּמוּ בַבֹּקֶר וַיִּשְׁתַּחֲווּ לִפְנֵי יְהֹוָה וַיָּשֻׁבוּ וַיָּבֹאוּ אֶל־בֵּיתָם הָרָמָתָה וַיֵּדַע אֶלְקָנָה אֶת־חַנָּה אִשְׁתּוֹ וַיִּזְכְּרֶהָ יְהֹוָה:

20 וַיְהִי לִתְקֻפוֹת הַיָּמִים וַתַּהַר חַנָּה וַתֵּלֶד בֵּן וַתִּקְרָא אֶת־שְׁמוֹ שְׁמוּאֵל כִּי מֵיְהֹוָה שְׁאִלְתִּיו:

Commentary

16. *Wicked woman.* בת־בליעל (*bat-beliya'al*). The expression was often mistakenly understood as "daughter of Beliya'al" (that is, "daughter of the Devil"). However, בת־בליעל derives from בלי, without, and יעל, having worth.

17. *Your request.* Note that שלתך (*sh'latech*) is written in an abbreviated form, without the *aleph*; the usual form would be שאלתך (*sh'elatech*).

19. *Knew his wife.* וידע (*vayeda*), he had intercourse with her. The word means both intellectual and physical knowledge, and appears first in the story of Adam and Eve. [11]

20. *Samuel.* The biblical etymology that explains the name fits Saul better than Samuel, for שאול (*sha'ul*, Saul) means "asked for."[12] But Hannah's comment was not a linguistic exercise; it was an outpouring of gratitude.[13] The actual etymology of the name is not clear. Most scholars derive it from *shem* (name) and *el* (God), "the one upon whom God's name is called"; or perhaps it comes from *shama* (has heard) and *el* (God), thus denoting "God has heard."

21. The man Elkanah went up with his household to offer up to the Eternal the yearly sacrifices and to execute his vow.

22. Hannah did not go up. She said to her husband: I will bring the child after he has been weaned. For when I bring him and he appears before the Eternal, he will have to stay there for good.

23. Elkanah her husband said to her: Do what seems good to you; stay until you've weaned him; only may the Eternal fulfill the divine promise. So the woman remained and nursed her son until she had weaned him.

24. When she had weaned him, she brought him up to the House of the Eternal at Shiloh—though he was still a child—together with a three-year-old bull, an ephah of meal, and a skin of wine.

25. They slaughtered the bull, and brought the lad to Eli.

26. Then she said: O my lord, I am the woman who stood near you right here, praying to the Eternal.

21 וַיַּעַל הָאִישׁ אֶלְקָנָה וְכָל־בֵּיתוֹ לִזְבֹּחַ לַיהוָה אֶת־זֶבַח הַיָּמִים וְאֶת־נִדְרוֹ:

22 וְחַנָּה לֹא עָלָתָה כִּי־אָמְרָה לְאִישָׁהּ עַד יִגָּמֵל הַנַּעַר וַהֲבִאֹתִיו וְנִרְאָה אֶת־פְּנֵי יְהוָה וְיָשַׁב שָׁם עַד־עוֹלָם:

23 וַיֹּאמֶר לָהּ אֶלְקָנָה אִישָׁהּ עֲשִׂי הַטּוֹב בְּעֵינַיִךְ שְׁבִי עַד־גָּמְלֵךְ אֹתוֹ אַךְ יָקֵם יְהוָה אֶת־דְּבָרוֹ וַתֵּשֶׁב הָאִשָּׁה וַתֵּינֶק אֶת־בְּנָהּ עַד־גָּמְלָהּ אֹתוֹ:

24 וַתַּעֲלֵהוּ עִמָּהּ כַּאֲשֶׁר גְּמָלַתּוּ בְּפָרִים שְׁלֹשָׁה וְאֵיפָה אַחַת קֶמַח וְנֵבֶל יַיִן וַתְּבִאֵהוּ בֵית־יְהוָה שִׁלוֹ וְהַנַּעַר נָעַר:

25 וַיִּשְׁחֲטוּ אֶת־הַפָּר וַיָּבִיאוּ אֶת־הַנַּעַר אֶל־עֵלִי:

26 וַתֹּאמֶר בִּי אֲדֹנִי חֵי נַפְשְׁךָ אֲדֹנִי אֲנִי הָאִשָּׁה הַנִּצֶּבֶת עִמְּכָה בָּזֶה לְהִתְפַּלֵּל אֶל־יְהוָה:

Commentary

23. *The divine promise*. A fragment of the Samuel books, found at Qumran, has: "May the Eternal fulfill the utterance of your mouth."

Until she had weaned him. We do not know how long this was, but it could have been up to four or five years.[14]

24. *Though he was still a child*. She did not wait any longer to fulfill her vow.

Three-year-old bull. So the Qumran fragment of the text, instead of "three bulls" in the masoretic text. The next verse speaks only of a single animal—and even this represented great economic value.

27. It was for this lad that I prayed, and the Eternal has granted my request.

28. I therefore dedicate him to the Eternal. So long as he lives he is dedicated to the Eternal. And there they worshipped the Eternal.

2:1. Then Hannah prayed, saying:

My heart exults in the Eternal,

My strength is exalted by the Eternal;

My mouth derides my foes,

As I rejoice in Your salvation.

2. There is none holy as the Eternal,

For there is none besides You;

There is no Rock like our God.

3. Make an end to your high-flown speech,

Let arrogance depart from your mouths!

For the Eternal is a God of [infinite]
   knowledge,

[a God] whose deeds are immeasurable.

4. The warrior's bows are shattered,

And those who stagger put on strength.

27 אֶל־הַנַּעַר הַזֶּה הִתְפַּלָּלְתִּי וַיִּתֵּן יְהוָה לִי
אֶת־שְׁאֵלָתִי אֲשֶׁר שָׁאַלְתִּי מֵעִמּוֹ:

28 וְגַם אָנֹכִי הִשְׁאִלְתִּהוּ לַיהוָה כָּל־הַיָּמִים
אֲשֶׁר הָיָה הוּא שָׁאוּל לַיהוָה וַיִּשְׁתַּחוּ שָׁם
לַיהוָה:

2:1 וַתִּתְפַּלֵּל חַנָּה וַתֹּאמַר
עָלַץ לִבִּי בַּיהוָה
רָמָה קַרְנִי בַּיהוָה
רָחַב פִּי עַל־אוֹיְבַי
כִּי שָׂמַחְתִּי בִּישׁוּעָתֶךָ:

2 אֵין־קָדוֹשׁ כַּיהוָה
כִּי אֵין בִּלְתֶּךָ
וְאֵין צוּר כֵּאלֹהֵינוּ:

3 אַל־תַּרְבּוּ תְדַבְּרוּ גְּבֹהָה גְבֹהָה
יֵצֵא עָתָק מִפִּיכֶם
כִּי אֵל דֵּעוֹת יְהוָה
וְלֹא [וְלוֹ] נִתְכְּנוּ עֲלִלוֹת:

4 קֶשֶׁת גִּבֹּרִים חַתִּים
וְנִכְשָׁלִים אָזְרוּ חָיִל:

Commentary

28. *Dedicated.* The same root שאל (sh-'-l) serves two complementary purposes: asking (for the gift of a son, verse 27) and dedicating him (to the One who responded favorably, verse 28).

And they worshipped. Eli, Hannah, and the child, and 2:11 suggests that Elkanah was also there.[15] Samuel later succeeded Eli.

2:1. *Then Hannah prayed.* See the essay below.

My mouth derides my foes. Rashi applies this to Peninah, who had so long taunted her.

5. Those who were full sell themselves for
   bread,
And those once hungry are full,
While the barren woman bears seven,
And the one with many children is
   bereaved.
6. The Eternal allots death and life,
Casts down to Sheol and lifts up.
7. The Eternal dispenses poverty and
   wealth,
Casts down and lifts up,
8. Lifting the poor from the dust,
Raising the needy from the dunghill,
Making them sit with the nobles,
Assigning them seats of honor.
For the earth's pillars are the Eternal's,
Who set the world upon them,
9. Who guards the steps of the faithful
While the wicked lie mute in darkness:
For not by might does one prevail.

5 שְׂבֵעִים בַּלֶּ֫חֶם נִשְׂכָּ֫רוּ
וּרְעֵבִים חָדֵ֫לּוּ
עַד־עֲקָרָה֙ יָלְדָ֣ה שִׁבְעָ֔ה
וְרַבַּ֥ת בָּנִ֖ים אֻמְלָֽלָה׃
6 יְהֹוָ֖ה מֵמִ֣ית וּמְחַיֶּ֑ה
מוֹרִ֥יד שְׁא֖וֹל וַיָּֽעַל׃
7 יְהֹוָ֖ה מוֹרִ֣ישׁ וּמַעֲשִׁ֑יר
מַשְׁפִּ֖יל אַף־מְרוֹמֵֽם׃
8 מֵקִ֨ים מֵעָפָ֜ר דָּ֗ל
מֵֽאַשְׁפֹּת֙ יָרִ֣ים אֶבְי֔וֹן
לְהוֹשִׁיב֙ עִם־נְדִיבִ֔ים
וְכִסֵּ֥א כָב֖וֹד יַנְחִלֵ֑ם
כִּ֤י לַֽיהוָה֙ מְצֻ֣קֵי אֶ֔רֶץ
וַיָּ֥שֶׁת עֲלֵיהֶ֖ם תֵּבֵֽל׃
9 רַגְלֵ֤י חֲסִידָו֙ יִשְׁמֹ֔ר
וּרְשָׁעִ֖ים בַּחֹ֣שֶׁךְ יִדָּ֑מּוּ
כִּֽי־לֹ֥א בְכֹ֖חַ יִגְבַּר־אִֽישׁ׃

Commentary

5. *Bears seven.* A round number; Hannah herself will have five or six children.[16]

6. *Allots death and life.* The words are repeated daily in the 2nd blessing of the *Amidah*.

Sheol. A common biblical image of the shadowy world of the dead. The language is poetic, connoting that God saves those for whom all hope has been abandoned. It does not imply immortality, for the ancient Israelites did not believe that the dead would actually return.

8. *Lifting the poor.* The first two lines of this verse also appear (in nearly identical form) in Psalm 113:7, which is recited as the opening of the *Hallel*.[17]

The earth's pillars. Poetic for the mountains upon which, ancients believed, the sky rested.

9. *For not by might.* So also the prophet Zechariah, "Not by might nor by power, but by My Spirit, says the Eternal."[18]

10. The foes of the Eternal shall be shat-
    tered
As God thunders against them in the heav-
    ens,
Judging the ends of the earth,
Endowing the king with strength,
Giving victory to the anointed.

יְהֹוָה יֵחַתּוּ מְרִיבָו [מְרִיבָיו] 10

עָלָו [עָלָיו] בַּשָּׁמַיִם יַרְעֵם

יְהֹוָה יָדִין אַפְסֵי־אָרֶץ

וְיִתֶּן־עֹז לְמַלְכּוֹ

וְיָרֵם קֶרֶן מְשִׁיחוֹ:

Essay

Hannah's prayer

This prayer, which is rich in oft-quoted poetic pearls, is considered by many modern scholars to have been composed in later times.[19] Indeed, at first reading it sounds like the song of a soldier like David who has been saved from his enemies,[20] and many of its references may seem inappropriate for Hannah. Still, there are others who would maintain that the words of the prayer fit the exulting spirit of a woman whose longed-for son now serves in the sanctuary of the Eternal. There is much to be said for this view, for Hannah can now be seen to "let go"—and all her pent-up sentiments finally find expression.

Hannah is known to us only through this haftarah and a few later verses. Like Rachel, who was beloved by Jacob, she had to endure her years of barrenness. In her day, childlessness—and especially the lack of a son—made her a semi-outcast, for in the absence of proper knowledge about the nature of conception, she was marked by society as one whom God had disdained. The biblical expression recalls this sentiment: "God had shut her womb." Hannah was taunted and distressed to the point of agony, yet managed to retain a deep spiritual feeling. She prays not only in order to appeal to God's mercy; she also raises her voice in gratitude for the divine gift.

When she is rewarded she is meticulous in fulfilling her pledge to dedicate her son to the service of the sanctuary. To her, the miracle of Samuel's birth is proof, if proof were needed, for the grace and power of God, and in her thanksgiving hymn she sings in phrases that later generations repeated time and again and made their own.

Thus, Hannah emerges indeed as a victor in the battle for life, and her son (so she hopes, while the reader already knows) will grow up to be a stalwart defender of the faith, one of the giants of biblical history.

Gleanings

Words to Remember

There is none holy as the Eternal,
For there is none besides You;
There is no Rock like our God. (2:2)

The Eternal dispenses poverty and wealth,
Casts down and lifts up,
Lifting the poor from the dust,
Raising the needy from the dunghill,
Making them sit with the nobles,
Assigning them seats of honor. (2:7-8)

Not by might does one prevail. (2:9)

The heroine

Hannah is a heroine of religious civilization, because she invents, out of her own urgent imagining, inward prayer. Without bringing a sacrifice, without requiring priestly attendance, soaring past every liturgical convention, she rides her words up into the holy air of the House of the Eternal; and in that instant she alters forever what we mean by "prayer."

Cynthia Ozick[21]

Elkanah had two wives

The reason for having two wives is found in the Israelite's terror of childlessness. A man could not look forward to personal survival after death, for the shadowy existence of Sheol was death rather than life.[22] But he could survive in his children who would keep his name alive among men.

George B. Caird[23]

The Talmud about Hannah

She had the stature of a prophet and therefore is given a place of honor in the Tanach. The Midrash tells us that she was married to her husband for ten years and, when she saw she could not bear children, persuaded him to take a second wife. That is how Peninah came into the family, and she bore ten sons. She constantly reminded Hannah of her childlessness, though one rabbinic source suggests that she did it in order to encourage Hannah to seek recourse in prayer.[24]

When Hannah went to Shiloh she reminded God that, after all, she had been endowed with breasts for the one purpose of nursing children.[25]

Her prayer was cited by the Sages as a model: she prayed with devotion, she moved her lips to pronounce the words, and she prayed in a low voice when she poured out her heart.

The fact that Eli thought her drunk and rebuked her teaches that one should not pray while drunk; and further, Eli did the right thing to confront Hannah when he thought she offended against public decency.[26]

About Elkanah

He too was a prophet and the descendant of prophets;[27] his name means "God has purchased [me]," for Providence had great plans for him. When the last judge had ruled Israel, lots were drawn to determine who would be the next to hold the office. After many fruitless tries the lot finally fell on Elkanah, but he refused the honor. When the elders prayed for guidance, God assured them that Elkanah's offspring would be their judge and prophet for many years to come.[28]

Hannah and the Rabbis

From Hannah's response to Eli, the Rabbis derived the rule that one must not let a false charge (in this case, of drunkenness) remain unanswered.

Talmud[29]

(So impressed were the Rabbis with Hannah's attitude that they enlarged the biblical story as follows: Hannah said to Eli, when he accused her of drunkenness:)

"You are no person of authority in this matter, and the Spirit of Holiness is not upon you, since you have been suspicious of me in this matter ... and have presumed me guilty rather than innocent. Are you not aware that I am a woman in anguish?"[30]

The bitter irony is that these very Rabbis, who showed much creativity in communal prayer, neglected to give Hannah's daughters—the women of Israel—a place in it.

Marcia Falk[31]

Reverberations

Part of Hannah's prayer (2:8) is paralleled in Psalm 113, which serves as the opening of the Hallel prayer for the festivals. The author of Mary's prayer in Christian scriptures (Luke 1:46-55) adapted the prayer; and the Latin version of the text serves as the "Magnificat," set to music by Monteverdi, Bach, and others.

* * *

Notes

[1] The other two were Sarah and Rachel; *B. Rosh Hashanah* 11a, which goes on to say that Rosh Hashanah is the Day of Remembrance and that the end of the women's barrenness was God "remembering" them (see 1:19). The choice of the haftarah for this day is recorded in *Megillah* 31a. See also Rashi's brief comment on the latter passage.

[2] I Samuel 9:15 and following.

[3] Radak favors the understanding of our translation, but Rashi says that Elkanah went to Shiloh for every festival.

[4] The second word, in the singular צבא (*tzava*), is the biblical and contemporary term for "army."

[5] See I. Finkelstein, *Anchor Bible Dictionary*, vol. 5, pp. 1069-1072.

[6] As told in I Samuel 2:12 and following. See there also for the further tale of Eli.

[7] Exodus 34:6, Numbers 14:18. It also occurs frequently in other parts of the Tanach when applied to humans. Literally, the Hebrew *apayim* denotes the two nostrils, and therefore came to signify "long breath," that is, patience.

[8] So also some moderns—for example, NEB.

[9] For the laws of the Nazir, see Numbers chapter 6; for an earlier example of lifelong dedication, see the haftarah for Naso and the story of Samson. (Although the word *Nazir* does not occur in the masoretic text, it is in the Samuel manuscript found among the Dead Sea Scrolls of Qumran.)

[10] See *B. Berachot* 31a.

[11] Genesis 4:1, and see the Torah Commentary (p. 39) on the term's importance for interpreting the tale of the Tree of Knowledge.

[12] From this, modern scholars have concluded that the explanation of the name was transposed in error from the story of Saul. The name Samuel is attested by the beginning of the second millennium B.C.E., when an Amorite king of Larsa (in Mesopotamia) bore the name "Sumuel," there meaning "suitable/appropriate/fitting to the god El."

[13] So Radak, who solves the problem by suggesting that the word "saying" (or "she said") has fallen out. Our translation follows Radak.

[14] A midrash speaks of her nursing Samuel for two years (Midrash Samuel, ed. S. Buber [1893], 3:53). In the story of another mother (also called Hannah by tradition) and her seven sons who gave their lives for the glorification of God, we learn that she had nursed her youngest for three years (II Maccabees 7:27; see also Koran 2:233). On Babylonian contracts for wet nurses and artistic depictions of nursing children, see M. Gruber, "Breast Feeding Practices in Biblical Israel and Old Babylonian Mesopotamia," *Journal of the Ancient Near Eastern Society*, vol. 19 (1989), pp. 61-83.

[15] *B. Berachot* 61a records that there was a manuscript of the book that said, "And Elkanah went after his wife." It probably stood before after verse 24.

[16] I Samuel 2:21. The text is not clear whether the five children mentioned there is the total number she bore.

[17] Psalms 113-118, recited on festivals.

[18] Zechariah 4:6; the selection is read as part of the haftarah on Shabbat Chanukah and Shabbat B'ha'alot'cha; see our comment on the latter.

[19] See Hertzberg, in his commentary *I and II Samuel*, p. 29.

[20] See the prayer of David, which appears both in II Samuel chapter 22 and as Psalm 18; it serves as the haftarah for Ha'azinu and also for the seventh day of Pesach.

[21] "Hannah and Elkanah: Torah as the Matrix for Feminism," p. 89.

[22] Belief in immortality arose in a much later, post-biblical age.

[23] *Interpreter's Bible*, vol. 2, p. 877.

[24] B. Baba Batra 16a, but most sources denigrate her motives.

[25] B. Berachot 31b.

[26] B. Berachot 31a-b.

[27] B. Megillah 14a.

[28] Pseudo-Philo 49 ff. brings this and other midrashim about Elkanah.

[29] B. Berachot 31b.

[30] Ibid.

[31] "Reflections on Hannah's Prayer," p. 99.

Jeremiah, chapter 31, verses 1 to 19

Introduction

Connection of haftarah and festival:

Penitence and forgiveness are the themes of the High Holy Days, and to these the Prophet speaks in this collection of admonitions.

The setting:

Jeremiah began his prophecies at a time when Josiah was king of Judah, in the last quarter of the 7th century B.C.E. A hundred years earlier, the kingdom of Israel (called Ephraim by Jeremiah, after its major tribe) had been destroyed by Assyria and its inhabitants had been deported. Now it was the Babylonians who threatened to overrun the Southern Kingdom (Judah and its capital, Jerusalem).

The haftarah consists of a number of separate poems, which seem to come from a time when the memory of the Northern Kingdom's destruction took on new relevance. The Prophet reassures his people that someday the exiles will return and the former two nations will become one once again. Our haftarah belongs to that part of Jeremiah's prophecies that has been called "the book of consolation."

For more on Jeremiah and his time, see our *General Introduction.*

The message:

1. The exiles will return and rejoin their southern relatives, and together they will worship in Jerusalem. (1-8)
2. A description of the joy that will then prevail. (9-13)
3. Mother Rachel weeps for her children, but God will comfort her. (14-16)
4. Ephraim repents and God takes the exiles back in love. (17-19)

HAFTARAH FOR THE SECOND DAY OF ROSH HASHANAH

Jeremiah, chapter 31, verses 1 to 19

31:1. Thus says the Eternal One:
A people who survived the sword
found favor in the wilderness;
I proceeded to give rest to Israel.
2. The Eternal appeared to Israel from afar
    [saying]:
with love everlasting have I loved you;
with faithful love I draw you (near) to Me.
3. I will build you up again,
O innocent daughter of Israel,
and you shall be rebuilt!
You shall take up your tambourines once
    more,
and dance among the merrymakers.
4. Again you shall plant vineyards on the
    hills of Samaria;
those who plant them shall enjoy the fruit.

31:1 כֹּה אָמַר יְהֹוָה

מָצָא חֵן בַּמִּדְבָּר

עַם שְׂרִידֵי חָרֶב

הָלוֹךְ לְהַרְגִּיעוֹ יִשְׂרָאֵל:

2 מֵרָחוֹק יְהֹוָה נִרְאָה לִי

וְאַהֲבַת עוֹלָם אֲהַבְתִּיךְ

עַל־כֵּן מְשַׁכְתִּיךְ חָסֶד:

3 עוֹד אֶבְנֵךְ וְנִבְנֵית

בְּתוּלַת יִשְׂרָאֵל

עוֹד תַּעְדִּי תֻפַּיִךְ

וְיָצָאת בִּמְחוֹל מְשַׂחֲקִים:

4 עוֹד תִּטְּעִי כְרָמִים בְּהָרֵי שֹׁמְרוֹן

נָטְעוּ נֹטְעִים וְחִלֵּלוּ:

Commentary

The numbering of this section differs slightly in various versions, which count verse 1 as the last of chapter 30 and begin the haftarah with verse 2 of chapter 31. Also, because the haftarot are read in public, the translation has at times been rephrased to reflect current standards (in Reform synagogues) of liturgical gender neutrality. As a result, the translation may say "You" when the Hebrew reads "He."

1. *In the wilderness.* Jeremiah evokes the image of Israel's wandering for forty years in the Sinai desert. God did not forsake them then and will not now forget those who have been saved from Assyria's sword.

2. *Appeared to Israel.* The Hebrew text has "to me."

From afar. From the remoteness of Sinai's peak.

3. *O innocent daughter.* Literally, "virgin," here used as a metaphor for innocence.

4. *Shall enjoy the fruit.* חללו (*chill'lu*, literally, "profane"): what was formerly set aside for sacred use may now be "profaned," that is, be enjoyed by all.

5. For a day is coming

when lookouts shall cry out on Ephraim's
hills:

Come, let us go up to Zion,

to the Eternal, our God!

6. For thus says the Eternal One:

Shout joyfully for Jacob,

raise a loud cry for the first of the nations,

exclaim in praise, and say:

Eternal One, save Your people,

the remnant of Israel.

7. Behold, I am bringing them from a
northern land,

gathering them from the ends of the earth,

the blind and the lame among them,

the woman with child and the woman in
labor,

a great company returning here.

8. Weeping shall they come;

and with compassion will I guide them.

I will bring them to streams of water,

on a smooth path, where they shall not
stumble.

For I am like a parent to Israel,

and Ephraim is My firstborn child.

כִּי יֶשׁ־יוֹם 5

קָרְאוּ נֹצְרִים בְּהַר אֶפְרָיִם

קוּמוּ וְנַעֲלֶה צִיּוֹן

אֶל־יְהוָה אֱלֹהֵינוּ:

כִּי־כֹה אָמַר יְהוָה 6

רָנּוּ לְיַעֲקֹב שִׂמְחָה

וְצַהֲלוּ בְּרֹאשׁ הַגּוֹיִם

הַשְׁמִיעוּ הַלְלוּ וְאִמְרוּ

הוֹשַׁע יְהוָה אֶת־עַמְּךָ

אֵת שְׁאֵרִית יִשְׂרָאֵל:

הִנְנִי מֵבִיא אוֹתָם מֵאֶרֶץ צָפוֹן 7

וְקִבַּצְתִּים מִיַּרְכְּתֵי־אָרֶץ

בָּם עִוֵּר וּפִסֵּחַ

הָרָה וְיֹלֶדֶת יַחְדָּו

קָהָל גָּדוֹל יָשׁוּבוּ הֵנָּה:

בִּבְכִי יָבֹאוּ 8

וּבְתַחֲנוּנִים אוֹבִילֵם

אוֹלִיכֵם אֶל־נַחֲלֵי מַיִם

בְּדֶרֶךְ יָשָׁר לֹא יִכָּשְׁלוּ בָּהּ

כִּי־הָיִיתִי לְיִשְׂרָאֵל לְאָב

וְאֶפְרַיִם בְּכֹרִי הוּא:

Commentary

5. *Ephraim's hills.* Israel, the (now destroyed) Northern Kingdom, whose capital was
Samaria.

Go up to Zion. North and south together. The division that occurred after Solomon's
death will be healed at last.

6. *First of the nations.* Israel, God's beloved.

7. *Northern land.* Assyria.

8. *Weeping.* Their emotion will overcome them as they return. Later, they will "revel in
dance." (verse 12)

Israel. Here meaning the people of Israel, the kingdom of Judah, whose counterpart is
Ephraim.

9. Hear the word of the Eternal, you
   peoples;

tell it to the islands from afar, and say:

The One who scattered Israel will gather
   them in,

and watch over them as a shepherd the
   flock.

10. For the Eternal has ransomed Jacob,

and redeemed him from one too strong for
   him.

11. Radiant at the Eternal's bounty—

the grain, the wine, the oil,

the young of the flock and the herd—

to Zion's height shall they come, shouting
   for joy;

and they shall be like a garden overflowing
   with water,

never again to languish.

12. Then girls shall revel in dance,

young and old as well.

I will turn their mourning into gladness,

I will comfort and cheer them out of their
   grief.

13. I will have the priests receive the best,

and My people shall be satisfied with My
   bounty,

says the Eternal One.

9 שִׁמְעוּ דְבַר־יְהֹוָה גּוֹיִם

וְהַגִּידוּ בָאִיִּים מִמֶּרְחָק וְאִמְרוּ

מְזָרֵה יִשְׂרָאֵל יְקַבְּצֶנּוּ

וּשְׁמָרוֹ כְּרֹעֶה עֶדְרוֹ:

10 כִּי־פָדָה יְהֹוָה אֶת־יַעֲקֹב

וּגְאָלוֹ מִיַּד חָזָק מִמֶּנּוּ:

11 וּבָאוּ וְרִנְּנוּ בִמְרוֹם־צִיּוֹן

וְנָהֲרוּ אֶל־טוּב יְהֹוָה

עַל־דָּגָן וְעַל־תִּירֹשׁ וְעַל־יִצְהָר

וְעַל־בְּנֵי־צֹאן וּבָקָר

וְהָיְתָה נַפְשָׁם כְּגַן רָוֶה

וְלֹא־יוֹסִיפוּ לְדַאֲבָה עוֹד:

12 אָז תִּשְׂמַח בְּתוּלָה בְּמָחוֹל

וּבַחֻרִים וּזְקֵנִים יַחְדָּו

וְהָפַכְתִּי אֶבְלָם לְשָׂשׂוֹן

וְנִחַמְתִּים וְשִׂמַּחְתִּים מִיגוֹנָם:

13 וְרִוֵּיתִי נֶפֶשׁ הַכֹּהֲנִים דָּשֶׁן

וְעַמִּי אֶת־טוּבִי יִשְׂבָּעוּ

נְאֻם־יְהֹוָה:

Commentary

10. *For the Eternal has ransomed Jacob.* From slavery.[1] This verse has become part of
the daily evening liturgy.[2]

621

14. Thus says the Eternal One:

A voice is heard in Ramah;

lamentation and bitter weeping!

Rachel is weeping for her children,

refusing to be comforted for her children,

for they are gone.

15. Thus says the Eternal One:

Hold back your voice from weeping,

your eyes from tears!

For your labor shall have its reward,

says the Eternal One:

They shall return from the land of the foe.

16. There is hope for your future:

your children shall return to their own
borders.

17. I can hear Ephraim bemoaning himself:

You have disciplined me,

I am disciplined like an untrained calf.

Help me to return, and I will return,

for You, O Eternal, are my God.

14 כֹּה אָמַר יְהֹוָה

קוֹל בְּרָמָה נִשְׁמָע

נְהִי בְּכִי תַמְרוּרִים

רָחֵל מְבַכָּה עַל־בָּנֶיהָ

מֵאֲנָה לְהִנָּחֵם עַל־בָּנֶיהָ

כִּי אֵינֶנּוּ:

15 כֹּה אָמַר יְהֹוָה

מִנְעִי קוֹלֵךְ מִבֶּכִי

וְעֵינַיִךְ מִדִּמְעָה

כִּי יֵשׁ שָׂכָר לִפְעֻלָּתֵךְ

נְאֻם־יְהֹוָה

וְשָׁבוּ מֵאֶרֶץ אוֹיֵב:

16 וְיֵשׁ־תִּקְוָה לְאַחֲרִיתֵךְ נְאֻם־יְהֹוָה

וְשָׁבוּ בָנִים לִגְבוּלָם:

17 שָׁמוֹעַ שָׁמַעְתִּי אֶפְרַיִם מִתְנוֹדֵד

יִסַּרְתַּנִי

וָאִוָּסֵר כְּעֵגֶל לֹא לֻמָּד

הֲשִׁיבֵנִי וְאָשׁוּבָה

כִּי אַתָּה יְהֹוָה אֱלֹהָי:

Commentary

14. *Ramah.* A number of places bore this name. Here it appears to refer to the town some 5 miles (8 kilometers) north of Jerusalem in the territory of Benjamin, where, according to one tradition, Rachel was buried.[3] But the accepted place for the Tomb of Rachel is near Bethlehem, a location mentioned in the story of her death, as told in the book of Genesis.[4]

Weeping for her children. Represented by the exiled of her offspring: Benjamin, her younger son, and Ephraim, her grandchild.

17. *Help me to return.* The phrase is cast in the plural in the book of Lamentations and in that form has entered the liturgy.[5]

18. *Now that I have strayed, I repent;*
now that I am made aware, I slap my thigh;
in shame and mortification I bear the dis-
grace of my youth.

18 כִּי־אַחֲרֵי שׁוּבִי נִחַמְתִּי
וְאַחֲרֵי הִוָּדְעִי סָפַקְתִּי עַל־יָרֵךְ
בֹּשְׁתִּי וְגַם־נִכְלַמְתִּי כִּי נָשָׂאתִי חֶרְפַּת נְעוּרָי:

19. *Is Ephraim My darling son?*
a babe of dear delights?
Yet even when I have disowned him
My thoughts have dwelt on him!
For My heart yearns for him,
[and] in love I will surely take him back,
says the Eternal One.

19 הֲבֵן יַקִּיר לִי אֶפְרַיִם
אִם יֶלֶד שַׁעֲשֻׁעִים
כִּי־מִדֵּי דַבְּרִי בּוֹ
זָכֹר אֶזְכְּרֶנּוּ עוֹד
עַל־כֵּן הָמוּ מֵעַי לוֹ
רַחֵם אֲרַחֲמֶנּוּ
נְאֻם־יְהוָה:

Commentary

18. *I slap my thigh.* In remorse; the English equivalent would be, "I beat my breast." In a Babylonian myth, the goddess of the underworld slaps her thigh as a gesture of derision. Remorseful over his past misconduct, Ephraim slaps his thigh in self-derision.[6]

19. *In love I will surely take him back.* Or, "I will surely show him love."
It has been shown that the verse contains three rhetorical questions:

　　1. Is Ephraim my darling son? (Answer: No, he has been terrible.)
　　2. Is he a babe of dear delights? (Answer: Hardly.)
　　3. Yet even when I have disowned him, why have My thoughts dwelt on him? (Answer: I can never get him out of My mind.)

"For My heart yearns for him (despite all his sins against Me) [and] in love I will surely take him back, says the Eternal One" (verse 19).[7]

Essay

The ingathering of the dispersed

Two themes pervade the poems found in our haftarah: God has caused the exile of Israel, and God will also will bring them back to their land. "The One who scattered Israel will gather them in" (verse 9).

This is the fundamental message that binds the prophetic books together. Israel's faithlessness has caused God to mete out severe punishment, but divine love will reverse the course of history and bring the people back to the land of their ancestors. It is a promise contained in the Torah itself: "Even if your outcasts are at the ends of the universe, the Eternal your God will gather you and fetch you from there. And the Eternal your God will bring you to the land your ancestors occupied, and you shall possess it ...."[8]

Thus God is seen as the motive power behind all that befalls the People of the Covenant, and even as their misdeeds caused their dispersion, so will their repentance move their severe Judge, yet merciful Guardian, to gather them in once again. This is the "ingathering of the exiles," known from talmudic times on as קבוץ גליות (*kibbutz galuyot*).[9]

The ingathering would comprise not only those who were forced into exile by their enemies, but also those who left their homeland voluntarily, in search of better opportunities. In Jeremiah's time, the largest of these voluntary *galuyot* was Egypt, where in fact Jeremiah himself spent his last days.[10]

The Prophets believed with all their hearts that God would cause the *kibbutz galuyot* in historic times. But, as the centuries rolled by, this hope receded more and more, and the divine promise was interpreted to refer to messianic, that is post-historic, days. For while God's intentions were ultimately hidden from human perception, the unity of the Jewish people was a reality that could not be doubted.

Was therefore the return of Jews to Eretz Israel part of a supernatural plan? Many have believed so and made Israel Independence Day a religious as well as a national celebration. But there remain two groups whose view of history is different: those who perceive it in secular terms, and those—at the other end of the scale—who consider the establishment of a Jewish state by human hands an intrusion into God's prerogative, for only the Eternal will bring the exiles back from the four corners of the earth.

Was Jeremiah's prophecy then a misreading of the divine will? After all, the northern exiles whom Assyria had taken away would never return (nor could they even be found). No, says tradition, for the Prophet, while hoping that *kibbutz galuyot* would take place in his

time, was sure that in God's own time the promise would be fulfilled. Meanwhile, he hoped, God would dry the tears that Rachel shed for Benjamin and Ephraim.

Jeremiah spoke what he perceived to be a message grounded in God's wisdom and will. His view of a God who managed history was shared by all biblical writers, though it is not widely shared today. Underlying it all was a belief in God's special relationship to Israel, and this has remained the dominant interpretation that Jews have given to their own history.

Gleanings

Words to Remember

A voice is heard in Ramah,
Rachel weeping for her children .... (verse 14)

Help me to return, and I will return,
for You, Eternal One, are my God. (verse 17)

Help us to return to You, Eternal One,
so that we may return;
renew our days as of old! (Lamentations 5:21)[11]

Rachel weeping for her children (31:15)

The text says that her voice was heard from Ramah, and Ramah is north of Jerusalem, while her tomb is at Bethlehem, south of Jerusalem (Genesis 35:19-20). The latter is in the territory of Judah, while Ramah is in the territory of Benjamin. Tradition felt obligated to resolve this contradiction, as indeed it tried hard to solve every apparent contradiction in the Tanach—for a contradiction in a divinely-inspired word appeared to be an oxymoron.

However, the Rabbis were not particularly successful in resolving this issue.[12]

Rashi, followed by Metzudat David, avoids the controversy by understanding the Ramah of our haftarah to mean "highland."

Rachel—a metaphor for Israel

The aforementioned midrash states that in this passage of Jeremiah, Rachel stands for all Israel. Thus the passage might be read: "A voice is heard in Ramah; lamentation and bitter weeping; Israel is weeping for her children, refusing to be comforted ...."

* * *

Notes

[1] See Leviticus 25:48, and the Torah Commentary, p. 950.

[2] It follows the recitation of the *Mi chamocha* (Who is like You...) and precedes the Hashkivenu (Cause us to lie down ...).

[3] I Samuel 10:2.

[4] 35:19-20. Genesis Rabbah 82:10.

[5] See Lamentations 5:21, cited in *Gleanings*. It is chanted after the scroll of the Torah is returned to the Ark.

[6] See James Pritchard, *Ancient Near Eastern Texts*, p. 108.

[7] See M. Held, "Rhetorical Questions in Ugaritic and Biblical Hebrew," *Eretz Israel*, vol. 9 (1969), pp. 71-79.

[8] Deuteronomy 30:4-5.

[9] B. Pesachim 88a and elsewhere.

[10] Jeremiah, however, was taken there against his will, after the assassination of Gedaliah (see our *General Introduction*).

[11] Note the somewhat different phrasing of Lamentations 5:21. The Sages attributed the book of Lamentations to Jeremiah.

[12] See Genesis Rabbah 82:10.

Hosea, chapter 14, verses 2 to 10 and Micah, chapter 7, verses 18 to 20 or Joel, chapter 2, verses 15 to 27

Introduction

Connection of haftarah and Shabbat:

The Shabbat between Rosh Hashanah and Yom Kippur is treated as a special day in the calendar, and therefore the haftarah has no connection with the sidra. Rather, the selections from Hosea and Micah or Joel deal with the theme of Repentance, appropriate for the High Holy Day season.[1]

Hosea

The setting:

Hosea lived in the 8th century B.C.E., and was a younger contemporary of Amos. He resided and preached in the Northern Kingdom, which bore the name of Israel. He addressed himself unsparingly to the social and religious ills of his society, though in the end he held out God's forgiveness if the people would mend their ways. (Note that the selection also forms part of the reading for Shabbat Vayeitzei.)

For more on Hosea and his time, see our *General Introduction*.

The message:

    1. The Prophet's call to repentance. (2-4)

    2. God's response. (5-9)

    3. A didactic postscript. (10)

HAFTARAH FOR SHABBAT SHUVAH

Hosea, chapter 14, verses 2 to 10 and Micah, chapter 7, verses 18 to 20 or Joel, chapter 2,
verses 15 to 27

Hosea

14:2. Return, O Israel, to the Eternal your
    God,

for you have stumbled in your iniquity.

3. Take words with you

and return to the Eternal,

and say:

Forgive all iniquity and accept the good;

and we will offer the fruit of our lips.

4. *Assyria cannot save us;*

we shall ride on horses no more;

never again shall we say "Our God"

to the works of our hands.

For in You [alone] the orphan finds a parent
    [again].

5. I will heal their disloyalty;

I will love them freely;

for My wrath has turned away from them,

6. I will be like dew to Israel.

They shall blossom like a lily

and strike roots like [the trees of] Lebanon.

14:2 שׁוּבָה יִשְׂרָאֵל עַד יְהֹוָה אֱלֹהֶיךָ
כִּי כָשַׁלְתָּ בַּעֲוֺנֶךָ:
3 קְחוּ עִמָּכֶם דְּבָרִים
וְשׁוּבוּ אֶל־יְהֹוָה
אִמְרוּ אֵלָיו
כָּל־תִּשָּׂא עָוֺן וְקַח־טוֹב
וּנְשַׁלְּמָה פָרִים שְׂפָתֵינוּ:
4 אַשּׁוּר לֹא יוֹשִׁיעֵנוּ
עַל־סוּס לֹא נִרְכָּב
וְלֹא־נֹאמַר עוֹד אֱלֹהֵינוּ
לְמַעֲשֵׂה יָדֵינוּ
אֲשֶׁר־בְּךָ יְרֻחַם יָתוֹם:
5 אֶרְפָּא מְשׁוּבָתָם
אֹהֲבֵם נְדָבָה
כִּי שָׁב אַפִּי מִמֶּנּוּ:
6 אֶהְיֶה כַטַּל לְיִשְׂרָאֵל
יִפְרַח כַּשּׁוֹשַׁנָּה
וְיַךְ שָׁרָשָׁיו כַּלְּבָנוֹן:

Commentary

2. *Return, O Israel.* The opening word, שובה (*shuvah*) has given the Shabbat its name.

Stumbled in your iniquity. Or, because of your iniquity.

3. *Take words with you.* Come prepared to confess your sins.

The fruit of our lips. Our earnest prayers. Reading פרי (*p'ri*, fruit) instead of פרים (*parim*, bulls).[2]

4. *On horses no more.* Alluding to the use of horses by Egypt's armies: Israel will no longer rely on an alliance with Egypt.[3]

5. *I will heal their disloyalty.* A wordplay on verse 2: I will heal your משובה (*m'shuvah*, disloyalty) if you heed My plea, שובה (*shuvah*, return).

From them. Here and in the following verse the Prophet uses the singular, apparently having in mind the word *am*, which is a singular for "people."

629

7. Their shoots shall spread out wide,

their splendor like an olive-tree's,

their fragrance like that of Lebanon.

8. Those who sit in their shade shall return
   [to Me],

they shall grow [their] corn,

and blossom like a vine,

renowned as the wine of Lebanon.

9. Ephraim   [shall say]: *What are idols to
   me now?*

[God will say:] *I will respond and look to
   him.*

[For] I am a luxuriant cypress,

from which your fruit is found.

10. The wise shall understand these things,

the discerning shall know them:

that straight are the ways of the Eternal;

while the righteous walk in them,

transgressors stumble on them.

7 יֵלְכוּ֙ יֹֽנְקוֹתָ֔יו

וִיהִ֥י כַזַּ֖יִת הוֹד֑וֹ

וְרֵ֥יחַ ל֖וֹ כַּלְּבָנֽוֹן׃

8 יָשֻׁ֙בוּ֙ יֹשְׁבֵ֣י בְצִלּ֔וֹ

יְחַיּ֥וּ דָגָ֖ן

וְיִפְרְח֣וּ כַגָּ֑פֶן

זִכְר֖וֹ כְּיֵ֥ין לְבָנֽוֹן׃

9 אֶפְרַ֕יִם מַה־לִּ֥י ע֖וֹד לָֽעֲצַבִּ֑ים

אֲנִ֥י עָנִ֖יתִי וַאֲשׁוּרֶ֑נּוּ

אֲנִי֙ כִּבְר֣וֹשׁ רַֽעֲנָ֔ן

מִמֶּ֖נִּי פֶּרְיְךָ֥ נִמְצָֽא׃

10 מִ֤י חָכָם֙ וְיָ֣בֵֽן אֵ֔לֶּה

נָב֖וֹן וְיֵֽדָעֵ֑ם

כִּֽי־יְשָׁרִ֞ים דַּרְכֵ֣י יְהֹוָ֗ה

וְצַדִּקִים֙ יֵ֣לְכוּ בָ֔ם

וּפֹשְׁעִ֖ים יִכָּ֥שְׁלוּ בָֽם׃

Commentary

9. *Ephraim*. The dominant tribe in the Northern Kingdom; Hosea often uses the name as a synonym for Israel. We understand this as Ephraim's repentance, while others believe it is part of God's speech.[4]

10. *The wise shall understand*. This verse concludes Hosea's prophecies and represents their summation, that worshipping the Eternal is Israel's true and only hope.

Micah

This selection from Micah is added when Shabbat Shuvah is the day on which the sidra Vayeilech is read; otherwise, the additional selection is from Joel; see below.

7:18. Who is a God like You,

forgiving iniquity, passing over transgres-
    sion;

You do not cling to Your anger with the
    remnant of Your people,

because You delight in showing love!

19. You will turn back [to us], You will take
    us back in love,

You will subdue our sins,

casting them into the depths of the sea.

20. You will show faithfulness to Jacob,

steadfast love to Abraham,

as You promised our ancestors from the
    days of old.

7:18 מִי־אֵל כָּמוֹךָ

נֹשֵׂא עָוֹן וְעֹבֵר עַל־פֶּשַׁע

לִשְׁאֵרִית נַחֲלָתוֹ לֹא־הֶחֱזִיק לָעַד אַפּוֹ

כִּי־חָפֵץ חֶסֶד הוּא:

19 יָשׁוּב יְרַחֲמֵנוּ

יִכְבֹּשׁ עֲוֹנֹתֵינוּ

וְתַשְׁלִיךְ בִּמְצֻלוֹת יָם כָּל־חַטֹּאותָם:

20 תִּתֵּן אֱמֶת לְיַעֲקֹב

חֶסֶד לְאַבְרָהָם

אֲשֶׁר־נִשְׁבַּעְתָּ לַאֲבֹתֵינוּ מִימֵי קֶדֶם:

The setting:

Micah was a younger contemporary of the First Isaiah and lived toward the end of the 8th century in a small town in Judah. Believing that his beloved country was headed for disaster because of the terrible injustices committed by its citizens, he preached repentance ere it was too late.

For more on Micah and his time, see our *General Introduction*.

The message:

Withal, God stands ready to forgive Israel's iniquities, for the divine love is unbounded.

Commentary

7:19. *Subdue our sins.* Literally, "step on our sins."[5]

Cast תשליך (*tashlich*). Micah's metaphor of God casting Israel's sins into the depth of the sea gave rise to the ceremony of Tashlich: on the afternoon of Rosh Hashanah (or, if the festival falls on Shabbat, on the second day), tradition summons Jews to go to a body of water and recite the three verses of this haftarah from Micah.

Joel

The following verses, rather than the selection from Micah, are added to the reading from Hosea when Shabbat Shuvah falls on a day when the weekly sidra is Ha'azinu and not Vayeilech, in which case the verses of Micah are added.

Joel uses a terrible plague of locusts (which may have devastated the land in his time) as a metaphor for God's punishment; and he speaks of a Day of Judgment that is to come—a theme to which the Ten Days of Repentance are devoted.

For more on Joel and his time, see our *General Introduction*.

2:15. Sound the shofar in Zion,

sanctify a fast-day,

call a sacred assembly!

16. Gather the people,

sanctify the congregation;

assemble the elders;

gather the children and babes at the breast.

Let the bridegroom come out of his chamber,

the bride from her canopy.

2:15 תִּקְעוּ שׁוֹפָר בְּצִיּוֹן

קַדְּשׁוּ־צוֹם

קִרְאוּ עֲצָרָה:

16 אִסְפוּ־עָם

קַדְּשׁוּ קָהָל

קִבְצוּ זְקֵנִים

אִסְפוּ עוֹלָלִים וְיֹנְקֵי שָׁדָיִם

יֵצֵא חָתָן מֵחֶדְרוֹ

וְכַלָּה מֵחֻפָּתָהּ:

The message:

  1. Assembling the people to call on God. (15-17)
  2. God's response. (19-20)
  3. Joel's joyous response to God's promise. (21-24)
  4. The Eternal's promise affirmed. (25-27)
  5. Thus, the selection speaks not of the need for repentance; rather, it paints the glorious picture of a people whose return to God will cause God to return to Israel.

Commentary

16. *Bridegroom ... bride.* The Torah [6] exempts the newlywed man for one year from military service; but here, both groom and bride are summoned to participate in the act of national supplication.

17. Between the vestibule and the altar,

let the priests, the ministers of the Eternal,
　　weep and say:

Have pity on Your people, Eternal One!

Let not Your heritage be mocked,

be a byword among the nations.

Why should they say among the peoples,

Where is their God?

18. Then the Eternal showed zeal for this
　　land,

and compassion for God's people.

19. The Eternal answered God's people,
　　saying:

Behold, I will send you grain, wine, and oil,

and it will satisfy you,

and I will no longer let you be put to
　　shame among the nations.

20. I will remove the northerner far from
　　you,

and drive it to a land parched and
　　desolate,

facing the eastern sea,

with the western sea at its rear.

17 בֵּין הָאוּלָם וְלַמִּזְבֵּ֫חַ

יִבְכּוּ הַכֹּהֲנִים מְשָׁרְתֵי יְהוָה וְיֹאמְרוּ

ח֫וּסָה יְהוָה עַל־עַמֶּ֫ךָ

וְאַל־תִּתֵּן נַחֲלָתְךָ לְחֶרְפָּה

לִמְשָׁל־בָּם גּוֹיִם

לָ֫מָּה יֹאמְרוּ בָעַמִּים

אַיֵּה אֱלֹהֵיהֶם:

18 וַיְקַנֵּא יְהוָה לְאַרְצוֹ

וַיַּחְמֹל עַל־עַמּוֹ:

19 וַיַּ֫עַן יְהוָה וַיֹּ֫אמֶר לְעַמּוֹ

הִנְנִי שֹׁלֵחַ לָכֶם אֶת־הַדָּגָן וְהַתִּירוֹשׁ וְהַיִּצְהָר

וּשְׂבַעְתֶּם אֹתוֹ

וְלֹא־אֶתֵּן אֶתְכֶם עוֹד חֶרְפָּה בַּגּוֹיִם:

20 וְאֶת־הַצְּפוֹנִי אַרְחִיק מֵעֲלֵיכֶם

וְהִדַּחְתִּיו אֶל־אֶרֶץ צִיָּה וּשְׁמָמָה

אֶת־פָּנָיו אֶל־הַיָּם הַקַּדְמֹנִי

וְסֹפוֹ אֶל־הַיָּם הָאַחֲרוֹן

Commentary

17. *Let the priests … weep.* Shedding tears of supplication. The priests represent the whole people's urgent appeal.

A byword. For mockery and contempt.

18. *God's people.* Literally, "His people."

20. *The northerner.* Traditionally believed to refer to a plague of locusts that devastated the land,[7] but more likely a reference to Israel's historic enemies coming from the north who—like the real locusts—devastated the land. There was also a folk belief that the north was infested with evil spirits, and such mythic thinking underlies the expulsion of the "northerner" into the western and eastern seas.[8]

Eastern sea … western sea. The Dead Sea[9] and the Mediterranean.

Its stench shall rise up, its foul smell shall
  ascend,

for [God] is doing great things.

21. Fear not, O soil, rejoice and be glad,

for the Eternal is doing great things.

22. Fear not, O beasts of the field;

for the pastures of the wilderness are green.
Every tree bears its fruit,

the fig-tree and the vine give their yield.

23. O children of Zion, rejoice

and be glad in the Eternal your God,

who in kindness is giving you the early
  rain,

pouring rain down for you,

the early rain and the later rain of the first
  month.

24. The threshing floors shall be heaped
  with grain,

the vats shall overflow with wine and oil;

וְעָלָה בָאְשׁוֹ וְתַעַל צַחֲנָתוֹ

כִּי הִגְדִּיל לַעֲשׂוֹת:

21 אַל־תִּירְאִי אֲדָמָה גִּילִי וּשְׂמָחִי

כִּי־הִגְדִּיל יְהוָה לַעֲשׂוֹת:

22 אַל־תִּירְאוּ בַּהֲמוֹת שָׂדַי

כִּי דָשְׁאוּ נְאוֹת מִדְבָּר

כִּי־עֵץ נָשָׂא פִרְיוֹ

תְּאֵנָה וָגֶפֶן נָתְנוּ חֵילָם:

23 וּבְנֵי צִיּוֹן גִּילוּ

וְשִׂמְחוּ בַּיהוָה אֱלֹהֵיכֶם

כִּי־נָתַן לָכֶם אֶת־הַמּוֹרֶה לִצְדָקָה

וַיּוֹרֶד לָכֶם גֶּשֶׁם

מוֹרֶה וּמַלְקוֹשׁ בָּרִאשׁוֹן:

24 וּמָלְאוּ הַגֳּרָנוֹת בָּר

וְהֵשִׁיקוּ הַיְקָבִים תִּירוֹשׁ וְיִצְהָר:

Commentary

[God]. Literally, "He."

23. *In kindness..* Or, "in vindication." [10]

Pouring rain down. מורה (*moreh*) can mean "early rain" as in the next line, or it can mean "teacher." Our translation follows the Talmud rather than most traditional commentators, who consider "teacher" a reference to the Messiah. [11] The heavy emphasis on rain underscores its crucial nature for the country's well-being, the early rain falling usually in October and the late rain in April.

25. I will repay you for what [you lost in]
the years when the swarmer ate your crops,
the hopper, the grub, the locust—
My great army that I sent against you.

26. You shall eat and be satisfied,
and praise the name of the Eternal your
    God,
who has done wondrous things for you.
My people shall never again be put to
    shame.

27. Then you shall know that I am in the
    midst of Israel,
and that I, the Eternal, am your God,
and there is no other.
My people shall never again be put to
    shame.

25 וְשִׁלַּמְתִּי לָכֶם
אֶת־הַשָּׁנִים אֲשֶׁר אָכַל הָאַרְבֶּה
הַיֶּלֶק וְהֶחָסִיל וְהַגָּזָם
חֵילִי הַגָּדוֹל אֲשֶׁר שִׁלַּחְתִּי בָּכֶם:

26 וַאֲכַלְתֶּם אָכוֹל וְשָׂבוֹעַ
וְהִלַּלְתֶּם אֶת־שֵׁם יְהֹוָה אֱלֹהֵיכֶם
אֲשֶׁר־עָשָׂה עִמָּכֶם לְהַפְלִיא
וְלֹא־יֵבֹשׁוּ עַמִּי לְעוֹלָם:

27 וִידַעְתֶּם כִּי בְקֶרֶב יִשְׂרָאֵל אָנִי
וַאֲנִי יְהֹוָה אֱלֹהֵיכֶם
וְאֵין עוֹד
וְלֹא־יֵבֹשׁוּ עַמִּי לְעוֹלָם:

Commentary

25. The fourfold sequence of pests appears only in Joel. It is unclear whether they are species of locust or different stages in the locust's life. The terrible damage done by these insects inspired deep fears among the peoples of the Near East. An Assyrian king wrote of his enemies: "One and all they were risen against me to offer battle like a spring invasion of countless locusts."

Essay

Return O Israel (Hosea 14:2)

Hosea's opening word, שובה (*shuvah*), is a challenge to return to God in true contrition. שובה contains both requisites of repentance: to turn from evil and turn to the good. The notion of turning implies that "sin is not an ineradicable stain but a straying from the right path." By the effort of turning all sinners can redirect their destiny. [12]

While today the Hebrew word for repentance is תשובה (*t'shuvah*), neither Hosea nor the entire Tanach knew the word in this sense. It was coined much later by the Rabbis and came into use only after the destruction of Jerusalem by the Romans (70 C.E.). For this event brought about not only the end of the Temple service but also of national existence, which required a radical restructuring of our religion.

When Hosea and the other prophets spoke, they addressed the need for *national* regeneration. It was Israel as a people living on its soil that had to turn to the Eternal, so that the nation might continue to live. It was a collective concept, which became an *individual* one only after the Temple and the commonwealth had been destroyed. The nation was gone, and the need for returning now rested on each person.

Of course, Hosea too had addressed himself to individuals, especially the leaders. They had to mend their ways, and their joint turning would accomplish the desired goal. While each one thus had a responsibility, there had to be enough of them to change the community's course. The focus of the prophets was on Israel's fate: the common decision to repent would spell well-being for all, even as the failure to heed the call for repentance would mean doom for the entire community, the guilty and the innocent.

In a democratic society, where each citizen has a share in the decision-making of the community, something of the biblical setting is re-created: we are all part of the need for turning. This applies wherever Jews live, in the Diaspora where they must exert whatever influence for good they can muster, and especially in Israel, where each citizen can help to shape the fate of the nation.

In this way, we can imagine Hosea speaking to our time, confronting us with our shortcomings and spelling out the consequences that await us if we fall short of our responsibilities and opportunities.

Gleanings

Words to Remember

Return, O Israel, to the Eternal your God,
for you have stumbled in your iniquity. (Hosea 14:2)

Who is a God like You,
forgiving iniquity, passing over transgression. (Micah (7:18a)

Before Creation

Repentance, say the Rabbis, was created before the world was created.

Talmud[13]

All your days

What does R. Eliezer mean when he says, "Repent one day before your death." How can one know when that day comes? Since no person can know this, one must repent every day of one's life.

Talmud[14]

The culminating idea

To act out of love and to be willing to bear the suffering which the good and true person must inevitably bear in a world like ours, in a world which is only partly divine and which must be won for God through our efforts—that is the deepest utterance of the Rabbis and the culminating idea of Jewish religiosity and of Jewish prayer.

Henry M. Slonimsky[15]

The role of Yom Kippur

If a person sins and expects that Yom Kippur will bring forgiveness, there will be no atonement. Similarly, if one says, "I will sin and then repent, and sin again and repent," such repentance will not be accepted.

Mishnah[16]

Hosea takes sides

The Prophet makes it clear that God has a controversy with Israel (4:1). Whose part does the Prophet take in the divine controversy? ... Hosea never tries to plead for the people or to dwell upon the reasons for the people's alienation from God. He has only one perspective: the divine partner. As a result there is little understanding for human weakness. ... God is in love with Israel, but also has a passionate love of right and a burning hatred of wrong.

Abraham J. Heschel[17]

* * *

Notes

[1] We follow here the prevalent tradition of North American Ashkenazim, while some, and especially western European, communities read Joel 2:15-17 instead of Micah.

[2] So the Septuagint and the Syriac translation.

[3] Compare II Kings 18:24; the same in Isaiah 36:9: "Relying on Egypt for chariots and horsemen."

[4] We follow Rashi and Radak, who also read the first part of verse 9 as coming from Ephraim, with the rest coming from God. Ibn Ezra considers God to be the speaker throughout (so also Andersen and Freedman, in *Anchor Bible*, Hosea).

[5] The same root is found in Akkadian (Assyro-Babylonian), and was regularly employed with words for sin and had the idiomatic sense of "forgive sins."

[6] Deuteronomy 24:5.

[7] So Ibn Ezra; M. Hirsch takes the expression to be a metaphor for an unwholesome, foreign distortion of Israel's character.

[8] See T. Gaster, *Myth, Legend and Custom in the Old Testament*, pp. 645-647.

[9] Compare Ezekiel 47:18.

[10] John A. Thompson, in *Interpreter's Bible* (commentary on Joel), translates: "[God] has given the early rain for vindication."

[11] Talmud: *B. Taanit* 6a; Rashi, Ibn Ezra and others understand it as "teacher." The Dead Sea community at Qumran used *moreh litzdakah* of this verse and the similar sounding *yoreh tzedek* in Hosea 10:12 for investing its hero with the title "teacher of righteousness."

[12] Jacob Milgrom, *Encyclopaedia Judaica*, vol. 14, p. 73.

[13] *B. Pesachim* 54a.

[14] *B. Shabbat* 153a.

[15] *Essays*, p.128.

[16] *M. Yoma* 8:9.

[17] *The Prophets*, pp. 49-50.

Isaiah, chapter 57, verse 14 to chapter 58, verse 14

Introduction

Connection of haftarah and holy day:

Repentance is the theme of Yom Kippur, and true repentance is the burden of the haftarah. Fasting and prayer mark the day, but they avail nothing if they are not accompanied by acts of social justice.

The setting:

The Second Isaiah, who is the author of this prophecy,[1] shared his people's exile in Babylon (6th century B.C.E.). We do not know his real name, and at some later time his writings were attached to those of the First Isaiah, who lived well over a century earlier (see our *General Introduction*).[2]

The haftarah is not one of consolation (such as the seven haftarot before Rosh Hashanah); rather, it is a ringing, poetic challenge to his people to reform their social and spiritual life. At the time of his preaching, his fellow exiles in Babylon had apparently developed a stratified social structure that allowed the rich to exploit the poor and thereby to distort their religious life. They still prayed and fasted, and thought that this was enough. For the Prophet, this was the surest way to alienate God and thereby put the redemption of the exiles ever farther into the future.

The message:

1. The people have sinned, but God stands ready to forgive them. (57:14-21)
2. God challenges the Prophet to rebuke the people. (58:1)
3. A sharp critique of the people's "religious" life, contrasted with true devotion and the fast that God really desires. (58:2-7)
4. The reward that God has laid up for those who do right. (58:8-14)

Gates of Repentance (Reform) omits 57:14-21

HAFTARAH FOR YOM KIPPUR MORNING

Isaiah, chapter 57, verse 14 to chapter 58, verse 14

57:14. [God] says:

Build up, build up, clear a way,

remove the obstacles from My people's
way!

15. For thus says the high and exalted
One,

who inhabits eternity, whose Name is holy:
I dwell in a place high and holy,

and with the contrite and humble in spirit:
to revive the spirit of the humble,

to revive the heart of the contrite.

16. I will not always accuse,

I will not be angry forever:

for before Me breath grows faint,

and [too] the spirits of those I created.

17. The sin of their ill-gotten gains angered
me;

I struck them, I withdrew, and [still] was
angry;

yet they strayed and went as they pleased.

18. I see their ways, yet I will heal them;

I will guide them;

them and the mourners among them

I will reward with consolation.

19. I [who] create the fruit of the lips [say]:
Peace, peace to the far and to the near,
says the Eternal One,

and I will heal them.

57:14 וְאָמַר

סֹלּוּ־סֹלּוּ פַּנּוּ־דָרֶךְ

הָרִימוּ מִכְשׁוֹל מִדֶּרֶךְ עַמִּי:

15 כִּי כֹה אָמַר רָם וְנִשָּׂא

שֹׁכֵן עַד וְקָדוֹשׁ שְׁמוֹ

מָרוֹם וְקָדוֹשׁ אֶשְׁכּוֹן

וְאֶת־דַּכָּא וּשְׁפַל־רוּחַ

לְהַחֲיוֹת רוּחַ שְׁפָלִים

וּלְהַחֲיוֹת לֵב נִדְכָּאִים:

16 כִּי לֹא לְעוֹלָם אָרִיב

וְלֹא לָנֶצַח אֶקְצוֹף

כִּי־רוּחַ מִלְּפָנַי יַעֲטוֹף

וּנְשָׁמוֹת אֲנִי עָשִׂיתִי:

17 בַּעֲוֹן בִּצְעוֹ קָצַפְתִּי

וְאַכֵּהוּ הַסְתֵּר וְאֶקְצֹף

וַיֵּלֶךְ שׁוֹבָב בְּדֶרֶךְ לִבּוֹ:

18 דְּרָכָיו רָאִיתִי וְאֶרְפָּאֵהוּ

וְאַנְחֵהוּ

וַאֲשַׁלֵּם נִחֻמִים

לוֹ וְלַאֲבֵלָיו:

19 בּוֹרֵא נוּב [נִיב] שְׂפָתָיִם

שָׁלוֹם שָׁלוֹם לָרָחוֹק וְלַקָּרוֹב

אָמַר יְהֹוָה

וּרְפָאתִיו:

Commentary

57:15. *High and exalted One, who inhabits eternity, whose Name is holy.* These words—
רם ונשא, שוכן עד, קדוש (ונורא) שמו (*rom v'nissa, shochein ad, kadosh v'nora sh'mo*)—have
become part of the Shabbat and holy day morning liturgy:[3]

16. *Grows faint.* Meaning, if God persists in anger, Israel will not recover.

20. The wicked are like the churning sea
   that cannot be still;

its waters toss up seaweed and mud.

21. There is no peace, says my God, for the
   wicked.

58:1. [God says:] Cry with a full throat, do
   not hold back,

let your voice resound like a shofar:

declare to My people their transgression,

and to the House of Jacob their sin.

2. Yes, they seek Me daily,

as though eager to learn My ways,

as if they were a people that does what is
   right,

and has not forsaken the way of its God.

They ask of Me the right way,

as though delighting in the nearness of
   God.

3. *When we fast,* you say,

why do You pay no heed?

Why, when we afflict ourselves,

do You take no notice?

Because on your fast day you pursue your
   own affairs,

while you oppress all your workers!

4. Because your fasting leads only to strife
   and discord,

while you strike with cruel fist!

—Such a way of fasting on this day

shall not help you to be heard on high.

כ וְהָרְשָׁעִים כַּיָּם נִגְרָשׁ כִּי הַשְׁקֵט לֹא יוּכָל
וַיִּגְרְשׁוּ מֵימָיו רֶפֶשׁ וָטִיט:
כא אֵין שָׁלוֹם אָמַר אֱלֹהַי לָרְשָׁעִים:
נח,א קְרָא בְגָרוֹן אַל־תַּחְשֹׂךְ
כַּשּׁוֹפָר הָרֵם קוֹלֶךָ
וְהַגֵּד לְעַמִּי פִּשְׁעָם
וּלְבֵית יַעֲקֹב חַטֹּאתָם:
ב וְאוֹתִי יוֹם יוֹם יִדְרֹשׁוּן
וְדַעַת דְּרָכַי יֶחְפָּצוּן
כְּגוֹי אֲשֶׁר־צְדָקָה עָשָׂה
וּמִשְׁפַּט אֱלֹהָיו לֹא עָזָב
יִשְׁאָלוּנִי מִשְׁפְּטֵי־צֶדֶק
קִרְבַת אֱלֹהִים יֶחְפָּצוּן:
ג לָמָּה צַּמְנוּ
וְלֹא רָאִיתָ
עִנִּינוּ נַפְשֵׁנוּ
וְלֹא תֵדָע
הֵן בְּיוֹם צֹמְכֶם תִּמְצְאוּ־חֵפֶץ
וְכָל־עַצְּבֵיכֶם תִּנְגֹּשׂוּ:
ד הֵן לְרִיב וּמַצָּה תָּצוּמוּ
וּלְהַכּוֹת בְּאֶגְרֹף רֶשַׁע
לֹא־תָצוּמוּ כַיּוֹם
לְהַשְׁמִיעַ בַּמָּרוֹם קוֹלְכֶם:

Commentary

58:1. *Cry with a full throat.* That is, loudly. The challenge is addressed to the Prophet: keep on rebuking them, and do it so insistently that they are forced to listen to you.

641

5. Is this the fast I have chosen?
A day of self-affliction?
Bowing your head like a reed,
and covering yourself with sackcloth and
   ashes?
Is this what you call a fast,
a day acceptable to the Eternal?

6. Is not *this* the fast that I have chosen:
to unlock the shackles of injustice,
to loosen the ropes of the yoke,
to let the oppressed go free,
and to tear every yoke apart?

7. Surely it is to share your bread with the
   hungry,
and to bring the homeless poor into your
   house;
when you see the naked, to cover them,
never withdrawing yourself from your own
   kin.

8. Then shall your light break forth like the
   dawn,
and your healing shall quickly blossom;
your Righteous One will walk before you,
the glory of the Eternal will be your rear
   guard.

9. Then, when you call,
the Eternal will answer;
when you cry, God will say: *Here I am.*

הֲכָזֶה יִהְיֶה צוֹם אֶבְחָרֵהוּ 5
יוֹם עַנּוֹת אָדָם נַפְשׁוֹ
הֲלָכֹף כְּאַגְמֹן רֹאשׁוֹ
וְשַׂק וָאֵפֶר יַצִּיעַ
הֲלָזֶה תִּקְרָא־צוֹם
וְיוֹם רָצוֹן לַיהוָה:

הֲלוֹא זֶה צוֹם אֶבְחָרֵהוּ 6
פַּתֵּחַ חַרְצֻבּוֹת רֶשַׁע
הַתֵּר אֲגֻדּוֹת מוֹטָה
וְשַׁלַּח רְצוּצִים חָפְשִׁים
וְכָל־מוֹטָה תְּנַתֵּקוּ:

הֲלוֹא פָרֹס לָרָעֵב לַחְמֶךָ 7
וַעֲנִיִּים מְרוּדִים תָּבִיא בָיִת
כִּי־תִרְאֶה עָרֹם וְכִסִּיתוֹ
וּמִבְּשָׂרְךָ לֹא תִתְעַלָּם:

אָז יִבָּקַע כַּשַּׁחַר אוֹרֶךָ 8
וַאֲרֻכָתְךָ מְהֵרָה תִצְמָח
וְהָלַךְ לְפָנֶיךָ צִדְקֶךָ
כְּבוֹד יְהוָה יַאַסְפֶךָ:

אָז תִּקְרָא 9
וַיהוָה יַעֲנֶה
תְּשַׁוַּע וְיֹאמַר הִנֵּנִי

Commentary

5. *A day of self-affliction.* The expression derives from the Torah's law of observing Yom Kippur.[4]

7. *Cover them.* Literally, "him."

If you remove lawlessness from your midst,
the pointing finger, the malicious word;
10. if you give yourself to the hungry,
and satisfy the needs of the afflicted;
then your light shall shine in the darkness,
and your night become bright as noon;
11. the Eternal will guide you always,
filling your throat in parched lands,
and renewing your body's strength;
you shall be like a garden overflowing with
    water,
like a spring that never fails.
12. Some of you shall rebuild the ancient
    ruins,
rebuilding the foundations of ages past.
You shall be called *Repairer of the breach,*
Restorer of streets to dwell in.

אִם־תָּסִיר מִתּוֹכְךָ מוֹטָה
שְׁלַח אֶצְבַּע וְדַבֶּר־אָוֶן:
10 וְתָפֵק לָרָעֵב נַפְשֶׁךָ
וְנֶפֶשׁ נַעֲנָה תַּשְׂבִּיעַ
וְזָרַח בַּחֹשֶׁךְ אוֹרֶךָ
וַאֲפֵלָתְךָ כַּצָּהֳרָיִם:
11 וְנָחֲךָ יְהוָה תָּמִיד
וְהִשְׂבִּיעַ בְּצַחְצָחוֹת נַפְשֶׁךָ
וְעַצְמֹתֶיךָ יַחֲלִיץ
וְהָיִיתָ כְּגַן רָוֶה
וּכְמוֹצָא מַיִם אֲשֶׁר לֹא־יְכַזְּבוּ מֵימָיו:
12 וּבָנוּ מִמְּךָ חָרְבוֹת עוֹלָם
מוֹסְדֵי דוֹר־וָדוֹר תְּקוֹמֵם
וְקֹרָא לְךָ גֹּדֵר פֶּרֶץ
מְשֹׁבֵב נְתִיבוֹת לָשָׁבֶת:

Commentary

9. *Lawlessness.* Reading מֻטֶּה (*mutteh*) instead of מוֹטָה (*motah,* yoke), which better fits the context.[5]

The pointing finger. Pointing the finger at someone means also in English "to accuse with (possibly malicious) words." The figure of speech is as old as the Code of Hammurabi, where it has legal significance.

10. *Satisfy the needs of the afflicted.* As opposed to the self-indulgent self-affliction of verse 5.

11. *Filling your throat in parched lands.* A speculative translation; the Hebrew text is unclear.

13. If you keep from trampling the
  Sabbath,

from pursuing your own affairs on My holy
  day;

if you call the Sabbath *a delight*,

the holy day of the Eternal *honored*;

if you honor it,

abstaining from your [old] ways,

from carrying on your own affairs or
  speaking of them—

14. then you shall delight in the Eternal.

I will cause you to ride upon the heights of
  the earth,

and I will feed you with the portion of
  Jacob your father

—The Eternal One has spoken.

13 אִם־תָּשִׁיב מִשַּׁבָּת רַגְלֶךָ

עֲשׂוֹת חֲפָצֶיךָ בְּיוֹם קׇדְשִׁי

וְקָרָאתָ לַשַּׁבָּת עֹנֶג

לִקְדוֹשׁ יְהֹוָה מְכֻבָּד

וְכִבַּדְתּוֹ

מֵעֲשׂוֹת דְּרָכֶיךָ

מִמְּצוֹא חֶפְצְךָ וְדַבֵּר דָּבָר:

14 אָז תִּתְעַנַּג עַל־יְהֹוָה

וְהִרְכַּבְתִּיךָ עַל־בָּמֳותֵי [בָּמֳתֵי] אָרֶץ

וְהַאֲכַלְתִּיךָ נַחֲלַת יַעֲקֹב אָבִיךָ

כִּי פִּי יְהֹוָה דִּבֵּר:

Commentary

13. *Trampling the Sabbath*. Seeing the Prophet's disdain for spurious fasting and praying, the mention of strict Sabbath observance comes as somewhat of a surprise. Consequently, some scholars have suggested that this passage was not part of the original text but added later on.[6] This view is usually connected with the supposition that the Second Isaiah was an anti-ritualist, who held fast days and Shabbatot in low esteem. However, this is a misreading of the Prophet (see the essay following), and in addition, Shabbat had an important social role by giving rest to the slaves.[7]

Call the Sabbath a delight. This phrase was taken by Jews who lived in British-mandated Palestine in the 1930s as proof text for creating an atmosphere of Shabbat joy, termed *Oneg Shabbat*; later on, Diaspora congregations took up the term and the practice with receptions, songs, and joyful celebrations.

Carrying on. דַּבֵּר דָּבָר (*dabber davar*), literally "talk about something," a wordplay with a negative connotation. In a modern Chanukah song, עוצו עצה (*utzu etzah*, make your plans), the words drawn from our verse and cast in plural form have the meaning of "planning something wicked."

14. *Ride upon the heights of the earth*. Similarly, a contemporary idiom would be "ride on cloud nine."

Essay

To fast or not to fast

The unequivocal condemnation of fasting on Yom Kippur while disregarding the requirements of living a righteous life gave traditional interpreters a difficult time. [8] After all, the mitzvah of fasting stands on its own feet and is to be observed by all, whether or not the rest of their existence conforms to the ideals of Judaism.

During the 19th century, when reforming zeal gripped German and North American Jews, these and similar prophetic passages were taken as clear proof that Isaiah was concerned with the deeds of his people rather than their ritual exercises like fasting and the like. Such interpretation encouraged disregard for ritual in general, which was replaced by a devotion to social justice, in accordance with the ringing denunciation of the Prophet: "Is this the fast I have chosen?" (58:5)

But what Isaiah says in fact is far from a derogation of cultic practices; rather, it is a denunciation of hypocrisy:

Because on your fast day you pursue your own affairs,

while you oppress all your workers!

... Such a way of fasting on this day

will not help you to be heard on high. (58:3-4)

Neither Isaiah nor the other prophets denounced ritual observance as such; quite the contrary: the trampling of the Sabbath aroused the ire of Isaiah in no small measure.

"Men may not drown the cries of the oppressed with the noise of hymns, nor buy off the Lord with increased offerings. The prophets disparaged the cult when it became a substitute for righteousness.

"One cannot doubt the sacred authenticity of the cult. It had a place and procedure of its own, a sacred nimbus, a mysterious glory. It differed from all other pursuits; exceptional, striking, set apart, it conferred unique blessings." [9]

Thus, overemphasis on ritual on the one hand, and derogation of ritual on the other, both distort what Judaism demands. To fast or not to fast is *not* the question; rather, to fast in order to increase one's love for the Eternal and one's concern for the needs of others— that is what is demanded of us.

Gleanings

Peace, peace to the far and to the near,
says the Eternal One,
and I will heal them. (57:19)

There is no peace ... for the wicked. (57:21)

Is this the fast that I have chosen? (58:5)

Share your bread with the hungry,
bring the homeless poor into your house;
when you see the naked, cover them.... (58:7)

Call the Sabbath a delight (*oneg*). (58:13)

"I will not be angry forever" (57:16)

The word *netzach* (forever) also means "victory." Therefore the verse could be understood: "I will not be angry in order [to gain] victory." God said: When I gain victory I lose. I defeated the generation of the flood by destroying the world—which means I really lost. So also with the Tower of Babel and the people of Sodom and Gomorrah. But when Israel sinned with the golden calf, Moses prevailed over Me, yet I won because Israel was not destroyed. So here too: "I will not always accuse/I will not be angry in order [to gain] victory."

Midrash[10]

"If you give yourself to the hungry" (58:10)

If you have nothing else to give, give comfort; say: "My heart goes out to you that I have nothing else to give you."

Midrash[11]

Peace, peace to the far and to the near" (57:19)

They are equal to one another. Those who, by devotion to Torah and service, have been near to Me since their youth, are like those who only now are turning to Me, for "I will heal them." But regarding those who refuse to be penitent, "there is no peace, says God, for the wicked" (57:21).

Rashi

Greater than fasting

Contrition for sin is a greater penance than fasting.

Nachman of Bratslav[12]

* * *

Notes

[1] According to many scholars, the last eleven chapters of the book (56-66) are by yet another unknown author, called Trito-Isaiah (Third Isaiah), but we have chosen not to enter this controversy and have distinguished merely between the First and the Second Isaiah (see our *General Introduction*).

[2] For the sake of brevity, Second Isaiah is simply called Isaiah in this haftarah.

[3] Recited shortly before the *Chatzi Kaddish* and the *Bar'chu*.

[4] Leviticus 16:31.

[5] So JPS, taking its cue from Ezekiel 9:9.

[6] So, for instance, J. L. McKenzie, *Anchor Bible*, Isaiah, p. 165.

[7] Deuteronomy 5:13-15, which fits Isaiah's thrust in 58:3-7. But Rashi reads the verse to mean: "If you walk beyond the *t'chum* ...." This is a reference to the permissible distance that (on the Sabbath) one may walk away from one's community.

[8] For a discussion of this theme see I. Jacobson, *Chazon Hamikra*, vol. 2, pp. 370-377.

[9] A. J. Heschel, *The Prophets*, p. 196.

[10] Pesikta Rabbati 9:3. In accordance with this teaching, the midrash goes on to interpret the frequent opening of psalms, *lam'natze'ach* (which is based on the root נצח, *n-tz-ch*), "To the one who wants to be conquered."

[11] Leviticus Rabbah 34.

[12] Quoted in סדר התפלה, *Forms of Prayer for Jewish Worship*, vol. III (London: The Reform Synagogues of Great Britain, 1985), p. 971.

יוֹנָה

The Book of Jonah

Introduction

Connection of haftarah and festival:

Jonah is bidden to preach to the sinful city of Nineveh, and its citizens listen to his message and repent of their evil ways. Repentance is of course the theme of the day.

The story and its message

Jonah receives the divine order to preach to Nineveh and tries to avoid the errand by fleeing to a far-distant land. In a storm brought on by God, Jonah is cast overboard and is swallowed by a great fish. He utters a prayer, and the fish—at God's order—spits Jonah out onto the land. Jonah once again receives the divine mission; this time he proceeds and predicts the city's destruction. But when Nineveh's people repent they are forgiven, and a disgruntled Jonah is rebuked by God.

For more on Jonah, see our *General Introduction* and the essay at the end of the haftarah.

HAFTARAH FOR YOM KIPPUR AFTERNOON

The Book of Jonah

1:1. The word of the Eternal came to Jonah son of Amittai:

2. Go at once to Nineveh, that great city, and proclaim judgment upon it; for their wickedness has come before Me.

3. Jonah started out, however, to flee to Tarshish from the service of the Eternal. He went down to Joppa and found a ship going to Tarshish. He paid the fare and went aboard to sail with the others to Tarshish, away from the service of the Eternal.

4. But the Eternal cast a mighty wind upon the sea, and such a tempest came upon the sea that the ship seemed likely to break up.

5. In their fright, the sailors cried out, each to his own god; and they flung the cargo overboard to make the ship lighter. Meanwhile, Jonah had gone into the hold of the vessel, where he lay down and fell asleep.

1:1 וַיְהִי֙ דְּבַר־יְהֹוָה֙ אֶל־יוֹנָ֥ה בֶן־אֲמִתַּ֖י לֵאמֹֽר׃

2 ק֠וּם לֵ֧ךְ אֶל־נִֽינְוֵ֛ה הָעִ֥יר הַגְּדוֹלָ֖ה וּקְרָ֣א עָלֶ֑יהָ כִּֽי־עָלְתָ֥ה רָעָתָ֖ם לְפָנָֽי׃

3 וַיָּ֤קׇם יוֹנָה֙ לִבְרֹ֣חַ תַּרְשִׁ֔ישָׁה מִלִּפְנֵ֖י יְהֹוָ֑ה וַיֵּ֨רֶד יָפ֜וֹ וַיִּמְצָ֧א אֳנִיָּ֣ה ׀ בָּאָ֣ה תַרְשִׁ֗ישׁ וַיִּתֵּ֨ן שְׂכָרָ֜הּ וַיֵּ֤רֶד בָּהּ֙ לָב֤וֹא עִמָּהֶם֙ תַּרְשִׁ֔ישָׁה מִלִּפְנֵ֖י יְהֹוָֽה׃

4 וַֽיהֹוָ֗ה הֵטִ֤יל רֽוּחַ־גְּדוֹלָה֙ אֶל־הַיָּ֔ם וַיְהִ֥י סַֽעַר־גָּד֖וֹל בַּיָּ֑ם וְהָ֣אֳנִיָּ֔ה חִשְּׁבָ֖ה לְהִשָּׁבֵֽר׃

5 וַיִּֽירְא֣וּ הַמַּלָּחִ֗ים וַֽיִּזְעֲקוּ֮ אִ֣ישׁ אֶל־אֱלֹהָיו֒ וַיָּטִ֨לוּ אֶת־הַכֵּלִ֜ים אֲשֶׁ֤ר בָּֽאֳנִיָּה֙ אֶל־הַיָּ֔ם לְהָקֵ֖ל מֵֽעֲלֵיהֶ֑ם וְיוֹנָ֗ה יָרַד֙ אֶל־יַרְכְּתֵ֣י הַסְּפִינָ֔ה וַיִּשְׁכַּ֖ב וַיֵּרָדַֽם׃

Commentary

1:1. *Jonah son of Amittai.* Mentioned in the book of Kings as a prophet;[1] see our *General Introduction.*

2. *Nineveh.* An ancient Mesopotamian city, which King Sennacherib made the capital of his Assyrian empire. A coalition of Medes and Babylonians destroyed it in 612 B.C.E. It was a large city, over 7 miles (11 kilometers) in circumference (but not as large as it is made out to have been in chapter 3 verse 3).[2]

3. *Tarshish.* Probably the Spanish city of Tartessus. Jonah wanted to flee to a place that he hoped would be out of reach of God's power.[3]

Joppa. The old translation of יפו (*yafo,* beautiful), now known as Jaffa, and still a splendidly located city on the Mediterranean, directly south of and adjacent to Tel Aviv. It was mentioned by King Thutmose III of Egypt in the 15th century B.C.E.

5. *Fell asleep.* The Hebrew verb comes from the same root as תרדמה (*tardeimah*), in the story of God putting Adam into a deep sleep so that Eve could be taken from his body.[4]

6. The captain went over to him and cried out: How can you be sleeping so soundly! Up! Call upon your god! Perhaps the god will be kind to us and we will not perish.

7. The men said to one another: Let us cast lots and find out on whose account this disaster has come upon us.
So they cast lots and the lot fell on Jonah.

8. They said to him: Tell us, you who have brought this disaster upon us, what is your business? Where do you come from? What is your country, and of what people are you?

9. I am a Hebrew, he replied. I worship the Eternal, the God of Heaven, who made both sea and dry land.

10. The men were greatly terrified, and they asked him: What have you done? And when the men learned that he was fleeing from the service of the Eternal—for so he told them—

11. they said to him: What must we do to you to make the sea calm around us?
For the sea was growing more and more stormy.

12. He answered: Heave me overboard, and the surrounding sea will quiet down: for I know that this terrible storm came upon you on my account.

13. Nevertheless, the men rowed hard to regain the shore, but they could not, for the sea was growing more and more stormy around them.

6 וַיִּקְרַב אֵלָיו רַב הַחֹבֵל וַיֹּאמֶר לוֹ מַה־לְּךָ נִרְדָּם קוּם קְרָא אֶל־אֱלֹהֶיךָ אוּלַי יִתְעַשֵּׁת הָאֱלֹהִים לָנוּ וְלֹא נֹאבֵד:

7 וַיֹּאמְרוּ אִישׁ אֶל־רֵעֵהוּ לְכוּ וְנַפִּילָה גוֹרָלוֹת וְנֵדְעָה בְּשֶׁלְּמִי הָרָעָה הַזֹּאת לָנוּ וַיַּפִּלוּ גּוֹרָלוֹת וַיִּפֹּל הַגּוֹרָל עַל־יוֹנָה:

8 וַיֹּאמְרוּ אֵלָיו הַגִּידָה־נָּא לָנוּ בַּאֲשֶׁר לְמִי־הָרָעָה הַזֹּאת לָנוּ מַה־מְּלַאכְתְּךָ וּמֵאַיִן תָּבוֹא מָה אַרְצֶךָ וְאֵי־מִזֶּה עַם אָתָּה:

9 וַיֹּאמֶר אֲלֵיהֶם עִבְרִי אָנֹכִי וְאֶת־יְהֹוָה אֱלֹהֵי הַשָּׁמַיִם אֲנִי יָרֵא אֲשֶׁר־עָשָׂה אֶת־הַיָּם וְאֶת־הַיַּבָּשָׁה:

10 וַיִּירְאוּ הָאֲנָשִׁים יִרְאָה גְדוֹלָה וַיֹּאמְרוּ אֵלָיו מַה־זֹּאת עָשִׂיתָ כִּי־יָדְעוּ הָאֲנָשִׁים כִּי־מִלִּפְנֵי יְהֹוָה הוּא בֹרֵחַ כִּי הִגִּיד לָהֶם:

11 וַיֹּאמְרוּ אֵלָיו מַה־נַּעֲשֶׂה לָּךְ וְיִשְׁתֹּק הַיָּם מֵעָלֵינוּ כִּי הַיָּם הוֹלֵךְ וְסֹעֵר:

12 וַיֹּאמֶר אֲלֵיהֶם שָׂאוּנִי וַהֲטִילֻנִי אֶל־הַיָּם וְיִשְׁתֹּק הַיָּם מֵעֲלֵיכֶם כִּי יוֹדֵעַ אָנִי כִּי בְשֶׁלִּי הַסַּעַר הַגָּדוֹל הַזֶּה עֲלֵיכֶם:

13 וַיַּחְתְּרוּ הָאֲנָשִׁים לְהָשִׁיב אֶל־הַיַּבָּשָׁה וְלֹא יָכֹלוּ כִּי הַיָּם הוֹלֵךְ וְסֹעֵר עֲלֵיהֶם:

Commentary

9. *I am a Hebrew.* The identification was an old one; in the Torah, Abraham is the first to be so called.[5] Usually, the word was used to contrast an Israelite with gentiles.[6]

14. [Before throwing him overboard,] they cried out to the Eternal: Please do not let us perish on account of this man. Do not compel us to kill an innocent person! For You, O Eternal One, by Your will, have brought this about.

15. And they heaved Jonah overboard, and the sea stopped raging.

16. Then the men were greatly in awe of the Eternal; they offered a sacrifice to the Eternal, and they made vows.

2:1. Then the Eternal ordained that a huge fish swallow Jonah; and Jonah remained in the fish's belly three days and three nights.

2. And Jonah prayed to his Eternal God from the bowels of the fish,

14 וַיִּקְרְאוּ אֶל־יְהוָֹה וַיֹּאמְרוּ אָנָּה יְהוָֹה אַל־נָא נֹאבְדָה בְּנֶפֶשׁ הָאִישׁ הַזֶּה וְאַל־תִּתֵּן עָלֵינוּ דָּם נָקִיא כִּי־אַתָּה יְהוָֹה כַּאֲשֶׁר חָפַצְתָּ עָשִׂיתָ:

15 וַיִּשְׂאוּ אֶת־יוֹנָה וַיְטִלֻהוּ אֶל־הַיָּם וַיַּעֲמֹד הַיָּם מִזַּעְפּוֹ:

16 וַיִּירְאוּ הָאֲנָשִׁים יִרְאָה גְדוֹלָה אֶת־יְהוָֹה וַיִּזְבְּחוּ־זֶבַח לַיהוָֹה וַיִּדְּרוּ נְדָרִים:

2:1 וַיְמַן יְהוָֹה דָּג גָּדוֹל לִבְלֹעַ אֶת־יוֹנָה וַיְהִי יוֹנָה בִּמְעֵי הַדָּג שְׁלֹשָׁה יָמִים וּשְׁלֹשָׁה לֵילוֹת:

2 וַיִּתְפַּלֵּל יוֹנָה אֶל־יְהוָֹה אֱלֹהָיו מִמְּעֵי הַדָּגָה:

Commentary

14. *They cried out.* Literally, "they called and said."

16. *They made vows.* To do or not do something pleasing to the Eternal if only they would be saved. Making vows was a firmly established part of biblical history,[7] and Jonah himself refers to his vows in 2:10.

2:1. *Huge fish.* Popular tradition identified this legendary creature as a whale, though the text uses the common word for "fish" (דג, *dag*). The tale of a sea monster swallowing and then disgorging a human is found in other cultures too. Greek myth tells of Heracles (in Rome known as Hercules) being swallowed by a whale near the port of Joppa and living in its belly for three days.[8]

Three days and three nights. Christian scripture applied this time span to Jesus and a visit to the "bowels of the earth."[9]

2. *And Jonah prayed.* He does not, however, pray for deliverance; rather, he thanks God for past help. For this reason, many scholars believe this to have been a later addition to the book. Traditional commentators suggest that Jonah did pray for deliverance (in an unreported prayer), and when it was granted he spoke the words that follow.[10]

Bowels of the fish. Although in the previous verse the male form דג (*dag*), was used, now that the fish is, so to speak, pregnant, a female form, דגה (*dagah*), describes it.[11]

3. saying:

In my distress I called to the Eternal,

who answered me;

from the belly of Sheol I cried out,

and You heard my voice.

4. You cast me into the depths,

into the heart of the seas;

the current enveloped me,

Your billows and waves passed over me.

5. And I said:

I am cast out from Your sight,

no more to look upon Your holy Temple.

6. The waters closed in on me,

up to my throat,

as the deep surrounded me,

and weeds twined about my head;

7. To the mountains' roots I sank,

and the bars of earth closed in on me

forever;

yet You brought me up from the pit,

O my Eternal God!

8. When my soul was about to faint away

I remembered the Eternal;

and my prayer came to You,

to Your holy Temple.

9. Those who keep to false gods

forsake their loyalty,

3 וַיֹּאמֶר

קָרָאתִי מִצָּרָה לִי אֶל־יְהֹוָה

וַיַּעֲנֵנִי

מִבֶּטֶן שְׁאוֹל שִׁוַּעְתִּי

שָׁמַעְתָּ קוֹלִי:

4 וַתַּשְׁלִיכֵנִי מְצוּלָה

בִּלְבַב יַמִּים

וְנָהָר יְסֹבְבֵנִי

כָּל־מִשְׁבָּרֶיךָ וְגַלֶּיךָ עָלַי עָבָרוּ:

5 וַאֲנִי אָמַרְתִּי

נִגְרַשְׁתִּי מִנֶּגֶד עֵינֶיךָ

אַךְ אוֹסִיף לְהַבִּיט אֶל־הֵיכַל קָדְשֶׁךָ:

6 אֲפָפוּנִי מַיִם

עַד־נֶפֶשׁ

תְּהוֹם יְסֹבְבֵנִי

סוּף חָבוּשׁ לְרֹאשִׁי:

7 לְקִצְבֵי הָרִים יָרַדְתִּי

הָאָרֶץ בְּרִחֶיהָ בַעֲדִי לְעוֹלָם

וַתַּעַל מִשַּׁחַת חַיַּי

יְהֹוָה אֱלֹהָי:

8 בְּהִתְעַטֵּף עָלַי נַפְשִׁי

אֶת־יְהֹוָה זָכָרְתִּי

וַתָּבוֹא אֵלֶיךָ תְּפִלָּתִי

אֶל־הֵיכַל קָדְשֶׁךָ:

9 מְשַׁמְּרִים הַבְלֵי־שָׁוְא

חַסְדָּם יַעֲזֹבוּ:

10. but I with thankful voice
will sacrifice to You;
I will fulfill my vows,
(for) deliverance comes from the Eternal.

11. Then the Eternal ordered the fish to
spew Jonah out upon dry land.

3:1. The word of the Eternal came to Jonah
a second time:

2. Go at once to Nineveh, that great city,
and proclaim to it what I tell you.

3. Jonah went at once to Nineveh in accordance with the word of the Eternal.
Nineveh was an enormously large city,
even on a divine scale, a three days' walk
across.

4. Jonah started out and made his way into
the city the distance of one day's walk, and
proclaimed: Forty days more, and Nineveh
shall be overthrown!

5. Then the people of Nineveh believed
God. They proclaimed a fast, and all alike,
great and small, put on sackcloth.

6. When the news reached the king of
Nineveh, he rose from his throne, took off
his robe, put on sackcloth, and sat in
ashes.

7. And he had the word cried through
Nineveh: By decree of the king and his nobles: Neither human nor beast shall taste
anything! They shall not graze, and they
shall not drink water!

10 וַאֲנִ֗י בְּק֤וֹל תּוֹדָה֙
אֶזְבְּחָה־לָּ֔ךְ
אֲשֶׁ֥ר נָדַ֖רְתִּי אֲשַׁלֵּ֑מָה
יְשׁוּעָ֖תָה לַיהוָֽה׃

11 וַיֹּ֥אמֶר יְהוָ֖ה לַדָּ֑ג וַיָּקֵ֥א אֶת־יוֹנָ֖ה אֶל־
הַיַּבָּשָֽׁה׃

3:1 וַיְהִ֧י דְבַר־יְהוָ֛ה אֶל־יוֹנָ֖ה שֵׁנִ֥ית לֵאמֹֽר׃

2 ק֛וּם לֵ֥ךְ אֶל־נִֽינְוֵ֖ה הָעִ֣יר הַגְּדוֹלָ֑ה וּקְרָ֤א
אֵלֶ֙יהָ֙ אֶת־הַקְּרִיאָ֔ה אֲשֶׁ֥ר אָנֹכִ֖י דֹּבֵ֥ר אֵלֶֽיךָ׃

3 וַיָּ֣קָם יוֹנָ֗ה וַיֵּ֛לֶךְ אֶל־נִֽינְוֵ֖ה כִּדְבַ֣ר יְהוָ֑ה
וְנִֽינְוֵ֗ה הָיְתָ֤ה עִיר־גְּדוֹלָה֙ לֵֽאלֹהִ֔ים מַהֲלַ֖ךְ
שְׁלֹ֥שֶׁת יָמִֽים׃

4 וַיָּ֤חֶל יוֹנָה֙ לָב֣וֹא בָעִ֔יר מַהֲלַ֖ךְ י֣וֹם אֶחָ֑ד
וַיִּקְרָא֙ וַיֹּאמַ֔ר ע֚וֹד אַרְבָּעִ֣ים י֔וֹם וְנִֽינְוֵ֖ה
נֶהְפָּֽכֶת׃

5 וַֽיַּאֲמִ֛ינוּ אַנְשֵׁ֥י נִֽינְוֵ֖ה בֵּֽאלֹהִ֑ים וַיִּקְרְאוּ־צוֹם֙
וַיִּלְבְּשׁ֣וּ שַׂקִּ֔ים מִגְּדוֹלָ֖ם וְעַד־קְטַנָּֽם׃

6 וַיִּגַּ֤ע הַדָּבָר֙ אֶל־מֶ֣לֶךְ נִֽינְוֵ֔ה וַיָּ֙קָם֙ מִכִּסְא֔וֹ
וַיַּעֲבֵ֥ר אַדַּרְתּ֖וֹ מֵֽעָלָ֑יו וַיְכַ֣ס שַׂ֔ק וַיֵּ֖שֶׁב עַל־
הָאֵֽפֶר׃

7 וַיַּזְעֵ֗ק וַיֹּ֙אמֶר֙ בְּנִֽינְוֵ֔ה מִטַּ֧עַם הַמֶּ֛לֶךְ וּגְדֹלָ֖יו
לֵאמֹ֑ר הָאָדָ֨ם וְהַבְּהֵמָ֜ה הַבָּקָ֣ר וְהַצֹּ֗אן אַל־
יִטְעֲמוּ֙ מְא֔וּמָה אַל־יִרְע֕וּ וּמַ֖יִם אַל־יִשְׁתּֽוּ׃

Commentary

3:3. *An enormously large city.* Literally, "a large city of God."

8. Let them be covered with sackcloth, human and beast, and cry mightily to God. Let all turn back from their evil ways and from the injustice of which they are guilty.

9. Who knows but that God may turn back and relent, so that we do not perish?

10. When God saw what they were doing, how they were turning back from their evil ways, God renounced the punishment planned for them, and did not carry it out.

4:1. This displeased Jonah greatly, and he was incensed.

2. He prayed to the Eternal, saying: Eternal One! Isn't this just what I said when I was still in my own country? This is why I fled beforehand to Tarshish. For I know that You are a compassionate and gracious God, endlessly patient, abounding in love, renouncing punishment.

3. Take my life, then, for I would rather die than live [to see this].

4. The Eternal replied: Is it right that you are angry?

5. Now Jonah had left the city and found a place east of the city. He made a booth there and sat under it in the shade, until he should see what happened to the city.

8 וְיִתְכַּסּוּ שַׂקִּים הָאָדָם וְהַבְּהֵמָה וְיִקְרְאוּ אֶל־אֱלֹהִים בְּחָזְקָה וְיָשֻׁבוּ אִישׁ מִדַּרְכּוֹ הָרָעָה וּמִן־הֶחָמָס אֲשֶׁר בְּכַפֵּיהֶם:

9 מִי־יוֹדֵעַ יָשׁוּב וְנִחַם הָאֱלֹהִים וְשָׁב מֵחֲרוֹן אַפּוֹ וְלֹא נֹאבֵד:

10 וַיַּרְא הָאֱלֹהִים אֶת־מַעֲשֵׂיהֶם כִּי־שָׁבוּ מִדַּרְכָּם הָרָעָה וַיִּנָּחֶם הָאֱלֹהִים עַל־הָרָעָה אֲשֶׁר־דִּבֶּר לַעֲשׂוֹת־לָהֶם וְלֹא עָשָׂה:

4:1 וַיֵּרַע אֶל־יוֹנָה רָעָה גְדוֹלָה וַיִּחַר לוֹ:

2 וַיִּתְפַּלֵּל אֶל־יְהֹוָה וַיֹּאמַר אָנָּה יְהֹוָה הֲלוֹא־זֶה דְבָרִי עַד־הֱיוֹתִי עַל־אַדְמָתִי עַל־כֵּן קִדַּמְתִּי לִבְרֹחַ תַּרְשִׁישָׁה כִּי יָדַעְתִּי כִּי אַתָּה אֵל־חַנּוּן וְרַחוּם אֶרֶךְ אַפַּיִם וְרַב־חֶסֶד וְנִחָם עַל־הָרָעָה:

3 וְעַתָּה יְהֹוָה קַח־נָא אֶת־נַפְשִׁי מִמֶּנִּי כִּי טוֹב מוֹתִי מֵחַיָּי:

4 וַיֹּאמֶר יְהֹוָה הַהֵיטֵב חָרָה לָךְ:

5 וַיֵּצֵא יוֹנָה מִן־הָעִיר וַיֵּשֶׁב מִקֶּדֶם לָעִיר וַיַּעַשׂ לוֹ שָׁם סֻכָּה וַיֵּשֶׁב תַּחְתֶּיהָ בַּצֵּל עַד אֲשֶׁר יִרְאֶה מַה־יִּהְיֶה בָּעִיר:

Commentary

4:2. *For I know.* Jonah knows God's compassion, while the king hopes for it and says, in verse 3:9 above, "Who knows ...."[12]

A compassionate and gracious God. Jonah repeats the words that Moses heard in his vision of God.[13] Note that the key word נחם (*n-ch-m*, to have compassion, relent, renounce) appears three times: in the mouth of the king, the narrator, and Jonah.[14]

6. The Eternal God provided a gourd, which grew up over Jonah, to provide shade for his head and save him from discomfort. Jonah was very happy about the plant.

7. But the next day at dawn God provided a worm, which attacked the plant so that it withered.

8. And when the sun rose, God provided a scorching east wind; the sun beat down on Jonah's head, and he became faint. He begged for death, saying: I would rather die than live.

9. Then God said to Jonah: Is it right that you are angry about the plant?
I am so angry that I want to die, he replied.

10. Then the Eternal said: You care about the plant, yet you did not work on it nor cultivate it; it appeared overnight and perished overnight.

11. And should I not care about Nineveh, that great city, in which there are more than a hundred and twenty thousand persons who do not [yet] know their right hand from their left, and also much cattle!

6 וַיְמַן יְהֹוָה־אֱלֹהִים קִיקָיוֹן וַיַּעַל מֵעַל לְיוֹנָה לִהְיוֹת צֵל עַל־רֹאשׁוֹ לְהַצִּיל לוֹ מֵרָעָתוֹ וַיִּשְׂמַח יוֹנָה עַל־הַקִּיקָיוֹן שִׂמְחָה גְדוֹלָה:

7 וַיְמַן הָאֱלֹהִים תּוֹלַעַת בַּעֲלוֹת הַשַּׁחַר לַמָּחֳרָת וַתַּךְ אֶת־הַקִּיקָיוֹן וַיִּיבָשׁ:

8 וַיְהִי כִּזְרֹחַ הַשֶּׁמֶשׁ וַיְמַן אֱלֹהִים רוּחַ קָדִים חֲרִישִׁית וַתַּךְ הַשֶּׁמֶשׁ עַל־רֹאשׁ יוֹנָה וַיִּתְעַלָּף וַיִּשְׁאַל אֶת־נַפְשׁוֹ לָמוּת וַיֹּאמֶר טוֹב מוֹתִי מֵחַיָּי:

9 וַיֹּאמֶר אֱלֹהִים אֶל־יוֹנָה הַהֵיטֵב חָרָה־לְךָ עַל־הַקִּיקָיוֹן וַיֹּאמֶר הֵיטֵב חָרָה־לִי עַד־מָוֶת:

10 וַיֹּאמֶר יְהֹוָה אַתָּה חַסְתָּ עַל־הַקִּיקָיוֹן אֲשֶׁר לֹא־עָמַלְתָּ בּוֹ וְלֹא גִדַּלְתּוֹ שֶׁבִּן־לַיְלָה הָיָה וּבִן־לַיְלָה אָבָד:

11 וַאֲנִי לֹא אָחוּס עַל־נִינְוֵה הָעִיר הַגְּדוֹלָה אֲשֶׁר יֶשׁ־בָּהּ הַרְבֵּה מִשְׁתֵּים־עֶשְׂרֵה רִבּוֹ אָדָם אֲשֶׁר לֹא־יָדַע בֵּין־יְמִינוֹ לִשְׂמֹאלוֹ וּבְהֵמָה רַבָּה:

Commentary

6. *Gourd*. Others, "ricinous plant."[15] Apparently, the booth that had provided shade (verse 5) was insufficient to shield him from the searing sun.

Essay

The message of the book

Despite the utter simplicity of the tale, its message is far from clear, and consequently it has been interpreted in a number of ways.[16]

1. It is a story composed in the 5th century B.C.E., designed to oppose the tribal and nationalistic policies of Ezra and Nehemiah. The gentile sailors and the people of Nineveh are open to the word of the universal God.

2. The Midrash makes a hero out of Jonah by suggesting that his motivation was to protect the good name of Israel. He knew that by announcing the destruction of Nineveh there would be immediate repentance, which in turn would cause God to reverse the decree. In consequence, Jonah and his people would be seen as foolish, and Israelite prophecy would be held in low esteem by other nations.

3. The book stresses divine forgiveness when sinners repent sincerely. It propounds the same theme as does Yom Kippur (when it is read to the congregation at afternoon services.)

4. Jonah appears to think that God's power ends at the borders of Israel, when in fact it reaches to the ends of the earth. It commands the mighty sea and its largest creatures as well as a simple plant and a lowly worm.

5. The book stresses the paradoxical nature of prophecy. The prophet foretells God's severe judgment, but if people listen and act accordingly, the prophecy will not be fulfilled.

6. Justice and mercy are always in tension. Divine forgiveness does not demonstrate God's weakness, even though the sinner is not punished as God's own law demands.

7. The book is essentially the personal story of Jonah, a prophet whose weaknesses along with his qualities acquaint us with his humanness.

8. There is a startling incongruity between the readiness of the sailors and the people of Nineveh to repent, while Jonah, the Israelite prophet, does not. The story thus becomes a metaphor for the unrepentant nature of the people of Israel as a whole, and it is to this that the author of the book addresses himself.

Most likely several of these themes entered the composition of the work and have made it into a prism: as one holds it up to the light it refracts in varying colors. Like the story itself, one is left with a question rather than an answer. That in itself adds to the eternal attraction of the book.

Gleanings

Midrashim about Jonah

Not surprisingly, midrashim abound about the highly popular tale. The following represent a few samples.[17]

Jonah did not want to preach to Nineveh because he loved Israel. He knew that the inhabitants of the wicked city would repent, something that Israel—despite its many God-sent prophets—had refused to do. Nineveh's repentance would make it more likely for God to proceed with punishing the covenant people.[18]

When Jonah asked the sailors to throw him overboard, they refused at first; then they lowered him partially into the water and when the sea subsided brought him back on deck. The storm, however, started again, and eventually, with much hesitation, they surrendered Jonah to the waters.[19]

Jonah was so comfortable in the fish that he felt no need to pray for deliverance; hence God sent another fish—this time a female with 365 small fish already in its belly—and Jonah was transferred there. (This midrash is based on the succeeding forms for "fish" in verses 2:1 and 2, one male and one female; see our commentary for these verses.)[20]

The people of Nineveh did repent, but a generation later they reverted to their old ways, and the city was destroyed forthwith.[21]

Jonah was blessed with an especially pious wife. Even though women were exempt from the duty to make three pilgrimages a year to the Temple, she insisted on fulfilling the mitzvah.[22]

* * *

Notes

[1] II Kings 14:25.

[2] A mound stemming from the ancient city (now part of Mosul) is called Nebi Yunus, that is "Prophet Jonah."

[3] See our comment on Isaiah 60:9; haftarah for Ki Tavo.

[4] Genesis 2:21.

[5] Genesis 14:13.

[6] See the Torah Commentary, p. 106; "Jew" (Hebrew *y'hudi*) first appears in the book of Esther 2:5 to describe Mordecai. The word passed via Greek and Latin into early English about 1000 C.E.

[7] See Numbers chapter 6 for the institution of the *Nazir*, which deals with a class of people who have made vows or for whom vows have been made (see the Torah Commentary, p. 1060).

[8] T. Gaster, *Myth, Legend and Custom in the Old Testament*, pp. 653-655.

[9] Matthew 12:40.

[10] His prayer recalls Psalm 107:23-32, where terrified sailors thank God for deliverance.

[11] The word appears in the Tanach both in its male and female forms. (See further under *Gleanings*.)

[12] Jonah 3:9.

[13] Exodus 34:6.

[14] Jonah 3:9, 10 and 4:2.

[15] So NJPS. Ibn Ezra cites Sephardic commentators who said that it was not important to know just what the plant was.

[16] For an overview, see *Interpreter's Dictionary of the Bible, Supplementary Volume*, pp. 488-491; for midrashic and other interpretations, see *Encyclopaedia Judaica*, vol. 10, pp. 170-178.

[17] A survey may be found in L. Ginzberg, *Legends of the Jews*, vol. 4, pp. 246 ff.

[18] J. Sanhedrin 11, 30b; see further Ginzberg, *Legends of the Jews*, vol. 6, p. 349, note 27.

[19] Pirkei deRabbi Eliezer 10.

[20] Midrash Jonah.

[21] Pirkei deRabbi Eliezer 43.

[22] B. Erubin 96a.

Zechariah, chapter 14, verses 1 to 21

Introduction

Why this haftarah was chosen:

Zechariah assigns to the festival of Sukkot (Tabernacles) a central place of importance in the religious calendar of the world. Beginning with verse 16, the Prophet describes how other nations will be obliged to make their pilgrimage to Jerusalem during the Sukkot festival.

The setting:

As our *General Introduction* points out, there is much scholarly debate over chapters 9-14 of the book of Zechariah. They appear to come from a different hand, probably from a "Second Zechariah" who lived after the new Temple had been built. The central sanctuary of the people was now functioning, but the hoped-for radical changes had not materialized. The focus shifts to a more distant future, even the very end of days, when God, Israel, and the rest of humanity will live in harmony, and Jerusalem becomes the religious center of the world.

For more on Zechariah and his time, see our *General Introduction.*

The message:

1. Jerusalem will be destroyed, but afterward a new Jerusalem will arise in a completely different landscape. (1-5)

2. The new Jerusalem lives peacefully under the rule of the Eternal, who is adored throughout the world. (6-11)

3. Reprise: Once more the enemies of Israel will arise, but they will suffer a dreadful fate. (12-15)

4. The survivors of all nations will make a yearly pilgrimage to Jerusalem in order to celebrate Sukkot. (16-21)

HAFTARAH FOR THE FIRST DAY OF SUKKOT

Zechariah, chapter 14, verses 1 to 21

14:1. Behold, a day is coming for the Eternal, and your plunder shall be divided by others in your midst.

2. For I will gather all the nations against Jerusalem to wage war, and the city shall be taken, and the houses ransacked, and the women raped. Half the city shall go out to exile, but the remaining folk shall not be cut off from the city.

3. Then the Eternal will go forth and wage war against those nations, fighting as on the day of battle.

4. On that day God's feet will stand on the Mount of Olives, which faces Jerusalem on the east, and the Mount of Olives will split in half, [making] a very great valley running east and west; and one half of the mountain shall move to the north, and the other half to the south.

14:1 הִנֵּה יוֹם־בָּא לַיהוָה וְחֻלַּק שְׁלָלֵךְ בְּקִרְבֵּךְ:

2 וְאָסַפְתִּי אֶת־כָּל־הַגּוֹיִם אֶל־יְרוּשָׁלַ͏ִם לַמִּלְחָמָה וְנִלְכְּדָה הָעִיר וְנָשַׁסּוּ הַבָּתִּים וְהַנָּשִׁים תִּשָּׁגַלְנָה [תִּשָּׁכַבְנָה] וְיָצָא חֲצִי הָעִיר בַּגּוֹלָה וְיֶתֶר הָעָם לֹא יִכָּרֵת מִן־הָעִיר:

3 וְיָצָא יְהוָה וְנִלְחַם בַּגּוֹיִם הָהֵם כְּיוֹם הִלָּחֲמוֹ בְּיוֹם קְרָב:

4 וְעָמְדוּ רַגְלָיו בַּיּוֹם־הַהוּא עַל־הַר הַזֵּיתִים אֲשֶׁר עַל־פְּנֵי יְרוּשָׁלַ͏ִם מִקֶּדֶם וְנִבְקַע הַר הַזֵּיתִים מֵחֶצְיוֹ מִזְרָחָה וָיָמָּה גֵּיא גְדוֹלָה מְאֹד וּמָשׁ חֲצִי הָהָר צָפוֹנָה וְחֶצְיוֹ־נֶגְבָּה:

Commentary

4. *God's feet.* Literally, "His feet."

Will stand on the Mount of Olives. הר הזיתים (*har ha-zeitim*), the only occurrence of the term in the Tanach (elsewhere the mountain is called by different names). It is located in East Jerusalem.

Will split in half. The historian Flavius Josephus (1st century C.E.) vividly describes the astonishing topographical changes wrought by the quake mentioned in the next verse.[1]

5. And you shall flee to the valley of the hills—for the valley of the hills shall reach as far as Azal—you shall flee as you fled because of the earthquake in the days of Uzziah king of Judah, and the Eternal my God will come, [and] all the holy beings [shall be] with You.

6. On that day, there shall be no light, only cold and frost;

7. and there shall be an endless day—its timing known only to God—neither day nor night, and at evening time it shall be light.

8. And on that day the living waters shall go forth from Jerusalem—one half to the Eastern sea, the other half to the Western sea: this shall happen in the summer and the winter.

9. And the Eternal shall reign over all the earth; on that day the Eternal shall be one, and known to be one.

5 וְנַסְתֶּם גֵּיא־הָרַי כִּי־יַגִּיעַ גֵּי־הָרִים אֶל־אָצַל וְנַסְתֶּם כַּאֲשֶׁר נַסְתֶּם מִפְּנֵי הָרַעַשׁ בִּימֵי עֻזִּיָּה מֶלֶךְ־יְהוּדָה וּבָא יְהוָה אֱלֹהַי כָּל־קְדֹשִׁים עִמָּךְ:

6 וְהָיָה בַּיּוֹם הַהוּא לֹא־יִהְיֶה אוֹר יְקָרוֹת יִקְפָּאוֹן [וְקִפָּאוֹן]:

7 וְהָיָה יוֹם־אֶחָד הוּא יִוָּדַע לַיהוָה לֹא־יוֹם וְלֹא־לָיְלָה וְהָיָה לְעֵת־עֶרֶב יִהְיֶה־אוֹר:

8 וְהָיָה בַּיּוֹם הַהוּא יֵצְאוּ מַיִם־חַיִּים מִירוּשָׁלַ͏ִם חֶצְיָם אֶל־הַיָּם הַקַּדְמוֹנִי וְחֶצְיָם אֶל־הַיָּם הָאַחֲרוֹן בַּקַּיִץ וּבָחֹרֶף יִהְיֶה:

9 וְהָיָה יְהוָה לְמֶלֶךְ עַל־כָּל־הָאָרֶץ בַּיּוֹם הַהוּא יִהְיֶה יְהוָה אֶחָד וּשְׁמוֹ אֶחָד:

Commentary

5. *Azal.* Probably northeast of Jerusalem.

Uzziah. Who reigned in the 8th century B.C.E.. The First Isaiah, Hosea, and Amos date their books by his reign. Amos (1:1) also mentions the earthquake.

All the holy beings [shall be] with you. The angels will stand on guard over you, that is, Jerusalem.[2]

8. *Living waters.* Fresh drinkable waters, used as an expression of the role of Zion as the cosmic center of the universe.[3] Similarly, God is "the fountain of life."[4]

Eastern sea ... Western sea. The Dead Sea and the Mediterranean.

9. *The Eternal shall reign.* The verse has been incorporated into all Jewish religious services, for it expresses a central messianic hope.[5] (See also the essay below.)

Shall be one, and known. Or, "there will be one YHVH with one name."[6]

10. Then the whole land shall be turned [into something] like the Aravah, from Geba to Rimmon south of Jerusalem— which will remain high up; people shall dwell under its wings from the Gate of Benjamin to the site of the First Gate, to the Corner Gate, and from the Tower of Hananel to the king's winepresses.

11. People shall dwell there, safe from further killing; Jerusalem shall dwell in safety.

12. Now with this plague will the Eternal strike all the nations who waged war against Jerusalem: their flesh shall rot as they stand on their feet; their eyes shall rot in their sockets; their tongues shall rot in their mouths.

13. On that day a great panic ordained by the Eternal will fall upon them: they shall each seize hold of the other's hand, and each one's hand shall be raised against the other's.

10 יִסּוֹב כָּל־הָאָרֶץ כָּעֲרָבָה מִגֶּבַע לְרִמּוֹן נֶגֶב יְרוּשָׁלָ͏ִם וְרָאֲמָה וְיָשְׁבָה תַחְתֶּיהָ לְמִשַּׁעַר בִּנְיָמִן עַד־מְקוֹם שַׁעַר הָרִאשׁוֹן עַד־שַׁעַר הַפִּנִּים וּמִגְדַּל חֲנַנְאֵל עַד יִקְבֵי הַמֶּלֶךְ:

11 וְיָשְׁבוּ בָהּ וְחֵרֶם לֹא יִהְיֶה־עוֹד וְיָשְׁבָה יְרוּשָׁלַ͏ִם לָבֶטַח:

12 וְזֹאת תִּהְיֶה הַמַּגֵּפָה אֲשֶׁר יִגֹּף יְהוָה אֶת־כָּל־הָעַמִּים אֲשֶׁר צָבְאוּ עַל־יְרוּשָׁלָ͏ִם הָמֵק בְּשָׂרוֹ וְהוּא עֹמֵד עַל־רַגְלָיו וְעֵינָיו תִּמַּקְנָה בְחֹרֵיהֶן וּלְשׁוֹנוֹ תִּמַּק בְּפִיהֶם:

13 וְהָיָה בַּיּוֹם הַהוּא תִּהְיֶה מְהוּמַת־יְהוָה רַבָּה בָּהֶם וְהֶחֱזִיקוּ אִישׁ יַד רֵעֵהוּ וְעָלְתָה יָדוֹ עַל־יַד רֵעֵהוּ:

Commentary

10. *Aravah*. In the Tanach, it denotes the deep valley rift that extends about 160 miles (258 kilometers) southward, consisting of three segments: from the Sea of Galilee, along the Jordan River to the Dead Sea; the Dead Sea itself (the lowest surface anywhere on the globe); and from there to the Red (Reed) Sea. In modern Israel only the last stretch carries the name Aravah, which is related to *arav*, Arabia. While this area has a minimal rainfall, it will be watered miraculously from the spiritual waters flowing out of Jerusalem and thus become highly fruitful.

Geba. A levitical town northwest of Jerusalem.[7]

Rimmon. Somewhere in the south, possibly near Beersheba.

11. *Safe from further killing*. The rendering follows the Targum.

14. Judah shall join the fighting in Jerusalem, and the wealth of all the surrounding nations—a great quantity of gold, silver, and apparel—shall be gathered up.

15. Such too shall be the plague that strikes the horses, mules, camels, asses; all the animals in those camps will suffer from this plague.

16. And the survivors of all the nations who came against Jerusalem, year by year shall go up to worship the Sovereign God of heaven's hosts and celebrate the festival of Sukkot.

17. But whoever from among the families of the earth does not go up to Jerusalem to worship the Sovereign God of heaven's hosts shall have no rain.

18. And if the family of Egypt does not go up, shall it not be struck by the same plague that shall strike the [other] nations that do not go up to celebrate the festival of Sukkot?

14 וְגַם־יְהוּדָה תִּלָּחֵם בִּירוּשָׁלִָם וְאֻסַּף חֵיל כָּל־הַגּוֹיִם סָבִיב זָהָב וָכֶסֶף וּבְגָדִים לָרֹב מְאֹד:

15 וְכֵן תִּהְיֶה מַגֵּפַת הַסּוּס הַפֶּרֶד הַגָּמָל וְהַחֲמוֹר וְכָל־הַבְּהֵמָה אֲשֶׁר יִהְיֶה בַּמַּחֲנוֹת הָהֵמָּה כַּמַּגֵּפָה הַזֹּאת:

16 וְהָיָה כָּל־הַנּוֹתָר מִכָּל־הַגּוֹיִם הַבָּאִים עַל־יְרוּשָׁלִָם וְעָלוּ מִדֵּי שָׁנָה בְשָׁנָה לְהִשְׁתַּחֲוֹת לְמֶלֶךְ יְהוָה צְבָאוֹת וְלָחֹג אֶת־חַג הַסֻּכּוֹת:

17 וְהָיָה אֲשֶׁר לֹא־יַעֲלֶה מֵאֵת מִשְׁפְּחוֹת הָאָרֶץ אֶל־יְרוּשָׁלִַם לְהִשְׁתַּחֲוֹת לְמֶלֶךְ יְהוָה צְבָאוֹת וְלֹא עֲלֵיהֶם יִהְיֶה הַגָּשֶׁם:

18 וְאִם־מִשְׁפַּחַת מִצְרַיִם לֹא־תַעֲלֶה וְלֹא בָאָה וְלֹא עֲלֵיהֶם תִּהְיֶה הַמַּגֵּפָה אֲשֶׁר יִגֹּף יְהוָה אֶת־הַגּוֹיִם אֲשֶׁר לֹא יַעֲלוּ לָחֹג אֶת־חַג הַסֻּכּוֹת:

Commentary

16-17. *Celebrate the festival of Sukkot.* In messianic times all peoples will participate in the water ceremony, for rain will be abundant everywhere, but whoever does not go up thereby shows disdain for God's bounty and will be treated accordingly.

18. T*he family of Egypt.* Probably so called here because there was a large Jewish colony in the country.

Shall it not be struck .... Egypt might be tempted not to go up to Jerusalem, because it is not dependent on rain and receives its sustenance from the Nile. Since being deprived of rain will be no punishment, it will be struck by the plague—an evocation of the ten plagues at the time preceding the Exodus.[8]

19. Such shall be the punishment of Egypt and the punishment of all the nations that do not go up to celebrate the festival of Sukkot.

20. On that day, the bells of the horses shall have *Holy to the Eternal* on them, and the pots in the House of the Eternal shall be like the basins before the altar,

21. and every pot in Jerusalem and in Judah shall be holy to the God of heaven's hosts. Then all who sacrifice shall come and take of them and boil [their sacrifices] in them; and on that day there shall no longer be any traders in the house of the God of heaven's hosts.

19 זֹאת תִּֽהְיֶה חַטַּאת מִצְרָיִם וְחַטַּאת כָּל־הַגּוֹיִם אֲשֶׁר לֹא יַעֲלוּ לָחֹג אֶת־חַג הַסֻּכּֽוֹת׃

20 בַּיּוֹם הַהוּא יִֽהְיֶה עַל־מְצִלּוֹת הַסּוּס קֹדֶשׁ לַֽיהוָה וְהָיָה הַסִּירוֹת בְּבֵית יְהוָה כַּמִּזְרָקִים לִפְנֵי הַמִּזְבֵּֽחַ׃

21 וְהָיָה כָּל־סִיר בִּירֽוּשָׁלַ͏ִם וּבִֽיהוּדָה קֹדֶשׁ לַֽיהוָה צְבָאוֹת וּבָאוּ כָּל־הַזֹּבְחִים וְלָקְחוּ מֵהֶם וּבִשְּׁלוּ בָהֶם וְלֹא־יִֽהְיֶה כְנַעֲנִי עוֹד בְּבֵית־יְהוָה צְבָאוֹת בַּיּוֹם הַהֽוּא׃

Commentary

20. *Holy to the Eternal.* The same words that were inscribed on the golden frontlet of Aaron.[9]

Pots ... basins. Even pots ordinarily used for menial tasks, such as carrying away ashes from the altar, will now obtain a special degree of sanctity and become like basins used for sacrifices.[10]

21. *Traders.* Literally, Canaanites.[11] Business dealings will be banned from the Temple precincts. This verse led Christian Scriptures to formulate the tale of Jesus expelling the money changers from the Temple.[12]

Essay

What did Zechariah try to teach?[13]

The modern reader is likely to ask questions about Zechariah's oracles, which are hard to understand today. If one wonders whether his own contemporaries were able to follow his message, the answer cannot be a straightforward yes or no.

Zechariah had extraordinary visions of things to come at the end of time. They told of happenings that no one had ever experienced; they put the familiar upside down and doubtlessly created astonishment among his listeners. Could everyone follow him? Probably not; but those able to read a transcript of his words could study his predictions and ponder hidden meanings.

The modern reader does the same, but in addition has to discover afresh what to the Prophet's audience were familiar allusions. They knew about "living waters" and about the rainfall in Egypt; words like Mount of Olives, Aravah, Geba, Rimmon, Eastern and Western seas did not have to be explained to them. The location of the gates in Jerusalem required no commentary, and Sukkot and its water festival were as much part of their lives as Thanksgiving Day is in North America.

Zechariah must have startled his contemporaries with his broad visions. He was a prophet who tied the fate of Israel closely to all humanity, and by doing so spoke of the future of Israel and that of nations far off in almost the same breath. With Jerusalem the spiritual capital of the world, and idolatry having disappeared, the Eternal would be the sole divinity whom people would adore.

The Prophet did not challenge his listeners to assist God so that this might come to pass. He did not think of missionaries traveling to the far ends of the globe in order to convert others to Judaism. If religious movements elsewhere were doing this, he did not know about them. For him, the sole motive power in this spiritual revolution was God, and none other. The time of the end would come when God was ready.

Zechariah's messianic vision became in time the religious property of his people. The Eternal's name would be on all lips, Zechariah foresaw, and by his vision, fortified a sense of pride and happiness in his contemporaries. The Temple was not just another building, it was a place of holy striving, where the flame of faith was kept burning for the time when God would make Jerusalem the goal of one vast human pilgrimage.[14]

Gleanings

Words to Remember

The Eternal shall reign over all the earth;
on that day, the Eternal shall be one, and known to be one. (14:9)

Rabbinic praise

Zechariah could interpret complex biblical passages;[15] he assisted Jonathan ben Uzziel in his translation of the prophetic books into Aramaic (Targum Jonathan);[16] and when he, Haggai, and Malachi died, prophecy ceased in Israel.[17]

A rabbinic critique

While Jeremiah was often compared to Moses, later prophets did not fare as well with some Rabbis, who ascribed full prophetic power only to the prophets between Moses and Jeremiah. Haggai, Zechariah, and Malachi possessed only a trace of the old inspiration.[18]

Another source goes further:

Jeremiah was the last of the prophets. But did not Haggai, Zechariah, and Malachi prophesy after him? Rabbi Eleazar said: Yes, but their their periods of prophecy were brief; and Rabbi Samuel bar Nachman said that, while the prophecies had been entrusted to them in Jeremiah's time, they did not utter them until he had died.[19]

Haggai and Zechariah

Since Haggai and Zechariah overlap in their ministries, and since Zechariah presupposes that temple work is already recommenced, Haggai's exhortation had apparently brought about the building efforts. Whereas Haggai is largely concerned with the reluctance of the people, because of their preoccupation with personal over national affairs, to respond to the Persian mandate, Zechariah addresses the meaning and symbolism of the temple as a legitimate and legitimizing expression of the new pattern of leadership that accompanies the temple project. For Zechariah the national focus of Yehud has already been transformed, or revitalized, by the initiation of work on the temple, which he relates to the lessons of the past that is evident in the destruction and exile of Judah. It is the progress of the rebuilding of the temple that inspires Zechariah to reflect on the world around them and to advise people how to operate within it.

Carol and Eric M. Meyers[20]

* * *

Notes

1 *Antiquities* IX 10:4.

2 So Ibn Ezra and, among the moderns, C. and E. Meyers (*Anchor Bible*, Zechariah). Septuagint and Peshitta presuppose a Hebrew "with Him" (that is, God).

3 C. and E. Meyers, in *Anchor Bible*, Zechariah, p. 435.

4 Psalm 36:10. In rabbinic literature, "living waters" was understood as a reference to the teachings of Torah.

5 It comes as the final declaration of the *Aleinu* (also known as Adoration).

6 So S. D. Sperling in private communication, basing himself on Kuntillet Ajrud inscriptions that speak of a Yhvh of Samaria and a Yhvh of Teman.

7 Joshua 21:17.

8 Our rendering is suggested by the Revised Version. By reading the verse as a rhetorical question one avoids the need for omitting the word "not"—an emendation adopted by some old versions.

9 Exodus 28:36.

10 C. and E. Meyers, in *Anchor Bible*, Zechariah, p. 486.

11 So used also in Proverbs 31: 24; Job 40:30. Traders were also called "Ishmaelites" and "Midianites"; see the Torah Commentary, p. 247.

12 See Matthew 21:12 and parallels.

13 For the purpose of this essay, no distinction is made between the First Zechariah (chapters 1-8) and the Second (chapters 9-14). See our *General Introduction*.

14 Except for a very brief period (during Roman times, 1st century B.C.E./C.E.) missionary attempts were foreign to Judaism.

15 B. Eruvin 21a-b.

16 B. Megillah 3a.

17 B. Yoma 9b.

18 *Midrash Aggada* 160, on Numbers 30:11; and see the discussion of this text in Ginzberg, *Legends of the Jews*, vol. 6, pp. 385-386.

19 *Pesikta deRab Kahana*, ed. Braude and Kapstein, 13:14 (p. 264). See there also on the alleged contradiction of two of his prophecies, 16:8 (p. 297).

20 *Anchor Bible Dictionary*, vol. 6, p. 1062.

סוכות ב

First Kings, chapter 8, verses 2 to 21

Introduction

This haftarah, which deals with the dedication of the First Temple in the days of King Solomon, is part of the haftarah for Pikudei. According to Rashi, it is re-read on Sukkot because the dedication exercises were held on the festival.[1]

For more on the books of Kings, see our *General Introduction*.

HAFTARAH FOR THE SECOND DAY OF SUKKOT

First Kings, chapter 8, verses 2 to 21

8:2. All the men of Israel came together before King Solomon at the festival (of Sukkot) in the seventh month, Etanim.

ב וַיִּקָּהֲל֞וּ אֶל־הַמֶּ֤לֶךְ שְׁלֹמֹה֙ כָּל־אִ֣ישׁ יִשְׂרָאֵ֗ל בְּיֶ֧רַח הָאֵֽתָנִ֛ים בֶּחָ֖ג ה֣וּא הַחֹ֣דֶשׁ הַשְּׁבִיעִֽי:

3. When all the elders of Israel had come, the priests took up the Ark.

ג וַיָּבֹ֕אוּ כֹּ֖ל זִקְנֵ֣י יִשְׂרָאֵ֑ל וַיִּשְׂא֥וּ הַכֹּהֲנִ֖ים אֶת־הָאָרֽוֹן:

4. The priests and levites together took up the Ark of God, the Tent of Meeting, and all the holy articles of the Tent.

ד וַֽיַּעֲל֞וּ אֶת־אֲר֤וֹן יְהֹוָה֙ וְאֶת־אֹ֣הֶל מוֹעֵ֔ד וְאֶת־ כָּל־כְּלֵ֥י הַקֹּ֖דֶשׁ אֲשֶׁ֣ר בָּאֹ֑הֶל וַיַּעֲל֣וּ אֹתָ֔ם הַכֹּהֲנִ֖ים וְהַלְוִיִּֽם:

Commentary

2. *In the seventh month.* In 6:38 we are told that the Temple was completed in the *eighth* month. Many suggestions have been made to explain this discrepancy, one being that the dedication ceremonies took place eleven months after the completion of the Temple.

Etanim. The writer makes two points: one, the festival is to be celebrated in the seventh month (a rule that the rebellious King Jeroboam I had defied);[2] and further, that the pre-exilic name of the month had been Etanim, as in Phoenician. Since the books of Kings were written after 587 B.C.E. (see our *General Introduction*), readers would have known only the later name, Tishri, on the fifteenth day of which the festival of Sukkot is celebrated.[3]

"Etanim" implies either strength (coming from a completed harvest that supplies one's needs) or running water (denoting the early rains of this season).

4. *Priests and levites.* This is the only time the levites are mentioned in the book of Kings, while in Chronicles their role is repeatedly emphasized. This notable difference reflects the changing status of the levites. In earlier days (reflected in Kings) all levites were priests, but later, only the Aaronide/Zadokite levites were recognized as such, and the other levites became their assistants. Their single mention in this verse must be considered a later gloss, designed to stress the distinction between the two groups of Temple servants.

Tent of Meeting. Tradition said that this was the same portable sanctuary that Moses had used during desert days.[4]

5. Meantime, King Solomon and all the community of Israel with him were sacrificing countless, innumerable sheep and oxen.

6. Then the priests brought the Ark of the Covenant of the Eternal to its place in the Inner Sanctuary of the Temple, the Holy of Holies, under the wings of the cherubim,

7. whose outstretched wings covered the place where the Ark was standing, so that they hid the Ark and its poles.

8. The poles were so long that their tops could be seen from the Sanctuary in front of the Innermost Sanctuary, but could not be seen from outside; they are [standing] there to this day.

5 וְהַמֶּ֣לֶךְ שְׁלֹמֹ֗ה וְכָל־עֲדַ֤ת יִשְׂרָאֵל֙ הַנּוֹעָדִ֣ים עָלָ֔יו אִתּ֖וֹ לִפְנֵ֣י הָֽאָר֑וֹן מְזַבְּחִים֙ צֹ֣אן וּבָקָ֔ר אֲשֶׁ֧ר לֹֽא־יִסָּפְר֛וּ וְלֹ֥א יִמָּנ֖וּ מֵרֹֽב:

6 וַיָּבִ֣אוּ הַכֹּהֲנִ֗ים אֶת־אֲרֹ֧ון בְּרִית־יְהֹוָ֛ה אֶל־מְקוֹמ֖וֹ אֶל־דְּבִ֣יר הַבַּ֑יִת אֶל־קֹ֣דֶשׁ הַקֳּדָשִׁ֑ים אֶל־תַּ֖חַת כַּנְפֵ֥י הַכְּרוּבִֽים:

7 כִּ֤י הַכְּרוּבִים֙ פֹּֽרְשִׂ֣ים כְּנָפַ֔יִם אֶל־מְק֖וֹם הָֽאָר֑וֹן וַיָּסֹ֧כּוּ הַכְּרֻבִ֛ים עַל־הָֽאָר֖וֹן וְעַל־בַּדָּ֥יו מִלְמָֽעְלָה:

8 וַיַּֽאֲרִ֘כוּ֮ הַבַּדִּים֒ וַיֵּרָאוּ֩ רָאשֵׁ֨י הַבַּדִּ֤ים מִן־הַקֹּ֨דֶשׁ֙ עַל־פְּנֵ֣י הַדְּבִ֔יר וְלֹ֥א יֵרָא֖וּ הַח֑וּצָה וַיִּ֣הְיוּ שָׁ֔ם עַ֖ד הַיּ֥וֹם הַזֶּֽה:

Commentary

5. *Community of Israel.* עדת ישראל (*adath yisrael*) describes the people as a religious community, and therefore many synagogues have been so named.

Innumerable sheep and oxen. These sacrifices during the procession replayed what had taken place in David's time, when he brought up the Ark. During the solemn processional, special sacrifices were offered.[5]

This is not the kind of celebratory rite that moderns would choose, but it must be understood as an expression of religious fervor in days when such offerings were an integral part of religious expression. Also, animals represented a substantial part of people's wealth, and giving them up for sacrifice was their way of showing how much the Ark meant to them.

6. *Cherubim.* Angelic, winged beings that protected the entrance to the Garden of Eden.[6] Images of two such creatures symbolized the throne of God and were mounted on the Ark in the Tent.[7] In Solomon's Temple they were given prominence: the Ark featured two large cherubim above it, and they also served as decorative motifs throughout the Sanctuary.[8] The word cherub(im) is probably related to the Akkadian *karabu*, meaning to pray or bless.

In poetic language, the Eternal could be depicted as riding a cherub (see the haftarah for Ha'azinu).

7. *Its poles.* They served originally to carry the Ark, and were left in place even though portability was no longer a problem.

To this day. That is, when the book of Kings was composed.[9]

9. There was nothing in the Ark but the two stone tablets that Moses had placed there at Horeb, where the Eternal had made a covenant with the people of Israel after they had come out of Egypt.

10. As soon as the priests filed out of the Sanctuary, the cloud [of God] filled the Temple of the Eternal—

11. for on account of the cloud the priests were unable to stand and do their service: the glory of God filled the Temple of the Eternal.

12. Then Solomon said: Eternal One, You have said: *I choose to dwell in thick darkness;*

13. now I have truly built for You a royal mansion, a place where You may dwell forever.

9 אֵ֣ין בָּֽאָר֔וֹן רַ֚ק שְׁנֵ֣י לֻח֣וֹת הָֽאֲבָנִ֔ים אֲשֶׁ֨ר הִנִּ֥חַ שָׁ֛ם מֹשֶׁ֖ה בְּחֹרֵ֑ב אֲשֶׁ֨ר כָּרַ֤ת יְהוָֹה֙ עִם־בְּנֵ֣י יִשְׂרָאֵ֔ל בְּצֵאתָ֖ם מֵאֶ֥רֶץ מִצְרָֽיִם:

10 וַיְהִ֕י בְּצֵ֥את הַכֹּֽהֲנִ֖ים מִן־הַקֹּ֑דֶשׁ וְהֶֽעָנָ֥ן מָלֵ֖א אֶת־בֵּ֥ית יְהוָֹֽה:

11 וְלֹא־יָֽכְל֧וּ הַכֹּֽהֲנִ֛ים לַֽעֲמֹ֥ד לְשָׁרֵ֖ת מִפְּנֵ֣י הֶֽעָנָ֑ן כִּֽי־מָלֵ֥א כְבֽוֹד־יְהוָֹ֖ה אֶת־בֵּ֥ית יְהוָֹֽה:

12 אָ֖ז אָמַ֣ר שְׁלֹמֹ֑ה יְהוָ֣ה אָמַ֔ר לִשְׁכֹּ֖ן בָּֽעֲרָפֶֽל:

13 בָּנֹ֥ה בָנִ֛יתִי בֵּ֥ית זְבֻ֖ל לָ֑ךְ מָכ֥וֹן לְשִׁבְתְּךָ֖ עֽוֹלָמִֽים:

Commentary

9. *The two stone tablets.* There were two major traditions about the inscription written on them: one, that it was the Ten Commandments; and another, that all 613 mitzvot were miraculously incised thereon.

Horeb. A synonym for Sinai. Many biblical scholars believe that Horeb and Sinai point to two different ancient traditions about the holy mountain.

10. *Cloud [of God].* Which had led the people through the wilderness years. It symbolized the Divine Presence, which was hidden from sight.[10]

12. *Then Solomon said.* The Septuagint here has an addition, saying that the king recited these lines from an otherwise unknown work, the Book of Song. Such a title would read in Hebrew, ספר השיר (*sefer hashir*). By transposing the letters י and שׁ in the Hebrew text that the translators used, השיר would become הישר, and one would obtain ספר הישר (*sefer hayashar*), a book that is elsewhere quoted in the Tanach.[11] It apparently contained war songs and other poetry, but no copies have survived.

In thick darkness. God cannot be seen.[12]

14. With all Israel standing there, the king turned around [to face them] and blessed them.

15. He said: Praised be the Eternal, the God of Israel, whose mouth made a promise to my father David and whose hand has fulfilled it.

16. God had said: *From the time I brought My people Israel out of Egypt, I did not choose a city from all the tribes of Israel for My Temple to be built there, for My Presence to be there; but I have chosen David to rule My people Israel.*

17. My father David set his heart on building a Temple for the Presence of the Eternal, the God of Israel.

18. But God said to my father David: *You have done well to set your heart on building a Temple for My Presence,*

19. *and yet it is not you, but your son, your own offspring, who will build that Temple for My Presence.*

20. See how that promise has now been kept! I have risen to succeed my father David, and I now sit on Israel's throne, as God promised, and I have built that Temple for the Presence of the Eternal, the God of Israel.

14 וַיַּסֵּב הַמֶּלֶךְ אֶת־פָּנָיו וַיְבָרֶךְ אֵת כָּל־קְהַל יִשְׂרָאֵל וְכָל־קְהַל יִשְׂרָאֵל עֹמֵד:

15 וַיֹּאמֶר בָּרוּךְ יְהוָה אֱלֹהֵי יִשְׂרָאֵל אֲשֶׁר דִּבֶּר בְּפִיו אֵת דָּוִד אָבִי וּבְיָדוֹ מִלֵּא לֵאמֹר:

16 מִן־הַיּוֹם אֲשֶׁר הוֹצֵאתִי אֶת־עַמִּי אֶת־יִשְׂרָאֵל מִמִּצְרַיִם לֹא־בָחַרְתִּי בְעִיר מִכֹּל שִׁבְטֵי יִשְׂרָאֵל לִבְנוֹת בַּיִת לִהְיוֹת שְׁמִי שָׁם וָאֶבְחַר בְּדָוִד לִהְיוֹת עַל־עַמִּי יִשְׂרָאֵל:

17 וַיְהִי עִם־לְבַב דָּוִד אָבִי לִבְנוֹת בַּיִת לְשֵׁם יְהוָה אֱלֹהֵי יִשְׂרָאֵל:

18 וַיֹּאמֶר יְהוָה אֶל־דָּוִד אָבִי יַעַן אֲשֶׁר הָיָה עִם־לְבָבְךָ לִבְנוֹת בַּיִת לִשְׁמִי הֱטִיבֹתָ כִּי הָיָה עִם־לְבָבֶךָ:

19 רַק אַתָּה לֹא תִבְנֶה הַבָּיִת כִּי אִם־בִּנְךָ הַיֹּצֵא מֵחֲלָצֶיךָ הוּא־יִבְנֶה הַבַּיִת לִשְׁמִי:

20 וַיָּקֶם יְהוָה אֶת־דְּבָרוֹ אֲשֶׁר דִּבֵּר וָאָקֻם תַּחַת דָּוִד אָבִי וָאֵשֵׁב עַל־כִּסֵּא יִשְׂרָאֵל כַּאֲשֶׁר דִּבֶּר יְהוָה וָאֶבְנֶה הַבַּיִת לְשֵׁם יְהוָה אֱלֹהֵי יִשְׂרָאֵל:

Commentary

15. *Whose mouth.* God speaking through the prophet Nathan. [13]

16. *My Presence.* Literally, "My Name." [14] So through verse 20.

19. *And yet it is not you.* Solomon delicately omits the reason why David was not permitted to build the Temple, namely, because he had committed adultery with Bathsheba (Solomon's own mother) and had her husband killed.

21. And I have made a place there for the Ark which contains the covenant that the Eternal, leading led them out of Egypt, made with our ancestors.

וָאָשִׂ֨ם שָׁ֜ם מָק֗וֹם לָֽאָרוֹן֙ אֲשֶׁר־שָׁ֣ם בְּרִ֣ית 21
יְהֹוָ֔ה אֲשֶׁ֥ר כָּרַ֖ת עִם־אֲבֹתֵ֑ינוּ בְּהוֹצִיא֣וֹ אֹתָ֔ם
מֵאֶ֖רֶץ מִצְרָֽיִם׃

Essay

The Ark

The אָרוֹן (*aron*) that David had brought to Jerusalem and that his son Solomon installed in the Temple, went by three names: Ark of the Eternal, Ark of God, and Ark of the Covenant. It contained the two stone slabs upon which the divine commandments were inscribed and, according to tradition, the fragments of the first tablets as well.[15] In some traditions, other objects as well were preserved there (see *Gleanings*); and some biblical scholars believe that it was the place where the Urim and Thummim were kept, which the High Priest used to search out the will of God.

With two cherubim guarding it from above, the Ark became the symbolic footstool of the Almighty (see the commentary on verses 6 and 7).

Popular belief invested the Ark with miraculous qualities. Armies took it with them into battle to vouchsafe victory, and it was carried around the walls of Jericho during Joshua's assault on the city.[16] Terrible punishment was visited on those who desecrated it in any fashion.[17]

The book of Samuel contains several chapters that deal with events affecting the Ark, including its capture by the Philistines.[18] When David defeated them he recaptured the Ark and brought it to his new capital.[19] There he housed it in a special tent, where it remained until Solomon made it the centerpiece of the Temple's dedication ceremonies.

After the Babylonians destroyed the Temple in 587 B.C.E., the Ark disappeared from extant historical annals, and Ezekiel, in his extended vision of the new Temple, does not foresee it as part of the reconstituted edifice.[20] Jeremiah, however, deals with it in a remarkable passage:

"[At some future time] people shall no longer speak of the Ark of the Eternal, and shall not give it any thought. They shall not mention it or miss it, nor shall they fashion another. At that time, they shall call Jerusalem "Throne of the Eternal," and all nations shall gather there ...."[21]

Meanwhile, the Ark has survived as a symbolic presence in every synagogue. It is usually placed in or by the wall that faces Jerusalem, and an Eternal Light burns nearby or above it. The Ark contains one or more handwritten scrolls of the Torah, and the beauty of their lettering and of their ornamentation has ever been a vivid testimony to the affection of the community for the sacred parchments. Most often the synagogue Ark is a recess in the wall, but in some places of worship it is a free-standing receptacle, like the portable shrine in the Tent or the permanent Ark in Solomon's Temple.

To this day it is the focus of the congregation, and the reading from the scroll remains at the center of the religious service.

Gleanings

Midrashic musings

After the destruction of the Temple, many legends were spun about the fate of the Ark. One, recorded in the Apocrypha, tells of Jeremiah hiding it in a secret place, where it will remain undiscovered "until God finally gathers the people [of Israel] together and shows mercy upon them."[22]

King Josiah, fearing that sometime soon the city and Temple would be destroyed, hid the Ark and holy objects, lest they be desecrated by the enemy. In addition, he also hid the holy oil, the jars of manna, the rod of Aaron, and other objects.[23]

Another tradition holds that Solomon provided a secret place in the newly erected Temple, so that in cases of emergency, holy objects could be hidden there.[24]

What the Ark contained

Beyond the second curtain was the tent called The Most Holy Place. Here was a golden altar of incense, and the ark of the covenant all plated over with gold, in which were a golden jar containing the manna, and Aaron's staff which once budded,[25] and the tablets of the covenant; and above it, the cherubim of God's glory.

Christian Scriptures[26]

The voice of the poet

> Lord, with what glory wast Thou served of old,
> When Solomon's temple stood and flourished!
> Where most things were of purest gold;
> The wood was all embellished
> With flowers and carvings, mystical and rare:
> All showed the builders, craved the seers care.

George Herbert[27]

* * *

Notes

[1] Other opinions are discussed by I. Jacobson, *Chazon Hamikra*, vol. 2, pp. 399-401. Thus, according to M. Hirsch's study, *Haftoroth*, the haftarah for the first day of Sukkot focuses on the future, while the present one recalls the past.

[2] I Kings 12:32.

[3] It was in ancient days characterized by water ceremonies, celebrating the rainy season.

[4] See Tosefta Sota 13:1; the Tent is described in Exodus 33:7-10; II Chronicles 1:3-4 states that it had been housed in Gibeon, while the Ark had already been brought up by David, who made a temporary Tent to house it.

[5] II Samuel 6:13.

[6] Genesis 3:24.

[7] Exodus 25:18-20

[8] I Kings 6:25.

[9] On the time of composition, see our *General Introduction*.

[10] See Exodus 33:9-11; 40:34.

[11] Joshua 10:13; II Samuel 1:18.

[12] The expression is also found in Psalms 18:12 and 97:2 (see *Gleanings* above). The Septuagint reads: "The Eternal One established the sun in the heavens, / but God said that thick darkness would be the divine abode. / I have built a royal house for You, / an established place for you forever." The Targum has still another version: "The Eternal One has been pleased to establish the Divine Presence in Jerusalem."

[13] II Samuel 7:11-15.

[14] See the corresponding rendering in II Chronicles 6:6.

[15] In the Torah (Deuteronomy 10:2,5), Moses tells how God asked him to deposit the tablets in the Ark, and how he had carried out the command. The story of the broken tablets is found in many rabbinic sources—for example, *B. Baba Batra* 14a-b; *Sh'kalim* 49b. But another tradition is cited in Talmud Yerushalmi, *Sotah* 8:22b-c, which says that there were two arks in the Tent, one with the whole tablets and one with the broken ones. Only the latter was carried into battle.

[16] Joshua chapter 6.

[17] I Samuel 6:19; II Samuel 6:6-7.

[18] I Samuel 4:1-7:2.

[19] II Samuel 6.

[20] Ezekiel 40-48.

[21] Jeremiah 3:15-17. Some biblical scholars believe that this was written in post-exilic times and inserted into the text.

[22] II Maccabees 2:4-8.

[23] This tradition is found frequently in the Talmudim—for example, *B. Yoma* 52b, *J. Sh'kalim* 6:59c.

[24] Reported by Radak on I Kings 6:19 and II Chronicles 35:3. However, the manuscript he used has been lost. See also Ginzberg, *Legends of the Jews,* vol. 6, pp. 377-378, footnote 118.

[25] Numbers 17:8.

[26] Hebrews 9:3-5 (NEB translation).

[27] *Chapters into Verse,* p. 235.

Ezekiel, chapter 38, verse 18 to chapter 39, verse 16

Introduction

Connection of haftarah and sidra:

The reasons for the choice of this haftarah are not clear. The best explanation has been offered by Issachar Jacobson, who suggests the following: While ordinarily the haftarah has a theme or expression related to the sidra or the holiday on which it is read, here the two are in contrast to one another. The Shabbat of Sukkot is centered around the Sukkah as a place of joyous and grateful contemplation of the past. The haftarah tells us of the future, and of the total upheaval that will accompany the ultimate Redemption.[1]

The setting:

Ezekiel lived in the days before and after the destruction of the First Temple and preached in the early part of the 6th century B.C.E. He was exiled to Babylon and lived through a period of great despair after the destruction of the Temple in 587. In his mystic vision he sees an Israel restored to its land, yet still beset by enemies. But these foes, represented by Gog, will be utterly destroyed.

For more on Ezekiel and his time, see our *General Introduction*.

The message:

The haftarah contains a single theme: the destruction of Gog and his hordes. The imagery of his downfall and its aftermath have led most commentators to suggest that the Prophet was not speaking of historical times but of the end of time, brought on by the Messiah.

HAFTARAH FOR CHOL HAMO-EID SUKKOT

Ezekiel, chapter 38, verse 18 to chapter 39, verse 16

38:18. On that day, the day when Gog attacks the land of Israel, the heat of My rage will boil over, says the Eternal God.

19. In My ardent and fiery rage I declare that on that day there shall be a great earthquake in the land of Israel.

20. The fish of the sea, the birds of the sky, the beasts of the field, all that creep on the earth, and every mortal on earth shall quake before Me. Then mountains shall be thrown down, the cliffs shall collapse, and every wall shall fall to the ground.

21. To all My mountains I will summon the sword against him, says the Eternal God, and every man's sword shall be against his brother.

22. I will pass sentence upon him with plague and bloodshed, and pour down torrents of rain and hail, fire and brimstone, on him and his troops and the many peoples with him.

18 וְהָיָה בַּיּוֹם הַהוּא בְּיוֹם בּוֹא גוֹג עַל־ 38:18
אַדְמַת יִשְׂרָאֵל נְאֻם אֲדֹנָי יֱהוִֹה תַּעֲלֶה חֲמָתִי
בְּאַפִּי:

19 וּבְקִנְאָתִי בְאֵשׁ־עֶבְרָתִי דִּבַּרְתִּי אִם־לֹא
בַּיּוֹם הַהוּא יִהְיֶה רַעַשׁ גָּדוֹל עַל אַדְמַת
יִשְׂרָאֵל:

20 וְרָעֲשׁוּ מִפָּנַי דְּגֵי הַיָּם וְעוֹף הַשָּׁמַיִם וְחַיַּת
הַשָּׂדֶה וְכָל־הָרֶמֶשׂ הָרֹמֵשׂ עַל־הָאֲדָמָה וְכֹל
הָאָדָם אֲשֶׁר עַל־פְּנֵי הָאֲדָמָה וְנֶהֶרְסוּ הֶהָרִים
וְנָפְלוּ הַמַּדְרֵגוֹת וְכָל־חוֹמָה לָאָרֶץ תִּפּוֹל:

21 וְקָרָאתִי עָלָיו לְכָל־הָרַי חֶרֶב נְאֻם אֲדֹנָי
יֱהוִֹה חֶרֶב אִישׁ בְּאָחִיו תִּהְיֶה:

22 וְנִשְׁפַּטְתִּי אִתּוֹ בְּדֶבֶר וּבְדָם וְגֶשֶׁם שׁוֹטֵף
וְאַבְנֵי אֶלְגָּבִישׁ אֵשׁ וְגָפְרִית אַמְטִיר עָלָיו וְעַל־
אֲגַפָּיו וְעַל־עַמִּים רַבִּים אֲשֶׁר אִתּוֹ:

Commentary

38:18. *Gog*. A mythic king; see the essay below.

The heat of My rage. The Hebrew is highly anthropomorphic: "My fury shall rise up in My nostrils."

20. *Mountains shall be thrown down.* A similar image is found in Joel 4:16.

22. *Fire and brimstone.* Fire and sulfur. Others translate as "sulfurous fire." The expression comes from the story of the destruction of Sodom and Gomorrah.[2]

21. *Against him.* Against Gog. The translation of the sentence is speculative.

23. I will manifest My greatness and My holiness, and make Myself known in the sight of many nations. Then they shall know that I am the Eternal.

39:1. And you, mortal, prophesy against Gog and say: Thus says the Eternal God: I am against you, Gog, prince of Rosh, Meshech, and Tubal.

2. I will turn you around and decimate you and bring you up from the far north and lead you to the mountains of Israel.

3. I will strike your bow from your left hand and spill your arrows from your right hand.

4. Upon the mountains of Israel shall you fall: you, your troops and the peoples with you; I am giving you as food for birds of prey of every kind and for the beasts of the field.

5. You shall fall in the open field, for I have spoken, says the Eternal God.

6. I will send fire on Magog and those who live in safety in the coastlands; then they shall know that I am the Eternal.

7. I will make My holy Name known to My people Israel; never again will I allow My holy Name to be diminished; and the nations shall know that I am the Eternal, holy in Israel.

23 וְהִתְגַּדִּלְתִּי֙ וְהִתְקַדִּשְׁתִּ֔י וְנ֣וֹדַעְתִּ֔י לְעֵינֵ֖י גּוֹיִ֣ם רַבִּ֑ים וְיָדְע֖וּ כִּֽי־אֲנִ֥י יְהוָֽה:

39:1 וְאַתָּ֤ה בֶן־אָדָם֙ הִנָּבֵ֣א עַל־גּ֔וֹג וְאָ֣מַרְתָּ֔ כֹּ֥ה אָמַ֖ר אֲדֹנָ֣י יְהוִ֑ה הִנְנִ֤י אֵלֶ֨יךָ֙ גּ֔וֹג נְשִׂ֕יא רֹ֖אשׁ מֶ֥שֶׁךְ וְתֻבָֽל:

2 וְשֹׁבַבְתִּ֙יךָ֙ וְשִׁשֵּׁאתִ֔יךָ וְהַעֲלִיתִ֖יךָ מִיַּרְכְּתֵ֣י צָפ֑וֹן וַהֲבִאוֹתִ֖ךָ עַל־הָרֵ֥י יִשְׂרָאֵֽל:

3 וְהִכֵּיתִ֥י קַשְׁתְּךָ֖ מִיַּ֣ד שְׂמֹאולֶ֑ךָ וְחִצֶּ֕יךָ מִיַּ֥ד יְמִֽינְךָ֖ אַפִּֽיל:

4 עַל־הָרֵ֨י יִשְׂרָאֵ֜ל תִּפּ֗וֹל אַתָּה֙ וְכָל־אֲגַפֶּ֔יךָ וְעַמִּ֖ים אֲשֶׁ֣ר אִתָּ֑ךְ לְעֵ֨יט צִפּ֧וֹר כָּל־כָּנָ֛ף וְחַיַּ֥ת הַשָּׂדֶ֖ה נְתַתִּ֥יךָ לְאָכְלָֽה:

5 עַל־פְּנֵ֥י הַשָּׂדֶ֖ה תִּפּ֑וֹל כִּ֚י אֲנִ֣י דִבַּ֔רְתִּי נְאֻ֖ם אֲדֹנָ֥י יְהוִֽה:

6 וְשִׁלַּחְתִּי־אֵ֣שׁ בְּמָג֔וֹג וּבְיֹשְׁבֵ֥י הָאִיִּ֖ים לָבֶ֑טַח וְיָדְע֖וּ כִּֽי־אֲנִ֥י יְהוָֽה:

7 וְאֶת־שֵׁ֨ם קָדְשִׁ֜י אוֹדִ֗יעַ בְּת֙וֹךְ֙ עַמִּ֣י יִשְׂרָאֵ֔ל וְלֹֽא־אַחֵ֥ל אֶת־שֵׁם־קָדְשִׁ֖י ע֑וֹד וְיָדְע֤וּ הַגּוֹיִם֙ כִּֽי־אֲנִ֣י יְהוָ֔ה קָד֖וֹשׁ בְּיִשְׂרָאֵֽל:

Commentary

23. *My greatness and My holiness*. "Holiness" reflects the Hebrew root קדש (*k-d-sh*), whose basic meaning is "set apart." The natural miracles that will accompany the destruction of Gog set the Divine author apart from other gods.

39:2. *Decimate you*. Our translation is based on Radak's suggestion, that the root of שִׁשֵּׁאתִיךָ (*shisheticha*) is שש (*shesh*), meaning six. God will cut Gog's forces in sixths (we would say, decimate them). Others render the word as "drive you."[3]

6. *Magog*. See the essay below.

7. *Diminished*. Or, profaned (see our comment on 36:20 in the haftarah for Shabbat Parah).

8. It is coming! It will happen! says the Eternal God. This is the day of which I spoke!

9. The people who live in Israel's cities shall go out and make fires and burn the weapons: shields, bucklers, bows and arrows, staves and spears, and the burning shall last for seven years.

10. They shall not need to bring firewood from the fields, or cut [trees] in the forest: the weapons shall be their fuel. They shall despoil their despoilers, they shall plunder their plunderers, says the Eternal God.

11. On that day I will give to Gog a famed place as a grave in Israel, in Traveler's Valley, east of the sea. It will block travelers from getting through. There Gog and all his horde shall be buried. They shall call it the Valley of Gog's Horde.

12. It will take the people of Israel seven months to bury them, in order to cleanse the land.

13. All the people will help bury them; and they will gain fame for it on the day that I gain glory, says the Eternal God.

8 הִנֵּה בָאָה֙ וְנִֽהְיָ֔תָה נְאֻ֖ם אֲדֹנָ֣י יֱהֹוִ֑ה ה֣וּא הַיּ֔וֹם אֲשֶׁ֖ר דִּבַּֽרְתִּי:

9 וְֽיָצְא֞וּ יֹשְׁבֵ֣י ׀ עָרֵ֣י יִשְׂרָאֵ֗ל וּבִֽעֲר֡וּ וְ֠הִשִּׂ֠יקוּ בְּנֶ֨שֶׁק וּמָגֵ֤ן וְצִנָּה֙ בְּקֶ֣שֶׁת וּבְחִצִּ֔ים וּבְמַקֵּ֖ל יָ֣ד וּבְרֹ֑מַח וּבִֽעֲר֥וּ בָהֶ֛ם אֵ֖שׁ שֶׁ֥בַע שָׁנִֽים:

10 וְלֹֽא־יִשְׂא֨וּ עֵצִ֜ים מִן־הַשָּׂדֶ֗ה וְלֹ֤א יַחְטְבוּ֙ מִן־הַיְּעָרִ֔ים כִּ֥י בַנֶּ֖שֶׁק יְבַֽעֲרוּ־אֵ֑שׁ וְשָׁלְל֣וּ אֶת־שֹׁלְלֵיהֶ֗ם וּבָֽזְזוּ֙ אֶת־בֹּ֣זְזֵיהֶ֔ם נְאֻ֖ם אֲדֹנָ֥י יֱהֹוִֽה:

11 וְהָיָ֣ה בַיּ֣וֹם הַה֡וּא אֶתֵּ֣ן לְ֠גוֹג֠ מְקֽוֹם־שָׁ֨ם קֶ֜בֶר בְּיִשְׂרָאֵ֗ל גֵּ֤י הָעֹֽבְרִים֙ קִדְמַ֣ת הַיָּ֔ם וְחֹסֶ֥מֶת הִ֖יא אֶת־הָעֹֽבְרִ֑ים וְקָ֣בְרוּ שָׁ֗ם אֶת־גּוֹג֙ וְאֶת־כָּל־הֲמוֹנ֔וֹ וְקָ֣רְא֔וּ גֵּ֖יא הֲמ֥וֹן גּֽוֹג:

12 וּקְבָרוּם֙ בֵּ֣ית יִשְׂרָאֵ֔ל לְמַ֖עַן טַהֵ֣ר אֶת־הָאָ֑רֶץ שִׁבְעָ֖ה חֳדָשִֽׁים:

13 וְקָֽבְרוּ֙ כָּל־עַ֣ם הָאָ֔רֶץ וְהָיָ֥ה לָהֶ֖ם לְשֵׁ֑ם י֗וֹם הִכָּ֣בְדִ֔י נְאֻ֖ם אֲדֹנָ֥י יֱהֹוִֽה:

Commentary

10. *Weapons will be their fuel.* Spear shafts, bows and arrows.

11. *Famed place.* Literally, a place with a name. Following some versions of the text, we read שֵׁם (*shem*) instead of שָׁם (*sham*, there).

Horde. Ordinarily, המון (*hamon*, horde) refers to any type of multitude. Abraham's name is derived by the Torah from it: "Father of a multitude" (Genesis 17:5). Here it has a clearly derogatory meaning, and there will even be a town called המונה (*hamonah*), to remind people of the dreadful events that took place (verse 16).

13. *All the people.* עם הארץ (*am ha-aretz*), literally, "the people of the land." The term eventually came to mean "peasants," but in the Bible it can mean a "landholder" of high or low rank.

14. And they shall set apart people to travel the land and bury [the bodies] still on the ground, in order to cleanse it. They will take seven months for the search.

15. As the travelers pass through land, anyone who finds a human bone shall set up a signpost alongside it, until the gravediggers can come and bury it in the Valley of Gog's Horde.

16. There shall also be a town there named Horde. Thus shall they cleanse the land.

14 וְאַנְשֵׁי תָמִיד יַבְדִּילוּ עֹבְרִים בָּאָרֶץ מְקַבְּרִים אֶת־הָעֹבְרִים אֶת־הַנּוֹתָרִים עַל־פְּנֵי הָאָרֶץ לְטַהֲרָהּ מִקְצֵה שִׁבְעָה־חֳדָשִׁים יַחְקֹרוּ׃

15 וְעָבְרוּ הָעֹבְרִים בָּאָרֶץ וְרָאָה עֶצֶם אָדָם וּבָנָה אֶצְלוֹ צִיּוּן עַד קָבְרוּ אֹתוֹ הַמְקַבְּרִים אֶל־גֵּיא הֲמוֹן גּוֹג׃

16 וְגַם שֶׁם־עִיר הֲמוֹנָה וְטִהֲרוּ הָאָרֶץ׃

Essay

Gog and Magog

The haftarah envisions God as destroying a great enemy who will invade Israel from the north. The ensuing struggle will end in the utter destruction of Gog and his hordes.

It is unlikely that Ezekiel had historical figures and places in mind when (at the beginning of chapter 38) he said: "Mortal, look toward Gog, the prince of Rosh, Meshech, and Tubal, in the land of Magog." Except for Rosh these names appear as mythic ancestors in the tables of prehistoric nations,[4] but not in any annals of recorded history.

There are those who believe that Ezekiel's prophecy was a veiled diatribe against his Babylonian captors. It would have been dangerous to pillory them outright, and therefore he hid his message behind inoffensive names, whose real identity his Jewish listeners—but not the authorities—were likely to understand. Thus, Gog seemed to hint at Gûgu (or Gyges), king of Lydia, for whom his audience silently substituted the king of Babylon (see also *Gleanings*, under "A cryptogram?").

Magog too was listed in Genesis 10 as a person, but Ezekiel appears to speak of Magog as the land from which Gog hailed. In post-biblical and Christian writings Magog was taken to be the name of a person or nation, and thus "God and Magog" entered mystical and messianic literature.

Post-biblical Jewish sources considered Gog and Magog as the quintessential enemies against whom God would wage the final battle for the redemption of humanity. However, despite some considerable aggadic material, Gog and Magog did not become subjects of sustained Jewish interest.[5]

It was different in Christian tradition. Gog and Magog are mentioned in Revelations 20:8-10, which says that after a thousand years Satan will team up with Gog and Magog to fight God's people and will be defeated by a fire from heaven. Medieval scholars speculated about the time when this would take place and about those who could be called "God's people."

Lately, interest in the wars of Gog and Magog has received renewed atttention through Christian revivalism. Videos have been created that portray in graphic and violent images the coming worldwide destruction, which can be averted only if people turn to God.

Thus, it is not the peaceful vision of an Isaiah that makes an impact on the modern public, but the mystical musings of Ezekiel whose oracles of Gog and Magog are newly packaged for the sake of attracting viewers to religion.

Of course, Ezekiel envisioned an Israel that would at last have surcease from its enemies. The question may well be asked: Did he think that this would happen only at the end of time? If so, it would reveal a streak of pessimism that is otherwise not apparent in his prophecies.

Gleanings

A cryptogram?

Reading the secret code in the name Magog, one sees that Ezekiel really aimed his oracle at Babylonia:

Write the consonants of Magog backward, and one obtains g-g-m, in Hebrew גגמ. Now take the preceding letters in the Hebrew alphabet and you obtain בבל (*b-b-l, Babel*, that is, Babylon).

Louis Finkelstein [6]

Such an interpretation is, of course, possible, yet if the prophet not only employed ciphers, but deliberately expressed himself in language so obscure as completely to mystify the Babylonian secret service, it can hardly be hoped that modern scholars may lift the veil and discover the true meaning of his words.

Robert H. Pfeiffer [7]

About Gog and Magog

Two prophets of the time of Moses, Eldad and Medad,[8] already predicted the coming of Gog and Magog at the end of time. Together they announced: All nations of the world will do homage to Gog, king of Magog. They together will make war on Israel after they return from exile. But God will protect Israel and wipe its enemies out, and especially Gog of Magog and his hosts. And in response the dead souls of Israel will be revived and join in rejoicing over the good that God has wrought.

Midrash [9]

* * *

Notes

1 *Chazon Hamikra,* vol. 2, pp. 408 ff.
2 Genesis 19:24; there the words appear in the reverse order: "brimstone and fire."
3 Based on a similar word in Ethiopian.
4 Genesis 10:2.
5 For examples see Louis Ginzberg, *Legends of the Jews,* vol. 1, p. 170; vol. 2, pp. 347, 356-357; vol. 3, pp. 47, 252, 443, 455; vol. 4, pp. 66, 267, 272; vol. 6, pp. 58, 266.
6 *The Pharisees,* pp. 335-341.
7 *Religion in the Old Testament,* rev. ed., p. 534, note 4.
8 Numbers 11:16, 26-30.
9 Numbers Rabbah 15:19.

שמיני עצרת

First Kings, chapter 8, verses 54 to 66

Introduction

Connection of festival and haftarah:

The dedication ceremonies of the new Temple in Jerusalem end with a public celebration on Sukkot, and it says that on the eighth day Solomon sent the people home.[1] The eighth-day connection forms the accepted link between Sh'mini Atzeret (the eighth day of Sukkot) and the haftarah, though other connections have been suggested.[2]

The setting:

Solomon acceded to the throne of David, his father, in the second third of the 9th century B.C.E. One of his first projects was the building of the Temple, and he completed the work in a remarkably short time. Our haftarah provides the final chapter of the joyful observances.

Two other haftarot deal with the dedication ceremonies, Vayakhel and Pikudei, the latter being taken from the earlier part of Kings chapter 8. Much of the chapter's phraseology is based on the book of Deuteronomy, in order to show that God's word in the Torah has indeed been fulfilled.

For more on the book of First Kings, see our *General Introduction*.

Content of the haftarah:

1. Solomon's challenge to the people. (54-61)
2. The celebratory sacrifices listed in detail. (62-64)
3. The two weeks of rejoicing, including the observance of Sukkot. (65)
4. Solomon sends the people home on the eighth day of Sukkot, on Sh'mini Atzeret. (66)

8:54. When Solomon finished offering to the Eternal all this prayer and entreaty, he rose up from kneeling before the altar of the Eternal with his hands spread out toward heaven.

55. He stood and, in a loud voice, blessed the whole community of Israel, saying:

56. Praised be the Eternal, who has given rest to Israel, God's people, in accordance with the divine promise; not one of the good things that God promised through Moses, servant of God, has failed.

57. May the Eternal our God be with us as with our ancestors, and never leave us or forsake us,

8:54 וַיְהִי כְּכַלּוֹת שְׁלֹמֹה לְהִתְפַּלֵּל אֶל־יְהוָה אֵת כָּל־הַתְּפִלָּה וְהַתְּחִנָּה הַזֹּאת קָם מִלִּפְנֵי מִזְבַּח יְהוָה מִכְּרֹעַ עַל־בִּרְכָּיו וְכַפָּיו פְּרֻשׂוֹת הַשָּׁמָיִם:

55 וַיַּעֲמֹד וַיְבָרֶךְ אֵת כָּל־קְהַל יִשְׂרָאֵל קוֹל גָּדוֹל לֵאמֹר:

56 בָּרוּךְ יְהוָה אֲשֶׁר נָתַן מְנוּחָה לְעַמּוֹ יִשְׂרָאֵל כְּכֹל אֲשֶׁר דִּבֵּר לֹא־נָפַל דָּבָר אֶחָד מִכֹּל דְּבָרוֹ הַטּוֹב אֲשֶׁר דִּבֶּר בְּיַד מֹשֶׁה עַבְדּוֹ:

57 יְהִי יְהוָה אֱלֹהֵינוּ עִמָּנוּ כַּאֲשֶׁר הָיָה עִם־אֲבֹתֵינוּ אַל־יַעַזְבֵנוּ וְאַל־יִטְּשֵׁנוּ:

Commentary

54. *Kneeling.* Solomon's prayer posture was most unusual, but then so were other aspects of the celebration when judged by post-biblical standards. This commentary takes the position that in Solomon's time the passages in the Torah that forbid the king's entrance to the holy precincts and similar prerogatives were not as yet known. Today, too, kneeling is not part of Jewish prayer, except for the Great Aleinu on Yom Kippur afternoon, when the liturgy calls for it. Standing was the usual prayer posture.

Hands spread out. Ancient Near Eastern art regularly depicts worshippers with their hands in front of their bodies, or raised heavenward.

55. *[Solomon] blessed the whole community.* In later years, when the books of Chronicles were being composed, none but a priest could assume this kind of function. Consequently, the verses dealing with his blessing and his offering sacrifices were omitted from the otherwise parallel account.

56. *God's.* Literally, "His." In this haftarah, as in others, when referring to God we use "God" as a substitute for the Hebrew text's masculine pronoun.

Rest. מנוחה (m'nuchah) signifies not only physical rest but the security of living in the Promised Land, which is called מנוחה in the Torah.[3]

58. inclining our hearts toward God, to walk in all God's ways, and to observe the commandments, statutes, and ordinances that God commanded our ancestors.

59. And may these words of mine with which I have entreated the Eternal be near to the Eternal our God day and night, so that the needs of God's servant and people, Israel, be fulfilled, as each day requires; [and]

60. so that all the peoples of the earth may know that the Eternal is [truly] God; there is no other.

61. And may you devote yourselves with a whole heart to the Eternal your God, following God's statutes and keeping God's commandments, as [you do] on this day.

62. Then the king, and all Israel with him, offered sacrifices before the Eternal.

63. Solomon offered as his offering of well-being to the Eternal twenty-two thousand oxen and one hundred and twenty thousand sheep; thus the king and all the people of Israel dedicated the House of the Eternal.

58 לְהַטּוֹת לְבָבֵנוּ אֵלָיו לָלֶכֶת בְּכָל־דְּרָכָיו וְלִשְׁמֹר מִצְוֹתָיו וְחֻקָּיו וּמִשְׁפָּטָיו אֲשֶׁר צִוָּה אֶת־אֲבֹתֵינוּ:

59 וְיִהְיוּ דְבָרַי אֵלֶּה אֲשֶׁר הִתְחַנַּנְתִּי לִפְנֵי יְהֹוָה קְרֹבִים אֶל־יְהֹוָה אֱלֹהֵינוּ יוֹמָם וָלָיְלָה לַעֲשׂוֹת מִשְׁפַּט עַבְדּוֹ וּמִשְׁפַּט עַמּוֹ יִשְׂרָאֵל דְּבַר־יוֹם בְּיוֹמוֹ:

60 לְמַעַן דַּעַת כָּל־עַמֵּי הָאָרֶץ כִּי יְהֹוָה הוּא הָאֱלֹהִים אֵין עוֹד:

61 וְהָיָה לְבַבְכֶם שָׁלֵם עִם יְהֹוָה אֱלֹהֵינוּ לָלֶכֶת בְּחֻקָּיו וְלִשְׁמֹר מִצְוֹתָיו כַּיּוֹם הַזֶּה:

62 וְהַמֶּלֶךְ וְכָל־יִשְׂרָאֵל עִמּוֹ זֹבְחִים זֶבַח לִפְנֵי יְהֹוָה:

63 וַיִּזְבַּח שְׁלֹמֹה אֵת זֶבַח הַשְּׁלָמִים אֲשֶׁר זָבַח לַיהֹוָה בָּקָר עֶשְׂרִים וּשְׁנַיִם אֶלֶף וְצֹאן מֵאָה וְעֶשְׂרִים אָלֶף וַיַּחְנְכוּ אֶת־בֵּית יְהֹוָה הַמֶּלֶךְ וְכָל־בְּנֵי יִשְׂרָאֵל:

Commentary

60. *The Eternal is [truly] God.* This the language of Deuteronomy.[4]

63. *Twenty-two thousand oxen.* These huge figures may simply mean "a very great number, with no expense spared."[5] Still, if a large portion of the people brought individual sacrifices and shared them with the priests and their own families, the number of offerings may indeed have been enormous.[6]

The exact place where the altar stood is not specified. An old tradition relates that the locus was the stone now found in the Mosque of Omar in Jerusalem.[7]

Dedicated. ויחנכו (*va-yachn'chu*) provided the root for חנכה (*chanukah*), the festival of dedication in Maccabean times.

64. On that day the king consecrated the middle of the court in front of the House of the Eternal, for there he sacrificed the (whole) burnt-offerings and the grain offerings, and the fat portions of the offerings of well-being, because the bronze altar that was before the Eternal was too small for the (whole) burnt-offerings and the grain-offerings, and the fat portions of the offerings of well-being.

64 בַּיּוֹם הַהוּא קִדַּשׁ הַמֶּלֶךְ אֶת־תּוֹךְ הֶחָצֵר אֲשֶׁר לִפְנֵי בֵית־יְהֹוָה כִּי־עָשָׂה שָׁם אֶת־הָעֹלָה וְאֶת־הַמִּנְחָה וְאֵת חֶלְבֵי הַשְּׁלָמִים כִּי־מִזְבַּח הַנְּחֹשֶׁת אֲשֶׁר לִפְנֵי יְהֹוָה קָטֹן מֵהָכִיל אֶת־הָעֹלָה וְאֶת־הַמִּנְחָה וְאֵת חֶלְבֵי הַשְּׁלָמִים:

65. At that time Solomon celebrated the Festival before the Eternal our God, for seven days, together with all Israel, a great throng coming from Lebo-Hamath to the Wadi of Egypt.

65 וַיַּעַשׂ שְׁלֹמֹה בָעֵת־הַהִיא אֶת־הֶחָג וְכָל־יִשְׂרָאֵל עִמּוֹ קָהָל גָּדוֹל מִלְּבוֹא חֲמָת עַד־נַחַל מִצְרַיִם לִפְנֵי יְהֹוָה אֱלֹהֵינוּ שִׁבְעַת יָמִים וְשִׁבְעַת יָמִים אַרְבָּעָה עָשָׂר יוֹם:

Commentary

65. *Offering of well-being.* We sometimes translate this as "peace-offerings." Both render the meaning of the root שלם (*shalem*).

65. *The Festival.* הֶחָג (*he-chag*) denotes the Sukkot festival as the festival par excellence.[8] Biblical scholars have long considered this observance as a kind of enthronement of God, which gave to Sukkot a place of special importance. It was observed for seven days.

Seven days. The translation follows the Septuagint, while the Hebrew text reads "fourteen days," which appears to include the preceding seven days of the dedication festivities. That, of course, raised a question early on: if the Sukkot observance started on the fifteenth of Tishri (as it always does), the seven days before must have included Yom Kippur (observed on the tenth of Tishri). This would indicate that either Yom Kippur with its solemn ritual and fasting was not observed in Solomon's days, or the people proceeded to bypass the solemnity and fasting and rejoiced as a onetime exception.[9] (See *Gleanings*.)

From Lebo-Hamath to the Wadi of Egypt. Meaning "from north to south."[10] The wadi is today known as El Arish. The Tanach contains several delineations of the "ideal" borders of Israel.[11]

66. Then, on the eighth day, he dismissed them, and they blessed the king and went to their tents rejoicing and contented because of all the good that the Eternal had done for David, God's servant, and Israel, God's people.

66 בַּיּוֹם הַשְּׁמִינִי שִׁלַּח אֶת־הָעָם וַיְבָרְכוּ אֶת־הַמֶּלֶךְ וַיֵּלְכוּ לְאָהֳלֵיהֶם שְׂמֵחִים וְטוֹבֵי לֵב עַל כָּל־הַטּוֹבָה אֲשֶׁר עָשָׂה יְהֹוָה לְדָוִד עַבְדּוֹ וּלְיִשְׂרָאֵל עַמּוֹ:

Commentary

66. *On the eighth day.* It would appear that Sh'mini Atzeret, the eighth day as a festival in its own right, was not as yet known.[12]

Essay

Celebration and sacrifice

The notation that twenty-two thousand oxen and one hundred and twenty thousand sheep were slaughtered to mark the joyous occasion seems at first blush to be thoroughly at variance with modern feeling. But is it in fact?

To begin with, we need to remember that animal sacrifice (which disappeared with the destruction of the Second Temple) had a dual function.

One, it was a significant surrender of valuable property, a giving up, which is the way we use the word sacrifice today.

Two, it was the means of sharing special occasions at a festive meal. On rare occasions the animal would be totally consigned to the fire, when the Torah asked for an *olah*, a holocaust.[13] Otherwise, animal and grain offerings were consumed at the celebration. The celebrants brought their families along and, when a large animal was sacrificed, they gave a portion to the priests, for whom it was a part of their sustenance. When local shrines were still in existence, such observances were usually the times when meat was consumed.

To be sure, we have not brought such sacrifices for the last two thousand years. But great occasions continue to be observed with special dinners or banquets, where large quantities of meat are served and consumed, though without the awareness that living creatures have been slaughtered for the festivity, and without the reverence that surrounded the ancient ritual. Most certainly, God does not figure in the modern setting.[14]

Vegetarians, of course, take a different view of all of such festivities, ancient or modern. They see the killing of living creatures for the purpose of human consumption as an affront to life itself, and they remind us that God's original purpose was to permit the human species to eat the products of the soil only.[15] We did not become carnivorous until after the Flood, when God gave permission for it: "Every creature that lives shall be yours to eat; as with the green grasses, I give you all these."[16] Thus the problem that the biblical story engenders does not lie in a contrast between ancient and contemporary perceptions with regard to eating animal flesh; it lies in the debate between vegetarians and the majority.

The focus of the biblical record is not on the festive meal but on the people's joy to have completed God's Temple and to have the Holy Ark in their midst. The listing of the number of animals killed for this purpose was a way of letting us know the extent of popular happiness. We have no description of the festivities themselves; we only know how many animals were killed so that humans could celebrate.

691

Gleanings

The fourteen-day celebration

Tradition was greatly puzzled about verses 65 and 66. The way the Rabbis read the text, the fourteen days started on the 8th of Tishri and continued for seven days, that is, to the 14th of the month; on the 15th day, the festival of Sukkot began and lasted for another seven days. On the 8th day the people were sent home.

The fact that this leave-taking occurred on Sh'mini Atzeret was of less concern to the Sages than that the first seven days of celebration included Yom Kippur, which always falls on the 10th of Tishri. But, so the tale goes, a heavenly voice proclaimed that the sin of transgressing the commands of Yom Kippur was forgiven, and that everyone who had participated was assured a portion in the world to come. Clearly, the rules were set aside for this singular event.

Talmud[17]

After the destruction

When the Temple was destroyed, all sacrifices ceased and prayer took their place. But the traditional prayer book still includes supplications for the return of Temple and sacrifice; and in Jerusalem, a group of priestly descendants scrupulously study all laws pertaining to sacrifice, so that they might be ready to resume the ancient practice the moment the Messiah gives the signal.

* * *

Notes

[1] I Kings 8:66.

[2] I. Jacobson, *Chazon Hamikra*, vol. 2, pp. 417-419.

[3] Deuteronomy 12:9.

[4] 4:35.

[5] Similar language is employed by Micah 6:7 (haftarah for Balak), when he criticizes a lavish cult that ignores what is truly important.

[6] So Gray, *I and II Kings*, pp. 318 ff.

[7] For the discussions concerning this matter, see R. de Vaux, *Ancient Israel*, pp. 318 ff.

[8] So also the Mishnah; see, for example, Ta'anit 1:1.

[9] Note that the parallel account in Chronicles 7:8 ff. also knows of fourteen days, while verse 66 in our haftarah continues with "the eighth day."

[10] Lebo-Hamath is specified in Numbers 13:22 and elsewhere as the northern boundary of the land.

[11] See the map in the Torah Commentary, p. 1106. Lebo is reflected in the name of modern Libweh, in Syria, where the Orontes River originates. David received tribute from one of the kings of Hamath; II Samuel 8:9-11.

[12] See also Numbers 29:36 and the Torah Commentary, p. 1214. In the view of many modern scholars, Leviticus 23:36 was the result of a later development. See J. Morgenstern, "The Three Calendars of Ancient Israel," *HUCA*, vol. 1 (1924), pp. 36 ff.

[13] On this, see the Torah Commentary, p. 756.

[14] Abraham Isaac Kook, the late chief rabbi of Israel, considered the code of Kashrut to be in part an atonement for taking the life of animals.

[15] Genesis 1:29-30.

[16] Genesis 9:3. To be sure, there were also creatures not allowed for human consumption.

[17] B. Mo'ed Katan 9a.

Joshua, chapter 1, verses 1 to 18

Introduction

Connection of sidra and haftarah:

On Simchat Torah the last chapter of the Torah is read (V'zot Hab'rachah), followed by Genesis 1:1-2:3, thus restarting the annual cycle of Scriptural readings. The haftarah, whose language and terminology are very much in the style of Deuteronomy, takes up the story of Joshua, Moses' successor, under whose guidance the conquest of Canaan will take place.

For text and commentary, see the haftarah for V'zot Hab'rachah.

Joshua, chapter 3, verses 5 to 7, chapter 5, verse 2 to chapter 6, verses 1, and 27

Introduction

Connection of festival and haftarah:

The connection is evident: the haftarah tells the tale of the first Passover in the Promised Land.

The setting:

Joshua's assumption of leadership and the beginning of the invasion occurred about the year 1200 B.C.E., which archaeologists also consider the beginning of the Iron Age.[1] The people were poised on the east side of the Jordan, and prepared to start the campaign. They then crossed the Jordan and were ready to lay siege to Jericho—their first battle in the country.

For more on the book of Joshua, see our *General Introduction;* on Joshua and his time, see the essay in the haftarah for V'zot Hab'rachah.

The message:

The text of the haftarah is taken from various portions of the book.
1. The consecration of the people for the ensuing battle is the first stage
of the conquest. (3:5-7)
2. The males of Israel are circumcised in preparation for the battle. (5:2-9)
3. Celebration of the first Passover in Canaan. (5:10-12)
4. Joshua's encounter with the angel. (5:13-15)
5. Two postscripts:
   Jericho under siege. (6:2)
   Joshua's spreading fame. (6:3)

HAFTARAH FOR THE FIRST DAY OF PESACH

Joshua, chapter 3, verses 5 to 7, chapter 5, verse 2 to chapter 6, verses 1 and 27

3:5. Joshua said to the people: Consecrate yourselves, for tomorrow the Eternal will work wonders in your midst!

6. Then Joshua said to the priests: Lift up the Ark of the Covenant and pass in front of the people. So they lifted up the Ark of the Covenant and paraded in front of the people.

7. The Eternal then said to Joshua: This day I begin to exalt you in the sight of all Israel, so that they may know that just as I was with Moses, so will I be with you.

5:2. At that time the Eternal said to Joshua: Make knives of flint and circumcise the people of Israel a second time.

3. Joshua made some knives of flint and circumcised the people of Israel at Gibeath-ha-aralot.

4. Joshua circumcised them because all the people who had gone out of Egypt, all the males, all the warriors, had died on the journey through the wilderness, after they had gone out of Egypt.

3:5 וַיֹּ֤אמֶר יְהוֹשֻׁ֙עַ֙ אֶל־הָעָ֔ם הִתְקַדָּ֑שׁוּ כִּ֣י מָחָ֗ר יַעֲשֶׂ֧ה יְהוָ֛ה בְּקִרְבְּכֶ֖ם נִפְלָאֽוֹת:

6 וַיֹּ֤אמֶר יְהוֹשֻׁ֙עַ֙ אֶל־הַכֹּהֲנִ֣ים לֵאמֹ֔ר שְׂא֙וּ אֶת־אֲר֣וֹן הַבְּרִ֔ית וְעִבְר֖וּ לִפְנֵ֣י הָעָ֑ם וַיִּשְׂאוּ֙ אֶת־אֲר֣וֹן הַבְּרִ֔ית וַיֵּלְכ֖וּ לִפְנֵ֥י הָעָֽם:

7 וַיֹּ֤אמֶר יְהוָה֙ אֶל־יְהוֹשֻׁ֔עַ הַיּ֣וֹם הַזֶּ֗ה אָחֵל֙ גַּדֶּלְךָ֔ בְּעֵינֵ֖י כָּל־יִשְׂרָאֵ֑ל אֲשֶׁר֙ יֵֽדְעוּן֙ כִּ֚י כַּאֲשֶׁ֣ר הָיִ֣יתִי עִם־מֹשֶׁ֔ה אֶהְיֶ֖ה עִמָּֽךְ:

5:2 בָּעֵ֣ת הַהִ֗יא אָמַ֤ר יְהוָה֙ אֶל־יְהוֹשֻׁ֔עַ עֲשֵׂ֥ה לְךָ֖ חַֽרְב֣וֹת צֻרִ֑ים וְשׁ֛וּב מֹ֥ל אֶת־בְּנֵֽי־יִשְׂרָאֵ֖ל שֵׁנִֽית:

3 וַיַּֽעַשׂ־ל֥וֹ יְהוֹשֻׁ֖עַ חַֽרְב֣וֹת צֻרִ֑ים וַיָּ֙מָל֙ אֶת־בְּנֵ֣י יִשְׂרָאֵ֔ל אֶל־גִּבְעַ֖ת הָעֲרָלֽוֹת:

4 וְזֶ֥ה הַדָּבָ֖ר אֲשֶׁר־מָ֣ל יְהוֹשֻׁ֑עַ כָּל־הָעָ֣ם הַיֹּצֵ֣א מִמִּצְרַ֗יִם הַזְּכָרִ֞ים כֹּ֣ל ׀ אַנְשֵׁ֣י הַמִּלְחָמָ֗ה מֵ֤תוּ בַמִּדְבָּר֙ בַּדֶּ֔רֶךְ בְּצֵאתָ֖ם מִמִּצְרָֽיִם:

Commentary

3:5. *Consecrate yourselves.* Literally, make yourselves holy. The text draws a compelling parallel with Israel at Sinai, where the people had to consecrate themselves in specific ways.[2] Thus, sexual relations had been prohibited during the days of "meeting God."

7. *So will I be with you.* In the days of your conquest. Taking possession of the Promised Land had a religious ambiance and therefore needed ritual fitness in every respect.

5:2. *Knives of flint.* Zipporah, Moses' wife, used such a knife when she circumcised her son.[3]

Gibeath-ha-aralot. Hill of foreskins.

5. The people who had gone out of Egypt had all been circumcised, but none of the people born on the journey through the wilderness after they had gone out of Egypt had been circumcised.

6. Forty years the people of Israel had trekked in the wilderness, until all that tribal army, the warriors who had gone out of Egypt, had perished; when they did not heed the divine command, the Eternal had sworn not to let them see the land that the Eternal had sworn to their ancestors to give us, a land flowing with milk and honey.

7. God thus raised up their children in their stead, and it is them that Joshua circumcised, for they were uncircumcised, not having been circumcised on the way.

8. And when the whole tribal army's circumcision had been completed, they remained in place in the camp until they were healed.

5 כִּי־מֻלִים הָיוּ כָּל־הָעָם הַיֹּצְאִים וְכָל־הָעָם הַיִּלֹּדִים בַּמִּדְבָּר בַּדֶּרֶךְ בְּצֵאתָם מִמִּצְרַיִם לֹא־מָלוּ:

6 כִּי אַרְבָּעִים שָׁנָה הָלְכוּ בְנֵי־יִשְׂרָאֵל בַּמִּדְבָּר עַד־תֹּם כָּל־הַגּוֹי אַנְשֵׁי הַמִּלְחָמָה הַיֹּצְאִים מִמִּצְרַיִם אֲשֶׁר לֹא־שָׁמְעוּ בְּקוֹל יְהוָה אֲשֶׁר נִשְׁבַּע יְהוָה לָהֶם לְבִלְתִּי הַרְאוֹתָם אֶת־הָאָרֶץ אֲשֶׁר נִשְׁבַּע יְהוָה לַאֲבוֹתָם לָתֶת לָנוּ אֶרֶץ זָבַת חָלָב וּדְבָשׁ:

7 וְאֶת־בְּנֵיהֶם הֵקִים תַּחְתָּם אֹתָם מָל יְהוֹשֻׁעַ כִּי־עֲרֵלִים הָיוּ כִּי לֹא־מָלוּ אוֹתָם בַּדָּרֶךְ:

8 וַיְהִי כַּאֲשֶׁר־תַּמּוּ כָל־הַגּוֹי לְהִמּוֹל וַיֵּשְׁבוּ תַחְתָּם בַּמַּחֲנֶה עַד חֲיוֹתָם:

Commentary

6. *All that tribal army.* Literally, all the people who were men of war. In the previous verse, the word for the circumcised people is עם (*am*); here, the word גוי (*goy*) and again so in verse 8 is used for those who were not yet circumcised. While in the Tanach *goy* signifies any nation, including Israel,[4] the variance in terms in this context is similar to biblical passages that identify *goy* with a gentile.

When they did not heed the divine command. Joshua and Caleb had been the two men who opposed the other ten spies' counsel against proceeding with the invasion.[5]

A land flowing with milk and honey. The biblical expression for agricultural wealth.[6]

7-8. The two verses repeat the story just told, a method characteristic of biblical times when traditions were transmitted orally and reaffirmed by repetition.

9. The Eternal then said to Joshua: This day I have rolled away from you the disgrace of Egypt.

So he called that place Gilgal, its name to this day.

10. The people of Israel camped in Gilgal, on the plains of Jericho, and on the evening of the fourteenth day of the month they celebrated the Passover.

11. On the day after the Passover offering, that very day, they ate of the yield of the land, unleavened bread and parched grain.

12. Once they had eaten of the produce of the land, the manna ceased: the people of Israel no longer got manna, and that year they ate of the yield of the land of Canaan.

13. When Joshua was near Jericho, he looked up and beheld a man standing before him, with a drawn sword in his hand. Joshua went to him and said: Are you one of us, or one of our foes?

14. He replied: Neither; I am here because I command the host of the Eternal. Now I have come [for battle]. Joshua then fell face down to the earth, prostrated himself, and said: What does my lord have to say to his servant?

9 וַיֹּאמֶר יְהֹוָה אֶל־יְהוֹשֻׁעַ הַיּוֹם גַּלּוֹתִי אֶת־חֶרְפַּת מִצְרַיִם מֵעֲלֵיכֶם וַיִּקְרָא שֵׁם הַמָּקוֹם הַהוּא גִּלְגָּל עַד הַיּוֹם הַזֶּה:

10 וַיַּחֲנוּ בְנֵי־יִשְׂרָאֵל בַּגִּלְגָּל וַיַּעֲשׂוּ אֶת־הַפֶּסַח בְּאַרְבָּעָה עָשָׂר יוֹם לַחֹדֶשׁ בָּעֶרֶב בְּעַרְבוֹת יְרִיחוֹ:

11 וַיֹּאכְלוּ מֵעֲבוּר הָאָרֶץ מִמָּחֳרַת הַפֶּסַח מַצּוֹת וְקָלוּי בְּעֶצֶם הַיּוֹם הַזֶּה:

12 וַיִּשְׁבֹּת הַמָּן מִמָּחֳרָת בְּאָכְלָם מֵעֲבוּר הָאָרֶץ וְלֹא־הָיָה עוֹד לִבְנֵי יִשְׂרָאֵל מָן וַיֹּאכְלוּ מִתְּבוּאַת אֶרֶץ כְּנַעַן בַּשָּׁנָה הַהִיא:

13 וַיְהִי בִּהְיוֹת יְהוֹשֻׁעַ בִּירִיחוֹ וַיִּשָּׂא עֵינָיו וַיַּרְא וְהִנֵּה־אִישׁ עֹמֵד לְנֶגְדּוֹ וְחַרְבּוֹ שְׁלוּפָה בְּיָדוֹ וַיֵּלֶךְ יְהוֹשֻׁעַ אֵלָיו וַיֹּאמֶר לוֹ הֲלָנוּ אַתָּה אִם־לְצָרֵינוּ:

14 וַיֹּאמֶר לֹא כִּי אֲנִי שַׂר־צְבָא־יְהֹוָה עַתָּה בָאתִי וַיִּפֹּל יְהוֹשֻׁעַ אֶל־פָּנָיו אַרְצָה וַיִּשְׁתָּחוּ וַיֹּאמֶר לוֹ מָה אֲדֹנִי מְדַבֵּר אֶל־עַבְדּוֹ:

Commentary

9. *The disgrace of Egypt.* Most commentators see this as a reference to the years of slavery. Now, the people have reaffirmed their freedom by submitting themselves voluntarily to circumcision.

Gilgal. A wordplay on גלל (g-l-l), "to roll away," used earlier in the verse.

10. *Evening of the fourteenth day.* As they did at the first Passover, in Egypt prior to their exodus.[7]

13. *A man standing before him.* Recalling the angel who met Jacob in a fateful hour.[8]

15. The commander of the host of the Eternal said to Joshua: *Remove your sandals from your feet, for the place on which you stand is holy.* And Joshua did this.

6:1. Now Jericho was shut tight because of the people of Israel; none could leave or enter.

27. And the Eternal was with Joshua, and his fame spread throughout the land.

15 וַיֹּאמֶר שַׂר־צְבָא יְהוָה אֶל־יְהוֹשֻׁעַ שַׁל־
נַעַלְךָ מֵעַל רַגְלֶךָ כִּי הַמָּקוֹם אֲשֶׁר אַתָּה עֹמֵד
עָלָיו קֹדֶשׁ הוּא וַיַּעַשׂ יְהוֹשֻׁעַ כֵּן:

6:1 וִירִיחוֹ סֹגֶרֶת וּמְסֻגֶּרֶת מִפְּנֵי בְּנֵי יִשְׂרָאֵל
אֵין יוֹצֵא וְאֵין בָּא:

27 וַיְהִי יְהוָה אֶת־יְהוֹשֻׁעַ וַיְהִי שָׁמְעוֹ בְּכָל־
הָאָרֶץ:

Commentary

15. *Remove your sandals.* Literally, "Remove your sandal from your foot." The same command that God gave to Moses at the thornbush.[9]

6:1. *Now Jericho was shut tight.* The chapter continues with the story of the city wall's collapse at the blowing of the shofar.

Essay

Freedom and circumcision

The entrance of the Israelites into the Promised Land was not just another event of their history. It was the end of a journey that began when Israel was finally was freed from Egyptian slavery. That happened long before the days of which we read in our haftarah, and it had been celebrated with the first Pesach ritual and the eating of matzot.

Since then, forty long years of wanderings had passed, and now the moment of fulfillment was finally at hand. It was marked by the people submitting themselves to circumcision—not just children but adult males as well.

Though the Torah has not recorded it, a rabbinic tradition says that similarly, before the Israelites celebrated their first Pesach before their exodus from Egypt, they had themselves circumcised. [10] A generation later, in Joshua's time, they completed the circle of redemption and once again observed the commandment. Circumcision was thus seen as the recurring sign that the people were truly free.

Is it a mere coincidence that the Pesach seder and the rite of circumcision remain the two most widely observed rituals of the Jewish people? Both are aspects of our connection to God and Covenant, and both continue as cornerstones of Jewish continuity.

Gleanings

Moses and Joshua

After the crossing of the Reed [Red] Sea, the Torah reports, the people believed in God and in Moses. After the miraculous crossing of the Jordan (with the waters standing aside for the holy Ark, just as they stood aside in the Reed Sea) the people recognized that even as God had been with Moses, the divine favor now rested on Joshua.

Issachar Jacobson[11]

The man with the drawn sword

The brief encounter is introduced abruptly, without any introduction, but its purport is clear: the campaign is about to begin, and again Joshua is admonished that his task has a sacred purpose, and is not another of the many sordid instances of conquest and plunder which fill the pages of history. He must approach it with awe and reverence, seeing himself as an agent to fulfill God's design.

Abraham Cohen[12]

The need for circumcision

The Children of Israel would never have been able to possess the Promised Land if they had not first submitted themselves to circumcision. The land had originally been promised to the Ancestors under the condition that the rite would be observed.

Midrash[13]

* * *

Notes

[1] On the dating of the invasion, see the essay for the haftarah to Sh'lach L'cha.

[2] Exodus 19:10-15.

[3] Exodus 4:25.

[4] In the verse that calls on Israel to be "a kingdom of priests and a holy nation" (Exodus 19:6) the term *goy* is used.

[5] See the sidra Sh'lach L'cha, Numbers 13.

[6] On the origin of the expression see the Torah Commentary on Numbers 13:27 (p. 1109).

[7] Exodus 12:6.

[8] Genesis 32:25 ff.

[9] Exodus 3:5.

[10] The tradition is found in various midrashim—see, for example, Exodus Rabbah 19:5.

[11] *Chazon Hamikra,* vol. 2, p. 244.

[12] Joshua (*Soncino Commentary*), p. 25.

[13] Midrash Aggadah, Genesis 17:8.

Second Kings, chapter 23, verses 1 to 9 and 21 to 25

Introduction

Connection of festival and haftarah:

The Torah selection speaks of the sacred occasions of the year and starts with Shabbat and Pesach; the haftarah, beginning with verse 21, deals with a notable Pesach celebration during the reign of King Josiah of Judah.

The setting:

The political power of Assyria, which had dominated the Near East for many years, was on the wane during the last half of the 7th century B.C.E. About the year 639, young Josiah (aged eight at the time) was chosen king of Judah, after his father had been assassinated. When he grew up he became the leader of a religious revolution, which did away with Baal worship and other unacceptable cultic practices, and reinstated the worship of the Eternal as the sole religion of the land.

For more on the book of Second Kings, see our *General Introduction*.

Content of the haftarah:

1. The king orders the newly found Book of the Covenant to be read to the people and enters into a solemn pact to observe its commandments henceforth. (23:1-3)

2. The abolition of the heathen cult and its priesthood. (4-9)

3. A nationwide Passover celebration takes place, something that had not happened for hundreds of years. (21-23)

4. The fate of the practitioners of idolatry. (24)

5. In praise of Josiah. (25)

23:1. At the king's behest, all the elders of Judah and Jerusalem assembled before him.

2. The king went up to the House of the Eternal with all the people of Judah and all the inhabitants of Jerusalem, the priests, the prophets, all the people, small and great, and he read to them all the words of the Book of the Covenant that had been found in the House of the Eternal.

3. The king stood at his place and entered into a covenant before God to follow the Eternal, observing the divine commandments, testimonies, and statutes with a whole heart and soul, fulfilling the terms of the covenant written in this scroll, and all the people accepted the covenant.

4. Then the king commanded Hilkiah the high priest and the priests of the second rank and the doorkeepers to remove from the House of the Eternal all the vessels made for [the worship of] Baal and Asherah and all the hosts of heaven; he had them burned outside Jerusalem in the fields of Kidron and brought the ashes to Bethel.

23:1 וַיִּשְׁלַח הַמֶּלֶךְ וַיַּאַסְפוּ אֵלָיו כָּל־זִקְנֵי יְהוּדָה וִירוּשָׁלָ͏ִם:

2 וַיַּעַל הַמֶּלֶךְ בֵּית־יְהֹוָה וְכָל־אִישׁ יְהוּדָה וְכָל־הָעָם לְמִקָּטֹן וְעַד־גָּדוֹל וְכָל־יֹשְׁבֵי יְרוּשָׁלַ͏ִם אִתּוֹ וְהַכֹּהֲנִים וְהַנְּבִיאִים וַיִּקְרָא בְאָזְנֵיהֶם אֶת־כָּל־דִּבְרֵי סֵפֶר הַבְּרִית הַנִּמְצָא בְּבֵית יְהֹוָה:

3 וַיַּעֲמֹד הַמֶּלֶךְ עַל־הָעַמּוּד וַיִּכְרֹת אֶת־הַבְּרִית לִפְנֵי יְהֹוָה לָלֶכֶת אַחַר יְהֹוָה וְלִשְׁמֹר מִצְוֺתָיו וְאֶת־עֵדְוֺתָיו וְאֶת־חֻקֹּתָיו בְּכָל־לֵב וּבְכָל־נֶפֶשׁ לְהָקִים אֶת־דִּבְרֵי הַבְּרִית הַזֹּאת הַכְּתֻבִים עַל־הַסֵּפֶר הַזֶּה וַיַּעֲמֹד כָּל־הָעָם בַּבְּרִית:

4 וַיְצַו הַמֶּלֶךְ אֶת־חִלְקִיָּהוּ הַכֹּהֵן הַגָּדוֹל וְאֶת־כֹּהֲנֵי הַמִּשְׁנֶה וְאֶת־שֹׁמְרֵי הַסַּף לְהוֹצִיא מֵהֵיכַל יְהֹוָה אֵת כָּל־הַכֵּלִים הָעֲשׂוּיִם לַבַּעַל וְלָאֲשֵׁרָה וּלְכֹל צְבָא הַשָּׁמָיִם וַיִּשְׂרְפֵם מִחוּץ לִירוּשָׁלַ͏ִם בְּשַׁדְמוֹת קִדְרוֹן וְנָשָׂא אֶת־עֲפָרָם בֵּית־אֵל:

Commentary

3. *The king stood at his place.* Reading עָמְדוֹ (*omdo*) instead of עַמּוּד (*ammud,* pillar), as in the parallel passage in Chronicles.[1] The king evidently had a special place in the Temple assigned to him.

4. *Fields of Kidron.* Outside of Jerusalem.

5. He made an end to the idolatrous priests whom the kings of Judah had appointed to make offerings on the shrines in the cities of Judah and the environs of Jerusalem, who had made offerings to Baal, to the sun and moon and constellations, to all the hosts of heaven.

6. He brought the Asherah from the House of the Eternal to the Wadi Kidron outside Jerusalem, burning it there and grinding it to dust, and throwing the dust into potter's field.

7. And he pulled down the apartments of the sacred prostitutes in the House of the Eternal, where the women would weave garments for Asherah.

8. Then he brought the priests from the cities of Judah and desecrated the shrines where the priests had made offerings— from Geva to Beersheba; and he pulled

5 וְהִשְׁבִּית אֶת־הַכְּמָרִים אֲשֶׁר נָתְנוּ מַלְכֵי יְהוּדָה וַיְקַטֵּר בַּבָּמוֹת בְּעָרֵי יְהוּדָה וּמְסִבֵּי יְרוּשָׁלָ͏ִם וְאֶת־הַמְקַטְּרִים לַבַּעַל לַשֶּׁמֶשׁ וְלַיָּרֵחַ וְלַמַּזָּלוֹת וּלְכֹל צְבָא הַשָּׁמָיִם:

6 וַיֹּצֵא אֶת־הָאֲשֵׁרָה מִבֵּית יְהוָה מִחוּץ לִירוּשָׁלַ͏ִם אֶל־נַחַל קִדְרוֹן וַיִּשְׂרֹף אֹתָהּ בְּנַחַל קִדְרוֹן וַיָּדֶק לְעָפָר וַיַּשְׁלֵךְ אֶת־עֲפָרָהּ עַל־קֶבֶר בְּנֵי הָעָם:

7 וַיִּתֹּץ אֶת־בָּתֵּי הַקְּדֵשִׁים אֲשֶׁר בְּבֵית יְהוָה אֲשֶׁר הַנָּשִׁים אֹרְגוֹת שָׁם בָּתִּים לָאֲשֵׁרָה:

8 וַיָּבֵא אֶת־כָּל־הַכֹּהֲנִים מֵעָרֵי יְהוּדָה וַיְטַמֵּא אֶת־הַבָּמוֹת אֲשֶׁר קִטְּרוּ־שָׁמָּה הַכֹּהֲנִים מִגֶּבַע

Commentary

5. *Idolatrous priests.* They are called כְּמָרִים (*k'marim*) instead of כֹּהֲנִים (*kohanim*), a term reserved for the Jewish priests. In modern Hebrew, *k'marim* denotes all non-Jewish religious officiants.

7. *Sacred prostitutes.* Who offered their services at shrines as part of pagan fertility rites. They are called קְדֵשִׁים (*k'deshim*), with the masculine plural ending, a term that probably includes both male and female prostitutes. The word has the same root as *kadosh*, holy, for the practice was considered sacred in pagan cults. It was specifically outlawed by the very book that the king had made his new religious guide.[2]

8. *Geva.* Formerly believed to be a place at the northern end of Judah, where it bordered on Benjamin, but now identified with a town in Assyrian-held territory farther north, in what formerly had been the kingdom of Israel. This would indicate that the reform had spread beyond Judah's borders, which led to a battle with Egypt, bent on supporting the Assyrians. Josiah died during the campaign.[3]

down the shrines of the gates, at the entrance of the gate of Joshua, the city governor, located on the left [as one enters] in the city gate.

9. The priests of the shrines, however, did not [dare to] ascend to the altar of the Eternal in Jerusalem, but they ate unleavened bread among their brethren.

21. The king commanded all the people, saying: Celebrate the Passover of the Eternal your God, as it is written in this Book of the Covenant.

22. Such a Passover had not been celebrated since the time when the Judges had led Israel, throughout the time of the kings of Judah and Israel.

23. Only in the eighteenth year of King Josiah's reign was the Passover of the Eternal so celebrated in Jerusalem.

עַד־בְּאֵר שֶׁבַע וְנָתַץ אֶת־בָּמוֹת הַשְּׁעָרִים
אֲשֶׁר־פֶּתַח שַׁעַר יְהוֹשֻׁעַ שַׂר־הָעִיר אֲשֶׁר־עַל־
שְׂמֹאול אִישׁ בְּשַׁעַר הָעִיר:

9 אַךְ לֹא יַעֲלוּ כֹּהֲנֵי הַבָּמוֹת אֶל־מִזְבַּח יְהוָה
בִּירוּשָׁלָ͏ִם כִּי אִם־אָכְלוּ מַצּוֹת בְּתוֹךְ אֲחֵיהֶם:

21 וַיְצַו הַמֶּלֶךְ אֶת־כָּל־הָעָם לֵאמֹר עֲשׂוּ פֶסַח
לַיהוָה אֱלֹהֵיכֶם כַּכָּתוּב עַל סֵפֶר הַבְּרִית
הַזֶּה:

22 כִּי לֹא נַעֲשָׂה כַּפֶּסַח הַזֶּה מִימֵי הַשֹּׁפְטִים
אֲשֶׁר שָׁפְטוּ אֶת־יִשְׂרָאֵל וְכֹל יְמֵי מַלְכֵי
יִשְׂרָאֵל וּמַלְכֵי יְהוּדָה:

23 כִּי אִם־בִּשְׁמֹנֶה עֶשְׂרֵה שָׁנָה לַמֶּלֶךְ יֹאשִׁיָּהוּ
נַעֲשָׂה הַפֶּסַח הַזֶּה לַיהוָה בִּירוּשָׁלָ͏ִם:

Commentary

Shrines of the gates. No such gates are known to have existed in Jerusalem; hence, this may refer to Beersheba.[4]

9. *Among their brethren.* They could share with the other priests all priestly dues (of which unleavened bread is one example), even though they were no longer allowed to participate in the sacrifices.

22. *Such a Passover.* That is, one that was ordered by the central authority.

Since ... the Judges. All the way back to the days of Joshua.[5]

24. Josiah also set ablaze the necromancers, soothsayers, the household gods and idols, all the abominations to be seen in Judah and Jerusalem, in order to fulfill the words of the Teaching written in the scroll that Hilkiah the priest had found in the House of the Eternal.

25. Before him there was no king like him, who turned to the Eternal with all his heart and soul and might, as taught by the Torah of Moses; nor did any like him arise after him.

24 וְגַם אֶת־הָאֹבוֹת וְאֶת־הַיִּדְּעֹנִים וְאֶת־הַתְּרָפִים וְאֶת־הַגִּלֻּלִים וְאֵת כָּל־הַשִּׁקֻּצִים אֲשֶׁר נִרְאוּ בְּאֶרֶץ יְהוּדָה וּבִירוּשָׁלַם בִּעֵר יֹאשִׁיָּהוּ לְמַעַן הָקִים אֶת־דִּבְרֵי הַתּוֹרָה הַכְּתֻבִים עַל־הַסֵּפֶר אֲשֶׁר מָצָא חִלְקִיָּהוּ הַכֹּהֵן בֵּית יְהוָה: 25 וְכָמֹהוּ לֹא־הָיָה לְפָנָיו מֶלֶךְ אֲשֶׁר־שָׁב אֶל־יְהוָה בְּכָל־לְבָבוֹ וּבְכָל־נַפְשׁוֹ וּבְכָל־מְאֹדוֹ כְּכֹל תּוֹרַת מֹשֶׁה וְאַחֲרָיו לֹא־קָם כָּמֹהוּ:

Commentary

24. *Set ablaze.* The religious revolution did not take place without violence.

25. *No king like him.* This was also said in praise of King Hezekiah.[6] Metzudat David explains this as follows: None was like Hezekiah when it came to trust in God; and none equaled Josiah when it came to repentance.

Essay

Josiah's reform

Traditional interpreters of the Josiah story hold that the book that the priest Hilkiah found in the Temple and brought to the king was the Torah—all five books of it. It had been transmitted by God to Moses and over the centuries had been forgotten by whole generations of Israel.

Modern scholarship considers the Torah to be a book that had a literary history stretching over many centuries—from the time of Moses down to Josiah and beyond. In this view, the book was not finalized until the 5th century or even later, and therefore what was found by Hilkiah could not have been the whole Torah but only a part of it. That part was the book of Deuteronomy (or the core of it), and represented a fairly new religious development.

In support of their theory these scholars point out the close relationship of Josiah's reforms to provisions contained only in Deuteronomy.

Some of these provisions differ with or at least vary from legislation contained in the other Torah books. For example, Josiah abolished the ancient practice of worshipping and offering sacrifices at the "high places" and established the Temple in Jerusalem as the sole sanctuary in which sacrifices could be properly offered. Deuteronomy is the only book of the Torah containing legislation to that effect.[7]

It is indeed difficult to imagine that the entire Torah had been totally forgotten, and that it took a chance discovery to bring it back to life. A new book, containing traditions and legislation hitherto unknown, would explain this remarkable development much better.

The timing of Josiah's reforms coincided with the weakening of the Assyrian empire, whose religious cult permeated the region, including Judah. It is therefore likely that religious reform was one side of the coin of national independence and, to be sure, it was so considered by the Assyrians and their allies the Egyptians. The ensuing military confrontation cost Josiah his life,[8] but his work endured, surviving the destruction of the Jewish state and the exile that followed. The prophet Jeremiah, who was Josiah's contemporary, composed laments on his death that were sung by the people, and he mentions him as one who dispensed justice and equity and upheld the rights of the poor and needy.[9] No wonder that the chronicler(s) who composed the books of Kings held him in the highest regard.

Gleanings

Only twenty years

The First Temple stood for four hundred and ten years, but Israel was free from idolatry for twenty years only. (These were most likely the years when King Josiah reintroduced the Torah to Israel.)

Midrash[10]

Precaution

Since Josiah knew, because of the prophecy of Huldah, that the Temple would be destroyed,[11] he hid the Holy Ark and all sacred appurtenances, so that they would not fall into the hands of the enemy.

Talmud[12]

The Pesach of Josiah

It can well be said of this special Pesach, in spite of the great days of David, Solomon and Hezekiah, that such a Pesach had never been celebrated from the era of the Judges on and during the reign of all the kings of Israel and Judah. For never had the defection and estrangement from Torah been as profound as in the time before Josiah undertook his reforms.

Mendel Hirsch[13]

* * *

Notes

[1] II Chronicles 34:31; so also Radak.

[2] Deuteronomy 24:18 and following. *K'deshim* had pursued their trade in Israel for centuries; see I Kings 14:24 and 22:47. See also E.A. Goodfriend, *Anchor Bible Dictionary*, vol. 5, p. 508.

[3] On the identification of Geva, see Cogan and Tadmor (*Anchor Bible*, II Kings), p. 286.

[4] A slight emendation of *she'arim*, "gates," to *se'irim*, "goat demons," would better fit the context. See Cogan and Tadmor (*Anchor Bible*, II Kings), p. 286.

[5] Joshua 5:10; see the haftarah for the First Day of Passover.

[6] II Kings 18:5.

[7] See also the Torah Commentary, pp. 1291 ff. and pp. 1297 ff. (an essay by William W. Hallo).

[8] It is reported in II Kings 23:29 (which is not included in the haftarah); another version of Josiah's death may be found in II Chronicles 35:23-24.

[9] II Chronicles 35:25 and Jeremiah 22:15. Tradition, which ascribes the authorship of the book of Lamentations (*Echa*) to Jeremiah, interpreted 4:20 of that book to be the reference to Josiah's mention in II Kings 23:25—see, for example, *B. Ta'anit* 22b, and also Josephus, *Antiquities* X 5:1.

[10] Seder Eliyahu Zuta (ed. Friedmann, 1900), 8:185. The identification of the "20 years" with Josiah is made by Ginzberg in *Legends of the Jews*, vol. 6, p. 280, note 12.

[11] II Kings 22:14 ff.

[12] *B. Yoma* 52b, which states that, aside from the Ark, he hid the holy oil, the jars of manna, and the rod of Aaron, as well as other items. Other traditions mention different objects; see Ginzberg, *Legends*, vol. 6, p. 377, note 118.

[13] Introduction to the haftarah (end).

Ezekiel, chapter 36, verse 37 to chapter 37, verse 14

Introduction

Connection of haftarah and Shabbat:

The extent of this haftarah is different in various traditions. Some begin with the last two verses of chapter 36, while others begin with chapter 37. (There are also congregations that extend the text and end with verses 15-17 in chapter 37.)

For those who begin with chapter 36:37, the connection is obvious: the two verses speak of the pilgrims who will visit the rebuilt Jerusalem during the festivals.

The connection of the Shabbat of Pesach and the main body of the haftarah (37:1-14) lies in the theme of Israel's deliverance: in the Torah it is delivered from slavery; in the haftarah, from death.

The setting:

Ezekiel lived in the days before and after the destruction of the First Temple and preached in the early part of the 6th century B.C.E. He was exiled to Babylon and experienced a period of great despair after the destruction of the Temple in 587. The hope that he gives his fellow exiles is clear: In time you will be returned to Jerusalem, like dry bones revived by God.

For more on Ezekiel and his time, see our *General Introduction*.

The message:

1. The celebration of the holidays in the future Jerusalem. (36:37-38)
2. The vision of the dry bones. (37:1-6)
3. The resurrection of the dead. (7-10)
4. The meaning of the vision. (11-14)

HAFTARAH FOR CHOL HAMO-EID PESACH

Ezekiel, chapter 36, verse 37 to chapter 37, verse 14

36:37. Thus says the Eternal God: This, [I will do] in addition: I will let Myself be sought out by the House of Israel to do [things] for them; I will increase their numbers like a human flock of sheep.

38. As Jerusalem is filled with flocks, flocks for sacrifice at her appointed festivals, so shall Israel's ruined cities be filled with flocks of people. Then they shall know that I am the Eternal.

37:1. The hand of the Eternal was upon me, leading me out by God's spirit and setting me down in the middle of a valley. It was full of bones.

2. God led me all around them. There were a great many of them spread on the surface of the valley, and they were very dry.

3. God said to me: Mortal, can these bones live? I answered: O God Eternal, You [alone] know.

36:37 כֹּה אָמַר אֲדֹנָי יְהוִֹה עוֹד זֹאת אִדָּרֵשׁ
לְבֵית־יִשְׂרָאֵל לַעֲשׂוֹת לָהֶם אַרְבֶּה אֹתָם כַּצֹּאן
אָדָם:

38 כְּצֹאן קָדָשִׁים כְּצֹאן יְרוּשָׁלַם בְּמוֹעֲדֶיהָ כֵּן
תִּהְיֶינָה הֶעָרִים הֶחֳרֵבוֹת מְלֵאוֹת צֹאן אָדָם
וְיָדְעוּ כִּי־אֲנִי יְהוָה:

37:1 הָיְתָה עָלַי יַד־יְהוָה וַיּוֹצִאֵנִי בְרוּחַ יְהוָה
וַיְנִיחֵנִי בְּתוֹךְ הַבִּקְעָה וְהִיא מְלֵאָה עֲצָמוֹת:

2 וְהֶעֱבִירַנִי עֲלֵיהֶם סָבִיב סָבִיב וְהִנֵּה רַבּוֹת
מְאֹד עַל־פְּנֵי הַבִּקְעָה וְהִנֵּה יְבֵשׁוֹת מְאֹד:

3 וַיֹּאמֶר אֵלַי בֶּן־אָדָם הֲתִחְיֶינָה הָעֲצָמוֹת
הָאֵלֶּה וָאֹמַר אֲדֹנָי יְהוִֹה אַתָּה יָדָעְתָּ:

Commentary

36:37. *I will let Myself be sought out.* Literally, "I can be asked," and I will tell you now that I will answer your prayer.

38. *Flocks for sacrifice.* Literally, "flocks for holy purposes." The Targum takes it to mean, "the holy flock," that is, Israel. Most commentators follow the literal meaning: the city will be filled with sacrificial animals during the holiday seasons, brought from a countryside that has been richly resettled.[1]

Flocks of people. The translation follows the Targum's interpretation.

37:1. *The hand of the Eternal was upon me.* God's overpowering Presence commanded me.[2]

2. *God led me.* Literally, "He," as elsewhere in this chapter. God shows the Prophet the multitude of bones.[3]

3. *Mortal.* The expression בֶּן־אָדָם (*ben-adam*) occurs often in Ezekiel; for an explanation, see the haftarah for Vayigash.

712

4. Then God said to me: Prophesy to these bones, and say to them: You dry bones, hear the word of the Eternal.

5. Thus says the Eternal God to these bones: Behold, I will cause breath to enter you, and you shall live.

6. I will put sinews on you, and cover you with flesh, and spread skin over you. I will put breath into you, and you shall live. Then you shall know that I am the Eternal.

7. I prophesied as I had been commanded. And as I prophesied, there was a loud noise, a sound, and the bones came together, bone to matching bone.

8. I looked and saw sinews and flesh and skin spread over them from above, but there was no breath in them.

9. Then God said to me: Mortal, prophesy to the breath, O prophesy! And say to the breath: Thus says the Eternal God: Come, breath, from the four quarters, and breathe into these slain [bodies], that they may live [again].

10. I prophesied as God had commanded me, and the breath came into them, and they came to life. They stood on their feet, an exceedingly great army.

4 וַיֹּ֣אמֶר אֵלַ֔י הִנָּבֵ֖א עַל־הָעֲצָמ֣וֹת הָאֵ֑לֶּה וְאָמַרְתָּ֣ אֲלֵיהֶ֔ם הָעֲצָמוֹת֙ הַיְבֵשׁ֔וֹת שִׁמְע֖וּ דְּבַר־יְהוָֽה׃

5 כֹּ֤ה אָמַר֙ אֲדֹנָ֣י יְהוִ֔ה לָעֲצָמ֖וֹת הָאֵ֑לֶּה הִנֵּ֨ה אֲנִ֜י מֵבִ֥יא בָכֶ֛ם ר֖וּחַ וִחְיִיתֶֽם׃

6 וְנָתַתִּי֩ עֲלֵיכֶ֨ם גִּדִ֜ים וְהַעֲלֵתִ֧י עֲלֵיכֶ֣ם בָּשָׂ֗ר וְקָרַמְתִּ֤י עֲלֵיכֶם֙ ע֔וֹר וְנָתַתִּ֥י בָכֶ֛ם ר֖וּחַ וִחְיִיתֶ֑ם וִידַעְתֶּ֖ם כִּֽי־אֲנִ֥י יְהוָֽה׃

7 וְנִבֵּ֖אתִי כַּאֲשֶׁ֣ר צֻוֵּ֑יתִי וַיְהִי־ק֤וֹל כְּהִנָּֽבְאִי֙ וְהִנֵּה־רַ֔עַשׁ וַתִּקְרְב֣וּ עֲצָמ֔וֹת עֶ֖צֶם אֶל־עַצְמֽוֹ׃

8 וְרָאִ֜יתִי וְהִנֵּֽה־עֲלֵיהֶ֤ם גִּדִים֙ וּבָשָׂ֣ר עָלָ֔ה וַיִּקְרַ֧ם עֲלֵיהֶ֛ם ע֖וֹר מִלְמָ֑עְלָה וְר֖וּחַ אֵ֥ין בָּהֶֽם׃

9 וַיֹּ֣אמֶר אֵלַ֔י הִנָּבֵ֖א אֶל־הָר֑וּחַ הִנָּבֵ֣א בֶן־אָדָ֗ם וְאָמַרְתָּ֣ אֶל־הָר֡וּחַ כֹּֽה־אָמַ֣ר ׀ אֲדֹנָ֣י יְהוִ֗ה מֵאַרְבַּ֤ע רוּחוֹת֙ בֹּ֣אִי הָר֔וּחַ וּפְחִ֛י בַּהֲרוּגִ֥ים הָאֵ֖לֶּה וְיִֽחְיֽוּ׃

10 וְהִנַּבֵּ֙אתִי֙ כַּאֲשֶׁ֣ר צִוָּ֔נִי וַתָּבוֹא֩ בָהֶ֨ם הָר֜וּחַ וַיִּֽחְי֗וּ וַיַּֽעַמְדוּ֙ עַל־רַגְלֵיהֶ֔ם חַ֖יִל גָּד֣וֹל מְאֹד־מְאֹֽד׃

Commentary

5. *Breath.* רוח (*ru-ach*) can have various meanings: wind (as in verse 9), or spirit (as in verse 1), or breath (as here).

7. *Loud noise.* As if an earthquake was occurring.[4]

9. *God said.* Literally, "He." Also in verses 10 and 11.

Breath from the four winds. The word רוח (*ru-ach*) is used here in two different meanings (see at verse 5): in the singular as "breath" and in the plural רוחות (*ruchot*) as "winds."

713

11. Then God said to me: Mortal, these bones are the whole House of Israel. They say: *Our bones are dried up, our hope is lost; we are cut off [from life]!*

12. Therefore prophesy to them and say: Thus says the Eternal God: I am going to open your graves, My people; I will lift you out of your graves and bring you [home] to the land of Israel.

13. And when I have opened your graves and lifted you out of them, My people, you shall know that I am the Eternal.

14. I will put My breath into you and you shall live [again], and I will place you in your own land. Then, says the Eternal One, you shall know that I, the Eternal, have spoken and acted.

11 וַיֹּאמֶר אֵלַי בֶּן־אָדָם הָעֲצָמוֹת הָאֵלֶּה כָּל־בֵּית יִשְׂרָאֵל הֵמָּה הִנֵּה אֹמְרִים יָבְשׁוּ עַצְמוֹתֵינוּ וְאָבְדָה תִקְוָתֵנוּ נִגְזַרְנוּ לָנוּ:

12 לָכֵן הִנָּבֵא וְאָמַרְתָּ אֲלֵיהֶם כֹּה־אָמַר אֲדֹנָי יֱהֹוִה הִנֵּה אֲנִי פֹתֵחַ אֶת־קִבְרוֹתֵיכֶם וְהַעֲלֵיתִי אֶתְכֶם מִקִּבְרוֹתֵיכֶם עַמִּי וְהֵבֵאתִי אֶתְכֶם אֶל־אַדְמַת יִשְׂרָאֵל:

13 וִידַעְתֶּם כִּי־אֲנִי יְהֹוָה בְּפִתְחִי אֶת־קִבְרוֹתֵיכֶם וּבְהַעֲלוֹתִי אֶתְכֶם מִקִּבְרוֹתֵיכֶם עַמִּי:

14 וְנָתַתִּי רוּחִי בָכֶם וִחְיִיתֶם וְהִנַּחְתִּי אֶתְכֶם עַל־אַדְמַתְכֶם וִידַעְתֶּם כִּי־אֲנִי יְהֹוָה דִּבַּרְתִּי וְעָשִׂיתִי נְאֻם־יְהֹוָה:

Commentary

11. *God said.* Literally, "He."
Cut off. It is not clear whom Ezekiel has in mind; see the essay below.
14. *I, the Eternal, have spoken and acted.* One would expect: "I ... have spoken and *will act* upon it." But for God, having spoken it is as good as if it had already occurred—a subtle emphasis that the divine promise is sure to be fulfilled.

Essay

The meaning of the vision

Who were the slain bodies whom God revived in Ezekiel's vision? In the first place, they were most likely the hundreds of thousands who were killed during their battle with the Babylonians and the destruction of the Holy City.

But, as always, the Prophet addressed himself also to his listeners, who were suffering captivity in Babylonian exile and whose lives were bereft of meaning. In his vision, they were included among those "slain," as if among those no longer alive. They were meant when he spoke of "the whole House of Israel" whose graves would be opened. The vision should therefore be seen as a metaphor—a preaching device used by all the prophets and especially by Ezekiel.

The message thus was: Israel as a people will be revived, and Israel comprises past and present. When it lives again as a nation, the innumerable dead of former generations are, so to speak, revived as well, for their religious hopes have been validated and their immortality is assured.

In the millennia after Ezekiel there was a strong tradition that the Prophet referred to messianic days, when indeed the whole House of Israel—all its generations—would be brought back to life. The effect of these interpretations was profound. For while the Torah nowhere speaks directly of resurrection,[5] Ezekiel's prophecy was seen as establishing its certainty, and in time it became a cornerstone of Jewish belief. The Mishnah established it as a religious principle,[6] as did Maimonides who included it among the 13 articles of faith. To this day, the traditional prayer book speaks of God as one who "revives the dead" (מחיה המתים, *mechayyeh ha-metim*).[7]

The Reform prayer book, having abandoned the belief in physical resurrection, has altered this phrase and addresses God as one who is the "Source of life" (מחיה הכל, *mechayyeh ha-kol*). The Reconstructionist prayer book too has removed the reference to resurrection, while Conservatives have maintained the traditional phrasing.

There are those in all camps who believe that "resurrection" never was a physical concept at all, but always a spiritual one. Instead of teaching physical revival, it betokens the hope of redemption for Israel and, by extension, for all humanity.[8]

Gleanings

God said to me: Mortal, can these bones live?
I answered: O God Eternal, You [alone] know. (37:3)

A dissident view

Rabbi Eliezer was among those who downplayed the extravagant visions of Ezekiel. Yes, he admitted the dead were revived, and when the divine breath entered into them, they stood on their feet and sang a song of praise to God. Having done this, they fell down and died again.

Talmud[9]

Ezekiel had doubts

When God asked him to assist in the miracle of reviving the dead, Ezekiel had his doubts. Because of his lack of faith, he was condemned to be buried not in Israel but on foreign soil.

Midrash[10]

Why did God ask him of all the prophets to have this vision? Because of his intense love for his people.

Midrash[11]

* * *

Notes

[1] So Rashi and Radak.

[2] Following Rashi. The metaphor occurs also in Ezekiel 1:3; 3:22; 8:1, and is reminiscent of the Torah's description of God as saving Israel "with a strong hand and an outstretched arm" (Deuteronomy 4:34).

[3] So Radak; but Rashi has a more complex explanation: Ezekiel was a priest, and as such he was not permitted to come in contact with the dead. To this day, a kohen (a member of the priestly clan) will not come close to a grave if he observes the traditional Halachah.

[4] So Eliezer of Beaugency.

[5] Some verses in the Tanach were taken to hint at it—for example, Deuteronomy 32:39: "I deal death and I give life."

[6] Sanhedrin 10:1.

[7] In the second benediction of the *Amidah*.

[8] See *B*. Sanhedrin 92b for the talmudic discussion. Among medieval commentators, Abarbanel championed the view that the Prophet combined metaphor and messianic resurrection. On the subject of resurrection, see *Encyclopaedia Judaica*, vol. 14, pp. 96 ff. There are also those who believe that the vision deals with a specific historical event, which the Prophet describes in metaphoric language.

[9] *B*. Sanhedrin 92b.

[10] Pirke deRabbi Eliezer 33.

[11] Seder Eliyahu Rabba 5:23.

Second Samuel, chapter 22, verses 1 to 51

Introduction

The selection for this festival is the same as for the sidra Ha'azinu. Why this choice?

Both the Torah reading for the festival and the haftarah are songs—one by Moses and one by David. The former celebrates the deliverance from Egyptian slavery, and the latter commemorates David's deliverance from his foes. See also Rashi's comment on *B.* Megillah 31a.

For text and commentary, see the haftarah for Ha'azinu.

Isaiah, chapter 10, verse 32 to chapter 12, verse 6

Introduction

Connection of haftarah and festival:

Isaiah 11:15 refers directly to the Exodus from Egypt. Furthermore, the message of the holy day is liberation brought on by God's doing, and the haftarah deals with the coming of days when Israel and the world will be liberated from the yoke of human strife and oppression.

The setting:

Isaiah lived during the second half of the 8th century B.C.E. in the kingdom of Judah (of which Jerusalem was the capital). The Assyrians, who were the major power in the Near East, had previously conquered the Northern Kingdom (Israel) and now, ten years later, were advancing on Jerusalem. King Hezekiah sought Isaiah's advice, who predicted that the city would be saved.

These events are related in detail in II Kings 18:13 and following. For more on Isaiah and his time, see our *General Introduction.*

The message:

1. Preamble (10:32-34): The Assyrian threat will be averted and will turn into eventual disaster for the enemy.

2. Part 1 (11:1-9): These oft-quoted passages describe a messianic era of universal peace, when "the wolf shall dwell with the lamb." (See the essay below.)

There is much debate among scholars whether these verses are indeed by Isaiah or by an earlier or later author, but an exposition of the arguments goes beyond the scope of this commentary. We treat them here as if they belong to the original text of the Prophet's work. However, they form a unit for themselves and appear unrelated to what comes before or after.

3. Part 2 (11:10-16): A further prophecy on the downfall of Assyria.

4. Part 3 (12:1-6): The grateful response of Isaiah and a hymn to the Eternal.

English	Hebrew
10:32. Even today he shall halt at Nob and wave his hand (at) the mount of fair Zion, the hill of Jerusalem.	10:32 עוֹד הַיּוֹם בְּנֹב לַעֲמֹד יְנֹפֵף יָדוֹ הַר בֵּית [בַּת־]צִיּוֹן גִּבְעַת יְרוּשָׁלָ͏ִם:
33. Behold, the Sovereign God of heaven's hosts will lop off boughs with violence: the tall ones shall be chopped down, the lofty brought low.	33 הִנֵּה הָאָדוֹן יְהֹוָה צְבָאוֹת מְסָעֵף פֻּארָה בְּמַעֲרָצָה וְרָמֵי הַקּוֹמָה גְּדוּעִים וְהַגְּבֹהִים יִשְׁפָּלוּ:
34. the forest thickets shall be struck down with iron and Lebanon shall fall to the Mighty One.	34 וְנִקַּף סִבְכֵי הַיַּעַר בַּבַּרְזֶל וְהַלְּבָנוֹן בְּאַדִּיר יִפּוֹל:
11:1. And a shoot shall sprout from the stock of Jesse, a branch grow out of his roots.	11:1 וְיָצָא חֹטֶר מִגֵּזַע יִשָׁי וְנֵצֶר מִשָּׁרָשָׁיו יִפְרֶה:

Commentary

10:32. *Shall halt at Nob*. Sennacherib, king of Assyria, will not advance beyond Nob (probably at the outskirts of Jerusalem).

Wave his hand. Disparagingly.[1]

33-34. An ironic reversal: Assyrians lacked wood and would march to Lebanon and obtain it there. Elsewhere, Isaiah mocks the boasting of Assyria about cutting down Lebanese timber,[2] and now turns the tables on them, for they will be like the trees that God will harvest.

34. *Bronze*. אדיר (*addir*) is related to the Akkadian *urudû*, which has this meaning.[3] This understanding provides the perfect parallel to the first half of the verse.

11:1. *Stock of Jesse*. The House of David (who was the son of Jesse[4]). Isaiah speaks elsewhere of a "holy seed" that would guarantee the future of the people;[5] here, the same metaphor is used. While earlier commentators considered this to be a reference to the Messiah who will redeem Israel and all creation,[6] modern scholars view this as a grand vision of an earthly ruler from the House of Jesse/David.

Radak connected the passage with its surrounding text: the threat to Jerusalem by the Assyrian army, which had been averted miraculously, was not a singular event, for the Almighty will work a still greater wonder and bring about the coming of the Messiah.

2. The spirit of the Eternal shall rest upon
   him:

the spirit of wisdom and understanding,

the spirit of counsel and might,

the spirit of knowledge and the fear of
God.

3. Reverence for the Eternal shall be his
   very breath.

He shall not judge by what he sees

or decide by what he hears,

4. but shall judge the poor with righteousness,

and decide with equity for the meek of the
earth.

He shall strike the ruthless with the rod of
his mouth,

and slay the wicked with the breath of his
lips.

5. Justice shall be a sash for his waist,

faithfulness a sash for his loins.

6. The wolf shall dwell with the lamb,

the leopard lie down with the kid;

calf and young lion and fatling together,

and a little child shall lead them.

2 וְנָחָ֥ה עָלָ֖יו ר֣וּחַ יְהֹוָ֑ה

ר֧וּחַ חׇכְמָ֣ה וּבִינָ֗ה

ר֤וּחַ עֵצָה֙ וּגְבוּרָ֔ה

ר֥וּחַ דַּ֖עַת וְיִרְאַ֥ת יְהֹוָֽה׃

3 וַהֲרִיח֖וֹ בְּיִרְאַ֣ת יְהֹוָ֑ה

וְלֹֽא־לְמַרְאֵ֤ה עֵינָיו֙ יִשְׁפּ֔וֹט

וְלֹֽא־לְמִשְׁמַ֥ע אׇזְנָ֖יו יוֹכִֽיחַ׃

4 וְשָׁפַ֤ט בְּצֶ֙דֶק֙ דַּלִּ֔ים

וְהוֹכִ֥יחַ בְּמִישׁ֖וֹר לְעַנְוֵי־אָ֑רֶץ

וְהִכָּה־אֶ֙רֶץ֙ בְּשֵׁ֣בֶט פִּ֔יו

וּבְר֥וּחַ שְׂפָתָ֖יו יָמִ֥ית רָשָֽׁע׃

5 וְהָ֥יָה צֶ֖דֶק אֵז֣וֹר מׇתְנָ֑יו

וְהָאֱמוּנָ֖ה אֵז֥וֹר חֲלָצָֽיו׃

6 וְגָ֤ר זְאֵב֙ עִם־כֶּ֔בֶשׂ

וְנָמֵ֖ר עִם־גְּדִ֣י יִרְבָּ֑ץ

וְעֵ֙גֶל֙ וּכְפִ֤יר וּמְרִיא֙ יַחְדָּ֔ו

וְנַ֥עַר קָטֹ֖ן נֹהֵ֥ג בָּֽם׃

Commentary

3. *Shall be his very breath.* Literally, "from the way he draws in his breath."[7] Older translations have "will be his delight."

4. *The ruthless.* This translation is based on restoring the text to its likely original. Instead of ארץ (*eretz*, earth) we would read עריץ (*aritz*, ruthless), which provides the intended parallel.

With the rod of his mouth. By the power of his word. שבט (*shevet*) also refers to the royal scepter.

6. *The wolf.* The images that follow project a return to the pristine state of creation, which did not know of carnivores.

7. The cow and the bear shall graze,

their young shall lie down together,

and a lion shall eat hay like an ox.

8. A nursing child shall play over a cobra's hole,

and a weaned child shall put its hand into a adder's nest.

9. They shall not hurt nor destroy

in all My holy mountain,

for the earth shall be full of the knowledge of the Eternal

as waters cover the sea.

10. On that day the root of Jesse, which still stands,

shall be an ensign for [the] peoples;

nations shall seek counsel of him,

and glorious shall be his resting-place.

11. And on that day the Eternal shall ready the divine hand to take possession yet a second time of the remnant of God's people, those who remain from Assyria, and from Egypt, and Pathros, and Kush, and Elam, and Shinar, and Hamath, and the coastlands.

7 וּפָרָה וָדֹב תִּרְעֶינָה

יַחְדָּו יִרְבְּצוּ יַלְדֵיהֶן

וְאַרְיֵה כַּבָּקָר יֹאכַל־תֶּבֶן:

8 וְשִׁעֲשַׁע יוֹנֵק עַל־חֻר פָּתֶן

וְעַל מְאוּרַת צִפְעוֹנִי גָּמוּל יָדוֹ הָדָה:

9 לֹא־יָרֵעוּ וְלֹא־יַשְׁחִיתוּ

בְּכָל־הַר קָדְשִׁי

כִּי־מָלְאָה הָאָרֶץ דֵּעָה אֶת־יְהוָה

כַּמַּיִם לַיָּם מְכַסִּים:

10 וְהָיָה בַּיּוֹם הַהוּא שֹׁרֶשׁ יִשַׁי אֲשֶׁר עֹמֵד

לְנֵס עַמִּים

אֵלָיו גּוֹיִם יִדְרֹשׁוּ

וְהָיְתָה מְנֻחָתוֹ כָּבוֹד:

11 וְהָיָה בַּיּוֹם הַהוּא יוֹסִיף אֲדֹנָי שֵׁנִית יָדוֹ

לִקְנוֹת אֶת־שְׁאָר עַמּוֹ אֲשֶׁר יִשָּׁאֵר מֵאַשּׁוּר

וּמִמִּצְרַיִם וּמִפַּתְרוֹס וּמִכּוּשׁ וּמֵעֵילָם וּמִשִּׁנְעָר

וּמֵחֲמָת וּמֵאִיֵּי הַיָּם:

Commentary

9. *In all My holy mountain.* Jerusalem's peace will be a model for the world, but such quiescence will not yet have become universal.

11-16. These six verses are separate from the messianic vision of the preceding passages. Assyria had destroyed Samaria (in 721), and much of its population had been exiled.

11. *God's people.* Literally "His." Similarly, verses 12, 16, and 12:4

A second time. The first time was the deliverance from Egypt, and since then quite a few members of the twelve tribes lived outside the Holy Land.[8] Except for Assyria and Egypt, the locations mentioned cannot be fixed with certainty. Thus, while Kush is usually identified with Ethiopia, it sometimes describes other locations.

12. God will raise an ensign for the nations, and assemble the outcasts of Israel, and gather the dispersed of Judah from the four corners of the earth.

13. Then Ephraim's envy shall depart, and those hostile to Judah shall be cut off; no more shall Ephraim envy Judah, and no more shall Judah be hostile to Ephraim.

14. But they shall swoop down upon the backs of the Philistines to the west; together they shall plunder the people of the east; Edom and Moab shall be within their grasp, and the people of Ammon shall obey them.

15. And the Eternal shall dry the tongue of the Egyptian sea, and with the might of the divine breath raise a hand over the Nile, breaking it into seven wadis, so that one can cross [it] in sandals.

12 וְנָשָׂא נֵס לַגּוֹיִם וְאָסַף נִדְחֵי יִשְׂרָאֵל וּנְפֻצוֹת יְהוּדָה יְקַבֵּץ מֵאַרְבַּע כַּנְפוֹת הָאָרֶץ:

13 וְסָרָה קִנְאַת אֶפְרַיִם וְצֹרְרֵי יְהוּדָה יִכָּרֵתוּ אֶפְרַיִם לֹא־יְקַנֵּא אֶת־יְהוּדָה וִיהוּדָה לֹא־יָצֹר אֶת־אֶפְרָיִם:

14 וְעָפוּ בְכָתֵף פְּלִשְׁתִּים יָמָּה יַחְדָּו יָבֹזּוּ אֶת־בְּנֵי־קֶדֶם אֱדוֹם וּמוֹאָב מִשְׁלוֹחַ יָדָם וּבְנֵי עַמּוֹן מִשְׁמַעְתָּם:

15 וְהֶחֱרִים יְהוָה אֵת לְשׁוֹן יָם־מִצְרַיִם וְהֵנִיף יָדוֹ עַל־הַנָּהָר בַּעְיָם רוּחוֹ וְהִכָּהוּ לְשִׁבְעָה נְחָלִים וְהִדְרִיךְ בַּנְּעָלִים:

Commentary

12. God will raise. Literally, "He." So also verse 16.

13. *Ephraim envy Judah*. After a remnant of the exiles will have returned home, the former animosity between north and south will be forgotten. Much later, the prophet Ezekiel will also express this thought.[9] Unfortunately, the hope of reconciliation was never put to the test, for no remnant of the northern ten tribes ever returned.

14. *The backs*. Literally, the shoulder; using the image of the Judean mountains from whence the reunited northern and southern Israelites will descend upon their old enemy.

15. *Shall dry*. Reading וְהֶחֱרִיב (v'hecheriv) for וְהֶחֱרִים (v'hecherim, shall destroy).

The tongue of the Egyptian sea. The Gulf of Suez.

On foot. Dry-shod. The exodus from Egypt and the crossing of the Reed (Red) Sea ("the first time") will be reenacted.[10]

16. And there shall be a highway from Assyria for the remnant left of God's people, as there was for Israel on the day it went up out of Egypt.

12:1. And you shall say on that day:
I give thanks to You, Eternal One,
for though You were angry with me,
Your anger has turned back,
and You have comforted me.

2. Behold, God is my salvation,
I will trust and will not fear.
For the Eternal God is my strength and my
   song,
and has become my salvation.

3. With joy you shall draw water
from the springs of salvation.

16 וְהָיְתָה מְסִלָּה לִשְׁאָר עַמּוֹ אֲשֶׁר יִשָּׁאֵר מֵאַשּׁוּר כַּאֲשֶׁר הָיְתָה לְיִשְׂרָאֵל בְּיוֹם עֲלֹתוֹ מֵאֶרֶץ מִצְרָיִם:

12:1 וְאָמַרְתָּ בַּיּוֹם הַהוּא
אוֹדְךָ יְהוָֹה
כִּי אָנַפְתָּ בִּי
יָשֹׁב אַפְּךָ
וּתְנַחֲמֵנִי:

2 הִנֵּה אֵל יְשׁוּעָתִי
אֶבְטַח וְלֹא אֶפְחָד
כִּי־עָזִּי וְזִמְרָת יָהּ יְהוָֹה
וַיְהִי־לִי לִישׁוּעָה:

3 וּשְׁאַבְתֶּם־מַיִם בְּשָׂשׂוֹן
מִמַּעַיְנֵי הַיְשׁוּעָה:

Commentary

16. *A highway*. There shall be a highway from Assyria for the remnant of God's people, just as there was when Israel left Egypt. The Second Isaiah will use the same thought in his prophecy.[11]

12:1. One of Isaiah's three hymns begins here; the other two are found in chapters 25 and 26.

Your anger has turned back. Assyria's threat to Jerusalem has ceased.[12]

2-3. These two verses form the beginning of the Havdalah liturgy recited at the end of Shabbat.

2. *The Eternal God*. יָהּ יְהוָֹה (*Yah Adonai*). יָהּ (a variant of יהוה) seldom occurs independently and is most often found as the last part of *hallelu-yah* (Praise the Eternal) or of personal names like *Yesha-yah* (Isaiah, The Eternal Will Redeem).

My song. Or "my might." The verse is virtually identical with Exodus 15:2, in the Song at the Sea, the Torah reading for the seventh day of Pesach.

3. *Draw water*. Most likely referring to the joyful water-drawing ceremony that marked the celebration of the Sukkot festival in ancient Israel.[13]

4. And you shall say on that day:

Give thanks to the Eternal,

Call on God's name,

Make known God's deeds among the peoples,

Declare that God's name is exalted.

5. Sing of the Eternal,

who has done glorious things;

make them known

in all the earth!

6. Shout and sing for joy,

you who dwell in Zion,

for great in your midst

is the Holy One of Israel!

4 וַאֲמַרְתֶּם בַּיּוֹם הַהוּא

הוֹדוּ לַיהוָה

קִרְאוּ בִשְׁמוֹ

הוֹדִיעוּ בָעַמִּים עֲלִילֹתָיו

הַזְכִּירוּ כִּי נִשְׂגָּב שְׁמוֹ:

5 זַמְּרוּ יְהוָה

כִּי גֵאוּת עָשָׂה

מְיֻדַּעַת [מוּדַעַת] זֹאת

בְּכָל־הָאָרֶץ:

6 צַהֲלִי וָרֹנִּי

יוֹשֶׁבֶת צִיּוֹן

כִּי־גָדוֹל בְּקִרְבֵּךְ

קְדוֹשׁ יִשְׂרָאֵל:

Commentary

4. *God's name … God's deeds.* Literally, "His."

Essay

Wolf and lamb together

Few passages of the Tanach have been quoted as often as Isaiah's vision of the ultimate future. All strife will cease, and nature itself will no longer be "red in tooth and claw." Former carnivores will lie peacefully next to their erstwhile prey, and children need no longer fear the bite of the poisonous snake. Human beings too will live by new rules and forswear strife—which is to say that messianic days will have arrived. They will be ushered in by a descendant of the House of David who will be wise and fair, and under his stewardship social justice will suffuse human society.

For the last two thousand years mainstream Christianity has seen these passages as prophecies foretelling the coming of Jesus of Nazareth and has identified his personality with that described by Isaiah.

Jews, on the other hand, while agreeing that Isaiah does indeed describe the time of the Messiah, have insisted that the Messiah has not yet come. The realities of our age are everything but messianic. War and hatred, violence and distrust are the order of the day, and neither does nature itself give signs of changing its ways. Christians explain this discrepancy by saying that, while Jesus was indeed the Messiah foretold in the Bible, he had to die in order to fulfill his fate, and that the days predicted by the Prophet will arrive only when the world will be ready for his "second coming."

Such religious differences cannot be settled by resorting to the biblical text. Orthodox Jews believe that God alone will decide the arrival of the Messiah, which may happen momentarily or thousands of years hence. Non-Orthodox Jews hesitate to speak of a personal Messiah and instead hope for "messianic days" and will apply the vision of Isaiah to post-historical times. Implied here is the thought that messianic days are an ideal and not a reality that human beings will experience in its fullness. We must strive to achieve a world of justice and love, even though we know that we will not live to see it.

How did Isaiah himself view the future? We cannot be certain; suffice it to say that the world he depicted burst the bonds of eons and continents, and became an ensign of hope. Human beings will never be perfect, but they must reach beyond themselves and strive to make life better in every way. The image of the wolf lying down with the lamb is a metaphor reminding us that everything is possible for God. Our human potential is less; yet it is large enough to create a world that has overcome the attractions of violence and injustice.

Gleanings

Words to Remember

The wolf shall dwell with the lamb. (11:6)

They shall not hurt nor destroy
in all My holy mountain. (11:9)

The Eternal God is my strength and my song,
and has become my salvation.
With joy you shall draw water
from the springs of salvation. (12:2-3)

Divergent views about the prophecy

Many commentators of past and present have seen this chapter as growing out of the conditions of Isaiah's time. He was bitterly disappointed with the reign of King Ahaz and hoped that his successor-in-waiting, Hezekiah, would reverse his father's policies and rule the land with righteousness.

The Targum, however, read the passage in messianic terms, and Rashi, Ibn Ezra, and Malbim, among others, followed this line. (See note 5.)

Christians, as indicated in the essay above, see in the prophecy a foretelling of the founder of their faith. [14]

Beyond the horizon

God's ultimate purpose revealed to the prophet indicates a proper rule, peace among nations who worship Israel's one Lord at Zion, and the full restoration of a creation wracked by bloodshed and the forces of chaos themselves. This day may live beyond the horizon of Isaiah's own time, but sufficient is the vision ....

Christopher R. Seitz [15]

Our insufficiency

Had the prophets relied on human resources for justice and righteousness, on human power to achieve redemption, they would not have insisted on the promise of messianic redemption. For messianism implies that any course of living must fail in redeeming the world. In other words, human history is not sufficient unto itself. Our conscience is timid, while the world is ablaze with agony. Our perception of justice is shallow, often defective, and our judgment liable to deception.

Abraham J. Heschel [16]

Israel singing (12:2)

[Israel says:] I sing—for when I sinned You were angry with me, but showed me mercy when I returned to the Torah.

Targum

727

Notes

[1] So Radak; the Assyrian king had conquered cities more heavily fortified, yet would fail against Jerusalem. See also Rashi.

[2] Isaiah 37:24. See also P. Machinist, *Journal of the American Oriental Society,* American Oriental Series, vol. 65 (1984), p. 103.

[3] So also the JPS translation.

[4] I Samuel chapter 16 contains the story of David's family.

[5] 6:13.

[6] So Rashi, Ibn Ezra, and Malbim. The Targum translates/interprets the verse: "A king will come from the House of Jesse, and the Messiah from its offspring." H. L. Ginsberg, in *Encyclopaedia Judaica,* vol. 9, p. 55, sees the Prophet combining his message of the perpetuity of the Davidic line with the Near Eastern notions of his time, that the well-being of plants and animals depends on the just rule of the king. Isaiah thus lays the foundations for post-biblical messianic ideas.

[7] The Hebrew word is related to רית (*re-ach*, odor). Ibn Ezra believes that Isaiah uses the term because he wants to contrast it with the senses of seeing and hearing. While the latter often deceive, the sense of smell, he says, never does.

[8] Medieval commentators were much puzzled over this verse. For, in their view, the Prophet must have foreseen the Babylonian exile (even though it would not happen until more than a hundred years later) and therefore the messianic ingathering should have been called "the third time." Our commentary does not ascribe such intention to Isaiah, who spoke from the perspective of his time.

[9] Ezekiel 37:11; see the haftarah for the Shabbat during Pesach.

[10] So Rashi.

[11] 40:3; haftarah for sidra Va'et-chanan (Shabbat Nachamu).

[12] The Targum and Rashi see the poem as a personal expression of the Prophet, who has been purified by suffering.

[13] Targum and Rashi take "water" to be the Living Waters of Torah.

[14] There is also considerable controversy among modern biblical scholars about the ascription of these verses to Isaiah altogether; they see them coming from a much later, exilic time.

[15] *Anchor Bible Dictionary,* vol. 3, pp. 472 ff., with an overview of various opinions.

[16] *The Prophets,* p. 184.

Ezekiel, chapter 1, verses 1 to 28 and chapter 3, verse 12

Introduction

Connection of haftarah and festival:

Shavuot is the festival of revelation, the giving of the Torah at Mount Sinai. The opening chapter of Ezekiel recalls his first personal revelation, when in his vision he beheld the heavenly chariot and the divine throne.

The setting:

Ezekiel lived in the days before and after the destruction of the First Temple and preached in the early part of the 6th century B.C.E. He was exiled to Babylon and experienced a period of great despair after the destruction of the Temple in 587. His vision assured the exiles that God was still enthroned on high and that therefore a return to the homeland was a realistic hope.

For more on Ezekiel and his time, see our *General Introduction.*

The message:

Despite the fact that this chapter was the most exhaustively studied text in the Tanach, its message is not at all clear. Medieval mystics saw endless meanings in it, for no other prophets had revealed their visions in such detail, yet so mysteriously. Our commentary tries to give the reader a broad idea of what the prophecy tries to convey, while taking note of its great complexity. We bring only a few interpretations, but do not attempt to paint a canvas of scholarly opinions, for there is wide disagreement on almost every phrase or image. (See the essay below.)

1. Time and place of the vision. (1:1-3)

2. The heavenly creatures. (4-14)

3. The chariot. (5-21)

4. The thunder of the Almighty. (22-25.)

5. A vision of God. (26-28.)

6. In praise of God. (3:12; an addition from another chapter, to end the haftarah on a majestic note.)

HAFTARAH FOR THE FIRST DAY OF SHAVUOT

Ezekiel, chapter 1, verses 1 to 28 and chapter 3, verse 12

1:1. On the fifth day of the fourth month of the thirtieth year, I was among the exiles by the river Kebar, when the heavens were opened and I saw visions of God.

2. On the fifth day of the month, in the fifth year of King Jehoiachin's exile,

1:1 וַיְהִי בִּשְׁלֹשִׁים שָׁנָה בָּרְבִיעִי בַּחֲמִשָּׁה לַחֹדֶשׁ וַאֲנִי בְתוֹךְ־הַגּוֹלָה עַל־נְהַר־כְּבָר נִפְתְּחוּ הַשָּׁמַיִם וָאֶרְאֶה מַרְאוֹת אֱלֹהִים:

2 בַּחֲמִשָּׁה לַחֹדֶשׁ הִיא הַשָּׁנָה הַחֲמִישִׁית לְגָלוּת הַמֶּלֶךְ יוֹיָכִין:

Commentary

1:1. *The thirtieth year.* Controversies about the chapter begin with this expression, for verse 1 presents a different time frame from verse 2. Verse 1 does not state the starting point of the thirtieth year, while verse 2 speaks of King Jehoiachin's exile, which happened in 597.

It seems that the key to the puzzle lies in the recognition that verse 2 is most likely an editorial insert. It speaks of Ezekiel in the third person, while verse 1 and the rest of the text have him speak of himself in the first person. Thus, the two verses do not belong together, a solution already suggested by the Midrash.[1] Shalom Spiegel believes that verse 1 was written at the end of the Prophet's career and then put at the head of his collected material. The "thirty year" notation thus would mean that Ezekiel started prophesying while still in Jerusalem, but that the vision related in the verses following belongs to the time of his exile.[2]

Visions of God. Traditional commentators emphasized that this expression makes it clear that Ezekiel was not like Moses. Ezekiel did not see real objects, nor did he actually see God as he would see persons or things.[3] The Torah states the difference clearly: "I make Myself known in a vision or appear in a dream to a prophet who arises among you. Not so with My servant Moses; he is trusted throughout My house. With him I speak mouth to mouth, plainly and not in riddles, and he beholds the likeness of the Eternal."[4] The prophet Hosea, who lived some two hundred years before Ezekiel, said that prophetic visions were like parables.[5]

Radak presents a totally different interpretation and points out that in the Tanach the word *elohim* has two major meanings: the God of Israel (read as a singular) and pagan gods (read as a plural). But in a few instances *elohim* can also mean something great, as in Jonah 3:3, which literally says that Nineveh was "a great city of God," a phrase that is generally understood to mean "an exceedingly great city." Also, in I Chronicles 12:23, the text speaks of "an encampment of God," meaning "a very large encampment." Thus, says Radak, do not read that Ezekiel saw "visions of God," but that he beheld "grand visions."

3. the word of the Eternal came to the priest Ezekiel son of Buzi in the land of the Chaldeans by the river Kebar, and there God's hand came upon him.

4. I looked and beheld a storm-wind coming from the north, a huge cloud with flashing fire and radiance all around it, and in the fire's center something like shining amber.

5. In its center were the shapes of four creatures. This was their appearance: they had human shape.

6. Each had four faces, and each of them had four wings.

7. Their legs were a single straight leg, and their feet had hoofs like a calf's hoof, sparkling like burnished bronze.

8. Under their wings were human hands. And the four had their faces and their wings on their four sides.

3 הָיֹה הָיָה דְבַר־יְהֹוָה אֶל־יְחֶזְקֵאל בֶּן־בּוּזִי הַכֹּהֵן בְּאֶרֶץ כַּשְׂדִּים עַל־נְהַר־כְּבָר וַתְּהִי עָלָיו שָׁם יַד־יְהֹוָה:

4 וָאֵרֶא וְהִנֵּה רוּחַ סְעָרָה בָּאָה מִן־הַצָּפוֹן עָנָן גָּדוֹל וְאֵשׁ מִתְלַקַּחַת וְנֹגַהּ לוֹ סָבִיב וּמִתּוֹכָהּ כְּעֵין הַחַשְׁמַל מִתּוֹךְ הָאֵשׁ:

5 וּמִתּוֹכָהּ דְּמוּת אַרְבַּע חַיּוֹת וְזֶה מַרְאֵיהֶן דְּמוּת אָדָם לָהֵנָּה:

6 וְאַרְבָּעָה פָנִים לְאֶחָת וְאַרְבַּע כְּנָפַיִם לְאַחַת לָהֶם:

7 וְרַגְלֵיהֶם רֶגֶל יְשָׁרָה וְכַף רַגְלֵיהֶם כְּכַף רֶגֶל עֵגֶל וְנֹצְצִים כְּעֵין נְחֹשֶׁת קָלָל:

8 וְיָדוֹ [וִידֵי] אָדָם מִתַּחַת כַּנְפֵיהֶם עַל אַרְבַּעַת רִבְעֵיהֶם וּפְנֵיהֶם וְכַנְפֵיהֶם לְאַרְבַּעְתָּם:

Commentary

3. *The priest Ezekiel.* This explains the Prophet's abiding interest in the priesthood and its duties and privileges, as well as his insistence that the new Temple must conform exactly to divinely ordained measurements (as found in the haftarah for Emor).

Chaldeans. Aramean people who lived in eastern Mesopotamia, whence Abraham's family came.[6] In Ezekiel's time Chaldeans had become a major factor in Babylonian politics, and King Nebuchadnezzar himself belonged to them. In several passages the Prophet uses the terms "Babylonians" and "Chaldeans" interchangeably.

Kebar. A river or canal that cannot be identified with certainty.

God's hand. A metaphor that expresses "the urgency, pressure and compulsion by which he is stunned and overwhelmed."[7]

4. *From the north.* "North" has a strong symbolic meaning in biblical and other Near Eastern literature, evoking fears of a foe coming from there—including the pest of locusts.[8]

Shining amber. חשמל (*chashmal*). Popular belief ascribed mythical qualities to the resinous substance, for the fire it seemed to emit reminded the ancients of lightning. The Septuagint translated the word as *electron*, and in modern Hebrew it stands for electricity.

9. Their wings touched one another; they moved without turning aside, each moving straight ahead.

10. Each of them had a human face, and all four had the face of a lion on the right side, all four the face of an ox on the left side, and all four had the face of an eagle.

11. Their wings were spread; from above, two wings of each creature touched the wing of another, while two covered their bodies.

12. Each one moved straight ahead; wherever the spirit was inclined to go, they would go, without turning as they went.

13. And the likeness of the creatures, their appearance, was like burning coals of fire, like the flare of torches; the fire was going about among the creatures, and the fire had a radiance; and from the fire went forth radiance.

14. The creatures ran to and fro, like lightning flashes.

15. As I looked at the creatures, I saw one wheel on the ground beside each of the four-faced creatures.

9 חֹבְרֹת אִשָּׁה אֶל־אֲחוֹתָהּ כַּנְפֵיהֶם לֹא־יִסַּבּוּ בְלֶכְתָּן אִישׁ אֶל־עֵבֶר פָּנָיו יֵלֵכוּ:

10 וּדְמוּת פְּנֵיהֶם פְּנֵי אָדָם וּפְנֵי אַרְיֵה אֶל־הַיָּמִין לְאַרְבַּעְתָּם וּפְנֵי־שׁוֹר מֵהַשְּׂמֹאול לְאַרְבַּעְתָּן וּפְנֵי־נֶשֶׁר לְאַרְבַּעְתָּן:

11 וּפְנֵיהֶם וְכַנְפֵיהֶם פְּרֻדוֹת מִלְמָעְלָה לְאִישׁ שְׁתַּיִם חֹבְרוֹת אִישׁ וּשְׁתַּיִם מְכַסּוֹת אֵת גְּוִיֹתֵיהֶנָה:

12 וְאִישׁ אֶל־עֵבֶר פָּנָיו יֵלֵכוּ אֶל אֲשֶׁר יִהְיֶה־שָׁמָּה הָרוּחַ לָלֶכֶת יֵלֵכוּ לֹא יִסַּבּוּ בְּלֶכְתָּן:

13 וּדְמוּת הַחַיּוֹת מַרְאֵיהֶם כְּגַחֲלֵי־אֵשׁ בֹּעֲרוֹת כְּמַרְאֵה הַלַּפִּדִים הִיא מִתְהַלֶּכֶת בֵּין הַחַיּוֹת וְנֹגַהּ לָאֵשׁ וּמִן־הָאֵשׁ יוֹצֵא בָרָק:

14 וְהַחַיּוֹת רָצוֹא וָשׁוֹב כְּמַרְאֵה הַבָּזָק:

15 וָאֵרֶא הַחַיּוֹת וְהִנֵּה אוֹפַן אֶחָד בָּאָרֶץ אֵצֶל הַחַיּוֹת לְאַרְבַּעַת פָּנָיו:

Commentary

5-14. Here begins the description of the fantastic chariot, the *merkavah*, as it is commonly referred to; in fact, the whole vision is frequently called by this name. (On its meaning, see the essay below.) However, neither in this chapter nor in chapter 10 (which is closely related) does the term occur.[9]

11. *Their wings*. Our translation follows the Septuagint, which omits "their faces." In Isaiah's vision,[10] the seraphim who were attending God had six wings: with two they covered their faces, with two they covered their legs, and with two they flew.

13-14. The vision contains a wordplay: in verse 13 the radiance is described as ברק (*barak*, lightning[11]), and in verse 14 as בזק (*bazak*, lightning flashes). In modern Hebrew, בזק (*bezek*) means telecommunication.

16. As for the appearance and structure of the wheels: they seemed to shine like topaz; and the four had the same form, their appearance and structure being something like a wheel within a wheel.

17. When they moved, they moved in any of their four quarters; they never turned aside from their course.

18. Their rims were tall and fearsome, for the rims of all four were full of eyes all around.

19. When the creatures went, the wheels went along beside them; and when the creatures lifted themselves from the earth, the wheels lifted themselves.

20. Wherever the spirit was inclined to go, they would go; wherever the spirit was inclined to go, the wheels lifted themselves along with them, for the spirit of the creatures was in the wheels.

21. When they went, the others went; when they stood still, the others stood still; and when they lifted themselves from the earth, the wheels lifted themselves along with them, for the spirit of the creatures was in the wheels.

22. Above the heads of the creatures there was a shape: something like a vault spread out above their heads, ice-like and awe-inspiring.

טז מַרְאֵה הָאוֹפַנִּים וּמַעֲשֵׂיהֶם כְּעֵין תַּרְשִׁישׁ וּדְמוּת אֶחָד לְאַרְבַּעְתָּן וּמַרְאֵיהֶם וּמַעֲשֵׂיהֶם כַּאֲשֶׁר יִהְיֶה הָאוֹפַן בְּתוֹךְ הָאוֹפָן:

יז עַל־אַרְבַּעַת רִבְעֵיהֶן בְּלֶכְתָּם יֵלֵכוּ לֹא יִסַּבּוּ בְּלֶכְתָּן:

יח וְגַבֵּיהֶן וְגֹבַהּ לָהֶם וְיִרְאָה לָהֶם וְגַבֹּתָם מְלֵאֹת עֵינַיִם סָבִיב לְאַרְבַּעְתָּן:

יט וּבְלֶכֶת הַחַיּוֹת יֵלְכוּ הָאוֹפַנִּים אֶצְלָם וּבְהִנָּשֵׂא הַחַיּוֹת מֵעַל הָאָרֶץ יִנָּשְׂאוּ הָאוֹפַנִּים:

כ עַל אֲשֶׁר יִהְיֶה־שָּׁם הָרוּחַ לָלֶכֶת יֵלֵכוּ שָׁמָּה הָרוּחַ לָלֶכֶת וְהָאוֹפַנִּים יִנָּשְׂאוּ לְעֻמָּתָם כִּי רוּחַ הַחַיָּה בָּאוֹפַנִּים:

כא בְּלֶכְתָּם יֵלֵכוּ וּבְעָמְדָם יַעֲמֹדוּ וּבְהִנָּשְׂאָם מֵעַל הָאָרֶץ יִנָּשְׂאוּ הָאוֹפַנִּים לְעֻמָּתָם כִּי רוּחַ הַחַיָּה בָּאוֹפַנִּים:

כב וּדְמוּת עַל־רָאשֵׁי הַחַיָּה רָקִיעַ כְּעֵין הַקֶּרַח הַנּוֹרָא נָטוּי עַל־רָאשֵׁיהֶם מִלְמָעְלָה:

Commentary

16. *Topaz*. תרשיש (*tarshish*) is the name both of a gem and also of a city (most likely Tartessus, in Spain) for which the prophet Jonah's ship was headed.[12] The Targum translates it as "sea color," probably meaning aquamarine.[13]

22. *Vault*. רקיע (*raki'a*). In the Creation story the word stands for firmament, evoking the image of a vault above the earth.[14]

23. Under the vault their wings were spread straight out, one toward another; and each of them had two wings covering its body.

24. And I heard the sound of their wings; when they moved, it was like the sound of mighty waters, like the thunder of the Almighty, a tumultuous sound like the sound of an armed camp; when they stood still, they let their wings drop.

25. Then came a voice from above the vault over their heads, as they stood still with folded wings.

26. And above the vault over their heads was what appeared like a sapphire in the shape of a throne; and above the throne-shape was something that appeared to have a human shape [sitting] on it from above.

27. Above what appeared like his loins, I saw something like shining amber, something that looked like fire enclosed all around; and below what appeared like his loins, I saw something that looked like fire, and there was a radiance all around.

28. Like a rainbow in the clouds on a rainy day, such was the appearance of the surrounding radiance. It was like the appearance of the Radiance [of the Presence] of the Eternal. When I saw it, I fell on my face, and I heard the voice of someone speaking.

23 וְתַ֣חַת הָרָקִ֗יעַ כַּנְפֵיהֶ֤ם יְשָׁרוֹת֙ אִשָּׁ֣ה אֶל־אֲחוֹתָ֔הּ לְאִ֗ישׁ שְׁתַּ֙יִם֙ מְכַסּוֹת֙ לָהֵ֔נָּה וּלְאִ֗ישׁ שְׁתַּ֣יִם מְכַסּוֹת֙ לָהֵ֔נָּה אֵ֖ת גְּוִיֹּתֵיהֶֽם׃

24 וָאֶשְׁמַ֣ע אֶת־ק֣וֹל כַּנְפֵיהֶ֡ם כְּקוֹל֩ מַ֨יִם רַבִּ֤ים כְּקוֹל־שַׁדַּי֙ בְּלֶכְתָּ֔ם ק֥וֹל הֲמֻלָּ֖ה כְּק֣וֹל מַחֲנֶ֑ה בְּעָמְדָ֖ם תְּרַפֶּ֥ינָה כַנְפֵיהֶֽן׃

25 וַיְהִי־ק֕וֹל מֵעַ֕ל לָרָקִ֖יעַ אֲשֶׁ֣ר עַל־רֹאשָׁ֑ם בְּעָמְדָ֖ם תְּרַפֶּ֥ינָה כַנְפֵיהֶֽן׃

26 וּמִמַּ֗עַל לָרָקִ֙יעַ֙ אֲשֶׁ֣ר עַל־רֹאשָׁ֔ם כְּמַרְאֵ֥ה אֶֽבֶן־סַפִּ֖יר דְּמ֣וּת כִּסֵּ֑א וְעַל֙ דְּמ֣וּת הַכִּסֵּ֔א דְּמ֞וּת כְּמַרְאֵ֥ה אָדָ֛ם עָלָ֖יו מִלְמָֽעְלָה׃

27 וָאֵ֣רֶא ׀ כְּעֵ֣ין חַשְׁמַ֗ל כְּמַרְאֵה־אֵ֤שׁ בֵּֽית־לָהּ֙ סָבִ֔יב מִמַּרְאֵ֥ה מָתְנָ֖יו וּלְמָ֑עְלָה וּמִמַּרְאֵ֤ה מָתְנָיו֙ וּלְמַ֔טָּה רָאִ֙יתִי֙ כְּמַרְאֵה־אֵ֔שׁ וְנֹ֥גַהּ ל֖וֹ סָבִֽיב׃

28 כְּמַרְאֵ֣ה הַקֶּ֡שֶׁת אֲשֶׁר֩ יִֽהְיֶ֨ה בֶעָנָ֜ן בְּי֣וֹם הַגֶּ֗שֶׁם כֵּ֣ן מַרְאֵ֤ה הַנֹּ֙גַהּ֙ סָבִ֔יב ה֕וּא מַרְאֵ֖ה דְּמ֣וּת כְּבוֹד־יְהוָ֑ה וָֽאֶרְאֶה֙ וָאֶפֹּ֣ל עַל־פָּנַ֔י וָאֶשְׁמַ֖ע ק֥וֹל מְדַבֵּֽר׃

Commentary

24. *Sound of mighty waters.* מַיִם רַבִּים (*mayim rabbim*), an expression evoking mythic memories.[15]

734

3:12. Then a spirit lifted me up, and behind me I heard a great quaking sound: *Praised be the Presence of the Eternal from its place!*

3:12 וַתִּשָּׂאֵנִי רוּחַ וָאֶשְׁמַע אַחֲרַי קוֹל רַעַשׁ
גָּדוֹל בָּרוּךְ כְּבוֹד־יְהֹוָה מִמְּקוֹמוֹ:

Commentary

3:12. *Praised be the Presence of the Eternal from its place.* These words have been incorporated into the daily liturgy and are recited in the third benediction of the *amidah* (during the *k'dushah*), where they follow shortly after the quotation from Isaiah, "Holy, holy, holy is the God of heaven's hosts, whose Presence fills all the earth."[16] In this way, the vision of Ezekiel becomes a daily response to the vision of Isaiah.

However, despite the familiarity of the phrase, its meaning is not clear. It is best to see it as a parallel to Psalm 135:21, which has a similar phrase: "Praised be the Eternal from Zion," meaning, God is praised by those who are in Zion. For Zion is God's place, and—says Ezekiel—when the exiles will return to it, God's Presence will once more be praised "from its place."[17]

735

Essay

The meaning of the vision

Innumerable attempts have been made to translate the descriptions of this complex vision into a comprehensible visual image, but none of them has been able to gain general support from the many scholars who have studied the text. Obviously, there are wheels and faces, but the way they move in all directions, and the wheels within wheels, present difficulties that cannot be overcome. This kind of vision, and especially the Prophet's desription of the divine throne, bursts the limits of the ordinary and has a reality all of its own.

No wonder, therefore, that those who believed that Ezekiel's experience had a deeper meaning endlessly explored the text for hidden allusions and mystical messages. A whole literature sprang up around this chapter, which has become known as מעשה מרכבה (*ma'aseh merkavah*, chariot mysticism).[18]

Students pored over the words—to such an extent that there was strong opposition to their introduction as the haftarah for Shavuot. In the end, Rabbi Judah's permissive opinion prevailed, for after all, what pious person would not wish to understand the secrets of such a religious vision![19]

Still, asking just exactly what Ezekiel had seen is asking the wrong question altogether. The Prophet had an overwhelming experience that he tried to convey to others. As a descriptive exercise his attempt failed, for his words could not manage to convey with any sense of clarity what his spiritual eye had seen. But, unwittingly perhaps, he thereby suggested to his contemporaries, and the thousands of others who studied his words, that the Presence of God is forever beyond human description.

Gleanings

Words to Remember

Praised be the Presence of the Eternal from its place. (3:12)

A comparison

Isaiah and Ezekiel had the same visions, but Isaiah was like one who lives in the city and sees the king often; while Ezekiel was like a farmer who sees the king rarely.

Talmud[20]

A contradiction

Ezekiel saw two different versions of the same vision: in 1:10 the chariot has an ox among its creatures, and in 10:14, the ox is changed to a cherub. The change took place at Ezekiel's request, for the ox represents Israel's sins, and the Prophet did not wish God to be constantly reminded of these transgressions. God agreed to the change—hence the difference in the two passages.

Talmud[21]

* * *

Notes

[1] Leviticus Rabbah 2:8; so also Rashi.

[2] Shalom Spiegel, "Ezekiel or Pseudo-Ezekiel," *Harvard Theological Review* (1931), vol. 24, pp. 245-321. Moshe Greenberg (see note 9), in his extensive commentary, suggests that perhaps the Prophet edited himself by inserting verse 2.

[3] See Rashi and the Talmud, *B. Yebamot* 49b, which says that Moses saw as if through a clear glass, and other prophets through a clouded glass. See also Maimonides, *Guide of the Perplexed*, vol. II, p. 42.

[4] Numbers 12:6-8.

[5] Hosea 12:11.

[6] Genesis 11:31.

[7] A. J. Heschel, *The Prophets*, p. 444.

[8] See, for example, Jeremiah 1:14 (haftarah for Matot). In Ugaritic mythology "North" (Tzafon) is the name of the mountain home of Baal, god of thunder and fertility.

[9] Moshe Greenberg (*Anchor Bible*, Ezekiel) p. 55, has pointed out that Ezekiel's creatures have their parallels in Mesopotamian iconography. The entrances of Assyrian palaces featured the statue of *lamassu*, a protective spirit with a bovine body, four or five legs, eagles' wings, and a crowned human head.

[10] Isaiah 6:2.

[11] Barak was also the name of Deborah's general; Judges 4 and 5.

[12] Jonah 1:3.

[13] For more on *tarshish*, see the Torah Commentary, p. 74, footnote 4; also, Isaiah 60:9 (haftarah for Ki Tavo).

[14] Genesis 1:7.

[15] See also H. May, *Journal of Biblical Literature*, vol. 74 (1955), pp. 9-21.

[16] Isaiah 6:3.

[17] But Luzzatto proposed that this difficult verse would be more easily understood if a scribal error were corrected. Instead of ברוך (baruch) we should read ברום (berum): "When the Presence of the Eternal rose from its place." Most scholars have adopted this suggestion, though Greenberg doubts it (pp.70-71). For the Jewish reader this possible restoration of the text has only academic value, since the accepted reading has become an important part of the liturgy.

[18] On the term *ma'aseh merkavah*, see S. D. Sperling, *Journal of Near Eastern Studies*, vol. 44 (1985), p. 153. For a survey, see *Encyclopaedia Judaica*, vol. 11, pp. 1386 ff., and, more recently, D. Halperin, *The Merkabah in Rabbinic Literature*.

[19] See *Mishnah* Megillah 4:10.

[20] *B. Hagigah* 13b.

[21] Ibid. The talmudic page contains many fanciful interpretations of the *merkavah*.

Habakkuk, chapter 3, verses 1 to 19

Introduction

Why this haftarah was chosen:

There is no obvious connection between this haftarah and the holy day that celebrates the Giving of the Torah at Sinai. Traditional interpreters base themselves on the obscure remark of Rashi, who sees in verse 3 the reason for the Rabbis' choice of this selection: "God will come from Teman," which Rashi seems to equate with God about to give the Torah on Mount Sinai.[1]

The setting:

As our *General Introduction* has pointed out, we do not know the historical challenges to which Habakkuk responded. Possibly he lived at the time of the destruction of Jerusalem by the Babylonians, who were commissioned by God to punish Israel because of its sins, though they in turn would pay the price for their cruelty. But perhaps it is not essential to know the historical setting, for the Prophet's poetry and commitment are supra-historical. His climactic declaration of unswerving faith in the face of adversity transcends all times and circumstances: "Yet I delight in the Eternal, rejoice in the God of my salvation" (verse 18).

For more on Habakkuk and his time, see our *General Introduction*.

The message:

1. An introductory, personal prayer. (1-2)
2. A celebration of God's awesome power, often referred to as a theophany, reminiscent of the final chapters of the book of Job. (3-17)

HAFTARAH FOR THE SECOND DAY OF SHAVUOT

Habakkuk, chapter 3, verses 1 to 19

3:1. *A prayer of Habakkuk the prophet in the manner of shigionot.*

2. O Eternal, I have heard of Your fame,

and am in awe of Your deed, O Eternal.

As the the years go by, tell it afresh,

throughout the years make it known;

[and even] in anger remember compassion!

3. God, You will come from Teman,

the Holy One from Mount Paran. Selah.

Your glory covers the heavens,

Your splendor fills the earth.

4. Your brightness is like the sun's,

rays of light came from Your hand;

the heavens are Your mighty palace.

תְּפִלָּה לַחֲבַקּוּק הַנָּבִיא עַל שִׁגְיֹנֽוֹת׃ 3:1

יְהֹוָה שָׁמַעְתִּי שִׁמְעֲךָ 2

יָרֵאתִי יְהֹוָה פָּעָלְךָ

בְּקֶרֶב שָׁנִים חַיֵּיהוּ

בְּקֶרֶב שָׁנִים תּוֹדִיעַ

בְּרֹגֶז רַחֵם תִּזְכּֽוֹר׃

אֱלוֹהַ מִתֵּימָן יָבוֹא 3

וְקָדוֹשׁ מֵהַר־פָּארָן סֶֽלָה

כִּסָּה שָׁמַיִם הוֹדוֹ

וּתְהִלָּתוֹ מָלְאָה הָאָֽרֶץ׃

וְנֹגַהּ כָּאוֹר תִּהְיֶה 4

קַרְנַיִם מִיָּדוֹ לוֹ

וְשָׁם חֶבְיוֹן עֻזֹּֽה׃

Commentary

The text presents great difficulties, mainly because it is a poem that uses allusions and figures of speech, some of which may have been readily comprehensible in Habakkuk's time but are no longer accessible. Modern poetry too is often hard to understand and will require added elucidation in the future.

1. *A prayer.* Which is found in verse 2.

Shigionot. A loanword from Akkadian (Assyro-Babylonian), where it refers to a genre of lament or complaint prayers. Here, verse 17 contains a lament over the failure of vegetation. The word occurs only once more in the Tanach, in Psalm 7:1.

3. *God, You will come.* From here through verse 6, our translation uses the second person, rather than the third, as in the Hebrew. A prayerful address to God continues the mode of verses 1 and 2.

Teman. Usually signifying the area of Edom, east of Israel, or meaning "south" in general. In modern Hebrew it is the name for Yemen, in southern Arabia. Inscriptions discovered in the Sinai peninsula speak of God as *Yhvh Tmn*, "the Eternal of Teman."[2]

Paran. The hill country along the eastern coast of the Gulf of Akaba. The blessing of Moses begins in a similar vein: "The Eternal came from Sinai … appearing from Mount Paran."[3] God is pictured as coming from the east to reveal the Divine Presence.

Selah. A concluding exclamation often appearing in Psalms, a kind of "Amen."

4. *The heavens are Your mighty palace.* A difficult verse; the translation follows N. Tur-Sinai.[4]

5 לְפָנָיו יֵלֶךְ דָּבֶר
וְיֵצֵא רֶשֶׁף לְרַגְלָיו:

6 עָמַד וַיְמֹדֶד אֶרֶץ
רָאָה וַיַּתֵּר גּוֹיִם
וַיִּתְפֹּצְצוּ הַרְרֵי־עַד
שַׁחוּ גִּבְעוֹת עוֹלָם
הֲלִיכוֹת עוֹלָם לוֹ:

7 תַּחַת אָוֶן רָאִיתִי אָהֳלֵי כוּשָׁן
יִרְגְּזוּן יְרִיעוֹת אֶרֶץ מִדְיָן:

8 הֲבִנְהָרִים חָרָה יְהוָה
אִם בַּנְּהָרִים אַפֶּךָ
אִם־בַּיָּם עֶבְרָתֶךָ
כִּי תִרְכַּב עַל־סוּסֶיךָ מַרְכְּבֹתֶיךָ יְשׁוּעָה:

9 עֶרְיָה תֵעוֹר קַשְׁתֶּךָ
שְׁבֻעוֹת מַטּוֹת אֹמֶר סֶלָה
נְהָרוֹת תְּבַקַּע־אָרֶץ:

5. Plague goes forth before You,
and Pestilence at Your heels.

6. You stand and shake the earth,
You gaze, and make the nations tremble:
the ancient mountains shatter,
the everlasting hills bow down;
the everlasting paths are smashed.

7. I see the tents of Cushan;
the tents [of Cushan] quiver,
Midian-Land is afraid.

8. Are You angry at the rivers, Eternal One?
or is Your wrath (directed at) Neharim,
Your fury against Yam,
that You ride Your steeds, Your chariots to
     victory?

9. You brandish Your naked bow,
the arrows [You] urge forth are sated;
into streams You split the earth. Selah.

Commentary

5. *Pestilence.* רשׁף (reshef). The prophet employs mythic language, denoting an ancient god of pestilence.[5]

At Your heels. That is, "behind You." God's power encompasses all creation.

6-7. The translation follows the suggestion of W. Albright.[6]

The everlasting paths. When the great earthquake occurred and the deep rift valley of the Aravah was formed.[7]

The tents of Cushan. Alluding to the people of a tribe in the Sinai peninsula.

8. *Or is Your wrath (directed at) Neharim.* A wordplay: in the previous line Neharim has the usual meaning of "rivers"; here it denotes a mythic sea monster in Canaanite folklore.

Yam. Another wordplay: in Hebrew it means sea, but in Canaanite lore it was the name of another sea monster.

9. *The arrows.* A conjectural translation.[8]

Selah. Transposed to the end of the verse.

10. The mountains see You and tremble;

a torrent of water passes by;

the deep gives forth its voice

it lifts its hands on high;

11. the sun [withholds its light],

the moon (stands still) at its zenith

at the light of Your flying arrows,

at the gleam of Your flashing spear.

12. In fury You tread the earth,

in wrath You trample nations.

13. You go forth for Your people's salvation,

the salvation of Your anointed.

You tear the roof from the house of the wicked,

laying it bare from bottom to top.

14. With his [own] staves You pierce

the leader of his troops,

who had stormed to scatter us,

whose delight it was

to devour the poor in ambush.

15. You tread the sea with Your steeds,

churning the mighty waters.

10 רָאוּךָ יָחִילוּ הָרִים

זֶרֶם מַיִם עָבָר

נָתַן תְּהוֹם קוֹלוֹ

רוֹם יָדֵיהוּ נָשָׂא׃

11 שֶׁמֶשׁ יָרֵחַ עָמַד זְבֻלָה

לְאוֹר חִצֶּיךָ יְהַלֵּכוּ

לְנֹגַהּ בְּרַק חֲנִיתֶךָ׃

12 בְּזַעַם תִּצְעַד־אָרֶץ

בְּאַף תָּדוּשׁ גּוֹיִם׃

13 יָצָאתָ לְיֵשַׁע עַמֶּךָ

לְיֵשַׁע אֶת־מְשִׁיחֶךָ

מָחַצְתָּ רֹּאשׁ מִבֵּית רָשָׁע

עָרוֹת יְסוֹד עַד־צַוָּאר סֶלָה׃

14 נָקַבְתָּ בְמַטָּיו

רֹאשׁ פְּרָזֹו [פְּרָזָיו]

יִסְעֲרוּ לַהֲפִיצֵנִי

עֲלִיצֻתָם

כְּמוֹ־לֶאֱכֹל עָנִי בַּמִּסְתָּר׃

15 דָּרַכְתָּ בַיָּם סוּסֶיךָ

חֹמֶר מַיִם רַבִּים׃

Commentary

10. *It lifts ...* A literal rendering of an obscure passage.

11. *The sun [withholds its light]* .... Some text is missing here; the bracketed words are supplied by the Septuagint.

13. *Your anointed.* Either Israel or the Davidic king who will reign over it.

From bottom to top. Literally, "from foundation to neck," an idiom occurring regularly in the royal Assyrian annals, in the descriptions of victories over enemies.

14. *Scatter us.* Literally, "scatter me." Habakkuk identifies himself with the agony of Israel.

15. *You tread the sea.* Not like the would-be god Pharaoh, who was engulfed by the waves. (See also *Gleanings* below.)

16. I hear, and my bowels shake;

my lips quiver at the sound.

Rottenness enters my bones,

I shake where I stand,

though I wait for the day of woe

to befall the people who attack us.

17. Though the fig-tree does not blossom,

and there is no fruit on the vine;

though the olive crop fails,

fields yield no food,

the flock is cut off from the fold,

and there are no cattle in the stalls,

18. yet I delight in the Eternal,

rejoice in the God of my salvation.

19. The Eternal God is my strength,

making my feet nimble as the doe's,

[so that] I can stride upon the heights.

For the leader: with musical instruments.

16 שָׁמַ֤עְתִּי ׀ וַתִּרְגַּ֨ז בִּטְנִ֜י

לְק֣וֹל צָלֲל֣וּ שְׂפָתַ֗י

יָב֣וֹא רָקָ֣ב בַּעֲצָמַ֔י

וְתַחְתַּ֖י אֶרְגָּ֑ז

אֲשֶׁ֤ר אָנ֙וּחַ֙ לְי֣וֹם צָרָ֔ה

לַעֲל֖וֹת לְעַ֥ם יְגוּדֶֽנּוּ׃

17 כִּֽי־תְאֵנָ֣ה לֹֽא־תִפְרָ֗ח

וְאֵ֤ין יְבוּל֙ בַּגְּפָנִ֔ים

כִּחֵשׁ֙ מַעֲשֵׂה־זַ֔יִת

וּשְׁדֵמ֖וֹת לֹא־עָ֣שָׂה אֹ֑כֶל

גָּזַ֤ר מִמִּכְלָה֙ צֹ֔אן

וְאֵ֥ין בָּקָ֖ר בָּרְפָתִֽים׃

18 וַאֲנִ֖י בַּיהוָ֣ה אֶעְל֑וֹזָה

אָגִ֖ילָה בֵּאלֹהֵ֥י יִשְׁעִֽי׃

19 יְהוִ֤ה אֲדֹנָי֙ חֵילִ֔י

וַיָּ֤שֶׂם רַגְלַי֙ כָּֽאַיָּל֔וֹת

וְעַ֥ל בָּמוֹתַ֖י יַדְרִכֵ֑נִי

לַמְנַצֵּ֖חַ בִּנְגִינוֹתָֽי׃

Commentary

16. *I hear, and my bowels shake.* The theophany ends in the way it began in verse 2: "I have heard of Your fame, and am in awe of Your work."

19. *Upon the heights.* Literally, my heights.

Essay

And yet ....

Habakkuk enters into his poem about God's greatness a note that tends to startle the modern reader:

Though the fig-tree does not blossom,
and there is no fruit on the vine;
though the olive crop fails,
fields yield no food,
the flock is cut off from the fold,
and there are no cattle in the stalls,
yet I delight in the Eternal,
rejoice in the God of my salvation. (verses 17 and 18)

This is a farmer speaking of a dismal season, when everything went wrong, when all investments were lost and the cash register was emptied. This is no mere prophetic imagination; it was then, and remains today, a calamity all too often repeated. The imagery applies to life in every age—but does the conclusion?

Almost triumphantly, Habakkuk announces that under no circumstances will he, for one, abandon his faith in God's goodness and providence. Transposed into the modern era, the poem resounds in the words of Maimonides that Jews bound for the gas chambers of Auschwitz put to song: "*Im kol zeh ani ma'amin,* yet will I believe!"

"Yet will I believe" is the refrain of the song, a chant of hope, trust, and faith. When people repeat it today, do they thereby affirm that this kind of belief is theirs as well?

Many chant the words but do it only as a tribute to history, to evoke the spirit of defiance. They themselves do not and cannot share the unconditional faith of a Habakkuk or of those singing their last song. They no longer see God as the *deus ex machina*, the power that controls everything. For them, God does not produce earthquakes; instead they see the interaction of huge plates shifting along the earth's faults. Nor do they believe in a God who commands the rain or its absence, or gives victory to one and hands defeat to another. If they still believe in God (and most say that they do), they think of the Divine Presence as a resource, but no longer as the Almighty of whom Habakkuk sings.

The haftarah is read on the second day of Shavuot, the festival that celebrates the Giving of the Torah at Sinai. That moment in history forged a partnership that did not lay an obligation of belief on the people, but rather an obligation of action. Judaism is a religion centered on mitzvot, the right kind of human behavior. The personal cry of Habakkuk has been an inspiration and example in past ages, but today many find themselves unable to repeat the Prophet's "and yet." Their inability does not remove them from the community, for belief is not the core of its existence. Faith is a diamond that sparkles with many colors.

Gleanings

The daring of Habakkuk

A famous talmudic figure, Choni the Circle Drawer—so called because when he wanted something of God he drew a circle and refused to leave it until God would heed his prayer—was given legitimacy by comparing him to Habakkuk. For in one of his prophecies he had said:

I will stand at my watch and take up my assigned station,
and wait to see what God will say to me in reply to my complaint.[9]

Choni was like the Prophet when he stood up to God in order to defend the welfare of his people.

Talmud[10]

Impatient prophet

Habakkuk's prophecy shows several characteristic features. The reader who comes to it by way of Amos, Micah, or Isaiah cannot but be surprised at the change which has come over the prophet's relationship to God. The roles seem to be reversed: the initiative lies with the prophet, for it is he who is discontented and impatient, while God is the one who is questioned.

Gerhard von Rad[11]

Literary parallel

[In the Babylonian *Creation Epic*[12]] we can follow precisely the movements and adventures ascribed to Marduk in that most famous and most influential liturgy in the ancient world .... The enemy of the Lord was the primeval foe, chaos and darkness; but he was also the ever recurring persecutor and oppressor of the Lord's people. Pharaoh, Amalek, Edom, or Nebuchadrezzar, and far down the centuries, Antiochus Epiphanes or even Adolf Hitler—all alike were but the demon of the primeval deep over whom the Lord triumphed at the beginning, over whom he is perennially and eternally triumphant.

William A. Irwin[13]

Against the idolatry of the gentiles

When, following the collapse of the Assyrian empire, a new pagan empire, no less powerful than Assyria, strode suddenly onto the stage of history, Israel was profoundly shaken. It had thought that Assyria's fall would mean the end of idolatrous power, and now this hope was disappointed. The terror and confusion of the time are expressed in Habakkuk's bitter outcry. Then, at that very moment, there is born something utterly new and heavy with consequence, the first direct assault on paganism addressed to the gentiles (2:18-20). The words are visionary. But words of this sort are here spoken for the first time to the gentiles, and not merely in a vision.[14]

Notes

[1] Issachar Jacobson, *Chazon Hamikra*, vol. 2, p. 315, cites the interpretation of his teacher, Rabbi J. Carlebach, who in 1933 (when the Nazis came to power) saw in Habakkuk proof that God's power would prevail to protect the Children of the Covenant. The Babylonians (whom Habakkuk excoriates in his earlier prophecies) were overcome, and so would the modern would-be conquerors of God's people.

[2] See J. Roberts, *Nahum, Habakkuk, and Zephaniah*, p. 132.

[3] Deuteronomy 33:2.

[4] *The Language and the Book II*, p.139.

[5] Attested in the third millennium B.C.E. at Ebla, in central Syria.

[6] "The Psalm of Habakkuk," in H. H. Rowley (ed.), *Studies in Old Testament Prophecy*, p. 11.

[7] See our comment on Zechariah 14:4 (haftarah for the first day of Sukkot).

[8] A most ingenious explanation was provided by H. S. J. Thackery in the *Journal of Theological Studies*, vol. 12 (1910-1911), pp. 191-210. He took the three words מטות אמר שבעות to be marginal notes, indicating that this chapter from Habakkuk was used as the haftarah for the festival of Shavuot as well as for the sidrot Matot and Emor, in communities that followed the triennial cycle of Torah readings.

[9] Habakkuk 2:1.

[10] B. Ta'anit 23a.

[11] *The Message of the Prophets*, p. 159.

[12] Early first millennium B.C.E.

[13] "The Psalm of Habakkuk," *Journal of Near Eastern Studies*, vol. 1 (1942), pp.10-42.

[14] Yehezkel Kaufmann, *The Babylonian Captivity*, p. 48.

Jeremiah, chapter 8, verse 13 to chapter 9, verse 23

Introduction

Connection of Tisha b'Av and the haftarah:

Tisha b'Av commemorates the tragedy of the Jewish people: the expulsion from its homeland and its subsequent exile. The haftarah brings us the dark vision of Jeremiah, who later on was destined to witness the destruction and its terrible aftermath. "No selection for this day could have been more appropriate than the one before us."[1]

The setting:

Jeremiah made himself increasingly unpopular when he inveighed against Jerusalem's religious and social corruption and against the king's wrong-headed policies. His dire predictions were proven true when the Babylonians plundered the city in 598 B.C.E., but did not destroy it at that time. Most likely the haftarah comes from the period after the invaders had left. Jeremiah warns of worse consequences if the people and their leaders will not reform their ways—prophecies that led to his incarceration.

For more on Jeremiah, see our *General Introduction.*

Content of the haftarah:

Many see the text as a collection of warnings and prophecies,[2] a view that seems plausible inasmuch as God, Israel, and Jeremiah alternate in speaking various verses. Since either Jeremiah's secretary, Baruch, or a later editor arranged the text, we can now read these seemingly disconnected lines as if they are a dialogue between God and Israel, and an occasional interjection by Jeremiah himself. For the underlying theme is the same: Israel's unfaithfulness and corruption have already led and will continue to lead to its utter destruction at the hands of a God who metes out just punishment.

Part 1

    1. God: I will make an end of this people. (8:13)
       Israel: We are lost, there is no hope. (14-16)

    2. God: Indeed, things will get worse. (17)
       Jeremiah: What will You answer the people? (18-19a)

    3. God: Why do they rely on other gods? (19b)
       Israel: Time passes and we are not saved. (20)

    4. God: Your doings have put Me too in mourning. (21)
       Jeremiah: Help! My anguish is too great to bear. (22-23)

Part 2

    5. Jeremiah: Alas for the people's corruption. (9:1-5)
       God: You are right; should they not be punished? (6-10)

6. A questioner: Why is all this happening? (11)

    Jeremiah: It is God's doing because of your evil ways. (12-15)

Part 3

7. God: The time for mourning has come. (16)

    Israel: Then we might as well call for the professional wailers. (17-18)

8. Jeremiah: Do it, and here is what they shall cry out .... (19-21)

    God's final word: Yet there is hope if you mend your ways. (22-23)

8:13. I will make an end of them,

says the Eternal,

[so that] there are no grapes on the vine,

no figs on the tree,

and the leaves wither,

and what I gave them will pass on [to the
enemy].

14. *Why are we sitting still?*

Let us assemble and go to the fortified cities,

there to meet our doom.

For the Eternal our God has doomed us,

making us drink poisoned waters,

because we have sinned against the Eternal.

15. *We hope for well-being but no good
comes;*

for a time of healing, and behold, terror.

אָסֹף אֲסִיפֵם 8:13

נְאֻם־יְהֹוָה

אֵין עֲנָבִים בַּגֶּפֶן

וְאֵין תְּאֵנִים בַּתְּאֵנָה

וְהֶעָלֶה נָבֵל

וָאֶתֵּן לָהֶם יַעַבְרוּם:

עַל־מָה אֲנַחְנוּ יֹשְׁבִים 14

הֵאָסְפוּ וְנָבוֹא אֶל־עָרֵי הַמִּבְצָר

וְנִדְּמָה־שָּׁם

כִּי יְהֹוָה אֱלֹהֵינוּ הֲדִמָּנוּ

וַיַּשְׁקֵנוּ מֵי־רֹאשׁ

כִּי חָטָאנוּ לַיהֹוָה:

קַוֵּה לְשָׁלוֹם וְאֵין טוֹב 15

לְעֵת מַרְפֵּה וְהִנֵּה בְעָתָה:

Commentary

8:13. *I will make an end of them.* The Hebrew is difficult, and it has been suggested that a change of vocalization would make the phrase into the perfect parallel to what follows. By reading אסוף אסיפם (*asuf asifam*), one would obtain, "their harvest has been gathered in."[3]

What I gave them. The yield of your fields.

... will pass on [to the enemy]. The Hebrew is difficult; our translation follows Radak.

15. *Well-being.* מרפה (*marpeh*). The Hebrew spelling is an example of the scrupulous care with which the scribes copied sacred texts. As it now appears, the word is misspelled, for the final letter should have been an aleph, and though the scribes knew this, they faithfully copied the mistake and wrote ה. (In Hebrew texts, a marginal note points this out.)

16. *From Dan is heard the snorting of his steeds;*

at the neighing of his stallions
the whole land quakes.
They come to consume the land and everything in it,
the city and all who dwell there.
17. For behold I send snakes among you,
adders against whom no charm is proof
when they bite you,
says the Eternal.
18. *My anguish has no cure;*
I am sick at heart.
19. *Hark! The cry of my people from a distant land!*
Is the Eternal not in Zion?
Is her Sovereign no longer in her midst?
Why have they angered Me with their idols,
their foreign no-gods?
20. *The harvest has passed,*
summer is over,
and we are not saved.
21. I am wracked by the wreckage of My (fair) people,
I [too] am in mourning: desolation has seized me.

16 מִדָּן נִשְׁמַע נַחְרַת סוּסָיו
מִקּוֹל מִצְהֲלוֹת אַבִּירָיו
רָעֲשָׁה כָּל־הָאָרֶץ
וַיָּבוֹאוּ וַיֹּאכְלוּ אֶרֶץ וּמְלוֹאָהּ
עִיר וְיֹשְׁבֵי בָהּ:
17 כִּי הִנְנִי מְשַׁלֵּחַ בָּכֶם נְחָשִׁים
צִפְעֹנִים אֲשֶׁר אֵין־לָהֶם לָחַשׁ
וְנִשְּׁכוּ אֶתְכֶם
נְאֻם־יְהֹוָה:
18 מַבְלִיגִיתִי עֲלֵי יָגוֹן
עָלַי לִבִּי דַוָּי:
19 הִנֵּה־קוֹל שַׁוְעַת בַּת־עַמִּי מֵאֶרֶץ מַרְחַקִּים
הַיהֹוָה אֵין בְּצִיּוֹן
אִם־מַלְכָּהּ אֵין בָּהּ
מַדּוּעַ הִכְעִסוּנִי בִּפְסִלֵיהֶם
בְּהַבְלֵי נֵכָר:
20 עָבַר קָצִיר
כָּלָה קָיִץ
וַאֲנַחְנוּ לוֹא נוֹשָׁעְנוּ:
21 עַל־שֶׁבֶר בַּת־עַמִּי הָשְׁבָּרְתִּי
קָדַרְתִּי שַׁמָּה הֶחֱזִקָתְנִי:

Commentary

16. *From Dan*. The tribe dwelt in the northernmost of the country, and it knew that the Babylonians were threatening to march again.[4]

His steeds. Babylon's war-horses.

The land and everything in it. The enemies have cast us out.[5]

19. *From a distant land*. In 598, Babylon had raided Jerusalem and exiled some of its people, who long to return to their homes.

20. *The harvest has passed*. Instead of being compensated for our toil, we are disappointed.[6]

21. *I [too] am in mourning*. Literally, in black.

22. Is there no balm in Gilead?

No healer there?

Why then does my people's wound remain
    unhealed?

23. Would that my head were water,

and my eyes a fountain of tears;

I would weep day and night

for the slain of my fair people.

9:1. Would that I could find

a lodging place for travelers in the wilder-
    ness

so that I could leave my people,

and go away from them—

for they are all adulterers,

a band of traitors.

2. They bend their tongues like bows

—to lie.

They are mighty in the land

—but not for truth,

as they proceed from evil to evil,

and Me they do not [want to] know,

says the Eternal One.

3. Let each beware of the other,

and do not depend on your kin,

הַצֳּרִי אֵין בְּגִלְעָד 22

אִם־רֹפֵא אֵין שָׁם

כִּי מַדּוּעַ לֹא עָלְתָה אֲרֻכַת בַּת־עַמִּי:

מִי־יִתֵּן רֹאשִׁי מַיִם 23

וְעֵינִי מְקוֹר דִּמְעָה

וְאֶבְכֶּה יוֹמָם וָלַיְלָה

אֵת חַלְלֵי בַת־עַמִּי:

מִי־יִתְּנֵנִי 9:1

בַמִּדְבָּר מְלוֹן אֹרְחִים

וְאֶעֶזְבָה אֶת־עַמִּי

וְאֵלְכָה מֵאִתָּם

כִּי כֻלָּם מְנָאֲפִים

עֲצֶרֶת בֹּגְדִים:

וַיַּדְרְכוּ אֶת־לְשׁוֹנָם קַשְׁתָּם 2

שֶׁקֶר

וְלֹא לֶאֱמוּנָה

גָּבְרוּ בָאָרֶץ

כִּי מֵרָעָה אֶל־רָעָה יָצָאוּ

וְאֹתִי לֹא־יָדָעוּ

נְאֻם־יְהֹוָה:

אִישׁ מֵרֵעֵהוּ הִשָּׁמֵרוּ 3

וְעַל־כָּל־אָח אַל־תִּבְטָחוּ

Commentary

22. *Is there no balm in Gilead?* The phrase became part of Hebrew speech, expressing hope in the midst of despair. But just what Jeremiah meant here by "Gilead" is not clear. Generally, the word denotes the territory east of the Jordan, assigned to Gad, Reuben, and half of the tribe of Manasseh.

for every brother is a heel-grabber,

and every friend goes about as a slanderer.

4. Each deceives the other,

no one speaks the truth;

they have trained their tongues to lie;

they are worn out with their own iniquity.

5. Amidst deceit is your dwelling,

[and] deceitfully they refuse to acknowledge Me,

says the Eternal One.

6. Therefore, thus says the God of heaven's
hosts:

Behold, I will refine and test them,

for what else can I do about My people?

7. Their tongues are deadly arrows,

speaking deceitfully through their mouths;

they speak cordially to their friends,

while inwardly setting traps for them.

8. Should I not punish them for these
things,

says the Eternal One?

Should I not avenge Myself

against such a nation?

9. For the hills

I take up weeping and wailing,

for the pastures of the wilderness

a dirge.

They are scorched,

so that no one can pass through,

כִּי כָל־אָח עָקוֹב יַעְקֹב

וְכָל־רֵעַ רָכִיל יַהֲלֹךְ:

4 וְאִישׁ בְּרֵעֵהוּ יְהָתֵלּוּ

וֶאֱמֶת לֹא יְדַבֵּרוּ

לִמְּדוּ לְשׁוֹנָם דַּבֶּר־שֶׁקֶר

הַעֲוֵה נִלְאוּ:

5 שִׁבְתְּךָ בְּתוֹךְ מִרְמָה

בְּמִרְמָה מֵאֲנוּ דַעַת־אוֹתִי

נְאֻם־יְהֹוָה:

6 לָכֵן כֹּה אָמַר יְהֹוָה צְבָאוֹת

הִנְנִי צוֹרְפָם וּבְחַנְתִּים

כִּי־אֵיךְ אֶעֱשֶׂה מִפְּנֵי בַּת־עַמִּי:

7 חֵץ שׁוֹחֵט [שָׁחוּט] לְשׁוֹנָם

מִרְמָה דִבֵּר בְּפִיו

שָׁלוֹם אֶת־רֵעֵהוּ יְדַבֵּר

וּבְקִרְבּוֹ יָשִׂים אָרְבּוֹ:

8 הַעַל־אֵלֶּה לֹא־אֶפְקָד־בָּם

נְאֻם־יְהֹוָה

אִם בְּגוֹי אֲשֶׁר־כָּזֶה

לֹא תִתְנַקֵּם נַפְשִׁי:

9 עַל־הֶהָרִים

אֶשָּׂא בְכִי וָנֶהִי

וְעַל־נְאוֹת מִדְבָּר

קִינָה

כִּי נִצְּתוּ מִבְּלִי־אִישׁ עֹבֵר

Commentary

9:3. *A heel-grabber.* A reference to Jacob, who was so named because at birth he held on to the heel of his twin brother, Esau.[7]

4. *They have trained their tongues to lie.* The art of lying is learned, not inborn.[8]

6. *I will refine and test them.* In the crucible of suffering.[9]

and the lowing of cattle is not heard.

Birds of the air, animals—

all have fled and are gone.

10. I will make Jerusalem a heap, a haunt of jackals,

and the towns of Judah will I make a wasteland

without inhabitants.

11. Who is wise enough to understand this?

To whom has God spoken, so they may impart it?

Why is the land destroyed, scorched like the desert,

without a passerby?

12. The Eternal One said:

Because they forsook My Teaching I had set before them,

and neither listened to My voice nor followed it,

13. but stubbornly followed their own hearts,

(followed) the Baals,

as their ancestors taught them.

14. Therefore, says the God of heaven's hosts,

the God of Israel:

Behold, I will give this people wormwood to eat and poison to drink,

וְלֹא שָׁמְעוּ קוֹל מִקְנֶה

מֵעוֹף הַשָּׁמַיִם וְעַד־בְּהֵמָה

נָדְדוּ הָלָכוּ:

10 וְנָתַתִּי אֶת־יְרוּשָׁלַ͏ִם לְגַלִּים מְעוֹן תַּנִּים

וְאֶת־עָרֵי יְהוּדָה אֶתֵּן שְׁמָמָה

מִבְּלִי יוֹשֵׁב:

11 מִי־הָאִישׁ הֶחָכָם וְיָבֵן אֶת־זֹאת

וַאֲשֶׁר דִּבֶּר פִּי־יְהוָה אֵלָיו וְיַגִּדָהּ

עַל־מָה אָבְדָה הָאָרֶץ נִצְּתָה כַמִּדְבָּר

מִבְּלִי עֹבֵר:

12 וַיֹּאמֶר יְהוָה

עַל־עָזְבָם אֶת־תּוֹרָתִי אֲשֶׁר נָתַתִּי לִפְנֵיהֶם

וְלֹא־שָׁמְעוּ בְקוֹלִי וְלֹא־הָלְכוּ בָהּ:

13 וַיֵּלְכוּ אַחֲרֵי שְׁרִרוּת לִבָּם

וְאַחֲרֵי הַבְּעָלִים

אֲשֶׁר לִמְּדוּם אֲבוֹתָם:

14 לָכֵן כֹּה־אָמַר יְהוָה צְבָאוֹת

אֱלֹהֵי יִשְׂרָאֵל

הִנְנִי מַאֲכִילָם אֶת־הָעָם הַזֶּה לַעֲנָה וְהִשְׁקִיתִים

מֵי־רֹאשׁ:

Commentary

11. *Who is wise enough.* We can't understand what is happening to us and need someone to tell us what is at the root of all our misfortunes.

753

15. and scatter them among nations
unfamiliar to them and their ancestors,
and make the sword pursue them
until I have consumed them.

16. Thus says the God of heaven's hosts:
Pay heed, and call to the wailing women to
come;
send for the skillful ones, and have them
come!

17. *Let them quickly raise a dirge for us,
that our eyelids may run with tears,
our eyes flow with water!*

18. *For out of Zion is heard a dirge:
How are we ruined, and greatly shamed!
For we have left our land,
for they have destroyed our dwellings!*

19. So hear, you women, the word of the
Eternal,
let your ears take [in] the word of God's
mouth;
teach a dirge to your daughters,
and each other a lament.

15 וַהֲפִצוֹתִים בַּגּוֹיִם
אֲשֶׁר לֹא יָדְעוּ הֵמָּה וַאֲבוֹתָם
וְשִׁלַּחְתִּי אַחֲרֵיהֶם אֶת־הַחֶרֶב
עַד כַּלּוֹתִי אוֹתָם:

16 כֹּה אָמַר יְהוָה צְבָאוֹת
הִתְבּוֹנְנוּ וְקִרְאוּ לַמְקוֹנְנוֹת וּתְבוֹאֶינָה
וְאֶל־הַחֲכָמוֹת שִׁלְחוּ וְתָבוֹאנָה:

17 וּתְמַהֵרְנָה וְתִשֶּׂנָה עָלֵינוּ נֶהִי
וְתֵרַדְנָה עֵינֵינוּ דִּמְעָה
וְעַפְעַפֵּינוּ יִזְּלוּ־מָיִם:

18 כִּי קוֹל נְהִי נִשְׁמַע מִצִּיּוֹן
אֵיךְ שֻׁדָּדְנוּ בֹּשְׁנוּ מְאֹד
כִּי־עָזַבְנוּ אָרֶץ
כִּי הִשְׁלִיכוּ מִשְׁכְּנוֹתֵינוּ:

19 כִּי־שְׁמַעְנָה נָשִׁים דְּבַר־יְהוָה
וְתִקַּח אָזְנְכֶם דְּבַר־פִּיו
וְלַמֵּדְנָה בְנוֹתֵיכֶם נֶהִי
וְאִשָּׁה רְעוּתָהּ קִינָה:

Commentary

16. *Wailing women.* It was an old custom to have women, rather than men, express personal and communal sorrow in an unrestrained and natural manner. In time, such authentic wailing became ritualized, and professional wailers accompanied the dead.

17. *Raise a dirge.* Note that ותשנה (vetissenah) lacks an aleph and should read ותשאנה. Though the ancient scribal error was obvious, it was nonetheless copied faithfully (see also note on 8:15).[10]

19. *God's mouth.* Literally, "His."

20. Death has come up through our
    windows,

has entered our palaces

to cut off children from the streets,

young people from the thoroughfares.

21. Thus shall you speak, says the Eternal
    One:

People's corpses shall fall

like dung on the field,

like sheaves after the harvester,

with no one to gather them up.

22. Thus says the Eternal One:

Let not the wise glory in their wisdom,

let not the mighty glory in their might,

let not the rich glory in their riches;

23. but let them who glory, glory in this:

that they understand and know Me,

that I, the Eternal, practice kindness,

justice, and righteousness in the earth,

for in these things do I delight,

says the Eternal One.

20 כִּי־עָלָה מָוֶת בְּחַלּוֹנֵינוּ

בָּא בְּאַרְמְנוֹתֵינוּ

לְהַכְרִית עוֹלָל מִחוּץ

בַּחוּרִים מֵרְחֹבוֹת:

21 דַּבֵּר כֹּה נְאֻם־יְהֹוָה

וְנָפְלָה נִבְלַת הָאָדָם

כְּדֹמֶן עַל־פְּנֵי הַשָּׂדֶה

וּכְעָמִיר מֵאַחֲרֵי הַקֹּצֵר

וְאֵין מְאַסֵּף:

22 כֹּה אָמַר יְהֹוָה

אַל־יִתְהַלֵּל חָכָם בְּחָכְמָתוֹ

וְאַל־יִתְהַלֵּל הַגִּבּוֹר בִּגְבוּרָתוֹ

אַל־יִתְהַלֵּל עָשִׁיר בְּעָשְׁרוֹ:

23 כִּי אִם־בְּזֹאת יִתְהַלֵּל הַמִּתְהַלֵּל

הַשְׂכֵּל וְיָדֹעַ אוֹתִי

כִּי אֲנִי יְהֹוָה

עֹשֶׂה חֶסֶד מִשְׁפָּט וּצְדָקָה בָּאָרֶץ

כִּי־בְאֵלֶּה חָפַצְתִּי

נְאֻם־יְהֹוָה:

Essay

The controversy about Tisha b'Av

The ninth of Ave has been a recurrent day of calamity for the Jewish people. Tradition says that both the First and Second Temples were destroyed on that day, and that the edict expelling the Jews from Spain was promulgated on Tisha b'Av as well. There was thus enough reason to mourn, and, indeed, in past centuries the unhappy day and the three weeks before were scrupulously observed by our people.

Not so today. With the emergence of Israel as an independent Jewish state, the whole idea of a God-enforced exile appears obsolete.

Nearly 150 years ago, David Einhorn, a German-American rabbi officiating in Baltimore, Maryland, preached a famous sermon in which he advocated the retention of Tisha b'Av as an important observance—albeit with a totally new message. God had willed the exile, he said, because Judaism's message was to be brought to the four ends of the earth. Instead of mourning the results of Divine Providence, we should be grateful for it, for we will now be enabled to be the harbingers of a new and better age, something that could never have been accomplished had we maintained our small state in its ancient land. Hence, the old day of mourning should be turned into a festival of joy.[11]

Though Einhorn's idea fell on deaf ears, the observance of Tisha b'Av slackened as the Jewish condition in the Diaspora improved. Today, with a vibrant Israel becoming the center of Jewish life in the world, with Jewish secularism spreading, and with democracy having made great strides in most of the lands where Diaspora Jews are living, the day of fasting and lamentation appears to many as an anachronism, best honored by indifference.

In addition there is now Yom ha-Shoah, observed on the 27th day of Nisan, which has captured the imagination of those who want to remember the Holocaust and all those who have fallen victim to anti-Jewish hatred. In Israel, Yom ha-Shoah has become a date in the official calendar of the state, and its observance has spread to the Diaspora.

There is also a theological problem that militates against the continued observance of the ninth of Av. The traditional rationale for the observance was the conviction that destruction was willed by God as a punishment of Israel, and that only God could signal the day when mourning would turn into joy and the Messiah would lead Jews and gentiles alike into an eternal era of peace. Indeed, our haftarah features Israel's sins and God's retribution in the harshest terms, though most believers do not lay the misfortunes that befall us at the

doors of either Israel or God. They look at the sins of those who hate and persecute Jews as the foremost reason for Jewish suffering.

Withal, Tisha b'Av continues to be observed by traditionalists and those others who want to identify themselves with Jewish history. The former will mark the day in the ancestral fashion, while the latter will reinterpret the day's message in the light of modern times and will do so with respect for the millennia of Jewish suffering and sacrifice for the honor of God's Name.

Gleanings

Words to Remember

Is there no balm in Gilead? (8:22)

Let not the wise glory in their wisdom,
let not the mighty glory in their might,
let not the rich glory in their riches;
but let them who glory, glory in this:
that they understand and know Me, that I, the Eternal,
practice kindness, justice, and righteousness in the earth,
for in these things do I delight, says the Eternal One. (9:22-23)

About these words

Maimonides devotes the last chapters of his *Guide to the Perplexed* to these verses, which to him represent the ladder of enlightenment toward human perfection. With variations, the same is the opinion of Radak and Abarbanel. They see the three examples of those who glory in what they represent, the three classes of society: the philosopher, the warrior, and the merchant.

The essence of traditional commentaries is that of all of human achievements, the knowledge of God's justice and essential purposes is the highest stage of enlightenment.

Solomon B. Freehof[12]

The Harvester [Gatherer] (9:21)

The Hebrew word for the one who gathers up the corpses left behind by the destruction is מאסף (*m'assef*). It was adopted in 1784 by the Society of the Friends of Hebrew Literature as the name for their magazine, *Ha-m'assef*, and was devoted to the revival of Hebrew as a modern idiom. It contained poetry, historical notes, philological questions, and book reviews, and represented in effect the beginning of the Haskalah, the enlightenment movement in Eastern Europe. [13]

A hardened position

We notice a certain hardening of the Prophet's position, as he moves from the hope of repentance to a sense of the inevitability of retribution. As this happens, we find increasing expression of prophetic and divine pathos—at first without distinction between the celestial and earthly perception; then, as the Prophet's social encounters increase, with a growing sense of the Prophet's isolation from God and man alike.

Joel Rosenberg[14]

* * *

Notes

[1] I. Jacobson, *Chazon Hamikra*, vol. 2, p. 336.

[2] So, for example, Bright (*Anchor Bible*, Jeremiah), p. 69.

[3] JPS seems to suggest this; similar re-vocalizations are also possible; see Bright (*Anchor Bible*, Jeremiah), p. 61, note b-b.

[4] Compare Jeremiah 4:15.

[5] So Rashi; Septuagint and others alter the verb form and arrive at a somewhat different meaning; see, for example, Bright (*Anchor Bible*, Jeremiah), p. 69, note j-j.

[6] So Luzzatto; Rashi explains it as a reference to Egypt, on whom Israel had relied.

[7] Genesis 27:36.

[8] Freedman calls attention to the prayer in the daily liturgy, which says: "The soul which You have given me, O God, came pure from You."

[9] So Rashi.

[10] In Hebrew texts, such an error is always pointed out in a marginal note.

[11] "Tisha b'Av and the Modern Jew," in W. G. Plaut, ed., *The Rise of Reform Judaism*, pp. 200-202.

[12] *Jeremiah*, pp. 74-75.

[13] See Plaut, ed., *The Rise of Reform Judaism*, p. 12. The magazine was published in Königsberg (the birthplace of Immanuel Kant); its leaders were intellectual followers of Moses Mendelssohn.

[14] "Jeremiah and Ezekiel," *The Literary Guide to the Bible*, ed. Robert Alter and Frank Kermode, pp. 186-187.

Isaiah, chapter 55, verse 6 to chapter 56, verse 8

Introduction

Connection of Tisha b'Av and Haftarah:

The haftarah is also read for the sidra Vayeilech. Why this choice?

The common explanation centers on Isaiah's call for *tz'dakah* (meaning both charity and doing what is just and right):

Thus says the Eternal One:

Maintain justice and do what is right (tz'dakah).

The Rabbis call attention to the custom of giving *tz'dakah* on public fast days, and therefore the reading of the haftarah is delayed from morning until the afternoon prayers so that everyone will have a chance to do something for the poor: See *B.* Megillah 31a and Berachot 6b, which contain the oft-cited saying: "The merit of a fast day is [giving] *tz'dakah*"; that is to say, fasting encourages practical compassion for the poor].

For the text and commentary, see the haftarah for Vayeilech.

Zechariah, chapter 2, verse 14 to chapter 4, verse 7

Introduction

The choice of this haftarah:

Chanukah is the festival of lights, and the haftarah ends with a vision of the candelabrum in the Jerusalem Temple. An additional reason for the choice lay in the memorable passage pronounced by the angel (4:6): "Not by might, nor by power, but by My Spirit ...." Political circumstances at the time were such that the Rabbis who chose the order of haftarot (centuries after Zechariah) wanted to infuse the festival of the Maccabean victory in 164 B.C.E. with a pacific note.

When there are two Shabbatot during the festival, Zechariah is read on the first Shabbat and a selection from the book of Kings on the second (see the next haftarah).

The haftarah from Zechariah is also read for the sidra B'ha-alot'cha; see there for text and commentary.

First Kings, chapter 2, verses 1 to 12

Introduction

The choice of this haftarah:

When there are two Shabbatot during the festival, the selection for the second one is the same as that for the sidra Vayakhel. Why this choice?

Various suggestions have been brought forward. The simplest is the explanation of Rashi [Commentary on *B.* Megillah 31a], who says that Chanukah is the festival of lights, and lights are one of the subjects of the haftarah (verse 49).

Issachar Jacobson [*Chazon Hamikra*, vol. 2, p. 177] calls attention to the comment of Rabbenu Nissim (14th century), who suggests the following reason for the choice of the haftarah: on the first Shabbat of Chanukah we read Zechariah's prophecy about lights; and on the second, we read about Solomon's. Zechariah (though he lived after Solomon) was placed first because his prophecy deals with the future.

For text and commentary, see the haftarah for Vayakhel.

Jeremiah, chapter 8, verses 19-23

Introduction

The day on which we remember the victims of the Holocaust (the 27th day of Nisan) recalls the years of terror and death, inflicted on European Jewry by the Nazis.

Jeremiah was present in 587 B.C.E., when the Babylonians destroyed the Temple, sacked Jerusalem, ravaged the population, and carried many away as prisoners. The Prophet's lamentation is the selection for Tisha b'Av morning, and a segment of it is our choice for Yom ha-Shoah as well. (See the relevant verses in the haftarah for Tisha b'Av morning.) It should be noted that many congregations read no haftarah on this day.

The questions raised by the Shoah have engendered a plenitude of books, whose discussion exceeds the limits of this commentary.

For more on Jeremiah and his time, see our *General Introduction.*

יום העצמאות

Isaiah, chapter 10, verse 32 to chapter 12, verse 6

Introduction

Israel Independence Day (fourth day of Iyar) has been acknowledged as a semi-festival in the Conservative and Reform movements, as well as in many Orthodox congregations. In Israel, the haftarah for the eighth day of Pesach is read, whether or not there is a Torah reading on that morning. That is our recommendation as well.

For text and commentary, see the haftarah for the eighth day of Pesach.

ADDITIONAL READINGS 1

First Kings, chapter 21, verses 1 to 20

King Ahab of Israel (9th century B.C.E.) and his wife Jezebel ruled the land autocratically, without regard to Jewish tradition. The story of Naboth and his vineyard, described in this haftarah, is an example of their corrupt practices which the prophet Elijah, the conscience of the nation, opposed. For more on the book of Kings from which the reading is taken, see our *General Introduction;* on Elijah, see the essay in the haftarah for Ki Tissa.

21:1. After these things, it happened that near the palace of Ahab, king of Samaria, was a vineyard owned by a man called Naboth the Jezreelite.

2. One day Ahab said to Naboth: Your vineyard is close to my palace: let me have it for a vegetable garden. I'll give you a better vineyard for it, or, if you prefer, I'll pay you a fair price.

3. But Naboth answered: Heaven forbid that I should give you what I have inherited from my ancestors.

4. Ahab went home downcast and furious over what Naboth had said to him. He lay on his bed with covered face and refused to eat.

5. His wife Jezebel went to him and said: Why are you so downcast? Why won't you eat?

6. He said to her: I said to Naboth, *Sell me your vineyard, or, if you like, I'll trade you another vineyard for yours,* but he said: *I won't let you have my vineyard!*

21:1 וַיְהִי אַחַר הַדְּבָרִים הָאֵלֶּה כֶּרֶם הָיָה לְנָבוֹת הַיִּזְרְעֵאלִי אֲשֶׁר בְּיִזְרְעֶאל אֵצֶל הֵיכַל אַחְאָב מֶלֶךְ שֹׁמְרוֹן:

2 וַיְדַבֵּר אַחְאָב אֶל־נָבוֹת לֵאמֹר תְּנָה־לִּי אֶת־כַּרְמְךָ וִיהִי־לִי לְגַן־יָרָק כִּי הוּא קָרוֹב אֵצֶל בֵּיתִי וְאֶתְּנָה לְךָ תַּחְתָּיו כֶּרֶם טוֹב מִמֶּנּוּ אִם טוֹב בְּעֵינֶיךָ אֶתְּנָה־לְךָ כֶסֶף מְחִיר זֶה:

3 וַיֹּאמֶר נָבוֹת אֶל־אַחְאָב חָלִילָה לִּי מֵיהֹוָה מִתִּתִּי אֶת־נַחֲלַת אֲבֹתַי לָךְ:

4 וַיָּבֹא אַחְאָב אֶל־בֵּיתוֹ סַר וְזָעֵף עַל־הַדָּבָר אֲשֶׁר־דִּבֶּר אֵלָיו נָבוֹת הַיִּזְרְעֵאלִי וַיֹּאמֶר לֹא־אֶתֵּן לְךָ אֶת־נַחֲלַת אֲבוֹתָי וַיִּשְׁכַּב עַל־מִטָּתוֹ וַיַּסֵּב אֶת־פָּנָיו וְלֹא־אָכַל לָחֶם:

5 וַתָּבֹא אֵלָיו אִיזֶבֶל אִשְׁתּוֹ וַתְּדַבֵּר אֵלָיו מַה־זֶּה רוּחֲךָ סָרָה וְאֵינְךָ אֹכֵל לָחֶם:

6 וַיְדַבֵּר אֵלֶיהָ כִּי־אֲדַבֵּר אֶל־נָבוֹת הַיִּזְרְעֵאלִי וָאֹמַר לוֹ תְּנָה־לִּי אֶת־כַּרְמְךָ בְּכֶסֶף אוֹ אִם־חָפֵץ אַתָּה אֶתְּנָה־לְךָ כֶרֶם תַּחְתָּיו וַיֹּאמֶר לֹא־אֶתֵּן לְךָ אֶת־כַּרְמִי:

7. Jezebel his wife said to him: Now is the time to exercise royal authority over Israel! Get up, eat something, and cheer up. I will get you the vineyard of Naboth the Jezreelite!

8. She then wrote some letters in Ahab's name, sealing them with his seal, to the elders and free citizens who dwelt in Naboth's town.

9. The letters said: Announce a fast-day, and seat Naboth at the head of the citizenry;

10. then give two corrupt men a place opposite him and let them testify against him, saying: *You cursed God and the king.* Then take him outside the town and stone him to death.

11. The elders and the free citizens who lived in his town followed Jezebel's orders.

12. They announced a fast-day, seated Naboth at the head of the citizens,

13. and two corrupt men accused him of having cursed God and the king. So it came about that they took him outside the town, and pelted him with stones until he died.

14. They then sent a message to Jezebel: Naboth has been stoned to death.

15. As soon as Jezebel heard that Naboth had been killed, she said to Ahab: Naboth lives no more! Go take over the vineyard that he refused to sell to you.

7 וַתֹּאמֶר אֵלָיו אִיזֶבֶל אִשְׁתּוֹ אַתָּה עַתָּה תַּעֲשֶׂה מְלוּכָה עַל־יִשְׂרָאֵל קוּם אֱכָל־לֶחֶם וְיִטַב לִבֶּךָ אֲנִי אֶתֵּן לְךָ אֶת־כֶּרֶם נָבוֹת הַיִּזְרְעֵאלִי:

8 וַתִּכְתֹּב סְפָרִים בְּשֵׁם אַחְאָב וַתַּחְתֹּם בְּחֹתָמוֹ וַתִּשְׁלַח הַסְּפָרִים [סְפָרִים] אֶל־הַזְּקֵנִים וְאֶל־הַחֹרִים אֲשֶׁר בְּעִירוֹ הַיֹּשְׁבִים אֶת־נָבוֹת:

9 וַתִּכְתֹּב בַּסְּפָרִים לֵאמֹר קִרְאוּ־צוֹם וְהוֹשִׁיבוּ אֶת־נָבוֹת בְּרֹאשׁ הָעָם:

10 וְהוֹשִׁיבוּ שְׁנַיִם אֲנָשִׁים בְּנֵי־בְלִיַּעַל נֶגְדּוֹ וִיעִדֻהוּ לֵאמֹר בֵּרַכְתָּ אֱלֹהִים וָמֶלֶךְ וְהוֹצִיאֻהוּ וְסִקְלֻהוּ וְיָמֹת:

11 וַיַּעֲשׂוּ אַנְשֵׁי עִירוֹ הַזְּקֵנִים וְהַחֹרִים אֲשֶׁר הַיֹּשְׁבִים בְּעִירוֹ כַּאֲשֶׁר שָׁלְחָה אֲלֵיהֶם אִיזָבֶל כַּאֲשֶׁר כָּתוּב בַּסְּפָרִים אֲשֶׁר שָׁלְחָה אֲלֵיהֶם:

12 קָרְאוּ צוֹם וְהֹשִׁיבוּ אֶת־נָבוֹת בְּרֹאשׁ הָעָם:

13 וַיָּבֹאוּ שְׁנֵי הָאֲנָשִׁים בְּנֵי־בְלִיַּעַל וַיֵּשְׁבוּ נֶגְדּוֹ וַיְעִדֻהוּ אַנְשֵׁי הַבְּלִיַּעַל אֶת־נָבוֹת נֶגֶד הָעָם לֵאמֹר בֵּרַךְ נָבוֹת אֱלֹהִים וָמֶלֶךְ וַיֹּצִאֻהוּ מִחוּץ לָעִיר וַיִּסְקְלֻהוּ בָאֲבָנִים וַיָּמֹת:

14 וַיִּשְׁלְחוּ אֶל־אִיזֶבֶל לֵאמֹר סֻקַּל נָבוֹת וַיָּמֹת:

15 וַיְהִי כִּשְׁמֹעַ אִיזֶבֶל כִּי־סֻקַּל נָבוֹת וַיָּמֹת וַתֹּאמֶר אִיזֶבֶל אֶל־אַחְאָב קוּם רֵשׁ אֶת־כֶּרֶם נָבוֹת הַיִּזְרְעֵאלִי אֲשֶׁר מֵאֵן לָתֶת־לְךָ בְכֶסֶף כִּי אֵין נָבוֹת חַי כִּי־מֵת:

766

16. The moment Ahab heard that Naboth was dead, he went down to take possession of Naboth's vineyard.

17. Now this word of the Eternal came to Elijah the Tishbite:

18. Speed your way down to Ahab king of Israel in Samaria. You will find him in Naboth's vineyard, about to take possession of it.

19. Tell him the word of the Eternal: *So you have murdered, and now you take possession? This is the word of the Eternal: In the very place where the dogs licked up Naboth's blood, they will lick up your blood—yours too!*

20. When Ahab saw Elijah, he said: So you have found me, O my enemy? And Elijah said: Yes, I have found you—you who have sold yourself out, by doing evil in the sight of the Eternal!

16 וַיְהִי כִּשְׁמֹעַ אַחְאָב כִּי מֵת נָבוֹת וַיָּקָם אַחְאָב לָרֶדֶת אֶל־כֶּרֶם נָבוֹת הַיִּזְרְעֵאלִי לְרִשְׁתּוֹ:

17 וַיְהִי דְּבַר־יְהוָֹה אֶל־אֵלִיָּהוּ הַתִּשְׁבִּי לֵאמֹר:

18 קוּם רֵד לִקְרַאת אַחְאָב מֶלֶךְ־יִשְׂרָאֵל אֲשֶׁר בְּשֹׁמְרוֹן הִנֵּה בְּכֶרֶם נָבוֹת אֲשֶׁר־יָרַד שָׁם לְרִשְׁתּוֹ:

19 וְדִבַּרְתָּ אֵלָיו לֵאמֹר כֹּה אָמַר יְהוָֹה הֲרָצַחְתָּ וְגַם־יָרָשְׁתָּ וְדִבַּרְתָּ אֵלָיו לֵאמֹר כֹּה אָמַר יְהוָֹה בִּמְקוֹם אֲשֶׁר לָקְקוּ הַכְּלָבִים אֶת־דַּם נָבוֹת יָלֹקּוּ הַכְּלָבִים אֶת־דָּמְךָ גַּם־אָתָּה:

20 וַיֹּאמֶר אַחְאָב אֶל־אֵלִיָּהוּ הַמְצָאתַנִי אֹיְבִי וַיֹּאמֶר מָצָאתִי יַעַן הִתְמַכֶּרְךָ לַעֲשׂוֹת הָרַע בְּעֵינֵי יְהוָֹה:

ADDITIONAL READINGS 2

Zephaniah, chapter 3, verses 9 to 14, 15b, and 20

Zephaniah preached in Jerusalem at the time of King Josiah (second half of the 7th century). He was in full accord with the king's religious reforms, which reversed the syncretistic practices in vogue during the long-term reign of King Manasseh. For more on these reforms, see the Torah Commentary, p. 1291.

The selections here presented reflect the optimistic mood of the Prophet.

3:9 כִּי־אָז אֶהְפֹּךְ אֶל־עַמִּים שָׂפָה בְרוּרָה לִקְרֹא כֻלָּם בְּשֵׁם יְהֹוָה לְעָבְדוֹ שְׁכֶם אֶחָד:

3:9. The day will come when I will restore a clear speech to the peoples, to summon them all in the name of the Eternal, so that they may serve God with one accord.

10 מֵעֵבֶר לְנַהֲרֵי־כוּשׁ עֲתָרַי בַּת־פוּצַי יוֹבִלוּן מִנְחָתִי:

10. From beyond the rivers of Nubia, those entreating me, My scattered people, shall bring My offering with a whole heart.

11 בַּיּוֹם הַהוּא לֹא תֵבוֹשִׁי מִכֹּל עֲלִילֹתַיִךְ אֲשֶׁר פָּשַׁעַתְּ בִּי כִּי־אָז אָסִיר מִקִּרְבֵּךְ עַלִּיזֵי גַאֲוָתֵךְ וְלֹא־תוֹסִפִי לְגָבְהָה עוֹד בְּהַר קָדְשִׁי:

11. You shall no longer bear the shame of your misdeeds when that day comes, for I will remove the arrogant boasters from among you; no more shall you go about all puffed up in My holy mountain!

12 וְהִשְׁאַרְתִּי בְקִרְבֵּךְ עַם עָנִי וָדָל וְחָסוּ בְּשֵׁם יְהֹוָה:

12. Instead, I will leave in your midst a people who are poor and humble, who shall find shelter in [the Presence of] the Eternal.

13 שְׁאֵרִית יִשְׂרָאֵל לֹא־יַעֲשׂוּ עַוְלָה וְלֹא־יְדַבְּרוּ כָזָב וְלֹא־יִמָּצֵא בְּפִיהֶם לְשׁוֹן תַּרְמִית כִּי־הֵמָּה יִרְעוּ וְרָבְצוּ וְאֵין מַחֲרִיד:

13. The survivors of Israel shall do no wrong and tell no lies; no words of deceit shall come from their tongues. They shall graze [like well-tended sheep], with none to make them afraid.

14 רָנִּי בַּת־צִיּוֹן הָרִיעוּ יִשְׂרָאֵל שִׂמְחִי וְעָלְזִי בְּכָל־לֵב בַּת יְרוּשָׁלָ͏ִם:

14. Sing for joy, fair Zion! Shout in gladness, O Israel! Rejoice and be glad with a whole heart, fair Jerusalem!

15b מֶלֶךְ יִשְׂרָאֵל יְהֹוָה בְּקִרְבֵּךְ לֹא־תִירְאִי רָע עוֹד:

15b. Israel's Sovereign, the Eternal, is in your midst; you have nothing more to fear.

20. At that time I will bring you [home], and at that time I will gather you up, and give you honor and glory in all the world, when I restore your fortunes before your very eyes. The Eternal One has spoken.

בָּעֵת הַהִיא אָבִיא אֶתְכֶם וּבָעֵת קַבְּצִי 20 אֶתְכֶם כִּי־אֶתֵּן אֶתְכֶם לְשֵׁם וְלִתְהִלָּה בְּכֹל עַמֵּי הָאָרֶץ בְּשׁוּבִי אֶת־שְׁבוּתֵיכֶם לְעֵינֵיכֶם אָמַר יְהֹוָה:

ADDITIONAL READINGS 3

Joshua, chapter 24, verses 1 to 11, 14 and 24

Joshua was the successor of Moses, and his task was to lead the people in their conquest of the Promised Land. For more on the book of Joshua, see our *General Introduction*; on Joshua the man, see the essay in the haftarah for V'zot Hab'rachah.

Joshua here recounts God's benefactions to Israel, and his challenge elicits the people's response: "It is the Eternal our God whom we shall serve and obey!"

24:1. Joshua gathered all the tribes of Israel at Shechem. He called all the elders, leaders, judges and officers, and they presented themselves before God.

2. Then Joshua said to all the people: Thus says the Eternal One, the God of Israel: Long ago your ancestors lived on the other side of the river Euphrates and worshipped other gods. One of your ancestors was Terach, the father of Abraham and Nahor.

3. Then I took your ancestor Abraham from across the Euphrates and led him through the whole land of Canaan. I gave him many descendants. I gave him Isaac,

4. and to Isaac I gave Jacob and Esau. I gave Esau the hill country of Se'ir to make his own, but Jacob and his children went down to Egypt.

5. Later I sent Moses and Aaron, and I plagued Egypt with [the wonders] I performed in its midst. Then I led you out.

6. I brought your parents out of Egypt and you came to the Sea. The Egyptians chased them with chariots and cavalry to the Reed [Red] Sea.

24:1 וַיֶּאֱסֹף יְהוֹשֻׁעַ אֶת־כָּל־שִׁבְטֵי יִשְׂרָאֵל שְׁכֶמָה וַיִּקְרָא לְזִקְנֵי יִשְׂרָאֵל וּלְרָאשָׁיו וּלְשֹׁפְטָיו וּלְשֹׁטְרָיו וַיִּתְיַצְּבוּ לִפְנֵי הָאֱלֹהִים:

2 וַיֹּאמֶר יְהוֹשֻׁעַ אֶל־כָּל־הָעָם כֹּה־אָמַר יְהוָה אֱלֹהֵי יִשְׂרָאֵל בְּעֵבֶר הַנָּהָר יָשְׁבוּ אֲבוֹתֵיכֶם מֵעוֹלָם תֶּרַח אֲבִי אַבְרָהָם וַאֲבִי נָחוֹר וַיַּעַבְדוּ אֱלֹהִים אֲחֵרִים:

3 וָאֶקַּח אֶת־אֲבִיכֶם אֶת־אַבְרָהָם מֵעֵבֶר הַנָּהָר וָאוֹלֵךְ אוֹתוֹ בְּכָל־אֶרֶץ כְּנָעַן וָאֶרֶב [וָאַרְבֶּה] אֶת־זַרְעוֹ וָאֶתֶּן־לוֹ אֶת־יִצְחָק:

4 וָאֶתֵּן לְיִצְחָק אֶת־יַעֲקֹב וְאֶת־עֵשָׂו וָאֶתֵּן לְעֵשָׂו אֶת־הַר שֵׂעִיר לָרֶשֶׁת אוֹתוֹ וְיַעֲקֹב וּבָנָיו יָרְדוּ מִצְרָיִם:

5 וָאֶשְׁלַח אֶת־מֹשֶׁה וְאֶת־אַהֲרֹן וָאֶגֹּף אֶת־מִצְרַיִם כַּאֲשֶׁר עָשִׂיתִי בְּקִרְבּוֹ וְאַחַר הוֹצֵאתִי אֶתְכֶם:

6 וָאוֹצִיא אֶת־אֲבוֹתֵיכֶם מִמִּצְרַיִם וַתָּבֹאוּ הַיָּמָּה וַיִּרְדְּפוּ מִצְרַיִם אַחֲרֵי אֲבוֹתֵיכֶם בְּרֶכֶב וּבְפָרָשִׁים יַם־סוּף:

7. They cried out for help to the Eternal, who put darkness between you and the Egyptians, and brought the Sea upon them. Your own eyes saw what I did to Egypt. You lived in the wilderness a long time.

8. Then I brought you to the land of the Amorites, who lived on the east side of the Jordan. When they fought you, I put them into your hand; you took possession of their land, as I wiped them out before you.

9. Then the king of Moab, Balak son of Tzippor, fought against you. He sent for Balaam son of Beor to put a curse on you,

10. but I would not listen to Balaam; he was compelled to bless you, and [in this way] I saved you from Balak.

11. You then crossed the Jordan and came to Jericho. The people of Jericho fought you, [namely,] the Amorites, Perizzites, Canaanites, Hittites, Girgashites, Hivites, and Jebusites. But I put them into your hand.

14. Now, then, said Joshua: Honor and serve the Eternal sincerely and faithfully. Get rid of the gods your ancestors used to worship in Mesopotamia and Egypt, and serve only the Eternal.

24. And the people declared to Joshua: *It is the Eternal our God whom we shall serve and obey!*

7 וַיִּצְעֲק֣וּ אֶל־יְהֹוָ֗ה וַיָּ֜שֶׂם מַֽאֲפֵל֮ בֵּינֵיכֶ֣ם וּבֵ֣ין הַמִּצְרִים֒ וַיָּבֵ֨א עָלָ֤יו אֶת־הַיָּם֙ וַיְכַסֵּ֔הוּ וַתִּרְאֶ֨ינָה֙ עֵֽינֵיכֶ֔ם אֵ֥ת אֲשֶׁר־עָשִׂ֖יתִי בְּמִצְרָ֑יִם וַתֵּשְׁב֥וּ בַמִּדְבָּ֖ר יָמִ֥ים רַבִּֽים:

8 וָֽאָבִ֣יאָה [וָֽאָבִ֣א] אֶתְכֶ֗ם אֶל־אֶ֤רֶץ הָֽאֱמֹרִי֙ הַיּוֹשֵׁב֙ בְּעֵ֣בֶר הַיַּרְדֵּ֔ן וַיִּֽלָּֽחֲמ֖וּ אִתְּכֶ֑ם וָֽאֶתֵּ֨ן אוֹתָ֤ם בְּיֶדְכֶם֙ וַתִּֽירְשׁ֣וּ אֶת־אַרְצָ֔ם וָֽאַשְׁמִידֵ֖ם מִפְּנֵיכֶֽם:

9 וַיָּ֨קָם בָּלָ֤ק בֶּן־צִפּוֹר֙ מֶ֣לֶךְ מוֹאָ֔ב וַיִּלָּ֖חֶם בְּיִשְׂרָאֵ֑ל וַיִּשְׁלַ֗ח וַיִּקְרָ֛א לְבִלְעָ֥ם בֶּן־בְּע֖וֹר לְקַלֵּ֥ל אֶתְכֶֽם:

10 וְלֹ֥א אָבִ֖יתִי לִשְׁמֹ֣עַ לְבִלְעָ֑ם וַיְבָ֤רֶךְ בָּרוֹךְ֙ אֶתְכֶ֔ם וָֽאַצִּ֥ל אֶתְכֶ֖ם מִיָּדֽוֹ:

11 וַתַּֽעַבְר֣וּ אֶת־הַיַּרְדֵּן֮ וַתָּבֹ֣אוּ אֶל־יְרִיחוֹ֒ וַיִּֽלָּֽחֲמ֣וּ בָכֶ֣ם בַּֽעֲלֵֽי־יְ֠רִיח֠וֹ הָֽאֱמֹרִ֨י וְהַפְּרִזִּ֜י וְהַֽכְּנַעֲנִ֣י וְהַֽחִתִּ֗י וְהַגִּרְגָּשִׁי֙ הַֽחִוִּ֣י וְהַיְבוּסִ֔י וָֽאֶתֵּ֥ן אוֹתָ֖ם בְּיֶדְכֶֽם:

14 וְעַתָּ֞ה יְר֧אוּ אֶת־יְהֹוָ֛ה וְעִבְד֥וּ אֹת֖וֹ בְּתָמִ֣ים וּבֶֽאֱמֶ֑ת וְהָסִ֣ירוּ אֶת־אֱלֹהִ֗ים אֲשֶׁ֨ר עָֽבְד֤וּ אֲבֽוֹתֵיכֶם֙ בְּעֵ֣בֶר הַנָּהָ֣ר וּבְמִצְרַ֔יִם וְעִבְד֖וּ אֶת־יְהֹוָֽה:

24 וַיֹּֽאמְר֥וּ הָעָ֖ם אֶל־יְהוֹשֻׁ֑עַ אֶת־יְהֹוָ֤ה אֱלֹהֵ֨ינוּ֙ נַֽעֲבֹ֔ד וּבְקוֹל֖וֹ נִשְׁמָֽע:

Isaiah, chapter 44, verses 1 to 8 and 21 to 23

The Prophet, who lived among the exiles in Babylon (6th century B.C.E.), tried to maintain the people's faith in the Eternal who would not forget Israel. For more on Isaiah, see our *General Introduction,* and especially the section dealing with the Second Isaiah, from whom this reading stems.

Our reading is an ode to faith and hope. Verse 6 is an oft-quoted affirmation, as is verse 22, which has become part of the Yom Kippur liturgy.

44:1. Listen to Me now, O Jacob My
    servant,

Israel, My chosen one:

2. Thus says the Eternal One, your Maker,

who formed you from the womb,

and will help you:

Have no fear, Jacob My servant,

Jeshurun, My chosen one.

3. As I pour water on thirsty soil,

and streams on dry ground,

so will I pour My spirit on your descen-
    dants,

My blessing upon your offspring.

4. They shall flourish amidst the grass,

like willows by flowing streams.

5. One shall say: *I am the Eternal's,*

and take the name *Jacob.*

Another shall write *For the Eternal* on his
    hand,

and be known as *Israel.*

6. Thus says the Eternal, Israel's Sovereign

and Redeemer, the God of heaven's hosts:

I am the first, I am the last;

there is no God but Me.

7. Who is like Me?

[If there is someone] declare it,

44:1 וְעַתָּה שְׁמַע יַעֲקֹב עַבְדִּי

וְיִשְׂרָאֵל בָּחַרְתִּי בֽוֹ:

2 כֹּה־אָמַר יְהֹוָה עֹשֶׂךָ

וְיֹצֶרְךָ מִבֶּטֶן יַעְזְרֶךָּ

אַל־תִּירָא עַבְדִּי יַעֲקֹב

וִישֻׁרוּן בָּחַרְתִּי בֽוֹ:

3 כִּי אֶצָּק־מַיִם עַל־צָמֵא

וְנֹזְלִים עַל־יַבָּשָׁה

אֶצֹּק רוּחִי עַל־זַרְעֶךָ

וּבִרְכָתִי עַל־צֶאֱצָאֶֽיךָ:

4 וְצָמְחוּ בְּבֵין חָצִיר

כַּעֲרָבִים עַל־יִבְלֵי־מָֽיִם:

5 זֶה יֹאמַר לַיהֹוָה אָנִי

וְזֶה יִקְרָא בְשֵׁם־יַעֲקֹב

וְזֶה יִכְתֹּב יָדוֹ לַיהֹוָה

וּבְשֵׁם יִשְׂרָאֵל יְכַנֶּֽה:

6 כֹּה־אָמַר יְהֹוָה מֶלֶךְ־יִשְׂרָאֵל

וְגֹאֲלוֹ יְהֹוָה צְבָאוֹת

אֲנִי רִאשׁוֹן וַאֲנִי אַחֲרוֹן

וּמִבַּלְעָדַי אֵין אֱלֹהִים:

7 וּמִי־כָמוֹנִי

יִקְרָא

proclaim it, and confront Me:

Since I founded the ancient people,

and [created] things yet to come,

let them foretell what they will be.

8. Do not be afraid; do not tremble.

You are My witnesses:

did I not tell you from of old?

Did I not declare [it]?

Is there any God or any Power but Me?

I know of none.

21. Remember these things, O Jacob,

for you are My servant, O Israel:

I formed you, You are My servant.

O Israel, do not forget Me!

22. I have swept away your transgressions

    like a cloud,

your sins like a thick cloud;

return to Me,

for I have redeemed you.

23. Shout for joy, you heavens,

for the Eternal has acted!

Shout in triumph, you depths of the earth!

Break out in joyful song, O hills,

O forests and all its trees!

For the Eternal has redeemed Jacob,

and is glorified in Israel.

וְיַגִּידֶהָ וְיַעְרְכֶהָ לִי

מִשּׂוּמִי עַם־עוֹלָם וְאֹתִיּוֹת

וַאֲשֶׁר תָּבֹאנָה יַגִּידוּ לָמוֹ:

8 אַל־תִּפְחֲדוּ וְאַל־תִּרְהוּ

הֲלֹא מֵאָז הִשְׁמַעְתִּיךָ וְהִגַּדְתִּי

וְאַתֶּם עֵדָי

הֲיֵשׁ אֱלוֹהַּ מִבַּלְעָדַי וְאֵין צוּר

בַּל־יָדָעְתִּי:

21 זְכָר־אֵלֶּה יַעֲקֹב

וְיִשְׂרָאֵל כִּי עַבְדִּי־אָתָּה

יְצַרְתִּיךָ עֶבֶד־לִי

אַתָּה יִשְׂרָאֵל לֹא תִנָּשֵׁנִי:

22 מָחִיתִי כָעָב פְּשָׁעֶיךָ

וְכֶעָנָן חַטֹּאותֶיךָ

שׁוּבָה אֵלַי

כִּי גְאַלְתִּיךָ:

23 רָנּוּ שָׁמַיִם

כִּי־עָשָׂה יְהֹוָה

הָרִיעוּ תַּחְתִּיּוֹת אָרֶץ

פִּצְחוּ הָרִים רִנָּה

יַעַר וְכָל־עֵץ בּוֹ

כִּי־גָאַל יְהֹוָה יַעֲקֹב

וּבְיִשְׂרָאֵל יִתְפָּאָר:

ADDITIONAL READINGS 5

First Kings, chapter 3, verses 5 to 15

King Solomon (10th century B.C.E.) was famous for his wide-ranging wisdom. The first example of his judicial capacity was his decision in the quarrel between two women, each of whom claimed that she was the rightful mother of a contested child. For more on Solomon, see the haftarah for Mikeitz; on the books of Kings, from which this reading is taken, see our *General Introduction*.

In his vision, Solomon is asked by God what kind of a gift he would choose for himself. His reply is "an open mind" (verse 9), to which God responds, "I am taking you by your word: I am giving you a wise and perceptive mind" (verse 12).

3:5. At Gibeon, the Eternal appeared to Solomon in a dream by night; and God said to him: What would you like Me to give you?

6. Solomon answered: You showed a constant love to my father David, Your servant, because in Your presence he lived a loyal and righteous life with upright mind; and You have continued this constant love to him to this day, by giving him a son to sit on his throne.

7. And now, Eternal my God, You have made Your servant king in place of my father David, though I am very young and inexperienced.

8. Your servant is in the midst of Your [own] people, whom You have chosen, a people that cannot be counted—so numerous are they.

9. Give Your servant an open mind to judge Your people, so that I can discern the difference between right and wrong; for who is equal to the task of ruling this great people of Yours?

10. It pleased the Eternal that Solomon had asked this,

3:5 בְּגִבְעוֹן נִרְאָה יְהֹוָה אֶל־שְׁלֹמֹה בַּחֲלוֹם הַלָּיְלָה וַיֹּאמֶר אֱלֹהִים שְׁאַל מָה אֶתֶּן־לָךְ:

6 וַיֹּאמֶר שְׁלֹמֹה אַתָּה עָשִׂיתָ עִם־עַבְדְּךָ דָוִד אָבִי חֶסֶד גָּדוֹל כַּאֲשֶׁר הָלַךְ לְפָנֶיךָ בֶּאֱמֶת וּבִצְדָקָה וּבְיִשְׁרַת לֵבָב עִמָּךְ וַתִּשְׁמָר־לוֹ אֶת־הַחֶסֶד הַגָּדוֹל הַזֶּה וַתִּתֶּן־לוֹ בֵן יֹשֵׁב עַל־כִּסְאוֹ כַּיּוֹם הַזֶּה:

7 וְעַתָּה יְהֹוָה אֱלֹהָי אַתָּה הִמְלַכְתָּ אֶת־עַבְדְּךָ תַּחַת דָּוִד אָבִי וְאָנֹכִי נַעַר קָטֹן לֹא אֵדַע צֵאת וָבֹא:

8 וְעַבְדְּךָ בְּתוֹךְ עַמְּךָ אֲשֶׁר בָּחָרְתָּ עַם־רָב אֲשֶׁר לֹא־יִמָּנֶה וְלֹא יִסָּפֵר מֵרֹב:

9 וְנָתַתָּ לְעַבְדְּךָ לֵב שֹׁמֵעַ לִשְׁפֹּט אֶת־עַמְּךָ לְהָבִין בֵּין־טוֹב לְרָע כִּי מִי יוּכַל לִשְׁפֹּט אֶת־עַמְּךָ הַכָּבֵד הַזֶּה:

10 וַיִּיטַב הַדָּבָר בְּעֵינֵי אֲדֹנָי כִּי שָׁאַל שְׁלֹמֹה אֶת־הַדָּבָר הַזֶּה:

11. and God said to him: Because this is what you asked, rather than long life, or wealth, or the life of your enemies; because you asked [only] for discernment in dispensing justice,

12. I am taking you at your word: I am giving you a wise and perceptive mind. There has never been anyone your equal, nor will there ever rise up one like you.

13. And I also grant you what you did not ask: both wealth and honor all your life—the like of which no king has ever had.

14. And if you walk in My ways and keep My statutes and commandments, as did your father David, I will also give you long life.

15. Then Solomon woke; it was a dream! He went to Jerusalem and stood before the Ark of the Covenant of the Eternal; there he offered (whole) burnt-offerings and peace-offerings. After that, he gave a feast for all his courtiers.

11 וַיֹּאמֶר אֱלֹהִים אֵלָיו יַעַן אֲשֶׁר שָׁאַלְתָּ אֶת־הַדָּבָר הַזֶּה וְלֹא־שָׁאַלְתָּ לְּךָ יָמִים רַבִּים וְלֹא־שָׁאַלְתָּ לְּךָ עֹשֶׁר וְלֹא שָׁאַלְתָּ נֶפֶשׁ אֹיְבֶיךָ וְשָׁאַלְתָּ לְּךָ הָבִין לִשְׁמֹעַ מִשְׁפָּט:

12 הִנֵּה עָשִׂיתִי כִּדְבָרֶיךָ הִנֵּה נָתַתִּי לְךָ לֵב חָכָם וְנָבוֹן אֲשֶׁר כָּמוֹךָ לֹא־הָיָה לְפָנֶיךָ וְאַחֲרֶיךָ לֹא־יָקוּם כָּמוֹךָ:

13 וְגַם אֲשֶׁר לֹא־שָׁאַלְתָּ נָתַתִּי לָךְ גַּם־עֹשֶׁר גַּם־כָּבוֹד אֲשֶׁר לֹא־הָיָה כָמוֹךָ אִישׁ בַּמְּלָכִים כָּל־יָמֶיךָ:

14 וְאִם תֵּלֵךְ בִּדְרָכַי לִשְׁמֹר חֻקַּי וּמִצְוֹתַי כַּאֲשֶׁר הָלַךְ דָּוִיד אָבִיךָ וְהַאֲרַכְתִּי אֶת־יָמֶיךָ:

15 וַיִּקַץ שְׁלֹמֹה וְהִנֵּה חֲלוֹם וַיָּבוֹא יְרוּשָׁלַם וַיַּעֲמֹד לִפְנֵי אֲרוֹן בְּרִית־אֲדֹנָי וַיַּעַל עֹלוֹת וַיַּעַשׂ שְׁלָמִים וַיַּעַשׂ מִשְׁתֶּה לְכָל־עֲבָדָיו:

ADDITIONAL READINGS 6

Psalm 72, verses 1 to 8, 12 to 14, and 17 to 19

The book of Psalms is found in *K'tuvim* ("Writings"), the third section of the Tanach. It contains 150 spiritual poems that exalt and call upon the Eternal as sovereign, friend, and savior. Tradition considers King David as the author of all the psalms that are either anonymous or ascribed to him, while modern scholarship assigns many of them to various later sources.

In our reading, King Solomon (10th century B.C.E.) is listed as the author. He sees God as the source of his own earthly power, but is concerned not with his own success. He prays also for the poor and oppressed.

72:1. A song of Solomon.
God, grant Your king justice,
share with [this] king's son Your righteousness,
2. that he may judge the people rightly,
and treat the poor with justice.
3. May the mountains and the hills bring
   prosperity to the people,
with righteousness.
4. May he do justice to the downtrodden,
save those who are needy,
and crush the one who takes by extortion.
5. Then Your people will revere You to all
   generations,
as long as there is sun,
as long as the moon [gives light].
6. Let him descend like rainfall on the
   meadows,
like showers on arid land.
7. Let the righteous flourish in his time,
let peace abound until the moon fades
   away.
8. Let him rule from sea to sea,
from the river Euphrates
to the ends of the earth.

72:1 לִשְׁלֹמֹה

אֱלֹהִים מִשְׁפָּטֶיךָ לְמֶלֶךְ תֵּן
וְצִדְקָתְךָ לְבֶן־מֶלֶךְ:
2 יָדִין עַמְּךָ בְצֶדֶק
וַעֲנִיֶּיךָ בְמִשְׁפָּט:
3 יִשְׂאוּ הָרִים שָׁלוֹם לָעָם
וּגְבָעוֹת בִּצְדָקָה:
4 יִשְׁפֹּט עֲנִיֵּי־עָם
יוֹשִׁיעַ לִבְנֵי אֶבְיוֹן
וִידַכֵּא עוֹשֵׁק:
5 יִירָאוּךָ עִם־שָׁמֶשׁ
וְלִפְנֵי יָרֵחַ
דּוֹר דּוֹרִים:
6 יֵרֵד כְּמָטָר עַל־גֵּז
כִּרְבִיבִים זַרְזִיף אָרֶץ:
7 יִפְרַח־בְּיָמָיו צַדִּיק
וְרֹב שָׁלוֹם עַד־בְּלִי יָרֵחַ:
8 וְיֵרְדְּ מִיָּם עַד־יָם
וּמִנָּהָר עַד־אַפְסֵי־אָרֶץ:

776

12. For he rescues the poor who cry out,
the weak who have no helper.

13. He pities the poor and the oppressed,
he saves the lives of the oppressed.

14. He saves them from lawless violence,
their life is precious to him.

17. Enduring be his fame;

let it flourish as long as the sun [shines],

a blessing for all the nations,

who themselves will call him blessed!

18. Blessed be the Eternal God, the God of
Israel,

who alone does wondrous things;

19. blessed be God's glorious Name forever,

and let all the earth be filled with God's
glory.

Amen and amen!

12 כִּי־יַצִּיל אֶבְיוֹן מְשַׁוֵּעַ

וְעָנִי וְאֵין־עֹזֵר לוֹ:

13 יָחֹס עַל־דַּל וְאֶבְיוֹן

וְנַפְשׁוֹת אֶבְיוֹנִים יוֹשִׁיעַ:

14 מִתּוֹךְ וּמֵחָמָס יִגְאַל נַפְשָׁם

וְיֵיקַר דָּמָם בְּעֵינָיו:

17 יְהִי שְׁמוֹ לְעוֹלָם

לִפְנֵי־שֶׁמֶשׁ יָנִין [יִנּוֹן] שְׁמוֹ

וְיִתְבָּרְכוּ בוֹ כָּל־גּוֹיִם

יְאַשְּׁרוּהוּ:

18 בָּרוּךְ יְהוָה אֱלֹהִים אֱלֹהֵי יִשְׂרָאֵל

עֹשֵׂה נִפְלָאוֹת לְבַדּוֹ:

19 וּבָרוּךְ שֵׁם כְּבוֹדוֹ לְעוֹלָם

וְיִמָּלֵא כְבוֹדוֹ אֶת־כָּל הָאָרֶץ

אָמֵן וְאָמֵן:

ADDITIONAL READINGS 7

Psalm 71, verses 1 to 2, 4 to 9, 14, and 17 to 23

The book of Psalms is found in *K'tuvim* ("Writings"), the third section of the Tanach. It contains 150 spiritual poems that exalt and call upon the Eternal as sovereign, friend, and savior. Tradition considers King David as the author of all the psalms that are either anonymous or ascribed to him, while modern scholarship assigns many of them to various later sources.

Our reading was composed by someone whose hair has already turned gray, and who looks back with gratitude on a life blessed by God. It is the kind of poem that may well have been authored by David (note, for instance, the mention of harp and lyre in verse 22). Verse 9 is among the oft-quoted passages of the book of Psalms.

71:1. In You, Eternal One, I trust: I shall never be put to shame.

2. In Your righteousness rescue and deliver me;

incline Your ear to me and save me.

4. O my God, deliver me from the hand of the wicked, from the grip of the cruel and unjust.

5. For You are my hope, O Eternal God, my trust since youth.

6. Before I was born, I relied on You;

You upheld me in my mother's womb;

I have gloried in You always.

7. I have been a sign to many,

for You are my mighty fortress.

8. My mouth has been full of Your praise,

glorifying You every day.

9. Do not cast me away in old age;

when my [own] strength fails, do not forsake me.

14. For I hope continually,

heaping praises upon You.

71:1 בְּךָ־יְהֹוָה חָסִיתִי

אַל־אֵבוֹשָׁה לְעוֹלָם:

2 בְּצִדְקָתְךָ תַּצִּילֵנִי וּתְפַלְּטֵנִי

הַטֵּה־אֵלַי אָזְנְךָ וְהוֹשִׁיעֵנִי:

4 אֱלֹהַי פַּלְּטֵנִי מִיַּד רָשָׁע

מִכַּף מְעַוֵּל וְחוֹמֵץ:

5 כִּי־אַתָּה תִקְוָתִי אֲדֹנָי יְהוִֹה מִבְטַחִי מִנְּעוּרָי:

6 עָלֶיךָ נִסְמַכְתִּי מִבֶּטֶן

מִמְּעֵי אִמִּי אַתָּה גוֹזִי

בְּךָ תְהִלָּתִי תָמִיד:

7 כְּמוֹפֵת הָיִיתִי לְרַבִּים

וְאַתָּה מַחֲסִי־עֹז:

8 יִמָּלֵא פִי תְּהִלָּתֶךָ

כָּל־הַיּוֹם תִּפְאַרְתֶּךָ:

9 אַל־תַּשְׁלִיכֵנִי לְעֵת זִקְנָה

כִּכְלוֹת כֹּחִי אַל־תַּעַזְבֵנִי:

14 וַאֲנִי תָּמִיד אֲיַחֵל

וְהוֹסַפְתִּי עַל־כָּל־תְּהִלָּתֶךָ:

17. You have taught me from my youth onward, O God;

and to this day I tell of Your wonders.

18. O God, even into old age and gray hair,

do not forsake me

till I proclaim Your might to the next generation,

Your power to all who come.

19. Your righteousness, O God, reaches high heaven,

You do great things:

O God, who is like You?

20. Having shown me many and grievous troubles,

You restore my life,

bringing me up again from the depths of the earth.

21. You increase my honor

and once more console me.

22. Therefore, my God, with the harp I thank You

for Your faithfulness,

and sing Your praises with the lyre,

O Holy One of Israel.

23. My lips shout for joy when I sing praise to You;

my spirit, too, that You have redeemed.

17 אֱלֹהִים לִמַּדְתַּנִי מִנְּעוּרָי
וְעַד־הֵנָּה אַגִּיד נִפְלְאוֹתֶיךָ:

18 וְגַם עַד־זִקְנָה וְשֵׂיבָה אֱלֹהִים
אַל־תַּעַזְבֵנִי
עַד־אַגִּיד זְרוֹעֲךָ לְדוֹר
לְכָל־יָבוֹא גְּבוּרָתֶךָ:

19 וְצִדְקָתְךָ אֱלֹהִים עַד־מָרוֹם
אֲשֶׁר־עָשִׂיתָ גְדֹלוֹת
אֱלֹהִים מִי כָמוֹךָ:
הָאָרֶץ תָּשׁוּב תַּעֲלֵנִי:

20 אֲשֶׁר הִרְאִיתַנוּ [הִרְאִיתַנִי] צָרוֹת רַבּוֹת
וְרָעוֹת
תָּשׁוּב תְּחַיֵּינוּ [תְּחַיֵּינִי]
וּמִתְּהֹמוֹת הָאָרֶץ תָּשׁוּב תַּעֲלֵנִי:

21 תֶּרֶב גְּדֻלָּתִי
וְתִסֹּב תְּנַחֲמֵנִי:

22 גַּם־אֲנִי אוֹדְךָ בִכְלִי־נֶבֶל
אֲמִתְּךָ אֱלֹהָי
אֲזַמְּרָה לְךָ בְכִנּוֹר
קְדוֹשׁ יִשְׂרָאֵל:

23 תְּרַנֵּנָּה שְׂפָתַי כִּי אֲזַמְּרָה־לָּךְ
וְנַפְשִׁי אֲשֶׁר פָּדִיתָ:

ADDITIONAL READINGS 8

Jeremiah, chapter 23, verses 1 to 8

Jeremiah was the fearless conscience of his people and paid for his courage with imprisonment, contumely, and threat of death. He survived the destruction of Jerusalem in 587 B.C.E., which he had foretold, and eventually was forced to migrate to Egypt, where he died. For more on the Prophet and his time, see our *General Introduction*.

Our reading shows how, despite his bitter disappointments, his belief was strong that in the end God would forgive Israel for its transgressions and return it to a state of spiritual and physical well-being.

23:1. This is the word of the Eternal One:
Woe on rulers who let the flock
that I care for
disperse and perish!

2. Therefore, thus says the Eternal One,
the God of Israel,
concerning the rulers who [should] tend
  My people:
You have scattered and driven away My
  flock,
and not attended to them—
but for the evil of your deeds
be sure that I will attend to you,
says the Eternal One.

3. I Myself will gather all that is left of My
  flock
from all the lands where I scattered them;
I will bring them back to their pasture,
where they shall be fruitful and grow in
  numbers.

4. I will appoint rulers to tend them,
and they shall no longer be fearful, or
  worried, or lost,
says the Eternal One.

23:1 הוֹי רֹעִים מְאַבְּדִים וּמְפִצִים
אֶת־צֹאן מַרְעִיתִי
נְאֻם־יְהֹוָה:

2 לָכֵן כֹּה־אָמַר יְהֹוָה
אֱלֹהֵי יִשְׂרָאֵל
עַל־הָרֹעִים הָרֹעִים אֶת־עַמִּי
אַתֶּם הֲפִצֹתֶם אֶת־צֹאנִי וַתַּדִּחוּם
וְלֹא פְקַדְתֶּם אֹתָם
הִנְנִי פֹקֵד עֲלֵיכֶם
אֶת־רֹעַ מַעַלְלֵיכֶם
נְאֻם־יְהֹוָה:

3 וַאֲנִי אֲקַבֵּץ אֶת־שְׁאֵרִית צֹאנִי
מִכֹּל הָאֲרָצוֹת אֲשֶׁר־הִדַּחְתִּי אֹתָם שָׁם
וַהֲשִׁבֹתִי אֶתְהֶן עַל־נְוֵהֶן
וּפָרוּ וְרָבוּ:

4 וַהֲקִמֹתִי עֲלֵיהֶם רֹעִים וְרָעוּם
וְלֹא־יִירְאוּ עוֹד וְלֹא־יֵחַתּוּ וְלֹא יִפָּקֵדוּ
נְאֻם־יְהֹוָה:

5. The time is coming,

says the Eternal One,

when I will raise up a righteous branch
   from David,

a wise ruler who will do what is just and
   right in the land.

6. In his time Judah shall be saved,

Israel shall rest securely;

and people will call him

Adonai Tzidkeinu—The Eternal is our Help.

7. The time is coming, says the Eternal
   One, when people shall no longer swear
   by Me as the living God who brought
   Israel out of Egypt,

8. but as the living God who brought the
   offspring of the House of Israel out of the
   north country, and out of all the lands
   where I scattered them. And they shall
   live on their own soil.

5 הִנֵּה יָמִים בָּאִים

נְאֻם־יְהֹוָה

וַהֲקִמֹתִי לְדָוִד צֶמַח צַדִּיק

וּמָלַךְ מֶלֶךְ וְהִשְׂכִּיל

וְעָשָׂה מִשְׁפָּט וּצְדָקָה בָּאָרֶץ:

6 בְּיָמָיו תִּוָּשַׁע יְהוּדָה

וְיִשְׂרָאֵל יִשְׁכֹּן לָבֶטַח

וְזֶה־שְׁמוֹ אֲשֶׁר־יִקְרְאוֹ

יְהֹוָה צִדְקֵנוּ:

7 לָכֵן הִנֵּה־יָמִים בָּאִים נְאֻם־יְהֹוָה וְלֹא־יֹאמְרוּ
עוֹד חַי־יְהֹוָה אֲשֶׁר הֶעֱלָה אֶת־בְּנֵי יִשְׂרָאֵל
מֵאֶרֶץ מִצְרָיִם:

8 כִּי אִם־חַי־יְהֹוָה אֲשֶׁר הֶעֱלָה וַאֲשֶׁר הֵבִיא
אֶת־זֶרַע בֵּית יִשְׂרָאֵל מֵאֶרֶץ צָפוֹנָה וּמִכֹּל
הָאֲרָצוֹת אֲשֶׁר הִדַּחְתִּים שָׁם וְיָשְׁבוּ עַל־
אַדְמָתָם:

ADDITIONAL READINGS 9

Ezra, chapter 6, verses 16 to 22

The book of Ezra is one of the last in the Tanach, part of the third section called *K'tuvim* ("Writings"). The man Ezra was considered by Jewish tradition to be second in importance only to Moses, for upon the exiles' return from Babylonian exile he presided over the re-emergence of Judaism as a viable religion. Estimates of the time when he was active vary from the latter part of the early 5th century B.C.E. to the middle of the 4th, and some consider him a pious construction of Maccabean times.

Our reading shows the difference between the dedication ceremonies of the First and Second Temples. The earlier one, in Solomon's time, took place in an era of prosperity in a well-established state, while in the days of Ezra the dedication was the modest effort of a reconstituted community, which was but a province in the Persian empire. (For comparison, see the haftarot for Vayakhel and Pikudei.)

6:16. The people of Israel—the priests, the levites, and all the other exiles [who had returned] celebrated the dedication of the Temple with joy.

17. At the dedication of this House of God they offered 100 bulls, 200 rams, and 400 lambs, and 12 goats as offerings for sin, according to the numbers of the tribes of Israel.

18. They also placed the priests in their divisions, and the levites in their sections, to supervise the service of God in Jerusalem, according to the instructions found in the book of Moses.

19. On the fourteenth day of the first month, the exiles [who had returned] celebrated Passover.

20. The priests and levites had purified themselves; one and all, they were pure, so they slaughtered the Passover sacrifice for all the [returned] exiles, for their fellow-priests, and for themselves.

6:16 וַעֲבַדוּ בְנֵי־יִשְׂרָאֵל כָּהֲנַיָּא וְלֵוָיֵא וּשְׁאָר בְּנֵי־גָלוּתָא חֲנֻכַּת בֵּית־אֱלָהָא דְנָה בְּחֶדְוָה:

17 וְהַקְרִבוּ לַחֲנֻכַּת בֵּית־אֱלָהָא דְנָה תּוֹרִין מְאָה דִּכְרִין מָאתַיִן אִמְּרִין אַרְבַּע מְאָה וּצְפִירֵי עִזִּין לְחַטָּיָא [לְחַטָּאָה] עַל־כָּל־יִשְׂרָאֵל תְּרֵי־עֲשַׂר לְמִנְיָן שִׁבְטֵי יִשְׂרָאֵל:

18 וַהֲקִימוּ כָהֲנַיָּא בִּפְלֻגָּתְהוֹן וְלֵוָיֵא בְּמַחְלְקָתְהוֹן עַל־עֲבִידַת אֱלָהָא דִּי בִירוּשְׁלֶם כִּכְתָב סְפַר מֹשֶׁה:

19 וַיַּעֲשׂוּ בְנֵי־הַגּוֹלָה אֶת־הַפָּסַח בְּאַרְבָּעָה עָשָׂר לַחֹדֶשׁ הָרִאשׁוֹן:

20 כִּי הִטַּהֲרוּ הַכֹּהֲנִים וְהַלְוִיִּם כְּאֶחָד כֻּלָּם טְהוֹרִים וַיִּשְׁחֲטוּ הַפֶּסַח לְכָל־בְּנֵי הַגּוֹלָה וְלַאֲחֵיהֶם הַכֹּהֲנִים וְלָהֶם:

21. All the people of Israel who had returned from exile, as well as those who had joined them, who had given up the unclean ways of the neighboring nations to follow the Eternal, the God of Israel, ate [of the sacrifice].

22. Joyfully they celebrated the Festival of Matzot for seven days, for the Eternal had given them cause for joy by moving the heart of the emperor of [of the lands once ruled by] Assyria to encourage their work on the Temple of God, the God of Israel.

21 וַיֹּאכְלוּ בְנֵי־יִשְׂרָאֵל הַשָּׁבִים מֵהַגּוֹלָה וְכֹל הַנִּבְדָּל מִטֻּמְאַת גּוֹיֵ־הָאָרֶץ אֲלֵהֶם לִדְרֹשׁ לַיהוָה אֱלֹהֵי יִשְׂרָאֵל:

22 וַיַּעֲשׂוּ חַג־מַצּוֹת שִׁבְעַת יָמִים בְּשִׂמְחָה כִּי שִׂמְּחָם יְהוָה וְהֵסֵב לֵב מֶלֶךְ־אַשּׁוּר עֲלֵיהֶם לְחַזֵּק יְדֵיהֶם בִּמְלֶאכֶת בֵּית־הָאֱלֹהִים אֱלֹהֵי יִשְׂרָאֵל:

ADDITIONAL READINGS 10

Joshua, chapter 3, verses 9 to 17 and chapter 4, verses 1 to 3 and 19 to 24

Joshua was the successor of Moses, and his task was to lead the people in their conquest of Canaan. For more on the book of Joshua, see our *General Introduction;* on Joshua the man, see the essay in the haftarah for *V'zot Hab'rachah.*

At the time of the exodus from Egypt, Israel experienced the wonder of crossing the Reed [Red] Sea on dry land, thereby escaping their pursuers. Now, as they are crossing the Jordan in order to take possession of the Promised Land, they become witness to a similar display of God's power.

3:9. Joshua said to the people of Israel: Come here and listen to the words of the Eternal your God.

10. He continued: By this you shall know that the living God is in your midst, who will certainly dispossess the Canaanites, Hittites, Hivites, Perizzites, Girgashites, Amorites, and Jebusites from before you:

11. the Ark of the Covenant of the Ruler of all the earth is crossing the [river] Jordan in front of you.

12. And now, pick twelve from the tribes of Israel, one from each tribe.

13. When the soles of the feet of the priests carrying the Ark of the Covenant of the Eternal, Ruler of all the earth, rest in the waters of the Jordan, the Jordan's waters shall stop flowing, and the water coming from upstream shall stand still in a great pile.

14. When the people decamped from their tents to cross the Jordan, the priests carrying the Ark of the Covenant were in front.

15. During the harvest season, the Jordan is in full flood. As soon as the Ark-bearers reached the Jordan and their feet dipped into the edge of the river,

3:9 וַיֹּאמֶר יְהוֹשֻׁעַ אֶל־בְּנֵי יִשְׂרָאֵל גֹּשׁוּ הֵנָּה וְשִׁמְעוּ אֶת־דִּבְרֵי יְהוָה אֱלֹהֵיכֶם:

10 וַיֹּאמֶר יְהוֹשֻׁעַ בְּזֹאת תֵּדְעוּן כִּי אֵל חַי בְּקִרְבְּכֶם וְהוֹרֵשׁ יוֹרִישׁ מִפְּנֵיכֶם אֶת־הַכְּנַעֲנִי וְאֶת־הַחִתִּי וְאֶת־הַחִוִּי וְאֶת־הַפְּרִזִּי וְאֶת־הַגִּרְגָּשִׁי וְהָאֱמֹרִי וְהַיְבוּסִי:

11 הִנֵּה אֲרוֹן הַבְּרִית אֲדוֹן כָּל־הָאָרֶץ עֹבֵר לִפְנֵיכֶם בַּיַּרְדֵּן:

12 וְעַתָּה קְחוּ לָכֶם שְׁנֵי עָשָׂר אִישׁ מִשִּׁבְטֵי יִשְׂרָאֵל אִישׁ־אֶחָד אִישׁ־אֶחָד לַשָּׁבֶט:

13 וְהָיָה כְּנוֹחַ כַּפּוֹת רַגְלֵי הַכֹּהֲנִים נֹשְׂאֵי אֲרוֹן יְהוָה אֲדוֹן כָּל־הָאָרֶץ בְּמֵי הַיַּרְדֵּן מֵי הַיַּרְדֵּן יִכָּרֵתוּן הַמַּיִם הַיֹּרְדִים מִלְמָעְלָה וְיַעַמְדוּ נֵד אֶחָד:

14 וַיְהִי בִּנְסֹעַ הָעָם מֵאָהֳלֵיהֶם לַעֲבֹר אֶת־הַיַּרְדֵּן וְהַכֹּהֲנִים נֹשְׂאֵי הָאָרוֹן הַבְּרִית לִפְנֵי הָעָם:

15 וּכְבוֹא נֹשְׂאֵי הָאָרוֹן עַד־הַיַּרְדֵּן וְרַגְלֵי הַכֹּהֲנִים נֹשְׂאֵי הָאָרוֹן נִטְבְּלוּ בִּקְצֵה הַמָּיִם וְהַיַּרְדֵּן מָלֵא עַל־כָּל־גְּדוֹתָיו כֹּל יְמֵי קָצִיר:

16. the waters flowing from upstream stood still in a great pile a long way off, from Adam, the town next to Zarethan. And [the waters] flowing downstream to the Sea of the Arabah—the Salt Sea—ran out completely; and the people crossed in front of Jericho.

17. The priests carrying the Ark of the Covenant of the Eternal stood firmly on dry ground in the middle of the Jordan, while all Israel crossed on dry ground until the whole nation had finished crossing.

4:1. When the whole nation had crossed the Jordan, the Eternal said to Joshua:

2. Choose twelve men, one from each tribe,

3. and have them take twelve stones out of the middle of the Jordan, from the very place where the priests are standing. You shall convey these stones with you and put them down where you camp tonight.

19. The people crossed the Jordan on the tenth day of the first month and camped at Gilgal, on the eastern edge of Jericho.

20. There Joshua placed the twelve stones taken from the Jordan.

21. And he said to the people of Israel: In the future, when children ask their parents, *What do these stones mean?*

22. Inform them about the time when Israel crossed the Jordan on dry ground.

16 וַיַּעַמְדוּ הַמַּיִם הַיֹּרְדִים מִלְמַעְלָה קָמוּ נֵד־אֶחָד הַרְחֵק מְאֹד מֵאָדָם [מֵאָדָם] הָעִיר אֲשֶׁר מִצַּד צָרְתָן וְהַיֹּרְדִים עַל יָם הָעֲרָבָה יָם־הַמֶּלַח תַּמּוּ נִכְרָתוּ וְהָעָם עָבְרוּ נֶגֶד יְרִיחוֹ:

17 וַיַּעַמְדוּ הַכֹּהֲנִים נֹשְׂאֵי הָאָרוֹן בְּרִית־יְהֹוָה בֶּחָרָבָה בְּתוֹךְ הַיַּרְדֵּן הָכֵן וְכָל־יִשְׂרָאֵל עֹבְרִים בֶּחָרָבָה עַד אֲשֶׁר־תַּמּוּ כָּל־הַגּוֹי לַעֲבֹר אֶת־הַיַּרְדֵּן:

4:1 וַיְהִי כַּאֲשֶׁר־תַּמּוּ כָל־הַגּוֹי לַעֲבוֹר אֶת־הַיַּרְדֵּן וַיֹּאמֶר יְהֹוָה אֶל־יְהוֹשֻׁעַ לֵאמֹר:

2 קְחוּ לָכֶם מִן־הָעָם שְׁנֵים עָשָׂר אֲנָשִׁים אִישׁ־אֶחָד אִישׁ־אֶחָד מִשָּׁבֶט:

3 וְצַוּוּ אוֹתָם לֵאמֹר שְׂאוּ־לָכֶם מִזֶּה מִתּוֹךְ הַיַּרְדֵּן מִמַּצַּב רַגְלֵי הַכֹּהֲנִים הָכֵן שְׁתֵּים־עֶשְׂרֵה אֲבָנִים וְהַעֲבַרְתֶּם אוֹתָם עִמָּכֶם וְהִנַּחְתֶּם אוֹתָם בַּמָּלוֹן אֲשֶׁר־תָּלִינוּ בוֹ הַלָּיְלָה:

19 וְהָעָם עָלוּ מִן־הַיַּרְדֵּן בֶּעָשׂוֹר לַחֹדֶשׁ הָרִאשׁוֹן וַיַּחֲנוּ בַּגִּלְגָּל בִּקְצֵה מִזְרַח יְרִיחוֹ:

20 וְאֵת שְׁתֵּים עֶשְׂרֵה הָאֲבָנִים הָאֵלֶּה אֲשֶׁר לָקְחוּ מִן־הַיַּרְדֵּן הֵקִים יְהוֹשֻׁעַ בַּגִּלְגָּל:

21 וַיֹּאמֶר אֶל־בְּנֵי יִשְׂרָאֵל לֵאמֹר אֲשֶׁר יִשְׁאָלוּן בְּנֵיכֶם מָחָר אֶת־אֲבוֹתָם לֵאמֹר מָה הָאֲבָנִים הָאֵלֶּה:

22 וְהוֹדַעְתֶּם אֶת־בְּנֵיכֶם לֵאמֹר בַּיַּבָּשָׁה עָבַר יִשְׂרָאֵל אֶת־הַיַּרְדֵּן הַזֶּה:

23. [Say to them:] *On dry land did Israel cross over the Jordan. The Eternal your God drained the water of the Jordan for you until you had crossed, just as God did to the Reed [Red] Sea for us, draining it before us, to [enable us to] cross,*

24. *so that all the peoples of the earth may know of the power of God's hand—for it is very great—and so that you may revere the Eternal your God forever.*

23 אֲשֶׁר־הוֹבִישׁ יְהֹוָה אֱלֹהֵיכֶם אֶת־מֵי הַיַּרְדֵּן מִפְּנֵיכֶם עַד־עָבְרְכֶם כַּאֲשֶׁר עָשָׂה יְהֹוָה אֱלֹהֵיכֶם לְיַם־סוּף אֲשֶׁר־הוֹבִישׁ מִפָּנֵינוּ עַד־עָבְרֵנוּ:

24 לְמַעַן דַּעַת כָּל־עַמֵּי הָאָרֶץ אֶת־יַד יְהֹוָה כִּי חֲזָקָה הִיא לְמַעַן יְרָאתֶם אֶת־יְהֹוָה אֱלֹהֵיכֶם כָּל־הַיָּמִים:

ADDITIONAL READINGS 11

Jeremiah, chapter 7, verses 4 to 11, 17 to 20, and 22 to 23

Jeremiah was the fearless conscience of his people and paid for his courage with imprisonment, contumely, and threat of death. He survived the destruction of Jerusalem in 587 B.C.E., which he had foretold, and eventually was forced to migrate to Egypt, where he died. For more on the Prophet and his time, see our *General Introduction*.

Our reading begins with a thrice-repeated phrase that was evidently popular in Jeremiah's day. People said, "The Temple of the Eternal" and said it over and over again, thereby expressing their belief that, since God's Temple stood in Jerusalem, the city was inviolable and safe, regardless of their immoral behavior.

7:4 אַל־תִּבְטְחוּ לָכֶם אֶל־דִּבְרֵי הַשֶּׁקֶר לֵאמֹר הֵיכַל יְהוָה הֵיכַל יְהוָה הֵיכַל יְהוָה הֵמָּה:

5 כִּי אִם־הֵיטֵיב תֵּיטִיבוּ אֶת־דַּרְכֵיכֶם וְאֶת־מַעַלְלֵיכֶם אִם־עָשׂוֹ תַעֲשׂוּ מִשְׁפָּט בֵּין אִישׁ וּבֵין רֵעֵהוּ:

6 גֵּר יָתוֹם וְאַלְמָנָה לֹא תַעֲשֹׁקוּ וְדָם נָקִי אַל־תִּשְׁפְּכוּ בַּמָּקוֹם הַזֶּה וְאַחֲרֵי אֱלֹהִים אֲחֵרִים לֹא תֵלְכוּ לְרַע לָכֶם:

7 וְשִׁכַּנְתִּי אֶתְכֶם בַּמָּקוֹם הַזֶּה בָּאָרֶץ אֲשֶׁר נָתַתִּי לַאֲבוֹתֵיכֶם לְמִן־עוֹלָם וְעַד־עוֹלָם:

8 הִנֵּה אַתֶּם בֹּטְחִים לָכֶם עַל־דִּבְרֵי הַשָּׁקֶר לְבִלְתִּי הוֹעִיל:

9 הֲגָנֹב רָצֹחַ וְנָאֹף וְהִשָּׁבֵעַ לַשֶּׁקֶר וְקַטֵּר לַבָּעַל וְהָלֹךְ אַחֲרֵי אֱלֹהִים אֲחֵרִים אֲשֶׁר לֹא־יְדַעְתֶּם:

10 וּבָאתֶם וַעֲמַדְתֶּם לְפָנַי בַּבַּיִת הַזֶּה אֲשֶׁר נִקְרָא־שְׁמִי עָלָיו וַאֲמַרְתֶּם נִצַּלְנוּ לְמַעַן עֲשׂוֹת אֵת כָּל־הַתּוֹעֵבוֹת הָאֵלֶּה:

7:4. Do not trust in false words like: *The Temple of the Eternal, the Temple of the Eternal, the Temple of the Eternal are these buildings.*

5. Rather, you must be sure to mend your ways and your actions; [for] if people treat each other fairly;

6. if you do not oppress the stranger, the orphan and the widow; if you do not shed innocent blood in this place nor follow other gods to your own harm—

7. then [and only then] will I dwell with you here in this place, in the land I gave to your ancestors from ancient days for all time.

8. Look, you are depending on illusions that get you nowhere.

9. Will you steal, murder, commit adultery, swear falsely, offer sacrifices to Baal and follow other gods you have not known [before],

10. and then come and stand before Me in this, My own Temple, and say: *We are saved*—in order to continue to do all these abominations?

11. Do you see this House, called after My Name, as a den of thieves? Be sure that I too can see, says the Eternal One!

17. Don't you see [Jeremiah] what they are doing in the cities of Judah and in the streets of Jerusalem?

18. The children gather sticks, the men build fires, and the women knead dough to make cakes for [Ishtar, the goddess they call] the Queen of Heaven. They also pour out libations to other gods, to spite Me.

19. But is it really Me they are spiting? No, they are spiting themselves, to their own ignominy.

20. Be sure, then, says the Eternal God: My burning anger will be poured over this place, on its people and its animals, on trees and crops. It shall burn, with none to quench it.

22. But when I brought your ancestors out of the land of Egypt, I neither spoke to them nor commanded them about burnt-offerings or sacrifices.

23. But this is the command I gave them: *Listen to Me, and I will be your God, and you shall be My people; walk only in the way that I have commanded you, and it shall go well with you.*

11 הַמְעָרַת פָּרִצִים הָיָה הַבַּיִת הַזֶּה אֲשֶׁר־נִקְרָא־שְׁמִי עָלָיו בְּעֵינֵיכֶם גַּם אָנֹכִי הִנֵּה רָאִיתִי נְאֻם־יְהֹוָה:

17 הַאֵינְךָ רֹאֶה מָה הֵמָּה עֹשִׂים בְּעָרֵי יְהוּדָה וּבְחֻצוֹת יְרוּשָׁלָ͏ִם:

18 הַבָּנִים מְלַקְּטִים עֵצִים וְהָאָבוֹת מְבַעֲרִים אֶת־הָאֵשׁ וְהַנָּשִׁים לָשׁוֹת בָּצֵק לַעֲשׂוֹת כַּוָּנִים לִמְלֶכֶת הַשָּׁמַיִם וְהַסֵּךְ נְסָכִים לֵאלֹהִים אֲחֵרִים לְמַעַן הַכְעִסֵנִי:

19 הַאֹתִי הֵם מַכְעִסִים נְאֻם־יְהֹוָה הֲלוֹא אֹתָם לְמַעַן בֹּשֶׁת פְּנֵיהֶם:

20 לָכֵן כֹּה־אָמַר אֲדֹנָי יֱהֹוִה הִנֵּה אַפִּי וַחֲמָתִי נִתֶּכֶת אֶל־הַמָּקוֹם הַזֶּה עַל־הָאָדָם וְעַל־הַבְּהֵמָה וְעַל־עֵץ הַשָּׂדֶה וְעַל־פְּרִי הָאֲדָמָה וּבָעֲרָה וְלֹא תִכְבֶּה:

22 כִּי לֹא־דִבַּרְתִּי אֶת־אֲבוֹתֵיכֶם וְלֹא צִוִּיתִים בְּיוֹם הוֹצִיא [הוֹצִיאִי] אוֹתָם מֵאֶרֶץ מִצְרָיִם עַל־דִּבְרֵי עוֹלָה וָזָבַח:

23 כִּי אִם־אֶת־הַדָּבָר הַזֶּה צִוִּיתִי אוֹתָם לֵאמֹר שִׁמְעוּ בְקוֹלִי וְהָיִיתִי לָכֶם לֵאלֹהִים וְאַתֶּם תִּהְיוּ־לִי לְעָם וַהֲלַכְתֶּם בְּכָל־הַדֶּרֶךְ אֲשֶׁר אֲצַוֶּה אֶתְכֶם לְמַעַן יִיטַב לָכֶם:

ADDITIONAL READINGS 12

Habakkuk, chapter 2, verses 9 to 12, 15 to 16, 19, 18, 20, and 14

The prophet Habakkuk was probably a contemporary of Jeremiah and lived at the time of the destruction of the Temple (587 B.C.E.). For more on him and his book, see our *General Introduction.*

Our reading reflects the main theme of his short book: the need to be aware of God's Presence. Verse 14 is a quotation from Isaiah 11:9 (see the haftarah for the eighth day of Pesach), and verse 20 became the opening of a popular hymn. The verses have been slightly reordered, for the sake of clarity.

2:9. Woe to you who rake in unjust gains
for the sake of your house,
setting your nest high
to escape harm!

10. You devise disgrace for your house,
shortening your life.

11. For [even] a stone cries out from the wall,
and a beam answers it from the paneling.

12. Woe to you who build towns with blood,
who establish cities with crime.

15. Woe to you who make your fellows drink
from the bowl of your anger
even to the point of being drunk,
to look on their nakedness!

16. You shall eat your fill—
not of glory but of contumely;
you too shall drink and stagger,
as the cup in God's hand
comes 'round to you,
and disgrace [supplants] your honor.

2:9 הֽוֹי בֹּצֵ֥עַ בֶּ֖צַע רָ֑ע
לְבֵית֑וֹ
לָשׂ֤וּם בַּמָּרוֹם֙ קִנּ֔וֹ
לְהִנָּצֵ֖ל מִכַּף־רָֽע׃

10 יָעַ֣צְתָּ בֹּ֔שֶׁת לְבֵיתֶ֑ךָ
קְצוֹת־עַמִּ֣ים רַבִּ֑ים וְחוֹטֵ֖א נַפְשֶֽׁךָ׃

11 כִּי־אֶ֖בֶן מִקִּ֣יר תִּזְעָ֑ק
וְכָפִ֖יס מֵעֵ֥ץ יַעֲנֶֽנָּה׃

12 הֹ֛וֹי בֹּנֶ֥ה עִ֖יר בְּדָמִ֑ים
וְכוֹנֵ֥ן קִרְיָ֖ה בְּעַוְלָֽה׃

15 הֹ֣וֹי מַשְׁקֵ֤ה רֵעֵ֙הוּ֙
מְסַפֵּ֣חַ חֲמָתְךָ֔
וְאַ֖ף שַׁכֵּ֑ר
לְמַ֥עַן הַבִּ֖יט עַל־מְעוֹרֵיהֶֽם׃

16 שָׂבַ֤עְתָּ
קָלוֹן֙ מִכָּב֔וֹד
שְׁתֵ֥ה גַם־אַ֖תָּה וְהֵעָרֵ֑ל
תִּסּ֣וֹב עָלֶ֔יךָ
כּ֖וֹס יְמִ֣ין יְהֹוָ֑ה
וְקִיקָל֖וֹן עַל־כְּבוֹדֶֽךָ׃

19. Woe to you who say to wood,
Wake up;
to silent stone, *Get up.*
Sheathed in gold and silver,
without the breath of life—
can that be your guide?

18. What good is an idol
when its maker has shaped it?
A molten image, a false guide—
why does its maker trust it,
who can only make a god that cannot talk?

20. But You, the Eternal, are in Your holy
  Temple—
let all the earth be silent in Your presence:

14. for the earth shall be filled
with the knowledge of the glory of God,
as water covers the sea!

19 הוֹי אֹמֵר לָעֵץ הָקִיצָה
עוּרִי לְאֶבֶן דּוּמָם
הוּא יוֹרֶה
הִנֵּה־הוּא תָּפוּשׂ זָהָב וָכֶסֶף
וְכָל־רוּחַ אֵין בְּקִרְבּוֹ:
18 מָה־הוֹעִיל פֶּסֶל
כִּי פְסָלוֹ יֹצְרוֹ
מַסֵּכָה וּמוֹרֶה שָׁקֶר
כִּי בָטַח יֹצֵר יִצְרוֹ עָלָיו
לַעֲשׂוֹת אֱלִילִים אִלְּמִים:
20 וַיהֹוָה בְּהֵיכַל קָדְשׁוֹ
הַס מִפָּנָיו כָּל־הָאָרֶץ:
14 כִּי תִּמָּלֵא הָאָרֶץ
לָדַעַת אֶת־כְּבוֹד יְהֹוָה
כַּמַּיִם יְכַסּוּ עַל־יָם:

ADDITIONAL READINGS 13

Zechariah, chapter 8, verses 7 to 13 and 16 to 17

The prophet Zechariah was intrumental in urging the people of Jerusalem who had returned from Babylonian captivity to rebuild the Temple. The structure was completed in the last part of the 6th centurv B.C.E. For more on Zechariah and his time, see our *General Introduction*.

The reading concerns the future of Israel and its Sanctuary. Both are secure and blessed by God if social justice reigns among the people, for then "they shall be My people, and I will be their God, in truth and righteousness" (verse 8).

8:7. This is the word of the God of heaven's hosts:

I will rescue My people from the east and from the land of sunset;

8. I will bring them home to live in Jerusalem.

They shall be My people, and I will be their God, in truth and righteousness.

9. This is the word of the God of heaven's hosts:

Take courage, as you hear the words spoken by the prophets when the foundations were laid for the rebuilding of the Temple, the House of the God of heaven's hosts.

10. Before that time, people got nothing for their work or for hiring out their animals; because of enemies it was unsafe to come and go; and I brought people into conflict with each other.

11. But now, says the God of heaven's hosts, I will not treat the remnant of My people as in the early days,

12. for I am planting the seed of well-being: the vine will give its fruit,

the ground its crop, the skies their dew—

כֹּה אָמַר יְהוָה צְבָאוֹת 8:7

הִנְנִי מוֹשִׁיעַ אֶת־עַמִּי מֵאֶרֶץ מִזְרָח

וּמֵאֶרֶץ מְבוֹא הַשָּׁמֶשׁ:

וְהֵבֵאתִי אֹתָם וְשָׁכְנוּ בְּתוֹךְ יְרוּשָׁלָ͏ִם 8

וְהָיוּ־לִי לְעָם

וַאֲנִי אֶהְיֶה לָהֶם לֵאלֹהִים

בֶּאֱמֶת וּבִצְדָקָה:

כֹּה־אָמַר יְהוָה צְבָאוֹת 9

תֶּחֱזַקְנָה יְדֵיכֶם הַשֹּׁמְעִים בַּיָּמִים הָאֵלֶּה אֵת

הַדְּבָרִים הָאֵלֶּה מִפִּי הַנְּבִיאִים אֲשֶׁר בְּיוֹם

יֻסַּד בֵּית־יְהוָה צְבָאוֹת הַהֵיכָל לְהִבָּנוֹת:

כִּי לִפְנֵי הַיָּמִים הָהֵם שְׂכַר הָאָדָם לֹא 10

נִהְיָה וּשְׂכַר הַבְּהֵמָה אֵינֶנָּה וְלַיּוֹצֵא וְלַבָּא אֵין־

שָׁלוֹם מִן־הַצָּר וַאֲשַׁלַּח אֶת־כָּל־הָאָדָם אִישׁ

בְּרֵעֵהוּ:

וְעַתָּה לֹא כַיָּמִים הָרִאשֹׁנִים אֲנִי לִשְׁאֵרִית 11

הָעָם הַזֶּה נְאֻם יְהוָה צְבָאוֹת:

כִּי־זֶרַע הַשָּׁלוֹם 12

הַגֶּפֶן תִּתֵּן פִּרְיָהּ

וְהָאָרֶץ תִּתֵּן אֶת־יְבוּלָהּ

I will give all these things to the remnant of
My people to possess.

13. And just as you were once considered
accursed among the nations, O House of
Judah and House of Israel, so as I save you
shall you become a blessing. Have no fear;
be strong!

16. These are the things you are to do:
speak the truth to one another;
render judgments in your gates that are
true and make for peace;

17. do not plan evil against your neighbor;
and approve no false oath;
for all these things I hate,
says the Eternal One.

וְהַשָּׁמַ֖יִם יִתְּנ֣וּ טַלָּ֑ם
וְהִנְחַלְתִּ֗י אֶת־שְׁאֵרִ֛ית הָעָ֥ם הַזֶּ֖ה אֶת־כָּל־אֵֽלֶּה׃
13 וְהָיָ֞ה כַּאֲשֶׁ֣ר הֱיִיתֶ֣ם קְלָלָ֗ה בַּגּוֹיִם֙ בֵּ֤ית
יְהוּדָה֙ וּבֵ֣ית יִשְׂרָאֵ֔ל כֵּ֚ן אוֹשִׁ֣יעַ אֶתְכֶ֔ם וִהְיִיתֶ֖ם
בְּרָכָ֑ה אַל־תִּירָ֖אוּ תֶּחֱזַ֥קְנָה יְדֵיכֶֽם׃
16 אֵ֥לֶּה הַדְּבָרִ֖ים אֲשֶׁ֣ר תַּעֲשׂ֑וּ
דַּבְּר֤וּ אֱמֶת֙ אִ֣ישׁ אֶת־רֵעֵ֔הוּ
אֱמֶת֙ וּמִשְׁפַּ֣ט שָׁל֔וֹם שִׁפְט֖וּ בְּשַׁעֲרֵיכֶֽם׃
17 וְאִ֣ישׁ ׀ אֶת־רָעַ֣ת רֵעֵ֗הוּ אַֽל־תַּחְשְׁבוּ֙
בִּלְבַבְכֶ֔ם
וּשְׁבֻ֥עַת שֶׁ֖קֶר אַֽל־תֶּאֱהָ֑בוּ
כִּ֧י אֶת־כָּל־אֵ֛לֶּה אֲשֶׁ֥ר שָׂנֵ֖אתִי
נְאֻם־יְהֹוָֽה׃

Psalm 43, verses 1 to 5

The book of Psalms is found in *K'tuvim* ("Writings"), the third section of the Tanach. It contains 150 spiritual poems that exalt and call upon the Eternal as sovereign, friend, and savior. Tradition considers King David as the author of all the psalms that are either anonymous or ascribed to him, while modern scholarship assigns many of them to various later sources.

The words of our reading are the outcry of a discouraged poet, who feels abandoned and betrayed. Still, there is one hope: "Trust in God, for I shall yet praise the One who is my help and my God" (verse 5).

<table>
<tr>
<td>

43:1. Vindicate me, O God, and defend my

    cause

against a disloyal nation;

deliver me from the deceitful, the unjust.

</td>
<td dir="rtl">

43:1 שָׁפְטֵנִי אֱלֹהִים וְרִיבָה רִיבִי

מִגּוֹי לֹא־חָסִיד

מֵאִישׁ־מִרְמָה וְעַוְלָה תְפַלְּטֵנִי:

</td>
</tr>
<tr>
<td>

2. For You are God my fortress:

Why do You reject me?

Why should I walk about downcast

at the taunts of foes?

</td>
<td dir="rtl">

2 כִּי־אַתָּה אֱלֹהֵי מָעוּזִּי

לָמָה זְנַחְתָּנִי

לָמָה־קֹדֵר אֶתְהַלֵּךְ

בְּלַחַץ אוֹיֵב:

</td>
</tr>
<tr>
<td>

3. Send forth Your light and Your truth;

let them lead me,

let them bring me to Your holy mountain,

to Your dwelling-place.

</td>
<td dir="rtl">

3 שְׁלַח־אוֹרְךָ וַאֲמִתְּךָ

הֵמָּה יַנְחוּנִי

יְבִיאוּנִי אֶל־הַר־קָדְשְׁךָ

וְאֶל־מִשְׁכְּנוֹתֶיךָ:

</td>
</tr>
<tr>
<td>

4. Then I shall come to the altar of God,

to the God of my delight, my joy,

and thank You with the lyre,

O God, my God.

</td>
<td dir="rtl">

4 וְאָבוֹאָה אֶל־מִזְבַּח אֱלֹהִים

אֶל־אֵל שִׂמְחַת גִּילִי

וְאוֹדְךָ בְכִנּוֹר

אֱלֹהִים אֱלֹהָי:

</td>
</tr>
<tr>
<td>

5. Why are you cast down, O my soul,

and why are you disquieted within me?

Trust in God,

for I shall yet praise the One

who is my help and my God.

</td>
<td dir="rtl">

5 מַה־תִּשְׁתּוֹחֲחִי נַפְשִׁי

וּמַה־תֶּהֱמִי עָלָי

הוֹחִילִי לֵאלֹהִים

כִּי־עוֹד אוֹדֶנּוּ

יְשׁוּעֹת פָּנַי וֵאלֹהָי:

</td>
</tr>
</table>

ADDITIONAL READINGS 15

Psalm 63, verses 1 to 6, 9, and 8

The book of Psalms is found in *K'tuvim* ("Writings"), the third section of the Tanach. It contains 150 spiritual poems that exalt and call upon the Eternal as sovereign, friend and savior. Tradition considers King David as the author of those psalms that are either anonymous or ascribed to him, while modern scholarship assigns many of them to various later sources.

Our reading identifies David as the author and notes the time of the poem's composition. David was fleeing from King Saul and was in hiding from the men sent out to find and kill him. His faith in God gave him hope and strength: "My soul stays close to You, Your hand holds me fast" (verse 9). The verses have been slightly reordered, for the sake of clarity.

63:1. A Psalm of David, when he was in the wilderness of Judah.

63:1 מִזְמוֹר לְדָוִד בִּהְיוֹתוֹ בְּמִדְבַּר יְהוּדָה:

2. God, You are my God; at first light I seek You.

2 אֱלֹהִים אֵלִי אַתָּה אֲשַׁחֲרֶךָּ

My soul thirsts for You, my flesh longs for You,

צָמְאָה לְךָ נַפְשִׁי כָּמַהּ לְךָ בְשָׂרִי

as in a dry and weary land, where there is no water.

בְּאֶרֶץ־צִיָּה וְעָיֵף בְּלִי־מָיִם:

3. So do I look for You in the Sanctuary,

3 כֵּן בַּקֹּדֶשׁ חֲזִיתִיךָ

to see Your power and Your glory.

לִרְאוֹת עֻזְּךָ וּכְבוֹדֶךָ:

4. Your love is better than life; my lips shall praise You.

4 כִּי־טוֹב חַסְדְּךָ מֵחַיִּים שְׂפָתַי יְשַׁבְּחוּנְךָ:

5. And I shall praise You with my life; I shall raise my hand [to bless] Your Name.

5 כֵּן אֲבָרֶכְךָ בְחַיָּי

בְּשִׁמְךָ אֶשָּׂא כַפָּי:

6. My soul is richly fed as from the fat of sacrifices;

6 כְּמוֹ חֵלֶב וָדֶשֶׁן

תִּשְׂבַּע נַפְשִׁי

my lips cry out for joy and my mouth shouts praise.

וְשִׂפְתֵי רְנָנוֹת יְהַלֶּל־פִּי:

9. My soul stays close to You, Your hand holds me fast,

9 דָּבְקָה נַפְשִׁי אַחֲרֶיךָ

בִּי תָּמְכָה יְמִינֶךָ:

8. You are my help, and in the shadow of Your wings I sing for joy.

8 כִּי־הָיִיתָ עֶזְרָתָה לִּי

וּבְצֵל כְּנָפֶיךָ אֲרַנֵּן:

ADDITIONAL READINGS 16

Psalm 106, verses 1 to 13, 19 to 23, and 48

The book of Psalms is found in *K'tuvim* ("Writings"), the third section of the Tanach. It contains 150 spiritual poems that exalt and call upon the Eternal as sovereign, friend, and savior. Tradition considers King David as the author of all the psalms that are either anonymous or ascribed to him, while modern scholarship assigns many of them to various later sources.

Our reading presents excerpts from what may be called a "national psalm," an ode to the God of a people who have not sufficiently apreciated divine wonders and guidance. (Verse 47, which is not included here, asks God to "gather us from among the nations." This suggests that the poem came from the time of the Babylonian exile.)

106:1. Halleluyah!

Give thanks to the Eternal,

who is good,

whose love is everlasting.

2. Who can describe the mighty acts of the
   Eternal?

Who can truly sing God's praise?

3. Happy is the one who executes justice,

the doer of righteousness at every turn.

4. Eternal One, as You favor Your people,

remember me,

visit me graciously

with Your salvation.

5. Let me enjoy the happiness of Your
   chosen ones,

rejoice in the joys of Your nation,

glory in [the people] You possess.

6. Like our ancestors before us,

we have sinned,

done wrong, done evil.

7. Our ancestors in Egypt

did not understand

[the meaning of] Your wonders;

they quickly forgot

Your many loving acts;

106:1 הַלְלוּיָהּ

הוֹדוּ לַיהוָה כִּי־טוֹב

כִּי לְעוֹלָם חַסְדּוֹ׃

2 מִי יְמַלֵּל גְּבוּרוֹת יְהוָה

יַשְׁמִיעַ כָּל־תְּהִלָּתוֹ׃

3 אַשְׁרֵי שֹׁמְרֵי מִשְׁפָּט

עֹשֵׂה צְדָקָה בְכָל־עֵת׃

4 זָכְרֵנִי יְהוָה בִּרְצוֹן עַמֶּךָ

פָּקְדֵנִי בִּישׁוּעָתֶךָ׃

5 לִרְאוֹת בְּטוֹבַת בְּחִירֶיךָ

לִשְׂמֹחַ בְּשִׂמְחַת גּוֹיֶךָ

לְהִתְהַלֵּל עִם־נַחֲלָתֶךָ׃

6 חָטָאנוּ עִם־אֲבוֹתֵינוּ

הֶעֱוִינוּ הִרְשָׁעְנוּ׃

7 אֲבוֹתֵינוּ בְמִצְרַיִם

לֹא־הִשְׂכִּילוּ

נִפְלְאוֹתֶיךָ

לֹא זָכְרוּ

אֶת־רֹב חֲסָדֶיךָ

they rebelled against You at the sea, by the
    Reed [Red] Sea.

8. For the sake of Your Name You saved
    them,

and made known Your power.

9. You roared at the Sea, and it dried up,

You led them across the deeps

as though it were a desert track.

10. You saved them from the hand of the
    foe,

You rescued them from the enemy's grip.

11. The waters covered their adversaries;

not one of them was left.

12. Then they believed Your promises;

they sang Your praise.

13. But they were quick to forget what You
    had done;

they would not wait for Your guidance.

19. They made a calf at Horeb;

[at Sinai] they worshipped a molten image,

20. exchanging their Glory

for the likeness of a bullock

that feeds on grass!

21. They forgot the God who had saved
    them

with great deeds in Egypt,

22. with wonders in the land of Ham,

awesome acts at the Reed [Red] Sea!

23. You would have made an end to them

had not Moses Your chosen one

stepped into the breach before You

to turn aside Your rage to destroy [them].

וַיַּמְרוּ עַל־יָם בְּיַם־סוּף:

8 וַיּוֹשִׁיעֵם לְמַעַן שְׁמוֹ
לְהוֹדִיעַ אֶת־גְּבוּרָתוֹ:

9 וַיִּגְעַר בְּיַם־סוּף וַיֶּחֱרָב
וַיּוֹלִיכֵם בַּתְּהֹמוֹת
כַּמִּדְבָּר:

10 וַיּוֹשִׁיעֵם מִיַּד שׂוֹנֵא
וַיִּגְאָלֵם מִיַּד אוֹיֵב:

11 וַיְכַסּוּ־מַיִם צָרֵיהֶם
אֶחָד מֵהֶם לֹא נוֹתָר:

12 וַיַּאֲמִינוּ בִדְבָרָיו
יָשִׁירוּ תְּהִלָּתוֹ:

13 מִהֲרוּ שָׁכְחוּ מַעֲשָׂיו
לֹא־חִכּוּ לַעֲצָתוֹ:

19 יַעֲשׂוּ־עֵגֶל בְּחֹרֵב
וַיִּשְׁתַּחֲווּ לְמַסֵּכָה:

20 וַיָּמִירוּ אֶת־כְּבוֹדָם
בְּתַבְנִית שׁוֹר
אֹכֵל עֵשֶׂב:

21 שָׁכְחוּ אֵל מוֹשִׁיעָם
עֹשֶׂה גְדֹלוֹת בְּמִצְרָיִם:

22 נִפְלָאוֹת בְּאֶרֶץ חָם
נוֹרָאוֹת עַל־יַם־סוּף:

23 וַיֹּאמֶר לְהַשְׁמִידָם
לוּלֵי מֹשֶׁה בְחִירוֹ
עָמַד בַּפֶּרֶץ לְפָנָיו
לְהָשִׁיב חֲמָתוֹ מֵהַשְׁחִית:

48. Blessed is the Eternal, the God of Israel

from of old and forever,

and let all the people say:

Amen.

Halleluyah!

48 בָּרוּךְ־יְהֹוָה אֱלֹהֵי יִשְׂרָאֵל

מִן־הָעוֹלָם וְעַד הָעוֹלָם

וְאָמַר כָּל־הָעָם

אָמֵן

הַלְלוּיָהּ:

Psalm 139, verses 1 to 12 and verses 23 to 24

The book of Psalms is found in *K'tuvim* ("Writings"), the third section of the Tanach. It contains 150 spiritual poems that exalt and call upon the Eternal as sovereign, friend, and savior. Tradition considers King David as the author of all the psalms that are either anonymous or ascribed to him, while modern scholarship assigns many of them to various later sources.

Our reading presents a poem of deep spiritual awareness of God's Presence—the God who is close to one's heart and at the same time the One whose Presence fills the world. The poem contains some of the best-known verses from the book of Psalms.

<table>
<tr><td>

139:1. Eternal One, You have searched me, and know me.

2. You know my sitting and my rising, You discern my thought from afar.

3. You observe my movement and my rest, and are acquainted with all my ways.

4. When there is not [yet] a word on my tongue, Eternal One, You know it already!

5. You compass me about behind and before, and lay Your hand upon me.

6. Such knowledge is too wonderful for me, too high—I cannot grasp it.

7. Whither can I go from Your spirit? Whither can I flee from Your presence?

8. If I ascend the heavens, You are there! If I make my bed in the lower depths, behold, You are there!

9. If I rise on the wings of the morning, [or] dwell on the ocean's farthest shore,

10. even there Your hand will lead me, Your hand will hold me.

</td><td dir="rtl">

139:1 יְהֹוָה חֲקַרְתַּנִי וַתֵּדָע:

2 אַתָּה יָדַעְתָּ שִׁבְתִּי וְקוּמִי
בַּנְתָּה לְרֵעִי מֵרָחוֹק:

3 אָרְחִי וְרִבְעִי זֵרִיתָ
וְכָל־דְּרָכַי הִסְכַּנְתָּה:

4 כִּי אֵין מִלָּה בִּלְשׁוֹנִי
הֵן יְהֹוָה יָדַעְתָּ כֻלָּהּ:

5 אָחוֹר וָקֶדֶם צַרְתָּנִי
וַתָּשֶׁת עָלַי כַּפֶּכָה:

6 פְּלִאיָה [פְּלִיאָה] דַעַת מִמֶּנִּי
נִשְׂגְּבָה לֹא־אוּכַל לָהּ:

7 אָנָה אֵלֵךְ מֵרוּחֶךָ
וְאָנָה מִפָּנֶיךָ אֶבְרָח:

8 אִם־אֶסַּק שָׁמַיִם שָׁם אָתָּה
וְאַצִּיעָה שְּׁאוֹל הִנֶּךָּ:

9 אֶשָּׂא כַנְפֵי־שָׁחַר
אֶשְׁכְּנָה בְּאַחֲרִית יָם:

10 גַּם־שָׁם יָדְךָ תַנְחֵנִי
וְתֹאחֲזֵנִי יְמִינֶךָ:

</td></tr>
</table>

11. If I say: Surely darkness will conceal
    me,

night will hide me from view,

12. even the darkness is not too dark for
    You,

the night is clear as the day;

darkness is as light [to You].

23. Search me, O God, and know my heart.

Try me; enter my thoughts.

24. Keep me from walking the path of pain,

and guide me in the way of eternity.

11 וָאֹמַר אַךְ־חֹשֶׁךְ יְשׁוּפֵנִי
וְלַיְלָה אוֹר בַּעֲדֵנִי:
12 גַּם־חֹשֶׁךְ לֹא־יַחְשִׁיךְ מִמֶּךָ
וְלַיְלָה כַּיּוֹם יָאִיר
כַּחֲשֵׁיכָה כָּאוֹרָה:
23 חָקְרֵנִי אֵל וְדַע לְבָבִי
בְּחָנֵנִי וְדַע שַׂרְעַפָּי:
24 וּרְאֵה אִם־דֶּרֶךְ־עֹצֶב בִּי
וּנְחֵנִי בְּדֶרֶךְ עוֹלָם:

Amos, chapter 5, verses 16 to 24

The prophet Amos lived in the 8th century B.C.E., and his central theme was the need for social justice. Without it, he preached, attention to ritual is meaningless. For more on Amos and his time, see our *General Introduction*.

Our reading is devoted to this theme, and verse 24 is its oft-quoted distillation. The Midrash explains verse 21 as follows: "I hate your feast-days"—for they are far removed from Mine, that is, the way I meant them to be observed: in an environment of social equity.

5:16. Thus says the Eternal One,	5:16 לָכֵן כֹּה־אָמַר יְהֹוָה
the Sovereign God of heaven's hosts:	אֱלֹהֵי צְבָאוֹת אֲדֹנָי
There shall be wailing in the squares,	בְּכָל־רְחֹבוֹת מִסְפֵּד
cries of woe in the boulevards;	וּבְכָל־חוּצוֹת יֹאמְרוּ הוֹ־הוֹ
farmers shall be called to mourn	וְקָרְאוּ אִכָּר אֶל־אֵבֶל
and the experts in lamentation to wail.	וּמִסְפֵּד אֶל־יוֹדְעֵי נֶהִי:
17. And there shall be mourning in every vineyard	17 וּבְכָל־כְּרָמִים מִסְפֵּד
when I pass through your midst,	כִּי־אֶעֱבֹר בְּקִרְבְּךָ
says the Eternal One.	אָמַר יְהֹוָה:
18. Are you hoping for the Day of the Eternal?	18 הוֹי הַמִּתְאַוִּים אֶת־יוֹם יְהֹוָה
What good will that day do you?	לָמָּה־זֶּה לָכֶם יוֹם יְהֹוָה
It is darkness, not light!	הוּא־חֹשֶׁךְ וְלֹא־אוֹר:
19. [It is] like running from a lion,	19 כַּאֲשֶׁר יָנוּס אִישׁ מִפְּנֵי הָאֲרִי
only to be met by a bear;	וּפְגָעוֹ הַדֹּב
like escaping into a house	וּבָא הַבַּיִת
and leaning one's hand against a wall,	וְסָמַךְ יָדוֹ עַל־הַקִּיר
only to be bitten by a snake!	וּנְשָׁכוֹ הַנָּחָשׁ:
20. Be sure of it—	20 הֲלֹא־
the Eternal God's day is darkness,	חֹשֶׁךְ יוֹם יְהֹוָה
not light,	וְלֹא־אוֹר
shrouded in gloom	וְאָפֵל
without a gleam of light!	וְלֹא־נֹגַהּ לוֹ:

21. I hate, I reject your feast-days [says
    God];

I take no pleasure in the scent of your
    solemn assemblies.

22. When you bring Me burnt-offerings
    and offerings of grain,

I will not accept them;

I will not look [with favor] upon your
    fatlings.

23. Spare Me your noisy songs;

I will not listen to the melody of your
    harps.

24. But let justice roll down like waters,

and righteousness like a mighty stream.

21 שָׂנֵאתִי מָאַסְתִּי חַגֵּיכֶם

וְלֹא אָרִיחַ בְּעַצְּרֹתֵיכֶם:

22 כִּי אִם־תַּעֲלוּ־לִי עֹלוֹת וּמִנְחֹתֵיכֶם

לֹא אֶרְצֶה

וְשֶׁלֶם מְרִיאֵיכֶם לֹא אַבִּיט:

23 הָסֵר מֵעָלַי הֲמוֹן שִׁרֶיךָ

וְזִמְרַת נְבָלֶיךָ לֹא אֶשְׁמָע:

24 וְיִגַּל כַּמַּיִם מִשְׁפָּט

וּצְדָקָה כְּנַחַל אֵיתָן:

ADDITIONAL READINGS 19

Hosea, chapter 6, verses 1 to 6

The prophet Hosea lived in the 8th century B.C.E. and spoke movingly of God's love for Israel, a love to which Israel must respond by its righteous deeds. For more on Hosea and his time, see our *General Introduction*.

In our selection, the Prophet excoriates those whose loyalty to God is "like swiftly vanishing dew" (verse 4). The Eternal has no use for sacrifices that are used as substitutes for the love of God.

6:1. Come, let us return to the Eternal,

who has wounded [us] and [now] will heal us,

who has smitten [us],

and [now] will bind us up.

2. In two days God will revive us,

on the third day raising us up

to live in God's presence.

3. Let us gain knowledge,

let us strive to know the Eternal,

whose appearance is sure as the dawn,

coming to us like rain,

like spring rain that waters the earth.

4. What must I do with you, Ephraim?

What must I do with you, Judah?

Your loyalty is like a morning cloud,

like swiftly vanishing dew.

5. Therefore have I cut down the prophets,

slaying them with the words of My mouth:

My judgment [of you] goes forth like light.

6. For it is steadfast love I desire, and not sacrifice,

the knowledge of God rather than burnt-offerings.

6:1 לְכוּ וְנָשׁ֙וּבָה֙ אֶל־יְהֹוָ֔ה

כִּ֛י ה֥וּא טָרָ֖ף וְיִרְפָּאֵ֑נוּ

יַ֖ךְ וְיַחְבְּשֵֽׁנוּ׃

2 יְחַיֵּ֖נוּ מִיֹּמָ֑יִם

בַּיּוֹם֙ הַשְּׁלִישִׁ֔י יְקִמֵ֖נוּ

וְנִחְיֶ֥ה לְפָנָֽיו׃

3 וְנֵדְעָ֣ה

נִרְדְּפָ֗ה לָדַ֙עַת֙ אֶת־יְהֹוָ֔ה

כְּשַׁ֖חַר נָכ֣וֹן מֽוֹצָא֑וֹ

וְיָב֚וֹא כַגֶּ֙שֶׁם֙ לָ֔נוּ

כְּמַלְק֖וֹשׁ י֥וֹרֶה אָֽרֶץ׃

4 מָ֚ה אֶֽעֱשֶׂה־לְּךָ֙ אֶפְרַ֔יִם

מָ֥ה אֶֽעֱשֶׂה־לְּךָ֖ יְהוּדָ֑ה

וְחַסְדְּכֶם֙ כַּעֲנַן־בֹּ֔קֶר

וְכַטַּ֖ל מַשְׁכִּ֥ים הֹלֵֽךְ׃

5 עַל־כֵּ֗ן חָצַ֙בְתִּי֙ בַּנְּבִיאִ֔ים

הֲרַגְתִּ֖ים בְּאִמְרֵי־פִ֑י

וּמִשְׁפָּטֶ֖יךָ א֥וֹר יֵצֵֽא׃

6 כִּ֛י חֶ֥סֶד חָפַ֖צְתִּי וְלֹא־זָ֑בַח

וְדַ֥עַת אֱלֹהִ֖ים מֵעֹלֽוֹת׃

Psalm 39, verses 2 to 11 and 13 to 14 and Psalm 63, verse 5

The book of Psalms is found in *K'tuvim* ("Writings"), the third section of the Tanach. It contains 150 spiritual poems that exalt and call upon the Eternal as sovereign, friend, and savior. Tradition considers King David as the author of all the psalms that are either anonymous or ascribed to him, while modern scholarship assigns many of them to various later sources.

Our reading is a meditation on the brevity of life and a plea for divine favor before the end comes. To the words of the 39th Psalm it adds one verse from Psalm 63.

39:2. I will watch my steps, I said,

lest I stumble over my tongue;

when the wicked are near me,

I will put a muzzle over my mouth.

3. I was speechless, [enveloped] in silence,

leaving unsaid even the good!

So my pain was stirred up.

4. My heart flared up,

my thoughts were ablaze,

and I gave tongue:

5. Tell me, Eternal One, when my end will
   be,

how many days I have;

let me know how evanescent I am.

6. You have made my days mere hand-
   breadths;

my life span is nothing before You;

those who stand

are but vapor. Selah.

7. They move about like shadows;

the noise they make comes to nothing;

they heap up riches,

without knowing who will gather them in.

8. What then can I hope for, Eternal One?

I can only trust in You.

39:2 אָמַרְתִּי אֶשְׁמְרָה דְרָכַי

מֵחֲטוֹא בִלְשׁוֹנִי

אֶשְׁמְרָה לְפִי מַחְסוֹם

בְּעֹד רָשָׁע לְנֶגְדִּי׃

3 נֶאֱלַמְתִּי דוּמִיָּה

הֶחֱשֵׁיתִי מִטּוֹב

וּכְאֵבִי נֶעְכָּר׃

4 חַם־לִבִּי בְּקִרְבִּי

בַּהֲגִיגִי תִבְעַר־אֵשׁ

דִּבַּרְתִּי בִּלְשׁוֹנִי׃

5 הוֹדִיעֵנִי יְהֹוָה קִצִּי

וּמִדַּת יָמַי מַה־הִיא

אֵדְעָה מֶה־חָדֵל אָנִי׃

6 הִנֵּה טְפָחוֹת נָתַתָּה יָמַי

וְחֶלְדִּי כְאַיִן נֶגְדֶּךָ

אַךְ כָּל־הֶבֶל

כָּל־אָדָם נִצָּב סֶלָה׃

7 אַךְ־בְּצֶלֶם יִתְהַלֶּךְ־אִישׁ

אַךְ־הֶבֶל יֶהֱמָיוּן

יִצְבֹּר

וְלֹא־יֵדַע מִי־אֹסְפָם׃

8 וְעַתָּה מַה־קִּוִּיתִי אֲדֹנָי

תּוֹחַלְתִּי לְךָ הִיא׃

9. Save me from the wrongs I do,   9 מִכׇּל־פְּשָׁעַי הַצִּילֵנִי

from the disgrace of being an impious fool.   חֶרְפַּת נָבָל אַל־תְּשִׂימֵנִי:

10. I am silent,   10 נֶאֱלַמְתִּי

I will not open my mouth,   לֹא אֶפְתַּח־פִּי

for [it is] You who must act.   כִּי אַתָּה עָשִׂיתָ:

11. Remove Your affliction from me;   11 הָסֵר מֵעָלַי נִגְעֶךָ

Your blows have brought me to my end.   מִתִּגְרַת יָדְךָ אֲנִי כָלִיתִי:

13. Hear my prayer, Eternal One;   13 שִׁמְעָה־תְפִלָּתִי יְהֹוָה

listen to my cry;   וְשַׁוְעָתִי הַאֲזִינָה

do not be deaf to my tears;   אֶל־דִּמְעָתִי אַל־תֶּחֱרַשׁ

for I am a stranger before You,   כִּי גֵר אָנֹכִי עִמָּךְ

an alien,   תּוֹשָׁב

like all my ancestors.   כְּכׇל־אֲבוֹתָי:

14. Turn Your gaze from me   14 הָשַׁע מִמֶּנִּי

and let me smile again,   וְאַבְלִיגָה

before I go away   בְּטֶרֶם אֵלֵךְ

and am no more.   וְאֵינֶנִּי:

63:5. And I will praise You with my life;   63:5 כֵּן אֲבָרֶכְךָ בְחַיָּי

I will raise my hand [to bless] Your Name.   בְּשִׁמְךָ אֶשָּׂא כַפָּי:

ADDITIONAL READINGS 21

Proverbs, chapter 6, verses 12 to 23

The book of Proverbs is found in *K'tuvim* ("Writings"), the third section of the Tanach. It contains proverbial sayings, warnings against excess, popular philosophy, and instructions for living a worthwhile life. While tradition has assigned its authorship to King Solomon (10th century B.C.E.), contemporary scholarship holds that it belongs to the genre of "wisdom literature," which flourished from the 4th century B.C.E. on under Greek influence.

The reading praises honesty and warns that the deceitful will come to a bad end. It commends the moral teaching of father and mother, and its last verse contains these oft-quoted words: "For a commandment is a lamp, and a teaching is a light."

6:12. The devilish and dissolute	אָדָם בְּלִיַּעַל אִישׁ אָוֶן 6:12
go about with lying lips,	הוֹלֵךְ עִקְּשׁוּת פֶּה:
13. with a wink, a shuffle, a pointing finger—	13 קֹרֵץ בְּעֵינָיו מֹלֵל בְּרַגְלָו מֹרֶה בְּאֶצְבְּעֹתָיו:
14. and in their hearts, unnatural things. They plot evil all the time, arousing discord.	14 תַּהְפֻּכוֹת בְּלִבּוֹ חֹרֵשׁ רָע בְּכָל־עֵת מְדָנִים [מִדְיָנִים] יְשַׁלֵּחַ:
15. Because of this, their doom will strike without warning, they will be suddenly broken, beyond repair.	15 עַל־כֵּן פִּתְאֹם יָבוֹא אֵידוֹ פֶּתַע יִשָּׁבֵר וְאֵין מַרְפֵּא:
16. There are six things the Eternal hates, seven that are abhorrent to God:	16 שֶׁשׁ־הֵנָּה שָׂנֵא יְהוָה וְשֶׁבַע תּוֹעֲבוֹת [תּוֹעֲבַת] נַפְשׁוֹ:
17. haughty eyes, a lying tongue, and hands that shed innocent blood;	17 עֵינַיִם רָמוֹת לְשׁוֹן שָׁקֶר וְיָדַיִם שֹׁפְכוֹת דָּם־נָקִי:
18. a mind that makes wicked plans, feet that are quick to run to evil;	18 לֵב חֹרֵשׁ מַחְשְׁבוֹת אָוֶן רַגְלַיִם מְמַהֲרוֹת לָרוּץ לָרָעָה:
19. a false witness who breathes out lies, and one who sows discord among kin.	19 יָפִיחַ כְּזָבִים עֵד שָׁקֶר וּמְשַׁלֵּחַ מְדָנִים בֵּין אַחִים:

20. Listen, my child,
to your father's precept,
and do not be deaf
to your mother's teaching;
21. bind them continually to your heart,
wind them continually around your neck;
22. when you go about, they shall guide
   you;
when you lie down to sleep, they shall
   protect you;
when you awake, they shall speak to you.
23. For [Your] commandment is a lamp,
and [Your] teaching a light,
and the admonitions of discipline are the
   way to life.

20 נְצֹר בְּנִי
מִצְוַת אָבִיךָ
וְאַל־תִּטֹּשׁ
תּוֹרַת אִמֶּךָ:
21 קָשְׁרֵם עַל־לִבְּךָ תָמִיד
עָנְדֵם עַל־גַּרְגְּרֹתֶךָ:
22 בְּהִתְהַלֶּכְךָ תַּנְחֶה אֹתָךְ
בְּשָׁכְבְּךָ תִּשְׁמֹר עָלֶיךָ
וַהֲקִיצוֹתָ הִיא תְשִׂיחֶךָ:
23 כִּי נֵר מִצְוָה
וְתוֹרָה אוֹר
וְדֶרֶךְ חַיִּים תּוֹכְחוֹת מוּסָר:

Jeremiah, chapter 22, verses 1 to 16

Jeremiah was the fearless conscience of his people and paid for his courage with imprisonment, contumely, and threat of death. He survived the destruction of Jerusalem in 587 B.C.E., which he had foretold, and eventually was forced to migrate to Egypt, where he died. For more on the Prophet and his time, see our *General Introduction*.

The reading concerns a visit by the Prophet to King Zedekiah, whom he warned to institute social justice in the nation, lest destruction would befall it. Unfortunately, the king did not listen, and the Babylonians conquered Jerusalem and destroyed city and Temple.

22:1. Thus says the Eternal One: Go down to the king of Judah's palace, and speak this word:

2. Listen to the word of the Eternal, king of Judah, you who sit on David's throne, you and your courtiers, and your people who pass through these gates.

3. The Eternal One says: Do what is just and right; rescue the victim from the extortionist's clutches; do not oppress or use violence against a stranger, an orphan, or a widow; and shed no innocent blood in this place.

4. If you faithfully fulfill this word, then kings who pass through the gates of this house shall be of David's royal line; they shall sit on his throne; they shall ride in chariots and on horses, they, their courtiers, and their people.

5. But if you do not listen to these words, says the Eternal One, I swear by Myself that this house shall become a ruin.

6. For thus says the Eternal One concerning the royal palace of Judah:
Though you are as dear to Me as Gilead,
or as the highest peaks of Lebanon,

22:1 כֹּה אָמַר יְהֹוָה רֵד בֵּית־מֶלֶךְ יְהוּדָה וְדִבַּרְתָּ שָׁם אֶת־הַדָּבָר הַזֶּה:

2 וְאָמַרְתָּ שְׁמַע דְּבַר־יְהֹוָה מֶלֶךְ יְהוּדָה הַיֹּשֵׁב עַל־כִּסֵּא דָוִד אַתָּה וַעֲבָדֶיךָ וְעַמְּךָ הַבָּאִים בַּשְּׁעָרִים הָאֵלֶּה:

3 כֹּה אָמַר יְהֹוָה עֲשׂוּ מִשְׁפָּט וּצְדָקָה וְהַצִּילוּ גָזוּל מִיַּד עָשׁוֹק וְגֵר יָתוֹם וְאַלְמָנָה אַל־תֹּנוּ אַל־תַּחְמֹסוּ וְדָם נָקִי אַל־תִּשְׁפְּכוּ בַּמָּקוֹם הַזֶּה:

4 כִּי אִם־עָשׂוֹ תַּעֲשׂוּ אֶת־הַדָּבָר הַזֶּה וּבָאוּ בְשַׁעֲרֵי הַבַּיִת הַזֶּה מְלָכִים יֹשְׁבִים לְדָוִד עַל־כִּסְאוֹ רֹכְבִים בָּרֶכֶב וּבַסּוּסִים הוּא וַעֲבָדָו [וַעֲבָדָיו] וְעַמּוֹ:

5 וְאִם לֹא תִשְׁמְעוּ אֶת־הַדְּבָרִים הָאֵלֶּה בִּי נִשְׁבַּעְתִּי נְאֻם־יְהֹוָה כִּי־לְחָרְבָּה יִהְיֶה הַבַּיִת הַזֶּה:

6 כִּי־כֹה אָמַר יְהֹוָה עַל־בֵּית מֶלֶךְ יְהוּדָה גִּלְעָד אַתָּה לִי רֹאשׁ הַלְּבָנוֹן

I will make you a desert,

[with] uninhabited towns.

7. I will consecrate marauders

each man with his weapons

to fell your choicest cedars

and throw them on the fire.

8. When other peoples pass by this city, they shall ask each other: Why did the Eternal do this to that great city?

9. And the answer shall come: Because they abandoned their covenant with the Eternal their God, and worshipped other gods and served them.

13. Woe to those who build their house by unjust means and their upper chambers by injustice; who make their neighbors work for nothing, and withhold their rightful wages;

14. who think to build themselves mansions with spacious upper chambers and cut out for themselves windows with cedar paneling and vermilion paint!

15. Do you rule because you compete with cedar?

Your father ate and drank,

and did justice and right.

Then it was well with him.

16. He judged the case of the poor and needy:

then it was well.

Is not this (what it means) to know Me? says the Eternal One.

אִם־לֹא אֲשִׁיתְךָ֙ מִדְבָּ֔ר

עָרִ֖ים לֹ֥א נוֹשָׁ֖בָה [נוֹשָֽׁבוּ]׃

7 וְקִדַּשְׁתִּ֥י עָלֶ֖יךָ מַשְׁחִתִ֑ים

אִ֖ישׁ וְכֵלָ֑יו

וְכָֽרְתוּ֙ מִבְחַ֣ר אֲרָזֶ֔יךָ

וְהִפִּ֖ילוּ עַל־הָאֵֽשׁ׃

8 וְעָֽבְרוּ֙ גּוֹיִ֣ם רַבִּ֔ים עַ֖ל הָעִ֣יר הַזֹּ֑את וְאָֽמְרוּ֙ אִ֣ישׁ אֶל־רֵעֵ֔הוּ עַל־מֶ֨ה עָשָׂ֤ה יְהֹוָה֙ כָּ֔כָה לָעִ֥יר הַגְּדוֹלָ֖ה הַזֹּֽאת׃

9 וְאָ֣מְר֔וּ עַ֚ל אֲשֶׁ֣ר עָֽזְב֔וּ אֶת־בְּרִ֖ית יְהֹוָ֣ה אֱלֹֽהֵיהֶ֑ם וַיִּֽשְׁתַּֽחֲו֛וּ לֵאלֹהִ֥ים אֲחֵרִ֖ים וַיַּֽעַבְדֽוּם׃

13 ה֣וֹי בֹּנֶ֤ה בֵיתוֹ֙ בְּלֹא־צֶ֔דֶק וַעֲלִיּוֹתָ֖יו בְּלֹ֣א מִשְׁפָּ֑ט בְּרֵעֵ֨הוּ֙ יַֽעֲבֹ֣ד חִנָּ֔ם וּפֹעֲל֖וֹ לֹ֥א יִתֶּן־לֽוֹ׃

14 הָֽאֹמֵ֗ר אֶבְנֶה־לִּי֙ בֵּ֣ית מִדּ֔וֹת וַעֲלִיּ֖וֹת מְרֻוָּחִ֑ים וְקָ֤רַֽע לוֹ֙ חַלּוֹנָ֔י וְסָפ֣וּן בָּאָ֔רֶז וּמָשׁ֖וֹחַ בַּשָּׁשַֽׁר׃

15 הֲתִֽמְלֹ֔ךְ כִּ֥י אַתָּ֖ה מְתַֽחֲרֶ֣ה בָאָ֑רֶז אָבִ֨יךָ֙ הֲל֣וֹא אָכַ֣ל וְשָׁתָ֔ה וְעָשָׂ֤ה מִשְׁפָּט֙ וּצְדָקָ֔ה אָ֖ז ט֥וֹב לֽוֹ׃

16 דָּ֛ן דִּֽין־עָנִ֥י וְאֶבְי֖וֹן אָ֣ז ט֑וֹב הֲלֽוֹא־הִ֛יא הַדַּ֥עַת אֹתִ֖י נְאֻם־יְהֹוָֽה׃

Job, chapter 31, verses 5 to 8, 13 to 17, 19 to 20, 24 to 25, 32, 34, and 38 to 40

The book of Job is found in *K'tuvim* ("Writings"), the third part of the Tanach. It presents the story of a man whose faith is tested by God and who tries to understand the inscrutable designs of the Almighty. The author of the book is unknown, and so is the time of its composition.

Our selection brings us the final self-justification of Job. He details his merits and thereby challenges God to tell him why he has been tried so sorely. (In the book God's answer follows. Job learns that human beings can never hope to grasp what the Eternal devises.)

31:5. Have I walked with vanity,

and have my feet rushed to deceive?

6. Were God to weigh me in the scales of justice,

God would know that I am innocent.

7. If my steps have deviated from the [right] way,

if my heart has followed my eyes,

if anything has stuck to my hands—

8. let others eat what I sow,

and let my offspring be pulled up by their roots!

13. If ever I spurned the claim of any servant of mine, man or woman,

when they contended against me,

14. what would I do when God rises up,

what would I answer when called to account?

15. Surely the One who formed me in the belly formed them,

molding us all in the same [divine] womb.

16. Did I ever grudge the poor their wish,

ever make a widow wear out her eyes with tears?

17. Did I ever eat my bread alone

and not let an orphan share it?

31:5 אִם־הָלַכְתִּי עִם־שָׁוְא

וַתַּחַשׁ עַל־מִרְמָה רַגְלִי:

6 יִשְׁקְלֵנִי בְמֹאזְנֵי־צֶדֶק

וְיֵדַע אֱלוֹהַּ תֻּמָּתִי:

7 אִם תִּטֶּה אַשֻּׁרִי מִנִּי הַדֶּרֶךְ

וְאַחַר עֵינַי הָלַךְ לִבִּי

וּבְכַפַּי דָּבַק מְאוּם:

8 אֶזְרְעָה וְאַחֵר יֹאכֵל

וְצֶאֱצָאַי יְשֹׁרָשׁוּ:

13 אִם־אֶמְאַס מִשְׁפַּט עַבְדִּי וַאֲמָתִי

בְּרִבָם עִמָּדִי:

14 וּמָה אֶעֱשֶׂה כִּי־יָקוּם אֵל

וְכִי־יִפְקֹד מָה אֲשִׁיבֶנּוּ:

15 הֲלֹא־בַבֶּטֶן עֹשֵׂנִי עָשָׂהוּ

וַיְכֻנֶנּוּ בָּרֶחֶם אֶחָד:

16 אִם־אֶמְנַע מֵחֵפֶץ דַּלִּים

וְעֵינֵי אַלְמָנָה אֲכַלֶּה:

17 וְאֹכַל פִּתִּי לְבַדִּי

וְלֹא־אָכַל יָתוֹם מִמֶּנָּה:

19. Did I ever see anyone dying for lack of clothing,

a pauper without a mantle,

20. but that such a one [had reason] to bless me

as he warmed himself with fleece from my flock?

24. Did I ever put my trust in gold,

ever think that gold would make me safe?

25. Did I ever gloat over my vast wealth,

the riches my hands had won?

32. No stranger ever had to sleep in the street—

for I would open my door to the traveler.

34. Was I ever afraid of the crowd,

or feared the scorn of the mob,

so that I was reduced to silence,

unwilling to go out the door?

38. Did my land ever cry out against me?

Did its furrows join in wailing?

39. Did I eat its yield without payment?

Did I snuff out the life of its landowners?

40. Then in place of wheat let there be thorns,

in place of barley, cockles!

(With this the words of Job are ended.)

19 אִם־אֶרְאֶה אוֹבֵד מִבְּלִי לְבוּשׁ

וְאֵין כְּסוּת לָאֶבְיוֹן:

20 אִם־לֹא בֵרְכוּנִי חֲלָצוֹ [חֲלָצָיו]

וּמִגֵּז כְּבָשַׂי יִתְחַמָּם:

24 אִם־שַׂמְתִּי זָהָב כִּסְלִי

וְלַכֶּתֶם אָמַרְתִּי מִבְטַחִי:

25 אִם־אֶשְׂמַח כִּי־רַב חֵילִי

וְכִי־כַבִּיר מָצְאָה יָדִי:

32 בַּחוּץ לֹא־יָלִין גֵּר

דְּלָתַי לָאֹרַח אֶפְתָּח:

34 כִּי אֶעֱרוֹץ הָמוֹן רַבָּה

וּבוּז־מִשְׁפָּחוֹת יְחִתֵּנִי

וָאֶדֹּם

לֹא־אֵצֵא פָתַח:

38 אִם־עָלַי אַדְמָתִי תִזְעָק

וְיַחַד תְּלָמֶיהָ יִבְכָּיוּן:

39 אִם־כֹּחָהּ אָכַלְתִּי בְלִי־כָסֶף

וְנֶפֶשׁ בְּעָלֶיהָ הִפָּחְתִּי:

40 תַּחַת חִטָּה יֵצֵא חוֹחַ

וְתַחַת־שְׂעֹרָה בָאְשָׁה

תַּמּוּ דִּבְרֵי אִיּוֹב:

ADDITIONAL READINGS 24

Isaiah, chapter 59, verses 1 to 14 and 20 to 21

The Prophet, who lived among the exiles in Babylon (6th century B.C.E.), tried to maintain the people's faith in the Eternal. The people wonder why their hoped-for return to their homeland is so slow in coming. In our selection, Isaiah answers that it is Israel's sins that have separated it from the Eternal, and these sins are recounted one by one. But, Isaiah assures the people, "a Redeemer will come to Zion, to those of Jacob who turn from transgression" (verse 20).

For more on Isaiah, see our *General Introduction*, and especially the section dealing with the Second Isaiah, from whom this reading stems.

59:1. Behold, the Eternal's arm is not too
short to save;

Nor is God's ear too dull to hear.

2. But your misdeeds have separated you
from your God,

and your sins have hidden [God's] counte-
nance from you,

so that God has not listened [to you].

3. Your hands are filthy with blood,

your fingers with wrongdoing;

your lips speak lies,

your tongues utter wickedness.

4. No one sues for just cause,

no one pleads in good faith;

they rely on empty words,

on lying speech,

conceiving mischief and begetting evil.

5. They hatch adders' eggs

and weave spider webs;

who eats their eggs dies,

the crushed egg hatches out a viper.

6. Their webs cannot serve as clothing;

they cannot dress themselves with what
they make;

their deeds are evil ones,

and their hands are turned to violence.

59:1 הֵ֤ן לֹֽא־קָצְרָה֙ יַד־יְהֹוָ֔ה מֵהוֹשִׁ֑יעַ
וְלֹא־כָבְדָ֥ה אָזְנ֖וֹ מִשְּׁמֽוֹעַ׃

2 כִּ֤י אִם־עֲוֺנֹֽתֵיכֶם֙
הָי֣וּ מַבְדִּלִ֔ים בֵּינֵכֶ֕ם לְבֵ֖ין אֱלֹֽהֵיכֶ֑ם
וְחַטֹּֽאותֵיכֶ֗ם הִסְתִּ֧ירוּ פָנִ֛ים מִכֶּ֖ם
מִשְּׁמֽוֹעַ׃

3 כִּ֤י כַפֵּיכֶם֙ נְגֹֽאֲל֣וּ בַדָּ֔ם
וְאֶצְבְּעוֹתֵיכֶ֖ם בֶּֽעָוֺ֑ן
שִׂפְתֽוֹתֵיכֶם֙ דִּבְּרוּ־שֶׁ֔קֶר
לְשׁוֹנְכֶ֖ם עַוְלָ֥ה תֶהְגֶּֽה׃

4 אֵין־קֹרֵ֣א בְצֶ֔דֶק
וְאֵ֥ין נִשְׁפָּ֖ט בֶּאֱמוּנָ֑ה
בָּט֤וֹחַ עַל־תֹּ֙הוּ֙
וְדַבֶּר־שָׁ֔וְא הָר֥וֹ עָמָ֖ל וְהוֹלֵ֥יד אָֽוֶן׃

5 בֵּיצֵ֤י צִפְעוֹנִי֙ בִּקֵּ֔עוּ
וְקוּרֵ֥י עַכָּבִ֖ישׁ יֶאֱרֹ֑גוּ
הָאֹכֵ֤ל מִבֵּֽיצֵיהֶם֙ יָמ֔וּת
וְהַזּוּרֶ֖ה תִּבָּקַ֥ע אֶפְעֶֽה׃

6 קֽוּרֵיהֶם֙ לֹא־יִהְי֣וּ לְבֶ֔גֶד
וְלֹ֥א יִתְכַּסּ֖וּ בְּמַעֲשֵׂיהֶ֑ם
מַֽעֲשֵׂיהֶם֙ מַֽעֲשֵׂי־אָ֔וֶן
וּפֹ֥עַל חָמָ֖ס בְּכַפֵּיהֶֽם׃

7. Their feet run to evil,

they rush to shed innocent blood;

their thoughts are thoughts of wickedness,

desolation and destruction are on their
  paths.

8. Of the way of peace they know nothing,

their steps do not aim for justice;

they have made their courses crooked;

those who tread on them know no peace.

9. Therefore is justice far from us,

and righteousness cannot reach us;

we hope for light, and, behold, there is
  darkness;

for brightness, and we walk in gloom.

10. We reach out, as the blind [grope]
  along a wall,

we reach, like those without eyes;

we stumble at noon as at dusk,

among the healthy as though we were
  dead.

11. We growl, all of us, like bears,

we moan like doves;

we hope for justice, but there is none;

for deliverance, but it is far from us.

12. Many are our transgressions before
  You,

and our sins accuse us;

yes, we are aware of our transgressions,

and we know our misdeeds:

13. transgression, unfaithfulness toward
  the Eternal,

turning away from our God,

planning oppression and revolt,

conceiving lies and telling them with
  conviction.

רַגְלֵיהֶם לָרַע יָרֻצוּ 7

וִימַהֲרוּ לִשְׁפֹּךְ דָּם נָקִי

מַחְשְׁבוֹתֵיהֶם מַחְשְׁבוֹת אָוֶן

שֹׁד וָשֶׁבֶר בִּמְסִלּוֹתָם:

דֶּרֶךְ שָׁלוֹם לֹא יָדָעוּ 8

וְאֵין מִשְׁפָּט בְּמַעְגְּלוֹתָם

נְתִיבוֹתֵיהֶם עִקְּשׁוּ לָהֶם

כֹּל דֹּרֵךְ בָּהּ לֹא יָדַע שָׁלוֹם:

עַל־כֵּן רָחַק מִשְׁפָּט מִמֶּנּוּ 9

וְלֹא תַשִּׂיגֵנוּ צְדָקָה

נְקַוֶּה לָאוֹר וְהִנֵּה־חֹשֶׁךְ

לִנְגֹהוֹת בָּאֲפֵלוֹת נְהַלֵּךְ:

נְגַשְׁשָׁה כַעִוְרִים קִיר 10

וּכְאֵין עֵינַיִם נְגַשֵּׁשָׁה

כָּשַׁלְנוּ בַצָּהֳרַיִם כַּנֶּשֶׁף

בָּאַשְׁמַנִּים כַּמֵּתִים:

נֶהֱמֶה כַדֻּבִּים כֻּלָּנוּ 11

וְכַיּוֹנִים הָגֹה נֶהְגֶּה

נְקַוֶּה לַמִּשְׁפָּט וָאַיִן

לִישׁוּעָה רָחֲקָה מִמֶּנּוּ:

כִּי־רַבּוּ פְשָׁעֵינוּ נֶגְדֶּךָ 12

וְחַטֹּאותֵינוּ עָנְתָה בָּנוּ

כִּי־פְשָׁעֵינוּ אִתָּנוּ

וַעֲוֹנֹתֵינוּ יְדַעֲנוּם:

פָּשֹׁעַ וְכַחֵשׁ בַּיהֹוָה 13

וְנָסוֹג מֵאַחַר אֱלֹהֵינוּ

דַּבֶּר־עֹשֶׁק וְסָרָה

הֹרוֹ וְהֹגוֹ מִלֵּב דִּבְרֵי־שָׁקֶר:

14. And so justice is turned back
and righteousness stands far off,
for truth stumbles in the square,
and uprightness cannot enter.

20. But a Redeemer shall come to Zion,
to those of Jacob who turn from transgression,
says the Eternal One.

21. And as for Me, this is My covenant
with them,
says the Eternal One:
My spirit that is upon you,
and the words that I have placed in your
mouth,
must not depart from your mouth,
and from your children's mouth,
and from your children's children's mouth,
says the Eternal One,
from now and forever.

14 וְהֻסַּג אָחוֹר מִשְׁפָּט
וּצְדָקָה מֵרָחוֹק תַּעֲמֹד
כִּי־כָשְׁלָה בָרְחוֹב אֱמֶת
וּנְכֹחָה לֹא־תוּכַל לָבוֹא:
20 וּבָא לְצִיּוֹן גּוֹאֵל
וּלְשָׁבֵי פֶשַׁע בְּיַעֲקֹב
נְאֻם יְהֹוָה:
21 וַאֲנִי זֹאת בְּרִיתִי אוֹתָם
אָמַר יְהֹוָה
רוּחִי אֲשֶׁר עָלֶיךָ
וּדְבָרַי אֲשֶׁר־שַׂמְתִּי בְּפִיךָ
לֹא־יָמוּשׁוּ מִפִּיךָ
וּמִפִּי זַרְעֲךָ
וּמִפִּי זֶרַע זַרְעֲךָ
אָמַר יְהֹוָה
מֵעַתָּה וְעַד־עוֹלָם:

Zechariah, chapter 7, verses 4 to 10 and chapter 8, verses 16 to 17, and 19

Zechariah was instrumental in urging the people of Jerusalem who had returned from Babylonian captivity to rebuild the Temple. Our selection is preceded by a notation (7:1) that this prophecy took place in the fourth year of King Darius of Persia—that is, the year 517 B.C.E. His empire included the province of Yehud, of which the rebuilt Jerusalem was the center.

Zechariah's words speak for themselves: God is concerned with the people's lack of justice and social compassion, truth and peace. For more on the Prophet and his time, see our *General Introduction.*

7:4. The word of the God of heaven's hosts, came to me:

5. Tell all the people of the land and the priests: When you fasted and lamented in the fifth and seventh months all these seventy years [since the Temple of Solomon was destroyed], did you fast for My sake?

6. And when you eat and drink, for whom are you eating, and for whom are you drinking (but for your own sake)?

7. When Jerusalem and the towns around her were at ease and filled with people, when the Negev and the lowlands were filled with people, what did I tell the people through the earlier prophets?

8. The word of the Eternal came to Zechariah, saying:

9. Thus says the God of heaven's hosts: See that true justice is done; treat each other with love and compassion;

10. do not oppress widows, orphans, strangers, or the poor; and plan no evil against each other.

7:4 וַיְהִי דְּבַר־יְהוָה צְבָאוֹת אֵלַי לֵאמֹר:

5 אֱמֹר אֶל־כָּל־עַם הָאָרֶץ וְאֶל־הַכֹּהֲנִים לֵאמֹר כִּי־צַמְתֶּם וְסָפוֹד בַּחֲמִישִׁי וּבַשְּׁבִיעִי וְזֶה שִׁבְעִים שָׁנָה הֲצוֹם צַמְתֻּנִי אָנִי:

6 וְכִי תֹאכְלוּ וְכִי תִשְׁתּוּ הֲלוֹא אַתֶּם הָאֹכְלִים וְאַתֶּם הַשֹּׁתִים:

7 הֲלוֹא אֶת־הַדְּבָרִים אֲשֶׁר קָרָא יְהוָה בְּיַד הַנְּבִיאִים הָרִאשֹׁנִים בִּהְיוֹת יְרוּשָׁלַם יֹשֶׁבֶת וּשְׁלֵוָה וְעָרֶיהָ סְבִיבֹתֶיהָ וְהַנֶּגֶב וְהַשְּׁפֵלָה יֹשֵׁב:

8 וַיְהִי דְּבַר־יְהוָה אֶל־זְכַרְיָה לֵאמֹר:

9 כֹּה אָמַר יְהוָה צְבָאוֹת לֵאמֹר מִשְׁפַּט אֱמֶת שְׁפֹטוּ וְחֶסֶד וְרַחֲמִים עֲשׂוּ אִישׁ אֶת־אָחִיו:

10 וְאַלְמָנָה וְיָתוֹם גֵּר וְעָנִי אַל־תַּעֲשֹׁקוּ וְרָעַת אִישׁ אָחִיו אַל־תַּחְשְׁבוּ בִּלְבַבְכֶם:

8:16. These are the things you are to do: speak the truth to one another; render judgments in your courts that are honest and make for peace;

17. do not plan evil against your neighbor; and approve no false oath; for all these things I hate, says the Eternal One.

19. [Instead,] you must love truth and peace.

8:16 אֵלֶּה הַדְּבָרִים אֲשֶׁר תַּעֲשׂוּ דַּבְּרוּ אֱמֶת אִישׁ אֶת־רֵעֵהוּ אֱמֶת וּמִשְׁפַּט שָׁלוֹם שִׁפְטוּ בְּשַׁעֲרֵיכֶם:

17 וְאִישׁ אֶת־רָעַת רֵעֵהוּ אַל־תַּחְשְׁבוּ בִּלְבַבְכֶם וּשְׁבֻעַת שֶׁקֶר אַל־תֶּאֱהָבוּ כִּי אֶת־כָּל־אֵלֶּה אֲשֶׁר שָׂנֵאתִי נְאֻם־יְהֹוָה:

19 וְהָאֱמֶת וְהַשָּׁלוֹם אֱהָבוּ:

Nehemiah, chapter 5, verses 1 to 13

Nehemiah has remained one of the lesser-known personages in Jewish history, although he was one of the most important. He had returned with the exiles from Babylon after 538 B.C.E. and became a driving force in reestablishing the community in their homeland. The book of Nehemiah reveals a successful man of action and of faith who provided inspired leadership in a crucial moment of his people's life. The book of Nehemiah is found in *K'tuvim* ("Writings"), the third section of the Tanach.

Our selection offers an example of his influence in a matter of moral and economic import. The community was still in flux, but already deep divisions between rich and poor had emerged. Nehemiah's radical appeal found a surprisingly ready acceptance.

5:1. Then the clamor of the people, men and women alike, was great against their Jewish kin.

2. Some said: With our sons and daughters we are many; let us obtain grain that we may eat and stay alive.

3. Others said: We have had to pledge our fields and vineyards and houses to get enough grain in this famine.

4. Still others said: We had to borrow money against our fields and vineyards to pay the royal tax.

5. Now, our flesh is just like our kindred's, and our children are just like theirs. Yet here we are reducing our sons and daughters to slavery. Some of our daughters have already been forced into bondage, and we could do nothing to prevent it because our fields and vineyards are in the hands of others.

6. When I [Nehemiah] heard their cries for help and their complaints, I grew extremely angry.

5:1 וַתְּהִ֞י צַעֲקַ֥ת הָעָ֛ם וּנְשֵׁיהֶ֖ם גְּדוֹלָ֑ה אֶל־
אֲחֵיהֶ֖ם הַיְּהוּדִֽים׃

2 וְיֵשׁ֙ אֲשֶׁ֣ר אֹמְרִ֔ים בָּנֵ֥ינוּ וּבְנֹתֵ֖ינוּ אֲנַ֣חְנוּ רַבִּ֑ים
וְנִקְחָ֥ה דָגָ֖ן וְנֹאכְלָ֥ה וְנִחְיֶֽה׃

3 וְיֵשׁ֙ אֲשֶׁ֣ר אֹמְרִ֔ים שְׂדֹתֵ֛ינוּ וּכְרָמֵ֥ינוּ וּבָתֵּ֖ינוּ
אֲנַ֣חְנוּ עֹרְבִ֑ים וְנִקְחָ֥ה דָגָ֖ן בָּרָעָֽב׃

4 וְיֵשׁ֙ אֲשֶׁ֣ר אֹמְרִ֔ים לָוִ֥ינוּ כֶ֖סֶף לְמִדַּ֣ת הַמֶּ֑לֶךְ
שְׂדֹתֵ֖ינוּ וּכְרָמֵֽינוּ׃

5 וְעַתָּ֗ה כִּבְשַׂ֤ר אַחֵ֙ינוּ֙ בְּשָׂרֵ֔נוּ כִּבְנֵיהֶ֖ם בָּנֵ֑ינוּ
וְהִנֵּ֣ה אֲנַ֡חְנוּ כֹבְשִׁים֩ אֶת־בָּנֵ֨ינוּ וְאֶת־בְּנֹתֵ֜ינוּ
לַעֲבָדִ֗ים וְיֵ֨שׁ מִבְּנֹתֵ֤ינוּ נִכְבָּשׁוֹת֙ וְאֵ֣ין לְאֵ֣ל יָדֵ֔נוּ
וּשְׂדֹתֵ֥ינוּ וּכְרָמֵ֖ינוּ לַאֲחֵרִֽים׃

6 וַיִּ֥חַר לִ֖י מְאֹ֑ד כַּאֲשֶׁ֤ר שָׁמַ֙עְתִּי֙ אֶת־זַעֲקָתָ֔ם
וְאֵ֖ת הַדְּבָרִ֥ים הָאֵֽלֶּה׃

7. After cudgeling my brains, I contended with the patricians and the heads [of the community] and declared to them: Every one of you is exacting usurious loans from your own kin! So I called a large assembly to deal with them.

8. I declared to them: We have done all we could to buy back our kindred, the Jews who have been sold to foreigners, yet you too are selling your kindred, and they must be sold [back] to us! They were silent; they found nothing to say.

9. I continued: You are doing wrong. You should live with reverence for God and avoid the defilement of the nations, our enemies.

10. Now, I and my companions and those who work for me have been lending the people money and grain. We shall give up our claims for interest.

11. And you—cancel all the debts they owe you: money or grain or wine or olive oil. And give them back their fields, vineyards, olive groves, and houses right now!

12. They answered: We shall make restitution. We shall not seek [anything] from them. Truly, we shall do as you say. I called the priests and made them swear to do as they had promised.

13. I also shook out the fold of my garment and declared: In this way may God shake any of you who fails to keep your promise! God will take away your houses and everything you own, and you shall be shaken out and empty [-handed].

Amen, said all the people, and they praised the Eternal. And the people kept their promise.

7 וַיִּמָּלֵךְ לִבִּי עָלַי וָאָרִיבָה אֶת־הַחֹרִים וְאֶת־הַסְּגָנִים וָאֹמְרָה לָהֶם מַשָּׁא אִישׁ־בְּאָחִיו אַתֶּם נֹשִׁאים וָאֶתֵּן עֲלֵיהֶם קְהִלָּה גְדוֹלָה:

8 וָאֹמְרָה לָהֶם אֲנַחְנוּ קָנִינוּ אֶת־אַחֵינוּ הַיְּהוּדִים הַנִּמְכָּרִים לַגּוֹיִם כְּדֵי בָנוּ וְגַם־אַתֶּם תִּמְכְּרוּ אֶת־אֲחֵיכֶם וְנִמְכְּרוּ־לָנוּ וַיַּחֲרִישׁוּ וְלֹא מָצְאוּ דָּבָר:

9 וַיֹּאמֶר [וָאֹמַר] לֹא־טוֹב הַדָּבָר אֲשֶׁר־אַתֶּם עֹשִׂים הֲלוֹא בְּיִרְאַת אֱלֹהֵינוּ תֵּלֵכוּ מֵחֶרְפַּת הַגּוֹיִם אוֹיְבֵינוּ:

10 וְגַם־אֲנִי אַחַי וּנְעָרַי נֹשִׁים בָּהֶם כֶּסֶף וְדָגָן נַעַזְבָה־נָּא אֶת־הַמַּשָּׁא הַזֶּה:

11 הָשִׁיבוּ נָא לָהֶם כְּהַיּוֹם שְׂדֹתֵיהֶם כַּרְמֵיהֶם זֵיתֵיהֶם וּבָתֵּיהֶם וּמְאַת הַכֶּסֶף וְהַדָּגָן הַתִּירוֹשׁ וְהַיִּצְהָר אֲשֶׁר אַתֶּם נֹשִׁים בָּהֶם:

12 וַיֹּאמְרוּ נָשִׁיב וּמֵהֶם לֹא נְבַקֵּשׁ כֵּן נַעֲשֶׂה כַּאֲשֶׁר אַתָּה אוֹמֵר וָאֶקְרָא אֶת־הַכֹּהֲנִים וָאַשְׁבִּיעֵם לַעֲשׂוֹת כַּדָּבָר הַזֶּה:

13 גַּם־חָצְנִי נָעַרְתִּי וָאֹמְרָה כָּכָה יְנַעֵר הָאֱלֹהִים אֶת־כָּל־הָאִישׁ אֲשֶׁר לֹא־יָקִים אֶת־הַדָּבָר הַזֶּה מִבֵּיתוֹ וּמִיגִיעוֹ וְכָכָה יִהְיֶה נָעוּר וָרֵק וַיֹּאמְרוּ כָל־הַקָּהָל אָמֵן וַיְהַלְלוּ אֶת־יְהוָה וַיַּעַשׂ הָעָם כַּדָּבָר הַזֶּה:

ADDITIONAL READINGS 27

Jeremiah, chapter 23, verses 13 to 29

Jeremiah was the fearless conscience of his people and paid for his courage with imprisonment, contumely, and threat of death. He survived the destruction of Jerusalem in 587 B.C.E., which he had foretold, and eventually was forced to migrate to Egypt, where he died. For more on the Prophet and his time, see our *General Introduction*.

Our selection is an example of Jeremiah's vigorous attacks on the establishment—the kind of preachments that earned him the enmity of the ruling classes and resulted in much personal suffering.

23:13. In Samaria's prophets I have seen a
repellent thing:
they have prophesied by Baal and misled
My people Israel.
14. And in the prophets of Jerusalem I have
[also] seen horrors:
they are adulterers who make their way by
dissembling;
they have so strengthened the hands of
evildoers,
so that no one turns from evil.
To Me, these [prophets] are like the people
of Sodom,
its [Jerusalem's] inhabitants are like
Gomorrah.
15. Be sure of this, says the God of
heaven's hosts, about the prophets:
I will give them wormwood to eat and
poisoned water to drink,
for ungodliness flows all over the land
from the prophets of Jerusalem.
16. The God of heaven's hosts has said:
Do not listen to these prophets who
prophesy to you:
they are ruining you.

23:13 וּבִנְבִיאֵי שֹׁמְרוֹן רָאִיתִי תִפְלָה

הִנַּבְּאוּ בַבַּעַל וַיַּתְעוּ אֶת־עַמִּי אֶת־יִשְׂרָאֵל:

14 וּבִנְבִאֵי יְרוּשָׁלַ͏ִם רָאִיתִי שַׁעֲרוּרָה

נָאוֹף וְהָלֹךְ בַּשֶּׁקֶר

וְחִזְּקוּ יְדֵי מְרֵעִים

לְבִלְתִּי־שָׁבוּ אִישׁ מֵרָעָתוֹ

הָיוּ־לִי כֻלָּם כִּסְדֹם וְיֹשְׁבֶיהָ כַּעֲמֹרָה:

15 לָכֵן כֹּה־אָמַר יְהוָה צְבָאוֹת עַל־הַנְּבִאִים

הִנְנִי מַאֲכִיל אוֹתָם לַעֲנָה וְהִשְׁקִתִים מֵי־רֹאשׁ

כִּי מֵאֵת נְבִיאֵי יְרוּשָׁלַ͏ִם

יָצְאָה חֲנֻפָּה לְכָל־הָאָרֶץ:

16 כֹּה־אָמַר יְהוָה צְבָאוֹת

אַל־תִּשְׁמְעוּ עַל־דִּבְרֵי הַנְּבִאִים הַנִּבְּאִים לָכֶם

מַהְבִּלִים הֵמָּה אֶתְכֶם

Their visions come out of their own minds,
not from the Eternal.

17. They reassure the people who scorn
My word, [saying:]

The Eternal says that all will be well;
to all who follow their own stubborn hearts
they say:

No harm will come to you.

18. But who has stood in the council of the
Eternal,

seeing and hearing [God's] word?
Who has listened to [God's] word
and announced it?

19. Observe the stormy [response] of the
Eternal!

[My] wrath goes forth,
and [like a] a whirling tempest
whirls down on the unjust.

20. The anger of the Eternal will not turn
back

until God has acted, bringing about God's
inner purposes.

In days to come you will fully understand.

21. I never sent those prophets, but they
rushed in;

I never spoke to them, but they spoke in
My name.

22. If only they had stood in My council,
they could have proclaimed My words to
My people,

and turned them back from their evil path
and wicked deeds.

23. Am I not a God who is nearby,
says the Eternal One,
rather than a God far off?

חֲזוֹן לִבָּם֙ יְדַבֵּ֔רוּ
לֹ֖א מִפִּ֥י יְהוָֽה׃

17 אֹמְרִ֤ים אָמוֹר֙ לִֽמְנַאֲצַ֔י
דִּבֶּ֣ר יְהוָ֔ה שָׁל֖וֹם יִֽהְיֶ֣ה לָכֶ֑ם
וְ֠כֹל הֹלֵ֞ךְ בִּשְׁרִר֤וּת לִבּוֹ֙ אָ֣מְר֔וּ
לֹֽא־תָב֥וֹא עֲלֵיכֶ֖ם רָעָֽה׃

18 כִּ֣י מִ֤י עָמַד֙ בְּס֣וֹד יְהוָ֔ה
וְיֵ֥רֶא וְיִשְׁמַ֖ע אֶת־דְּבָר֑וֹ
מִֽי־הִקְשִׁ֥יב דְּבָרִ֖י [דְּבָר֥וֹ]
וַיִּשְׁמָֽע׃

19 הִנֵּ֣ה ׀ סַעֲרַ֣ת יְהוָ֗ה
חֵמָה֙ יָֽצְאָ֔ה
וְסַ֖עַר מִתְחוֹלֵ֑ל
עַ֛ל רֹ֥אשׁ רְשָׁעִ֖ים יָחֽוּל׃

20 לֹ֤א יָשׁוּב֙ אַף־יְהוָ֔ה
עַד־עֲשֹׂת֖וֹ
וְעַד־הֲקִימ֥וֹ מְזִמּ֖וֹת לִבּ֑וֹ
בְּאַחֲרִ֣ית הַיָּמִ֔ים תִּתְבּ֥וֹנְנוּ בָ֖הּ בִּינָֽה׃

21 לֹא־שָׁלַ֥חְתִּי אֶת־הַנְּבִאִ֖ים וְהֵ֣ם רָ֑צוּ
לֹא־דִבַּ֥רְתִּי אֲלֵיהֶ֖ם וְהֵ֥ם נִבָּֽאוּ׃

22 וְאִֽם־עָמְד֖וּ בְּסוֹדִ֑י
וְיַשְׁמִ֤עוּ דְבָרַי֙ אֶת־עַמִּ֔י
וִֽישִׁב֛וּם מִדַּרְכָּ֥ם הָרָ֖ע
וּמֵרֹ֥עַ מַֽעַלְלֵיהֶֽם׃

23 הַאֱלֹהֵ֧י מִקָּרֹ֛ב אָ֖נִי נְאֻם־יְהוָ֑ה
וְלֹ֥א אֱלֹהֵ֖י מֵֽרָחֹֽק׃

24. If you hide yourself in secret places,

says the Eternal One,

do you think I won't see you?

Surely I fill heaven and earth

—says the Eternal One.

25. I have heard those false prophets,

the ones who tell lies in My name.

They say: *I've had a dream! I have had a dream!*

26. How long will those lying prophets,

prophets who speak with the intent to deceive,

27. tell these dreams of theirs to one another,

hoping to make My people forget My Name,

as did their ancestors who forgot My Name through Baal?

28. Let The prophet who has a dream admit that it was [only] a dream;

let the one who has My message tell it faithfully!

What does straw have in common with clean, threshed grain? says the Eternal One.

29. The Eternal One says: My word is like fire,

like a hammer that shatters a rock!

24 אִם־יִסָּתֵר אִישׁ בַּמִּסְתָּרִים

וַאֲנִי לֹא־אֶרְאֶנּוּ

נְאֻם־יְהֹוָה

הֲלוֹא אֶת־הַשָּׁמַיִם וְאֶת־הָאָרֶץ אֲנִי מָלֵא

נְאֻם־יְהֹוָה:

25 שָׁמַעְתִּי אֵת אֲשֶׁר־אָמְרוּ הַנְּבִאִים

הַנִּבְּאִים בִּשְׁמִי שֶׁקֶר

לֵאמֹר חָלַמְתִּי חָלָמְתִּי:

26 עַד־מָתַי הֲיֵשׁ בְּלֵב הַנְּבִאִים נִבְּאֵי הַשָּׁקֶר

וּנְבִיאֵי תַּרְמִת לִבָּם:

27 הַחֹשְׁבִים לְהַשְׁכִּיחַ אֶת־עַמִּי שְׁמִי

בַּחֲלוֹמֹתָם אֲשֶׁר יְסַפְּרוּ אִישׁ לְרֵעֵהוּ

כַּאֲשֶׁר שָׁכְחוּ אֲבוֹתָם אֶת־שְׁמִי בַּבָּעַל:

28 הַנָּבִיא אֲשֶׁר־אִתּוֹ חֲלוֹם יְסַפֵּר חֲלוֹם

וַאֲשֶׁר דְּבָרִי אִתּוֹ יְדַבֵּר דְּבָרִי אֱמֶת

מַה־לַתֶּבֶן אֶת־הַבָּר נְאֻם־יְהֹוָה:

29 הֲלוֹא כֹה דְבָרִי כָּאֵשׁ נְאֻם־יְהֹוָה

וּכְפַטִּישׁ יְפֹצֵץ סָלַע:

820

Psalm 107, verses 1 to 16 and 35 to 43

The book of Psalms is found in *K'tuvim* ("Writings"), the third section of the Tanach. It contains 150 spiritual poems that exalt and call upon the Eternal as sovereign, friend, and savior. Tradition considers King David as the author of all the psalms that are either anonymous or ascribed to him, while modern scholarship assigns many of them to various later sources.

Our psalm extols God as the refuge for those in need. Verse 2 sets the theme: "Let this be the song of those saved by the Eternal, whom God has saved from their foes."

107:1. Give thanks to the Eternal,

who is good,

whose love is everlasting.

2. Let this be the song of those saved by
   the Eternal,

whom God has saved from their foes,

3. bringing them back from far-off lands,

from east and west, from north to south.

4. Some could not find a path in the
   wilderness,

could not find a settled town;

5. they were hungry and thirsty,

their lives were fading away;

6. in their trouble they cried out to the
   Eternal,

who saved them from their plight,

7. leading them on a straight path,

right to a settled place.

8. Let them thank the Eternal,

who showed them steadfast love,

who does wonders for human beings,

9. satisfying the dried-up soul,

and filling the hungry soul with good.

10. Some dwell in darkness, [in] the
    shadow of death,

prisoners in painful fetters,

107:1 הֹדוּ לַיהֹוָה

כִּי־טוֹב

כִּי לְעוֹלָם חַסְדּוֹ:

2 יֹאמְרוּ גְּאוּלֵי יְהֹוָה

אֲשֶׁר גְּאָלָם מִיַּד־צָר:

3 וּמֵאֲרָצוֹת קִבְּצָם

מִמִּזְרָח וּמִמַּעֲרָב מִצָּפוֹן וּמִיָּם:

4 תָּעוּ בַמִּדְבָּר בִּישִׁימוֹן דָּרֶךְ

עִיר מוֹשָׁב לֹא מָצָאוּ:

5 רְעֵבִים גַּם־צְמֵאִים

נַפְשָׁם בָּהֶם תִּתְעַטָּף:

6 וַיִּצְעֲקוּ אֶל־יְהֹוָה בַּצַּר לָהֶם

מִמְּצוּקוֹתֵיהֶם יַצִּילֵם:

7 וַיַּדְרִיכֵם בְּדֶרֶךְ יְשָׁרָה

לָלֶכֶת אֶל־עִיר מוֹשָׁב:

8 יוֹדוּ לַיהֹוָה חַסְדּוֹ

וְנִפְלְאוֹתָיו לִבְנֵי אָדָם:

9 כִּי־הִשְׂבִּיעַ נֶפֶשׁ שֹׁקֵקָה

וְנֶפֶשׁ רְעֵבָה מִלֵּא־טוֹב:

10 יֹשְׁבֵי חֹשֶׁךְ וְצַלְמָוֶת

אֲסִירֵי עֳנִי וּבַרְזֶל:

11. because they rebelled against God's
    commands,

rejecting the counsel of the Most High,

12. who brought them low through suffer-
    ing,

[so that] they stumbled, with none to help;

13. [then,] in their trouble, they cried out to
    the Eternal,

who saved them from their plight,

14. bringing them out of that deathly
    darkness

and snapping their chains.

15. Let them thank the Eternal,

who showed them steadfast love,

who does wonders for human beings:

16. breaking down gates of bronze,

cutting through doors barred with iron;

35. turning desert into reedy pools,

dry ground into flowing springs;

36. settling there the hungry,

who establish a city to dwell in.

37. They sow fields and plant vineyards,

and gather in the fruit of their yield.

39. Once few in numbers, and crushed

by oppression, misery, and sorrow,

38. their numbers grow by God's blessing,

and their herds do not decrease.

40. God pours contempt on the mighty,

and makes them lose their way

in a trackless waste,

41. but lifts up the poor out of their poverty

and makes their families prosper.

כִּי־הִמְרוּ אִמְרֵי־אֵל 11

וַעֲצַת עֶלְיוֹן נָאָצוּ:

וַיַּכְנַע בֶּעָמָל לִבָּם 12

כָּשְׁלוּ וְאֵין עֹזֵר:

וַיִּזְעֲקוּ אֶל־יְהֹוָה בַּצַּר לָהֶם 13

מִמְּצֻקוֹתֵיהֶם יוֹשִׁיעֵם:

יוֹצִיאֵם מֵחֹשֶׁךְ וְצַלְמָוֶת 14

וּמוֹסְרוֹתֵיהֶם יְנַתֵּק:

יוֹדוּ לַיהֹוָה 15

חַסְדּוֹ

וְנִפְלְאוֹתָיו לִבְנֵי אָדָם:

כִּי־שִׁבַּר דַּלְתוֹת נְחֹשֶׁת 16

וּבְרִיחֵי בַרְזֶל גִּדֵּעַ:

יָשֵׂם מִדְבָּר לַאֲגַם־מַיִם 35

וְאֶרֶץ צִיָּה לְמֹצָאֵי מָיִם:

וַיּוֹשֶׁב שָׁם רְעֵבִים 36

וַיְכוֹנְנוּ עִיר מוֹשָׁב:

וַיִּזְרְעוּ שָׂדוֹת וַיִּטְּעוּ כְרָמִים 37

וַיַּעֲשׂוּ פְּרִי תְבוּאָה:

וַיְבָרֲכֵם וַיִּרְבּוּ מְאֹד 38

וּבְהֶמְתָּם לֹא יַמְעִיט:

וַיִּמְעֲטוּ וַיָּשֹׁחוּ 39

מֵעֹצֶר רָעָה וְיָגוֹן:

שֹׁפֵךְ בּוּז עַל־נְדִיבִים 40

וַיַּתְעֵם בְּתֹהוּ

לֹא־דָרֶךְ:

וַיְשַׂגֵּב אֶבְיוֹן מֵעוֹנִי 41

וַיָּשֶׂם כַּצֹּאן מִשְׁפָּחוֹת:

42. The righteous see this and are glad,

while the unjust close up their mouths.

43. The wise will take note of these things,

and pay heed to God's steadfast love.

42 יִרְא֖וּ יְשָׁרִ֣ים וְיִשְׂמָ֑חוּ

וְכָל־עַ֝וְלָ֗ה קָ֣פְצָה פִּֽיהָ׃

43 מִי־חָכָ֥ם וְיִשְׁמָר־אֵ֑לֶּה

וְ֝יִתְבּֽוֹנְנ֗וּ חַֽסְדֵ֥י יְהֹוָֽה׃

Psalm 4, verses 2 to 9

The book of Psalms is found in *K'tuvim* ("Writings"), the third section of the Tanach. It contains 150 spiritual poems that exalt and call upon the Eternal as sovereign, friend, and savior. Tradition considers King David as the author of all the psalms that are either anonymous or ascribed to him, while modern scholarship assigns many of them to various later sources.

Our psalm sings of the joy that faith can bring to us. Though we may be in trouble or be wracked by despair, know that God is there to help: "You alone, Eternal One, make me dwell secure" (verse 9).

4:2. When I call, be my Answer, O God,
my Champion.
In my straits You have widened my
borders:
be gracious to me now, and hear my
prayer.

3. O mortals,
how long will you turn my honor into
insult?
How long will you love emptiness and run
after falsehood?

4. Know that the Eternal does wonders for
the faithful:
the Eternal will listen when I call.

5. Tremble, then, and sin no more;
look into your heart as you lie abed,
and hold your peace. Selah.

6. Let your sacrifices be fitting,
and trust in the Eternal.

7. There are many who say,
Who will show us good?
Cause the light of Your presence to rise
upon us, Eternal One!

4:2 בְּקָרְאִי עֲנֵנִי אֱלֹהֵי צִדְקִי

בַּצָּר הִרְחַבְתָּ לִּי

חָנֵּנִי וּשְׁמַע תְּפִלָּתִי:

3 בְּנֵי אִישׁ

עַד־מֶה כְבוֹדִי לִכְלִמָּה

תֶּאֱהָבוּן רִיק תְּבַקְשׁוּ כָזָב סֶלָה:

4 וּדְעוּ כִּי־הִפְלָה יְהוָה חָסִיד לוֹ

יְהוָה יִשְׁמַע בְּקָרְאִי אֵלָיו:

5 רִגְזוּ וְאַל־תֶּחֱטָאוּ

אִמְרוּ בִלְבַבְכֶם עַל־מִשְׁכַּבְכֶם

וְדֹמּוּ סֶלָה:

6 זִבְחוּ זִבְחֵי־צֶדֶק

וּבִטְחוּ אֶל־יְהוָה:

7 רַבִּים אֹמְרִים

מִי־יַרְאֵנוּ טוֹב

נְסָה־עָלֵינוּ אוֹר פָּנֶיךָ יְהוָה:

8. For You have put joy in my heart,
more than some have
when their corn and their wine abound.
9. Now I shall lie down in peace, and
  sleep;
for You alone, Eternal One, make me dwell
  secure.

8 נָתַתָּה שִׂמְחָה בְלִבִּי

מֵעֵת דְּגָנָם וְתִירוֹשָׁם רָבּוּ:

9 בְּשָׁלוֹם יַחְדָּו אֶשְׁכְּבָה וְאִישָׁן

כִּי־אַתָּה יְהֹוָה לְבָדָד לָבֶטַח תּוֹשִׁיבֵנִי:

ADDITIONAL READINGS 30

Judges, chapter 16, verses 4 to 22

Samson was the last of the leaders mentioned in the book of Judges. He was a Nazirite, that is, someone dedicated to God and bound to certain rules, one of them being that he was never to cut his hair. As long as he observed the Nazirite restriction he would be blessed wIth superhuman power. For more on the book of Judges, see our *General Introduction;* on Samson, see the haftarah for Naso.

Israel was then ruled by the Philistines, and Samson, with his unpredictable actions and enormous physical strength, was a thorn in their side. They aimed to kill him and prevailed upon Delilah, one of Samson's lovers, to learn the secret of his strength. The story does not end where this reading concludes, but continues with the final revenge that Samson wreaks upon his enemies.

16:4. Afterward, Samson fell in love with a woman named Delilah, who lived in the Valley of Sorek.

5. The Philistine lords went to her and said: Trick Samson into telling you what makes him so strong and how we can overpower him, so that we may bind him and torture him; then we shall each give you eleven hundred shekels of silver.

6. So Delilah said to Samson: Please tell me what makes you so strong. If someone wanted to tie you up and torment you, how could it be done?

7. Samson answered: If they tied me up with seven fresh, moist sinews, I would be as weak as anyone else.

8. So the Philistine lords brought her seven fresh moist sinews that had not been dried, and she tied Samson up

9. while a band of men waited in her room, to ambush him. Then she cried: *Samson! The Philistines are upon you!* And he snapped the sinews as tow breaks when it smells fire. So the secret of his strength remained a secret.

16:4 וַיְהִי אַחֲרֵי־כֵן וַיֶּאֱהַב אִשָּׁה בְּנַחַל שֹׂרֵק וּשְׁמָהּ דְּלִילָה:

5 וַיַּעֲלוּ אֵלֶיהָ סַרְנֵי פְלִשְׁתִּים וַיֹּאמְרוּ לָהּ פַּתִּי אוֹתוֹ וּרְאִי בַּמֶּה כֹּחוֹ גָדוֹל וּבַמֶּה נוּכַל לוֹ וַאֲסַרְנֻהוּ לְעַנֹּתוֹ וַאֲנַחְנוּ נִתַּן־לָךְ אִישׁ אֶלֶף וּמֵאָה כָּסֶף:

6 וַתֹּאמֶר דְּלִילָה אֶל־שִׁמְשׁוֹן הַגִּידָה־נָּא לִי בַּמֶּה כֹּחֲךָ גָדוֹל וּבַמֶּה תֵאָסֵר לְעַנּוֹתֶךָ:

7 וַיֹּאמֶר אֵלֶיהָ שִׁמְשׁוֹן אִם־יַאַסְרֻנִי בְּשִׁבְעָה יְתָרִים לַחִים אֲשֶׁר לֹא־חֹרָבוּ וְחָלִיתִי וְהָיִיתִי כְּאַחַד הָאָדָם:

8 וַיַּעֲלוּ־לָהּ סַרְנֵי פְלִשְׁתִּים שִׁבְעָה יְתָרִים לַחִים אֲשֶׁר לֹא־חֹרָבוּ וַתַּאַסְרֵהוּ בָּהֶם:

9 וְהָאֹרֵב יֹשֵׁב לָהּ בַּחֶדֶר וַתֹּאמֶר אֵלָיו פְּלִשְׁתִּים עָלֶיךָ שִׁמְשׁוֹן וַיְנַתֵּק אֶת־הַיְתָרִים כַּאֲשֶׁר יִנָּתֵק פְּתִיל־הַנְּעֹרֶת בַּהֲרִיחוֹ אֵשׁ וְלֹא נוֹדַע כֹּחוֹ:

10. Then Delilah said to Samson: Oh, you fooled me and didn't tell me the truth! Now please tell me how you could be tied up.

11. He said: If I were tied up with new ropes that have never been used, I would be as weak as anyone else.

12. So Delilah took new ropes and tied him up, while a band of men waited in another room, to ambush him. But when she cried: *Samson, the Philistines are upon you!* he snapped them off his arms as though they were threads.

13. Delilah then said to Samson: You keep fooling me and lying to me! Tell me how you could be tied up! He said to her: If you weave seven plaits of my hair with the warp-threads (of a loom), I would be as weak as anyone else.

14. [Delilah then lulled him to sleep, took his seven plaits of hair, and wove them into the warp-threads of a loom]. She fastened [them] with a peg and cried: *Samson! The Philistines are upon you!* He woke up and pulled out both peg and warp-threads .

15. She then said to him: How can you say you love me, when you won't tell me the truth? This is the third time you've made a fool of me and not told me where you get your strength.

16. Finally, after she had nagged him and importuned him day by day, he became sick to death of it,

10 וַתֹּאמֶר דְּלִילָה אֶל־שִׁמְשׁוֹן הִנֵּה הֵתַלְתָּ בִּי וַתְּדַבֵּר אֵלַי כְּזָבִים עַתָּה הַגִּידָה־נָּא לִי בַּמֶּה תֵּאָסֵר:

11 וַיֹּאמֶר אֵלֶיהָ אִם־אָסוֹר יַאַסְרוּנִי בַּעֲבֹתִים חֲדָשִׁים אֲשֶׁר לֹא־נַעֲשָׂה בָהֶם מְלָאכָה וְחָלִיתִי וְהָיִיתִי כְּאַחַד הָאָדָם:

12 וַתִּקַּח דְּלִילָה עֲבֹתִים חֲדָשִׁים וַתַּאַסְרֵהוּ בָהֶם וַתֹּאמֶר אֵלָיו פְּלִשְׁתִּים עָלֶיךָ שִׁמְשׁוֹן וְהָאֹרֵב יֹשֵׁב בֶּחָדֶר וַיְנַתְּקֵם מֵעַל זְרֹעֹתָיו כְּחוּט:

13 וַתֹּאמֶר דְּלִילָה אֶל־שִׁמְשׁוֹן עַד־הֵנָּה הֵתַלְתָּ בִּי וַתְּדַבֵּר אֵלַי כְּזָבִים הַגִּידָה לִי בַּמֶּה תֵּאָסֵר וַיֹּאמֶר אֵלֶיהָ אִם־תַּאַרְגִי אֶת־שֶׁבַע מַחְלְפוֹת רֹאשִׁי עִם־הַמַּסָּכֶת:

14 וַתִּתְקַע בַּיָּתֵד וַתֹּאמֶר אֵלָיו פְּלִשְׁתִּים עָלֶיךָ שִׁמְשׁוֹן וַיִּיקַץ מִשְּׁנָתוֹ וַיִּסַּע אֶת־הַיְתַד הָאֶרֶג וְאֶת־הַמַּסָּכֶת:

15 וַתֹּאמֶר אֵלָיו אֵיךְ תֹּאמַר אֲהַבְתִּיךְ וְלִבְּךָ אֵין אִתִּי זֶה שָׁלֹשׁ פְּעָמִים הֵתַלְתָּ בִּי וְלֹא־הִגַּדְתָּ לִּי בַּמֶּה כֹּחֲךָ גָדוֹל:

16 וַיְהִי כִּי־הֵצִיקָה לּוֹ בִדְבָרֶיהָ כָּל־הַיָּמִים וַתְּאַלְצֵהוּ וַתִּקְצַר נַפְשׁוֹ לָמוּת:

17. and he spoke honestly to her. No razor has ever touched my head, he told her, for I have been dedicated to God as a Nazirite from the time I was conceived. If my hair were shaved, my strength would leave me and I would be as weak as anyone else.

18. Seeing that he had spoken honestly to her, Delilah sent for the Philistine lords, with this message: This is the time to come up; he has told me his secret. The Philistine lords came up, bringing the money with them.

19. She lulled him to sleep on her lap and called a man in, who cut off his seven plaits of hair. Then she began to torment him, for his strength had left him.

20. And when she cried: *Samson! The Philistines are upon you!* he woke up not knowing that the Eternal had left him, and thought he would break loose and free himself as he had done the other times.

21. But [this time] the Philistines took him captive and gouged out his eyes. They took him to Gaza, bound him in bronze chains, and put him to work [as a slave] grinding [at the mill] in the prison.

22. But his hair, after it had been cut off, began to grow back.

17 וַיַּגֶּד־לָהּ אֶת־כָּל־לִבּוֹ וַיֹּאמֶר לָהּ מוֹרָה לֹא־עָלָה עַל־רֹאשִׁי כִּי־נְזִיר אֱלֹהִים אֲנִי מִבֶּטֶן אִמִּי אִם־גֻּלַּחְתִּי וְסָר מִמֶּנִּי כֹחִי וְחָלִיתִי וְהָיִיתִי כְּכָל־הָאָדָם:

18 וַתֵּרֶא דְּלִילָה כִּי־הִגִּיד לָהּ אֶת־כָּל־לִבּוֹ וַתִּשְׁלַח וַתִּקְרָא לְסַרְנֵי פְלִשְׁתִּים לֵאמֹר עֲלוּ הַפַּעַם כִּי־הִגִּיד לָהּ [לִי] אֶת־כָּל־לִבּוֹ וְעָלוּ אֵלֶיהָ סַרְנֵי פְלִשְׁתִּים וַיַּעֲלוּ הַכֶּסֶף בְּיָדָם:

19 וַתְּיַשְּׁנֵהוּ עַל־בִּרְכֶּיהָ וַתִּקְרָא לָאִישׁ וַתְּגַלַּח אֶת־שֶׁבַע מַחְלְפוֹת רֹאשׁוֹ וַתָּחֶל לְעַנּוֹתוֹ וַיָּסַר כֹּחוֹ מֵעָלָיו:

20 וַתֹּאמֶר פְּלִשְׁתִּים עָלֶיךָ שִׁמְשׁוֹן וַיִּקַץ מִשְּׁנָתוֹ וַיֹּאמֶר אֵצֵא כְּפַעַם בְּפַעַם וְאִנָּעֵר וְהוּא לֹא יָדַע כִּי יְהוָה סָר מֵעָלָיו:

21 וַיֹּאחֲזוּהוּ פְלִשְׁתִּים וַיְנַקְּרוּ אֶת־עֵינָיו וַיּוֹרִידוּ אוֹתוֹ עַזָּתָה וַיַּאַסְרוּהוּ בַּנְחֻשְׁתַּיִם וַיְהִי טוֹחֵן בְּבֵית הָאֲסִירִים [הָאֲסוּרִים]:

22 וַיָּחֶל שְׂעַר־רֹאשׁוֹ לְצַמֵּחַ כַּאֲשֶׁר גֻּלָּח:

Joel, chapter 2, verse 21 to chapter 3, verse 2

The prophet Joel was possibly a contemporary of Amos, but in fact we cannot determine the time of his activity with any certainty. For more on Joel, see our *General Introduction* and the haftarah for Shabbat Shuvah.

In our reading Joel paints a vision of the Day of the Eternal, when the divine spirit shall rest upon everyone, when "your old shall dream dreams, your young shall see visions" (3:1).

2:21. Fear not, O soil, rejoice and be glad,
for the Eternal is doing great things.

22. Fear not, O beasts of the field;
for the pastures of the wilderness are
   covered with grass.
Every tree bears its fruit,
the fig-tree and the vine give their yield.

23. O children of Zion, rejoice
and be glad in the Eternal your God,
who in kindness is giving you the early
   rain,
pouring rain down for you,
the early rain; and the later rain of the first
   month.

24. The threshing floors shall be heaped
   with grain,
the vats shall overflow with wine and oil;

25. I will repay you for what [you lost in]
the years when the swarmer ate your crops,
the hopper, the grub, the locust—
My great army that I sent against you.

26. You shall eat and be satisfied,
and praise the name of the Eternal your
   God,
who has done wondrous things for you.
My people shall never again be put to
   shame.

אַל־תִּירְאִי אֲדָמָה גִּילִי וּשְׂמָחִי 2:21
כִּי־הִגְדִּיל יְהוָה לַעֲשׂוֹת:
אַל־תִּירְאוּ בַּהֲמוֹת שָׂדַי 22
כִּי דָשְׁאוּ נְאוֹת מִדְבָּר
כִּי־עֵץ נָשָׂא פִרְיוֹ
תְּאֵנָה וָגֶפֶן נָתְנוּ חֵילָם:
וּבְנֵי צִיּוֹן גִּילוּ 23
וְשִׂמְחוּ בַּיהוָה אֱלֹהֵיכֶם
כִּי־נָתַן לָכֶם אֶת־הַמּוֹרֶה לִצְדָקָה
וַיּוֹרֶד לָכֶם גֶּשֶׁם
מוֹרֶה וּמַלְקוֹשׁ בָּרִאשׁוֹן:
וּמָלְאוּ הַגְּרָנוֹת בָּר 24
וְהֵשִׁיקוּ הַיְקָבִים תִּירוֹשׁ וְיִצְהָר:
וְשִׁלַּמְתִּי לָכֶם 25
אֶת־הַשָּׁנִים אֲשֶׁר אָכַל הָאַרְבֶּה
הַיֶּלֶק וְהֶחָסִיל וְהַגָּזָם
חֵילִי הַגָּדוֹל אֲשֶׁר שִׁלַּחְתִּי בָּכֶם:
וַאֲכַלְתֶּם אָכוֹל וְשָׂבוֹעַ 26
וְהִלַּלְתֶּם אֶת־שֵׁם יְהוָה אֱלֹהֵיכֶם
אֲשֶׁר־עָשָׂה עִמָּכֶם לְהַפְלִיא
וְלֹא־יֵבֹשׁוּ עַמִּי לְעוֹלָם:

27. Then you shall know that I am in the
   midst of Israel,

and that I, the Eternal, am your God,

and there is no other.

My people shall never again be put to
   shame.

3:1. And then I will pour out My spirit

on the whole human race:

your sons and daughters will speak as
   prophets,

your old shall dream dreams,

your young shall see visions.

2. In those days I will pour out My spirit

even on servants, men and women alike.

27 וִידַעְתֶּ֗ם כִּ֣י בְקֶ֤רֶב יִשְׂרָאֵל֙ אָ֔נִי

וַאֲנִ֛י יְהֹוָ֥ה אֱלֹהֵיכֶ֖ם

וְאֵ֣ין ע֑וֹד

וְלֹא־יֵבֹ֥שׁוּ עַמִּ֖י לְעוֹלָֽם׃

3:1 וְהָיָ֣ה אַחֲרֵי־כֵ֗ן אֶשְׁפּ֤וֹךְ אֶת־רוּחִי֙

עַל־כָּל־בָּשָׂ֔ר

וְנִבְּא֖וּ בְּנֵיכֶ֣ם וּבְנוֹתֵיכֶ֑ם

זִקְנֵיכֶם֙ חֲלֹמ֣וֹת יַחֲלֹמ֔וּן

בַּח֣וּרֵיכֶ֔ם חֶזְיֹנ֖וֹת יִרְאֽוּ׃

2 וְגַ֥ם עַל־הָֽעֲבָדִ֖ים וְעַל־הַשְּׁפָח֑וֹת

בַּיָּמִ֣ים הָהֵ֔מָּה אֶשְׁפּ֖וֹךְ אֶת־רוּחִֽי׃

Joshua, chapter 14, verses 6 to 15

The book of Joshua, from which this reading is taken, deals with the long and torturous campaign of conquering the Land of Promise. For more on the book, see our *General Introduction*.

Our reading deals with the reward that Caleb son of Jephunneh finally obtains. In the Torah we meet him as one of the twelve spies whom Moses sent out to reconnoiter Canaan, and he with Joshua were the only two who came back with a positive report. The other ten swayed the majority of the people, and in consequence the whole generation of adult Israelites were condemned to die in the desert, except Caleb and Joshua (see the story in Numbers chapter 13).

14:6. One day, [some people of] the tribe of Judah came to Joshua at Gilgal. One of them, Caleb son of Jephunneh, said: You know what the Eternal said in Kadesh Barnea about you and me to Moses, the man of God.

7. I was forty years old when Moses, the servant of the Eternal, sent me from Kadesh Barnea to spy out this land. I brought back a report [telling him] exactly what was in my mind.

8. While my companions who went with me took the heart out of the people, I dedicated myself to the Eternal my God.

9. That day Moses swore: The land on which you set foot shall surely be a possession for you and your children forever, because you have dedicated yourself to the Eternal my God.

10. Well now, just as promised, the Eternal has sustained me. It is forty-five years since the Eternal made that promise to Moses. That was when Israel was going

14:6 וַיִּגְּשׁוּ בְנֵי־יְהוּדָה אֶל־יְהוֹשֻׁעַ בַּגִּלְגָּל וַיֹּאמֶר אֵלָיו כָּלֵב בֶּן־יְפֻנֶּה הַקְּנִזִּי אַתָּה יָדַעְתָּ אֶת־הַדָּבָר אֲשֶׁר־דִּבֶּר יְהוָה אֶל־מֹשֶׁה אִישׁ־הָאֱלֹהִים עַל אֹדוֹתַי וְעַל אֹדוֹתֶיךָ בְּקָדֵשׁ בַּרְנֵעַ:

7 בֶּן־אַרְבָּעִים שָׁנָה אָנֹכִי בִּשְׁלֹחַ מֹשֶׁה עֶבֶד־יְהוָה אֹתִי מִקָּדֵשׁ בַּרְנֵעַ לְרַגֵּל אֶת־הָאָרֶץ וָאָשֵׁב אֹתוֹ דָּבָר כַּאֲשֶׁר עִם־לְבָבִי:

8 וְאַחַי אֲשֶׁר עָלוּ עִמִּי הִמְסִיו אֶת־לֵב הָעָם וְאָנֹכִי מִלֵּאתִי אַחֲרֵי יְהוָה אֱלֹהָי:

9 וַיִּשָּׁבַע מֹשֶׁה בַּיּוֹם הַהוּא לֵאמֹר אִם־לֹא הָאָרֶץ אֲשֶׁר דָּרְכָה רַגְלְךָ בָּהּ לְךָ תִהְיֶה לְנַחֲלָה וּלְבָנֶיךָ עַד־עוֹלָם כִּי מִלֵּאתָ אַחֲרֵי יְהוָה אֱלֹהָי:

10 וְעַתָּה הִנֵּה הֶחֱיָה יְהוָה אוֹתִי כַּאֲשֶׁר דִּבֵּר זֶה אַרְבָּעִים וְחָמֵשׁ שָׁנָה מֵאָז דִּבֶּר יְהוָה אֶת־הַדָּבָר הַזֶּה אֶל־מֹשֶׁה אֲשֶׁר־הָלַךְ יִשְׂרָאֵל

through the wilderness. I am now eighty-five years old,

11. and just as strong today as on the day Moses sent me. I am strong enough for battle, or for anything else.

12. So let me have this hill country as the Eternal promised back then. As you heard that day, the [giant] Anakites are there, and the cities are large and well fortified; but if the Eternal is with me, I will drive them out, just as the Eternal said.

13. Joshua blessed him and gave Caleb son of Jephunneh the city of Hebron as a (hereditary) possession.

14. Therefore, Hebron still belongs to the descendants of Caleb son of Jephunneh the Kenizzite, because he dedicated himself to the Eternal, the God of Israel.

15. Before this, Hebron was called Kiryat Arba (City of Arba), after the man who was the greatest of the [giant] Anakites.

And now the land had rest from war.

בַּמִּדְבָּר וְעַתָּה הִנֵּה אָנֹכִי הַיּוֹם בֶּן־חָמֵשׁ וּשְׁמוֹנִים שָׁנָה:

11 עוֹדֶנִּי הַיּוֹם חָזָק כַּאֲשֶׁר בְּיוֹם שְׁלֹחַ אוֹתִי מֹשֶׁה כְּכֹחִי אָז וּכְכֹחִי עַתָּה לַמִּלְחָמָה וְלָצֵאת וְלָבוֹא:

12 וְעַתָּה תְּנָה־לִּי אֶת־הָהָר הַזֶּה אֲשֶׁר־דִּבֶּר יְהוָה בַּיּוֹם הַהוּא כִּי אַתָּה־שָׁמַעְתָּ בַיּוֹם הַהוּא כִּי־עֲנָקִים שָׁם וְעָרִים גְּדֹלוֹת בְּצֻרוֹת אוּלַי יְהוָה אוֹתִי וְהוֹרַשְׁתִּים כַּאֲשֶׁר דִּבֶּר יְהוָה:

13 וַיְבָרֲכֵהוּ יְהוֹשֻׁעַ וַיִּתֵּן אֶת־חֶבְרוֹן לְכָלֵב בֶּן־יְפֻנֶּה לְנַחֲלָה:

14 עַל־כֵּן הָיְתָה־חֶבְרוֹן לְכָלֵב בֶּן־יְפֻנֶּה הַקְּנִזִּי לְנַחֲלָה עַד הַיּוֹם הַזֶּה יַעַן אֲשֶׁר מִלֵּא אַחֲרֵי יְהוָה אֱלֹהֵי יִשְׂרָאֵל:

15 וְשֵׁם חֶבְרוֹן לְפָנִים קִרְיַת אַרְבַּע הָאָדָם הַגָּדוֹל בָּעֲנָקִים הוּא וְהָאָרֶץ שָׁקְטָה מִמִּלְחָמָה:

First Kings, chapter 12, verses 1 to 14 and 16

Rehoboam, son of Solomon, hoped to be crowned king of the united monarchy, after his father Solomon's death (latter part of the 10th century B.C.E.). The northern tribes, led by Jeroboam son of Nebat, were willing to acknowledge Rehoboam, but only on condition that he lighten the "heavy yoke" of taxation and forced labor. This demand he rejected. In consequence, the northerners went home and shortly thereafter (as described in the text following this reading) split from the south, elected Jeroboam king and established the state called Israel; the south was henceforth known as Judah.

For more on the book of Kings from which the reading is taken, see our *General Introduction*.

12:1. Rehoboam went to Shechem, where all Israel had gathered to crown him king.

וַיֵּ֥לֶךְ רְחַבְעָ֖ם שְׁכֶ֑ם כִּ֥י שְׁכֶ֛ם בָּ֥א כָל־ 12:1
יִשְׂרָאֵ֖ל לְהַמְלִ֥יךְ אֹתֽוֹ:

2. When Jeroboam son of Nebat heard this news, he was still living in Egypt, for he had fled there to escape King Solomon.

2 וַיְהִ֞י כִּשְׁמֹ֣עַ ׀ יָרָבְעָ֣ם בֶּן־נְבָ֗ט וְהוּא֙ עוֹדֶ֣נּוּ
בְמִצְרַ֔יִם אֲשֶׁ֣ר בָּרַ֔ח מִפְּנֵ֖י הַמֶּ֣לֶךְ שְׁלֹמֹ֑ה וַיֵּ֥שֶׁב
יָרָבְעָ֖ם בְּמִצְרָֽיִם:

3. The people sent for him; and Jeroboam went with the people to Rehoboam and said to him:

3 וַיִּשְׁלְחוּ֙ וַיִּקְרְאוּ־ל֔וֹ וַיָּבֹ֥אוּ [וַיָּבֹ֖א] יָרָבְעָ֖ם
וְכָל־קְהַ֣ל יִשְׂרָאֵ֑ל וַֽיְדַבְּר֔וּ אֶל־רְחַבְעָ֖ם
לֵאמֹֽר:

4. Your father's yoke was heavy; if you make easier the hard labor he laid on us, and [lighten] his heavy yoke, we will serve you.

4 אָבִ֖יךָ הִקְשָׁ֣ה אֶת־עֻלֵּ֑נוּ וְאַתָּ֡ה עַתָּ֣ה הָקֵל֩
מֵעֲבֹדַ֨ת אָבִ֜יךָ הַקָּשָׁ֗ה וּמֵעֻלּ֛וֹ הַכָּבֵ֖ד אֲשֶׁר־נָתַ֥ן
עָלֵ֖ינוּ וְנַעַבְדֶֽךָ:

5. He said: Come back in three days and I will give you my answer.

So the people left.

5 וַיֹּ֣אמֶר אֲלֵיהֶ֗ם לְכ֥וּ עֹ֛ד שְׁלֹשָׁ֥ה יָמִ֖ים וְשׁ֣וּבוּ
אֵלָ֑י וַיֵּלְכ֖וּ הָעָֽם:

6. King Rehoboam consulted the elders who had stood before his father Solomon during his lifetime. What answer do you advise me to give these people? he asked.

6 וַיִּוָּעַ֞ץ הַמֶּ֣לֶךְ רְחַבְעָ֗ם אֶת־הַזְּקֵנִים֙ אֲשֶׁר־הָי֣וּ
עֹמְדִ֗ים אֶת־פְּנֵי֙ שְׁלֹמֹ֣ה אָבִ֔יו בִּֽהְיֹת֥וֹ חַ֖י לֵאמֹ֑ר
אֵ֚יךְ אַתֶּ֣ם נֽוֹעָצִ֔ים לְהָשִׁ֥יב אֶת־הָֽעָם־הַזֶּ֖ה
דָּבָֽר:

7. They answered: If now you become a servant to this people, and serve them, and you return a kind answer to them, they will be your servants for all time.

7 וַיְדַבֵּ֨ר [וַיְדַבְּר֣וּ] אֵלָיו֮ לֵאמֹר֒ אִם־הַיּ֤וֹם
תִּֽהְיֶה־עֶ֨בֶד֙ לָעָ֣ם הַזֶּ֔ה וַֽעֲבַדְתָּ֖ם וַֽעֲנִיתָ֑ם
וְדִבַּרְתָּ֨ אֲלֵיהֶ֜ם דְּבָרִ֣ים טוֹבִ֗ים וְהָי֥וּ לְךָ֛
עֲבָדִ֖ים כָּל־הַיָּמִֽים:

8. But he ignored the advice of the elders and consulted the young men who had grown up with him, and who stood before him.

9. What do you advise me to answer the people who said to me, *Lighten the heavy yoke your father laid on us?* he asked.

10. The young men who had grown up with him said: This is what you should tell those people who said, *Your father's rule was heavy; make it lighter for us*—say to them: My little finger is thicker than my father's loins.

11. Heavy as was the yoke my father laid on you, I will add to your yoke. My father lashed you with whips, but I will lash you with scorpions.

12. Three days later Jeroboam and all the people returned to King Rehoboam, as he had instructed them, saying: Come back to me on the third day.

13. Ignoring the advice of the elders, the king spoke harshly to the people.

14. Following the advice of the young men, he said: My father made your yoke heavy, I will add to your yoke. My father lashed you with whips, but I will lash you with scorpions.

16. When all Israel saw that the king had not listened to them, they replied in kind: We have no part in David, no share in Jesse's son! To your tents, Israel; now look to your own house, David!

And the people of Israel returned to their homes.

8 וַיַּעֲזֹב אֶת־עֲצַת הַזְּקֵנִים אֲשֶׁר יְעָצֻהוּ וַיִּוָּעַץ אֶת־הַיְלָדִים אֲשֶׁר גָּדְלוּ אִתּוֹ אֲשֶׁר הָעֹמְדִים לְפָנָיו:

9 וַיֹּאמֶר אֲלֵיהֶם מָה אַתֶּם נוֹעָצִים וְנָשִׁיב דָּבָר אֶת־הָעָם הַזֶּה אֲשֶׁר דִּבְּרוּ אֵלַי לֵאמֹר הָקֵל מִן־הָעֹל אֲשֶׁר־נָתַן אָבִיךָ עָלֵינוּ:

10 וַיְדַבְּרוּ אֵלָיו הַיְלָדִים אֲשֶׁר גָּדְלוּ אִתּוֹ לֵאמֹר כֹּה־תֹאמַר לָעָם הַזֶּה אֲשֶׁר דִּבְּרוּ אֵלֶיךָ לֵאמֹר אָבִיךָ הִכְבִּיד אֶת־עֻלֵּנוּ וְאַתָּה הָקֵל מֵעָלֵינוּ כֹּה תְּדַבֵּר אֲלֵיהֶם קָטָנִּי עָבָה מִמָּתְנֵי אָבִי:

11 וְעַתָּה אָבִי הֶעְמִיס עֲלֵיכֶם עֹל כָּבֵד וַאֲנִי אוֹסִיף עַל־עֻלְּכֶם אָבִי יִסַּר אֶתְכֶם בַּשּׁוֹטִים וַאֲנִי אֲיַסֵּר אֶתְכֶם בָּעַקְרַבִּים:

12 וַיָּבוֹ [וַיָּבֹא] יָרָבְעָם וְכָל־הָעָם אֶל־רְחַבְעָם בַּיּוֹם הַשְּׁלִישִׁי כַּאֲשֶׁר דִּבֶּר הַמֶּלֶךְ לֵאמֹר שׁוּבוּ אֵלַי בַּיּוֹם הַשְּׁלִישִׁי:

13 וַיַּעַן הַמֶּלֶךְ אֶת־הָעָם קָשָׁה וַיַּעֲזֹב אֶת־עֲצַת הַזְּקֵנִים אֲשֶׁר יְעָצֻהוּ:

14 וַיְדַבֵּר אֲלֵיהֶם כַּעֲצַת הַיְלָדִים לֵאמֹר אָבִי הִכְבִּיד אֶת־עֻלְּכֶם וַאֲנִי אֹסִיף עַל־עֻלְּכֶם אָבִי יִסַּר אֶתְכֶם בַּשּׁוֹטִים וַאֲנִי אֲיַסֵּר אֶתְכֶם בָּעַקְרַבִּים:

16 וַיַּרְא כָּל־יִשְׂרָאֵל כִּי לֹא־שָׁמַע הַמֶּלֶךְ אֲלֵיהֶם וַיָּשִׁבוּ הָעָם אֶת־הַמֶּלֶךְ דָּבָר לֵאמֹר מַה־לָּנוּ חֵלֶק בְּדָוִד וְלֹא־נַחֲלָה בְּבֶן־יִשַׁי לְאֹהָלֶיךָ יִשְׂרָאֵל עַתָּה רְאֵה בֵיתְךָ דָוִד וַיֵּלֶךְ יִשְׂרָאֵל לְאֹהָלָיו:

ADDITIONAL READINGS 34

Psalm 73, verses 1 to 3, 13 to 17, and 21 to 28

The book of Psalms is found in *K'tuvim* ("Writings"), the third section of the Tanach. It contains 150 spiritual poems that exalt and call upon the Eternal as sovereign, friend, and savior. Tradition considers King David as the author of all the psalms that are either anonymous or ascribed to him, while modern scholarship assigns many of them to various later sources.

The psalm describes the author's struggle with faith and how, having rediscovered the Divine Presence, the poet can say: "… nearness to God is my good; I have made the Eternal God my shelter, telling of all Your works" (verse 28).

73:1. God is truly good to Israel,
to all the pure in heart.

73:1 אַךְ טוֹב לְיִשְׂרָאֵל אֱלֹהִים
לְבָרֵי לֵבָב:

2. My feet nearly slipped,
my legs very nearly tripped,

2 וַאֲנִי כִּמְעַט נָטוּי [נָטָיוּ] רַגְלָי
כְּאַיִן שֻׁפְּכָה [שֻׁפְּכוּ] אֲשֻׁרָי:

3. for I envied the boastful,
as I saw the wicked prosper.

3 כִּי־קִנֵּאתִי בַּהוֹלְלִים
שְׁלוֹם רְשָׁעִים אֶרְאֶה:

13. [I thought:]
*In vain I cleanse my heart
and in innocence rinse my hands,*

13 אַךְ־רִיק זִכִּיתִי לְבָבִי
וָאֶרְחַץ בְּנִקָּיוֹן כַּפָּי:

14. *yet I am hurting all day long,
and am reproved every morning.*

14 וָאֱהִי נָגוּעַ כָּל־הַיּוֹם
וְתוֹכַחְתִּי לַבְּקָרִים:

15. Had I said, This is the way I will tell it,
I would have betrayed the assembly of
    Your children.

15 אִם־אָמַרְתִּי אֲסַפְּרָה כְמוֹ
הִנֵּה דוֹר בָּנֶיךָ בָגָדְתִּי:

16. So I struggled to understand,
but it seemed to me a [hopeless] labor,

16 וָאֲחַשְּׁבָה לָדַעַת זֹאת
עָמָל הִיא [הוּא] בְעֵינָי:

17. until I entered God's sanctuary
to think about [the wicked and] their fate.

17 עַד־אָבוֹא אֶל־מִקְדְּשֵׁי־אֵל
אָבִינָה לְאַחֲרִיתָם:

21. My mind was bitter,
my heart was stunned,

21 כִּי יִתְחַמֵּץ לְבָבִי
וְכִלְיוֹתַי אֶשְׁתּוֹנָן:

22. I was a fool, ignorant,
[like] a beast in Your sight.

22 וַאֲנִי־בַעַר וְלֹא אֵדַע
בְּהֵמוֹת הָיִיתִי עִמָּךְ:

23. Yet I was always with You,
and You held me by the hand;

23 וַאֲנִי תָמִיד עִמָּךְ
אָחַזְתָּ בְּיַד־יְמִינִי:

24. Your counsel guided me,

and then You brought me honor.

25. Whom have I in heaven but You?

and having You, I want nothing else on
earth.

26. Though body and mind will fail,

God is the rock of my heart, and my
portion forever.

27. Those who keep far from You will
perish;

You make an end to all who are unfaithful
to You.

28. As for me, nearness to God is my good;

I have made the Eternal God my shelter,

telling of all Your works!

24 בַּעֲצָתְךָ תַנְחֵנִי

וְאַחַר כָּבוֹד תִּקָּחֵנִי:

25 מִי־לִי בַשָּׁמָיִם

וְעִמְּךָ לֹא־חָפַצְתִּי בָאָרֶץ:

26 כָּלָה שְׁאֵרִי וּלְבָבִי

צוּר־לְבָבִי וְחֶלְקִי אֱלֹהִים לְעוֹלָם:

27 כִּי־הִנֵּה רְחֵקֶיךָ יֹאבֵדוּ

הִצְמַתָּה כָּל־זוֹנֶה מִמֶּךָּ:

28 וַאֲנִי קִרֲבַת אֱלֹהִים לִי־טוֹב

שַׁתִּי בַּאדֹנָי יֱהֹוִה מַחְסִי

לְסַפֵּר כָּל־מַלְאֲכוֹתֶיךָ:

ADDITIONAL READINGS 35

Psalm 34, verses 2 to 5, 7 to 9, and 12 to 15

The book of Psalms is found in *K'tuvim* ("Writings"), the third section of the Tanach. It contains 150 spiritual poems that exalt and call upon the Eternal as sovereign, friend, and savior. Tradition considers King David as the author of all the psalms that are either anonymous or ascribed to him, while modern scholarship assigns many of them to various later sources.

In our psalm the poet issues an invitation to those who still have not found God: "Come, children, and listen to me: I will teach you reverence for God" (verse 12).

34:2. I will praise the Eternal at all times;
Your praise, [O God,] shall be ever on my
lips.

3. My soul delights in the Eternal;
the needy hear and rejoice.

4. O magnify the Eternal with me;
together let us exalt God's name.

5. I sought the Eternal, who answered me;
and rescued me from all my troubles.

7. This poor wretch called, and the Eternal
listened,
and saved me from all my distresses.

8. The angel of the Eternal is on guard for
all who revere God,
and succors them.

9. Taste and see that the Eternal is good;
happy is the one who trusts in God.

12. Come, children, and listen to me:
I will teach you reverence for God.

13. Who among you desires life,
who longs for days of seeing good?

14. Then keep your tongue from evil,
and your lips from speaking guile;

אֲבָרְכָה אֶת־יְהֹוָה בְּכָל־עֵת 34:2
תָּמִיד תְּהִלָּתוֹ בְּפִי:

בַּיהֹוָה תִּתְהַלֵּל נַפְשִׁי 3
יִשְׁמְעוּ עֲנָוִים וְיִשְׂמָחוּ:

גַּדְּלוּ לַיהֹוָה אִתִּי 4
וּנְרוֹמְמָה שְׁמוֹ יַחְדָּו:

דָּרַשְׁתִּי אֶת־יְהֹוָה וְעָנָנִי 5
וּמִכָּל־מְגוּרוֹתַי הִצִּילָנִי:

זֶה עָנִי קָרָא וַיהֹוָה שָׁמֵעַ 7
וּמִכָּל־צָרוֹתָיו הוֹשִׁיעוֹ:

חֹנֶה מַלְאַךְ־יְהֹוָה סָבִיב לִירֵאָיו 8
וַיְחַלְּצֵם:

טַעֲמוּ וּרְאוּ כִּי־טוֹב יְהֹוָה 9
אַשְׁרֵי הַגֶּבֶר יֶחֱסֶה־בּוֹ:

לְכוּ־בָנִים שִׁמְעוּ־לִי 12
יִרְאַת יְהֹוָה אֲלַמֶּדְכֶם:

מִי־הָאִישׁ הֶחָפֵץ חַיִּים 13
אֹהֵב יָמִים לִרְאוֹת טוֹב:

נְצֹר לְשׁוֹנְךָ מֵרָע 14
וּשְׂפָתֶיךָ מִדַּבֵּר מִרְמָה:

15. depart from evil and do good;
seek peace and pursue it.

15 סוּר מֵרָע וַעֲשֵׂה־טֽוֹב
בַּקֵּשׁ שָׁלוֹם וְרָדְפֵֽהוּ:

Joshua, chapter 23, verses 1 to 8 and 11 to 14

Joshua was the successor of Moses, and his task was to lead the people in their conquest of the Promised Land. For more on the book of Joshua, see our *General Introduction;* on Joshua the man, see the essay in the haftarah for V'zot Hab'rachah.

At the end of his life Joshua gives two farewell addresses, of which this reading presents the first. Observance of the teachings of Moses, avoidance of mixed marriages, and firm belief in God are set forth as the secure foundations of Israel's future.

23:1. Many years had passed since the Eternal had given Israel rest from all the enemies who surrounded them, and Joshua was now an old man, coming to [the end of] his days.

2. Joshua called all Israel, their elders, leaders, judges, and officials, and said to them: I am aged, I am coming to [the end of] my days.

3. You have seen what the Eternal has done for your sake to all these nations, for the Eternal your God has fought for you.

4. See, I have assigned as the possession of your tribes [the land of] the nations that are still left, as well as of all the nations that I have already cut down, from the Jordan [in the east] to the Mediterranean Sea, where the sun sets.

5. The Eternal will drive them from before you, and will dispossess them from before you. So their land shall be yours, as the Eternal your God has promised you.

6. Be firm, then, to carry out and do everything that is written in the Book of the Teaching of Moses, never swerving from it to the right or the left,

וַיְהִי֩ מִיָּמִ֨ים רַבִּ֜ים אַחֲרֵ֗י אֲשֶׁר־הֵנִ֨יחַ 23:1
יְהֹוָ֤ה לְיִשְׂרָאֵל֙ מִכׇּל־אֹֽיְבֵיהֶ֣ם מִסָּבִ֔יב וִיהוֹשֻׁ֣עַ
זָקֵ֔ן בָּ֖א בַּיָּמִֽים:

וַיִּקְרָ֤א יְהוֹשֻׁ֨עַ֙ לְכׇל־יִשְׂרָאֵ֔ל לִזְקֵנָ֖יו 2
וּלְרָאשָׁ֗יו וּלְשֹׁפְטָיו֙ וּלְשֹׁ֣טְרָ֔יו וַיֹּ֖אמֶר אֲלֵהֶ֑ם
אֲנִ֣י זָקַ֔נְתִּי בָּ֖אתִי בַּיָּמִֽים:

וְאַתֶּ֣ם רְאִיתֶ֗ם אֵ֤ת כׇּל־אֲשֶׁר֙ עָשָׂ֜ה יְהֹוָ֤ה 3
אֱלֹֽהֵיכֶם֙ לְכׇל־הַגּוֹיִ֣ם הָאֵ֔לֶּה מִפְּנֵיכֶ֑ם כִּ֚י יְהֹוָ֣ה
אֱלֹֽהֵיכֶ֔ם ה֖וּא הַנִּלְחָ֥ם לָכֶֽם:

רְא֗וּ הִפַּ֤לְתִּי לָכֶם֙ אֶת־הַגּוֹיִ֣ם הַנִּשְׁאָרִ֜ים 4
הָאֵ֤לֶּה בְּנַחֲלָה֙ לְשִׁבְטֵיכֶ֔ם מִן־הַיַּרְדֵּ֖ן וְכׇל־
הַגּוֹיִם֙ אֲשֶׁ֣ר הִכְרַ֔תִּי וְהַיָּ֥ם הַגָּד֖וֹל מְב֥וֹא
הַשָּֽׁמֶשׁ:

וַֽיהֹוָ֣ה אֱלֹֽהֵיכֶ֗ם ה֚וּא יֶהְדֳּפֵ֣ם מִפְּנֵיכֶ֔ם 5
וְהוֹרִ֥ישׁ אֹתָ֖ם מִלִּפְנֵיכֶ֑ם וִֽירִשְׁתֶּם֙ אֶת־אַרְצָ֔ם
כַּֽאֲשֶׁ֥ר דִּבֶּ֛ר יְהֹוָ֥ה אֱלֹֽהֵיכֶ֖ם לָכֶֽם:

וַחֲזַקְתֶּ֣ם מְאֹ֔ד לִשְׁמֹ֣ר וְלַעֲשׂ֔וֹת אֵ֥ת כׇּל־ 6
הַכָּת֔וּב בְּסֵ֖פֶר תּוֹרַ֣ת מֹשֶׁ֑ה לְבִלְתִּ֥י סוּר־מִמֶּ֖נּוּ
יָמִ֥ין וּשְׂמֹֽאול:

7. never mixing with these nations that are left among you, never calling on their gods nor swearing by them, never serving or bowing to them.

8. Instead, cling to the Eternal your God, as you have done till now.

11. Take very great care to love the Eternal your God.

12. For if you join with the nations that are still left among you and intermarry with them; if you join with them and they with you,

13. you may be sure that the Eternal your God will not continue to dispossess these nations from before you; they will be a trap and a snare for you, like a scourge to your sides or like thorns in your eyes, till you vanish from the good land that the Eternal your God has given you.

14. I am now going the way of all the earth. You know in your hearts and souls that not one of the good things that the Eternal your God has promised you has failed to happen; they have all come true for you, not a single one has failed.

7 לְבִלְתִּי־בוֹא בַּגּוֹיִם הָאֵלֶּה הַנִּשְׁאָרִים הָאֵלֶּה אִתְּכֶם וּבְשֵׁם אֱלֹהֵיהֶם לֹא־תַזְכִּירוּ וְלֹא תַשְׁבִּיעוּ וְלֹא תַעַבְדוּם וְלֹא תִשְׁתַּחֲווּ לָהֶם:

8 כִּי אִם־בַּיהוָה אֱלֹהֵיכֶם תִּדְבָּקוּ כַּאֲשֶׁר עֲשִׂיתֶם עַד הַיּוֹם הַזֶּה:

11 וְנִשְׁמַרְתֶּם מְאֹד לְנַפְשֹׁתֵיכֶם לְאַהֲבָה אֶת־יְהוָה אֱלֹהֵיכֶם:

12 כִּי אִם־שׁוֹב תָּשׁוּבוּ וּדְבַקְתֶּם בְּיֶתֶר הַגּוֹיִם הָאֵלֶּה הַנִּשְׁאָרִים הָאֵלֶּה אִתְּכֶם וְהִתְחַתַּנְתֶּם בָּהֶם וּבָאתֶם בָּהֶם וְהֵם בָּכֶם:

13 יָדוֹעַ תֵּדְעוּ כִּי לֹא יוֹסִיף יְהוָה אֱלֹהֵיכֶם לְהוֹרִישׁ אֶת־הַגּוֹיִם הָאֵלֶּה מִלִּפְנֵיכֶם וְהָיוּ לָכֶם לְפַח וּלְמוֹקֵשׁ וּלְשֹׁטֵט בְּצִדֵּיכֶם וְלִצְנִנִים בְּעֵינֵיכֶם עַד־אֲבָדְכֶם מֵעַל הָאֲדָמָה הַטּוֹבָה הַזֹּאת אֲשֶׁר נָתַן לָכֶם יְהוָה אֱלֹהֵיכֶם:

14 וְהִנֵּה אָנֹכִי הוֹלֵךְ הַיּוֹם בְּדֶרֶךְ כָּל־הָאָרֶץ וִידַעְתֶּם בְּכָל־לְבַבְכֶם וּבְכָל־נַפְשְׁכֶם כִּי לֹא־נָפַל דָּבָר אֶחָד מִכֹּל הַדְּבָרִים הַטּוֹבִים אֲשֶׁר דִּבֶּר יְהוָה אֱלֹהֵיכֶם עֲלֵיכֶם הַכֹּל בָּאוּ לָכֶם לֹא־נָפַל מִמֶּנּוּ דָּבָר אֶחָד:

ADDITIONAL READINGS 37

First Samuel, chapter 8, verses 1 to 22

Samuel was for many years the undisputed leader of the tribes of Israel, and his life is described in the books named for him. For details on the books and the Prophet, see our *General Introduction.*

Our reading tells how late in his life Samuel's sons disappoint him, and so does the people's request to have a king rule over them. Samuel, at the behest of God, yields to them, though with great reluctance. Note than in verse 16 we follow the Septuagint and read "cattle" instead of "young men." For a continuation of the story told in our reading, see the haftarah for Korah.

8:1. When Samuel grew old, he made his sons judges over Israel.

2. The older son was named Joel and the younger one Abijah; [they sat as] judges in Beersheba.

3. But they did not follow in his footsteps; they went after unjust gain, so they took bribes and perverted justice.

4. Then all the leaders of Israel came together. They approached Samuel in Ramah,

5. and said to him: You have grown old, and your sons are not following your example. Therefore [we want you to] appoint a king for us, to rule us like all other nations.

6. Samuel thought it a bad business that they said, *Give us a king to rule us,* so he prayed to the Eternal.

7. But the Eternal One said to Samuel: Listen to what the people are saying to you. You are not the one they have rejected; I am the one they have rejected as their ruler.

8. This is typical of their behavior since I raised them up out of Egypt: they forsook Me and served other gods, exactly as they are behaving toward you as well.

8:1 וַיְהִ֗י כַּאֲשֶׁ֤ר זָקֵן֙ שְׁמוּאֵ֔ל וַיָּ֧שֶׂם אֶת־בָּנָ֛יו שֹׁפְטִ֖ים לְיִשְׂרָאֵֽל׃

2 וַיְהִ֞י שֶׁם־בְּנ֤וֹ הַבְּכוֹר֙ יוֹאֵ֔ל וְשֵׁ֥ם מִשְׁנֵ֖הוּ אֲבִיָּ֑ה שֹׁפְטִ֖ים בִּבְאֵ֥ר שָֽׁבַע׃

3 וְלֹֽא־הָלְכ֤וּ בָנָיו֙ בְּדַרְכָ֔ו [בִּדְרָכָ֔יו] וַיִּטּ֖וּ אַחֲרֵ֣י הַבָּ֑צַע וַיִּקְחוּ־שֹׁ֔חַד וַיַּטּ֖וּ מִשְׁפָּֽט׃

4 וַיִּֽתְקַבְּצ֔וּ כֹּ֖ל זִקְנֵ֣י יִשְׂרָאֵ֑ל וַיָּבֹ֥אוּ אֶל־שְׁמוּאֵ֖ל הָרָמָֽתָה׃

5 וַיֹּאמְר֣וּ אֵלָ֗יו הִנֵּה֙ אַתָּ֣ה זָקַ֔נְתָּ וּבָנֶ֕יךָ לֹ֥א הָלְכ֖וּ בִּדְרָכֶ֑יךָ עַתָּ֗ה שִֽׂימָה־לָּ֥נוּ מֶ֛לֶךְ לְשָׁפְטֵ֖נוּ כְּכָל־הַגּוֹיִֽם׃

6 וַיֵּ֤רַע הַדָּבָר֙ בְּעֵינֵ֣י שְׁמוּאֵ֔ל כַּאֲשֶׁ֣ר אָמְר֔וּ תְּנָה־לָּ֥נוּ מֶ֖לֶךְ לְשָׁפְטֵ֑נוּ וַיִּתְפַּלֵּ֥ל שְׁמוּאֵ֖ל אֶל־יְהוָֽה׃

7 וַיֹּ֤אמֶר יְהוָה֙ אֶל־שְׁמוּאֵ֔ל שְׁמַע֙ בְּק֣וֹל הָעָ֔ם לְכֹ֥ל אֲשֶׁר־יֹאמְר֖וּ אֵלֶ֑יךָ כִּ֣י לֹ֤א אֹֽתְךָ֙ מָאָ֔סוּ כִּֽי־אֹתִ֥י מָאֲס֖וּ מִמְּלֹ֥ךְ עֲלֵיהֶֽם׃

8 כְּכָֽל־הַֽמַּעֲשִׂ֣ים אֲשֶׁר־עָשׂ֗וּ מִיּוֹם֩ הַעֲלֹתִ֨י אֹתָ֜ם מִמִּצְרַ֗יִם וְעַד־הַיּ֣וֹם הַזֶּ֔ה וַיַּ֣עַזְבֻ֔נִי וַיַּֽעַבְד֖וּ אֱלֹהִ֣ים אֲחֵרִ֑ים כֵּ֛ן הֵ֥מָּה עֹשִׂ֖ים גַּם־לָֽךְ׃

9. So do as they say, but give them a stern warning and explain to them how their kings will treat them.

10. Samuel told the people who were asking him for a king everything that the Eternal had said to him.

11. This shall be the practice of the king once he rules over you, he explained. He shall take your sons and assign them to his chariots and his cavalry, and [others] shall run before his chariot.

12. He shall appoint officers in charge of a thousand, and others in charge of fifty. Some will be designated to plow his fields, harvest his crops, and make his weapons and the equipment for his chariots.

13. Your daughters he shall take to be mixers of ointments, cooks, and bakers.

14. He shall take your best fields, vineyards, and olive groves, and give them to his courtiers.

15. He shall take a tenth of your seed crops and your grapes for his eunuchs and courtiers.

16. He shall take your male and female slaves, your best cattle and donkeys, and put them to work for him.

17. He shall take a tenth of your flocks, and you yourselves will become his slaves.

18. The day will come when you shall cry out because of the king whom you yourselves have chosen, but on that day the Eternal will not answer.

19. The people would not listen to Samuel's warning. No, they said, we want a king;

9 וְעַתָּה שְׁמַע בְּקוֹלָם אַךְ כִּי־הָעֵד תָּעִיד בָּהֶם וְהִגַּדְתָּ לָהֶם מִשְׁפַּט הַמֶּלֶךְ אֲשֶׁר יִמְלֹךְ עֲלֵיהֶם:

10 וַיֹּאמֶר שְׁמוּאֵל אֵת כָּל־דִּבְרֵי יְהוָה אֶל־הָעָם הַשֹּׁאֲלִים מֵאִתּוֹ מֶלֶךְ:

11 וַיֹּאמֶר זֶה יִהְיֶה מִשְׁפַּט הַמֶּלֶךְ אֲשֶׁר יִמְלֹךְ עֲלֵיכֶם אֶת־בְּנֵיכֶם יִקָּח וְשָׂם לוֹ בְּמֶרְכַּבְתּוֹ וּבְפָרָשָׁיו וְרָצוּ לִפְנֵי מֶרְכַּבְתּוֹ:

12 וְלָשׂוּם לוֹ שָׂרֵי אֲלָפִים וְשָׂרֵי חֲמִשִּׁים וְלַחֲרֹשׁ חֲרִישׁוֹ וְלִקְצֹר קְצִירוֹ וְלַעֲשׂוֹת כְּלֵי־מִלְחַמְתּוֹ וּכְלֵי רִכְבּוֹ:

13 וְאֶת־בְּנוֹתֵיכֶם יִקָּח לְרַקָּחוֹת וּלְטַבָּחוֹת וּלְאֹפוֹת:

14 וְאֶת־שְׂדוֹתֵיכֶם וְאֶת־כַּרְמֵיכֶם וְזֵיתֵיכֶם הַטּוֹבִים יִקָּח וְנָתַן לַעֲבָדָיו:

15 וְזַרְעֵיכֶם וְכַרְמֵיכֶם יַעְשֹׂר וְנָתַן לְסָרִיסָיו וְלַעֲבָדָיו:

16 וְאֶת־עַבְדֵיכֶם וְאֶת־שִׁפְחוֹתֵיכֶם וְאֶת־בַּחוּרֵיכֶם הַטּוֹבִים וְאֶת־חֲמוֹרֵיכֶם יִקָּח וְעָשָׂה לִמְלַאכְתּוֹ:

17 צֹאנְכֶם יַעְשֹׂר וְאַתֶּם תִּהְיוּ־לוֹ לַעֲבָדִים:

18 וּזְעַקְתֶּם בַּיּוֹם הַהוּא מִלִּפְנֵי מַלְכְּכֶם אֲשֶׁר בְּחַרְתֶּם לָכֶם וְלֹא־יַעֲנֶה יְהוָה אֶתְכֶם בַּיּוֹם הַהוּא:

19 וַיְמָאֲנוּ הָעָם לִשְׁמֹעַ בְּקוֹל שְׁמוּאֵל וַיֹּאמְרוּ לֹא כִּי אִם־מֶלֶךְ יִהְיֶה עָלֵינוּ:

20. we want to be like the other nations. Let a king rule us and lead us to fight our battles.

21. Samuel listened to the people's words, and reported them to the Eternal.

22. And the Eternal One said to Samuel: Do as they say and give them a king. Samuel then told the Israelites to go back to their homes.

20 וְהָיִינוּ גַם־אֲנַחְנוּ כְּכָל־הַגּוֹיִם וּשְׁפָטָנוּ מַלְכֵּנוּ וְיָצָא לְפָנֵינוּ וְנִלְחַם אֶת־מִלְחֲמֹתֵנוּ:

21 וַיִּשְׁמַע שְׁמוּאֵל אֵת כָּל־דִּבְרֵי הָעָם וַיְדַבְּרֵם בְּאָזְנֵי יְהֹוָה:

22 וַיֹּאמֶר יְהֹוָה אֶל־שְׁמוּאֵל שְׁמַע בְּקוֹלָם וְהִמְלַכְתָּ לָהֶם מֶלֶךְ וַיֹּאמֶר שְׁמוּאֵל אֶל־אַנְשֵׁי יִשְׂרָאֵל לְכוּ אִישׁ לְעִירוֹ:

ADDITIONAL READINGS 38

Joshua, chapter 20, verses 1 to 9

Joshua was the successor of Moses, and his task was to lead the people in their conquest of the Promised Land. For more on the book of Joshua, see our *General Introduction;* on Joshua the man, see the essay in the haftarah for V'zot Hab'rachah.

In our reading, Joshua proceeds to enact the prescription of the Torah to establish cities of refuge (Numbers 35:6 and following). See the essay on this subject in the Torah Commentary ("The Blood Avenger," p. 1249).

20:1. The Eternal One said to Joshua:

2. Speak to the people of Israel, saying: Pick out the cities of refuge of which I spoke to you through Moses,

3. to which a person may escape who kills anyone accidentally, and unintentionallly. These shall be places of refuge from a victim's relative who seeks revenge.

4. One [who kills by accident] may run away to one of these cities, show up at the entrance to the city gate, and explain to the town leaders what happened; they must gather that person into the city and give him a place to live.

5. If someone looking for revenge follows him there, the people of the city must not hand the slayer over to him, since he killed the other person unintentionally and had not been his enemy in the past.

6. Let him live in that city until he has received a public trial, [and remain there] until the death of the current high priest. Then the slayer may go back to his home in his own town, from which he had run away.

20:1 וַיְדַבֵּ֥ר יְהֹוָ֖ה אֶל־יְהוֹשֻׁ֥עַ לֵאמֹֽר׃

2 דַּבֵּ֛ר אֶל־בְּנֵ֥י יִשְׂרָאֵ֖ל לֵאמֹ֑ר תְּנ֤וּ לָכֶם֙ אֶת־עָרֵ֣י הַמִּקְלָ֔ט אֲשֶׁר־דִּבַּ֥רְתִּי אֲלֵיכֶ֖ם בְּיַד־מֹשֶֽׁה׃

3 לָנ֣וּס שָׁ֗מָּה רוֹצֵ֙חַ֙ מַכֵּה־נֶ֥פֶשׁ בִּשְׁגָגָ֖ה בִּבְלִי־דָ֑עַת וְהָי֤וּ לָכֶם֙ לְמִקְלָ֔ט מִגֹּאֵ֖ל הַדָּֽם׃

4 וְנָ֞ס אֶל־אַחַ֣ת ׀ מֵהֶעָרִ֣ים הָאֵ֗לֶּה וְעָמַד֙ פֶּ֚תַח שַׁ֣עַר הָעִ֔יר וְדִבֶּ֛ר בְּאׇזְנֵ֛י זִקְנֵ֥י הָעִיר־הַהִ֖יא אֶת־דְּבָרָ֑יו וְאָסְפ֙וּ אֹת֤וֹ הָעִ֙ירָה֙ אֲלֵיהֶ֔ם וְנָתְנוּ־ל֥וֹ מָק֖וֹם וְיָשַׁ֥ב עִמָּֽם׃

5 וְכִ֥י יִרְדֹּ֞ף גֹּאֵ֤ל הַדָּם֙ אַחֲרָ֔יו וְלֹא־יַסְגִּ֥רוּ אֶת־הָרֹצֵ֖חַ בְּיָד֑וֹ כִּ֤י בִבְלִי־דַ֙עַת֙ הִכָּ֣ה אֶת־רֵעֵ֔הוּ וְלֹא־שֹׂנֵ֥א ה֛וּא ל֖וֹ מִתְּמ֥וֹל שִׁלְשֽׁוֹם׃

6 וְיָשַׁ֣ב ׀ בָּעִ֣יר הַהִ֗יא עַד־עׇמְד֞וֹ לִפְנֵ֤י הָֽעֵדָה֙ לַמִּשְׁפָּ֔ט עַד־מוֹת֙ הַכֹּהֵ֣ן הַגָּד֔וֹל אֲשֶׁ֥ר יִהְיֶ֖ה בַּיָּמִ֣ים הָהֵ֑ם אָ֣ז ׀ יָשׁ֣וּב הָרוֹצֵ֗חַ וּבָ֤א אֶל־עִירוֹ֙ וְאֶל־בֵּית֔וֹ אֶל־הָעִ֖יר אֲשֶׁר־נָ֥ס מִשָּֽׁם׃

7. So they set aside Kedesh in the hill country of Naphtali in Galilee, Shechem in the hill country of Ephraim, and Kiriat-Arba (also called Hebron) in the hill country of Judah.

8. And across the (river) Jordan, on the desert plateau east of Jericho, they chose Bezer in the territory of Reuben; Ramot in Gilead, in the territory of Gad; and Golan in Bashan, in the territory of Menasseh.

9. Those were the appointed cities of refuge for all Israel and for any foreigner living among them. Anyone who killed a person accidentally could run away and be safe there from revenge; he could not be killed by the blood avenger (but remained there) until his trial by the community.

7 וַיַּקְדִּשׁוּ אֶת־קֶדֶשׁ בַּגָּלִיל בְּהַר נַפְתָּלִי וְאֶת־שְׁכֶם בְּהַר אֶפְרָיִם וְאֶת־קִרְיַת אַרְבַּע הִיא חֶבְרוֹן בְּהַר יְהוּדָה:

8 וּמֵעֵבֶר לְיַרְדֵּן יְרִיחוֹ מִזְרָחָה נָתְנוּ אֶת־בֶּצֶר בַּמִּדְבָּר בַּמִּישֹׁר מִמַּטֵּה רְאוּבֵן וְאֶת־רָאמֹת בַּגִּלְעָד מִמַּטֵּה־גָד וְאֶת־גָּלוֹן [גּוֹלָן] בַּבָּשָׁן מִמַּטֵּה מְנַשֶּׁה:

9 אֵלֶּה הָיוּ עָרֵי הַמּוּעָדָה לְכֹל בְּנֵי יִשְׂרָאֵל וְלַגֵּר הַגָּר בְּתוֹכָם לָנוּס שָׁמָּה כָּל־מַכֵּה־נֶפֶשׁ בִּשְׁגָגָה וְלֹא יָמוּת בְּיַד גֹּאֵל הַדָּם עַד־עָמְדוֹ לִפְנֵי הָעֵדָה:

Psalm 25, verses 1 to 11 and 16 to 22

The book of Psalms is found in *K'tuvim* ("Writings"), the third section of the Tanach. It contains 150 spiritual poems that exalt and call upon the Eternal as sovereign, friend, and savior. Tradition considers King David as the author of all the psalms that are either anonymous or ascribed to him, while modern scholarship assigns many of them to various later sources.

Psalm 25 is a plea for help in a time of trouble. It asks for the salvation that comes from knowing God's ways (verses 4 and 5).

25:1. To You, Eternal One, I lift up my soul.

2. In You I trust, O my God;

let me not be put to shame—

let not my foes exult over me.

3. Let none who hope in You be put to shame—

let the faithless be shamed and empty-handed.

4. Make me to know Your ways, Eternal One;

teach me Your paths.

5. Lead me in Your truth and teach me,

for You are the God of my salvation;

in You I hope all day long.

6. Be mindful of Your mercy and Your steadfast love,

Eternal One, for they are from of old.

7. The sins of my youth and transgressions do not remember;

remember me [instead] in Your steadfast love, Eternal One,

[remember me] because of Your goodness.

8. Good and upright is the Eternal,

who therefore teaches sinners the way,

9. leading the humble in what is right,

teaching the humble [God's] way.

אֵלֶיךָ יְהֹוָה נַפְשִׁי אֶשָּׂא: 25:1

אֱלֹהַי בְּךָ בָטַחְתִּי 2

אַל־אֵבוֹשָׁה

אַל־יַעַלְצוּ אֹיְבַי לִי:

גַּם כָּל־קֹוֶיךָ לֹא יֵבֹשׁוּ 3

יֵבֹשׁוּ הַבּוֹגְדִים רֵיקָם:

דְּרָכֶיךָ יְהֹוָה הוֹדִיעֵנִי 4

אֹרְחוֹתֶיךָ לַמְּדֵנִי:

הַדְרִיכֵנִי בַאֲמִתֶּךָ וְלַמְּדֵנִי 5

כִּי־אַתָּה אֱלֹהֵי יִשְׁעִי

אוֹתְךָ קִוִּיתִי כָּל־הַיּוֹם:

זְכֹר־רַחֲמֶיךָ יְהֹוָה וַחֲסָדֶיךָ 6

כִּי מֵעוֹלָם הֵמָּה:

חַטֹּאות נְעוּרַי וּפְשָׁעַי אַל־תִּזְכֹּר 7

כְּחַסְדְּךָ זְכָר־לִי־אַתָּה

לְמַעַן טוּבְךָ יְהֹוָה:

טוֹב־וְיָשָׁר יְהֹוָה 8

עַל־כֵּן יוֹרֶה חַטָּאִים בַּדָּרֶךְ:

יַדְרֵךְ עֲנָוִים בַּמִּשְׁפָּט 9

וִילַמֵּד עֲנָוִים דַּרְכּוֹ:

10. All the paths of the Eternal are
    steadfast love and truth,
to those who keep [God's] covenant,
    [God's] decrees.

11. For Your Name's sake, Eternal One,
pardon my sin, though it be grave.

16. Turn to me and be gracious to me,
for I am lonely and afflicted.

17. My heart grows ever more grieved;
take me out of my distress.

18. Behold my affliction and my pain,
and forgive all my sins.

19. See how many are my foes,
how violently they hate me.

20. Protect me and rescue me,
that, taking refuge in You, I am not put to
    shame.

21. May innocence and uprightness
    preserve me,
for I hope in You.

22. Redeem Israel, O God, out of all its
    troubles.

10 כָּל־אָרְחוֹת יְהֹוָה חֶסֶד וֶאֱמֶת
לְנֹצְרֵי בְרִיתוֹ וְעֵדֹתָיו:

11 לְמַעַן־שִׁמְךָ יְהֹוָה
וְסָלַחְתָּ לַעֲוֹנִי כִּי רַב־הוּא:

16 פְּנֵה־אֵלַי וְחָנֵּנִי
כִּי־יָחִיד וְעָנִי אָנִי:

17 צָרוֹת לְבָבִי הִרְחִיבוּ
מִמְּצוּקוֹתַי הוֹצִיאֵנִי:

18 רְאֵה עָנְיִי וַעֲמָלִי
וְשָׂא לְכָל־חַטֹּאותָי:

19 רְאֵה־אוֹיְבַי כִּי־רָבּוּ
וְשִׂנְאַת חָמָס שְׂנֵאוּנִי:

20 שָׁמְרָה נַפְשִׁי וְהַצִּילֵנִי
אַל־אֵבוֹשׁ כִּי־חָסִיתִי בָךְ:

21 תֹּם־וָיֹשֶׁר יִצְּרוּנִי
כִּי קִוִּיתִיךָ:

22 פְּדֵה אֱלֹהִים אֶת־יִשְׂרָאֵל מִכֹּל צָרוֹתָיו:

ADDITIONAL READINGS 40

Psalm 119, verses 1 to 2, 10, 34 to 35, 72, 99, and 165

The book of Psalms is found in *K'tuvim* ("Writings"), the third section of the Tanach. It contains 150 spiritual poems that exalt and call upon the Eternal as sovereign, friend, and savior. Tradition considers King David as the author of all the psalms that are either anonymous or ascribed to him, while modern scholarship assigns many of them to various later sources.

Psalm 119, composed as a multiple alphabetical acrostic, is the longest of all psalms. Our selection emphasises the importance of Torah.

119:1. Happy are those whose way is blameless,
who walk in the Torah of the Eternal.

2. Happy are those who keep God's guidance,
who seek God with a whole heart.

10. With all my heart I seek You,
do not let me wander from Your commandments.

34. Give me understanding, that I may keep Your Torah
and observe it with a whole heart.

35. Lead me in the path of Your commandments,
for that is my delight.

72. The Torah You teach is better to me than a thousand gold or silver coins.

99. I gain understanding from all my teachers,
as Your precepts are my [constant] concern.

165. Great peace have they who love Your Torah;
nothing can make them stumble.

119:1 אַשְׁרֵי תְמִימֵי־דָרֶךְ
הַהֹלְכִים בְּתוֹרַת יְהֹוָה:

2 אַשְׁרֵי נֹצְרֵי עֵדֹתָיו
בְּכָל־לֵב יִדְרְשׁוּהוּ:

10 בְּכָל־לִבִּי דְרַשְׁתִּיךָ
אַל־תַּשְׁגֵּנִי מִמִּצְוֹתֶיךָ:

34 הֲבִינֵנִי וְאֶצְּרָה תוֹרָתֶךָ
וְאֶשְׁמְרֶנָּה בְכָל־לֵב:

35 הַדְרִיכֵנִי בִּנְתִיב מִצְוֹתֶיךָ
כִּי־בוֹ חָפָצְתִּי:

72 טוֹב־לִי תוֹרַת־פִּיךָ מֵאַלְפֵי זָהָב וָכָסֶף:

99 מִכָּל־מְלַמְּדַי הִשְׂכַּלְתִּי
כִּי עֵדְוֹתֶיךָ שִׂיחָה לִי:

165 שָׁלוֹם רָב לְאֹהֲבֵי תוֹרָתֶךָ
וְאֵין־לָמוֹ מִכְשׁוֹל:

Psalm 1, verses 1 to 6

The book of Psalms is found in *K'tuvim* ("Writings"), the third section of the Tanach. It contains 150 spiritual poems that exalt and call upon the Eternal as sovereign, friend, and savior. Tradition considers King David as the author of all the psalms that are either anonymous or ascribed to him, while modern scholarship assigns many of them to various later sources.

This reading contains the first six verses of the book of Psalms. Our selection praises those who study Torah and delight in it.

1:1. Happy are those who do not follow the counsel of the wicked,	1:1 אַשְׁרֵי־הָאִישׁ אֲשֶׁר לֹא הָלַךְ בַּעֲצַת רְשָׁעִים
or take the path of sinners,	וּבְדֶרֶךְ חַטָּאִים לֹא עָמָד
or sit in the seat of cynics,	וּבְמוֹשַׁב לֵצִים לֹא יָשָׁב:
2. but whose delight is the Eternal's Teaching,	2 כִּי אִם בְּתוֹרַת יְהוָה חֶפְצוֹ
and whose study day and night is God's Teaching.	וּבְתוֹרָתוֹ יֶהְגֶּה יוֹמָם וָלָיְלָה:
3. They are like a tree planted by streams of water	3 וְהָיָה כְּעֵץ שָׁתוּל עַל־פַּלְגֵי מָיִם
that yields its fruit in due season	אֲשֶׁר פִּרְיוֹ יִתֵּן בְּעִתּוֹ
and whose leaves do not wither;	וְעָלֵהוּ לֹא־יִבּוֹל
they prosper in all that they do.	וְכֹל אֲשֶׁר־יַעֲשֶׂה יַצְלִיחַ:
4. Not so the wicked—	4 לֹא־כֵן הָרְשָׁעִים
who are like chaff driven by the wind.	כִּי אִם־כַּמֹּץ אֲשֶׁר־תִּדְּפֶנּוּ רוּחַ:
5. Therefore the wicked cannot survive judgment,	5 עַל־כֵּן לֹא־יָקֻמוּ רְשָׁעִים בַּמִּשְׁפָּט
nor sinners [survive] in the assembly of the righteous.	וְחַטָּאִים בַּעֲדַת צַדִּיקִים:
6. For the Eternal watches over the way of the righteous,	6 כִּי־יוֹדֵעַ יְהוָה דֶּרֶךְ צַדִּיקִים
but the way of the wicked is doomed.	וְדֶרֶךְ רְשָׁעִים תֹּאבֵד:

Joshua, chapter 8, verses 30 to 35

Joshua was the successor of Moses, and his task was to lead the people in their conquest of the Promised Land. For more on the book of Joshua, see our *General Introduction;* on Joshua the man, see the essay in the haftarah for V'zot Hab'rachah.

In our reading, Joshua prepares to carry out the instructions of Moses (Deuteronomy 11:26 ff.). Mount Gerizim and Mount Ebal represent the choice between life and death that Israel is called upon to make. See the analysis in the Torah Commentary, p. 1418.

8:30. Then Joshua built an altar for the Eternal, the God of Israel, on Mount Ebal.

31. As Moses the servant of the Eternal had commanded the people of Israel, as it is written in the Book of the Torah of Moses, [it was] an altar of whole stones, upon which no iron tool had been wielded. Then he offered (whole) burnt-offerings to the Eternal, and sacrificed peace-offerings.

32. There, in the presence of the people of Israel, he [Joshua] inscribed on the stones the copy of Moses' Teaching, which he had written.

33. All Israel—its elders, officials, and judges—stranger and citizen alike, stood on either side of the Ark opposite the levitical priests, who were carrying the Ark of the Covenant of the Eternal, one half facing Mount Gerizim and one half facing Mount Ebal, as Moses the servant of the Eternal had instructed of old, [for them] to bless the people of Israel.

34. Afterward he read [aloud] all the words of the Teaching, blessing and curse, all as written in the Book of the Teaching.

8:30 אָ֣ז יִבְנֶ֤ה יְהוֹשֻׁ֙עַ֙ מִזְבֵּ֔חַ לַֽיהוָ֖ה אֱלֹהֵ֣י יִשְׂרָאֵ֑ל בְּהַ֖ר עֵיבָֽל׃

31 כַּאֲשֶׁ֣ר צִוָּה֩ מֹשֶׁ֨ה עֶֽבֶד־יְהוָ֜ה אֶת־בְּנֵ֣י יִשְׂרָאֵ֗ל כַּכָּתוּב֙ בְּסֵ֙פֶר֙ תּוֹרַ֣ת מֹשֶׁ֔ה מִזְבַּח֙ אֲבָנִ֣ים שְׁלֵמ֔וֹת אֲשֶׁ֛ר לֹֽא־הֵנִ֥יף עֲלֵיהֶ֖ן בַּרְזֶ֑ל וַיַּעֲל֤וּ עָלָיו֙ עֹלוֹת֙ לַֽיהוָ֔ה וַֽיִּזְבְּח֖וּ שְׁלָמִֽים׃

32 וַיִּכְתָּב־שָׁ֖ם עַל־הָאֲבָנִ֑ים אֵ֗ת מִשְׁנֵה֙ תּוֹרַ֣ת מֹשֶׁ֔ה אֲשֶׁ֣ר כָּתַ֔ב לִפְנֵ֖י בְּנֵ֥י יִשְׂרָאֵֽל׃

33 וְכָל־יִשְׂרָאֵ֡ל וּזְקֵנָ֡יו וְשֹׁטְרִ֣ים ׀ וְשֹׁפְטָ֡יו עֹמְדִ֣ים מִזֶּ֣ה ׀ וּמִזֶּ֣ה ׀ לָאָר֡וֹן נֶגֶד֩ הַכֹּהֲנִ֨ים הַלְוִיִּ֜ם נֹשְׂאֵ֣י ׀ אֲר֣וֹן בְּרִית־יְהוָ֗ה כַּגֵּר֙ כָּֽאֶזְרָ֔ח חֶצְיוֹ֙ אֶל־מ֣וּל הַר־גְּרִזִ֔ים וְהַֽחֶצְי֖וֹ אֶל־מ֣וּל הַר־עֵיבָ֑ל כַּאֲשֶׁ֨ר צִוָּ֜ה מֹשֶׁ֣ה עֶֽבֶד־יְהוָ֗ה לְבָרֵ֛ךְ אֶת־הָעָ֥ם יִשְׂרָאֵ֖ל בָּרִאשֹׁנָֽה׃

34 וְאַֽחֲרֵי־כֵ֗ן קָרָא֙ אֶת־כָּל־דִּבְרֵ֣י הַתּוֹרָ֔ה הַבְּרָכָ֖ה וְהַקְּלָלָ֑ה כְּכָל־הַכָּת֖וּב בְּסֵ֥פֶר הַתּוֹרָֽה׃

35. Joshua did not fail to read a single word of all that Moses had commanded, before the whole assembly of Israel, including the women and children, and the strangers who were accompanying them.

35 לֹא־הָיָה דָבָר מִכֹּל אֲשֶׁר־צִוָּה מֹשֶׁה אֲשֶׁר
לֹא־קָרָא יְהוֹשֻׁעַ נֶגֶד כָּל־קְהַל יִשְׂרָאֵל
וְהַנָּשִׁים וְהַטַּף וְהַגֵּר הַהֹלֵךְ בְּקִרְבָּם:

Psalm 15, verses 1 to 5

The book of Psalms is found in *K'tuvim* ("Writings"), the third section of the Tanach. It contains 150 spiritual poems that exalt and call upon the Eternal as sovereign, friend, and savior. Tradition considers King David as the author of all the psalms that are either anonymous or ascribed to him, while modern scholarship assigns many of them to various later sources.

The five verses of our reading make righteous conduct the condition of obtaining God's favor.

15:1. A Psalm of David.

Eternal One, who may abide in Your tent?

Who may dwell on Your holy mounain?

2. Those who walk with integrity and do
   what is right,

and speak truth from their heart;

3. who have no slander on their tongue,

who do no evil to their neighbor

or bring shame upon their kin;

4. who despise the dishonorable

but show respect for the God-fearing;

who give their word and, come what may,
   do not retract;

5. who lend without taking advantage,

who take no bribes against the innocent.

Those who do all this shall never be
   shaken.

15:1 מִזְמוֹר לְדָוִד

יְהֹוָה מִי־יָגוּר בְּאָהֳלֶךָ

מִי־יִשְׁכֹּן בְּהַר קׇדְשֶׁךָ:

2 הוֹלֵךְ תָּמִים וּפֹעֵל צֶדֶק

וְדֹבֵר אֱמֶת בִּלְבָבוֹ:

3 לֹא־רָגַל עַל־לְשֹׁנוֹ

לֹא־עָשָׂה לְרֵעֵהוּ רָעָה

וְחֶרְפָּה לֹא־נָשָׂא עַל־קְרֹבוֹ:

4 נִבְזֶה בְּעֵינָיו נִמְאָס

וְאֶת־יִרְאֵי יְהֹוָה יְכַבֵּד

נִשְׁבַּע לְהָרַע וְלֹא יָמִר:

5 כַּסְפּוֹ לֹא־נָתַן בְּנֶשֶׁךְ

וְשֹׁחַד עַל־נָקִי לֹא לָקָח

עֹשֵׂה־אֵלֶּה לֹא יִמּוֹט לְעוֹלָם:

Proverbs, chapter 28, verses 1 to 7 and 9 to 14

The book of Proverbs is found in *K'tuvim* ("Writings"), the third section of the Tanach. It contains proverbial sayings, warnings against excess, popular philosophy, and instructions for living a worthwhile life. While tradition has assigned its authorship to King Solomon (10th century B.C.E.), contemporary scholarship holds that it belongs to the genre of "wisdom literature," which flourished from the 4th century B.C.E. on under Greek influence.

Our selection presents the kind of collected wisdom that forms the basis of the book of Proverbs.

28:1 נָסוּ וְאֵין־רֹדֵף רָשָׁע וְצַדִּיקִים כִּכְפִיר יִבְטָח׃

28:1. The wicked run when none pursue, but the righteous are confident as lions.

2 בְּפֶשַׁע אֶרֶץ רַבִּים שָׂרֶיהָ וּבְאָדָם מֵבִין יֹדֵעַ כֵּן יַאֲרִיךְ׃

2. When a nation is in rebellion, it has many [would-be] rulers. But one who is discerning and wise rules a long time.

3 גֶּבֶר רָשׁ וְעֹשֵׁק דַּלִּים מָטָר סֹחֵף וְאֵין לָחֶם׃

3. The poor who extort from the weak are a driving rain that destroys the crops.

4 עֹזְבֵי תוֹרָה יְהַלְלוּ רָשָׁע וְשֹׁמְרֵי תוֹרָה יִתְגָּרוּ בָם׃

4. Those who renounce the law praise the wicked; while those who keep the law strive against them.

5 אַנְשֵׁי־רָע לֹא־יָבִינוּ מִשְׁפָּט וּמְבַקְשֵׁי יְהֹוָה יָבִינוּ כֹל׃

5. Evil people do not know what justice is, but those who seek the Eternal understand it fully.

6 טוֹב־רָשׁ הוֹלֵךְ בְּתֻמּוֹ מֵעִקֵּשׁ דְּרָכַיִם וְהוּא עָשִׁיר׃

6. Better [to be] a pauper who walks a blameless path than to be rich and choose crooked paths.

7 נוֹצֵר תּוֹרָה בֵּן מֵבִין וְרֹעֶה זוֹלְלִים יַכְלִים אָבִיו׃

7. A wise child listens to instruction, while those who run with the depraved shame their parents.

9 מֵסִיר אָזְנוֹ מִשְּׁמֹעַ תּוֹרָה גַּם־תְּפִלָּתוֹ תּוֹעֵבָה׃

9. Those who refuse to listen to instruction, even their prayers are abhorrent.

10 מַשְׁגֶּה יְשָׁרִים בְּדֶרֶךְ רָע בִּשְׁחוּתוֹ הוּא־יִפּוֹל וּתְמִימִים יִנְחֲלוּ־טוֹב׃

10. Those who misdirect the upright onto an evil path fall into their own pit, while the virtuous obtain good fortune.

11. Rich people think themselves wise, but a poor person sees through them.

12. When the good rise to power, everyone celebrates; but when the wicked rise to power, the people hide.

13. Those who conceal their sins cannot succeed, while those who confess and desist find compassion.

14. Happy are those who tremble continually [before God]; but those who harden their hearts fall into ruin.

11 חָכָם בְּעֵינָיו אִישׁ עָשִׁיר וְדַל מֵבִין יַחְקְרֶנּוּ:

12 בַּעֲלֹץ צַדִּיקִים רַבָּה תִפְאָרֶת וּבְקוּם רְשָׁעִים יְחֻפַּשׂ אָדָם:

13 מְכַסֶּה פְשָׁעָיו לֹא יַצְלִיחַ וּמוֹדֶה וְעֹזֵב יְרֻחָם:

14 אַשְׁרֵי אָדָם מְפַחֵד תָּמִיד וּמַקְשֶׁה לִבּוֹ יִפּוֹל בְּרָעָה:

Isaiah, chapter 35, verses 1 to 2, and 5, 6, 8, 9, 10

Most of the first 39 chapters of Isaiah were authored by a prophet who lived in the 8th century B.C.E. in Jerusalem. For more on Isaiah and his time, see our *General Introduction*.

The Prophet foresees a glorious future for Israel if it treads the "Road of Holiness." It is a prophecy rich in metaphors; thus, the blind shall able to see and the deaf shall hear.

35:1. The desert and the dry land shall rejoice,
the wilderness shall bloom like the crocus.

2. Luxuriantly shall it blossom
and sing, even shout for joy;
it shall take on the glory of the mountains of Lebanon,
the splendor of the fields of Carmel and Sharon.
Everyone shall see the glory of the Eternal,
the splendor of our God.

5. The blind shall be able to see,
and the deaf shall hear.

6. The lame shall leap like a deer,
and those who cannot speak shall shout for joy.
Water shall pour into the desert,
streams [shall flow] into the wilderness.

8. There shall be a highway and a road,
called the Road of Holiness.

9. No lion shall be there;
no rapacious animal shall pass that way;
but those whom God has rescued
shall travel [home] by that road.

35:1 יְשֻׂשׂוּם מִדְבָּר וְצִיָּה
וְתָגֵל עֲרָבָה וְתִפְרַח כַּחֲבַצָּלֶת:
2 פָּרֹחַ תִּפְרַח
וְתָגֵל אַף גִּילַת וְרַנֵּן
כְּבוֹד הַלְּבָנוֹן נִתַּן־לָהּ
הֲדַר הַכַּרְמֶל וְהַשָּׁרוֹן
הֵמָּה יִרְאוּ כְבוֹד־יְהוָה
הֲדַר אֱלֹהֵינוּ:
5 אָז תִּפָּקַחְנָה עֵינֵי עִוְרִים
וְאָזְנֵי חֵרְשִׁים תִּפָּתַחְנָה:
6 אָז יְדַלֵּג כָּאַיָּל פִּסֵּחַ
וְתָרֹן לְשׁוֹן אִלֵּם
כִּי־נִבְקְעוּ בַמִּדְבָּר מַיִם
וּנְחָלִים בָּעֲרָבָה:
8 וְהָיָה־שָׁם מַסְלוּל וָדֶרֶךְ
וְדֶרֶךְ הַקֹּדֶשׁ יִקָּרֵא לָהּ
9 לֹא־יִהְיֶה שָׁם אַרְיֵה
וּפְרִיץ חַיּוֹת בַּל־יַעֲלֶנָּה לֹא תִמָּצֵא שָׁם
וְהָלְכוּ גְאוּלִים:

10. Those whom the Eternal has ransomed
    shall return,
in jubilation advancing on Zion,
perpetual joy on their crowns,
joy and gladness overtaking them,
[as] sorrow and groaning flee away.

10 וּפְדוּיֵי יְהֹוָה יְשֻׁבוּן
וּבָאוּ צִיּוֹן בְּרִנָּה
וְשִׂמְחַת עוֹלָם עַל־רֹאשָׁם
שָׂשׂוֹן וְשִׂמְחָה יַשִּׂיגוּ
וְנָסוּ יָגוֹן וַאֲנָחָה:

Joshua, chapter 4, verses 1 to 24

Joshua was the successor of Moses, and his task was to lead the people in their conquest of the Promised Land. For more on the book of Joshua, see our *General Introduction;* on Joshua the man, see the essay in the haftarah for V'zot Hab'rachah.

Our reading tells of Israel's army crossing the Jordan, and the miracle of the Reed [Red] Sea being repeated.

4:1. When the whole nation had crossed the Jordan, the Eternal addressed Joshua, saying:

2. Choose twelve men, one from each tribe,

3. and have them take twelve stones out of the middle of the Jordan, from the very place where the priests are standing. You shall convey these stones with you and put them down where you camp tonight.

4. Then Joshua called the twelve men he had chosen, one from each tribe,

5. and told them: Go into the Jordan, first passing in front of the Ark of the Covenant of your Eternal God. Each one of you take a stone on his shoulder, one for each of the tribes of Israel.

6. These stones shall be a reminder to you. In the future, when your children ask: *What do these stones mean to you?*

7. tell them that the waters of the Jordan were cut off when the Ark of the Covenant of the Eternal crossed the river. These stones shall be a reminder to the people of Israel forever.

א וַיְהִי כַּאֲשֶׁר־תַּמּוּ כָל־הַגּוֹי לַעֲבוֹר אֶת־
הַיַּרְדֵּן וַיֹּאמֶר יְהוָֹה אֶל־יְהוֹשֻׁעַ לֵאמֹר:

ב קְחוּ לָכֶם מִן־הָעָם שְׁנֵים עָשָׂר אֲנָשִׁים אִישׁ־
אֶחָד אִישׁ־אֶחָד מִשָּׁבֶט:

ג וְצַוּוּ אוֹתָם לֵאמֹר שְׂאוּ־לָכֶם מִזֶּה מִתּוֹךְ
הַיַּרְדֵּן מִמַּצַּב רַגְלֵי הַכֹּהֲנִים הָכִין שְׁתֵּים־
עֶשְׂרֵה אֲבָנִים וְהַעֲבַרְתֶּם אוֹתָם עִמָּכֶם
וְהִנַּחְתֶּם אוֹתָם בַּמָּלוֹן אֲשֶׁר־תָּלִינוּ בוֹ הַלָּיְלָה:

ד וַיִּקְרָא יְהוֹשֻׁעַ אֶל־שְׁנֵים הֶעָשָׂר אִישׁ אֲשֶׁר
הֵכִין מִבְּנֵי יִשְׂרָאֵל אִישׁ־אֶחָד אִישׁ־אֶחָד
מִשָּׁבֶט:

ה וַיֹּאמֶר לָהֶם יְהוֹשֻׁעַ עִבְרוּ לִפְנֵי אֲרוֹן יְהוָֹה
אֱלֹהֵיכֶם אֶל־תּוֹךְ הַיַּרְדֵּן וְהָרִימוּ לָכֶם אִישׁ
אֶבֶן אַחַת עַל־שִׁכְמוֹ לְמִסְפַּר שִׁבְטֵי בְנֵי־
יִשְׂרָאֵל:

ו לְמַעַן תִּהְיֶה זֹאת אוֹת בְּקִרְבְּכֶם כִּי־יִשְׁאָלוּן
בְּנֵיכֶם מָחָר לֵאמֹר מָה הָאֲבָנִים הָאֵלֶּה לָכֶם:

ז וַאֲמַרְתֶּם לָהֶם אֲשֶׁר נִכְרְתוּ מֵימֵי הַיַּרְדֵּן
מִפְּנֵי אֲרוֹן בְּרִית־יְהוָֹה בְּעָבְרוֹ בַּיַּרְדֵּן נִכְרְתוּ
מֵי הַיַּרְדֵּן וְהָיוּ הָאֲבָנִים הָאֵלֶּה לְזִכָּרוֹן לִבְנֵי
יִשְׂרָאֵל עַד־עוֹלָם:

8. The men followed Joshua's orders. As the Eternal had commanded Joshua, they took twelve stones from the middle of the Jordan, one for each tribe of Israel, carried them to the night's camping-place, and deposited them there.

9. Joshua also set up twelve stones in the middle of the Jordan, where the priests carrying the Ark of the Covenant had stood. The stones are still there.

10. Now the priests had stood in the middle of the Jordan until everything was done that the Eternal had commanded Joshua to tell the people to do, just as Moses had commanded Joshua. Then the people hurried across the river.

11. When the people finished crossing, the priests passed before the people, carrying the Ark of the Covenant of the Eternal.

12. The men of the tribes of Reuben and Gad and of half the tribe of Menasseh, arrayed for battle, crossed ahead of the rest of the people, as Moses had told them to do.

13. In the presence of God about 40,000 battle-ready men crossed over to the plains of Jericho.

14. That day the Eternal magnified Joshua in the sight of all Israel. They revered him all his life, as they had revered Moses.

15. Then the Eternal told Joshua:

16. *Command the priests carrying the Ark of the Covenant to come up out of the Jordan.*

17. Joshua ordered the priests with the words, *Move up out of the Jordan,*

8 וַיַּעֲשׂוּ־כֵן בְּנֵי־יִשְׂרָאֵל כַּאֲשֶׁר צִוָּה יְהוֹשֻׁעַ וַיִּשְׂאוּ שְׁתֵּי־עֶשְׂרֵה אֲבָנִים מִתּוֹךְ הַיַּרְדֵּן כַּאֲשֶׁר דִּבֶּר יְהוָה אֶל־יְהוֹשֻׁעַ לְמִסְפַּר שִׁבְטֵי בְנֵי־יִשְׂרָאֵל וַיַּעֲבִרוּם עִמָּם אֶל־הַמָּלוֹן וַיַּנִּחוּם שָׁם:

9 וּשְׁתֵּים עֶשְׂרֵה אֲבָנִים הֵקִים יְהוֹשֻׁעַ בְּתוֹךְ הַיַּרְדֵּן תַּחַת מַצַּב רַגְלֵי הַכֹּהֲנִים נֹשְׂאֵי אֲרוֹן הַבְּרִית וַיִּהְיוּ שָׁם עַד הַיּוֹם הַזֶּה:

10 וְהַכֹּהֲנִים נֹשְׂאֵי הָאָרוֹן עֹמְדִים בְּתוֹךְ הַיַּרְדֵּן עַד תֹּם כָּל־הַדָּבָר אֲשֶׁר־צִוָּה יְהוָה אֶת־יְהוֹשֻׁעַ לְדַבֵּר אֶל־הָעָם כְּכֹל אֲשֶׁר־צִוָּה מֹשֶׁה אֶת־יְהוֹשֻׁעַ וַיְמַהֲרוּ הָעָם וַיַּעֲבֹרוּ:

11 וַיְהִי כַּאֲשֶׁר־תַּם כָּל־הָעָם לַעֲבוֹר וַיַּעֲבֹר אֲרוֹן־יְהוָה וְהַכֹּהֲנִים לִפְנֵי הָעָם:

12 וַיַּעַבְרוּ בְּנֵי־רְאוּבֵן וּבְנֵי־גָד וַחֲצִי שֵׁבֶט הַמְנַשֶּׁה חֲמֻשִׁים לִפְנֵי בְּנֵי יִשְׂרָאֵל כַּאֲשֶׁר דִּבֶּר אֲלֵיהֶם מֹשֶׁה:

13 כְּאַרְבָּעִים אֶלֶף חֲלוּצֵי הַצָּבָא עָבְרוּ לִפְנֵי יְהוָה לַמִּלְחָמָה אֶל עַרְבוֹת יְרִיחוֹ:

14 בַּיּוֹם הַהוּא גִּדַּל יְהוָה אֶת־יְהוֹשֻׁעַ בְּעֵינֵי כָּל־יִשְׂרָאֵל וַיִּרְאוּ אֹתוֹ כַּאֲשֶׁר יָרְאוּ אֶת־מֹשֶׁה כָּל־יְמֵי חַיָּיו:

15 וַיֹּאמֶר יְהוָה אֶל־יְהוֹשֻׁעַ לֵאמֹר:

16 צַוֵּה אֶת־הַכֹּהֲנִים נֹשְׂאֵי אֲרוֹן הָעֵדוּת וְיַעֲלוּ מִן־הַיַּרְדֵּן:

17 וַיְצַו יְהוֹשֻׁעַ אֶת־הַכֹּהֲנִים לֵאמֹר עֲלוּ מִן־הַיַּרְדֵּן:

18. and when the priests, bearers of the Ark of the Covenant of the Eternal, clambered out of the Jordan, and the soles of their feet touched dry land, the waters of the Jordan returned to their place and flowed as before along its banks.

19. The people crossed the Jordan on the tenth day of the first month and camped at Gilgal, on the eastern edge of Jericho.

20. There Joshua placed the twelve stones taken from the Jordan.

21. And he said to the people of Israel: In the future, when children ask their parents, *What do these stones mean?*

22. inform them about the time when Israel crossed the Jordan on dry ground.

23. [Say to them:] *On dry land did Israel cross over the Jordan. The Eternal your God drained the water of the Jordan for you until you had crossed, just as God did to the Reed [Red] Sea for us, for God drained it before us, until we had crossed,*

24. *so that all the peoples of the earth may know of the power of God's hand—for it is very great—and so that you may revere the Eternal your God forever.*

18 וַיְהִי בַּעֲלוֹת [כַּעֲלוֹת] הַכֹּהֲנִים נֹשְׂאֵי אֲרוֹן בְּרִית־יְהוָה מִתּוֹךְ הַיַּרְדֵּן נִתְּקוּ כַּפּוֹת רַגְלֵי הַכֹּהֲנִים אֶל הֶחָרָבָה וַיָּשֻׁבוּ מֵי־הַיַּרְדֵּן לִמְקוֹמָם וַיֵּלְכוּ כִתְמוֹל־שִׁלְשׁוֹם עַל־כָּל־גְּדוֹתָיו:

19 וְהָעָם עָלוּ מִן־הַיַּרְדֵּן בֶּעָשׂוֹר לַחֹדֶשׁ הָרִאשׁוֹן וַיַּחֲנוּ בַּגִּלְגָּל בִּקְצֵה מִזְרַח יְרִיחוֹ:

20 וְאֵת שְׁתֵּים עֶשְׂרֵה הָאֲבָנִים הָאֵלֶּה אֲשֶׁר לָקְחוּ מִן־הַיַּרְדֵּן הֵקִים יְהוֹשֻׁעַ בַּגִּלְגָּל:

21 וַיֹּאמֶר אֶל־בְּנֵי יִשְׂרָאֵל לֵאמֹר אֲשֶׁר יִשְׁאָלוּן בְּנֵיכֶם מָחָר אֶת־אֲבוֹתָם לֵאמֹר מָה הָאֲבָנִים הָאֵלֶּה:

22 וְהוֹדַעְתֶּם אֶת־בְּנֵיכֶם לֵאמֹר בַּיַּבָּשָׁה עָבַר יִשְׂרָאֵל אֶת־הַיַּרְדֵּן הַזֶּה:

23 אֲשֶׁר־הוֹבִישׁ יְהוָה אֱלֹהֵיכֶם אֶת־מֵי הַיַּרְדֵּן מִפְּנֵיכֶם עַד־עָבְרְכֶם כַּאֲשֶׁר עָשָׂה יְהוָה אֱלֹהֵיכֶם לְיַם־סוּף אֲשֶׁר־הוֹבִישׁ מִפָּנֵינוּ עַד־עָבְרֵנוּ:

24 לְמַעַן דַּעַת כָּל־עַמֵּי הָאָרֶץ אֶת־יַד יְהוָה כִּי חֲזָקָה הִיא לְמַעַן יְרָאתֶם אֶת־יְהוָה אֱלֹהֵיכֶם כָּל־הַיָּמִים:

Joel, chapter 2, verses 15 to 19a and 21 to 27

The prophet Joel was possibly a contemporary of Amos, but we cannot determine the time of his activity with any certainty. For more on Joel, see our *General Introduction* and the haftarah for Shabbat Shuvah.

In our reading, the Prophet tries to bring solace to a stricken people who have lost their faith in God.

2:15. Sound the shofar in Zion,	2:15 תִּקְעוּ שׁוֹפָר בְּצִיּוֹן
set a fast-day aside,	קַדְּשׁוּ־צוֹם
call a sacred assembly!	קִרְאוּ עֲצָרָה:
16. Gather the people,	16 אִסְפוּ־עָם
sanctify the congregation;	קַדְּשׁוּ קָהָל
assemble the elders;	קִבְצוּ זְקֵנִים
gather the children and the suckling babes.	אִסְפוּ עוֹלָלִים וְיֹנְקֵי שָׁדָיִם
Let the bridegroom come out of his chamber,	יֵצֵא חָתָן מֵחֶדְרוֹ
the bride from her canopy.	וְכַלָּה מֵחֻפָּתָהּ:
17. Between the vestibule and the altar,	17 בֵּין הָאוּלָם וְלַמִּזְבֵּחַ
let the priests, the ministers of the Eternal, weep and say:	יִבְכּוּ הַכֹּהֲנִים מְשָׁרְתֵי יְהוָה וְיֹאמְרוּ
Have pity on Your people, Eternal One!	חוּסָה יְהוָה עַל־עַמֶּךָ
Let not Your heritage be mocked	וְאַל־תִּתֵּן נַחֲלָתְךָ לְחֶרְפָּה
and be a byword among the nations.	לִמְשָׁל־בָּם גּוֹיִם
Why should they say among the peoples,	לָמָּה יֹאמְרוּ בָעַמִּים
Where is their God?	אַיֵּה אֱלֹהֵיהֶם:
18. Then the Eternal showed zeal for this land,	18 וַיְקַנֵּא יְהוָה לְאַרְצוֹ
and compassion for this people.	וַיַּחְמֹל עַל־עַמּוֹ:
19a. The Eternal answered the people, saying:	19 וַיַּעַן יְהוָה וַיֹּאמֶר לְעַמּוֹ
21. Fear not, O soil, rejoice and be glad,	21 אַל־תִּירְאִי אֲדָמָה גִּילִי וּשְׂמָחִי
for the Eternal is doing great things.	כִּי־הִגְדִּיל יְהוָה לַעֲשׂוֹת:

22. Fear not, O beasts of the field,

for the pastures of the wilderness are covered with grass;

every tree bears its fruit,

the fig-tree and the vine give their yield.

23. O children of Zion, rejoice

and be glad in the Eternal your God,

who in kindness is giving you the early rain,

pouring rain down for you,

the early rain; and the later rain of the first month.

24. The threshing floors shall be heaped with grain,

the vats shall overflow with wine and oil;

25. I will repay you for what [you lost in]

the years when the swarmer ate your crops,

the hopper, the grub, the locust—

My great army that I sent against you.

26. You shall eat and be satisfied,

and praise the name of the Eternal your God,

who has done wondrous things for you.

My people shall never again be put to shame.

27. *Then you shall know that I am in the midst of Israel,*

and that I, the Eternal, am your God,

and there is no other.

My people shall never again be put to shame.

22 אַל־תִּירְאוּ בַּהֲמוֹת שָׂדָי

כִּי דָשְׁאוּ נְאוֹת מִדְבָּר

כִּי־עֵץ נָשָׂא פִרְיוֹ

תְּאֵנָה וָגֶפֶן נָתְנוּ חֵילָם:

23 וּבְנֵי צִיּוֹן גִּילוּ

וְשִׂמְחוּ בַּיהוָה אֱלֹהֵיכֶם

כִּי־נָתַן לָכֶם אֶת־הַמּוֹרֶה לִצְדָקָה

וַיּוֹרֶד לָכֶם גֶּשֶׁם

מוֹרֶה וּמַלְקוֹשׁ בָּרִאשׁוֹן:

24 וּמָלְאוּ הַגֳּרָנוֹת בָּר

וְהֵשִׁיקוּ הַיְקָבִים תִּירוֹשׁ וְיִצְהָר:

25 וְשִׁלַּמְתִּי לָכֶם

אֶת־הַשָּׁנִים אֲשֶׁר אָכַל הָאַרְבֶּה

הַיֶּלֶק וְהֶחָסִיל וְהַגָּזָם

חֵילִי הַגָּדוֹל אֲשֶׁר שִׁלַּחְתִּי בָּכֶם:

26 וַאֲכַלְתֶּם אָכוֹל וְשָׂבוֹעַ

וְהִלַּלְתֶּם אֶת־שֵׁם יְהוָה אֱלֹהֵיכֶם

אֲשֶׁר־עָשָׂה עִמָּכֶם לְהַפְלִיא

וְלֹא־יֵבֹשׁוּ עַמִּי לְעוֹלָם:

27 וִידַעְתֶּם כִּי בְקֶרֶב יִשְׂרָאֵל אָנִי

וַאֲנִי יְהוָה אֱלֹהֵיכֶם

וְאֵין עוֹד

וְלֹא־יֵבֹשׁוּ עַמִּי לְעוֹלָם:

Psalm 78, verses 1 to 7

The book of Psalms is found in *K'tuvim* ("Writings"), the third section of the Tanach. It contains 150 spiritual poems that exalt and call upon the Eternal as sovereign, friend, and savior. Tradition considers King David as the author of all the psalms that are either anonymous or ascribed to him, while modern scholarship assigns many of them to various later sources.

The name of Asaph is attached to twelve psalms, but what this means is not clear: was it the name of the author or of a musical tradition borne by people called "Asaphites"? Maskil is also a difficult term; it probably means "instructional psalm." Here, the teaching concerns trust in God.

78:1. A maskil of Asaph.

Hear my teaching, O my people;

incline your ears

to the words of my mouth.

2. I will open my mouth with a parable,

expounding riddles from time past,

3. things we have heard and know,

things our ancestors have told us.

4. We will not hide them from their children,

telling to the coming generations

the praiseworthy deeds, the mighty acts,

the wonders done by the Eternal,

5. who established a testimony in Jacob

and ordained a Teaching in Israel,

commanding it to our ancestors,

to make it known to their children,

6. so that the next generation might know it—children yet unborn—

and rise up and tell it to their children,

7. that they may put their trust in God,

and not forget God's deeds,

but keep God's commandments.

78:1 מַשְׂכִּיל לְאָסָף

הַאֲזִינָה עַמִּי תּוֹרָתִי

הַטּוּ אָזְנְכֶם לְאִמְרֵי־פִי:

2 אֶפְתְּחָה בְמָשָׁל פִּי

אַבִּיעָה חִידוֹת מִנִּי־קֶדֶם:

3 אֲשֶׁר שָׁמַעְנוּ וַנֵּדָעֵם

וַאֲבוֹתֵינוּ סִפְּרוּ־לָנוּ:

4 לֹא נְכַחֵד מִבְּנֵיהֶם

לְדוֹר אַחֲרוֹן מְסַפְּרִים

תְּהִלּוֹת יְהוָה וֶעֱזוּזוֹ

וְנִפְלְאוֹתָיו אֲשֶׁר עָשָׂה:

5 וַיָּקֶם עֵדוּת בְּיַעֲקֹב

וְתוֹרָה שָׂם בְּיִשְׂרָאֵל

אֲשֶׁר צִוָּה אֶת־אֲבוֹתֵינוּ

לְהוֹדִיעָם לִבְנֵיהֶם:

6 לְמַעַן יֵדְעוּ דּוֹר אַחֲרוֹן בָּנִים יִוָּלֵדוּ

יָקֻמוּ וִיסַפְּרוּ לִבְנֵיהֶם:

7 וְיָשִׂימוּ בֵאלֹהִים כִּסְלָם

וְלֹא יִשְׁכְּחוּ מַעַלְלֵי־אֵל

וּמִצְוֹתָיו יִנְצֹרוּ:

Second Kings, chapter 2, verses 1 to 14

The final journey of Elijah into heaven by means of a fiery chariot is the climactic tale about the most popular of all prophets.

For more on the books of Kings, see our *General Introduction;* on Elijah, see the haftarah for Ki Tissa; on Elisha, the haftarah for Vayeira.

2:1. When the Eternal was about to take Elijah up to heaven in a whirlwind, Elijah and Elisha were on their way from Gilgal.

2. Elijah said to Elisha: Stay here; the Eternal has sent me to Beth El. But Elisha said: As the Eternal lives, and as you live, I shall not leave you.

So they went down to Beth El.

3. The band of prophets [located] in Beth El went to Elisha and said to him: Do you know that today the Eternal is taking your master away from you?

He said: Yes, I do know; be silent.

4. Elijah then said to Elisha: Stay here; the Eternal has sent me to Jericho. But Elisha said: As the Eternal lives, and as you live, I shall not leave you.

So they went to Jericho.

5. The band of prophets [located] in Jericho went to Elisha and said to him: Do you know that today the Eternal is taking your master away from you?

He said: Yes, I do know; be silent.

6. Elijah then said to Elisha: Stay here; the Eternal has sent me to the Jordan. But Elisha said: As the Eternal lives, and as you live, I shall not leave you.

So they went [to the Jordan],

וַיְהִ֗י בְּהַעֲל֤וֹת יְהֹוָה֙ אֶת־אֵ֣לִיָּ֔הוּ בַּֽסְעָרָ֖ה 2:1
הַשָּׁמָ֑יִם וַיֵּ֧לֶךְ אֵלִיָּ֛הוּ וֶאֱלִישָׁ֖ע מִן־הַגִּלְגָּֽל:

וַיֹּ֩אמֶר֩ אֵלִיָּ֨הוּ אֶל־אֱלִישָׁ֜ע שֵֽׁב־נָ֣א פֹ֗ה כִּ֤י 2
יְהֹוָה֙ שְׁלָחַ֣נִי עַד־בֵּֽית־אֵ֔ל וַיֹּ֣אמֶר אֱלִישָׁ֗ע חַי־
יְהֹוָ֤ה וְחֵֽי־נַפְשְׁךָ֙ אִם־אֶעֶזְבֶ֔ךָּ וַיֵּֽרְד֖וּ בֵּֽית־אֵֽל:

וַיֵּצְא֨וּ בְנֵֽי־הַנְּבִיאִ֤ים אֲשֶׁר־בֵּֽית־אֵל֙ אֶל־ 3
אֱלִישָׁ֔ע וַיֹּאמְר֣וּ אֵלָ֗יו הֲיָדַ֙עְתָּ֙ כִּ֣י הַיּ֔וֹם יְהֹוָ֛ה
לֹקֵ֥חַ אֶת־אֲדֹנֶ֖יךָ מֵעַ֣ל רֹאשֶׁ֑ךָ וַיֹּ֛אמֶר גַּם־אֲנִ֥י
יָדַ֖עְתִּי הֶחֱשֽׁוּ:

וַיֹּ֩אמֶר֩ ל֨וֹ אֵלִיָּ֜הוּ אֱלִישָׁ֣ע שֵֽׁב־נָ֣א פֹ֗ה כִּ֤י 4
יְהֹוָה֙ שְׁלָחַ֣נִי יְרִיח֔וֹ וַיֹּ֕אמֶר חַי־יְהֹוָ֖ה וְחֵֽי־נַפְשְׁךָ֑
אִם־אֶעֶזְבֶ֖ךָּ וַיָּבֹ֥אוּ יְרִיחֽוֹ:

וַיִּגְּשׁ֨וּ בְנֵֽי־הַנְּבִיאִ֥ים אֲשֶׁר־בִּירִיחוֹ֮ אֶל־ 5
אֱלִישָׁע֒ וַיֹּאמְר֣וּ אֵלָ֗יו הֲיָדַ֙עְתָּ֙ כִּ֣י הַיּ֔וֹם יְהֹוָ֛ה
לֹקֵ֥חַ אֶת־אֲדֹנֶ֖יךָ מֵעַ֣ל רֹאשֶׁ֑ךָ וַיֹּ֛אמֶר גַּם־אֲנִ֥י
יָדַ֖עְתִּי הֶחֱשֽׁוּ:

וַיֹּ֩אמֶר֩ ל֨וֹ אֵלִיָּ֜הוּ שֵֽׁב־נָ֣א פֹ֗ה כִּ֤י יְהֹוָה֙ 6
שְׁלָחַ֣נִי הַיַּרְדֵּ֔נָה וַיֹּ֕אמֶר חַי־יְהֹוָ֖ה וְחֵֽי־נַפְשְׁךָ֑
אִם־אֶעֶזְבֶ֖ךָּ וַיֵּלְכ֖וּ שְׁנֵיהֶֽם:

7. and fifty members of the guild of prophets went and stood at a distance, as the two of them stood by the Jordan.

8. Elijah then took his mantle and rolled it up, and struck the water so that it split into two parts, and the two of them crossed on dry ground.

9. As they were crossing, Elijah said to Elisha: What can I do for you before I am taken from you? Elisha replied: Let a double portion of your spirit be mine.

10. He said: You have asked a hard thing: if you see me being taken from you, it shall be granted you; but if not, it shall not be so.

11. They were going along and talking, and behold! a fiery chariot and fiery horses separated the two of them, and Elijah went up to heaven in a whirlwind.

12. But Elisha saw it, and he cried: Father! Father! The chariots of Israel and its horsemen! But when he could no longer see him, he took hold of his [own] clothes and tore them in half.

13. Then he picked up the mantle of Elijah that had dropped from him, turned back and stood at the shore of the Jordan.

14. Taking the mantle that had dropped from Elijah, he struck the water and said: *Where is the Eternal, the God of Elijah?* When he had struck the water, it split into two parts and Elisha passed through.

7 וַחֲמִשִּׁים אִישׁ מִבְּנֵי הַנְּבִיאִים הָלְכוּ וַיַּעַמְדוּ מִנֶּגֶד מֵרָחֹוק וּשְׁנֵיהֶם עָמְדוּ עַל־הַיַּרְדֵּן:

8 וַיִּקַּח אֵלִיָּהוּ אֶת־אַדַּרְתּוֹ וַיִּגְלֹם וַיַּכֶּה אֶת־הַמַּיִם וַיֵּחָצוּ הֵנָּה וָהֵנָּה וַיַּעַבְרוּ שְׁנֵיהֶם בֶּחָרָבָה:

9 וַיְהִי כְעָבְרָם וְאֵלִיָּהוּ אָמַר אֶל־אֱלִישָׁע שְׁאַל מָה אֶעֱשֶׂה־לָּךְ בְּטֶרֶם אֶלָּקַח מֵעִמָּךְ וַיֹּאמֶר אֱלִישָׁע וִיהִי־נָא פִּי־שְׁנַיִם בְּרוּחֲךָ אֵלָי:

10 וַיֹּאמֶר הִקְשִׁיתָ לִשְׁאֹול אִם־תִּרְאֶה אֹתִי לֻקָּח מֵאִתָּךְ יְהִי־לְךָ כֵן וְאִם־אַיִן לֹא יִהְיֶה:

11 וַיְהִי הֵמָּה הֹלְכִים הָלֹוךְ וְדַבֵּר וְהִנֵּה רֶכֶב־אֵשׁ וְסוּסֵי אֵשׁ וַיַּפְרִדוּ בֵּין שְׁנֵיהֶם וַיַּעַל אֵלִיָּהוּ בַּסְעָרָה הַשָּׁמָיִם:

12 וֶאֱלִישָׁע רֹאֶה וְהוּא מְצַעֵק אָבִי אָבִי רֶכֶב יִשְׂרָאֵל וּפָרָשָׁיו וְלֹא רָאָהוּ עֹוד וַיַּחֲזֵק בִּבְגָדָיו וַיִּקְרָעֵם לִשְׁנַיִם קְרָעִים:

13 וַיָּרֶם אֶת־אַדֶּרֶת אֵלִיָּהוּ אֲשֶׁר נָפְלָה מֵעָלָיו וַיָּשָׁב וַיַּעֲמֹד עַל־שְׂפַת הַיַּרְדֵּן:

14 וַיִּקַּח אֶת־אַדֶּרֶת אֵלִיָּהוּ אֲשֶׁר־נָפְלָה מֵעָלָיו וַיַּכֶּה אֶת־הַמַּיִם וַיֹּאמַר אַיֵּה יְהוָה אֱלֹהֵי אֵלִיָּהוּ אַף־הוּא וַיַּכֶּה אֶת־הַמַּיִם וַיֵּחָצוּ הֵנָּה וָהֵנָּה וַיַּעֲבֹר אֱלִישָׁע:

Psalm 90, verses 1 to 6, 10, 12, and 14 to 17

The book of Psalms is found in *K'tuvim* ("Writings"), the third section of the Tanach. It contains 150 spiritual poems that exalt and call upon the Eternal as sovereign, friend, and savior. Tradition considers King David as the author of all the psalms that are either anonymous or ascribed to him, while modern scholarship assigns many of them to various later sources.

This psalm, ascribed to Moses, has become one of the oft-cited poems in the synagogue, and Rabbis will frequently use it when they eulogize the departed. It reminds us of the fleeting nature of our lives: "The days of our years are threescore and ten, or, if we have strength, fourscore years .... Teach us, then, to number our days, that we may get us a heart of wisdom."

90:1. A prayer of Moses, the man of God.
Eternal One, You have been our dwelling
  place in all generations.

2. Before the mountains were born,
before You bought forth the earth and the
  world,
from eternity to eternity You are God.

3. You turn us back to dust, saying,
Turn back, you mortals!

4. For a thousand years in Your sight
are as yesterday when it is past,
or as a watch in the night.

5. You sweep them away:
they are like a dream at daybreak,
like grass renewed in the morning;

6. In the morning it is renewed:
in the morning it flourishes and is renewed,
in the evening it fades and withers.

10. The days of our years are threescore
  and ten,
or, if we have strength, fourscore years,
yet toil and trouble fill their span:

תְּפִלָּה לְמֹשֶׁה אִישׁ־הָאֱלֹהִים 90:1
אֲדֹנָי מָעוֹן אַתָּה הָיִיתָ לָּנוּ בְּדֹר וָדֹר:

2 בְּטֶרֶם הָרִים יֻלָּדוּ
וַתְּחוֹלֵל אֶרֶץ וְתֵבֵל
וּמֵעוֹלָם עַד־עוֹלָם אַתָּה אֵל:

3 תָּשֵׁב אֱנוֹשׁ עַד־דַּכָּא
וַתֹּאמֶר שׁוּבוּ בְנֵי־אָדָם:

4 כִּי אֶלֶף שָׁנִים בְּעֵינֶיךָ
כְּיוֹם אֶתְמוֹל כִּי יַעֲבֹר
וְאַשְׁמוּרָה בַלָּיְלָה:

5 זְרַמְתָּם
שֵׁנָה יִהְיוּ בַּבֹּקֶר
כֶּחָצִיר יַחֲלֹף:

6 בַּבֹּקֶר יָצִיץ וְחָלָף
לָעֶרֶב יְמוֹלֵל וְיָבֵשׁ:

10 יְמֵי־שְׁנוֹתֵינוּ בָהֶם שִׁבְעִים שָׁנָה
וְאִם בִּגְבוּרֹת שְׁמוֹנִים שָׁנָה

they are soon gone,

and we fly away.

12. Teach us, then, to number our days,

that we may get us a heart of wisdom.

14. Satisfy us in the morning with Your loyal love,

that we may rejoice and be glad all our days.

15. Cause us to rejoice as many days as we were afflicted,

as many years as we saw evil.

16. Let Your work be manifest to Your servants,

Your glory to their children.

17. Let the favor of our Eternal God be upon us,

and prosper the work of our hands.

O prosper the work of our hands!

וְרָהְבָּם עָמָל וָאָוֶן

כִּי־גָז חִישׁ וַנָּעֻפָה:

12 לִמְנוֹת יָמֵינוּ כֵּן הוֹדַע

וְנָבִא לְבַב חָכְמָה:

14 שַׂבְּעֵנוּ בַבֹּקֶר חַסְדֶּךָ

וּנְרַנְּנָה וְנִשְׂמְחָה בְּכָל־יָמֵינוּ:

15 שַׂמְּחֵנוּ כִּימוֹת עִנִּיתָנוּ

שְׁנוֹת רָאִינוּ רָעָה:

16 יֵרָאֶה אֶל־עֲבָדֶיךָ פָעֳלֶךָ

וַהֲדָרְךָ עַל־בְּנֵיהֶם:

17 וִיהִי נֹעַם אֲדֹנָי אֱלֹהֵינוּ עָלֵינוּ

וּמַעֲשֵׂה יָדֵינוּ כּוֹנְנָה עָלֵינוּ

וּמַעֲשֵׂה יָדֵינוּ כּוֹנְנֵהוּ:

BIBLIOGRAPHY

Aharoni, Yohanah. In *New Directions in Biblical Archaeology*. David Noel Freedman, ed. Garden City, N.Y.: Doubleday, 1969.

Ahituv, S. *Handbook of Ancient Hebrew Inscriptions*. Jerusalem: Bialik Institute, 1992.

Alter, Robert, and Frank Kermode. *A Literary Guide to the Bible*. Cambridge: Harvard University Press, 1987.

Anchor Bible. William Foxwell Albright and David Noel Freedman, eds. Garden City, N.Y.: Doubleday, from 1964. (Various authors for the individual books.)

Anchor Bible Dictionary. David Noel Freedman, ed. 6 vols. Garden City, N.Y.: Doubleday, 1992.

Bamberger, Bernard J. *Proselytism in the Talmudic Period*. New York: KTAV, 1968.

Beit Hamidrash. A. Jellinek, ed. 6 vols., Jerusalem: Bamberger and Wahrmann, 1938

Blake, William, *Milton*. London: Trianon Press, 1968.

Blank, Sheldon H. *Understanding the Prophets*. New York: UAHC,1969.

Braude, William G. and Israel J. Kapstein. *Pesikta deRab Kahana*, Philadelphia: Jewish Publication Society, 1975.

— *Pesikta Rabbati*. 2 vols. New Haven/London: Yale University Press, 1968

Buber, Martin. *The Prophetic Faith*. New York: Macmillan, 1949.

Buttenwieser, Moses. *The Psalms*. Chicago: University of Chicago Press, 1938.

Carlebach, Joseph. *Die drei grossen Propheten*. Frankfurt: Kaufmann, 1932.

Chapters into Verse: Poetry in English Inspired by the Bible, Vol. 1. Robert Atwan and Laurance Wieder, eds. New York: Oxford University Press, 1993.

Childs, Brevard S. *Introduction to the Old Testament as Scripture*. Philadelphia: Fortress Press, 1979.

Church, Brooke Peters. *The Private Lives of the Prophets*. New York and Toronto: Holt, Rinehart and Co., 1953.

Cogan, Mordechai, and U. Simon. *Mikra LeYisrael*. Tel Aviv: Am Oved, 1992.

Cogan, Mordechai, and,Hayim Tadmor. *II Kings* (in *Anchor Bible*; see there).

Cross, Frank Moore, and David Noel Freedman. "A Royal Song of Thanksgiving: II Samuel 22=Psalm 18," *Journal of Biblical Literature*, vol. 72 (1953), pp. 15-34.

De Vaux, Roland. *Ancient Israel*. London: Darton, Longham & Todd, 2nd ed., 1973.

Duhm, Bernhard. *Das Buch Jesaia*. Göttingen: Vandenhock & Ruprecht, 1968.

— *Das Buch Jeremia*. Tübingen: Mohr, 1901.

Ehrlich, Arnold B. *Mikra ki-Pheshuto III*. Reprint. New York: Ktav, 1969.

Elbogen, Ismar. *Jewish Liturgy: A Comprehensive History* (trl. by R. Scheindlin from the 1931 German ed.). New York: Jewish Theological Seminary of America, 1993.

Encyclopaedia Judaica. 16 vols. Jerusalem and New York: Keter./Macmillan, 1972.

Encyclopaedia Mikra'it. 8 vols. Tel Aviv: Mosad Bialik, 1955-1982.

Encyclopedia of Religion. New York: Macmillan, 1987.

Falk, Marcia. "Reflections on Hannah's Prayer," in *Out of the Garden: Women Writers on the Bible*. C. Büchmann and C. Spiegel, eds. New York: Fawcett Columbine, 1994.

Finkelstein, Louis. *The Pharisees*. Philadelphia: Jewish Publication Society. 2nd ed., 1940.

Freehof, Solomon B. *Book of Psalms*. Cincinnati: UAHC, 1938.

— *Book of Isaiah*. New York: UAHC, 1972.

— *Book of Jeremiah*. New York: UAHC 1977.

— *Book of Ezekiel*. New York: UAHC, 1978

Gaster, Theodore. *Myth, Legend and Custom in the Old Testament*. New York: Harper & Row, 1975.

Gates of Repentance. Chaim Stern, ed. New York: Central Conference of American Rabbis, 1978.

Ginzberg, Louis. *The Legends of the Jews*. 7 vols. Philadelphia: Jewish Publication Society. 1909-1946.

Glueck, Nelson. "Explorations in Eastern Palestine," *Annual of the American Schools of Oriental Research*, XXV-XXVIII (1951).

Gordon, Cyrus H. *Introduction to Old Testament Times*. Ventnor, N.J.: Ventnor Publishers, 1953.

Gray, John. *I and II Kings*. Old Testament Library. Philadelphia: Westminster, 3rd ed., 1979.

Greenberg, Sidney, ed. *A Treasury of Comfort*. New York: Crown Publishers, 1954.

Gruber, Mayer I. "The Motherhood of God in Second Isaiah," *Revue Biblique* 90 (1983), pp. 351-359.

Hallo, William W., and others, eds. *Scripture in Context II*. Winona Lake: Eisenbrauns, 1983.

Halperin, David. *The Merkabah in Rabbinic Literature*. New Haven: American Oriental Society, 1980.

Hamilton, Edith. *Spokesmen for God*. New York: W. W. Norton, 1936/1949.

Herbert, A. S. *The Book of the Prophet Isaiah*. Cambridge, 1975.

Herodotus. *Historiae*. trl. George Rawlinson. London: Dent, 1912.

Hertz, Joseph H. ed. *Pentateuch and Haftorahs*. Oxford: Oxford University Press, 1929-1936.

Hertzberg, Wilhelm H. *I and II Samuel*. Philadelphia: Westminster Press, 1964

Heschel, Abraham J. *God in Search of Man*. New York: Straus and Cudahy, 1955.

— *The Prophets*. Philadelphia: Jewish Publication Society, 1955.

High Holiday Prayer Book. Morris Silverman, ed. Hartford: Prayer Book Press, 1939.

Hillers, Delbert R. *Micah*. Philadelphia: Fortress Press, 1984.

Hirsch, Mendel. *Haftoroth*. New York: Judaica Press, 1971 (tr. from the 1896 German edition).

— *Die zwölf Propheten*. Frankfurt: A. J. Hofmann, 1900.

Holladay, William Lee. *Jeremiah 1*. Philadelphia: Fortress Press, 1986.

— *Jeremiah 2*. Philadelphia: Fortress Press, 1989.

Honor, Leo L. *Book of Kings 1*. New York: UHAC, 1955.

Hooker, Morna D. *The Influence of the Servant Concept of Deutero-Isaiah in the New Testament*. London: 1959.

Interpreter's Bible. George A. Buttrick, ed. 12 vols. New York and Nashville: Abingdon Press; commentaries (various authors) from 1953 on.

Interpreter's Dictionary of the Bible. George A. Buttrick, ed. New York and Nashville: Abingdon Press, 4 vols. and supplementary vol., 1962-1972.

Jacobs, Louis. *A Jewish Theology*. London: Darton, Longmans and Todd, 1973.

Jacobson, Issachar. חזון המקרא (*Chazon Hamikra*). 2 vols. Tel Aviv: Sinai, 1959.

JPS Torah Commentary. Nahum M. Sarna and Chaim Potok, eds. Philadelphia: Jewish Publication Society from 1989.

Kaufmann, Yehezkel. *The Babylonian Captivity and Deutero-Isaiah.* New York: Ktav, 1970.

— *Toledot ha-emunah ha-yisra'elit.* 4 vols. Tel Aviv: Devir, 1960.

King, Philip J. *Amos, Hosea, Micah—An Archaeological Commentary.* Louisville: Westminster, 1988.

— *Jeremiah: An Archaeological Companion.* Louisville: Westminster, 1993.

Kittel, Rudolf. *Great Men and Movements in Israel.* New York: Macmillan, 1929.

Klein, A[braham]. M. *Collected Poems.* Ottawa: University of Ottawa Press, 1975.

— *Poems.* Philadelphia: Jewish Publication Society, 1944.

Krauss, Samuel. *Isaiah.* In A. Kahana, *Torah, Nevi'im u-Khetuvim.* Jerusalem: Makor, 1968.

Kugel, James L. *The Idea of Biblical Poetry.* New Haven: Yale University Press, 1981.

Levenson, Jon Douglas. *Sinai and Zion.* Minneapolis: Winston Press, 1985.

Loewenstamm, Samuel E. *Comparative Studies in Biblical and Ancient Oriental Literatures.* Nuekirchen-Vluyn: Neukirchener Verlag, 1980.

Marcus, David. *Jephthah and His Vow.* Lubbock: Texas Tech, 1986.

Mattuck, Israel I. *The Thought of the Prophets.* London: Allen & Unwin, 1953.

McKane, William. *A Critical and Exegetical Commentary on Jeremiah I.* Edinburgh: T. & T. Clark, 1986.

Modern Poems on the Bible: An Anthology. David Curzon, ed. Philadelphia: Jewish Publication Society, 1994.

New Century Classical Handbook. New York: Appleton-Century-Crofts, 1962.

Noth, Martin. *The History of Israel.* London: Ackroyd (rev. ed.), 1960.

Olam HaTanach (עולם התנך). Tel Aviv: Davidon-Iti, 1994.

Oppenheim, A. Leo. *Ancient Mesopotamia.* Chicago: University of Chicago (rev. ed), 1977.

Orlinsky, Harry M. "The So-called 'Servant of the Lord' and 'Suffering Servant' in Second Isaiah." *Supplements to Vetus Testamentum,* XIV (1967), pp. 1-133.

— *Essays in Biblical Culture and Biblical Translation.* New York: Ktav, 1974.

— "The Origin of the Kethib-Qere System: A New Approach," in Shnayer Z. Leiman. *The Canon and Masorah of the Bible*. New York: Ktav, 1974.

Ozick, Cynthia. "Hannah and Elkanah: Torah as the Matrix for Feminism," in *Out of the Garden: Women Writers on the Bible*. C. Büchmann and C. Spiegel, eds. New York: Fawcett Columbine, 1994.

Pfeiffer, Robert H. *Religion in the Old Testament*. New York: Harper & Row, 1961.

Philippson, Ludwig. *Das Buch der Haphthoroth*. Leipzig: Baumgärtners Buchhandlung, 1859.

Plaut, W. Gunther, ed. *The Torah—A Modern Commentary*. New York: UAHC, 1994 [1981].

— *The Book of Proverbs*. New York: UAHC, 1961.

— *The Rise of Reform Judaism*. New York: World Union for Progressive Judaism, 1963.

— *The Case for the Chosen People*. New York: Doubleday, 1965.

Polish, David. *Give Us a King*. Hoboken, N.J.: Ktav, 1989.

Pritchard, James. *Ancient Near Eastern Texts*. Princeton: Princeton University Press, 1969.

Pseudo-Philo. *Biblical Antiquities of Philo*. English tr. by M. R. James. 1917.

Roberts, Jimmy J. M. *Nahum, Habakkuk, and Zephaniah*. Louisville: Westminster/ John Knox, 1991.

Sarna, Nahum. *The JPS Torah Commentary, Genesis*. Philadelphia: Jewish Publication Society, 1989.

Skinner, John. *Kings*. Edinburgh: T. & T. Clark, 1900.

Slonimsky, Henry M. *Essays*. New York: Hebrew Union College Press, 1967.

Snaith, Norman H. "Isaiah 40-66: A Study of the Second Isaiah and Its Consequences," in *Supplements to Vetus Testamentum*, XIV (1967), pp. 135-264.

Soncino Books of the Bible. A. Cohen, ed. Hindhead and London: Soncino Press, from 1947. (Also referred to as *Soncino Commentary*; various authors for individual books.)

Standard Prayer Book. S. Singer, ed. New York: Bloch Publishing Company, 1957.

Stern, Chaim. *Gates of Repentance* (see there).

Stern, Philip D. *The Biblical Herem*. Atlanta: Scholars Press, 1991.

Studies in Old Testament Prophecy Presented to Theodore H. Robinson. Harold H. Rowley, ed. Edinburgh: T. & T. Clark, 1950.

Tov, Emanuel. *Textual Criticism of the Hebrew Bible.* Minneapolis: Fortress Press, 1992.

Tur-Sinai, Naphtali Herz. *The Language and the Book II* (הלשון והספר). Jerusalem: Bialik Institute, 1959.

Union Hymnal (Central Conference of American Rabbis). New York: Case, 1965.

Von Rad, Gerhard. *The Message of the Prophets.* London: SCM Press, 1968.

Weinfeld, Moshe. *Deuteronomy and the Deuteronomic School.* Oxford: Oxford University Press, 1972.

Weiss, Andrea L. "Female Imagery in the Book of Isaiah," *CCAR Journal* (Winter 1994), pp. 65-70.

Westermann, Klaus. *Isaiah 40-66.* Philadelphia: Westminster Press, 1969.

Williamson, Hugh G. M. *The Book Called Isaiah.* Oxford: Clarendon, 1994.

Women's Bible Commentary. Carol A. Newman and Sharon H. Ringe, eds. London and Louisville: Westminster/John Knox, 1992.